Footprint Chile

Janak Jani
5th edition

A ribbon stretching for nearly two and a half thousand miles, bleached by tropical suns in the north, and frayed into innumerable, windswept shreds of islands and fjords in the south.

Stephen Clissold, *Chilean Scrap-book*

Chile Highlights

See colour maps at back of book

1 Altiplano national parks
Shy vicuñas set against a background of snow-capped volcanoes

2 La Tirana
Dance for a week at the famous fiesta

3 San Pedro de Atacama
A desert town surrounded by geysers and salt pans

4 Parque Nacional Pan de Azúcar
Where sea lions hang out on beautiful beaches

5 Elqui and Limarí valleys
Star-filled skies and wild countryside

6 Valparaíso
A UNESCO World Heritage site, just waiting to be explored

7 Cerro La Campana
Some of Chile's most stunning views can be enjoyed from the summit in winter

8 Ski resorts
The best skiing and boarding in Latin America, within easy reach of Santiago

9 Wine routes
Chile's finest vintages come from the Central Valley

10 Pucón
One of the top destinations in the Lake District, with volcanoes, fishing and whitewater rafting all nearby

11 Lago Llanquihue
The third largest lake in South America is a haven of peace and tranquillity

12 Lakes route to Bariloche
Travelling by boat and bus to Argentina is one of the region's most beautiful journeys

13 Parque Pumalín
Native temperate rainforest preserved for posterity

14 Chiloé
A magical island of fishing, forests and mythical creatures

15 Futaleufú
The country's mecca for whitewater rafting

16 Carretera Austral
Cycle, hike or fish your way through spectacular scenery between Puerto Montt and Villa O'Higgins

17 Laguna San Rafael
Cruise to the mighty glacier before it disappears

18 Torres del Paine
Quite simply one of the world's greatest national parks

19 Isla Navarino
Trek through wild forests and beaver dams south of Tierra del Fuego

20 Easter Island
A remote dot in the Pacific ocean with a fascinating cultural heritage

4

Contents

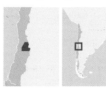
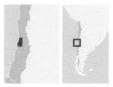

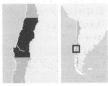

The Lake District

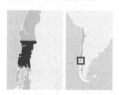

Chiloé

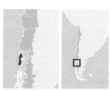

Carretera Austral

The Far South

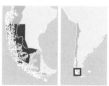

A team of riders prepares to enter the medialuna at the national rodeo finals.

Sun, sea and stairs
A colourful view from Cerro Alegre, Valparaíso: "a blend of amaranth and yellow, crimson and cobalt, green and purple" (Pablo Neruda).

A foot in the door

With an almost comical geographical shape, virtually every climate imaginable, and the political earthquake of the Pinochet affair to compliment its geological shudders, Chile is a country that, in recent years, has forced the world to sit up and take notice. Here, you can ski in the mountains in the morning and be drinking *pisco sours* on the beach come sundown. This beautiful, memorable corner of the world is a place of extremes and contradictions, in terms of geography – and politics.

For a start, few countries in the world have quite such a split geographical personality. Here, you can often glimpse the snows of the high Andes from the Pacific Ocean. To the south, the country is hemmed in by thick temperate rainforest, while to the north is the uniquely memorable Atacama Desert, with its endless spaces and pristine skies. The desert's geoglyphs bear testament to the ingenuity of some of prehistoric America's most complex civilizations, while an intermingling of the old world with the new has led to some of the most enduring aspects of ancient and modern Chilean culture; these range from the legend of the Inca princess La Tirana, which spawned the country's biggest religious fiesta, to the political militancy, which arose among the nitrate mines in the early 20th century and played a big part in forging Salvador Allende's Popular Unity government of 1970-1973, later to be overthrown by Augusto Pinochet.

10 Politics and poetry

Like it or not, Chile is most famous today for the legacy of the Pinochet government. A decade ago, the very mention of politics was likely to lead to an embarrassed silence but, these days, people are much freer with their opinions. The constraints of the military government on people's conversations have gone and the result is an increasing cultural dynamism. Many avant-garde writers (such as Roberto Bolaño and Raul Zurita) hail from Chile, perpetuating the country's long and distinguished artistic tradition. With its remarkable geography and an enduring sense of isolation, it is perhaps no surprise that poetry has flourished here. The country is rightly proud of its two Nobel laureates, the poets Gabriela Mistral and Pablo Neruda, whose writings reveal something of the essence of Chile. But the country's poetic output is not limited to these two international names: Chileans have a saying that there is a poet hidden under every stone...

The heart of Chile
A vineyard in Santa Cruz, a typical vista in the Central Valley.

Isolation and identity

It has long been said (in Chile and elsewhere) that the Chileans are the 'English of South America'. The roots of this surprising assertion cut to the heart of much of what it once meant to be Chilean. Inaccessible for centuries, except by sea or over the passes of the high Andes, Chileans developed a highly distinct and slightly isolationist identity; an insularity and indomitable national pride that meant that they could empathize all too easily with a place such as England. These days, however, with the collapse of the dictatorship and the resulting cultural liberation, Chileans are increasingly self-confident and outward-looking. They might still call their high tea '*onces*' (Chilean for 'elevenses'), but other vestiges of supposed 'Englishness' – old-fashioned ceremoniousness and the modelling of the Chilean Navy on the British one – are of less and less importance to the psyche. This is an increasingly confident nation, with no need to look elsewhere for its national pride.

Torres del Paine
A rare still day in Chile's most stunning park, where the views of peaks, glaciers and icebergs change constantly.

1 Traditional ways of life die hard in southern Chile. ▸▸ See page 433.

2 High in the Andes the geysers at El Tatio, over 4000 m above sea level, are at their most impressive first thing in the morning. ▸▸ See page 220.

3 Between Santiago and Tierra del Fuego there are over a dozen excellent rivers for whitewater rafting; the Petrohué is one of the most beautiful. ▸▸ See page 63.

4 The churches and monasteries of Santiago give a vivid sense of the thriving arts scene in colonial Spanish America. ▸▸ See page 537.

5 In many areas hunted to extinction, an estimated 20,000 guanaco now survive in the far north and parts of the far south. ▸▸ See page 557.

6 In the the northern altiplano, the brilliant quality of the light gives colours an intensity that is not easily forgotten. ▸▸ See page 256.

7 Palafitos, or traditional wooden houses built on stilts over the water, were once popular in all the main ports, but are now mostly found at the northern end of Castro, Chiloé. ▸▸ See page 379.

8 The Magellanic penguin is one of the nine penguin species living in Chile. ▸▸ See page 557.

9 There are several good fish restaurants in Caleta Membrillo, Valparaíso. ▸▸ See page 133.

10 Molten lava bubbles in the crater of Volcán Villarrica, Chile's most-climbed volcano, which erupted 10 times in the 20th century. ▸▸ See page 319.

11 The Feria de Temuco is one of the most fascinating markets in Chile. ▸▸ See page 314.

12 Los penitentes, giant wind-formed ice sculptures at the Paso San Francisco. ▸▸ See page 187.

In a microcosm

Most visitors are attracted to Chile for its serenity and natural beauty. Travelling from north to south and with only a little exertion it is possible to see the highest geyser, the driest desert and one of the highest lakes in the world; a flowering desert; schools of dolphins; the Andes; forests of monkey puzzle trees; temperate rainforest; the Patagonian ice-field; the glaciers of Tierra del Fuego; and the islands near Cape Horn. More vigorous visitors can climb active volcanoes where the crater bubbles away beneath them, ride galloping horses along wild and empty beaches, ski in some of South America's finest mountain resorts, go whitewater rafting, canoeing or kayaking and trek in one of the world's finest national parks, Torres del Paine in Patagonia.

Highs of metropolitan life

This cornucopia of wilderness should be reason enough to come to Chile. Yet while the country wears its beautiful scenery on its sleeve, peel away the layers of urban life and an equally intriguing animal lurks below. Chile is perhaps more 'European' than some of its Andean neighbours and it possesses some fascinating cities. Santiago is a sophisticated capital with a vibrant cultural life, including an underground rock scene and some of South America's most experimental modern artists. The nearby port city of Valparaíso, with its warrens of streets and brightly painted houses, is a place where it is possible to spend weeks and not even scratch the surface. To the south, Chillán has wonderful galleries and museums that provide an

The spectacular San Rafael glacier is inexorably on the retreat and is likely to have disappeared entirely by 2011.

The other-worldly landscapes of the Valle de la Luna were created by the erosion of salt mountains.

insight into life in Chile's heartland, while Iquique – one of the driest cities on earth – gives a sense of life on a forbidding frontier.

Mapuche to Moai

Away from material considerations, one of Chile's greatest attractions is its people – warm, courteous and generous to a fault. You will find an effusive welcome all over the country, especially if you speak Spanish. In the south, particularly in the region around Temuco, you can also gain first-hand experience of the fierce pride of the Mapuche people and understand something of their heritage and tragic history. Meanwhile, to confirm the strength of Chile's indigenous cultures, it is only necessary to look westwards to Easter Island, where the mysterious *moai* figures have fascinated anthropologists for decades.

Doubts and witches

But just in case you are still doubtful that Chile is anything more than a European country disguised as a South American one, take a short boat trip to the island of Chiloé in the southwest of the country. Here the islanders have developed an entire mythology all of their own, peopled with goblins, ghost ships and mermaids, not to mention witches, who fly to the graveyards at night and eat the bodies of the recently interred.

A homage to the ancestors
Moai at Rano Raraku, Rapa Nui (Easter Island).

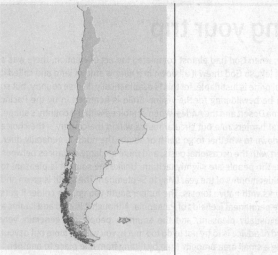

Planning your trip

Chileans say that, when God had almost completed the act of creation, there was a little of everything left, so God threw it all down in a narrow strip of land and called it Chile. The national pride is justifiable, for this is a fantastically diverse country, but so much choice can be bewildering for the visitor. Chile is hemmed in by the Pacific Ocean, the Atacama Desert and the Andes. When combined with the country's shape, these geographical barriers rule out circular routes within the country – the choice therefore comes down to whether to go north or south. The north is generally drier. Much of it is desert with the occasional oasis, and there are large distances between places of interest. The people are slightly taciturn. Unlike the south it is pleasant to visit during the colder months of the year (May to September). The south is green and full of national parks with native forests. The further south you go, the colder it gets until you reach the permanent icefields of Patagonia. Although it is cold and it rains a lot, summers are usually pleasant, and the southern people are generally very welcoming. A word of advice is to try not to do too much; you will get more out of your travels by covering a small area properly than by flitting from one place to another.

Where to go

With such variety to explore, this guide makes no attempt to be prescriptive. There are, however, a number of places that stand out. These itineraries are suggested for those who want to see as much of the country as they can in the time available; but those with more time to spare could easily devote several weeks to each area of the country without running out of things to see and do.

The south

One week Those with just a week to see something of the south are probably best advised to use a **LanChile** South American airpass (see page 44) to fly straight from Santiago to Puerto Montt, allowing two or three days to visit either the beautiful island of **Chiloé** or the southern Lake District. In Chiloe you could see the penguins at **Pumillahue**, the town of **Ancud** and many of the island's Jesuit churches. Visiting Chiloé in 1835, Charles Darwin found that the rolling hills reminded him of England. It has changed little since and, with its rich mythology and close-knit agricultural communities, it still evokes a bygone age. Just north of Chiloé and Puerto Montt is the **Lake District**. The German-founded town of **Puerto Varas** could be used as a base to visit the area around **Lago Llanquihue**, where the Osorno volcano provides a spectacular backdrop to the third-biggest lake in South America. The impressive Petrohué waterfalls are an hour to the east. Travellers could then fly south to **Punta Arenas**, where four days could be spent visiting the mountains and eerie blue glaciers of the **Parque Nacional Torres del Paine**, one of the world's great national parks, before flying back to Santia.

Two weeks With a little more time, several great additions could be made to the one-week itinerary. Rather than flying straight to Puerto Montt, travellers might want to make the journey by bus, spending a few days in the Central Valley. This is the heart of Chile and a visit here is essential for a deeper understanding of the country. The high mountains around **Vilches**, east of Talca, could be visited, or the **Parque Nacional de las Siete Tazas**, near Curicó. Wine-buffs might want to sample some of Chile's best wines on the **Ruta del Vino**, near San Fernando, while beach lovers might prefer surfing at **Pichilemu**, or visiting beautiful and deserted resorts such as **Iloca** or **Curanipe**. After four or five days move on to the famous forests and hills in the northern Lake District around

Lago Villarrica, perhaps climbing the famous volcano nearby, doing a day trek in the Araucaria forests of Huerquehue or Cañi, braving a day of whitewater rafting and relaxing in natural thermal springs, before flying from Puerto Montt to Punta Arenas to visit the **Torres del Paine** (as above) and then heading straight back to Santiago. go.

One month A month is enough time for a truly memorable trip. Spend a further two or three days on **Chiloé**, visiting the **Parque Nacional de Chiloé** at Cucao, and **Castro**. A boat could then be caught to **Chaitén**, from where you could spend the next eight or nine days exploring the fabulous region of the **Carretera Austral**. See giant alerce forests in the **Parque Pumalín**, experience some of the world's best whitewater rafting around **Futaleufú** and hike around **Cerro Castillo** or **Cochrane**, before making for **Puerto Chacabuco** and (if money is no object) taking a two-day cruise to the **Laguna San Rafael glacier**. After this you could fly down to **Puerto Natales**, and complete the itinerary at **Torres del Paine** (see above), adding the wilds of **Tierra del Fuego** or the **Glaciares National Park** in Argentina, before flying back to Santiago.

> ✷ *The two-week itineraries could be combined into a one-month exploration of the country as a whole.*

The north

One week With just a week to see the best of northern Chile, you will again probably want to take advantage of the **LanChile** South American airpass, flying first to **La Serena** to spend perhaps three days exploring the area around the city. Pick two attractions from among the **Elqui Valley** and the public observatory there, the **Parque Nacional Fray Jorge**, the penguins, dolphins and sea lions at **Isla Damas**, the cave paintings at the **Valle del Encanto** or the **Limarí Valley**. Fly on to **Calama**, gateway to the Atacama, to visit the small town of **Chiu Chiu**. The next day, travel to the oasis of **San Pedro de Atacama** and spend three days visiting the geysers, altiplano lakes, the salt flat and the Valley of the Moon, before flying back to Santiago.

Two weeks Those with a fortnight to spend in the north will probably want to avoid flying. A bus north to **Ovalle** provides a good introduction to the beauties of the mountains of the semi-desert, before visiting the attractions around **La Serena** mentioned above. From La Serena, it's worth travelling to Chañaral to see the spectacular **Parque Nacional Pan de Azúcar**, before moving on to Calama to continue with the itinerary suggested above. After exploring the area around **San Pedro**, travel to **Arica**, and spend two days visiting the spectacular **Parque Nacional Lauca** and the world's highest lake, **Chungará**, before the flight back to the capital.

One month A month allows you to visit some fascinating additional destinations in the north of the country. Two or three days should be spent exploring the hinterland around **Illapel**, **Salamanca** and **Combarbalá**, for example, which is spectacularly rugged country and full of minerals and ancient rock art. Heading north from Chañaral, break your journey at the eerie, attractive coast town of **Taltal** and then use one of your extra days to visit **Chuquicamata**, the largest opencast copper mine on earth. With two extra days at **San Pedro de Atacama**, you should tour the beautiful altiplano villages, before travelling north to the city of **Arica**. Take a four-day altiplano tour, visiting **Lauca**, **Surire** and **Isluga** parks and ending in **Iquique** where you can relax on the beach for a couple of days and visit the nearby thermal baths at **Mamiña**.

Other options

The itineraries suggested above incorporate the most popular destinations for visitors to Chile, but those who have more time available (or who want to experience other aspects of the country) will find their travel plans equally busy. Since over one third of Chileans live in **Santiago**, it is a shame to avoid the capital completely;

travellers who enjoy nightlife and/or urban living will thrive here, though it is best to try and avoid the incapacitating heat of summer and the worst days of the winter smog. Just 90 minutes away, **Valparaíso** is perhaps the most interesting city in Chile, acknowledged to be its cultural and artistic capital. Nearby, the summit of the **Cerro La Campana** offers some of the best views in the whole country. The beach resorts to the north and south of Valparaíso are also attractive, though busy in summer.

Two final suggestions would be the **Juan Fernández Islands**, where Alexander Selkirk was marooned for almost five years, and **Rapa Nui (Easter Island)**, the remotest inhabited island on earth, with its famous archaeological heritage; both are easy (if expensive) to reach from Santiago by plane.

When to go

When planning your trip you should take into account the time of year. High season throughout the country is during the summer (especially January and February), when most areas are open to visitors, though the altiplano (the high plain of the Andes east of the Atacama) can experience heavy rain. It is also worth bearing in mind that many destinations are busy with Chilean and Argentine tourists at this time, especially in the far south, and bus fares and hotel prices are up to 50% higher. The north of the country has another high season in June, July and August, but these are winter months in the south, meaning that many services here are closed and transport links are reduced. Probably the ideal seasons for a visit, therefore, are spring (October to December) and autumn (March to April) when many facilities in the south are open, but less crowded, and temperatures in the northern and central regions are lower.

It is also worth arranging your travel plans to coincide with certain festivals (see page 58). In this case, it is best to book transport and accommodation well in advance. The period around the national Independence festivals on 18 September will be especially busy wherever you are.

Tour operators

UK and Ireland
Austral Tours, 20 Upper Tachbrook St, London SW1V 1SH, T020-7233 5384, www.latinamerica.co.uk. Specialist company with a wide range of activity holidays.

Condor Journeys and Adventures, 2 Ferry Bank, Colintraive, Argyll PA22 3AR, T01700-841318, www.condorjourneys-adventures.com. A wide range of specialist tours available – website in French.

Essentials Planning your trip

Cox & Kings Travel, Gordon House, 10 Greencoat Place, London SW1P 1PH, T020-78735000, www.coxandkings.co.uk. Exclusive set tours all over the continent.

Exodus Travels, Grange Mills, Weir Rd, London SW12 0NE, T0870-2405550, www.exodus. co.uk. Experience in adventure travel around the world; good trips to all parts of Chile.

Journey Latin America, 12-13 Heathfield Terrace, Chiswick, London W4 4JE, T020-8747 8315; 12 St Ann's Sq (2nd floor), Manchester M2 7HW, T0161-832 1441, www.journeylatin america.co.uk. Long-established company running escorted and bespoke tours throughout the region, and offering a wide range of flight options.

Last Frontiers, Fleet Marston Farm, Aylesbury, Buckinghamshire HP18 0QT, T01296-653000, www.lastfrontiers.co.uk. Tailor-made Latin American travel.

New Worlds, Northway House, 1379 High Rd, London N20 9LP, T020-8445 8444, www.newworlds.co.uk. Specialist company offering tailor-made itineraries.

Pura Aventura, 18 Bond St, Brighton, East Sussex BN11 1RD, T0845-2255058, www.Pura-aventura.com. Small Chilean specialist with a wide range of organized and tailor-made tours.

Scott Dunn (formerly Passage to South America), Fovant Mews, 12a Noyna Rd, London SW17 7PH, T020-86825030, www.scottdunn.com. Wide range of tailor-made packages throughout the region.

Select Latin America, 79 Maltings Place, 169 Tower Bridge Road, London SE1 3LJ, T020-7407 1478, www.selectlatinamerica.co.uk. Specialist in tours to Latin America.

South American Experience, 47 Causton St, Pimlico, London SW1P 4AT, T020-79765511, www.southamericanexperience.co.uk. Apart from booking flights and accommodation, also offers tailor-made trips.

Steppes Latin America, 51 Castle St, Cirencester, Gloucester GL7 1QD, T01285-885333, www.steppestravel.co.uk. Tailor-made holidays including Patagonia escorted tours, horse riding trips and birdwatching.

Trips Worldwide, 14 Frederick Place, Clifton, Bristol, BS8 1AS, T0117-311 4400, www.tripsworldwide.co.uk. Specialists in tailor-made holidays.

4 Star South America, 3003 Van Ness, NW Suite S-823, Washington, DC 20008, T1-800 7474540 (North America)/0870-7115370 (UK)/+49-700-4444 7827 (rest of Europe), www.4starsouthamerica.com. Tour operator and flight consolidator.

Chile For Less, 7201 Wood Hollow Drive, Austin, TX 78731, T877-269 0309 (toll-free), www.chileforless.com. Offers travel packages to Chile and other South American countries.

Discover Chile Tours, 5775 Blue Lagoon Drive Suite 190, Miami, FL 33126. T305-2665827 (local), T1-800 826 4845 (toll-free), www.discover-chile.com. Has a range of tours, including good ski trips.

International Expeditions, 1 Environs Park, Helena, AL35080, USA, T1-800 633 4734, www.internationalexpeditions.com. Travel company specializing in nature tours.

Ladatco Tours, 2200 South Dixie Highway Suite 704, Coconut Grove, FL 33133, T1-800 327 6162, www.ladatco.com. Specialist operator based in Miami, runs explorer tours themed around mysticism, wine, etc.

Essentials Planning your trip

Mila Tours, T1-800-367 7378, www.mila tours.com. Arranges a wide variety of tours from rafting to photography.

Mountain Travel Sobek, 6420 Fairmount Av, El Cerrito, CA 94530, T1-888-MTSOBEK (toll-free)/T1-510-527 8100, www.mtsobek. com. A specialist in Chile, offering a range of trekking tours.

Myths and Mountains, 976 Tee Court, Incline Village, NV 89451, T1-800-670-6984, www.mythsandmountains.com. Cultural, wildlife and environmental trips.

South American Explorers Club, 126 Indian Creek Rd, Ithaca, NY 14850, T1-607- 2770488, 1-800-2740568 (toll free in USA), www.samexplo.org. Gives good advice.

Wilderness Travel, 1102 Ninth St, Berkeley, CA 94710, T510-5582488, T1-800-368 2794 (toll free), www.wildernesstravel.com. Organizes trips worldwide, including very good tours of Patagonia.

South America
CAT Argentina and Chile, Av Presidente Roque Saenz Peña 615, Of 718, Buenos Aires, www.cat-travel.com. With offices in several Latin American countries, this Dutch-owned and run company offers tailor-made trips.
Exploranter, Rua Joaquim Antunes 232, Jardim Paulistano, São Paulo, SP 05415 000, T+55(11)3085 2011, www.hotelsobrerodas. com.br. Overlanding trips with fully equipped vehicles in Patagonia, Atacama and Brasil.

Australia and New Zealand
Australian Andean Adventures, Suite 201 level 6, 32 York St, Sydney, T02-92999973, www.andeanadventures.com.au. Specialists in trekking in South America for Australians.
South America Travel Centre, 104 Hardware St, Melbourne, T03-96425353, www.satc.com.au. Good, individual, tailor-made trips to Chile.

Finding out more

For general information contact **Tourism Promotion Corporation of Chile** ① *Antonio Bellet 77, Oficina 602, Providencia, Santiago, T02-2350105, www.visit-chile.org.*

Useful websites
There are a great many sites about Chile that surfers may wish to explore, but note that you may have to weed out the sites related to chilli peppers!
Useful sites specifically covering all Chile:
www.visit-chile.org, **www.sernatur.cl** and **www.gochile.cl**
Other sites dealing with specific destinations in Chile include, from north to south:
www.arica.cl
www.infoarica.cl

www.iquique.co.cl
www.sanpedroatacama.com
 www.laserena.cl
www.vinadelmarchile.cl
www.vinadelmar.cl
www.municipalidad devalparaisochile.cl
www.ciudad.cl
www.pucon.com
www.gopucon.com
www.pucon turismo.cl
www.ptovaras.cl
www.puertovaras.org

Essentials Planning your trip

www.puerto monttchile.cl
www.chiloe.cl
www.chiloemagico.cl
www.chileaustral.com
www.pat agoniachile.cl
www.patagonia-chile.com
www.rapanui.co.cl

www.chile-hotels.com Reservations for many hotels in Chile (particularly upmarket ones); prices may be cheaper booking direct.
www.hostel world.com Useful for finding cheaper accommodation.
www.backpackerschile.com and

www.backpackersbest.cl For finding good hostels and guesthouses.
www.trekkingchile.com For trekking in central Chile.
www.ccv.cl Website of the Chilean wine-making association, for wine enthusiasts.
www.surf.cl For surfers
www.greenpeace.cl Up-to-date information on environmental issues.
www.desaparecidos.org/chile and www.rem ember-chile.org Background on the Pinochet years and human rights situation.
www.mapuche.cl Information on Chile's Mapuche people.

Language

Although English is understood in many major hotels, tour agencies and airline offices (especially in Santiago), travellers are strongly advised to learn some Spanish before setting out. Chilean pronunciation – very quick and lilting, with final syllables cut off – can present difficulties to the foreigner. Chileans have a wide range of idioms that even other Latin Americans find difficult to understand. Visitors may want to buy *How to Survive in the Chilean Jungle* by John Brennan and Alvaro Taboada, a handbook for English speakers on Chilean colloquialisms and slang, available in bookshops in larger cities. In some rural areas travellers will encounter indigenous languages – Mapudungu (the Mapuche language) in the south; Aymará in the north – but most people usually also speak Spanish. ▶▶ *For a list of Spanish words and phrases, see page 564.*

For Spanish courses in Chile contact **Amerispan** ① *PO Box 58129, 117 South 17 St, 14th floor, Philadelphia, PA19103, USA, T1-215 751 1100, www.amerispan.com*, or **Spanish Abroad** ① *5112 N 40th St, Suite 103, Phoenix, AZ85018, T1-888 722 7623 (toll free)/1-602 778 6791/0800-028 7706 (UK freephone), www.spanishabroad.com*, which offers courses in Santiago, with tailor-made programmes, airport pickup and excursions. Many people will prefer to study somewhere other than Santiago. **Contact Chile** ① *Huelén 219 piso 2, Providencia, Santiago, T02-2641719, www.contactchile.cl*, offers courses throughout the country. As well as this several hostels in the provinces have Spanish schools attached. Details are given thoughout the text in the Directory sections.

Disabled travellers

Chileans are usually very courteous, and disabled travellers will be helped and assisted where possible. The 2002 census found that 334,000 Chilean citizens had some form of disability, but the **National Fund for the Disabled** (**FONDIS**) estimates that the actual number is closer to one million. Congress passed a law in 1994 to promote the integration of people with disabilities into society and **FONDIS** has a US$1.5 million budget. However, the disabled still suffer some forms of legal discrimination; for example, blind people cannot become teachers or tutors. Although the law now requires that new public buildings provide disabled access and the more expensive hotels usually have dedicated facilities, transport provision is a different matter. The línea 5 subway line in Santiago has no facilitated access for the disabled and, although bus companies will certainly be helpful, and the new **Transsantiago** buses are supposed to be disabled friendly, the rest do not have any dedicated services. Where possible, therefore, disabled travellers might be better off hiring their own transport, especially since reserved parking for the disabled is now reasonably common.

Useful organizations

Directions Unlimited,123 Green Lane, Bedford Hills, NY 10507, T1-800 533 5343. A tour operator specializing in tours for disabled US travellers.

Disability Action Group, 2 Annadale Av, Belfast BT7 3JH, T01232-491011. Information about access for British disabled traveller.

Disabled Persons' Assembly, PO Box 27-524, Wellington 6035, New Zealand, T04-801-9100, www.dpa.org.nz. Has lists of tour operators and travel agencies catering for the disabled.

Gay and lesbian travellers

In a macho culture, it is no surprise that there is quite a lot of homophobia in Chile, and gay and lesbian travellers should be aware that derogatory jokes about homosexuals (especially men) are widespread. Having said that, attitudes are beginning to loosen up, and there is a lively gay scene in most large cities. A mine of information is the website **www.gaychile.com**, where you can make gay-friendly hotel reservations and seek out gay-friendly shops and establishments up and down the country. There is also a specialist travel agency for gays and lesbians in Chile called **Novellus** ① *Almirante Pastene 7, Oficina 54, Providencia, Santiago, T02-2518547, novellus@tempotravel.cl.*

Student travellers

If you are planning to study in Chile for a long period it is essential to get a student visa in advance, which you obtain by contacting a Chilean consulate (see page 31); you will be asked for proof of affiliation to a Chilean university. Note that students are not allowed to undertake paid employment in Chile.

If you are in full-time education you are entitled to an International Student Identity Card, which is distributed by student travel offices and travel agencies in 116 countries. The **ISIC** gives you special prices on all forms of transport, and access to a variety of other concessions and services. To find the location of your nearest ISIC office, look at www.isic.org. In Chile, student ID cards can be obtained from the ISIC offices ① *Hernando de Aguirre 201, Oficina 602, Providencia, Santiago, T02-411 2000, www.isic.cl*, and cost US$15 (photo and proof of status required). If you are a holder of an ISIC card and get into trouble, you can make a reverse-charge call to the helpline on T+44-20-8762-8110. If travelling with a student card, it is always worth asking for discounts for museum entry and bus tickets, although all student ID cards must carry a photograph if they are to be of any use.

Travelling with children

Chile is a good place for travelling with children as there are few health risks and children are very popular. Officials tend to be more amenable where children are concerned, and even thieves and pickpockets seem to have retained the traditional respect for families and may leave you alone because of it.

However, given Chile's geography, a lot of time can be spent travelling. On bus journeys, if the children are good at amusing themselves, or can readily sleep while travelling, the problems can be considerably reduced. Train journeys are easier, as they allow more scope for moving about, but there are few of these in Chile. On all long-distance buses you pay for each seat; there are no half-fares, so it is cheaper, if less comfortable, to seat small children on your knee for shorter trips. On urban and local buses, small children generally do not pay a fare, but are not entitled to a seat if paying customers are standing. On sightseeing tours you should always bargain for a family rate; often children can go free. All civil airlines charge a third less for children under 12.

Food can be a problem if your children are not adaptable. It is easier to take biscuits, drinks, bread, etc with you on longer trips than to rely on meal stops. A small immersion heater and jug for making hot drinks is invaluable. You will find that people will be very friendly to children in restaurants. As far as **health** is concerned, remember to be very careful about sunburn in the south, due to the lack of ozone.

In **hotels,** try to negotiate family rates. If charges are per person, always insist that two children will only occupy one bed, therefore counting as one tariff. If rates are per bed, the same applies. You can often get a reduced rate at cheaper hotels.

Women travellers

Chile presents no special problem for women travellers. Most Chileans are courteous and helpful. The following useful tips have been supplied by women (although most apply to any single traveller).

When you set out, err on the side of caution until your instincts have adjusted to the customs of the country. Unless actively avoiding foreigners like yourself, don't go too far from the beaten track; there is a very definite 'gringo trail' that you can join. This can be helpful when looking for safe accommodation, especially if arriving after dark. Remember that a taxi at night can be as dangerous as wandering around on your own, particularly in Santiago. At borders, dress as smartly as possible. Buses are much easier than trains for a person alone; on major routes seats are reserved and bags are locked in the hold.

Women may, though, be subject to much unwanted attention. To help minimize this, do not wear suggestive clothing. Some readers advise not flirting. By wearing a wedding ring and carrying a photograph of your 'husband' and 'children' you may dissuade an aspiring suitor. If politeness fails, do not feel bad about showing offence and departing. When accepting a social invitation, make sure that someone knows the address and the time you left. Ask if you can bring a friend (even if you do not intend to do so). A good rule is always to act with confidence, as though you know where you are going, even if you do not. Someone who looks lost is more likely to attract unwanted attention. Finally, be aware that anywhere calling itself a 'nightclub' is in fact a brothel.

Working in Chile

It is not difficult to find short-term or temporary work as a foreigner in Chile. The most obvious opening is as a teacher of English as a foreign language; even those without the appropriate TEFL qualification should be able to find this kind of work, especially in Santiago, but also in other cities such as Viña del Mar, Concepción and La Serena. Teachers are expected to be clean-cut and well-dressed, and to have the correct paperwork. The pay is often poor; as low as US$4 per hour after tax for those without the appropriate qualification. Prospective English-language teachers should apply in mid- February/early March with a full CV and photo. A work visa should be obtained as soon as you have found a contract (see below); beware that, without this, you will be liable to deportation and fines if discovered. We have received reports of more unscrupulous institutes employing teachers with 90-day tourist visas and then 'discovering', as this expires, that the teacher is not entitled to work, at which point unpaid wages may be withheld. The best-paid work for English language teachers is almost invariably private, one-to-one tuition, mainly found through word of mouth (although it may also be worth placing an advertisement in a newspaper such as *El Mercurio*).

The main obstacle to anyone seeking to work in Chile is the problem of obtaining and maintaining a working visa. All sorts of extraordinary pieces of paper may be asked for, and, at the very least, you will need proof of employment before the visa is issued. Those planning to work may enter Chile on a tourist visa and then get a working visa on presentation of a contract with a minimum wage of 100,000 Chilean pesos per month after tax (approximately US$180).

Business people face no special problems when doing short-term business in the country, and may enter on a tourist visa. It is recommended to carry a good supply of business cards, as the first thing which many business people will do at a meeting is ceremoniously present you with their card. Business visas must be applied for by those who are buying a going concern, or are investing a minimum of US$5000 in Chile, and who wish to reside in the country. ▶▶ *For further information, see Visas and immigration, page 30.*

Volunteering

Opportunities for work are not limited to language teaching. There is considerable scope for volunteer work in Chile, both in inner cities and on environmental projects. Those with appropriate skills and experience may also find work by approaching foreign companies (especially engineering or financial service firms) with offices in Chile (usually in Santiago). There is a large expatriate community in Santiago; try visiting some favourite local haunts, particularly **The Phone Box Pub**, Providencia 1670; Metro Manuel Montt, or **Flannery's Irish Pub**, Encomenderos 83, Las Condes, and asking around.

Volunteer organizations
Earthwatch, 126 Bank St, South Melbourne, Victoria 3205, Australia, T03-96826828, www.earthwatch.org. Organizes volunteer work on scientific and cultural projects around the world (also has associated offices in Oxford, UK).
Project Trust, Hebridean Centre, Isle of Coll,

Argyll PA78 6TE, UK, T01879-230441, www. projecttrust.org.uk. Volunteer work for foreigners.
Raleigh International, 27 Parsons Green Lane, London SW6 4HZ, UK, T0207-3718585, www.raleigh.org.uk. Volunteer projects for young travellers.

Before you travel

Visas and immigration

Regulations change frequently, so it is imperative to check visa requirements before you travel. At the time of writing, **visas** are required by citizens of Cuba, Guyana, Haiti; all African and Middle-Eastern countries, except Israel, Morocco and South Africa; all Asian and Pacific countries, except Fiji, Indonesia, Japan, Malaysia, Singapore, Tonga and Turkey; all former Communist countries except for Croatia, the Czech Republic, Estonia, Hungary, Lithuania, Poland, the Slovak Republic and Slovenia.

A **passport**, valid for at least six months, and a **tourist card** are required for entry by all other foreigners, except for citizens of Argentina, Bolivia, Brazil, Colombia, Paraguay, Peru and Uruguay, who require national identity cards only. Those entering with just a passport and tourist card may all stay for a period of 90 days, except for citizens of Belize, Costa Rica, Malaysia and Singapore (30 days only), and citizens of Greece, Indonesia and Peru (60 days only). Tourist cards are handed out as a matter of routine at immigration offices at major land borders and Chilean airports. It is essential that you keep the tourist card safe, since you must surrender it on departure. Onward travel tickets are officially required for entry but these are rarely asked for. On arrival you may be asked where you are staying in Chile; just give the name of any hotel. Remember that it is your responsibility to ensure that your passport is stamped in and out when you cross borders. The absence of entry and exit stamps, or passports stamped with the wrong date of entry can cause serious difficulties, so seek out the proper immigration offices if the stamping process is not carried out as you cross. The vast majority of border crossings, though, are trouble-free.

Ninety-day **visa extensions** (costing US$100) can be obtained from the **Ministerio del Interior** (Extranjería) in Santiago or from any local *gobernación* (government office). The procedure is often time-consuming and is officially supposed to include providing proof of funds and having an international record check (although these are usually missed out). To avoid hours of queuing and excessive punctiliousness when you are finally dealt with, you are advised to obtain extensions from smaller provincial offices rather than from Santiago; every provincial capital has a *gobernación*. If you must get the extension in Santiago, arrive at **Extranjería** early and consider bringing lunch. If you wish to stay longer than 90 days as a tourist, it is often easier to make a short trip into Argentina, or Peru if near Arica, and return with a new tourist card, rather than to apply for an extension. An obvious advantage of this is that the US$100 fee does not need to be paid. However, if you do this once too often officials may become difficult. Usually, after nine months or so of obvious one-day trips to Argentina, you will be given a final warning to get a residency visa within the next 90 days or leave.

In theory, there are entry taxes (officially called reciprocity charges) to be paid in dollars at all international borders, for nationals of Australia (US$52), Canada (US$132), Mexico (US$15) and the USA (US$100); however, in practice, this tax is only charged at airports and is valid for the lifetime of the passport. These charges vary according to the how much is charged to Chilean citizens for tourist visas to these countries.

Finally, on a general note, Chilean officials are very document-minded, but also often exceptionally hospitable and helpful. In remote areas, you should register your documents with the *carabineros* (police), not only as a matter of courtesy, but also because the local police are usually a mine of information about local conditions, and may be able to help you find accommodation and transport. If staying for a while, it is also worth registering at your embassy or consulate. Then, if your passport is stolen, the process of replacing it is simplified and speeded up. Keeping photocop essential documents, including flight ticket, and some additional passport-size photographs, is recommended; always carry a photocopy of your passport on your person as, legally, some form of identification must be carried at all times.

Chilean embassies

For a full and updated list, see www. minrel.gov.cl, and look under *misiones*.
Argentina, Tagle 2762, Capital Federal (1425), T54-11-48088601, www.embajada dechile.com.ar. Also consulates up and down the country.
Australia, 10 Culgoa Circuit, O'Malley Act 2606, Canberra, T61-6-62862430, www.embachile-australia.com. Also consulates in Melbourne and Sydney.
Austria, Lugeck 1/3/10, Vienna A-1010, T43-1-5129208, echileat1@chello.at.
Belgium, 160 rue des Aduatiques, 1040 Brussels, T32-2-7433660, www.embachile.be.
Bolivia, Av San Martín Esq 2 anillo, Edif Torres Equipetrol, piso 9, Santa Cruz, T591-3-3341251, www.consulado-chile.scz.com. Note this is only a consulate; there are other consulates in La Paz and Cochabamba.
Brazil, Ses, Av Das Nacoes, q 803, Lote 11, CEP 70.407-900, Brasília, T55-61-21035151, embchile@embchile.org.br. Consulates throughout the country.
Canada, 50 O'Connor St, Suite 1413, Ottawa, Ontario K1P 6L2, T1-613-2354402, www. chile.ca. Also consulates in several other cities .
Colombia, Calle 100 No 11 B-44, Apdo Aéreo 90061, Bogotá, T57-1-6206613, www.embajadadechile.com.co.
Denmark, Kastelsvej 15, III, 2100 Copen-hagen, T45-35385834, www.chiledk.dk.
Ecuador, Juan Pablo Sanz 3617 y Amazonas, Edificio Xerox, piso 4, Quito, T593-2-249403. Also consulate in Guayaquil.
France, 2 Av de la Motte Picouet, 75007 Paris, T33-1-44185960, www.amb-chili.fr.
Germany, Mohrenstrasse 42, 10117 Berlin, T49-30-7262035, www.embajada consuladoschile.de. Also consulates in Frankfurt, Hamburg, Munich.
Ireland, 44 Wellington Rd, Ballsbridge, Dublin 4, T353-1-6675094 www.embachile-irlanda.ie.
Israel, Beit Sharbat, 8th floor, Kaufman 4 St, Tel Aviv 68012, T972-3-5102750, consulad@inter.net.il.

Italy, Via Po 23, 00198 Roma, T39-6- 884 1449, www.chileit.it Consulate in Milan.
Japan, Nihon Seimei Akabanebashi Building 8F, 3-1-14 Shiba, Minato-ku, Tokyo 105-0014, T81-3-34527561, www.chile.or.jp.
Mexico, Andrés Bello 10, Edificio Forum, piso18, Col Polanco, CP11560, DF, T52-55-2809681, www.embajadadechile.com.mx. Also consulates in Guadalajara and Monterrey.
Netherlands, Mauritskade 51, 2514 HG, The Hague, T31-70-3123640, www.e chile.nl. Also a consulate in Amsterdam.
New Zealand, 19 Bolton St, Wellington, T64-4-4716270, www.embchile.co.nz.
Norway, Meltzers Gate 5, 0244 Oslo, T47-22448955, www.chile.no.
Paraguay, Capital Emilio Nudelman 351, Esquina Campos Cervera, Asunción, T595-21-662 756, echilepy@conexion.com.py.
Peru, Av Javier Prado Oeste 790, San Isidro, Lima, T51-1-6112200, www.embajada chileperu.com.pe. Also consulate in Tacna.
South Africa, 235 Veale St, Brooklyn Gardens Building, corner of Veale St and Middel St, Block B – 1st floor, New Muckleneuk 0181, Pretoria, T27-12-4608090, www.embchile. co.za. Also consulate in Cape Town.
Spain, Lagasca 88, 6 Planta, 28001 Madrid, T34-91-4319160, echilees@tsai.es. Consulate in Barcelona.
Sweden, Sturegatan 8, 3rd floor, Stockholm 114 35, T46-8-6798280, www.chileemb.se Also a consulate in Gothenburg.
Switzerland, Eigerplatz 5, 3007 Berne, T41-31-3700058, embajada@embachile.ch.
UK, 12 Devonshire St, London, W1G 7DS, T44-20-75801023, www.echileuk.demon.co.uk.
Uruguay, 25 de Mayo 575, Montevideo, T598-2-9164090, echileuy@netgate.com.uy.
USA, 1732 Massachusetts Av NW, Washington DC 20036, T1202-7851746, www.chile-usa.org. Also consulates across the country.
Venezuela, Paseo Enrique Eraso, Torre la Noria piso 10, OF 10-A Las Mercedes, Sector San Román, Caracas, T58-212-9531485, www.embachileve.org.

...ty free and export allowances

...ay be brought into Chile duty free: 500 cigarettes or 100 cigars or 500 ...lus three bottles of liquor, and all articles for personal use, including ...os, portable tape recorders, cameras, personal computers, and similar ...'s agricultural sector is free of many diseases, and so fruit, vegetables, ...ers and milk products may not be imported; these will be confiscated at all ...where there are thorough searches. This applies even to those who have had to travel through Argentina in the far south to get from one part of Chile to another. There are also internal customs checks for all travellers going south from Región I. This is mainly to inspect for duty-free goods from Iquique but fruit, vegetables, meat, flowers and milk products may also be confiscated.

Vaccinations

Before you travel make sure the medical insurance you take out is adequate. Have a check-up with your doctor, if necessary, and arrange your immunizations well in advance; children should, of course, also be up-to-date with any immunization programmes in their country of origin. It is also advisable to know your blood group. There is no malaria in Chile. ➤➤ *For further information, see Health, page 64.*

What to take → *Take twice as much money as you think you might need.*

Everybody has their own list but here are a few suggestions to help you pack for your trip to Chile. As far as clothing is concerned, be prepared for the desert heat and mountain snow. You'll need fully waterproof clothing (essential for the south at any time of year), very warm clothes for the northern highlands and the far south, light clothing for the summer, plus a sun hat, a pair of strong shoes/boots and a pair of sandals (outside Santiago sizes over 10½/44 are very hard to find!). A sarong is very useful as it can be used as a skirt, curtain, bedsheet or a towel.

Other items that you might want to take (especially budget travellers) include an inflatable travel pillow for neck support, a small first-aid kit and handbook, earplugs and airline-type eye mask to help you sleep in noisy and poorly curtained hotel rooms, a sheet sleeping bag and pillowcase, a clothes line, a nailbrush (useful for scrubbing dirt off clothes as well as off oneself), a universal plug, a Swiss Army knife, an alarm clock or watch and a torch or headlamp. Remember not to throw away spent batteries containing mercury or cadmium; take them home to be disposed of, or recycled properly. Good clothes are also available in Chile, usually at prices which are half those in Europe or North America.

It's a good idea to travel with pre-moistened wipes (such as Wet Ones) and toilet paper – cheap hotels and restaurants do not supply it. Obviously these, as well as all basic toiletries, are readily available in Chile.

Insurance

It is vital to take out fully comprehensive travel insurance (including medical insurance) for the duration of your stay overseas. Numerous companies offer travel insurance, including many high-street travel agents. As well as full medical insurance (including evacuation by air ambulance where necessary), it is important to check that you are covered for any special activities, as many policies exclude so-called dangerous sports (including, in some cases, trekking). Also, many cases there's a limit of cover per item, so, if you are taking something valuable and want it fully insured, you may need to pay extra.

If you do have the misfortune to be robbed (or even just to lose something), you need to make a report to the police and get a police certificate within 24 hours in order to make a successful claim on your insurance. Be prepared for a bureaucratic nightmare. Police will either want you to make a *denuncia* (complaint), or a *constancia* (report).

Exchange rates

£1 = 1013 pesos
US$1 = 538 pesos
€1 = 684 pesos
(September 2006)

Beware of making a *denuncia* as you will be making a formal request to the police to follow up on the theft. As a consequence of this, if a case eventually comes to court you will be subpoenaed, and by failing to attend the trial you will be breaking the law and may well face serious problems should you visit Chile again. In most cases you should make a *constancia*. However, usually you will be presented with a stamped receipt which has no reference to the items you have reported stolen. The document you really require is called a *certificado*, and it should list all your missing goods. You may find that outside popular tourist areas the local police may not know what the *certificado* is, and you will need to explain your situation to a superior officer. Note also that every policy will have an excess amount, which you will have to pay; this varies. There is no substitute for reading the small print of a policy before signing up to it.

Money

Currency

The unit is the peso, its sign is $. Notes are for 1000, 2000, 5000, 10,000 and 20,000 pesos; coins come in denominations of 1, 5, 10, 50, 100 and 500 pesos. Inflation is low. Official exchange rates for many currencies are quoted in *La Tercera*, and the best rates are to be had in Santiago. Travellers to rural areas should carry supplies of 1000- and 2000-peso notes; higher denominations are difficult to change. This is also good advice when travelling on local transport or when shopping in small stores early in the day. In many cities and towns changing cash and/or traveller's cheques is simpler and quicker at *casas de cambio* than at banks, although exchange rates vary, so shop around.

Exchange

ATMs The easiest way to obtain cash in Chile is by using automatic telling machines (ATMs). These are situated at the major banks and often in other locations, especially in shopping malls, bus stations, at the larger supermarkets and at most Esso petrol stations. You can choose to be guided through the transaction in English. ATMs operate under the sign **Redbanc**; both Cirrus (MasterCard) and Plus (Visa) are accepted for daily transactions of up to US$500. The exception to this is the **Banco del Estado** whose Redbanc machines accept MasterCard but not Visa. A full list of **Redbanc** machines in Chile is listed by town at www.redbanc.cl.

Cash Most major currencies can be readily exchanged in tourist centres, but rates for the US dollar and, increasingly commonly, the euro, remain much better than for any other currency. US dollars and euros are widely accepted by banks, *casas de cambio* (exchange shops) and some hotels, but rarely if ever by shops and other establishments. Outside the larger cities, currencies other than US dollars and euros are rarely accepted. Foreign notes are often scrutinized carefully and rejected if torn or marked in any way. Before changing any currency check whether any commission is charged. If crossing to Argentina take some low-value US dollar bills: the Argentine currency crisis means that the 'greenback' remains widely accepted.

Credit cards Visa and MasterCard are readily accepted but American Express and Diners' Club are less useful. Credit card use does not usually incur a commission or higher charge in Chile. In shops, identification is usually necessary to use credit cards; places accepting Visa and MasterCard usually display a **Redcompra** sticker in the window. In case of loss or theft of your card make sure that you carry the phone numbers necessary to report this; make a photocopy of the numbers and keep them in a safe place. Some travellers have reported problems with their credit cards being frozen by their bank when a charge is incurred in a foreign country. To avoid this problem, notify your bank before departure that you will be making charges in Chile (and other countries, where applicable). To avoid charges from your bank, top up your credit card account with sufficient cash before departure. If you will need to make very expensive one-off purchases, you may want to specify that your daily spending limit should not be applied to the amount by which your account is in credit, although this will prove dangerous if your card is stolen.

Traveller's cheques Exchanging traveller's cheques is possible in most large cities, although the rate will be about 2% lower than for cash. In Santiago, **American Express Bank**, Andrés Bello 2711, piso 9, will change AmEx traveller's cheques to dollars without commission. However, it is generally not advisable to change cash or traveller's cheques in banks as the rate is much worse than at *casas de cambio*.

Transferring money
Before leaving your home country, find out whether any Chilean bank is correspondent to your own bank. Then, when you need funds, arrange for your bank to transfer the money to the local bank (confirming by fax). Be sure to provide the exact details of the SWIFT code of the receiving bank. Funds can be received within 48 banking hours. This is useful for transferring large amounts. Otherwise, money can be sent within minutes (and with a very large commission) through **Western Union** (in Chile operated by Chile Express, www.chilexpress.cl); if collecting money in a city with more than one Western Union agent, you can go to any one of them to receive the money.

Cost of living
The minimum wage in Chile is approximately US$240 per month, while the wage for relatively senior office workers may be around US$750 per month. This is low considering the general cost of living in the country. The cost of accommodation or rent is higher in Santiago than elsewhere – around US$220 per month for a basic two-room unfurnished flat as compared to half that in the provinces. Many office workers eat out for lunch, and you can usually find a basic meal for US$2.50 or US$3. City bus fares are US$0.70 in Santiago, less in the provinces. Someone living in Santiago and earning a reasonable salary (by Chilean standards) will find that they have little spare change at the end of the month; holidays and weekends away are a definite luxury.

Cost of travelling
Prices for food and other consumables tend to rise in proportion to the distance from central Chile (being highest in Punta Arenas), although accommodation is cheaper outside the capital. In Santiago itself, the eastern part of the city, encompassing Vitacura, Las Condes and to a lesser extent Providencia are much more expensive than the rest of the city.

Chile is more expensive than much of South America , and you should budget on a minimum of US$250 per week per person for basic accommodation, food,overland transport and an occasional tour. Cheap accommodation in Santiago costs US$10 per person or more, while north and south of the capital *alojamiento* in private houses (bed, breakfast and often use of the kitchen) costs US$8-15 per person (bargaining is sometimes possible off season). *Colaciones* (a single dish offered at cheaper restaurants at lunchtime) are available for about US$3 in most places. Long-distance bus fares are reasonable (around US$2 plus US$2 per 100 km). Southern Chile is more expensive from 15 December to 15 March. With a budget of US$500 a week, you will be able to stay in nice hotels, eat in smart restaurants and not stint yourself on excursions and nightlife.

Getting there

Air

On long-haul flights, airlines now generally allow one piece of luggage which may not weigh more than 32 kg; you are likely to be charged extra for more. If you know you are over the limit, arrive early. Weight limits for internal flights are usually 30 kg for first class and 20 kg for economy class.

Flights from the UK

Flights from the UK take 16 to 20 hours, including a change of plane. It is impossible to fly directly to Santiago from London, so connections have to be made on one of the following routes: **Aerolíneas Argentinas**, www.aerolineas.com.ar, via Madrid and Buenos Aires, three per week, and direct via Buenos Aires, three per week; **Air France**, www.airfrance.com, via Paris, daily; **British Airways**, www.ba.com, connecting through LanChile in Buenos Aires, daily; **Iberia**, www.iberia.com, via Madrid or Barcelona, daily; **LanChile**, www.lan.com, via Madrid, daily; **Lufthansa**, www.lufthansa.com, code sharing with Swiss International Airlines (www.swis.com), via Frankfurt or Zurich, four or five per week; **Varig**, www.varig.com, via Rio or São Paulo, daily.

Alternatively, there are daily connecting flights on one of the American carriers via New York or Miami (see below).

Flights from North America

Flights from Miami to Santiago take nine hours and are operated by **American Airlines**, www.aa.com, direct from Miami, daily; LanChile direct from Miami, daily. LanChile also has daily flights to Santiago from New York, 12 hours, and from Los Angeles, with connections from Boston, Chicago, Dallas, San Francisco and Washington. **American Airlines** flies from Dallas Fort Worth to Santiago daily, while **Delta**, www.delta.com, connects daily through Atlanta to Santiago. Additional flights from Los Angeles, Miami and New York to Santiago are operated by **Copa** (via Panama City), www.copaair.com. **Taca** (via San José or San Salvador) www.taca.com, and **Aero Mexico** (via Mexico City), www.mexicana.com, have flights from several US cities.

From Canada, **Air Canada**, www.aircanada.com, has the only direct flights, daily from Toronto, connecting from all other major cities. **LanChile** offers connections with sister airlines from Vancouver to Los Angeles and thence to Santiago, or from Toronto to New York and on to Santiago. Both American and Delta also have services via the US.

Flights from Australia and New Zealand

LanChile flies twice a week from Tahiti (connections to Japan, Australia and New Zealand) to Santiago, with a stop at RapaNui/Easter Island. **Qantas**, www.qantas.com, and **LanChile** have a code-sharing agreement on the five weekly flights between Sydney and Santiago via Auckland. There are also several weekly flights from Auckland to Santiago via Buenos Aires with **Aerolíneas Argentinas**.

Flights from the rest of Europe

There are direct flights from many European destinations to Santiago. From Paris with **Air France** (daily); from Madrid with **Iberia** and **LanChile** (each daily) and **Air Madrid**, www.airmadrid.com, three per week (also from Barcelona); from Frankfurt with **Lufthansa** (four or five per week) and **LanChile** (daily); from Lisbon with **Varig** via Rio or São Paulo (daily); from Rome with **Varig** via São Paulo.

Flights from South Africa

From South Africa it is possible to connect to Santiago through Rio de Janeiro or São Paulo on **South African Airways** (twice weekly from Johannesburg). **Varig** also has flights from some African destinations connecting to Santiago through São Paulo, including **Luanda** (Angola), **Maputo** (Mozambique) and **Sal** (Cape Verde).

Flights from other Latin American countries

There are about 75 flights per week to Santiago from Buenos Aires (Argentina), operated by **LanChile**, **Aerolíneas Argentinas**, **Air France**, **American** or **Avianca** (many depart at the same time, check carefully). There are also two daily flights by **LanChile** from Bariloche, Córdoba, Mendoza and Rosario, and summer flights from Ushuaia. **LanChile** and **Pluna** run eight weekly flights from Montevideo (Uruguay). **TAM** has four flights a week from Asunción (Paraguay). Flights from Rio de Janeiro (Brazil) are run by **Iberia** (four weekly), **LanChile** (two daily), or **Varig** (three daily). There are also services from São Paulo by **LanChile** (three non-stop daily), **Varig** (four daily). Flights from La Paz (Bolivia) are offered by **Lloyd Aéreo Bolivian** (www.labairlines.com; five weekly) and daily with **LanChile**. **LAB** also has flights from Cochabamba and Santa Cruz; **LanChile** three a week from Santa Cruz. There are 23 flights per week from Lima (Peru) by **LanPeru**, **TACA** and **LanChile**. (**LanChile** also flies daily from Arequipa, Cuzco, Juliaca and Puerto Maldonado through its sister airline **LanPeru**.) From Ecuador, **LanChile**, **Tame** and **Saeta** fly non-stop from Guayaquil (**Saeta** and **Tame's** flights start in Quito). **Avianca**, **Aeroméxico** and **LanChile** have nine weekly services between them from Bogotá (Colombia). **LanChile** and **Viasa** both have two weekly flights from Caracas (Venezuela). There are also two weekly flights from Havana (Cuba) with **LanChile** and **Cubana**; six flights weekly from Mexico City with **Aeroméxico** and **LanChile** and two weekly from Cancún with **LanChile**.

Flights to other Chilean destinations

There are flights to Arica and Iquique from La Paz and Santa Cruz with **LAB** and **LanChile**. **LanChile** flies to Santiago from Port Stanley on the Falkland Islands (Malvinas) via Punta Arenas. In summer **DAP** flies between Punta Arenas and Ushuaia.

Prices and discounts

The very busy seasons are 7 December to 15 January (until the end of February for flights within South America) and 10 July to 10 September. If you intend travelling during those times, book as far ahead as possible. From February to May and September to November special offers may be available. Fares vary from airline to airline, destination to destination and according to time of year. In the low season it may be possible to get a return flight from London to Santiago for as little as £580 (plus over £100 airport departure taxes), but in the high season this may rise to £800 return. Prices are comparable for flights from the US, but from Australia and New Zealand they may rise to £1000 return or more. Most airlines offer discounted fares of one sort or another on scheduled flights. These are not offered by the airlines direct to the public, but through agencies who specialize in this type of fare. If you buy discounted air tickets always check the reservation with the airline concerned to make sure the flight still exists.

Excursion (return) fares Restricted validity eg seven to 90 days. Most carriers have introduced flexibility into these tickets, permitting a change of dates on payment of a fee.

Yearly fares May be bought on a return basis. Some airlines require a specified return date, changeable upon payment of a fee. If staying for a whole year, you may find that the airline is not yet booking return flights that far ahead; in that case it may be possible to secure one free change of date on your ticket, even if buying through a discount operator. To leave the return completely open is possible for an extra fee. You must fix the route (some of the cheapest flexible fares now have six months' validity). If you foresee returning home at a busy time, such as Christmas or August, a booking is advisable on any type of open return ticket.

Student (or under 26) fares Do not assume that student tickets are the cheapest; though they are often very flexible, they can be more expensive than excursion or yearly fares. Some airlines are flexible on the age limit, others are strict.

Round-the-world fares Many airlines now offer code-sharing round-the-world fares. Although the cheapest ones tend to miss out South America, the Buenos Aires-Wellington and Santiago-Tahiti-Sydney flights mean that, for around £1200, it is possible to include Chile on a round-the-world trip.

Open-jaw fares For people intending to travel a linear route, arriving at and departing from different airports. Open jaws are available as student, yearly or excursion fares. Many require a change of plane at an intermediate point, and a stopover may be permitted, or even obligatory, depending on schedules. Simply because a flight stops at a given airport does not mean you can break your journey there; the airline must have traffic rights to pick up or set down passengers between points A and B before it will be permitted. This is where dealing with a specialized agency (such as **Journey Latin America**) will really pay dividends. On multi-stop itineraries, the specialized agencies can often save clients hundreds of pounds.

Flight agents

In the UK
Just the Ticket, Level 2, 28 Margaret St, London W1W 8RZ, T08700-275076, www.justtheticket.co.uk. All-purpose cheap ticket agency, often with excellent deals.
STA Travel, Priory House, 6 Wrights Lane, London W8 6TA, T08701-630026, www.statravel.co.uk. Good-value youth and student fares.
Trailfinders, 194 Kensington High St, London W8 7RG, T0845-0585858, www.trailfinders.com. Sometimes has good deals to Latin America, especially at peak times. Also at 48 Earl's Court Rd, London W8 6EJ, T020-7938 3366.

Also check out websites such as www.cheapflights.com; www.dialaflight.com; www.ebookers.com; www.flynow.com; and www.lastminute.com.

In North America
Air Brokers International, 323 Geary St, Suite 411, San Francisco, CA 94102, T1-800 883 3273, www.airbrokers.com. Specialist on RTW and Circle Pacific tickets.
Airtech, 588 Broadway, Suite 204, New York, NY 10012, T212-219 7000, www.airtech.com.
Exito Travel, 1212 Broadway Suite 910, Oakland CA 94618, T1-800-6554053 (toll-free), www.exitotravel.com.
STA Travel, 10 Downing St, New York, NY 10014, T1-800-781-4040 (toll-free), www.statravel.com.

Travel CUTS, 234 College St, Toronto, ON
M5T 1P7, T1-866-246 9762 (toll-free),
www.travelcuts.com. Also in many other
Canadian cities.

Online agents include www.expedia.com;
www.priceline.com; www.travelocity.com;
www.cheaptickets.com; and
www.etn.nl/discount.htm.

In Australia and New Zealand
Anywhere Travel, 345 Anzac Parade,
Kingsford, Sydney, T02-96630411,
www.anywheretravel.com.au.
Budget Travel, 600 Hurtsmere Rd,

Takapuna, Box 336620, Auckland,
T09-366-4665.
Destinations Unlimited, 13 Clyde Rd,
PO Box 35-573, Browns Bay, T09-4785042,
www.etravelnz.com.
Flight Centre, 82 Elizabeth St, Sydney, T02-
133133, www.flightcentre.com.au. Also at
350 Queen St, Auckland, T09-3584310, and
in many other antipodean cities.
STA Travel, 702 Harris St, Ultimo, Sydney
T1300-733035, www.statravel.com.au.
Also in other major cities and towns.
Travel.com.au, 80 Clarence St, Sydney,
T130-1300481, www.travel.com.au.

Road and rail

There are good **road** connections between Chile and Argentina, from Santiago and Valparaíso to Mendoza via Los Andes (see page 130), from Osorno and Puerto Montt to Bariloche (see pages 347 and 367) and from Punta Arenas to Río Gallegos (see page 441); there is also a reasonable road from Arica to La Paz in Bolivia (see page 249), and a good road from Arica to Tacna in Peru (see page 249). All of these routes are served by buses. There are less good road connections north and south of Santiago. Note that any of the passes across the Andes to Argentina can be blocked by snow from April onwards (including the main Mendoza crossing, where travellers are occasionally stranded at the border posts). Travelling to or from Argentina anywhere north of Mendoza is likely to be an adventure you will not forget in a hurry.

Chile has international **rail** links from Arica to Tacna and from Calama to Uyuni and Oruro in Bolivia; for further details, see page 216.

Sea

Around 50 cruise ships, operated by the major cruise lines, visit Chilen every summer. Enquiries regarding sea passages to Chile should be made through agencies in your own country. In the UK, try **Strand Voyages** ① *Charing Cross Shopping Concourse, The Strand, London WC2N 4HZ, T020-7836 6363*, or ① **The Cruise People**, *88 York St, London W1H 1DP, T020-7723 2450 (reservations T0800-526313)*. In the USA contact **Freighter World Cruises** ① *180 South Lake Av, Pasadena, CA 91101, T1-818 449 3106, www.freighterworld.com*.

Touching down

Airport information

Aeropuerto Arturo Merino Benítez ① *26 km northwest of Santiago at Pudahuel, international terminal information T02-6901900/6018758, flight information T02-6763149/6763297, www.aeropuertosantiago.cl*, handles both international and domestic flights, and is the only airport in Chile with intercontinental connections. It is a modern, safe and efficient terminal, recently voted the best airport in Latin America

Touching down

Business hours Banks: Monday-Friday 0900-1400. Government offices: Monday-Friday 1000-1230 (the public is admitted for a few hours only). Businesses: Monday-Friday 0830-1230, 1400-1800. Shops (Santiago): Monday-Friday 1030-1930, Saturday 0930-1330.
International dialling code +56.

Official time GMT minus four hours; minus three hours in summer. Clocks change from mid-September or October to early March.
Voltage 220 volts AC, 50 cycles.
Weights and measures The metric system is obligatory but the *quintal* of 46 kg (101.4 lb) is used.

from a sample of 70,000 international businessmen. Domestic and international flights leave from different sections of the same terminal. Procedures at customs (*aduana*) are quick and efficient. Facilities include ATMs accepting both Visa and MasterCard, fast-food outlets, a Sernatur tourist information office which offers an accommodation booking service, a *casa de cambio* for changing money near the baggage reclaim area (poor rates) and several car hire offices. Left luggage is US$8 per item per day (much more expensive than in the city centre) and items can be left for a maximum of 60 days. Outside customs there are kiosks for minibus and taxi companies serving Santiago, as well as car hire companies; you are likely to be approached by people offering taxi and bus services as you emerge from the customs area. ▶▶ *For further details, see Ins and outs, page 72.*

Check-in time for international flights is two hours before departure, one hour for domestic flights. Some airlines will perform check-in at their offices in the city the previous day, after which they require you to be at the airport just 45 minutes before departure. Remember that some airlines require you to reconfirm bookings on international flights 72 hours in advance. Airport **departure tax** is US$18 for international flights; US$8 for domestic flights. There is also a tourist tax of 2% on single air fares and 1% on return fares beginning or ending in Chile, and a sales tax of 5% on all transport within Chile. All these taxes will be included in the price of the ticket when bought by the traveller.

Tourist information

The national secretariat of tourism, **Sernatur** ① *Av Providencia 1550 (Casilla 14082), Santiago, T02-2362420, www.sernatur.cl,* has offices throughout the country (addresses are given throughout this guide). Most of the larger tourist offices around the country are run by Sernatur and can provide town maps, leaflets and other useful information, otherwise contact the head office. **CONAF** (Corporación Nacional Forestal) ① *Presidente Bulnes 291, piso 1, Santiago, T/F02-697-2273, www.conaf.cl,* manages national parks throughout Chile (see box page 61). CONAF's staff are dedicated and knowledgeable, though their offices in the parks themselves are usually much more helpful than the regional head offices. CONAF also publishes a number of leaflets and has documents and maps about the national park system that can be consulted or photocopied in its Santiago office; but these are not very useful for walking. **Ancient Forest International** ① *Box 1850, Redway, CA 95560, T/F707-3233015, USA, www.ancientforests.org,* can be contacted regarding Chilean forests. ▶▶ *For details of other useful organizations and their publications, see also page 560.*

Local customs and laws

Codes of conduct

Politeness – even a little ceremoniousness – is much appreciated in Chile. Men should always remove any headgear and say 'permiso' when entering offices, and be prepared to shake hands; always say 'buenos días' (until midday) or 'buenas tardes' (in the afternoon and evening) and wait for a reply before proceeding further. Remember that the traveller from abroad has enjoyed greater advantages in life than most Chilean minor officials, and should be friendly and courteous in consequence. Never be impatient, and do not criticize situations in public: the officials may know more English than you think (especially when it comes to swearwords) and they can certainly interpret gestures and facial expressions. You should be aware that the stereotype of the corrupt Latin American official does not apply in Chile, where most officials are scrupulously honest.

Politeness should also be extended to street traders; saying 'No, gracias' with a smile is better than an arrogant dismissal. Bargaining is not as commonplace in Chile as in some other South American countries, and very low offers will be seen as contemptuous, even in markets. Begging is rare outside Santiago. Whether you give money to beggars is a personal matter, but locals may provide an indication of whether people are begging out of genuine need. In Santiago, beggars get onto buses and sing or sell tiny religious calendar cards; Santiaguinos are often generous towards them. There are occasions where giving away food in a restaurant may be appropriate, but first inform yourself of local practice.

Dress

Urban Chileans are very fashion conscious. You should dress reasonably smartly in the towns and cities as scruffiness will make things needlessly difficult. People tend to dress smartly at nightclubs in urban centres – Santiago, Viña del Mar, La Serena and Iquique being particularly swish. Away from the cities, though, and in areas where there are many foreign tourists, people are less concerned about such matters.

Tipping

In restaurants 10% is a good tip, but you should only leave about 100 pesos (US$0.15) in bars and *fuentes de soda*. Cloakroom attendants should get about US$0.20. Taxi drivers are not tipped.

Prohibitions and getting out of trouble

There are several types of police operating in Chile: *Carabineros* (green uniforms) handle all tasks except immigration; *Investigaciones* (in civilian dress) are the detectives, and deal with everything except traffic; *Policía Internacional*, a division of the *Investigaciones*, handle immigration and customs.

If you get into trouble with the police, the worst thing that you can do is offer a bribe to get yourself out of trouble. Chilean police are very proud of their office and will assume any attempt to bribe them is both an insult and an admission of guilt. Legal penalties for most offences are fairly similar to what you might expect in a western European or North American country, although be advised that the attitude towards possession of soft drugs, such as cannabis, is very strict. If you get into trouble, your first call should be to your consulate, which should be able to put you in touch with a lawyer who speaks your language.

⦂ How big is your footprint?

1 Where possible choose a destination, tour operator or hotel with a proven ethical and environmental commitment, and if in doubt ask.
2 Spend money on locally produced (rather than imported) goods and services and use common sense when bargaining – your few dollars saved may be a week's salary to others.
3 Consider staying in local-, rather than foreign-owned, accommodation – the economic benefits for host communities are far greater and there are many more opportunities to learn about local culture.
4 Use water and electricity carefully – travellers may receive preferential supply while the needs of local communities are overlooked.
5 Learn about local etiquette and culture – consider local norms and behaviour – and dress appropriately for local cultures and situations.
6 Protect wildlife and other natural resources – don't buy souvenirs or goods made from wildlife unless they are clearly sustainably produced and are not protected under CITES legislation.
7 Always ask before taking photographs or videos of people.

Responsible tourism

Travel to the furthest corners of the globe is now commonplace and the mass movement of people for leisure and business is a major source of foreign exchange and economic development in Chile. Towns such as Puerto Natales, San Pedro de Atacama and Pucón depend almost exclusively on tourism for their livelihoods, while every town south of Temuco is awash with people letting out private rooms in their homes.

The benefits of international travel are self-evident for both hosts and travellers: employment, increased understanding of different cultures, and business and leisure opportunities. At the same time there is clearly a downside to the industry. Where visitor pressure is high and/or poorly regulated, adverse impacts on society and the natural environment may be apparent. This is as true in undeveloped and pristine areas (where culture and the natural environment are less 'prepared' for even small numbers of visitors) as in major resort destinations.

The travel industry is growing rapidly and its impact is becoming increasingly apparent: air travel is clearly implicated in global warming and damage to the ozone layer, while resort location and construction can destroy natural habitats and restrict traditional rights and activities. Although these effects can seem remote and unrelated to an individual trip or holiday, a traveller's attitude and choices can make a big difference to his or her own impact on the region (see box page 41). And, collectively, travellers have a significant role in shaping a more responsible and sustainable industry.

Travel and tourism in a region can also have beneficial effects. Chile's national parks, for example, are part funded by receipts from visitors. Travellers can promote the patronage and protection of important heritage sites through their interest and contributions via entrance and performance fees. They can also support small-scale enterprises by staying in locally run hotels and hostels, eating in local restaurants and by purchasing local goods, supplies and arts and crafts.

In an attempt to promote awareness of responsible tourism, UK organizations such as **Green Globe** (T020-7930 8333, greenglobe@compuserve.com), the **Centre for Environmentally Sustainable Tourism** (CERT; T01268-795772) and **Tourism Concern** (T020-7753 3330, www.tourismconcern.org.uk) now offer advice on destinations and sites that have made certain commitments to conservation and sustainable development. Generally these are larger mainstream destinations and resorts, although efforts are being made to also provide information on smaller operations.

Ecotourism

Ecotourism has expanded astronomically in Chile over the past decade, and is probably the fastest-growing sector of the travel industry today, providing access to a vast range of destinations and activities, from the Atacama to Tierra del Fuego. While the eco-authenticity of some operators needs to be interpreted with care, there is clearly both a huge demand for this type of activity and also significant opportunities for travellers to support worthwhile conservation and social development initiatives. Organizations such as **Tourism Concern** (see above), **Planeta** (www.planeta.com), the **International Eco-Tourism Society** (T001-802-447 2121, www.ecotourism.org) and **Conservation International** (T001-202-429 5660, www.ecotour.org) have begun to develop and/or promote ecotourism projects and their websites are an excellent source of information. Additionally, **Earthwatch** (T01865-311601, www.earthwatch.org) and **Discovery International** (T020-7229 9881, www.discoveryinitiatives.com) offer opportunities to participate directly in scientific and development projects throughout the region.

Safety

While Chileans will delight in building up the prowess of Chilean thieves to nervous visitors, Chile is generally a safe country to visit. Police stations in rural areas very rarely have people in their one cell. Like all major cities, though, Santiago and Valparaíso do have crime problems. Avoid the *poblaciones* (shanty towns) of Santiago – notably Pudahuel and parts of the north (such as Conchalí) – especially if you are travelling alone or have only recently arrived. The following suggestions are particularly applicable in central Santiago, in some of the hills of Valparaíso and in Coquimbo, which has a reputation for theft. ▸▸ *See also Women travellers, page 28.*

Keep valuables out of sight Cameras should be kept in bags when not in use, and expensive watches or jewellery should not be worn. It is best to leave any valuables you don't need in the hotel safe deposit when sightseeing locally. Always keep an inventory of what you have deposited. If you lose valuables, always report to the police and note details of the report for insurance purposes. ▸▸ *See Insurance, page 32.*

Keep all documents and money secure When travelling with all your gear, hide your main cash supply in different places or under your clothes; you may wish to use extra pockets sewn inside shirts and trousers, pockets closed on the outside with a zip or safety pin, moneybelts (best worn under clothes, below the waist rather than around the neck), neck or leg pouches or elasticated support bandages for keeping money and cheques above the elbow or below the knee.

Try not to appear nervous Nervous behaviour is a clear sign to any thief that you are carrying valuables or that you are unsure where you're going. Walking confidently, but without excessive speed, is a sure way of showing that you are at home in a place – even if you are not.

Look out for tricks Petty thieves may employ tricks to distract your attention and separate you from your possessions. One common ruse in large city centres is 'the mustard trick': the victim is sprayed with mustard, ketchup or some other substance, apparently accidentally, and an accomplice offers sympathy and helps to clean your jacket, removing your wallet at the same time.

⁞ Quake, rattle and roll

It is impossible to spend much time in Chile without becoming aware of the fragility of the land beneath your feet. Earth tremors and violent quakes are a part of everyday life, and raising the matter with Chilean friends tends to lead to quick changes of the subject. The most severe earthquake in recent decades occurred in 1960, causing devastation to the Lake District around Valdivia, see box page 336.

Quite apart from the terror of the earthquakes, tremors really are commonplace. These are most often felt at night, owing to the fact that everything is quieter. If sleeping, your first feeling may be that someone is gently shaking your bed and interfering with your dream. The vibrations of crockery and swaying flowers should alert you to the fact that this is something more. Once the tremor has passed, frightened dogs start barking, thought to be because – owing to their more sensitive hearing – they can hear the creaks and groans of the earth below.

While it is likely that visitors passing through the region will experience nothing more sinister than tremors, they should be aware that a severe earthquake is expected in Central Chile at some point in the next 10 to 15 years. There is no way of telling, at the beginning of a tremor, whether it will develop into a full-scale earthquake. If you are unfortunate enough to experience an earthquake, do not panic. Rushing outside into the street leaves you vulnerable to falling masonry and objects such as flower pots. In fact, the safest place to hide really is beneath the lintel of a doorway, as in the old wives' tale.

Don't fight back If you are attacked, remember your assailants may well be armed, so it is better to hand over your valuables rather than risk injury.

Other risks Finally, bear in mind that safety awareness is not just a matter of avoiding theft or violent attack. While Chile is no worse than any other South American country as far as sexually transmitted diseases are concerned, travellers should always practise safe sex.

Getting around

Internal transport is usually straightforward. Most of Chile is linked by one road, the paved **Pan-American Highway** (or Panamericana), marked on maps as Ruta 5, which runs from the Peruvian border south to Puerto Montt and the island of Chiloé. However, some of the most popular destinations in Chile lie to the south of Puerto Montt, and travelling to this part of the country requires careful planning. Though much of this area can be reached by the **Carretera Austral**, a gravel road marked on maps as Ruta 7, bus services here are far less reliable than elsewhere in the country. Furthermore, the Carretera Austral is punctuated by three ferry crossings, with a further crossing at Villa O'Higgins for those on the direct overland route from the Carretera to the far south; the latter is only open in the summer. Alternatives are to travel by sea and air from Puerto Montt. Ferries provide vital links in this region: notably from Chiloé to both Puerto Montt and Chaitén for the Carretera Austral; from Puerto Montt to Puerto Chacabuco (and Coyhaique); and from Puerto Montt to Puerto Natales in the far south.

Air

Travellers with very limited time to spare should consider flying. Air travel can offer fantastic views stretching from the Andes to the sea, but the disadvantage, of course, is that it reduces your knowledge of the bits in between. LanChile (www.lan.com) flies between Santiago and major cities under the banner Lan Express. There are two other main domestic airlines Sky (T600-6002828, www.skyairline.cl) and Aerolíneas del Sur, a subsidiary of Aerolínes Argentinas. Details of useful flights are given throughout the guide.

Check with the airlines for matrimonial, student and other discounts. LanChile has cheap rates for flights bought more than three weeks in advance, and also sells good-value last-minute return flights, published on the internet on Tuesdays, while the best-value one-way tickets are generally with Aerolíneas del Sur. Passengers travelling to Chile with LanChile can obtain reductions on subsequent internal flights (see below). Note that with some fares it may be cheaper to fly long distance than take a *salón cama* bus, and also that flight times may be changed without warning; always double check the time of your flight when reconfirming. You should book several months in advance for flights to Easter Island in January and February.

‼ Confirm domestic flights at least 24 hrs before departure.

LanChile sells a **South America Airpass** which can be used on all LAN routes within South America including 16 Chilean cities and 31 other destinations throughout the continent. The airpass can only be purchased outside South America and in conjunction with a ticket to South America. It is valid for a maximum of six months, and must include a minimum of three single flights. There is no maximum. If bought with a LAN intercontinental flight the domestic single flights cost between US$85 and US$127, while international flights will set you back between US$85 and US$177. Flights to Easter Island cost US$257 each way. If you are using the airpass together with an intercontinental flight with another airline the coupons are about 20% more expensive. Air taxes must be paid in addition for each flight. Reservations should be made well in advance since many flights are fully booked. Route changes and cancellations may be made prior to the flight date on payment of a penalty. ▸▸ *See domestic air routes, page 580.*

‼ For the best views of the Andes sit on the left when flying south and on the right when flying north.

Rail

There are 4470 km of line, of which most are state owned. Most of the privately owned 2130 km of line are in the northern deserts where only two lines, from Arica to Tacna (Peru) and from Calama to Uyuni (Bolivia) carry passengers. The main passenger service south from Santiago runs to Temuco; this journey is more tranquil than travelling by road along the Panamericana, and between Santiago and Chillán it is faster than the bus. During his recent term of office, President Lagos promised to extend the line to its original terminus, Puerto Montt, by 2009, and work is well under way. There are also suburban passenger trains around Santiago and inland from both Concepción and Valparaíso, as well as the scenic line from Talca along the valley of the Río Maule to Constitución (see page 279), and a tourist steam train inland from Valdivia on Sundays in summer.

Trains in Chile are moderately priced, and snacks are available on the main Temuco line. There is a 15% discount on return tickets and a 10% discount for senior citizens aged 60 or over. For further information on all domestic lines, visit www.efe.cl.

⁞ Ticket to ride

The following is intended to provide an idea of single bus fares from Santiago. Fares given are for standard *servicio clásico* to the south and *semi cama* on longer journeys northwards; other services such as *salón cama* and *premium* are more expensive. Lower fares than those shown are often available, especially at the last minute, but much higher fares are charged in summer (January-February) and during the Independence celebrations in September. Prices quoted are in US dollars.

Northbound		Southbound	
Valparaíso	4-6	Talca	5-7
La Serena	10-15	Temuco	10-13
Copiapó	20-25	Pucón	12-15
Antofagasta	33-38	Valdivia	12-16
Iquique	40-45	Puerto Montt	15-20
Arica	45-50	Ancud	20-25
		Chiloé	20-30

Road

About half of the 79,593 km of roads in Chile can be used all year round, though a large proportion is unimproved and only about 15,000 km are paved. Many other roads are described as *ripio*, meaning the surface is unmade gravel and/or stones; speed limits on these roads are usually slower. The region round the capital and the Central Valley has the best road connections. The main road is the Pan-American Highway (Ruta 5; see also page 43), which is now dual carriageway from La Serena to Puerto Montt. This is a toll road; the toll includes towing to the next city and free ambulance in case of an accident. Good toll motorways also link Santiago with Valparaíso and Viña del Mar, and Chillán with Concepción. A paved coastal route running the length of Chile is under construction, and should be completed in time for Chile's bicentenary celebrations in 2010.

Bus

Bus services in Chile are frequent and, on the whole, good. Buses tend to be punctual, arriving and leaving when they say they will. Apart from at holiday times, there is little problem getting a seat on a long-distance bus and there is no need to reserve far in advance out of season. Services are categorized as *salón-cama* meaning 25 seats, *semi-cama* meaning 34 seats and *salón-ejecutivo* or *clásico* meaning 44 seats. There are also *premium* services with seats that fully recline into flat beds. *Premium* and *salón-cama* services run between main cities and stops are infrequent; **TurBus** and **Pullman Bus** have nationwide coverage and are among the best companies.

> ⁞ *Avoid back seats near the toilet due to bad smells and the disruption of passing passengers.*

Since there is lots of competition between bus companies, you may be able to bargain for a lower fare, particularly just before departure, out of season. Prices are highest between December and March, while fares from Santiago double during the Independence celebrations in September. Students with ISIC cards may get discounts, which vary in amount, but these are not usually available in high season; discounts are also often available for return journeys. Most bus companies will carry bicycles, but may ask for payment.

The best way of sending luggage around Chile is by *Encomienda*: your package is taken by bus from terminal to terminal and stored for up to one month at the destination (**TurBus** can deliver to a specified address). This means you can *Encomienda* bags when you don't need them, and pick them up when you do, which is great if you only need camping or cold-weather gear for, say, Torres del Paine .

Car

Documents Always carry your passport and driving licence. According to the Chilean **Ley de Tránsito**, a national driver's licence is acceptable, but *carabineros* may demand an international driver's licence (in the north especially). To avoid problems, obtain one before leaving home. Car drivers require a Chilean *Relaciones de pasajeros* document, available at borders, and the original registration document of their vehicle. Motorcyclists require the bike registration document and are also advised to carry an international *carnet de passages* (see below). In the case of a car registered in someone else's name, carry a notarized letter of authorization.

Taking a vehicle into Chile Officially, if you wish to take a vehicle into South America you must have one of the following three documents, although in practice, none is required: a *carnet de passages* issued by the **Fedération Internationale de l'Automobile** (FIA – Paris); a *carnet de passages* issued by the **Alliance Internationale de Tourisme** (AIT-Geneva), or the *Libreta de Pasos por Aduana* issued by the **Féderación Interamericana de Touring y Automóvil Clubs** (FITAC). The *carnet de passages* is available only in the country where the vehicle is registered. In the UK it can be obtained from the **RAC** and the **AA**. In the USA the **AAA** seems not to issue the carnet, although the organization's headquarters in Washington DC may be able to give advice. It is, however, available from the **Canadian Automobile Association** ① *1775 Courtwood Crescent, Ottawa, K2C 3JZ, T613-2267631, F2257383*.

Buying a vehicle in Chile It is possible to buy a vehicle privately or through a dealer in Chile, although you will be responsible for repairs, maintenance and road taxes. Buying through a dealer may involve a 'buy-back' guarantee. Reports of the efficiency of companies offering this service are mixed. All Chilean cars have to undergo an annual technical revision (*revision técnica*) to ensure road-worthiness; the month when this is due will be shown on a sticker on the windscreen. If your vehicle fails the technical revision you are given one month to carry out repairs. Technical revisions can be carried out in any of the larger cities; it is worth enquiring locally about the best centres as standards vary. If hiring a car, or buying through an agent with buy-back arrangements, check when its technical revision is due and who is responsible for it. In most cases it will be the hire company. Note also that all Chilean car taxes are payable in March each year; again, check who is responsible for paying tax. Failure to keep the tax up to date can lead to trouble with the police.

Car hire Car hire is an increasingly popular way of travelling around Chile, although it tends to reduce your contact with Chileans. Many agencies, both local and international, operate in the country. Note that the **Automóvil Club de Chile** (see below) has a car-hire agency (with discounts for members or affiliates), although the office may not be at the same place as the Club's regional delegation. Vehicles may be rented by the day, the week or the month, usually with unlimited mileage. Rates quoted should include insurance and 19% VAT, but always check first. A small car, with unlimited mileage costs about US$250 a week in high season around Santiago, a pickup much more, but shop around for a deal, as there is plenty of competition. In the Lake District prices are about 50% higher, while in Patagonia they can be double. In some areas rates are much lower off season, while at peak holiday times, eg for the Independence celebrations, car hire is very difficult. Note that a few agencies are unwilling to rent cars to people holding driving licences from countries where cars drive on the left. Holders of (for example) UK driving licences are advised to travel with an international licence. If intending to leave the country in a hired car, you must obtain an authorization from the hire company, otherwise you will be turned back at the frontier. When leaving Chile this is exchanged for a quadruple form, one part of which is surrendered at each border control. If you plan to leave more than once you will need to photocopy the authorization.

Insurance This is obligatory and can be bought at borders. It is very expensive and increasingly difficult to insure against accident, damage or theft. If the car/motorbike is stolen or written off you will be required to pay very high import duty on its value. Get the legal minimum cover, not expensive, as soon as you can, because if you should be involved in an accident and are uninsured, your vehicle could be confiscated. If anyone is hurt, do not pick them up (you may become liable). Seek assistance from the nearest police station or hospital if you are able to do so.

Information and maps Members of foreign motoring organizations may join the **Automóvil Club de Chile** ① *Av Andrés Bello 1863, Santiago, T02-431-1000, www.automovilclub.cl, US$58 for 3 months*, and obtain discounts and roadside assistance. Road maps are available at the Santiago headquarters, or from other regional offices. Several individual maps provide greater detail than the Club's road atlas. Reasonable maps are available from many Copec filling stations, while **Turistel** maps mark police posts; make sure you are not speeding when you pass them, as *carabineros* are strict about speed limits. ▸▸ *For details of other maps, see page 562.*

Fuel Petrol (Benzina) costs about US$1.10 per litre, but becomes more expensive the further north and further south you go. Petrol is unleaded, 93, 95 or 97 octane. Diesel fuel (confusingly known as Petróleo) is widely available and much cheaper. Most service stations accept credit cards, except perhaps those in isolated rural areas, and the standard of facilities is generally good. When driving in the south (on the Carretera Austral particularly) and in the northern desert and altiplano, always top up your fuel tank and carry spare fuel in a steel container; a siphon pipe is also essential for those places where fuel is sold out of the drum. Car hire companies may not have fuel cans and they are not obtainable from service stations, although some supermarkets may stock them.

Preparing a car This is largely a matter of common sense. Obviously any part that is not in first-class condition should be replaced. Tyres need to be hard-wearing and to have tubes, since air plugs are hard to find. Always take spare tubes, an extra spare tyre, spare plugs, fanbelts, radiator hoses and headlamp bulbs. Driving long distances on *ripio* roads usually requires a high-clearance vehicle, and the number of *ripio* roads outside the main cities means that normal street cars are of limited use if heading way off the beaten track, although they should be able to cope with roads designated as *buen ripio*. If you intend to drive on *ripio* roads, especially the Carretera Austral, fit a good windscreen protector. It is also wise to carry a spade, jump leads, tow rope, an air pump, spare fuel (see above), water and a neon light, and to fit tow hooks. In Santiago car parts are available from many shops on Calle 10 de Julio. For car and motorcycle tyres try Calle Serrano 32, Santiago, reported to have the best stock in South America.

Safety and security Chile is much safer than most South American countries, and you need do no more to protect your vehicle than you would at home. Remove all belongings and leave the empty glove compartment open when a car is unattended. Try not to leave a fully laden bike on its own, and always secure your bike with a D-lock or chain. Be sure to note down key numbers and carry spares of the most important ones (but don't keep all spare keys inside the vehicle). Wheels should be secured by locking nuts. Driving at night is not recommended; be especially careful on major roads into and out of cities in the early evening because people tend to cross the highway without warning. Watch out for cyclists without lights at night in rural areas.

Cycling

At first glance a bicycle may not appear to be the most obvious vehicle for a major journey, but given ample time and reasonable energy it is certainly one of the best. It can be ridden, carried by almost every form of transport from an aeroplane to a canoe, and lifted across your shoulders over short distances. Cyclists can be the envy of travellers using more orthodox transport, since they can travel at their own pace, explore more remote regions and meet people who are less commonly in contact with tourists.

Choosing a bicycle A mountain bike is essential. Good-quality mountain bikes (and the cast-iron rule is never to skimp on quality) are incredibly tough and rugged, with low gear ratios for difficult terrain, wide tyres with plenty of tread for good road-holding, cantilever brakes, and a low centre of gravity for improved stability. Although imported spares are available in the larger cities, locally manufactured parts are of a lower quality and rarely last. Buy everything you possibly can before you leave home.

Luggage and equipment Be sure to have a small but comprehensive tool kit, a spare tyre and inner tubes, a puncture repair kit, a set of brake blocks, brake and gear cables and all types of nuts and bolts, at least 12 spokes, a light oil for the chain, tube of waterproof grease, a pump secured by a pump lock, a Blackburn parking block (a most invaluable accessory, cheap and virtually weightless), a cyclometer, a loud bell, and a secure lock and chain. Strong and waterproof front and back panniers are essential, and must be mounted on the strongest racks available. A top bag-cum-rucksack makes a good addition for use on and off the bike. A front bag (or any other bar bag) is good for maps, camera, compass, etc. Waterproof and wind-resistant goretex jacket and overtrousers are invaluable. All equipment and clothes should be packed in plastic bags to give extra protection against dust and rain.

Useful tips Wind, not hills, is the enemy of the cyclist. Try to make the best use of the times of day when there is little; mornings tend to be best but there is no steadfast rule. Take care to avoid dehydration. In northern Chile, where supplies of water are scarce between towns, be sure to carry an ample supply. Give your bicycle a thorough daily check for loose nuts or bolts or bearings, and to see that all parts run smoothly. A good chain should last 3000 km or more but be sure to keep it as clean as possible and to oil it lightly from time to time. Most towns have a bicycle shop of some description, but it is best to do your own repairs and adjustments whenever possible. Most cyclists agree that the main danger comes from other traffic. A rearview mirror has been frequently recommended to forewarn you of vehicles which are too close behind. Make yourself conspicuous by wearing bright clothing. Wearing a helmet is a legal requirement. Several good handbooks on long-distance cycle touring are available in larger bookshops. In the UK there is also the **Cyclist's Touring Club** (CTC) ① *Cotterell House, 69 Meadrow, Godalming, Surrey, GU7 3HS, T0870-8700060, cycling@ctc.org.uk*, for touring and technical information.

Hitchhiking

Hitchhiking in Chile is relatively easy and safe, and when a lift does come along it is often in the shape of an exhilarating open-air ride in the back of a pickup truck. However, in some regions – especially in the south – traffic is sparse, and roads in places like Tierra del Fuego rarely see more than two or three vehicles per day. Drivers will sometimes make hand-signals if they are only going a short distance beyond – this is not a rude gesture.

Motorbike

The bike should be off-road capable. Fit heavy duty front fork springs and the best quality rebuildable shock absorber you can afford. Fit lockable luggage or make some detachable aluminium panniers. Fit a tank bag and tank panniers for better weight distribution. A large capacity fuel tank is essential if going off the beaten track. A washable air filter is a good idea, also fuel filters, fueltap rubber seals and smaller jets for high altitude Andean motoring. A good set of trails-type tyres as well as a high mudguard are useful. If riding a chain driven bike, a fully enclosed chaincase is useful. A hefty bash plate/sump guard is invaluable.

Take oil filters, fork and shock seals, tubes, a good manual, spare cables (taped into position), a plug cap and spare plug lead. A spare electronic ignition is a good idea. A first-class tool kit is a must and, if riding a bike with a chain, then a spare set of sprockets and an 'o' ring chain should be carried. Spare brake and clutch levers should also be taken as these break easily in a fall. Recommended mechanics are given throughout the guide. You should wear a tough waterproof jacket, comfortable strong boots, gloves and a good helmet. If you're going to camp, take the best-quality tent and camping gear that you can afford and a petrol stove that runs on bike fuel.

▶▶ *For further details, see the Car section page 46.*

Taxis and colectivos

Taxis usually have meters and can be engaged either in the street or by phoning, though they tend to be more expensive when booked from a hotel. A minimum fare is shown on a large sticker in the windscreen, with increments (usually per 200 m or 60 seconds) below. A surcharge (typically around 50%) is applied after 2100 and on Sunday. Agree beforehand on fares for long journeys out of city centres or for special excursions; also compare prices among several drivers for this sort of trip. There is no need to give a tip unless some extra service is performed. Bear in mind that taxi drivers may not know the location of streets away from city centres.

Colectivos (collective taxis) operate on fixed routes (identified by numbers and destinations) and are a good way of getting around cities. They are usually flagged down on the street corner, although in some cities such as Puerto Montt there are signs. The fixed charges are normally advertised in the front windscreen and increase at night and weekends. It is best to use small denominations when paying, as the driver takes the money and offers change while driving along. Yellow *colectivos* also operate on some interurban routes (especially in the north), leaving from a set point when full. On interurban routes they compete favourably with buses for speed but not for comfort.

Sea

In the south of Chile, maritime transport is very important. Vital routes are, from north to south: Puerto Montt to Chiloé (many daily); Puerto Montt to Chaitén (several weekly in summer) and Puerto Chacabuco (weekly); Puerto Montt to Puerto Natales (weekly in summer); Castro or Quellón to Chaitén (several weekly in summer, fewer in winter); Castro to Puerto Chacabuco (once weekly); Punta Arenas to Porvenir (five times weekly); Punta Arenas to Puerto Williams (twice monthly).

The main operators are **Transmarchilay**, **Navimag** and **Catamaranes del Sur**. Reservations are essential for the ferries in high summer. Details of all routes and booking information are given under the relevant chapters. Note that routes and timetables change frequently.

Maps

A good map of **Santiago** is the *Plano de Santiago*, published annually by **Publiguías** ①*Av Santa María 0792, Providencia, Santiago*; this contains sectional maps of the city and a street index. Maps of Santiago are also available at kiosks in the capital. Maps of the major tourist and trekking areas are published by **Matasi**, and are sold locally at newspaper kiosks and good bookshops. However, they do contain the odd error which can be rather serious if you are stuck off the beaten path. Two good trekking maps for central Chile can be ordered from www.trekkingchile.com.

Geophysical and topographical maps (US$14) are available from **Instituto Geográfico Militar** ① *Dieciocho 369, T02-6987278, Mar-Dec Mon-Fri 0900-1800; Jan and Feb Mon-Fri 0800-1400*. The **Instituto Geográfico** has published a *Guía Caminera*, with roads and city plans (not 100% accurate). It is only available at IGM offices, although the **Biblioteca Nacional** in Santiago has an excellent collection of IGM maps, sections of which can be photocopied. The **Turistel** guidebooks contain good general maps (see page 562). Turistel also publish an annual road map, as do COPEC service stations.

Stanfords ① *12-14 Long Acre, Covent Garden, London, WC2E 9LP, T020-7836 1321, www.stanfords.co.uk*, with over 80 well-travelled staff and 40,000 titles in stock, is the world's largest map and travel bookshop. It also has branches at 29 Corn Street, Bristol, BS1, and at 39 Spring Gardens, Manchester, M2.

Sleeping

Chile is still relatively behind the times with accommodation, so the swisher hotels are often part of uninspiring international chains, while the 'historic' hotels are often run down. Some characterful B&Bs are cropping up, but there are hardly any places that make you think 'wow!'. In most parts of Chile, however, accommodation is plentiful and finding a room to suit your budget should be easy. During the summer holiday months of January and February, rooms can be more scarce – especially in upmarket hotels in the more popular holiday venues of the south. This is also true during Easter, and at the time of the Independence Day holidays in mid-September. Even so, you should rarely have a problem in getting a roof over your head. In larger cities, the cheapest and often the nastiest hotels tend to be situated around bus terminals. If you arrive late and are just passing through, they may be OK, but better quality accommodation is often to be found near the main plaza.

Types of accommodation

The term **hotel** implies an expensive establishment in the south (but not in the north). Top-class hotels are available in Santiago and major cities, but elsewhere choice is more limited. **Hosterías** tend to be in rural areas and may have many of the facilities of a hotel, while the terms **hostal**, **residencial** and **hospedaje** usually refer to a small family-run establishment with limited facilities and services. A **motel**, especially if it is situated on the outskirts of a city, is likely to rent rooms by the hour. In the south, many families offer bed and breakfast, which may be advertised by a sign in the window. People here often meet buses to offer rooms, but the quality is variable.

Backpackers should consult www.backpackerschile.com and www.backpackers best.cl for information on suitable accommodation around the country. The former focuses on hostels charging around US$15 per person and are all of a good standard, while the latter features lots of hostels in a broad price range. For people who want to learn Spanish while they travel, a group of hostels offer the same syllabus in different parts of the country; consult www.spanish-for-travellers.com for further details.

⦂ Hotel price codes explained

LL US$150 and above Top-of-the-range hotels with all amenities, mainly in Santiago.

L US$100-150 Very luxurious business-style hotels.

AL US$66-99 Good city or resort hotels, sometimes with gym, pool and restaurant.

A US$46-65 Upper-range hotels with most facilities in minor cities and smaller resorts.

B US$31-45 Mid-range hotels with mod cons, private bathrooms and TV.

C US$21-30 Comfortable small hotels with few luxuries but decent facilities.

D US$16-20 Basic *hospedajes* in small towns.

E US$12-15 Generally single rooms in decent *hospedajes*.

F US$7-11 Price per person in shared rooms or singles in simple *hospedajes*.

G USS$6 and under Price per person in remote *hospedajes*.

Essentials Sleeping

Camping → Turistel publishes an annual guide, listing campsites.

Camping is not always cheap at official sites. A common practice is to charge US$12 or more for up to five people, with no reductions for fewer than five; however, if a site is not full, owners will often give a pitch to a single person for around US$6. A few hostels (indicated in the text) allow camping in their garden and offer very good value per person rates. **Camping Gaz International** stoves are recommended, since green replaceable cylinders are available throughout the country (white gas – *benzina blanca* – is available in hardware shops; for good value try the **Sodimac** or **Easy** chains of DIY stores). Cheap gas stoves can be bought in camping shops in Santiago and popular trekking areas. Campsites are very busy in January and February.

Camping wild is easy and safe in remote areas of the far south and in the *cordillera* north of Santiago. However, in much of central and central-southern Chile the land is fenced off, and it is often necessary to ask permission to camp. In Mapuche and Aymará communities it is both courteous and advisable to make for the primary school or some other focal point of a village to meet prominent members of the community first. Camping wild in the north is difficult, because of the absence of water. Note that officially it is illegal to camp on private land without permission.

Albergues (youth hostels)

Albergues spring up in summer all over the south of Chile. These are usually schools earning extra money by renting out floor space. They are very cheap (rarely more than US$6 per person) and are excellent places to meet young Chileans. Do not go to them if you want a good night's sleep, though; guitars often play on into the small hours. There is no need for an International Hostelling card to stay in *albergues*, but there is rarely much in the way of security either.

Official youth hostels throughout Chile cost about US$10-20 per person. The Hostelling International card (US$30) is usually readily accepted, but as an alternative you can obtain a Chilean YHA card (US$5) from the **Asociación Chilena de Albergues Turísticos Juveniles** (ACHATJ) ① *Hernando de Aguirre 201, Oficina 602, T02-4112050, www.hostelling.cl*, together with a guidebook of all youth hostels in Chile, *Guía Turística de los Albergues Juveniles*. In practice, HI hostels in Chile, while generally decent, are not necessarily better than any other hostel. Better value can often be had elsewhere.

Accommodation is more expensive in Santiago than in most other parts of the country, although prices also tend to be higher in Patagonia, as well as in some northern cities such as Antofagasta. In tourist areas, prices rise in the high season (January/February, plus any local festivity), but off season you can often bargain for a lower price, though you will usually have to stay for two or more days to be successful; ask politely for a discount (*descuento*). Single travellers do not come off too badly in Chile compared to some other Latin American countries. In the south, *hospedajes* charge per person (although you may have to share your room), while in the north, single rooms are about 60-70% the price of a double.

Value Added Tax (known as **IVA**) at 19% is charged on hotel bills and should be included in any price quoted in pesos. The government waives the VAT charge for hotel bills paid in dollars (cash or traveller's cheques) but only for hotels that have an agreement (*convenio*) with the government. As a result, larger hotels (but few other establishments) can offer you much lower tariffs if you pay in dollars than those advertised in pesos. However, they will often have such a poor dollar exchange rate that you can end up paying more in dollars than in pesos. Ask for prices in both currencies and see which is cheaper. Establish clearly in advance what is included in the price.

Rooms and facilities

Many hotels, but few budget places, have restaurants serving lunch and dinner. Most *hospedajes* offer breakfast, which usually consists of instant coffee or tea with bread and jam; but in the north, fewer hotels offer breakfast. An increasing number of cheaper establishments have kitchen facilities for guest use, but if you are relying on these you should check them out first. Most establishments will not allow you to wash and dry clothes in your room, but some offer facilities for you to do your own laundry. Many hotels have parking facilities, though in large cities this may be a few blocks from the hotel itself. Motorcycle parking is widely available.

Reception areas in hotels can be very misleading, so it is a very good idea to see the room before booking. If you are shown a dark room without a window, ask if there are rooms with windows (*con ventana*). In large cities the choice may be between an inside room without a window and a room with a window over a noisy street. Many middle-range establishments have rooms with private bathroom (*con baño privado*) and without (*con baño compartido*) so it is often worth asking whether there is anything cheaper than the price initially quoted. If you are not satisfied, do not be afraid of walking away and trying elsewhere.

Many hotels, restaurants and bars have inadequate water supplies. Without exception used toilet paper should not be flushed down the pan, but placed in the receptacle provided. This applies even in expensive hotels. Failure to observe this custom will block the pan or drain, causing a considerable health risk. Remember to carry toilet paper with you, as cheaper establishments as well as restaurants, bars, etc, frequently do not supply it.

Eating

Chile's cuisine is varied and often delicious. The Mediterranean climate of the central regions is perfect for growing a wide variety of fruit and vegetables – avocados are especially delicious. The semi-tropical climate of northern Chile supplies mangoes, papayas, *lúcumas* and *chirimoyas* (custard apples). In the central valley, grapes, melons and watermelons abound. The lush grasslands of the south are ideal for dairy and beef farming as well as for growing grains, apples, cherries and plums, while in Patagonia, sheep roam the plains and rhubarb grows wild.

⋮ Restaurant price codes explained

🍴🍴🍴 Elegant and/or fashionable restaurants. Mostly Mediterranean or other international cuisine. Many, but not all, will have a decent wine list. US$10 and over for a main dish or set meal.
🍴🍴 Slightly more upmarket fish and

meat restaurants. Variable decor, from tasteful and intimate to plastic chairs and tables. US$5-10 for a main dish or set meal.
🍴 Usually basic Chilean fare, no frills but hearty meals. Under US$5 for a main dish or set meal

Although Chilean cuisine is mostly rooted in the Spanish tradition, it has also been influenced by the immigrant groups who have settled in the country. The pastry-making skills of the Germans have produced '*onces Alemanas*', a kind of high tea with *Küchen*. *Pan de Pascua*, a traditional Christmas fruit loaf, also derives from Germany.

The main meals are breakfast (*desayuno*), lunch (*almuerzo*) and dinner (*cena*). Lunch is eaten any time from 1300 to 1530, and dinner between 2000 and 2230. *Las onces* (literally elevenses) is the name given to a snack usually including tea. In cafés and restaurants this is served at around 1700 but many Chileans also call their evening meal *once*. Breakfast usually consists of bread, butter and jam, served with coffee or tea. Lunch tends to be the main meal of the day, and many restaurants serve a cheaper fixed-price meal at lunch time; when this consists of a single dish it is known as *la colación*, whereas if there is more than one course it is called *el menú*. In more expensive places, this may not be referred to on the menu. ▸▸ *For simple vocabulary related to food and drink, see page 564.*

Food

Seafood

Perhaps the most outstanding ingredient is the seafood. Although there are good fish restaurants in Santiago, and fine seafood can be found at the Mercado Central, naturally the best seafood and fish is found on the coast. The excellent fish restaurants between Playa Ancha and **Concón**, near Valparaíso, are especially popular with Santiaguinos. Almost every port on the Chilean coast has a small market or a row of seafood restaurants where excellent seafood can be eaten very cheaply; in smaller harbours, it is often possible to eat with the fishermen. Most of these seafood restaurants receive their supplies of fish and shellfish from local fishing boats which land their catch every morning in the harbours. Watching the unloading at a port such as **Talcahuano** can be fascinating. If you have the courage to bargain you may be able to pick up some delicious, fresh fish from the boats or from the stalls along the harbour; whole crates of shellfish go for the equivalent of a few dollars.

In the north, great seafood can be had at **Caleta Hornos**, north of La Serena, and at **Huasco**. In the centre and south the best seafood is to be had at Valparaíso, **Constitución**, Talcahuano, **Angelmó** (Puerto Montt) and on **Chiloé**, where you should try the famous *curanto*, a stew of shellfish, pork, chicken and other ingredients. Beware of eating seafood that you have bought unofficially in the far south because of the poisonous *marea roja* (see page 444).

The most popular fish are *merluza* (a species of hake inferior to European hake), *congrio* (kingclip or ling), *corvina* (bass), *reineta* (a type of bream), *lenguado* (a large kind of sole), *albacora* (sword fish) and *salmón*. *Merluza*, which is usually fried, is an inexpensive fish, found in ordinary restaurants. *Congrio* is very popular, and particularly delicious served as *caldillo de congrio*, a soup containing a large *congrio* steak. *Albacora* is a delicious fish, available mainly in quality restaurants. *Ceviche*, fish marinated in lemon juice, is usually made with *corvina*.

There is an almost bewildering array of shellfish. Look out for *choritos*, *cholgas* and *choros maltón* (varieties of mussel), *ostiones* (queen scallops), *ostras* (oysters) and *erizos* (sea urchins). Prawns are known as *camarones*, but these are often imported from Ecuador and can be tasteless and expensive. Chile's most characteristic products are the delicious *erizos*, *machas*, *picorocos* and *locos*, which are only found in these seas. *Machas a la parmesana* are a kind of razor clam prepared in their shells with a parmesan cheese sauce, grilled and served as a starter, or as a canapé with *pisco sour*. *Picorocos* (giant barnacles), which are normally boiled or steamed in white wine, are grotesque to look at but have a very intense taste: it may be very disconcerting to be presented with a plate containing a rock with feathery fins but it is well worth taking up the challenge of eating it. Note, only the white fleshy part is edible. *Locos*, a kind of abalone, are the most popular Chilean mollusc, but because of overexploitation its fishing is frequently banned. This situation has led to an extensive illegal trade, both nationally and internationally, with *locos* being exported illegally to parts of Asia (especially Japan). The main crustaceans are *jaiba* (crab), *langosta* (lobster) and the local *centolla*, an exquisite king crab from the waters of the south.

Packages of dried seaweed, particularly *cochayuyo* (which looks like a leathery thong), are sold along coastal roads. Both *cochayuyo* and *luche* are made into a cheap, nutritious stew with vegetables, and eaten with potatoes or rice; these dishes are rarely available in restaurants. Until recently salmon was available only in the south where the rivers and lakes are full of 'wild' salmon that has escaped from farms. It is now farmed extensively in the south and can be found on menus in many parts of the country.

Other specialities

Away from seafood, savoury Chilean dishes tend to be creative. Specialities include *humitas* (mashed sweetcorn mixed with butter and spices and baked in sweetcorn leaves), *pastel de papas* (meat pie covered with mashed potatoes), and *cazuela*, either *de ave* (chicken) or *de vacuno* (beef); it's a nutritious stew with pumpkin, potato, coriander and rice, and maybe onions and green peppers – the most common everyday dish. In central and southern Chile stews with beans (*porotos*) are common. A typical (and unhealthy) dish from Valparaíso is the *chorillana*: chips covered with sliced steak, fried onions and scrambled eggs. *Valdiviano* is another stew, common in the south, with beef, onion, sliced potatoes and eggs. *Pastel de choclo* is a casserole of meat and onions with olives, topped with polenta, baked in an earthenware bowl. *Prieta* is a blood sausage stuffed with cabbage leaves. *Bife* or *lomo a lo pobre* (a poor man's steak) is just the opposite: it is a steak topped by two fried eggs, chips, onions and salad. A *paila* can take many forms (the *paila* is simply a kind of serving dish), but the commonest are made of eggs or seafood. In the north, *paila de huevos* (two fried eggs with an *hallulla* – a kind of bread) is common for breakfast. *Paila chonchi* is a kind of bouillabaisse, while a *paila marina* is a delicious shellfish stew.

Chileans tend to have a very sweet tooth, and their **desserts** can be full of *manjar* (caramelized condensed milk).

Snacks

Among the many snacks sold in Chile, the most famous are **empanadas**, pastry turnovers made *de pino* (with meat, onions, egg and an olive), *queso* (cheese) or *mariscos* (shellfish). The quality of *empanadas* varies: many are full of onions rather than meat; by the coast the *empanadas de mariscos* are delicious and usually better value.

Chilean sandwiches tend to be fairly substantial: the *churrasco* is a minute steak in a bun with and can be ordered with any variety of fillings. *Chacareros* contain thinly sliced steak and salad; *barros lucos* have steak and grilled cheese; and *barros jarpas* have grilled cheese and ham.

⦂ Pisco sour

What is important in making *pisco sour* is the balance between the ingredients; once the mixing is done you can add extra sugar, *pisco* or lemon to taste. The egg white is purely for presentation. Most Chileans have their own recipe for this famous drink.

Ingredients Half a litre of decent *pisco*; 250 ml lemon juice (use one or two limes for extra flavour); a handful of ice cubes; 150g icing sugar; a dash of egg white.

Method Put all the ingredients except the ice in liquidizer and mix for a few seconds, until the sugar is well dissolved, then add the ice and mix some more. You may use water instead of ice but you will need to chill the final mixture. For an extra kick add a drop of angostura bitters to each full glass.

Completos are the cheapest and most popular snacks: betraying the German influence on everyday food, these are hot dogs served with plenty of extras, including mustard, sauerkraut, tomatoes, mayonnaise and *ají* (chilli sauce). An *Italiano* is a *completo* with avocado and without the sauerkraut. Avocado is very popular at family *onces*, mashed up and served on bread. Bread itself is plentiful and cheap, and comes in pairs of fluffy rolls (*maraquetas*) or as a crisper slim roll (*hallullas*). Most large cities have many ice cream stands doing a roaring trade.

Drink

Coffee and tea While Argentine cafés have excellent real coffee, if you ask for **coffee** in many places in Chile you will get a cup of boiling water and a tin of instant coffee, even in quite high-class restaurants. There are espresso bars in major cities, elsewhere specify *café-café, espresso*. A *cortado* is an expresso with hot frothed milk served in a glass. **Tea** is usually served with neither milk nor lemon. If you order *café*, or *té, con leche'*, it will come with all milk; to have just a little milk ask for your tea or coffee '*con un poco de leche'*. After a meal, instead of coffee, try an *agüita* – hot water in which herbs such as mint, or aromatics such as lemon peel, have been steeped. A wide variety of refreshing herbal teas is available in sachets.

Wine The international reputation of Chilean wine continues to grow every year. The last 20 years have seen radical modernization and innovation in production techniques and processes putting Chile firmly on the world wine map. Chilean reds tend to be full bodied with lots of tannins and high alcohol content. Production centres around the great Bordeaux grapes, Cabernet Sauvignon, Merlot and Chilean wine's latest claim to fame, the lost Carmenère grape, wiped out in France over a century ago and rediscovered in Chile a decade ago. Pinot Noir is also now being successfully produced. Chilean whites are also getting better every year. Sauvignon Blancs from Casablanca and San Antonio tend to be crisp and fruity and are excellent when drunk young, while the Chardonnays have been winning awards for years. The very best wines can sell for upwards of US$30 a bottle, while a good reserve wine might set you back around US$10. Anything over US$3 should be perfectly drinkable, and even cheaper wine sold in tetrapacks (US$2 to US$2.50 a litre) can sometimes be surprisingly good. Anything cheaper than this should be avoided. ➤➤ *For more on wine, see page 558.*

Beer The emergence in recent years of several small independent breweries means that Chilean beer is no longer as bland as it used to be, and makes a fresh change from the previous situation whereby CCU, the country's largest brewery had bought out the regional competition one by one and either discontinued or standardized their beers. Chile's best-selling beer is the rather insipid *Cristal*. *Escudo* is slightly more full bodied, while *Royal Guard* has a more flowery flavour. *Austral* brewed in Patagonia is good, but mediocre elsewhere. *Baltica* is good, stong and cheap. *Heineken* and *Brahma* are also good, but *Dorada* is best left for the drunks. *Kunstmann* is the best of the nationwide beers. *Malta*, a dark beer, is recommended for those wanting a British-type beer; however, there are different breweries, and the *Malta* north of Temuco is more bitter than that to the south. Of the regional beers, *Cerveza del Puerto* (Valparaíso), *HBH* and *Capital* (Santiago), *Kross* (Buín), *Los Colonos* (Llanquihue) and *Imperial* (Punta Arenas) are all recommended. European beers are increasingly available. A refundable deposit is required for litre beer bottles (about US$0.50). Disposable bottles are sold, but these are more expensive, as are cans and smaller bottles. Draught lager is generically known as *Schop*.

Pisco and other spirits The most famous spirit is *pisco*, made with grapes, usually drunk with lemon or lime juice as *pisco sour* (see box page 55). *Pisco* is also often mixed with coca cola or sprite. *Pisco* is graded in strength from 30-46°; surprisingly, the stronger versions are much more pleasant and easy to drink, as they have generally had more time to mature in the barrel. Recommended brands of *pisco* are *Alto del Carmen* and *Gabriela Mistral*; avoid the ironically named *Pisco Control*, especially at 30°C. Reasonably good *anís* and crème de menthe are all bottled in Chile, and good gin is also produced. Local rum and brandy are very cheap and tend to lead to poisonous hangovers. *Manzanilla* is a local liqueur, made from *licor de oro* (like Galliano); *crema de cacao*, especially Mitjans, has been recommended. Two delicious drinks are *vaina*, a mixture of brandy, egg and sugar and *cola de mono*, a mixture of *aguardiente*, coffee, milk and vanilla served very cold at Christmas. There are many seasonal fruit liqueurs which are delicious; *eguindado*, made from cherries, is particularly recommended. *Chicha* is any form of alcoholic drink made from fruit; *chicha cocida* is three-day-old fermented grape juice boiled to reduce its volume and then bottled with a tablespoonful of honey, while *chicha fresca* is fresh fermented grape juice. Cider (*chicha de manzana*) is popular in the south.

Other drinks Away from alcoholic drinks, Chile does not perhaps take as much advantage of its variety of fruits as it should. Unlike in Mexico, say, cheap and freshly squeezed juices are uncommon, though of course there is nothing to stop you buying a job lot of fruit from the market and preparing juices for yourself. Note that a *jugo natural* is fresh fruit liquidized with water and sugar added. If you want a 100% pure fresh juice you should ask for a *vitamina*. *Mote con huesillo*, made from wheat hominy and dried peaches, is very refreshing in summer. Families tend to drink a lot of sugary soft drinks, picking up on the usual international brands.

Eating out

Fashionable Chilean society has seen something of a gastronomic boom over the last few years. An increasing number of boutique restaurants have been opening in Santiago (and to a lesser extent in other major cities). Typically, with upper class Chile's insecurity with its own identity they almost all shun Chilean food in favour of the flavour of the month, whether it be sushi or 'ethnic fusion'. Many of these are clichéed copies of northern hemisphere new cuisine. Occasionally there are new restaurants that try to fuse uniquely Chilean ingredients with international styles and these are worth looking out for. The older established elegant restaurants rarely offer typical Chilean food either, tending to stick to Mediterranean fare.

The focal point for life in towns is the plaza, in which there will typically be a number of slightly upmarket cafés, where people tend to have a beer and snacks, but rarely go for a full meal. If you are travelling in small villages off the beaten track, it is usually possible to find someone who will cook for you; ask around. Those on a budget will want to stick to the cheaper eateries, where simple and very tasty meals can be had at a very reasonable price; a *colación* need not cost you more than US$3. The cheapest restaurants in urban areas tend to be by the transport terminals and markets or, in coastal areas, by the port. These restaurants may well have a wide choice of food for very reasonable prices, and often there is very little difference in the quality of the food between cheaper and more expensive places, the main differences being the service and the elegance (or pretensions) of the surroundings. More expensive places will, though, have a wider range of starters and desserts, which are often non-existent in cheaper eateries. Among the cheaper eating places are the *casinos de bomberos* (firemen's canteens) in most towns. Fire stations are not paid for by the state, and firemen are all voluntary. Eating at a canteen helps fund their work, and the food is usually cheap and good.

> ‡ *When ordering from the menu note that vegetables, other than potatoes, are not usually included in the price.*

Although there are **vegetarian restaurants** in major cities, vegetarians will find that their choice of food is severely restricted, especially in smaller towns and away from tourist areas. To confuse matters, '*carne*' is understood to mean red meat, so asking if a dish has meat in it is likely to lead to disaster; or chicken, at the very least. Vegetarians should explain which foods they cannot eat rather than saying '*Soy vegetariano*' (I'm a vegetarian) or '*No como carne*' ('I don't eat meat'). To make matters worse, the bread known as *hallulas* is often made with lard (*manteca*); ask first. There are fewer problems for vegetarians if they can cook for themselves, and they may be best off looking for accommodation which has cooking facilities.

Entertainment

Bars and clubs

Nightlife in Chile varies enormously depending on where you are. Santiago and other university towns as well as major tourist resorts have a thriving nightlife. In the latter case bars may get busy at around 2000 or 2100, whereas in major cities nightlife rarely gets going before midnight. Bohemian nightlife in Santiago centres around Barrio Bellavista, below Cerro San Cristóbal, where you can listen to anything from 1980s pop to salsa, jazz or the latest fashions in both Latin and European music, and the streets are crowded with night birds until after 0500 in the morning. Valparaíso has become a centre for the Electronic music scene and in summer there are several events. Most villages of any size will have a disco open at weekends and at least one bar, although invariably this will be populated by no more than two old drunks sharing a tetrapack of cheap wine. There is quite a severe alcoholism problem, especially on Chiloé and in the far south. There are numerous bars in every town, and often many bars even in small villages.

Cinema

With the expansion of mall culture in Chile most of the larger cities are home to multiplex cinemas. These generally show Hollywood blockbusters and the occasional South American film. Prices are usually cheaper on weekday afternoons, and student discounts are common. Santiago has a thriving arts cinema scene and there are several repertory cinemas in the capital. Outside the capital there is an arts cinema in Viña and another in Valparaíso, where there are also several film clubs with several screenings a week. Many universities throughout the country also show films. In summer there are important film festivals in Santiago, Valparaíso, Viña del Mar and Valdivia.

Dance

There are occasional performances by both Chilean and visiting groups in the capital and other culturally important cities such as Valparaíso.

Music

Concerts are common, especially in summer. Each year there are always two or three Superstars (in 2006 for example U2) who play the national stadium. The music festival in Viña also occasionally attracts rising stars. Other than that, there are several Chilean rock, pop and folk groups who are seemingly constantly on tour throughout the country. Chileans are very musical and if you go to a party in someone's house do not be surprised if someone pulls out a guitar for everyone to sing along to classic pop and folk songs.

Classical concerts are less prevalent, with Santiago naturally being the focus. In the provinces there are a few good chamber orchestras, and in summer there is a good classical festival in Frutillar as well as a series of concerts in Viña del Mar.

Theatre

Santiago is definitely the hub of Chile's theatre culture. There are dozens of small theatres showing both classic and contemporary works. Booking is best done in advance, but unless an internationally renowned group is performing, a day or two should suffice.

Festivals and events

Festivals

Festivals are held in all of Chiloé's towns, rotating from week to week, Jan and Feb (see page 376).

Fiesta de la Piedra Santa Mapuche festival of the Holy Stone in the Lake District, 20 Jan (see page 295).

Fiesta de la Candelaria One of northern Chile's most important religious festivals, first Sun in Feb (see page 186).

Festival de la Canción Viña del Mar hosts the dreaded (and often dreadful) international music festival, Feb (see page 145).

Campeonato Nacional de Rodeo National rodeo competition in Rancagua (see page 272).

Fiesta de San Pedro Processions, dancing and lots of fish eating in all coastal towns and villages in celebration of the patron saint of fishermen.

La Tirana This festival near Iquique, celebrating the Virgin del Carmen, is an exhilarating combination of indigenous and Catholic folklore, attended by people from all over Chile and from neighbouring Bolivia and Peru, 16 Jul (see page 238).

La Pampilla The week-long independence celebrations in Coquimbo are the biggest in the country, 13-20 Sep (see page 175).

Fiesta de la Virgen de Lo Vásquez The main Santiago-Valparaíso highway is closed as 80,000 faithful make the pilgrimage on foot (and sometimes even on hands and knees) to the church at Lo Vásquez.

Día de la Virgen Pilgrimage to Quinchao, off Chiloé, 8 Dec (see page 386).

Fiesta Grande Vast pilgrimage to Andacollo, 23-27 Dec (see page 162). Most towns in the south of Chile have a week of festivities in January or February.

Public holidays

New Year's Day 1 Jan
Easter 2 days in Mar/Apr
Labour Day 1 May
Navy Day 21 May
Assumption 15 Aug
Day of National Unity 1st Mon in Sep
Independence 18, 19 Sep
Columbus Day 12 Oct
All Saints' Day 1 Nov
Immaculate Conception 8 Dec
Christmas Day 25 Dec

Shopping

What to buy

There is an excellent variety of handicrafts: woodwork, pottery, copperware, leather-work, indigenous woven goods including rugs and ponchos. However, many of the goods sold in main handicraft markets are from elsewhere in South America, in some cases with the country of origin labels cut off; if going on a wider South American tour, these goods are almost always cheaper in the northern Andean countries. Among the most interesting purchases will be jewellery made with the semi-precious lapis lazuli stone. There are also less well known stones unique to Chile (such as the *combarbalita*, found around Combarbalá, near Illapel), and many fine jewels and knick-knacks (such as paperweights) made with stones such as onyx. People returning home may want to buy typical Chilean foods or drinks: *pisco*, *aji chileno* or *manjar*, for instance.

Where to buy

Bargaining is rare in Chile, and often seen as impolite. You can't try the usual 'offer a half, go up to two thirds' formula, and asking for a *descuento* may be seen as implying that the goods you want to buy are defective. Instead you should ask for 'una atención', and you will often do well to knock more than the equivalent of US$1 off the asking price. If you want to get the cheapest possible price your best bet is to go directly to the area where the object you have in mind is made, since craft specialities tend to be specific to particular places in Chile (see page 535); once there, do not go to the first craft shop you find (those nearest to the entry to the town), but look for those that are tucked away. The past decade has seen the growth of mall culture, especially in parts of Santiago, such as Las Condes.

Sport and activities

Chile might well have been designed for adventure tourism. In a country where you can often see the Andes from the coast, you are never more than a few hours' drive away from mountains, so a wide range of adventure activities can be practised year round. In the high summer month of January, for instance, although Parinacota volcano in the north is shrouded in cloud, the Torres del Paine in Patagonia enjoy their main season. Some destinations are unusually versatile: the mountain resorts near Santiago are famous for their skiing, but they are also good for mountain biking and trekking in high summer.

The infrastructure for 'soft' adventure tourism, such as a half-day's rafting on a Grade 3 river (quite a thrill), or a day spent climbing a volcano, is quite good in Chile, particularly in the Lake District. Agencies in centres such as Pucón and Puerto Varas organize combinations of activities, many for one day but some for longer durations. Parapenting can be organized from Santiago, but is best in Arica or Iquique. Santiago is well placed for short trips, especially for horse riding in the central *cordillera* and visits to the ski resorts nearby. Some of the world's top rafting and fishing is also easily accessible.

'Tougher' adventure tourism, often involving camping at high altitudes, is also possible. Chile offers boundless opportunities for well-equipped independent adventurers; the best way to see the Atacama Desert is on your own in a rented 4WD vehicle; and a mountain bike is the best form of transport on the Carretera Austral. Multi-day treks are an option throughout the country. It is important to check the experience of agencies offering expeditions to remote areas.

Among the organizations involved in adventure tourism several deserve special mention: **CATA** (Consejo de Autorregulación de Aventura) ① *Arzobispo Casanova 3, Providencia, Santiago, T02-7358034, www.catachile.cl*, is an organization formed by the more reputable agencies to try (with mixed success) to regulate adventure tourism, ensure safety and exclude 'cowboy' operators. It works closely with **CONAF** ① *T02-2361416, www.conaf.cl; see also box page 61*), which regulates adventure activities within the national parks, following CATA's written guidelines on matters such as guide experience, types of activity, size of groups and safety requirements. **Sernatur** (the National Tourist Board, www.sernatur.cl) has a separate section in its head office in Santiago specialising in adventure tourism and ecotourism (see page 39). ►► *For further information, see also Books, page 560.*

Climbing

Rock climbing This is not organized on a national basis, though **ENAM** (Escuela Nacional de Montaña de Santiago) runs courses in rock and ice climbing, and adventure tourism agencies are beginning to offer rock climbing activities. The three granite towers in the **Parque Nacional Torres del Paine** are the best known and most difficult climbs, but they are in such demand that a climbing fee is levied. There are also very high cliffs (800 m) at the eastern en end of **Lago Todos Los Santos** and at Cerro Picada (800 m) on the northwest shore.

Mountain climbing High mountains such as **Tupungato** and **Ojos del Salado** rival the Argentine peak of Aconcagua for climbers. Like the latter they pose few technical difficulties, but the weather can be vicious and the altitude should be taken very seriously. Moreover, Ojos del Salado is not easily accessible.

Ice climbing Some of the most important high-altitude ice climbs are easily reached from Santiago: the **Loma Larga** and **Plomo** massifs are two to three hours' drive from the capital. The **Federación de Andinismo** can advise on the better known and more difficult climbs such as El Plomo, El Altar and El Morado, though it is less useful for information of mountains further afield and its offices are often closed.

Volcano climbing There are hundreds of volcanoes to choose from, ranging from the high-altitude **Parinacota** in the far north and remote **Licancábur** on the Bolivian border near San Pedro to the chain of much lower cones in the Lake District and along the Carretera Austral. Some of these, such as **Puntiagudo** and **Corcovado** with their precipitous plugs, are difficult climbs. The easiest and most popular are **Villarrica** and **Osorno**, though CONAF rightly controls access to these because the crevasses are hazardous. Osorno, with its seracs and ice caves, is a more attractive climb, but Villarrica has the dubious advantage of being more active and hiring guides for this trek is much cheaper. Note that Osorno and Villarrica are still not easy climbs, and even well-equipped and experienced climbers have suffered fatal accidents on them.

Canyoning The southern bank of the **Río Petrohué** in the Lake District offers many fantastic canyons for climbing. Nearby rope ladders have been fixed in the canyon of the Río Leon, 30 minutes by boat from Petrohué on the southern shore of **Lago Todos Los Santos**.

Formalities To climb many mountains in border areas, permission must be obtained from the **Dirección de Fronteras y Límites** ① *piso 5, Ministerio de Relaciones Exteriores, Bandera 52, Santiago, T02-6714210, F6971909*. Preferably apply three months in advance; Chilean embassies abroad can help. In the case of Ojos del Salado, Sernatur in Copiapó can help organize a permit at short notice. In addition,

⁞ Park life

Chile has an extensive system of protected natural areas, covering seven million hectares in all. These areas are divided into national parks, forest reserves, natural monuments and natural sanctuaries, although these distinctions are of little importance for the visitor. Most of the areas have public access and details are given in the text. Camping areas are usually clearly designated and wild camping is discouraged and frequently banned.

The first forest reserve was the Reserva Forestal Malleco in 1907; the first national park was the Parque Nacional Vicente Pérez Rosales in 1926. The expansion of the system has been based on the desire to preserve natural resources and to provide access for the public to areas of outstanding beauty.

All of these protected areas are managed by CONAF (the Corporación Nacional Forestal), a dependency of the Ministry of Agriculture which also has responsibility for forestry development. See page 39 for CONAF's head office address in Santiago. It maintains an office in each of the regions of the country and kiosks in some natural areas and other locations. It publishes an illustrated guide to the parks and maps of the major protected areas which can be obtained from its head office and from some regional offices, the addresses of which are given in the text. CONAF publishes a useful little book on native trees, *Arboles nativas de Chile, Guía de Reconocimiento*, by Claudio Donoso Zegers (1983).

climbers require permits for some mountains, such as Torres del Paine and Volcán Osorno; further information from the **Federación de Andinismo** (see below).

Mountain rescue services are provided by the **Cuerpo de Socorro Andino,** based in Santiago, and by rescue groups in popular climbing areas: if organizing a climb register with them, often at the entry control to the mountain and with the local *carabineros*. Away from the popular areas you are on your own, which can also be one of Chile's main attractions.

Further information The national climbing club is the **Federación de Andinismo de Chile** ① *Almte Simpson 77A, Santiago, T02-2220888, www.feach.cl, office open daily in theory but frequently closed, especially in Jan and Feb; museum daily 1100-1330, 1700-2000, free; library Mon, Tue, Thu-Sat 1930-2100.* It organizes training for local climbers, runs some expeditions and hires out equipment to members. The shop in the foyer sells climbing guides and equipment and is often open when the office is closed. **Escuela Nacional de Montaña** (ENAM) ① *T02-2220799, www.enamchile.cl*, is based at the same address. It holds seminars and conferences on climbing, runs rock- and ice-climbing courses, plus qualification courses for guides in Santiago and elsewhere. It also administers the *Carnet de La Federación de Chile*, a card which is often required to climb mountains especially where CONAF control access. The *carnet* can be renewed through CONAF offices.

Fishing

The lakes and rivers of Regions IX (Araucanía), X (Los Lagos) and XI (Aisén) offer great opportunities for fishing, especially trout (rainbow, brown and fario) and salmon (coho and chinook). Organized fly-fishing with a guide gets more expensive the further south you go: trolling and spinning are the more widely practised methods.

The Lake District is popular for **trout** fishing. Both rainbow and fario trout are found in all major lakes; the largest fish are found in Lago Llanquihue, while Lago Todos Los Santos, on which very few boats are permitted, is noted for quantity. Apart from the main lakes, Lago Maihue and Lagunas El Toro, El Encanto and Paraíso (all in the Parque Nacional Puyehue) have been recommended. In the southern Lake District the main rivers for **salmon** fishing include the Pescado, Petrohué, Puelo and Maullín rivers and, on Chiloé, the Chepu and Pudeto.

The greatest fishing area in Chile lies along the Carretera Austral: Lago Yelcho and the Ríos Futaleufú and Palena are important areas for **fly-fishing**, while further south the rivers and lakes around Coyhaique offer some of the best fishing in the world; Lago Blanco on Tierra del Fuego is also a good destination.

Sea fishing is popular between Puerto Saavedra in the IX Region and Maullín in the X Region: the main centres are Mehuín, the coast from Niebla to Curiñanco near Valdivia, Maicolpue, Llico and Maullín itself, where salmon may be caught in the sea. In Villarrica a lot of fishing guides offer trips down the Tolten river.

Formalities and further information A licence is required, whether for one day or a longer period, and is usually obtained from the local Municipalidad, though some tourist offices also sell them. For details on licences and regional seasons, contact the **Servicio Nacional de Pesca** (Sernap) ① *Victoria 2832, Valparaiso, T032-819441, www.sernap.cl (see the section on pesca deportiva), Mon-Fri 0900-1400*.

Horse riding

There is more of an equine culture south of Santiago than further north, but some of the best riding country is to the north and east of Santiago, where the narrow tracks over mountain passes provide spectacular terrain. Saddles are narrow and covered with sheepskins, but Argentine saddles are wider and tend to be more comfortable.

Horse treks are organized in Santiago, in Ritoque near Valparaíso, in the Elqui and Hurtado valleys, in the Lake District and on Chiloé, and in numerous remote areas of the south. One of the best places for hiring and riding horses is along the west coast of Chiloé; expect to pay US$8 per hour. The biggest danger to riders is from cars and trucks.

Mountain biking

Mountain biking is a popular activity, particularly on descents from the Andes and from *refugios* on volcanoes such as Antillanca and Osorno. Touring the length of the **Carretera Austral** by mountain bike is also an excellent way of seeing this part of the country. Bikers might also wish to explore coastal areas anywhere between Valparaíso and Puerto Montt. In resorts such as Pucón and San Pedro, reasonable quality mountain bikes can be hired (prices from US$12 per day). The best place in Santiago for bikes is on Calle San Diego, south of the Alameda. Every year, in late summer, there is an international urban downhill mountain bike competition in Valparaíso.

Sailing and yachting

Sailing, both wind and motor powered, is popular in Chile. Protected harbours, yacht clubs and racing fleets can be found at most sizeable coastal towns. The biggest regatta in Chile's sailing calendar is the biennial event in January (2008, 2010, etc) from Puerto Montt around the coast of **Chiloé**. There are also important annual regattas, plus weekly events on **Lagos Llanquihue** and **Villarrica** every Saturday, racing Lasers, Vagabonds and catamarans. Sailing is best south of Puerto Montt. You should allow at least a week to begin to do justice to Chiloé and the islands off its eastern shore. Three weeks or more are required to reach the glaciers of **Laguna San Rafael**.

Skiing

Chile's major international ski resorts lie in the Andes near Santiago (see page 113), but skiing is possible from Santiago to Punta Arenas. **Sernatur** produces a leaflet on all Chilean ski resorts. Skiing elsewhere is mostly on the volcanoes to the south of Santiago, although back-country ski-mountaineering is quite possible on the volcanoes of the northern *altiplano* where a guide is essential and expertise required. The larger resorts in the south are **Termas de Chillán**, **Villarrica/Pucón** and **Antillanca**, all of which have accommodation on or near the slopes. There are, however, alternatives to these: many suitable volcanoes close to towns have a small base lodge and a lift which functions at weekends or peak periods (eg Antuco near Los Angeles; Llaima and Lonquimay further south). Here prices tend to be very reasonable and basic equipment rental is usually possible in the nearest town. Hitching is often the only form of transport, though it is sometimes possible to arrange transport with the local **Club Andino**. After all the effort to reach the snow, the atmosphere is happy-go-lucky and the skiing is great.

In the southern resorts skiing is for the laid-back and adventurous only. Snow conditions tend to become more slushy the further south you go. Lift systems are not the most modern, fast or well-maintained, piste preparation is mediocre and the weather is often more rainy than snowy. Despite all these disadvantages skiing on an active volcano looking down onto five huge lakes, as is the case at Villarrica/Pucón, is a memory which will truly last a lifetime.

Trekking

Chile offers limitless possibilities for both short and long treks in vastly differing landscapes: a one-day hike to the **Valle de la Luna** near San Pedro de Atacama is half a continent away from the famous week-long circuit of the **Parque Nacional Torres del Paine**. Over 1000 km of hiking opportunities have been opened up by the building of the Carretera Austral, though bad weather outside summer in this area can be a drawback. Within the national parks there are often short two- to three-hour signposted nature trails, starting from a visitors' centre, supplemented, in season, by lectures (usually only in Spanish), on flora and fauna and other highlights of the park.

The latest plan is the **Sendero de Chile**, a walking route stretching all the way from the Peruvian border to Tierra del Fuego, supposedly due to be completed during the next decade. Whether this ambitious undertaking will ever be realized remains to be seen: it seems likely that the authorities in the Atacama and Aysen regions may have particular difficulties, although pilot sections are now open in each region. For more information, see www.visit-chile.org or www.senderodechile.cl, or ask at any **Sernatur** office.

Watersports

Water sports, such as diving and surfing, are generally practised in northern Chile. An exception is **Pichilemu**, a resort three hours to the southwest of Santiago, which is famous for surfing. ▶▶ *For Sailing and yachting, see page 62.*

Rafting Over a dozen rivers between Santiago and Tierra del Fuego are excellent for whitewater rafting. Apart from the Maipo, which is the most easily accessible from Santiago, the main ones are the Trancura, Fuy, Bueno, Rahue and Petrohué; the Yelcho, Futaleufú, Corcovado, Palena and Baker and the Serrano and Tyndall. One of the most beautiful rivers is the Río Petrohué, which flows between the Osorno and Calbuco volcanoes with lush temperate rainforest along its banks.

Rafting is generally well organized and equipment is usually of high quality. Access to the headwaters of most rivers is easy. Agencies, particularly in Pucón and Puerto Varas, offer half-day trips to Grade 3 rivers for beginners, US$40-69 per person. Rafts should ideally carry six people and certainly no more than seven plus guide. The Futaleufú in northern Patagonia offers some of the most exciting and challenging whitewater in the world. Several agencies offer trips down long stretches of Grade 5 water.

Kayaking The most attractive waters for sea kayaking are around the islands off eastern **Chiloé** or around **Hornopirén** in the fjords of the sheltered Gulf of Ancud. Adventurous and experienced sea kayakers will be tempted by the prospect of circumnavigating the island of Cape Horn in the far south. The highlight for lake kayaking is the open competition on **Lago Llanquihue**, involving five stages totalling 310 km around the lake shore. Whitewater kayaking is usually available in the same areas as whitewater rafting, although you will generally have to show some kayaking accreditation or take lessons.

Kayaks can be hired from **Oceanic** ① *Isidora Goyenehcea, 3120, Piso 7, T02-2442020, info@oceanic.cl*, and **Kayak Equipment** ① *San Vicente de Paul 5831, La Reina, T/F02-2775288*, both in Santiago, and from **Canoas Tours** ① *Rosario 1305, T02-233587*, in Puerto Varas. Courses are available at the **Chiloé Sea Kayaking Centre** near Dalcahue and are bookable through **Altué Expeditions** in Santiago.

Health

Before you go

Ideally, you should see your GP/practice nurse or travel clinic at least six weeks before your departure for general advice on travel risks and recommended vaccinations. Your local pharmacist can also be a good source of readily accessible advice. Make sure you have travel insurance, get a dental check (especially if you are going to be away for more than a month), know your own blood group and if you suffer a long-term condition such as diabetes or epilepsy make sure someone knows or that you have a Medic Alert bracelet/necklace with this information on it.

Recommended vaccinations

Vaccinations for rabies, hepatitis B and tuberculosis are commonly recommended for Chile. The final decision, however, should be based on a consultation with your GP or travel clinic. You should also confirm your primary courses and boosters are up to date (diphtheria, tetanus, poliomyelitis, hepatitis A, typhoid). A yellow fever certificate is required if entering from an endemic area and travelling to Easter Island.

A-Z of health risks

Altitude sickness

Acute mountain sickness can strike from about 3000 m upwards and in general is more likely to affect those who ascend rapidly (for example by plane) and those who over-exert themselves. Acute mountain sickness takes a few hours or days to come on and presents with heachache, lassitude, dizziness, loss of appetite, nausea and vomiting. Insomnia is common and often associated with a suffocating feeling when lying down in bed. You may notice that your breathing tends to wax and wane at night and your face is puffy in the mornings – this is all part of the syndrome. If the symptoms are mild, the treatment is rest and painkillers (preferably not aspirin-based) for the headaches. Should the symptoms be severe and prolonged it is best to descend to a lower altitude immediately and reascend, if necessary, slowly and in stages. The symptoms disappear very quickly – even after a few hundred metres of descent.

The best way of preventing acute mountain sickness is a relatively slow ascent. When trekking to high altitude, some time spent walking at medium altitude, getting fit and acclimatising is beneficial. When flying to places over 3000 m a few hours' rest and the avoidance of alcohol, cigarettes and heavy food will go a long way towards preventing acute mountain sickness.

Bites and stings

This is a very rare event indeed for travellers, but if you are unlucky (or careless) enough to be bitten by a venomous snake, spider, scorpion or sea creature, try to identify the culprit, without putting yourself in further danger (do not try to catch a live snake).

Snake bites in particular are very frightening, but in fact rarely poisonous – even venomous snakes bite without injecting venom. Victims should be taken to a hospital or a doctor without delay. It is not advised for travellers to carry snake bite antivenom as it can do more harm than good in inexperienced hands. Reassure and comfort the victim frequently. Immobilize the limb with a bandage or a splint and get the patient to lie still. Do not slash the bite area and try to suck out the poison. This also does more harm than good. You should apply a tourniquet in these circumstances, but only if you know how to. Do not attempt this if you are not experienced.

Certain tropical fish inject venom into bathers' feet when trodden on, which can be exceptionally painful. Wear plastic shoes if such creatures are reported. The pain can be relieved by immersing the foot in hot water (as hot as you can bear) for as long as the pain persists.

Diarrhoea and intestinal upset

Diarrhoea can refer either to loose stools or an increased frequency of bowel movement, both of which can be a nuisance. Symptoms should be relatively short-lived but if they persist beyond two weeks specialist medical attention should be sought. Also seek medical help if there is blood in the stools and/or fever.

Adults can use an antidiarrhoeal medication such as loperamide to control the symptoms but only for up to 24 hours. In addition keep well hydrated by drinking plenty of fluids and eat bland foods. Oral rehydration sachets taken after each loose stool are a useful way to keep well hydrated. These should always be used when treating children and the elderly.

Bacterial traveller's diarrhoea is the most common form. Ciproxin (Ciprofloxacin) is a useful antibiotic and can be obtained by private prescription in the UK. You need to take one 500 mg tablet when the diarrhoea starts. If there are so signs of improvement after 24 hours the diarrhoea is likely to be viral and not bacterial. If it is due to other organisms such as those causing giardia or amoebic dysentery, different antibiotics will be required.

The standard advice to prevent problems is to be careful with water and ice for drinking. Ask yourself where the water came from. If you have any doubts then boil it or filter and treat it. There are many filter/treatment devices now available on the market. Food can also transmit disease. Be wary of salads (what were they washed in, who handled them), re-heated foods or food that has been left out in the sun having been cooked earlier in the day. There is a simple adage that says wash it, peel it, boil it or forget it. Also be wary of unpasteurised dairy products as these can transmit a range of diseases.

A bout of diarrhorea/ intestinal upset is almost inevitable. A study showed up to 70% of travellers may suffer during their trip.

Hepatitis

Hepatitis means inflammation of the liver. Viral causes of the disease can be acquired anywhere in the world. The most obvious symptom is a yellowing of your skin or the whites of your eyes. However, prior to this all that you may notice is itching and tiredness. Pre-travel hepatitis A vaccine is the best bet. Hepatitis B (for which there is a vaccine) is spread through blood and unprotected sexual intercourse, both of which can be avoided.

Rabies

Rabies is endemic throughout certain parts of the world so be aware of the dangers of the bite from any animal. Rabies vaccination before travel can be considered but if bitten always seek urgent medical attention – whether or not you have been previously vaccinated – after first cleaning the wound and treating with an iodine base disinfectant or alcohol.

Sun

Take good heed of advice regarding protecting yourself against the sun. Overexposure can lead to sunburn and, in the longer term, skin cancers and premature skin aging. The best advice is simply to avoid exposure to the sun by covering exposed skin, wearing a hat and staying out of the sun if possible, particularly between late morning and early afternoon. Apply a high factor sunscreen (greater than SPF15) and also make sure it screens against UVB. A further danger in tropical climates is heat exhaustion or more seriously heatstroke. This can be avoided by good hydration, which means drinking water past the point of simply quenching thirst. Also when first exposed to tropical heat take time to acclimatize by avoiding strenuous activity in the middle of the day. If you cannot avoid heavy exercise it is also a good idea to increase salt intake.

Underwater health

If you plan to dive make sure that you are fit do so. The **British Sub-Aqua Club (BSAC)** ① *Telford's Quay, South Pier Rd, Ellesmere Port, Cheshire CH65 4FL, UK, T01513-506200, www.bsac.com*, can put you in touch with doctors who will carry out medical examinations. Check that any dive company you use are reputable and have appropriate certification from BSAC or **Professional Association of Diving Instructors (PADI)** ① *Unit 7, St Philips Central, Albert Rd, St Philips, Bristol, BS2 0TD, T0117-3007234, www.padi.com*.

Water

There are a number of ways of purifying water. Dirty water should first be strained through a filter bag and then boiled or treated. Bring water to a rolling boil for several minutes. There are sterilising methods that can be used and products generally contain chlorine (eg Puritabs) or iodine (eg Pota Aqua) compounds. There are a number of water sterilizers now on the market available in personal and expedition size. Make sure you take the spare parts or spare chemicals with you and do not believe everything the manufacturers say.

Other diseases and risks

There are a range of other insect borne diseases that are quite rare in travellers, but worth finding out about if going to particular destinations. Examples are sleeping sickness, river blindness and leishmaniasis. Fresh water can also be a source of diseases such as bilharzia and leptospirosis and it is worth investigating if these are a danger before bathing in lakes and streams. Also take heed of advice regarding protecting yourself against the sun (see above) and remember that unprotected sex always carries a risk and extra care is required when visiting some parts of the world.

Further information

Websites

Foreign and Commonwealth Office (FCO) (UK), www.fco.gov.uk
The National Travel Health Network and Centre (NaTHNaC) www.nathnac.org/
World Health Organisation, www.who.int

Books

Dawood R (editor). *Travellers' health*, 3rd Ed. Oxford University Press, 2002.

Warrell, David and Sarah Anderson (editors) *Expedition Medicine*, The Royal Geographic Society, ISBN 1 86197 040-4.

Keeping in touch

Communications

Internet

You will have no problem locating an internet café in tourist centres, cities and towns; they are everywhere. This means that prices tend to be competitive, ranging from US$0.50-2 per hour. Other than dealing with slow connection speeds (in rural areas) and Spanish keyboards, the services are perfectly adequate, and should suit most people's needs. To access the @ symbol, you usually press the ctrl and alt keys together with 'q'. Website addresses are given wherever possible throughout the guide.

Post

The Chilean postal system is usually efficient. Airmail takes around a week from both the UK and the US. Seamail takes eight to 12 weeks from the UK. There is a daily airmail service to Europe. Letters to Europe/North America cost US$0.80. To register a letter costs US$1. Airmail rates for parcels to Europe cost US$20 for less than 1 kg; US$25 for 1-3kg; US$150 for 10 kg. There is no overseas surface mail service from Chile. The poste restante service ('*lista de correo*') only holds mail for 30 days, then returns it to sender. The *Lista de Correo* in the Central Post Office in Santiago is good and efficiently organized, but letters are kept separately for men and women so envelopes should be marked Señor or Señora/Señorita.

Telephone

National and international calls have been opened up for competition in Chile. For those with their own phoneline, there are a dozen or so main companies (*carriers*) offering competing rates. If you do not have your own phone, though, it is best to make a call from a **centro de llamados**, or call centre. National calls cost around US$0.12 per minute. However, **telephone boxes** can be used for making local, long-distance and collect calls and for receiving calls. They are programmed to direct calls via one carrier: to make a local call, simply dial the number you require and pay the rate charged by the carrier who owns the booth. To make an inter-urban call, dial 'o' plus the area code (DD) and the number;

The prefix 09 indicates a mobile phone. Bolivia +591, Peru +51; Argentina +54.

if you wish to select a carrier, dial its code before the area code (leaving out 'o'), then the number. Phone cards only charge for the duration of the call rather than for the normal three-minute minimum. A call to a mobile costs US$0.20 per 30 seconds. For international calls, call centres in the larger urban centres often have very good value rates (as low as US$0.20 per minute to fixed lines in Europe). Check around as prices vary. If you will be travelling to more remote areas it may be worth buying an international phone card which may be used from any phonebox. These are available in newspaper kiosks in the larger cities. Try and find a card that has a good rate for the country you wish to call.

Most **mobile phone** networks in Chile operate on the GSM 1900 system. If you have a compatible phone you can use it in Chile, either with its original sim-card or buying a new one in Chile(US$12), giving you a Chilean number. Alternatively mobile phones using prepaid phonecards can be purchased for as little as US$50 and will allow friends and family to keep in touch. The main operators are Movistar, Entel and Smartcom. Phones and sim-cards can be bought from their sales offices in most cities.

Media

Newspapers and magazines

Santiago daily papers are *El Mercurio* (centre-right, a heavyweight broadsheet), *La Nación* (the official state newspaper, liberal-left and worth buying on a Sunday), *La Segunda* (middle-market tabloid), *La Tercera* (more serious tabloid), *La Cuarta* (salacious and gossip-mongering) and *Las Ultimas Noticias*. Look out for *The Clinic*, a satirical weekly paper named after the hospital at which General Pinochet was arrested in 1998. *News Review* ① T02-6651237, newsreview.cl, US$1.20, a weekly in English, is published on Fridays, and is on sale at selected kiosks. Recent international newspapers can be bought at kiosks on the Paseo Ahumada in Santiago. Magazines published weekly include *Hoy*, *Qué Pasa*, *Ercilla*, *Rocinante* (art, culture, society).

Radio

South America has more community radio stations than practically anywhere else in the world. Visitors to the region are recommended to bring or buy a compact portable radio, with digital tuning and a full range of short-wave bands, as well as FM, long and medium wave, as a practical means to brush up on the language, sample popular culture and absorb some regional music. International broadcasters such as the **Voice of America** (6130 or 7370 KHz), **Monitor Radio International** (operated by Christian Science Monitor in Boston, Mass (15.30 or 9.755 MHz) and the Quito-based evangelical station, **HCJB**, keep the traveller abreast of news and events, in both English and Spanish. Unfortunately the **BBC World Service** has stopped broadcasting to Chile, although it can be heard over the internet. In small regional centres, the local radio station is a very effective medium for sending a message to someone else in the area; go to the studio and make the request in person.

Television

TV channels include **TVUC** (Universidad Católica) on Channel 13, the leading station; **TVN** (government operated) on Channel 7; **Mega** (private) on Channel 9, **La Red** (private) on Channel 4 and **Chilevisión** (owned by former presidential hopeful Sebastián Piñera) on Channel 11. Soap operas (*teleseries*) and soccer constitute the most popular programmes. Cable television is widely available. Channels vary from region to region, but there are usually some channels in English, French, Italian and German.

Santiago Region

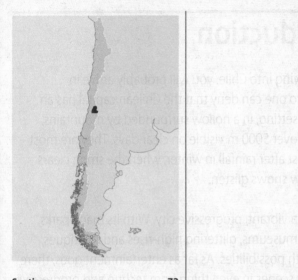

⦂ Footprint features

Introduction

If you are flying into Chile, you will probably arrive in Santiago. No one can deny that the Chilean capital has an impressive setting, in a hollow surrounded by mountains, with peaks over 5000 m visible on clear days. They are most dramatic just after rainfall in winter, when the smog clears and the new snows glisten.

Santiago is a vibrant, progressive city. With its many parks, interesting museums, glittering high-rises and boutiques, it bursts with possibilities. As far as entertainment goes, there are popular scenes in everything from techno and progressive rock to Bohemian hang-outs and most of the bits in between. Certainly, those who spend an extended period of time in Santiago soon find plenty of things to do at night and at the weekends.

The region around the capital encompasses several of the country's highlights. The resorts on the coast are less than two hours away and also within easy reach are the best ski resorts in South America, which are great spots for weekend hikes in summer. Meanwhile, the area south of Santiago is perhaps the best wine-producing area in Chile. Autumn, when the grapes are being harvested, is a particularly good time to visit the vineyards.

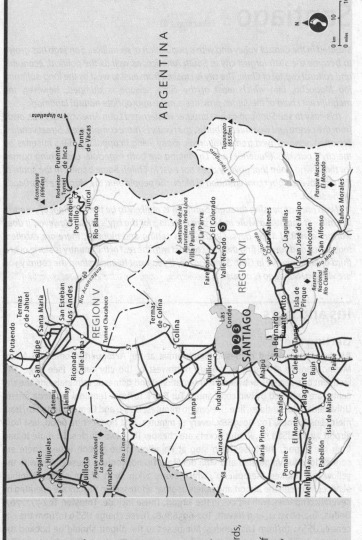

★ Don't miss...

1 Museo Chileno de Arte Precolombino Visit one of the world's most important collections of Native South American artefacts, page 78.

2 Mercado Central Have lunch at this market and discover weird and wonderful varieties of shellfish, pages 78 and 98.

3 Cerro San Cristóbal Take in a panoramic view of the city and the Andes (smog permitting) from the top of Cerro San Cristóbal, page 83.

4 Maipo Valley Take a tour then sip wine at some of Chile's best vineyards, page 111.

5 Valle Nevado Probably the best of several fine ski resorts in the Andes, just a stone's throw from Santiago, page 113.

Santiago → Colour map 3, B3.

Situated in the Central Valley and with a population of six million, Santiago has grown to become the sixth largest city in South America, as well as the political, economic and cultural capital of Chile. The city is crossed from east to west by the long-suffering Río Mapocho, into which most of the city's sewage is dumped; however, the magnificent chain of the Andes provides a more appropriate natural landmark.

It is easy to see Santiago as just another westernized Latin American city but, away from the centre and wealthier suburbs, the reality is more complicated. Street vendors are often newly arrived from rural areas, many living in appalling villas miserias on the city's outskirts (Pudahuel and La Pintana are both especially chastening barrios for those who claim that poverty does not exist in Chile). Some barrios in the south of the city have a higher concentration of Mapuche people than the Mapuche heartlands of the south.

If you are just passing through, Santiago is unlikely to be the highlight of your trip to Chile – it can take a while to get a real feeling for the city's pulse. However, it does warrant a visit of a few days. On top of its setting and nightlife, there are excellent museums, and you will find that the contrast with the rest of the country is stark; over a third of Chileans live in Gran Santiago, so, if you want to understand the country you are visiting, Santiago is a must. ▸▸ *For Sleeping, eating and other listings, see pages 88-109.*

Ins and outs

Getting there

Air International and domestic flights arrive at the Aeropuerto Comodoro Arturo Merino Benítez at Pudahuel, 26 km northwest of the city centre (see page 38). Frequent bus services between the international and domestic terminals and the city centre are operated by two companies: **Tur Bus I** to/from Terminal Alameda (metro Universidad de Santiago, line 1), every 30 minutes, US$3; and **Centropuerto I** to/from metro Los Héroes, T02-6019883, every 15 minutes, first from centre 0600, last from airport 2230, US$2.50. Return tickets are cheaper than two singles. En route to and from the airport, the buses also stop at Pajaritos metro station (where there are connections for Valparaíso and Viña del Mar). Do not confuse these buses with the yellow bus marked 'Aeropuerto', which stops 2 km short of the airport. Minibus services between the airport and hotels or other addresses in the city are operated by several companies with offices in the airport. These include: **Transfer,** T02-7777707; **Delfos,** T02-6011111, and **Navett,** T02-6956868. These charge US$9 to/from the city centre, US$11 to/from Las Condes. Minibuses to the airport should be booked the previous day, but taxis are cheaper if flagged down in the street. There is a taxi office inside the international terminal. Taxis to/from the centre should cost around US$20, to/from Providencia US$25; agree the fare beforehand. It is also possible to negotiate taxi fares from the airport to quite distant cities such as Melipilla and Valparaíso; rates to Valparaíso start from around US$70.

Bus and train Intercity buses arrive at one of four terminals, all located close to each other, just west of the centre and not far from the train station, along Avenida Libertador Bernardo O'Higgins. This is the main east-west avenue through the city and is within easy reach of line 1 of the metro. ▸▸ *For further details, see Transport, page 102.*

Getting around

The city's main avenue, Avenida Libertador Bernardo O'Higgins, is almost always referred to as the Alameda, while Plaza Baquedano, one of the city's main squares, is

Moving mountains

While Santiago's smog is not too bad in spring, summer and autumn, those who arrive here during winter could be in for an unpleasant shock. It might not take more than half an hour for your throat to begin to itch and your eyes to water due to one of Santiago's biggest problems – pollution. In 2001, it was rated the eighth most polluted city in the world. When Pedro de Valdivia founded the city in 1541, between the coastal mountains and the Andes, it must have seemed like a perfect site; he could never have imagined that the city would one day engulf the whole valley, and that the mountains would become a serious problem.

The principal reason for Santiago's high levels of pollution is that it lies in a bowl, encircled by mountains, which means that the smog is trapped. This, combined with the centralization of Chilean industry in Santiago, the fact that many buses are not equipped with catalytic converters and the sheer volume of cars that choke the city's highways, conspires to create a problem that cannot easily be resolved. It is a serious issue: asthma rates are high and older people sometimes die during the winter *emergencias*, when the pollution gets particularly bad.

Over the years, all sorts of solutions have been proposed. A team of Japanese scientists once even suggested blowing up the part of the Andes nearest the city, so that the pollution could disperse more easily. Each weekday, cars that have number plates ending in one of two digits are prohibited from circulating. But, until the government finds a means of dispersing the population more widely throughout the country, the problem is likely to remain.

almost always known as Plaza Italia (in both instances, this book follows suit). Most of the more expensive accommodation is situated in the city centre or further east in the neighbourhoods of Providencia and Las Condes. Most budget accommodation is located in the city centre or further west in the vicinity of the bus terminals. Although parts of the centre can be explored on foot, you will need to master the city's transport system, which is well organized, if crowded and slow in peak periods. ▸▸ *For a map of the metro, see page 105.*

Tourist information

Sernatur (Servicio Nacional de Turismo) ① *Av Providencia 1550, metro Manuel Montt, T02-7318336, www.sernatur.cl, Mon-Fri 0845-1830, Sat 0900-1400*. The national tourist board has maps, many brochures and posters. English, German and some French are spoken. Good notice board. There is also an information office at the airport I 0900-2100 daily. **Municipal Tourist Board** ① *Casa Colorada, Merced 860, metro Plaza de Armas, T02-336700, www.munistgo.cl/colorada*, offers walking tours of the city. There is also a good free booklet on historic buildings in the city, available in English and Spanish, *Historical Heritage of Santiago: A Guide for Tourists*. Many tourist offices in small towns, particularly in the south, are closed in winter, so stock up on information here. **CONAF (Corporación Nacional Forestal)** ① *Paseo Presidente Bulnes 285 piso 1 (metro Moneda), T02-3900125 , www.conaf.cl*, publishes a number of leaflets and has documents and maps about the national park system that can be consulted or photocopied (not very useful for walking). **CODEFF (Comité Nacional Pro-Defensa de la Fauna y Flora)** ① *Luis Uribe 2620, Ñuñoa, T02-2747461, www.codeff.cl*, can also provide information on environmental questions.

Security

Like all large cities, Santiago has problems of theft. However, it has to be said that these tend to be exaggerated by Santiaguinos. While the central area is frequented by pickpockets and bag snatchers (who are often well dressed) – operating mostly on the metro, around the Plaza de Armas, in Barrio Brasil, near Cerro Santa Lucía and around the restaurants in Bellavista – these are easily avoided with a little common sense. The biggest risk is in unwittingly entering a dangerous *barrio* away from the centre. Parts of Pudahuel and Cerro Navia in the west, Conchalí and Renca in the north and Macul, El Bosque and La Pintana in the south have a big drug and crime problem and can be dangerous. At night, it is best to take a public bus (*micro*) rather than a taxi, as you will be watched over by your fellow passengers; better still, call for a radio taxi.

Best time to visit

The Santiago area enjoys a Mediterranean climate, with long dry summers and daytime temperatures rising to over 30ºC, when the heat can be uncomfortable. Rainfall is heaviest from May to August and often falls in bands lasting for two or three days at a time. In summer, rainfall is almost unknown. Snowfall is rare, although frost is not uncommon, and, as houses in Santiago rarely have central heating, you will feel the cold on winter nights. There is usually less wind in winter, making smog a more serious problem over the city (forecast levels of smog are published in the daily papers, during television weather forecasts, inside underground stations and at www.sitios.cl). Pollution levels vary; the west and the old city centre are much worse affected than the more expensive areas around Las Condes. Pollution is usually at its worst in July and at its lightest in September and October and after rainfall.

Santiago orientation

• 24 hours in the city

First, try to make sure you are here on a Saturday. Assuming you are staying in the centre, get up early and walk down to Calle San Diego for breakfast. Afterwards, walk down San Diego to the **Iglesia de los Sacrementinos** – Santiago's answer to Sacré Coeur – and then west through gardens until you reach the **Palacio Cousiño** in time for the first tour at 0930. This extraordinary building (see page 80) gives a real insight into the lives, customs and belief systems of the Chilean aristocracy and the opulence to which the upper classes became accustomed. Once the tour has finished, stroll to Toesca metro and head a few stops south to Franklin. Here you will find swarms of people all making their way to the **Mercado Bío Bío**. This market will show you how most of Santiago lives and it provides a striking contrast to Palacio Cousiño.

When you start feeling hungry, head back to Franklin metro and take the train north to Cal y Canto. On the opposite side of the Río Mapocho is the **Vega Central**, where you will find some of the best **seafood restaurants** in Santiago. Don't be put off by the choice – take your time and enjoy some of the best shellfish the world has to offer.

After lunch, it's time to remind yourself that Santiago has one of the most dramatic settings of any of the world's major cities. Cross back over the Río Mapocho and stroll east towards the conical hill of **Cerro San Cristóbal**. If it's summer, the heat may be making you feel a little tired by now – if so, you could go up the hill on the **funicular railway**. If you are lucky and it is a clear day, you will have an unforgettable view of the Andes. Here you can stroll through lanes that are lined with trees – a world away from the clutter of the city. There are even swimming pools to cool off in and the chance to do some wine tasting. Towards dusk, have a drink in the café near the funicular railway station and watch the sun go down over the coastal mountain range, lighting up the snows of the Andes.

After dark, go back down the hill by funicular railway (it's not advisable to walk here in the evening) in time to sample Santiago's nightlife. At the foot of Cerro San Cristóbal is **Barrio Bellavista**. Here you can take your pick of any one of dozens of excellent (and expensive) restaurants, before going out to one of the area's buzzing *salsotecas*. These don't really get going until midnight and you'll usually find that you don't leave much before five, so perhaps head back to your hotel room for some sleep after dinner and then go out dancing later on.

Santiago Region Santiago

History

Santiago was founded by Pedro de Valdivia on 12 February 1541 on the site of a small indigenous settlement between the southern bank of the Río Mapocho and the Cerro Santa Lucía. During the colonial period, it was only one of several Spanish administrative and cultural centres; also important were Concepción to the south and La Serena in the north. Nevertheless, by 1647 there were 12 churches in the city but, of these, only San Francisco (1618) survived the earthquake of that year. A further earthquake destroyed most of the city in 1730.

Following Independence, the city became more important. In the 1870s, under the Intendente (regional governor) Benjamín Vicuña MacKenna, an urban plan was drafted, the Cerro Santa Lucía was made into a public park and the first trams were introduced. As the city grew at the end of the 19th century, the Chilean elite, wealthy from mining and shipping, built their mansions west of the centre around Calle Dieciocho, Avenida España and República. One of these families was the Cousiños, who built the Palacio Cousiño and later donated this and what became the Parque O'Higgins to the city. Expansion east towards Providencia began in 1895. Until the 1930s, much of the city centre had colonial buildings in the style of Quito or Lima, but expansion and modernization meant that these were gradually replaced. In the latter

Santiago centre

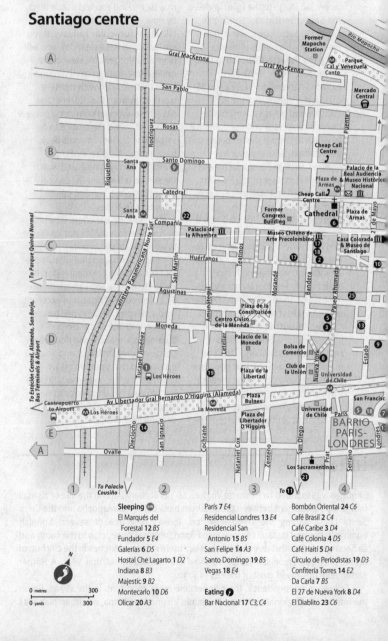

0 metres 300
0 yards 300

Sleeping 🛏
El Marqués del
 Forestal **12** *B5*
Fundador **5** *E4*
Galerías **6** *D5*
Hostal Che Lagarto **1** *D2*
Indiana **8** *B3*
Majestic **9** *B2*
Montecarlo **10** *D6*
Olicar **20** *A3*

París **7** *E4*
Residencial Londres **13** *E4*
Residencial San
 Antonio **15** *B5*
San Felipe **14** *A3*
Santo Domingo **19** *B5*
Vegas **18** *E4*

Eating 🍴
Bar Nacional **17** *C3, C4*

Bombón Oriental **24** *C6*
Café Brasil **2** *C4*
Café Caribe **3** *D4*
Café Colonia **4** *D5*
Café Haití **5** *D4*
Círculo de Periodistas **19** *D3*
Confitería Torres **14** *E2*
Da Carla **7** *B5*
El 27 de Nueva York **8** *D4*
El Diablito **23** *C6*

part of the 20th century, like most Latin American capital cities, Santiago spread rapidly. Many older Santiaguinos who live in areas that are now relatively central tell how, when they first arrived in the city, their homes were right on the outskirts. In general, the more affluent moved east into new neighbourhoods in the foothills of the Andes, and poorer neighbourhoods were established to the west of the centre. This geographic division of wealth continues today.

Sights

The centre of the old city lies between the Río Mapocho and the city's main avenue, Alameda. From **Plaza Italia**, in the east of the city's central area, the river flows to the northwest and the Alameda runs to the southwest. From Plaza Italia, Calle Merced runs due west to the **Plaza de Armas**, the heart of the city, which lies five blocks south of the Río Mapocho.

Around the Plaza de Armas 🍴🛏 ▶ pp88-94.

The shadiness and tranquillity of the Plaza de Armas has been disturbed by a recent remodelling of the square. Some of the taller trees were stripped away to make way for new stonework but most Santiaguinos are unhappy with the barer plaza that has resulted. On the eastern and southern sides, there are arcades with shops and cheap restaurants; on the northern side is the post office and the Municipalidad; and on the western side the cathedral and the archbishop's palace. The **cathedral**, much rebuilt, contains a recumbent statue in wood of San Francisco Javier and the chandelier that lit the first meetings of Congress after Independence; it also houses an interesting museum of religious art and historical pieces. The **Museo Histórico Nacional** ⓘ *Plaza de Armas 951, T02-4117000, www.museohistorico nacional.cl, Tue-Sun 1000-1730, US$1, free on Sun*, is located in the Palacio de la Real Audiencia and covers the period from the Conquest until 1925 and contains a model of colonial Santiago.

A block west of the cathedral is the **former Congress building**, now occupied by the Ministry of Foreign Affairs (the new Congress building is in Valparaíso). Nearby are the law courts and the **Museo Chileno**

El Naturista 9 *D4*
El Rápido 18 *C4*
El Vegetariano 10 *C4*
Faisan d'Or 6 *C4*
Gelato's 25 *D4*
Govindas 22 *C2*
Las Tejas 11 *E3*
Les Assassins 15 *C6*
Los Adobes del
  Argomedo 1 *E6*

Los Braseros de
  Lucifer 18 *C4*
Lung Fung 12 *D5*
Masticón 21 *E4*
Nuria 16 *D5*
Opera Catedral 20 *C6*
Salón de Té
  Cousiño 13 *D4*

de Arte Precolombino ⓘ Bandera 361, *www.precolombino.cl, Tue-Sun 1000-1800, US$4, students and children free, booklet US$0.80*. Housed in the former Real Aduana, this is one of the best museums in Chile with an excellent representative exhibition of objects from the pre-Columbian cultures of Central America and the Andean region. Displays are well labelled in English. A visit is highly recommended. A further two blocks west is **Palacio de la Alhambra** ⓘ *Compañía 1340, To2-6890875, www.snba.cl, Mon-Fri 1100-1300, 1700-1930*, a national monument sponsored by the Society of Arts. It stages exhibitions of paintings as well as having a permanent display.

A few metres east of the Plaza de Armas is the Casa Colorada. Built in 1769, it was the home of the Governor in colonial days and then of Mateo de Toro y Zambrano y Ureta, president of Chile's first national governing council . It now holds the **Museo de Santiago** ⓘ *Merced 860, www.munistgo.cl/colorada, Tue-Sat 1000-1800, Sun and holidays 1100-1400, US$3, students free, booklet US$0.60*, which covers the history of Santiago from the Conquest to modern times with excellent displays, models and guided tours.

From the Plaza de Armas, Paseo Ahumada runs south to the Alameda, four blocks away. **Ahumada** is a pedestrianized street and is the commercial heart of the centre. This is always an interesting place to come for a stroll, especially at night, when those selling pirated CDs or playing the three-card trick mix with evangelist preachers and exorcists. One block south of the Plaza de Armas, Ahumada crosses **Calle Huérfanos**, which is also pedestrianized and presents a similar spectacle, as does Calle Estado, one block east of Paseo Ahumada.

Four blocks north of the Plaza de Armas is the interesting **Mercado Central** ⓘ *Av 21 de Mayo y San Pablo*. The central market is the best place to come for seafood in Santiago (see page 91), and is so prominent in the Chilean psyche that it was the setting for a recent national soap opera, *Amores del Mercado*. The building faces the **Parque Venezuela**, on which is the Cal y Canto metro station and, at its western end, the **former Mapocho railway station**, now one of the capital's most important cultural centres and concert venues. If you head east from Mapocho station, along the river, you arrive at the **Parque Forestal**. Although the park is prettily laid out, the proximity of many busy roads means that few people stroll here for long. The **Museo Nacional de Bellas Artes** ⓘ *www.mnba.cl, Tue-Sun 1000-1900, US$1.20*, is located in the wooded grounds and is an extraordinary example of neoclassical architecture. Inside is a large display of Chilean and foreign painting and sculpture; contemporary art exhibitions are held several times a year. In the west wing of the building is the **Museo de Arte Contemporáneo** ⓘ *US$1.20, Bellas Artes metro*.

Along and around the Alameda ⬤⬤ ›› *pp88-94*.

On the Alameda

The Alameda runs through the heart of the city for over 3 km. It is 100 m wide, choked full of *micros*, taxis and cars day and night and ornamented with gardens and statuary. The most notable are the equestrian statues of generals O'Higgins and San Martín; the statue of the Chilean historian Benjamín Vicuña MacKenna who, as mayor of Santiago, beautified Cerro Santa Lucía; and the great monument in honour of the battle of Concepción in 1879 during the war of the Pacific.

At the eastern end of the Alameda is **Plaza Italia**, where there is a statue of General Baquedano and the Tomb of the Unknown Soldier. Four blocks south is the **Museo Nacional Benjamín Vicuña MacKenna** ⓘ *Av V MacKenna 94, Mon-Sat 0930-1300, 1400-1750, US$1.20*, which records the life and works of the 19th-century Chilean historian and biographer who became one of Santiago's most important mayors. It also has occasional exhibitions.

Between the Parque Forestal, Plaza Italia and the Alameda is the **Calle Lastarria** neighbourhood (Universidad Católica metro). For those interested in antique furniture, pieces of art and old books, the area is worth a visit, especially the **Plaza Mulato Gil de Castro**. Occasional shows are put on in the plaza, and surrounding it are restaurants, a lot of cafés, bookshops, handicraft and antique shops, an art gallery, the **Museo de Artes Visuales** and the **Museo Arqueológico de Santiago** ① *Lastarria 307, Tue-Sun 1030-1830, US$2, free on Sun*, with temporary exhibitions of Chilean archaeology, anthropology and pre-Columbian art. The museum also houses the **Museo de Artes Visuales** ① *Tue-Sun 1030-1830*.

Nearby on Calle Lastarria are the the **Cine Biógrafo** (No 131) and, at the corner with Calle Merced, the **Instituto Chileno-Francés**.

From here, the Alameda skirts Cerro Santa Lucía on the right and the Universidad Católica on the left. **Cerro Santa Lucía**, a cone of rock rising steeply to a height of 70 m, can be scaled from the Caupolicán esplanade, past the statue of the Mapuche leader, but the ascent from the northern side of the hill – where there is an equestrian statue of Diego de Almagro – is easier.

On clear days you can see across to the Andes from Cerro Santa Lucía. Even on smoggy days, the view of the sunset is good.

Santiago Region Santiago Sights

There are views of the city from the top, which is reached by a series of stairs. There is a fortress, the **Batería Hidalgo** (closed to visitors) on the summit, but only its platform survives from the colonial period. The hill closes at 2100; visitors must sign a register at the entrance, giving their ID card number. It is best to descend the eastern side, to see the small **Plaza Pedro de Valdivia** with its waterfalls and **statue of Valdivia**. The area is known to be dangerous after dark. Travellers should beware of thieves here, although, with the new need to register ID cards, security in the area has been tightened up.

Beyond the hill, on the right, the Alameda goes past the **Biblioteca Nacional** ① *Av Libertador Bernardo O'Higgins 651, Santa Lucía metro, www.dibam.cl, Mon-Fri 0900-1900, Sat 0910-1400, free*, which contains the national archives as well as exhibitions of books, book illustrations, documents and posters. Concerts and lectures also take place here, entry to which is often free.

Beyond, on the left, between Calle San Francisco and Calle Londres, is the oldest church in Santiago: the red-walled church and monastery of **San Francisco** (1618). Inside is the small statue of the Virgin that Valdivia carried on his saddlebow when he rode from Peru to Chile. Free classical concerts are sometimes given in the church in summer; arrive early for a seat. Annexed to the church, near the cloisters, is the **Museo Colonial** ① *Londres 4, T02-6398737, www.museosanfrancisco.cl, Tue-Sat 1000-1300, 1500-1800, Sun 1000-1400, US$1.50*. Containing displays of religious art, one of the rooms here has 54 paintings of the life of Saint Francis. In the cloisters is a room containing Gabriela Mistral's Nobel Prize medal and there is also a collection of locks. Some of the information is in English. Universidad de Chile metro, line 1, south exit.

South of San Francisco is the attractive **Barrio París-Londres**, built in 1923-1929, now restored and pedestrianized, while two blocks north of the Alameda is the **Teatro Municipal** ① *C Agustinas, www.municipal.cl, guided tours Tue 1300-1500 and Sun 1100-1400, US$4*. A little further west along the Alameda is the **Universidad de Chile** and the **Club de la Unión**, an exclusive social club founded in 1864. The current building dates from 1925 and houses a restaurant where wonderful meals are served at exorbitant prices. Nearby, on Calle Nueva York, is the **Bolsa de Comercio** (stock exchange). The public are allowed access to view the trading, but you will have to show your passport to get inside.

One block further west there are three plazas: **Plaza de la Libertad** to the north of the Alameda with a monument to the former President Arturo Alessandri Palma, **Plaza Bulnes** in the centre and **Plaza del Libertador O'Higgins** to the south where Chile's founding father is buried. To the north of Plaza de la Libertad, hemmed in by the skyscrapers of the Centro Cívico, is **Palacio de la Moneda** (the presidential palace) containing historic relics,

80 paintings, sculptures and the elaborate Salón Rojo used for official receptions. Although the Moneda was damaged by air attacks during the military coup of 11 September 1973, the 1805 building has been fully restored. The courtyards are open to the public (access from north side) ① *Mon-Fri 1000-1800 unless important state business is being carried out, guided tours of the palace 0900-1300 final Sun of every month*. Ceremonial changing of the guard every other day at 1000.

Just behind the Moneda is the Plaza de la Constitución home to the underground Centro Cívico de la Moneda. Like a mini version of London's Tate Modern, it houses temporary exhibitions as well as an arts cinema and an interesting gallery of Chilean handicrafts.

South of the Alameda

Four blocks south of Plaza del Libertador O'Higgins is **Parque Almagro**, notable for the **Iglesia de los Sacramentinos**, a Gothic church loosely designed in imitation of Sacré Coeur in Paris, which is best viewed from the nearby Palacio Cousiño against the backdrop of the *cordillera*. **Palacio Cousiño** ① *Dieciocho 438, Toesca metro, line 2 (www.palaciocousino.co.cl), admission by guided tour only (Spanish or English), Tue-Fri 0930-1330, 1430-1700 (last tour 1600), Sat, Sun and holidays 0930-1330, US$3*, on the west side of the Parque Almagro and five blocks south of the Alameda, is a large mansion in French rococo style. It was built by Luis and Isadora Cousiño, part

Santiago west of centre

Sleeping 😴
Conde Ansúrez **2**
Ducado **16**
Happy House Hostel **1**
Hostal Americano **5**

Hostal Che Lagarto **3**
Hostal Río Amazonas **7**
La Casa Roja **9**
Majestic **4**
Residencial Alemana **10**

Residencial Mery **11**
Residencial Sur **6**
Residencial Turístico **13**
SCS Habitat **18**
Tur Hotel Express **12**

0 metres   200
0 yards   200

of a wealthy Chilean dynasty that made its money in the coal and silver mining industries. Furnished with tapestries, antiques and pictures imported from France, the palace startled Santiago society with its opulence and its advanced technology, including its own electricity generators and the first lift in the country. Even today, the word luxurious falls short when describing the palace: one of the chandeliers is made with 13,000 pieces of crystal and the superb Italian staircase was built using 20 different types of marble. Look out also for the *indiscretos*, three-seater armchairs designed for courting couples and a chaperone. The family monogram can be seen on the curtains, mirrors and doors. Now owned by the Municipalidad, the palace is used for official receptions but is also open as a museum. A visit is highly recommended.

> ‡ Try to get to Palacio Cousiño in time for the first tour of the morning or afternoon, as later groups tend to be rushed.

Parque O'Higgins lies about 10 blocks south of the Alameda. It has a small lake, playing fields, tennis courts, a swimming pool (open in summer), an open-air stage for local song and dance, a disco, the racecourse of the **Club Hípico**, and an amusement park, **Fantasilandia** ① *daily in summer, Sat and Sun only in winter, adults US$10, children US$7.50, unlimited rides*. There are kite-flying contests on Sundays and, during the Independence celebrations around 18 September, there are many good *peñas*. There is also a group of about 20 basic restaurants, some craft shops, and three small museums: **Acuario Municipal** ① *Local 9, T02-5565680, daily 1000-2000, small charge*; **Museo de Insectos y Caracoles** ① *Local 12, daily 1000-2000, small charge*, with a collection of insects and shellfish; and **Museo del Huaso** ① *T02-5561927, Mon-Fri 1000-1700, Sun and holidays 1000-1400, free*, which houses a small, interesting collection of *criollo* clothing and tools. Cars are not allowed in the park, which can be reached by metro line 2 to Parque O'Higgins station or by bus from Parque Baquedano via Avenida MacKenna and Avenida Matta.

Barrio Brasil

On the northern side of the Alameda, immediately to the west of the Panamericana, is the Barrio Brasil, a tranquil area in which many of the houses are brightly painted. At the end of the 18th century, this historic part of the city was the first area to be colonized by Santiaguinos away from the centre. The area is rich in colonial architecture and is also a centre for nightlife with many underground bars, clubs and restaurants and Santiago's most radical shop, **La Lunita**, stocking feminist books and Santiago's only gay monthly, *Lambda News*.

The heart of the *barrio* is **Plaza Brasil**, easily reached by walking straight up Calle Concha y Toro from the República metro stop (line 1). This is a narrow, winding cobbled street that passes elegant old stone homes in rococo and German Gothic styles before reaching the plaza, which is shaded by palms, lime trees and silk cottons. Just east

Eating ⓪
El Puente de Chabuca **3**
Las Vacas Gordas **1**
Los Buenos Muchachos **2**
Los Chinos Ricos **4**

Ocean Pacific **6**
Ostras Azócar **5**

of the plaza, on Huérfanos, is the **Basílica del Salvador**, a striking yellow- and rose-coloured church built between 1870 and 1872, with stained glass and a statue of the Virgen del Carmen. A little further along Compañía is the **Iglesia Preciosa Sangre**, a bright red church of neoclassical design, with impressive reliefs and twin towers. You could then walk one block north to Calle Catedral, where there are some fine old buildings with tall double windows, wooden balconies and stone pallisades.

> ❊ In 1981, a thief made off with the statue of the Virgen, but returned it the next day after an earthquake rocked the city.

Around Estación Central

The Alameda continues westwards across the Pan-American Highway towards the impressive railway station, **Estación Central**, which is surrounded by several blocks of market stalls. Opposite Estación Central is the **Planetarium** ① *US$6*, while to the north on Avenida Matucana y Diego Portales is **Parque Quinta Normal**, Quinta Normal metro, line 5. The park was founded as a botanical garden in 1830, and is a pleasant, popular spot, which gets very crowded on Sundays with families and the street entertainers who vie with one another to get their pesos.

The park contains several museums. **Museo Ferroviario** ① *www.corpdicyt.cl, Tue-Fri 1000-1800, Sat and Sun 1100-1900, US$2, free to over 60s*, contains the former

Bellavista

Sleeping 🛏
Bellavista Hostel **8**
Casa Condell **7**
Hostal Casa Grande **1**
Montecarlo **3**
Patio Suizo **2**
Presidente **5**
Principado **6**
Santa Victoria **4**

Eating 🍴
Ají Verde **3**
Azul Profundo **22**
Café de la Dulcería
   Las Palmas **3**
Café Universitario **30**
Como Agua para
   Chocolate **23**
Eladio **8**

El Antojo de Gauguin **5**
El Diablito **7**
El Kilometro 11.680 **24**
El Otro Sitio **6**
El Tablao **18**
El Viejo Verde **20**
Gatopardo **10**
Il Siciliano **12**
La Divina Comida **14**

presidential stagecoach and 13 steam engines built between 1884 and 1953, including a rare surviving Kitson-Meyer. **Museo Nacional de Historia Natural**, ① www.mnhn.cl, Tue-Sat 1000-1730, Sun and holidays 1100-1830, US$1.20, Sun free, students free, was founded in 1830 and is one of Latin America's oldest museums. Housed in a neoclassical building, it has exhibitions on zoology, botany, mineralogy, anthropology and ethnography. **Museo Artequín** ① Av Portales 3530, T02-6825367, www.artequin.cl, Tue-Fri 0900-1700, Sat, Sun and holidays 1100-1800, US$1.60, is housed in the Chilean pavilion built for the 1889 Paris International Exhibition. It contains prints of famous paintings and explanations of the techniques of the great masters. Recommended. Two blocks east of the park is the **Museo de la Solidaridad Salvador Allende** ① Herrera 360, T02-6817542, www.mssa.cl, Tue-Sun 1000-1900, US$1.20. Located in a beautiful listed building with a cobbled patio and palm trees with nesting birds, it houses a collection of over 400 art works produced by Chilean and foreign artists in support of the Unidad Popular government and in opposition to the Pinochet dictatorship. Artists include Alexander Calder, Joan Miró, Oswaldo Guayasamín and Roberto Matta. There are also videos of interviews (in Spanish) with survivors of the 1973 coup and an information sheet in English. You need to give four days' notice for guided tours, but they are recommended. The café serves a cheap set lunch. The museum is due to be relocated during 2007-2008.

La Pergola de la Plaza 21
Les Assassins 15
Michelle's 17
Off the Record 25
Opera Catedral 26
Tercera Compañía
 de Bomberos 29
Venezia 19
Zen 2

Bars & clubs 🎵
HBH 11
La Bodega de Julio 13
La Casa en el Aire 1
Libro Café
 Mediterráneo 16
Restaurant/Pub Evelyn 9

Bellavista and Cerro San Cristóbal 🍴🎵🏨 ➤ pp88-95.

Santiago's Bohemian face is most obvious in the Bellavista district, on the north bank of the Río Mapocho at the foot of Cerro San Cristóbal. This is the main focus of nightlife in the old city; the area around Pío Nono and Antonia López de Bello hums and buzzes, especially at weekends. In the bars you can see everything from live Cuban music to local imitations of Georges Brassens, while eating options range from classic Italian dishes to sushi and West African palm-nut stew. There are also theatres, art galleries and craft shops specializing in lapis lazuli, as well as **La Chascona** ① Fernando Márquez de la Plata 0192, T02-7778741, www.uchile.cl/neruda/chascona.html, Tue-Sun 1000-1300, 1500-1800, US$3 guided visits only, English guides can be booked. This is one of the homes of the poet Pablo Neruda. There are really three houses, built on a steep hillside and separated by gardens. La Chascona was completed in 1955 and thereafter Neruda lived here whenever he was in the capital. It is basically in the same condition as when he lived here (it was restored after being damaged in the 1973 coup) and is also now the headquarters of the **Fundación Pablo Neruda**.

Parque Metropolitano

The sharp, conical hill of **San Cristóbal** to the northeast of the city, forms the Parque Metropolitano ⓘ *daily 0900-2100, vehicles US$4*, the largest and most interesting of the city's parks. On a clear day it provides excellent views over the city and across to the Andes. More usually, however, the views provide a graphic demonstration of Santiago's continuing smog problem. There are two sectors, **Sector Cumbre** on Cerro San Cristóbal and, further east, **Sector Tupahue**. There are three entrances: west from Pío Nono in Bellavista, south from Pedro de Valdivia Norte and east from La Pirámide and Avenida Américo Vespucio. When the weather is good, the walk up the access road from Bellavista is very pleasant, providing unexpected views of distant and little-visited northern parts of the city. On Cerro Cumbre (300 m above the city), there is a colossal statue of the Virgin, which is floodlit at night; beside it is the astronomical observatory of the Catholic University, which can be visited on application to the observatory's director. Near the Bellavista entrance is the **Jardín Zoológico** ⓘ *www.zoologico.cl, Tue-Sun 1000-1800, US$4*, which has a well cared for collection of animals.

The Tupahue sector is reached by taxi either from the Bellavista entrance (much cheaper from inside the park as taxis entering the park have to pay the entrance fee) or alternatively you could walk the kilometre from Pedro de Valdivia metro. This section of the park contains terraces, gardens and paths. One building houses the **Camino Real** ⓘ *T02-2321758, www.eventoscaminoreal.cl*, a good, expensive restaurant with a splendid view from the terrace, especially at night, and an *enoteca* or exhibition of Chilean wines from a range of vineyards. You can taste one of the six 'wines of the day' ⓘ *US$2 per glass*, and buy if you like, although prices are higher

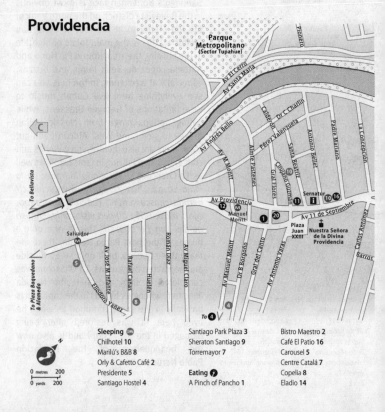

Providencia

Sleeping		
Chilhotel 10	Santiago Park Plaza 3	Bistro Maestro 2
Marilú's B&B 8	Sheraton Santiago 9	Café El Patio 16
Orly & Cafetto Café 2	Torremayor 7	Carousel 5
Presidente 5		Centre Catalá 7
Santiago Hostel 4	**Eating**	Copelia 8
	A Pinch of Pancho 1	Eladio 14

0 metres 200
0 yards 200

than in shops. Nearby is the **Casa de la Cultura**, which has art exhibitions and free concerts at midday on Sunday. There are also two good **swimming pools** in the park (see page 101). East of Tupahue are the **Botanical Gardens** ① *daily 0900-1800, guided tours available*, with a collection of Chilean native plants.

If you don't want to walk to the top of Cerro San Cristóbal, you can take the **funicular** ① *Plaza Caupolicán at the northern end of C Pío Nono, every few mins 1000-2000 daily, US$2 return, US$1.35 one way*. Or, from the Tupahue sector, take the **teleférico** ① *Estación Oasis, Av Pedro de Valdivia Norte via Tupahue, summer only, Mon 1430-1830, Tue-Fri 1030-1830, Sat and Sun 1030-1900, US$4 combination ticket including funicular*. An open bus also operated by the *teleférico* company runs to San Cristóbal and Tupahue from the Bellavista entrance with the same schedule.

Cementerio General

From the top of Cerro San Cristóbal the Cementerio General can be seen, situated in the *barrio* of La Recoleta to the north. This cemetery contains the mausoleums of most of the great figures in Chilean history and the arts, including Violeta Parra, Victor Jara and Salvador Allende. There is also an impressive monument to the victims of the 1973-1990 military government; their names, ages and dates of detention or disappearance are listed in two sections: those who disappeared and those executed for political reasons. See www.cementeriogeneral.cl for more details. The cemetery can be reached by any Recoleta bus from Calle Miraflores or by metro, Cementerios, line 2.

El Giratorio **14**
El Huerto **9**
Gatsby **6**
Kimomo **11**
La Pez Era **20**
Oriental **4**

Osadía **15**
Salvaje **12**

Phone Box Pub **10**

Bars & clubs
Brannigan's Pub **3**
Louisiana River Pub **18**

East to Providencia and Las Condes 🍴🏛🚶 ›› pp88-95.

East of Plaza Italia, the main east-west axis of the city becomes known as **Avenida Providencia**, as it heads out towards residential areas at the eastern and upper levels of the city. On the south bank of the Mapocho, beneath Parque Metropolitano is **Parque Balmaceda**. It is one of the more attractive parks in Santiago with well laid-out gardens and fountains. The park houses the **Museo de los Tajamares** ① *Av Provi-dencia 222, To2-3407329, Mon-Fri 0900-1400, 1500-2100*, an exhibition of the 17th- and 18th-century walls and subsequent canalization developed to protect the city from flooding.

Providencia

The neighbourhood of Providencia is the upmarket commercial centre of Santiago, a busy area of shops, offices and smart restaurants, mostly congregated around Pedro de Valdivia and Los Leones metro stations, line 1. The head office of Sernatur, the national tourist board, are located here. **Calle Suecia**, near Los Leones, is the focal point for nightlife in this part of the city, with over a dozen 'pubs' offering European beers on tap, Tex-Mex food and live music.

Las Condes

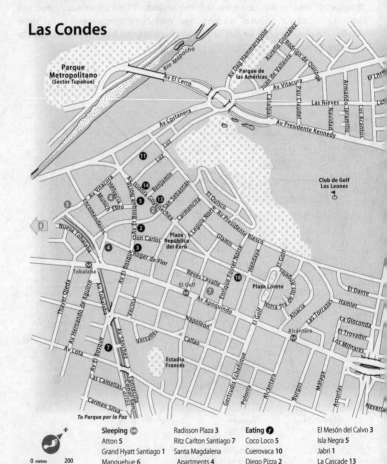

Santiago Region Santiago Sights

Sleeping 🛏	Radisson Plaza 3	Eating 🍴	El Mesón del Calvo 3
Atton 5	Ritz Carlton Santiago 7	Coco Loco 5	Isla Negra 5
Grand Hyatt Santiago 1	Santa Magdalena	Cuerovaca 10	Jabri 1
Manquehue 6	Apartments 4	Diego Pizza 2	La Cascade 13
Montebianco 2	Urania's B&B 8	El Madroñal 11	Le Fournil 12

0 metres 200
0 yards 200

At Tobalaba metro, Avenida Providencia becomes **Avenida Apoquindo**, which heads on past Avenida Américo Vespucio – Santiago's ring road – and out towards the exclusive neighbourhoods of Las Condes, Vitacura, Lo Curro, Lo Barnechea and La Dehesa. Here you will find walled residential compounds, houses with servants and top of the range cars, and expensive US-style shopping malls, such as **Alto Las Condes** and **Parque Arauco**. Anyone who is anyone in Chilean society lives in this part of town.

Las Condes is home to two museums. **Museo de la Escuela Militar** ① *Los Militares 4500, Mon-Fri 0900-1230*, has displays on Bernardo O'Higgins, the Conquest and the Pacific War. **Museo Ralli** ① *Alonso Sotomayor 4110, Vitacura, Tue-Sun 1100-1700, closed in summer, free,* has an excellent collection of works by modern artists, including Dalí, Chagall, Bacon and Miró. Recommended. There are art galleries on Avenida Nueva Costanera and Alonso de Córdova, Vitacura, in the Barrio Alto. Here, four or five private galleries showcase contemporary Chilean and Latin American art. All galleries are within a couple of blocks of each other. Try **Galería Tomas Andreu** ① *Av Nueva Costanera 3731, T02-2289952*; **Galería de Arte Isabel Aninat** ① *Alonso de Córdova 3053, T02-2632729*; and **AMS Marlborough** ① *Av Nueva Costanera 3723, T02-2288696*.

South of Las Condes

Parque por la Paz ① *Av Arrieta 8200, www.villagrimaldi.cl*, the new peace park in the southeastern suburb of Peñalolén, stands on the site of **Villa Grimaldi**, the most notorious torture centre during the Pinochet regime. The Irish missionary, Sheila Cassidy, has documented the abuses that she underwent when imprisoned without trial in this place. The walls are daubed with human rights graffiti and the park makes a moving and unusual introduction to the conflict that has eaten away at the heart of Chilean society for the past 30 years. To reach the park, take a metro to Tobalaba and then any bus marked Peñalolén heading south down Tobalaba. Get off at the junction of Tobalaba y José Arrieta and then walk five minutes up Arrieta towards the mountains.

La Florida

To the southeast of the centre, La Florida is a typical lower middle class residential neighbourhood that would not merit a visit were it not for the excellent **Museo Interactivo Mirador (MIM)** ① *Punta Arenas 6711, Mirador metro, line 5, T02-2807800, www.mim.cl, Mon 0930-1330, Tue-Sun 0930-1830, US$6, concessions US$4*. This is a fun interactive science and technology museum, a perfect place for a family outing. There is also an aquarium in the grounds.

To Museo Ralli

Av Vitacura
El Coigue
El Ulmo
Nieves
Las Nipas
Matico
Los Coligües
El Ciruelillo
Los Laureles
El Clonqui
Espangue
La Lima
Av Circumvalación Américo Vespucio
Cerro Colorado
Los Talaveras
Artilleros
Los Cadetes
Los Estandartes
Tungay
Av Presidente Riesco

Escuela Militar

Los Militares
Escuela Militar
Av Apoquindo
Luis Rodríguez
Puerta del Sol

To 1
To 8
To 6 & Plaza Artesanos de Manquehue

Osadía **7**	Bars & clubs 🎵
Pinpilinpausha **14**	Flannery's Irish
Puerto Mariskо **18**	Geo Pub **4**
Sakura **16**	

Maipú

The suburb of Maipú, 10 km southwest of Santiago, is a 45-minute bus ride from the Alameda. Here, a monument marks the site of the Battle of the Maipú, 5 April 1818, which resulted in the final defeat of the Spanish royalist forces in mainland Chile. Nearby is the monolithic **National Votive Temple of Maipú** ① *daily 0830-2000; in summer mass Mon-Fri 1700, Sat and Sun 1200 and 1700; in winter mass Mon 1830, Tue-Sun 1200 and 1830*. This is a fine example of modern architecture and stained glass (best viewed from the inside). It is located on the site of an earlier temple, built in 1818 on the orders of Bernardo O'Higgins to commemorate the battle. The walls of the old construction stand in the forecourt, having fallen into ruin due to successive earthquakes. Pope John Paul II gave a mass here on his visit to Chile in 1987. The **Museo del Carmen** ① *Tue-Sun 1000-1800*, is part of the same building and contains carriages, furniture, clothing and other items from colonial times and later.

● Sleeping

Most of the more expensive accommodation is situated in the city centre or further east in the neighbourhoods of Providencia and Las Condes. The expensive hotels listed tend to be slightly characterless but with good service. Most budget accommodation is located in the city centre or further west in the vicinity of the bus terminals. There are many basic hotels on Morandé, Gral MacKenna, San Martín and San Pablo in the centre, particularly on Gral MacKenna 1200 block, but bear in mind that this is the red-light district. Another good option is to stay in a family-run guesthouse.

Accommodation here is generally about 30% more expensive than elsewhere in the country. Check if breakfast is included in the price quoted. Most 3-, 4- and 5-star hotels do not charge the 18% tax to foreigners who pay in US$ cash. However, the exchange rate given is often so punitive that it may be cheaper to pay in pesos. Several websites offer hotel booking services for Santiago and the rest of Chile, but most charge a sizeable commission.

If you are staying for weeks or months rather than days, staying with a family is an economical and interesting option. For private rentals, see the classified ads in *El Mercurio* – where flats, homes and family *pensiones* are listed by district – or in *El Rastro* (weekly), or try the notice board at the tourist office. Rates for 2-bed furnished apartments in a reasonable neighbourhood start at around US$200 per month. A month's rent and a month's deposit are normally required. Some offer daily and weekly lets. Estate agents handle apartments. The 3 agencies here are recommended:
Edificio San Rafael, Miraflores 264, T02-6330289, F2225629.
Nancy Lombardo, MacIver 175, oficina 42, T02-6382009, F6330210.
Tempo Rent, Santa Magdalena 116, T02-2311608, tempo.rent@chilnet.cl.

It's worth getting a list of addresses around the country from the **Asociación Chilena de Albergues Turísticos Juveniles** (ACHATJ), Hernando de Aguirre 201, oficina 602, T02-2333220, www.hostelling.cl.

Around the Plaza de Armas
p77, map p76
AL **Majestic**, Santo Domingo 1526, T02-6958366, www.hotelmajestic.cl. With breakfast, pool, US-chain standard. The rooms, while spacious, retain their 1970s decor, although there are internet connection ports in the rooms. Excellent Indian restaurant. English spoken.
D **Indiana** (no sign), Rosas 1339, T02-6880008, hostal_indiana@hotmail.com. F singles. Very basic, kitchen facilities, friendly, internet.
D **Olicar**, San Pablo 1265, T02-6730837, hotel_olicar@chile.com. F singles. Basic, cooking facilities.
D **Residencial San Antonio**, San Antonio 811, T02-6384607, ressnant@ctcinternet.cl. F singles. Good place, decent value.
D **Residencial Sur**, Ruiz Tagle 055, T02-7765533. F singles. Clean, meals available.

D **San Felipe**, Gral MacKenna 1248, T02-6714598. F singles. Cheap laundry service, kitchen, noisy (2nd floor quieter), luggage stored.
D **Santo Domingo**, Santo Domingo 755, T02-6396733, santodomingoinn@hotmail. com. F singles. Cleanish, basic, gloomy.

Along and around the Alameda *p78, maps p76, p80 and p82*

LL **Fundador**, Paseo Serrano 34, T02-3871200, www.hotelfundador.cl. In a nice area, central, with helpful staff, conference rooms and banqueting halls. Pool, bar, restaurant, internet connections. Some rooms on the small side. Universidad de Chile metro, line 1, south exit.
L **Galerías**, San Antonio 65, T02-4707400, www.hotelgalerias.cl. Large rooms, good location, generous breakfast, 5-star. Excellent value if booked over the internet.
AL-A **Principado**, Vicuña MacKenna 30, 1 block south of Plaza Baquedano, T02-2228142, www.hotelesprincipado.com. Reasonable if nondescript 3-star standard.
A **El Marqués del Forestal**, Ismael Valdés Vergara 740, T02-6333462, www.apart -hotel-elmarques.cl. Good value, apartments.
A-B **Montecarlo**, Victoria Subercaseaux 209, T02-6392945 , www.hotelmontecarlo.cl. At foot of Cerro Santa Lucía in quiet street, modern but with nice art deco touches, restaurant, stores luggage, helpful. Recommended.
A-B **Vegas**, Londres 49, T02- 6322514, www.hotelvegas.net. Standard 3 star. Nice location, very convenient for centre. Slightly brusque staff.
B-C **Hostal Che Lagarto**, Tucapel Jiménez 24, T02-6991493, www.chelagarto.com. E per person in dorms. Some rooms with bath. Newish branch of the South American chain hostel. Comfortable common areas, kitchen facilities, internet.
B-C **París**, París 813, T02-6640921, www. hotelparis.cl. With bath, quiet, clean, no-frills but good value, breakfast extra, luggage store. Book in advance in summer. Recommended.
C **Residencial Londres**, Londres 54, T02-6382215, unico54@ctcinternet.cl. E singles. Near San Francisco Church, former mansion, large old-fashioned rooms and furniture, some rooms with bath, few singles, no

heating so cold in winter, some English spoken, book exchange, great value, very popular, highly recommended, usually full, no advance bookings high season, arrive early.

Barrio Brasil *p81, map p80*
A **Happy House Hostel**, Catedral 2207, metro Cumming or República, T02-6884849, www.happyhousehostel.cl. E per person in dorms. In a completely refurbished mansion, this is one of the best hostels in the country. High-ceilinged spacious rooms, excellent fully equipped kitchen, internet, bar, pool room. One room even has an en suite sauna. Friendly and informative staff who speak English. The only downside is that some rooms facing the main street can be a little noisy. Expensive, but still highly recommended.
B **Ducado**, Agustinas 1990, T02-6969384, hotelducado@entelchile.net. With breakfast. Reasonable value, clean, quiet at back. Secure parking. Also self-contained apartments.
B **Hostal Río Amazonas**, Rosas 2234, T02-6984092, www.hostalrioamazonas.cl. With breakfast and bath, internet, good value if paying in US dollars or euros. Recommended.
C **Hostal Americano**, Compañia 1906, T02-6981025, www.hostalamericano.cl. Nondescript brick and concrete building. Clean, comfortable rooms, some with private bathroom. Friendly atmosphere, some English spoken. There is a pleasant garden at the back. Better value if paying in US dollars. Recommended.
C **La Casa Roja**, Agustinas 2113, T02-6964241, www.lacasaroja.cl. F per person in dorms. Huge old house slowly being restored. Without breakfast, kitchen facilities, internet, Spanish lessons. Large garden with table tennis and other games. Australian run. Can be noisy. Recommended if you want to party, not if you want to sleep. Camping available.
D **Residencial Turístico**, Catedral 2235, T02-6954800. F singles. Basic, clean, hot showers, quiet location, good value.

Around Estación Central *p82, map p80*
Staying in this area is convenient for those on a lightening visit or for those with an early or late start.

A **Conde de Anzúrez**, Av República 25, T02-6960807, www.ansurez.cl. República metro. Convenient for airport, central station and bus terminals, clean, helpful, safe, luggage stored, good car hire deals and occasional special offers.

A **Tur Hotel Express**, Av Libertador Bernardo O'Higgins 3750, piso 3, in the Turbus Terminal, T02-6850100, www.turbus.com/html/turhotel_stgo.html . Comfortable business standard with breakfast, cable TV, a/c, free internet. Particularly useful if you need to take an early flight as buses leave for the airport from here.

B-C **Residencial Mery**, Pasaje República 36, off 0-100 block of República, T02-6968883, www.resid encialmery.virtuabyte.cl. Art deco building down an alley, some rooms with bath, breakfast extra, friendly owners, quiet. Recommended.

C **Residential Alemana**, República 220 (no sign), T02-6712388, ralemana@entelchile. net. República metro. **E** singles. Without bath, clean, with breakfast, pleasant patio, central, heating on request, good cheap meals available. Also long term rentals. Recommended.

D **SCS Habitat**, San Vicente 1798, T02-6833732, scshabitat@yahoo.com. **F** per person in dorms. English spoken, lots of information, hot showers, laundry facilities, bicycle rental, internet, maps, guidebooks and camping equipment sold/rented, safe parking for bikes and motorbikes, book exchange, not central, frequently recommended but some mixed reports. Camping available.

Bellavista and Cerro San Cristóbal *p83, map p82*

AL **Presidente**, Eliodoro Yáñez 867, almost at Providencia, T02-2358015, www. Presidente.cl. Salvador metro. Slightly soulless, medium-sized chain hotel. Good value and good location.

B **Bellavista Hostel**, Dardignac 0184, T02-7328737, www.bellavistahostel.com. **E** per person in dorms. Fun hostel in the heart of this lively area. European-style hostel, sheets provided but make your own bed. With breakfast. Kitchen facilities, free

internet, satelite TV in common area, bicycles lent to guests. Good meeting place.

C **Hostal Casa Grande**, Vicuña MacKenna 90, T02-2227347, www.hostalcasagrande.cl. Baquedano metro. **E** singles. Laberinthine *hostal* on the 2nd floor of an old high-ceilinged building. Some rooms with bath and TV, quiet, good value.

Providencia *p86, map p84*

LL **Santiago Park Plaza**, Av Ricardo Lyon 207, T02-3724000, www.parkplaza.cl. 5-star, another typical 'luxury hotel' geared towards business travellers.

LL **Sheraton Santiago**, Santa María 1742, T02-2335000, www.sheraton.cl. 5-star, one of the best in town, good restaurant, good buffet lunch, all facilities.

AL **Orly**, Pedro de Valdivia 027, T02-2318947, www.orlyhotel.com. Pedro de Valdivia metro. Small, comfortable, excellent location. Also more expensive suites, small café attached with reasonable food. Recommended.

AL **Torremayor**, Av Ricardo Lyon 322, T02-2342000, www.hoteltorremayor.cl Clean, modern, good service, restaurant, good location.

A-B **Marilú's Bed and Breakfast**, Rafael Cañas 246 C, T02-2355302, www.bedand breakfast.cl. Salvador metro. Comfortable, no credit cards, very friendly, good beds, English and French spoken. Reservations essential. Recommended.

A **Chilhotel**, Cirujano Guzmán 103, T02-2640643, www.chilhotel.cl. Run of the mill small hotel. Good value. Manuel Montt metro.

A **Patio Suizo**, Condell 847, Bustamante metro (line 5), T02-4941214, www.patiosuizo. com. Comfortable and pleasant Swiss-run B&B in a quiet area. Some rooms with bath. Breakfast included, English, German spoken, Spanish classes. Recommended.

B-C **Casa Condell**, Condell 114, T02-2092343 Salvador metro, www.casacondell.cl. Also 4-bed dorms, **E-F** per person. Pleasant old house, central, quiet, nice roof terrace. Shared baths, no breakfast, kitchen facilities, free local phone calls, friendly, English spoken. Recommended.

C **Santa Victoria**, Santa Victoria 6, metro Santa Isabel, line 5, T02-2220031. Quiet, small, safe, family run.

E **Santiago Hostel**, Barros Borgoño 199, Manuel Montt metro, T02-2649899. Price per person in dorms. European-style youth hostel. With breakfast, kitchen facilities, garden, internet, excellent skiing information.

Las Condes *p87, map p87*

LL **Grand Hyatt Santiago**, Av Kennedy 4601, T02- 9501234, www.santiago.grand.hyatt. com. Superb, beautifully decorated, large outdoor pool, gymnasium, Thai restaurant. Recommended.

LL **Ritz Carlton Santiago**, El Alcalde 15, T02-4708500, www.ritzcarlton.com/hotels/ santiago. New 5-star plus hotel. All services. The most luxurious hotel in Santiago and also the most expensive.

LL-L **Radisson Plaza**, Av Vitacura 2610, T02-2036000, www.radisson.cl. 5-star, excellent, disabled access.

AL **Atton**, Alonso de Córdova 5199, T02-4227979, www.atton.cl. Comfortable, 4-star, disabled-friendly, good value.

AL **Manquehue**, Esteban Dell'Orto 6615, T02-4301100, www.hotelmanquehue.com. Very good with new wing, new pool, 4 star.

AL **Montebianco**, Isidora Goyenechea 2911, T02-2331808, www.hotelmontebianco.cl. Small, smart hotel. Good value. Can arrange tours to vineyards and trips to the ski centres.

AL **Santa Magdalena Apartments**, office at Helvecia 244, Las Condes, T02-3746875, www.santamagdalena.cl. Apartment rental (for 1-4 people) 1 block from metro stations (Tobalaba or Los Leones), a/c.

B **Urania's Bed and Breakfast**, Boccaccio 60, T02-2012922, uraniae@hotmail.com. Comfortable, friendly, good beds, English and French spoken. Good value. Recommended, though not particularly convenient for public transport.

❼ Eating

Luxury hotels have computerized information on the more expensive restaurants, particularly useful if you are not sure what to eat. There is also an excellent guide to the more exclusive restaurants at www.emol.com, *El Mercurio*'s online entertainment guide.

For excellent cheap seafood lunches make for the Mercado Central (Cal y Canto metro), or the Vega Central market on the opposite bank of the Mapocho. Budget travellers should make the *almuerzo* their main meal. For cheap meals in the evening try the *fuentes de soda* and *schoperias* scattered around the centre.

Around the Plaza de Armas
p77, map p76

₮₮₮-₮₮ **Da Carla**, MacIver 577, T02-6333739. Intimate old-time Italian trattoria, good service and has maintained it quality over the years.

₮₮₮-₮₮ **Les Assassins**, Merced 297, T02-6384280. Small family-run French bistro. Excellent food with friendly service and a decent wine list. Good value set lunches. Recommended.

₮₮₮-₮₮ **Los Adobes del Argomedo**, Argomedo 411 y Lira, T02-2222104. Good Chilean food, floor show (Mon-Sat) includes *cueca* dancing, salsa and folk.

₮₮₮-₮₮ **Majestic**, Santo Domingo 1526. This hotel has an excellent Indian restaurant, good range of vegetarian dishes.

₮₮ **El Naturista**, Moneda 846. Excellent vegetarian, serving quiches, tortillas, a wide range of soups and wholemeal sandwiches. Also serves organic coffee, fruit and vegetable juice as well as beer and wine. Closes 2100.

₮₮ **Faisan d'Or**, Plaza de Armas. Good *pastel de choclo*, pleasant place to have a drink and watch the world go by.

₮₮ **Lung Fung**, Agustinas 715. The oldest Chinese restaurant in Santiago. Pricey but serves decent food. There is a large cage in the centre with noisy parrots.

₮₮-₮ **Nuria**, Agustinas y MacIver. This was a well-known Bohemian hang-out in the 1960s. Now past its heyday, it still serves a wide variety of decent food.

₮ **Bar Nacional**, Bandera 317. Good restaurants, popular, local specialities. There is another branch at Huérfanos 1151.

₮ **El Rápido**, C Bandera, next door to **Bar Nacional**. Famed for its *empanadas* and *completos*, cheap, quick service, popular.

El Vegetariano, Huérfanos 827, Local 18. Popular vegetarian fast food, good juices. There are other branches in the centre.
Govindas, Compañía 1489, Santa Ana metro. Indian vegetarian restaurant in a Hari Krishna centre.

Cafés
Bombón Oriental, Merced 345, T02-6391069, www.bombonoriental.cl. Superb Turkish coffee, arabic snacks and sweets.
Café Caribe and **Café Haití**, Paseo Ahumada, institutions among Santiago's business community and good places to see the people who make Chile tick; also branches throughout the centre and in Providencia.
Café Colonia, MacIver 133. Splendid variety of cakes, pastries and pies, efficient if some-what brusque service by staff who haven't changed for decades. Recommended.
Gelato's, Agustinas 941. Very good. For ice cream in the centre try here.
Salón de Té Cousiño, Matías Cousiño 107. Good coffee, snacks and onces, very popular, not cheap.

Along and around the Alameda *p78, maps p76, p82 and p80*
†††-†† Opera Catedral , José Miguel de la Barra 407, Bellas Artes metro, line 5, T02-6645491, www.operacatedral.cl. Very good, if expensive, French restaurant on the ground floor. Upstairs there is a minimalist pub-restaurant, usually packed at night, serving fusion food at reasonable prices.
†† El 27 de Nueva York, Nueva York 27, a stone's throw from the Alameda. T02-6991555. Large and slightly soulless restaurant serving international cuisine, good and varied menu. Tends to fill up with the lunchtime executive crowd.
†† Gatopardo, Lastarria 192, opposite the plaza Mulato Gil de Castro, T02-6336420. A mixture of Bolivian and Mediterranean cuisine. Good value lunch buffet. Recommended.
†† La Pérgola de la Plaza, Plaza Mulato Gil de Castro, Lastarria, French specialities.
††-† El Diablito , 336, Local 2, Bellas Artes metro, line 5. Fashionable somewhat Bohemian bar-restaurant serving sandwiches and a wide range of beer.

Círculo de Periodistas, Amunátegui 31, piso 2. Unwelcoming entrance, good value lunches. Recommended.
Confitería Torres, Av Libertador Bernardo O'Higgins 1570. Chile's oldest bar/restaurant dating from 1570, good atmosphere, live tango music at weekends. Cheap lunches are served in a large underground *comedor*.

Cafés
Café Universitario, Alameda 395 y Subercaseaux (near Santa Lucía), Lastarria. Good, cheap *almuerzos*, lively at night, separate room for lovers of rock videos, very pleasant.
Tip-Top Galletas, for freshly baked biscuits, there are 2 branches on the Alameda just east of the Moneda, take-away only.

South of the Alameda *p80*
Those on a very tight budget should make straight for C San Diego, where there are the following:
††-† Los Braseros de Lucifer, No 397. Excellent *parrilladas*, also seafood, popular, recommended. A little more expensive than the ones listed below.
† Las Tejas, No 234. Lively, rowdy crowd, very cheap cocktails and drinks such as *pisco sour* and *pipeño*, excellent *cazuelas* and other typical dishes.
† Masticón, No 152. Good service, excellent value, popular, wide range.
† Tercera Compañía de Bomberos, Vicuña Mackenna 097, near the junction with Diagonal Paraguay. Good food, very cheap, recommended.

Barrio Brasil *p81*
†††-†† Las Vacas Gordas, Cienfuegos 280, T02-6971066. Excellent *parrillada*. Very popular, so book in advance.
†††-†† Ocean Pacific's, Cumming 221, T02-6972413. Extremily kitsch seafood restaurant with ship and submarine themed rooms. You can find better food elsewhere, but for over the top exuberance this is hard to beat.
†† El Puente de Chabuca, Brasil 72, T02-6967962. Average Peruvian fare in an impressive colonial building.
†† Los Buenos Muchachos, Cumming 1031, T02-6980112, www.losbuenosmuchachos.cl. Cavernous hall seating over 400 and serving

traditional Chilean food in abundant portions. Very popular, especially at night when shows of traditional Chilean dances are held.

Los Chinos Ricos, Brasil 373, T02-6963778, www.chinosricos.cl, on the plaza. Famed Chinese. The restaurant used to be called Los Chinos Pobres, but was so popular it had to change its name. Fills up with noisy families on Sun lunchtimes.

Ostras Azócar, Bulnes 37. Specializes in oysters. Several reasonable seafood restaurants on the same street.

Bellavista and Cerro San Cristóbal
p83, map p82

Most restaurants in Bellavista close on Sun and public holidays, but this is one of the liveliest places to come out and eat at night, with many excellent and costly restaurants. There are dozens more restaurants than those listed below, with a new place seeming to open every few weeks.

Azul Profundo, Constitución 111. Fish and seafood with a touch of invention. Good range of cocktails.

Como Agua Para Chocolate, Constitución 88. Mexican and Mediterranean. Slightly pretentious presentations but excellent service.

El Kilometro 11.680, Dardignac 0145, T02-7770410. French restaurant with one of Chile's best wine lists.

El Otro Sitio, Antonia López de Bello 053. Upmarket Peruvian. Good service, excellent range of starters. If you are feeling brave try the Rocoto relleno. Recommended.

El Viejo Verde, Antonia López de Bello 94. Excellent vegetarian food.

Il Siciliano, Dardignac y Constitución. Elegant trattoria serving excellent pasta and seafood. Extensive wine list.

La Divina Comida, Purísima 093. Italian with 3 rooms: Heaven, Hell and Purgatory. Recommended.

Off the Record, Antonia López de Bello 0155, T02-7777710, www.offthe record.cl. Bar-restaurant. Period design, nice atmosphere with live music on Fri-Sat nights, cheaper set lunch.

Zen, Dardignac 175, Bellavista. Sushi restaurant. Recommended.

Ají Verde, Constitución 284, T02-7353329. Specializes in Chilean food, open for lunch.

El Antojo de Gaugin, Pío Nono 069. Arabic. Good *brochetas a la plancha*.

El Tablao, Constitución 110, T02-7378648. Traditional Spanish restaurant. The food is reasonable, but the main attraction is the live flamenco show on Fri-Sat nights.

Eladio, Pío Nono 251. Argentine cuisine, good steaks, bingo.

Michelle's, C del Arzobispo 0615, T02-7779919. Mediterranean bistro, excellent seafood and fish dishes. Recommended.

Venezia, Pío Nono y Antonia López de Bello, Bellavista. Traditional Chilean home-cooked fare. Large servings, good value. One of Neruda's favourite haunts.

Cafés

Café de la Dulcería Las Palmas, Antonia López de Bello 190. Good pastries and lunches.

Cafetería La Nona, Pío Nono 099. Real coffee, good *empanadas* and cakes, fresh fruit juices. Recommended.

Empanatodos, Pío Nono 153. Serves 25 different types of *empanadas*.

Green, Constitución 042. Excellent healthy sandwiches and snacks.

Providencia *p86, map p84*

Carousel, Los Conquistadores 1972, T02-2321728. Fine French cuisine, exceptionally smart, nice garden, very expensive.

Centre Catalá, Av Suecia 428 near Lota. Elegant Catalan restaurant, quiet street, nice decor, cheaper set lunch.

El Giratorio, 11 de Septiembre 2250, piso 16, T02-2321827. Good French food eaten while the whole city rotates outside your window. Recommended for the view.

El Huerto, Orrego Luco 054, T02-2332690. Recommended. Open daily, live music Fri and Sat evenings, varied menu, very good, popular.

Osadía, Tobalaba 477, T02-2322732. Celebrated French restaurant, very pricey.

Salvaje, Av Providencia 1177. Excellent international menu, open-air seating, good-value lunches. Recommended.

ⓉⓉⓉ-ⓉⓉ A Pinch of Pancho, Gral del Canto 45, T02-2351700. Seafood and fish specialities, very good.

ⓉⓉⓉ-ⓉⓉ Oriental, M Montt 584, T02-352389. One of the best Chinese restaurants in Santiago. Excellent service.

ⓉⓉ Bistro Maestro, Las Urbinas y Providencia. Russian food, good.

ⓉⓉ Café El Patio, Providencia 1652, next to Phone Box Pub. Tofu and pasta as well as fish dishes, nice sandwiches, popular. Good drinks. Internet. Very pleasant.

ⓉⓉ Eladio, 11 de Septiembre 2250, piso 5. Reasonably priced, good meat dishes. There is often karaoke on Fri and Sat nights.

ⓉⓉ Gatsby, Providencia 1984, T02-2330732. Nationwide chain serving American food, all-you-can-eat buffet and lunch/dinner, also coffees and snacks, open till 2400, tables outside in warm weather, good.

ⓉⓉ La Pez Era, Providencia 1421. Seafood, smart but reasonably priced.

Ⓣ Kimomo, Av Providencia 1480, Vegetarian. Tofu, miso soup, good snacks.

Cafés

Cafetto, Pedro de Valdivia 030, next to **Hotel Orly**. Upmarket café with a wide variety of sandwiches.

There are several good places for snacks and ice cream on Av Providencia including: **Copelia**, No 2211; **Bravissimo**, No 1406; **El Toldo Azul**, No 1936. Also, **Salón de Té Tavelli**, Drugstore precinct, No 2124.

Las Condes *p87, map p87*

This area has many first-class restaurants, including grills, serving Chilean (often with music), French and Chinese cuisine. They tend to be more expensive than central restaurants. Lots of expensive eateries are located on El Bosque Norte, near the Tobalaba metro stop.

ⓉⓉⓉ Coco Loco, El Bosque Norte 0215, T02-2313082. Fish, seafood, good.

ⓉⓉⓉ Cuerovaca, El Mañío 1659, Vitacura, T02-2468936. Serves fantastic steaks, both Argentine and Chilean cuts. Recommended.

ⓉⓉⓉ El Madroñal, Vitacura 2911, T02-2336312. Excellent, Spanish cuisine, one of the best restaurants in town, booking essential.

ⓉⓉⓉ El Mesón del Calvo, El Bosque Norte y Roger de Flor. Seafood specials.

ⓉⓉⓉ Isla Negra, next door to Coco Loco, El Bosque Norte. Seafood a speciality.

ⓉⓉⓉ La Cascade, Isidora Goyenechea 2930. French, expensive, long established, closed Sun.

ⓉⓉⓉ Pinpilinpausha, Isidora Goyenechea 2900, T02-2325800. Basque specialities, good.

ⓉⓉⓉ Sakura, Vitacura 4111. Renowned sushi restaurant. Recommended.

ⓉⓉⓉ-ⓉⓉ Diego Pizza, El Bosque Norte y Don Carlos. Friendly, good cocktails, popular. Recommended.

ⓉⓉⓉ-ⓉⓉ Puerto Marisko, Isidora Goyenechea 2918, T02-2332096. Good seafood.

ⓉⓉ Jabri, Vitacura 6477. Arab cuisine.

ⓉⓉ Le Fournil, Vitacura 3841, opposite Cuerovaca, T02-2280219. Excellent French bakery and restaurant. Particularly popular at lunchtime. Good soups. Service can be poor.

Ⓞ Bars and clubs

As in most of South America, a night out in Santiago begins late. Arrive in a restaurant before 2100 and you may be eating alone, while bars and clubs are often empty before midnight. Clubs and bars playing live music will generally charge an entry fee of between US$2 (for student-orientated places) and US$10 (for upmarket clubs), usually with some sort of drink included in the price.

Santiago has a good selection of varied restaurants, bars, discos and *salsotecas* from the reasonably priced in Bellavista (Baquedano metro) to the smarter along Av Suecia and G Holley in Providencia (Los Leones metro).

In Las Condes, El Bosque Norte is lined with chic bars and expensive restaurants for the Chilean jet-set (Tobalaba metro).

Barrio Brasil has a number of bars and restaurants dotted around Plaza Brasil and on Av Brasil and Cumming. The area is popular with Chilean students (República metro).

In the middle-class suburb of Ñuñoa is Plaza Ñuñoa, around which a number of good bars are dotted.

Clubs in Las Condes and Providencia can be expensive, up to US$20 or more to get in. Clubs in Bellavista are cheaper and more downmarket than those in Providencia.

Bellavista *p83, map p82*

Bogart, Antonia López de Bello 34. Rock music.

Café Mistral, C del Arzobispo 0635, T02-7776173. Owned by French mountain-climber, free climbing wall, internet.

Caribbean, Antonia López de Bello 40. Reggae.

Club 4-40, Santa Filomena 081. Named after popular singer Juan Luis Guerra's backing group from the Dominican Republic, live Cuban music, packed at weekends.

Disco Salsa, Pío Nono 223. Good atmosphere, also salsa dance classes downstairs.

Emmanuelle, Andrés Bello 2857. Shows at 0100 and 0300.

HBH Bar, Purísima y Antonia López de Bello. Good beer, good atmosphere.

Heaven, Recoleta 345. Thu-Sat 2330-0500, US$15 per person.

La Bodega de Julio, Constitución 256. Cuban staff and Cuban cocktails, excellent live music and dancing possible, very popular, free entry before 2300, very good value. Highly recommended.

La Casa en el Aire, Antonia López de Bello 125. Pleasant atmosphere, live music. Recommended.

La Otra Puerta, Pío Nono 348. Lively *salsoteca* with live music. Recommended.

Libro Café Mediterráneo. Popular with students, lively, expensive. US$4.50 charge on Mon nights, when a local man does good Georges Brassens impressions.

Peña Nano Parra, San Isidro 57. Good folk club, cheap.

Restaurant/Pub Evelyn, Purísima 282. Austrian beers on tap, good atmosphere, not cheap.

Tu Tu Tanga, Pío Nono 127. Busy at night, cheap, good value.

Providencia *p86, map p84*

Brannigan's Pub, Suecia 35, T02-2327869. Good beer, live jazz, lively.

Golden Bell Inn, Hernando de Aguirre 27. Popular with expats.

Ilé Habana, Bucaré just off Suecia. Bar with salsa music, often live, and a good dance floor.

Louisiana River Pub, Suecia y General Holley. Live music.

Phone Box Pub, Providencia 1670, T02-2350303. Very popular with expats, serves numerous European beers including Pilsener Urquell, and canned British beers including Newcastle Brown Ale, Beamish Stout and Old Speckled Hen. A good place to go if you are missing home.

Las Condes *p87, map, p87*

Country Village, Av Las Condes 10680. Mon-Sat from 2000, Sun from lunch onwards, live music Fri and Sat.

Flannery's Irish Geo Pub, Encomenderos 83, T02-2336675, www.flannerys.cl. Irish pub, serving Guinness on draft, good lunches including vegetarian options, popular among gringos and Chileans alike.

Las Urracas, Vitacura 9254. US$20 but free before 2300 if you eat there. Huge variety of cocktails.

Morena Pizza and Dance Bar, Av Las Condes 10120. Good sound system, live music at weekends, happy hour before 2200.

Tequila, Av Las Condes at Paseo San Damián. One of a few popular bar-restaurants in the area.

⊙ Entertainment

For all entertainment, nightclubs, cinemas, restaurants, concerts, *El Mercurio* website, www.emol.com, has listings and a good search feature. Look under the *tiempo libre* section. There are also listings in weekend newspapers, particularly *El Mercurio* and *La Tercera*, and in *Santiago What's On*.

Cinemas

A good guide to daily cinema listings across the city is provided by the 2 free newspapers, *La Hora* and *tmg*, which are given out at metro stations early on weekday mornings. Seats cost US$4-7 with reductions on Mon, Tue and Wed (elsewhere in the country the day varies). Some cinemas offer discounts to students and over 60s (proof required).

There are many mainstream cinemas showing international films, usually in original English with Spanish subtitles. Multiplex cinemas include:

CineHoyts Huérfanos, Huérfanos 735, T02-600-5000400, www.cinehoyts.cl.

CineHoyts San Agustín, Moneda 835, T02-600-5000400, www.cinehoyts.cl.

CineHoyts Estación Central, Exposición 155, www.cinehoyts.cl, in the shopping mall next to the train station. T02-6005000400.

CineHoyts La Reina, Av Ossa 655, T02-600-5000400, www.cinehoyts.cl. Simón Bolívar metro, line 4.

Cinemark Alto Las Condes, Av Kennedy 9001, Las Condes, T02-600-6002463, www.cinemark.cl. Attached to the mall.

Showcase Parque Arauco, Av Kennedy 5413, Las Condes, T02-5657010. Attached to the shopping malls.

'CineArte' (art-house cinemas that show quality foreign films) are also very popular and include the following:

Casa de Extensión Universidad Católica, Av B O'Higgins 390, T02-6351994. Universidad Católica metro, south exit, line 1.

Centro Arte Alameda, Av Bernado O'Higgins 139, Baquedano metro, line 1, T02-6648821, www.centroartealameda.cl.

Cine Arte Normandie, Tarapacá 1181, T02-6972979. Varied programme, altered frequently, films at 1530, 1830 and 2130 daily, students half price. Moneda metro, south exit, line 1.

El Biógrafo, Lastarria 181, T02-6334435. Universidad Católica metro, north exit, line 1.

Tobalaba, Av Providencia 2563, T02-2316630. Tobalaba metro, line 1.

Cultural centres

Centro Cultural Estación Mapocho, Cal y Canto metro, line 2, T02-787 0000. www.estacionmapocho.cl. Regular art exhibitions, concerts, shows.

Centro Cultural Palacio La Moneda, Plaza de la Ciudadanía, Moneda metro, north exit, line 1, T02-3556500, www.ccplm.cl. Cinema and good temporary exhibitions.

Corporación Cultural de Las Condes, Av Apoquindo 6570, near beginning of Av Las Condes. T02-3669393. Also art exhibitions, concerts, lectures, etc.

Instituto Cultural de Providencia, Av 11 de Septiembre 1995. T02-2232700. Pedro de Valdivia metro, north exit, line 1. Art exhibitions, concerts, theatre, worth checking out the programme.

Instituto Cultural del Banco del Estado de Chile, Alameda 123. Regular art exhibitions, concerts, theatrical performances.

Performing arts

Teatro Municipal, Agustinas y San Antonio, www.municipal.cl. Stages international opera, concerts by the Orquesta Filarmónica de Santiago and performances by the Ballet de Santiago, throughout the year. On Tue at 2100 there are free operatic concerts in the Salón Claudio Arrau. Tickets range from US$10 for a very large choral group with a symphony orchestra, and US$12 for the cheapest seats at the ballet, to US$100 for the most expensive opera seats. Some cheap seats are often sold on the day of concerts.

Teatro Municipal de Ñuñoa, Av Irarrázaval 1564, www.ccn.cl, T02-2777903. Dance, art exhibitions, cinema, children's theatre.

Teatro Universidad de Chile, Plaza Baquedano, www.teatro.uchile.cl, T02-9782203. Home of the Orquesta y Coro Sinfónica de Chile and the Ballet Nacional de Chile.

A great number of more minor theatres around the city stage plays, including **Abril**, Huérfanos 786; **Camilo Henríquez**, Amunátegui 31; **Centro Arrayán**, Las Condes 14891; **El Galpón de los Leones**, Av Los Leones 238; **El Conventillo**, Bellavista 173 and **La Comedia**, Merced 349. Events are listed in *El Mercurio* and *La Tercera*.

☻ Festivals and events

Mar/Apr Religious festivals and ceremonies continue throughout **Holy Week**, when a priest ritually washes the feet of 12 men.

End of May A food festival called **Expo gourmand**. Its location changes every year.

16 Jul The image of the **Virgen del Carmen** (patron saint of the armed forces) is carried through the streets by cadets.

18 Sep Chile's **Independence Day** when many families get together or celebrate in *fondas* (small temporary constructions made of wood and straw where people eat traditional dishes, drink *chicha* and dance *cueca*).

19 Sep **Armed Forces Day** is celebrated with an enormous military procession through the Parque O'Higgins. It takes 4 hrs.

Nov A free **art fair** lasting a fortnight is held in the Parque Forestal on the banks of the Río Mapocho.

O Shopping

There are many shopping areas in Santiago. The shops in the centre and to the north of the Plaza de Armas are cheaper and more downmarket than the countless arcades and boutiques strung along Providencia, especially near Av Ricardo Lyon. Specialist shops tend to be grouped together, eg bikes, computer hardware and second-hand books on San Diego, new bookshops on Providencia, opticians on MacIver, lapis lazuli in Bellavista. Some kiosks on Paseo Ahumada/Huérfanos sell overseas newspapers and journals.

Bookshops

Book prices are very high compared with Europe, even for second-hand books. There are many bookshops in the Pedro de Valdivia area on Av Providencia. Much better value but with a smaller selection are the bookshops in the shopping mall at Av Providencia 1114-1120. Those looking for cheap English-language books should also try the many second-hand book kiosks on San Diego, 4 blocks south of Plaza Bulnes, next to the Iglesia de los Sacramentinos.

Apostrophes, Merced 324, www.apostrophes.cl, specializes in foreign-language publications including literature.

Books, Providencia 1652, Local 5, in a courtyard beside the **Phone Box Pub** and **Café El Patio**. Wide selection of English-language books for sale or exchange, English spoken. On the expensive side.

Feria Chilena del Libro, Huérfanos 623. Largest bookstore in Santiago, good for travel books and maps; also at Nueva York 3, Agustinas 859, Mall Parque Arauco and Providencia 2124.

Librairie Française, Estado 337. French books and newspapers.

Librería Chile Ilustrado, Providencia 1652 local 6, next door to **Books**, T02-2358145, chileil@tnet.cl. Specializes in books (nearly all in Spanish) relating to Chile, particularly flora and fauna, history and anthropology.

Librería Eduardo Albers, Vitacura 5648, Las Condes, T02-2185371, F2181458. Spanish, English and German – good selection, cheaper than most, helpful, also German and Swiss newspapers.

Librería Inglesa, Huérfanos 669, local 11, Pedro de Valdivia 47, Vitacura 5950, Providencia 2653, T02-2319970, www.libreria inglesa.cl. Sells only books in English, good selection, stocks the *South American Handbook*.

Librería Lila, Providencia 1652, local 3. Mind/body/spirit specialists, best in Santiago in this field.

Librería Universitaria, Av Bernado O'Higgins 1050, T02-6951529, F6956387. Particularly for books in Spanish.

LOM Ediciones, Estación Mapocho, Mon-Fri 1000-2000, Sat 1000-1400. Sells a stock of literature, history, sociology, art and politics from its own publishing house. Also a bar and a reading room with recent Chilean newspapers and magazines.

South American Way, Av Apoquindo 6856, Las Condes, T02-2118078. Sells books in English.

Camping and outdoors equipment

Bertonati Hnos, Manuel Montt 2385. Equipment for camper vans.

Casa Italiana, Tarapacá 1120. Repairs camping stoves.

Club Andino and **Federación de Andinismo** (see page 100). Expensive products as the stocked articles are imported.

Fabri Gas, Bandera y Santo Domingo. Camping gas cartridges.

Industria Yarur, Rosas 1289 y Teatinos, T02-6723696. Good value for money, discounts available.

Juan Soto, Silva Vildosola 890, Paradero 1, Gran Avenida, San Miguel, T02-5558329. For tent repairs.

La Cumbre, Apoquindo 5258, Las Condes, T02-2209907, la_cumbre@email.com. Climbing equipment.

Luz Emperatriz Sanhuela Quiroz, Portal de León, Loc 14, Providencia 2198. Los Leones metro. Second-hand equipment.

Outdoors & Travel, Encomenderos 206, Las Condes, T02-3357104. For wide range of imported and locally made camping goods.

Patagonia, Helvecia 210, Providencia, T02-3351796. Good range of clothing and equipment, comparatively expensive.

Unisport, Av Providencia 2503. Camping gas cartridges.

Those wishing to spend a reasonable amount of money buying good-quality crafts may wish to travel to Pomaire (see page 110), where goods from all over Chile are for sale at prices cheaper than those in Santiago.

The gemstone, lapis lazuli, can be found in a few expensive shops in Bellavista but is cheaper in the arcades on the south side of the Plaza de Armas. Antique stores can be found in Plaza Mulato Gil de Castro and elsewhere on Lastarria (Merced end).

Plaza Artesanos de Manquehue, Av Manquehue Sur, block 300-600, just off Apoquindo in Las Condes. This is the biggest craft market in Chile. A good range of modern Chilean crafts from ceramics to textiles, a pleasant central piazza, and places where the artisans can be seen working on wood, silver, glass and so on. Although more expensive than, for instance, the market in Santa Lucía, this is a good and attractive place to come; take any bus east from Providencia or Escuela Militar which goes via Apoquindo.

Aldea de Vitacura, Vitacura 6838, T02-7353959. 1000-2000.

Amitié, Av Ricardo Lyon y Av Providencia. Los Leones metro. Recommended.

Centro Artesanal Santa Lucía, Santa Lucía metro, south exit. Lapis lazuli can be bought here cheaply. Also has a wide variety of woollen goods, jewellery etc.

Chile Vivo, Dardignac 15, Bellavista, T02-7350227, chilevivo@latinmail.com. Shopping centre with café, handicraft shop, internet, art gallery and jewellery workshop.

Dauvin Artesanía Fina, Providencia 2169, local 69. Los Leones metro. Recommended.

El Almacén Campesino, Purísima 303, Bellavista. Cooperative association in a colonial building. Sells handicrafts from all over Chile, including attractive Mapuche weavings, woodcarvings, pottery and beautiful wrought copper and bronze. Prices similar to those in Temuco. Ask about shipping.

El Pueblo de Artesanos, daily except Mon, 1130-1900. All types of ware on sale, classes given in some shops, interesting.

Marita Gil, Los Misioneros 1991, Pedro de Valdivia Norte, T02-2326853. A cheaper craft market is next to the bridge of Pío Nono in Bellavista, best at weekends.

Prisma de los Andes, Santo Domingo 1690, T02-6730540. Santa Ana metro. A women's social project, sells distinctive high-quality textiles made in the organization's cooperative workshops (which can be visited).

Other craft stalls can be found in an alleyway 1 block south of Av O'Higgins between A Prat and San Diego; on the 600 to 800 blocks of Santo Domingo and at Pío Nono y Av Santa María in Bellavista.

Maps

Automóvil Club de Chile, Av Andrés Bello 1863, Pedro de Valdivia metro, line 1, T02-4311000, www.automovilclub.cl). Mon-Thu 0900-1815, Fri 0900-1700. Route maps of Chile, US$6 each, free to members of affiliated motoring organizations; very helpful.

CONAF, see page 73. Maps of national parks.

Instituto Geográfico Militar, Dieciocho 369, near Toesca metro, T02-4109463. Detailed geophysical and topographical maps of the whole of Chile, very useful for climbing. Expensive (about US$15 each), but **Biblioteca Nacional**, Av Libertador Bernardo O'Higgins 651, T02-3605200, stocks them and will allow you to photocopy parts of each map.

Librería Australis, Av Providencia 1670, local 5. All sorts of local, regional and trekking maps.

Markets

For details of the city's craft markets, see Handicrafts.

Bío Bío flea market, C Bío Bío. Every Sat and Sun morning. This is the largest and cheapest flea market in the city and sells everything from spare parts for cars and motorbikes to second-hand furniture. Those trying to do up a new flat on the cheap, a car on the hoof, or who are simply interested in sharing a street with tens of thousands of others, should find their way here; just go to Franklin metro, line 2 and follow the crowds. Beware of rip-offs.

Mercado Central, Puente y 21 de Mayo by the Río Mapocho. Cal y Canto metro. Brilliant for seafood, with many places to eat cheaply, **Donde Augusto** is recommended. Otherwise an excellent range of goods, but quite expensive. See also page 78.

Vega Central, on the opposite bank of the river, is cheaper than Mercado Central.

Music
There are many small shops selling CDs in Paseo Las Palmas, Ricardo Lyon and Av 11 de Septiembre.
Billboard, Providencia 2314 and at La Bolsa 75 (downtown). Good source for rock, jazz and alternative music.
Feria del Disco, Paseo Ahumada. The biggest chain. Also sell tickets for rock concerts. Branches in numerous malls.
Funtrucks, Parque Arauco Mall.
Su Música, many branches in the centre of Santiago.

Opticians
Those needing a new pair of glasses should head for MacIver 0-100 block, where there are many opticians to choose from, and prices are lower rates in Europe or North America.

Wine
There's a good selection of wines at **Jumbo**, **Líder** and **Santa Isabel** supermarkets.
El Mundo del Vino, Isidora Goyenechea 2929. Also in the Alto Las Condes and Plaza Vespucio malls.
Vinopolis, Pedro de Valdivia 036, Pedro de Valdivia metro, line 1. Mon-Fri 0900-2300, Sat 1000-2300, Sun 1000-2200. Exclusively Chilean wines. Good selection.
The Wine House, Portada de Vitacura 2904.

Shopping malls
Generally open 7 days a week 1000-2100.
Apumanque, Apoquindo y Manquehue, Las Condes.
Centro Comercial Alto Las Condes, Av Kennedy, east of Las Condes. This is the largest and most modern mall in the city.
Parque Arauco, Av Kennedy 5413, Las Condes. Similar to Alto Las Condes but more variety. There is a boulevard with cafés, good restaurants and an ice trail.
Mall del Centro, C Rosas 900-block, just north of the Plaza de Armas. Brings US mall culture to the centre of Santiago.
Plaza Vespucio, Bellavista de La Florida metro, line 5. The next most convenient after Mall del Centro.

Bowling
Bowling Center, Av Apoquindo 5012. Ten-pin bowling, lots of lanes. Recommended. A 15-min walk east of Escuela Militar metro, line 1.

Cricket
Club Príncipe de Gales, Las Arañas 1901, right by the junction of Bilbao and Vespuccio. Matches held on Sat in summer at this snooty ground. Admission US$5, membership not required (just tell the doorman you are there for the cricket), lots of drinks included in the price.

Football
There are 3 big clubs; see also box, page 100. If you decide to visit the Estadio Nacional, where international matches are played, find a space high up on the terraces and you will be able to watch the sun set over the mountains behind Santiago.
Colo Colo, play at the Estadio Monumental, reached by any bus to Puente Alto or Pedrero metro, line 5; tickets from Av Marathon 5300, Macul, T02-2947300.
Universidad Católica, play at San Carlos de Apoquindo, reached by bus from Escuela Militar metro; tickets from Andrés Bello 2782, Providencia, T02-2312777.
Universidad de Chile, play at Estadio Nacional, Av Grecia 2001 Ñuñoa, Ñuble metro, line 5. Tickets from Av General Miranda 2094, Ñuñoa.

Gymnasiums
Gimnasio Alicia Franke, Moneda 1481, T02-6961681. Central location for aerobics and fitness classes (women only). Another at Huérfanos 1313, T02-6711562.
Sésamo, Los Leones 2384, Providencia, T02-2042770. With pool, aerobics. Recommended.

Racecourses
Betting is a growing industry, with increasing numbers of **Teletrak** betting shops around the city.
Club Hípico, Blanco Encalada 2540. Racing every Sun and every other Wed afternoon, worthwhile even if only to watch dusk fall over the Andes, entry to main stand US$5, card of up to 18 races.

Santiago Region Santiago Listings

Soccer nation

Football arrived in Chile towards the end of the 19th century, courtesy of the British. The role of British workers – most of whom were employed in the construction of the railway system – is reflected in the names of several of the leading teams, notably Santiago Wanderers (who are based in Valparaíso), Everton (based in Viña) and Rangers (based in Talca). The game's popularity grew rapidly; by the 1940s most large towns boasted their own team and stadium. In 1962, Chile's importance as a soccer nation was recognized internationally when it hosted the World Cup and the national side finished third. The quarter final between Chile and Italy became known as the 'Battle of Santiago', one of the most vicious games in the sport's history (Chile won 2-1).

Although Chilean football may not enjoy the worldwide recognition given to Argentina and Brazil, Chileans follow 'the beautiful game' with as much passion as their illustrious neighbours.

The local season is split into two tournaments, the *apertura* running from March to June and the *clausura* from August to December. Most of the support (and money) goes to the big three clubs, all based in Santiago: Universidad de Chile (known as 'La U'), Colo-Colo and Universidad Católica (which tends to be favoured by the well-off). The greatest rivalry is between La U and Colo-Colo (who are also known as Los Indios, as their strip carries an image of the great Mapuche leader after whom they were named). The most fervent supporters of the former are known as *los de abajo* (the underdogs), while those of the latter are called *la garra blanca* (the white claw).

A visit to a match, especially either an international game or a *clásico* (local derby), is an unforgettable experience. Watching football is still very much a family affair and the supporters dance, sing and wave their team colours beneath a non-stop rain of confetti, fireworks and coloured smoke. Cheap tickets cost around US$5.

Hipódromo Chile, Av Hipódromo Chile 1715, Independencia. T02-2709237. Every Sat afternoon. Pari-mutuel betting.

Sightseeing tours

Ace Turismo, Av Libertador Bernardo O'Higgins 949, piso 16, T02-3600350. City tour, US$20 for half a day.
Maysa, Ejército 294, oficina 103, T/F02-6968986, maysa@mi-mail.cl. Good tours of wine bodegas and Valparaíso, US$50.
Nicole Aventuras, T02-225 6155/T8241277 (mob), www.fis.puc.cl/~gtarrach/avenic. Excursions in Santiago region, including wildlife and glacier tours.

Skiing and climbing

The 2 main climbing areas near Santiago are the Grupo Loma Larga near the Cajón del Maipo and the Grupo Plomo near the ski resort of La Parva. For ski resorts in the Santiago area, see page 113. Ski equipment hire is much cheaper in Santiago than in the resorts.

Club Alemán Andino, El Arrayán 2735, Providencia, T02-2324338, www.dav.cl. May-Jun Tue and Thu 2000.
Club Andino de Chile, Av Libertador Bernardo O'Higgins 108, local 215, T02-2749252, www.skilagunillas.cl. Ski club.
Federación de Andinismo de Chile, Almte Simpson 77A, T02-2220888, www.feach.cl. Open daily. It has the addresses of all the mountaineering clubs in the country and runs a mountaineering school.
La Cumbre Ltda, Av Apoquindo 5258, T02-2209907, www.lacumbreonline.cl. Mon-Fri 1100-2000, Sat 1100-1600. Dutch proprietors very helpful, good climbing and trekking equipment.
Mountain Service, Santa Magdalena 75, T02-2343439, Providencia, www.mountain

service.cl. English spoken, tents, stoves, clothing, equipment rental. Recommended.
Panda Deportes, Paseo Las Palmas 2217, T02-2321840. Los Leones metro.
Skitotal, Av Apoquindo 4900, of 40-42, T02-2460156. Rents equipment, organizes accommodation and lessons. English and German spoken. Transport also provided to the ski resorts of Farellones, El Colorado, La Parva and Valle Nevado.

Swimming pools
Antilen, Cerro San Cristóbal. Open Tue-Sun 1000-1500 in summer; closed Apr-Oct, US$10. Fine panoramic view over the city.
Parque Araucano, near Parque Arauco Shopping Centre, Escuela Militar metro. Nov-Mar Tue-Sat 0900-1900. Olympic pool.
Parque O'Higgins, T02-5569612. Two pools (one for children), open summer only, US$4.
Tupahue, Cerro San Cristóbal. Large pool with cafés, US$7; 2 for the price of 1 on Wed.

Tennis
There are municipal courts in Parque O'Higgins; the national stadium, **Estadio Nacional**, Av Grecia con Av Marathon, has a tennis club that offers classes.
Also, **Club de Tenis Universidad Católica Santa Rosa**, Andrés Bello 3782, T02-2312777; and **Club de Tenis Stade Français**, Sánhcez Fontecilla y Tobalaba, T02-2337216.

Tour operators
Altue Expediciones, Encomenderos 83, piso 2, Las Condes, T02-2321103, www.altue.com. For wilderness trips including tour of Patagonia and sea-kayaking in Chiloé.
Andina del Sud, Av El Golf 99, Las Condes, T02-3880101, www.andinadelsud.com. Climbing and trekking in the Lake District and other areas.
Azimut 360, General Salvo 159, Providencia, T02-2351519, www.azimut.cl. Salvador metro. Reasonable prices. Adventure and eco-tourism throughout Chile, including tours to the Atacama Desert. Aconcagua base camp services and mountaineering expeditions to Parinacota and Sajama. Highly recommended.
Cascada Expediciones, Camino al Volcán 17710, T02-8611777, www.cascada-exped iciones.cl. Specialize in activity tours in remote areas.

Mountain Service, Paseo Las Palmas 2209, T02-2330913, info@mountainservice.cl, Los Leones metro. Recommended climbing trips.
Patagonia Connection SA, Fidel Oteíza 1921, of 1006, Providencia, T02- 2256489, www.patagonia-connection.com, Pedro de Valdivia metro. For cruises to Patagonia.
Rapa-Nui, Huérfanos 1160, oficina 912, piso 9, T02-6721050. www.rapanuiturismo.cl. Specializes in trips to Easter Island.
Southern Cross Adventure, Victor Rae 5994, Las Condes. T02-6396591, www.sc adventure.com. Offers mountaineering, biking, horse riding, trekking, high-altitude archaeology, visits to volcanoes, fishing in the Andes. English, French, German and Spanish-speaking guides, camping gear provided.
Sportstours, Moneda 970, piso 18 T02-5495200, www.sportstour.cl. German-run, helpful, 5-day trips to Antarctica. Another branch at **San Cristóbal Tower**, Av Santa María 1742.
Turismo Cabo de Hornos, www.turismo cabodehornos.cl. Agustinas 814, oficina 706, T02-6643458. For DAP flights and Tierra del Fuego/Antarctica tours.

Travel agents
4 Star South America, T1-800 747 4540 (US)/0871-711 5370 (UK)/+49-700-4444 7827 (rest of the world), http://4starSouth America.com (tours to South America), http://4starFlights.com (flight consolidator tickets to South America). Tour operator and flight consolidator with internet- and catalogue-based marketing.
Asatej Student Flight Centre, Hernando de Aguirre 201, oficina 401, T02-3350395, chile@asatej.com.ar. For cheap flights and youth travel, also tours, car rental, ISIC cards, medical insurance and hotels.
Passtours, Huérfanos 886, oficina 111, T02-6393232, www.passtours.com. Many languages spoken, helpful.
Turismo Grant, Av Vitacura 2771, oficina 806, Las Condes, T02-2365301. Helpful, English spoken.
Turismo Tajamar, Orrego Luco 023, Providencia, T02-3368000, www.tajamar.cl. Good for flights, helpful. Recommended.
VMP Ltda, Huérfanos 1160, local 19, T/F02-6967829. For all services. Many languages spoken, helpful. Recommended.

● Transport

Air

For details of the Aeropuerto Comodoro Arturo Merino Benítez, see page 38. For domestic flights from Santiago see under relevant destinations.

Aerolíneas Argentinas, oficina Generales Roger de Flor 2921 y 2907, Las Condes, Tobalaba metro, T02-2109000, www.aero lineasargentinas.com; **Aeroméxico**, Isidora Goyenechea 2939, oficina 602, Las Condes, Tobalaba metro, T02-3901000, www.aero mexico.com; **Air France**, Av Américo Vespucio Sur 100, oficina 202, Las Condes, Escuela Militar metro, T02-2909330, www.airfrance.cl; **Alitalia**, El Bosque Norte 107, oficina 21, www.alitalia.cl, T02-3788230; **American**, Huérfanos 1199, Universidad de Chile metro, www.american airlines.cl, T02-6790000; **British Airways**, Ebro 2743, piso 1, oficina 1 T02-2329563 or Don Carlos 2939, Las Condes, Tobalaba metro, airport T02-6901845, www.ba.com; **Continental** (Chilean agents are Copa Airlines) Fidel Oteíza 1921, oficina 703, Pedro de Valdivia metro, south exit, T02-2002100, www.continental.com; **Delta**, Isidora Goyenechea 2939, oficina 601, Las Condes, Tobalaba metro, T02-2801600, www.delta.com; **Iberia**, Bandera 206, piso 8, Universidad de Chile metro, north exit, T02-8701000, reservations T02-8701070, www.iberia.com; **KLM**, San Sebastián 2839, oficina 202, Las Condes, Tobalaba metro, T02-2330011 (sales), T02-2330991 (reservations), www.klm.com; **LACSA**, Dr Barros Borgoño 105, piso 2, Providencia, Manuel Montt metro, south exit, T02-2355189 , www.grupotaca.com; **LanChile**, Huérfanos 926, Santiago, Universidad de Chile metro, north exit. Also at Av Providencia 2006, Providencia, Los Leones or Pedro de Valdivia metro and Isidora Goyenechea 2888, Las Condes, Tobalaba metro, T02-6005262000, www.lanchile.com; **Lufthansa**, Av El Bosque Norte 500, piso 16, Las Condes, Tobalaba metro, T02-6301655, airport 6901112, www.lufthansa.cl; **South African Airways** (Chilean agents, Space, Adriana Frugone), 11 de Septiembre 1881, oficina 713, Providencia, Pedro de Valdivia metro, south exit, T02-3769042; **Sky Airline**, Andrés de

Fuenzalida 55, Providencia, Los Leones metro, north exit, T02-600-6002828, www.skyair line.cl; **United**, Av Andrés Bello 2687, piso 16, Las Condes, Tobalaba metro, www.united.com, T02-3370000; **Varig**, El Bosque Norte 0177, oficina 903, piso 9, Las Condes, Tobalaba metro, T02-7078020, www.varig.cl.

Bicycle

For parts and repairs the only place to go is C San Diego, south of the Alameda. The 800 and 900 blocks have scores of bicycle shops with spare parts, new models and repairs all offered at prices much cheaper than you will find in Providencia or Las Condes.

Bicicletas Wilson, C San Diego 909; **El Supermercado de las Bicicletas**, C San Diego 921, good stock; **Importadora Caupolicán**, C San Diego 863, T02-6972765, wide range, helpful, has been recommended; **Luis Cabalin**, Coquimbo 1114, T02-6984193, is good for maintenance and repairs; **Terrabike**, C San Diego 896, does repairs.

Bus

Local In Santiago, buses are known as *micros*, with each *micro* displaying its particular route on a board in the window. Over the past decade, the system has progressed from one of utter chaos (in which buses could stop anywhere at all and no routes were numbered) to a curious combination of chaos and efficiency. Now routes are all numbered and, on most main roads, buses will only stop at bus stops. On the Alameda, Providencia and Apoquindo, different bus stops serve different destinations (eg Pudahuel, Las Condes, Maipú) – these destinations are clearly marked on the stops. The chaos is provided by the new ticket machines. Theoretically, on getting onto the bus, you are supposed to put exact change into the machine to get a printed ticket, but in practice any one of several things may happen: you may give the money to the driver who will then arrange a printed ticket; or you may give the money to the driver who will give you a paper ticket of the type that were used before the machines were brought in. Whatever happens, the driver will expect you to be expecting his particular way of doing things. The fare is about US$0.75, but there are frequent rises.

Long distance There are frequent, good inter-urban buses to all parts of Chile. Prices are much lower outside the peak summer season. You should always book ahead in Jan and Feb, Jul, and other peak times such as Easter and on and around Chile's Independence Day (18 Sep). At other times of the year, departures are so frequent that it is usually possible to just turn up and go. Check if student rates are available, or reductions for travelling on the same day as purchasing the ticket; it is worth bargaining over prices, especially shortly before departure and out of the summer season. Also take a look at the buses before buying the tickets (there are big differences in quality among bus companies); ask about the on-board services, as many companies offer drinks, sometimes complimentary, and luxury buses have meals and videos. Reclining seats are the norm and there are also *salón cama* sleeper buses. Fares from/to the capital are given in the text, see the Transport sections in each destination.

There are 4 terminals, all located close to each other near the city centre. Tur Bus has two booking offices throughout the centre, including at Universidad de Chile and Tobalaba metro stations , and at Av Apoquindo 6421, T02-2126435, and in the Parque Arauco and Alto Las Condes malls for those beginning their journeys in Las Condes. Bear in mind that on Fri evenings in summer, when the night buses are preparing to depart, the terminals are nightmarishly chaotic and busy in the extreme.

Terminal Alameda, Av Libertador Bernardo O' Higgins 3712, T02-27071500, Universidad de Santiago metro, has a modern extension with a shopping centre called Mall Parque Estación, several Redbanc ATMs and internet. This has the best left-luggage facilities in the city, and is a good choice as two of the best companies, Tur Bus (www.turbus.com) and Pullman Bus (www.pullman.cl), leave from here (serving all main destinations from **Arica** to **Puerto Montt**), and there are also Pullman del Sur buses to less frequented parts of the central valley, eg **Chanco** (US$9), **Iloca** (US$7).

Terminal Santiago, O'Higgins 3878, T02-3761755, just west of Terminal Alameda, Universidad de Santiago metro. Sometimes referred to as the 'Terminal Sur', this is used by services to and from the **south**, as well as buses to **Valparaíso** and **Viña del Mar**. It is the only terminal with services to **Punta Arenas** (48 hrs), and is also the centre for some international services (see below). There is a Redbanc ATM.

Terminal San Borja, O'Higgins y San Borja, T02-7760645, 1 block west of Estación Central, 3 blocks east of Terminal Alameda. Estación Central metro. There are buses to destinations in the **Santiago area**, such as **Melipilla**, and many companies serving **northern Chile**. Booking offices are arranged according to destination. The entrance is, inconveniently, located through the shopping centre next to the station, and is not immediately apparent from the Alameda.

Terminal Los Héroes, Tucapel Jiménez, just north of the Alameda, T02-4200099. Los Héroes metro. A smaller terminal with 8 companies, but useful destinations such as **Mendoza**, **Vicuña** with **Diamantes de Elqui** and **Chiloé** with **Cruz del Sur**. Note that some long-distance bus services also call at **Las Torres de Tajamar**, which is much more convenient if you are planning to stay in Providencia.

International Most international buses leave from the Terminal Santiago.
To Argentina There are frequent services through the Cristo Redentor tunnel to **Mendoza**, 6-7 hrs, US$15, many companies, eg Ahumada (recommended), Andesmar, CATA, TAC (recommended), Tas Choapa, departures around 0800, 1200 and 1600, touts approach you in Terminal Santiago. Most of these services continue on to **Buenos Aires**, 24 hrs, US$50. There are also minibuses to **Mendoza** from the Terminal Santiago, 5-6 hrs, US$20; Chi-Ar Ltda is recommended (pickup from hotels), shorter waiting time at customs.

Companies in the Terminal Santiago have connections to many other Argentine cities: Andesmar to **Bahía Blanca**, US$60, change in Mendoza, 24 hrs; TAC and Tas Choapa direct to **Córdoba**, US$35, 18 hrs (El Rápido not recommended); to **San Juan**, TAC, Tas

Choapa, US$25. If going to destinations such as **Bariloche** or **Neuquén** in Argentine Patagonia, it is better to travel south to Temuco or Osorno and connect there.

To other destinations To **Montevideo** (Uruguay), most involving a change in Mendoza, **Tas Choapa** and others, 27 hrs, including meals. To **São Paulo** and **Rio de Janeiro** (Brazil), Chilebus and Pluma, Tue, Thu, Sat, 72 hrs, US$110. To **Asunción** (Paraguay), 4 a week, 28 hrs, US$85. The biggest company serving Andean destinations is the Peruvian **Ormeño** in Terminal Santiago, whose buses leave on Tue and Fri at 0900 to **Lima** (Peru), where connections are made to **Guayaquil** and **Quito** (Ecuador), **Cali** and **Bogotá** (Colombia) and **Caracas** (Venezuela) – buses are good and comfortable and there are meal stops. To **Lima**, 51 hrs, US$90 (it is cheaper to take a bus to Arica, a *colectivo* to Tacna (US$3), then bus to Lima); to **Guayaquil**, 80 hrs, US$130; to **Quito**, 88 hrs, US$150; to **Cali**, 4½ days, US$200; to **Bogotá**, US$210, 5 days; to **Caracas**, US$230, 7 days. Those heading for Bolivia are best advised to travel to one of the northern cities and then go by frequent bus from Iquique or Arica, or via the weekly train from Calama.

Car
As in most big cities, traffic and pollution are major problems: driving is restricted according to licence plate numbers; each day, plates ending in 1 of 2 digits are prohibited from circulating (prohibited registration numbers are published in the press as well as on TV and radio).

Car hire
Prices of car hire vary widely so shop around. Tax of 18% is charged but check if it is included in the price quoted. A credit card is usually asked for when renting a vehicle. Hertz, Avis, Budget and others are available from the airport; **Alameda**, Av Bernado O'Higgins 4332, T02-7790609, www.alameda rentacar.cl, San Alberto Hurtado metro (ex Pila del Ganso), line 1, also in the airport, very good value; **ANSA**, Av Eleodoro Yáñez 1198, Providencia , T02-2510256; **Automóvil Club de Chile**, Av Vitacura 9511, Providencia, T02-4311106, 25% discount for members of

associated motoring organizations; **Avis**, San Pablo 9900, T02-3310121, poor service reported; **Hertz**, Costanera Andrés Bello 1469, T02-6010477, and at Hotel Hyatt T02-2455936, has a good network in Chile and cars are in good condition; **Rosselot**, Francisco Bilbao 2032, Providencia, T02-3813690, www.rosselot.cl, and airport, T02-6901374, reputable Chilean firm with national coverage; **Seelmann**, www.seel mann.cl, Monseñor Edwards 1279, La Reina , T02-2779259; **Verschae**, Manquehue Sur 660, T02-2027266, www.verschae.cl, good value, branches throughout the country.

Colectivo
Collective taxis, which operate on fixed routes between the centre and the suburbs, are a convenient form of transport. They ply the streets and carry destination signs and route numbers. Fares vary, depending on the length of the journey, but are usually between US$1-2. Higher fares at night.

Ferry
Check schedules with shipping lines rather than the national tourist office, Sernatur. Specific details are given throughout the guide under Transport.
Cruceros Australis, El Bosque Norte 0440, T02-4423110, www.australis.com, for trips from **Punta Arenas** to **Puerto Williams**, **Cape Horn** and **Ushuaia**; M/N Skorpios, Augusto Leguía Norte 118, Las Condes, El Golf metro, north exit, line 1, T02-4771900, www.skorpios.cl, for luxury cruise out of **Puerto Montt** to **Laguna San Rafael**; **Navimag**, Av El Bosque Norte 0440, piso 11, Las Condes, T02-4423120, www.navimag. com. For services from **Puerto Montt** to **Puerto Natales** and vice versa; Patagonia Connection SA, Fidel Oteíza 1921, oficina 1006, Providencia, T02-2256489, www.patagonia-connection.com, Pedro de Valdivia metro, for services **Puerto Montt-Coyhaique/Puerto Chacabuco-Laguna San Rafael**; Transmarchilay, Agustinas 715, oficina 403, T02-6335959, www.transmarchilay.cl, for reservations www.navieraustral.cl, for services between **Chiloé** and the mainland and ferry routes on the **Camino Austral**.

Hitchhiking

Hitchhiking is generally safe, although the normal common-sense rules apply. To **Valparaíso**, take the metro to Pajaritos and walk 5 mins to west – you'll have no difficulty hitching a lift. To hitch **south**, take Buses del Paine from outside the Terminal San Borja as far as possible on the highway to the toll area, about US$1.50, 75 mins.

To hitch **north** is not easy, but take blue Metrobus marked 'Til-Til' (frequent departures from near the Mercado Central as far as the toll bridge (*peaje*), 40 mins, US$130), then hitch from just beyond the toll bridge; you may be better off getting a bus north to the town of La Calera, 2 hrs, and trying from there.

To **Buenos Aires** (and **Brazil**) take a bus to Los Andes (Buses Los Andes leave from Tucapel Jiménez y Moneda, behind Terminal Los Héroes), then go to Copec station on the outskirts (most trucks travel overnight).

Metro

Line 1 of the underground railway system runs west-east between Escuela Militar and San Pablo, under the Alameda. Line 2 runs north-south from Vespucio Norte to La Cisterna. Line 5 runs northwest-southeast from Quinta Normal to Vicente Valdés. The new Line 4 runs north – south from Tobalaba to Plaza de Puente Alto with a branch to La Cisterna. There are interchanges at Los Héroes, Baquedano, Santa Ana, Tobalaba, Vicente Valdés and La Cisterna.

The trains are modern, fast, quiet and very full during rush hour. The first train is at 0630 (Mon-Sat), 0800 (Sun and holidays), the last about 2245. Fares vary according to time of journey; there are two charging periods: high 0715-0900 and 1800-1930, US$0.80; low all other times, US$0.60. The simplest solution is to buy a **Tarjeta Multivía**, which costs US$3 (and can be topped up subsequently). Metrobus services (blue buses, fare US$0.70) connect the metro stations of Lo Ovalle, San Pablo, Las Rejas, Cal y Canto, Salvador,

Santiago metro

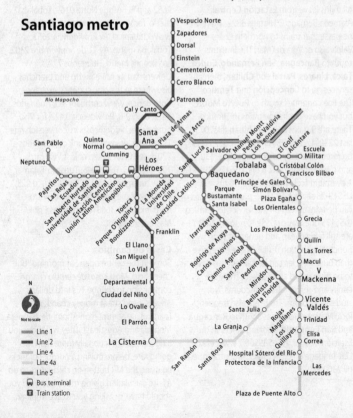

N

Not to scale

— Line 1
— Line 2
— Line 4
— Line 4a
— Line 5
🚌 Bus terminal
🚆 Train station

Escuela Militar, Pedrero and Bellavista de la Florida with outlying parts of Gran Santiago. For more information on the metro, see www.metrosantiago.cl.

Taxi

Taxis (black with yellow roofs) are abundant, and not expensive, with a minimum charge of US$0.40, plus US$0.15 per 200 m. Higher charges are permitted to charge more at night, but in the daytime check that the meter is set to day rates. Taxis are more expensive at bus terminals and from the ranks outside hotels – best to walk a block and flag one down. Avoid taxis with more than one person in them, especially at night. For journeys outside the city arrange the charge beforehand. **Radio Taxis Andes Pacífico**, T02-2253064, www.andespacifico.cl, and **Rigoberto Contreras**, T02-6381042, ext 4215, are recommended, but rates are above those of city taxis.

Train

All trains leave from **Estación Central**, Alameda Bernado O'Higgins 3322. There are no passenger trains to northern Chile, Valparaíso or Viña del Mar. The line runs south to **Rancagua**, **San Fernando**, **Curicó**, **Talca**, **Linares**, **Parral** and **Chillán**, thereafter services go to **Concepción** and **Temuco**. The line continues south to **Puerto Montt**, but you have to change trains in Temuco. There are 9 trains daily to **Chillán** (first 0730, last 2230, 4½ hrs, US$17 turista, US$25 clase preferente), 2 daily to **Concepción** (1130 and overnight at 2230, 8 hrs, US$17-22) and 1 overnight to **Temuco** (2200, 10 hrs, US$19-26 salón, US$22-35 preferente). Cars can be transported on the service to Temuco (US$175 one way or US$230 return). Trains are still fairly cheap and generally very punctual, although usually more expensive than buses. Cycles can be carried, but have to be dismantled and packed. There are family and senior citizen discounts. No student discounts. There are also frequent local **Metrotren** services south to **Rancagua** and **San Fernando**. Booking offices in the Estación Central, T02-5855000, www.efe.cl. Left-luggage office at Estación Central, open till 2300.

● Directory

Banks

Banks are open from 0900 to 1400, but close on Sat. Official daily exchange rates are published in *El Mercurio* and *La Nación*. There is never a problem in finding a Redbanc ATM. Look for **Banco SantanderSantiago** and others with Redbanc sign, for Cirrus ATMs.

American Express, Av Isidora Goyenechea 3621, piso 10, Las Condes, T02-3506700, Tobalaba metro, also at Blanco Viajes, San Sebastián 2881, Las Condes, Tobalaba metro, T02-3354632, no commission, poor rates (better to change TCs into dollars – no limit – and then into pesos elsewhere); **Banco de Chile**, www.bancodechile.cl, Ahumada 251, Av Providencia 1912, Pedro de Valdivia metro, Av 11 de Septiembre 2303, Los Leones metro, demands the minimum of formalities, but may charge commission; **Banco SantanderSantiago**, www.santander santiago.cl, Av 11 de Septiembre 1877, local 01, Pedro de Valdivia metro , Av Providencia 2652 and El Bosque Norte 0169, Tobalaba metro, for Visa, no commission; **Citibank**, www.citibank.cl, Av Providencia 2653, Tobalaba metro, Av 11 de Septiembre 2302, Los Leones metro, Huérfanos 770, Universidad de Chile metro and branches elsewhere in the city, currency exchange; **Corp Banca**, www.corpbanca.cl, Huérfanos 1072, or 770-B, Providencia 1422, for Visa but beware hidden costs in 'conversion rate'; **Transbank**, www.transbank.cl, Huérfanos 770, piso 10, for stolen or lost Visa cards, T02-6386383, F6317945; **Turismo Tajamar**, www.turismo tajamar.cl, Orrego Luco 023, Los Leones or Pedro de Valdivia metro, north exit, T02-3668165, Thomas Cook/ MasterCard agent.

Casas de cambio

Some in the centre open Sat morning (but check first). Most *casas de cambio* charge 3% commission to change TCs into dollars. Always avoid street money changers (particularly common on Ahumada, Bandera, Moneda and Agustinas). They will show you a figure that is fractionally more than the going rate, before pulling a number of tricks, eg using the MR button on calculators to do a false calculation giving much less than you should have, or asking you to accompany them to somewhere obscure. Muggings or the passing of forged notes have also been reported.

Afex, Moneda 1148 , Agustinas 1050, Pedro de Valdivia 012, Parque Arauco, good rates for TCs; Alfa, Agustinas 1052; Cambios Andino, Ocho, Agustinas 1062; Cambios Manquehue, Huérfanos 1160, local 5 (Galería Alessandri); Guiñazú, Matías Cousiño 170, all major currencies can be bought or sold; Exprinter, Bombero Ossa 1053, good rates, low commission; Intermundi, Moneda 896. Also several around Av Pedro de Valdivia, Providencia, eg at Gral Holley 66, good rates; Inter, Andrés de Fuenzalida 47, Los Leones metro, north exit; Casa de Cambio Blancas, opposite Hotel Orly, Pedro de Valdivia; Mojakar, Pedro de Valdivia 059.

Dentists
Antonio Yazigi, Vitacura 3082, apto 33, T02-2087962/2085040, English spoken, recommended; Dr Torres, Av Providencia 2330, dept 23, excellent, speaks English.

Embassies and consulates
Embassies Argentina, Miraflores 285, T02-5822500, www.embargentina.cl; Australia, Isidora Goyenechea 3621, Torre B (piso 12-13), Las Condes, T02-5503500; Austria, Barros Errázuriz 1968, piso 3, Providencia, T02-2234774; Belgium, Av Providencia 2653, piso 11, dept 1103-04, T02-2321070; Bolivia, Av Santa María 2796, Providencia, T02-2328180, Los Leones metro; Brazil, Alonso Ovalle 1665, piso 15, T02-6982486, www.embajadade brasil.cl; Canada, Nueva Tajamar 481, Torre Norte, piso 12 (Edificio World Trade Center), www.dfait-maeci.gc.ca/latin-america/chile/, T02-3629660; Colombia, Av Presidente Errázuriz 3943, T02-2061999; Denmark, Jacques Cazotte 5531, Vitacura, T02-2185949; Ecuador, Av Providencia 1979, piso 5, T02-2315073; Finland, Alcántara 200, of icina 201, T02-2634917, embajada@finlandia. co.cl; France, Condell 65, www.france.cl/ francais/, T02-4708000; Germany, Las Hualtatas 5677, T02-4632500; Greece, Jorge VI 306, Las Condes, T02-2127900; India, Triana 871, Providencia, T02-2352633; Israel, San Sebastián 2812, piso 5, Las Condes, T02-7500500; Italy, Clemente Fabres 1050, Providencia,

T02-4708400; Japan, Av Ricardo Lyon 520, piso 1, T02-2321807; Mexico, Félix de Amesti 128, T02-5838400; Netherlands, Apoquindo 3500, piso 13, Las Condes, El Golf metro, T02-7569200; New Zealand, El Golf 99, oficina 703, Las Condes, T02-2909800; Norway, San Sebastián 2839, oficina 509, Las Condes, T02-2342888; Panama, La Reconquista 640, Las Condes, T02-2026318; Paraguay, Huérfanos 886, oficina 514 , T02-6394640; Peru, Av Andrés Bello 1751, Providencia, T02-2352356; South Africa, Av 11 de Septiembre 2353, piso 17, Torre San Ramón , T02-2312862; Spain, Av Andrés Bello 1895, Providencia, T02-2352755; Sweden, Av 11 de Septiembre 2353, Torre San Ramón, piso 4, Providencia, T02-9401700, www.embajadasuecia.cl; Switzerland, Av Américo Vespucio Sur 100, piso 14, Las Condes, T02-2634211; UK, El Bosque Norte 0125, piso 6, Casilla 72-D, T02-3704100, F3704160, will hold letters; Uruguay, Av Pedro de Valdivia 711, Providencia, T02-2047988 ; USA, Av Andrés Bello 2800, T02-2322600, www.embajadaeeuu.cl.

Consulates For the consulate, contact the embassies above with the exception of the following: Argentina, Vicuña MacKenna 41, T02-5822608, F5822606, 0900-1400, if you need a visa for Argentina, get it here or at the consulates in Concepción, Puerto Montt or Punta Arenas, there are no facilities at the borders; Australians will need a letter from their embassy to get a visa for Argentina. Bolivia, Av Santa María 2796, Providencia, T02-2328180, Mon-Fri 0900-1330; Brazil, MacIver 225, piso 15, T02-6398867, Mon-Fri 0930-1330 , visa takes 2 days, take passport, 2 photos, ticket in and out of Brazil, photo-copy of first 2 pages of passport, tickets, credit card and tourist card; Paraguay, Huérfanos 886, oficina 515, T02-6394640, 0900-1300, 2 photos and copy of first page of passport required for visa; Peru, Padre Mariano 10, Oficina 309, Providencia, T02-2354600, Mon-Fri 0900-1400; US, Av Andrés Bello 2800, Las Condes, T02-2322600, Mon-Fri 0830-1300, visa obtainable there. Uruguay, Av Pedro de Valdivia 711, Providencia, T02-2238398, Mon-Fri 1000-1600.

If you need to get to a hospital, it is better to take a taxi than wait for an ambulance. **Clínica Central**, San Isidro 231-243, Santa Lucía metro, T02-4631400, 24 hrs, German spoken; **Emergency hospital (Hospital Clínico de la Universidad Católica)**, Marcoleta 367 , Universidad Católica metro, T02-3543266 emergency, T02-6332051 general; **Hospital de Urgencia (Posta Central)**, Portugal 125, cheapest hospital open to the public; **Hospital del Salvador**, Av Salvador 334 or J M Infante 551, Providencia, T02-2740093 emergency, T02-3404000 general, Mon-Thu 0800-1300 and 1330-1645, Fri 0800-1300 and 1330-1545; **Vaccinatoria Internacional**, Hospital Luis Calvo, MacKenna, Antonio Varas 360, Providencia, Manuel Montt metro, south exit, children's hospital, T02-3401600.

Other medical services Dr Sergio Majlis Drinberg, T02-2320853, physician available 1430-1900; **Emergency pharmacy**, Portugal 155, Universidad Católica metro, T02-6313005. You can consult www.farmaciasahumada.cl for other emergency pharmacies.

Internet

Internet cafés are ubiquitous. Prices around US$0.60 to US$1 per hr. **463@café**, Av Brasil 463, Barrio Brasil; **Anditel**, Bandera y Catedral, 1 block from the Plaza de Armas, quiet; **c@fe.com**, Av Bernado O'Higgins 0145, near Plaza Italia, good snacks; **Café Phonet**, San Sebastián 2815, Providencia, also very cheap international phone calls; **Ciberia**, Pío Nono 015, Bellavista; **Cybercafe**, Santa Lucía 0120, next to Instituto Chileno-Británico; **Cybercafe**, Cienfuegos 161, near junction with Moneda, just west of Panamericana, Barrio Brasil, cheap; **easy@net**, Ricardo Lyon y Providencia, Providencia; **ES Computación**, Salvador Sanfuentes 2352, Barrio Brasil, República metro, helpful staff; **Internet Virtual**, Santo Domingo 1091, also very cheap call centre; **Sonnets Ltda**, Londres 043, tea, coffee, book exchange, owner speaks Spanish, English, Dutch and German, helpful. There is also access at the **Terminal de Buses Alameda**, on the upper floor of the terminal building.

Language schools

Amerispan, PO Box 58129, 117 South 17 St, 14th floor, Philadelphia, PA19103, USA, T1-215 715 1100, www.amerispan.com, provides information about the affiliated Amerispan school in Santiago; **Carolina Carvajal**, Miraflores 113, dept 26, T02-3810000, T/F02-381000, ccarvajal@inter activa.cl, Spanish taught to individuals and small groups, intensive/business courses offered, recommended ; **Centro de Idiomas Bellavista**, C del Arzobispo 0609, Providencia, Salvador metro, T02-7323443, www.escuelabellavista.cl; **Escuela de Idiomas Violeta Parra**, Ernesto Pinto Lagarrigue 362-A, Recoleta-Barrio Bellavista, T02-7358211, www.tandemsant iago.cl, courses aimed at budget travellers, information programme on social issues, arranges accommodation and visits to local organizations and national parks; **Instituto Chileno de la Lengua**, Ernesto Riquelme 226, 2nd floor, Santa Ana metro, line 2, walk to the south, T02-6972728, www.ichil.cl; **Instituto Chileno Suizo de Cultura**, José Victorino Lastarria 93, Universidad Católica metro, line 1, north exit, T02-6385414, www.chilenosuizo.cl, courses in Spanish, French, Portuguese, German, Italian, Mandarin Chinese and English taught by native speakers, also computer courses, internet access, café, library, art gallery, accommodation can be arranged; **Natalislang Language Centre**, Vicuña Mackenna 06, piso 7, oficina 4, Providencia, Baquedano metro, line 1, to the south, T02-2228721, info@natalislang.com, 2-week courses are recommended as good value; **Pacífica**, Guillermo Acuña 2884, Providencia, Francisco Bilbao metro, line 4, walk 10 mins to the east along F Bilbao, T02-2055129, pacifica@netline.cl, Anglo-Chilean agency offering cultural programmes to students, will also find accommodation with families and arrange Spanish classes either in language schools or with private teachers, minimum 1 month, US$70 commission charged; **Top Language Services**, Huérfanos 886, oficina 1107, T/F02-6390321, offers Spanish in groups and individually, accommodation organized.

Many private teachers: **Silvia Pöltl**, T02-2353463, T09-3536835 (mob), silviapol793 @hotmail.com, well qualified and very experienced, recommended. **Patricia Vargas Vives**, José Manuel Infante98 , departamento 308, Salvador metro, line 1, south exit, Providencia, T02-2442283, qualified and experienced.

Laundry

Dry cleaning At the corner of Providencia and Dr Luis Middleton there are several self-service dry cleaners (Pedro de Valdivia metro, 11 de Septiembre exit (south)). Also several just south of Universidad Católica metro including **American Washer**, Portugal 71, Torre 7, local 4, 0900-2100 including Sun, US$3, can leave washing and collect it later.

Wet-wash Lava Fácil, Huérfanos 1750, Mon-Sat 0900- 2000, US$4 per load; **Lavandería Lola**, Av Ricardo Cumming y Moneda, very busy so get there before 1100, US$6 per load; **Laverap**, Av Providencia 1600 block, Manuel Montt 67; **Marva**, Carlos Antúnez 1823, Pedro de Valdivia metro, south exit, wash and dry US$10; Av Providencia 1039, full load, wet-wash, US$7, 3 hrs; **Nataly**, Bandera 572.

Post office

The main office is on the Plaza de Armas (0800-1900), poste restante is well organized (though only kept for 30 days), passport essential, list of letters and parcels received in hall of central post office (one list for men, another for women, indicate Sr or Sra/Srta on envelope).

Also sub offices in Providencia, Av 11 de Septiembre 2092, Luis Thayer Ojeda 0146, Pedro de Valdivia 1781, oficina 52, Providencia 1466, Moneda 1155 (downtown) and in Estación Central shopping mall. These are open Mon-Fri 0900-1800, Sat 0900-1230.

If sending a parcel, the contents must first be checked at the post office. Paper, tape, etc on sale, Mon-Fri 0800-1900, Sat 0800-1400.

Telephone

The cheapest call centres are on C Bandera, Catedral and Santo Domingo, all near the Plaza de Armas. International calls from here are half the price of the main company offices: to the US, US$0.25 per min, to Europe, US$0.35 per min, eg at Catedral 1033 and Santo Domingo 1091. The main company offices are **Telefónica CTC Chile**, Moneda 1151, closed Sun, Bandera 168, Terminal San Borja and **ENTEL**, Huérfanos 1133, Mon-Fri 0830-2200, Sat 0900-2030, Sun 0900-1400, calls cheaper 1400-2200, fax upstairs. Also Torre Entel, Moneda metro.

Fax also available at the Telefónica office in **Mall Panorámico**, 11 de Septiembre y Av Ricardo Lyon, Los Leones metro, line 1, 3rd level (phone booths are on level 1). There are also **Telefónica** phone offices at some metro stations including La Moneda, Escuela Militar, Tobalaba, Universidad de Chile and Pedro de Valdivia for local, long-distance and international calls.

Useful address

Ministerio del Interior, Departamento de Extranjería, Agustinas 1235, 1 block north of the Moneda, T02-6744000, www.extranjeria. gob.cl. Mon-Fri 0900-1200. Visit for an extension of tourist visa or any enquiries regarding legal status. Expect long queues.

Around Santiago → *Colour map 3, B3.*

This region can be divided into three: to the east are the peaks of the Andes; to the west is the coastal range; and between is the Central Valley. On the eastern edge of the Central Valley lies Santiago, its more affluent suburbs spreading east into the foothills of the Andes. Some of the highest peaks in the range lie in this region: just over the border in Argentina, Aconcagua is the highest mountain in the world outside Asia, rising to 6964 m. There is a mantle of snow on all the high mountains, while the lower slopes are covered with dense forests. Between the forest and the snowline there are pastures; during the summer, cattle are driven up there to graze. In this area you can ski in winter, hike in summer and soothe your limbs in thermal springs year round. The less energetic may opt for a tour of the vineyards, sampling the yield en route. ▸▸ *For Sleeping, Eating and other listings, see pages 116-118.*

Pomaire

A small town, 65 km west of Santiago, Pomaire is in a charming setting surrounded by high grassy hills dotted with algarrobo bushes. The town is famous for its ceramics; the main street is brimful with shops selling dark clay pots and kitchenware, as well as diverse *artesanía* from all over Chile including fine basketwork from the Central Valley and some lovely items made from the *combarbalita* stone from the north. There are probably few better places in Chile in which to buy general souvenirs and presents (although bargaining is not really entered into); pottery can be bought and the artists can be observed at work, before visitors retire to any one of numerous restaurants serving traditional dishes such as *humitas*, giant *empanadas* and *pastel de choclo*.

Reserva Nacional Río Clarillo

① *Reached by paved road via Av Vicuña Mackenna to Puente Alto, where it continues as Av Concha y Toro, turn right at the T-junction where the road leads to El Principal after 2 km. Open all year. US$5.*

This reserve covers 10,185 ha and is situated 45 km southeast of Santiago in the *precordillera* at between 850 m and 3000 m. It offers excellent views of the higher mountains and of the surprisingly green pastures of the foothills. The information centre is at the entrance, 2 km southeast of El Principal. There are guided trails and wildlife, including the endangered Chilean iguana, salamanders and the rare bird, torcaza. The reserve is also the only remaining home to *sclerophyllous* (hard leaved) trees in central Chile. In summer it is very hot and horse flies are a nuisance. There are no places to stay and camping is forbidden. If you are in the city for a while it is a good place to get away from the bustle for a day.

Santuario de la Naturaleza Yerba Loca

① *Park administration office, Villa Paulina, 4 km north of Route G21, 25 km northeast of Santiago, T02-3216285, Sep-Apr, US$7.*

Reached via a *ripio* side road off the paved Route G21, 25 km northeast of Santiago towards Farellones, this park covers 39,000 ha of the valley of the Río Yerba Loca, ranging in altitude between 900 and 5500 m. It was founded in 1973. From the park administration office a four-hour walk leads north to **Casa de Piedra Carvajal**, which offers fine views. Further north are two hanging glaciers, **La Paloma** and **El Altar**. You may spot eagles and condors in the park. Native tree species include the mountain olive. Maps and information available from CONAF. There is no accommodation here.

¿Huevón, Señor?

If you spend any time in Chile, it is almost impossible not to come across *huevón*. This versatile word is used by all classes of Chilean society to describe a person.

Literally meaning 'big egg', it is by turns an expression of endearment ('mate', 'buddy') and a slang expression of disgust ('idiot', 'fool'), and is used equally often in both senses. In some conversations, virtually every other word may seem to be *huevón*.

Legend has it that an expatriate living in Santiago a few years ago made the mistake of ordering a sandwich with *huevón* rather than *huevo* (egg). The waiter was so overcome that he had to finish

his shift early. The hilarity with which mistakes of this sort are greeted can work to the visitor's advantage, however: tell any Chilean acquaintance that you have been to the shop to buy *huevón* and your friendship will be secured for life.

The use of *huevón* is symptomatic of the distinctiveness of Chilean Spanish, which has an unusually wide range of idioms and slang not used elsewhere in Latin America.

Anyone who is serious about getting to grips with Chilean Spanish, should get hold of a copy of *How to Survive in the Chilean Jungle*, by John Brennan and Alvaro Taboada (Ventriloc Dolmen, 2001), a handbook of Chilean colloquialisms.

Maipo Valley vineyards

The Maipo Valley is considered by many experts to be the best wine-producing area in Chile. Several vineyards in the area can be visited and this makes a good excuse to get away from the smog:

Cousiño-Macul ① *Av Quilin 7100, on the eastern outskirts of the city, T02-3514175, www.cousinomacul.cl, US$10*, offers tours in English and Spanish at 1100 and 1500 from Monday to Friday. Call in advance if you wish to visit.

Concha y Toro ① *Virginia Subercaseaux 210, Pirque, near Puente Alto, 40 km south of Santiago, T02-4765269, www.conchaytoro.cl, US$12*, offers short tours (three a day in Spanish, four daily in English). Reserve two days in advance and enquire about the specific time of tours in your language of choice.

‡ Note that prices on the outskirts of town are twice as high as those charged in the centre.

Undurraga ① *Santa Ana, 34 km southwest of Santiago, T02-3722850, contact Patricia Jerez, wwwundurraga.cl, US$10*, allows vistors who have made a prior reservation two days in advance. Tours are given by the owner-manager, Pedro Undurraga on weekdays, 1000-1530.

Viña Santa Rita ① *Padre Hurtado 0695, Alto Jahuel, Buin, 45 km south of Santiago on the Camino a Padre Hurtado, T02-3622520, www.santarita.cl, US$10*, offers good tours in both English and Spanish (Tuesday to Friday at 1215 and 1500, Saturday and Sunday at 1200 and 1530). You must reserve three days in advance. The vineyard has a good restaurant. Weekend tours only available to those with reservations at the restaurant (lunch US$40 per head).

Cajón del Maipo ⬤🅕🅕🅕 ↠ *pp116-118.*

pp116-118.

This rugged and green valley southeast of Santiago provides an easy escape from the smog and bustle of Santiago. The valley is lined by precipitous mountains and the snows of the high Andes can easily be seen. There are many interesting and beautiful side tracks, such as to Lagunillas (see page 114) or Los Maitenes, but the upper reaches of the valley around El Volcán and Baños Morales are amazingly deserted.

The road into the valley runs east from Puente Alto via Las Vizcachas, where the most important motor racing circuit in Chile is located, towards **San José de Maipo**. The mountain town of **Melocotón** is 6 km south of San José de Maipo and **San Alfonso** is 4 km further on. The walk from San Alfonso to the **Cascada de las Animas** is pleasant; ask at the campsite for permission to cross the bridge.

The road continues up the valley and divides 14 km southeast of San Alfonso. One branch forks northeast along a very poor road (4WD essential) via Embalse El Yeso to **Termas del Plomo**, Km 33, thermal baths with no infrastructure, but stunning scenery. The other branch continues and climbs the valley of the Río Volcán. At **El Volcán** (1400 m), 21 km from San Alfonso, there are astounding views, but little else. It is possible to cross the river and camp in the wild on the far side, surrounded by giant rock walls and with a real sense of isolation. If visiting this area or continuing further up the mountain, be prepared for military checks: passport and car registration numbers may be taken. From El Volcán the poor road runs 14 km east to Lo Valdés, a good base for mountain excursions. Nearby are warm natural baths at **Baños Morales** ① *open from Oct, US$4*. This is a wonderful area to come and get away from it all and it is possible to spend days here exploring the paths that lead high into the mountains. (This is the old southerly horse trail linking Santiago and Mendoza, with a path still leading over into Argentina.) Some 12 km further east up the mountain is **Baños Colina** (not to be confused with Termas de Colina, see page 114) with free, hot thermal springs and horses for hire. This area is popular at weekends and holiday times, but is otherwise deserted. There are no shops so take food. Try the local goat's cheese if you can, it may be sold by the roadside or at farmhouses.

Situated north of Baños Morales, **Parque Nacional El Morado** ① *Oct-Apr, US$4, administration near the entrance*, covers an area of 3000 ha including the peaks of El Morado (5060 m), El Mirador del Morado (4320 m) and El Morado glacier. It is in an

Cajón del Maipo

SANTIAGO

La Florida
Las Vizcachas
Puente Alto
Pirque
San José de Maipo
El Principal
Reserva Nacional Río Clarillo
Río Clarillo
Papagayo (2317m)
Melocotón
San Alfonso
Cascada de las Animas
San Lorenzo (3902m)
Pedro Nolasco (3216m)
Río Maipo
Río Colorado
Lagunillas
Punta Negra (4090m)
Laguna Negra
Embalse El Yeso
Laguna Encantado
Aparejo (4794m)
Termas del Plomo
Río Yeso
Río Manzanito
Parque Nacional El Morado
Río Volcán
El Volcán
Baños Morales
Lo Valdés
Baños Colina

N

0 km 5
0 miles 5

exceptionally secluded and beautiful place with wonderful views, well worth making the effort to reach. There is a good day hike from the park entrance to the glacier and back. Lakeside camping is possible near the glacier.

Ski resorts ⬛🚹🚾 ⇥ *pp116-118.*

There are six main ski resorts near Santiago, four of them around the mountain village of Farellones. All have modern lift systems, international ski schools, rental shops, lodges, mountain restaurants and first-aid facilities. The season runs from June to September/October, weather permitting, although some resorts have equipment for making artificial snow. Many professional skiers from the northern hemisphere come here to keep in practice during the northern summer. Altitude sickness can be a problem, especially at Valle Nevado and Portillo, so avoid over-exertion on the first day or two.

Farellones
ⓘ *32 km east of Santiago, daily lift ticket US$42 (allows access to El Colorado).*
The first ski resort built in Chile, Farellones is situated on the slopes of Cerro Colorado at 2470 m and is reached by road from the capital in under 1½ hours. From the resort there are incredible views for 30 km across 10 Andean peaks. It is a service centre for the three other resorts and provides affordable accommodation and several large restaurants. It also has a good beginners' area and is connected by lift to El Colorado. Perhaps the most popular resort for residents of Santiago, it is busy at weekends. One-day excursions, US$10, are available from **Ski Club Chile** ⓘ *Candelaria Goyenechea 4750, Vitacura (north of Los Leones Golf Club), T02-2117341.*

El Colorado
ⓘ *8 km from Farellones, www.elcolorado.cl, daily lift ticket US$42 (including Farellones ski lifts).*
Further up Cerro Colorado along a circuitous road, El Colorado has a large but expensive ski lodge at the base, which offers all facilities, and a mountain restaurant higher up. There are 16 lifts in total, giving access to a large intermediate ski area with some steeper slopes. La Cornisa and Cono Este are two of the few bump runs in Chile. This is a good centre for learning to ski.

La Parva
ⓘ *Daily lift ticket US$40.*
Situated nearby at 2816 m, La Parva is the upper-class Santiago weekend resort with 30 pistes and 14 lifts, running from 0900 to 1730. Accommodation is in a chalet village and there are some good bars in high season. Although the runs vary, providing good intermediate to advanced skiing, skiers face a double fall-line so it is not suitable for beginners. Connections with Valle Nevado are good. Equipment rental is from US$20-35 depending on quality. In summer, this is a good walking area, with a trail that leads to the base of Cerro El Plomo, which can be climbed.

Valle Nevado
ⓘ *16 km from Farellones, T02-2060027, www.vallenevado.com, daily lift ticket US$40 Mon-Fri, US$52 Sat and Sun.*
Owned by **Spie Batignolles** of France, Valle Nevado was the site of the 1993 Pan-American winter games and offers the most modern ski facilities in Chile. It has been described as a deluxe hotel complex high up in the mountains. Although not to everyone's taste, it is highly regarded and efficient. There are 40 km of slopes accessed by 41 lifts. The runs are well prepared and are suitable for intermediate skiers and beginners. There's also a ski school and excellent heli-skiing.

① *145 km north of Santiago, www.skiportillo.cl, daily lift ticket US$40.*

Situated at 2855 m, Portillo lies 62 km east of Los Andes, near the customs post on the route to Argentina, and is one of Chile's best-known resorts. The 23 pistes (including one of the fastest in the world) are varied and well prepared, equipped with snow machines and connected by 12 lifts, two of which open up the off-piste areas. This is an excellent family resort, with a very highly regarded ski school, and there are some gentle slopes for beginners near the hotel. The major skiing events are in August and September. Cheap packages can be arranged at the beginning and out of season; equipment hire costs US$30.

Nearby, at an altitude of 2835 m, is the **Laguna del Inca**, 5½ km long, 1½ km wide and surrounded on three sides by accessible mountain slopes. This lake, frozen over in winter, has no outlet and its depth is not known. From **Tío Bob's** there are magnificent views of the lake and condors may be spotted from the terrace. There are boats for fishing; but beware, the afternoon winds often make the homeward pull three or four times as long as the outward pull. Mules can be hired for stupendous expeditions to the glacier at the head of the valley or to the Cerro Juncal.

Lagunillas

① *67 km southeast of Santiago, www.skilagunillas.cl, tow fees US$30, daily ski lift ticket US$25.*

Lagunillas lies in the Cajón del Maipo (see page 112), 17 km east of San José de Maipo, along a beautiful *ripio* road clinging to the edge of a chasm with stunning views of the far reaches of the Andes. It is more basic than the other ski centres in the region, with less infrastructure, but the skiing is good. It is owned by the **Club Andino de Chile**, and is the only not-for-profit ski centre in the country. There are 13 pistes and four ski lifts. In winter, the *carabineros* insist that drivers have snowchains, and rent them out at US$10. Being lower than the other resorts, its season is shorter but it is also cheaper.

From Santiago to Argentina ⬤⬤⬤⬤ » pp116-118.

The route across the Andes via Los Andes and the Redentor tunnel is one of the major crossings into Argentina. Route 57 runs north of Santiago through the rich Aconcagua Valley, known as the Valle de Chile. The road forks at the Santuario de Santa Teresa, the west branch going to San Felipe, east to Los Andes and Mendoza. Before travelling, you should always check on weather and road conditions beyond Los Andes. It is difficult to hitchhike over the border, and Spanish is essential; try getting a ride on trucks leaving from the Aduana building in Los Andes.

Termas de Colina

Based at **Hotel Termas de Colina** at 915 m, 43 km north of Santiago (see page 117), this is an attractive, popular spa in the mountains. The temperature of the water is on the cool side (25°C) but it is supposedly good for rheumatism and nervous disorders. There is a large swimming pool, plus individual baths that can be filled with the thermal water, and a sauna. There are some pleasant short walks in the area. The springs are in a military-controlled area, so do not take photos or even show your camera when passing the military base.

San Felipe and around

The capital of Aconcagua Province, 96 km north of Santiago, San Felipe is an agricultural and mining centre with an agreeable climate. Part of the Inca Highway has recently been discovered in the city; previously, no traces had been found south of La Serena. **Curimón**, 3 km southeast of San Felipe, is the site of the

Convento de Santa Rosa de Viterbo (1727), which has a small museum attached. A paved road (13 km) runs north from San Felipe to the old town of **Putaendo**; in its church there is an 18th-century baroque statue of Christ. Situated high in the *cordillera*, **Termas de Jahuel** lies 18 km by road northeast of San Felipe; see Sleeping for details. The mountain scenery includes a distant view of Aconcagua.

Los Andes

Some 16 km southeast of San Felipe and 77 km north of Santiago, Los Andes is situated in a wealthy agricultural, fruit-farming and wine-producing area, but is also the site of a large car assembly plant. It is a good place for escaping from Santiago and a convenient base for skiing at nearby Portillo, see page 114. There are monuments to José de San Martín and Bernardo O'Higgins in the Plaza de Armas and a monument to the Clark brothers, who built the Transandine Railway to Mendoza (now disused although there are tentative plans to re-establish it). There are good views from El Cerro de la Virgen, reached in an hour via a trail from the municipal picnic ground on Independencia.

The road to the border: Los Libertadores

The road to Argentina follows the Aconcagua Valley for 34 km until it reaches the village of **Río Blanco** (1370 m), where the ríos Blanco and Juncal meet to form the Río Aconcagua. There is a fish hatchery with a small botanical garden at the entrance to the Andina copper mine. East of Río Blanco the road climbs until Juncal where it zigzags steeply through 29 hairpin bends at the top of which is the ski resort of Portillo (see page 114). This is the location of the Chilean border post. If entering Chile, there may be long delays during searches for fruit, meat and vegetables, which may not be imported. Put all camera film in your hand luggage as this is not X-rayed.

Traffic crosses the border through the 4-km **Redentor tunnel** ① *Sep-May 24 hrs, Jun-Aug 0700-2300, toll US$5*. Note that this pass is closed after heavy snowfall, when travellers are occasionally trapped at the customs complex on either side of the border.

Above the tunnel is the old pass, used before the tunnel was built, and above this again, at 3854 m, is the statue of **El Cristo Redentor** (Christ the Redeemer), which was erected jointly by Chile and Argentina in 1904 to commemorate King Edward VII's decision in the boundary dispute of 1902. It is completely dwarfed by the landscape. The old road over the pass is in a very poor state, especially on the Chilean side, and is liable to be blocked by snow even in summer. When weather conditions permit, the statue can be reached on foot from **Las Cuevas**, a modern settlement on the Argentine side (4½ hours up, two down). There are also 12-hour excursions to the statue from Mendoza.

Into Argentina → *Argentine phone code: +54*

Just beyond Argentine customs and immigration is **Puente del Inca**, a sports resort named after the natural bridge which crosses the Río Mendoza. The bridge, apparently formed by sulphur-bearing hot springs, is 19 m high, 27 m wide and has a span of 21 m. At the resort are **Hostería Puente del Inca** and **Residencial Vieja Estación** (much cheaper), as well as camping, transport to Mendoza and information and access for climbing **Aconcagua** (6964 m), the highest mountain peak on earth outside Asia.

Some 17 km further east is **Punta de Vacas**, from where there is a good view of Tupungato (6550 m). The only town of any size between the border and Mendoza is **Uspallata**, from where two roads lead to Mendoza: the paved, southern branch of Route 7, via Potrerillos; and the unpaved, northern branch via Villavicencio.

⊜ Sleeping

Cajón del Maipo *p112, map p112*

L-AL Hostería Millahue, El Melocotón, T02-8612020, T09-98176833, www.hosteria millahue.com. Accommodation in *cabañas* including full board. There is also a games room and an outdoor heated swimming pool.

A Refugio Alemán Lo Valdés, Lo Valdés, T02-2207610 , T09-92208525, www.refugio lovaldes.com. E per person in dorm. Stone-built chalet accommodation. Good restaurant. Lots of trekking and climbing information. Recommended.

A-B Cabañas Corre Caminos, Estero Morales 57402, Baños Morales, T02-2692283, www.loscorrecaminos.com. Cabins sleeping 2-5 people. Food available, activities including horse riding and massages.

B Hostería Los Ciervos, Camino al Volcán 31411, San Alfonso, T/F02-8611581. With breakfast, full board also available, good.

C Alojamiento Inesita, Comercio 301, San José, T02-8611012. Good, excellent chips.

C Residencial España, Av Argentina 711, San Alfonso, T02-8611543. Clean, comfortable, with restaurant.

C Residencial Los Chicos Malos, Baños Morales, T02-6241887, T09-93236424, www.banos morales.cl. Comfortable, fresh bread, good meals. There are also *cabañas* and a campsite.

C Residencial Pensión Díaz, Manzana C, sitio 10, Lo Valdés, T02-8611496. F singles. Basic, friendly.

Camping

Comunidad Cascada de las Animas, 500 m off the main road, San Alfonso, T02-8611303. US$30 per site (up to 6 people). Also cabins with hot water, cooking equipment etc, sauna and horse riding. There are a dozen or so other campsites throughout the valley.

Farellones *p113*

LL Farellones, Las Bandurrias 11, T02-3211081, www.hotelfarellones.cl. Half board. Slightly careworn, heated swimming pool. Half price in summer.

LL La Cornisa, Los Cóndores 636, T02-3211172, www.lacornisa.cl. Half board, good restaurant. Reasonably basic but comfortable, chalet style. Much cheaper in summer.

LL Posada de Farellones, T02-2013704, www.skifarellones.com. Cosy and warm, Swiss style, satellite TV and games room. Transport service to slopes. Decent restaurant. Price includes half board.

AL Refugio Alemán, Los Cóndores 1451, T02-2649899, www.refugioaleman.cl. B per person in shared rooms. Rooms with shared bathrooms. Includes half board. English spoken. Good value.

B Refugio Universidad de Chile, Los Cóndores 879, T02-3211595, www.dta.cl/ refugio-u.htm. Price per person in shared rooms with half board. Standard *refugio*, often fills up with students from the university at weekends.

El Colorado *p113*

LL Colorado Apart Hotel, Av Apoquindo 6275, oficina 88, Las Condes, T02-2453401, www.skiandes.co.cl. Fully furnished apartments, half board. Also has cheaper cabins.

LL-L Edificio Monteblanco, bookings from Av Apoquindo 5555, of 905, T02-2073700, www.ceciliawilson propiedades.cl. Apart- ments that can be rented by the day or week. Food and room service available at extra cost.

La Parva *p113*

LL-L Condominio Nueva La Parva, reservations in Santiago, El Bosque Norte 0177, piso 2, T02-3398482 www.skilaparva.cl. Good hotel and restaurant. 3 other restaurants.

Valle Nevado *p113*

LL Apart Hotel Mirador del Inca, T02-3813000, www.miradordelinca.cl. Fully furnished apartments and 2 restaurants serving everything from gourmet to fast food.

LL Valle Nevado, T02-4777000, www.valle nevado.com. 5-star resort, full board, lift ticket included. The same company runs 2 other hotels at the complex, both slightly cheaper but still LL. See website for details.

Portillo *p114*

LL-AL Hotel Portillo, Renato Sánchez 4270, Las Condes, T02-2630606, www.skipor tillo.com. On the shore of Laguna del Inca. Accommodation ranges from lakeside suites with full board and fabulous views, to family apartments, to bunk rooms without bath. Self-service lunch, open all year, minibus to

Santiago US$70 each. Cinema, nightclub, swimming pool, sauna and medical service.

Lagunillas *p114*
AL Cabañas Pura Vida, Camino a Lagunillas, T02-2084234, Km 4 from San José on the Lagunillas road. Beautiful spot in a fantastic gorge, swimming pool, completely calm and off the beaten track. Highly recommended.
AL Club Andino de Chile, bookings at Av Bernado O'Higgins 108, local 215 , Santiago, T02-6380497, www.skilagunillas.cl. Cabins with full board.

Termas de Colina *p114*
AL Hotel Termas de Colina, T/F02-8440990. Modern, expensive thermal baths, a beautiful swimming pool (closed Fri), US$8. Formal restaurant. Facilities open to public, crowded at weekends.

San Felipe and around *p114*
LL Termas de Jahuel, T034-582323, www.jahuel.cl, northeast of San Felipe. Newly refurbished luxury health resort with thermal pool, spa, gym and tennis courts.

Los Andes *p115*
LL Baños El Corazón, San Esteban 2 km north of Los Andes, T034-482852, www.termaselcorazon.cl. Full board, swimming pool, thermal baths, take bus San Esteban/El Cariño (US$0.50).
A Plaza, Esmeralda 367, T034-421929. Good, expensive restaurant.
C Central, Esmeralda 278, T034-421275. Reasonable and very friendly (excellent bakery opposite, try the *empanadas*).
C Estación, Rodríguez 389, T034-421026. Without breakfast. Basic. Cheap restaurant.
C Residencial Italiana, Rodríguez 76, T034-423544. Clean rooms without bath.
D Residencial Maruja, Rancagua 182. Clean.

The road to the border *p115*
See above for accommodation in Portillo.
A Hostería Guardia Vieja, 8 km east of Río Blanco. Expensive but untidy, campsite.
B Hostería Luna, 4 km west of Río Blanco, T034-421026. Good value, clean, helpful, good food.

❼ Eating

Cajón del Maipo *p112, map p112*
❬❬ El Rancho del Ché, on the road between Puente Alto and San José, El Canelo. Excellent Argentine meat dishes.
❬❬ La Petite France, on the road between Puente Alto and San José, nearer San José. Good French food, not cheap.
❬❬ Restaurant El Campito, Camino al Volcán 1841, San José. Very good.
❬❬ Restaurant La Isidora, on the plaza, San José. Smart, good, meat dishes.

Portillo *p114*
❬❬❬-❬❬ Restaurant La Posada, opposite Hotel Portillo. Cheaper than the hotel, but open evenings and weekends only.

San Felipe and around *p114*
❬❬ La Piedra del Molino, in the Sector Almendral, a couple of kilometres east of San Felipe on the road to Santa María. Excellent traditional food.

❽ Transport

Pomaire *p110*
From **Santiago** take the **Melipilla** bus from behind Estación Central metro station, every few mins, US$1.50 each way, Rutabus 78 goes on the motorway, 1 hr, other buses via Talagante take 1 hr 25 mins. Alight at the side road to Pomaire, 2-3 km from town; from here there are *colectivos* and *micros* every 10-15 mins (there are also *colectivos* linking Pomaire and Melipilla) – this route is easier than taking one of the direct buses from Santiago. En route, delicious *pastel de choclo* can be obtained at **Mi Ranchito**.

Santuario de la Naturaleza Yerba Loca *p110*
Colectivos with **Taxis Transarrayán Ltda** leave from Plaza San Enrique in Lo Barnechea. Take any bus for **Barnechea** from Alameda or Providencia in Santiago.

Reserva Nacional Río Clarillo *p110*
Bus from **Puente Alto** in Cajón del Maipo (see below) to **El Principal**, 1 hr, US$3.50.

For **Cousiño-Macul**, take either bus 390 from Alameda or bus 391 from Merced, both marked to **Peñalolén**. For **Concha y Toro**, take the metro to **La Florida**, then catch Metrobus 74 to **Pirque** and ask the driver to let you off by the vineyard, or take the *colectivo* from Plaza Baquedano, US$2.50. For **Undurraga**, take a Talagante bus from the Terminal San Borja to the entrance. For **Viña Santa Rita**, get a bus direct to Alto Jahuel from Terminal San Borja, T02-7760645.

Cajón del Maipo *p112, map p112*
Buses leave Santiago from the Plaza Italia, every 15 mins to **San José**, 2 hrs, US$1.50; or take línea 5 metro to Bellavista de la Florida and catch a Metrobus. Línea 27 *colectivos* also run from the plaza in Puente Alto as far as **San Alfonso**. On weekdays hitching from San José is possible on quarry trucks.

From Plaza Italia, to **El Volcán** and to **Baños Morales**, 1 bus daily, leaves Plaza Italia at 1200 (San José at 1345), returns at 1745; buy return on arrival to ensure seat back. This service goes through **San José**, **El Melocotón** and as far as **San Gabriel**. Between **Baños Morales** and **Baños Colinas** you may be able to arrange a lift on one of the summer tour buses.

Ski resorts *p113*
Air
Services are run by **Alfa Helicópteros**, T02-2739999, www.alfa-helicopteros.com, 45 mins.

Bus
Services from Santiago to **Farellones**, **El Colorado**, **La Parva** and **Valle Nevado** are run by **Ski Total**, Av Apoquindo 4900, Edificio Omnium, oficinas 40-42, T02-2466881, www.skitotal.cl, and leave from outside their offices, daily from 0730 in season, book in advance, US$10 return. **Centro de Esquí El Colorado**, T02-2463344, www.elcolorado.com, departs from here to **Farellones** and **El**

Colorado daily from 0800 in season.
Manzur Expediciones, Sótero del Río 475, oficina 507, Santiago, T02-7774284, leave for **Farellones**, **Valle Nevado**, **El Colorado**, **Lagunillas** and **Portillo**, Wed, Sat and Sun 0830 from Baquedano metro. Except in bad weather, **Portillo** is also reached by any bus from Santiago, Valparaíso or Los Andes to Mendoza; you may have to hitch back.

It is easy to hitch from the junction of Av Las Condes/El Camino Farellones (YPF petrol station in the middle).

Termas de Colina *p114*
From Santiago take the bus from Av La Paz 302 (40 mins). From here a rough road leads through countryside 6 km; last return bus at 1900. Taxi from Colina to the hotel, US$8.

Los Andes *p115*
Los Héroes terminal has services to **Mendoza** (Argentina) with **Tas Choapa**, **Fenix Pullman Norte**, **Cata** and **Ahumada**. Any of these will drop passengers off at **Portillo**, US$10.

The road to the border *p115*
Saladillo buses hourly from Los Andes to **Río Blanco**; there are also services from Santiago, Ahumada, 1930 daily, direct, 2 hrs, US$2. For Transport into Argentina, see page 103.

❶ Directory

San Felipe has similar facilities to Los Andes, but there is little infrastructure elsewhere.

Los Andes *p115*
Banks ATMs on the Plaza de Armas. Cambio Inter, Plaza Hotel, good rates, changes TCs, also *casa de cambio* in Portillo customs building and at **Ingeniero Roque Carranza**, 13 km from tunnel.
Telephone Telefónica, O'Higgins 405.
Useful address Automóvil Club de Chile, Chacabuco 33, T034-422790.

Valparaíso & Viña del Mar

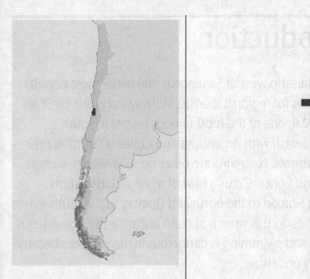

⁞ Footprint features

Introduction

The coastal strip west of Santiago is one of the most popular destinations for regional tourists. Midway along the coast is Viña del Mar, one of the most famous resorts in South America, awash with Argentines and Chileans strutting their stuff in summer. Near Viña are other popular resorts, such as Reñaca and Concón, plus a host of more secluded spots, including Horcón to the north and Quintay to the south. While the beaches on this stretch of coast are attractive, the water is very cold and swimming is dangerous in many places because of a heavy undertow.

The place that makes this part of Chile really worth visiting is Valparaíso, once the south Pacific's most important port and now the most beguiling city in the country, the capital of Región V and seat of the Chilean house of parliament, part of which has been declared a UNESCO World Heritage site. Nearby is the lumpy summit of Cerro La Campana, a high hill between the coast and the Central Valley, which offers some of the best views in Chile and can be climbed in a day. South of Valparaíso, towards the mouth of the Río Maipo, are a number of other centres, including Algarrobo, perhaps the most affluent resort along this coast, and Isla Negra, a village famous as the home of Pablo Neruda, in which the Nobel laureate gathered together a collection of objets d'art from around the world.

★ Don't miss...

1 **Cerros Alegre and Concepción** Enjoy the architectural anarchy of Valparaíso's hills, page 127.
2 **Cerro La Campana** Climb to the top for some of the best views in Chile, page 130.
3 **Viña del Mar** Sun yourself along with the rich and famous on the beach at Chile's premier resort, page 138.
4 **Concón** Enjoy some of the best cuisine in Chile at one of the resort's many restaurants, page 140.
5 **Horcón** Watch horses towing the fishing boats ashore, ready for the catch to be unloaded at this small fishing village on the coast, page 140.

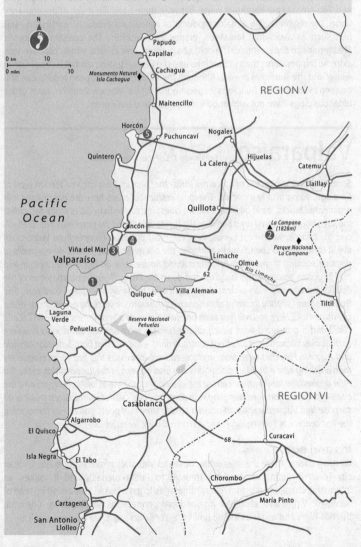

Background

This was one of the first areas to be settled by the Spanish, the lands being assigned to prominent *conquistadores* during the 16th century. For most of the colonial period this region was an important exporter of wheat and other foodstuffs to Peru. With Independence and the ending of trade restrictions in the 19th century Valparaíso rose to become the most important port on the Pacific coast of South America, but there were few other large centres of population along this coastline until the 1880s, when the fashion for holidaying near the sea spread from southern Europe. Viña del Mar was established in 1880 and several other resorts followed between 1880 and 1900: Algarrobo, Cartagena, Las Cruces, Zapallar and Papudo, all owing part of their popularity to the building of railway lines linking them to the capital.

Today, this area is one of the major economic centres of the country. Valparaíso and San Antonio are important ports, between them handling much of the country's trade. The region is also a major producer of agricultural products, particularly soft fruit such as avocados, tomatoes, grapes and peaches. The coastline enjoys a Mediterranean-style climate: the cold sea currents and coastal winds produce less extreme temperatures than in Santiago and the Central Valley; rainfall is moderate in winter and the summers are dry. Although the influence of European resorts can still be seen in some of the buildings, especially in Viña del Mar and Zapallar, most of the older buildings have not withstood earthquakes and bulldozers.

Valparaíso → *Colour map 3, B2. Population: 300,000.*

Sprawling over a crescent of 42 cerros (hills) that rear up from the sea 116 km west of Santiago, Valparaíso is a one-off. The main residential areas here are not divided into regimented blocks, as in all other Chilean cities; instead Valparaíso is really two cities: the flat, vaguely ordered area between the bus terminal and the port known as 'El Plan', and the chaotic, wasp-nest cerros, in which most porteños (people from Valparaíso) live. It is possible to spend weeks exploring the alleyways of the cerros, where packs of dogs lie sunning themselves, brightly painted houses pile on top of one another and half-forgotten passageways head up and down the hills, offering fantastic views of the Pacific, the city and – on a clear day – right over to the snow-capped cordillera. The Bohemian and slightly anarchic atmosphere of the cerros reflects the urban chaos of the city as a whole. Here you will find such unusual sights as a 'monument to the WC' (Calle Elias) and a graveyard from which all the corpses were shaken out during a severe earthquake. Valparaíso is all about contradictions – the fact that both Salvador Allende and Augusto Pinochet were born and raised here expresses this fact more eloquently than anything else – but the oppositions can also be seen in the juxtaposition of the flat Plán against the labyrinthine cerros; the sea against the views of Aconcagua; and the city's grandiose mansions mingling with some of Chile's worst slums. Given this it is no surprise that Valparaíso has attracted a steady stream of poets and artists throughout the last century. ►► *For Sleeping, Eating and other listings, see pages 131-138.*

Ins and outs

Getting there There are inter-urban buses to Valparaíso from every major Chilean city (even including connections through to Punta Arenas), and it makes an interesting change to most travellers' itineraries to get a bus to Valparaíso instead of Santiago. Valparaíso also has international connections to Mendoza, Córdoba, Buenos Aires and as far as Rio de Janeiro. ►► *For further details, see Transport page 136.*

Getting around You should never have to wait more than 30 seconds to travel anywhere within El Plán (between Plaza Aduana and Avenida Argentina): buses along Pedro Montt are cheap but slow; Errázuriz buses are faster. Valparaíso is the only city in Chile still to have trolleybuses; they are mostly Swiss and from the 1950s, ply the length of El Plán and cost the same as a local bus fare. Buses to Cerro Alegre and the top of Cerro Concepción leave from outside the bus terminal (142) or Avenida Argentina (D3), both via Plazuela Ecuador. Taxis and *colectivos* usually wait around at the bottom of each *cerro*; otherwise, you can use the *ascensores* (funicular railways). If you are going to Viña or one of the nearby towns to the north, catch a *micro* from Errázuriz or Brasil; *colectivos* to Viña leave from the same place. Taxis serving a particular cerro do not use their meters but are generally reasonable and, if there are three or four of you, sharing a taxi can be cheaper than taking a *colectivo*. Taxis from the bus terminal are metered and can be quite expensive.

Security Robbery is an occasional problem in El Puerto and around the *ascensores* on Avenida Argentina. The upper outskirts of town, while offering amazing views, are not the safest of places. The poorer and rougher districts tend to be those furthest from the centre. Also be aware that Calle Chacabuco (on which some hotels are located) is the pickup point for local rent boys. Beware of the mustard trick (see page 42).

Tourist information Offices are located in the Municipalidad ① *Condell 1490, oficina 102, Mon-Fri 0830-1400, 1530-1730*, and at Muelle Prat ① *Nov-Mar only, Mon-Fri 1030-1430, 1600-2000*. However, the building is currently being refurbished and meanwhile there are kiosks by the Plaza Sotomayor and the Plaza Aníbal Pinto. There are also two information offices in the bus terminal, but these are privately run on a commission basis and hence do not give impartial advice.

History

Founded in 1542, Valparaíso became, in the colonial period, a small port used for trade with Peru. It was raided at least seven times during the colonial era by pirates and corsairs, including Drake. The city prospered from Independence more than any other Chilean town. It was used in the 19th century by commercial agents from Europe and the US as their trading base in the southern Pacific and became a major international banking centre as well as the key port for shipping between the northern Pacific and Cape Horn. Until the 1840s, the journey from the port to El Almendral (site of the congress and the old road to Santiago) took several hours and passed over wild hills but, as the city's wealth and importance grew, part of the original bay was filled in, creating the modern day Plán. Fine buildings were erected here, including several banks, South America's first stock exchange and offices of *El Mercurio*, the world's oldest newspaper in the Spanish language, first printed in 1827 and still in publication. (The impressive Mercurio building, built in 1900, stands on the site of a famous pirates' cave.) Wealthy European merchants began to populate Cerro Concepción and Cerro Alegre in this period, building churches and fine mansions in every conceivable architectural style.

The city's decline was the result of two factors: the development of steam ships, which stopped instead for coaling at Punta Arenas and Concepción, and the opening of the Panama Canal in 1914. Further decline followed the development of a container port in San Antonio, the shift of banks to Santiago and the move of the middle classes to nearby Viña del Mar. Recently money has been pumped in through UNESCO, the Inter-American Development bank and to some extent tourism, and the city is slowly being restored to its former splendour.

● *Recognizing the city's cultural and architectural importance, UNESCO took the decision in 2002 to declare Cerro Alegre and Cerro Concepción as well as part of El Plan towards El Puerto, a World Heritage site.*

Neruda on Valparaíso

"The hills of Valparaíso decided to dislodge their inhabitants, to let go of the houses on top, to let them dangle from cliffs that are red with clay, yellow with gold thimble flowers, and a fleeting green with wild vegetation. But houses and people clung to the heights, writhing, digging in, worrying, their hearts set on staying up there, hanging on, tooth and nail, to each cliff. The port is a tug-of-war between the sea and nature, untamed on the *cordilleras*. But it was man who won the battle little by little. The hills, and the sea's abundance gave the city a pattern, making it uniform, not like a barracks, but with the variety of spring, its clashing colours, its resonant bustle. The houses became colours: a blend of amaranth and yellow, crimson and cobalt, green and purple."

Pablo Neruda, *Memoirs*, Penguin, 1978.

Little of the city's colonial past survived the pirates, tempests, fires and earthquakes, but a remnant of the old colonial city can be found in the hollow known as El Puerto, grouped round the low-built stucco church of La Matriz. Very few wooden buildings predate the devastating earthquake of 1906, which was followed by a series of fires.

Valparaíso west

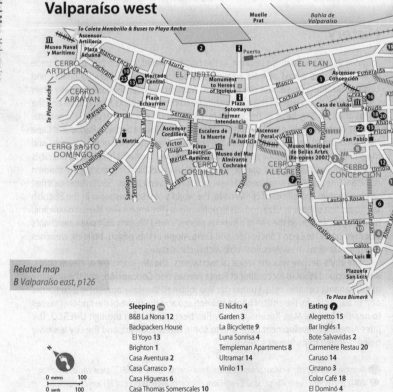

Related map
B *Valparaíso east, p126*

Sleeping	El Nidito **4**	Eating
B&B La Nona **12**	Garden **3**	Alegretto **15**
Backpackers House	La Bicyclette **9**	Bar Inglés **1**
El Yoyo **13**	Luna Sonrisa **4**	Bote Salvavidas **2**
Brighton **1**	Templeman Apartments **8**	Carmenère Restau **20**
Casa Aventura **2**	Ultramar **14**	Caruso **14**
Casa Carrasco **7**	Vinilo **11**	Cinzano **3**
Casa Higueras **6**		Color Café **18**
Casa Thomas Somerscales **10**		El Dominó **4**

Sights

The lower part of the city, known as **El Plan**, is the business centre, with fine office buildings on narrow streets that are strung along the edge of the bay and cluttered with buses. Above, covering the hills or *cerros* is a fantastic agglomeration of buildings in every conceivable shape that seem literally to tumble down the slopes. Part of the charm of the *cerros* is the lack of order. It is as if every individual bought a plot of land and built whatever they saw fit, resulting in a hotchpotch of size, style and colour. Spanish colonial mansions lie alongside adobe shacks and neoclassical monoliths.

Superb views over the bay are offered from most of the *cerros*, each of which provides its own unique vista and distinct atmosphere. It is enjoyable to spend an afternoon exploring the hills and, however lost you might feel, a few minutes' walk downhill will always lead you back to El Plan. The lower and upper cities are connected by steep winding roads, flights of steps and 15 *ascensores* or funicular railways dating from the period 1883-1914.

Plaza Sotomayor and El Puerto

The old heart of El Plan is the **Plaza Sotomayor**, dominated by the former **Intendencia** (Government House), now the seat of the admiralty. Be careful when crossing the plaza, which, although it appears pedestrianized, is in fact criss-crossed by busy roads. Opposite is a fine monument to the 'Heroes of the Battle of Iquique', which also serves as a mausoleum housing the bodies of all who fought in the battle. Visitors are occasionally allowed inside and on 21 May it is the focus of a massive procession of the armed forces through the city celebrating the anniversary of the battle. While excavating under Plaza Sotomayor in order to build a new underground car park, parts of Valparaíso's original **old quay** were uncovered; they can be visited in summer. Alternatively, they can be viewed from above ground through the glass ceiling, although the glass tends to mist up. Look out, too, for the bronze plaques on the ground illustrating the movement of the shoreline over the centuries.

The area around Plaza Echaurren in El Puerto can be dangerous at night; it is inadvisable to seek accommodation here.

One block away from Plaza Sotomayor is the port entrance (take a boat trip from here around the bay, recommended if sunny; see Activities and tours, page 136) and the **railway station**, from which passenger services run on the newly modernized metropolitan line to Viña del Mar and Limache.

One block northwest of Plaza Sotomayor, on Calle Serrano, is the **Ascensor Cordillera** and the Escalera de la Muerta (the Stairs of Death; just try climbing them to find out why). At the top, on Plazuela Eleuterio Ramírez, take Calle Merlet to the left and you will find the **Museo del Mar Almirante Cochrane**

Gloria Vuscovic 7
Hamburg 8
La Colombina 9
La Costeñita 10
La Tertulia 11
Le Filou de Montpellier 12
Los Porteños 13
Mastodonte 21
Pasta e Vino 22

Pizza Napolitana 6
Puerto Viejo 23
Turri 16

Bars & clubs
La Piedra Feliz 19
Vinilo 17

Valparaíso & Viña del Mar Valparaíso

ⓘ *Merlet 195, Tue-Sun 1000-1800, free*, which hosts temporary art exhibitions in a small colonial house with excellent views over the bay (the New Year fireworks are filmed from here). Note that pickpockets are known to work in this area.

Back in El Plan, continue another block along Serrano into the heart of El Puerto to reach **Plaza Echaurren**, Valparaíso's oldest square, tree-lined and with a picturesque fountain. It was once the height of elegance but is now surrounded by cheap restaurants and frequented by a sizeable population of local drunks. Near Plaza Echaurren stands the church of **La Matriz**, built in 1842 on the site of the first church in the city and unusual for its sloping nave and stained-glass windows all depicting Valparaíso themes. Further northwest, along Bustamante, lies Plaza Aduana, named after the customs building, from where the **Ascensor Artillería** takes you up to the Mirador 21 de Mayo and the imposing **Museo Naval y Marítimo** ⓘ *Tue-Sun 1000-1730, US$1*, in the old Naval Academy, which documents naval history 1810-1880, and includes exhibitions on Chile's two naval heroes, Lord Cochrane (see box, page 341) and Arturo Prat.

Playa Ancha and around

To the west of **Cerro Artillería**, the Avenida **Gran Bretaña** winds its way to the municipal stadium on Cerro Playa Ancha, which seats 20,000 people and is home to the local football team Santiago Wanderers. The buildings on Avenida Gran Bretaña are a good example of the suburb's eccentric architecture. Past the stadium the road continues downhill to the foot of Cerro Playa Ancha at **Las Torpederas**, a small

Valparaíso east

Bahía de Valparaíso

Muelle Barón

Sleeping		Eating
Hostal El Rincón	O'Higgins Plaza 4	Bambú 1
Universal 9	Puerta de Alcalá 8	Bogarín 13
Hostal Kolping 5	Puerto Natura 1	Casino Social JJ Cruz 3
Hostal Patricia 2	Robinson Crusoe 11	Coco Loco 4
Hostelling International	Sra Mónica Venegas 12	Empanadas
Valparaíso 3		Famosas's de Adali 5

bathing beach. Just beyond the beach is a promontory topped by the **Faro de Punta Angeles**, which was the first lighthouse on the west coast of South America. There is a picturesque coastal road back to town, the Avenida Altamirano, passing **Caleta Membrillo**, which has a number of good seafood restaurants.

Around Cerros Alegre and Concepción

Southeast of Plaza Sotomayor, calles Prat, Cochrane and Esmeralda run through the old banking and commercial centre to **Plaza Aníbal Pinto**, around which are some of the city's oldest bars and cafes. Above this part of El Plan are **Cerro Alegre** and **Cerro Concepción**, the heart of the UNESCO-designated area and for many the undisputed symbols of the city. Both are filled with brightly painted mansions and high-ceilinged 19th century houses, some falling down but many now being restored to their former glory and some being extended upwards, despite supposedly restrictive planning regulations, a contentious issue for many in the local community. Cerro Concepción is as posh as Valparaíso gets, while Cerro Alegre has a more artistic, bohemian feel: brightly coloured murals abound, most of the shops seem to double as art galleries and, during university term, students can be seen on practically every street corner sketching buildings or the panoramic views. The two hills are connected to El Plan by three *ascensores*, of which **Ascensor Concepción**, inaugurated on 1st December 1883, is the oldest in Valparaíso. Three *miradores* offer views of the bay, over to Viña and beyond.

    Museo Municipal de Bellas Artes ① *Paseo Yugoslavo, closed for refurbishment till mid-2007, then Tue-Sun 1000-1800, free*, is housed in Palacio Baburizza, and has displays of Chilean land- and seascapes and some modern paintings. A visit is highly recommended and, if you are lucky, you may get to see the whole of this interesting rococo mansion; the games room, drawing room, shower and servants' quarters provide an insight into the contrasting lifestyles of *porteños* in the early part of the 20th century.

    Also worth a visit is the **Casa de Lukas** ① *Paseo Mirador Gervasoni 448, Cerro Concepción, T032-2221344, www.lukas.cl, Tue-Sun 1100-1900, US$1.80*, dedicated to the work of Chile's most famous caricaturist. Lukas (real name Renzo Pecchenino) was originally from Italy but spent most of his life in Valparaíso. The museum holds a permanent exhibition of his work, which gives a humorous insight into the political and social history of Valparaíso and Chile. There are also temporary exhibitions and occasional films.

Avenida Alemania and around

Walking uphill along any of the main streets of Cerro Alegre will lead you to the Plazuela San Luis, from where **Avenida Alemania** runs southeast, following the contours of Valparaíso's hills. This is the only road that connects all the hills above Valparaíso and makes a pleasant walk, with ever-changing views, one of the best of which is to be had from **Plaza Bismark**. Calle Cumming heads back down to the Plán from Plaza Bismark passing the former prison (now a cultural

To Viña del Mar & Caleta Portales

Related map
A Valparaíso west, p124

Ascensor Barón

Ascensor Lechero

Ascensor Larraín

Congreso Nacional

Rawson

Av España

Av Argentina

Wed/Sat Fruit & Veg Market, Sun Flea Market

Ascensor Polanco

Simpson

To Santiago

Gato Tuerto **14**
Gioco **6**
Hon San **7**
La Mangiata **8**
La Otra Cocina **9**
La Puerta del Sol **10**
Nuevo O'Higgins **11**

San Carlos **12**
Valle de Quintil **2**

⁝ A walk over the cerros Alegre and Concepción

From the **Plaza Aníbal Pinto** walk up Calles Cumming and Elias and take the **Ascensor Reina Victoria** up to a viewing point. Walk along Paseo Dimalow to the end, then head down Urriola (opposite). After one block, turn right onto **Calle Templeman**. On the left are two alleyways: Pasaje Templeman has a couple of art workshops, while Pierre Loti has typical English-style houses. Further along Calle Templeman is the Anglican church of **San Pablo**, built in 1858, which has organ recitals every Sunday at 1230. Follow the church round past the entrance on Pilcomayo and head down to the end of that street, where steps lead down to **Paseo Pastor Schmidt**, with views of the cemetery opposite. Carry on past the Lutheran church (1897) and along the revamped **Paseo Atkinson**, once home to merchants and ships' captains and with expansive views. At the end of the walkway, turn right onto Papudo. The next right leads to the **Paseo Gervasoni**, overlooking the port and the Turri clock tower, and

home to the Lukas museum. Following the paseo round, take the steps down to the labyrinthine **Pasaje Galvez**, past restaurants, bars and art galleries.

Cross Calle Urriola, and head up **Pasaje Bavestrello**, ahead and to the right. At the top is an unusual building, four storeys high and 3 m wide. Turn right here onto the **Paseo Yugoslavo** and the Palacio Baburizza, with views of the Cochrane museum to the left and Playa Ancha beyond. Walk past the Ascensor Peral and follow the road up and round into **Pasaje Leighton**. The second road on the right is **Miramar**. Climb 100 m and turn left onto **Lautaro Rosas**, an avenue lined with fine houses and mansions. After two blocks the road crosses the stair-lined **Calle Templeman**, boasting one of Valparaíso's classic views.

If you still have any energy left you can climb three blocks to the **Plazuela San Luis** and begin exploring other hills along the Avenida Alemania.

centre housing temporary exhibitions and occasional concerts – worth a visit) and three cemeteries, all of which can be visited: **Cementerios I** and **II** are the city's two oldest Catholic cemeteries, while the third, **Cementerio de los Disidentes**, holds the graves of Protestant immigrants. Back on Avenida Alemania, meanwhile, a 20-minute walk will bring you to the former home of Pablo Neruda, **La Sebastiana** ① *Ferrari 692, off Av Alemania, Altura 6900, Cerro Florida, T032-2256606, www.lasebastiana- neruda.cl, Tue-Sun 1030-1430, 1530-1800 (until 1900 in summer), US$4.50, students half price Tue-Fri, bus O from Av Argentina, US$0.50, or colectivo from Plazuela Equador, US$0.60.* It now houses an art gallery as well as a collection of some of his objets d'art, showing his eccentric tastes to the full, and there is a small café in the garden, with fine views.

⁝ *The best way to enjoy this avenida is to board to 'O' bus between Avenida Argentina and El Puerto which winds up and down the cerros!*

Plaza de la Victoría and around

From **La Sebastiana**, walk down **Cerro Bellavista** along Calle Ferari and Calle Hectór Calvo to arrive at the **Museo al Cielo Abierto**. Opened in 1992, this open-air museum consists of large-scale murals painted on the outside walls of buildings throughout Cerro Bellavista by 17 of Chile's leading artists. Look out in particular for the 6 m by 3 m mural by Chile's most famous contemporary artist, Roberto Matta, which is situated just before you reach the Ascensor Espíritu Santo; it's a typical example of

Matta's later work with sharp-toothed monsters hurtling through space. At the bottom of the *museo*, in El Plan, is **Plaza de la Victoria** with the cathedral on its east side and the municipal library on Plaza Simón Bolívar just to the north. Plaza Victoria is the official centre of Valparaíso and commemorates Chile's victory in the War of the Pacific; the statues and fountain were looted from Peru during the war.

One block west, on Calle Condell in the 19th-century Palacio Lyon is the **Museo de Historia Natural** ① *Condell 1546, T032-2257441, www.dibam.cl/subdirec_museos/ mhn_valpo/home.asp, Tue-Fri 1000-1300, 1400-1800, Sat 1000-1800, Sun 1000-1400, US$1.10*, which hosts exhibitions. Next door is the **Galería de Arte Municipal** ① *Condell 1550, T032-2220062, Mon-Sat 1000-1900, free*.

Plaza O'Higgins and further east

East of Plaza de la Victoria, Pedro Montt leads to the Parque Italia and **Plaza O'Higgins**. The latter is dominated by the imposing **Congreso Nacional**, a monolithic arch in neo-fascist style, thoroughly out of keeping with the rest of the city. (Now that the congress is possibly about to return to Santiago, the municipality is in a quandary as to what to do with the construction.) Opposite is the bus terminal, while four blocks north on Errázuriz is the Barón train station and the **Muelle Barón**, the new terminal for cruise ships. A walk to the end of this pier, past kite-flying children, gives a different view of Valparaíso, clearly showing the amphitheatre-like form of the city. Just off the pier is a small colony of sea-lions, and at the pier's base, kayaks can be hired to paddle in the bay. A new coastal walkway has recently been built running northeast from here past several small beaches as far as Caleta Portales, a small fishing harbour with several seafood restaurants that lies almost at the border between Valparaíso and Viña del Mar.

To the east of the Congress building, Avenida Argentina runs south past four *ascensores* including **Ascensor Polanco** (entrance from Calle Simpson, off Avenida Argentina a few blocks southeast of the bus terminal). This is the most unusual *ascensor* in the city as it is in two sections: walk along a 160-m horizontal tunnel through the rock, then take a vertical lift to the summit on which there is a mirador. Note that the lower entrance is in an area that can be unsafe after dark: do not go alone and do not take valuables. Beyond Polanco the road branches left towards Santiago or continues straight on to Cerro O'Higgins, where there are several mansions built by the British in the 19th century. Nearby is the **Mirador O'Higgins**, from which the Supreme Director, Bernardo O'Higgins, saw the arrival of Cochrane's liberating squadron (see box, page 341) and proclaimed "On those four craft depends the destiny of America".

South of Valparaíso

Laguna Verde, 12 km south of Valparaíso, is a picturesque bay with a huge beach that's peaceful and perfect for picnics, although the wind can get quite fierce in the afternoons and strong undercurrents make swimming dangerous.

Further south, **Quintay** is the least known of the villages on the central *littoral* (there is no direct route here from Santiago), and also one of the most picturesque. In its heyday, the village's whaling station, which is open to visitors ① *Tue-Sun 0900-1800, US$0.70*, employed over 1000 workers, mostly from Chiloé, but now only the fishermen remain. Most people ignore the threatening sign warning you not to climb up to the lighthouse. If you take the risk, the view is worth the short climb; sit on the rocks and watch the sunset.

Quintay has two beaches, the larger of which is being overrun by a housing development. The other, **Playa Chica**, is accessed via an unsignposted route through a eucalyptus wood (entry by the *carabineros*). It is wild and deserted off season and is definitely worth the 20-minute walk.

East of Valparaíso

Towards Santiago

Reserva Nacional Peñuelas ① *US$2*, encompasses 9260 ha around the artificial Lago Peñuelas and is open to visitors for walking and fishing. The park, which is covered by pine and eucalyptus forest, is situated 30 km southeast of Valparaíso near the main road to Santiago (Route 68). Buses between the two cities pass the entrance where the park administration is located. Beyond the park, Route 68 passes through two tunnels, the first of which is 51 km southeast of Valparaíso and charges a US$3 toll. On the journey east, this can be avoided by turning off about 1 km before the tunnel onto the old road over the mountains, which has good views of the surrounding countryside (*toll US$1.50*). There is another tunnel with a toll further east, 56 km west of Santiago.

Towards Argentina

Route 62 (better known as 'El Troncal') runs through Viña del Mar, climbs out of the bay and passes through **Quilpué**, Km 16, a dormitory town for Valparaíso and Viña, with an interesting municipal zoo. It crosses a range of hills and reaches the Aconcagua Valley at **Limache**, a sleepy market town, famous for its tomatoes, 40 km from Valparaíso. Route 62 joins Route 60 just before **Quillota**, another fruit-growing centre, continuing to La Calera, Km 88, where it joins the Pan-American Highway; turn southeast and east for Llaillay, San Felipe, Los Andes and the Redentor tunnel to Mendoza.

Parque Nacional La Campana

Situated north of Olmué (8 km east of Limache), the **park** ① *US$2.75 per person*, covers 8000 ha and includes **Cerro La Campana** (1828 m), which Darwin climbed in 1835, and **Cerro El Roble** (2200 m). It is divided into three main sections, each with its own entrance: in the south are **Sector Granizo** ① *paradero 45, 5 km east of Olmué*, from which the Cerro La Campana is climbed, and **Sector Cajón Grande** ① *paradero 41, reached by unpaved road off the Olmué-Granizo road*, while to the north is **Sector Ocoa** ① *reached by unpaved road (10 km) off the Pan-American Highway between Hijuelas and Llaillay*, which is where the main concentration of Chilean coconut palms (*kankán*) can be found. This native species is now found in natural woodlands in only two locations in Chile. The park can be crossed on foot (six hours) between Ocoa and Cajón Grande along well-marked trails through the gamut of Chilean natural vegetation, from cactuses and palm trees to southern beech and lingue. A number of shorter trails lead from all three entrances.

A fair amount of agility is required to climb **Cerro La Campana**; visitors without much climbing and scrambling experience may wish to seek advice or take a guide. Allow a whole day there and back from Olmué, although fit and experienced hikers could probably do it in around seven hours. There are three places where fresh water is available on the climb, but you should take your own food and drink. From the entrance at Granizo, a path leaves the road to the left just past the CONAF *guardería*, and climbs steeply through forest, fording a clear, rushing stream and providing increasingly fine views of the Andes until reaching an old mining area (two hours from the *guardería*). From here the path is well marked, but becomes more testing; after passing a plaque dedicated by the British community to Charles Darwin on the centenary of his visit, it climbs over loose rock to a pass to the northeast, before doubling back and rising over rocks (where scrambling and a little very basic climbing is required) to the summit. The wonderful views from the top of the Cerro la Campana take in a 300-km stretch of the Andes (including Aconcagua), as well as the rugged outline of the central *cordillera* losing itself in the haze to the north, the gentler scenes of the southern hills, and, when the haze is not too great, Valparaíso and the Pacific Ocean to the west. It is also possible to ascend La Campana from Quillota, but this route is more difficult and definitely requires a guide.

● Sleeping

Plaza Sotomayor and El Puerto
p125, map p124

D **Garden**, Serrano 501, T032-252776.
F singles. Friendly, large rooms, gloomy
and run down but cheap, use of kitchen.
Not the safest area at night.

Playa Ancha and around *p126*

B **Villa Kunterbunt**, Av Quebrada Verde 192,
Playa Ancha, T032-2288873. Lovely building
– the tower room has panoramic views –
breakfast, very friendly, Chilean-German run,
garden, English and German spoken. Highly
recommended. Buses 1, 2, 5, 6, 17, 111, N,
and *colectivos* 150, 151, 3b all pass by.

Around Cerros Alegre and
Concepción *p127, map p124*

There are several *hostales* in the
neighbourhood; shop around.

LL-L **Casa Higueras**, Higuera 133,
Cerro Alegre, T032-2497900, www.hotelcasa
higueras.cl. New luxury boutique hotel.
Not open at time of going to press but
set to be a small intimate affair, wooden
interiors restored, talk of luxuries such
as a pool.

L-AL **Casa Thomas Somerscales**, San
Enrique 446, Cerro Alegre, T032-2331006,
www.hotelsomerscales.cl. Spacious
rooms in a restored mansion with period
furniture. Basic English spoken. Wifi areas.
The rooms on the top floor have lovely
views over the bay, although some
question whether building an extra
storey on a historic building in a protected
area can be justified.

AL **El Nidito**, Templeman 833, piso 2, Cerro
Alegre, T032-2734117, www.elnidito.cl.
Spacious luxury apartment recently restored
with high ceilings, large fully equipped
kitchen and bathtub with views over the bay.
English spoken, lots of info, advance booking
advised. Highly recommended.

AL-A **Brighton**, Paseo Atkinson 151, Cerro
Concepción, T032-2223513, www.brigh
ton.cl. Bills itself as a typical building in a
historic part of Valparaíso, although it's
barely 10 years old. Small rooms, mixed
reports on service, one room has a balcony
with excellent views. There is live tango and
bolero music in the bar at weekends.

A **Templeman Apartments**, Pierre Loti 65,
Cerro Concepción, T032-2257067, chantal
derementeria@hotmail.com. Fully equipped,
stylish, self-contained apartments sleeping
3-4, one uses an old weaving loom as table
and has a wardrobe painted Mondrian style;
good if you want a little peace away from
the gringo trail. Book in advance for
weekends. Highly recommended.

A-B **Casa Carrasco**, Abato 668, Cerro
Concepción, T032-2210737, www.casa-
carrasco.cl. D singles. Some rooms with bath,
but some are dark. Good location, terrace
with fine views, good meeting place,
although somewhat overpriced.

B **Vinilo**, Urriola, Cerro Concepción, T032-
2230665, www.cafevinilo.cl. Minimalist
doubles and twins with shared bathrooms.
Also studio flats, A.

B-C **Luna Sonrisa**, Templeman 833,
Cerro Alegre, T032-2734117,
www.lunasonrisa.cl. E singles, F per person
in shared rooms. Some rooms with bath.
Newly restored, bright, comfortable, large
kitchen, lots of information, excellent
breakfast including wholemeal bread
and real coffee, tours arranged, English
and French spoken, friendly and helpful,
and run by the author of this guide.
Highly recommended – of course!

C **B&B La Nona**, Galos 660, Cerro Alegre,
T032-2495706. E singles. Small, friendly
family run bed and breakfast. English spoken.
Recommended.

C **Casa Aventura**, Pasaje Gálvez 11,
off C Urriola, Cerro Concepción,
T032-2755963, www.casaventura.cl.
F per person in shared rooms. One of
Valparaíso's longest established backpackers'
hostels, in a restored traditional house,
with good breakfast, German and English
spoken, Spanish classes offered, tours,
helpful, friendly, informative, kitchen
facilities. Highly recommended.

C **La Bicyclette**, Almte Montt 213, Cerro
Alegre. T032-2222215, www.bicyclette.cl.
E singles. With breakfast. Basic, bright rooms,
lovely patio, French run, hires out bicycles.
There are several more *hostales*, generally
B or C in Cerro Concepción.

Avenida Alemania and around
p127, maps p124 and p126

AL **Puerto Natura**, Héctor Calvo 850,
Cerro Bellavista, T032-2224405, www.puerto
natura.cl. In a restored mansion set in large
grounds with fruit trees and small swimming
pool. Excellent views. There is also a holistic
centre with sauna, massages and yoga
classes. Recommended.

L-AL **Ultramar**, Pérez 173, Cerro Cárcel,
T032-2210000, www.hotelultramar.cl.
A-B singles. Old brick warehouse tastefully
refurbished as an upmarket bed and
breakfast. The more expensive rooms are
spacious and have fantastic views, although
they can feel a little stuffy in summer. Rooms
are centrally heated, café/bar downstairs.
Friendly attentive staff. English and Greek
spoken. Slightly isolated from the main
points of interest.

Plaza de la Victoria and around
p128, maps p124 and p126

L-AL **Robinson Crusoe** , Hector Calvo 389,
Cerro Bellavista, T032-2495449, www.hotels.
tk/robinson. Down the hill from the
Sebastiana Museum in a large restored old
house. Lovely roof terrace with views,
peaceful, nice suites with bathrooms, but
most rooms have shared bath and these
are overpriced.

A **Puerta de Alcalá**, Pirámide 524,
T032-2227478, www.hotelpuertadealcala.cl.
Everything you would expect of a standard
3-star without being spectacular.

B-C **Hostelling International Valparaíso**,
B Vera 542, Cerro San Juan de Dios,
T032-2734336, www.hivalparaiso.cl. F per
person in dorms. Large youth hostel in a
former mansion in a pleasant residential
district.

C **Hostal Kolping**, Valdés Vergara 622 y
Independencia, T032-2216306, kolping
valparaiso@yahoo.es. Rooms without bath,
pleasant, quiet, a nice choice in El Plan.

F **Backpackers House El Yoyo**, Ecuador 355,
T032-2591087, ktyoyo@hotmail.com. Price
per person in somewhat cramped dorms.
Fun youth hostel for the younger crowd.

Plaza O'Higgins and further east
p129, map p126

The area near the bus terminal can be
unsafe, especially at night.

A **O'Higgins Plaza**, Retamo 517, T032-
2235616, www.restaurantohiggins.cl/hotel.
html. A good business standard, next to the
Congress building but not the most
interesting part of town.

C **Hostal El Rincón Universal**, Argentina
825, T032-2235184, www.elrinconuniversal.
cl. E singles. With breakfast, laundry, study,
cable TV and internet access a good,
reasonably priced alternative in this part
of town; the area can be intimidating at
night, though.

C **Hostal Patricia**,12 de Febrero 315,
T032-2220290. E singles, F per person in
dorms. Family accommodation, hot showers,
laundry and kitchen facilities, good local
knowledge. Not the nicest area, but very
convenient for the bus terminal.

C-D **Sra Mónica Venegas**, Av Argentina 322,
Casa B, T032-2215673. F singles, 2 blocks
from bus terminal, often booked up.

South of Valparaíso *p129*

Camping is possible at Laguna Verde at
Camping Los Olivos, which has good
facilities and is well run and friendly.

Parque Nacional La Campana *p130*

There are places to stay in all price categories
in Olmué for easy access to the Granizo
sector of the park.

AL **El Copihue**, Diego Portales 2203, Olmué ,
T033-441544, www.copihue.cl. Small resort
set in pleasant gardens, with gym, games
room, indoor and outdoor pools. Half and
full board available.

C **La Alondra**, Granizo 8459, Olmué,
T033-441163. F singles. A reasonable
budget choice.

C **Sarmiento**, Blanco Encalda 4689, Olmué,
T033-442838. E singles. Cheap and cheerful.

Camping

It is possible to camp in all sectors of the
park, US$11 per site with cold showers. In
summer reserve in advance, T033-2441342.

● Eating

Plaza Sotomayor and El Puerto
p125, map p124

⑪⑪⑪ Bote Salvavidas, Muelle Prat s/n, piso 2, T032-2251477. Upmarket seafood restaurant overlooking the port.

⑪⑪ La Costeñita, Blanco 86. Good seafood restaurant, with incredibly kitsch decor. Try the *pastel de jaivas*.

⑪⑪ Los Porteños, Cochrane 102. Perennial favourite for fish and shellfish, terse service but good food.

⑪ Puerto Viejo, Cochrane y Valdivia. Very good-value set lunch fish dishes.

There are countless *fuentes de soda* throughout El Plan and in the market, where the portions are large (closed in the evenings).

⑪ Sandrita, 2nd floor of the market (off Plaza Echaurren). Good *carbonada de mariscos*, friendly, recommended.

Playa Ancha and around *p126*

There are several good fish restaurants at Caleta Membrillo, 2 km west of Plaza Sotomayor (take any Playa Ancha bus).

⑪⑪ Club Social de Pescadores, Altamirano 1480. A concrete monstrosity by the harbour, redeemed by views. Busy at weekends.

⑪⑪ El Membrillo, Caleta Membrillo. The oldest restaurant in the Caleta. Opposite the Club Social.

Around Cerros Alegre and Concepción *p127, map p124*

⑪⑪⑪-⑪⑪ Carmenère Restau, Concepción 280, Cerro Concepción , T032-2493319. New restaurant using local ingredients in surprising and innovative ways. Good fish dishes. Recommended.

⑪⑪⑪-⑪⑪ Pasta e Vino, Templeman 352, Cerro Cocepción, T032-2496187. Upmarket trendy restaurant serving fresh pasta with a twist. Giant salmon raviolis with curry are a perennial favourite. Closed Mon. Book 2 days in advance at weekends.

⑪⑪⑪-⑪⑪ La Colombina, Paseo Yugoslavo 15, Cerro Alegre, T032-2236254. Good food, wide range of wines, fine views, the *ostiones* in particular are recommended.

⑪⑪⑪-⑪⑪ Turri, Templeman 147, on Cerro Concepción, T032-2259198. Wonderful views, reasonable food but a bit of a tourist trap.

⑪⑪ Alegretto, Pilcomayo 529, Cerro Concepción, T032-2968839. British owned pizzeria with excellent bases and unusual toppings. Also gnocchi.

⑪⑪ Bar Inglés, Cochrane 851 (entrance also on Blanco Encalada), El Plan, T032-2214625. Historic bar/restaurant dating from the early 1900s; a chart shows the ships due in port. Good food and drink, traditional, not cheap.

⑪⑪ Café Vinilo, Almirante Montt 448, Cerro Alegre, T032-2230665. Good value inventive lunchtime menus. Also a lively bar at night.

⑪⑪ Caruso, Cumming 201, Cerro Cárcel, T032-2594039. Mostly seafood and fish with a Peruvian touch. Uses inshore fish not found in other restaurants. Good wine list and regular tastings.

⑪⑪ Cinzano, Plaza Aníbal Pinto 1182, El Plan, T032-2213043. The oldest bar in Valparaíso, also serving food. Flamboyant live music at weekends, noted for tango performances but no dancing by guests allowed. Service can be awful.

⑪⑪ Le Filou de Montpellier, Almte Montt 382, T032-2224663. French run. Set lunch menu very popular and deservedly so. Also open weekends for dinner. Good value. Recommended.

⑪⑪ Pizza Napolitana, Lautaro Rosas 510, Cerro Alegre. T032-2594851. Good all round Italian. The pizzas are excellent. Delivery service within the neighbourhood.

⑪⑪-⑪ La Tertulia, Esmeralda 1083, El Plan, T032-2210905. Good vegetarian options.

⑪ El Dominó, Cumming 67, El Plan. Traditional basic *porteño* restaurant serving *empanadas*, *chorrillanas* and the like.

⑪ Mastodonte, Esmeralda 1139, El Plan, T032-2251205. No nonsense, very good value, traditional food in incredibly kitsch surroundings. Often crowded but still excellent service and cheap locally brewed draught beer.

⑪ Gloria Vuscovic, Montealegre 280. Good set lunches in a delightful old house.

Cafés

Both the Turri restaurant and the Hotel Brighton have terraces where you can drink coffee while enjoying the views.

Café con Letras, Almte Montt 316, Cerro Concepción. Cosy and friendly no smoking café with books, magazines and newspapers. Excellent coffee, also soup in winter.

Color Café, Papudo 526, Cerro Concepción.
Eclectic, arty café serving tea and real coffee,
fresh juice, good cakes and snacks, regular
live music, art exhibits, and local art and craft
for sale. Slow service.

El Desayunador, Almte Montt 399, Cerro
Alegre, T032-2755735. Wide range of teas
and real coffee, also vegetarian dishes.
Opens early for breakfast.

Pan de Magia, Almte Montt 738 y
Templeman, Cerro Alegre, T032-2227868.
Cakes, cookies and by far the best
wholemeal bread in town, all take away.

Riquet, Plaza Aníbal Pinto, El Plan. One of
the oldest cafes in Valparaíso, good coffee
and breakfast.

Plaza de la Victoria and around
p128, map p124

¶¶¶ **Coco Loco**, Blanco 1781, pisos 21 y 22,
T032-2227614. Plush revolving restaurant
70 m above the bay. Extensive menu.

¶¶¶-¶¶ **Gato Tuerto**, Héctor Calvo 205, Cerro
Bellavista, T032-2220867. Thai food, great
views. Downhill from La Sebastiana, or take
ascensor Espíritu Santo from the Plán.

¶¶ **Hamburg**, O'Higgins 1274, T032-
2597037. Owned by an elderly German
emigré. Right-wing military memorabilia
abounds. The food is apparently good.

¶¶ **Hon San**, Donoso y Huito. Chinese.
Nothing special, but the best of the bunch
nevertheless.

¶¶ **Valle de Quintíl**, Rodolfo 254, Cerro
Bellavista, T032-2469631. At the top of the
ascensor Espíritu Santo. Good fish dishes with
extensive views over the city and the bay.

¶ **Bambú**, Pudeto 450, T032-2234216.
Vegetarian lunches only, closed Sun.

¶ **Casino Social JJ Cruz**, Pasaje Condell 1466,
T032-2250319. A Valparaíso institution:
restaurant-cum-museum, famous for its
chorrillanas, and for being open when
everything else is not. Not to be missed
unless you are vegetarian.

¶ **Empanadas Famosas's de Adali**,
S Donoso 1381, T032-2227497. Among the
best *empanadas* in Valparaíso. Wide range of
fillings available.

¶ **Gioco**, Molina 586-B (in yoga centre). No
sign. Excellent-value vegetarian set lunches
with fruit juices.

¶ **San Carlos**, Las Heras y Independencia.
Traditional family run restaurant with lots of
character that hasn't changed in years.
Lunch only. Good food guaranteed. Always
full of locals. Recommended.

Cafés
Bogarín, Plaza Victoria 1670. Great juices
and good sandwiches and ice cream.

Cioccolata, Condell 1235. Good coffee,
excellent cakes.

Plaza O'Higgins and further east
p129, map p126

¶¶¶ **Portofino**, Bellamar 301, Cerro Esperanza
(above caleta Portales), T032-2629939. Fine
restaurant with excellent views. One of the
best in Valparaíso. The tártaro de Avestruz is
worth a try. Take colectivo 6 from Plaza
Victoria.

¶¶¶-¶¶ **Caleta Portales**, Av España s/n,
T032-2625814, www.restaurantcaleta
portales.cl. Good seafood restaurant on
the road to Viña. There are several other
restaurants nearby, mostly ¶¶.

¶¶ **La Otra Cocina**, Yungay 2250. Seafood
specialities, cosy, good food and service.

¶¶ **Nuevo Restaurant O'Higgins**, Almte
Barroso 506, behind the congress. Not to be
confused with Restaurant O'Higgins around
the corner, specializes in meat and
parrilladas, good.

¶¶-¶ **La Mangiata**, Rodríguez 538, off Pedro
Montt. Italian, simple decor, very good food.

¶ **La Puerta del Sol**, Pedro Montt 2033,
T032-2235158. Traditional Chilean dishes,
great chips are served outside.

Cafés
Hesperia, Victoria 2250. A classic old-time
coffee emporium With huge comfy bar
stools.

South of Valparaíso *p129*
El Galeón restaurant in Laguna Verde serves
good simple food. In Quintay try the local
speciality *congrio arriero* (fish stew with chips
on top!) at any of the reasonably priced
restaurants on the harbour (**Miramar** is
especially recommended for its huge
portions, fresh fish and good service.)

Plaza Sotomayor and El Puerto
p125, map p124

Playa, Serrano 567. An old-fashioned bar, similar to **Bar Inglés**, but cheaper, frequented by students and run by slightly snooty staff. There are several bars attracting a similar crowd nearby.

Liberty, Almte Rivero 9, Plaza Echaurren. A real dingy old-timers' bar, where you can see local characters drinking and singing all day. Good cheap food is served.

Pagano, Blanco 236, El Puerto. 80s music and 'anything-goes' atmosphere.

Proa Al Canaveral, Errázuriz 304. Seafood restaurant downstairs, bar upstairs with dancing from 0100, poetry reading on Thu, Latin pop music, mostly students.

Playa Ancha and around *p126*

Bar Roma, Playa Ancha. The unofficial drinking hole of the crazier students from the university down the street.

Around Cerros Alegre and Concepción *p127, map p124*

Hotel Brighton (see Sleeping, above) has a small bar with live music at weekends 2300 to 0300. There are also good bars at **Cinzano** and **Bar Inglés** (see Eating, above).

Axe Bahía, Errázuriz 1084. Cuban salsoteca.

El Cielo, Errázuriz 1152. Disco for the technopop generation.

La Piedra Feliz, Errázuriz 1054. Incorporates 3 areas, each with different decor: a large pub, a live music area and a dance floor, serving up everything from jazz to salsa, bossanova and tango depending on the evening, entrance US$9.

Poblenou, Urriola 476, Cerro Alegre, T032-2495245. Intimate winebar serving tapas and other snacks. Open Sun.

Vinilo, Almte Montt 448, Cerro Alegre. Café/bar attracting a friendly 20- and 30-something crowd, good place to meet locals and other travellers. Extensive vinyl record collection and occasional live music at weekends. Serves food.

p128, map p126

El Huevo, Blanco 1386. One of Valparaíso's most popular nightspots with 3 levels of dancing and drinking.

El Irlandés, Blanco 1279, T032-2593675. Irish owned pub with a huge variety of bottled beer as well as Bitter and Stout from Britain and Ireland on draught. Live music at weekends. Good fun.

There are many bars on Subida Ecuador, but be careful which ones you go into, as in some of them you risk being eaten alive (only enter **El Muro**, for example, if you are into methylated spirits and the sordid elements of life). **El Coyote Quemado** is by far the best.

Entertainment

It is worth checking out the 'Invite' supplement, inside the *Mercurio de Valparaíso* every Fri. For live music venues, see Bars and clubs above.

Cinema

Cinehoyts, Pedro Montt 2111, T032-594709. Mainstream movies, most from Hollywood.

8½, Almte Montt 642, Cerro Alegre, T032-2598213, www.8ymedio.cl. Small arts cinema showing DVD projection films.

Instituto Chileno-Norteamericano de Cultura (see below) also shows films, as do smaller film clubs. The 'Invite' supplement, inside the *Mercurio de Valparaíso* every Fri has details of these.

Galleries

In addition to the **Galería de Arte Municipal** and the **Museo Municipal de Bellas Artes**, occasional free exhibitions are held at the following galleries:

Camara Lucida, Plaza Echaurren, T032-2597466, www.camaralucida.cl. Photographic exhibitions and workshops.

Cult-Art, Almte Montt y Galos, Cerro Alegre. Contemporary art by local artists.

Fundación Valparaíso, Héctor Calvo, Cerro Bellavista (between La Sebastiana and ascensor Espíritu Santo). Local contemporary art.

Instituto Chileno-Norteamericano, Esmeralda 1069. Temporary exhibitions of photos and paintings from all over Chile.

Wenteche, Templeman523, Cerro Concepción. Features work by Valparaíso artists.

⊛ Festivals and events

New Year is celebrated by a 3-day festival culminating in a superb 40-min firework display on the bay, which is best seen from the *cerros*. Over a million visitors and locals take supper and champagne to celebrate from vantage points around the bay. Accommodation can double or even triple in price at this time and needs to be booked well in advance.

◉ Shopping

Books

CRISIS, Pedro Montt by the bus terminal. An excellent new and second-hand bookshop.
Cummings no 1, Cumming 1, just off Plaza Aníbal Pinto. Wide selection of new and used books in English and other languages.
Librería Ivens, Plaza Aníbal Pinto. The oldest bookshop in Valparaíso with periodicals in English, French and German, and lots of literature about the city and its history.
Librería Universitaria, Esmeralda 1132. Good selection of regional history.

Crafts

Handicraft shops on the quay are expensive and poor quality. There are several small workshops on cerros Alegre and Concepción selling interesting hand-made objects:
Design for Valparaíso, Concepción 154, Cerro Concepción . Small textile workshop.
Taller Atiquina, San Enrique y Templeman, Cerro Alegre. Good quality rustic leather goods ranging from chairs to tea coasters.
Valarte, Pasaje Fischer 68, off Pasaje Gálvez, Cerro Concepción. Glass ornaments as well as paintings in the naïve style.
Victor Hugo, Pasaje Templeman y C Templeman, Cerro Concepción. Silver and lapiz lazuli jewellery.

Department stores

Falabella and **Ripley**, both by the Plaza Victoria.

Markets

The **fruit and veg** market on Av Argentina, Wed and Sat, is colourful and worth a visit; a **flea market** is held on the same site on Sun. There is also a large **antiques market** around Plaza O'Higgins on Sun mornings.

▲ Activities and tours

A number of tour companies have cropped up recently offering city tours, but it is hard to say if any will last the distance. The best advice is to ask at the place you are staying, but bare in mind that your hosts may recommend the operator that pays the highest commission.

Boat trips

Launches run trips around the harbour from Muelle Prat, 30 mins, US$1.80 per person or US$18 to hire an entire boat, offering a pleasant view of the city, especially when it is sunny. Beware that groups of foreign tourists are liable to be overcharged. Other boats can be hired for fishing. Don't photograph naval ships or installations.

Diving

Austral Divers, Caleta Quintay, T09-98855099, www.australdivers.cl. Diving courses and trips for qualified divers.

Horse riding

Ritoque Expediciones, north of Concón, T032-2816344, www.ritoqueexpediciones.cl. Excellent day trips over a variety of terrain. Galloping encouraged. Also night time rides under the full moon. Recommended. Pickup service from Valparaíso and Viña del Mar.

Parque Nacional la Campaña *p130*
Paredón, Granizo sector, T033-443741, www.paredonadventure.com. Good tours of the park in Spanish, English and French.

⊖ Transport

Air

Santiago airport is 1½ hours away. A taxi will cost around US$75. To get to Valparaiso from the airport by public transport take the airport bus going to Santiago and get off at the Pajaritos station on the outskirts of the city, from where there are direct buses to Valparaiso and Viña. The total journey time is around 2 hrs, cost about US$7 per person. **LanChile**, Esmeralda 1048, T600-5622000.

Ascensores

Very cheap at US$0.20-0.30 per journey; going uphill is slightly more expensive;

sometimes you pay on entrance, sometimes on exit.

Bus

Buses and trolley buses, US$0.45 within El Plan, US$0.55 to the *cerros*. There are plenty of buses between the long-distance terminal and Plaza Sotomayor.

Local An excellent and incredibly frequent bus and *colectivo* service from Plaza Aduana, passes along Av Errázuriz to **Viña del Mar**, 20 mins, $0.70. Buses serving **Lago Peñuelas**, **Isla Negra** and **San Antonio** leave every 30 mins from the main terminal, US$3.

Long distance The terminal is at Pedro Montt y Rawson, 1 block from Av Argentina. To **Santiago**, frequent, 1¾ hrs, US$4-6; shop around for the best prices, book on Sat to return to the capital on Sun. There are also daily services to the following destinations: to **Chillán**, 7 hrs, US$11; to **Concepción**, 8 hrs, US$13; to **Puerto Montt**, 14 hrs, US$18; to **La Serena**, 7 hrs, US$11 semi cama; to **Calama**, 24 hrs, US$28 semi cama; to **Arica**, 30 hrs, US$32 semi cama. La Porteña and **Intercomunal** run several buses daily north leaving from the Plaza Victoria to **Pichidangui** and **Los Vilos**, Intercomunal continuing on to **Illapel** and **Salamanca**, although it may be easier to catch any bus to **La Calera** from Errázuriz/Brasil (every few minutes) and make a connection there.

To Argentina To **Mendoza**, 5 companies, 8 hrs, US$13, leaving early morning. Also overnight service summer only, **Pluma** continuing on Tue, Fri and Sun to Buenos Aires, Florianopolis, São Paulo and Rio. To **Córdoba**, Tas Choapa, daily, US$40.

Car

Colón Rent a Car, Colón 2581, T032-2256529; **Suzuval**, Colón 2537, T032-2255505; many more options in Viña.

Ferry

For boat services from Valparaíso to the Juan Fernández Islands, see page 507.

Taxi

Colectivos, which pickup and set down passengers anywhere en route, operate along the same routes as buses and offer a cheap and quick form of transport. Taxis are more expensive than Santiago.

Train

Regular service on **Merval**, the Valparaíso metropolitan line, to **Viña del Mar**, every 10 mins, 15 mins, US$0.60, and on to **Quilpué** and **Limache**. A special card is needed to travel which can be purchased at any station.

South of Valparaíso *p129*

Buses to **Laguna Verde** can be caught from Pedro Montt via Playa Ancha every 30 mins, 40 mins, US$1. A yellow *colectivo* from C 12 de Febrero behind the bus terminal in Valparaíso runs to **Quintay**; it won't go until it's full, but if you're in a hurry you can pay for the extra seats, 45 mins, US$2.20.

Parque Nacional La Campana *p130*

The entrances at **Granizo** (paradero 45) and **Cajón Grande** (paradero 41) are reached in summer by **Euro Express** bus from Calle Errázuriz in Valparaíso, via Viña and Limache, otherwise by local bus/*colectivo* from Limache. There is no public transport to the entrance at **Palmar de Ocoa** to the north; bargain with *colectivo*/taxi drivers in La Calera, expect to pay around US$15-20 for the trip, arrange return transport if necessary.

● Directory

Banks Banks open 0900-1400, closed on Sat; many **Redbanc** ATMs on Prat, also one in the bus terminal; best exchange rates from **Marin Orrego**, 3rd floor of the stock exchange building, Prat y Urriola, only changes US$ and euro cash; for other currencies, there are several casas de cambio along Prat and Esmeralda.

Consulates Argentina, Blanco 890, oficina 204, T032-2213691; **Belgium**, Prat 827, piso 12, T032-2213494; **Bolivia**, Serrano 579, T032-2259906; **Brazil**, Blanco 951, piso 2, T032-2217856; **Denmark**, Errázuriz 940, T032-2268379; **Ecuador**, Blanco Encalada 1623, oficina 1740, T032-2222167; **Germany**, Blanco 1215, oficina 1102, T032-2256749; **Guatemala**, Blanco 1199, Local 4, T032-2255214; **Norway**, Freire 657, T032-2252219; **Panama**, Blanco 1623, oficina 1103, T032-2213592; **Peru**, Errázuriz 1178, oficina 71, T032-2253403; **Spain**, Brasil 1589, piso 2, T032-2214466; **Sweden**, Errázuriz 940, T032-2250305; **UK**, Blanco 1199, piso 5, T/F032-2213063. **Internet** There are dozens, scattered all over El Plán; in Cerro Alegre, on Templeman y Urriola. **Language schools** Escuela Español Interactivo, Pasaje Gálvez 25, Cerro Concepción, www.interactive-spanish.cl. **Laundry** Las Heras 554, good and cheap; Lavanda Café, Almirante Montt 454, Cerro Alegre, enjoy a coffee while you wait for your clothes, US$3 wash, US$3 dry, full service US$1 extra. **Medical services** Dr Walther Meeden Bella, Condell 1530, Depto 44, T032-2212233, dentist; Hospital Alemán,

G Munich 203, Cerro Alegre, often has English-speaking staff on duty. **Post office** North side of Pedro Montt, between San Ignacio & Bolívar. **Telephone** There are cheap call centres all over the plan and a couple on cerros Alegre and Concepción. **Useful addresses** YMCA (Asociación Cristiana de Jóvenes), Blanco Encalada 1117; YWCA (Asociación Cristiana Feminina), Blanco 967.

Viña del Mar and around → *Colour map 3, A/B2.*

Nine kilometres northeast of Valparaíso via the Avenida España, which runs along a narrow belt between the shore and precipitous cliffs, is Viña del Mar, one of South America's leading seaside resorts. Viña is also famous throughout Chile for its annual international music festival, during which the attention of the entire country is focused on the city; the festival used to bring in some top performers from all over Latin America, but this is no longer the case. In fact, neither the festival nor Viña itself are as wonderful as Chileans like to make out. This is the only place in Chile where road signs are in English as well as Spanish and much of the city feels like suburban North America. That said, with pleasant beaches and shady parks, Viña is a nice enough city to visit, especially if you have some pesos to burn, and makes an interesting contrast to nearby Valparaíso.

North of Viña strung along the coast are several smaller settlements. Reñaca, now a suburb of Viña del Mar, is a well-to-do resort with extensive beaches, while further north, Maitencillo and Zapallar are fashionable seaside destinations, overflowing with tourists in summer. In between are the fishing towns of Concón, famous for its seafood, and Horcón, where horses are still used to tow the fishing boats onto land.
▶▶ For Sleeping, Eating and other listings, see pages 141-146.

Ins and outs

Getting there There are inter-urban buses to Viña del Mar from many Chilean cities. The city also has daily connections through to Mendoza in Argentina.

Getting around Frequent *micros* linking Viña and Valparaíso depart from Plaza Vergara. *Colectivos* also serve this route, as well as running to many of the city's outlying neighbourhoods and there are numerous buses along the coast. Taxis are plentiful and usually reasonably priced.

Tourist information Sernatur is at ① *Valparaíso 507, oficina 303, T032-2683355, infovalparaiso@sernatur.cl*. The municipal tourist office is on the corner of Plaza Vergara and can arrange the rental of private homes in the summer season; there's also a kiosk on calle Valparaíso y Villanelo.

Viña del Mar ⬤🚻🎭🎡🎿⚓🚊🏨 *pp141-146.*

The older part of Viña del Mar is situated on the banks of a creek, the Marga Marga, which is crossed by bridges. Around Plaza Vergara and the smaller Plaza Sucre are the **Teatro Municipal** (1930) and the exclusive **Club de Viña**, built in 1910. It's a private club, but sometimes hosts public concerts and events. The municipally owned

Quinta Vergara, formerly the residence of the shipping entrepreneur Francisco Alvarez, lies two blocks further south. The superb grounds include a double avenue of palm trees and encompass a children's playground and a large outdoor amphitheatre where the music festival takes place in February; it also hosts concerts and events throughout the year. Also here is the **Palacio Vergara** ① *To32-2680618, Tue-Sun 1000-1400, 1500-1800, US$1*, which houses the **Museo de Bellas Artes** and the **Academia de Bellas Artes**. You can take a tour of the city in a horse drawn carriage from the Plaza Vergara for around US$30 depending on the length of the trip.

Calle Libertad runs north from the plaza, lined with banks, offices and shops. At the junction with 4 Norte is the **Palacio Carrasco**, now a cultural centre housing temporary exhibitions. In the same grounds is the **Museo Sociedad Fonk** ① *Calle 4 Norte 784, Tue-Fri 1000-1800, Sat and Sun 1000-1400, US$1.80*, an interesting archaeological museum, with objects from Easter Island and the Chilean mainland, including Mapuche silver. East of this is the **Palacio Rioja** ① *Quillota 214, To32-689665, Tue-Sun 1000-1400, 1500-1800*, built in 1906 by a prominent local family and now used for official municipal receptions. The ground floor is preserved in its original state and is well worth a visit. Four blocks further east is the **Valparaíso Sporting Club** with a racecourse and playing fields, while to the north, in the hills, are the **Granadilla Golf Club** and a large artificial lake, the **Laguna Sausalito** ① *US$4, children under 11 US$3, colectivo 19 from Viana*, which has an excellent tourist complex open in summer with swimming pools, boating, tennis courts and sandy beaches. Nearby is the **Estadio Sausalito**, home to Everton football club.

West of the plaza, on a headland overlooking the sea, is **Cerro Castillo**, the president's summer palace; its gardens can be visited. Below, on the coast, Castillo

Viña del Mar

N

0 metres 200
0 yards 200

Wolff houses the **Museo de la Cultura del Mar** ① *T032-262542, Tue-Sat 1000-1300, 1430-1800, Sun 1000-1400*, which contains a collection devoted to the life and work of the novelist and maritime historian, Salvador Reyes. Just north, on the other side of the Marga Marga, is the **casino** ① *open all year, US$2.50*, built in the 1930s and set in beautiful gardens. North of this are the main beaches, **Acapulco** and **Las Salinas** (see below), while south of Cerro Castillo is another popular beach at **Caleta Abarca**.

Jardín Botánico Nacional ① *8 km southeast of the city, US$1.80, bus 20 from Plaza Vergara*, was formerly the estate of the nitrate magnate Pascual Baburizza and is now administered by CONAF. Covering 405 ha, it contains over 3000 species from all over the world and is a good picnic spot. Within the gardens is a large collection of Chilean cacti; it's very pretty, but unfortunately the different species are not labelled. There is also a canopy adventure tourism site with ziplines linking trees within the park.

Resorts north of Viña del Mar ⬤🔆🔆✳🔺🖥 *pp141-146.*

North from Viña del Mar

North of Viña del Mar the coast road runs past **Las Salinas**, a popular beach set between two towering crags. The suburb of **Reñaca** is a popular resort with access to excellent beaches, while to the north at Cochoa, there are giant sand dunes and a large sea lion colony 100 m offshore. This route affords lovely views over the sea, but there is also a much faster inland road between Reñaca and Concón.

Concón

Concón lies on the southern shore of a bay 18 km north of Viña del Mar at the mouth of the Río Aconcagua. The town claims to be the oldest settlement in Chile, having been founded by Pedro de Valdivia in 1541, prior to his arrival at what is now Santiago. Concón is famous for its restaurants and is rightly known as the culinary capital of the V region. The area is very popular among Santiaguinos, who often come here for the weekend. A series of six beaches stretches along the bay between Caleta Higuerilla at the western end and La Boca at the eastern end. These beaches include **Playa Amarilla**, which is good for sunbathing; the very peaceful **Playa Higuerillas**, where there are lots of shells; **Playa Los Lilenes**, backed by sand dunes, and **Playa La Boca** itself, which is by far the largest of the six, and excellent for beach sports (horses US$5 for 30 mins; also kayaks for hire). Helpful **tourist office** ① *annexed to the municipal museum, Maroto 1030, www.concon.cl*, can provide maps of the resort.

✱ *Most buses to Concón drop passengers off at the main roundabout near La Boca. The Nandu bus from Viña follow the coast road and passes all six beaches.*

Quintero

Another 23 km north of Concón, Quintero is a fishing town situated around a rocky peninsula with 16 small beaches, all of varying character and quality. The path running along the north side of the peninsula offers a good view of the sunset over the ocean from the Cueva del Pirata at its western end. Good fishing and windsurfing are available at **Playas Loncura** and **Ritoque** to the north of the town, while horses can be hired on **Playa Albatros**. Note that there are many touts and beggars in Quintero in the high season, when the atmosphere can become a little tense. On the opposite side of the bay is **Las Ventanas**, where a power station and copper processing plant rather spoil the outlook from the beach.

Horcón

Set back in a cove surrounded by cliffs, Horcón, also known locally as Horcones, is a pleasant small village, mainly of wooden houses. Although overcrowded in season, during the rest of the year it is a charming place, populated by fishermen and artists, with a tumbledown feel unlike the more well-to-do resorts to the north and south. Across the headland to the south of the village is **Playa Cau Cau**; scramble down a steep flight of log steps to reach the sandy, frequently deserted, tree-lined cove, sadly now dominated by a condominium development.

Maitencillo

Maitencillo, 19 km north of Las Ventanas, is an upmarket resort consisting mainly of chalets and frequented mainly by well-to-do Santiaguinos. There is a wonderful long beach here but the sea is notorious for its strong undercurrents. It is usually deserted off season.

Zapallar

A fashionable resort with a lovely beach, 33 km north of Las Ventanas, Zapallar is an expensive place to stay. The number of fine mansions along Avenida Zapallar are a clue to its luxurious heritage. At **Cachagua**, 3 km south, there are clear views of a colony of penguins on an offshore island from the northern end of the beach; take binoculars.

Papudo

Ten kilometres further north is the site of a naval battle in November 1865, in which the Chilean vessel *Esmeralda* captured the Spanish ship *Covadonga* during the War of Independence. Following the arrival of the railway Papudo rivalled Viña del Mar as a fashionable resort but it has declined a great deal since its heyday in the 1920s. Among the buildings surviving from that period is the **Casa Rawlings**, now the Casa de la Cultura. There are two fine beaches, which are empty except in high summer .

● Sleeping

Viña del Mar *p138, map p139*
There are a great many more places to stay in addition to those listed here, particularly in the AL-A range, although many are in the business district and not convenient for the beaches. In season, it is generally cheaper to stay in Valparaíso and commute to the beaches around Viña. Note that during the music festival in Feb, accommodation is almost impossible to find. Out of season, furnished apartments can be rented through agencies (with commission).
LL Hotel del Mar, Av Perú y Los Héroes, casino complex, T032-2500600, www.hoteldelmar.cl. Very expensive luxurious hotel on the upper floors of the casino. Panoramic views. suites, pool, spa, tours, several restaurants.
LL Sheraton Miramar, Av Marina N 15, T032-2838799, www.starwoodhotels.com. Viña's newest upmarket hotel with exceptional views as well as a swimming pool, gym and restaurant.
LL-L Gala, Arlegui 273, Local 10, T032-2321500, www.galahotel.cl. Excellent, suites, all mod cons and wide ranging business facilities.

L-AL Cap Ducal, Av de la Marina 51, T032-2626655, www.capducal.cl. Ship-shaped building literally overhanging the sea. Recommended for its location although services are also reasonable. There is a good restaurant at street level (see below).
L-AL San Martín, San Martín 667, T032-2689191, www.hotelsanmartin.cl. Slightly decrepit exterior. Small rooms, some with sea view and small balcony. Also café, bar, sauna. Not great value.
AL-A Albamar, San Martín 419, T032-2975274, www.hotelalbamar.cl. Standard hotel with little charm but well located. Cheaper rooms are on the small side.
A Agora, 5½ Poniente 253, T032-2694669, www.hotelagora.cl. On a quiet side street. Brightly coloured clean rooms, most with full size bath tub. Wifi in all rooms, English spoken, friendly staff. 4 floors but no lifts.
A Andalué, 6 Poniente 124, T032-2684147, hotelandalue.cl. Good location, decent carpeted rooms. Restaurant downstairs and heated pool on the roof. Good value.
A Hostal Girasoles de Agua Santa, Pasaje Monterrey 78, off Agua Santa, T032-2482339, bandngirasoles@vtr.net. **E** per person in

shared rooms. Old wooden house with small but pleasant garden. Internet, information, basic cooking facilities, tours arranged, English spoken. A little overpriced for what is on offer.

A **Offenbacher Hof**, Balmaceda 102, Cerro Castillo, T032-2621483, www.offenbacher -hof.cl. Large wooden house in a quiet residential district overlooking the city crentre. The best rooms, with bath and cable TV, are spacious and have views. Good breakfast served on a bright terrace, German and some English spoken. Cheaper to pay in pesos than in dollars. Recommended.

A-B **Genross**, Paseo Monterrey 18, off Agua Santa, T032-2661711, genrosshotel@hot mail.com. Located in a beautiful old mansion, clean airy rooms with bath, garden patio and sitting room, very friendly and informative, homely atmosphere, good breakfast, Canadian-Chilean owned, recommended. Closed in winter.

A-B **Residencia 555**, 5 Norte 555, T032-2739035, residencial555@vtr.net. C singles Characterful wooden house with antique furniture. Rooms ranging widely in size have bath and cable TV. Good value. Advance reservations difficult as a deposit is required but credit cards not accepted.

B **Hostal El Escorial**, 4 Norte 535, T032-2907919, www.escorial.cl. Basic rooms with bath and small TVs. Some could do with a little refurbishment. Grumpy owner.

B **Vancouver Viña**, 5 Norte 650, T032-2482983, www.hotelvancouvervina.cl. Clean carpeted modest rooms with bath and cable TV. Room 12 is the nicest. Friendly, good value. Also cafeteria downstairs. There are 2 similar hotels opposite.

There are lots of cheap *residenciales* around the junction of Von Schroeders and Valparaíso, but this is the red-light district and is particularly insalubrious at night. The best options here are probably the following:

C **Residencial Blanchait**, Valparaíso 82A, T032-2974949, www.blanchait.cl. E singles. Some rooms with bath. Clean, good service. Breakfast extra.

C **Residencial Capric**, von Schroeder 39, T032-2978295, hotelcapric@yahoo.com. E-F per person in shared rooms. Run-down rooms with bath and TV, breakfast included, special rates for YHA members.

Camping

Reñaca Center, town centre, T032-833207. Good facilities on the river bank, US$20 per site.

Reñaca *p140*

Accommodation here is much cheaper out of season.

L **Cabañas Don Francisco**, Torreblanca 75, T032-2834802. Helpful service, *cabañas* only available for week-long bookings.

L **Montecarlo**, V MacKenna 136, T032-2830397. Very modern and comfortable.

AL **Piero's**, Av Central y Segunda, T032-2830280. Comfortable, with café, pool, some rooms with sea view.

Concón *p140*

AL **Hostería Edelweiss**, Av Borgoño 19200, T032-2814043, www.edelweiss.cl. Modern *cabañas* sleeping 2-6, clean, sea views, pool, kitchenette (cheaper cabins without), including breakfast, excellent food in attached restaurant, German spoken. Recommended.

B **Cabañas Los Romeros**, T032-2813671. Cabins for up to 3 people.

B **Cabañas Río Mar**, T/F032-2814644. Many other *cabañas* in this price range.

Camping

Mantagua, 3 km north, T032-811415, www.mantagua.cl. Well equipped but very expensive, also *cabañas*.

Quintero *p140*

There are lots of cheap *residenciales* here.

AL-A **Yachting Club**, Luis Acevedo 1736, T032-2930061, www.hotelyachting.cl. Hotel with pool and large gardens on the seafront.

B-C **Monaco**, 21 de Mayo 1530, T032-2930939. Run down but interesting and good views.

B-C **Residencial Brazilian**, 21 de Mayo 1336, T032-2930590, clilo3@msn.com. With breakfast, large windows but no view, clean, well maintained, warm seawater baths for US$6.

Horcón *p140*

There are many *cabañas* around the village; shop around for the best price, especially off season. Rooms are also available in private houses and, although there's no campsite, camping is possible in people's gardens.

B-C El Ancla, by the harbour. Pleasant
cabañas, also serves good food.

C Cabañas Arancibia, T032-2796169. Cabins
with or without bath, pleasant gardens,
good food, friendly. Recommended.

C Juan Esteban, Pasaje Miramar, Casa 2,
T032-2796056, www.geocities.com/jeste
banc. E singles. English, Portuguese and
Italian spoken, nice terrace with view.
Recommended. Also fully equipped
cabañas (A) for 4 people.

Maitencillo *p141*

LL Marbella Resort, 2 km south,
T032-2772020, www.marbella.cl. 5-star
resort, conference centre, restaurants, golf
course, tennis courts, pools, and everything
else you would expect.

A Cabañas La Mar, Av de la Mar 524,
T032-2771036. One of several options in
this price range.

Zapallar *p141*

Accommodation is expensive especially in
the centre where it is sparse. There is no
campsite.

L Isla Seca, T033-741224, islasec@ctc
internet.cl. Small, with pool and very
expensive suites, good restaurant.

AL César, T033-741259. Nice but expensive.

A-B Hostal Villa Real. Large rooms, with
breakfast. Recommended.

A-B Residencial Villa Alicia, Moises Chacón
280, T033-741176, good, and one of the
cheapest.

Papudo *p141*

There are several cheap *residenciales* on
Chorillos 100-150.

A Carande, Chorillos 89, T033-791105.
Best in town.

A De Peppino, No 609, T033-791108.
Cabañas for 4-6 people.

C Armandini, F Concha 525.

● Eating

Viña del Mar *p138, map p139*

There are dozens of restaurants in the
triangle formed by San Martín, 5 Poniente

and 2 Norte, ranking from Mexican to Italian,
Austrian, Argentinian and Chinese.

¶¶¶ Cap Ducal, in the Cap Ducal hotel (see
above). Good seafood, elegant surroundings,
excellent views.

¶¶¶ Savinya, Peru 199. Elegant restaurant
above the casino.

¶¶¶-¶¶ Diego Pizza, San Martín y 8 Norte,
T032-22681105. Good pizzas but overpriced.
Home delivery service.

¶¶¶-¶¶ El Otro Estilo, 6 Norte357,
T032-2883144. Delightful tiny bistro, serving
good value set lunch and more adventurous
à la carte dishes at night. Simple decor but
good food and service.

¶¶¶-¶¶ Enjoy del Mar, Av Peru s/n,
T032-2500785. Modern restaurant serving
everything from gourmet dishes to
barbeques and fast food, all on an open
terrace on the seafront.

¶¶¶-¶¶ Fellini, 3Norte 88, T032-2975742. Wide
range of fresh pasta in delicious sauces.

¶¶¶-¶¶ Las Delicias del Mar, San Martín 459.
Award-winning basque seafood restaurant.
Slightly hackneyed menus but good
nevertheless.

¶¶¶-¶¶ Mastrantonio, 8 Norte y 4 Poniente.
Good Italian.

¶¶¶-¶¶ Ruby Tuesdays, in the mall, 14 Norte.
For those of you who can't do without a
US-style sports bar.

¶¶ La Dieta de Nos, 3 Norte y 5 poniente,
T032-2460235. For people with special
dietary needs. Dishes for diabetics,
hypertensives and vegetarians.

¶¶ Las Gaviotas, 14 Norte 1248. Chilean meat
dishes, inexpensive.

¶ Africa, Valparaíso 324. Extraordinarily kitsch
facade, cheap lunches with a wide range of
dishes including soups and salads.

¶ Café Alemán, Arlegui 228. Good set lunch.

¶ Café Journal, Agua Santa y Alvarez.
Excellent value set lunch, recommended.

¶ Cevasco, Valparaíso 700, on the corner of
Plaza Vergara. Super-sized fast food. Similar
at **El Guatón** next door.

¶ Club Giacomo, Villanelo 131. A Viña
institution. Traditional set lunches with a
pool hall annex.

¶ Jerusalem, Quinta 259. Excellent falafel to
eat in or take away.

● *For an explanation of sleeping and eating price codes used in this guide, see inside the*
● *front cover. Other relevant information is found in Essentials, see pages 50-57.*

¶ **La Flor de Chile**, 8 Norte 607 y 1 poniente. Good, typically Chilean food.

¶ **Le Fondue**, Arlegui 394. Cheap dishes including vegetarian options. Doubles as a bar at night with occasional poetry readings.

¶ **Shawerma Kabab**, Ecuador 255. Kebabs, stuffed vineleaves and other Arabic specialities.

Cafés

Alster, Valparaíso 225. Elegant, but pricey.

Enjoy Cafe, Av Peru by the casino. Bright café on the seafront. Live jazz outside on sat evenings.

Samoiedo, Valparaíso 637. Old-time café.

Reñaca p140

¶¶¶ **Hotel Oceanic**, Av Borgoño. Very good.

¶¶¶ **Rincón Marino**, Av Borgoño 17120. Good seafood.

¶¶¶ **El Pancho**, Av Borgoño 16180. Excellent seafood and service.

Concón p140

Seafood is the name of the game here. Both Caleta Higuerilla and La Boca are renowned for their restaurants.

¶¶¶ Among the most upmarket are located along Av Borgoño, one side fronting onto the road, the other onto the beach, including the following in Caleta Higuerilla: **Albatross**, No 21295; **Aqui Jaime**, No 21303; **Bellamar**, No 21505; **Don Chico**, No 21410; **Edelweiss**, No 19200; and **Vista al Mar**, No 21270.

¶¶-¶ Mid-range options include **La Picá de Emeterio**, and **Las Deliciosas**, both on Borgoño in La Boca, while cheaper eateries are to be found in Alto Higuerillas, where *picadas* have been converted by the fishermen into good-value restaurants: try **La Cava de Franz**, San Pedro 345; **La Picá de Juan Segura**, Illapel 15; **La Picá El Horizonte**, San Pedro 120, and **La Picá Los Delfines**, San Pedro 130. Look out, too, for tasty seafood *empanadas* served in the resort's bars.

Quintero p140

There are several cheap seafood restaurants down by the harbour.

Horcón p140

Seafood lunches made from the catch of the day are sold at any number of stalls on the seafront, where there also a number of restaurants.

¶¶ **Bahía**. Good food, pleasant atmosphere.

¶¶ **El Ancla**. Recommended.

¶¶ **Santa Clara**. Try the *chupe de mariscos* (cheesy shellfish soup) and *pastel de jaivas* (crabmeat cooked in cheese and breadcrumbs). Recommended.

¶ **Reina Victoria**. Cheap and good quality.

¶ **Roty Schop**. Acclaimed for its *empanadas*.

Maitencillo p141

¶¶¶ **Bar Rest La Canasta**, Av del Mar 592. Mediterranean and Moroccan cuisine served in elegant surroundings, expensive but worth it.

¶¶¶ **Bar Tsunami**, Av del Mar 1366. Mid-range seafood.

¶ **Café Entre Rocas**, Av del Mar s/n. Good drinks and snacks.

Zapallar p141

¶¶¶ **Isla Seca**, see Sleeping above. Expensive, excellent seafood.

¶¶¶ **César**, see Sleeping above. Good food and reasonable prices.

¶ **La Culebra**. Cheap eaterie.

¶ **Los Troncos**. Good-value grub.

¶ **Natón**, Cachagua, south of Zapallar. Cheap restaurant with disco.

Papudo p141

¶¶¶ **Cava del Mar**. Pricey international cuisine.

¶¶¶ **Gran Azul**. Expensive seafood.

¶¶ **La Abeja**. Mid-range.

¶¶ **La Maison des Fous**, Blanco 151. Unusual bar-restaurant in lovely old house. Friendly staff, good food and atmospheric candlelit piano bar with graffiti-covered pillars.

¶ **Don Rota**. Cheap seafood.

Bars and clubs

Viña del Mar p138, map p139

There are dozens of bars and clubs in the triangle formed by San Martín, 5 Poniente and 2 Norte. They tend to change name and style every other year.

Barlovento, 2 Norte y 5 Poniente. The designer bar in Viña, set over 3 floors with a roof terrace, serves great pizzas and good beer.

Café Journal, Agua Santa y Alvarez. Good beer. Full of students at night.

Oh! Cerveza, 7 Norte y 3 Poniente. Wide variety of draught beer.

Sikaru, 3 Poniente 660. Huge range of bottled beers from all over the world. Also serves pizzas and snacks.
Twister, Av Borgoño. One of many discos. Also try **Kamikaze** and **Neverland** east of town.

Reñaca *p140*
El Ciervo, Av Central y Segunda. Bar/café with live music in evenings. Recommended.

Papudo *p141*
Help, Glorias Navales 409. Disco with music from techno to salsa.
La Maison des Fous, see Eating above.

⊙ Entertainment

Viña del Mar *p138, map p139*
Cinemas
Cine Arte, Plaza Vergara 42. Also a multiplex in the shopping mall on Libertad (see Shopping, below).

Galleries
Fodigliani, 5 Norte 168.
Mar Pau, Valparaíso 595, local 18.
Palacio Carrasco, Libertad 250.
Sala de Arte Viña del Mar, Arlegui 683.

⊛ Festivals and events

Viña del Mar *p138, map p139*
Feb Festival Internacional de la Canción, which attracts an audience from all over Chile. Tickets are available from the Municipalidad and should be bought ahead of time; you should also reserve any accommodation well in advance.

Resorts north of Viña del Mar *p140*
29 Jun Since this area comprises coastal communities, it is no surprise that the **Fiesta de San Pedro** (the patron saint of fishermen) is an important event.

◎ Shopping

Viña del Mar *p138, map p139*
The **market** is held on Wed and Sat at the intersection of Av Sporting and the river. There is a huge new **mall** on Libertad between 14 and 15 Norte, open till 2300. A good range of Chilean Wine is available from **La Vinoteca**, San Martín 545 y 6 Norte

▲ Activities and tours

Viña del Mar *p138, map p139*
Bowling
Available in the shopping mall on Libertad y 14 Norte (see Shopping above).

Diving
Octopus, Libertad 1154, T032-973857, octopus@entelchile.net. Scuba diving along the central coast, with lots of shipwrecks to explore. Courses for US$200.

Maitencillo *p141*
Paragliding
Parapente Aventura, Maitencillo, T09-2330349, www.parapente.cl. Single tandem flight, US$70; 13 classes, US$500.

Surfing
Café Entre Rojas, see Eating, above. Surfing classes and biplane tours (US$60 for 20 mins).

◉ Transport

Viña del Mar *p138, map p139*
Air
Aerolíneas Argentinas, Ecuador y Marina, T800-610200; **Aerolíneas del Sur**, Ecuador y Marina, T800-710300; **Air France**, Ecuador 125, T032-2710976; **Air Madrid**, Ecuador y Arlegui, T032-2381070; **American**, 8 Norte 492, T032-2990997; **LanChile**, Valparaíso 280, T600-5262000, www.lanchile.cl; **Sky**, Ecuador 78, T032-600-6002828, www.skyairline.cl.

Bus
Bus terminal is 2 blocks east of Plaza Vergara at Av Valparaíso y Quilpué. To **Santiago**, frequent, 1¾ hrs, many companies, US$5-6, heavily booked in advance for travel on Sun afternoons, at other times some buses pick up passengers opposite the train station; to **La Serena**, 6 daily, 7 hrs, US$11; to **Antofagasta**, 20 hrs, US$25 (semi-cama); to **Temuco**, 9 hrs, US$14. To **Mendoza** (Argentina), 5 companies, all leave in the morning and some also at night in summer, 7 hrs, US$13. Buses north from Valparaíso for destinations **La Calera**, **La Ligua**, **Cabildo**, **Pichidangui** and **Los Vilos** all pass through Viña, and can be caught on Libertad.

Car hire from **Euro Rent-A-Car**, in Hotel O'Higgins, clean cars, efficient; **Flota Verschae**, Libertad 10, T032-2267300, www.verschae.cl, good value, recommended; **Hertz**, Quillota 766, T032-2971625; **Rosselot**, Libertad 892, T032-2382373, www.rosselot.cl, well regarded nationwide agency. A recommended car mechanic is **Luis Vallejos**, 13 Norte 1228, recommended.

Train

Services on the Valparaíso Metropolitan line (**Merval**) stop at Viña (see page 136).

Resorts north of Viña del Mar *p140*

Buses run from Av Errázuriz in Valparaíso and from Av Libertad in Viña del Mar: to **Concón**, bus 1 or 10 (much slower), very frequent, 20-30 mins, US$0.70; to **Quintero** and

Horcón, Sol del Pacífico, every 30 mins, 2 hrs, US$1.50; to **Zapallar** and **Papudo**, Sol del Pacífico, 4 a day (2 before 0800, 2 after 1600), US$4.

❶ Directory

Viña del Mar *p138, map p139*

Banks Several casas de cambio on calles Arlegui and Valparaíso; shop around for best rates, and avoid changing money on the street; many banks (with ATMs) on Arlegui, Valparaíso and Libertad; ATMs also in the mall; **Western Union** money transfer, Libertad 715 (also has DHL).
Internet Several all along C Valparaíso, prices around US$0.60 per hr. **Post office** North of Plaza Vergara, by the bridge. **Telephone** Several on C Valparaíso. **Useful address** Automóvil Club de Chile, 1 Norte 901, T032-2689509.

Resorts south of Valparaíso

This cluster of resorts stretches along the coast from the mouth of the Río Maipo north towards Valparaíso. The resorts here are not as upmarket as those north of Viña, but every summer tens of thousands of Chileans flock to them from the capital. Beaches range from classic wide white-sand affairs to secluded coves, and a wild, rocky zone around Isla Negra; off season, most are deserted. ➤➤ *For Sleeping, Eating and other listings, see pages 148-148.*

Ins and outs

Road links between Valparaíso and the resorts to the south are poor, but there are two good routes from Santiago: one from the main Santiago-Valparaíso highway to Algarrobo and the other, Route 78, direct to San Antonio. Buses link the resorts in this area, but a hire car will allow you to explore more secluded coves.

San Antonio

Situated near the mouth of the Río Maipo, 112 km south of Valparaíso, San Antonio was at the epicentre of a large earthquake in 1985. Subsequently, the harbour was rebuilt and has now taken over from Valparaíso as the main container port for this part of the coast. It is the terminal for the export of copper brought by rail from the large mine at El Teniente, near Rancagua (see page 268) as well as being an important fishing port. Many restaurants buy their fish and seafood here and a visit to the docks just after the catch has been unloaded is an interesting experience. **Museo Municipal de Ciencias Naturales y Arqueología** ① *Av Barros Luco, Mon-Fri 0900-1300, 1500-1900*, has displays on nature, precolonial culture and geology. There is also a botanical garden.

Nearby to the south are two resorts: **Llolleo,** 4 km, famous for the treatment of heart diseases, and 7 km further **Rocas de Santo Domingo**, the most attractive and exclusive resort in this area with 20 km of beaches and a golf course; even in high season it is not very crowded.

Cartagena

Eight kilometres north of San Antonio, Cartagena is the biggest resort on this part of the coast, but is a quieter place than San Antonio. It is filled with fish restaurants and ice cream shops and has lovely views sweeping north around the bay towards Isla Negra. In the early years of this century, it was a fashionable summer retreat for the wealthy of Santiago; a number of mansions survive, notably the **Castillo Foster** overlooking the bay. The centre lies around the **Plaza de Armas**, situated on top of the hill. To the south is the picturesque **Playa Chica**, overlooked by many of the older hotels and restaurants; to the north is **Playa Larga**. Between the two a promenade runs below the cliffs; high above hang old houses, some in disrepair but offering spectacular views. Cartagena is a very popular resort in summer but out of season it is a good centre for visiting nearby points of interest; there are many hotels and bus connections are good. For more information on Cartagena, look at www.cartagena.cl

North of Cartagena

The road to Algarrobo runs north along the coast through several small resorts including **Las Cruces**, **El Tabo** and **El Quisco**, a small fishing port with two beautiful white-sand beaches (crowded during Chilean holidays). Just south of Las Cruces is **Laguna El Peral** ① *Sep-Apr daily 0900-1400, 1500-1800; May-Aug daily 0900-1300, 1400-1800*, a nature reserve that protects a wide range of aquatic birds.

Isla Negra

Four kilometres south of El Quisco in the village of Isla Negra is the beautifully restored **Museo-Casa Pablo Neruda** ① *T035-461284, Tue-Sun 1000-2000 in summer; Tue-Fri 1000-1400, 1500-1800, entry only with guided tours in Spanish, English or French US$6, call in advance for opening hours or to book an English guide*. Bought by Neruda in 1939, this house, overlooking the sea, was the poet's writing retreat in his later years, and became the final resting place of Neruda and his last wife Mathilde. The house contains artefacts gathered from all over the world and the café specializes in Neruda's own recipes. The museum conveys a powerful sense of the poet and is well worth a visit. However, some Chileans feel that the **Fundación Pablo Neruda** should not be charging such high admission prices. For further information about Pablo Neruda, visit his Santiago house, La Chascona, page 83, and La Sebastiana in Valparaíso, page 128; see also box page 544.

Algarrobo

Algarrobo is the largest resort north of Cartagena and the most chic, with large houses, a yacht club and a marina. Conveniently located for Santiago, it was the retreat of politicians in the 1960s; both Salvador Allende and Eduardo Frei had summer residences here. Today, it remains one of the most popular spots on the central coast: its shallow waters and sheltered bay ensure that sea temperatures here are much warmer than at most other resorts along the central Chilean coast, while good beaches are supplemented by activities such as fishing, surfing and sailing. From **Playa Canelo** there are good views of pelicans and boobies in a seabird colony on an offshore island. Boat tours circle round it in summer, departing from the jetty.

● *The celebrated 1994 film* Il Postino *was based on Antonio Skármeta's novel* Ardiente
● Paciencia, *which is set on Isla Negra during the last years of Neruda's life. After the success of the film, the novel was retitled* El Cartero de Neruda *(Neruda's Postman).*

Sleeping

San Antonio and around *p146*
AL Rocas de Santo Domingo, La Ronda 130, Santo Domingo, south of San Antonio, T035-444356, F444494. Clean, friendly, with restaurant, cable TV. Good breakfast included in price. Also suites.
B Jockey Club, 21 de Mayo 202, T035-211777, F212922. Best accommodation in town, good views, restaurant.
F Residencial El Castillo, Providencia 253, Llolleo, south of San Antonio, T035-373821. Price per person.

Cartagena *p147*
D Violeta, Condell 110, T035-450372. With swimming pool, good views.
E Residencial Carmona, Playa Chica, T035-450485. Small rooms, basic, clean, good value.
F El Estribo, just off Plaza de Armas. Rooms with breakfast, basic, cheap comedor.
F Residencial Paty's, Alacalde Cartagena 295, T035-450469. Nice spot, good value.

North of Cartagena *p147*
Accommodation is generally more expensive in El Quisco.
A Motel Barlovento, El Quisco, T035-471030. 3-star accommodation.
C Gran Italia, Dubournais 413, El Quisco, T/F035-481631. Good beds and pool. Recommended.
C Hotel El Tabo, El Tabo, T035-433719. Good accommodation.
C La Posada, Las Cruces, T035-421280. With bath and breakfast, good birdwatching.
D Cabañas Pozo Azul, Capricornio 234, El Quisco, T035-471401. Southeast of town, quiet.
D El Quisco, Dubournais 166, El Quisco, T035-481923. With breakfast, clean, open weekends only, with seafood restaurant.
D Motel El Tabo, next door to the hotel El Tabo, T035-212719. Very crowded in Jan-Feb.

D Residencial Julia, Aguirre 0210, El Quisco, T035-471546. Very clean, quiet, good value.
E Residencial Oriental, near the beach, El Quisco, T035-471662. Price per person with breakfast, good, clean, hot water.

Isla Negra *p147*
B Hostería Santa Elena, T035-213439. Beautiful building and location, but some rooms damp and gloomy, also restaurant.
F Casa Azul, Av Santa Luisa, T035-461154. Price per person with breakfast, kitchen and living room, English spoken, camping. Recommended.

Algarrobo *p147*
A Uribe, behind Costa Sur, T035-481035. Pleasant, quiet.
E-F Residencial Vera, Alessandri 1521, T035-481131. Price per person with breakfast, good.
G Residencial San José, Av Principal 1598, T035-481131. Price per person. Basic, no hot water.

⊙ Transport

Bus
Pullman Lago Peñuelas operates direct buses from Valparaíso to **San Antonio**, every 30 mins until 2000, 2 hrs, US$3. The coastal service from Valparaíso to **Algarroba** and **Isla Negra**, every 30 mins, 2 hrs, US$3, also continues to San Antonio. **Empresa de Buses San Antonio** and **Empresa Robles** run frequent services from Algarroba to **San Antonio**, until 2000, 30 mins.
Pullman Bus runs services from Santiago to **San Antonio**, every 20 mins in summer, US$3. There are also frequent services from the capital with **Pullman Bus** (from Terminal Alameda) and other companies (from Terminal Sur) to **Isla Negra** and **Algarrobo** (via Cartagena and other resorts).

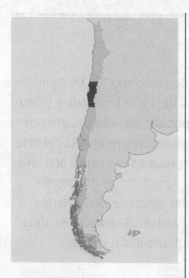

⁝ Footprint features

Introduction

This is a little-known part of Chile, stretching 500 km from Santiago north to La Serena and the fertile Elqui Valley. While some of the coastal towns are popular, the interior between La Ligua and Vicuña is almost universally overlooked. Yet here there are rich rewards for those prepared to rough it and take a few risks – one of the world's highest concentrations of petroglyphs, spectacular mountainsides speckled different colours by rich mineral deposits and desolate tracks winding through some of Chile's best high-mountain scenery.

The largest resort is La Serena, the usual centre for visiting the *pisco* distilleries of the Elqui Valley. This valley is one of the world's most important astronomical centres, with four observatories, including one built especially for visitors – it is also the focal point of Chile's New Age movement, and was the birthplace of Nobel laureate Gabriela Mistral. South of La Serena is the lively city of Ovalle, an ideal centre for forays into the *cordillera* and for visiting the Parque Nacional Fray Jorge, a temperate rainforest that survives in this dry region due to the sea mists that hang almost constantly over its hills.

★ Don't miss...

1 **Petroglyphs** Explore and imagine the pre-Hispanic past of the Diaguitas and Molle people, etched poignantly into the area's beautiful mountainsides, pages 152 and 158.

2 **Pacific beaches** Get away from it all in places such as Pichidangui, La Herradura and Tongoy, pages 153 and 168.

3 **Parque Nacional Fray Jorge** A temperate rainforest amid semi-desert that survives due to dense fogs, page 158.

4 **Observatories** Budding astronomers and those who are simply curious will want to visit at least one of the star-gazing institutes near La Serena, page 166.

5 **Reserva Nacional Pingüino de Humboldt** Take a boat trip among dolphins, penguins and sea-lions, page 171.

6 **La Pampilla** Take in Chile's biggest independence day celebrations in Coquimbo, a week of constant revelry in September, page 175.

Background

Stretching north from the Río Aconcagua to the Río Elqui, this area is a transitional zone between the fertile heartland and the northern deserts. Rainfall is rare, and only occurs in winter, while temperatures are relatively stable, with little seasonal variation. North of the Aconcagua, the Andes and the coastal *cordillera* merge in a spectacular lattice of mountains and are crossed by river valleys separated by high ridges. The valleys of the Choapa, Limarí and Elqui rivers are green oases, where the land is intensively farmed using irrigation to produce fruit and vegetables. Elsewhere, the vegetation is characteristic of semi-desert, except in those areas where frequent sea mists provide sufficient moisture to support temperate rainforest. The coastline is generally flat, with many beautiful coves, both rocky and sandy, and good surf, although the water is very cold.

Archaeological finds indicate that the river valleys were inhabited at an early stage in prehistory. The rise of the Molle culture happened around the same time as the rise of Christianity in Europe; sharing links with northern Argentina, the Molle people produced intricate ceramics and worked with copper. They were superseded by the Diaguitas, who crossed the Andes around AD 900 and settled throughout the area. The pre-Hispanic peoples left their mark in the form of petroglyphs (rock carvings).

Soon after the arrival of the Spanish and the foundation of Santiago, Pedro de Valdivia attempted to secure control over northern Chile by founding La Serena in 1544. Due to the arid climate and the more testing living conditions, the indigenous people here were less numerous than the Mapuche in the south and, despite a few setbacks for the Spanish, they were soon subjugated and wiped out. Throughout the colonial period, La Serena dominated the rest of the region; although small, it was the only city in the north and its leading families had close ties to the main Spanish landowners in the other valleys. After Independence, the area became an important mining zone, producing large amounts of silver, copper and gold.

Mining remains an important industry in this area: El Indio, inland from La Serena is the biggest gold producer in Chile, as well as a source of copper, and El Romeral, north of La Serena, is the most important iron ore deposit in the country. Quartz and the semi-precious stones lapis lazuli and combarbalita are also mined. Despite the dry climate, much of the region's industry is linked to its agricultural produce, notably the distilling of *pisco* from grapes; by law, only grapes grown in the regions of Atacama and Coquimbo can be used to make *pisco*.

North of Santiago → *Colour map 3, A2/3.*

The first stretch of the Pan-American Highway from Santiago heads inland through green valleys with rich blue clover and wild artichokes. North of La Ligua, it follows the coast, and the first intimations of the northern deserts appear. From Los Vilos, a paved road turns off the Panamericana towards Illapel, climbing steeply up to a pass, from which there are staggering views of the Andes and the Choapa River.

Illapel is surrounded by barren hills, with good views of the cordillera *to the east. While the town is not wildly interesting in itself, it is close to wonderful mountain country, best explored by the adventurous or those with their own transport. The Illapel region is largely ignored by travellers, yet it has some worthwhile attractions. This is the narrowest part of Chile, between Arica and Aysén, and the Andes are never far away, with valleys carving right up towards the snowline. There are many examples of pre-Hispanic petroglyphs for those who take the trouble to find them.* ▶▶ *For Sleeping, Eating and other listings, see pages 155-157.*

Ins and outs

Illapel is easily reached by regular buses from Los Vilos, Santiago, La Serena and other destinations as far north as Calama. However, those travelling by bus in this region should note that bus companies take advantage of the remoteness of the Choapa Valley and double their prices for the return journey from Illapel to Los Vilos. Without your own transport, there's no alternative means of leaving the area.

Los Vilos and the coast

Los Vilos, a former mineral port 216 km north of Santiago, is now a small seaside resort. Set in a wide bay, it is a peaceful, windswept place, disturbed mainly by the noise of the kelp gulls and the waves. There are several attractive *plazuelas* on the *costanera*, with stone benches from which you can watch the fishing boats bobbing in the sea; the water is cold for bathing.

> ♣ In the evenings there is a craft market in Los Vilos at Caupolicán y Purén selling relatively cheap woollens and semi-precious stones.

Offshore are two islands reached by frequent launches: **Isla de Los Huevos**, situated in the bay, and, 5 km south, **Isla de Los Lobos**, where there is a colony of seals. There is a **tourist office** ① *Caupolicán 278, www.losvilos.cl, open summer only.*

Pichidangui, 26 km south, is a popular resort on a rocky peninsula, with a beautiful beach to the north. **Los Molles**, 10 km south of Pichidangui, is a fishing village where many wealthy residents of Santiago have their summer homes. Nearby are the **Puguén blow holes** ① *US$1.50, free off season*, and the **Piscina Los Molles**, a natural swimming pool.

Illapel

Nearly 480 km north of Santiago, Illapel is a poor town that depends on mining in the surrounding mountains for its survival. The lives of the *pilquineros* in the nearby hills provide a sobering illustration of the lifestyle that miners in the north of Chile have endured since colonial times. The workers drag rocks from the mine-face in rusting wheelbarrows, living without power, fresh water or even public transport, and many of them die tragically young from lung cancer or chagas disease. If you do venture up into these remote areas, bring gifts and humility in abundance.

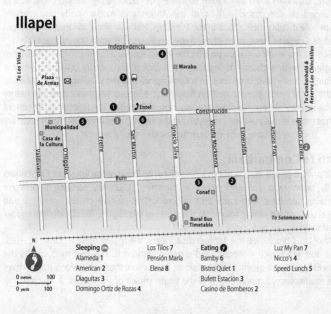

Illapel

To Los Vilos · Plaza de Armas · Independencia · Marabu · Entel · Constitución · Municipalidad · Casa de la Cultura · Valdivieso · O'Higgins · Freire · San Martín · Ignacio Silva · Vicuña Mackenna · Esmeralda · Arturo Prat · Ignacio Carrera · To Combarbalá & Reserva Las Chinchillas · Buin · Conaf · To Salamanca · Rural Bus Timetable

N · 0 metres 100 · 0 yards 100

Sleeping
Alameda 1
American 2
Diaguitas 3
Domingo Ortíz de Rozas 4

Los Tilos 7
Pensión María Elena 8

Eating
Bamby 6
Bistro Quiet 1
Bufett Estación 3
Casino de Bomberos 2

Luz My Pan 7
Nicco's 4
Speed Lunch 5

Mineral heaven

If you are at all interested in geology, you could spend months in this part of Chile and still not be satisfied. The mountains of the *cordillera* here are brimful of minerals that are easily visible to the naked eye. Near Combarbalá, the colours are white and red, showing that the combarbalita – a marble-type rock found nowhere else in the world – is nearby. In the high mountains inland from Ovalle is one of the world's two mines of the brilliant blue stone, lapis lazuli; while at Andacollo, you may have your only chance in Chile to see small-scale gold mining in operation, although the number of miners working here has declined rapidly in recent years.

Miners in these areas often work independently and they are known as *pilquineros*. They process their findings in two types of small mills. The *trapiche* consists of two heavy vertical wheels in a container half filled with water. As the ore is ground between the wheels, the mineral sticks to mercury, which is spread on the sides of the container. The other type of mill, the *maray*, resembles a large mortar and pestle and is hand driven. Both the *trapiche* and the *maray* are rented by the miner, the rent being paid as a share of the ore.

Illapel is a small town, and can easily be covered on foot. There is a small archaeological museum next to the library in the **Casa de la Cultura** ① *Valdivieso y Constitución, just off the Plaza de Armas, Mon-Fri 0900-1300 and 1400-1800, free*, with a bizarre and disordered collection of arrowheads, jewellery, pottery, miners' boots and newspapers so dusty you almost choke. There is no tourist office (although you could try asking for information at the Municipalidad on the Plaza), but there is a very helpful office run by **CONAF** ① *Vicuña Mackenna 93, open Mon-Sat 0830-1730*.

Salamanca and around
This small, friendly town lies 32 km southeast of Illapel along the Río Choapa. It is surrounded by the dusty foothills of the Andes and has a shady plaza where craftspeople display their goods in the evenings. Halfway along the road from Illapel is the **Los Cristales Pass**, from where there are views of distant snowy mountains.

Some 2 km north of Salamanca on the Illapel road is a turning for the small town of **Chalinga**, with a church dating from 1750 (ask at the nearby convent if entry is possible). A dusty road continues from Chalinga up into the Chalinga valley, passing plantations of *pisco* grapes, fruit orchards and irrigated vegetable patches before heading up into barren mountain scenery around **Zapallar**. The teacher at the school here has made a study of the petroglyphs in the surrounding area – of which there are many – and may be able to help interested parties seek them out.

North to Combarbalá
From Illapel, a paved road leads 15 km north to the **Reserva Nacional Las Chinchillas** ① *daily 0900-1700 (or until 1800 in summer), US$3.50*, passing impressive mountains speckled with cacti and minerals. The reserve covers 4229 ha and protects the last remaining colony of chinchillas in this region. The chinchillas and six related species can be viewed from behind two-way mirrors.

After Las Chinchillas, the asphalt disappears, the mountainsides close in – red, purple and white with minerals, and covered with cacti. The bad road climbs the **Cuesta El Espino** to a height of over 2000 m, from where there are unforgettable views of the multicoloured mountains and the white snows of the Andes. A much worse road – suitable for riders and cyclists only – branches off at the junction for Las Chinchillas and follows the old railway track on an even more remote and dramatic route to Combarbalá, via mining settlements at Farellón Sánchez and Matancillas. Eventually, it rejoins the main road below Cuesta El Espino and reaches the small town of Combarbalá, 73 km north of Illapel.

Combarbalá is set in a dusty bowl surrounded by mountains. The town is famous as the home of the *combarbalita*, a semi-precious stone that was declared the National Stone of Chile in 1993. However, the town is little known, even to Chileans – the **Senatur** office in Santiago told a caller to "phone the appropriate embassy" when asked about Combarbalá in 2001. *Combarbalita* is similar in appearance to marble and is found nowhere else in the world. There are lots of workshops on the north side of town, particularly on Calle Flores, where you can see the craftsmen at work and buy their goods. An astronomical observatory, the **Cruz del Sur** is currently being built near the town, and will be open to the public for astronomical tours from mid 2007.

● Sleeping

Los Vilos and the coast *p153*
Pichidangui has various hotels and pensiones at every price.
A Pichidangui, Francis Drake s/n, Pichidangui, T053-531114, www.hotel pichdangui.cl. Hotel with swimming pool and restaurant.
B American Motel, Km 224, T053-541163. Right on the highway and a convenient stopping place between Viña del Mar or Santiago and La Serena, good value. There are several other motels here as well.
C El Conquistador, Caupolicán 210, Los Vilos, T053-541663. Very nice rooms with bath, TV and refrigerator, big breakfast, pleasant patio, sauna, friendly, worth bargaining off season, excellent value, highly recommended. Also *cabañas*.
C Hostería Puquen, 2 Poniente s/n, Pichidangui, T053-531104. **F** singles. Attractive and good value.
C Lord Willow, Hostería 1444, Los Vilos, T053-541037, information T02-8572930. Overlooking beach and harbour, collection of old firearms, with breakfast and bath, pleasant, friendly, parking, weekend disco next door.
C-D Bellavista, Rengo 20, Los Vilos, T053-541073. **F** singles. With breakfast, bath and TV in carpeted rooms, hot water, sea views, no curtains.
D There are 3 cheap, central *residenciales* on Caupolicán in Los Vilos, **Drake**, at No 435, **Turismo**, No 437, and **Residencial Angélica**, No 627. The latter is cold and has lumpy beds.

Camping
Bahía Marina de Pichidangui, Pichidangui, T053-531120. Sports facilities and *cabañas*.
Campomar, Campusano s/n, Los Vilos, T053-541049. Campsite plus *cabañas* near the town centre.

Illapel *p153, map p153*
A Domingo Ortíz de Rozas, Ignacio Silva 241, T053-522127, www.hotelortizderozas.cl. Spacious rooms with all mod cons at this attractive 3-star.
B Diaguitas, Constitución 276, T053-522587, www.hoteldiaguitas.cl. Noisy, with swimming pool, internet connection in rooms.
B American, Carrera 128, T053-523361. Nice courtyard, with breakfast, bath and TV.
C Los Tilos, Ignacio Silva 45, T053-523335, hotellostiloss@hotmail.com. With bath, breakfast and TV, friendly, but small rooms. Laundry service and internet.
C-D Alameda, Ignacio Silva 20, T053-522355, hotelalameda@hotmail.com. **E** singles. With bath and TV, without breakfast, friendly, clean, nice patio with lemon and orange trees, cheap laundry service, recommended.
D Pensión María Elena, Esmeralda 54. **F-G** singles. Best of the cheapies, very basic but warm and friendly.

Salamanca and around *p154*
B Hostal Vasco, Bulnes 120, T053-551119. With bath and breakfast, swimming pool.
D Residencial O'Higgins, O'Higgins 430. **F-G** singles. Breakfast extra, friendly, clean, basic, patio.

There are several basic campsites in the Chalinga Valley, including one at Zapallar.

North to Combarbalá *p154*

C Yagnam, Comercio 252, Combarbalá, T053-741329, hotelyagnam@hotmail.com. Clean, new hotel, friendly, room service, good value, recommended.

C Reserva Nacional Las Chinchillas. Well-equipped *cabañas*, with kitchen facilities, also a campsite.

D Residencial La Golondrina, Chacabuco y Libertad, Combarbalá. Basic but cheap.

❶ Eating

Los Vilos and the coast *p153*

Restaurants in Pichindangui tend to be pricey, although there is a food shop.

❦❦ Alisio, Caupolicán 298, Los Vilos. Seafood and fish, good value.

❦❦ Restaurant Turístico Costanera, Purén, Los Vilos. Good views over ocean, good meals and choice of wines, nice warm bread. Also serves a cheap menu.

❦ El Rey de la Paila Marina, Purén, Los Vilos. Good-value seafood.

❦ El Rey de la Paila Marina Vileña, Purén, Los Vilos. Fish and seafood.

❦ Pastelería/Heladería Roma, Caupolicán 712, Los Vilos. Excellent cakes and ice creams. The very helpful owners both speak English.

❦ Restaurant Crucero del Amor, Los Vilos. One of countless places on the seafront.

Illapel *p153, map p153*

❦❦ Bistro Quiet, Constitución 200 block. Smart, fills up at weekends.

❦❦ Bufett Estación, Buín 452. Smartest in town, good food.

❦❦ Nicco's, Ignacio Silva 219. Good pizzas, fancy decor, vegetarian options.

❦ Bamby Restaurant, Constitución 340. Not great quality but very cheap.

❦ Casino de Bomberos, Buín 590. Incredibly friendly, excellent value, good views of the town, highly recommended.

❦ Luz My Pan, San Martín, opposite the bus station. Good bread and cakes.

❦ Speed Lunch, Constitución 160. Friendly, some vegetarian possibilities (ask for lentils), not as bad as the name suggests.

Salamanca and around *p154*

❦ El Americano, O'Higgins y M de Montepio. Good lunches, also has information on the surrounding area.

❦ Restaurant Crillón, on the Plaza on M de Montepio. Friendly, excellent value *almuerzos*, serves Grolsch.

❦ Restaurant Salamanca, Echavarría 340, seafood and meat, clean.

There are cheap ice creams at a shop next to **ENTEL** on the plaza.

❶ Bars and clubs

Los Vilos and the coast *p153*

Piel Morena, Rengo s/n, Los Vilos. Summer only.

Dino's Disco, Caupolicán, Los Vilos. Popular.

Zone Beach, Rengo 86, Los Vilos. A favourite hangout in summer.

Illapel *p153, map p153*

Pub Marabú, Ignacio Silva 260. US$3. Bar with free drink, salsa and merengue at the weekends.

❋ Festivals and events

Salamanca *p154*

Feb/Mar Holy Week is a big event in Salamanca, with horse races a la Chilena and costumed processions through the town.

▲ Activities and tours

Illapel *p153, map p153*

Turismo Libuca, Independencia 099, T053-522155. Specializes in tours of the south for those from Illapel, but can also arrange visits to Las Chinchillas.

❶ Transport

Los Vilos and the coast *p153*

Bus There is only 1 bus daily between Pichidangui and Santiago, but north-south buses on the Highway (for example **Inca Bus**) also pass Los Vilos and Pichidangui.

The main companies serving Los Vilos are **Pullman Bus**, **Turbus** and **Tas Choapa**, each with at least 5 buses daily to **Santiago**, 3½ hrs, US$7, and **La Serena** (usually at night), 4½ hrs, US$8, as well as frequent buses to **Illapel**, 1 hr, US$1, and **Salamanca**, US$2.

Illapel *p153, map p153*

Bus The bus station is at San Martín, on the 200 block. Illapel is best served by **Pullman Bus**, which has services to **Santiago**, US$7, and **La Serena**, US$8, via Los Vilos. **Intercomunal** has 4 buses daily to **Viña** and **Valparaíso**, US$8. Buses to rural destinations leave from Independencia y Ignacio Silva; the timetables are posted at the greengrocer's at the bottom end of Ignacio Silva.

Salamanca and around *p154*

Bus The bus company offices are on O'Higgins. There are one or two rural buses daily from Salamanca to the mountain communities, as well as *colectivos* to Illapel and Chalinga. Further afield, 2 buses an hour, from 0800 to 1800, US$1, run to **Illapel**, continuing either north to **La Serena** or south to **Santiago**.

North to Combarbalá *p154*

Bus Combarbalá is reached by buses from **Ovalle** (page 162), or with **Buses Combarbalá** from **Santiago**, **La Calera**, **La Ligua** and **Los Vilos**. Pullman Bus has a daily service to **Illapel** via reserva nacional **Las Chinchillas**.

● Directory

Los Vilos and the coast *p153*

Dentist Juan Rubio, Lautaro 435, Los Vilos, T053-541683. **Post office** Lincoyán, Los Vilos. **Telephone** ENTEL, Caupolicán 873, Los Vilos.

Illapel *p153, map p153*

Banks Banco de Chile, Tarcifio Valderrama s/n. **Dentist** Vicuña Mackenna 183, T053-521010. **Hospital** Independencia s/n, T053-522312. **Laundry** Alondra, Ignacio Silva 370, only one in town. **Post office** Plaza de Armas, Western Union money transfers. **Telephone** ENTEL San Martín y Constitución, and at Constitución 161.

Salamanca and around *p154*

The following are in Salamanca.

Banks BCI, O"Higgins y Montepio. **Post office** Bulnes, on the plaza. **Telephone** CTC Veronica, on the plaza. ENTEL, M de Montepio y Bulnes, on the pla3za.

Limarí Valley → *Colour map 2, C1.*

The Limarí Valley contains much of the north of Chile in a microcosm: beaches at Tongoy, the mysteriously lush Parque Nacional Fray Jorge, countless examples of ancient rock art and wonderful mountain scenery. With remote tracks through the mountains and giant hillsides sprinkled with cacti and multicoloured minerals, it is a fine place to wander for a week or more. ▸▸ *For Sleeping, Eating and other listings, see pages 160-162.*

Ins and outs

Getting there and around Ovalle is easily reached by regular buses: north from La Serena and destinations as far north as Arica; south from Illapel and Santiago. Note that, although Ovalle is a small city, confusingly it has two bus terminals: the Terrapuerto Limarí and the Terminal Media Luna. The Terrapuerto Limarí is by far the more important and is the only one used by all major companies. Numerous local buses link Ovalle with outlying communities. Most *colectivos* leave from Avenida Ariztía. ▸▸ *For further details, see Transport, page 162.*

Ovalle and around

Situated inland in the valley of the Río Limarí – a fruit-growing and mining district – this lively town is a focal point for the numerous communities in the surrounding mountains. Edged by dusty hills, which are lined with vines for *pisco* grapes and orchards of avocado trees, it gets busy on market days, when local *campesinos* throng around the market area. It is famous for its *talabarterías* (saddleries) and for its products made of locally mined lapis lazuli, as well as *queso de cabra* (goat's cheese) and dried fruits (sold in the market). The central part of town can easily be covered on foot. **Museo del Limarí** ① *Covarrubias y Antofagasta, Tue-Fri 0900-1300, 1500-1900, Sat and Sun 1000-1300, US$1, Sun free,* is housed in the old railway station and has displays of petroglyphs and a good collection of Diaguita ceramics and other artefacts (replicas on sale). There is an unofficial **tourist information** kiosk on the Plaza de Armas.

Embalse La Paloma, the largest reservoir in Chile, is 26 km southeast. On the northern shore is the small town of **Monte Patria**, with a *pisco* distillery that can be visited. From Monte Patria, a paved road leads to Chilecito and Carén, where there is the **Parque Ecológico La Gallardina** ① *T053-726009, US$2 (US$3 at weekends),* containing a beautiful collection of roses and other plants and flowers amid the dry mountains.

Monumento Nacional Valle del Encanto ① *about 22 km southwest of Ovalle, open all year 0800-1800, US$2,* is one of the most important archaeological sites in northern Chile. Artefacts from hunting peoples from over 2000 years ago have been found, but the most visible remains date from the Molle culture (AD 700). There are over 30 petroglyphs as well as great boulders, distributed in over sites.

Termas de Socos ① *Pan-American Highway, 35 km southwest of Ovalle, www.termasocos.cl, US$9,* is a very popular resort among Chileans. There are swimming pools and individual bath tubs fed by thermal springs, as well as a sauna, Jacuzzi and water massage.

Parque Nacional Fray Jorge

① *T053-620058, Sat, Sun and public holidays 0900-1800, last entry 1600, US$4.*
Situated 90 km west of Ovalle and 110 km south of La Serena at the mouth of the Río Limarí, this UNESCO Biosphere Reserve covers 9959 ha and contains original temperate rainforests, which contrast with the otherwise barren surroundings. Receiving no more than 113 mm of rain a year, the forests survive because of the almost constant fog and mist covering the hills, the result of the discharge of the warm waters of the Río Limarí into the cold waters of the Pacific. The increasingly arid climate of this part of Chile has brought the habitat under threat and hence visits are

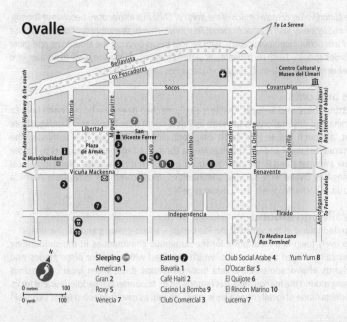

Ovalle

Sleeping	Eating	Club Social Arabe 4	Yum Yum 8
American 1	Bavaria 1	D'Oscar Bar 5	
Gran 2	Café Haiti 2	El Quijote 6	
Roxy 5	Casino La Bomba 9	El Rincón Marino 10	
Venecia 7	Club Comercial 3	Lucerna 7	

closely controlled by **CONAF**. Scientific groups may obtain permission to visit otherwise inaccessible parts of the park from the Director of CONAF in La Serena ① *Cordovez 281, To51-211124, www.conaf.cl*. All visitors should take particular care to leave no trace of their presence behind them. The park is reached by a dirt road leading off the Pan-American Highway. The entrance and administration are at Km 18, from where it is 10 km further to the summit of the coastal hills (known as the Altos de Talinay), which rise to 667 m. Waterproof clothing is essential. There is no public transport to the park, but tours are offered from La Serena.

Along the Río Limarí

From Ovalle, a road leads 77 km northeast, following the course of the Río Limarí to the village of Hurtado. The route passes the Recoleta Reservoir and then follows the valley, where fat horses graze on alfalfa, vines with *pisco* grapes are strung out across what flat land there is, and the glades are planted with orchards of orange and avocado trees.

The road is paved as far as Samo Alto; shortly after is the turn-off (to San Pedro) for the **Monumento Natural Pichasca** ① *0800-1800, US$43*. Some 47 km northeast of Ovalle at an altitude of 1350 m, this park contains petrified tree trunks and archaeological remains, including a vast cave, comparable to the Cueva Milodón outside Puerto Natales, with remnants of ancient roof paintings. Gigantic rock formations can be seen on the surrounding mountains. Encouraged by the local mayor, a bright green model of a dinosaur has been erected here. Sure to be a magnet for groups of local schoolchildren, the dinosaur is supposed to be the north's answer to the sloth in the Milodon Cave near Puerto Natales, but as yet it is too early to claim that Jurassic Park has come to Pichasca. Note that it is 3 km to the park from the turn-off and about 2 km further to sites of interest.

Beyond the village of **Pichasca** are several plantations, where rickety wooden suspension bridges cross to the far side of the Río Limarí. It is a further 32 km to Hurtado and the road continues winding along the side of the valley, with the Andes now easily visible at the head of the valley. At **Vado Morrillos**, 4 km before Hurtado, is the **Hacienda Los Andes** ① *To53-691 822, www.haciendalosandes.com*, a centre for horse riding excursions in the area, set in a very pretty location, with a 7 km nature trail. The hacienda is run by a German/Austrian couple with previous experience of running horseback trips, English and German spoken. Horse riding tours from one to eight days are offered in the surrounding mountains, starting at US$93. If coming by bus to the hacienda, ask the driver to let you off at the bridge at Vado Morrillos – the entrance to the hacienda is just before the bridge on the right.

The road continues on to **Hurtado**, a village set at 1300 m. Excellent accommodation is available at **Tambo de Limarí** (see Sleeping below), a *hospedaje* owned by Señora Orieta. Near Hurtado is the only petroglyph in Chile depicting the sun, hinting at possible links to the Incas, and it is also possible to climb the Cerro Gigante (2825 m) and visit the site o a Diaguita cemetry.

The extremely adventurous may consider continuing from Hurtado into **Argentina** (permission must be sought

Valley of the Limarí

La Serena
Vicuña
To Monte Grande & Pisco Elqui
Hurtado
Andacollo
Monumento Natural Pichasca
Río Limarí
Las Breas
Embalse La Recoleta
Pichasca
Pan-American Highway
Path to Argentina
Ovalle
Monte Patria
Carén
Termas de Socos
Valle del Encanto
Embalse La Paloma
To Combarbalá
To Argentina

N

0 km   20
0 miles   20

Sleeping
Hacienda Juntas 1
Hacienda Los Andes 2
Tambo de Limarí 3

Eating
Flor del Valle 1

from the *carabineros* in Hurtado). It is three days by horse to the pass into Argentina (4229 m); near the pass are the corrals of El Ternero, where a wall built by pre-Hispanic peoples climbs up into the snows. On the far side of the border, the path descends to the Laguna de los Patos, where the Argentines have a police post. However, it is then a further seven to 10 days by horse to the nearest settlement in Argentina and there is no road. It may be possible to find guides for this trip in the village of Las Breas, 22 km beyond Hurtado, where there is a small restaurant.

An easier option is to continue from Hurtado north to **Vicuña** in the Elqui Valley (see page 169) only 46 km away. This is a desolate road; there is very little traffic and no public transport, but pickups can be hired in Hurtado to make the trip for US$35-40.

To Andacollo

The good road inland between Ovalle and La Serena makes an interesting contrast to Ruta 5, the Pan-American Highway, with a fine pass and occasional views of snowcapped Andes across cacti-covered plains and semi-desert mountain ranges. Some 66 km north of Ovalle, a winding side road runs 27 km southeast, to **Andacollo**.

Situated in a gorge, Andacollo has been a mining centre since before the arrival of the Spanish (see box page 154). Ruins of mines and waste tips dot the area. Two mines, one copper and one gold, still operate and there are many independent mines and *trapiches*, small processing plants, which can be visited; the gold has, however, begun to run out and, in recent years, many miners have moved away. Andacollo, however, is more famous as one of the great pilgrimage sites in Chile. In the enormous **Basilica** (1893), 45 m high and with a capacity of 10,000, is a small, carved wooden statue of the Virgen del Rosario de Andacollo, brought from Peru in the 17th century and credited with miraculous powers. Nearby is the **Templo Antiguo**, smaller and dating from 1789. There is also a museum, **Museo de Andacollo** ⓘ *open daily 0900-1300, 1500-1900*. The tourist office on the Plaza de Armas can arrange tours to the Basilica and to mining operations.

● Sleeping

Ovalle and around *p157, map p158*
Accommodation is poor in Ovalle itself.
AL Termas de Socos, Panamericana, 35 km southwest of Ovalle, T053-1982505, www.termasocos.cl. Reasonable hotel offering full board and access to thermal pools.
AL Hotel Hacienda Juntas, near Monte Patria, Km 41, T053-711290. Stands in 90 ha of vineyards, with spectacular views and a swimming pool.
A-B Hotel Turismo, Victoria 295, T053-623258. Parking, modern, friendly.
B Gran Hotel, Mackenna 210 (entrance through Galería Yagnam), T053-621084, yagnam@terra.cl. Decent rooms. Bargain, ask to be away from the main road.
B Hotel American, Mackenna 169, T053-620159, F053-620722. Friendly, small

rooms, overpriced.
C Roxy, Libertad 155, T053-620080. Constant hot water, big rooms, clean, friendly, patio, slightly run down. Recommended.
D Hotel Venecia, Libertad 261, T053-620968. **F-G** singles. Clean, safe, friendly. Recommended.

Camping
There are camping facilities at **Monumento Nacional Valle del Encanto** (price per tent) and near the **Termas de Socos**.

Parque Nacional Fray Jorge *p158*
A There is 1 *cabaña* sleeping 5 people, which may be hired.
C Basic accommodation is also available in an old hacienda, and at 2 campsites in the national park, one at the administra-

● *For an explanation of sleeping and eating price codes used in this guide, see inside the front cover. Other relevant information is found in Essentials, see pages 50-57.*

tion centre, the other 3 km away at
El Arrayancito.

Along the Río Limarí p159, map p159
AL **Hacienda Los Andes**, Vado Morrillos,
T053-691 822, www.haciendalosandes.com.
Bed and breakfast. All the rooms have a
private bath and there is a sauna and a
jacuzzi that overlooks the river. Camping
(including hot showers) is also available,
US$4 per person, as well as horse riding,
trekking and other outdoor activities.
C **Tambo de Limarí**, Caupolican 27, Hurtado,
T053-1982121. F singles. Excellent *hospedaje*
with wonderful breakfast. Owner Señora
Orieta is very friendly. There is an interesting
collection of ancient riding spurs, stirrups
and Spanish padlocks. Recommended.

To Andacollo p160
There are no hotels, but some *pensiones*.
During the festival, private houses rent beds
and some let you pay for a shower. Contact
the tourist office for details.

❶ Eating

Ovalle and around p157, map p158
❙❙ **Bavaria**, MacKenna 161. Usual range
of plastic-tasting sandwiches and main
dishes, overpriced.
❙❙ **Club Social Arabe**, Arauco 255.
Spacious glass-domed premises, limited
selection of Arab dishes, not cheap.
❙ **Casino La Bomba**, Aguirre 364.

Very good value *almuerzos*, run by the
fire brigade.
❙ **Club Comercial**, Aguirre 244 (on plaza).
Open Sun for general Chilean fare.
❙ **El Quijote**, Arauco 294. Intimate
atmosphere, good seafood, inexpensive,
Ovalle's 'Bohemian' hangout.
❙ **El Rincón Marino**, Victoria 400-block.
One of the better seafood restaurants
beside the market.
❙ **La Bocca Restaurant**, Benavente 110.
Specializes in shellfish.
❙ **Restaurant Lucerna**, Independencia 339
(opposite the market). Opens early for
breakfast, popular, interesting place
doubling as a doss house for campesinos.
Next door is **Las Tejas**, of a similar ilk.

Cafés
Café Caribe Express, MacKenna 241.
For drinks and snacks.
Café Haiti, Victoria 307. Opens early
for breakfast.
D'Oscar Bar, Plaza de Armas. Serves
good real coffee and is open late.
Panadería Victoria, MacKenna 60.
Mouthwatering cakes.
Pastelería Josti, Libertad 427. Good cakes.
Yum Yum, MacKenna 21. Good, cheap,
lively.

Along the Río Limarí p159, map p159
❙ **Restaurant Flor del Valle**, Pichasca.
Cheap meals and basic accommodation.

☻ Entertainment

Ovalle and around *p157, map p158*
Cine Cervantes, Centro Comercial G Corral.
Cinema on the plaza.
Eskla Discotheque, Mackenna 100-block.
Nightclub, often featuring live music.

☻ Festivals and events

To Andacollo *p160*
23-27 Dec Fiesta Grande attracts 150,000
pilgrims from northern Chile (most important
day 26 Dec). The ritual dances date from a
pre-Spanish past. Transport is available from
La Serena and Ovalle but 'purists' walk (torch
and good walking shoes essential). Two
villages are passed on the route, which starts
on the paved highway, then goes along a
railway track and lastly up a steep, dusty hill.
1st Sun of Oct Fiesta Chica is a smaller
festival.

○ Shopping

Ovalle and around *p157, map p158*
Market days are Mon, Wed, Fri and Sat, till
1600; the market, **feria modelo**, is off
Benavente, east of the town centre. There
are many *talabarterías* nearby on Benavente.
For articles made of lapis lazuli, try **Sr
Wellington Vega Alfaro**, T053-620797,
although his workshop, on the northern
outskirts, is difficult to reach without
transport. Phone ahead for directions.

▲ Activities and tours

Ovalle and around *p157, map p158*
Tres Valles, Libertad 496, T053-629650,
torrejonhnos@adsl.tie.cl. Worth a try for trips
to Fray Jorge, Valle del Encanto and other
destinations in the area.

☻ Transport

Bus
Local Rural buses – of which there are
many – leave from a terminal outside the
feria modelo, next to the Terrapuerto Limarí.
Hourly buses to Carén serve the **Parque
Ecológico La Gallardina**. However, there is
no service to the **Nacional Valle del
Encanto**; instead you must take a long-

distance southbound bus and ask to be
dropped off; it's a 5 km walk to the valley;
flag down a bus to return. The journey from
Ovalle to **Andacollo** costs US$3 by *colectivo*
and US$2 by bus.

Long distance Ovalle's 2 bus terminals
are the **Terrapuerto Limarí** (next to the feria
modelo near Benavente 500-block) and the
Terminal Media Luna (by the rodeo ring on
Ariztía Oriente). The Terrapuerto Limarí is the
only one used by all major companies (most
buses using the Terminal Media Luna have
departed from the Terrapuerto Limarí).
There are buses to **Santiago**, mostly
mid-morning or late at night, 6½ hrs, US$9;
to **La Serena**, 20 a day, 1½ hr, US$2.50
(Horvitur and Via Elqui); also to **Valparaíso**,
6 hrs, US$9, **Antofagasta**, 14 hrs, US$20, and
Arica, 24 hrs, US$28, mostly at night (Tur
Bus, Pullman Bus, Fenix Norte). Pullman
and **Expreso Norte** serve Illapel, US$4.
Buses M&R, T053-1982121, T09-98220320,
has an erratic schedule linking Ovalle with
Hurtado. On Ovalle's market days (Mon,
Wed, Fri, Sat), 3 buses leave Hurtado
between 0600 and 0630; on Tue and Thu,
the buses leave Hurtado at 1000 and 1015,
on Sun, at 1230 and 1245. From Ovalle, there
are 3 buses to Hurtado on market days
(1200, 1230 and 1500), except for Sat, when
there is just 1 bus at 1400. On Tue and Thu,
buses leave Ovalle at 1615 and 1645, on Sun
at 1700 and 1730. The fare is US$3. These
buses pass the turn-off to the **Monumento
Natural Pichasca** about 42 km from the city.

Taxi
Abel Olivares Rivera, T053-620352.
Recommended. The round trip to **Parque
Nacional Fray Jorge** costs US$50.

● Directory

Ovalle *p157, map p158*
Banks Many Redbanc ATMs on the Plaza de
Armas, including **Banco de Chile** and **Banco
Santander. Internet** Several in and around
the centre. **Post office** MacKenna on the
Plaza de Armas. **Telephone** Telefónica,
Victoria y Vicuña MacKenna, on the Plaza de
Armas. **Useful address** Automóvil Club de
Chile, Libertad 144, T053-620011, helpful,
with overnight parking.

Elqui Valley

A dramatic cleft in the heart of the mountains, the Elqui Valley is home to two of the north's most important cities, Coquimbo and La Serena. Inland, you will find star-filled nights lit up by shooting stars, pisco distilleries and villages in the mountains. The valley of the Río Elqui is one of the most attractive oases in this part of Chile. There are mines, orchards and vineyards set against imposing arid mountains. The contrast between the immense rock formations and the lush valley floor is overwhelming. ➤➤ *For Sleeping, Eating and other listings, see pages 171-176.*

Ins and outs

Getting there The cities of Coquimbo and La Serena are easily reached by countless buses from both north and south, from any one of more than 10 companies. Several flights daily from Santiago to Copiapó, Antofagasta and Iquique stop off at La Serena. For transfers to the airport, call To51-295058, US$1.80 per person, or take any Vicuña-bound bus and get off at airport entrance.

Getting around La Serena and Coquimbo are linked by buses that pass down Avenida Francisco de Aguirre in La Serena before travelling along the Panamericana. Taxis are plentiful and cheap.

La Serena ⊕⊘⊘⊕⊕⊜⊕ ➤➤ *pp171-176.*

Situated nearly 500 km north of Santiago, La Serena is the capital of Región IV and is one of the most attractive cities in northern Chile. Built on a hillside 2 km inland from the Bahía de Coquimbo, the city is famous for its numerous churches, while the centre is made up of white buildings of neo-colonial style. Beneath this façade, however, La Serena has a more ancient history and residents often claim to stumble across indigenous burial sites in their backyards. The city has rapidly become a major tourist centre, being popular for its long sandy beach and its proximity to the Elqui Valley – it is full of Chilean holidaymakers in January and February.

Ins and outs

Helpful tourist information is available from **Sernatur** ① *Edificio de Servicios Públicos (next to the post office on the Plaza de Armas), T/Fo51-225199, infocoquimbo@ sernatur.cl, Mon-Fri 0845-1830 (0845-2030 in summer), Sat and Sun 1000-1400 (1000-1400 and 1600-2000 in summer).* Sernatur also has a kiosk at the bus terminal (summer only) which is helpful and has accommodation information.

History

La Serena was founded by Juan de Bohón, aide to Pedro de Valdivia, in 1544, destroyed by the Diaguita in 1546 and rebuilt by Francisco de Aguirre in 1549. The city was sacked by the English pirate Sharpe in 1680. In the colonial period, it was the main staging-post on the route north to Peru; many of the religious orders built churches and convents here providing accommodation for their members. In the 19th century, the city grew prosperous from copper-mining; the neo-classical mansions of successful entrepreneurs from this period can still be seen. The characteristic neo-colonial style of architecture in the centre, however, dates only from the 1950s, when the city was remodelled under the instructions of President González Videla, a lawyer, diplomat and Radical party politician, who was eager to leave his mark on his native city. González Videla ordered the drafting of an urban plan, under which Avenida Francisco de Aguirre was modernized and the Pedro de Valdivia gardens, west of the city, were built. All new buildings in the centre were constructed in Californian colonial style, although his regulation has since been modified, permitting the erection of some modern buildings.

Sights

Around the attractive Plaza de Armas, most of the official buildings can be found, including the post office and the **Casa González Videla**, the great man's residence from 1927 to 1977, which now houses the **Museo Histórico Regional** ⓘ *www.dibam.cl/subdirec_museos/mhr_videla/home.asp, Mon-Fri 1000-1800, Sat 1000-1300, US$1 (ticket also valid for Museo Arqueológico)*, with several rooms dedicated to his life and the history of La Serena. Opposite is the **cathedral**, built in 1844 and featuring a carillon which plays every hour. There are 29 other churches, several of which have unusual towers. **Santo Domingo**, half a block southwest of the Plaza de Armas, built in 1755 with a clock tower dating from 1912, is fronted by a small garden with statues of sea-lions. Southeast of the plaza, on Balmaceda y de La Barra, is **San Francisco**, built between 1586 and 1627, which has a baroque façade and faces a small plaza with arcades. It is home to the **Museo De Arte**

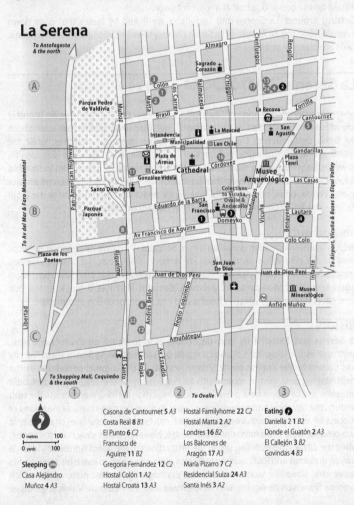

La Serena

Sleeping 🛏
Casa Alejandro
  Muñoz *4 A3*
Casona de Cantournet *5 A3*
Costa Real *8 B1*
El Punto *6 C2*
Francisco de
  Aguirre *11 B2*
Gregoria Fernández *12 C2*
Hostal Colón *1 A2*
Hostal Croata *13 A3*
Hostal Familyhome *22 C2*
Hostal Matta *2 A2*
Londres *16 B2*
Los Balcones de
  Aragón *17 A3*
María Pizarro *7 C2*
Residencial Suiza *24 A3*
Santa Inés *3 A2*

Eating 🍴
Daniella *2 1 B2*
Donde el Guatón *2 A3*
El Callejón *3 B2*
Govindas *4 B3*

The clear skies of northern Chile

With its large expanses of uninhabited desert and its dry, relatively thin atmosphere, northern Chile has become one of the great astronomical centres of the world. In the Elqui Valley alone, there are no fewer than three large observatories, built by international organizations with important backing from Europe or the USA.

One, **La Silla**, is owned by European Southern Observatory (ESO), which is financed by the governments of some 10 European governments. The other two are **El Tololo**, which belongs to a consortium of US and Chilean universities, and **Las Campanas**, which is owned by the Carnegie Institute. Visitors are welcome at all these sites, but are not allowed to use the telescopes (see page 166). For this experience, you should go to **Mamalluca**, a smaller observatory in the valley built specifically for the public. It offers night-time visits and provides an opportunity to view the southern skies from the vantage point of the Elqui Valley.

The great powers of astronomy have continued to expand their operations in northern Chile. A new observatory was opened by ESO in March 1999 at **Cerro Paranal**, 120 km south of Antofagasta (see page 202). Known as the VLT ('very large telescope'), it consists of four 8-m telescopes that together are capable of picking out items on the moon as small as 1 m long. When the lenses arrived at the port of Antofagasta, the entire city centre had to be closed down to allow them to be transported to their final destination. Planning is now under way on an even larger project at Chajnantor, over 5000 m up in the Andes; this giant observatory, with 64 12-m radio telescopes, is being financed by ESO along with the governments of the USA and Japan.

These new developments are not without controversy, however. Construction of Cerro Paranal was held up by local landowners, who refused to renounce their rights to permit mining activity on their land (which would threaten the observatory with increased dust). Eventually, the Chilean government was forced to introduce some new legislation permitting it to buy out the landowners to enable the project to go ahead.

Religiosa ① *Mon-Fri 1000-1300, 1600-1800, Sat 1000-1300, US$0.80*, which includes the funeral mask of Gabriela Mistral.

San Augustín, northeast of the plaza at Cantournet y Rengifo, originally a Jesuit church, dates from 1755 but has been heavily modified. Opposite this church is **La Recova**, the market, which includes a large display of handicrafts and, upstairs, several seafood restaurants. One block south is **Museo Arqueológico** ① *Cordovez y Cienfuegos, T051-224492, www.dibam.cl/subdirec_museos/m_laserena/home.asp, Tue-Fri 0930-1750, Sat 1000-1300, 1600-1900, Sun 1000-1300, US$1*, which has an outstanding collection of Diaguita and Molle Indian exhibits, especially of attractively decorated pottery, although they are poorly labelled. There are also some exhibits from Easter Island. Further from the centre, in the University of La Serena, is the **Museo Mineralógico Ignacio Domeyko** ① *A Muñoz 870, Mon-Fri 0930-1230, US$0.80*, for those with a particular interest in geology.

One block west of the Plaza de Armas is the **Parque Pedro de Valdivia** ① *1000-2000*, with the Parque Japonés just south of it. Avenida Francisco de Aguirre, a pleasant boulevard lined with statues and known as the **Alameda**, runs from the centre to the coast, skirting the Parque Japonés and terminating at Faro Monumental, a neo-colonial mock-castle and lighthouse, now a pub. A string of beaches stretch from here to **Peñuelas**, 6 km south, linked by the Avenida del Mar. Many apartment blocks, hotels, *cabañas* and restaurants have been built along this part of the bay.

Visiting the observatories

The clear skies and dry atmosphere of the valleys around La Serena have led to the area becoming one of the astronomical centres of the world (see box, page 165). There are four observatories, one built specially to receive visitors. Personal applications for visitors' permits to the other three observatories can be made at the office at Colina Los Pinos, on a hill behind the new university ① T051-207301. It is critical to reserve tours to these three in advance – up to three or four months ahead during holiday periods, although off season a few days notice may be enough. Most tour operators in La Serena and Coquimbo arrange tours to Mamalluca. If you can arrange tickets directly with the observatory, taxi drivers will provide transport.

Some visitors to the three large observatories complain that they do not get as much of an insight as they had expected. Bear in mind that trained astronomers have to reserve years in advance to use the equipment and that a day tour will not be the beginning of your astronomical career – it will, though, give you a window onto the workings of some of the most important telescopes on earth.

El Tololo ① *www.ctio.noao.edu, open to visitors by permit Sat 0900 and 1300. For (free) permits write to Casilla 603, La Serena, T051-205200, ctiorecp@noao.edu. Pick your it up before 1200 on the day before your visit from the office at Colina Los Pinos.*
Situated at 2200 m, 87 km southeast of La Serena in the Elqui valley, 51 km south of Vicuña, this observatory belongs to Aura, an association of US and Chilean universities. It possesses what was until recently the largest telescope in the southern hemisphere (diameter 4 m), six other telescopes and a radio telescope. During holiday periods apply for a visitor's permit well in advance; at other times it is worth trying for a cancellation the day before. The administration will insist that you have private transport; you can hire a taxi, US$55, but you will require the registration number when you book. Motorcycles are, apparently, not permitted to use the access road.

La Silla ① *www.ls.eso.org, open Sat except in Jul and Aug, 1330-1700. For permits, register in advance at Alonso de Córdoba 3107, Santiago, T02-4633101, mbauerle@eso.org, or write to Casilla 567, La Serena, T051-224527.*
Located at 2400 m, 156 km northeast of La Serena, this belongs to ESO (European Southern Observatory), is financed by eight EU countries and comprises 14 telescopes. To reach La Silla, head north from La Serena for 120 km along the Panamericana to the turn-off, then another 36 km.

Las Campanas ① *www.lco.cl, open Sat 1430-1730. For permits, write to Casilla 601, La Serena, T051-207301.*
This observatory is at 2510 m, 162 km northeast of La Serena, 30 km north of La Silla. It belongs to the Carnegie Institute, has five telescopes and is altogether a smaller facility than the other two. To get to Las Campanas, follow the Panamericana, take the turning for La Silla and then turn north after 14 km.

Mamalluca ① *bookings from Gabriela Mistral 260, La Serena, T051-411352, www.mamalluca.org, visits daily at 2100, 2300, 0100 in summer, 1800, 2000, 2200 in winter, US$7.50 plus transport (US$3) per person.*
Situated at 1500 m, 6 km north of Vicuña, this recent observatory was built specifically for the public and is the only one where visitors can actually look through

⁞ Buccaneers of the Chilean coast

Sir Francis Drake was one of the first Europeans to commit piracy along the west coast of South America but his example was soon widely followed. By the second half of the 17th century, free-booting renegades – mostly English, French and Dutch – were roaming the South Seas preying on Spanish coastal towns and shipping in the hope of getting rich quick.

Basil Ringrose has a special place among these desperadoes because he left a fascinating first-hand account of his activities. Towards the end of 1679, he set out, under the command of a Captain Sharp, to take and plunder what Ringrose describes as the "vastly rich town of Arica". On finding the Spanish defence of Arica too strong to overcome, however, they had to continue south to nearby Hilo where they managed to land and occupy the sugar factory. The besieged Spaniards agreed to supply Ringrose and his comrades "four score of beeves" on the condition that they didn't burn the sugar factory to the ground. After several days of waiting for the "beeves" to arrive, the pirates began to smell a rat and decided to burn the factory

down regardless and retreated to their ship. It was as well they did because they had no sooner re-embarked than they saw 300 Spanish horsemen advancing on their encampment. But Ringrose was still impressed by Hilo, describing it as "a valley very pleasant being all over set with figs, olives, oranges, lemons, and lime trees, and many other fruits agreeable to the palate". What Ringrose most remembered Hilo for, however, was its "good chocolate" of which they "had plundered some small quantity".

After the double disappointment of Arica and Hilo, the pirates continued south to the Bay of Coquimbo where they discovered the city of La Serena, "most excellent and delicate, and far beyond what we could expect in so remote a place". Ringrose was particularly impressed by the town's seven churches which he and his companions hoped to loot, but again news of their activities preceded them and the Spaniards had already removed the churches' treasures. Instead they "found strawberries as big as walnuts and very delicious to the taste".

a telescope at the night sky. The first telescope, diameter 30 cm, was donated by El Tololo. There is also a multimedia centre here. Advance booking is strongly recommended. Spanish- and English-speaking guides are available for groups of five or more with advance notice.

Coquimbo and the coast 🈺🏍❀🚌🅒 ➤ pp171-176.

Coquimbo

On the same bay as La Serena and only 84 km from Ovalle, Coquimbo was used during the colonial period as a port for La Serena, attracting attention from English pirates, including Francis Drake, who visited in 1578. A statue to Drake was erected in the city in 1998. Legends of buried treasure at Bahía la Herradura de Guayacán persist to this day. From these small beginnings, Coquimbo grew into a city in the 19th century, when it – and the separate centre of Guayacán – became important in the processing of copper. By 1854, there were two large copper foundries in Coquimbo and in 1858 the largest foundry in the world was built in Guayacán.

Today, the city depends on the port for its vitality and economic solvency. It has one of the best harbours on the coast and several major fish-processing plants. The city is strung along the north shore of a peninsula, with most of the commercial life centred on three streets that run between the port and the steep hillside on which are perched many of the poorer houses. The 19th-century mansions of the **Barrio Inglés** along Aldunate to the north of the Plaza de Armas have recently been restored and these are home to much of the city's nightlife. On the south shore of the peninsula lies the suburb of **Guayacán**, where there is an iron-ore loading port, a steel church designed by Eiffel, an English cemetery and a huge cross, the **Cruz del Tercer Milenio**, erected to mark the millennium. It is possible to climb the 83-m cross for a charge of US$2. In 1981, heavy rain uncovered 39 tenth-century burials of humans and llamas, which had been sacrificed; the exhibits are on display in the **Museo del Sitio** ① *Plaza Gabriela Mistral, Jan and Feb only, Mon-Sat 0930-2030, Sun 0930-1400, free.* It doubles as a tourist information office. Travellers should be aware that Coquimbo has a reputation for theft. In summer, it is possible to take boat trips around the harbour and to Punta Lobos on the bay ① *regular departures, US$4.*

The coastal resorts

The coast around Coquimbo has some great beaches; the closest is at **La Herradura**, 2½ km from Coquimbo, a slightly upmarket suburb that has the best beaches in the bay and numerous *cabañas* and restaurants. Also nearby is a resort complex called **Las Tacas**, with beach, swimming pool, tennis and apartments. Heading south, there are good swimming beaches at **Totoralillo**, 12 km beyond Coquimbo, and a 10-km beach east of **Guanaqueros**, a fishing village on the southern coast of a large bay,

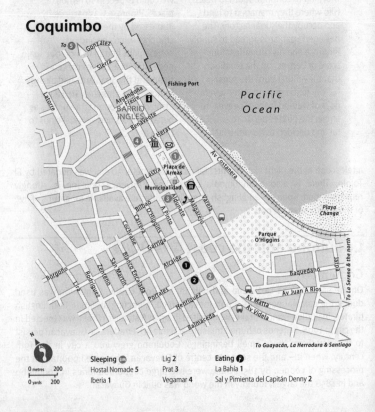

Coquimbo

Sleeping	Lig 2	Eating
Hostal Nomade 5	Prat 3	La Bahía 1
Iberia 1	Vegamar 4	Sal y Pimienta del Capitán Denny 2

37 km south of Coquimbo. **Tongoy**, 13 km further on is an old fishing port occupying the whole of a small peninsula. It is now a rapidly growing resort and well worth a visit, with two large beaches: the Playa Grande to the south (14 km long) and the Playa Socos to the north.

Vicuña and the Upper Elqui Valley

» pp171-176.

Vicuña, the main town in the Elqui Valley, lies 66 km east of La Serena. The road is paved for another 37 km beyond, as far as Pisco Elqui. Most of the tiny towns here have but a single street. Many tour operators in La Serena offer day trips as far as Pisco Elqui, but you really need to stay overnight to experience the wonder of the upper valley. The valley is the centre of *pisco* production: of the nine distilleries in the valley, the largest is Capel in Vicuña. *Huancara*, a delicious fortified wine introduced by the Jesuits, is also produced in the valley. The Río Elqui has been dammed east of El Molle, 30 km east of La Serena. This has forced the relocation of five small towns in the valley and has also led to increased winds in the valley, according to locals.

Vicuña

This small, friendly town was founded in 1821. On the west side of the plaza is the Municipalidad, built in 1826 and topped in 1905 by a medieval-style tower – the **Torre Bauer** – prefabricated in Germany and imported by the German-born mayor of the time. Inside the Municipalidad is a gallery of past local dignitaries as well as the tourist office. Also on the plaza is the **Iglesia Parroquial**, dating from 1860.

Museo Gabriela Mistral ① *Gabriela Mistral 759, www.dibam.cl/subdirec_ museos/mgm_vicuna/home.asp, Mon-Sat 1000-1840, Sun 1000-17400, shorter hrs off season, US$1, students half price*, contains manuscripts, books, awards and many other details of the poet's life. Next door is the house where the poet was born. **Museo Entomológico** ① *C Chacabuco 334, daily 1000-2100 in summer; Mon-Fri 1030-1330 and 1530-1930, Sat-Sun 1030-1900 in winter, US$0.50*, has over 3000 insect species displayed. **Solar de los Madariaga** ① *Gabriela Mistral 683, open Jan, Feb and*

From Santiago to La Serena **Elqui Valley**

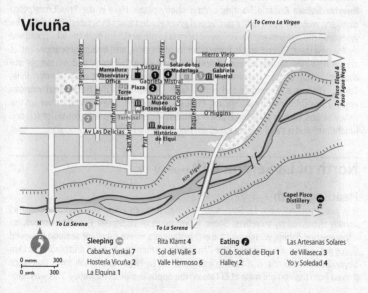

Vicuña

Sleeping
Cabañas Yunkai 7
Hostería Vicuña 2
La Elquina 1
Rita Klamt 4
Sol del Valle 5
Valle Hermoso 6

Eating
Club Social de Elqui 1
Halley 2
Las Artesanas Solares de Villaseca 3
Yo y Soledad 4

holidays, Mon-Fri 1000-1900, intermittently off season, US$0.70, is a former residence containing artefacts belonging to a prominent local family. There are good views from Cerro La Virgen, north of town.

The **Capel Pisco distillery** ① *open Dec-May Mon-Sat 1000-1800, no booking required, free, guided tours (in Spanish),* lies 1½ km east of Vicuña, to the right of the main road. **Mamalluca** observatory is 6 km north of Vicuña.

The valley

From Vicuña a *ripio* road (high clearance vehicle necessary) runs south via Hurtado (Km 46), Pichasca (Km 85) and the Monumento Natural Pichasca to Ovalle (Km 120); see pages 157-159. The main road through the Elqui Valley continues east another 18 km to **Rivadavia**, where the rivers Turbio and Claro meet. Here the road divides, the main route (Route 41) winds through the mountains on a good, partly paved road to the Argentine border at **Paso Agua Negra** (4775 m). Chilean immigration and customs ① *open 0800-1700,* are at Juntas, 84 km west of the border (88 km east of Vicuña), where there is also a turning to Baños del Toro and the **Mina el Indio**. The mine can be visited only with a permit (obtainable from **Compañía Minería del Indio**, Baño Industrial Piñuelas, La Serena), and may be forced to close in the coming years because of pollution concerns.

The other branch of the road runs through Paihuano to **Monte Grande**, where the schoolhouse in which Gabriela Mistral lived and was educated by her sister is now a museum ① *C Principal s/n, T051-415015, Tue-Sun 1000-1300, 1500-1800 (until 1900 in Jan and Feb), US$0.80.* The poet's tomb is situated at the edge of town, opposite the **Artesanos de Cochiguaz** *pisco* distillery, which is open to the public. Here the road forks, one branch leading to the **Cochiguaz Valley**. There is no public transport along this road, but there are several New Age settlements – it is said that the valley is an important energy centre – and a number of campsites. At night, there is no better place on earth to star gaze. When the moon is new, or below the horizon, the stars seem to be hanging in the air; spectacular shooting stars can be seen every couple of seconds, as can satellites crossing the night sky. Back on the main road, just south of Montegrande is the **Cavas del Valle** organic winery with free tastings and a salesroom.

Pisco Elqui, with a population of 500, is situated 2 km south of Monte Grande along the main road. It is an attractive village with the newly restored **Iglesia de Nuestra Señora Rosario** fronting onto a shady plaza. Here is the **Tres Erres** *pisco* distillery, which is open to the public and gives guided tours in Spanish for US$4; the vineyards themselves are now covered by nets to protect them from the winds caused by the new dam. Pisco Elqui is famous for its night skies and beautiful scenery and is also a New Age centre, where all sorts of alternative therapies and massages are available. Horses can be hired, for exploring the surrounding area. Ramón Luis, T051-451168, is a recommended guide. At the **Astropub** in the **Hotel Elqui** you can enjoy a few drinks while stargazing through telescopes. Some 4 km further up the valley at **Los Nichos** is a small *pisco* distillery open to the public for visits (closed lunchtime) and a store selling excellent dried fruit and other local products.

North of La Serena 🍴🚌 ➤➤ *pp171-176.*

Heading north

It is 218 km north from La Serena to Vallenar, through a sparsely populated district usually bypassed by travellers. Some 35 km north of La Serena is **Caleta Hornos**, an impoverished fishing village with several restaurants where excellent seafood is served (*locos* are sometimes available). The Panamericana then climbs to an arid plateau; 21 km beyond Caleta Hornos is a turning eastwards to **La Higuera**, a small town that once thrived from the iron ore mine at **El Tofo** on the opposite side of the valley. This was once

● The Elqui Valley in the words of its poet

"It is a heroic slash in the mass of mountains, but so short as to be little more than a green-banked torrent, yet small as it is one comes to love it as perfect. It contains in perfection all that man could ask of a land in which to live: light, water, wine and fruit. And what fruit! The tongue which has tasted the juice of its peaches and the mouth which has eaten of its purple figs will never seek sweetness elsewhere.

The people of the Elqui take remarkable pride in their green soil.

Whenever there is a hump, a ridge or bare patch without greenery, it is because it is naked rock. Wherever the Elquino has a little water and three inches of soil, however poor, he will cultivate something: peaches, vines or figs. That the leafy, polished vines climb only a little way up the mountainsides is because if they were planted higher, they would wither in the pitiless February sun."

Gabriela Mistral, quoted in Jan Reed, *The Wines of Chile* (Mitchell Beazley, 1994).

one of the largest iron ore mines in the world; the mine stacks can clearly be seen from the Panamericana, as can the eerie eucalyptus trees on top of the hill, kept alive by the coastal fog. Only the guardian of the mine lives here now, but it is worth driving up to El Tofo to see the ghost town and for the spectacular views down to the coast.

To Reserva Nacional Pinguino de Humboldt

Sixteen kilometres north of the turn-off for El Tofo, a road heads westwards from the Panamericana, signposted for **Punta de Choros**. This *ripio* road leads through a rugged dry river valley for 20 km before reaching the small village of **Los Choros Bajos**, where the main activity is growing olives; the groves of olive trees provide a beautiful green backdrop to the harshness of the desert. There is a restaurant serving basic meals here, but it is better to continue a further 22 km towards the coast to **Punta de Choros**, the departure point for visiting the reserve.

Reserva Nacional Pinguino de Humboldt consists of three islands: **Chañaral**, **Choros** and **Damas**. It was founded to preserve the coast's marine life, which includes many penguins, sea lions and dolphins, as well as wonderful birdlife. The combination of this and the coast's rugged isolation means that visits here will not be quickly forgotten. To visit the reserve, tours are available from La Serena and Vallenar or you can hire a boat with the local fishermen (around US$80 for up to 10 people). Isla Damas is the only island at which it is possible to disembark (entrance to the island costs US$3.50) and here camping is allowed, but before visiting or camping on the island you must seek permission from CONAF in Punta de Choros (T051-272798); there is also a toilet on Isla Damas but no drinking water. From the turning to Punta de Choros, the Panamericana continues north, passing several small mining towns. At Domeyko, 165 km north of La Serena, a *ripio* road leads west to the coast towards the northern sector of the reserve, based around the small *caleta* at Chañaral.

● Sleeping

La Serena *p163, map p164*
The Panamericana from La Serena to Coquimbo is lined with cheaper accommodation and restaurants. There are also hotels and other accommodation along Av del Mar, 500 m off the highway.

L **Costa Real**, Av de Aguirre 170, T051-221010, www.costareal.cl. 5-star although without most of the features of a hotel in this category. Good restaurant, bar, unheated pool and conference centre. Probably the best hotel in town.

AL **Francisco de Aguirre**, Cordovez 210, T051-222991, www.diegodealmagro hoteles.cl. 4-star, recently refurbished with pool and reasonable restaurant.

AL **La Serena Plaza**, Fransisco de Aguirre 0660, T051-225665, www.hotelserena plaza.cl. Upmarket hotel by the beach with spacious rooms, swimming pool gym and restaurant. Good value.

AL-A **Los Balcones de Aragón**, Cienfuegos 289, T051-212419, www.losbalconesde aragon.cl. Standard 3-star with rooms arranged around a small courtyard.

A **Cabañas Bahia Drake**, Av del Mar 1300, T051-223367, cabanasbahiadrake.cl. Pleasant fully equipped cabins on the seafront with swimming pool.

A-B **Hostal Colón**, Colón 371, T051- 223979, www.hostaldecolonlaserena.cl. Rooms around a small central courtyard. Nothing exceptional but better value than others in this category, discounts for payment in dollars and for stays of more than 1 night.

A-B **Hostal Del Mar**, Cuatro Esquinas 0680 (south of town centre, near beach), T051-225559, www.hostaldelmar.cl. Also apartments, clean, friendly. There are several more motels along Av del Mar.

A-B **Londres**, Cordovez 550, T051-219066, www.hotellondres.cl. Simple hotel. Bright rooms with good beds, cable TV and decent bathrooms. The rooms backing on to the Din shop can be noisy during the day.

A-B **Santa Inés**, Matta 196 y Colón, T051-228117. Another slightly run-down, no frills hotel. Rooms vary enormously in size. The suites are bright, spacious and reasonable value.

B-C **El Punto**, Andrés Bello 979, T051-228474, www.punto.de. D-E singles, F per person in shared rooms. Recently refurbished rooms with or without bath, with breakfast, tasteful, comfortable, café, laundry, book exchange, parking, English and German spoken, wifi area, information given and tours arranged, highly recommended.

C **Casa Alejandro Muñoz**, Brasil 720, T051-211619. F singles. Accommodation in family home in old part of town, hot showers, good breakfast, garden, English and French spoken, friendly atmosphere.

C **Casona de Cantournet**, Cantournet 815, T051-213070, correo.lacasonacantournet@ gmail.com. With bath, huge rooms in old mansion, comfortable.

C **Gregoria Fernández**, Andrés Bello 1067, T051-224400, gregoria_Fernández@hotmail. com. E-F singles. Clean, friendly and very helpful (good local information), good beds, some rooms with bath, 3 blocks from bus terminal, garden, decent breakfast, price per person. Highly recommended. Fills up quickly so book ahead.

C **Hostal Matta**, Matta 234, T051-210014, www.hostalmatta.cl. E singles. Pleasant family run bed and breakfast. Simple but clean high ceilinged rooms, some with bath and cable TV. Small garden with barbeque area.

C **Hostal Croata**, Cienfuegos 248, T/F051-224997, hostalcroata@entelchile.net. F singles. Some rooms with bath or without, with breakfast, kitchen and laundry facilities, cable TV, patio, hospitable, some English spoken, good value.

C **Hostal Familyhome**, Av Santo 1056, T/F051-224059, www.familyhome.cl. Near bus terminal, some rooms with bath, ample kitchen facilities, Quiet despite being on a main road. F singles.

C **Residencial Suiza**, Cienfuegos 250, T051-216092, residencial.suiza@terra.cl. With bath and breakfast, good beds, recommended.

C-D **María Pizarro**, Las Rojas 18, T051-229282, hostalmariacasa.cl. E-F singles. Very welcoming, near bus terminal, laundry facilities, garden, camping, very helpful. Good value. Highly recommended.

Coquimbo *p167, map p168*
Accommodation is cheaper than La Serena.

B **Lig**, Aldunate 1577, T051-311171, F313717. Comfortable, friendly, with breakfast, overpriced, near bus terminal.

C **Hostal Nomade**, Regimento Coquimbo 5, T051-315665, www.hostalnomade.cl. E singles, F per person in dorms. New HI affiliated hostel. Kitchen and laundry facilities, internet, tours arranged, also camping. English spoken.

C **Prat**, Bilbao y Aldunate, T/F051-311845. Comfortable, with breakfast, pleasant.

C-D **Iberia**, Lastra 400, T051-312141, F326307. Cheaper without bath. Friendly. Recommended.

D **Vegamar**, Las Heras 403, T051-311773. Shared bath, basic.

The coastal resorts *p168*

B Cabañas Bahia Club, Guanaqueros, T051-395819, camping1@entelchile.net *Cabañas* for 3 people with kitchens, on the waterfront. Recommended. Camping also available.

C La Herradura, Av La Marina 200, La Herradura, T/F051-261647. Rooms with bath, restaurant attached.

Camping
Camping La Herradura, La Herradura, T051-263867, mac-food@ctcinternet.cl. Price for up to 5 people.
Camping Oasis, Guanaqueros, T051-395319. On the beach; price per site.

Vicuña *p169, map p169*
Prices are higher in Jan and Feb.

AL Cabañas Yunkai, O'Higgins 72, T051-411195, yunkai@latinmail.com. *Cabañas* for 4/6 persons, pool, restaurant.

A Hostería Vicuña, Sgto Aldea 101, T051-411144, www.hosteriavicuna.cl. In spacious grounds. Swimming pool, tennis court, poor restaurant, parking.

C La Elquina, O' Higgins 65, T051-411317. Lovely garden, laundry and kitchen facilities.

C Rita Klamt, Condell 443, T051-419611, rita_klamt@yahoo.es. **E** single. Impeccably kept bed and breakfast. Excellent breakfast, ample kitchen facilities, pleasant garden with pool. Friendly and helpful. German and some English spoken. Highly recommended.

C Sol del Valle, Gabriela Mistral 741. T051-411078. With breakfast, bath, TV, vineyard, restaurant, swimming pool, recommended.

C Valle Hermoso, Gabriela Mistral 706, T/F051-411206. Clean, comfortable, parking. Recommended.

Camping
G Gabriela Mistral 152, T09-94286158. Hot showers, kitchen.
G Las Tinajas, east end of Chacabuco. Swimming pool, restaurant.

The valley *p170*
Accommodation in the valley is much cheaper outside Jan and Feb. If you're heading for the Argentine border, there is basic, clean accommodation at **Huanta** (Guanta on many maps), Km 46 from Vicuña;

ask for Guillermo Aliaga. Huanta is also the last chance to buy food. The following options are all in Pisco Elqui.

L Los Mistérios de Elqui, A Prat s/n, Pisco Elqui, T051-1982544, www.misteriosde elqui.cl. Plush *cabañas*, sleep 4, swimming pool, good expensive restaurant.

A-B El Tesoro del Elqui, Pisco Elqui, T051-451069, www.tesoro-elqui.cl. *Cabañas* for up to 4, also shared rooms, **F** per person, pleasant gardens, pool, English and German spoken. Tours arranged, food served. Recommended.

A-B Los Dátiles, A Prat s/n, Pisco Elqui, T051-451226, losdatileselqui.cl. *Cabañas* with kitchenette, sleep 5, good sized swimming pool, good restaurant serving Chilean country cooking.

C Elqui, O'Higgins s/n, Pisco Elqui, T051-451130. **E-F** singles. Hot shower, good restaurant and bar. Recommended.

C La Casa de Don Juan, Prat s/n, Pisco Elqui. **F** singles. Rickety wooden mansion. The upstairs room has spectacular views.

E Hospedaje, Prat 27, Pisco Elqui. **G** singles. Cheapest option, friendly, watch out for fleas.

Camping
El Olivo, Pisco Elqui. Small restaurant, pool, excellent facilities. Well-stocked supermarket 1 block from the plaza.
Sol de Barbosa, Pisco Elqui. Showers, open all year, price per site.

North of La Serena *p170*
B Cabañas Los Delfines, Pilpilen s/n, sitio 33, Punta de Choros, T09-96396678. Cabins for up to 6 people. There are other eating and accommodation options in the area.

● Eating

La Serena *p163, map p164*
Eating tends to be expensive in La Serena – Coquimbo is cheaper. For good cheapish fish lunches, try the restaurants on the upper floor of the Recova market where you will be immediately assailed by numerous waiters. The quality of restaurants, especially on Av del Mar, varies considerably; often many dishes on the menu are not available.

♦♦♦-♦♦ Tololo Beach, Av del Mar 5200, Sector Las Gaviotas. On the beach about 4 km south of town. Extensive menu mostly of meat and seafood. You will have to travel a long way to get a better steak!

Donde El Guatón, Brasil 750. Parrillada, paradise for meat eaters, also good seafood, one of the better places in the town centre.

La Mía Pizza, O'Higgins 360, T051-215063. Italian, good value pizzas and also fish dishes, good winelist (another branch on Av del Mar 2100 in summer, T051-212232).

Diavoletto, Prat 565 and O'Higgins 531. Fast food, popular.

El Callejón, O'Higgins 635. Bohemian student hangout serving cheap dishes. Popular bar at night.

Daniela 2, F de Aguirre 460. Typical Chilean home cooking.

Govindas, Lautaro 841, T051-224289. Incredibly cheap vegetarian food served in a Hari Krishna yoga centre. Open Mon-Fri lunchtime only.

For seafood the best place to go is the Sector de los Pescadores in Peñuelas on the coast halfway between La Serena and Coquimbo. Take any bus to Coquimbo and get off at the junction with Los Pescadores, opposite a mini zoo. Walk 300 m to the coast and there are a dozen or so restaurants. Prices generally ⛛-⛛.

Cafés

Café Colonial, Balmaceda 475. Sandwiches fast food and coffee. Also serves breakfast.

Café do Brasil, Balmaceda 461. Good coffee.

Café Morocco, Prat 566. Good coffee and fresh juices.

Tahití, Cordovez 540, local 113. Real coffee, pastries. Recommended.

Coquimbo *p167, map p168*

According to the tourist office in La Serena, the best seafood is to be had at Coquimbo; it is especially cheap in the municipal market, Melgarejo, entre Bilbao y Borgoño.

Sal y Pimienta del Capitán Denny, Aldunate 769. One of the best in town: pleasant, old fashioned, mainly fish cooked in Chilean style.

Crucero, Valera. Excellent seafood.

La Picada, Costanera. Excellent, good pebre. Near statue of O'Higgins.

Mai Lai Fan, Av Ossandón 1. Reasonable Chinese food.

La Bahía, Pinto 1465. Excellent, good value.

La Barca, Ríos y Varela. Modest but good.

Vicuña *p169, map p169*

Club Social de Elqui, Gabriela Mistral 435. Very good, attractive patio, good value *almuerzo*, real coffee.

Halley, Gabriela Mistral 404. Specialists in local meat dishes including rabbit and huge portions of goat. The side rooms are more pleasant than the central patio.

Las Artesanas Solares de Villaseca, 8 km east of Vicuña in Villaseca. A unique restaurant, pioneers in the use of solar ovens.

Pizzería Virgos, Prat 234 on the plaza. Mid-range pizzas.

Mistral, Gabriela Mistral 180. Very good, popular with locals, good value *almuerzo*.

Yo Y Soledad, Gabriela Mistral 364. Inexpensive hearty Chilean food, good.

The upper valley *p170*

Miraflores, Camino a Los Nichos. Excellent meat dishes. Off season open weekends only.

Donde la Elke, O'Higgins y Rodríguez. Well prepared meat fish and pasta. Recommended.

El Rincón Chileno, O'Higgins s/n. Chilean country fare including roast goat.

Los Jugos, on the plaza. Light snacks and fresh juices.

🔾 Bars and clubs

La Serena *p163, map p164*

Most of the clubs are on the Av del Mar and in Peñuelas but in town, you should try:

B-Cool, Av 4 Esquinas s/n. Recommended.

El Callejón, O'Higgins 635. Relaxed atmosphere with a lounge bar and patio. Young crowd. Fills up with students at weekends.

El Faro, Av del Mar y Av Francisco Aguirre. A pricey but good pub.

El Nuevo Peregrino, Peni y Andrés Bello. Intimate bar with live music at weekends.

Pub-Discosalsa Kamanga, Costanera 4785. University crowd, fun, recommended.

🎭 Entertainment

La Serena *p163, map p 164*
Cine Centenario, Cordovez 399. There is also a multiplex cinema complex in the **Mall Plaza** (see Shopping below).

🎊 Festivals and events

Coquimbo *p167, map p168*
14-21 Sep Coquimbo hosts **La Pampilla**, by far the biggest Independence Day celebrations in Chile. Between 200,000 and 300,000 people come from all over the country for the fiesta, which lasts for a week. Things get going on 14 Sep, and the partying does not stop until 21 Sep. It costs a nominal US$1.50 to gain access to the area where the main dancing tents are to be found, as well as much typical Chilean food and drink. You have to pay to enter the *peñas*, but there also free communal areas. Big bands such as Illapu and La Ley have played here in recent years, as well as cumbia bands from Argentina and Colombia.

⭕ Shopping

La Serena *p163, map p164*
For handicrafts try **Cema-Chile**, Los Carrera 562, or **La Recova** handicraft market on Cantournet and Cienfuegos, though many items sold here are imported from Peru and Bolivia.

Good supermarkets include **Las Brisas**, Cienfuegos y Cordovez, open 0900-2200, and **Rendic**, Balmaceda 561, open 0900-2300. There is also a big new shopping centre, the **Mall Plaza**, on the Panamericana, next to the bus station.

Tintos y Blancos, Prat 630, has a good selection of fine wines and good quality *piscos*.

Librería Inglesa, Cordovez 309, on the plaza. English-language bookshop.

🔺 Activities and tours

La Serena *p163, map p164*
Several agencies offer similar tours of the region. Approximate tour prices: Valle del Elqui US$25, Parque Nacional Fray Jorge US$40, Tongoy US$35, city tour US$15, Mamalluca observatory US$22, Reserva

Nacional Los Pingüinos and the Isla Damas US$42. Some operators also offer tours to Valle del Encanto, Andacollo and Isla Chañaral.

Quality varies enormously. The more responsible operators will not lead tours to Mamalluca or Isla Damas in bad weather. Many hostels will arrange tours with the agency that pays them the highest commission, so their recommendations are not always to be taken at face value.

The following are recommended and offer a range of local tours including trekking and climbing options:
Chile Safari, Matta 367, T051-50434, www.chilesafari.com
Delfines, Matta 591, T051-223624, www.turismoaventuradelfines.cl
Elqui Valley Tour, Los Carrera 515, T051-214846, www.elquivalleytour.cl.
Talinay Adventure Expeditions, Prat 470, in the courtyard, T051-218658, www.talinaychile.com.

The Upper Valley.
Mundo Elqui, O' Higgins s/n, Pisco Elqui, T051-451290, www.mundoelqui.cl, offer trekking and mountainbiking trips as well as horse riding trips in the Cochihuaz Valley.

⭕ Transport

La Serena *p163, map p164*
Air
Aeropuerto La Florida, 5 km east of the city, T051-271812. To **Santiago** and **Copiapó**, Lan Chile, 45 mins.

Bicycle
Repairs from **Mike's Bikes**, Av de Aguirre 004, T051-224454, sales, hire, repairs, English spoken, helpful.

Bus
Local The bus terminal is at El Santo y Amunátegui (about 8 blocks south of the centre). City buses cost US$0.50. To **Coquimbo**, bus No 8 from Av Aguirre y Cienfuegos, US$0.75, every few mins; to **Vicuña**, with **Vía Elqui** and **Servitur**, every ½ hr, 1 hr, US$2, most buses continue to **Pisco Elqui**, US$3, last one at 2000. *Colectivos* to **Coquimbo** from Av Aguirre y Balmaceda; to **Vicuna** from Domeyko y Balmaceda, US$3;

to **Andocollo** and **Ovalle**, yellow *colectivos* from Domeyko. *Colectivos* also operate on fixed routes throughout city.

Long distance Buses daily to **Santiago**, several companies, 7-8 hrs, US$10 classic, US$12 semi cama, US$20 cama; to **Arica**, 20 hrs, US$28; to **Calama**, 16 hrs, US$24; to **Vallenar**, 3 hrs, US$5; to **Valparaíso**, 7 hrs, US$12; to **Caldera**, 6 hrs, US$9; to **Antofagasta**, several companies, 12 hrs, US$16, and to **Iquique**, 17 hrs, US$25.

Car
Hire from **Avis**, Av de Aguirre 063, T051-227171; **Budget**, Balmaceda 3820, T051-290241; **Daire**, Balmaceda 3812, T051-226933, recommended, good service; **Flota Verschae**, Fransisco de Aguirre 0240, T051-27645, good value, recommended; **Hertz**, Av de Aguirre 068, T051-227171, prices range from US$40 to US$80 per day; **La Florida**, at airport, T051-271947.

Taxi
City taxis charge a flat rate of US$0.55 plus US$0.20 for every 200 m.

Coquimbo and the coast *p167, map p168*
Bus
Terminal at Varela y Garriga. To **La Serena**, every few mins, US$0.75; to **Guanaqueros**, 45 mins, US$1; to **Tongoy**, 1 hr, US$1.50, with **Ruta Costera**, frequency varies according to day (more on Sun) and season. There are also *colectivos* to **Guanaqueros**, US$2 and to **Tongoy**, US$2.50.

Upper Elqui Valley *p169*
Bus
Buses depart from Pisco Elqui to **La Serena**, US$3, on the hour, via Vicuña. From Vicuña to **La Serena**, about 10 a day (more in summer), mostly with **Via Elqui** or **Servitur**, 1st 0800, last 1930, 1 hr, US$2, also *colectivo* from the bus terminal, US$3; to **Santiago** via La Serena, with **Via Elqui** and **Turbus**, US$13; to **Pisco Elqui**, hourly, with **Vía Elqui** and

Servitur, 1 hr, US$2. There is no public transport beyond towards the border past Rivadavia, although El Indio mine transport may give lifts as far as Juntas.

North of La Serena *p170*
There is no public transport to Punta de Choros, but tours are readily available from La Serena; traffic on the road between Punta de Choros, and the Panamericana is relatively frequent, especially at weekends, so hitching is also possible.

---

❶ Directory

La Serena *p163, map p164*
Banks Several throughout the city centre. There is an ATM in the bus termina. Casas de cambio at **Inter**, Balmaceda 431; **Cambio Fides**, Caracol Colonial, Balmaceda 460, good rates, changes TCs; also **Cambio Caracol** in the same building. **Cultural centres** Centro Latino- Americano de Arte y Cultura, Balmaceda 824, T051-229344. Offers music and dance workshops, art gallery, handicraft workshops. **Nueva Acropolis**, Benavente 692, T051-21214. Lectures, discussions, free entry. **Internet** Ubiquitous. **Laundry** Vicky, Peni 363, T051-222746 will pick up and deliver. **Telephones** Lots of call centres in the town centre. **Useful address** Automóvil Club de Chile, E de la Barra 435, T051-225279.

Coquimbo and the coast
p167, map p168
Casa de cambio Cambios Maya, Portales 305. Also many Redbancs in the centre. **Internet** Aldunate 1196, open until 2330. **Telephone** CTC, Aldunate 1633.

Upper Elqui Valley *p169*
Banks There are 2 banks in Vicuña but none further up the valley. **Useful information** CODEFF, the environmental organization, has an office on the outskirts of Vicuña.

Into the Atacama

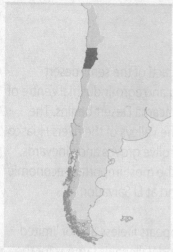

⁞ Footprint features

Introduction

From La Serena, the shrubs and cacti of the semi-desert stretch north as far as the mining and agro-industrial centre of Copiapó. Beyond this city, the Atacama Desert begins. The main population centres are in the valleys of the rivers Huasco and Copiapó, which are oases of olive groves and vineyards, and in the Salado Valley, where the most important economic activity is mining, especially inland at El Salvador.

Although much of this region appears lifeless and of limited interest to visitors, the area around Vallenar is famous for the flowering of the desert following the rare occasions when there is heavy rainfall; the upper reaches of the Huasco Valley are beautiful and tranquil, and make a good resting point en route to or from the Atacama, as does the beach resort of Bahía Inglesa, while the port of Huasco itself has excellent seafood. All along the coast of this region a variety of excellent inshore fish known as *pescado de roca* are caught. There are also three national parks: the Parque Nacional Pan de Azúcar, which protects a wide range of marine life; the Parque Nacional Llanos de Challe, which safeguards the habitat of one of the very rare flowers that bud with rainfall; and the Parque Nacional Tres Cruces, which covers extensive areas of salt flats northeast of Copiapó. East of the Parque Nacional Tres Cruces is the Paso San Francisco, a desolate yet spectacular border crossing into Argentina; near the pass are some of the highest peaks in the Andes, although most are best tackled from the Argentinian side.

★ Don't miss...

1 **Desierto florido** When it rains, go to the desert around Vallenar and witness the kaleidoscopic assortment of flowers, whose buds lie dormant in the sand waiting for moisture. An unforgettable sight, page 182.

2 **Alto del Carmen and Horcón Quemado distilleries** Sample Chile's best liqueur, *pisco*, at these distilleries near Vallenar, page 182.

3 **Tránsito Valley** Explore the high Andean valleys, page 182.

4 **Ojos del Salado** Climb the tallest mountain in Chile and the highest volcano in the world, page 186.

5 **Pan de Azúcar** Visit a park with stunning beaches and a wide variety of wildlife, page 192.

Into the Atacama

Background

Although small groups of Spanish settlers took over the fertile lands in the Huasco and Copiapó valleys in the 16th century, no towns were founded until late in the colonial period. Even the valleys were sparsely populated until the 19th century when the development of mining led to the creation of the ports of Caldera, Chañaral and Huasco and encouraged the building of railways. Mining remains a major economic activity: one of the largest copper mines is at El Salvador and over 50% of all Chilean iron ore is mined around Vallenar. Agriculture is limited to the valleys; the Copiapó Valley is an important producer of grapes, while the lower Huasco Valley is Chile's main olive-growing area. Fishing is centred on Caldera and, on a smaller scale, Chañaral and Huasco.

This part of the country can be divided into two: between the Río Elqui and the Río Copiapó the transitional semi-desert zone continues; north of the Copiapó the Atacama Desert begins and drivers should beware high winds and blowing sand. The valleys of the rivers Huasco, Copiapó and Salado form oases in this barren landscape. On the coast, temperatures are moderated by the sea and mist is common in the mornings. Inland temperatures are higher by day and cooler by night; Vallenar and the upper valleys of the Copiapó and Huasco can be especially cold on winter evenings. Rainfall is sparse and occurs in winter only, with amounts decreasing as you go north.

East of Copiapó the Andes divide between the eastern range (Cordillera de Claudio Gay) and the western range (Cordillera de Domeyko); a basin collects the waters from the Andes. Here there are salt flats, the most extensive being the Salar de Pedernales. The eastern range has some of the highest peaks in Chile: Ojos del Salado (6893 m/6864 m), Incahuasi (6615 m), Tres Cruces (6749 m) and San Francisco (6020 m).

Huasco Valley

This valley (known as the Jardín de Atacama) is an oasis of olive groves and vineyards. It is rugged and spectacular, reminiscent of the Cajón del Maipo near Santiago. At Alto del Carmen, 39 km east of Vallenar, the valley divides into the Carmen and Tránsito valleys. There are pisco distilleries at Alto del Carmen and San Félix, both of which have basic residenciales. A sweet wine known as pajarete is also produced. Today the Río Huasco is the last of the unpolluted rivers in the north. However, there is a huge goldmining project in the upper valley, which, if given the green light, will get underway in 2007 to the displeasure of many locals. ►► *For Sleeping, Eating and other listings, see pages 182-184.*

Ins and outs

The Huasco Valley's main town and transport hub is Vallenar, which is easily reached by regular buses from both north and south. Tourist information for the valley is available from the Municipalidad on the Plaza de Armas in Vallenar as well as the Municipalidades in Huasco and Alto del Carmen.

Vallenar → *Phone code: 051. Colour map 2, B2. Population: 47,000.*

Nearly 200 km north of La Serena is Vallenar, the chief town of the Huasco Valley. It was founded in 1789 as San Ambrosio de Ballenary to commemorate the birthplace in Ireland of Ambrosio O'Higgins. The town is centred on a pleasant Plaza de Armas, in which all the benches are made of Chile's purest marble, extracted from the Tránsito Valley. The plaza is dominated by the church, a kitsch monstrosity with its iron girder steeple and electric chimes on the hour. There is a summer-only information kiosk on the plaza. **Museo del Huasco** ① *Sgto Aldea 742, Tue-Fri 1500-1800, US$1*, contains historic photos and artefacts from the valley. Opposite is the northernmost Chilean palm tree in the country.

Freirina, founded in 1752, was the most important town in the valley, its prosperity based upon the nearby Capote goldmine and on later discoveries of copper. The pleasant main plaza with the Municipalidad (1870) and the Santa Rosa church (1869) is flanked by streets of multicoloured houses. There are scattered olive groves either side of town, and both olives and olive oil are sold from farmhouses and by the side of the road. It is easily reached by *colectivo*, 36 km west of Vallenar.

Situated at the mouth of the river, **Huasco** lies 56 km west of Vallenar. Those arriving from the desert north will appreciate the change of scenery – poplars and olive groves with an occasional glimpse of the river below. Destroyed by an earthquake in 1922, Huasco is a modern town with a large beach that is popular in summer, and a further expanse of deserted beach curves round to the north. There is a new coastal promenade with shaded benches looking out to sea and an esplanade for occasional concerts in summer. The port is interesting, as the fishermen unload their catches and hundreds of pelicans hover, waiting to snatch the fish that slip off the crates into the sea. There is a thriving sea-lion colony on the small islands offshore, and fishermen may be willing to take people there for a small charge. However, the best reason to come to Huasco is undoubtedly the seafood. There is good tourist information in the Municipalidad.

Some 9 km east of Huasco, a road branches north at the settlement of Huasco Bajo, near which are the **Humedal de Huasco** wetlands, known for their variety of marine birdlife (there are over 100 species). Some 50 km further north (37 of them *ripio*) is the small *caleta* of **Carrizal Bajo**. Carrizal Bajo is the best place from which to visit the **Parque Nacional Llanos de Challe**, set up to preserve the habitat of the *garra de león* and other flowers during the rare occasions when the desert is in bloom. The park is also home to Copiapoa cacti and guanacos. Tracks follow the coastline north of Carrizal Bajo, passing a series of small *caletas* en route to Caldera, including the beautiful beach at Puerto Viejo.

Vallenar

Sleeping
Cecil **2**
Hostal Camino del Rey **1**
Hostal Real Quillahue **8**
Hostal Vall **6**
Hostería de Vallenar **3**
Residencial La Oriental **5**
Residencial Mary 2 **4**
Viña del Mar **7**

Eating
Bavaria **1**
Corona del Inca **3**
La Pica **4**
Moros y Cristianos **5**
Pizza Il Boccato **2**
Shanghai **6**

Into the Atacama Huasco Valley

⦂ The flowering of the desert

The average annual rainfall in this region declines as you travel north: in Vallenar it is 65 mm, in Copiapó 20 mm. Most years, the semi-desert appears to support only bushes and cacti and these become sparser as you continue north. However, in years of heavier than usual winter rainfall, this semi-desert breaks into colour as dormant seeds and bulbs germinate to produce blankets of flowers, while insects that normally hide underground emerge to enjoy the foliage.

Although the *desierto florido* (flowering of the desert) used to occur every seven years or so, changing climatic conditions have led to an increase in the phenomenon.

Although the first traces of the *desierto florido* can be seen as far south as La Ligua and Los Molles, it is particularly worth seeing around Vallenar. From La Serena northwards, the Pan-American Highway is fringed with expanses of different colours: there are great stretches of violet *pata de guanaco*, yellow *corona del fraile* and blue *suspiro del campo*. Not all of these species can be seen at the same time: as the brief spring unfolds, the colours change and new species push through to replace others.

Around Vallenar, however, the colours are more varied as different species compete to celebrate this ever more frequent coming of spring: the Pan-American Highway north of the city as far as Copiapó and the coastal road north of Huasco are both recommended for a prime view. For guided tours, contact Roberto Alegría, T051-613865, Vallenar, and for further information, contact Vallenar tourist office (see page 180).

East of Vallenar

East of Vallenar, a paved road leads 39 km to **Alto del Carmen**, the site of the distillery of one of the best *piscos* in Chile. The road clings to arid hillsides sprinkled with cacti and *maitén* bushes, passing the Santa Juana Reservoir, which was created following the damming of the Río Huasco in 1995 and has transformed agriculture in the area. The valley is filled with grapevines for *pisco* and with groves of pepper and eucalyptus trees.

At Alto del Carmen, the road forks: left for the **Tránsito Valley**, right for the **Carmen Valley**. The Tránsito Valley is wilder and extends further into the heart of the mountains, while the Carmen Valley is greener and more populous: both valleys are unlikely clefts in the rocky Andes and reward the traveller who is prepared to make the effort to get to know them. Some 21 km beyond Alto del Carmen along the Tránsito Valley is the *mina de mármol blanco*, where Chile's finest marble is quarried. The peaceful village of **El Tránsito**, where there is basic accommodation and a cheap restaurant, is a further 10 km on. The village has a pleasant shady plaza, with snow-capped mountains as a backdrop in winter. The Carmen Valley stretches 25 km from Alto del Carmen to **San Félix**, the largest town of the valley, and the site of the distillery for Horcón Quemado *pisco*. A 39-km path connects the two valleys, from San Félix to the Quebrada de Pinte, 7 km south of El Tránsito, forming part of the Sendero de Chile. Allow two to three days for the trek. The tourist information office in Alto del Carmen's Municipalidad is helpful.

⊜ Sleeping

Vallenar *p180, map p181*
A Hostería de Vallenar, Ercilla 848, T051-614379, hotval@ctcinternet.cl.

Excellent accommodation with pool, parking, good breakfast and **Hertz** car hire office. Worth bargaining.

A-B **Cecil**, Prat 1059, T051-614071, F614400. Modern and clean with bath and hot water, and swimming pool. Recommended.
B **Hostal Real Quillahue**, Prat 70, T/F051-619992. With breakfast, modern, friendly. Recommended.
C **Hostal Camino del Rey**, Merced 943, T/F051-613184. Clean, cheaper rooms without bath; friendly, good value. Worth bargaining for longer stays. Recommended.
D **Hostal Vall**, Aconcagua 455, T051-613380, hostal_vall@yahoo.es. Rooms with breakfast and bath. Friendly, parking, good value.
D-E **Residencial Mary 2**, Ramírez 631. F singles. With private bath, friendly.
E **Residencial La Oriental**, Serrano 720, T051-613889. F singles. Pleasant, friendly, cheap meals, decent value. There are also several *residenciales* in the town.
E **Viña del Mar**, Serrano 611, T051-611478. Clean, *comedor*, nice rooms. Recommended.

West of Vallenar *p181*
There is no accommodation in Freirina but you'll find options in Huasco.
B **Hostería Huasco**, Carrera Pinto 110, Huasco, T051-531026. Parking, conference room, with TV and all mod cons.
C-D **Hostal San Fernando**, Pedro de Valdivia 176, Huasco, T051-531726. F singles. Some rooms with bath. Parking, restaurant. The owner lived for several years in Norway.
D **Cabañas Skitniza**, Craig 833, Huasco, T051-531596. Parking available.

Camping
Tres Playitas , 12 km north of Huasco along the coast towards Carrizal Bajo. Also in Huasco near the post office, US$2 per site.

East of Vallenar *p182*
F **Cabañas Camino al Oro**, Serrano y Larraín, San Félix, T051-983173. Cabins, per person.
F **Residencial El Azadón del Valle**, Alonso García s/n, Alto del Carmen, T051-617695. Price per person.
    There is no accommodation in the Tránsito Valley but camping wild is easy.

🍴 Eating

Vallenar *p180, map p181*
🍴🍴 **Bavaria**, Serrano 802. Reasonable chain, attentive service.

🍴🍴 **Moros y Cristianos**, Panamericana, junction with Huasco road. A good choice.
🍴🍴 **Pizza Il Boccato**, Prat 750. T052-614609. Good coffee, clean but lacking in style. At the slightly upmarket end for this town.
🍴 **Corona del Inca**, Prat 900-block in *local* set aside from road. Cheap meals, good cocktails.
🍴 **La Pica**, Brasil y Faez. Seriously cheap but good, serves meals, cocktails and seafood. There are other cheap places along the south end of Av Brasil.
🍴 **Shanghai**, Ramírez 1267. Chinese.

West of Vallenar *p181*
Aficionados of Chile's seafood should take a trip to Huasco for lunch; the journey takes only 45 mins from Vallenar. Some of the best seafood in the country is served at many cheap restaurants near Huasco's port. Heading north up the coast, there is also a seafood restaurant at Carrizal Bajo.

🎭 Entertainment

Vallenar *p180, map p180*
Bar Bogart, Serrano 925. Popular old-timers' bar with the fattest roundest bar stools you have ever seen. **Billboard Pub**, Prat 920. Popular with locals. It is also worth checking out the **Centro Cultural Vallenar**, Vallenar y Colchagua, for cultural events, and occasional exhibitions and concerts.

🎉 Festivals and events

29 Jun Fiesta de San Pedro is celebrated by the fishing community in Huasco.
19 Jul Fiesta del Carmen, Alto del Carmen.
15 Aug Fiesta del Tránsito in Alto del Carmen with a rodeo, market and famous for its ice creams made of snow.

🛍 Shopping

Local products are sold in Vallenar's market. **Horcón Quemado**, Ercilla 660, Vallenar, T051-610985, sells some of Chile's finest *pisco*.

▲ Activities and tours

Agrotur, Maule 742, Vallenar, T051-617549, 09-2879425. Tours of the Huasco Valley as well as the northern section of the Reserva Nacional Humboldt.

⊖ Transport

Bus

Operators to/from Vallenar include **Tur Bus**, Merced 561, and **Pullman Bus**, opposite. Next door is Vallenar's bus terminal, from which **TasChoapa** and **Flota Barrios** depart. To **Copiapó**, 2 hrs, US$6; to **Chañaral**, 5 hrs,US$11; to **La Serena**, 2 hrs, US$6. Buses to **Junta de Valeriano** (Tránsito Valley) and **San Félix** (Carmen Valley), as well as the intermediate points such as **Alto del Carmen**, leave from Marañon 1289, at 0730, 1100, 1430, 1630, 1730. **Turbus** runs a daily service between **Huasco** and **Santiago**.

There are also *colectivos* in Vallenar, which may be useful for those with heavy luggage making their way to the bus terminals (catch them on Serrano). *Colectivos* from Vallenar to Huasco leave when full, 1 hr 20 mins, US$3.

❶ Directory

Vallenar *p180, map p181*
Banks Several on Prat, east of the plaza.
Clinic Consulta Médico y Laboratorio Clínico, Pje Nicolás Naranjo 341, T051-616012.
Internet Several, US$0.75 per hr. **Laundry** Lavaseco Rodier, Verdaguer y Ramírez.
Telephone ENTEL, Prat 1000-block.

Copiapó Valley

From Vallenar it is 148 km north to Copiapó, the largest city in the valley of the Río Copiapó, generally regarded as the southern limit of the Atacama Desert. This valley is a surprisingly green cleft in the desert, an oasis of farms, vineyards and orchards about 150 km long. ▸▸ *For Sleeping, Eating and other listings, see pages 188-191.*

Ins and outs

Getting there The Copiapó Valley's main centre is Copiapó, which is easily reached by regular buses from both north and south. There are several daily flights serving Copiapó from Santiago and La Serena, continuing on to El Salvador. For a transfer to the airport call To52-218889. ▸▸ *For further details, see Transport, page 191.*

Getting around There are many *colectivos* and public buses in Copiapó, which may be useful for those heading for some of the out-of-town sites, such as the Santuario de la Candelaria; the fare for buses is US$0.50.

Tourist information The **Sernatur** office in Copiapó is on the north side of Plaza de Armas ① *Los Carrera 691, To52-212838, infoatacama@sernatur.cl, Mon-Fri 0830-1930, Sat 1030-1430, 1630-1930, Sun 1030-1430; out of season Mon-Fri 0830-1730 only,* and is extremely helpful. English is spoken. There is also a **CONAF** office in Copiapó ① *Juan Martínez 55, To52-210282.*

Copiapó and around ▣❶❶❶❀▲▣❶

▸▸ *pp188-191. Colour map 2, B2.*

The capital of Región III Atacama, Copiapó, with a population of 127,000, is an important mining centre with a big mining school and a backdrop of arid hills to the north. Founded in 1744, Copiapó became a prosperous town after the discovery in 1832 of the third largest silver deposits in South America at Chañarcillo. The wealth from Chañarcillo formed the basis of the fortunes of several famous Chilean families – most notably, the Cousiños – and helped finance the first railway line in South America, linking Copiapó to Caldera (1851). Although quite a poor city in itself, Copiapó's economy thrives on the large numbers of lone miners who descend to the city in order to seek distraction and spend their pay cheques. On cool summer nights, people flock to the pleasant, shady Plaza de Armas to chat and watch the world go by.

The neoclassical **cathedral**, on Plaza Prat, dating from 1851, was designed by William Rogers. Mass is held here every evening. The **Museo Mineralógico** ① *Colipí y Rodríguez, a block east of the plaza, Mon-Fri 1000-1300, 1530-1900, Sat 1000-1300, US$0.80,* is the most impressive museum of its type in Chile. It possesses a collection of weird, beautiful minerals from Chile and also from Asia, Europe and North America, plus a decent set of fossils. There is an unfortunate lack of narrative or explanation but a visit is highly recommended nonetheless; it is extraordinary how, although there are minerals from all over the world, the most colourful or striking are almost always Chilean.

Three blocks further north, at Infante near Yerbas Buenas, is the colonial Jesuit **Iglesia de Belén** ① *Mon-Fri 1630-1830*, remodelled in 1856. Further west, at Atacama y Rancagua, you'll find the **Museo Regional del Atacama** ① *murea@entelchile.net, Mon 1400-1745, Tue-Fri 0900-0745, Sat 1000-1245, 1500-1745, Sun 1000-1245, US$1 (free Sun),* containing collections on local

> ✱ *On Plaza Prat, at the corner of Colipi y Los Carrera, is a stall selling exquisite minerals from the Atacama, a uniquely Chilean souvenir.*

history, especially from the 19th century up to the time of the War of the Pacific; it is also notable for its collection of artefacts from the Huentelauquén people, thought to have flourished 10,000 years ago. On the opposite corner of the same block, at Matta y O'Higgins, is the **Monument to Juan Godoy**, the muleteer, who, in 1832, discovered silver at Chañarcillo. Behind is the **Iglesia de San Francisco**, built in 1872 (the nearby convent is from 1662), which is a good example of a 19th-century construction using Pino Oregón and Guayaquil cane, popular materials of the day. The wealth of the 19th-century mining families is reflected in the **Villa Viña de Cristo**, built in Italian Renaissance style, three blocks northwest on Calle Freire. A few blocks further on, the Norris Brothers steam locomotive and carriages used in the inaugural journey between Copiapó and Caldera in 1851 can be seen at the **Universidad de Atacama**; also at the university is an example of an old *trapiche* (see box page 154). Nearby, in the old railway station on Calle Ramírez, is the **Museo Ferroviario**, which has photos and artefacts from the railway age, but it opens only sporadically.

Copiapó

Sleeping	
Archi 1	
Chagall 2	
Copa de Oro 21	
Corona del Inca 3	
Diego de Almeida 4	
Duna Apart Hotel 23	
El Sol 5	
España 6	
Inti 8	
La Casona 9	
Miramonti 10	
Montecatini I 11	
Montecatini II 7	
Palace 12	
Residencial Benbow 13	
Residencial Casagrande 14	
Residencial Chacabuco 22	
Residencial Nuevo Chañarcillo 15	
Residencial Eli 16	
Residencial Nuevo Chañarcillo 5	
Residencial Rocío 17	
Residencial Rodríguez 5	
Residencial Torres 18	
Roca D'Argento 19	
San Francisco de la Selva 20	

Eating
Bavaria 1
Café Colombiano 8
Chifa Hao Hwa 2
Don Elias 3
Empanadopolis 6
Entre Yuntas 7
La Pizza di Tito 4
La Vitrola 8
Nuevo Quincho 5

0 metres 200
0 yards 200

On the other side of the city, 3 km southeast of the centre, the **Santuario de la Candelaria** is the site of two churches, the older built in 1800, the other in 1922; inside the latter is the Virgen de la Candelaria, a stone image discovered whole in the Salar de Maricunga by the muleteer Mariano Caro in 1780. The Virgin is said to protect miners, hence her local importance, and is celebrated in the Fiesta de la Candelaria every February (see page 190).

Around Copiapó

The **Centro Metalúrgico Incaico** is a largely reconstructed Inca bronze foundry, the most complete example in existence, 90 km up the Copiapó Valley by paved road. Further up the valley at Km 98 is the 19th-century **Aquaducto de Amolana**, hidden 300 m off the main road. There is no accommodation in the nearby villages of Valle Hermoso or Las Juntas but there are *cabañas* at Los Loros, which was the site of a clinic for pulmonary diseases at the beginning of the 20th century, attended by the rich and unhealthy from Santiago.

South of Copiapó, about 59 km on the Pan-American Highway, is a signpost for the turning to the ghost town and former silver mine of **Chañarcillo**, along a very poor road. When Chañarcillo was at its peak, the town had a population of 7000; the mine was closed in 1875 but the tips have been reworked and this has destroyed many of the ruins. Now that the silver has gone, only a few goatherds live here among the ruins of dry stone walls. Note there are dozens of dangerously unmarked and unprotected mineshafts, and if you have an accident you are far from help.

East to Paso San Francisco ●▲ ▸▸ pp188-191.

The Argentine border can be crossed at **Paso San Francisco** (4726 m), which is situated just north of **Ojos del Salado** (see below). The pass can be reached by three poor *ripio* roads (high-clearance vehicle necessary) from Copiapó and by another *ripio* road that runs south and east from El Salvador. All these routes meet up near the northern sector of the **Parque Nacional Tres Cruces** (see below). The road from El Salvador meets the main *camino internacional* from Copiapó near the Salar de Maricunga, 96 km west of Paso San Francisco. The other two routes from Copiapó are branches off the *camino internacional*: the first forks off 10 km east of the Copiapó-Diego de Almagro road and continues southeast through the Quebrada San Miguel to reach the Laguna del Negro Francisco in the southernmost sector of the Parque Nacional Tres Cruces, before turning north. This is a very poor road, where drivers can easily get lost. The second runs through the Quebrada de Paipote and then on through the northernmost sector of the park. Travellers taking either of these alternatives en route to Argentina should note that they will need to deviate north to pass through the Chilean immigration post at the Salar de Maricunga (see page 187). Before setting off it is advisable to speak to the *carabineros* in Copiapó as they will be able to give you information about the state of the various roads.

Climbing Ojos del Salado

Ojos del Salado is considered to be the third highest peak in the Americas and the highest active volcano in the world. Its true height is still under debate, with estimates ranging from 6864 m to 6893 m. Most experts believe the latter figure is more accurate, and a definitive survey is planned in the near future. A permit is required to climb it, available free from the **Dirección de Fronteras y Límites** ① *Bandera 52, piso 4, T02-6714110, F6971909*, taking two or three days to issue. Permits can also be arranged at short notice from the **Sernatur** office in Copiapó. The ascent is best attempted between January and March, though it is possible between November and April. In November, December and April it can be hit by the *Invierno Boliviano*, a particularly nasty weather pattern coming from the northeast. Temperatures have been known to drop to -40°C with high winds up to 150 km per hour.

Access to the volcano is via a turning off the main Chile-Argentina road at the former **Hostería Murray** (burned down). Base camp for the climb is at the old Argentine frontier post (4500 m). There are two *refugios*: **Refugio Atacama** (four to six beds) at 5100 m and **Refugio Tejos** (better, 12 beds) at 5750 m. The spur to the former is not easy to find, but can be reached with a high clearance 4WD vehicle. From **Refugio Tejos** it is 10 to 12 hours' climb to the summit. The climb is not very difficult (approximately grade three), except the last 50 m, which is moderate climbing on rock to the crater rim and summit. Take large quantities of water for the ascent. Guides and equipment can be hired in Copiapó.

Parque Nacional Tres Cruces

Extending over 59,082 ha, this newly designated park is in two sectors: the largest part, the northern sector, includes **Laguna Santa Rosa** and parts of the **Salar de Maricunga**, an expanse of salt flats covering 8300 ha at 3700 m; the southern sector covers the area around **Laguna del Negro Francisco**, a salt lake covering 3000 ha at 4200 m. The lakes are home to some 47 bird species, including all three species of flamingo found in Chile, as well as guanacos and vicuñas. The park is stunningly beautiful and, owing to its isolation, rarely visited. The park administration ⓘ *summer only 0830-1230, 1400-1800, US$8 (US$5 for Chileans)*, is located at a *refugio* southeast of Laguna del Negro Francisco.

Paso San Francisco

Although officially open all year, this pass is liable to closure after snow in winter. Call T052-1981009 for reports of the road's condition. **Chilean customs** ⓘ *0900-1900, US$2 per vehicle for crossing Sat, Sun and holidays*, are near the Salar de Maricunga, 100 km west of the border. From here a *ripio* road continues along the southern shore of Laguna Verde, where there are thermal springs and a reasonable campsite, en route to the border. On the Argentine side, a paved road continues to Tinogasta. The **Argentine border post** ⓘ *0700-1900*, is at Fiambalá, 210 km beyond the border, but there is also a police post at La Gruta, 24 km after the border.

Caldera and around 🍴⚡🏔🚌 ▸▸ *pp188-191. Colour map 2, B2.*

Caldera, 73 km northwest of Copiapó, is a port and terminal for the loading of iron ore, with a population of 12,000. In the late 19th century, it was a major railway engineering centre and was the terminus of the first railway in South America. The train station has recently been restored to its former glory and now houses a cultural centre and tourist information office (summer only, T052-316076). The **Iglesia de San Vicente de Paul** (1862), on the revamped Plaza de Armas, was built by English carpenters working for the railway company. Caldera is home to the earliest non-denominational cemetery in Chile, where vestiges of a prouder past can be glimpsed in the crumbling graves of European settlers.

Bahía Inglesa, 6 km south of Caldera and 6 km west of the Pan-American Highway, is popular with Chileans for its beautiful white sandy beaches and unpolluted, crystal-clear sea. Although the bay is now dominated by an oyster farm, this is not too noticeable from the beach. The water in this sheltered bay is warmer than around the neighbouring coast and it is safe to swim. Bahía Inglesa is rather expensive and can get crowded in January and February and at weekends, but off season makes a perfect, deserted retreat. It was originally known as Puerto del Inglés after the visit in 1687 of the English pirate, Edward Davis.

● Sleeping

Copiapó and around *p184, map p185*
There is often a shortage of accommodation in Copiapó. Advance booking advisable. All the below are in Copiapó.
AL Duna Apart Hotel, O'Higgins 760, T052-240203, www.dunapart.cl. Comfortable cosy apartments – bathroom, living room, fully equipped kitchen (no oven but there is a microwave). Cheaper if you ask for a *doble factura*.
AL-A Miramonti, Freire 731, T/F052-210440, www.miramonti.cl. All facilities but slightly cold atmosphere. Book in advance as it fills up with business travellers. That said, there are occasionally cheap walk-in dollar rates. The suites have hydromassage baths.
A Chagall, O'Higgins 760, T052-213775, www.chagall.cl. The best of the executive hotels, central, some rooms with king-size beds and desk, modern fittings, internet, spacious lounge and bar open to public. Recommended.
A Diego de Almeida, Plaza Prat, T052-212075, www.diegodealmagrohoteles.cl. Cable TV, good restaurant, spacious bar, pool.
A-B Montecatini II, Atacama 374, T052-211516. Not much character but spacious and comfortable. Cable TV and patio. 10% discount for cash payment. Cheaper when paying in US$.
B Hotel Copa de Oro, Infante 530, T052-211309, hotelcopadeoro@hotmail.com. Big rooms with all mod cons.
B Hotel San Francisco de la Selva, Los Carrera 525, T052-217013, hosanco@entel chile.net. Nice rooms, central, with breakfast, modern cafeteria/bar.
B Inti Hotel, Freire 180, T/F052-217756. Nice modern rooms, friendly.
B La Casona, O'Higgins 150, T052-217278, www.lacasonahotel.cl. Clean, friendly, desert colours, restaurant and bar, internet access plug in rooms, good beds, cable TV, pleasant garden, more like home than a hostel. A little overpriced. English spoken. Cheaper for foreigners paying in US dollars. Recommended.
B Rocca D'Argento, Maipú 580, T052-218744, hotelrocca@atacamachile.com. Ugly exterior. Rooms vary in size. Some very spacious doubles are good value, but there are some overpriced pokey singles. Cable TV, heating, tours and car hire arranged, better prices in dollars, worth bargaining off season.

B-C Corona del Inca, Las Heras 54, T052-217019, F213831. With breakfast, big rooms, friendly, quiet, good value, worth bargaining. No restaurant.
B-C España, Yerbas Buenas 571, T/F052-217198. With breakfast, friendly, small rooms, a little overpriced.
B-C Montecatini I, Infante 766, T052-211363, h.montecatini@terra.cl. Large rooms around beautiful courtyard, swimming pool. Some smaller rooms without TV are cheaper. Helpful, best value in this price bracket. The only downside is that the beds have foam mattresses. Cheaper to pay in dollars. Ask for tax free rate.
C El Sol, Rodríguez 550, T/F052-215672. Smallish rooms leading off from a central corridor. Rooms with bath and cable TV, quiet, breakfast included, parking.
C Palace, Atacama 741, T052-212852. Comfortable, breakfast extra, parking, central, nice patio. Good value.
D Residencial Chacabuco, Salas 451, T052-213428. Cheaper rooms with shared bath, with breakfast, simple, quiet, clean.
D Residencial Nuevo Chañarcillo, Rodríguez 540, T052-212368. **E** singles. Dozens of rooms branching off from a seemingly endless corridor, some with bath. Bright central patio. Minimal service, a little stuffy.
E Hotel Archi, Vallejos 111, T/F052-212983. Without bath, ugly setting, convenient for bus terminal.
E Residencial Benbow, Rodríguez 541, T052-217634. Basic rooms, some with bath, but the best value of the many *residenciales* on this part of Rodríguez. Usually full of mine workers. Excellent value full-board deals.
E Residencial Casagrande, Infante 525, T052-244450. **F-G** singles. Tumbledown colonial building with covered portico around a central courtyard with bougainvillea. Cluttered, with TV in big rooms. Extremely grumpy unhelpful owner, but browbeaten staff more friendly.
E Residencial Eli, Maipú 739, T052-219650. **F-G** Singles. Friendly, simple rooms, good beds, decent choice.
E Residencial Rocío, Yerbas Buenas 581, T052-215360. **F** singles. Some rooms with bath and cable TV, common area, clean, patio. Good budget option. Recommended.
E Residencial Rodríguez, Rodríguez 528, T052-212861. **F-G** singles. Basic, poky rooms, good *comedor*.

E **Residencial Torres**, Atacama 230, T052-240727. F-G singles. Without bath, hot water, friendly, quiet. Recommended.
F-G **Residencial Chañarcillo**, O'Higgins y Vallejos, T052-213281. With breakfast, central, parking, rooms with and without bath. Price per person.

There are also several cheap places (**F-G**) per person around the local bus terminal.

East to Paso San Francisco *p186*
F 2 **CONAF** *refugios* in the Parque Nacional Tres Cruces: one southeast of Laguna Santa Rosa, very basic, another southeast of Laguna del Negro Francisco, with bunk beds, heating, electric light and hot water. Price per person.

Caldera and around *p187*
AL **Rocas de Bahía**, El Morro 888, Bahía Inglesa, T052-316005, www.rocasdebahia.cl. 4-star hotel with all facilities, good restaurant and swimming pool on the roof.
A **Hostería Puerta del Sol**, Wheelwright 750, Caldera, T052-315205, F315507. *Cabañas* with kitchen, all mod cons, laundry service, view over bay.
A **Los Jardines de Bahía Inglesa**, Av Copiapó, Bahía Inglesa, T052-315359. *Cabañas*, open all year, good beds, comfortable.
A **Portal del Inca**, Carvallo 945, Caldera, T052-315252. Fully equipped 4-star *cabañas* with kitchen, English spoken, restaurant not bad, order breakfast on previous night.
A-B **Cabañas**, Playa Paraíso, Av Costanera 6000, Bahía Inglesa, T09-8867666, www.cabanasparaiso.cl. On the shore about 6 km south of town. Cosy cabins with kitchenettes and barbecues. Idyllic location, almost like having your own private beach. No public transport, but the owners usually go into town once a day. Reiki and massages available. Recommended.
B **Blanco Encalada**, Copiapó y Pacífico, Bahía Inglesa, T/F052-315345. Comfortable, some rooms with balcony, roof terrace with great view, English spoken. Cheap per person deals in low season. Recommended.
B **Costanera**, Wheelwright 543, Caldera, T/F052-316007. Takes credit cards, simple rooms, friendly.
B **El Coral**, Av El Morro, Bahía Inglesa, T052-315331. Overlooking sea, good seafood, open all year. Also *cabañas*.

C **Domo Chango Chile**, Av El Morro 610, Bahía Inglesa, T052-316168. Comfortable accommodation in geodesic domes overlooking the bay. Decent restaurant and lots of activities offered, including surfing, bike rental and tours. English spoken. Recommended.
D **Restaurant Hospedaje Mastique**, Panamericana Norte Km 880, outside Caldera. Cabin accommodation, hot showers, breakfast included, comfortable.
F **Residencial Millaray**, main plaza, Cousiño 331, Caldera, T052-315528. Friendly, good value, basic. Price per person.

Camping
Camping Bahía Inglesa, Playa Las Machas, T052-315424. Price per site. Also fully equipped *cabañas* for up to 6 persons.

❶ Eating

Copiapó and around *p184, map p185*
♦♦ **Bavaria**, Plaza Prat. Pricey restaurant upstairs, cafeteria downstairs (open 0800 for breakfast), *salón de té* around the corner in Los Carrera.
♦♦ **Chifa Hao Hwa**, Yerbas Buenas 334, also Colipí 340. One of several reasonably priced *chifas* (Chinese restaurants) in town. Terse service and the typical mix of muzak and western pop, but the food is decent.
♦♦ **Entre Yuntas**, Vallejos 226. Somewhat rustic but cosy. Peruvian/Chilean food, friendly service, live music Fri and Sat nights.
♦♦ **La Carreta**, Av Copayapu. Expensive *parrillada*.
♦♦-♦ **La Vitrola**, Cosmocentro Plaza Real, 2nd floor. Self-service lunch buffet, good range, reasonably priced, good views overlooking Plaza Prat.
♦♦ **Nuevo Restaurante Quincho**, Atacama 109. Range of meat, dancing on Fri and Sat.
♦ **Benbow**, Rodríguez 543. Very good value *almuerzo*, extensive menu. Recommended.
♦ **Don Elias**, Los Carrera y Yerbas Buenas. Excellent seafood, popular. Recommended.
♦ **Empanadopolis**, Colipí 310. Snack bar serving *empanadas*, pizza, fresh juice. Eat in or takeaway. Cheap and good.
♦ **La Pizza di Tito**, Chacabuco 710, T052-240253. Pizzas (bog standard crispy bases but good toppings), sandwiches, cheap *almuerzos*.

There are several juice bars dotted around the town centre.

Café Colombiano, Cosmocentro Plaza Real 215. Real coffee, snacks, overlooks Plaza Prat, popular meeting place.

Don Gelato, Colipí 506 (northeast corner of plaza). Real coffee, ice cream and fresh juices.

El Bramador, Paseo Julio Aciares (part of Casa de la Cultura). Real coffee, good meeting place. Recommended.

Panadería La Industrial, O'Higgins 984. Good cakes.

Caldera and around *p187*

₸₸₸-₸₸ Belvedere, Hotel Rocas de Bahía, Bahía Inglesa. Reasonably elegant Italian/Chilean restaurant, with good service and views.

₸₸ Chango Chile, El Moro 610, on the Costanera, Bahía Inglesa, T052-316168. Chilean/international fusion served in a geodesic dome with views over the bay. Good wine list.

₸₸ El Pirón de Oro, Cousiño 218, Caldera. Good but not cheap.

₸₸ El Plateao, Costanera, Bahía Inglesa. Local specialities, mostly fish and shellfish, friendly service, recommended.

₸₸ El Teatro, Gana 12, Caldera, T052-316768. Generally considered to be the best restaurant in Caldera.

₸ Miramar, Gana 090, Caldera. Good seafood at the pier.

❶ Bars and clubs

Copiapó and around *p184, map p185*

Arte Pub, Maipú 641. Intimate bar with wooden interior and tables on 2 levels. Live music every night from 2300, ranging from rock to jazz. US$2 cover charge. Also serves cheap healthy meals at lunchtime.

Costa Cuervos and **Kamikaze**, Circun-valación. 2 discos on the edge of town.

La Tabla, Los Carrera y Salas. Good pub, live music, very popular with locals.

❷ Entertainment

Copiapó and around *p184, map p185*

Alhambra, Atacama 455, T052-212187. Copiapó's single-screen cinema.

Casa de la Cultura, Plaza Prat, T052-217866. This green colonial-style mansion has a

gallery devoted to plastic arts, occasional film screenings and concerts and also organizes workshops. An annexe houses the Café El Bramador, and hosts theatre productions and recitals.

Club de Ajedrez, Plaza Prat. Join the locals for a friendly game of chess on the south side of the plaza.

Sala de Cámara, M A Matta 292. New cultural centre hosting exhibitions, concerts, seminars.

❸ Festivals and events

Copiapó and around *p184, map p185*

Feb Fiesta de la **Candelaria** begins on the **1st Sun in Feb** and lasts for 9 days. Up to 50,000 pilgrims and 3000 dancers congregate at the Santuario de la Candelaria in Copiapó (see page 186) from all over the north of Chile for this important religious festival.

▲▲ Activities and tours

Copiapó and around *p184, map p185*

A full list of guides, specializing in mountain trekking and climbing, is available from Sernatur in Copiapó (see page 184).

Alejandro Aracena, Tierra Amarilla, near Copiapó, T052-320098. Personal tours of small working mines, starting from a town in the valley. You must provide your own transport.

Aventurismo, Mall Plaza Real, oficina 212, Copiapó, T052-235340, www.aventurismo.cl. Mountaineering experts, concession holders for Ojos del Salado, experienced in trips to all of the higher peaks in the region.

Cristian Irribarren, T099-884 5836. Sandboarding trips. Based in Copiapó.

Gran Atacama, Mall Plaza Real, oficina B122, Copiapó, T052-219271, www.granatacama.cl. The largest of the regional operators. Offers trips throughout the region, horse riding, mountain climbing, altiplano trips etc.

East to Paso San Francisco *p186*

See also above for details of tour operators based in Copiapó operating in the area.

Azimut 360, Arzobispo Casanova 3, Providencia, Santiago, T02-7358034, www.azimut.cl. Based in the capital, this French-run adventure and ecotourism company offers mountaineering expeditions to Ojos del Salado and Incahuasi.

Caldera and around *p187*
Océano Aventura, Gabriela Mistral 57,
Caldera, T099-5469848. Diving trips.

⊖ Transport

Air
Desierto de Atacama Airport is 45 km north
west of Copiapó and 15 km east of Caldera.
LanChile, Colipí 484, Copiapó, outside the
mall, T052-213512, airport T052-214360.
Buses Casther (T052-218889) has a minibus
service to Copiapó (US$9 per person). Book in
advance. Taxis to Caldera. LanChile flies daily
to/from **Santiago**, also to **El Salvador**.

Bus and colectivo
Local Although the major companies run
between Copiapó and **Caldera**, the cheapest
services are provided by Buses Recabarren
and Buses Casther, every 30 mins, US$1,
leaving from the street 1 block west of the
main bus terminal in Copiapó. *Colectivos* to
Caldera also leave from this point. They are
much quicker than the bus, cost US$2.50, and
will take you to **Bahía Inglesa** for an extra
US$0.75. Otherwise, *colectivos* between **Bahía
Inglesa** and **Caldera** cost US$1.50. There are
also buses in summer for US$0.50. *Colectivos*
run from **Copiapó** to **Chañaral** and **Vallenar**
and serve the upper valley as far as the
Nantoco; you will have to arrange a price if
you wish to go higher up the valley. Note that
there are no public transport connections to
the **Parque Nacional de Tres Cruces**.
Long distance Copiapó's main bus
terminal is 3 blocks southwest of the centre
on Freire y Chacabuco. To **Santiago** 12 hrs,
US$15; to **La Serena** 5 hrs, US$6.50; to

Antofagasta 8 hrs, US$13; to **Calama**
11 hrs, US$17; to **San Pedro de Atacama**
13 hrs, US$19. **Pullman Bus** has its own
terminal next door, where there is a good
left-luggage store. Turbus and Tas Choapa
are 1 block away in Chañarcillo.
There are bus services from Caldera to
Santiago, several daily, and to **Antofagasta**, 7
hrs, US$11, although to travel north it may be
better to take a bus to **Chañaral** (Inca-bus
US$2), then change.

Car and bicycle
The following companies are in Copiapó.
Car hire Avis, Peña 102, T/F052-213966.
Budget, Freire 4 66, T052-218802. Flota
Verschae, Luis Flores y Copayapu, T052-
227898. Hertz, Copayapu 173, T052-213522.
Rodaggio, Colipí 127, T052-212153. **Bike
repairs** Bicicletería Biman, Las Carrera
998A, T052-217391. Sales, repairs, parts.

⊕ Directory

Copiapó and around *p184, map p185*
Banks Cambio Fides, Mall Plaza Real, oficina
B123. Mon-Fri 1000-1400, 1600-1900 (closed
Sat and Sun). Reasonable rates.There are
several banks with Redbanc ATMs around the
plaza as well as ATMs in the Plaza Real
shopping centre and supermarkets. **Dentist**
Eduardo Cáceres, Salas 385, T052-211902.
Hospital Los Carrera s/n, T052-212023.
Laundry Lavandería Añañucas, Chañarcillo
612. **Internet** Several in and around the
centre. US$0.60 per hr. **Post office** Los
Carrera y Colipí, on Plaza Prat. Mon-Fri
1000-1400, 1600-2000. **Telephone** Several
centros de llamados in town centre.

Salado Valley

*It is 93 km north from Caldera to Chañaral, the port of the valley of the Río Salado. Until
Chañaral, there are some vestiges of vegetation in the desert, but thereafter there is
nothing but unremitting pampa until Antofagasta. The course of the Río Salado itself is
always dry and the valley is less fertile and prosperous than the Copiapó or Huasco
valleys to the south.* ⏵⏵ *For Sleeping, Eating and other listings, see pages 193-194.*

Chañaral → *Colour map 2, B2. Population: 12,000.*
This is a small, sad town with wooden houses perched on the hillside. In its heyday,
Chañaral was the processing centre for ore from the nearby copper mines of El Salado
and Las Animas, but those mines have declined, and the town now ekes out a living

processing the ores from other mines in the interior. Stone walkways climb up the desert hills behind the main street, Merino Jarpa, reaching platforms where you'll find several stone benches from which to watch the sea; behind the benches are religious murals daubed with the graffiti of impoverished, angry urban youth. There is a beautiful and often deserted white-sand beach just beyond the Panamericana, created by waste minerals from the old copper processing plant, and stained green by its pollution. There is an ongoing project to cover the beach with clean sand. Swimming is dangerous here.

Museo de Historia Natural ① *Buín 818, Mon-Fri 0900-1300 and 1530-1900, free*, has exhibits on the mineralogy, hydrobiology and entomology of the region; interesting for naturalists. There is a municipal **tourist information** kiosk on the Panamericana, south of town, in summer.

There are two alternative routes from Copiapó to Chañaral: west to Caldera and then north along the coast, 167 km; or the inland route, known as the Inca de Oro, via Diego de Almagro and then west to meet the Panamericana near Chañaral, 212 km.

Parque Nacional Pan de Azúcar
① *CONAF office, Caleta Pan de Azúcar, daily 0830-1800 (but don't expect anyone to be there at lunchtime), park admission US$6 (US$3 for Chileans).*
This jewel of a national park north of Chañaral manages to combine four incredibly contrasting sets of geographical and ecological features in a strech of land just 20 km from east to west. Offshore, the **Isla Pan de Azúcar** is home to Humboldt penguins and other sea birds, while fantastic white-sand beaches line the coast; they are popular at weekends in summer. A series of valleys run west to east. In pre-Columbian times they were inhabited by the Chango, a semi-nomadic coastal people. Occasionally archaeological artefacts such as pottery and arrowheads can be found. Dominating the park are coastal hills rising to 800 m, providing spectacular views. To the east the park extends into the desert. The park is inhabited by 103 species of birds as well as guanacos and foxes, and a sea lion colony can be observed by following the signs marked *loberías* from the park entrance. The *camanchaca* (coastal fog) ensures that the park has a unique set of flora that belies its desert location; after rain tall *alstroemerias* of many colours bloom in some of the gullies. The park is also one of the best places in Chile to see the flowering desert (see box, page 182), as well as extremely rare species of cacti.

There are two entrances to the park: either along a side road 20 km from the Pan-American Highway, 45 km north of Chañaral, or by a good secondary road north from Chañaral, 28 km from the village of **Caleta Pan de Azúcar**. The **CONAF** office here has an exhibition room and cactarium. Basic maps are available, as well as entrance tickets to the park. It's a 2½-hour walk from the office to a *mirador* with extensive views over the southern section but, to experience the park fully, transport is needed. Although the penguins are sometimes visible from the mainland, for a closer look take a boat trip round Isla Pan de Azúcar from Caleta, US$8.50 per person (minimum total US$85).

Towards El Salvador → *Colour map 2, A2.*
Some 67 km from Chañaral on the El Salvador road is the smaller mining town of **Diego de Almagro**. About 12 km north of here, on a mining track through the desert, is the interesting **Pampa Austral** project, where Codelco, the state mining company, has used water resulting from the process of extracting copper from nearby mines to irrigate the desert, producing a 4-ha extension of plantations in the middle of the desert *pampa*.

El Salvador itself is a modern town, built near one of the biggest copper mines in Chile. Located 120 km east of Chañaral, just north of the valley of the Río Salado, it is reached by a road that branches off the Pan-American Highway, 12 km east of Chañaral. All along the valley people are extracting metal ore from the water with primitive settling tanks. Further east, 60 km by unpaved road is the **Salar de Pedernales**, salt flats 20 km in diameter and covering 30,000 ha at an altitude of 3350 m, where pink flamingos can be seen.

Situated 25 km off the Pan-American Highway and 146 km north of Chañaral, Taltal is the only town between Chañaral and Antofagasta, a distance of 420 km. Along Avenida Prat are several wooden buildings, including the impressive church, dating from the late 19th century when Taltal prospered as a mineral port of 20,000 people, exporting nitrates from 21 mines in the area. The town is now a fishing port with a mineral processing plant. **Museo Augusto Capdeville** ① *Av Prat 5*, free, is a good local museum in the former *gobernación*, with rooms on prehistory, local history and the saltpetre industry, European immigration, and an exhibition on the Paranal observatory. The curator is very friendly. On Calle O'Higgins is an old steam engine with a pair of carriages. The pleasant tree-lined plaza is laid out in the form of the Union Jack in honour of the historical importance of the British community in the town. Just north of town is the cemetery, where the European influence can clearly be seen.

Excellent and deserted beaches line the coast both north and south of Taltal, the best known of which is **Cifuncho**, some 40 km south. There's no accommodation here, but camping is easy. North along the coast by 72 km is the **Quebrada El Médano**, a gorge with ancient rock paintings along the upper valley walls.

⊜ Sleeping

Chañaral *p191*
B Hostería Chañaral, Müller 268, T052-480050. Slightly dated, but spacious and attentive service, decent restaurant in beautiful dining room, pool room, parking.
B Portal Atacama, Merino Jarpa 1420, T052-489799, portalatacama@hotmail.com. Cold and disinterested staff, but newly refitted to a decent standard. Rooms with bath, TV. Also apartments, AL, sleeping 6.
B-C Nuria, Costanera 302, T052-480903. With bath and breakfast, parking, friendly, but a little basic and overpriced. Worth bargaining.
C Carmona, Costanera 402, T052-480522. With bath and TV, friendly, decent value.
C-D Hostal Sutivan, Comercio 365, T052-489123, hostalsutivan@terra.cl. E-F singles. Very friendly, clean, nice rooms, good beds, excellent value. Rooms with or without bath. Highly recommended. Also arranges tours to Pan de Azúcar.
C-D Hotel Jiménez, Merino Jarpa 551, T052-480328. Friendly, patio with lots of birds, clean rooms, modern bathrooms (some shared), good-value restaurant, convenient for **Pullman Bus**. Recommended.
D Residencial Molina, Pinto 583, T052-480075. F singles. Rooms in a family home. Reasonably basic, but very friendly. Owner Sergio does very good tours of the park and offers good-value lodging plus tour combos.

E-F La Marina, Merino Jarpa 562. G singles. Basic, many parakeets, no hot water.

Parque Nacional Pan de Azúcar *p192*
AL-A CONAF cabañas, T052-213404 (reservations advised). Perfectly placed *cabañas* on a deserted beach behind the *caleta*. However, slightly run-down, poor beds and price for 2 people same as for 6. Some of the fishermen in the Caleta let out rooms. They are generally quite basic and around the F per person range.

Camping
There's a campsite on the beach with showers and 20 litres of drinking water. Price per person. Book through **CONAF**.

Towards El Salvador *p192*
AL Camino del Inca, El Tofo 330, El Salvador, T052-475252. The upmarket choice.
C-G Hostería El Salvador, Potrerillos 003, El Salvador, T052-475749. Cheaper rooms here are without bath.

Taltal *p193*
B Cabañas Caleta Hueso, Camino a Paposo 2 km from Taltal, T055-612251, m.finger@entelchile.net. Good cabins.
C Hostería Taltal, Esmeralda 671, T055-611173, btay@entelchile.net. Sea view, excellent restaurant, good value *almuerzo*.
C Mi Tampi, O'Higgins 138, T055-613605. Recommended.

C-D **Hostal del Mar**, Carrera 250, T/F055-611612. Modern, comfortable.

F-G **Residencial Paranal**, O'Higgins 106. Next door to **Hostal del Mar**. Good. Price per person.

G **San Martín**, Martínez 279, T055-611088, F268159. Without bath, good *almuerzo*.

🍴 Eating

Chañaral *p191*

🍴 **Capely**, Merino Jarpa 1140, T052-480477. Simple, but slightly more upmarket than the rest. Serves good fish and usual Chilean fare.

🍴-🍴 **Restaurant Nuria**, Yungay 434, on the plaza, T052-489199. Good fresh seafood, clean, friendly service, open at night.

🍴 **Restaurante de los Pescadores**, La Caleta. Good fish, clean, cheap.

🍴 **Rincón Porteño**, Merino Jarpa 567, T052-480070. Good and inexpensive sandwiches, etc.

There are also a couple of restaurants on the Panamericana, open 24 hrs.

Parque Nacional Pan de Azúcar *p192*

In Jan and Feb, there is a restaurant in **Caleta**. Otherwise, buy fish straight from the boats at around 1700 Tue-Sun and prepare it yourself. Take all other food with you.

Taltal *p193*

🍴 **Club Social Taltal**, Torreblanca 162. Excellent, good value. The former club of the British community, with poker room, billiard table and ballroom.

🍴 **Caverna**, Martínez 247. Good seafood.

🍴 **Las Brisas**, by the *caleta*. Large servings, good and cheap.

🎉 Festivals and events

Chañaral *p191*

15 Jul The people of Chañaral celebrate the **Fiesta de la Virgen del Carmen** (the same fiesta for which La Tirana is so famous, see page 238). This is a scaled-down version of La Tirana, but still involves plenty of drumming and dancing around the plaza. The religious groups are dressed in elaborate costumes and vie with one another for the loudest band and the most complex dance; it's a moving manifestation of the faith of this impoverished but proud town.

▲ Activities and tours

Chañaral *p191*

Chango Turismo, Panamericana Norte s/n, T052-480484, changoturismo@hotmail.com. Offers tours to the park as well as kayak trips to the island (entirely at your own risk).

Sergio Molina, T09-720077, takes very interesting and informative day tours of the Parque Nacional Pan de Azúcar. He is often found outside the **Pullman Bus** terminal.

🚌 Transport

Chañaral *p191*

There is no main bus terminal. The **Pullman Bus** terminal is at Los Baños y Costanera, **Tur Bus** is on the Panamericana, opposite Copec. Frequent services to **Antofagasta**, US$12 *semi cama*, 5 hrs, and **Santiago**, US$21. To **Copiapó**, US$4. To **Taltal**, 3 daily, US$5; *colectivos* to Copiapó depart from Merino Jarpa y Los Baños, US$5, try to leave early in the morning.

Parque Nacional Pan de Azúcar *p192*

Taxi from Chañaral, US$15. Both tour operators also offer a transport-only service. Gates control vehicles in the park, but keys are available from the **CONAF** office. There are fines for driving in restricted areas.

Towards El Salvador *p192*

Lan Chile flies to/from **Santiago** and **Copiapó**. There are **Pullman Bus** services daily to **Santiago**, **Copiapó** and **Chañaral**.

Taltal *p193*

Bus services to **Santiago**, 3 a day; to **Antofagasta**, Tur Bus, US$7. There are many more bus services from the Pan-American Highway (taxi US$10).

① Directory

Chañaral *p191*

Banks Poor rates for cash in BCI on the plaza. Nowhere to change TCs; Redbanc ATMs in the supermarket and ESSO; in summer, money exchange is offered at the ironmonger's, Consuelo y Merino Jarpa. **Telephone** CTC, Merino Jarpa 506; ENTEL Merino Jarpa 700-block, next to the municipal health centre.

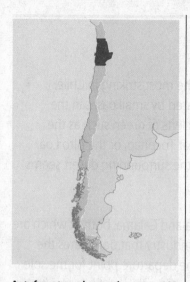

Antofagasta, Calama & San Pedro de Atacama

⦂ Footprint features

Introduction

This desolate region is one of the most striking in Chile. The Atacama Desert is punctuated by small oases in the all-encompassing yellowness; clefts of green such as the beautiful Quebrada de Jere, near Toconao, or the Alto Loa, from where the lifelessness of the surrounding desert seems somehow impossible.

The main cities are Antofagasta and Calama, both of which are service centres for the mining industry that dominates the region's economy. Calama is the departure point for the sole remaining passenger train service in northern Chile, the 'tren de la muerte' to Uyuni in Bolivia. Most visitors, however, head straight to San Pedro de Atacama, an ancient centre of civilization in the region since well before the Spanish conquest, and the base for excursions to spectacular desert landscapes such as the Valle de la Luna and the Salar de Atacama, as well as to the El Tatio geysers and altiplanic lakes. San Pedro is home to one of the north's most important archaeological museums, and excursions can also be made over the er into Bolivia to the Salar de Uyuni and to two beautiful lakes, Laguna Colorada and Laguna Verde.

★ Don't miss...

1 **La Portada** The rock arch near Antofagasta is famous throughout the country, page 200.
2 **Chuquicamata** The enormity of the mine makes for a very interesting trip, page 210.
3 **Quebrada de Jere** A beautiful green oasis that provides a memorable contrast with the desert. The Río Loa, near Lasana, is equally lovely, pages 212 and 221.
4 **Valle de la Luna** Extraordinary desertscape near San Pedro, page 219.
5 **El Tatio geysers** Set at over 4000 m, these are the highest geysers in the world, page 220.
6 **Volcán Licancábur** A popular choice among the many remote tracks through the altiplano that the adventurous and well-equipped trekker might want to take, page 224.

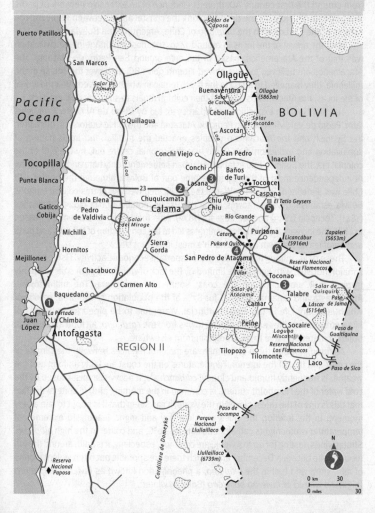

Background

The Atacama Desert stretches 1255 km north from the Río Copiapó to the Chilean border with Peru. The Cordillera de la Costa, at its highest in this region (the highest peak is Cerro Vicuña (3114 m), runs close to the coast, an inhospitable and spectacular cliff face rising sheer from the waters to a height of up to 900 m. Below this cliff, on the edge of the Pacific, is a ledge on which the city of Antofagasta and some smaller towns are situated. In the eastern branch of the Andes, several peaks rise to around 6000 m: Llullaillaco (6739 m), Socompa (6051 m), Licancábur (5916 m), Ollagüe (5863 m). The western branch of the Andes ends near Calama. In between these two ranges the Andean Depression includes several salt flats, including the Salar de Atacama and the smaller Salar de Ascotán.

Before the Spanish conquest, this part of Chile was populated both on the coast and inland. The Chango people fished in the Pacific out of boats made from the pelts of sea lions. They traded fish with the peoples of the interior, from whom they bought coca leaves and quinoa (the staple grain before the arrival of those from Europe); from around the first century AD, there is evidence of an extensive network of paths and trade routes crossing the desert, linking the coastal areas between Taltal and the estuary of the Río Loa with the *altiplano* of Chile, Argentina and Bolivia.

Until the arrival of the Incas in around 1450, the most important inland civilization was that of the Atacameños, based in the area around San Pedro de Atacama. The Atacameños are believed to have arrived around 9000 BC and, over the course of the millennia, they managed to adapt to the harsh terrain in which they lived. After the arrival of the Incas, the Atacameños adapted their cultural rituals to suit their new masters.

The first Spanish expedition arrived in 1536, led by Diego de Almagro. Four years later, Pedro de Valdivia took San Pedro de Atacama and the fort at Quitor and, thereafter, the Spanish and the Atacameño peoples enacted the familiar and tragic pattern of subjugation and extinction. San Pedro was the colonial centre but, by the end of the colonial era, the Spanish had established urban settlements only here and in Chiu Chiu. At independence most of the region became part of Bolivia, although the border with Chile was ill-defined. Before the War of the Pacific deprived her of this coastal territory, Bolivia established several towns along the Pacific, notably Cobija (1825), Mejillones (1841), Tocopilla (1843) and Antofagasta (1872). After the war, when the territory passed to Chile, the increased exploitation of nitrates led to the construction of railways and ports and Antofagasta's growth into the north's most important city.

These days, mining is by far the most important economic activity. Fishing is also a major industry, with agriculture limited by the lack of water and poor soils to mainly tropical fruit production on the coast south of Antofagasta. The main towns, Antofagasta and Calama, account for 87% of the population of the area, 97.6% of which is urban. Life in the area is artificial. Water has to be piped for hundreds of kilometres to the cities and the mining towns from the *cordillera*; all food and even all building materials have to be brought in from elsewhere.

As throughout northern Chile, there are major differences between the climate of the coast and that of the interior. Temperatures on the coast are fairly uniform and the weather is frequently humid and cloudy; *camanchaca*, a heavy sea mist caused by the cold water of the Humboldt current, is common in the morning and, in spite of the fact that this is one of the driest places in the world, it can seem that it is about to rain at any moment. In the interior, the skies are clear day and night, leading to extremes of temperature; winter nights can often be cold as -10°C, and colder in the high *altiplano*. Strong winds, lasting for up to a week, are common, especially, it is said, around the full moon, while between December and March there are sporadic but often violent storms of rain, snow and hail in the *altiplano*, a phenomenon known as *invierno altiplánico* (highland winter) or *invierno boliviano* (Bolivian winter).

Archaeology of the Atacama

From early times, people settled along the northern coast of Chile, sustained by the food supply from the Pacific Ocean. Since about 7600 BC, fisherfolk and foragers lived in large groups in permanent settlements, such as the Quebrada de Conchas, just to the north of Antofagasta. They fished with fibre nets, sometimes venturing inland to hunt for mammals.

About 2000 years later, the successors of these people, the 'Chinchorros', developed one of the deepest characteristics of Andean cultures, veneration for their ancestors. The role of the dead in the world of the living was vital to the earliest Andean people. As a link between the spiritual and the material world, the ancestor of each local kin group would protect his clan. The expression of these beliefs came in the form of veneration of the ancestors' bodies; sacrifices were made to them, funeral rites were repeated, and precious grave offerings were renewed. In the arid climate of the Atacama, the people observed how bodies were naturally preserved. The skilled practice of mummification was thus developed, over a period of 3000 years, preserving the dead as sacred objects and spiritual protectors.

Another major cultural practice of northern Chile was the use of hallucinogens. Grave remains found in the region, dating from about AD 1000, include leather bags containing organic powder, wooden tablets and snuffer tubes. The tablets and snuffers were often decorated with supernatural figures, such as bird-headed angels, winged humans, star animals and other characters familiar in *altiplano* cultures. Although the origins and function of taking hallucinogens is not known for certain (see page 518), it is thought that the practice may have been brought down to the coast by traders from the highlands. There were also 'medicine men' who travelled throughout the central and south central Andes dispensing the drugs and healing the sick. As with cures practiced in the Andes and Amazonia, it is possible that the drugs were taken as part of religious rituals, and often for a combination of spiritual and physical healing.

Antofagasta → *Colour map 1, C1.*

Situated on the edge of a bay, nearly 700 km south of Arica, Antofagasta is the largest city in northern Chile and the fourth largest in the country (its population numbers 225,316). It is not a terribly attractive place, perhaps only worth stopping at to break a long journey. That said, the combination of the tall mountains and the ocean is dramatic, and after a week in the desert interior it is pleasant to breath the sea air. Apart from the lack of rain, the climate is pleasant; the temperature varies from 16°C in June and July to 24°C in January and February, never falling below 10°C at night. The city's economy depends on the enormous mine at La Escondida in the interior, where 8000 people work, doing week-long shifts at the mine before spending a week in the city; the city's port also acts as the processing point for the copper from La Escondida and Chuquicamata. As well as being the capital of Region II, Antofagasta is also an important commercial centre and the home of two universities. ▶▶ *For Sleeping, Eating and other listings, see pages 202-205.*

Getting there Antofagasta is served by many regular buses from both north and south. All major companies serving the north stop here and there are frequent flights with **LanChile, Aerolíneas del Sur** and **Sky** south to Santiago and north to Calama, Iquique and Arica. Taxis to/from the airport cost US$12 but may be cheaper if ordered from a hotel. For airport transfers, call T055-262727.

Getting around Antofagasta is one of Chile's largest cities, and you may need to take some of the *colectivos* or buses to get to more out-of-the-way places, particularly the discos and bars in the south and the university campuses.

Tourist office ① *Prat 384, in the intendencia on Plaza Colón, T055-451818, infoanto fagasta@sernatur.cl, Mon-Fri 0930-1730, Sat 1000-1400*. There is also a kiosk on Balmaceda near **Hotel Antofagasta** ① *Mon-Fri 0930-1300, 1530-1930, Sat and Sun 0930-1300*, and a kiosk at the airport (open summer only).

Sights

In the main square, **Plaza Colón**, there is a clock tower donated by the British community in 1910. It is a miniature of Big Ben with a carillon that produces similar sounds. Two blocks north of Plaza Colón, near the old port, is the former **Aduana**, built as the Bolivian customs house in Mejillones and moved to its current site after the War of the Pacific. Inside is **Museo Regional de Antofagasta** ① *Balmaceda 2786, www.dibam.cl/subdirec_museos/m_antofagasta/, Tue-Fri 0900-1700, Sat, Sun and holidays 1100-1400, US$1, children half price, free on Sun*, which includes displays on the geology and natural history of the north, as well as sections on the War of the Pacific and the nitrate era. The explanations are in Spanish only. Opposite are the former offices of the **Capitanía del Puerto** (harbourmaster) and the **Resguardo Marítimo** (coastguard).

East of the port are the buildings of the **Antofagasta and Bolivia Railway Company** (FCAB) dating from the 1890s and beautifully restored, but still in use and difficult to visit. These include the former railway station, company offices, workers' housing and the **Museo del Ferrocarril a Bolivia** ① *Bolívar 255, T055-206311, jlyons@fcab.cl (reservations must be made 48 hours in advance)*, which has an interesting collection relating to the history of the Antofagasta-Bolivia railway, with photographs, maps, instruments and furniture. Just north of the port is the **Terminal de Pescadores**, where there are markets selling seafood, fruit and vegetables. Pelicans sit on the fish market roof and sea lions swim in the harbour; there are half-hour tours of the port available from **La Cabaña de Mario** ① *Aníbal Pinto s/n, US$5*.

The former main plaza of the **Oficina Vergara**, a nitrate town built in 1919 and dismantled in 1978, can be seen in the campus of the University of Antofagasta, 4 km south of the centre (take *colectivo* 114 or 333 from the town centre). Also on the university campus is the **Museo Geológico de la Universidad Católica del Norte** ① *Angamos 610, gchong@socompa.ucn, Mon-Fri 0930-1300, 1530-1800, free*. On a hill to the south of town (reached by bus B) are the ruins of **Huanchaca**, a Bolivian silver refinery built after 1868 and closed in 1903. From below, the ruins resemble a fortress rather than a factory.

Excursions

La Portada, 16 km north of the city, is a natural arch with fantastic rock formations that are the symbol of Region II and are often seen on postcards up and down the country. From the main road it is 2 km to the beach which, although beautiful, is too dangerous for swimming. However, a number of bathing beaches are within easy reach.

A windsurfers' paradise, **Juan López**, is 38 km north of Antofagasta. The sea is alive with birds, including Humboldt penguins, especially opposite Isla Santa María. If you have your own transport, follow the road out of Juan López to the beautiful cove at Conchilla. Keep on the track to the end at Bolsico.

Antofagasta

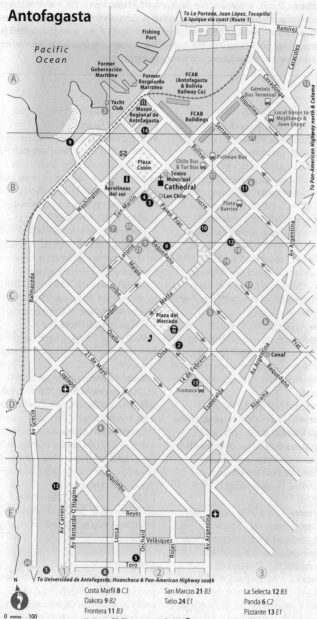

Antofagasta, Calama & San Pedro de Atacama **Antofagasta**

Located on Cerro Paranal, 2600m high in the coastal *cordillera*, 132 km south of Antofagasta, this is, at present, the most powerful **telescope** in the world, although it will soon be usurped by a rival telescope that is currently being built near La Serena. The site at **Cerro Paranal** was chosen as 350 clear nights a year were guaranteed (see also box, page 165). Visits to the public have been discontinued, but for more information on the observatory, see www.eso.org/paranal.

Sleeping

Antofagasta *p199, map p201*
Budget hotels are scarce and of poor quality.
L-AL Antofagasta, Balmaceda 2575, T055-228811, www.hotelantofagasta.cl. 4-star, parking, pool, lovely view of port and city, reasonable, if expensive restaurant (bar serves cheaper snacks), convention centre, beach, rooms facing the city are noisy due to all-night copper trains. Understaffed, not great service. English spoken. Rack rates are overpriced.
A Ancla Inn, Baquedano 516, T055-224814, www.anclainn.cl. One of the city's larger hotels with restaurant, pool and sauna. Reasonably good value but avoid the interior rooms.
A Tatio, Av Grecia 1000, T055-419111. 1970s concrete construction on the main road south out of town by a small beach. All rooms have a balcony and sea view. Cheaper in dollars than pesos. 10 mins' bus ride from the centre.
B Colón, San Martín 2434, T055-261851. With breakfast, quiet, clean, reasonable value.
B Costa Marfil, Prat 950, T055-225569, hotelcostamarfil@yahoo.es. With breakfast, good service, friendly, English spoken. The rooms are clean though some are a little gloomy. The nicer rooms have full bath tubs.
B Horizonte, Latorre 2450, T055- 221886, www.hotelhorizonte.cl. Cable TV, bar, friendly and pleasant, good value though lacking in character, recommended.
B Marsal, Prat 867, T055-268063, www.marsal.cl. Modern, very comfortable, bright and spacious rooms, some with a balcony. Catalan owner, friendly atmosphere, internet access, recommended. **B Rocomar**, Baquedano 810, T055-261139. Decent sized bright rooms with bath. All have rooms out onto the street. With breakfast and room service. A nice option.
B San Marcos, Latorre 2946, T055-251763 . Comfortable rooms with bath and cable TV,

parking, avoid rooms at the back (loud music), slightly overpriced.
C Ciudad de Avila, Condell 2840, T/F055-221040. E singles. Very clean, with bath, TV, basic restaurant, excellent value. Highly recommended considering the alternatives.
C Dakota, Latorre 2425, T055-251749. With breakfast and cable TV, friendly, popular, good value, recommended.
C Frontera, Bolívar 558, T055-281219. Basic but with bath and decent beds. TV in rooms. Breakfast at extra cost. Rooms on upper floors are brighter. Recommended.
C-D Brasil, Ossa 1978, T055-267268. Dark rooms around a central patio. Some rooms have bath and Cable TV. Nothing special.
C-D Residencial El Cobre, Prat 749, T055-225162. E-F Singles. Some rooms with bath. Bright but tatty. Set around a central courtyard.
D Hostal del Norte, Latorre 3162, T055-251265, hostaldelnorte_aft@hotmail.com. Some rooms with bath, clean, comfortable, quiet, brighter annex at the back.
D-E Residencial La Riojanita, Baquedano 464, T055-381056. F singles. Friendly, basic. Older rooms have high ceilings but are run down. Newer rooms with bath but smaller. Not a bad budget option.
E-F Rawaye, Sucre 762, T055-225399. F-G singles. Very basic. Shared bathrooms but rooms have sinks. Hot water morning only, no towels.

Camping
Las Garumas, Km 6, south of the city on the road to Coloso, T055-247763 ext 42. Also cabins (sleep 4), cold showers and beach. For reservations contact Av Angamos 601, Casilla 606. Price per site (bargain for lower price out of season), wild camping is possible on the beach nearby.
Rucamóvil, Km 11, south of the city on the road to Coloso, T055-223929. Open year round.

Around the coast *p200*

A **La Rinconada**, 10 km from Juan López, T055-261139. This is a *cabaña* and camping complex, prices for up to 5 people.

C **Hostería Sandokan**, Juan López, T055-223022. Standard facilities.

Eating

Antofagasta *p199, map p201*

Note that many bars and restaurants are closed on Sun.

†††† **Club de la Unión**, Prat 474, 2 piso, T055-268371. Excellent *almuerzo*, good service, traditional atmosphere.

†††† **Club de Yates**, on the costanera. Exclusive, great sea views and great seafood.

†††† **Marina Club**, Av Ejército 909. Good fish and seafood dishes and a view, expensive but worth it.

†††-†† **Don Karl's**, A Toro 1093, T055- 419401. Decent German cuisine. Decor a poor attempt at rustic elegance.

†† **Bavaria**, Ossa 2424, T055-266567. Plastic Chilean chain serving well-prepared meat and salad dishes. Good service.

†† **D'Alfredo**, Condell 2539. Reasonable pizzas, good value, popular.

†† **El Arriero**, Condell 2644, T055-264371. Grills and traditional hearty criollo food. Good service, cheaper set lunch, popular, live music.

†† **Panda**, Condell 2505, T055-254827. Self- service, all you can eat for US$8. A mixture of Chinese and Chilean dishes on offer.

†† **Pizzante**, Carrera 1857, T055-223344 . Good pasta and seafood. Vegetarian options.

†† **Rincón Oriental**, Washington 2432. Excellent Cantonese, pricey, 'over the top' decor. Recommended.

†† **Tío Jacinto**, Uribe 922. Friendly and serves good seafood.

† **Bundes Schop**, Latorre 2655. Cheap and open late.

† **Chicken House Center**, Latorre 2660. Chicken, beef and daily specials. Open till 2400.

† **El Curicano**, Simon Bolívar 607. Very good value basic set menu lunches and dinners.

† **La Selecta**, Sucre 720. Basic food, but cheap and open for *cenas*.

Above the market are several good places selling cheap seafood *almuerzos* and super-cheap set lunches, including **El**

Mariscal and **Toledo**. Good fish restaurants are also to be found in Terminal Pesquero Centro and at Caleta Coloso, 8 km south.

Cafés

Note that it is difficult to find coffee or breakfast before 0900.

Café Bahía, Prat 474. Open 0900 for real coffee.

Café Haití, Galería, Prat 482. Serves real coffee.

Chez Niko's, Ossa 1951. Bakery, pastelería, good pizzas, *empanadas* and bread.

Heladería Latorre, Baquedano y Latorre. For ice creams.

Along the coast *p200*

†††† **La Portada**, Camino a la portada, T055-226423. Excellent, expensive seafood restaurant and café, open lunchtime only.

Bars and clubs

Antofagasta *p199, map p201*

Thanks to Antofagasta's large student population, the nightlife is thriving. The most popular bars and clubs are 16 km south of the town in Balneario El Huascar. Take Micro 2 from C Matta to get there.

Bar Picadillo, Av Grecia 1000. Lively atmos- phere, serves good food. Recommended.

Castillo Pub, Pasaje Carrera 884. Live music, tasty food and good value *almuerzo*, fun. Recommended.

Pub En Vivo, O'Higgins 1998. Often has live music, popular.

Wally's Pub, Toro 982. British expat-style with pool, darts and beer, closed Sun.

Club Happy, **Entre Negros**, **La Terraza**, **Vox**, Camino Coloso. Popular clubs on the road south along the coast past the universities.

Entertainment

Antofagasta *p199, map p201*

Teatro Municipal, Sucre y San Martín, T055-264919. Modern, state-of-the-art theatre.

Teatro Pedro de la Barra, Condell 2495. Run by University of Antofagasta, this theatre has a regular programme of high-quality plays, reviews, concerts and more; details in press.

✿ Festivals and events

Antofagasta *p199, map p201*
29 Jun The image of **San Pedro**, patron saint of the fishermen, is taken out by launch to the breakwater to bless the first catch of the day.
Last weekend of Oct The city's immigrant communities put on a joint festival on the seafront with national foods, dancing and music.

ⵔ Shopping

Antofagasta *p199, map p201*
Antiques
Galería de Arte Imagen, Uribe 485, sells antiques including artefacts from former nitrate plants.

Bookshops
Librería Andrés Bello, Condell 2421. Excellent selection.
Multilibro, opposite Librería Universitaria. Contemporary Latin American literature, also English-language authors. Recommended.

Food and drink
Korlaert, Ossa y Maipú block. Supermarket.
Las Brisas, Baquedano 750. Supermarket with ATM.
Lider A Pinto, north of the port. Supermarket.
Naturista, Condell 2394. Health food specialist.
Infante, Baquedano 800 block. Supermarket.

Markets
Feria Modelo O'Higgins, Av Pinto, next to the fish market. Excellent fruit and vegetables as well as restaurants.
Fish market, Av Pinto, next to the Feria Modelo.
Municipal market, Matta y Uribe.

▲ Activities and tours

Antofagasta *p199, map p201*
Club de Tenis Antofagasta, Av Angamos 906, T055-247756. Phone for details of temporary membership.
Geyser, Chillán 1245, T055-255278. Genuine sauna plus Turkish bath, hydro-massage, health suite.
Olympic Swimming Pool, Condell y 21 de Mayo. For when the sea is too cold.

Tour operators
Tour companies in Antofagasta offer general adventure tourism, including packages to the Atacama, but, on the whole, it is much better value to book directly with an operator in San Pedro (page 227).
Atacama Wüstereisedienst, Apartado Postal 55, T055-243322. Alex Joseph Valenzuela Thompson guides German-speakers around the area.
Intitour, Baquedano 460, T055-266185, intitour@dtl.net. English-speaking guides.
Tatio Travel, Washington 2513, T055-263532. English spoken, tours arranged for groups or individuals. Highly recommended.
Turismo Nomade, Los Inmigrantes 762, T055-243636, www.turismonomade.cl. Diving and sea kayaking trips.

⊜ Transport

Air
Cerro Moreno Airport is 22 km north of the city. LanChile, Aerolíneas del Sur and Sky fly daily to **Santiago**, **Iquique** and **Arica**.
Airline offices LanChile, Prat 445, T055-265151, 600-5262000; **Aerolíneas del Sur**, Washington 2548, T055-228779, 800-710300; **American**, Washington 2507, T055-410781; **Lufthansa**, Copiapó 654, T055-263399; **Sky**, Velaquez 890, T055-459090.

Bicycle
Bicycle spares from **Rodrigo Baez Banda**, Condell 3071, also repairs; **Cicles Miranda**, Matta 2795, T055-223867.

Bus
No main terminal; each company has its own office in town, some at quite a distance from the centre.
Local La Portada is reached by minibuses from Latorre y Sucre (US$4 return), or on Corsal buses for Mejillones from Condell, between Sucre and Bolívar. Taxis charge US$18. Hitching is easy. Buses go to **Juan López** at weekends in the summer only; there are also minibuses daily in summer from Latorre y Sucre.
Long distance Except for services to Mejillones (see page 209), buses depart from the company offices as follows: **Flota Barrios**, Condell 2682, T055-268559; **Géminis** and

Camus, Latorre 3055, T055-251796; **Pullman Bus**, Latorre 2805, T055-262591; **Tur Bus**, Latorre 2751, T055-264487; **Condor Bus**, Bolívar y Latorre.

Numerous companies run services to **Santiago**, 18 hrs, US$35 semi-cama, US$55 cama, US$80 premium, occasional student discounts. Book 2 days in advance during high season. If all seats to the capital are booked, catch a bus to **La Serena**, 12 hrs, US$25 semi-cama, US$35 cama, then re-book.

To **Valparaíso**, 16 hrs, US$35 semi-cama; to **Arica**, 11 hrs, US$20 semi-cama, **Tur-Bus**; to **Chuquicamata**, frequent, 3 hrs, US$6; to **Calama**, several companies, 3 hrs, US$6; to **San Pedro de Atacama**, Tur Bus, 7 daily, 5 hrs, US$8, or via Calama; to **Copiapó**, US$18; to **Iquique**, 6 hrs, frequent, US$15.

To **Salta and Argentina**, Pullman Bus and Géminis, Tue, Fri, Sun at dawn, change at Calama, via San Pedro, Paso Sico and Jujuy, US$38. Immigration check at San Pedro de Atacama. Book in advance for this service, take food and as much warm clothing as possible. There is nowhere to change Chilean pesos en route; take small denomination dollar bills to use in Argentina.

Car

Car rental from **Avis**, Balmaceda 2499, T055-221073; **Budget**, Balmaceda 2584, Of 6, T055-251745; **First**, Bolívar 623, T055-225777; **Hertz**, Balmaceda 2492, T055-269043, offers city cars and jeeps (group D, Toyota Landcruiser) and does a special flat rate, with unlimited mileage; IQSA, Latorre 3033, T055-264675.

Andrés Ljubetic Romo, Atacama 2657, T055-268851, is a recommended mechanic.

Hitchhiking

If hitching south from Antofagasta, go to the checkpoint, restaurant and gas station at **La Negra**, about 15 km south of the city. If hitchhiking to Mejillones or Tocopilla try starting at the police checkpoint on the Mejillones road north of Antofagasta.

Antofagasta *p199, map p201*

Banks It is difficult to change TCs south of Antofagasta until you reach La Serena; major banks around Plaza Colón include **Banco Santiago Santander** and **Banco BCI**; all have ATMs; there are also ATMs at Las Brisas supermarket (see Shopping above). **Casas de cambio** These are mainly on Baquedano, such as **Ancla**, Baguedano 524, Mon-Fri 0900-1400, 1600-1900, Sat 0900-1400, poor rates (if closed try the ice cream shop next door); several exchange agents in the shopping centre at Baquedano 482-498; nearby is also **Nortour**, Baquedano 474; **AFEX**, Latorre 668, open Mon-Fri 0830-2000, Sat 0830-1400, better rates for TCs than Ancla. **Consulates** Argentina, Blanco Encalada 1933, T055-220440; **France** and **Belgium**, Baquedano 299, T055-268669; **Bolivia**, Washington 2675, piso 13, oficina 1301, T055-225010; **Germany**, Pérez Zujovic 4940, T055-251691; **Holland**, Washington 2679, of 902, T055-266252; **Italy**, Matta 1945, oficina 808, T055-227791; **Spain**, Rendic 4946, T055-269596. **Cultural centres** Centro Cultural Nueva Acropolis, Condell 2679, T055-222144, talks Wed 2100, also tai chi, yoga, archaeological and philosophical discussions; Instituto Chileno-Alemán de Cultura, Bolívar 769, T055-225946; Instituto Chileno-Norte americano de Cultura, Carrera 1445, T055-263520.

Internet Cheapest is **Intitour** (see Activities and tours, above), US$0.60 per hr; also try Cybercafé, Maipú y Latorre, US$1/hr, or Sucre 671, US$0.80/hr. **Laundry** Clean clothes, G Lorca 271; La Ideal, Baguedano 660; **Laverap**, 14 Febrero 1802, efficient, not cheap; **París**, Condell 2455, laundry and dry cleaning, expensive, charges per item. **Post office** Plaza Colón, 0830-1900, Sat 0900-1300. **Telephones** CTC, Condell 2529; **Entel Chile**, Condell 2451; on Sun, the only call centre to open is CTC, Condell 2750. **Useful addresses** Automóvil Club de Chile, Condell 2330, T055-225332; CONAF, Argentina y Baquedano.

North of Antofagasta

There are two routes north from Antofagasta: to Iquique along the Pan-American Highway or along the coastal road, Ruta 1, towards Tocopilla and beyond. The coastal route is more picturesque and makes a beautiful alternative to the sterility that accompanies large stretches of the Panamericana. ➤ *For Sleeping, Eating and other listings, see pages 208-209.*

Along the Pan-American Highway ●● ➤ *pp208-209.*
Colour map 1, C1/2 & B2.

From Antofagasta, the Panamericana continues north via Baquedano (Km 68) and **Carmen Alto** (Km 101), where there is a turning to Calama. Four kilometres' walk from the junction is **Chacabuco** (100 km northeast of Antofagasta), a large abandoned nitrate town, opened in 1924 and closed in 1938. It was used as a concentration camp by the Pinochet government between 1973 and 1975. Workers' housing, the church, theatre, stores and the mineral plants can be visited and there is a free guided tour in Spanish. If you visit Chacabuco, be sure to take water and set out early in the morning as you will probably be hitching back.

Another turning 69 km north of Carmen Alto leads to **Pedro de Valdivia**, a nitrate town abandoned in 1996, which has been declared a National Monument and can be visited. From here, a road runs north, parallel to the Pan-American Highway, crossing the Salar del Mirage to **María Elena**, the only nitrate town still functioning. After a half-century or more in the doldrums, the nitrate business is now profitable once again, because the nitrates extracted from the Atacama Desert are thought to be better for the soil than the chemical version. **Museo Arqueológico y Histórico** ① *on the main plaza, US$1,* has exhibits on pre-Hispanic cultures.

Some 20 km southeast of María Elena, just off the Pan-American Highway, is the **Balneario Chacance**, where bathing and camping are available on the banks of the Río Loa. North of María Elena, meanwhile, the Highway crosses the Tocopilla-Calama road 107 km north of Carmen Alto. At **Quillagua**, Km 81, there is a customs post where all vehicles heading south are searched. Situated 111 km further north is the southernmost and largest section of the **Reserva Nacional Pampa del Tamarugal**, which contains the **Geoglifos de Pintados**, about 400 figures of humans, animals and geometric shapes on the hillside 3 km west of the highway; the other sections are near La Tirana (see page 237) and 60 km north of Pozo Almonte (see page 220).

Along the coastal road ●🚲🏍🚗🏔🚌🚐 ➤ *pp208-209.*
Colour map 1, C1/2.

Mejillones and beyond
Located 60 km north of Antofagasta, Mejillones stands on a good natural harbour protected from westerly gales by high hills. Until 1948, it was a major terminal for the export of tin and other metals from Bolivia. Remnants of that past include a number of fine wooden buildings: the Intendencia Municipal, the Casa Cultural, built in 1866, and the church, 1906, as well as the Capitanía del Puerto. The town has been

● *In 2000, a British TV programme visited Quillagua in the Atacama and found sufficient*
● *meteorological records to prove that this small town really is the driest on earth.*

Nitrates

The rise and fall of the nitrate industry played an important role in opening up the northern desert areas between Iquique and Antofagasta to human settlement. In the second half of the 19th century, nitrates became important in Europe and the USA as an artificial fertilizer and for making explosives. The world's only known deposits of nitrates were in the Atacama Desert provinces of Antofagasta in Bolivia and Tarapacá in Peru. After the War of the Pacific, Chile gained control of all the nitrate fields, giving her a monopoly over world supply. Ownership was dominated by the British who controlled 60% of the industry by 1900. Taxes on the export of nitrates provided Chilean governments with around half their income for the next 40 years.

The processing of nitrates was labour intensive: at its height over 60,000 workers were employed. Using a combination of dynamite and manual labour, the workers dug the nitrate ore from the desert floor. It was then transported to nitrate plants, known as *oficinas*, crushed and mixed with water, allowing pure nitrates to be extracted. The mining and refining processes were dangerous and cost many lives. Wages were relatively high, but workers were paid in special tokens valid only for the particular *oficina* in which they worked. This not only meant that they had no means of leaving the *oficina* with ready cash, but also that they had to buy all their goods from the company stores which were, of course, controlled by the *oficina*.

The development of the Haber-Bosch process, a method of producing artificial nitrates, in Germany during the First World War, dealt a severe blow to the nitrate companies and many mines closed in the 1920s. New techniques were introduced by the Guggenheim company, but the world depression after 1929 led to a collapse in demand and with it the Chilean nitrate industry. Traces of the nitrate era can, however, still be seen: the mining ghost towns of Chacabuco, north of Antofagasta, and Humberstone, near Iquique, can be visited, as can Baquedano, the most important junction of the nitrate railways; most of the other *oficinas* are marked only by piles of rubble at the roadsides north of Antofagasta. Only one mine survives today, at María Elena; paradoxically, its future is secure, as the nitrates from the Atacama are believed to be much better for the soil than those created by the artificial process and demand has increased in recent years.

transformed in recent years by the building of the largest port in South America here – on completion the port will link Argentina, southern Brazil and Paraguay with the lucrative markets of the Asian Pacific Rim. Although the large port buildings now dominate the northern end of the town, fishing remains important, and Mejillones comes alive in the evening when the fishermen prepare to set sail. The sea is very cold around Mejillones because of the Humboldt current.

From Mejillones, the road runs at the foot of 500-m cliffs, with constantly shifting views of the mountains and of the glistening ocean. Where the cliffs break down into jagged rocks on the shoreline, hundreds of cormorants can be seen swarming all over the pinnacles. There are good weekend beach resorts at **Hornitos**, 88 km north of Antofagasta, and **Poza Verde**, 117 km north.

There is no fuel between Mejillones and Tocopilla.

Behind the mountains, the coastal sierra is extensively mined for copper, often by *pilquineros*, small groups of self-employed miners. There are larger mines, with the biggest concentration inland at Michilla. Reminders of the area's mining past can be seen, principally at the ruins of **Cobija**, 127 km north of Antofagasta, founded by order of Simón Bolívar in 1825 as Bolivia's main port. A prosperous little town handling silver exports from Potosí, it was destroyed by an earthquake in 1868 and again by a tidal wave in 1877 before losing out to the rising port of Antofagasta. Adobe walls, the rubbish tip right above the sea and the wreckage of the port are all that remains. The haunting ruins of the port of **Gatico** are at Km 144, just a little way beyond, and about 4 km further north there is an amazing ransacked cemetery. About 152 km north of Antofagasta, a very steep zigzag road winds up the cliffs a further 18 km to the mine at **Mantos de la Luna**. At the top, there are rather dead-looking groves of giant cactus living off the sea mist that collects on the cliffs. Wildlife includes foxes, or *zorros*.

Tocopilla

Tocopilla lies 187 km north of Antofagasta via the coast road (or 365 km via the Pan-American Highway), and has one of the most dramatic settings of any Chilean town, sheltering at the foot mountains that loom inland at heights of 500 m. Tocopilla is dominated by a thermal power station, which supplies electricity to much of the far north, and by the port facilities used to unload coal and to export nitrates and iodine from María Elena. There is a run-down and slightly menacing air to the place and a prolonged stay is not recommended. There are, however, some interesting early 20th-century buildings with wooden balustrades and façades, while the sloping plaza is an unlikely fiesta of palms and pepper trees amid the otherwise unremitting desert. There are two good beaches: **Punta Blanca**, 12 km south, and **Caleta Covadonga**, 3 km south, which has a swimming pool. A colony of some 20 to 30 sea turtles can oftend be seen about 3 km norh of the town. There is also fine deep-sea fishing here, if you can find a boat and a guide. For a spectacular view, head up Calle Baquedano as far as possible until you reach a stone stairway. Walking up this, you reach a minor road, which climbs up behind the town, giving views of the cliffs to the north, the mountains reaching inland and the fishing boats bobbing up and down in the harbour.

Routes north and east of Tocopilla

The coastal road runs north from Tocopilla to Iquique, 244 km away, and is a highly recommended journey, offering views of the rugged coastline, sea lions and tiny fishing communities. The customs post at Chipana-Río Loa (Km 90) searches all southbound vehicles for duty-free goods; this can take up to half an hour. Basic accommodation is available at **San Marcos**, a fishing village (Km 131). At **Chanaballita** (Km 184), there is a hotel, *cabañas*, camping, restaurant, shops. There are campsites at the former salt mining town of **Guanillos** (Km 126), **Playa Peruana** (Km 129) and **Playa El Aguila** (Km 160).

East of Tocopilla a good paved road climbs a steep, narrow valley 72 km to the Pan-American Highway. From here, the road continues eastwards to **Chuquicamata** (see page 210). Chuquicamata lies 16 km away from Calama, the main city of the interior.

● Sleeping

Along the Pan-American Highway *p206*
D Posada Los Arbolitos, 122 km north of Carmen Alto. Rooms, *cabañas* and meals but no running water.

D Residencial Chacance, María Elena, T055-632749. Run-down but the same owners provide nicer rooms round the corner and cheap meals are available at Casino Social.

Mejillones *p206*

AL Hotel Mejillones, M Montt 086, T055-621590, www.hotelmejillones.cl. New 4-star.
C París, Pje Iquique 095, T055-623061, iseghe @hotmail.com. **D** singles. Clean, modern, good.
D Residencial Elisabeth, Alte Latorre 440, T055-621568. **F** singles. Friendly, basic, with restaurant. Price per person.
D Residencial Marcela, Borgoño 150, T055-621464. **F** singles. With bath, pleasant.
Wild camping is possible on the beach.

Tocopilla *p208*

B-C Atenas, 21 de Mayo 1448, T/F055-813651. Charterless but comfortable. With bath and cable TV. Restaurant.
C Croacia, Bolívar 1332, T055-812783. Modern, helpful. Cheaper without bath. Opposite on Bolívar is the **Sucre**, same ownership, same price.
C-D Hotel Colonial, 21 de Mayo 1717, T055-811621, F811940. With bath, breakfast and cable TV, friendly, helpful.
D Hostal Central, A Pinto 1241. Huge rambling place like something out of a Hitchcock film, very basic, friendly, vast rooms, no hot water.

⑦ Eating

Mejillones *p206*

₮₮ Sion-Ji, Alte Latorre 718. Good-value Chinese cuisine.
₮ Juanito, Las Heras 241. Excellent *almuerzo* and cheap eats.

Tocopilla *p208*

₮₮ Club de la Unión, Prat 1354. Pleasant atmosphere. Good value *almuerzo*.
₮₮ Oregón, Rodríguez 1280. Cafeteria, fine sea views from veranda.

₮ El Chilenito, 21 de Mayo 2042. Few places open early for breakfast; this is the first up.

⊕ Transport

Along the Pan-American Highway *p206*
Buses between Antofagasta and Calama stop at the **Carmen Alto** junction, 1½ hrs, US$4. **María Elena** is served by **Tur Bus** from Iquique, 6 hrs, US$10.

Mejillones *p206*
Buses depart every half hour from the Corsal terminal, Condell y Sucre in Antofagasta for Mejillones, 1 hr, US$2. There are also **minibuses** to Mejillones departing from Latorre 2730.

Tocopilla *p208*
There is no bus terminal in Tocopilla. Bus offices are located on 21 de Mayo, including **Pullman Bus**, **Tur Bus**, **Flota Barrios** and **Pullman Carmelita**, all serving the following destinations: **Antofagasta**, many daily, 2½ hrs, US$5; **Iquique**, frequent, 3 hrs, US$6. **Tur Bus** also runs services to **Chuquicamata** and **Calama**, 3 a day, 3 hrs, US$7. All the above companies also serve Santiago.
Note that most buses to southern destinations are en route from Iquique, so you're unlikely to be able to leave Tocopilla before mid-morning.

⊕ Directory

Tocopilla *p208*
Banks BCI, Baquedano y Prat, has a Redbanc ATM. **Internet** 21 de Mayo 1721, US$1.20 per hr. **Post office** 21 de Mayo y A Pinto. **Telephone** CTC call centre near the post office; also ENTEL, 21 de Mayo 2066.

Calama and around → *Colour map 1, B3 & C2.*

Calama is a seedy city, set at 2265 m in the oasis of the Río Loa, with beautiful views of volcanoes in the Ollagüe area. An expensive and modern town, roughly 200 km northeast of Antofagasta, it acts as a service centre for the large nearby mines of Chuquicamata and Radomiro Tomic. Initially a staging post on the silver route between Potosí and Cobija, Calama superseded San Pedro de Atacama in importance with the development of mining activities at Chuquicamata. Most travellers use Calama as the departure point for San Pedro de Atacama and the weekly train to Bolivia, however, football fans will certainly want to make sure that their visit coincides with a home match of Cobreloa, the most successful Chilean football team outside Santiago in the past 20 years or so. Nearby are oasis villages such as Chiu Chiu and Caspana with their historic churches and altogether slower pace of life. ▸▸ *For Sleeping, Eating and other listings, see pages 214-217.*

Ins and outs

Getting there Calama is easily reached by regular buses from Antofagasta and the south, and by less frequent buses from Iquique and Arica, which often travel overnight. For those heading to Uyuni in Bolivia, there is a weekly train (see box page 217) and two weekly buses. There are also three weekly buses to Salta in Argentina. The airport is served by daily flights to/from Antofagasta and Santiago. It is about 5 km from the city centre. Taxis to/from the airport cost US$8. Airport transfers are also available. The more expensive hotels may offer courtesy vans.

Getting around The central part of Calama is relatively compact and you should not need to take public transport. There are, however, many *colectivos*, most of which pick up on Abaroa or Vargas.

Tourist office ⓘ *Latorre 1689, T055-345345, www.calamacultural.cl, Mon-Fri 0830-1300, 1400-1800*. Provides map of town, English spoken, helpful staff.

Calama

The centre of Calama is Plaza 21 de Mayo, a shady spot in which to relax. The peach-coloured **Catedral San Juan Bautista** on the west side with its copper clad spire makes a pleasant contrast to the colours of the desert. On the northeastern side, the pedestrian walkway of Ramírez continues two blocks east, where visitors will not be able to miss the bright red, phallic statue of **El Minero**, erected as a tribute to the bravery of the region's miners, but also an unlikely piece of kitsch in the Atacama.

This area comes alive at night. In the plaza, teenagers flirt with one another, while Argentine backpackers down on their luck ponder their next move. The pedestrian walkways of Ramírez are awash with young and old, beggars and hippies, not to mention an old man winding a barrel organ, watched by his pet parakeet.

On Avenida Bernado O'Higgins, 2 km from the centre, is the **Parque El Loa** ⓘ *1000-1800*, which contains a reconstruction of a typical colonial village built around a reduced-scale reproduction of Chiu Chiu church. In the park is the **Museo Arqueológico y Etnológico** ⓘ *Tue-Fri 1000-1300, 1400-1800, Sat-Sun 1400-1830, US$0.40*, which has an exhibition of local pre-Hispanic cultural history. Nearby is the new **Museo de Historia Natural** ⓘ *1000-1300, 1500-1830, US$0.90*, which has an interesting collection devoted to the *oficinas* and the region's ecology and palaeontology.

Chuquicamata

A visit here is truly memorable. Some 16 km north of Calama, Chuquicamata is the site of the world's largest open-cast copper mine, employing 8000 workers and operated by **Codelco**, the state copper corporation. Although copper has been mined here since pre-Inca times, it was the Guggenheim brothers who introduced modern mining and processing techniques after 1911 and made Chuquicamata into the most important single mine in Chile. In other parts of the plant, 60,000 tonnes of low-grade ore are processed a day to produce refined copper of 99.98% purity. Output is over 600,000 tonnes a year, but the diggers are having to cut ever deeper into the desert, making the extraction process increasingly expensive. In 2005 the town that surrounds the mine was closed and the families moved to Calama, leaving only a small historic centre for visitors. This will enable Codelco to exploit the copper that is buried in the earth beneath the houses and will make Chuquicamata the latest and the largest in the Atacama's long line of ghost towns. The latest plan is to link the three mines in the area, Chuquicamata, mina sur and Radomiro Tomic to create a hole in the earth 14 km long producing 10% of the world's copper supplies.

A visit to the mine at Chuquicamata is highly recommended for the insight it gives into the industry that bankrolls Chile's economy. It also gives fantastic views of the desert pampa and the volcanoes to the east. Guided bus tours (Monday-Friday 1400, less frequently in low season, 1 hour, US$2 donation, passport essential) depart from the office of Chuqui Ayuda (a local children's charity) near the entrance at the top end of the plaza. The tours are in Spanish (although guides usually speak reasonable English). Places on tours need to be booked in advance, either by calling the office in Chuquicamata (T055-327469) or from the tourist office in Calama. Covered shoes, long trousers and long sleeves must be worn. Arrive 30 minutes early.

North and east of Calama

Chiu Chiu was one of the earliest centres of Spanish settlement in the area. Set in the shadow of the Volcán San Pedro, it is a peaceful oasis village and a nice contrast to the bustle of Calama. In the glades nearby, horses graze on surprisingly lush grasses and the local people cultivate alfalfa. Chiu Chiu's plaza, fringed with pepper trees and opposite the church, is a pleasant place to while away a few hours. The church of **San Francisco**, dating from 1611, has roof beams of cactus and walls over 1 m thick – please leave a donation. Some 10 km away on the road to Caspana is a unique, perfectly circular, very deep lake, also called **Chiu Chiu** or **Icacoia**.

Calama

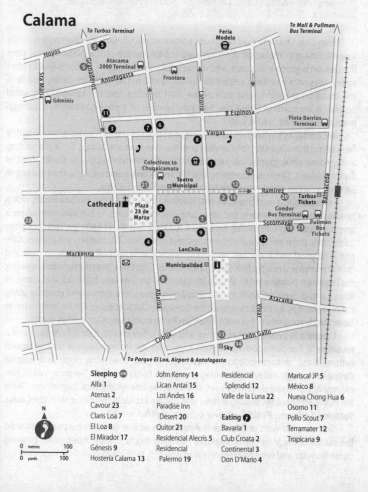

Sleeping
Alfa 1
Atenas 2
Cavour 23
Claris Loa 7
El Loa 8
El Mirador 17
Génesis 9
Hostería Calama 13

John Kenny 14
Lican Antai 15
Los Andes 16
Paradise Inn
 Desert 20
Quitor 21
Residencial Alecris 5
Residencial
 Palermo 19

Residencial
 Splendid 12
Valle de la Luna 22

Eating
Bavaria 1
Club Croata 2
Continental 3
Don D'Mario 4

Mariscal JP 5
México 8
Nueva Chong Hua 6
Osorno 11
Pollo Scout 7
Terramater 12
Tropicana 9

Farewell to Chuqui

The town of Chuquicamata has always been famous in Chile. Quite apart from the fact that the mine is responsible for a large part of Chile's GDP, miners at 'Chuqui' are treated differently, with free healthcare in a special modern hospital and guaranteed housing close to the mine. The decision to move all those living in Chuqui down to Calama is very sad for those who have grown up and lived in the town, and will have a severe impact on both the people of Chuqui and on those living in nearby Calama.

Some 2500 families have recently been moved from Chuqui to new neighbourhoods on the outskirts of Calama, near the road to Chiu Chiu. The town's famous hospital has also been transferred to Calama, and is now of great benefit to the city as a whole. The two reasons for the change are the reserves of copper lying beneath the town of Chuqui and the pollution risks for those living there. Certainly, anyone approaching Calama only has to look at the great cloud that hangs to the north to appreciate the dangers of pollution in Chuqui. Nevertheless, the death of the town was a momentous and sad event in the history of northern Chile.

From Chiu Chiu, the road continues north towards Ollagüe. Just beyond the oasis, a small turning branches off the main road and follows the course of the Río Loa. Here the canyon is green with crops, and donkeys plough the earth – it seems like a secret valley. This area has been settled for millennia and petroglyphs are clearly visible in the rocks on the right-hand side of the road heading towards **Lasana**. This small hamlet, 8 km north of Chiu Chiu, has striking ruins of a pre-Inca *pukará*, a national monument; drinks are on sale.

At **Conchi**, 25 km north of Lasana, the road crosses the Río Loa via a bridge dating from 1890; there is a spectacular view over the river from the bridge, but it is a military zone, so no photographs are allowed. Access to the river is by side tracks, best at Santa Bárbara. There is interesting wildlife and flower meadows and trout fishing in season; you can obtain a permit from Gobernación in Calama.

From Conchi, a road branches east following the valley of the **Río San Pedro**, which has been a route for herders and silver caravans for centuries, to **Inacaliri**, from where a very poor road (4WD essential) runs south to Linzor and the **El Tatio geysers** (see page 220). While there are several direct routes east from Chiu Chiu towards the geysers, only one is in good condition: just north of Chiu Chiu, turn right off the Ollagüe road and continue until you reach a fork some 22 km east of Chiu Chiu. Take the right fork, ignoring the large sign pointing left to El Tatio (this leads to another very bad track via Linzor). At Km 47 a track turns off north to Caspana; again, ignore this turning and continue along the main road as it climbs steeply up the Cuesta de Chita. At about Km 80, branch left to Tatio; this branch meets the main Tatio-San Pedro road some 5 km further north.

Caspana is beautifully set among hills with a tiny church dating from 1641 and a **museum** ① *Tue-Sun 1000-1300, 1500-1730*, with interesting displays on Atacameño culture. Basic accommodation is available. A poor road runs north and east of Caspana through valleys of pampas grass with llama herds to **Toconce**, which has extensive pre-Hispanic terraces set among some interesting rock formations. There are many archaeological sites nearby and the area is ideal for hiking, with the **Cerros Toconce**, **León** and **Paniri** – all over 5500 m – within reach.

Some 20 km west of Toconce is **Ayquina**, in whose ancient church is enshrined the statue of the Virgin of Guadalupe. Her feast day is 8 September, when pilgrims come from far and wide to celebrate and worship. ▸▸ *See Festivals and events, page 215.*

Turi and the ruins of a 12th-century *pukará* that was once the largest fortified town in the Atacama mountains. Close to the village of **Cupo** is a large, ruined pre-Hispanic settlement at **Paniri**, with extensive field systems, irrigation canals (including aqueducts) and a necropolis. Some of the fields are still in use. The area around Cupo is one of the best for seeing the Atacama giant cactus (*Notocereus atacamensis*); flamingos are also visible on the mudflats. Surrounding the *baños* is an oasis of ancient pastoral land, the **Vega de Turi**, now drying up due to the water consumption of the mines. It remains an important site for the llama- and sheep-herders, who believe it has curative properties. At several times in the year, especially September, herders from a wide area congregate here with their flocks.

Ollagüe

Situated 198 km north of Calama on the dry floor of the Salar de Ollagüe at 3696 m, Ollagüe is surrounded by a dozen volcanic peaks of over 5000 m. It is a cold, dusty, windswept place, but remarkable for its sense of remoteness. At this altitude, nights are cold, while the days are warm and sunny, there are only 50 mm of rain a year and water is very scarce.

The road to Ollagüe from Chiu Chiu runs north to Estación San Pedro. This first section is in poor condition, however, from Estación San Pedro to a *carabinero* checkpoint at **Ascotán**, it is worse. This is the highest point of the road at 3900 m. Ask at Ascotán or Ollagüe about weather conditions before setting out, especially in December and January or August. North of Ascotán, the road improves as it crosses the Salares de Ascotán and de Carcote and Ollagüe. There are many llama flocks along this road and flamingos on the *salares*. There is no petrol between Calama and Uyuni in Bolivia, although if you completely run out, you could try buying some from the *carabineros* at Ollagüe or Ascotán, the military at Conchi or the mining camp at Buenaventura.

Some 5 km south of Ollagüe is the sulphur mining camp of **Buenaventura**, which is situated at an altitude of 5800 m, only 150 m short of the summit of Ollagüe Volcano. Camping is possible and there are amazing views over the volcanoes and salt flats. A road leads to the sulphur camp but be wary of walking the route if not coming from Bolivia, as you will not yet be acclimatized for exercise at this altitude. You should also bear in mind that temperatures can drop as low as -37°C.

A road runs west from Ollagüe to the sulphur mines, now closed, of **Aucanquilcha**, where there are the ruins of an aerial tram system. A high-clearance vehicle is needed to drive to the mine but from there you can scramble to the summit of Aucanquilcha, at 6176 m, from which there are superb views. An interesting excursion can also be made north from Ollagüe to the village of **Coska** with its traditional agriculture and herds of llamas and alpacas.

Into Bolivia → *Bolivian phone code: +591.*

A poor road leads across the Bolivian border ① *immigration and customs 0800-2000*, from Ollagüe and runs to **Uyuni**, 170 km east. Trucks take a more northerly route across the Salar de Uyuni but motorists are warned against using this latter route into Bolivia. As well as the danger of getting lost on the many tracks leading over the salt lakes, there's no petrol between Calama and Uyuni and little hope of help with a breakdown on the Bolivian side, unless you don't mind waiting for days. After rain the route is impassable and even experienced guides get lost. Maps give widely differing versions of the route. Where the road has been built up, never forsake it for the appealing soft salt beside it. The salt takes a person's weight but a vehicle breaks through the crust into unfathomable depths of plasticine mud below.

● Sleeping

Calama *p210, map p211*

L Park , Camino Aeropuerto 1392, T055-319900, www.parkplaza.cl/calama. On the edge of town by the airport. First class, pool, bar and restaurant.

L-AL Lican Antai, Ramírez 1937, T055-341621, hotellicanantai@terra.cl. With breakfast, central, good service and good restaurant, TV. Recommended.

AL Hostería Calama, Latorre 1521, T055-341511, hcalama@tie.cl. Comfortable, good cafeteria and service. Buffet breakfast. Rooms have heating, some with king size beds. There is also a gym and a small pool.

AL Hotel Paradise Inn Desert, Ramírez 1867, T/F055-341618, paradise_hotel@hotmail.com. Internet, more expensive rooms with jacuzzi, excellent views, nice terrace, good for business people.

AL El Mirador, Sotomayor 2064, T/F055-340329, www.hotelmirador.cl. With bath, good atmosphere, clean, helpful. Internet access. Recommended.

A Alfa, Sotomayor 2016, T055-342496, hotelalfa@entelchile.net. Comfortable and with good service. Some rooms a little stuffy. Could do with a revamp. Overpriced.

A Quitor, Ramírez 2116, T055-341716, hotelquitor@entelchile.net. Central, pleasant, helpful, internet access. Good.

B John Kenny, Ecuador 1991, T055-341430. Modern, clean, friendly, parking.

B Residencial Alecris, Felix Hoyos 2143, T055- 341616. **C** without bath. No breakfast. Single, double and triple rooms. Well maintained, very clean, family atmosphere, popular with miners. Sunny courtyard. Chatty owner, Alejandro.

C Atenas, Ramírez 1961, T055-342666 . With bath and cable TV, small, somewhat stuffy rooms, pricey laundry service, breakfast extra.

C El Loa, Abaroa 1617, T055-341963. Cheaper rooms without bath. English spoken.

C Residencial Splendid, Ramírez 1961, T055- 341841. Central, clean, friendly, hot water, often full, good, cheaper without bath.

C-D Cavour, Sotomayor 1841, T055-314718. With bath and cable TV. No breakfast. Basic, bright and friendly. Slightly run-down.

C-D Claris Loa, Granaderos 1631, T055-341293. **F** singles. With bath. Clean, quiet.

C-D Genesis, Granaderos 2148, T055-

319075. **F** singles. Without bath, near Géminis bus terminal, clean.

C-D Residencial Palermo, Sotomayor 1889, T055-341283. **F** singles. Some rooms with bath. Friendly, central, very dark.

D Valle de la Luna, Sotomayor 2326, T055-312114. **F** singles. More expensive rooms with bath. Clean, central.

D-E Los Andes, Vivar 1920, T055-341073. F Singles. As basic as it gets. Decent beds.

North and east of Calama *p211*

B Hostal Chiu Chiu, Esmeralda s/n, Chiu Chiu, T055- 326386. Friendly and helpful. Three rooms are also available at the community tourism project in **Toconce**, providing accommodation for up to 12 people, with full board.

Ollagüe *p213*

There is nowhere official to stay in Ollagüe, but police and border officials will help travellers to find unofficial lodgings.

● Eating

Calama *p210, map p211*

ᵀᵀᵀ Terramater, Vivar 1797, T055-312010. An unlikely elegant restaurant in the city centre. Intimate surroundings and a good wine list. Slightly overattentive staff and a little overpriced, but this is probably Calama's best restaurant.

ᵀᵀ Bavaria, Sotomayor 2093, T055-3414965. Good restaurant with cafeteria downstairs, real coffee, open 0800, very popular, also at Latorre 1935.

ᵀᵀ Mariscal JP, Félix Hoyos 2127, T055-312559. Best seafood in town, not cheap but worth it.

ᵀᵀ México, Latorre 1986. Mexican cuisine, fairly expensive. Doubles as a pub with live music at weekends.

ᵀᵀ Osorno, Espinosa 2198 y Ganaderos, T055-341035. Grill, with live Chilean folk music.

ᵀᵀ Patagonia, Granaderos 2549. Lots of meat. Good wine list.

ᵀᵀ-ᵀ Continental, Vargas 2180. Good seafood and fish, cheaper than **Mariscal JP** but less charm.

ᵀᵀ-ᵀ Club Croata, Abaroa 1869, Plaza 23 de Marzo, T055-342126. Excellent value 4-course *almuerzo*.

♈-♈ **Nueva Chong Hua**, Abaroa 2006.
The best Chinese. Recommended.
♈ **Don D'Mario**, Abaroa 1756-A. Basic *picada*,
cleaner than most and serving hearty
Chilean food.
♈ **Jugo Camelot**, Abaroa 1968. Good fruit juice.
♈ **Pollo Scout**, Vargas 2102. Clean, friendly,
popular, reasonable.
♈ **Tropicana**, Sotomayor 2043. Good fruit juice.
There are also many very cheap eateries
in the **Féria modelo** (see below).

Chuquicamata *p210*
♈ Cheap lunches are available at the **Club de
Empleados** and at **Arco Iris** both facing the
bus terminal.

Chiu Chiu *p211*
♈♈ **Café Tambo**. A nice place with old
wooden furniture. Mid-range meals.

🌗 Bars and clubs

Calama *p210, map p211*
Karka's Pub, Latorre 1986B. Swish, good.
Schoperia Ché Carlitos, Abaroa 1901.
Central, popular.
Calama's nightclubs are all out of town on
Av Circunvalación. There are over 10 of them,
including **Kamikaze**, very expensive, and
Vox, both recommended.

☸ Festivals and events

Calama *p210, map p211*
Early Feb Calama's **annual festival** is a riot
of activities and celebrations –
recommended for those in the area.

North and east of Calama *p211*
8 Sep The feast day of the **Virgen de
Guadalupe** is celebrated in Ayquina, with
day-long group dancing to indigenous
rhythms on flute and drum. Towards sunset
the Virgin is carried up a steep trail to a small
thatched shrine, where the image and the
people are blessed before the dancing
recommences, continuing all the way back
to the village. The poor people of the hills
gather stones and make toy houses all along
the route: miniatures of the homes they
hope to have some day.
19 Mar The **fiesta** of San José is clebrated in
Cupo, southwest of Ayquina.

Ollagüe *p213*
19 Jun Fiesta de San Antonio de Padua
celebrates the patron saint of Ollagüe, with
dancing and Quechua customs, such as the
sacrifice of llamas.

○ Shopping

Calama *p210, map p211*
Económico, Grecia 2314. Supermarket.
El Cobre, Vargas 2148. Supermarket.
Féria Modelo, Antofagasta between Latorre
and Vivar. The market sells fruit juices and
crafts. There are also craft stalls on Latorre
1600-block.
Shopping mall , Baquedano, north of centre.
Reached by bus 1M, *colectivos* 11B and 18B.

▲ Activities and tours

Calama *p210, map p211*
Several agencies in Calama run 1-day and
longer tours to the Atacama region, including
San Pedro; these are usually more expensive
than tours from San Pedro and require a
minimum number for the tour to go ahead.
Reports of tour quality are mixed – watch out
for poorly maintained vehicles and poor
guides – but the following have received
positive recommendations. The tourist office
(see above) also offers tours of the area.
Atacama Explorer, Lascar 4182, Villa
Ayquina, 055-335527. Atacama tours, plus
trips to the old nitrate mines and the upper
Loa Valley.
Atacama Park Adventure, Camino al
Aeropuerto 1392, T055-440100. Atacama
tours and other expeditions.
Azimut 360, T/F055-333040, www.azimut.cl.
Tours to the Atacama desert, plus mountaineering to Licanábur and Llullaillaco.
Recommended.
Colque Tours, Caracoles, T055-851109,
colquetours@terra.cl. 4WD tours of Andes
and salt plains into Bolivia. Guides, vehicles,
food and accommodation better than most,
although that is not saying much. Main
office is in San Pedro de Atacama.
Keps Turismo , Sotomayor 1812-A, T055-
318983, kepsturismo@terra.cl. A variety of
day tours around Chiu Chiu and San Pedro.
Turismo Buenaventura, T/F055-341882,
buenventur@entelchile.net. Recommended
for tours of Atacama region.

Calama *p210, map p211*

Air

LanChile to **Santiago** via Antofagasta, 5 daily, from US$230 return. **Sky Airline** is slightly cheaper. Transfer services from the airport are offered by Transfer city express, T055-341022, US$6 per person.

Airline offices LanChile, Latorre 1726, T600-5262000 and airport, T055- 311331; Sky, Latorre 1497, T055-310190.

Bus

No main terminal, buses leave from the company offices: **Tur Bus**, Granaderos, about 12 blocks north of centre; tickets from Ramírez y Balmaceda; **Pullman Bus**, Balmaceda 1802; **Atacama 2000**, Abaroa 2106;**Frontera**, Antofagasta 2041;**Géminis**, Antofagasta 2239; **Kenny Bus**, Vivar 1954; **Flota Barrios**, Ramírez 2298.

To **Santiago**, 22-24 hrs, US$35, sálon cama US$55, premium US$80; to **Antofagasta**, 3 hrs, several companies, US$6; to **Arica**, usually overnight, 9 hrs, US$16, or change in Antofagasta; to **Valparaíso/Viña del Mar**, US$35; to **Iquique**, Tur Bus, 3 daily, 6 hrs, via Chuquicamata and Tocopilla, US$13. To **La Serena**, usually with delay in Antofagasta, 16 hrs, US$28. To **Chuquicamata** (see below). To **San Pedro de Atacama**, 1½ hrs, US$3, **Tur Bus**, several daily, **Atacama 2000**, 3 a day, **Frontera**, 9 a day, last bus 2030, often leaves late, but does have a driver who likes to dress up as spiderman.

To **Salta** (Argentina), 15 hrs, services with both companies leave early morning Tue, Fri and Sun, US$38, **Géminis**, US$45, **Pullman Bus**.

To **Bolivia**, Buses Frontera, 0700 on Wed and Sun to Uyuní, US$12, also serving Ollagüe for US$6 (see below).

Car

Car hire is not reliable in San Pedro de Atacama, so you're better off picking up a vehicle in Calama. A high-clearance vehicle (necessary for the desert) costs around US$100 per day. Rates are sometimes much lower at weekends. A hired car, shared between several people, is an economic alternative for visiting the Atacama region. ...ire companies include **Alamo**, Hoyos ..., T055-364543; **Avis**, Gallo 1985A,

T055-319757; **Budget**, Granaderos 2925, T341076; **Hertz**, Latorre 1510, T055-341380; **IQSA**, O'Higgins 877, T055-310281.

Train

To **Uyuni** (Bolivia), weekly service, departing Wed 2300 (in theory), up to 24 hrs, US$13. Remember that between Oct and Mar, Chilean time is 1 hr later than Bolivian. Station closes for lunch 1300 to 1500, no luggage store. Book seats in advance (passport essential) from railway station (Balmaceda y Sotomayor, T055-348900) after 1530 on the day before travel. Catch the train as early as possible: although seats are assigned, the designated carriages may not arrive; passengers try to occupy several seats to sleep on but will move if you politely show your ticket. Sleeping bag and/or blanket essential. Restaurant car serves cheap food and drinks, with waiter service; food is also available at Ollagüe (see also box, page 217).

Chuquicamata *p210*

Yellow *colectivos* (marked 'Chuqui') depart from Abaroa just north of the Plaza 23 de Marzo in Calama, US$1.60. Chuqui is on the main road north from Calama and is served by buses to **Arica** at 2200 (weekends at 2300), 9 hrs, US$16; to **Antofagasta**, US$6; to **Iquique**, US$11; to **Santiago**, 24 hrs, US$35.

Chiu Chiu *p211*

Served by minibuses to/from **Calama**, about 6 a day, US$3. To catch one, either ring ahead in Calama, T055-343400, or take the Línea 80 *colectivo* on Abaroa to the end of the line in Calama and then catch the next vehicle to Chiu Chiu. If arranged in advance, the minibuses will continue on to Lasana for an extra charge – you will have to book the return trip, or walk back to Chiu Chiu.

Ollagüe *p213*

There is no fuel in Ollagüe. **Buses Frontera** from **Calama**, Wed & Sun at 0700, 5 hrs, US$6; returns next day. Ollagüe can also be reached by taking the **Calama-Uyuni train** (see above) but, if you stop off, you will have to hitch back as the daily freight trains are not allowed to carry passengers. Hitching by road is difficult but the police may help you to find a truck.

The 'tren de la muerte' from Calama to Uyuni

The line between Calama and Uyuni in Bolivia is the only section of the old Antofagasta and Bolivia railway line still open to passenger trains. It is a long journey, often taking up to 36 hours to Uyuni. It is one of the world's great train journeys but uncomfor- table – if your idea of fun is standing still at a border post for up to 10 hours, this is the trip for you. The journey is cold, both during the day and at night (-15°C). From Calama the line climbs to reach its highest point at Ascotán (3960 m); it then descends to 3735 m at Cebollar, skirting the Salar de Ascotán. Chilean customs are at Ollagüe, where there is a delay of five to six hours while an engine is sent from Uyuni. Immigration formalities are conducted on the train but passengers are required to disembark with their luggage, to be searched on the Bolivian side. There are money changers on the train but beware of forged notes. From the border, the line runs to Uyuni, 174 km northeast, crossing the Salar de Chiguana and running at an almost uniform height of 3,660 m. Uyuni is the junction with the line south to the Argentine frontier at Villazón.

A personal account: "A few years back, I was travelling with two friends in Bolivia and decided to take the train back from Uyuni to Calama. We were told that the train would arrive in Uyuni at 2300, so we sat in the waiting room until 0230, when the train finally arrived. The 'train' in fact consisted of several different sections, each heading in a different direction – some carriages only to Potosí, others on to Villazón, and only two carriages to Chile. After running frantically up and down in the freezing temperatures, we finally found the right carriage. However, the train went nowhere until dawn...

"We reached Ollagüe at 1000, and then spent the entire day waiting there as the Chilean border guards searched every bag of every passenger for contraband goods – Bolivians travel with a lot of bags and so the train did not leave Ollagüe until 2000.

"As we pulled out, the Chilean border guard remarked that the train was ahead of schedule. It arrived in Calama at 0300 the next morning, when, of course, most of the hotels were shut."

◐ Directory

Calama *p210, map p211*
Banks Rates are generally poor especially for TCs. Tere are several banks with ATMs on Latorre and Sotomayor. **Casas de cambio** Moon Valley Money Exchange, Vivar 1818, and also another exchange at Sotomayor 1837; also on Ramírez, next to Centro Comercial Gala, most open Sat.
Consulates Bolivia, Centro Boliviano, Latorre 1395, T055-341976, open (in theory) 0900-1230 Mon-Fri, friendly, helpful.

Hospital Hospital del Cobre, Chorrillos 689, T055-, T055-342769. **Internet** There are several throughout the centre. Prices US$1 per hour. **Laundry** Universal, Vargas 2178 (cheapest); Lavexpress, Sotomayor 1887, good, speedy. **Post office** Granaderos y V Mackenna, open 0830-1300, 1530-1830, Sat 0900-1230, will not send parcels over 1 kg. **Telecommunications** CTC, Sotomayor 1825; Entel, Sotomayor 2027. **Useful address** Automóvil Club de Chile, Av Ecuador 1901, T/F055342770.

San Pedro de Atacama and around → *Colour map 1, C3.*

Situated 103 km by paved road southeast of Calama, San Pedro is an oasis town in the valley of the Río San Pedro at 2436 m. While it is now famous among visitors as the base for excursions in this part of the Atacama, it was important as the centre of the Atacameño culture long before the arrival of the Spanish. There is a definite sense of history in the shady streets and the crumbling ancient walls that drift away from the town into the fields and on into the dust. Owing to the clear atmosphere and isolation, there are wonderful views of the night sky from just outside town. Despite being in the desert, it does rain in San Pedro about three or four times a year, usually around March, as a result of the invierno altiplánico. *San Pedro is a good base from which to visit Toconao, the Salar de Atacama and the geysers of El Tatio. Entry charges are levied at most of the natural attractions (around US$4), with the money going to the local communities.* ➤ *For Sleeping, Eating and other listings, see pages 225-228.*

Ins and outs

Getting there San Pedro can be reached by 16 buses a day to/from Calama and six daily from Antofagasta. There are three companies: **Atacama 2000, Frontera** and **Tur Bus.** If driving be aware there is no food, water or fuel along the Calama-San Pedro road.
Getting around San Pedro is small so taxis (from by the football field) are only needed for out-of-town trips.
Tourist office Sernatur has an office in the plaza (closed on Thursdays). It is worth going there to check out previous travellers' observations on the merits of the various tour companies in the complaints and suggestions book.
Climate Be prepared for the harsh climate and high altitudes of the interior. Gloves, a hat and a warm coat are essential for excursions from San Pedro, especially for the early morning trip to El Tatio. High-factor suncream and a hat are necessary for the burning daytime sun. Take plenty of water, sunglasses and lip balm on any excursion.

Background

The main centre for the Atacameño culture, which flourished in this region before the arrival of the Incas around 1450, San Pedro was defended by a *pukará* (fortress) at Quitor, 3 km north. The cultivable land around was distributed in 15 *ayllos* (socio-economic communities based on family networks) and irrigation channels were built. San Pedro was visited by both Diego de Almagro and Pedro de Valdivia and the town became a centre of Spanish colonial control; a mission was established in 1557. After Independence, the town became an important trading centre on the route between Cobija on the coast and Salta in Argentina, but the decline of Cobija and the rise of copper-mining led to San Pedro being superceded as an economic centre by Calama.

In the early 20th century, San Pedro's economy was based around mining, with salt mines in the Valle de la Luna (whose ruins are easily visible today) and sulphur mines in the high mountains. Since the 1970s, tourism has been of increasing importance and the town is now dependent on the annual influx of Chilean and foreign visitors. However, travellers should be aware that tourism is a somewhat divisive issue in San Pedro. In many ways the town has lost much of it's atacameño feel, and with more tourists than locals you may well feel that on entering San Pedro you are leaving Chile behind. Moreover, the tour companies are often run by outsiders and the glut of travel agencies has led to a tenfold increase in rents in the past ten years. Many of the local people still work in agriculture, having lower incomes than those who work with tourism, and, with over 25 tour companies there are dark (and doubtless somewhat exaggerated) rumours that some of these operations are fronts for money laundering and drug running, especially with Bolivia so close.

The road from Calama

At **Paso Barros Arana** (Km 58) there is an unpaved turning to the left, which leads through interesting desert scenery to the small, mud-brick village of **Río Grande**. Look out for guanacos on the pass. The main road continues skirts the Cordillera de la Sal about 15 km from San Pedro. There are spectacular views of the sunset over the western *cordilleras*. The old unpaved road to San Pedro turns off the new road at Km 72 and crosses this range through the Valle de La Luna (see below), but should only be attempted by 4WD vehicles. This road is partly paved with salt blocks.

San Pedro de Atacama

The **Iglesia de San Pedro**, dating from the 17th century, is supposedly the second oldest church in the country. It has been heavily restored and the tower was added in 1964. The roof is made of cactus; inside, the statues of Mary and Joseph have fluorescent light halos. Nearby, on the shady Plaza, is the **Casa Incaica**, the oldest building in San Pedro.

Museo Arqueológico ① www.ucn.cl/museo, Mon-Fri 0900-1200, 1400-1800, Sat and Sun 1000-1200, 1400-1800, US$3.50, contains the collection of Padre Gustave Le Paige, a Belgian missionary who lived in San Pedro between 1955 and 1980. It is now under the care of the Universidad Católica del Norte. One of the most important museums in northern Chile, it traces the development of pre-Hispanic Atacameño society. It is well organised, each display having a card with explanations in English. Graham Greene observed "the striking feature of the museum is the mummies of Indian women with their hair and dresses intact dating from before the Conquest, and a collection of paleolithic tools which puts the British Museum in the shade". No heating: wear warm clothing.

The **Pukará de Quitor**, 3 km north of San Pedro along the river, is a pre-Inca fortress which was restored in 1981 and covers 2.5 ha on a hillside on the west bank of the river. It was stormed by the Spanish under Pedro de Valdivia, 1000 defenders being overcome by 30 horsemen who vaulted the walls. The road to Quitor involves fording the river several times, until the *pukará* comes into view on the hill on the left-hand side of the valley. There is a new plaza here, built as a homage to the indigenous people of the region and set amid thorn trees. The road continues along the valley of the Río San Pedro as the canyon climbs further into the Atacama, passing a couple of small farmsteads sheltered by pepper trees where sheep graze in the desert sun. A further 4 km up the river, there are ruins at **Catarpe**, which was the Inca administrative centre for this region. The ruins are on top of a hill on the east side of the valley, and are difficult to find without a guide; archaeological tours are offered in San Pedro.

There's another archaeological site 12 km southwest of San Pedro at **Tulor**, where parts of a village (dated 500-800 BC) have been excavated. The road is *ripio*, and fine for 4WD vehicles. You can sleep in two reconstructed huts or take a tour, US$8. Nearby are the ruins of a 17th-century Spanish-style village, abandoned in the 18th century because of the lack of water.

Baños de Puritama ① US$9, just under 30 km north of San Pedro, are pleasant thermal baths. Taxis will drop you and wait for two hours.

Valle de la Luna

Some 12 km west of San Pedro, this is a valley of fantastic landscapes caused by the erosion of salt mountains. The valley is crossed by the old San Pedro-Calama road. Although buses on the new road will stop to let you off, where the old road branches off 13 km northwest of San Pedro (signposted to Peine), it is far better to travel from San Pedro on the old road, either on foot (allow three hours there, three hours back), by bicycle or high-clearance vehicle. The Valle is best seen at sunset. Take water, hat, camera and a torch. Note that camping is prohibited. Agencies in San Pedro offer tours, departing around 1530, returning after sunset, US$8-10 per person, but make sure the agency departs in time for arrival in the Valle before sunset as they do not always do so. Tours usually include a visit to the **Valle de la Muerte**, a crevice in the Cordillera de la Sal near San Pedro, with red rock walls, contorted into fantastic shapes.

The geysers of El Tatio

At an altitude of 4321 m, the geysers of El Tatio (① *US$4*) are a popular attraction. From San Pedro, they are reached by a road in variable state of repair that runs northeast, past the **Baños de Puritama**, then on for a further 94 km. The geysers are said to be at their best in the morning between 0630 and 0830, although the spectacle varies; locals say the performance is best when weather conditions are stable. A swimming pool has been built nearby. From here, you can hike to surrounding volcanoes if you are adapted to altitude, although it is advisable to take a guide because of the dangers of minefields.

San Pedro de Atacama

Sleeping 🛏
Camping Kunza 1 *B1*
Camping Los Perales 13 *D2*
Casa Corvatsch 15 *B1*
Casa de Norma 25 *C2*
...Tatio 2 *C2*

Hostal Edén Atacameño 3 *C3*
Hostal Inti Kamac 4 *B1*
Hostal Katarpe 7 *C1*
Hostal Lickana 17 *C1*
Hostal Mamatierra 18 *C3*
Hostal Martita 21 *D2*
Hostal Puritama 20 *C1*
Hostal Sonchek 22 *B2*
Hostal Sumaj Jallpa 23 *B3*
Hostal Takha-Takha 5 *C1*
Hostelling
  International 24 *C3*

Hostería San Pedro 6 *C3*
Kimal 8 *C1*
La Casa de Don Tomás 9 *D2*
Residencial Chiloé 10 *B1*
Residencial Don Raul 11 *C1*
Residencial La Florida 12 *B2*
Residencial Vilacoyo 16 *B2*
Tulor 19 *C1*

Eating 🍴
Adobe 9 *C2*
Café Étnico 10 *C2*

Café Export 2 *C3*
Café Tierra Todo
  Natural 7 *C2*
Casa Piedra 1 *C2*
Cuna 4 *B2*
La Casona 5 *C2*
Quitor 11 *B1*

Bars & clubs 🍸
Estaka 6 *C2*

There is no public transport and hitching is impossible. If going in a hired car, make sure the engine is suitable for very high altitudes and is protected with anti-freeze; 4WD is advisable. If driving in the dark, it is almost impossible to find your way: the sign for El Tatio is north of the turn-off. Following recent accidents a series of stone walls and wooden walkways has been built around the geysers, which some say has taken away from the spectacle.

From San Pedro to Toconao

From San Pedro to Toconao, a 37-km journey south, the paved road runs through occasional groves of acacia and pepper trees. There are many tracks leading to the wells (*pozos*), which supply the intricate irrigation system. Most have thermal water but bathing is not appreciated by the local farmers. The groves of trees are havens for wildlife, especially rheas (*ñandu*) and Atacama owls; there are also some llamas.

Toconao and around

This village, at an altitude of 2600 m, is on the eastern shore of the Salar de Atacama. Unlike San Pedro, Toconao's economy is based on agriculture, not tourism. All houses are built of bricks of white volcanic stone, which gives the village an appearance totally different from San Pedro. The 18th-century church and bell tower are also built of volcanic stone. Food is available and there are small shops selling handicrafts. The local church is cared for by nuns who give liturgies. There are no priests.

East of the village is a beautiful gorge called the **Quebrada de Jere** ① *US$2*, which is almost unimaginably verdant and filled with fruit trees and grazing cattle. At the bottom of the gorge a crystal-clear stream cuts down towards Toconao. There are picnic sites but camping is prohibited. Near the head of the valley on the East side is a petroglyph of a llama. Nearby is the quarry where the stone *sillar* is worked; it can be visited. The stones sound like bells when struck. Also worth visiting are the vineyards, which produce a unique sweet wine.

About 4 km before Toconao, vehicle tracks head east across the sand to a hidden valley 2 km from the road where there is a small settlement called **Zapar**. There are some well-preserved pre-Hispanic ruins on the rocky cliffs above the cultivated valley here. The sand is very soft and a 4WD vehicle is essential.

Around the Salar de Atacama

South of Toconao is one of the main entrances to the Salar de Atacama. Formed by deglaciation some 12,000 years ago it encompasses some 300,000ha, making it the third largest expanse of salt flats in the world; the air is so dry here that you can usually see right across the Salar, 100 km to the north. Rich in minerals, including borax, potassium and an estimated 40% of world lithium reserves, the Salar is home to three of the world's five species of flamingos – the Andean, Chilean and James – as well as other birds including sandpipers, the Andean gull, and the Andean avocet (although these can only be seen when lakes form in winter). The flamingos live by eating algae and tiny shellfish that subsist in the small saline pools in the Salar. Three areas of the Salar are part of the seven-sector **Reserva Nacional de los Flamencos** ① *US$5*, totalling 73,986 ha, administered by **CONAF** in conjunction with local communities. There is a walkway over part of the salar with information boards in Spanish. You should not leave the path.

From Toconao, a road runs 67 km along the eastern edge of the Salar de Atacama to the attractive village of **Peine**, where you'll find the offices of the lithium extraction company. It is worth asking if the company's access road can be used to visit the Salar de Atacama's spectacular salt formations. Nearby are some prehistoric cave paintings. Local guides in the village offer tours for around US$5 per person. There is also a thermal pool where you can swim. Woollen goods and knitwear are made here. To the east of the village lies a group of beautifully coloured hills, whose colours are more vibrant at sunset, with good views over the Salar de Atacama. A path leads

❖ Minefields: Beware

An indication of the nature of General Pinochet's geopolitics in the 1970s and 1980s is provided by the numerous minefields that were placed along Chile's border with Bolivia and northern Argentina at that time. The minefields were put down to forestall any possible invasion from Chile's neighbours, which was then perceived to be a very real threat.

Following the Ottowa convention, Chile has begun the slow process of dismantling its extensive minefields. Meanwhile, the danger remains. It is not unknown for people to have

been killed or maimed (often while attempting to smuggle drugs across the border). It is very unwise to make any lone forays into the *altiplano* without a knowledgeable local guide.

Minefields are known to affect the new **Parque Nacional Llullaillaco** (see page 222) and the Chilean side of **Volcán Licancabur** (see box, page 224) to give just two examples – and there may be other areas that are not known about. Always ask first before heading off into the northern wilderness, keeping in mind that local people are often more knowledgable than officials.

across these hills to **Socaire**; allow two days. Other villages worth visiting include **Tilomonte** and **Tilopozo**, south and west of Peine.

From Peine, a road (64 km) crosses the Salar de Atacama and joins the road that runs from San Pedro down the west side of the Salar, continuing south to **Pan de Azúcar**, an abandoned railway station. Here it meets the paved road that runs east-west from the Pan-American Highway south of Antofagasta to Socompa on the Argentine border, via the vast **La Escondida** copper mine, which has an output of copper higher than any other mine in the world. Ten kilometres east of La Escondida at Imilac, a poor road turns off south to the **Parque Nacional Llullaillaco**. This recently created park covers 263,000 ha and includes **Cerro Llullaillaco** at 6739 m, the second highest peak in Chile, as well as three other peaks over 5000 m: Cerro de la Pena at 5260 m, Guanaqueros, 5131 m, and Aguas Calientes, 5070 m. The park is inhabited by large numbers of guanacos and vicuñas. Visits are by arrangement only with CONAF in Antofagasta, owing to the dangers of minefields in the area. Further along the Pan de Azúcar-Socompa road (poor condition) is **Monturaqui**, the source of the green onyx that is used for carving.

❖ *The Escondido-Pan de Azúcar-Peine route is a good way of travelling from Antofagasta to San Pedro for those without their own transport.*

Southeast of Toconao

From Toconao, another road heads south through the villages of **Camar**, where handicrafts made from cactus may be bought, and **Socaire**, which has llama wool knitwear for sale and a recently restored church built from volcanic rock. From the top of the tchurch tower you can see agricultural land planted on traditional terraces. There are also a couple of places that serve basic lunches. The road is paved as far as Socaire. About 20 km further south, a rough road leaves the main route to the Paso Sico and climbs a hill to the beautiful **Laguna Miscanti** (4240m asl), a lake that is part of the **Reserva Nacional Los Flamencos** (① US$4). 'Miscanti' means 'toad' in Atacameño, and refers to when the lake was full of toads. In the 1940s and 1950s, trout were introduced for American fishermen working in Chuquicamata, resulting in the decline of the toad population; today there are none left. There is a path around the lake. Allow 4 hours for the circuit.

Nearby is the **Laguna Miñiques**. The lakes are on the site of ancient Atacameño ʃting grounds and arrowheads can still be found on the shores, which are edged ɹ whorls of calcium salt crystals. The rare Hornet coot can often be seen here.

There are clear views of the volcanoes behind the lakes, often snowcapped between april and june, as well as fantastic views down to the Salar.

After the turning to the lakes, the road goes on to the mine at Laco, before proceeding to the **Paso de Sico**, which has replaced the higher, more northerly Guaytiquina pass, at 4295 m (also spelt Huaytiquina) to Argentina (see below).

Some 10 km south of Toconao, the old road branches east towards Guaytiquina. In a deep *quebrada* below Volcán Láscar is the now deserted settlement of **Talabre**, with terracing and an ancient threshing floor. Above the *quebrada* is an isolated, stone-built cemetery. Large flocks of llamas graze where the stream crosses the road below the Láscar Volcano at 5154 m. After a steep climb on a very bad road, you reach the **Laguna Lejía** at 4190 m, once full of flamingos. Mysteriously, the colony declined rapidly immediately after the eruption of Volcán Láscar in 1993. You then pass through the high plains of **Guaytiquina** (4275 m), where only a few herdsmen are found. The Guaytiquina crossing to Argentina is not open to road traffic.

Argentine border crossings from San Pedro

There are three crossings: the best is the most northerly, the **Paso de Jama** at 4200 m, 165 km southeast of San Pedro, which is reached by a paved road that runs via the Salar de Tara, which forms a sector of the Reserva Nacional de los Flamencos. The main alternative to this, **Paso de Sico** at 4079 m, lies further south, 207 km southeast of San Pedro, and is reached by a very poor road which runs via Toconao and Socaire (see above, page 222). This pass has replaced the higher **Paso de Guaytiquina** at 4275 m. The most southerly crossing is **Paso de Socompa**, 3865 m, which is reached by another very poor road from Pan de Azúcar (see page 222).

South of San Pedro de Atacama

Into Bolivia: the Salar de Uyuni and other sights

East of San Pedro, on the border with Bolivia, lies **Volcán Licancábur** (5916 m), a sacred site for the Incas and the focal point of three Inca paths that crossed the *altiplano* and the Salar de Atacama. The volcano can be climbed only from the Bolivian side, at any time of the year except January and February. At the foot of the volcano on the Bolivian side is **Laguna Verde** (4400 m), which extends over 17 sq km; its wind-lashed waters are an impressive jade, the result, it is said, of magnesium, calcium carbonate, lead or arsenic. There is a *refugio* near the lake (US$2, small, mattresses, running water).

Further north is the equally impressive **Laguna Colorada** (4278 m), which covers 60 sq km; its flaming red waters are the result of the effects of the wind and afternoon sun on the numerous micro-organisms that live in it (up until midday the water is a fairly ordinary colour). The water is less than a metre deep but the mud is very soft,

and the shores are encrusted with borax, which provides an arctic white contrast with the waters of the lake. The pink algae in the lake provides food for the rare James flamingos, along with the more common Chilean and Andean flamingos. Some 40 other bird species can also be seen.

Further north still, beyond Ollagüe, is the **Salar de Uyuni**, the largest and highest salt lake in the world and an increasingly popular attraction for visitors. Situated at an altitude of 3650 m and covering 9000-12,000 sq km (depending on who you believe), the Salar is twice as big as the Great Salt Lake in the United States. The depth of the salt varies from 2 to 20 m. Driving across it is one of the most fantastic experiences in South America, especially in June/July when the bright blue skies contrast with the blinding-white salt (be sure to bring good sunglasses). After particularly wet rainy seasons the Salar is covered in water, which adds to the surreal experience.

There is a Chilean post for **immigration and customs** ⓘ *0800-2300*, at Paso de Socompa. Immigration and customs formalities for Paso de Jama and Paso de Sico are dealt with in San Pedro de Atacama ⓘ *0800-2300*. Incoming vehicles are searched for meat, fruit and dairy products. If crossing by private vehicle, check road conditions with the *carabineros* and at immigration in San Pedro, as these crossings are liable to be closed by heavy rain in summer and blocked by snow in winter. If hitching, try the immigration post in San Pedro; Spanish is essential.

On the Argentine side of the border, all these roads link up and continue to **San Antonio de los Cobres** (where Argentine customs and immigration formalities take place) and **Salta**. Transport using the Paso de Jama crossing usually follows a more northerly alternative via **Susques**, where there is accommodation, and **Jujuy**. The most southerly route via Paso de Socompa is perhaps the most spectacular, crossing salt flats and wide expanses of desert, but this route is virtually unused.

Bolivian border crossings from San Pedro

There are two crossings, the more northerly of which, via Ollagüe, is described above (see page 213). The more southerly crossing is at **Hito Cajones**, 45 km east of San Pedro via a poor road that turns off the paved road towards Paso de Jama at La Cruz, 8 km ...thwest of the border. Laguna Verde (see box, above) is 7 km north of Hito Cajones. ... an **immigration and customs** ⓘ *0800-2300*, are in San Pedro. Incoming vehicles ... arched for fruit, vegetables and dairy products.

There is no public transport: do not be tempted to hitch to the border as you risk being stranded without water or shelter at sub-zero temperatures. The most practical method of crossing this border is on a tour from San Pedro (see page 227). If you intend to travel independently in this region do not underestimate the dangers of getting stuck without transport or accommodation at this altitude. Do not travel alone and seek full advice in advance.

● Sleeping

San Pedro de Atacama *p218, map p220*
San Pedro is an expensive town; accommodation rates rise in Jan and Feb when it may also be scarce.
LL Explora, Av Américo Vespucio Sur 80, 5 piso, Santiago, T055-2066060, www.explora.com. Luxury full board and excursion programme, 3 nights, 4 nights and 8 nights, advance booking only.
L Hostería San Pedro, Toconao 460, T055-851011, hsanpedro@chilesat.net. The town's oldest luxury hotel. Pool (residents only), petrol station, cabins. Some rooms with satellite TV. Reasonably comfortable but nothing special for the price.
L Tulor, Atienza 523, T/F055-851027, www.tulor.cl. Rooms with cane roofs and balconies. Good service, swimming pool, heating, parking, laundry service, bar and restaurant. English spoken. Slightly overpriced.
L Kimal, Atienza 452 y Caracoles, T055-851030, www.kimal.cl. Comfortable, nice living room. Some rooms are bigger than others and some have their own terrace. Small swimming pool with jacuzzi and spa. Good restaurant (open to the public). Recommended.
AL La Casa de Don Tomás, Tocopilla s/n, T055-851055, www.dontomas.cl. Good accommodation, very pleasant inside, bright and spacious lounge, quiet, swimming pool, snacks served. English spoken.
A El Tatio, Caracoles 219, T055-851092, eltatio@sanpedroatacama.com. Slightly run-down, the outside rooms at the back are much brighter. Tiny swimming pool, some English spoken.
A Hostal Katarpe, Atienza 441, T055-851033, www.katarpe.com. Comfortable and quiet, nice patio, friendly. Some staff speak English. Breakfast extra. Not great value.
A-C Hostal Takha-Takha, Caracoles s/n, T055-851038, takhatakha@terra.cl. Pretty, lovely garden, pleasant shady patio with tall

trees and flowers, clean rooms with or without bath (D singles). Also camping (US$7 per person). Laundry facilities. Friendly staff. Recommended.
B Casa Corvatsch, Le Paige 178, T/F055-851101, corvatsch@entelchile.net. Pleasant views, but several bad reports about the owner. Also has much cheaper rooms.
B Hostal Inti Kamac, Atienza, T055-851200. D singles. Pleasant veranda, with bath. Friendly and good value.
B Hostal Lickana, Caracoles y Atienza, T055-851940. New hostel. Impeccable rooms with bath. Friendly staff. No breakfast. Good choice.
B Hostal Sonchek, Le Paige 170, T/F055-851112, soncheksp@hotmail.com. E singles, F per person in dorms. Decent value hostel with kitchen and laundry facilities, a ping pong table and a café attached. The more expensive rooms have private bathrooms. English and French spoken.
B-C Hostal Puritama, Caracoles 113, T055-851540. Simple but comfortable, with large patio, kitchen facilities, good showers, camping available.
B-C Hostal Mamatierra, Pachamama 615, T055-851418. F per person in shared rooms. 5 mins' walk from the centre. Will pick you up from the bus terminals. Some rooms with bath. Kitchen facilities, peaceful, friendly, recommended.
B-C Hostal Sumaj Jallpa, Volcán el Tatio 703, Sector Licancabur, T055-851416, sumajjallpa@sanpedroatacama.com. Pleasant peaceful Swiss-Chilean run hostel east of town. Free pickup from bus terminals. The hostel is about a half hour walk from town, but it rents bikes.
B-C Residencial Chiloé, Atienza 404, T055-851017. Rooms with bath much nicer than those without. Sunny veranda, good clean bathrooms, breakfast extra, laundry facilities, good beds but no single rooms, luggage store.

B-C **Residencial Don Raul**, Caracoles 130-A, T055-851138, www.donraul.cl. With bath. E singles without bath. Pleasant rooms with tiled floors and slightly airier than most. Kitchen facilities. Breakfast extra.

B-D **Hostal Edén Atacameño**, Toconao 592, T055-851154. D-F singles. Friendly. Rooms without bath are basic. Internet facilities. Unkempt kitchen available for cooking. Also camping.

C **Hostal Martita**, Palpana 4. F singles. 5 mins' walk from town centre. Some rooms with bath. Good beds, friendly. Good value.

C **Hostelling International**, Caracoles 360, T055-851426, www.hostellingatacama.com. E per person in dorms. Lively hostel. Cramped shared rooms with lockers. Shoddy construction. Bicycle rental.

D **Casa de Norma**, Tocopilla, T055-851114. F singles. Very basic family accommodation, simple rooms, patio. Kitchen facilities. Slightly aloof owners.

D **Residencial La Florida**, Tocopilla 406, T055- 851021. F-G per person in shared rooms. Without bath, basic, intermittent hot water, kitchen and laundry facilities. Hammock in courtyard.

D **Residencial Vilacoyo**, Tocopilla 387, T055-851006. F singles. Rooms without bath. Friendly, good kitchen facilities, recommended.

There are a number of informal, unregistered hostels, usually F-G per person, but security is often lax, and thefts have been reported.

Camping

Camping Kunza, Antofagasta y Atienza, T055-851183. Disco next door at weekends. Also **Camping Los Perales** and **Camping Terracota**. **Alberto Terrazas oasis Camping** at Pozo 3, 5 km east of town, has the best facilities including a swimming pool.

The geysers of El Tatio p220

There is a workers' camp at El Tatio, which is empty apart from one guard, who might let you sleep in a bed in one of the huts; bring food and a sleeping bag.

Toconao and around p221, map p223

There are basic *residenciales* in the village. Cheap accommodation is also offered at the **Restaurant Lascar**, which has good, simple food. Camping is not possible along the Quebrada de Jere.

① Eating

San Pedro de Atacama p218, map p220

Few places are open before 1000. Restaurants in the centre close at midnight. Drink bottled water as, owing to its high mineral content, the local supply is not recommended for those unaccustomed to it.

♔ **Adobe**, Caracoles. A good meeting place with an open fire, where you can watch the moon rise. Loud music and somewhat supercilious service. Greenwich Village/ Islington in the Atacama.

♔ **Café Export**, Toconao y Caracoles. Nice decor, vegetarian options, real coffee, English spoken, loud music.

♔ **Casa Piedra**, Caracoles s/n. Open fire, friendly service, also has a cheap menu, many of the waiters are musicians who, if in the mood, will play Inti Illimanni or Victor Jara songs on panpipes and queñas late at night, good food and cocktails. Warmly recommended.

♔ **Cuna**, Tocopilla 359, T055-851999. Understated and warm. Interesting menu. Good service. Spacious patio open in summer.

♔ **La Casona**, Caracoles. Good food, vegetarian options, cheap lunchtime menu, large portions, interesting Cubist-style paintings of the desert, popular. Recommended.

♔ **Milagro**, Caracoles. Good food, vegetarian options, attentive service.

♔-♔ **Café Etnico**, Tocopilla 423, T055-851377. Good-value set lunch, juice and sandwiches, internet access. Book exchange.

♔ **Quitor**, Licancabur y Domingo Atienza, T055-851056. Good, basic home-cooked Chilean food, inexpensive (3 courses for US$3).

There are several stalls on Licancabur by the football pitch offering a variety of inexpensive lunches.

● *For an explanation of sleeping and eating price codes used in this guide, see inside the*
● *front cover. Other relevant information is found in Essentials, see pages 50-57.*

Cafés

Café Tierra Todo Natural, Caracoles.
Much the best choice for breakfast, serving
excellent fruit juices and the best bread in
the Atacama, plus real coffee and yoghurt.
It also opens earliest.

◐ Bars and clubs

San Pedro de Atacama *p218, map p220*
Many San Pedro restaurants double as bars
at night, although they close at midnight. A
'pueblo turístico' has been built just east of
town with several late night bars and clubs.
Estaka, Caracoles. Lively watering hole after
2300, where the Chilean New Age scene
congregates. Also very good cuisine and
service. Recommended.

◯ Shopping

San Pedro de Atacama *p218, map p220*
There is a good craft market one block east
of the plaza.

▲ Activities and tours

San Pedro de Atacama *p218, map p220*
San Pedro is awash with tour operators and,
with competition so stiff, prices are low.
Approximate prices for tours are as follows:
Valle de la Luna US$6-8 (plus US$3
entrance); **Salar de Atacama** US$10-12 (plus
US$4 entrance); **Geysers of Tatio** US$20-25
(plus US$4 entrance); **Altiplano Lakes**
(including **Toconao** and **Salar de Atacama**)
US$35-40 (plus US$10 in entrance fees).

The following advice should help those
trying to pick through the glut of operators:
avoid cut-price operators and try to check out
vehicles and guides before booking; if
travelling to high altitude make sure that
oxygen is being carried; report any complaints
to the Municipalidad or to Sernatur; if in
doubt, check through the book with travellers'
complaints at the Sernatur office.

Spanish speakers may prefer to go with
one of the smaller operators to experience
better the vastness of the desert, although all
the more responsible operators do try to stay
away from the well-trodden routes used by
the majority. There are about 25 agencies,
but some are temporary and/or open for
only part of the year.

Atacama Connection, Toconao 460,
T055-851548. Usual range of tours.
Professional if somewhat impersonal.
Atacama Inca Tour, Toconao 421-A, T055-
581062, atacamaincatour@starmedia.com.
Recommended but not always open.
Ázimut 360, T02-2351519 www.azimut.cl.
A long-established nationwide operator that
also offers adventure tours. Book in advance.
Bernardo Flores, T099-98771102 . Local
guide recommended for horse riding trips.
Cactus Tour, Atienza 419, T055-851524,
www.cactustour.cl. One of the reputable
agencies. Good vehicles. Occasionally offer
tours to Bolivia. Most guides speak English.
Recommended.
Cosmo Andino Expediciones, Caracoles,
T/F055-851069, cosmoandino@entelchile.
net. One of the best tour agencies. English,
French, German, Dutch spoken, good
vehicles, good drivers, experienced guides,
excellent book exchange for tour customers
only, highly recommended for non-Spanish
speakers. Dutch owner Martin Beeris is very
knowledgeable about the region.
Desert Adventures, Caracoles s/n,
T/F055-851067, www.desertadventure.cl.
Offers excursions to all the major sites,
modern fleet of vehicles, large numbers,
mostly good reports.
Expediciones Corvatsch, Tocopilla,
T055-851087, ccorvatsch@entelchile.net
Operated by Residencial Corvatsch and
Residencial Florida, good vehicles, casual
service, offer discounts for package tours
with accommodation.
La Herradura, Tocopilla s/n, T055-851087,
laherraduraatacama@yahoo.es. Horseback
tours with good local guides, repeatedly
recommended.
Space, Caracoles 166, T055-851935,
www.spaceobs.com. Astronomical tours
given by a Frenach astronomer who has set
up a small observatory in the village of Solor,
south of San Pedro. Tours are interesting and
informative and compare favourably with
those in Mamalluca in the Elqui valley. Tours
in English, French and Spanish. US$17. Book
in advance from the office where you are
picked up in the evening. Wear warm
clothing. Recommended.
Turismo Colque, Caracoles, T055-851109,
www.colquetours.com. Specialists for tours
to Bolivia, including 1-day tour to Laguna

Verde and 3-day tours to Laguna Colorado and the Salar de Uyuni (US$90 per person, see below); TCs, Visa and MasterCard all accepted, more reliable than most, hires sleeping bags, often recommended but some mixed reports. Has agencies in Uyuni and La Paz. Two or three other tour companies in San Pedro offer similar tours.
Turismo Ochoa, Caracoles y Toconao, T055-851022. Oldest operator in San Pedro, knowledgeable local guides who are a bit taciturn, inexpensive.
Vulcano, Caracoles 317, 055-851023, www.vulcanochile.cl. Mountain climbs, guided cycle trips, sandboarding and other adventure tours to infrequently visited areas including bespoke tours, also hire out mountain bikes, English speaking guides, recommended.

The geysers of El Tatio p220
Tours to El Tatio depart around 0400, arriving at the geysers at 0700, US$20-25, including breakfast. There are opportunities to swim in the hot thermal pool and to visit the Baños de Puritama on the return journey. Take warm clothing and a swimming costume. Some agencies offer tours to El Tatio and on to Calama, via the villages of the *altiplano*.

Around the Salar de Atacama p221
Agencies in San Pedro offer excursions to Toconao and the Salar, returning via the Quebrada de Jere, US$12-15 plus park entry, usual departure 1530, but note that the flamingos are best seen in the morning, so try to get a morning tour, or combine with visiting the *altiplano* lakes.

Bolivia tours
The Salar de Uyuni, Laguna Colorada and Laguna Verde are usually visited by tours from the Bolivian town of Uyuni, where accommodation, money exchange and transport to La Paz, Oruro and Potosí are all available. However, **Turismo Colque** (among others) in San Pedro (see above) also offers this tour and will drop passengers off in Uyuni, although some report that, to see the colour changes on Laguna Colorada, the trip is best done from Uyuni.

⊖ Transport

San Pedro de Atacama *p218, map p220*
Bicycle
Several agencies offer cycle hire, check prices and condition of bicycles carefully, as quality varies.

Bus
To **Calama**, Tur Bus, several daily (6 continue on to Antofagasta), also **Frontera** 7 a day, 1½ hrs, first 0900, last 1900, US$2.50. Frequencies vary with more departures in Jan/Feb and some weekends, fewer out of season. Book in advance if you want to return from San Pedro on Sun evening.
  Frontera also run to **Toconao**, 4 daily at 1240, 1600, 1930, 2030, US$1.20, and to **Peine** and **Socaire** 2 or 3 weekly to each destination, US$3.
  To **Arica**, daily direct service with **Tur Bus**, US$24. **Pullman Bus** and **Géminis** services from Calama to **Salta**, Argentina (see page 216) also stop in San Pedro.

Car
Some agencies in San Pedro offer vehicle hire, but you should check vehicle condition and insurance very carefully as there are reports of accidents involving uninsured and badly serviced vehicles; it is better to hire cars in Calama.

❶ Directory

San Pedro de Atacama *p218, map p220*
Banks ATMs appear and then disappear with no discernable pattern. Better to bring pesos from Calama or elsewhere. **Cambio Atacama**, Toconao, daily 1030-1800, rates posted outside, good rates for US$ cash, poor rates for TCs; best not to try changing TCs in San Pedro; bring Chilean pesos from Calama. The **Géminis** bus terminal will change Bolivianos. **Internet** Ubiquitous, including **Café Étnico**, on Tocopilla, book exchange. **Laundry** Alana, Caracoles, near Atienza. **Post office** Padre Le Paige, opposite Museo Archaeológico.
Telephone CTC, Caracoles y Toconoa; Entel on the plaza, Mon-Fri 0900-2200, Sat 0930-2200, Sun 0930-2100.

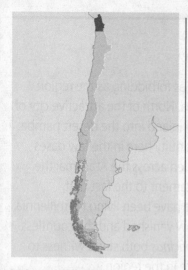

Iquique, Arica & the Far North

⁝ Footprint features

Introduction

The far north of Chile is equally as forbidding as the region around Antofagasta and Calama. North of the attractive city of Iquique, transport arteries head inland into the desert pampa. There is a palpable sense of antiquity here in the few oases and settlements that are sprinkled across the Atacama; the profusion of geoglyphs are testament to the fact that, wherever there is water, people have been living for millennia. These geoglyphs of peoples now vanished and the countless ghost towns of former nitrate *oficinas* both stand witness to the harshness and fragility of life in the region.

Further inland still, towards the *altiplano*, are some beautiful spots. Mamiña and Pica are two thermal springs resorts near Iquique, each of them remarkable for their tranquillity. There are four remote national parks in the high Andes, the northernmost of which – the Parque Nacional Lauca – offers some of the most stunning scenery in Chile, with a necklace of high lakes, snow-capped volcanoes, lava fields and varied bird life. It is easily reached from Arica, Chile's northernmost city, along the international road to Bolivia. Near Parque Nacional Lauca are small Andean villages, such as Visviri and Parinacota, where most people speak Aymará, and Spanish remains a foreign language.

★ Don't miss...

1 **Iquique** Wander among the city's well preserved 19th-century architecture built with the wealth of the nitrate era, page 233.
2 **Humberstone and Santa Laura** These abandoned towns are ghostly reminders of the region's nitrate industry, page 236.
3 **Mamiña** Relax in a thermal bath at the hot springs of this small Andean village, famous for the restorative powers of its waters, page 237.
4 **Cerro Unitas, Pintados or Tiliviche** Be amazed by the geoglyphs carved in the desert by pre-Hispanic people at three of the best-known sites, page 240.
5 **The altiplano national parks** Take a four-day trip from Arica to Iquique via Lauca, Las Vicuñas, Surire and Isluga, escaping the modern world in unforgettable, pristine natural environments, page 256.

Iquique, Arica & the Far North

Background

As elsewhere in northern Chile, there was a widespread and highly developed network of pre-Hispanic cultures in this region. The geoglyphs at sites such as Pintados and Tiliviche are thought to have been markers for caravans of traders making their way from the *altiplano* to the coast and back again. Circles marked in the hillsides signalled the presence of water. The coastal peoples traded furs and fish with the more highly developed cultures of the interior, maintaining links with Tiahuanaco and the Incas.

Even after the Spanish conquest, the early Spanish settler population was small in numbers. Settlement was concentrated largely in the oases of the sierra, where the climate was easier and where malaria, the scourge of the coast, was not found. From an early date, Arica became one of the principal ports for the silver trade from Potosí, but the coast remained sparsely inhabited until the 19th century. At the time of Independence, the whole of this area became the Peruvian provinces of Tarapacá and Arica, with the provincial capital at the now ruined city of Tarapacá, near Huara. The region became the focal point for the War of the Pacific (1879-1883), with decisive naval battles fought at Iquique on 21 May 1879, and at Angamos, near Mejillones, on 8 October of the same year. After the war, the area as far north as Tacna came under Chilean control, and became the country's economic powerhouse following the sudden growth of the nitrate industry.

The poor conditions of workers in the nitrate mines led to the development of early left-wing and trade unionist movements in the far northern part of Chile. In 1907, a group of miners from one of the nitrate *oficinas* was executed by the army in the Santa María school in Iquique for campaigning to be paid in hard cash instead of *oficina* tokens. The legacy of the far north's radicalism can be seen in the now infamous 'caravan of death' executed in seven northern cities by one of General Pinochet's henchmen in the days following the 1973 coup (see page 530).

The region's borders were finally delineated in 1929: Tacna voted in a referendum to return to Peru, while Arica opted to remain Chilean. The collapse of the nitrate industry in the 1930s and 1940s was a regional crisis but the quick growth of the fishing industry saved the area from disaster.

The sea still provides the main source of wealth in this region: Iquique is the principal fishing port in Chile, unloading 35% of the total national catch, and has important fish processing industries. Nowadays, mining is much less important than in other parts of northern Chile; however, silver and gold are mined at Challacollo and copper at Sagasca, near Tarapacá, while the new copper mine at Collahuasi has made a big difference to the region's economy. Over 90% of the population lives in the two coastal cities, Arica and Iquique.

Geography and climate

The Atacama Desert extends over most of the far north. The Cordillera de la Costa slowly loses height north of Iquique, terminating at the Morro in Arica: from Iquique northwards it drops directly to the sea and, as a result, there are few beaches along this coast. Inland, the central depression, the *pampa*, 1000 to 1200 m high, is arid and punctuated by salt flats south of Iquique. Between Iquique and Arica, it is crossed from east to west by numerous gorges, formed by several rivers flowing west from the sierra; the more northerly of these, the Ríos Lluta and San José, provide water for Arica and for the Valle de Azapa. The source of the former is snowmelt from Volcán Tacora. Its sulphurous waters can only support crops such as corn, alfalfa and onions. In contrast the San José brings crystal fresh water from the altiplano to the Azapa Valley which is well known for its olive crop and tropical fruit. On the coast, temperatures are moderated by the Pacific Ocean but, in the *pampa,* variations of temperature between day and night are extreme, ranging between 30°C and 0°C. Coastal regions receive *camanchaca* (sea mist) but the *pampa* is permanently rainless.

⦂ Behind the wheel

Do not think of visiting the *altiplano* in a cheap hire car. A 4WD is essential, with the highest clearance possible. Tyres should not be inflated to more than 30lbs at sea level. Take extra fuel: cars are much less fuel efficient at high altitude. During the climb from Arica, you should stop several times to release excess pressure in fuel cans and tyres if necessary. There is a private petrol pump at the chemical plant at the Salar de Surire that will nearly always sell petrol or diesel in an emergency.

In the rainy season water levels rise. If a bridge is washed away or the road/path goes through a river or laguna, get out, check the depth and make sure the height of your car's air vents are higher than this. At the Río Lauca crossing this can be as high as 1 m. Drive through the shallowest part. Do not leave the road or well travelled tracks. Drive slowly and watch out for potholes. On the main road lorry drivers can be erratic. If a vehicle is approaching in the other direction on a *ripio* track, apply pressure to the windscreen with your hand. This will prevent the windscreen from shattering if hit by a stone.

East of the central depression lies the sierra, the western branch of the Andes, beyond which is a high plateau, the *altiplano* (3500-4500 m), from which rise volcanic peaks, including Parinacota (6350 m), Pomerape (6250 m), Guayatiri (6064 m), Acotango (6050 m), Capurata (5990 m), Tacora (5988 m) and Tarapacá (5825 m). There are also a number of lakes in the *altiplano*, the largest of which, Lago Chungará, is one of the highest in the world. The main river draining the *altiplano*, the Río Lauca, flows eastwards into Bolivia. Temperatures in the sierra average 20°C in summer and 9°C in winter. The *altiplano* is much colder, averaging just 10°C in summer and -5°C in winter. Both the sierra and the *altiplano* are affected by storms of rain, snow and hail (*invierno boliviano*), usually between January and April.

Iquique and around → *Colour map 1, B2.*

Iquique is the the capital of Región I (Tarapacá) and one of the main ports of northern Chile (with a population of around 20,000). The city is situated on a rocky peninsula at the foot of the high coastal mountain range, sheltered by the headlands of Punta Gruesa and Cavancha. Iquique is perhaps the most attractive city in northern Chile, with a well-preserved collection of historical buildings in the centre, whose bright wooden façades make a surprising contrast to the lifeless desert and the grey coastal mist.

Inland from Iquique are several small towns that were the early centres of Spanish colonial settlement. They are less crowded than villages near Calama and Arica and are well worth visiting. The rainy season in this area is mainly in January. ▸▸ *For Sleeping, Eating and other listings, see pages 240-246.*

Iquique ⬤🚗🏨🏤🎡❄🅾🔺🏛🎵 *pp240-246.*

Although the site was used as a port in pre-Hispanic times, it remained sparsely populated throughout the colonial period. Even in 1855, when Iquique had begun to export nitrates, the population was only about 2500. The nitrate trade transformed the city, bringing large numbers of foreign traders and creating a wealthy elite.

Although partly destroyed by an earthquake in 1877, the city became the centre of this trade after its transfer from Peru to Chile at the end of the War of the Pacific. Today, the fabulous wealth the nitrate industry brought to the town can be seen in some wonderful buildings. Its coastal position also means that you can enjoy some relaxing days sunning, surfing and swimming.

Ins and outs → *492 km north of Antofagasta.*

Getting there Iquique is served by all major bus companies from the south and from Arica – most southbound buses take the coastal road to Tocopilla. There are also daily buses up to Oruro and La Paz in Bolivia. National flights to Arica, Antofagasta and Santiago; international to La Paz. The airport transfer service, US$5, is unreliable; it can be just as cheap to get a taxi if there are a few of you, US$12.

Getting around The best way to get around in Iquique is by *colectivo.*

Tourist information Sernatur ① *Aníbal Pinto 436, T057-312238, infoiquique@sern atur.cl, Mon-Fri 0830-1630*, is very helpful.

Sights

The old town stretches south and west from **Plaza Prat** with a clock tower and bell dating from 1877. The plaza has recently been remodelled to good effect, with shady benches and newly planted trees. Every Sunday at midday there is a military parade lasting 45 minutes, while on Friday and Saturday nights there are often free theatrical or musical events. On the northeast corner of the plaza is the **Centro Español**, built in Moorish style by the local Spanish community in 1904, and unique in Chile. The ground floor is a restaurant but the upper floors show paintings of scenes from Don Quixote and from Spanish history by the Spanish artist, Vicente Tordecillas. The extravagance of its construction shows the fabulous wealth that nitrates once brought to the region. On the south side of the plaza is the **Teatro Municipal**, built as an opera house in 1890 with a façade featuring four women representing the seasons; in its heyday it played host to such famous names as Carruso. Three blocks north of the plaza is the old **Aduana** (customs house) built in 1871 and the scene, in 1891, of an important battle in the Civil War between supporters of President Balmaceda and congressional forces. Part of it now houses the **Museo Naval de Iquique** ① *Esmeralda 250, Tue-Fri 1000-1300, 1600-1900, Sat 1000-1400, US$0.40*, dedicated to the War of the Pacific, and more specifically, to the naval battle of Iquique. Nearby, is the harbour; there are **cruises** ① *45 mins, US$4, minimum 10 people*, from the passenger pier . Sea lions and pelicans can be seen.

Five blocks east along Calle Sotomayor is the **railway station**, now disused, built in 1883 and displaying several old locomotives. Two blocks south of the railway station, on Bolívar, is the **cathedral**, dating from 1885. It is painted bright yellow and blue and has interesting stained-glass windows. On Amunátegui, behind the **Escuela Santa María** on Zégers, there is a memorial to the workers from the nitrate mines who were killed by the army while sheltering in the school during the strike of 1907.

On Calle Baquedano, which runs south from Plaza Prat, is the highly recommended **Museo Regional** ① *Baquedano 951, T057-411214, Mon-Fri 0830-1300, 1530-1830, Sat 1030-1300, Sun (in summer) 1000-1300 and 1600-2000, free*, which has an excellent collection of pre-Hispanic artefacts (including several mummies). The archaeological section is very well set out, although explanations are in Spanish only, tracing the development of pre-Hispanic civilizations in the region and containing an important ethnographical collection of the Isluga culture of the *altiplano* (circa AD 400) and of contemporary Aymará cultures. There is also a section devoted to the nitrate era, with exhibits including a collection of *oficina* tokens, a model of a nitrate *oficina* and the collection of the nitrate entrepreneur, Santiago Humberstone.

● *The name of the town is derived from the Aymará word 'ique-ique', meaning 'place of rest and tranquillity'.*

Elsewhere on the street are the attractive former mansions of the 'nitrate barons'. Adorned with columns, balconies and impressive old doors, these buildings date from between 1880 and 1903 and were constructed from timber imported from

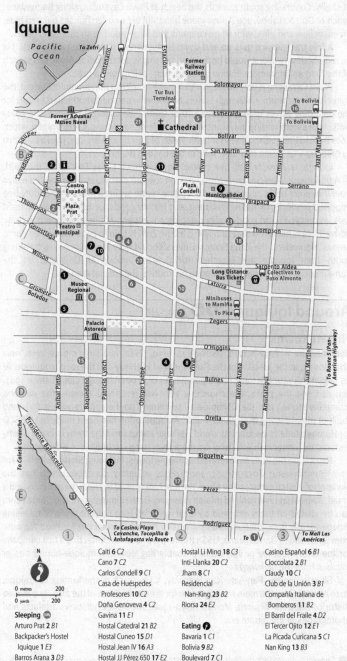

Iquique

Pacific Ocean

To Zofri

Former Railway Station

Tur Bus Terminal

Former Aduana/ Museo Naval

Cathedral

Centro Español

Plaza Prat

Teatro Municipal

Museo Regional

Palacio Astoreca

To Caleta Cavancha

To Casino, Playa Cavancha, Tocopilla & Antofagasta via Route 1

To Mall Las Américas

To Route 5 (Pan- American Highway)

Long Distance Bus Tickets

Sargento Aldea Colectivos to Poso Almonte

Minibuses to Mamiña

To Pica

Solomayor

Esmeralda

To Bolivia

Bolívar

San Martín

Serrano

Tarapacá

Thompson

Latorre

Zegers

O'Higgins

Bulnes

Orella

Riquelme

Pérez

Rodríguez

Plaza Condell

Municipalidad

N

0 metres 200
0 yards 200

Sleeping 🛏
Arturo Prat **2** *B1*
Backpacker's Hostel
  Iquique **1** *E3*
Barros Arana **3** *D3*
Buenos Aires **5** *B2*

Caiti **6** *C2*
Cano **7** *C2*
Carlos Condell **9** *C1*
Casa de Huéspedes
  Profesores **10** *C2*
Doña Genoveva **4** *C2*
Gavina **11** *E1*
Hostal Catedral **21** *B2*
Hostal Cuneo **15** *D1*
Hostal Jean IV **16** *A3*
Hostal JJ Pérez 650 **17** *E2*
Hostal Juan López **14** *E2*

Hostal Li Ming **18** *C3*
Inti-Llanka **20** *C2*
Jham **8** *C1*
Residencial
  Nan-King **23** *B2*
Riorsa **24** *E2*

Eating 🍴
Bavaria **1** *C1*
Bolivia **9** *B2*
Boulevard **7** *C1*
Brasileña **8** *D2*

Casino Español **6** *B1*
Cioccolata **2** *B1*
Claudy **10** *C1*
Club de la Unión **3** *B1*
Compañía Italiana de
  Bomberos **11** *B2*
El Barril del Fraile **4** *D2*
El Tercer Ojito **12** *E1*
La Picada Curicana **5** *C1*
Nan King **13** *B3*

California. The finest of these is the **Palacio Astoreca** ① *O'Higgins 350, Tue-Fri 1000-1300, Sat 1000-1330, Sun 1100-1400, US$1*, built in 1903, subsequently the Intendencia and now a museum with fine late 19th-century furniture and exhibitions of shells. Continuing south towards the beach at Playa Cavancha, along Baquedano, Lynch or Obispo Labbé, you'll pass many beautiful old wooden houses painted blue, green, yellow and pink, with white columns and large wooden shutters and doors.

A free tram service runs up and down Baquedano (1000-1400, 1700-2000). It is incredibly slow (walking would be quicker) but that is not the point. Along this stretch of the road an impromptu market often appears, selling bric-a-brac.

Playa Cavancha is very popular in summer – in spite of the Humboldt Current, the water is almost warm – although surfers and other watersports enthusiasts make for the pounding waves of **Playa Brava** further south (see page 245). Those who enjoy walking or sandboarding may want to climb the large sand dune, **Cerro Dragón**, which rises behind Iquique and gives fantastic views of the city and the sea; take a *colectivo* to Chipana y La Tirana and then walk to the base of the hill.

Iquique is a major duty-free centre. North of town is the Free Zone, the **Zofri**, ① *Amuñategui, Mon-Sat 1100-2100, limit on tax-free purchases US$1000*, colectivo *from the centre US$0.70*. It is a giant shopping centre selling a wide range of duty-free imported products, including electronic and leather goods, perfumes, new and used cars, motorcycles and good-quality camping equipment. At Christmas, people come from all over Chile to do their shopping, as the Zofri is said to be cheaper than Punta Arenas' equivalent, the Zona Franca. Drivers should note that all vehicles travelling south from Iquique are searched for duty-free goods at Quillagua on the Pan-American Highway and at Chipana on Route 1, the coastal road.

Around Iquique ●❼⊟ *pp240-246.*

Nitrate towns

Humberstone ① *T057-751213, visits 0830-1830, US$2*, is a large nitrate town, now abandoned, at the junction of the Pan-American Highway and the road to Iquique. At its height in 1940, the town had a population of 3700. Although closed since 1961, you can see the plaza, the church, a very well-preserved theatre, the *pulpería* (company stores) and the Olympic-size swimming pool complete with grandstand (built of metal plating from ships' hulls). An application has been made to UNESCO for Humberstone to be granted World Heritage status, and the town is being slowly restored by former residents who are more than happy to reminisce with visitors.

Nearby are the ruins of several other mining towns, including **Santa Laura** ① *2 km from Humberstone, T057-751981, 1000-1800, voluntary donation*, which has the skeleton of a nitrate processing plant, the machinery used to crush the minerals and a small, somewhat disorganized mining museum. Both Humberstone and Santa Laura can be visited on tours arranged by local agencies (see below). If you're travelling independently from Iquique, take any bus to Arica or a *colectivo* for Pozo Almonte from Sgto Aldea y Barros Arana, US$3 (there is a phone for contacting a taxi company for the return journey or you could probably flag down an Iquique-bound bus or minibus from the highway).

Situated on the Pan-American Highway, 5 km south of the turning to Iquique, Pozo Almonte was the main service centre for the nitrate fields of the area. The **Museo Histórico Salitrero** ① *plaza, Mon-Fri 0830-1300, 1600-1900*, displays artefacts and photographs of the nitrate era.

● *General Augusto Pinochet has been known to visit Mamiña to relieve the aches and pains*
● *of old age.*

South of Pozo Almonte, the Pan-American Highway runs to **Quillagua**, 172 km, where there is a customs post. All southbound vehicles, including buses, are searched. The road continues towards Antofagasta. At Km 24, the road runs through the largest section of the **Reserva Nacional Pampa del Tamarugal** (the other two sections are around La Tirana and north of Huara), which is administered by CONAF. Covering a total of 100,650 ha, the reserve includes plantations of tamaruga, a tree species adapted to the dry climate and saline soils.

The **Geoglifos de Pintados**, some 400 figures on the hillsides, representing humans, animals and birds, as well as abstract designs, are situated some 3 km west of the Pan-American Highway; take any bus south, US$3.50, and get off at Km 43. Many other sites around Iquique, including the Gigante del Atacama (see box, page 240), are difficult to visit without a vehicle.

Mamiña

A very popular thermal springs resort, Mamiña is reached by a good paved road, which runs 74 km east from Pozo Almonte. Situated on a ridge at 2,750 m, this is a delightful and very friendly village and would be an ideal place to relax for a few days after more strenuous activities in Bolivia or San Pedro de Atacama.

Mamiña has pre-Hispanic origins – its name means 'the girl of my eyes' in Aymará – and is inhabited mainly by people of Aymará origin. If you stand on the hill above the village, a circular geoglyph indicating the presence of water is clearly visible on the opposite side of the valley. The Aymará cultural centre, **Kaspi-Kala** ① *1000-1400, 1600-2000*, near the **Hotel Los Cardenales** (see page 242), includes an *artesanía* workshop and a sales outlet. Legend has it that one of Mamiña's thermal pools once cured an Inca princess; an Inca *pukará* stands on a hilltop 3 km east marked by a white cross that can be seen from the village (it's probably best to hire a guide if you want to visit it). There are also said to be the ruins of a pre-Hispanic settlement further down the valley towards the *pampa*.

The church, built in 1632, is the only colonial Andean church in Chile with twin towers, each topped by a bell tower; ascend the church by steps at the side for a view of the bells linked together by a single rope. Mamiña's abundant thermal springs and unique mud spring have meant that it has been a popular health resort since the nitrate era; the **Hotel Termas** dates from this period. The thermal springs, classified as being radioactive, are rich in sodium, potassium, sulphur, chlorides and silicates, and are acknowledged to be valuable in treating ailments, such as rheumatoid arthritis and sciatica, as well as respiratory and digestive problems. There is also a mud bath, the **Baño Los Chinos** ① *0930-1300*, which is considered valuable in the treatment of many skin diseases, such as psoriasis. The bath contains radioactive mud with natural deposits of vegetal mineral mud activated by the fermentation of certain algae; the mud is allowed to dry on the skin after the bath and then washed off in one of the thermal springs.

La Tirana

Situated 10 km east of the Pan-American Highway, on a turning 9 km south of Pozo Almonte, La Tirana is famous for a religious festival dedicated to the **Virgen del Carmen**, held annually from 10 to 16 July (see box, page 238), which attracts some 150,000 pilgrims and merrymakers (catapulting the population from around 550). Over 100 groups dance night and day decked out in colourful costumes and spectacular masks, starting on 12 July. All the dances take place in the main plaza in front of the church; no alcohol is served.

At other times of year, the church is well worth a visit, and there is a small museum, the **Museo de la Virgen de La Tirana** ① *Mon-Fri 0900-1300, 1600-1930, Sat-Sun 0900-2100, US$0.25*, which contains gifts to the virgin.

⦂ La Tirana

The legend of La Tirana is an intriguing mix of Andean traditions and Catholicism. It is said that, when Diego de Almagro made the first Spanish foray into Chile, one of his companions was an Inca princess. She was a fierce warrior who loathed everything to do with the Spanish and escaped into the pampa to wage war against them. She was so fierce that she became known as 'La Tirana' ('The Tyrant').

La Tirana's techniques were overthrown when she fell in love with Vasco de Almeyda, a Portuguese soldier enlisted by the Spanish, who persuaded her to convert to Christianity. When her companions discovered her treachery, both the Inca princess and the warrior were killed. The legend goes that a priest, coming some years later to the area to evangelize, discovered a cross on the spot where the couple had died, and built a church there.

Today, the fiesta treads a fine line between commercialism and maintaining these hybrid traditions.

The most important day and night occur on 16 July but, for up to a week beforehand, the town is awash with travelling salesmen, who come from all over Chile to sell everything that you could possibly need – clothes, music, bags, hats, cheap meals, ice creams and so on. At the same time, troupes of religious dancers and their accompanying brass bands come from as far away as Peru and Argentina to pay homage to the Virgen del Carmen. Eclecticism is the order of the day: as well as traditional Andean groups, there are also dancers who imitate the Sioux Indians from North America, as well as the 'Ali Baba Christians' dancing with imitation wooden sphinxes. The noise is deafening, day and night, as the brass bands vie with one another to produce the greatest racket. There is even an office set up by the church to perform marriages, and one of the most touching sights at the fiesta is that of happy couples being carried towards the church, amid the dancing, music and the chaos.

Matilla

Some 38 km east of La Tirana, Matilla is an oasis settlement founded in 1760 by settlers from Pica (see below). The village declined after 1912 when the waters of the Quebrada de Quisma were diverted to Iquique. The church (1887) is built of blocks of borax and rears up from over the arid plain like a version of the Sacré Coeur in the desert. It was damaged by an earthquake in 2005 but is being restored. Nearby is a **museum** ① *Lagar de Matilla, daily 0900-1700*, used in the 18th century for fermenting wine. Get a key from the kiosk in the plaza. Near Matilla, an unpaved, rough road runs southwest to meet the Pan-American Highway.

Pica

Four kilometres northeast of Matilla, Pica, with a current population of 3000, was the most important centre of early Spanish settlement in this region. In colonial times, it produced a famous wine sold as far away as Potosí. Most of the older buildings, including the church, date from the nitrate period when it became a popular resort. It is a leafy oasis, famous for its thermal baths and the fruit grown here – one of the highlights of a stay is drinking fresh fruit juices from any one of numerous stalls near the thermal springs, which lie about 1 km from the centre of the town at **Cocha Resbaladero** ① *0700-2000, US$3*. There are changing rooms, a snack bar and a beautiful pool on site and a small tourist information office opposite.

A few kilometres east of Pica on the road to the altiplano, there is a *mirador* with fine views. There is also a map showing where to find some fossilized dinosaur footprints. Tours are available from Pica.

From Iquique to the Bolivian border

Some 30 km north of Pozo Almonte, **Huara** was once a town of 7000 people, serving as a centre for the nearby nitrate towns. Today, the population is reduced to 400 and little evidence remains of the town's former prosperity, apart from the railway station, which is a national monument, and a small museum preserving a pharmacy from the nitrate era with all the cures and remedies that were then on offer. The church is also worth a look. The town was badly damaged by the 2005 earthquake and much of it is still in ruins.

At Huara, a road turns off the Pan-American Highway and runs to Colchane, 173 km northeast on the Bolivian frontier. Some 13 km east of Huara, the road passes, on the right, the **Geoglifos de Cerro Unitas**, the most outstanding of which is the **Gigante del Atacama**, a human figure 86 m tall, reported to be the largest geoglyph in the world and best viewed from a distance.

At Km 23, an unpaved road branches off south to **Tarapacá**, settled by the Spanish around 1560 and capital of the Peruvian province of Tarapacá until 1855, now largely abandoned except for the **Fiesta of the Virgen de la Candelaria** on 2 and 3 February. The major historic buildings, the Iglesia de San Lorenzo and the Palacio de Gobierno, are in ruins. At **Chusmisa** (Km 77), there are thermal springs producing water that is bottled and sold throughout northern Chile. The forlorn and windy border town of **Colchane** livens up for the market, which takes place every other Saturday, and provides access to the southern entrance of the **Parque Nacional Volcán Isluga**, some 6 km northwest. The border is open 0800-2000 daily; on the Bolivian side, an unpaved road leads to Oruro, 233 km northeast.

North towards Arica

The Pan-American Highway runs across the Atacama Desert at an altitude of around 1000 m, with several steep hills, best tackled in daylight. At night, sea mist, *camanchaca*, can reduce visibility.

At Zapiga, 47 km north of Huara, a road heads west for 41 km to **Pisagua**, formerly an important nitrate port, now reduced to a small fishing village. Several of the old wooden buildings are national monuments, including the **Municipal Theatre** (1892) and the **Clock Tower** (1887), but the town is now largely abandoned, although a handful of fish restaurants make it a pleasant stop for a meal. Pisagua was the site of a detention centre after the 1973 military coup; mass graves from that period were discovered near here in 1990.

Heading east from Zapiga, meanwhile, a poor road (deep sand and dust) leads 67 km to **Camiña**, a picturesque village in an oasis. From here, a terrible road runs to the **Tranque de Caritaya**, a dam 45 km further northeast, which supplies water for the coastal towns and which is set in splendid scenery with lots of wildlife and interesting botany (especially *llareta*).

About 10 km north of Zapiga is an interesting British cemetery dating from the 19th century: note the fine wrought-iron gates. Nearby, stop for a view of the **Geoglifos de Tiliviche**, representing a group of llamas (signposted to the left and easily accessible). Further north at Km 111, the **Geoglifos de Chiza** can be seen from the bridge that carries the highway over the Quebrada de Chiza. At Km 172, a road runs east to **Codpa**, an agricultural community in a deep gorge surrounded by interesting scenery, with poor roads continuing north and east towards Putre (see page 258), through Tignamar and **Belén**.

This tiny village was founded by the Spanish in 1625 on the silver route between Potosí and the coast. It has two colonial churches: the older one, the **Iglesia de Belén** is one of the oldest (and smallest) churches in Chile; the other, the **Iglesia de Carmen**,

Set in stone

Found as far south as the Río Loa and as far north as the Río Azapa near Arica, as well as along the Peruvian coast as far as Nazca, geoglyphs or *geoglifos* are one of the most visible traces left by ancient civilizations in the Atacama. Dating from an estimated AD 1000-1400, these designs were made on the rocks using two different techniques: by scraping away the topsoil to reveal different coloured rock beneath or by arranging stones to form a kind of mosaic. They exhibit three main themes: geometrical patterns; images of animals, especially camelids, birds and snakes; and humans, often holding or carrying instruments or weapons, such as a bow and arrows. They are easily visible because they were intended to be seen. They are generally located on isolated hills in the desert, on the western slopes of the Cordillera de la Costa or on the slopes of *quebradas* (gorges). Their significance is thought by some experts to be ritual, but the more current theory is that they were often a kind of signpost pointing out routes between the coast and the sierra.

The largest site is at **Pintados**, 96 km south of Iquique, reached by turning off the Pan-American Highway towards Pica and then following a 4 km track from which several panels can be seen, including representations of animals, birds and a large number of humans dressed in ponchos and feather head-dresses, as well as geometrical designs.

Although there are several more sites, the other most important ones are at **Tiliviche**, 127 km north of Iquique, some 600 m south of the Pan-American Highway, where, on the southern side of the *quebrada*, a 300 m panel can be seen representing a drove of llamas moving from the *cordillera* to the coast; at **Cerro Rosita**, 20 km north of Huara near the Pan-American Highway,where the 'Sun of Huara' (an Aymara sun emblem) is visible on the eastern side of the hill; and at **Cerro Unitas**, 15 km east of Huara, where geoglyphs are visible on the western and southern sides of an isolated hill. On the western slope of Cerro Unitas is the *Gigante del Atacama* or Giant of the Atacama, probably the most famous of all the images: 86 m high, this is a representation of an indigenous leader with a head-dress of feathers and a feline mask; to his left is a reptile, thought to link him to the earth god Pachamama, to his right is his staff of office.

dates from the 18th century. There are many pre-Hispanic ruins in the area, with four *pukarás* and a well-preserved stretch of the Camino del Inca. At Tignamar Viejo, an abandoned village 14 km south, there is another colonial church.

Sleeping

Iquique *p233, map p235*
Accommodation is scarce in the weeks before Christmas as many Chileans visit Iquique to shop at the Zofri. At other times, it is always worth bargaining for better rates. There's no campsite in Iquique but wild camping is possible on La Brava beach.

L-AL Terrado Suites, Los Rieles 126, Península de Cavancha, T057-488000, www.terrado.cl. Good sea-view suites with balconies, most expensive, rooftop restaurant, all mod cons. Near beaches but away from the centre.
AL Cavancha, Los Rieles 250, T057-434800, hotelcavancha.cl. 4-star, expensive

restaurant, pleasant inside but ugly exterior, south of city on the water's edge.

AL Gavina, Prat 1497, T057-413030, www.gavina.cl. Upmarket with bar, pool, sauna and jacuzzi. Good rooms, the best are on the upper floors with balconies overlooking the sea. English spoken.

AL-A Arturo Prat, Aníbal Pinto 695, T057-427000, www.hotelarturoprat.cl. 4-star, pool, health suite, games room, internet, restaurant, tours arranged. Some rooms have a balcony. Reserve in advance for a room with a view over the plaza. Attentive service, good value. Some staff speak English.

A Atenas, Los Rieles 738, Cavancha, T057-431100, atenashotel2000@yahoo.es. Pleasant, personal, good value, good service and food, pool.

A-B Barros Arana, Barros Arana 1302, T057-412840, www.hotelbarrosarana.cl. In two parts. The old part is nothing special. The new section has very large rooms and is much more comfortable. Internet, swimming pool, friendly, good value. In a quiet part of town. Recommended.

A-B Cano, Ramírez 996, T057-315580, www.iqq.cl/hotelcano. Friendly, nice atmosphere, decent rooms. Typical 2-star plus.

A-B Jham, Latorre 426, T057-415457, www.hoteljham.cl. Smart, modern, not much character but near the centre. The matrimonial suite has a jacuzzi.

B Carlos Condell, Baquedano 964, T/F057-3113027, hotel-carlos-condell@entelchile.net. The impressive façade hides a bog standard hotel with a modern, though slightly run-down exterior. Poor breakfast, erratic service. Okay choice if you can get one of the original rooms at the front.

B Inti-Llanka, Obispo Labbé 825, T057-311104, www.inti-llanka.cl. Nice rooms with good beds and spacious bathrooms, clean, laundry, good value. Wi-Fi, luggage store. Reduced prices off season. Terse service.

B Riorsa, Vivar 1542, T057-420153. Friendly, reasonable rooms with breakfast bath and TV, overpriced but good for the beach. Worth bargaining off season.

B-C Doña Genoveva, Latorre 458, T057-411578, hgenoveva@gtdmail.com. Spacious rooms with breakfast table and cable TV. The rooms with windows onto the street are bright and sunny. Bog standard but very good value if you pay in dollars.

C Buenos Aires, Esmeralda 713, T057-472229. **E** singles. With bath, breakfast and cable TV. Meals served. Clean but basic and slightly tatty. A good option if arriving late with Turbus as it is by the terminal.

C Casa de Huéspedes Profesores, Ramírez 839, T057-314475, iquiquealojamiento@123mail.cl. **F** singles. With breakfast, doubles with bath. Helpful, old building with high ceilings and lots of character. Nice garden, help with tours, recommended.

C Hostal Catedral, Labbé 253, T057-426372. **D-E** singles. Most rooms with bath and cable TV, quiet, nice balcony and bright patio with plants and seating area, interesting building. Recommended.

C Hostal Cuneo, Baquedano 1175, T057-428654, hostalcuneo@hotmail.com. **E-F** singles. Clean with lots of common areas. Some rooms with bath. Lots of 1950s-1970s furnishings. There is a stand up piano in the living room. Good value.

C Hotel Caiti, Gorostiaga 483, T/F057-423038. Pleasant, with bath, breakfast and all mod cons, interior rooms are stuffy. No luggage storage. Recommended if you can get a room with an outside window.

C-D Backpacker's Hostel Iquique, Amunategui 2075, T057-320223, www.hosteliquique.cl. **E** singles, **F** per person in dorms. With breakfast. Typical lively backpackers' affiliated to HI. Kitchen facilities, internet, games room, activities arranged. Convenient for the beach, south of town centre.

C-D Hostal JJ Pérez 650, JJ Perez 650, T057-421820. **F** singles. With breakfast, rooms with bath and cable TV, good value, simple and clean. The downstairs rooms are somewhat on the dark side.

C-D Hostal Li Ming, Barros Arana 705, T057-421912, www.hostal.cl. **F** singles. Clean, simple, some rooms with bath and cable TV, good value, kitchen and laundry facilities, internet, small rooms. Recommended.

D Hostal Jean IV, Esmeralda 936, T510855, hostaljeaniv@yahoo.es. **F** singles. With bath, breakfast and cable TV, clean, friendly, nice lounge and nice patio, with bath, convenient for buses to Bolivia, excellent value. Highly recommended.

D Hostal Juan López, Rodríguez 550, T/F057-427524. **F** singles. Near beach, basic and tatty with shared bath, unhelpful.

D **Residencial Nan-King**, Thompson 752, T057- 423311. **E-F** singles. Clean, small but nice rooms with bath and Cable TV. No breakfast.

Nitrate towns *p236*

C **Estancia Inn**, Comercial, Pozo Almonte. Basic, geared towards mineworkers.
C **Hotel Anakana**, Comercio 053, Pozo Almonte, T057-751201. Same as **Estancia**.

Mamiña *p237*

All the following are recommended, and all have rooms with private bath and thermal water available. Prices are for full board; as there are so many hotels in Mamiña, it is always worth bargaining.
L **Refugio del Salitre**, Latorre 766, T057-319655, www.refugiodelsalitre.cl. **AL-A** singles. Secluded, pretty terrace, lovely views, swimming pool, nice rooms, games room, helpful, interesting older part where the top brass from the nitrate *oficinas* stayed. Recommended.
AL **Los Cardenales**, Av Barros Chinos s/n, T057-517000, slvezendy@yahoo.com. **B** singles. 4-star, thermal baths, swimming pool with spring water, excellent cuisine in attractive restaurant, games room, lovely gardens and outlook, English, German spoken, delightful. Highly recommended.
A **Bellavista**, Av El Tambo s/n, T057-474506. **C** singles. Secluded, aviary in garden, games room, friendly, good cooking (including vegetarian options), sun terrace, basic but good rooms with bath and TV, worth bargaining.
AL **La Coruña**, Santa Rosa 687, T057-420645. **B** singles. Good Spanish cuisine, games room, swimming pool, very friendly and helpful, lots of local knowledge, parking and cable TV. Highly recommended. Children half price. Cheaper rates for bed and breakfast only.
AL **Llama Inn**, Sulumpa 85, T057-419893, llamainn@vtr.net. **B** singles. Pool tables, casino table, massage, terrace, friendly, cook will produce vegetarian meals if asked. Highly recommended. Cheaper rates for bed and breakfast only.

La Tirana *p237*

During the festival, a bed is difficult to find other than in organized campsites (take your own tent), which have basic toilets and showers, and through a few families who rent out rooms for over US$30 a night.

Matilla *p238*

Complejo Turístico El Parabien, T057-431645. Fully furnished *cabañas* and a pool.

Pica *p238*

The hotels get full at weekends and at holidays, as well as during La Tirana – it is best to ring ahead. The following places are all near the Cocha Resbaladero.
B-C **Hostal Suizo**, Ibáñez 210, T057-741551. With bath, popular, modern, very comfy.
C **Hostal Casablanca**, Ibáñez 75, T057-741410. **E** singles. Smallish rooms with bath and cable TV. Friendly, comfortable, cooking facilities, bright patio with pool, parking.
D **Residencial El Tambo**, Ibáñez 68, T/F057-741041. **F** singles. Without bath, meals served, very popular, hospitable. Also 4-person *cabañas*. Recommended.

Options in the town centre include:
C **Camino del Inca**, Esmeralda 14, T/F057-741008, hotelcaminodelinca@hotmail.com. With breakfast, shady patio, table football, good value. Recommended.
C **Los Emilios**, Cochrane 201, T057-741126. **F** singles. With bath and breakfast, friendly, nice lounge, small pool, interesting old building with photos of the nitrate era, lovely patio. Highly recommended.
C **O'Higgins**, Balmaceda 6, T057-741524, hohiggins@123mail.cl. **E-F** singles With bath, modern.
D **San Andrés**, Balmaceda 197, T057-741319, gringa733@hotmail.com. **F** singles. With bath and breakfast, basic but clean, good restaurant with cheap 4-course *almuerzos*.

Iquique to the Bolivian border *p239*

Basic accommodation is available in the **Restaurant Frontera** in Huara and in 4 simple *residenciales* in Colchane.

North towards Arica *p239*

Belén Food and lodging from **María Martínez**, General Lagos y San Martín.
Camiña A simple *hostal* on the plaza.
Pisagua D **Restaurant Acuario**, friendly, also has beds. Also there is a **campsite** at the northern end of the beach.

❷ Eating

Iquique *p233, map p235*

Beware of the expensive and poor-value tourist restaurants on the wharf on the opposite side of Av Costanera from the bus terminal. Several good, cheap and super-cheap seafood restaurants can be found on the 2nd floor of the central market, Barros Arana y Latorre. There are a number of restaurants near Cavancha beach in Caleta Cavancha, including **Neptuno**, in **Hostería Cavancha**, see Sleeping, above.

♆♆♆ **Club Náutico**, Los Rieles 110, T057-432951. Seafood, exclusive. Live music on Sat nights.

♆♆♆ **El Sombrero**, Los Rieles 704, T057-312410. Quality fish and seafood cuisine, elegant setting, not cheap. Buffet lunches.

♆♆♆-♆♆ **Casino Español**, Plaza Prat 584, T057-423284. Good meals well served in a 1904 Moorish-style palace, which in itself is a reason to eat there.

♆♆ **Bavaria**, Aníbal Pinto 926, T057-427888. German-Chilean chain steakhouse restaurant, reasonably priced café, serving real coffee, snacks and *almuerzo*.

♆♆ **Boulevard**, Baquedano 790, T057-413695, www.boulevard.cl. Excellent French and Mediterranean food.

♆♆ **Brasileña**, Vivar 1143, T057-423236. Friendly Brazilian-run restaurant serving seafood during the week and Brazilian food on Sat.

♆♆ **Club de la Unión**, Plaza Prat 278, piso 4, T057-413236. Roof terrace with panoramic views, open lunchtimes only, reasonable value.

♆♆ **Colonial**, Plaza Prat. Fish and seafood, popular, good value.

♆♆ **El Barril del Fraile**, Ramírez 1181, T057-390334. Good seafood, nice atmosphere, doubles as a lively bar at night.

♆♆ **La Picada Curicana**, Zegers 204, T057-428200. Hearty central Chilean country cooking – Pernil, costillar, arrollado etc. oven roasted and served in clay pots. Large portions, very good value. A meat-eaters paradise.

♆♆ **La Tarantella**, Tarapacá y Baquedano. Small portions, Italian-style, smart, cheap *almuerzo*.

♆♆ **Las Tejas de Barros Arana**, Barros Arana 684. Peruvian *parrillada*.

♆♆ **Nan King**, Amunategui 533, T057- 420434. Deservedly known as the best Chinese in town. Large portions, good value.

♆♆ **Pizzeria d'Alfredo**, Los Molles 2290 (Playa Brava). Large variety of pizzas, well-prepared pastas, not cheap, reasonably priced *almuerzo*.

♆♆-♆ **Compañía Italiana de Bomberos**, Serrano 520. Authentic Italian cuisine, excellent value *almuerzo*, otherwise more expensive. Recommended.

♆♆-♆ **El Tercer Ojito**, Patricio Lynch 1420, T057-426517 Peruvian specialities along with a vegetarian menu.

♆ **Bolivia**, Serrano 751. *Humitas* and *salteñas*. Recommended. Several other cheap Bolivian restaurants nearby.

♆ **Claudy**, Lynch 749. Simple but hearty lunches at a more than reasonable price.

♆ Many Chinese *chifas* on Tarapacá 800/900 blocks, including **Win Li**, San Martín 439, and **Sol Oriental**, Martínez 2030.

There are lots of cheap restaurants on the upper floor of the **Mercado Municipal**, Barros Arana s/n.

Cafés

Café Estación Iquique, Lynch 787, T057-321437. Cultural café with temporary art exhibitions and occasional live music.

Capuccino, Baquedano y Gorostiaga. Coffee and good ice cream. Pleasant to sit outside and watch the world go by.

Cioccolata, Pinto 487 (another branch in the Zofri). Good coffee and cakes.

Jugos Tarapacá, Tarapacá 380. Good juices.

Salon de Té Ricotta, Vivar y Latorre. Very popular for *onces*, quite expensive.

Splendid, Vivar 795. Good *onces*, cheap.

Tropical, Baquedano y Thompson. Juices and snacks. Recommended.

Via Pontony, Baquedano y Zegers. Fruit juices and *empanadas*. Recommended.

Mamiña *p237*

Most hotels (see Sleeping above) operate on a full-board basis only, but there are also some cheap independent eateries.

● *For an explanation of sleeping and eating price codes used in this guide, see inside the front cover. Other relevant information is found in Essentials, see pages 50-57.*

Cafetería Ipla. Excellent fruit juices, vegetarian options.
Los Chacras de Pasquito. Clean, good.
Restaurant Cerro Morado. Good variety, traditional dishes, including rabbit.

Pica *p238*

Pica is famous for its *alfajores* filled with cream and honey, and you cannot leave without trying some of the fruit juices. Hotels **San Andrés** and **El Tambo** (see Sleeping, above) both have good cheap restaurants.
El Edén de Pica, Riquelme 12. Best in town, speciality dishes, fine ice cream, lovely surroundings.
Los Naranjos, Esmeralda y Barbosa. Nice decor, good food.
La Mía Pappa, Balmaceda. Good selection of meat and juices, attractive location near plaza.
La Palmera, Balmaceda 115. Excellent *almuerzo*, popular with locals, near plaza.
La Viña, Ibáñez 70, by Cocha de Resbaladero. Good cheap *almuerzo*.
Oasis, Balamaceda, by the plaza. Ridiculously cheap. Recommended for *alfajores* and fruit juice.

Bars and clubs

Iquique *p233, map p235*
Most discos are out of the town on the road south to the airport.
Hotel Gavina (see Sleeping, above) has a good club on Fri and Sat nights, quite smart.
La Caldera del Sabor, Bajo Molle, south of the city. Most popular Iquique club, Thu-Sat. Plays salsa and merengue, with dance classes.
Pharo's, Av Costanera Sur 3607, Playa Brava. Enormous club with an elaborate design, popular, good.
Rumba, Bolívar y Lynch, T057-318123. Salsatheque with salsa classes on Fri nights.
Santa Fe, Mall Las Américas, locales 10-11-193. Mexican, live music, great atmosphere, very popular. Highly recommended.
Taberna Barracuda, Gorostiaga 601. Nice decor, good atmosphere, recommended for late night food, drink, video entertainment, dancing.
Taberna Van Gogh, Ramírez y Latorre. Live music Fri and Sat nights.

Entertainment

Iquique *p233, map p235*
There are occasional recitals in the cathedral.
Casino, Balmaceda 2755. Nightly, *salón* US$3.
Cine Tarapacá, Serrano 202. Foreign films.
Mall las Américas, Av Héroes de la Concepción, T057-432500. 6 screens.
Teatro Municipal, Plaza Prat, T057-411292. Plays, ballet, dance and concerts.

Festivals and events

Iquique *p233, map p235*
10-16 Jul For details of the festival of the **Virgen del Carmen** in La Tirana, 70 km east of Iquique, see page 237. There are numerous other, smaller religious festivals in the area – ask in Iquique's tourist office for information.

Shopping

Iquique *p233, map p235*
Most of the city's commerce is in the **Zofri** duty-free zone.
Andrés Bello, Héroes de la Concepción 2855, which stocks an excellent range of books.
Mall Las Américas, south of the centre on Av Héroes de la Concepción.
Camping equipment is sold at **Tunset**, Zofri, and **Lombardi**, Serrano 447.

Activities and tours

Iquique *p233, map p235*
Fishing
Fishing for broadbill swordfish, striped marlin, yellowfin tuna and bonito is a popular pastime from Mar till end of Aug. Equipment can be bought from:
Ferretería La Ocasión, Sgto Aldea 890.
Ferretería Lonza, Vivar 738, T057-415587.

Hang-gliding and landsailing
There are also 2 hang-gliding clubs: **Altazar**, Serrano 145, of 702, T057-431382; and **Manutara**, T057-418280.
Civet Adventure, Bolívar 684, T057-428483, civetcor@ctcinternet.cl. Landsailing. English and German spoken.

Paragliding
The cliffs directly behind Iquique are a great place from which to launch off down

towards the coast. Several agencies offer 30 to 40-min tandem flights from around US$50. **Frank Valenzuela**, T057-329041, www.paraventura.cl, is recommended.

Surfing
Iquique offers some of the best surfing in Chile with numerous reef breaks on **Playa Brava**, south of the city. Surfboard rental and surf classes are available from a number of agencies. Lessons cost roughly US$9 per hr. **Club de Surf**, Av Héroes de la Concepción 1939, T057-447070.

Swimming
The beach at **Cavancha**, just south of the town centre, is good, and popular Nov-Mar. There's another bathing beach at **Huaiquique**, 5 km south, and a freshwater pool, **Piscina Godoy**, Av Costanera at Aníbal Pinto and Riquelme, open evening, US$1.50.

Tennis
Club de Tenis Tarapacá, Bulnes 140, T057-412489. Temporary membership available.

Tour operators
Avitours, Baquedano 997, T057-473775, www.avitours.cl. Tours to Pintados, La Tirana, Humberstone, Pica, etc, some bilingual guides, day tours start at US$20. **Iquitour**, Lynch 563, T/F057-412415. Tours of saltpeter *oficinas* and Pica oasis. English spoken. **Viatours**, Baquedano 736, T/F057-417197, viatours@entelchile.net. Local tours.

Tours are also offered by the **Arturo Prat** (see Sleeping). The tourist office maintains a list of other operators.

⊖ Transport

Iquique *p233, map p235*
Air
Diego Aracena International Airport, 35 km south at Chucumata. **Sky, Aerolíneas del Sur** and **LanChile** fly south to **Santiago**, via Antofagasta, and north to **Arica** – some flights continue on to **La Paz** in Bolivia. **Airline offices** Iberia, Vivar 630, T057-411878; **KLM**, Pinto 515, T057-423009. **LAB**, Serrano 442, T057-407015; **LanChile**, Tarapacá 465, T057-427600, and in the Mall Las Américas; **Sky**, Tarapacá 530, T600-526200; **TAM**, Serrano 430, T057-390600.

Bus
The bus terminal is at the north end of Patricio Lynch but not all buses leave from here; **Tur Bus** has its own terminal, Ramírez y Esmeralda, with a Redbanc ATM and a good luggage store. Bus company offices are near the market on Sgto Aldea and Barros Arana. All southbound buses are stopped for a luggage check on leaving the duty-free zone of Region I at Quillagua on the Pan-American Highway and at Chipana/Río Loa on the coastal Route 1.

To **Arica**, buses and *colectivos*, frequent, 4½ hrs, US$7; to **Antofagasta**, 6 hrs, US$14; to **Calama**, 6 hrs, US$14; to **Tocopilla** along the coastal road, 3 hrs, US$8; to **La Serena**, 18 hrs, US$25; to **Valparaíso** and **Viña del Mar**, 25 hrs, US$36; to **Santiago**, 25 hrs, US$36 (US$56 for salón cama and US$72 for cama prémium).

Most bus companies for international services to **Oruro** and **La Paz** (Bolivia) leave from Esmeralda, near the junction of Juan Martínez (note that some buses go via Arica and Tambo Quemado to La Paz, not via Colchane and Oruro). **Litoral Buses**, T057-423670, daily at 2200 to **Oruro**, US$12, to **La Paz**, US$15; **Salvador Buses** at 2300, same price; **Géminis** from the bus terminal to **La Paz**, via Oruro, more expensive. **Delta**, **Tata Sabaya** and **Comet** all leave from Esmeralda y Juan Martínez 2100-2300 to **Oruro** (via Colchane), bargain for a good price.

Car/bicycle/motorbike
Car hire from **Continental**, 18 de Septiembre 105, T057-441426; **Hertz**, A Pinto 1303, T057-510432; airport office T057- 407020; **IQSA**, Labbé 1089, T057-417068. **Jofamar**, Libertad 1156, T057-411639; **Procar**, Serrano 796, T057-413470, at airport T057-410920. Motorcycle mechanic, **Sergio Cortez**, Civet, Bolívar 684, is recommended. **Bianchi**, Bulnes 485, for bike parts, repairs; for sales try the Zofri.

Colectivos/taxis
Any car that looks like a taxi serves is a *colectivo* unless it says 'sólo taxi'. Tell the driver where you are going and, if your destination can combine with that of other passengers, he will take you; if you are the first passenger, tell the driver you want to hire the car as a *colectivo* and he will fit the journeys of subsequent passengers around

your destination. The fare is US$0.70 (a little more late at night). Taxi fares are US$1.90 for journeys within the city centre.

Mamiña p237

Two companies run minibuses between **Iquique** and Mamiña; best to book the day before: **Transportes Tamarugal**, Barros Arana 897, departs Iquique daily 0800, 1600, 2½ hrs, US$6 one-way, returns from Mamiña 0800, 1800; **Turismo Mamiña**, Latorre 779, departs Iquique Mon-Sat 0800-1600, also Sun 1600, 2½ hrs US$6, returns from Mamiña Tue-Sat 0830, Mon-Sat 1800.

La Tirana p237

In ordinary times, buses from Iquique to Pica stop here; during the festival, virtually every taxi and *colectivo* in Iquique seems to be heading for La Tirana, leaving from Sargento Aldea by the market; some bus companies also have services from Antofagasta and Arica.

Pica p238

Three bus companies run between **Iquique** and Pica: **Santa Rosa**, Barros Arana 777, departs Iquique daily 0830 and 0930, 2 hrs, US$3.50, returns from Pica 1700 and 1800; **San Andrés**, Sgto Aldea y Barros Arana, departs Iquique daily 0930, returns from Pica daily 1800, US$3.50; **Pullman Chacón**, Barros Arana y Latorre, many daily, US$3.50, first return bus from Pica leaves at about 1100.

From Iquique to the Bolivian border p239

Pullman La Paloma runs daily bus services to **Colchane** at 2300 from Esmeralda y Juan Martínez, US$8.

North towards Arica p239
From Arica, **Buses La Paloma**, German Riesco 2071,T058-222710, runs a service to **Belén**, departing Tue and Fri at 0645, US$5.

❶ Directory

Iquique p233, map p235
Banks Numerous Redbanc ATMs in the centre; lots of ATMs in the Zofri. Casas de cambio at **AFEX**, Serrano 396, changes TCs; **Cambio Cambio's**, Lynch 548, Local 1-2; **Wall Street**, in the Zofri, sells AmEx TCs and changes them. **Consulates** Bolivia, Gorostiaga 215, Departamento E, T057-421777, Mon-Fri 0930-1200; **Netherlands**, Tarapacá 123, T057-390900; **Italy**, Serrano 447, T057-421588; **Paraguay**, O'Higgins 480, T057-419040; **Peru**, Zegers 570, T057-411466; **Spain**, Manzana 2, Sitio 5 y 9, ZOFRI, T057- 422330. **Dentist** Clinica Dental Lynch, Lynch y Orella, T057-413060. **Hospitals** Centro Médico, Orella 433, T/F057-414396; also at Héroes de la Concepción 502, T057-415555. **Internet** Several in and around the centre, US$1 per hr. **Language schools** Academia de Idiomas del Norte, Ramírez 1345, T057-411827, idiomas@chilesat.net. Swiss-run, Spanish classes, accommodation for students. **Laundry** Nicos, Bulnes 485; **Cruz del Sur**, Thompson 553. **Post office** In the Zofri, there is another branch in the **Mall de las Américas**. **Telephone** CTC, Serrano 620; Entel, Tarapacá 476; Correos, CTC, Chilexpress, Chilesat and Entel all have offices in the Plaza de Servicios in the Zofri. **Useful address** Automóvil Club de Chile, Serrano 154, T057-426772.

Arica and around → *Colour map 1, A1.*

Arica is the northernmost city in Chile, just 19 km south of the Peruvian border. With Peru so close and Arica being the main port for Bolivian trade, the city has a distinct half-way house sort of feel. It is less ordered than most Chilean cities, with hundreds of street vendors and indoor markets selling cheap, imported goods. The city centre itself is quite attractive, with long beaches, pleasant gardens and extensive networks of sand dunes all nearby. Rearing up to the south is El Morro, the rock that marks the end of the Chilean coastal range. Inland is the verdant valle de azapa with olive groves and a museum housing the world's oldest mummies. Day trips can easily be made across the border to Tacna, the southernmost city in Peru. ►► *For Sleeping, Eating and other listings, see pages 251-256.*

Getting there Arica is a long way from most of Chile. All major bus companies serving the north make this their final stop; buses take up to 30 hours to reach Santiago to the south. Arica is a centre for connections to Bolivia and Peru, with a train and frequent *colectivos* north to Tacna in Peru and buses east to La Paz in Bolivia. There is also quite a wide-ranging bus service to villages in the sierra and the *altiplano*. **Sky**, **Aerolíneas del Sur** and **LanChile** fly south to Santiago via Iquique and Antofagasta, with some flights continuing on to La Paz in Bolivia. A taxi to town from the airport costs US$10, *colectivos* cost US$5 per person from Lynch y 21 de Mayo.

Getting around Arica is quite a large city, and you may need to take some of the *colectivos* or buses to get to more out-of-the-way places, particularly the discotheques, many of which are on the road out to the Azapa Valley.

Tourist information Sernatur ① *Marcos 101 y Parque Baquedano, T058-232101, Mon-Fri 0830-1300, 1500-1830*, is very helpful and can supply a list of tour companies and a good map.

Background

During the colonial period, Arica was important as the Pacific end of the silver route from Potosí. Independence from Spain and the re-routing of Bolivian trade through Cobija led to a decline, but the city recovered with the building of rail links to Tacna (1855) and La Paz (1913) when it became the port of choice for those two cities. The city came under Chilean control at the end of the War of the Pacific. The Morro in Arica was the site of an important Chilean victory over Peru on 7 June 1880.

Arica remains an important route centre and port. Now linked to the Bolivian capital La Paz by road and an oil pipeline, it handles 47% of Bolivia's foreign trade and attracts Bolivians, as well as locals, to its beaches. There are also road and rail connections with the Peruvian city of Tacna, 54 km north. Most of the large fishmeal plants have moved to Iquique, leaving several rusting hulks of trawlers in the bay, now home to a significant local crow population. Regrettably, there are indications that Arica is also becoming a key link in the international drugs trade.

Arica

Unlike in most Chilean cities, life is not centred around the main square, but Avenida 21 de Mayo, a mostly pedestrianized street full of banks, shops, restaurants and cafés. Just south of this is the **Plaza Colón**, on which stands the Gothic-style cathedral of **San Marcos**, built in iron by Eiffel. Although small, it is beautifully proportioned and attractively painted. It was brought to Arica from Ilo in Peru as an emergency measure after a tidal wave swept over Arica in 1868 and destroyed all its churches; inside the cathedral is a Christ figure dating from the 12th century. Eiffel also designed the nearby Aduana (customs house), which is now the **Casa de la Cultura** ① *0830-2000*. Just north of the Aduana is the La Paz railway station; outside is an old steam locomotive (made in Germany in 1924) once used on this line, while inside is a memorial to John Roberts Jones, builder of the Arica portion of the railway.

To climb **El Morro**, 110 m high, walk to the southernmost end of the Calle Colón, and then follow the pedestrian walkway up to the summit; there are fine views of the city from here. **Museo Histórico y de Armas** ① *0830-2000, US$1.50*, on the summit, contains weapons and uniforms from the War of the Pacific.

Valle de Azapa

A highly recommended excursion is up the Azapa Valley, a beautiful oasis east of Arica. At Km 12 is the **Museo Arqueológico San Miguel de Azapa** ① *T058-205555, museo@uta.cl, 0900-2000 (2 Jan-28 Feb), 1000-1800 (1 Mar-31 Dec), US$2*, part of the University of Tarapacá and well worth a visit. Set in a pleasant, shady part of the valley, the museum contains a fine collection of pre-Columbian tools, weaving,

Arica

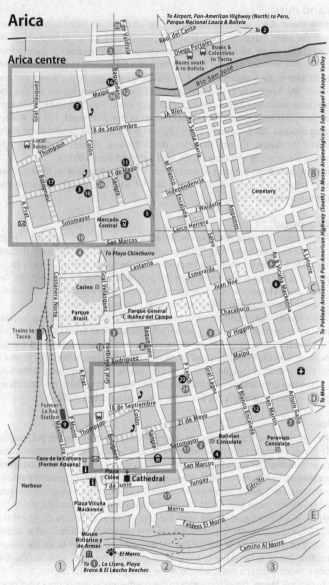

Arica centre

To Airport, Pan-American Highway (North) to Peru,
Parque Nacional Lauca & Bolivia

N

0 metres 200
0 yards 200

Sleeping
Almagro **2** *D2*
Aragón **28** *Arica centre*
Arica **1** *E1*
D'Marie-Jeanne y David **3** *C1*
El Paso **4** *C1*
Hostal Jardín del Sol **7** *D3*

Hostal Venecia **8** *D2*
King **26** *Arica centre*
Lynch **29** *D2*
Maison de France **5** *A1*
Plaza Colón **10** *Arica centre*
Residencial América **11** *D2*
Residencial Blanquita **12**
    Arica centre
Residencial Don Pepé **14** *D1*
Residencial Ecuador **6** *C3*
Savona **17** *E2*
Sunny Days **20** *A2*
Surf House **9** *C2*

Tarapacá **16** *Arica centre*

Eating
Caffelatte **3** *Arica centre*
Chifa Chin Huang Tao **4** *D2*
Cyclo Public **2** *A3*
D'Aurelio **5** *Arica centre*
Di Mango **3** *Arica centre*
Don Floro **6** *C3*
El Andén **9** *D1*
El Arriero **11** *Arica centre*
El Rey del Marisco **7**
    Arica centre

La Bomba **10** *Arica centre*
Los Aleros del 21 **12** *D3*
San Fernando **16**
    Arica centre
Scala **17** *Arica centre*
Yuri **20** *D2*

Bars & clubs
France Tropicale Pub **8**
    Arica centre

pottery, woodcarving and basket work from the coast and the valleys as well as four mummified humans from the Chinchorro culture (8000-10,000 BC), the most ancient mummies yet discovered. In the final room there is an exhibition about the olive oil produced in the valley, including a huge old press. In the forecourt of the museum are several boulders with pre-Columbian petroglyphs and opposite is a garden full of tropical plants and birds. Comprehensive explanations are provided by booklets in English, French, German and Spanish, loaned free at the entrance.

On the road between Arica and San Miguel several groups of geoglyphs of humans and llamas can be seen to the south of the road. On the opposite side of the valley at San Lorenzo are the ruins of a *pukará* (pre-Inca fortress) dating from the 12th century.

In the nearby village of San Miguel, there are several restaurants with a wide range of prices. A good walk in the area is to climb the desert hill behind the valley, 45 minutes, giving wonderful views of the green oasis and the desolation beyond – running back down the hill takes three minutes and is an exhilarating experience.

Into Peru

Chilean immigration at the border post of **Chacalluta** ⓘ *Sun-Thu 0800-2400, 24 hrs Fri and Sat*, is usually fairly uncomplicated, although crossing the border into Peru with a hire car is difficult: make sure you have the correct papers. The Peruvian side of the border is open 0900-2200. There are no exchange facilities at the border. Good rates are generally available at Tacna's bus station or in the city centre.

> ⁞ *Chilean time is one hour ahead of Peruvian time between October and March, and two hours ahead from October to February or March (varies annually.*

Drivers of private vehicles entering Chile are required to file a form, *Relaciones de Pasajeros* (four copies; eight if planning to return to Peru via this crossing), giving details of passengers. The form can be obtained from a stationery store in Tacna, or at the border in a kiosk near customs. You must also present the original registration document for your car from its country of registration. The first checkpoints outside Arica on the road to Santiago also require the *Relaciones de Pasajeros* form, but the form is not required when travelling south of Antofagasta. If you can't buy the form (available from some service stations), write the details on a piece of paper.

Tacna is 36 km north of the border. The city was in Chilean hands from 1880 to 1929, when its citizens voted by plebiscite to return to Peru. There is a wide variety of hotels and restaurants here, as well as bus and air services to the rest of Peru. Many Chileans travel to Tacna for optical and dental treatment, which is much cheaper than in Chile. There is a **tourist office** ⓘ *Av Bolognesi 2088*.

Into Bolivia

Vía Chungará and Tambo Quemado There are two routes from Arica to the Bolivian border. **Route 11** (paved to La Paz, although seriously worn in places by overloaded juggernauts) turns off the Pan-American Highway, 12 km north of Arica, and runs through the Lluta Valley, where the **Geoglifos de Lluta** – four groups of geoglyphs representing llamas and humans – can be seen on the hillsides between Km 14 and Km 16. At Km 35 at Pocon Chile there is a Hari Krishna community offering accommodation and good vegetarian food (www.ecotruly-arica.org). Further on, at Km 73 is a *centro magnético*, an optical illusion which makes the climbing road seem as if it going downhill. There is a stunning Mirador overlooking Copaquilla (Km 89), and Km 99 there is a turnoff for the village of Belén, see page 239. The village of Socoroma lies 9 km up the valley, 4 km north of the main road. At an altitude of 3000m It is a pretty Aymara settlement with a well ordered plaza with bright flowers. The traditional houses look odd with their corrugated zinc roofs. The traditional straw and leather was replaced as it was all too often home to the bug that causes Chaga's disease. Past Socoroma the road continues via Putre and Parinacota through the

⁞ Animal magic

Although the park lies very close to the lifeless Atacama desert, its altitude ensures it receives more rain, which creates a fairyland of volcanoes and highland lakes surrounded by brilliant-green wetlands and vast expanses of puna grassland. The Río Lauca rises near Lago Chungará, then laces slowly through the park leaving marshy cushion bogs and occasional raceways and providing an array of habitats for the varied wildlife of the *altiplano*.

The **camelids** are the stars of the park; thousands of domesticated llamas and alpacas, as well as the dainty, graceful, wild vicuña which now number over 18,000. The charming viscacha, seemingly a long-tailed rabbit, but in fact belonging to the chinchilla family, can be seen perched sleepily on the rocks in the mornings, backside toward the rising sun.

Pumas, huemules (deer), foxes, skunks and armadillos are the more elusive **mammals**, some nocturnal, occupying the more remote reaches.

Lauca **bird life** is spectacular with more than 120 species either resident or migrant here. Lago Chungará is home to more than 8000 giant coots, distinguished by their bright orange legs, never-ending nest building and primordial cackling. In addition to coots, ducks and grebes, the wetlands provide a fine habitat for the puna plover, the rare diademed sandpiper plover, the puna ibis, Andean species of avocet, goose and gull, and an assortment of migratory shorebirds. Occasionally three species of flamingo can be seen at once: the Andean, the James (locally called *parinas*) and the more common Chilean flamingo.

Trips through the drier grasslands can produce glimpses of the puna tinamou, always in groups of three, and the puna rhea, seen in October and November with 20 or 30 miniatures scooting along behind. Passerines occupy all the habitats in the park, some to 5000 m and above. There are also Sierra finches, black siskins, earthcreepers, miners, canasteros, cinclodes, tit-spinetails – new names for most birders. And in the skies above, keep your eyes peeled for Andean condors, mountain caracaras, aplomado falcons, black chested buzzard eagles and buteo hawks.

Parque Nacional Lauca to the border at Chungará. This is the route followed by most transport to Bolivia, including buses and trucks. Estimated driving time to La Paz is six hours. Chilean **immigration** formalities are 7 km west of the border ① *0800-2000*. Bolivian immigration and customs are at Tambo Quemado, just over the border (where there is a local barter market every other Friday). This is a relatively speedy crossing, but very cold; if you're travelling by bus (see page 254), take a blanket or sleeping bag, food, water and a sense of humour.

Vía Visviri and Charaña The road to Oruro and La Paz (Route 108) is unpaved and should not be attempted in wet weather. It follows the La Paz–Arica railway line to the

⁞ *Visviri can also be reached by road from Putre, see page 258.*

Chilean immigration post at **Visviri** (altitude 4069 m) ① *3 km from the Bolivian border and 12 km from Peru (no crossing), T058-261486, 0800-2000.* There is no fuel or accommodation here. Bolivian formalities are conducted behind the railway station at **Charaña**, 10 km east. Cheap accommodation is available at **Alojamiento Aranda**. There are two routes, both poor, continuing from Charaña towards La Paz, both of which meet at Viacha. Over the border, the route passes through the **Parque**

Nacional Sajama, which covers 60,000 ha and contains the world's highest forest, consisting mainly of the rare Kenua tree, which survives at altitudes of up to 5200 m. The scenery is wonderful and includes views of three volcanos: Parinacota (6342 m) and Pomerape (6282 m), both of which are on the border, and Sajama (6530 m), which is Bolivia's highest peak, but can be seen from the Lauca national park in Chile. Park administration is at Sajama village, 14 km off Route 108 (altitude 4200 m), where there is basic accommodation. There is also accommodation at Carahuara de Carangas, 111 km northeast of Tambo Quemado, and at **Patacamaya**, 104 km south of La Paz, where Route 108 joins the main Oruro-La Paz highway.

● Sleeping

Arica *p246, map p248*

L Arica, San Martín 599, 2 km south on coast (frequent buses, *colectivos*), T058-254540, www.panamericanahoteles.cl. 4-star. Restaurant, tennis court, pool, lava beach (not safe for swimming). Not great value. Better rates sometimes available off season.

L-AL El Paso, Gral Velásquez 1109, T/F058-231965, www.hotelpaso.cl. Bungalow style, excellent restaurant, lovely gardens, nice suites, tennis court, pool.

A Savona, Yungay 380, T058-231000, www.hotelsavona.cl. Recently refurbished but maintaining much of the original furnishings. Rooms on the upper floors are bigger. A/c. Some have giant TV, full bathtub and/or bidet. Airport transfer service, casino voucher included. Internet access, Wi-Fi. Airy terrace area. Attentive service. Eglish spoken. Highly recommended.

A-B Sol de Arica, Avalos 2041, T058-246050, www.hotelsoldearica.cl. Set in large grounds on the edge of the city on the way to Azapa. Sauna, jacuzzi, pool. Recommended.

B Plaza Colón, San Marcos 261, T058-254424, www.hotelplazacolon.cl. Good location opposite the cathedral. Modern, comfortable, internet.

B Saucache, Sánchez 621, Valle de Azapa, T/F058-241458, desierto300@123click.cl. Fully equipped *cabañas*, sleep 2 or 4.

B-C Aragón, Maipú 344, T/F058-252088, www.hoteleranortegrande.com. **D** singles. Bog standard concrete costruction. Clean rooms with ceramic floors, cable TV, bath and breakfast.

B-C King, Colón 376, T058-232094, hotelking@chilenet.cl. With bath and breakfast. Incredibly kitsch and seemingly stuck in a 1970s timewarp. Linoleum floor, turquoise wallpaper and a fantastic lamp in the lobby. Some rooms are bigger than others and the brightest face the street.

C Almagro, Sotomayor 490, T058-224444, F221240. With breakfast, helpful, comfy, parking, stores luggage. Recommended.

C D'Marie-Jeanne y David, Velásquez 792, T058-258231, hoteldmariejeanneydavid@ hotmail.com. **D-E** singles. Fairly comfortable and clean rooms with bath. Some with cable TV. Good location but on a main road so some rooms can be a little noisy. French spoken.

C Hostal Jardín del Sol, Sotomayor 848, T058-232795, hostaljardindelsol@ hotmail.com. **E** singles. With bath and breakfast, comfortable,beds with duvets, friendly, good value, free internet, stores luggage, some info, bike hire. Large kitchen area (US$1 charge) . Highly recommended.

C Lynch, Lynch 589, T058-231581. **E** singles. Basic rooms with bath and cable TV.

C Residencial Ecuador, Juan Noé 989, T/F058-251934.**F** singles. With bath and breakfast, kitchen and laundry facilities, recently renovated. Recommended.

C Sunny Days, Tomas Aravena 161 y Pedro de Valdivia, pob. Chinchorro, T058-241038, www.sunny-days-arica.cl. **F** singles. Run by a New Zealander and his Chilean wife, laundry facilities, some rooms with bath, English spoken, nice atmosphere, lots of information on the area, book exchange, bike rental, will pick you up from the terminal. Convenient for the beach. Highly recommended.

C-D Maison de France, Aurelio Valdivieso 152, pob Chinchorro, T058-223463, atchumturist@hotmail.com. **F** singles. Friendly hostel owned by Christian, a larger than life Frenchman. Breakfast US$2. Good meals served. Kitchen facilities, bright patio, info about tours or self guided trips to the altiplano. Good location for beach and nightlife. Recommended.

C-D **Tarapacá**, Maipú 455, T058-252680, hoteltarapaca@hotmail.com. With bath (cheaper without), clean, friendly, helpful.

D-E **Hostal Venecia**, Baquedano 741, T058-252877, hostal_venecia@hotmail.com. F-G singles. Spotless, hot water, small rooms, some with bath, friendly, good value, laundry service. Recommended.

D-E **Residencial América**, Sotomayor 430, T058-254148, www.residencialamerica.com. Some rooms with bath, clean, hospitable, good value. E-F singles.

D-E **Residencial Blanquita**, Maipú 472, T058-232064, residencialblanquita@ hotmail.com. F-G singles. Clean, pleasant, good value.

E **Residencial Don Pepe**, Velásquez 755, T058- 253996. F-G singles. Basic but friendly and clean. A good budget option.

E **Surf House**, O'Higgins 661, T058-312213, www.aricasurfhouse.cl. F-G singles. Budget hostel aimed, as the name suggests, at surfers. Decent beds and showers, large common areas, kitchen facilities. Tours, jet-ski rental. Good value.

Camping

El Refugio de Azapa, 3½ km from Arica, T058-227545. Full facilities including a restaurant. Also *cabañas*.

Gallinazos, Villa Frontera, 15 km north of Arica, T058-232373. One of many campsites at Villa Frontera. Full facilities, pool. Can get rowdy on summer nights.

Basic camping (no water or facilities) is also possible at **Playa Las Machas**, 5 km north, **Playa Chinchorro**, north of town, and **Playa Corazones**, 8 km south, but this is risky as there have been reports of daylight mugging and robbery.

Valle de Azapa p247

L-AL **Azapa inn**, Sánchez 660, T058-244537, www.azapainn.cl. Set in 4 ha of attractive grounds out of town in the Azapa Valley, pleasant location, also cheaper *cabañas*, good restaurant. Often used for large conferences.

● Eating

Arica p246, map p248

♙♙♙-♙♙ **El Arriero**, 21 de Mayo 385, T058-232636. *Parrillada*, also seafood and fish. Large portions, recommended.

♙♙ **Bavaria**, Colón 613, T058-251679. Another branch of the German Chilean rotisserie chain. Also coffee and cakes.

♙♙ **Chifa Chin Huang Tao**, Patricio Lynch 224. Good-value Chinese food, diners welcome to take away 'leftovers'.

♙♙ **Cyclo Public**, Diego Portales 1364 T058-262098. Fashionable seafood and pasta restaurant, reasonably priced. Vegetarian options. Recommended.

♙♙ **D'Aurelio**, Baquedano 369, T058-231471. Italian specialities, good pasta, seafood. Also vegetarian options.

♙♙ **Don Floro**, V MacKenna 847. Popular little seafood restaurant. Also serves steaks, etc, good service. Recommended.

♙♙ **El Rey del Marisco**, Maipú y Colón, 2 piso. Excellent seafood, though more expensive than others in the area. Not always welcoming.

♙♙ **Los Aleros del 21**, 21 de Mayo 736, T058-254641. One of the cities oldest established restaurants specializing in Southern Chilean cuisine. Large portions and lots of pork. Good service. Recommended.

♙♙-♙ **El Andén**, In the former La Paz railway station. Good-value inventive menu Mon-Fri, à la carte weekends. An old train carriage is used as one of the dining areas. Service is attentive but a little slow.

♙♙-♙ **Mata Rangi**, on the pier. Good food in fishy environment, good value *menú de casa*.

♙ **Capricho Latino**, 18 de Septiembre 250. Good-value *almuerzo*.

♙ **La Bomba**, Colón 357, at fire station, T058-255626. Good value simple Chilean food. Friendly service, with the chatter of the on duty firemen in the background.

♙ **San Fernando**, Baquedano 601. Simple breakfast, good value *almuerzo*. One of several cheap restaurants on this block.

♙ **Yuri**, Maipú y Lynch. Good service, cheap Chinese lunches. Recommended.

♙ **Mercado Colón**, Maipú y Colón. Several stalls offering good lunches and fresh juices.

Cafés

There are 3 good places on 21 de Mayo, all offering real coffee and outdoor seating: **Caffelatte**, No 248; **Carlos Díaz León Snack Place**, No 388; and **Di Mango**, No 244, which also serves juices and lovely ice cream.

Also try **Mi Viejo**, Maipú 436, for cheap meals and snacks, and **Scala**, 21 de Mayo 201, for excellent fruit juices and real coffee.

Valle de Azapa *p247*

🍴 **Las Tejas de Azapa**, Km 1.5, No 4301, T058-246817. *Parrillada* and other options.

🎶 Bars and clubs

Arica *p246, map p248*
Carpaccio, Velásquez 510. Restaurant and bar with live music from 2330 Wed-Sat.
France Tropicale Pub, 21 de Mayo 384. Open till dawn, live music weekends, nice atmosphere. Food also served (pizza, pasta, etc). French and English spoken.
Puerto Navarrón, Paseo Bolognesi. Open till 0400, live music at weekends.
Soho, Buenos Aires 209. For rock 'n' roll.

Valle de Azapa *p247*
Sunset and **Swing**, both 3½ km out of town. Open weekends 2300-0430 (taxi US$3).

🎭 Entertainment

Arica *p246, map p248*
Casino
Casino Municipal de Arica, Velásquez 955. 1200-0300. US$3.50 to enter which includes a welcome drink. Formal dress not required.

Cinemas
Cine Arte, Biblioteca Publíca , Yungay.
Colón, 7 de Junio 190, T058-231165.

Music
A *peña folklórica* of Andean music is held in the **Poblado Artesanal**, Fri and Sat 2130.

Theatre
Teatro Municipal de Arica, Baquedano 234. Theatrical and musical events, exhibitions.

🎉 Festivals and events

Arica *p246, map p248*
Jan Arica hosts a miniature version of the Festival de la Canción famous in Viña del Mar, with performances by Andean musicians.
Feb The Ginga is another festival of Andean dance and music, a slightly more debauched version of the famous festival at La Tirana.
Jun The festival of Arica and the national Cueca championships. On 7 Jun, it's the anniversary of the Chilean victory in the Battle of the Morro, with parties and fireworks.

🛍 Shopping

Arica *p246, map p248*
Crafts
Feria Turística Dominical, Chacabuco, between Velásquez and Mackenna, Sun market, good prices for llama sweaters.
Poblado Artesanal, Plaza Las Gredas, Hualles 2825 (take bus 2, 3 or 7). Expensive but especially good for musical instruments, open Tue-Sun 0930-1300, 1500-1930. Not always open out of season.

Markets
Mercado Central, Sotomayor y Sangra. Recently renovated, fruit and vegetables, mornings only.
Terminal del Agro, southeastern edge of town; take bus marked 'Agro' along 18 de Septiembre. Fruit, vegetables and old clothes. An interesting experience.

Supermarkets
There are supermarkets at Baquedano y 18 de Septiembre, San Martín y 18 de Septiembre and at Chacabuco y Lagos.

Into Bolivia *p249*
There are markets in **Visviri** on Wed and Sat mornings; a Sun morning market is held from 0900 north of the town at the border of the 3 countries.

⛰ Activities and tours

Arica *p246, map p248*
Boat trips
Raúl, owner of the **Mata Rangi** restaurant on the pier, turismomarino@yahoo.es, organizes boat trips to nearby sea lion and penguin colonies. Recommended.

Surfing
There's good surfing at **Playa Las Machas** and **Playa Chinchorro**, north of the city, and at **La Isleta** and **Playa Corazones**, 9 km south along coast road (take bus or *colectivo*).

Swimming
The best beach for swimming is **Playa Chinchorro**, north of town (bus 24). **Playa Las Machas**, further north, has strong currents. Buses 7 and 8 run to beaches south of town; the first two, **La Lisera** and **El**

Iquique, Arica & the Far North Arica & around *Listings*

Laucho, are both small and mainly for sunbathing. **Playa Brava**, also south, is popular for sunbathing but is too dangerous for swimming.

There's an Olympic pool in **Parque Centenario**, Tue-Sat; bus No 5A from 18 de Septiembre (buy a ticket on Thu mornings).

Tennis
Club de Tenis Centenario, Av España 2640. Open daily.

Tour operators
Most of the following offer local tours and excursions to the *altiplano* at similar prices: **city tour** US$13; **Valle de Azapa** US$16; **Parque Nacional Lauca**, 1 day US$25, 2 days US$100 including food and accommodation; **Parque Nacional Lauca** and the **Salar de Surire**, 3 days US$180. **Parques Nacional Lauca and Isluga** and the **Salar de Surire**, 4 days, ending in Iquique or Arica, US$280.

Some agencies pay up to 25% commission to hotels and *residenciales* that refer travellers; to get a lower price form a group of 5 or 6 travellers and negotiate direct with agencies. Make sure that tours advertised as, say, 2 days are 2 full days and do not leave in the afternoon. Shop around as not all operators have the full variety of tours leaving on any specific day. Very few tours leave on Mon. If you want an English speaking guide you may have to book a couple of days ahead and be prepared to pay a little extra.

Clinamen Safaris y Expediciones, Sotomayor 361, piso 2, T058-232281, www.clinamen.cl. Bespoke small group expeditions (maximum 3 people) to the Altiplano. Guide Christian Rolf speaks fluent English, German and French.

Ecotour Expediciones, Bolognesi 362, T058-250000, www.ecotourexpediciones.cl.

Geotour, Bolognesi 421, T058-253927, www.geotour.cl. Good *altiplano* tours.

Globo Tour, 21 de Mayo 260, T/F058-232807, globotour@entelchile.net. Good for international flight bookings.

Latinorizons, Bolognesi 449, T/F058-250007, www.latinorizons.com. Specializes in tours to Lauca and the other altiplano national parks. Not cheap, but one of the better agencies. English and French spoken. Recommended.

Parinacota Expeditions, Thompson y Bolognesi, T/F058- 256227, www.parinacota expediciones.cl. Reasonable reports.

Raices Andinas, Paseo Thompson, local 21, T/F058- 233305, www.raicesandinas.com. Well-designed 2- to 4-day trips to the *altiplano* plus bespoke longer trips. Tours generally involve a fair amount of walking as well as contact with local people in the villages. More expensive than most but definitely worth it. English and French spoken in the office, thogh most guides speak Spanish only. Highly recommended.

Ruta de las Aceitunas, Manual Castillo Ibaceta 3689, T/F058-244485, www.rutadela aceituna.com. Day tours of Arica and Azapa valley including an olive oil processing plant.

Suma Inti, Gonzalo Cerda 1366, T058-225685, www.sumainti.cl. Tours to the *alti plano*. Recommended guide Freddy Torrejón.

Turismo Lauca, Thompson 200 y Bolognesi, T/F058-252322, www.turismolauca.cl. The biggest of the *altiplano* agencies. OK for 1-day tours. Not the best option for multi-day trips.

Valle de Azapa p247
Golf
18-hole course, daily except Mon.

⊖ Transport

Arica p246, map p248
Air
Arica airport, 18 km north of city, Chacalluta, T058-211116. Flights to **La Paz**, LanChile; to **Santiago**, Sky, Aerolíneas del Sur and LanChile all via Iquique (some via Antofagasta), book well in advance; to **Lima**, LanPerú and others from Tacna (Peru), enquire at travel agencies in Arica.

Airline offices LanChile, 21 de Mayo 345, T058-251641, F252600; Lloyd Aéreo Boliviano, P Lynch 371, T058-216411; Sky, Chacabuco 314, local 52, T058-251816.

Bicycle/motorbike
Bicicletas Wilson, 18 de Sept 583, repairs, parts, sales, ATB specialists.
Pablo Fernández Davils, El Salitre 3254, T058-212863, for motorbike repairs.

Bus
Local City buses run from Maipú, US$0.45. *Colectivos* run on fixed routes within city

limits, US$0.50 per person (US$0.80 per person after 2000). To reach **Valle de Azapa**, take a yellow *colectivo* from P Lynch y Chacabuco, US$1.50.

Long distance There are 2 terminals, both northeast of the centre at Av Portales y Santa María, reached by many buses, *colectivos* (including No 8 and 18, US$0.45 or US$0.50) and taxis, US$2 (terminal tax US$0.40).

The main terminal is for national services and services to La Paz with Chilean companies (see page 255). Next door is the terminal for *colectivos* to Tacna (see page 256) and Bolivian services to La Paz. It is advisable to arrive 30 mins before departure for all services.

Apart from the following, bus company offices are located at the bus terminals: **Buses La Paloma**, Germán Riesco 2071 (bus U from centre); **Martínez**, 21 de Mayo 575, T058-232265; **Bus Lluta**, Chacabuco y V Mackenna. **Litoral**, Chacabuco 454, T058-254702; **Andes-Mar**, Galerín Río San José, Av Santa María 2010, T058-248200.

To **Antofagasta**, 11 hrs, US$18; to **Calama** and **Chuquicamata**, 10 hrs, US$17, several companies, all between 2000 and 2200; to **San Pedro de Atacama**, daily 2200, 11½ hrs, US$19; to **Iquique**, frequent, 4½ hrs, US$7, also *colectivos*, several companies, all with offices in the terminal; to **Santiago**, 30 hrs, a number of companies, including **Carmelita**, **Turbus**, **Pullman Bus**, **Fénix** and **Flota Barrios**, US$40, also *salón cama* services, US$55 (most serve meals though these vary in quality; generally better on more expensive services; student discounts available); to **La Serena**, 23 hrs, US$30 (salon cama US$40); to **Viña del Mar** and **Valparaíso**, 29 hrs, US$40. Note that all southbound luggage is carefully searched for fruit prior to boarding and is then searched again at Cuya on the Pan-American Highway. If you are travelling south of Iquique on an evening bus you may well have to get off the bus in the middle of the night.

Car
Car hire from **American**, Gral Lagos 571, T/F058-257752; **Cactus**, Baquedano 635, Loc 40, T058-257430, reasonable service; **GP**, Copacabana 628, T058-252594, good reports; **Hertz**, Baquedano 999, T058-231487, reliable; **Klasse**, Velásquez 760, Piso 2, Loc 25, T058-254498. OK.

Hertz provides the most reliable vehicles but check any rental vehicle for jack and lug wrench, and check the condition of both the fan belt (often dry and cracked) and the spare tyre.

It is periodically forbidden to take fruit products south of Arica (generally whenever there is a fruit fly infestation): vehicles may be searched at Cuya, 105 km south, and at Huara, 234 km south. There are service stations between the Peruvian border and Santiago at Arica, Iquique, Pozo Almonte, Oficina Victoria, Tocopilla, Oficina María Elena, Oficina Blanco Encalada, Chuquicamata, Calama, Carmen Alto, Antofagasta, La Negra, Agua Verde, Taltal, Chañaral, Caldera, Copiapó, Vallenar, La Serena, Termas de Socos, Los Vilos, and then every 30 km to the capital.

Hitchhiking
It's not easy to hitch south: try **Terminal del Agro** off the Pan-American Highway (trucks leave Mon, Thu and Sat before 0700) and the **Copec station** opposite (reached by bus from Arica marked 'Agro' or *colectivo* No 8).

Taxi
Taxis cost US$2 within the city centre. Try **Radiotaxis Chacalluta**, T058-254812, for journeys to/from the airport.

Into Peru *p249*
Car
Crossing to Tacna with a hire car can be difficult; the hire firm **Klasse** (see Arica, above) can arrange the paperwork for this.

Colectivo
Regular service from the international terminal in Arica, Diego Portales 1002, to **Tacna**, 1½ hrs, drivers take care of all the paperwork. Bargaining is fierce. Chilean operators generally charge US$4 per person, while Peruvians charge US$3. Supply and demand means that lower prices than these are often on offer. A bus from the terminal, US$2, takes much longer than a *colectivo*.

Train
There is a regular service to the centre of Tacna; Arica train station is on Maximo Lira, by the port, and trains leave Mon-Sat 1000 and 1900, 1½ hrs, US$2. Return from Tacna

Mon-Sat 0600, 1600. To be safe, buy your ticket at least a day in advance and arrive early. It is interesting to note the different attitudes to border defence adopted by the Chilean and Peruvian governments.

Into Bolivia *p249*
Bus
There are 3 or 4 buses daily between Arica and **La Paz**, via the border towns of Chungará (Chile) and Tambo Quemado (Bolivia), 8-10 hrs: **Humire**, Tue-Fri at 0900, US$20; **Geminis**, Mon, Wed, Fri 1000, US$20 without lunch; **ChileBus**, daily 1000, US$20; **Transalvador**, Tue, Thu, Sat, 0900, US$15. If you are going to Putre, these will drop you off 4 km away.

Paloma runs services from Arica to **Putre**, daily, 07000, US$5, via several villages. Book the day before and arrive half an hour early.

Humire buses also runs services from Arica to **Visviri**, Tue and Fri at 1030, US$10, from where you can take a jeep across the border to **Charaña**. From Charaña, buses to **La Paz** leave before 1000, US$6, 6 hrs.

Hitchhiking
The Chungará border post is a good place for hitching to La Paz; truck transport leaves in the afternoon. Trucks from Arica to La Paz rarely give lifts, and in any case are excruciatingly slow, but another place to try is at the **Poconchile** control point, 37 km from Arica.

⊙ Directory
Arica *p246, map p248*
Banks Several all along the pedestrian part of 21 de Mayo, some with ATMs open 24 hrs. Casas de cambios include **Marta Daguer**, San Martín 258, slow service, high commission for TCs; **Yanulaque**, 21 de Mayo 175, Mon-Fri 0900-1400, 1600-2000, Sat 0930-1330; most large hotels also change cash; rates for TCs are universally better in Iquique.
Consulates Bolivia, Lynch 270, T058-231030; **Peru**, 18 de Septiembre 1554, T057-231020, T058-231020; **Germany**, Prat 391, oficina 101, T058-254663. **Hospital** 18 de Setiembre 1000, T058- 232242. **Internet** Several in centre, US$.80 per hr. **Laundry** Lavandería A Kilo, Santa Isabel shopping centre, US$6 per 5 kg; **Lavandería La Moderna**, 18 de Septiembre 457, US$4 per kg, open Sat till 2200. **Post office** Prat 375 to send parcels abroad, contents must be shown to Aduana (1st floor of post office), Mon-Fri 0800-1200, packaging sold but take your own tape. **Telephone** CTC, Colón 430 and at 21 de Mayo 211; **Entel-Chile**, 21 de May 345, 0900-2200; **VTR Telecommunications**, 21 de Mayo 477 and Colón 301, fax etc too.
Useful addresses Automóvil Club de Chile, Chacabuco 460, T058-252878, F232780; **CONAF**, MacKenna 820, T/F058-250570, Mon-Fri 0830-1730.

Altiplano national parks → *Colour map 1, A2.*

In the Andes and stretching from the border with Bolivia, Parque Nacional Lauca is one of the most spectacular national parks in Chile. Declared a Biosphere Reserve by UNESCO, it is renowned for its bird life, but is equally remarkable for the extraordinary views of snow-capped volcanoes set against the backdrop of Lago Chungará, one of the world's highest lakes, and the profusion of vicuñas and viscachas that live here. The brilliant quality of the light gives colours an intensity that is not easily forgotten and there are many deserted tracks across the altiplano, which provide a unique sense of the space and beauty of this remote corner of the world.

South of Parque Nacional Lauca are three further parks, covering areas of the western range of the Andes. They are best visited from Arica or Putre, as this permits acclimatization in Putre (Colchane and Enquelga, the alternatives, are too high). Furthermore, moving from north to south means you will not have the sun in your eyes as you travel. Tours in this area, lasting two or four days, can also be arranged from here. Guides in Putre charge a fixed price per vehicle per day, so for groups of three or four, arranging a tour from here can be better value than from Arica. ⋙ For Sleeping, Eating and other listings, see pages 260-262.

⁍ Acclimatization for the altiplano

Unless you are entering Chile from Bolivia, the high altitude of the *altiplano* encountered in the national parks presents specific health problems for the traveller. The risks should not be underestimated; anyone with circulation or respiratory problems should avoid the area. Visitors to the park are advised to spend at least one night, preferably more, in Putre before moving on to higher altitudes. Drinking lots of water and/or *mate de coca* is also advised to compensate for the loss of body fluid. You should, of course, take it easy, limiting exercise before you get that familiar headache associated with *soroche* (altitude sickness), avoid smoking and take steps to get as much fresh air as possible, particularly if spending the night in a *refugio*. In popular *refugios* there can be six to 10 people breathing the same air all night in a small room: to avoid the 0300 headache that often develops in such conditions leave a window open and keep the water bottle nearby. Sleeplessness is a common first night problem but is not a cause for concern. One-day trips to the national park from Arica cannot really be recommended, either for health or for enjoyment: what should be an unforgettable trip amid incredible scenery can become an unpleasant endurance exercise in a minibus full of passengers all suffering from the dreaded *soroche*.

To minimize symptoms the following tips should be followed during the day before climb to the altiplano. Eat plain food, avoiding anything that could be hard to digest such as shellfish or rich sauces. Do not eat any dairy products or drink any fizzy drinks. A glass of wine is fine but travelling to the altiplano with a hangover is a recipe for disaster. Take lip balm, sunblock, a sun hat, woolly hat and windproof clothing with you.

In and outs

Getting there and around Access to Parque Nacional Lauca is easy as Route 11, the main Arica–La Paz road, runs through the park. In January and February, during the rainy season, and in August, when snowfall can occur, some roads in the park may be impassable; check in advance with **CONAF** or the *carabineros* in Arica or Putre. Maps are available from the **Instituto Geográfico Militar** in Santiago. Much of the water in the park is drinkable but you should take bottled water as well.

Parque Nacional Lauca 🖥️🚻🔞⛰️🚌🛈 *pp260-262.*

Situated 145 km east of Arica, the park covers 137,883 ha and includes a large lake, **Lago Chungará**, a system of smaller lakes, the **lagunas Cotacotani**, and lava fields. Ranging in altitude from 3200 m to four peaks of over 6000 m, Lauca brings significant risks of *soroche*, or altitude sickness (unless you are coming from Bolivia). Because of the extreme height, it is best to rise in stages, spending a night in Putre before going on to Lago Chungará; for this reason one-day tours from Arica are not the best way of seeing the park.

Often, when climbing the road from Arica, it may seem as though the weather is overcast; but vehicles soon gain altitude, climbing through the mist into a sort of lost world above, where the sky is a piercing blue colour and you can gaze down at the grey clouds huddled in the valley as if looking into a different plane of reality. On the way from Arica, at Km 90, there is a pre-Inca *pukará* (fortress) and, a few kilometres further, there is an Inca *tambo* (inn).

Putre is a scenic Aymará village, 15 km west of the park entrance at 3500 m, and provides an ideal base for exploring and acclimatization. Situated at the base of **Volcán Tarapacá** (Spanish name Nevadas de Putre; 5824 m), it is surrounded by terracing dating from pre-Inca times, which is now used for cultivating alfalfa and oregano. It has a church dating from 1670. The main street, Baquedano, has several shops, restaurants and *residenciales*, and there is a tourist information office on the plaza which will help arrange tours (some English is spoken). The village, with a popuation of 1200, is a good centre for hiking: an extensive network of trails lead to numerous villages in the mountains, which provide great opportunities to explore, for those with the necessary time and fitness. In the vicinity, there are four archaeological sites with cave paintings up to 6000 years old. About 11 km east by road are the hot springs of **Jurasi** ① *US$2*, with very hot water, a red mud bath, and views of vicuñas and alpacas. Transport can be organized in Putre. Weather can be poor in January and February, with fog and rain.

Exploring the park

From Putre, the road continues to climb and soon enters the park. Some 23 km from Putre is the *sector* **Las Cuevas**, where there is a path and a wooden bridge leading to some rustic thermal springs with water at 40°C. Vizcachas are a common sight. A little furter on there is a CONAF ranger station. **Parinacota** (4392 m), a small village of whitewashed adobe houses, lies 26 km into the park and 41 km from Putre on two ancient trading routes, one from Potosí to Arica and the other from Belén into Bolivia. The interesting **17th-century church** – rebuilt in 1789 – has frescoes, silver religious objects and the skulls of past priests. Señor Sipriano keeps the key: ask for him at the kiosks and make sure you leave a donation. The CONAF office ① *0900-1200, 1230-1700*, which administers the national park is also here. There is a small shop in Parinacota with basic supplies, but most of the handicrafts sold in Parinacota are from Bolivia or Peru: a better place to buy locally made products is **Chucuyo**, 36 km further east, where local residents weave and knit from their own high-quality alpaca wool.

Cerro Guaneguane (5300 m) can be climbed from Parinacota; ask one of the villagers to accompany you as a guide (and pay them). There is also a path to the **Lagunas de Botocatani**, a walk that would make a good day hike. CONAF maintains a nature trail that covers most plant and bird habitats, beginning at the CONAF pond in Parinacota and ending back in the village. Some 20 km southeast of Parinacota is **Lago Chungará**, one of the highest lakes in the world, at 4512 m, a must for its views of the Parinacota, Pomerape, Sajama and Guallatire volcanoes. Overlooking the lake, there is a CONAF *refugio* and campsite; vicuñas, llamas and alpacas can be seen grazing nearby. From here, it is 3 km to the Chilean passport control point at Chungara and 10 km to the Bolivian border at **Tambo Quemado** (see page 249). The border can also be reached via an unpaved road from Parinacota to **Visviri**, 90 km further north.

Heading south ▣⬤⬤ *pp260-262.*

A dirt road (A235) turns south off the Arica–La Paz highway, 1 km east of **Las Cuevas**, park ranger post. It is signed to Chilcaya and Colchane and ends at Huara on the Pan-American Highway, near Iquique (see page 239). There is no public transport on this route and between Las Cuevas and Isluga the only traffic you will generally see is the occasional tour guide with his group and the odd truck from the Borax plant (see below). The road is open all year round but, between December and February and in August, it may be impassable because of deep mud and water, which can wash out the bridges. If you are planning to travel then, you will find a spade useful. Four-wheel drive is essential; take sleeping bags and stock up on fuel, drinking water and food for emergencies.

66 99 Climb through the mist into a sort of lost world above, where the sky is a piercing blue colour, and gaze down at the grey clouds huddled in the valley as if looking into a different plane of reality...

Although many maps show roads descending from the *altiplano* from Surire to the Pan-American Highway and from Colchane to Camiña, do not be tempted to follow them. These roads are terrible in the dry season, dangerous and impassable in the rainy season; if stranded you could wait weeks for help to arrive. The only two safe routes between the *altiplano* and the Pan-American Highway are the international routes to Arica through Parque Nacional Lauca (see page 249), from Colchane to Huara (see page 239), and from the Salar de Huasco to Pica or Pozo Almonte.

Reserva Nacional Las Vicuñas

Split off from Parque Nacional Lauca in order to permit mining, this reserve, reached by Route A235 (entrance free), stretches across 209,131 ha, most of it rolling *altiplano* at an average altitude of 4300 m. The reserve is bisected by the Río Lauca, along which riverine vegetation alternates with puna tola/grasslands and many camelids can be seen. Keep an eye open, too, for condors, rheas and migrating peregrine falcons. **Mina Choquelimpie** (not operating), one of the world's highest gold and silver mines, can be reached by a 7-km detour (clearly marked) off Route A235. The park administration is in **Guallatire**, a village 96 km south of Las Cuevas at the foot of the smoking Guallatire Volcano (6060 m); the village has a lovely 17th-century *altiplano* church and a *carabinero* control post. At Km 139, the road reaches the Salar de Surire.

Monumento Natural Salar de Surire

Situated at 4300 m and covering 17,500 ha, the Salar de Surire is a desolate, spectacular drying salt lake split into two sections. The first, with windy and sulphurous thermal springs (together with picnic site) and a year-round population of 12,000 to 15,000 flamingos of three species (nesting season is January) is protected and administered by CONAF. It is open all year, but see advice above. Administration is in **Surire**, 45 km south of Guallatiri and 138 km south of Putre. The other half of the *salar* is mined for borax; sometimes Surire may be reached by getting a ride in a borax truck from Zapahuira, a road junction at Km 100 on the road from Arica to La Paz.

Parque Nacional Volcán Isluga

This park includes some of the best volcanic scenery of northern Chile and covers 174,744 ha at altitudes above 2100 m. Although the lower parts of the park, at its southwestern end, lie in the hills of the *precordillera*, the heart of the park is situated between **Laguna Aravilla** with its flamingoes and the village of **Isluga**, where there is a beautiful 18th-century Andean church and bell tower. Route A235 crosses the park, from the northern entrance, 40 km south of Surire, to the southern near Isluga. Northeast of Isluga under the smoking **Volcán Isluga** (5501 m) is the village of **Enquelga**, where Aymaran weavers can be seen working in the sand behind wooden wind breaks. This is also the location of the park administration but there are seldom *guardaparques* there. 1 km south of the village is a turn off to some warm natural thermal springs with changing rooms and a picnic area. Three other peaks over

5000 m in the park are Quimsachata (5400 m), Tatajachura (5252 m) and Latamara (5207 m). Wildlife varies according to altitude; there are large numbers of camelids and birds but fewer than in Parque Nacional Lauca.

South of the park is the border village of Cochrane with basic services and transport to Iquique and Oruro in Bolivia. From here a mostly good road runs southwest 180 km to join the Panamericana at Huara. Alternatively a *ripio* road continues south. After 20 km or so there is a turning to the right leading to a hill of giant *Cardón* cactuses. Towering up to 8 m, they flower in September and produce an edible fruit, like a cross between a kiwi and a prickly pear. The road south passes the village of Cariquima and continues on to Lirima through a pass at over 5000 m. This road is new and may not be marked on some maps, but has some of the most spectacular views of the altiplano over the shrubland below. Lodging is available in Lirima, and there are thermal springs 6 km west, with accommodation with a thermal pool in each room. The road from Lirima continues south for 53 km, with microplants turning the flat terrain a radioactive green, before arriving at the **Salar de Huasco**. On the west side there is a radio station in contact with Iquique, and a *refugio* is being built. The view of the sun or full moon rising here is spectacular. In theory it is possible to continue south on the *altiplano* to Ollage and on to San Pedro, but there are also decent roads west to Pica or Pozo Almonte.

● Sleeping

Note that many villages marked on maps in the *altiplano* are uninhabited. Do not expect even the most basic services.

Putre *p258*
AL Las Vicuñas, T058-228564, www.chileanaltiplano.cl. Half board, bungalow-style, heating, restaurant, does not accept TCs, US$ cash or credit cards.
B Hostal Pachamama, Cochrane s/n, T058-251354, www.chileanaltiplano.cl. Reasonable cabins with en suite bathrooms and cooking facilities, also dorms without bath, **F** per person.
C Residencial Calí, Baquedano 399, T099-88566091, krlos_team@hotmail.com. **E** singles. Clean, rooms with bath.
C Residencial Rosamel, Putre. **E** singles. Clean, pleasant, with hot water and restaurant.
C-D Residencial La Paloma, O'Higgins 353, T099- 91979319, lapalomahugopaco@hotmail.com. Same owners as the bus company. Newly renovated, indoor parking, some rooms with bath, no heating, also restaurant.
D Baquedano 250, no sign (blue garage door). **F-G** singles. Basic, clean, hot water, good value. Recommended.
D Residencial Oasis, Putre. **F-G** singles. Basic, no showers, good food, very friendly.

Camping
Sra Clementina Caceres, blue door, Lynch, Camping in the garden and lunch.
Turismo Taki, Copaquilla, 45 km west of Putre (100 km east of Arica). Campsite with a restaurant (serving homemade bread). English and Italian spoken. Also runs excursions to nearby *pukaras* (fortress), the Inca *tambo* (inn) and cemetery and the Inca trail, which connected the highlands with the coast.

Parque Nacional Lauca *p257*
D Casa Barbarita, Parinacota, T058-300013. 2 bedrooms, cooking facilities, heating, naturalist library.
F CONAF refugio, Parinacota. Many beds, cooking facilities. Price per person. Also camping. Best to reserve in Putre.
F CONAF refugio, Lago Chungará. 8 beds, cooking facilities, camping, prices as in Parinacota, reserve in Putre. Take a sleeping bag, food and candles. CONAF *refugios* do not provide sheets or blankets.
F-G Residencial Copihue de Oro, Chucuyo. Price per person. 1 room, 4 beds, no showers, restaurant.
F-G Residencial Doña Mati, Chucuyo. Price per person. 1 room, 5 beds, no shower, restaurant.
F-G Sra Francisca, Parinacota. Price per person. 3 beds, cooking facilities.

F-G Sr Gumercindo Gutierrez, Lagunillas, 10 km north of Parinacota on road to Visviri, turn left near lake. Price per person. Accommodation and guide.

F-G Uta Maillko, Parinacota. The name means 'home of the condor' in Aymara. Price per person. Dormitory, home-cooked Aymara food.

Reserva Nacional Las Vicuñas *p259*
There is accommodation for up to 7 people at the park administration in Guallatire, T058-250570. Imperative to reserve at least 5 days in advance or it will be closed.
F Don Julian, Guallatire. Price per person. Basic accommodation, with half board, hot water and electricity.
F-G Sra Clara Blanca, 1 km east off A235, 10 km after Chuquelimpie turnoff. Price per person. An Aymaran weaver offers overnight accommodation, food typical of the region and allows travellers to help with llamas and alpacas.

Salar de Surire *p259*
F CONAF refugio, Surire, 8 km past the borax mine. 15 beds, heating and cooking facilities. Sleeping bags necessary. Advance booking at CONAF in Arica advised (page 256).

In an emergency, food and lodging will almost always be given at the **Borax mine**.

Camping
Polloquere, 17 km south of Surire. No facilities, no water. Price per site.

Parque Nacional Volcán Isluga *p259*
CONAF refugio, Enculega. 6 beds and cooking facilities, reservation in Arica advised (see page 256).
Residencial El Volcán, Enculega. Basic. There are also several basic *residenciales* in Colchane, which lies 6 km south of the southern entrance (see page 239).

🍴 Eating

Other eating options are given under Sleeping, above.

Parque Nacional Lauca *p257*
🍴 **Restaurant Kuchamarka**, Baquedano s/n, Putre. Serves local specialities including alpaca and vegetarian options, good value.

🍴 **Restaurant Los Payachatas**, Chucuyo. Tasty alpaca dishes.

Reserva Nacional Las Vicuñas *p259*
🍴 **Restaurant Sánchez** (no sign), 1 block from *carabineros*, Guallatire. Good lunch stews in an *altiplano* truckstop.

❀ Festivals and events

Putre *p258*
Nov Feria de la voz Andina takes place in Putre every year, attracting top Andean groups, as well as cultural exhibitions. If going, book accommodation in advance.

⦿ Shopping

Putre *p258*
Buy all food for the park in Putre, which has markets where bottled water, fresh bread, vegetables, meat, cheese and canned foods can be obtained. The **Cooperativo** on the plaza is usually cheapest. Fuel is available from the **Cali** and **Paloma** supermarkets, but is cheaper at **ECA**, next to the post office. **Sra Daria Condori**'s shop on C O'Higgins sells locally made artesanía and naturally coloured alpaca wool. Organically grown vegetables are available from **Freddy Blanco**, opposite the Banco del Estado.

▲ Activities and tours

Putre *p258*
Birding Alto Andino, Baquedano 299, T099-92826195, www.birdingaltoandino.com. Specialist birdwatching tours of the area and also walking tours along the Camino del Inca. English spoken, owner is an Alaskan biologist/naturalist, recommended.
Freddy Torrejón, Gonzalo Cerda 1366, Arica, T058-225685, www.sumainti.cl. Accommodation in Putre and tours of the surrounding area, including Lago Chungará and the village of Parinacota, as well as trips to the more out-of-the-way places, such as the Salar de Surire and ancient rock paintings.
Justino Jirón, T099-90110702, www.tourandino.com. Recommended guide based in Putre. There are several other guides, some more knowledgeable than others.

Tours are offered by many agencies in **Arica** (see page 253), daily in season, according to demand at other times, US$20 with light breakfast and lunch; all 1-day tours make Parinacota their last stop. It is better to spend more than 1 day in the park. Longer tours are also available. You can leave the tour and continue on another day as long as you ensure that the company will collect you when you want (tour companies try to charge double for this).

Climbing

The best season for climbing is Aug-Nov; avoid Jan-Feb. Permits are required for climbing Parinacota, Pomerape, Tarapacá and Guallatire volcanoes; these can be obtained from the governor's office in Putre. The procedure is routine (passport required) but expect a delay of 1 or 2 days. To obtain a permit in advance, contact **Departamento de Fronteras y Limites (DIFROL)**, Banderas 52, piso 5, Santiago, T02-6794200, listing the mountains you wish to climb.

Arturo Gómez, who lives next to the Lipigas propane shop in Putre, is a climbing guide and local plant expert.

⊙ Transport

Bus

La Paloma leaves Arica from its own terminal daily at 0700 for **Putre**, US$3.50, returning from Putre at 1330. The bus often leaves full, so buy your ticket the day before. The journey takes you through several villages on the way. Alternatively, any bus heading to **La Paz** (page 256) will drop you on the main

road, 3 km from Putre. Hitching from here is usually easy with the army or *carabineros*. If you walk, take it easy until you have acclimatized to the altitude.

Jurasi *colectivos*, T058-222813, leave Arica daily at 0700, picking up at hotels, US$10.

Buses Humire run services 1030 Tue and Fri from Arica to **Parinacota**, US$7, slow.

Car

For 5 or more, the most economical proposition is to hire a vehicle in Arica but take at least 1 spare fuel can with a tightly fitting cap. During the climb from Arica, you should stop several times to release excess pressure in fuel cans. For tyre repairs, ask for Andrés in Putre. For the Parque Nacional Lauca, 4WD and antifreeze are essential; if you wish to cross from the park into Bolivia you will need a permit from the hire company.

Hitchhiking

Most trucks for Bolivia pass **Parinacota** between 0700-1100. Hitching back to Arica is not difficult and you may be able to bargain with one of the tour buses.

The **Salar de Surire** can sometimes be reached by getting a ride in a borax truck from Zapahuira, Km 100 on the Arica–La Paz road; trucks run sporadically depending on rainfall. The drop-off point is on the mine side of the Salar, 30 km from the hot springs.

☉ Directory

Putre *p258*
Bank No ATM. May changes US cash to pesos, but no TCs. **Internet** on the plaza.

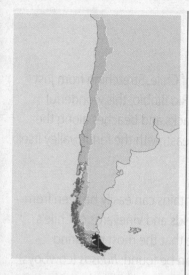

Central Valley

⁖ Footprint features

Introduction

The Central Valley is the heart of Chile. Stretching from just north of Santiago south to the Río Biobío, this wonderful region climbs from secluded tracks and beaches along the coast to the high Andes in the east, with the fertile valley itself in between.

On clear days, the snowy mountains can easily be seen from the coast, across the woods, fields and vineyards of Chile's agricultural heartland. It is here that the most enduring images of Chilean village life can be found: *huasos* (cowboys) with their long spurs, green valleys speckled with grazing horses and whitewashed houses in colonial style, hinting at that bygone age before cars and motorbikes sounded the death knell for the horse.

★ Don't miss...

1 **Rodeos** The highlight being the National Rodeo championships in Rancagua at the end of March, page 269.
2 **The beach at Pichilemu** One of the best surfing strands in Chile, page 270.
3 **Pacific coast resorts** Iloca, Curanipe and Lebu are the favourites, but there are countless others along the beautiful and largely deserted Pacific coast, pages 275, 281 and 292.
4 **Trekking** Trek in the mountains near the resort of Vilches, east of Talca, page 279.
5 **Vineyards** Wine tasting is a pleasure in the vineyards around Santa Cruz and the Maule Valley, page 280.

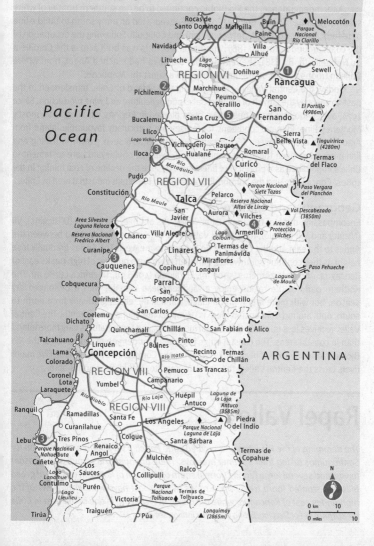

Central Valley

Background

The peoples of the Central Valley did not prove as fierce as their Mapuche neighbours. They were conquered by the Incas in about 1470. On his second visit to Chile, Pedro de Valdivia led an expedition southwards, founding Concepción in 1550 and a further seven cities south of the Río Biobío. The Mapuche insurrection of 1598 and the Spanish defeat at Curalabo in 1599 led the Spanish to withdraw north of the Río Biobío and concentrate their efforts in the Central Valley.

Here, the land and its inhabitants were divided up among the colonists to create the forerunner of the hacienda, which was to dominate social and economic life in Chile. The hacienda was a self-contained unit, producing everything it needed. There were no towns in the area but, from the 1740s, the Spanish crown attempted to increase its control over the region by founding settlements, including Rancagua (1743), San Fernando (1742), Curicó (1743), Talca (1742), Cauquenes (1742) and Linares (1755).

After Independence, the Río Biobío continued to be the southern frontier of white settlement until, in 1862, Colonel Cornelio Saavedra led an army south to build a line of 10 forts, each 4 km apart, between Angol and Collipulli. Following the occupation of the coast around Arauco in 1867, another line of forts was built across the Cordillera de Nahuelbuta. By 1881, the railway from Santiago had reached Angol, from where Chilean troops set out on the final campaign against the Mapuche.

Today, the Central Valley is the agricultural heartland of Chile, transformed in the past 30 years by the growth of commercial export agriculture and wine production. Since 1974, over 1,500,000 ha of trees have been planted in Regions VII, VIII and IX, mostly Monterrey Pine. Climatic conditions for forestry are particularly favourable inland from Arauco. The coast between Dichato and Arauco has also seen growth in fishing and fish-processing since the 1980s, while inland, swathes of vineyards are testament to Chile's importance as a producer of fine wines. Despite the decline of coal mining in the 1980s, Concepción and the surrounding area are an important industrial area in Chile.

Geography and climate

Encompassing three of the administrative regions of Chile, Regions VI (O'Higgins), VII (Maule) and VIII (Biobío), the Central Valley is a wide depression located between the Andes to the east and the Cordillera de la Costa to the west. The Andes gradually lose height as they continue southwards, although there are a number of high peaks east of Rancagua: Alto de los Arrieros (5000 m), El Palomo (4986 m), Tingiririca (4280 m). The northern parts of the region enjoy a Mediterranean climate, with a prolonged dry season, but with more rain than Santiago. Rainfall increases gradually from north to south, until around Concepción there is usually some rainfall each month. The Central Valley receives less rain than the coastal mountains, but temperatures vary more inland than in coastal areas. The coastal range is generally under 500 m, but south of the Río Biobío it forms a range of high peaks known as the Cordillera de Nahuelbuta. Five major rivers cross the Central Valley: the Rapel, Mataquito, Maule, Itata and Biobío.

Rapel Valley → Colour map 3, B3.

The damming of the Río Rapel has created Lago Rapel, a very popular destination for Santiaguinos taking their summer holidays. There are numerous small and pleasant towns, and several large fundos (farms) south of the town of Rapel, in an area of green hills and stunted thorn trees. Open roads by the coast have wonderful views of the high Andes east of Rancagua, while the beach at Pichilemu is one of the best in Chile for surfing. ▶▶ For Sleeping, Eating and other listings, see pages 270-273.

Rancagua ⬛🏍️🎑🎡⬛🔺⬛🚌 » pp270-273.

The capital of Región VI, Rancagua lies 82 km south of Santiago, on the Río Cachapoal. The city was founded in 1743 and in October 1814 was the scene of an important battle during the Wars of Independence, when Bernardo O'Higgins and his 1700 Chilean patriots were surrounded in the centre of the town by 4500 Royalist (pro-Spanish) troops. O'Higgins managed to break out and escape but was forced into exile in Argentina, only to return within a few years finally to defeat the Spanish forces in Chile (see also page 525).

Ins and outs

Getting there Rancagua is accessible by bus and train from Santiago (both hourly). There are also connections to the towns further south, especially Talca, Chillán, Concepción, Temuco and Puerto Montt (several daily).

Getting around While the centre of Rancagua is compact, some of the outlying *barrios* are quite a distance and you may wish to take one of the numerous *colectivos*.

Tourist information ① *Germán Riesco 277, T072-230413, info_ohiggins@serna tur.cl, English spoken. Also municipal office in the Municipalidad on Plaza de los Héroes.*

Sights

At the heart of the city is an attractive tree-lined plaza, the **Plaza de los Héroes** and several streets of single-storey colonial-style houses. In the centre of the plaza is an equestrian statue of O'Higgins. The double-spired cathedral on the south side of the plaza was restored in the 1860s, the original building having been destroyed in the battle of Rancagua, together with most of the other buildings around the plaza. There are several plaques in the city centre marking the sites of the battle and a diagram in the

Sleeping 🛏️
Aguila Real 1
Camino del Rey 2
España 3
Hostal Yaiman 4
Rancagua 5
Residencial Ahumada 7
Santiago 6

Eating 🍴
Bravíssimo 1
Geo Algas 2
La Cocina
Artesanal 6
Lasagna 4

plaza shows the disposition of the troops. One block north is the **Merced** church, from where O'Higgins commanded his beleaguered forces. It dates from 1758 but has been restored several times. The main commercial area lies along Avenida Independencia, which runs west from the plaza towards the bus and rail terminals. **Museo Histórico** ① *Estado 685 y Ibieta, T/F072-221524, www.museorancagua.cl, Tue-Fri 1000-1800, Sat and Sun 0900-1300, US$1.50 (Tue free)*, housed in a colonial mansion, contains collections of religious art and late 19th-century furniture.There is also a **Casa de la Cultura** ① *corner of Milán and Cachapoal, T072-230976, daily 0830-1330, 1500-1700*, directly south of Plaza de Los Héroes, which houses temporary exhibitions. In the station there is a small gallery with paintings by local artists for sale.

Around Rancagua ⬤🔋🛈⬤⬤⬤ ➤ *pp270-273.*

Lago Rapel
West of Rancagua, this lake is 40 km long and feeds the Rapel hydroelectric plant. Most facilities at this popular summer resort are on the east shore around El Manzano, the main town, while the tourist information office is in Las Cabras. There are watersports at Bahía Skorpios, including windsurfing, yachting, waterskiing and fishing.

East of the city
The **El Teniente** copper mine, one of the biggest in the country, is 67 km east of Rancagua. Owned by **Codelco**, it can only be visited by prior arrangement with the company. Nearby, on a private road above El Teniente, is the small **Chapa Verde** ski resort ① *T072-294255, www.chapaverde.cl, lift tickets US$23 per day Mon-Fri, US$29 per day Sat, Sun, obtainable only from resort office, Del Sol shopping centre, north of Rancagua, online reservations also available*. The resort is owned by **Codelco**, but is open to the public in season (June-September). Equipment can be hired, but there's no accommodation.

South of El Teniente and 28 km east of Rancagua are the thermal springs of **Cauquenes** ① *T072-899010, www.termasdecauquenes.cl*, with a colonial hotel, visited by Charles Darwin in 1835. A bath in the springs costs US$8, massages start at US$13 and a jacuzzi costs US$19. Some 5 km north is the village of **Coya**, where the Chilean President has a summer residence, while to the south is the **Reserva Nacional Río de los Cipreses** ① *T072-297505, US$5*. Situated 50 km southeast of Rancagua, the reserve covers 36,882 ha of the valley of the Río de los Cipreses at altitudes ranging from 900 m to 4900 m. Park administration is at the entrance at the north end of the park.

San Fernando and around
San Fernando lies on the Río Tingiririca, 51 km south of Rancagua. Founded in 1742, it is capital of Colchagua Province and a service town for this fertile valley. There is a small local museum in the **Casa Patronal de Lircunlauta** ① *Jiménez y Alameda, closed Mon, US$3*, a 17th-century colonial mansion, with local history exhibits.

From San Fernando, a road runs east towards the *cordillera* and divides: the southern branch of the road goes to the resort of **Sierra Bellavista**, a private *fundo* where many Santiago businesspeople have holiday houses, and where there are rodeos in October and November. The northern branch, a treacherous 75 km, runs to the **Termas del Flaco** near the Argentine border, where there are camping facilities, *cabañas* and several hotels and *hospedajes*. The thermal springs (US$2) are open only in the summer when they attract large numbers of visitors. Some 500 m from the Termas del Flaco are 'Las huellas de dinosaurios', dinosaur footprints preserved in the rock, dating from over 120 million years ago. There are good one-day treks starting from the baths, and a four-hour horseride leads to the site of the Uruguayan plane crash immortalised in the film *Alive*.

☷ Ride 'em cowboy

During the summer months, rodeo is one of the most popular sports in central and southern Chile, second only to the inevitable: football. Teams (or *colleras*) of two riders on horseback compete throughout the season, culminating in the national championships in Rancagua at the end of March. Eliminatory rounds are held in Osorno, Temuco, San Carlos, San Fernando, Vallenar and Los Andes, but most small towns in central southern Chile have their own *media lunas* (stadia, with their own corrals and horseboxes), often used once a year only.

Rodeo owes its origins to the colonial period, when cattle roamed openly and were rounded up once annually to be identified and marked by their owners in a rodeo. Based on the traditional view that heifers need to be broken in, the modern sport of rodeo is a test of the ability of two horses and their riders to work together and control the cattle.

The event takes place inside a stockade of thick upright timbers; although now circular, this is known as a *media luna* (crescent) after the design of the early rings: at two points the walls of the ring are covered by padded sections, with a flag at either end of the section. Each *collera* competes by manoeuvring a heifer around the edge of the ring between the padded sections, stopping it at each padded section by pinning its hindquarters against the fence, before turning it in the opposite direction. This is done three times before the animal is released from the ring.

Three judges give points (on a scale of one to seven) for elegance and horsemanship. It is one of the principles of rodeo that no heifer should be put through this performance more than once; the event should come as a complete surprise to the animal.

Rodeo is a good opportunity to see traditional Chilean rural customs: the *huasos* (cowboys) wearing brightly coloured ponchos, wide-brimmed hats and carved wooden stirrups that were common in the 19th century; the fine horses, and the *cuecas* (traditional dances) that sometimes follow the main event.

Los Lingues ① *Panamericana Sur, Km 124, www.loslingues.com*, is a private *hacienda*, 20 km northeast of San Fernando, where the 'best' horses in Chile are bred. Visits can be arranged to the 17th-century house, a gift of the King of Spain, and one-day tours, including transport, rodeo and lunch, are also available.

Heading west ☐☐☐☐☐ ⇒ *pp270-273*.

West of San Fernando, tracks branch off the main road to Pichilemu southwards through quiet hill country towards **Lago Vichuquén** (see page 275). Dry thorn trees gradually give way to more fertile land, with the first signs of *copihues* and forests, while ridges high above the valleys provide beautiful routes for cyclists, walkers and horse riders.

Santa Cruz

Fifty kilometres southwest of San Fernando, Santa Cruz is surrounded by some of the country's best vineyards and is the site of the offices of the **Ruta del Vino del Valle de Colchagua** ① *Plaza de Armas 140, Of 6, T072-823199, www.rutadelvino.cl* Also in the town is **Museo de Cochagua** ① *Errazuriz 145, T072-821050, www.museocolchagua.cl, Tue-Sun 1000-1900, US$5, concessions US$2*, an excellent small museum with exhibits on local history and prehistory as well as winemaking. In summer, a steam train links Santa Cruz with many of the wineries in the Colchagua valley. For reservations, see www.trendelvinochile.cl.

Pichilemu

Pichilemu is a coastal resort with a great many hotels and *residenciales*, 120 km west of San Fernando. It was founded by Agustín Ross Edwards in the 19th century in the style of a European resort. The town is on two levels, one at sea level with the main town above. In summer it is a popular destination for Chileans. During the rest of the year there is a steady flow of foreigners who come to enjoy some of the best surf in South America. This is reflected in the number of shops along the main drag selling surfing accessories.

There is a small go-kart style motorbike circuit on the south end of the *costanera*, and further along there are three surf schools that also hire out equipment. Among several beaches is **Punta Los Lobos**, where international surfing competitions are held. The former train station, made of wood in 1925, is a national monument, and now home to the tourist information office. There is also a small museum, the **Museo del Niño Rural de Ciruelos**, a few kilometres south of town, with three rooms of interesting exhibits from the pre-Hispanic cultures of the region. Fishing is good in nearby lakes. Some 20 km southeast along a *ripio* road is Pañul, where interesting pottery is produced using the local clay. Nearby is a watermill, dating from 1904 and which locals still use to grind their wheat into flour. It can be visited for US$1. Unless you go by taxi or with a guide, prepare to get lost on the way.

● Sleeping

Rancagua *p267, map p267*

AL Camino del Rey, Estado 275, T072-232314, hotelcaminodelrey@terra.cl. 4-star, suites, full facilities, best in town.

AL Santiago, Brasil 1036, T072-230860, www.hotelsantiago.cl. One of the city's oldest hotels, and it is showing its age. There is a restaurant and swimming pool. Overpriced.

A Rancagua, San Martín 85, T072-232663, F241155. Drab but clean rooms with bath and TV, quiet, secure parking.

A-B Aguila Real, Brasil 1045, T072-222047, hsamour@ctcinternet.cl. Modern 3-star. With breakfast, cable TV, laundry, restaurant. Some English spoken.

B España, San Martín 367, T072-230141, noraberriosf@latinmail.com. Bath, cheaper without, central, hot water, pleasant, clean, laundry, food served.

B-C Hostal Yaiman, Bueras 655, T072-641773. **D-E** singles. Some rooms with bath. Laundry facilities, food served.

C Residencial Ahumada, Mujica 125, T072-225892. **F** singles. Kitchen facilities, secure.

Lago Rapel *p268*

L-AL Punta Verde, Bahía Skorpios, T072-591434. 4-star resort with full facilities.

C Hostería L Finca, Sector La Carmen caminio Llallauquén, Km 3, T02-2896676. Pleasant hostel with a pool and restaurant.

Camping

The eastern shore of Lago Rapel around El Manzano is lined with campsites.

Camping Punta Arenas, 3 km north of El Manzano. Basic and cheap.

East of the city *p268*

L-AL Hotel Termas de Cauquenes, Cauquenes, T072-899010, www.termasdecauquenes.cl. Housed in a colonial building. Excellent food is served in the hotel restaurant (full board available). It also has a chapel and gardens.

Camping

There is a site at **Los Maitenes**, 12 km south of the entrance to the Reserva Nacional Río de los Cipreses, prices per site.

● *For an explanation of sleeping and eating price codes used in this guide, see inside the*
● *front cover. Other relevant information is found in Essentials, see pages 50-57.*

San Fernando and around *p268*
LL Hacienda Los Lingues, Panamericana Sur, Km124, 22 km north of San Fernando, www.loslingues.com (see page 269). The very expensive accommodation starts at US$250 with an extra charge for breakfast or full board. The hacienda is a member of the French Hotels et Relais et Chateaux.
B Español, Av Rodríguez 959, San Fernando, T072-711098. 3-star, with parking and pool.
C Imperio, Av Rodríguez 770, San Fernando, T072-714595. With breakfast and bath (cheaper without), clean, cable TV, parking.
D Pérez, Av Rodríguez 1028, San Fernando, T072-713328. **F** singles, without bath.

Santa Cruz *p269*
Prices are cheaper Apr-Dec.
L Santa Cruz Plaza, Plaza de Armas 286, T072-209600, www.hotelsantacruzplaza.cl. Four-storey building in colonial style on the Plaza. There is a gym, pool and spa as well as a fine restaurant. Spacious rooms and luxurious suites. Disabled friendly. Tours and visits to wineries arranged.
A Hostal Casa Familia, Los Pidenes 421, T072-825766, www.valledecolchagua.cl/casafamilia. **B** singles. Charming upmarket bed and breakfast. Some rooms a little on the small side.
B Hostal Santa Cruz, JJ Carvacho 40, T072-822046, hostalsantacruz@terra.cl. **D-E** singles. Standard rooms with TV and bath. Internet access, tours arranged.

Pichilemu *p270*
There are dozens of very cheap places to stay.
A-B Rocas del Pacífico, Gaete 244, T072-841346, www.hotelrocasdelpacifico.cl. With breakfast. Spacious rooms with good bathrooms. Some rooms on the top floor have a decent sea view. Comfortable, if a little plastic.
B-C Asther, Ortúzar 540, T072-841072, www.hotelasther.cl. Traditional hotel dating from the 1930s but redesigned since then. Small comfortable rooms with bath and cable TV. The best rooms back on to the terrace with extensive views to the north. There is a pleasant bar/breakfast area where meals are served in summer and an unheated pool outside. Recommended.
E Rex, Ortúzar 34, T072-841003. Price per person. Good breakfast, good value.

B-C Chile-España, Ortúzar 255, T072-841270, hotelchileespana@terra.cl. **E** singles. Good option close to the beach. Ample space for storing surf boards. The rooms with bath have cable TV and electric blankets. There is also a café attached.
B-C Waitara, Av Costanera 1039, T072-841331, waitara@costapichilemu.cl. **E** singles. Cabins on the seafront with fully equipped kitchens. Also slightly cheaper rooms with bath. Discounts for longer stays.
F Bahía, Ortúzar 262. Price per person with breakfast, clean.

Camping
Pichilemu has several campsites, but at US$12 per site, these are more expensive than the cheaper *residenciales*.

Eating

Rancagua *p267, map p267*
▼ **Bravissimo**, Astorga 307. Recommended for ice cream.
▼ **Geo Algas**, Independencia 677, 2nd floor. Vegetarian food.
▼ **La Cocina Artesanal**, O´Carrol 60. Traditional meat and seafood dishes.
▼ **Lasagna**, west end of plaza. Good for bread and *empanadas*.

San Fernando and around *p268*
▼ **Club Social San Fernando**, Rodríguez 787. Good local food.
▼ **Restaurante La Carreta**, Rancagua 759. Traditional cuisine.
▼ **Rigoletto**, Rodríguez 751. Pizzas.

Pichilemu *p270*
▼▼ **La Balaustra**, Ortúzar 289, T072-842458. Has the most innovative menu in town, ranging from lamb ribs with mashed Quínoa to fish in garlic sauce. Also serves coffee, sandwiches, pancakes and fresh juice.
▼ There a number of basic restaurants serving fish and traditional Chilean dishes.

Bars and clubs

Rancagua *p267, map p267*
La Notta, Illanes 303-A. Bar with restaurant.
Pub Restaurant Puerto Girón, Bueras 358. Expensive.
Varadero, O´Carrol 1109. Disco.

Toscano Pub Disco, Quechereguas 966.
Fri and Sat night disco.

Pichilemu *p270*
Many people come here for the nightlife;
there is a good atmosphere after dark, with a
dozen or so discos open in summer, and
weekends off season.
Delerium Tremens, Ortúzar 215.
One of a small but growing number of
micro-brew pubs in Chile.

⊛ Festivals and events

Rancagua *p267, map p267*
Beginning Feb Beans are the most
important staple food for *campesinos* in the
area and are celebrated at the Festival del
Poroto (Bean Festival).
End Mar National Rodeo Championships
are held in the Complejo Deportivo, north of
the centre, US$15 per day. There are plenty
of opportunities for purchasing cowboy
items; watch out especially for the fantastic
spurs, which are much more important to
horsemanship in Chile than elsewhere in
Latin America.

Santa Cruz *p269*
First weekend in Mar Fiesta de la
Vendimia (harvest celebration) is held in
Santa Cruz around the town's main plaza,
where local wine and food can be sampled.

○ Shopping

Rancagua *p267, map p267*
There's a shopping mall at Cuevas 483,
and a supermarket at **Hipermercado
Independencia**, Av Miguel Ramírez 665.

▲ Activities and tours

Rancagua *p267, map p267*
Andes Sur Expediciones, T072-491157,
www.andes-sur.cl. Regional operator
specializing in mountaineering, trekking,
horse riding and fishing in the Andes.
Recommended.
Ruta del Vino del Valle del Cachapoal,
Panamericana, Km 110 (20 km south of
Rancagua), T072-522085, www.chilean
wineroute.com. See box, page 558.

⊙ Transport

Rancagua *p267, map p267*
Air
Airline offices in town include **Iberia**,
Lacsa and **United Airlines**, Cuevas No 744,
T072-220288 ; **LanChile**, Astorga 223B,
T600-5622000.

Bus
Main terminal in Rancagua is at Doctor
Salinas y Calvo just north of the market but
most buses for **Santiago** leave from the **Tur
Bus** terminal at Calvo y O'Carrol. Many
services from further south stop on the
Pan-American Highway, 2 km outside town.

Local There are far too many local buses to
list here, but destinations include **Lago
Rapel** with Sextur, T072-231342, or Galbus
T072-230640, every 20 mins, US$2.75;
Pichilemu, US$5 one-way, many companies;
and **Termas Del Flaco**, US$16 return with
Buses Amistad, T072-229358, booking
required 2 days in advance.

Long distance Frequent services to
Santiago, 1¼ hrs, US$4. To **Valparaíso** and
Viña del Mar, Tur Bus, US$7. Viatur, T072-
234502, have a nightly bus to **Valdivia**,
Osorno and **Puerto Montt** (US$16), and
another to **Chillán** and **Los Angeles** (US$9).
Buses Lit, T072-239800, also run southbound
services.

Car/bicycle
Car hire with **Weber Rentacar**, Membrillar
40, Of 2, T072-226005, autorentasweber
@tie.cl; **Comercial O'Carrol**, O'Carrol 1120,
T072-230041, ocarrolrentacar@yahoo.com.
For parts try **Aucamar**, Brasil 1177,
T072-223594, and several others around
Brasil 1100-1200, although the selection and
prices are better in Santiago. Bike spares at
Gustavo Sepúlveda, Bueras 481,
T072-241413.

Train
Rancagua station is at Av La Marina,
T072-230361, www.efe.cl. Mainline services
between **Santiago** and **Chillán** stop here.
Also regular services to/from **Santiago**, 1¼
hrs, and **San Fernando**, 35 mins, on
Metrotren, 10-19 a day, US$2.75.

East of the city *p268*

Chapa Verde ski resort can only be reached by mine-transport bus from **Del Sol** shopping centre on the northern outskirts of Rancagua, daily 0900, plus every 15 mins 0800-0930 during weekends in season. The thermal springs of **Cauquenes** are served by 5 daily buses from Rancagua with **Buses Termas**, US$1.50, or a colectivo from Rancagua market.

San Fernando and around *p268*

Bus

Many companies have buses to **Santiago**, US$4.50, including **Andimar**, T072-711817 and **Pullman del Sur**, T072-714076. To **Pichilemu**, US$4, with **Nilahue**, T072-711937 and **Galbus**, T072-712983; to **Termas del Flaco**, US$12 return, with **Amistad**, T072-710348, **Andibus**, T072-711817, and others. Lots of competition to the south, with services running as far as **Chiloé**, US$19, with **Cruz** del Sur, T072-710348, and most intermediate destinations with **Turbus**, T072-712923, and **Buses Lit**, T072-711679.

Train

The station is at Quecheregua s/n, T072-711087. **Metrotren** runs 10 trains daily to Santiago, US$3.25.

Pichilemu *p270*

Andimar and **Nilahue** buses to **Santiago**, 4 hrs, US$7.

Directory

Rancagua *p267, map p267*

Banks Exchange at **Cambios Afex**, Av Campos 363, open every day; also several banks on Independencia. **Internet** There are several around the Plaza de Armas **Useful address** Automóvil Club de Chile, Ibieta 09, T072-239930, F239907.

Mataquito Valley → *Colour map 3, C2.*

The Río Mataquito, formed by the confluence of the Ríos Lontué and Teno, flows through the peaceful heart of Chilean wine country, reaching the Pacific at a wide and serene estuary near Iloca. The Andes can clearly be seen from the cliffs above the largely deserted coast. ▸▸ *For Sleeping, Eating and other listings, see pages 275-277.*

Curicó ▸▸ *pp275-277.*

Curicó, which means 'black water' in the Mapuche language, lies between the rivers Lontué and Teno, 54 km south of San Fernando. Founded in 1743, it is the only town of any size in the Mataquito Valley and is the service centre for the region's vineyards. The bustling town centre offers good views towards the mountains and a friendly atmosphere after dark.

Ins and outs

Getting there Curicó is easily accessible by bus from Santiago (many times daily). There are also some connections to the towns further south, especially Talca, Chillán, Temuco and Puerto Montt (several daily).

Getting around While the centre of Curicó is quite compact, some of the outlying *barrios* are quite a distance away, and you may wish to take one of the numerous *colectivos*.

Tourist information Gobernación Provincial ⓘ *Plaza de Armas, Mon-Fri 0900-1330, 1600-1800,* helpful, has street map. **CONAF** ⓘ *Gobernación Provincial building, piso 1, Plaza de Armas, daily 0900-1430.*

The **Plaza de Armas** is surrounded by about 40 Canary Island palms and has lovely fountains with sculptures of nymphs, black-necked swans and a monument to the Mapuche warrior, Lautaro, carved from the trunk of an ancient beech tree. The steel **bandstand** was built in New Orleans in 1904 and is now a national monument. On the western side of the plaza is the church of **La Merced**, which was badly damaged by an earthquake in 1986, and is slowly being restored. Five blocks east is the neo-Gothic church of **San Francisco**, a national monument, which contains the 17th-century Virgen de Velilla, brought from Spain. At the junction of Carmen and Avenida San Martín is the imposing **Iglesia del Carmen**.

To the east of the city is the Avenida Manso de Velasco, with statues of various national heroes, and also a bust of Mahatma Gandhi. Nearby is **Cerro Condell** offering fine views of the surrounding countryside and across to the distant Andes; it is an easy climb to the summit, from where there are a number of short walks.

The **Miguel Torres bodega** ① *5 km south of the city, T075-564100, www.torres.es/ eng/asp/vav_curico.asp, daily 1000-1700 in autumn and winter, daily 1000-1900 in spring and summer, tours in Spanish only*, is one of the biggest wine *bodegas* in Chile and well worth a visit. To get there, take a bus for Molina from the local terminal or from outside the railway station and get off at Km 195 on the Pan-American Highway. There's a good restaurant on the site, open Tuesday to Sunday. For details of other *bodegas* and vineyards in the area, contact the **Ruta del Vino del Valle de Curicó** ① *Merced 331, piso 2, T075-328972, www.rvvc.cl.*

Curicó

To ⑥

Sleeping 🛏

Comercio 1
Prat 3
Residencial Colonial 6
Residencial Ensueño 7

Residencial Rahue 9
Turismo 11

Eating 🍴

American Bar 1

Café-Bar Maxim 2
Centro Italiano
  Club Social 3
Club de la Unión 4
El Fogón Chileno 5

Los Cisnes 6
Sant' Angelo 7

Area de Proteccíon Radal Siete Tazas
① *Oct-Mar, US$3.*

This park is in two sectors, one at **Radal**, 65 km east of Curicó, the other at **Parque Inglés**, 9 km further east and the site of the park administration. The most interesting sector is at Radal, where the Río Claro flows through a series of seven rock 'cups' (the *siete tazas*), each with a pool emptying into the next by means of a waterfall. The river then passes through a canyon, 15 m deep but only 1½ m wide, which ends abruptly in a cliff and a beautiful waterfall. There are several well-marked trails in the area.

Towards the coast
From Curicó, a road runs west through the small town of **Licantén** towards the mouth of the Río Mataquito and the popular resort of **Iloca**, set in a wide bay with great views south along the coastline. Some 5 km north of Iloca is **Puerto Duao**, a fishing village with a good campsite, while beyond is the resort of **Llico**, a long narrow one street town with a pleasant dark sand beach and windsurfing facilities. It is reached either by the coastal route or by an unpaved inland road, which branches off at Hualañe, 74 km east of Curicó.

Six kilometres west of Licantén a bridge crosses the Río Mataquito, leading to a road south along the coast to **Putú**, past kilometres of rolling sand dunes, a kind of mini Sahara. Further south, the road reaches the Río Maule, where a ferry crosses to Constitución (see page 279).

Lago Vichuquén and around
Just east of Llico and 114 km west of Curicó, Lago Vichuquén is a large, peaceful lake, set in a bowl surrounded by pinewoods. It is very popular with the wealthy and with watersports enthusiasts and, although parts of the eastern shore of the lake are inaccessible by road, there are full facilities on the western shore, particularly at Aquelarre. The nearby town of **Vichuquén** has some well-preserved colonial architecture and a recommended small **museum** ① *US$1.80*, set in a beautiful porticoed house in the town centre.

Just north of Lago Vichuquén, 120 km west of Curicó, is the **Reserva Nacional Laguna Torca** ① *administration and campsite 4 km east of Llico, open Sep-Apr*. The reserve covers 604 ha and is a natural sanctuary for over 80 species of birds, especially black-necked swans and other water fowl. To get there take any bus from Curicó to Llico and get out near the administration.

⬤ Sleeping

Curicó *p273, map p274*
AL Turismo, Carmen 727 y Prat, T075-543440, www.hotelturismocurico.cl. Curicó's best hotel, suites, pleasant garden, good restaurant with an extensive wine list.
A Comercio, Yungay 730, T075-310014, www. Hotelcomercio.cl. 3-star, newly refurbished with pool, gym, restaurant, wifi and car hire.
C-D Residencial Ensueño, Rodríguez 442, T075- 312648. Basic lodging, some rooms with bath. Includes breakfast.
C-D Prat, Peña 427, T075-311069. **F** singles.

Rooms with or without bath. Pleasant patio with grapevines and fig trees, friendly, clean, hot water, laundry facilities, breakfast extra, parking. Recommended.
D Residencial Colonial, Rodríguez 461, T075- 314103, resicolonial@terra.cl. **F** singles. Clean, patio, friendly, some rooms with bath. Good value.
D Residencial Rahue, Peña 410, T075-312194. **F** singles. Basic, with bath, meals, hot water, the cheaper annex rooms without bath have no ventilation.

C Hostería La Flor de la Canela, Parque Inglés, 3 km west of *siete tazas*, T075-491613. Breakfast extra, good food. Good value. Highly recommended.

Camping

There's a dirty campsite near the entrance with a shop, US$2 per person. Inside the park is **Camping Las Catas**, US$17 per site, no shop.

Towards the coast *p275*

B Hostería Atlántida 2000, Llico, T075-400264. Near beach, small rooms, with breakfast.

B Hotel Iloca, Besoain 221, Iloca, T075-1983751. Recently restored, with bath. Breakfast, good views. Several *cabañas*, many open in summer only.

B-C Hospedaje El Capricho del Corazón, 35 km west of Curicó on road to Hualañe and Iloca, T09-96391086. Swiss run, English, French and German spoken, tours arranged. Recommended.

C Residencial Miramar, Carrera Pinto 48, Llico, T075-400032. At the far end of town. Good seafood restaurant, small rooms with bath, excellent value, full board available.

C-D Hospedaje Marilla, opposite the *carabineros*, Iloca. **F** singles. Simple but clean and friendly. Some rooms with bath.

Camping

El Peñón, 6 km south of Iloca, T072-471026, T02-6336099. US$15 per site. Phone ahead for reservation.

La Puntilla, 2 km north of Iloca, T09-97415585. US$12 per site, also *cabañas*.

Lago Vichuquén and around *p275*

L-AL Marina Vichuquén, T075-400265, www.marinavichuquen.cl. Fully equipped resort, good. Lots of activities including watersports, tennis, mountain biking, horse riding.

AL Hostería Vichuquén, Lago Vichuquén, T075-400018, www.lagovichquen.cl. Spacious rooms with views across the lake. Well-equipped, with good food. Rents out bicycles and kayaks.

Camping

Vichuquén, east shore of lake, T075-400062. Full facilities.

El Sauce, north shore of lake, T075-400203. Good facilities, US$25 per site.

🍴 Eating

Curicó *p273, map p274*

There are several seriously cheap restaurants with varying standards of cleanliness outside the market on C Donoso. **Hotel Turismo** and **Comercio** both have decent restaurants.

🍴🍴-🍴🍴 **Club de la Unión**, Plaza de Armas. Innovative food in elegant surroundings. Recommended.

🍴 **American Bar**, Yungay 647. Real coffee, small pizzas, open daily morning to evening.

🍴 **El Fogón Chileno**, M Montt 399. For meat and wines.

🍴 **Los Cisnes**, Rodríguez 1186. Parilladas and cheaper *almuerzos*.

🍴 **Café-Bar Maxim**, Prat 617. Light meals, beer and wine.

🍴 **Centro Italiano Club Social**, Estado 531. Good, cheap meals.

🍴 **Sant' Angelo**, Prat 430. Excellent patisserie, also serving good value set lunches.

🍸 Bars and clubs

Curicó *p273, map p274*

The following are fairly basic drinking holes, and are likely to be shut during the day:

Bar Deportivo, Montt 446.

Crazy Horse, Manso de Velasco.

Scram Pub, Velasco 451.

⊛ Festivals and events

Curicó *p273, map p274*

Mid-Mar Fiesta de la Vendimia (wine harvest festival) has displays on traditional winemaking and the chance to try local food and wine. A similar event is also held in nearby Molina at the same time.

⊖ Transport

Curicó *p273, map p274*

Bus

The **main bus terminal** is on Prat y Maipú. Local buses, including those to coastal towns as well as some long-distance services use

Terminal Plaza, Prat y Maipú. Turbus stop on M De Velasco; their office is also on M De Velasco, 1 block south. Pullman del Sur have their own terminal at Henríquez y Carmen. Many southbound buses by-pass Curicó, but can be caught by waiting outside town.

To Santiago several companies, frequent, 2½ hrs, US$5. To Temuco, Alsa and Tur Bus, US$8. To Llico, Buses Díaz, regular in summer, 2 daily off season, 3 hrs, US$3.50. To Iloca, every hour in summer, less frequently off season, 2 hrs, US$3.50.

Motorbike

Motorcycle spares from Chaleco López Motos, San Martín 171, T075-316191.

Train

The railway station is at the west end of Prat, 4 blocks west of Plaza de Armas, T075-310028, www.efe.cl. To/from Santiago, 6 a day, 2 hrs, US$10-20; to/from Chillán, 6 a day, 2¼ hrs, US$12-24.

Area de Protección Siete Tazas *p275*

Access by car is easy as the road through the park is paved. If you're travelling by public transport, take a minibus from Terminal Plaza to Molina, 26 km south of Curicó; from Molina 4 buses run daily to the Parque Inglés in summer (last return 1700), 3 hrs, US$3. There's also a daily bus from Curicó in summer at 1330 Mon-Sat (returns 0745) and at 0700 Sun (returns 1900), 4½ hrs.

❶ Directory

Curicó *p273, map p274*
Banks Major banks located around Plaza de Armas. Casa de Cambio, Merced 255, Local 106, no TCs. **Internet** Several in the city centre. **Laundry** Ecológico, Yungay 411; Lavacentro, Yungay 437; expensive, good. **Post office** Plaza de Armas.
Telephones Call centres are expensive in Curicó, but try O'Higgins 877 or Prat 74; also CTC, Peña 650-A. **Useful address** Automóvil Club de Chile, Chacabuco 759, T075-311156.

Maule Valley → *Colour map 3, C2.*

The Río Maule flows for 240 km from Laguna Maule in the Andes to the sea at Constitución. Its waters have been dammed east of Talca, providing power for the region and creating Lago Colbún. The river itself is particularly beautiful near the coast at Constitución. ►► *For Sleeping, Eating and other listings, see pages 282-284.*

Talca ⬛🚋🏠🎡☀🔺📻☎ ►► *pp282-284.*

Situated on the south bank of the Río Claro, a tributary of the Maule, Talca lies 56 km south of Curicó. The most important city between Santiago and Concepción, it is a major manufacturing centre and the capital of Region VII, Maule. Founded in 1692, it was destroyed by earthquakes in 1742 and 1928. Today, it is a busy, dusty town, with a lively atmosphere day and night.

Ins and outs

Getting there Talca is easily accessible by bus and train from Santiago (both many times daily). There are also frequent connections to the towns further south, especially Chillán, Concepción, Temuco and Puerto Montt (several daily).
Getting around Talca is a sizeable city, and some of the *barrios* are quite a distance from the centre. Buses and *colectivos* ply the routes to these areas, with their destinations marked in the window.
Tourist information Sernatur ① *1 Poniente 1281, T071-233669, infomaule@sern atur.cl, winter Mon-Fri 0830-1730, summer Mon-Fri 0830-1930.*

In the **Plaza de Armas** are statues that were looted by the Talca Regiment from Peru during the War of the Pacific. Just off the plaza is a colonial mansion that belonged to Juan Albano Pereira, tutor to the young Bernardo O'Higgins, who lived here as a child. The house was later the headquarters of O'Higgins' Patriot Government in 1813-1814, before his defeat at Rancagua and is now **Museo O'Higginiano** ① *1 Norte 875, T071-210428, www.dibam.cl/subdirec_museos/moba_talca/home.asp, Tue-Fri 1030-1300, 1430-1845, Sat and Sun 1000-1300, free*. In 1818, O'Higgins signed the declaration of Chilean Independence here: the room Sala Independencia is decorated and furnished in period style. The museum also houses a collection of regional art. The **Casino de Bomberos** ① *2 Sur y 5 Oriente*, has a small museum room with two old fire engines, old firefighting equipment and, for those with an interest in little-known conflagrations, information on important fires in Talca's history.

About 8 km southeast of the centre is **Villa Huilquilemu** ① *T071-242474, Tue-Fri 1500-1830, Sat 1600-1830, Sun 1100-1400, US$1, San Clemente bus*, a 19th-century hacienda, now part of the Universidad Católica del Maule, housing four museums of religious art, handicrafts, agricultural machinery and wine. It is also the office for the **Ruta de Vino del Valle del Maule**, www.valledelmaule.cl.

East of Talca ⊞▲⊜ ➤➤ *pp282-284.*

Lago Colbún and around

From Talca a road runs 175 km southeast along **Lago Colbún** and up the valley of the Río Maule, passing through some of the finest mountain scenery in Chile to reach the Argentine border at **Paso Pehuenche** ① *open Dec-Mar 0800-2100; Apr-Nov 0800-1900*. On the Argentine side the road continues to Malargüe and San Rafael.

At the western end of Lago Colbún is the town of **Colbún**, from where another road leads south and west to eventually join the Pan-American Highway at Linares. After 5 km it passes through **Panimávida**, where there are thermal springs. While at Panimávida, try the local 'Bebida Panimávida', made from spring water, still or

Talca

To Pan-American Highway (North)

Av B O'Higgins
Av B O'Higgins

To Río Claro & Las Viejas Cochinas

3 Norte
2 Norte
1 Norte
1 Sur
2 Sur
3 Sur

1 Oriente · 2 Oriente · 3 Oriente · 4 Oriente · 5 Oriente · 6 Oriente · 7 Oriente · 8 Oriente · 9 Oriente · 10 Oriente · 11 Oriente

Museo O'Higginiano
Municipalidad
Museo Municipal
Plaza de Armas

To Pan-American Highway (South)

N

0 metres 200
0 yards 200

Sleeping		Eating	
Amalfi 1	Hostal del Puente 11	Bavaria 1	Posada de la Luna 6
Casa Chueca 4	Hostal del Río 12	Casino de Bomberos 3	Rubén Tapia 8
Cordillera 2	Residencial Maule 9	El Toro Bayo 2	
Hostal Alcázar 3	Terrabella 10	La Casa del Esquina 7	
	Terranova 5		

Central Valley Maule Valley

here than in Linares. Further on towards Linares is **Quinamávida**, 12 km south of Colbún, where there are more thermal springs, and an upmarket hotel.

Vilches and around
Some 63 km east of Talca, Vilches is the starting point for the climb to the volcanoes **Quizapu** (3050 m) and **Descabezado** (3850 m). For walks on Descabezado Grande and Cerro Azul, ice axe, crampons and an experienced guide are required (see page 284). There is also great horse riding in this area.

Situated just east of Vilches, the **Reserva Nacional Altos del Lircay** ① *US$2*, covers 12,163 ha and includes peaks up to 2228 m as well as several small lakes. Much of the park is covered with mixed forest including lenga, ñirre, coigüe, roble, raulí and copihue. Near the entrance are the administration and visitors' centre; nearby are the **Piedras Tacitas**, a stone construction supposedly built by the indigenous inhabitants of the region, and the **Mirador Del Indio** from where there are fine views over the Río Lircay. There are also two good hikes: to **Laguna del Alto**, eight hours via a lagoon in a volcanic crater; and to **El Enladrillado**, 12 hours, a high basalt plateau from where there are great views. ▸▸ *For Sleeping, Eating and other listings, see pages 282-284.*

South of Talca ⊜⊘▲⊜⊖ ▸▸ *pp282-284.*

Linares
Fifty-three kilometres south of Talca on the Panamericana, Linares is a peaceful town with a distinctly *huaso* feel. It boasts the remarkable **Cathedral de San Ambrosio**, built between 1934 and 1967 in a Byzantine romantic style. On Letelier 572, in the middle of a row of colonial houses, is the **Museo de Arte y Artesania Nacional** ① *www.dibam.cl/subdirec_museos/maya_linares/home.asp, Tue-Fri 1000-1730, Sat 1000-1700, Sun 1200-1700, US$1, Sun free*. Here there are exhibits of local, military and prehistoric history, including a 2-ft-long decorative curved spanner, an exploded cannon, horsehair artefacts from the village of Rari, local paintings, petrified wood, old toys and everyday utensils. In the **Mercado Municipal** on Chacabuco, it is possible to buy horsehair art from Rari. Tourist information is available from the Gobernación and Municipalidad, both on the plaza.

> ⁝ *There is a cycle path much of the way between Linares and Panimávida.*

West of Talca ⊜⊘⊜ ▸▸ *pp282-284.*

Constitución
Lying west of Talca at the mouth of the Río Maule, Constitución is reached by road (89 km) and by a **narrow-gauge railway** line from Talca, which offers fine views over the wooded Maule Valley. The railway, packed with chatting locals (and as often as not their goats and chickens) is unique in Chile and offers travellers a microcosm of life in the Central Valley. It is not unusual for trains to be flagged down like buses and for the driver to stop in order to share gossip and a coffee with a farmer.

Founded in 1794, the city is situated in a major commercial logging area; there are naval shipyards here and a giant cellulose factory, whose pungent odour hangs over the town on windless days; fishing is also important. Constitución's main appeal, however, is as a seasonal seaside resort. While the town itself is relatively uninteresting, the beach, an easy walk from the centre, is surrounded by picturesque rocks, and the coast both to the north and south is beautiful.

There are good views from **Cerro Mutrún**, at the mouth of the river, accessed via Calle O'Higgins; the **Playa El Cable**, with *cabañas*, is 5 km south. For a pleasant walk

Wine tasting in the Central Valley

The Central Valley offers ample scope for visits to vineyards and winetasting, whether independently, or on a tour on one of several "*rutas del vino*" (wine routes). There are four main areas producing quality wines here, each with distinctive characteristics, based on slight variations in soil and climate. Independent visits can be made to a number of vineyards, although a day's notice is usually required. Most give free tours with bilingual guides, or charge a small fee, with visitors paying for each wine they taste; some may provide lunch for an additional charge. For further information, consult the vineyard's own website.

The **Cachapoal Valley** (around Rancagua) produces a wide variety of wine, especially fruity Merlot and Carmenère. Tours of the valley's wine route start from Km 109 of the Panamericana, some 16 km south of Rancagua, T072-522085, www.chileanwineroute.com, and mix visits to local vineyards with local food and culture. They are not cheap, starting at about US$100 per person (less for large groups or if you have your own transport). Vineyards offering independent tours include: **Chateau Los Boldos**, Camino Los Boldos s/n, Requínoa, T072-551230, www.chateaulosboldos.com. **Gracia**, Camino Totihue s/n, Requínoa, T02-2067868, www.gracia.cl. **La Roncière**, Cousiño s/n, Graneros, T072-471571, www.laronciere.com **Santa Mónica**, Camino Doñihue Km 5, Rancagua, T072-231444, www.santamonica.cl. **Torreón de Paredes**, Camino Las Nieves s/n, Rengo, T072-512551, www.torreon.cl

The **Colchagua Valley** (around San Fernando and Santa Cruz) is one of the great success stories of modern Chilean wine, with the Apalta region producing some world-beating Cabernet Sauvignons. The Colchagua valley wine route's office is on the plaza at Santa Cruz, 37 km west of San Fernando, T072-823199, rv@uva.cl, and offers tours of three, four or six hours, from around US$40-70 per person. The longer tours include lunch or a visit to the wine museum in Santa Cruz. Vineyards offering independent tours include:

or drive, take the quiet track along the south bank of the Maule 8 km east of Constitución to a disused railway bridge over the river; the bridge is open to vehicles, and has great views of the river valley.

Chanco and around

A paved road runs from Constitución along the coast, through thick forest and past a large logging factory, via deserted beaches and fishing villages to the small, peaceful town of Chanco. Chanco is famous for its cheese and its traditional colonial architecture, including the charming **Iglesia San Ambrosia**. There is a pleasant 3-km walk to the coast and the unspoilt **Playa Monolito** (camping The land just north of Chanco is the prettiest in this area, with rolling hills, small farmsteads and two small parks: the **Area Silvestre Laguna Reloca** ① *8 km north of Chanco, Mon-Fri 1430-1800, Sat and Sun 0830-1800, free*, is a private park covering 245 ha. Some 130 bird species have been identified including flamingoes and black-necked swans. Closer to Chanco, the **Reserva Nacional Federico Albert** ① *Apr-Nov 0830-1800, Dec-Mar 0830-2000, US$1*, covers 145 ha of dunes planted with eucalyptus and cypresses in experiments to control the shifting sands. It has a visitors' centre and campsite. facilities).

La Posada, R Casanova 570, Sta Cruz, T072-822589, www.puebloantiguo.cl.

Pueblo Antiguo, F Valdez 236, Nancagua, T072-858296, www.puebloantiguo.cl.

Selentia, Villa Angostura s/n, San Fernando, T072-913081, www.vinaselentia.cl.

Viu Manent, San Carlos de Cunaco s/n, Sta Cruz, T072-858350, www.viumanent.cl.

The **Curico Valley** is where the Chilean wine revolution began in 1980. It now produces fruity reds, and quality Sauvignon Blancs. The valley office is in Curico's plaza, on the second floor of the Club de la Unión, T075-328972, www.rvvc.cl There are various circuits, ranging from basic half-day tours, taking in a couple of wineries, to multi-day tours including trips to thermal springs or horse riding.

Vineyards offering independent tours include:

Miguel Torres, R5 sur, Km 195, T075-564100, www.torres.es/eng/asp/vav_curico.asp.

San Pedro, R5 sur, Km 205, T075-491517, www.sanpedro.cl.

The **Maule Valley** (around Talca and San Javier), traditionally the home of the insipid *Pais* grape, has now been replanted with noble varieties, and produces well-balanced reds of a decent standard. The wine route's offices are in the Villa Cultural Huilquilemu, 7 km southeast of Talca, on the road to San Clemente, T071-246460, www.chilewineroute.cl

Tours cost US$14 per person for half a day (two vineyards) and US$38 for a full day (two vineyards, plus lunch and museum visit). Vineyards offering independent tours include:

Balduzzi, Av Balmaceda 1189, San Javier, T072-322138, *www.balduzzi.cl.*

Casa Donoso, Camino Palmira Km 3.5, Talca, T071-241980, www.casadonoso.cl.

Gillmore Estate, Camino Constitución, Km 20, SJ, T073-1975539, www.gillmore.cl.

Hugo Casanova, Camino Las Rastras s/n, Talca, T071-266540, vcasanov@ctcinternet.cl.

Martínez de Salinas, Camino Cauquenes a Parral, T073-512505, www.martinezdesalinas.cl.

Further south

South of Chanco are two more small resorts at **Pelluhue** and **Curanipe**, 83 km south of Constitución. One kilometre south of Pelluhue a path leads down to a hidden beach, beautiful and deserted even in summer, while Curanipe has a lovely stretch of black sand. From Curanipe a poorly maintained track leads 50 km through wild country to the small seaside town of **Cobquecura**. A tranquil, friendly town with slate-roofed colonial buildings, it has a good beach, a pretty plaza, accommodation, several good seafood restaurants and well-preserved colonial-style houses. About 1 km north of the village is a long curved beach with a large colony of sea lions offshore. At low tide the beach almost extends as far as the rock on which they live and their yelps can clearly be heard. It is worth a detour to see. About 5 km to the north is an impressive *portada* or arch in the cliffs. There are also a few good surfing beaches nearby.

This coast can also be reached by paved road from Parral via Cauquenes. Just north of the road between Cauquenes and Chanco is the **Reserva Nacional Los Ruiles** ① *Dec-Mar 0830-2000, Apr-Nov 0830-1800, US$1.50, buses from Constitución or Cauquenes*, which covers 45 ha of native flora, including the *ruil* (Nothofagus alessandri), an endangered species of southern beech.

🔘 **Sleeping**

Talca *p277, map p278*

AL Terrabella, 1 Sur 641, T071-226555, www.hotelterrabella.cl. The best hotel in town. Business standard with conference rooms and swimming pool. English spoken.

A Casa Chueca, Camino Las Rastras, 4 km from city centre, T071-1970096, trekking chile.com. **F** per person in shared rooms. European-run colonial-style house with swimming pool, great views, large gardens, mountain bikes, games room. Price includes breakfast, nice rooms with private bathrooms or cheaper rooms with shared bath. Good dinner on request. Trekking and horse riding tours organized, Spanish classes also available. English, German, French, Portuguese and Swedish spoken. Highly recommended. Call for instructions on how to get there.

A Terranova, 1 Sur 1026, T071-239608, www.hotelterranova.cl. Another decent business standard with conference room and sauna. Buffey breakfast.

B Cordillera, 2 Sur 1360, T071-221817, www.cordillerahotel.cl. Decent no frills hotel, serves good breakfast.

B Hostal del Puente, 1 Sur 407, T071-220930, hostaldelpuente@adsl.tie.cl. Lovely gardens, English spoken, parking, with bath, cable TV, breakfast extra.

B-C Amalfi, 2 Sur 1265, T071-239292. **E** singles. Old-fashioned, central, good breakfast, cheaper rooms do not have bath.

B-C Hostal del Río, 1 Sur 411, T071-225448, www.amarillas.cl/hostaldelrio. Opened by the feuding brother of the owner of the **Hostal del Puente** next door, and designed to be just a little better and a little cheaper.

C Hospedaje Santa Margarita, Pellarco, 18 km northeast of Talca, T09-3359051. **F** singles. Swiss-run, meals served, open Dec-Mar only, reservation advised.

C Hostal Alcázar, 6 Oriente 1449, T071-233587. **F** singles. Without bath, quiet, good value.

C Residencial Maule, 2 Sur 1381, T071-220995. **F** singles. Without breakfast, basic, overpriced.

Lago Colbún and around *p278*

L-AL Hotel Quinamávida, Quinamávida, T073- 213887, www.termasdequina mavida.cl. In the hotel there are thermal baths, Turkish baths, reflexology, and massage.

L-AL Hotel Termas de Panimávida, Panimávida, 073-211743, liceocolbun@hot mail.com. Full board and access to thermal pools. A once grand hotel now partly restored but retaining a feeling of decaying grandeur. In the grounds is a small fountain, where you can drink the sulphourous 'agua de la mona'.

B-C Posada Rabones, Km 10 on Linares-Rabones road, Quinamávida, T09-97520510, www.posadarabones.cl. Price per person. Large *estancia* with forest trails and beaches, offering full board and bed and breakfast deals. English spoken. Highly recommended.

Camping

There are several campsites about 12 km east of Colbún on the south shore of Lago Colbún. There are also 3 sites near Panimávida.

Vilches and around *p279*

AL-A Complejo Turístico El Roble, Vilches (Sector Seminario), T071-242148/09-7411065, www.turismoelroble.com. Fully furnished comfortable *cabañas* sleeping up to 6, with swimming pool.

C Refugio Ecológico Biota Maule, T09-903 26105, www.ayacara.org. A wooden house in the middle of a forest, with excellent value for money accommodation. Meals available.

Linares *p279*

A Hotel Curapalihue, Curapalihue 411, Linares, T/F073-212516. Breakfast and bath, cable TV, conference facilities.

B Hotel Turismo, Manuel Rodríguez 522, Linares, T073-210636, F214128. Breakfast and bath, restaurant, cable TV.

C Hotel Real, Freire 482, Linares, T/F073-210834. Bath, without breakfast, cable TV.

D Hotel Londres, Rodríguez 456, Linares, T073-210177, F213720. **F-G** singles. Without bath or breakfast.

D Hostal Linares, Freire 442, Linares, T073-210695. **F-G** singles. With breakfast.

Constitución *p279*

A-B Hostería Constitución, Echeverria 460, T071-671450 . Overpriced and not as good as it was, but still the best equipped hotel in town. Good lunches.

C Avendaño, O'Higgins 681. **F** singles. Pleasant patio, restaurant, friendly, safe.

C **Ruta Verde**, 12 km east of town, off the road to Talca, T02-6884849/09-82946472, www.turismorutaverde.cl. E singles. Call for free pick up from Constitución. Pleasant house in the woods with lots of animals and powered by solar panels. Very friendly and helpful, English and Italian spoken, excellent tours of the region on horse or in a 4WD. Highly recommended.

There are many other *residenciales* on Freire 100-300 blocks, including **Residencial López** at No 153; **Residencial Familiar** at No 160 and **Residencial Ramírez** at No 209. Book in advance from Jan to Mar.

Further south *p281*

A **Cabañas Campomar**, north of Curanipe, T073-541000, campomar@ctcinternet.cl. Prices for up to 6 people, kitchen, English spoken.
B **Hostería Blanca Reyes**, Prat 615, Pelluhue, T073-541061, blancareyes@123mail.cl. With good restaurant, best in town.
C **Pacífico**, Comercio 509, Curanipe, T073-556016. Pleasant, clean.
D **Pensión Rocas**, Condell 708, Pelluhue, T073-541017. Basic.
D **Residencial La Playa**, Prat 510, Pelluhue, T09-8714538. Meals served. Also has *cabañas*.

● Eating

Talca *p277, map p278*
‼ **Bavaria**, 1 Sur 1370. Plastic Chilean chain serving reasonable steaks and sandwiches.
‼ **El Toro Bayo**, Camino Las Rastras, 2 km east of town, T071-247643. The best in the area, offering a wide and inventive menu, closed Sun evenings, recommended.
‼ **La Casa del Esquina**, 1 Poniente 708. Spanish food, good.
‼ **Los Ganaderos**, Panamericana, 10 km south of Talca. Great food, a good place to stop for lunch for those with transport.
‼ **Posada de la Luna**, 1 Sur 626. Slightly upmarket restaurant with attractive garden, good seafood.
‼ **Rubén Tapia**, 2 Oriente 1339. Excellent modern cuisine. Good service and very reasonable prices.
‼ **Café al Grano**, Galería Zaror, local 10. Cosy, good coffee and snacks.
‼ **Casino de Bomberos**, 2 Sur y 5 Oriente. Good value. There is an interesting museum annexed.

‼ **Las Viejas Cochinas**, on the banks of the Río Claro, just over the bridge. Famous *picada* serving very good typical Chilean food. Large portions and more than reasonable prices. Lots of others nearby.

There are many cheap restaurants in the **municipal market**, 3 blocks east of the plaza and several kiosks selling completos on 5 Oriente 900 block; some are open 24 hrs.

Linares *p279*
‼ **Fay Chy**, Rodríguez 398. Chinese.
‼ **Las Parrillas de Linares**, Lautaro 350. Typical grill.
‼ **Estadio Español**, León Bustas 01242. Traditional food.

Constitución *p279*
Some of the town's *posadas* and *hosterías* provide meals. In addition, you should try:
‼ **El Rancho Astillero**, open in summer only, on the banks of the river and accessible only by boat. Wonderful fish cooked over hot coals between 2 terracotta tiles.

Further south *p281*
Pelluhue is more expensive than **Curanipe**; it has seafood restaurants and **Omas Küchen**, Condell 823, which sells wonderful cakes.

● Bars and clubs

Talca *p277, map p278*
Varadero, 5 Oriente 985. Good Cuban-themed pub.
Wurlitzer, 5 Oriente 960. Deservedly popular pub above a pool hall.

Linares *p279*
El Tablón, Ibáñez y Chacabuco. Basic bar.
Refugio, V Letelier 480. Basic bar.

● Entertainment

Talca *p277, map p278*
Mainstream **cinema** at 1 Sur 1271 and Sur 770. Arts cinema at 1 poniente 685. Also in Mall Plaza Maule, east of centre.

● Festivals and events

Talca *p277, map p278*
1st week of Jan Regional folklore festival.
4 Oct Fiesta San Francisco, an important

huaso festival, takes place in Huerta del Maule (southwest of Talca).

First week of Nov Feria del Vino y la Viticultura (TECVIN) is enjoyable for those with an interest in Chilean wine.

Last week in Nov Feria Regional de Folklore y Artesanía is held at Villa Cultural Huilquilemu.

▲ Activities and tours

Talca *p277, map p278*
La Casa Chueca, see Sleeping, above and www.trekkingchile.com. Excellent touring information, plus kayaking, trekking and horse riding trips.
Leonardo Cáceres Rencoret, T09-98923625. Good mountain guide, works for CONAF.

Vilches and around *p279*
La Casa Chueca in Talca (see above). Two recommended horse guides in Vilches are **Don Pancho**, T09-97635447, and **Don Eladio**, T09-93418064.

Linares *p279*
Achibueno Expediciones, 8 km southeast of Linares, T073-375098, www.achibuenoexpediciones.cl. Bespoke horse riding trips in the cordillera from US$100 per day per person.
Expediciones Cordillera, Rodríguez 712, T073-210240, calesi@mi.terra.cl. Tours around the region in a 4WD.

⊖ Transport

Talca *p277, map p278*

Bicycle
Cycle repairs from **Bicimotora Burgos**, 5 Oriente 1185.

Bus
Talca bus terminal is at 12 Oriente y 2 Sur.

Local To **Lago Colbún**, Pullman del Sur, 2 daily, US$1.50; to **Vilches**, Buses Vilches, 5 daily, 2-2½ hrs, US$2.50; to **Linares**, many companies, frequent, US$1.50; to **Constitución**, Empresa O'Higgins and Contimar, every 20 mins, 2 hrs, US$1.50. There are hourly buses to **Chanco**, **Curanipe** and **Pelluhue** with Buses Bonanza, US$4, also 3 daily with Contimar, US$4, and 10 daily with Pullman del Sur, US$3.50.

Long distance To **Chillán**, frequent service, US$3. To **Puerto Montt**, US$14, 9 hrs. To **Temuco**, US$8, 5½ hrs. Many buses to **Santiago**, US$5, 3½ hrs, and direct services to destinations as far north as Copiapó.

Train
Talca railway station is at 2 Sur y 11 Oriente, T071-226254. Trains run to **Santiago**, 8 a day, US$11-US$22; to **Chillán**, 7 a day, US$9-US$22; to **Temuco**, nightly; to **Concepción**, nightly; to **Constitución**, 2 a day, 2½ hrs, US$2.50.

Lago Colbún and around *p278*
Buses Villa Prat runs direct services to **Quinamávida** from Santiago's Terminal Sur. For services to/from **Talca** see above.

Linares *p279*
Linares' **bus** terminal is at Espinoza 530. To **Colbún** via Quinimávida and Panimávida, US$1.50. For services to/from **Talca**, see above.

The **railway** station is at Brasil y Independencia, T073-216352. Trains run to **Santiago**, 7 a day, 3¼ hrs, US$12-US$24; to **Chillán**, 7 a day, 1 hr, US$5-US$7.

Constitución *p279*
Empresa Amigo runs buses to **Cauquenes**, 2½ hrs, US$3. For services to/from **Talca**, see above.

⊙ Directory

Talca *p277, map p278*
Banks Banco Santander, 1 Sur y 4 Oriente; Edificio Caracol, Oficina 15, 1 Sur 898. For US$ cash. **Internet** several around the city centre. **Laundry** Lavaseco Donini, 6 Oriente 1120; Lavaseco Flash, 1 Norte 995. **Post office** 1 Oriente s/n. **Telephone** CTC, 1 Sur 1156 and 1 Sur 835. **Useful address** Automóvil Club de Chile, 1 Poniente 1267, T071-2232774.

Linares *p279*
Banks Banco A Edwards, on plaza; Banco Santander, Independencia 555. **Internet** Chacabuco 491. **Post office** Rodríguez 610. **Telephone** Call centre, Independencia 488A.

Itata Valley → Colour map 3, C2.

The Río Itata and its longer tributary, the Río Ñuble, flow west reaching the Pacific some 60 km north of Concepción. This is a tranquil valley with some native woods along the banks near the mouth of the river at the tiny hamlet of Vegas de Itata. There is no bridge here, although boats can be hired to make the short crossing in summer; in winter the river swells and no one attempts the crossing. ►► *For Sleeping, Eating and other listings, see pages 287-289.*

Chillán 🎗️🚲❄️🏠🚍🏢 ►► pp287-289. Colour map 3, C2.

Chillán, 150 km south of Talca, is a busy but friendly place. Founded in 1580 and destroyed by the Mapuche, the city has been moved several times, most recently following an earthquake in 1833. Although the older site, now known as Chillán Viejo, is still occupied, further earthquakes in 1939 and 1960 ensured that few old buildings have survived. Nevertheless, this is one of the more interesting cities south of Santiago and has a shady plaza, numerous interesting churches and several museums, as well as a mural of the life of Bernardo O'Higgins. Pleasantly hot in summer, the city is filled with local *campesinos* on market days, creating an atmosphere that is the essence of the Central Valley.

Ins and outs
Getting there Chillán is served by several trains and buses daily from Santiago. There are also frequent connections to the towns further south, especially Concepción, Temuco and Puerto Montt.

Getting around Chillán is a reasonably large city, and some of the outlying *barrios* and attractions are quite a distance from the centre. Buses and *colectivos* are numerous, with their destinations marked in the window, but taxis are most useful for arranging excursions out of the city.

Tourist information The municipal office ① *18 de Sept 455, at side of Gobernación, T042-223272*, can provide a street map of the city and various leaflets on skiing, Termas de Chillán etc.

Sights
Chillán was the birthplace of Bernardo O'Higgins and today's city is centred around the Plaza O'Higgins and its modern **cathedral**, designed to resist earthquakes. The **San Francisco** church, three blocks northeast contains a **museum** ① *Tue-Sun 1600-1800, US$1.50*, of religious and historical artefacts. Above the main entrance is a mural by Luis Guzmán Molina, a local artist, which is an interpretation of the life of San Francisco but placed in a Chilean context. The adjoining **convent** (1835) was a big centre for missionary work among the Mapuche.

Five streets west of the plaza is the neo-Gothic **Iglesia Padres Carmelita**, while to the northwest, on Plaza Héroes de Iquique, is the **Escuela México** ① *daily 1000-1300, 1500-1830*, donated to the city after the 1939 earthquake. In its library are outstanding murals by the great Mexican artists David Alvaro Siqueiros and Xavier Guerrero depicting allegories of Chilean and Mexican history. Three blocks further south is the **Museo Naval El Chinchorro** ① *Collin y I Riquelme, Tue-Fri 0930-1200, 1500-1730*, which contains naval artefacts and models of Chilean vessels.

🎈 *In 2003, the centenary year of the birth of the local pianist Claudio Arrau, Chillán was*
● *made American city of culture.*

In Chillán Viejo, southwest of the centre, is a monument and park marking the birthplace of Bernardo O'Higgins; a 60-m-long mural depicts his life (an impressive, but sadly faded mosaic of various native stones), while the **Centro Histórico y Cultural** ① *0830-2000* has a gallery of contemporary paintings by regional artists. Halfway between the centre and Chillán Viejo on Avenida O'Higgins is the **Capilla San Juan de Dios**, a small chapel dating from 1791.

Around Chillán ⊜⊜ » *pp287-289.*

Quinchamalí

Quinchamalí is a small village of little houses hidden under large fruit trees, located 27 km southwest of Chillán, at the halfway point of the new motorway to Concepción. The village is famous for the originality of its crafts in textiles, basketwork, guitars, primitive paintings and especially black ceramics (see box page 287). These are all on sale in Chillán market and at a handicraft fair in the village during the second week of February.

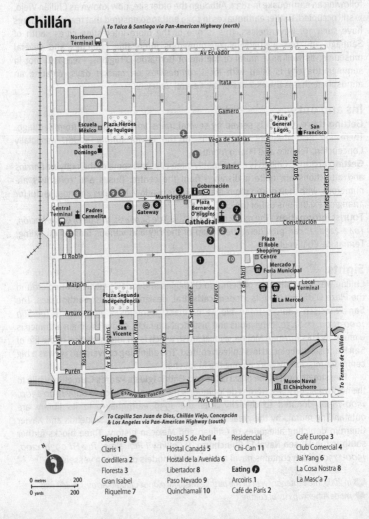

Chillán

Sleeping ⊜	Hostal 5 de Abril 4	Residencial	Café Europa 3
Claris 1	Hostal Canadá 5	Chi-Can 11	Club Comercial 4
Cordillera 2	Hostal de la Avenida 6		Jai Yang 6
Floresta 3	Libertador 8	Eating ⑦	La Cosa Nostra 8
Gran Isabel	Paso Nevado 9	Arcoiris 1	La Masc'a 7
Riquelme 7	Quinchamali 10	Café de París 2	

0 metres 200
0 yards 200

⁝ Earth and wares

Quinchamalí is one of the two most famous villages in Chile for producing black ceramic ware; the other, Pomaire, near Santiago, is much more influenced by tourism. While the men work on the land, women work with clay, mixing it with sand to make it porous and to prevent it breaking when it is heated. The mixture is worked in two halves, which are then joined and allowed to dry. The characteristic white patterns are made by incising with an old needle before the piece is wrapped in straw and heated over an open fire. Apart from items for domestic use, the women produce a wide range of other pieces, including roosters, three legged pigs and women with children, but the most popular object is the *guitarrera* (a woman playing the guitar).

Termas de Chillán

Situated 82 km east of Chillán by good road (paved for the first 50 km), 1850 m up at the foot of the double-cratered Chillán volcano, are two open-air thermal pools, officially for hotel guests only, and a health spa with jacuzzi, sauna, mud baths and other facilities. There are several trekking oportunities from the *termas*, including a good one- or two-day return hike past some natural hot mud baths (free of charge) to the **Valle de Aguas Calientes**, where there are yet more hot springs, spectacular scenery and solitude.

Above the thermal baths is the largest **ski resort** in southern Chile, with 10 ski lifts and 28 ski runs (the longest is 13 km in length), rental shops, restaurants, bars, ski school, first aid and a nursery. Experienced skiers can take advantage of nordic skiing, alpine randonnée and heli-skiing, but Chillán is also suitable for families and beginners and is cheaper than centres nearer Santiago. For further information, contact the **Chillán Ski Centre** ① *Barros Arana 261, www.termaschillan.cl, lift pass US$35 per day, US$27 half day, equipment hire US$30 per day.*

San Fabián de Alico

This pleasant mountain village on the banks of the Río Ñuble lies 67 km northeast of Chillán (via San Carlos, daily buses). In summer it is very lively and full of young Chileans. There are several campsites and *hospedajes*, and many opportunities for trekking up the valley. Horses can readily be hired for about US$12 per day. Tourist information is available in the plaza or from the Municipalidad.

● Sleeping

Chillán *p285, map p286*

AL Gran Hotel Isabel Riquelme, Constitución 576, T042-213663, hotelir@ termaschillan.cl. Slightly overpriced, with cable TV, restaurant, laundry and parking.

A Paso Nevado, Libertad 219, T042-237666, www.hotelpasonevado.cl. Nice rooms, internet, conference room, bar, tours arranged. A good option in this price range.

A Quinchamalí, El Roble 634, T042-223381, www.hotelquinchamali.cl. 5-storey building in the city centre, quiet, clean, hot water, heated lounge.

B Hostal de la Avenida, O'Higgins 398 y Bulnes, T042-230256. 2-star facilities, including cable TV, café, bar and laundry.

A Cordillera, Arauco 619, on Plaza de Armas, T042-215211, www.hotelcordillera.cl. Small friendly 3-star.

B-C Floresta, 18 de Septiembre 278, T/F042-222253. Quiet, old fashioned, friendly.

C Hostal 5 de Abril, 5 de Abril y Constitución. **F** singles. Without bath.

C Hostal Canadá, Libertad 269, T042-234515. **F** singles. Without breakfast or bath.

Central Valley Itata Valley Listings

C **Libertador**, Libertad 85, T042-223255.
F singles. Without breakfast, parking,
clean, good.

C-D **Claris**, 18 de Septiembre 357, T042-
221980. F singles. Clean, friendly, run down,
with bath or without.

D **Residencial Chi-Can**, Constitución 34.
F singles. Basic and noisy, but near the
central terminal.

There are lots more cheap *hospedajes* on
Constitutión 1-300.

Termas de Chillán *p287*

The following are all located at Las Trancas
on the road to the *termas*, 70 km southeast
of Chillán. Several *cabañas* are also available
in the village, usually A for up to 6 people,
see www.vallelastrancas.cl for more details.
Camping is available 2 km from the slopes.

LL **Gran Termas de Chillán**, information
T02-2331313, www.termaschillan.cl. 5-star,
sports facilities, sauna, thermal pool and
spa centre.

L **Pirigallo**, information T042-434200,
www.termaschillan.cl. 3-star. Same
ownership as above.

AL **Parador Jamón, Pan y Vino**,
T042-222682, www.nevadosdechillan.cl.
Arranges recommended horse riding trips.

AL **Robledal**, T042-214407, hotelrobledal.cl.
Pleasant rooms, including some suites, bar,
restaurant, sauna and Jacuzzi. Wide variety
of tours offered.

A **Los Pirineos**, T042-293839. Fully-
furnished cabins.

B-C **Hostelling International**, T042-244628,
j.bocaz@ctcinternet.cl. E per person in
dorms. Basic European-style youth hostel.

❷ Eating

Chillán *p285, map p286*

The Chillán area is well known for its *pipeño*
wine (very young) and its *longanizas*
(sausages).

❤ **Arcoiris**, El Roble 525. Vegetarian.

❤ **Café de París**, Arauco 666. Good bar
and fine restaurant upstairs.

❤ **Café Europa**, Libertad 475.
Recommended.

❤ **La Cosa Nostra**, Libertad 398. Italian
cuisine, German and Italian spoken, very
good and reasonably priced.

❤ **Los Adobes**, Parque O'Higgins, Chillán
Viejo. Tasty food and good service at
reasonable prices.

❤ **Club Comercial**, Arauco 745. Popular at
lunchtime, good value *almuerzo*, popular bar
at night. Recommended.

❤ **Jai Yang**, Libertad 250. Good value
Chinese.

❤ **La Copucha**, 18 de Septiembre y
Constitución. Inexpensive meals and
sandwiches.

❤ **La Masc'a**, 5 de Abril 544. Excellent cheap
meals, *empanadas de queso*, drinks.
Recommended.

There are also many cheap restaurants in
and around the **mercado municipal**.

❂ Festivals and events

Chillán *p285, map p286*

Jan Encuentro International de Teatro,
with plays being performed in public spaces
around the city.

Thirs week in Mar Fiesta de la Vendemia is
an annual wine festival.

◔ Shopping

Chillán *p285, map p286*

Mercado y Feria Municipal, Riquelme y
Marpón. This large market sells regional arts
and crafts.

Plaza El Roble, El Roble y Riquelme.
A modern shopping centre.

◕ Transport

Chillán *p285, map p286*
Bus

Buses to **Yumbel** and **Quinchamalí**, 30
mins, US$1.50, leave from the terminal
near the market, Maipón y Sgto Aldea.
There are 2 long-distance terminals: **Tur Bus**,
Línea Azul, **Tas Choapa** and **Alsa-LIT** all use
the central terminal at Brasil y Constitución.
Other companies use the modern northern
terminal at O'Higgins y Ecuador. To
Santiago, 5 hrs, US$9; to **Concepción**, Tur
Bus and Línea Azul every 30 mins, 1¼ hrs,
US$4; to **Curicó**, US$5; to **Tecumo**, US$6.

Motorbike

Motorcycle spares from **Roland Spaarwater**,
Ecuador 275, T/F042-232334.

Train
The station is on Brasil opposite Libertad, 5 blocks west of Plaza de Armas, T042-222424, www.efe.cl. To **Santiago**, 7 daily, 4¼ hrs, US$16.

Termas de Chillán *p287*
Dedicated ski buses run Jun-Sep from Libertador 1042 to the slopes at 0800 and from Chillán Ski Centre, subject to demand, US$40 (including lift pass). In summer (Jan-mid Mar) there's a bus service from **Anja**, 5 de Abril 594, Thu, Sat, Sun only at 0730, US$9 return, book in advance. Taxis cost US$40 one way, 1½ hrs. At busy periods hitching may be possible from Chillán Ski Centre.

⊙ Directory

Chillán *p285, map p286*
Banks On the Plaza de Armas are Banco BCI, Banco Santander and Banco de Chile, with ATMs, better rates than banks at Casa de cambio, Constitución 550. **Internet** Ubiquitous. **Post office** Gobernación, Plaza de Armas. **Telephone** Entel, 18 de Septiembre 746; CTC, Arauco 625; also call centre at 5 de Abril 607. **Useful address** Automóvil Club de Chile, O'Higgins 677, T042-212550.

Biobío Valley → *Colour map 3, C1; Colour map 4, A1/2.*

The Río Biobío flows northwest from the Andes to reach the sea near Concepción. At 407 km, it is the second longest river in Chile. Its more important tributaries include the Ríos Laja, Duqueco and Renaico. Apart from Concepción and Talcahuano on the coast, the valley includes several other important cities, notably Los Angeles. This is the southernmost end of the central valley, and while you will find grapes and other Mediterranean fruit being cultivated, there are also hints of what the Lake District has to offer to the south, with forests of Araucaria and snowcapped volcanoes inland. ▸▸ *For Sleeping, Eating and other listings, see pages 296-300.*

Concepción and around ⊟🖊🚻🛈▲🛉🛈 → *pp296-300.*

The capital of Región VIII (Biobío), Concepción is the third biggest city in Chile, with a population of nearly a quarter of a million. Founded in 1550, it was a frontier stronghold in the war against the Mapuche after 1600. The city was destroyed by an earthquake in 1751 and moved to its present site in 1764, but suffered another destructive earthquake and a tidal wave in 1835. Today, although it is one of the country's major industrial centres, Concepción is not in itself a wildly beautiful or fascinating place. Those staying for a long period or getting involved with students at the important university will find doors opening, but otherwise a visit to the port of Talcahuano, Chile's most important naval base (15 km north), is the highlight.

‡ *The weather is very pleasant in Concepción during the summer months, but from April to September it rains heavily.*

Ins and outs
Getting there Concepción is 15 km from the estuary of the Río Biobío, 516 km south of Santiago. There are flights daily to Concepción from Santiago and Puerto Montt, one or two of which continue on to Punta Arenas. Taxi to airport US$6. Concepción is the transportation hub of the region, and is served by buses to and from Santiago,

● *The 1835 earthquake that devastated Concepción was so severe that some cows, grazing on an island in the bay, rolled into the sea.*

Central Valley Biobío Valley

Temuco, Valdivia and Puerto Montt, as well as to and from other smaller destinations such as Cañete and Lota. There are two long-distance bus terminals and neither is located in the city centre. To get to nearby destinations such as Dichato and Talcahuano, it is easiest to take a *colectivo*.

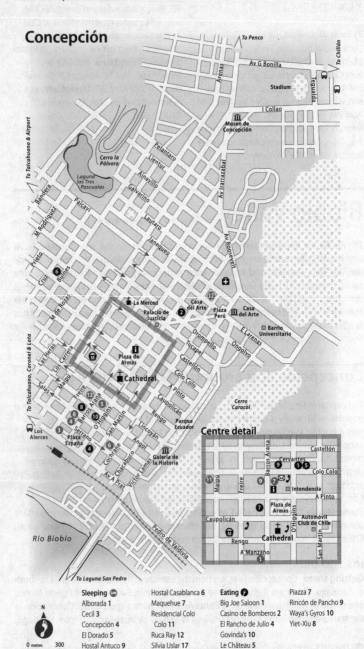

Concepción

Centre detail

N

| 0 metres | 300 |
| 0 yards | 300 |

Sleeping
Alborada 1
Cecil 3
Concepción 4
El Dorado 5
Hostal Antuco 9
Hostal Bianca 8

Hostal Casablanca 6
Maquehue 7
Residencial Colo
Colo 11
Ruca Ray 12
Silvia Uslar 17

Eating
Big Joe Saloon 1
Casino de Bomberos 2
El Rancho de Julio 4
Govinda's 10
Le Château 5
Mar y Tierra 6

Piazza 7
Rincón de Pancho 9
Waya's Gyros 10
Yiet-Xiu 8

Colectivos and buses abound; the destinations are signed on the
window or roof. Fares are US$0.30 for buses, slightly more for *colectivos*.
Tourist information Sernatur ① *Aníbal Pinto 460 on Plaza de la Independencia,
T041-2741337, infobiobio@sernatur.cl*, provides regional information.

Sights

In the centre of the city is the attractive **Plaza de la Independencia**, where, in January
1818, Bernardo O'Higgins proclaimed the Independence of Chile. Nearby are many
official buildings, including the modern cathedral, the Municipalidad and the Palacio
de la Justicia. Also on the plaza is the **Museo de Arte Sagrado** ① *Caupolicán 441,
Tue-Fri 1000-1330, 1600-2000, Sat-Sun, 1100-1400, US$0.75*, containing many fine
sacred Christian objects, including priests robes embroidered with gold, and a
marble Christ. Southeast of the plaza is the **Parque Ecuador**, where the **Galería de la
Historia** ① *Tue-Sun 1000-1330, 1500-1830, free*, contains a pictorial history of the
region; upstairs is a collection of Chilean painting. A few blocks north is the **Casa del
Arte** ① *Chacabuco y Paicaví, by the Plaza Perú, T041-2204290 Tue-Fri 1000-1800, Sat
1000-1600, Sun 1000-1300, free*, which contains the University art collection and
temporary exhibitions; the entrance hall is dominated by *La Presencia de América
Latina* by the Mexican Jorge González Camerena (1965), an impressive allegorical
mural depicting Latin American history, famous throughout Chile and often depicted
on postcards. Note especially the pyramid representing the continent's wealth, the
figures of an armoured warrior and an Indian woman and the wounded cactus with
parts missing, representing Mexico's defeat by the USA in 1845-1848. University art
students are on hand to provide explanations. There is another fine mural in the
entrance hall of the railway station, *La Historia de Concepción* by Gregorio de la
Fuente. From the Parque Ecuador you can climb **Cerro Caracol**, to the south, from
where there are views over the city and the river.

Sixteen kilometres from Concepción, **Museo y Parque Hualpen** ① *Tue-Sun
1000-1300, 1400-1900, free*, is a house and garden that is now a national monument.
Built around 1885, the house contains beautiful exhibits from all over the world. To
get there take a city bus to Hualpencillo from Freire; ask the driver to let you out then
walk for 40 mins (or hitch) along Av Las Golondrinas to the Enap oil refinery, turn left,
then right (it is signed). Further west in the park, near the mouth of the Río Biobío,
there are good opportunities for walking on the hills and several fine beaches
including **Playa Rocoto**.

North of Concepción

A road (nightmare for cyclists) runs north from Concepción along the coast through
the suburbs of **Penco** (Km 12), where there is a fine beach, and **Lirquén**, Km 15, a
small, old, pretty town of wooden houses with a beach that can be reached by
walking along the railway. There is plentiful cheap seafood for sale here. **Tomé**, 13 km
further north, is a small town set in a broad bay with long beaches and an interesting
cemetery, Miguel Gulán Muñoz, on the cliff overlooking the ocean.

Dichato, 9 km further north along a hilly road offering fine views, is a beautiful
fishing village and a busy summer holiday resort. It is also the site of the
oceanographic centre of the University of Concepción. From Dichato you can take a
local bus around the wide horseshoe bay to the tiny village of **Cochölgüe**.

Talcahuano

Situated at the neck of Península de Tumbes, Talcahuano has the best harbour in Chile. It
is Chile's main naval station and an important commercial and fishing port, where crowds
of fishermen unload their catches of seafood before a seething mass of buyers,
stevedores and hoary, old sailors, snaffling molluscs as they are carried past. In the naval
base you can visit the great ship **Huáscar** ① *Tue-Sun 0900-1300, 1400-1700, US$1.50*, a

relic of the War of the Pacific. Photography is permitted, but passports must be handed in at the main gate. Along the peninsula is **Parque Tumbes** ① *information from Codeff, Caupolicán 346, T041-2226649, free*, with paths leading along the coast.

The coastal route south of Concepción

🏨🍴🎓🚗 ▸▸ *pp296-300.*

South of the Río Biobío is the **Costa del Carbón**, until recently the main coal-mining area of Chile. The road is busy, noisy and polluted by trucks plying to and from the numerous local industries; it is linked with Concepción by two bridges over the Biobío.

Towards Lota

Just across the Río Biobío from Concepción is the **Laguna Grande**, a watersports centre, and **Laguna San Pedro Chica**, which is good for swimming. **Coronel**, 29 km from Concepción, was the scene of a British naval defeat in 1914, when the *Good Hope* and *Monmouth* were sunk by the German ship *Scharnhorst*. A monument commemorating the defeat was erected in November 1989. The defeat was later avenged at the Battle of the Falklands/Malvinas with the destruction of the German squadron. Close to town on the Bahía de Coronel are the small **Playa Negra**, which has few people and black sand, and **Playa Blanca**, which is bigger with white sand and more crowds, as well as bars, cafés, seafood restaurants and a free campsite.

Forty-two kilometres south of Concepción, **Lota** was, until recently, the site of the most important coal mine in Chile, originally the property of the Cousiño family (see page 80). Even before the mine's closure in April 1997, the town was known to be one of the poorest in Chile and, although the government has invested in retraining for the miners and in trying to open up Lota to tourism, the city still suffers greatly from poverty and neglect. The town is in two parts: **Lota Alto**, on the hill, is the original mining town, while **Lota Bajo**, below, is more recent.

♆ *The church on the main plaza in Lota contains a statue of the Virgin made of coal.*

The **Parque de Lota Isidora Cousiño** ① *1000-1800, till 2000 in summer, US$3.50*, covering 14 ha on a promontory to the west of the town, was the life's work of Isadora Cousiño. Laid out by English landscape architects in the 19th century, it contains plants from all over the world, ornaments imported from Europe, romantic paths and shady nooks offering views over the sea; peacocks and pheasants roam freely; no picnicing allowed. The mansion, which was Isadora's home during her stays in Lota, was destroyed in the 1960 earthquake. Near the entrance to the park is the **Museo Historíco de Lota** ① *1000-2000 Nov-Mar, 1000-1800 Apr-Oct, US$1.50.*

The tunnels of the **coal mine** ① *T041-2870682, 1000-1700, US$7*, run almost entirely under the sea (the longest is 11 km) and can be visited on guided tours led by former miners; at the entrance is a small Museo Minero. Offshore is an island, **Isla Santa María**, which has basic accommodation and good beaches.

Towards Lebu

South of Lota the road runs past the seaside resort of **Laraquete**, where there are miles of golden sands and lots of Chilean holidaymakers in summer. The road passes a large cellulose factory and then, at Carampangue, Km 64 south of Concepción, it forks: one branch running west to **Arauco**, the site of a great beach but also two pungent cellulose factories; the other branch continuing south, 52 km, to Tres Pinos, where there is a turning towards Lebu.

A fishing port and coal washing centre, **Lebu** lies at the mouth of the Río Lebu, 149 km south of Concepción, and is the capital of Arauco province. There are enormous beaches to both the north and south, popular on summer weekends. About 3 km north, at **Playa Millaneco**, are steep hills and caves offering good walks and majestic views.

Twenty-four kilometres south of Tres Pinos is the small town of Cañete. It is located on the site of the historic **Fort Tucapel** (now being restored), where Pedro de Valdivia and 52 of his men were killed by Mapuche warriors in 1553. About 1 km south on the road to Contulmo, in a modern building supposedly inspired by the traditional Mapuche *ruca*, is the **Museo Mapuche Juan Antonio Ríos** ① *T041-2611093, www.dibam.cl/ subdirec_museos/mm_canete/home.asp summer Mon-Fri 0930-1830, Sat and Sun 1100-1900, closed Mon in winter, US$2*. Displays include Mapuche ceramics and textiles. Behind the museum is a reconstruction of a *ruca*.

South of Cañete, **Lago Lanalhue** is surrounded by forested hills from which there has been extensive logging. Much less popular than the Lake District, this area offers good opportunities for walking. A road runs south from Cañete along the north side of the lake to **Contulmo**, a sleepy village at the foot of the *cordillera*. The **Monumento Natural Contulmo**, 8 km south of the village and administered by CONAF, covers 82 ha of native forest. Access to the lake shore is restricted, as much of it is private property, but **Playa Blanca**, 10 km north of Contulmo, is a popular beach in summer (take any bus between Contulmo and Cañete). The wooden **Casa y Molino Grollmus**, 3 km along the southern side of the lake, are well worth a visit. The splendid garden has a fine collection of *copihue*, the national flower, and the mill, built in 1928, still contains its original wooden machinery. From here, the track runs 9 km north to the **Posada Campesina Alemana**, an old German-style hotel in a fantastic spot at the water's edge.

Twenty kilometres further east, **Purén** is reached by crossing the *cordillera* through dense forest (do this journey in daylight). Located in a major logging area, Purén was the site of a fortress built by Pedro de Valdivia in 1553 and destroyed soon after. It was again a key stronghold of the Chilean army in the last campaign against the Mapuche (1869-1881) and there is now a full-scale reconstruction of the wooden fort on the original site.

Lago Lleulleu and Tirúa

Lago Lleulleu lies 34 km south of Cañete. It is a peaceful lake covering 4300 ha and offers sandy beaches, many opportunities for camping, fine views of the coastal mountain range and the chance to interact with the local Mapuche community, but there are few facilities. Further south, at the mouth of the Río Tirúa is the town of **Tirúa**, unremarkable in itself, but close to some wonderful country for walking and riding and with a beach that is calm and deserted. The island of **Mocha**, visited by Juan Bautista Pastenes in 1544 and later by Sir Francis Drake, lies 32 km offshore. Most of the island's 800 inhabitants live around the coast, the interior being forest. The main settlement is **La Hacienda** where accommodation is available with families.

Los Angeles and around ⊖❼▲⊖❶ ▸▸ *pp296-300.*

Situated on the Pan-American Highway, 110 km south of Chillán, Los Angeles is the capital of Biobío province and lies at the heart of a wine, fruit and timber-producing district. Founded in 1739 as a fort, it was destroyed several times by the Mapuche.

Ins and outs

Getting there Los Angeles is easily accessible from north and south by bus; the most common destinations are Santiago, Puerto Montt and Concepción, but all intermediate destinations are also served.

Getting around Los Angeles is not as big as some of the other cities of the central valley, and as a result it is not necessary to take public transport quite as often as in, say, Chillán or Talca.

Tourist information The tourist office is on Caupolicán close to post office; also try **CONAF** ① *Ercilla 936, daily 0900-1300.*

Los Angeles

Most visitors find themselves in Los Angeles on their way to Parque Nacional Laguna de Laja and, although there isn't much here in the way of sights, it is a pleasant, expanding city, with a large Plaza de Armas. Colón is the main shopping street and there is a good daily market. The **Museo de la Alta Frontera** ① *Colón 195, Mon-Fri 0815-1830, free*, has some Mapuche silver and colonial artefacts. Swimming is possible in the nearby **Río Duqueco**, 10 minutes south by bus, US$0.80.

Salto del Laja, 25 km north of Los Angeles, is a spectacular waterfall where the Río Laja plunges 15 m over the rocks. Numerous tour groups stop here, and the place is filled with tourist kiosks selling pap. Boat trips are available in the *Buenaventura* ① *T09-94181247.*

Parque Nacional Laguna de Laja

A road, paved for the first 64 km, runs east from Los Angeles for 93 km, past the impressive rapids of the Río Laja, to the Parque Nacional Laguna de Laja. Covering 11,600 ha, the park is dominated by the scree slopes of the **Antuco Volcano** (2985 m), which is still active, and the glacier-covered **Sierra Velludac**. There is no clear path to the summit of Antuco. Start out early (0500) from the Refugio Digeder at 1400 m to allow about six hours to ascend and leave plenty of time for the descent, which is exhausting. The volcano slopes are made of black scorias blocks, which are razor sharp, so wear good strong boots and take water; be warned that this sort of terrain is very demanding and can catch out those who are unaware of its severity. From the sulphur fume-cloaked summit of the volcano are fine views over the glaciers and south to the smoking Villarrica Volcano. The valley below is green and wooded, very pleasant and sparsely visited, even in high season. The **visitors' centre** is 1 km from the park administration (4 km from the entrance).

Club de Esquí de los Angeles ① *May-Aug*, has two ski-lifts, giving a combined run of 4 km on the Antuco Volcano. Passing the ski station, the road reaches the turquoise waters of the **Laguna de la Laja**, with views of the Andes stretching towards

Los Angeles

To Long Distance Bus Terminal & Pan-American Highway (North) Local

Convento San Francisco
Tucapel

Av. Ercilla
Mendoza
Valdivia
Rengo
Colón
Almagro
Villagrán
Manso de Velasco

To 5 & Pan-American Highway

Local

Estero Quilque

Colo Colo

Laguna Esmeralda

Lautaro

Plaza de Armas

Caupolicán

Municipalidad

Museo de la Alta Frontera

Ricardo Vicuña

To Pan-American Highway (South)

N

0 metres 100
0 yards 100

Sleeping 🛏   Gran Müso **3**   **Eating** 🍴   Julio's Pizzas **3**
Caupolicán 651 **1**   Residencial Santa   Di Leone **5**   Rancho de Julio **1**
De Villena **2**   María **4**   El Arriero **2**

Fiesta de la Piedra Santa

The ancient festival of the Holy Stone is celebrated in Lumaco, near Purén every year on 20 January. The women dress in their traditional costumes, with colourful belts and silver jewellery. Each family carries a fowl, which is sacrificed, covering the stone with blood, while they ask for favours or give thanks for favours received. A few drops of wine are also poured onto the stone before the rest is drunk. The stone is illuminated by hundreds of candles and crosses made of straw or grass are placed over the blood, which sticks to them. *Machis* (shamans), surrounded by people from their communities, go up to the stone and, accompanied on their sacred instrument, the *kultrung*, they sing, dance and recite, while passing their knives over the diseased parts of the bodies of the sick. The festival continues through the night with singing, dancing, music and prayers.

Abridged and translated from *Lengua y Costumbres Mapuches* by Orietta Appelt Martin, Temuco, 1995.

Argentina; note, however, that it is a walk of several hours from the park entrance to the lake and there is very little passing traffic. The laguna was created by the damming of the Río de Laja by a lava flow and is surrounded by stark scenery. Trees include a few surviving araucarias, and there are 47 species of birds including condors and the rare Andean gull. From the lake, the road continues to the Argentine border at **Paso Pichachén** ① *Oct-Apr, depending on amount of snow.*

Angol

Although of limited interest to travellers, Angol is the main base for visiting the Parque Nacional Nahuelbuta, further west. Reached from the Pan-American Highway by roads from Los Angeles and Collipulli, the town is situated at the confluence of the Ríos Rehue and Picolquén, at the foot of the Cordillera de Nahuelbuta, and is the capital of the province of Malleco. It was founded by Pedro de Valdivia in 1552 and was destroyed seven times by the Mapuche.

Northwest of the attractive Plaza de Armas is the church and convent of **San Buenaventura**. Built in 1863, it became the centre for missionary work among the Mapuche. Also worth visiting is **El Vergel** ① *5 km southeast of Angol, Mon-Fri 0900-1900, Sat and Sun 1000-1900, US$1.50, colectivo No 2*, which was founded in 1880 as an experimental fruit-growing nursery but now incorporates an attractive park with a wide range of trees and the Museo Dillman Bullock with displays on archaeology and natural history. There's an excellent **tourist office** ① *O'Higgins s/n, across bridge from bus terminal, T045-711255*, and an office of **CONAF** ① *Prat 191, piso 2, T045-711870*.

Parque Nacional Nahuelbuta

① *Open all year (snow Jun-Sep).* Situated in the coastal mountain range at an altitude of 800-1550 m, the park covers 6832 ha of forest and offers views over both the sea and the Andes. There are some good walks: one heads 4 km west of visitors centre to the **Piedra el Aguila** at 1158 m, where there is a *mirador* on top of a huge boulder; another goes to **Cormallín**, 5 km north of visitors' centre, from where you may continue to Cerro Anay, 1402 m, and another *mirador*. Although the forest includes many species of trees, the araucaria is most striking; some are over 2,000 years old, 50 m high and with trunks 2 m in diameter. There are also seven species of orchid. Animals include pudu, Chiloé foxes, pumas, kodkod, black woodpeckers and parrots. There is a **visitors' centre** ① *spring and summer daily 0800-1300, 1400-2000*, at Pehuenco, 5 km from the entrance. Rough maps are available for US$0.25.

● Sleeping

Concepción *p293, map p290*

Good budget accommodation
is hard to find.

AL Alborada, Barros Arana 457, T041-2911121, www.hotelalborada.cl. Good 4-star
with all mod cons. Large rooms and suites
with king size beds. Disabled friendly. Tours
offered.

AL-A El Dorado, Barros Arana 348, T041-2229400, hoteleldorado.cl. Comfortable
business standard, central, spacious rooms,
bar and cafeteria, parking.

A-B Concepción, Serrano 512, T041-2228851, hotelconcepcion@entelchile.net.
Central, comfortable, heating, English spoken.

B Maquehue, Barros Arana 786, piso 7,
T041-2911966, www.hotelmaquehue.cl.
Clean, with bath and cable TV, restaurant,
laundry service, parking. Recommended.

B-C Cecil, Barros Arana 9, near railway
station, T041-2739981. With bath and
breakfast, clean, quiet. Recommended.

B-C Hostal Antuco, Barros Arana 741, apart
31-33 (entry via the Galería Martínez),
T/F041-2235485. Some rooms with bath.
Simple and spartan but clean and
reasonable value.

B-C Hostal Bianca, Salas 643-C,
T041-2252103, www.hostalbianca.cl.
Some rooms with bath. With breakfast, food
available, parking, student discounts.

C Hostal Casablanca, Cochrane 133,
T041-2226576. Some rooms with bath,
clean. Good value.

C Residencial Colo Colo, Colo Colo 743,
T041-2227118. **E** singles, with bath and
breakfast. Meals available.

C Ruca Ray, Barros Arana 317B,
T041-2238942. **E** singles. With breakfast,
slightly old fashioned but comfortable and
clean. Cable TV in room.

C Silvia Uslar, Edmundo Larenas 202,
T041-2227449. **F** singles. Good breakfast,
quiet, clean, comfortable. Usually lets rooms
to university students.

North of Concepción *p291*

B Bahía Velero, P Aguirre Cerda 760,
Dichato, T041-2683014. Clean and pleasant
rooms with bath and breakfast. Friendly
owners. Right by the beach. Parking.

C De la Costa, M Montt 923, Tomé, T041-

2653379. **F** singles. With bath and breakfast.

C Vista Hermosa, Costanera 1135, Tomé,
T041-2650280. On the seafront, with bath,
without breakfast.

C-D Residencial Santa Inés, República 540,
Dichato. **F** singles. Without bath, basic.

Talcahuano *p291*

B De La Costa, Colón 630, T041-2545913.
Rooms with breakfast.

B France, Av Pinto 44, T041-2920090,
www.hotelfrance.cl. Standard 2-star hotel
with café and internet access.

B-D Residencial San Pedro, Rodríguez 22,
T041-2542145. **E-F** singles. With breakfast.
some rooms with bath.

Towards Lota *p292*

C-D Angel de Peredo, Alessandri 169, Lota,
T041-2876824. With bath and breakfast.
Good value.

D Residencial Roma, Galvarino 233, Lota,
T041-2876257. **F** singles. Clean, friendly,
some rooms with bath. No breakfast.

Towards Lebu *p292*

B Hostería Arauco, Esmeralda 80, Arauco,
T041-2551131, itafesa@hotmail.com. Good
restaurant, bar, laundry and parking.

B-C Plaza, Chacabuco 345, Arauco, T041-2551265. Cheaper rooms without bath.

C-D Central, Pérez 183, Lebu, T/F041-2511904. **E-F** singles. Most rooms with bath,
clean, parking. Recommended.

C-D Hostal La Quinta, Laraquete, T041-2571993. **F** singles. Helpful, basic,
good breakfast.

D Residencial Los Abedules, Los Abedules
144, Laraquete, T041-2571953. **F-G** singles.
Friendly, small rooms, poor bathrooms.

Cañete, Contulmo and Lanalhue *p293*

Lanalhue Turismo, T041-2613537,
www.lanalhueturismo.cl, is an
agglomeration of local hotel and *cabaña*
owners who also offer tours and information.
There are several *cabañas* on the lakeshore.
Real coffee is served at **Café Nahuel**, off the
plaza in Cañete.

L Hostería Lanalhue, Lago Lanalhue,
T041-2234981. On the south side of the lake,
many facilities, good.

A Hotel Licahue, Lago Lanalhue, 4 km north
of Contulmo, T09-98702822. Full board,

attractively set overlooking lake, with pool. Highly recommended. Also owns *cabañas* nearby (connected by boat).

B-C Nahuelbuta, Villagrán 644, Cañete, T041-2611073, hotelnahuelbuta@lanalhue turismo.cl. Clean, pleasant, parking. Cheaper without bath.

C Central, on the plaza, Purén. Excellent meals, rooms in tourist season only.

C-D Derby, Mariñán y Condell, Cañete, T0412-611960. **F** singles. Without bath, clean, basic, restaurant.

C-D Gajardo, 7 de la Línea 817 (1 block from plaza), Cañete. **F** singles. Without bath, old fashioned, friendly, pleasant.

D Central, Millaray 131, Contulmo, T041-2618089, hotelcentral@lanalhue turismo.cl. **F** singles, no sign, hospitable.

D Contulmo, Millaray 116, Contulmo, T041-2894903. **F** singles. Some rooms without bath, an attractive retreat, friendly and hospitable. Recommended.

D Don Juanito, Riquelme 151, Cañete. **F-G** singles. Very good, friendly. Recommended by the locals, cheap.

Camping

Camping Elicura, Contulmo. Clean, US$6. Recommended.

Camping Huilquehue, 15 km south of Cañete. Lakeside site.

Camping Playa Blanca, Lago Lanalhue.

Lago Lleulleu and Tirúa *p293*

C Residencial Elimar, T041-894902. One of 3 *hospedajes* in Tirúa.

Los Angeles *p293, map p294*

AL Gran Hotel Müso, Valdivia 222 (Plaza de Armas), T043-313183, www.hotelmuso.cl. 3-star business standard. Good restaurant open to non-residents.

A Hostería Salto del Laja, T043-321706, www.saltodellaja.cl. With fine restaurant, 2 swimming pools and chalet-type rooms on an island overlooking the falls, fishing trips arranged, also cabañas, for up to 6.

B Complejo Turístico Los Manantiales, Salto del Laja, T/F043-314275. Also camping.

B Hospedaje El Rincón, Panamericana Sur Km 494, El Olivo, 2 km east,18 km north of Los Angeles, T09-94415019, www. Elrinconchile.cl. Beautiful property beside a small river, restful. Good breakfast. South

American and European cuisine, including vegetarian, tours arranged, Spanish classes, horse riding, rafting, English, French and German spoken, kitchen facilities.

B-C Residencial Santa María, Plaza de Armas, T043-328214. Hot shower, TV, friendly but run-down and overpriced.

C-D Hotel de Villena, Lautaro 579, T043-321643. With breakfast.

C-D Caupolicán 651. **F** singles. Private house offering good value rooms and large breakfast. Opposite is another, also No 651, basic, cheaper.

There are also several cheap *residenciales* around Colo Colo and Almagra.

Parque Nacional Laguna de Laja *p294*

In Antuco, most places are fully occupied by local workers. Take your own food as little is available in Abanico or inside the park. Camping is not permitted on lake shore.

B Cabañas Lagunillas, T043-321086, 2 km from park entrance. Open all year, cabins sleep 6, lovely spot close to the river among pine woods, restaurant, also camping US$2.50 per person.

B Refugio Chacay, 21 km from the lake, T043-222651. Food, drink and beds, closed in summer.

C Hostería El Bosque, Abanico. With restaurant and good campsite.

D Refugio Digeder, 11 km from the park entrance, T041-2229054. *Refugio* on slopes of Antuco Volcano.

D Refugio Universidad de Concepción, Of O'Higgins 740, T041-2229054. *Refugio* on slopes of Antuco Volcano.

Angol *p295*

B La Posada, El Vergel, T045-712103. With full board, clean, friendly.

C Casa de Huéspedes, Dieciocho 465. **F** singles, with breakfast, friendly.

C Josanh-Paecha, Caupolicán 579, T045-711771. With breakfast, clean, good food.

Camping

There are 2 campsites on the road to Parque Nacional Nahuelbuta at Km 21 and Km 20.

Parque Nacional Nahuelbuta *p295*

There's a campsite near the visitors' centre, US$11, and many free campsites along the road from El Cruce to the entrance.

● Eating

Concepción *p293, map p290*

♯♯♯ **Le Château**, Colo Colo 340. French, seafood and meat, closed Sun.

♯♯♯ **Rincón de Pancho**, Cervantes 469. Excellent meat, also pasta and *congrio*, good service and ambience, closed Sun.

♯♯ **Big Joe Saloon**, O'Higgins 808, just off plaza. Popular at lunchtime, open Sun evening, good breakfasts, vegetarian meals, snacks and pizzas.

♯♯ **El Rancho de Julio**, O'Higgins 36. Argentine *parrillada*.

♯♯ **Novillo Loco**, Portales 539. Traditional food. Good, efficient service.

♯♯ **Piazza**, Barros Arana 631, 2nd floor. Good pizzas.

♯ **Casino de Bomberos**, O'Higgins y Orompello. Good-value lunches.

♯ **Govinda's**, Angol 451. Good value vegetarian dishes.

♯ **Mar y Tierra**, Colo Colo 1182. Seafood and fish.

♯ **Waya's Gyros**, Angol 441. Excellent value kebabs. Recommended. Also on Plaza Perú.

♯ **Yiet-Xiu**, Angol 515. Good, cheap oriental food.

Cafés and snack bars

Café Colombia, Aguirre Cerda. Good coffee, pleasant atmosphere.

Café El Dom, Caupolicán 415. One of several cafés near the Plaza de Armas. Open Sun morning.

Café Haiti, Caupolicán 515. Open Sun morning, good coffee.

Fuente Alemana, Caupolicán 654. *Fuente de soda* near the Plaza de Armas. Recommended.

Gelatería Dimarco, Plaza de Armas. Popular for ice creams.

La Capilla, Vicuña MacKenna 769. Good ponches, popular, crowded.

Nuria, Barros Arana 736. Very good breakfasts and lunches, good value.

QuickBiss, O'Higgins between Tuscapel and Castellón. Salads, real coffee, good service, good lunches.

Royal Pub, O'Higgins 790. Posh snack bar.

Saaya 1, Barros Arana 899. Excellent *panadería/pastelería/rotisería*.

Treinta y Tantos, Prat 356. Nice bar, good music, wide selection of *empanadas*, good breakfasts and lunches. Recommended.

North of Concepción *p291*

There are several seafood restaurants on P Aguirre Cerda 600 and 700 blocks in Dichato.

♯♯ **Casino Oriente**, Penco. Good seafood restaurant.

♯♯ **Munot**, Baquedano 1690, Tomé. Swiss food.

♯♯ **Villa Marina**, Riquelme 55, Tomé. Traditional food.

Talcahuano *p291*

The market abounds with fine seafood.

♯♯ **Club Talcahuano**, Colón 446. For meat.

♯♯-♯ **Benotecas**, on seafront. A row of 4 restaurants facing the harbour. Superb fish and seafood. Recommended.

♯♯-♯ **Domingo Lara**, Aníbal Pinto 450. Seafood specialities, excellent.

♯♯-♯ **La Aguada**, Colón 912. Shellfish dishes.

Lota *p292*

♯ **El Greco**, P Aguirre Cerda 422, Lota. Traditional food, cheap.

Los Angeles *p293, map p294*

♯♯ **Di Leone**, Av Alemania 606. Italian with good lasagne on the menu.

♯♯ **El Arriero**, Colo Colo 235. Good *parrillas* and international dishes.

♯♯ **Rancho de Julio**, Colón 720. Excellent *parrilla*. Recommended.

♯ **Julio's Pizzas**, Colón 542. Good pizzeria.

Angol *p295*

♯ **Carloncho**, Lautaro 447. Simple food, popular with locals.

● Bars and clubs

Concepción *p293, map p290*

El Caríno Malo, Barros Arana y Salas. Popular bar and disco with live music, not cheap.

⊛ Festivals and events

Cañete, Contulmo and Lanalhue *p293*

Jan Semana Musical (music week) is held in Contulmo.

20 Jan Fiesta de Piedra Santa is a major Mapuche festival, held in Lumaco (see box, page 295).

O Shopping

Concepción *p293, map p290*
Feria Artesanal, Freire 757. Craft market.
Galería Internacional, Caupolicán y Barros Arana. Worth a visit; **El Naturista** vegetarian restaurant is at local 22.
Las Brisas, Freire y Lincoyán. Supermarket.
Mercado Municipal, 1 block west of the Plaza de Armas. Seafood, fruit and veg.
Plaza del Trebol, near the airport. Large modern shopping mall and multiplex cinema. Take any bus for Talcahuano.

▲ Activities and tours

Concepción *p293, map p290*
Alta Luz, S Martín 586, Piso 2, T041-2217727. Tours to national parks.
Aventuratur, Ejército 599, T041-2819634. Tours.
Chile Indomito Adventure, Serrano 551, oficina 3, T041-2221618. Trekking.
Ram, T041-2256161. City and local tours.
South Expeditions, O'Higgins 680, piso 2, oficina 218D, T/F041-232290. Rafting, horse riding, fishing and trekking expeditions.
Viajes Publitur, A Pinto 486, oficina 202, T041-240800. City and local tours.

Los Angeles *p293, map p294*
Senderos Chile Expediciones,
T09-7143958. Trekking, mountain biking.
Strong Visión, Caupolicán 506, T09-312295. Trekking, mountain biking, rafting, kayaking, bungee-jumping, fishing.

☻ Transport

Concepción *p293, map p290*
Air
Concepción airport is north of the city, off the main road to Talcahuano. In summer, flights daily to and from **Santiago** (fewer in winter); connections to **Temuco**, **Puerto Montt** and **Punta Arenas**. **Airline offices**: LanChile, Barros Arana 560, T041-2248824; Aerolíneas Argentinas, O'Higgins 650, of 602.

Bus
Local Línea Azul and Costa Azul buses from Concepción pass through the villages north of the city, which can also be reached cheaply by *colectivo* (every 15-20 mins).

To **Talcahuano**, frequent service from Plaza de Armas (bus marked 'Base Naval'), 1 hr, US$0.70, express 30 mins, US$1; *colectivos* leave San Martín every 2 mins.
Services to **Coronel**, US$0.70, **Lota**, **Lebu**, **Cañete**, **Tirúa** and **Contulmo** are run by J Ewert (next to railway station on Prat), Los Alerces (terminal at Prat y Maipú) and Jeldres, who leave from the main terminal.

Long distance The main terminal is known as **Terminal Collao**, 2 km east, Av Gral Bonilla, next to athletics stadium. To reach the city centre take a bus marked 'Hualpencillo' from outside the terminal and get off in Freire, US$0.60, taxi US$4.
Tur Bus, Línea Azul and Buses Bío Bío services leave from **Terminal Camilo Henríquez**, 2 km northeast of main terminal on J M García, reached by buses from Av Maipú in centre, via Terminal Collao.
To **Santiago**, 8 companies, 6½ hrs, US$10; to **Valparaíso**, 8 hrs, US$12 (most go via Santiago). Estrella del Sur have buses to **La Serena** and **Iquique**. To **Puerto Montt** several companies, about 9 hrs, US$13 (cama US$26); to **Pucón** direct, 7 hrs, US$10, in summer only; to **Valdivia**, 7 hrs, US$10, Tur Bus only; to **Los Angeles**, every ½ hr, US$3.
Best direct bus to **Chillán** is Línea Azul, 2 hrs, US$3. For a longer, more scenic route, take the Costa Azul bus, which follows the old railway line, through Tomé, Coelemu and Nipas on to Chillán (part dirt-track, takes 5½ hrs).

Car/bicycle
Car hire Avis, Chacabuco 726, T041-2235837; **Budget**, Castellón 134, T041-2225377; **Dollar**, at airport, T041-483661; **Full famas**, O'Higgins 1154, T041-2248300, F2242385, airport T09-94403300; **Hertz**, Prat 248, T041-2230341. Bicycle repairs from **Martínez**, Maipú y Lincoyán, very helpful.

Train
The station is at Prat y Barros Arana, T041-226925, www.efe.cl. To **Santiago**, Rápido del Bío Bío one daily and one overnight, 10 hrs, US$16-21. Also local services to **Laja** and **Yumbel**, and suburban trains to **Talcahuano** and **Chiguayante**. Booking offices at the station and at **Galería Alessandri**, Aníbal Pinto 478, local 3, T041-225286.

Towards Lota *p292*
Buses to **Concepción**, 1½ hrs, US$1. Many buses bypass the centre of Lota: catch them from the main road. See also above.

Cañete, Contulmo and Lanalhue *p293*
In Cañete: J Ewert, Inter Sur and Thiele use the bus terminal at Riquelme y 7° de la Línea; Jeldres, Erbuc and other companies use the Terminal Municipal, Serrano y Villagrán.

To **Santiago**, Inter Sur, daily, 12 hrs; to **Contulmo**, frequent, US$1.50; to **Purén**, US$2, sit on right for views of Lago Lanalhue; to **Concepción**, 3 hrs, US$4.50; to **Lebu** US$2; to **Angol** US$4.50; to **Tirúa**, Jeldres, frequent, and J Ewert, 3 a day, 2 hrs, US$3.

Contulmo is also served by buses to/from **Concepción**, Thiele, 4 hrs, US$6, and **Temuco**, Thiele and Erbuc, US$7, see above.

Tirúa *p293*
Buses run from Cañete to Tirúa, from where there are ferries to **Mocha**, 0600 daily, US$20. Alternatively, you can also ask the police to radio the plane to Mocha, US$100.

Los Angeles *p293, map p294*
Long-distance bus terminal on northeastern outskirts of town, local terminal at Villagrán y Rengo in centre (most services to Ralco and Santa Bárbara).

To **Santiago**, 6½ hrs, US$11, cama US$24. To **Viña del Mar** and **Valparaíso**, 8 hrs, US$14; to **Concepción**, US$3, 2 hrs; to Valdivia, US$8; to **Chillán**, US$3.50. To **Temuco**, US$6, hourly; to **Curacautín**, daily, 3 hrs, US$5. **Salto del Laja** is served by Bus Biobío from Los Angeles, frequent, 30 mins, US$1.50, and from Chillán, US$2.75.

Parque Nacional Laguna del Laja *p294*
Take ERS Bus, Villagrán 507, from Los Angeles to **Abanico**, then walk 4 km to park entrance. Alternatively take a bus to **Antuco**, 2 hrs, 5 daily Mon-Sat, 2 daily Sun, US$2, then hitch the remaining 24 km to the park.

Angol *p295*
Local buses use **Terminal Rural**, Ilabaca y Lautaro. Long-distance bus terminal is at Chorrillos y Caupolicán. To **Santiago**, US$10; to **Los Angeles**, US$1.80; to **Temuco**, Trans Bío-Bío, frequent, US$3.50. Car hire from Christopher Car, Ilabaca 421, T/F045-715156.

Parque Nacional Nahuelbuta *p295*
There is a direct bus to park entrance from Angol, Dec-Feb, Sun 0800, return 1700. Otherwise, take a bus to **Vegas Blancas** (27 km west of Angol) 0700 and 1600 daily, return 0900 and 1600, 1½ hrs, US$1.80, and get off at El Cruce, for a 7-km walk to the park entrance (US$6). Access is also possible via a dirt road from Cañete, 4WD only Jun-Sep.

❶ Directory

Concepción *p293, map p290*
Banks ATMs at banks on Av O'Higgins; high commission; several cambios in Galería Internacional, Barros Arana 565 and Caupolicán 521, check rates first: Afex, local 57, no commission on TCs; Cambios Fides, local 58, good rates for TCs; Inter-Santiago, local 31, T041-2228914. **Consulates** Argentina, San Martín 472, oficina 52, T041-2230257. **Cultural centres** Alliance Française, Colo Colo y Lamas, library, concerts, films, cultural events; Chilean-British Cultural Institute, San Martín 531, British newspapers, library; Chilean-North American Institute, Caupolicán 301 y San Martín, library. **Internet** Barros Arana 541, Caupolicán 567, English spoken. Many others. **Laundry** American Cleaning, Freire 817; Lavandería Radiante, Salas 281, open 0900-2030, very good; also at Lincoyán 441. **Post office** O'Higgins y Colo Colo. **Telephone** CTC, Colo Colo 487, Angol 483; Entel, Barros Arana 541, Caupolicán 567, piso 2, Colo Colo 487. **Useful addresses** Automóvil Club de Chile, O'Higgins 630, Of 303, T041-2245884; Codeff, Caupolicán 346, piso 4, T041-2226649.

Los Angeles *p293, map p294*
Banks Banco Santander, Colón 500. MasterCard; Corp Banca, Colón 300, Visa. ATMs at banks; reluctant to change TCs or cash; best rates at Agencia Interbruna, Caupolicán 350. **Post office** Plaza de Armas. **Telephone** CTC, Colo Colo; Entel, Colo Colo 393. **Useful address** Automóvil Club de Chile, Villagrán y Caupolicán, T043-322149.

Angol *p295*
Banks Banco Bice, Chorrillas 364; Banco Santander, Lautaro 399.

Lake District

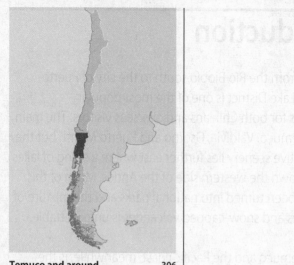

Footprint features

Introduction

Extending from the Río Biobío south to the city of Puerto Montt, the Lake District is one of the most popular destinations for both Chileans and overseas visitors. The main cities are Temuco, Valdivia, Osorno and Puerto Montt, but the most attractive scenery lies further east where a string of lakes stretches down the western side of the Andes. Much of this region has been turned into national parks and the mixture of forests, lakes and snow-capped volcanoes is unforgettable.

Between Temuco and the Pacific coast, meanwhile, is the indigenous heartland of Chile, home to the largest Mapuche communities. Here you will find *rucas* (traditional thatched houses) and communities still fiercely proud of their traditions, hinting at the sort of country that the first *conquistadors* might have found.

The major resorts include Pucón on Lago Villarrica and Puerto Varas on Lago Llanquihue. The cities of Temuco and Puerto Montt are also popular: Temuco for excursions into the Mapuche communities towards the coast and Puerto Montt as a base for longer voyages south to Puerto Natales, Puerto Chacabuco and the San Rafael glacier, as well as east across the lakes and mountains to the Argentine resort of Bariloche.

★ Don't miss...

1 **Parque Nacional Conguillio** The best place in Chile to see the *araucarias* (monkey puzzle trees), in the shadow of Volcán Llaima, page 310.

2 **Temuco's feria** This is one of the biggest and most fascinating markets in Chile, filled with Mapuche men and women who have come by ox cart to the city to sell their produce, page 314.

3 **Volcán Villarrica** An active volcano where molten lava bubbles in the crater, page 319.

4 **Corral** Visit this old fortified settlement near Valdivia and then take the coastal path south through wild forest clinging to cliffs above the ocean, page 338.

5 **The journey from Puerto Montt to Bariloche in Argentina** Cross the emerald waters of the Lago Todos Los Santos, overlooked by the Osorno volcano, and then take a narrow pass over the Andes, page 364.

6 **Eating at Angelmó** This harbour near Puerto Montt has some of the best seafood in Chile (and, by extension, in the world), page 367.

Lake District

Background

After the Mapuche rebellion of 1598, Spanish settlement south of the Río Biobío was limited to Valdivia, although the Spanish had a right of way north from Valdivia along the coast to Concepción. At independence the only other Spanish settlement in this region was Osorno, refounded in 1796. The Chilean government did not attempt to extend its control into the Lake District until the 1840s. In 1845, all land south of the Río Rahue was declared the property of the state and destined for settlement and, in 1850, Vicente Pérez Rosales was sent to Valdivia to distribute lands to arriving European colonists.

The southern Lake District was settled from the 1850s onwards, mainly by German immigrants (see box, page 352). Further north, Chilean troops began occupying lands south of the Biobío after 1862, but the destruction of Mapuche independence did not occur until the early 1880s when Chilean forces led by Cornelio Saavedra founded a series of forts in the area including Temuco (1881), Nueva Imperial (1882), Freire (1883) and Villarrica (1883). A treaty ending Mapuche independence was signed in Temuco in 1881.

White settlement in the area was further encouraged by the arrival of the railway, which reached Temuco in 1893, reducing the journey time from Santiago to 36 hours; the line was later extended to Osorno (1902) and Puerto Montt (1912). In the 1930s the area became popular as a destination for rich Santiaguinos, and also as an important fishing destination for foreigners.

Today, agriculture is the most important sector of the local economy and the main industries are connected to the region's produce. Proof of Chile's position as a timber producer of international standing is provided by wood-chip piles and cellulose plants dotted along the coast. Fishing is particularly important in the south of the region, where farmed salmon regularly appears on restaurant menus. Tourism is a mainstay in summer (from mid-December to mid-March), when Chileans flock to the Lake District resorts, prices are high, and it is best to book well in advance, particularly for transport. Out of season, however, many facilities are closed.

Geography

The region between the cities of Temuco and Puerto Montt is one of the most picturesque lake regions in the world. There are 12 great lakes, and dozens of smaller ones, as well as imposing waterfalls and snowcapped volcanoes. This landscape has been created by two main geological processes: glaciation and volcanic activity. The main mountain peaks are volcanic: the highest are Lanín (3747 m) and Tronador (3460 m), both on the Argentine border. The most active volcanoes include Llaima and Villarrica, which erupted 22 and 10 times respectively in the 20th century.

❢ *Enormous horseflies (tábanos) are a problem between mid-December and mid-Juary, especially in the Parque Nacional Vicente Pérez Rosales: cover up as much as possible and do not wear dark clothing.*

Seven main river systems drain the Lake District, from north to south the ríos Imperial, Toltén, Valdivia, Bueno, Maullín, Petrohué and Puelo. The Río Bueno drains Lago Ranco and is joined by the ríos Pilmaiquén and Rahue, thus receiving also the waters of Lagos Puyehue and Rupanco: it carries the third largest water volume of any Chilean river. In most of the rivers there is excellent fishing.

Rain falls all the year round, most heavily further south, but decreases as you go inland: some 2500 mm of rain fall on the coast compared to 1350 mm inland. There is enough rainfall to maintain heavy forests, mostly of southern beech and native species, though there are increasingly large areas of eucalyptus and other introduced varieties to cater for the booming timber industry.

The Mapuche

The largest indigenous group in southern South America, the Mapuche take their name from the words for 'land' (*mapu*) and 'people' (*che*). They were known as Araucanians by the Spanish.

Never subdued by the Incas, the Mapuche successfully resisted Spanish attempts at conquest. At the time of the great Mapuche uprising of 1598 they numbered some 500,000, concentrated in the area between the Río Biobío and the Reloncaví estuary. After 1598, two centuries of intermittent war were punctuated by 18 peace treaties. The 1641 Treaty of Quilín recognized Mapuche autonomy south of the río Biobío.

Although tools and equipment were privately owned, the Mapuche held land in common, abandoning it when it was exhausted by repeated use. This relatively nomadic lifestyle helps explain their ability to resist the Spanish. Learning from their enemies how to handle horses in battle, they became formidable guerrilla fighters. They pioneered the use of horses by two men, one of whom handled the animal, while the other was armed with bow and arrows. Horses also enabled the Mapuche to extend their territory to the eastern side of the Andes and the Argentine *pampas*.

The conquest of the Mapuche was made possible by the building of railways and the invention of new weapons, especially the breach-loading rifle (which had a similarly disquieting effect in Africa and Asia). The settlement of border disputes between Chile and Argentina enabled Argentine troops to occupy border crossings, while the Chileans subjugated the Mapuche.

Under the 1881 treaty, the Mapuche received 500,000 ha from the government, while 5000,000 ha were kept for Chile. The Mapuche were confined to reservations, most of which were situated near large estates for which they provided a labour force. By the 1930s, the surviving Mapuche, living in more than 3000 separate reservations, had become steadily more impoverished and dependent on the government.

The agrarian reforms of the 1960s provided little real benefit to the Mapuche since they encouraged private landholding – indeed some communal lands were sold off at this time – and the military government made continued encroachments on Mapuche communities, which remain among the poorest in Chile.

It is estimated that the Mapuche now occupy only about 1.5% of the lands they inhabited at the time of the Spanish conquest, mainly in communities south of the Biobío and in reserves in the Argentine *cordillera* around Lago Nahuel Huapi. July 2001 saw repeated clashes with the police over land rights.

Lake District Background

Crossing to Argentina

There are five main routes from the Lake District into Argentina:

1 From Curacautín and Lonquimay to Zapala via Paso Pino Hinchado (see page 311).
2 From Pucón and Curarrehue to Junín de los Andes via Paso Tromen (see page 322).
3 From Panguipulli via Choshuenco and Lago Pirehueico to San Martín de los Andes via Paso Huahum (see page 334).
4 From Osorno and Entrelagos via the Parque Nacional Puyehue and Paso Puyehue to Bariloche (see page 347).
5 The lakes route, from Puerto Montt or Osorno via Ensenada, Petrohué and Lago Todos los Santos to Bariloche (see page 364).

Temuco and around → *Colour map 4, A2/3.*

At first sight, Temuco may appear a grey, forbidding place. However in reality it is a lively industrial and university town. For visitors, it is perhaps most interesting as a contrast to the more European cities in other parts of Chile. Temuco is proud of its Mapuche heritage, and it is this that gives it a distinctive character, especially around the feria (outdoor market). North and east of the city are five national parks and reserves, and several hot springs, while to the west, in the valley of the Río Imperial, are the market towns of Nueva Imperial and Carahue and, on the coast, the resort of Puerto Saavedra. ▸▸ For Sleeping, Eating and other listings, see pages 311-316.

Ins and outs

Getting there Manquehue Airport is 6 km southwest of city. There are several daily flights north to Santiago and Concepción, and south to Puerto Montt. Taxis from airport to Temuco city centre cost US$6.50; there is no airport bus service. Temuco is the transport hub for the Lake District, and its municipal bus station serves much of the region, as well as the communities towards the coast. The long-distance terminal is on the northern outskirts of town. The city is easily accessible by bus from Santiago (many daily) and has connections to large towns both north and south, especially Talca, Chillán, Concepción, Valdivia and Puerto Montt (many daily). There are also train connections to Santiago and south as far as Puerto Montt.

Getting around Temuco is a large city. *Colectivos* and buses serve the outlying *barrios*. However, the centre is relatively compact, and few places are more than a half-an-hour walk away in this area. When looking for a specific address, be careful not to confuse the streets Vicuña MacKenna and General MacKenna.

Tourist information Sernatur ① *Bulnes 586, T045-211969, infoaraucania@serna tur.cl, summer daily 0830-2030, winter Mon-Fri 0900-1200, 1500-1700,* has good leaflets in English. There is also a tourist information kiosk in the municipal market and an office of **CONAF** ① *Bilbao 931, T045-234420.*

Temuco

The city is centred on the recently redesigned **Plaza Aníbal Pinto**, around which are the main public buildings including the cathedral and the municipalidad; the original cathedral was destroyed by the 1960 earthquake, when most of the old wooden buildings in the city were also burnt down. On the plaza itself is a monument to La Araucanía featuring figures from local history. Nearby are fountains and a small Sala de Exposiciones, which stages exhibitions. More compelling, though, is the huge produce **market** at Lautaro y Aníbal Pinto, always crammed with people (many of them Mapuche), who have come from the countryside to sell their produce (see page 314).

West of the centre, the **Museo de la Araucanía** ① *Alemania 084, Mon-Fri 0900-1700, Sat 1100-1700, Sun 1100-1300, US$1.50, bus 1 from centre,* houses a well arranged collection devoted to the history and traditions of the Mapuche nation; there's also a section on German settlement.

A couple of kilometres northeast of the centre is the **Museo Nacional Ferroviario Pablo Neruda** ① *Barros Arana 0565, T045-227613, www.temucochile.com, Tue-Sun 0900-1800, US$1.90, concessions US$0.50, bus 1 variante or Taxi (US$2.50 from the centre).* Exhibits include over 20 engines and carriages (including the former presidential carriage) dating from 1908 to 1953. The grounds contain rusting hulks and machinery, while the annex houses temporary exhibitions.

● *The final treaty between the Chilean army and the Mapuche was signed on Cerro Ñielol in 1881, under La Patagua, a tree that can still be seen.*

On the northern edge of the city is the **Monumento Natural Cerro Ñielol** offering views of the city and surrounding countryside. It is a good spot for a picnic. There is an excellent visitors' centre ① *0830-2030, US$1.50*, run by CONAF and a fine collection of native plants in their natural environment, including the *copihue rojo*, the national flower. A tree marks the spot where peace was finally made with the Mapuche. Note that the hill has a one-way system for drivers (entry by Prat, exit by Lynch) and that bicycles are only allowed in before 1100.

Padre las Casas is a predominantly Mapuche suburb, southeast of the centre, on the other side of the Río Cautín, where you will find the **Casa de la Mujer Mapuche** ① *in the Gymnasium, between calles Corvalín and Almte Barroso, To9-1694682, Mon-Fri 0930-1300, 1500-1830, bus 8a or 10, colectivo 13a*. Crafts and textiles made by a cooperative of 135 Mapuche weavers are sold here. The items are very good quality, but correspondingly expensive.

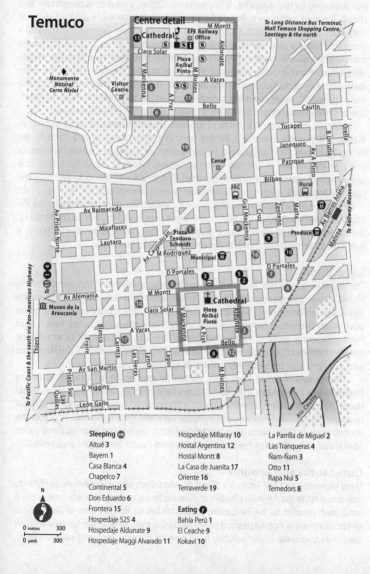

Temuco

To get a flavour of the life of the Mapuche, it is well worth making a trip to this dusty, friendly country town in the heart of Mapuche country. Daily buses, laden with corn, vegetables, charcoal and animals as well as locals make the 30-km journey by paved road from Temuco across rolling countryside, with views of five volcanoes on a clear day. You will see people travelling by ox cart on the tracks nearby, and a few traditional round *rucas* (thatched houses). There are also several cheap bars in the town, as well as a small museum dedicated to Mapuche culture.

Puerto Saavedra and around

From Temuco a paved road follows the Río Imperial 35 km west to the market town of **Nueva Imperial**, where cattle auctions are held on Mondays and Tuesdays. From here the road continues to **Carahue**, the site of the Spanish colonial city of Imperial which was destroyed by the Mapuche. It has accommodation, a market, supermarkets and shops. The road continues to **Puerto Saavedra**, which lies behind a sandspit south of the mouth of the Río Imperial. Founded in 1897, the town was destroyed in 1960 by a *maremoto* (tidal wave; see box, page 336). Fortunately the local population were warned of the disaster by the sight of water draining from the bay, and so few people were killed. However, the impact of the *maremoto* on folktales cannot be over-estimated. A local man commented to the author of this book, "We thought it was the end of the world, so we spent two months drunk on the hills until the water receded". One of Chile's most famous films in recent years, *La Frontera*, was filmed here.

After the *maremoto*, the centre of the town moved inland and its former site at **Maule**, 2 km south, became a fishing port. Just beyond Maule is a track to the incredibly narrow sandspit created by the *maremoto*. It stretches several kilometres north to the mouth of the Río Imperial, where there's a beautiful beach and uninterrupted views of the ocean. The third distinct area of Puerto Saavedra is the resort of **Boca Budi**, 4 km south, where there's an enormous beach.

From Puerto Saavedra a track leads north 2 km to a free ferry crossing over the Río Imperial to **Nehuentue**, on the north bank. From here launches may be chartered up the Río Moncul to the pleasant tour of **Trovolhue**, four hours. Alternatively there is a half paved half *ripio* road north to the town of **Tirúa**, 70 km away.

Lago Budi

The only inland saltwater lake in Chile, Lago Budi lies south of Puerto Saavedra and is visited by over 130 species of water bird, including black-necked swans. Although the lake is marked on maps as having an outlet to the sea, this is dried up for most of the year, when there is a continuous track along the expanses of sandy beach from Puerto Saavedra south to Porma and Toltén. This was the old right of way for the Spanish between Concepción and Valdivia before their final defeat of the Mapuche; wild and remote, it passes many isolated Mapuche communities.

On the east shore of Lago Budi, 40 km by road south of Carahue, is **Puerto Domínguez**, a picturesque little town famous for its fishing. On the west shore is **Isla Huapi** (also spelt Guapi), a peninsula with a Mapuche settlement of *rucas* (traditional thatched houses) and fine views of both the lake and the Pacific. This is one of the poorest spots in Chile, but is ideal for camping. It can be reached by *balsa* (ferry) either from about 10 km south of Puerto Saavedra or from Puerto Domínguez (see below).

Curacautín and around

Thirty kilometres north of Temuco a paved road branches off the Pan-American Highway and runs east to the Argentine border at Pino Hachado, passing through Curacautín. A small town situated on the Río Cautín, Curacautín lies 84 km northeast of Temuco and 56 km southeast of Victoria by good paved roads. Deprived by new, stricter deforestation laws of its traditional timber industry (until recently there were several sawmills here),

⁞ The monkey puzzle tree

The Araucaria Araucana, known in Chile as the *araucaria* or *pehuén* and elsewhere called variously the Chilean pine, the umbrella tree, the parasol tree and the monkey puzzle tree, is the Chilean national tree and has flourished in this area for 200 million years. Very slow growing, it can grow up to 40-m high; and live for 1200 years. The characteristic cones can weigh up to 1 kg so take care sitting underneath! Though its natural habitat is on both sides of the Andes between 37° and 39° south, it is much more widespread in Chile than in Argentina.

The *araucaria* was revered by the Mapuche, who ate both its cones and its sharp leathery leaves. Some isolated trees are still seen as sacred by the Mapuche who leave offerings to the tree's spirit.

Curacautín is trying to recreate itself as a centre for tourism; it is a useful base for visiting the nearby national parks and hot springs, including the indoor and sadly run-down **Termas de Manzanar** ⓘ *17 km east of Curacautín, open all year, US$8*. On the way, at Km 6, the road passes a turn-off to **Laguna Blanca** (25 km north, take fishing gear) and the **Salto del Indio** ⓘ *Km 13, US$1.20*, a 30-m high waterfall, where there are *cabañas*. Some 3 km beyond Manzanar is the **Salto de la Princesa**, a 50-m waterfall, with camping and *hostería*. ➤➤ *For Sleeping, Eating and other listings, see pages 311-316.*

Termas and Parque Nacional Tolhuaca

The beautiful pine-surrounded **Termas de Tolhuaca** ⓘ *open all year, US$6*, are 35 km to the north of Curacautín by *ripio* road, or 57 km by unpaved road from just north of Victoria; a high-clearance 4WD is essential out of season. Two kilometres further north is the **Parque Nacional Tolhuaca** ⓘ *open Dec-Apr*, which covers 6374 ha of the valley of the Río Malleco at altitudes of 850 to 1830 m and includes the waterfalls of Malleco and Culebra, and two lakes, Laguna Malleco and Laguna Verde. There's superb scenery and good views of the volcanoes from Cerro Amarillo. Park administration is near Laguna Malleco and there is a campsite nearby. Unfortunately, much of the park, together with the neighbouring **Reserva Nacional Malleco**, was damaged by forest fires in 2002, and will take several decades fully to recover.

Reserva Nacional Malalcahuello-Nalcas

Situated northeast of Curacautín, this 31,305 ha park lies on the slopes of the **Lonquimay Volcano** (2865 m), and is much less crowded than the nearby Parque Nacional Conguillío. The volcano began erupting on Christmas day 1988 and the crater produced was named Navidad. Useful information about the park is available from the **CONAF** office on the main road in Malalcahuello (east of Curacautín) and from **La Suizandina** (see Sleeping below), which is also a good base for treks and for the ascent of the volcano. Several marked trails (varying from one hour to two days) leave from the CONAF office. From Malalcahuello it is a one-day hike to the Sierra Nevada (see below), or a two-day hike to Conguillío national park; less experienced climbers should hire a guide.

Los Arenales ski resort ⓘ *To45-891071, www.arenalespark.cl, season Jun-Sep, Sat-Tue only, winter access from Lonquimay town only, ski pass US$17, equipment hire US$15*, is at Las Raíces Pass on the road from Malalcahuello to Lonquimay town. It is a pleasant, small resort with a nice restaurant and four lifts that go up to 2,500 m

● *Lonquimay Volcano began erupting on Christmas Day 1988. The resulting crater is known as Navidad.*

with great views. In winter the pass is usually snowed out, and the road from Malalcahuello to Lonquimay town is diverted via the **Túnel Las Raices** ① *toll US$2*. This former railway tunnel was, until recently, the longest in South America at 4.8 km. There is talk of repairing the tunnel, but for the moment it is in poor condition, unlit and with constant filtration. If travelling by bicycle it is wiser to hitch through the tunnel in a pickup than cycling through yourself.

Access to **climb Lonquimay** is either from Malalcahuello, 15 km south, or from from the ski resort from where it is a one-hour walk to the municipal *refugio* at the base of the mountain. Walk towards the ski lift and from there head to the spur on the left. Allow four hours for the ascent, one hour for the descent. Crampons and ice-axe are necessary in winter, but in summer it is a relatively simple climb.

Parque Nacional Conguillio

① *Entry US$6, each entrance has an information centre. There is also a visitors' centre (open Dec-Mar) at the park administration by Lago Conguillio. CONAF runs free slide lectures and short guided walks during the summer, covering flora and fauna, Volcán Llaima and other subjects.*

Covering 60,833 ha, the park, situated 80 km east of Temuco, is one of the most popular in Chile though it is deserted outside January and February and at weekends. In the centre is the **Llaima Volcano** (3125 m), which is still active and can be climbed. There are two craters: the western crater was blown out in 1994 and began erupting again in March 1996. There are two large lakes, Laguna Verde and Lago Conguillio, and two smaller ones, Laguna Arco Iris and Laguna Captrén. North of Lago Conguillio rise the snow-covered peaks of extinct volcano **Sierra Nevada**, which reaches 2554 m.

Much of the park is covered in forests of southern beech but it is also the best place in Chile to see native **araucaria forest**, which used to cover extensive areas of land in

Parque Nacional Conguillio

To Curacautín ▼
To Curacautín ◄

Termas del Río Blanco

Sierra Nevada

Río Captrén

Laguna Captrén

Lago Conguillio

Laguna Quepe

Laguna Arco Iris

To Vicún ◄

Laguna Verde

Ski Club Refugio

Volcán Llaima (3050m)

Río Calbuco

Parque Nacional Conguillio

Río Rilpe

Saltos de Truful-Truful

To Argentina via Paso Icalma ▼

Río Truful-Truful

N

0 km   5
0 miles 5

To Cunco ◄   Melipeuco

☐ Park administration posts
🏠 Park warden posts

this part of the country (see box, page 309). Mature araucaria forest can be found around Lago Conguillio and on the slopes of Llaima. Other trees include cypresse and *canelo* (winter's bark). Among the park's wildlife are condors, black woodpeckers, the marsupial *monito del monte*, pumas, foxes, *pudú* and many waterfowl.

There are three **entrances** to the park: the northern entrance is reached by *ripio* road from Curacautín, 28 km north; the southern entrance at Truful-Truful is reached by a *ripio* road from Melipeuco, 13 km southwest, while the western entrance is reached by *ripio* road from Cherquenco (high-clearance vehicle essential). Close by is the **Araucarias ski resort** ① *T045-211314, US$13 Mon-Fri, $18 Sat, Sun*, with two ski lifts, a café, restaurant, bar, *refugio* and equipment rental.

Trails within the park range from 1 to 22 km in length. Details are available from the park administration or from CONAF in Temuco. One of the best trails is a path round the east side of Lago Conguillio and north towards the Sierra Nevada (allow a full day for the round trip). The first 10 km are reasonably easy, with two or three *miradores* offering spectacular views. After this the going gets much more difficult for the final 5-km climb. From the western entrance it is a two- to three-day hike around Volcán Llaima to Lago Conguillio – a dusty route, but with beautiful views of Laguna Quepe – then on to the Laguna Captrén *guardería*.

Climb **Llaima** south from **Guardería Captrén**, avoiding the crevassed area to the left of the ridge and keeping to the right of the red scree just below the ridge. From the ridge it is a straight climb to the summit. Beware of sulphur fumes at the top. Allow five hours to ascend, two hours to descend. Crampons and ice-axe are essential except in summer; less experienced climbers should also hire a guide. Further information on the climb is available from **Guardería Captrén**.

Border with Argentina

Paso Pino Hachado (1884 m) can be reached either by a paved road 73 km southeast from Lonquimay or by a mostly unpaved road 129 km east from Melipeuco. On the Argentine side this road continues to Zapala; some buses from Temuco to Zapala and Neuquén use this crossing. **Immigration and customs** at Liucura ① *22 km west of the frontier, Sep to mid-May 0800-2000; winter 0800-1900*, can involve very thorough searches, especially when entering Chile.

An alternative route is via **Paso de Icalma** (1298 m) reached by *ripio* road, 53 km east of Melipeuco, south of Parque Nacional Conguillio, and continuing on the Argentine side to Zapala. This route is often impassable in winter. To see if the pass is open contact the **Policía Internacional** in Temuco (Prat 19, T045-293890). **Chilean immigration** ① *open mid-Oct to mid-Mar 0800-2000; winter 0800-1900*.

◉ Sleeping

Temuco *p306, map p307*
Many cheaper *residenciales* and *pensiones* can be found in the market area.
L Terraverde, Prat 0220, T045-239999, www.panamericanahoteles.cl. This 5-star is the best in town.
AL Frontera, Bulnes 726, T045-200400, www.hotelfrontera.cl. Good business standard. Large conference room.
A Aitué, A Varas 1048, T045-212512, www.hotelaitue.cl. Another business standard. Central, bar, English spoken, comfortable.
A Hotel Don Eduardo, Bello 755, T045-214133, www.hoteldoneduardo.cl. Parking,

suites with kitchen, recommended.
A-B Bayern, Prat 146, T045-276000, www. hotelbayern.cl. Standard 3-star. Small rooms, clean, helpful, buffet breakfast, parking. Cheaper if paying in US dollars.
B Continental, Varas 708, T045-238973, www.turismochile.cl/continental. With breakfast, charming old-fashioned building (this is the oldest hotel in Temuco). Large rooms with antique furniture, decent restaurant, the bar is popular with locals in the evening, cheaper rooms available without bath. Neruda stayed here once. Recommended.

B Hostal Montt, Manuel Montt 637, T045-910400, www.hostalmontt.cl. Comfortable and clean. Some rooms with cable TV and bath. With breakfast. Gym downstairs. Overpriced.

B Luanco, Aldunate 821, T045-213749, luanco@surnet.cl. Apartments with kitchenette.

B-C La Casa de Juanita, Carrera 735, T045-213203. Quiet bed and breakfast. Hot water, laundry, heating, parking. Cheaper rooms without bath. Several similar places on Bello, west of the plaza.

B-C Oriente, M Rodríguez 1146, T045-233232, h-oriente@123mail.cl. Old, but clean and friendly. Good value rooms with bath, cheaper without (these rooms do have sinks). Heating, TV, parking, laundry. Some rooms with no windows. Recommended.

C Blanco Encalada 1078, T045-234447. Use of kitchen, friendly, good breakfast.

C Chapelco, Cruz 401, T045-749393 www.hotelchapelco.cl. Airy, has seen slightly better days. Rooms with bath and cable TV. Breakfast, internet in lobby, comfortable, good service, recommended.

C Hospedaje Aldunate, Aldunate 187, T045-270057, cristorresvalenzuela@hotmail.com. **E-F** singles. Friendly, cooking facilities. Some rooms with TV and bath.

C Hostal Argentina, Aldunate 864, T045-624238. Run down. With breakfast, hot water, parking and TV.

C-D Casa Blanca, Montt 1306 y Zenteno, T045-277799, www.hostalcasablanca.cl. **F** singles. With breakfast, friendly, slightly run down, but good value for rooms with bath.

C Hospedaje Maggi Alvarado, Recreo 209, off Av Alemania, T045-409804, cppacl@gmail.com. **E** singles. Small rooms, but very clean, friendly, helpful, in a pleasant part of town. Also has a good value *cabaña* sleeping 4.

C-D Hospedaje 525, Zenteno 525, T045-233982. **F** singles. Without breakfast, some rooms with bath, large rooms, clean, poor beds but good value. TV lounge.

D Hospedaje Millaray, Claro Solar 471, T045- 645720, hostalmillaray_tco@yahoo.es. **F** singles. Simple, basic, unfriendly. Other private houses on this street in the same price range.

Puerto Saavedra and around *p308*
The following are in Puerto Saavedra.

B-C Cabañas Miramar, Miramar 4, Puerto Saavedra, T045-634290, www.miramarchile.com. Fully equipped *cabañas* for 2-8 people, with picnic and barbeque areas. Also camping, US$10 per site.

C Hotel Boca Budi, Boca Budi, T045-352990/09-4532107. With bath and breakfast. Sea views, heating, room service. Tours offered. Mid-price restaurant.

D Lago Los Cisnes, Boca Budi, T045-251891. Cheap option with restaurant.

D Sra Rita Sandoval Muñoz, Las Dunas 01511. **F** singles. Lovely, knowledgeable host.

Lago Budi *p308*
C Hostería Rucaleufú, Alessandri 22, Puerto Domínguez. With good meals, clean, lake views. Highly recommended.
The only other accommodation is the **Puaucho** campsite on Isla Huapi.

Curacautín and around *p308*
L-A Termas de Manzanar, Termas de Manzanar, 17 km from Curacautín, T045-881200, www.termasdemanzanar.cl. Simple rooms with bath. Overpriced. Includes access to thermal pools. Full board available.

A-B Anden Rose, 5 km west of Manzanar (Km 68) on the banks of the river Cautín, T09-98691700, www.andenrose.com. Rooms with bath and central heating. With breakfast, restaurant, bike, horse, kayak rental, tours arranged, camping, German owners.

C Hostería Abarzúa, Termas de Manzanar, 18 km from Curacautín, T045-870011. Simple, friendly, cheaper without bath. Full Board available (good food).

C Hostería La Rotunda del Cautín, Termas de Manzanar, 17 km from Curacautín, T045-1971478. Rooms and good mid-range restaurant, friendly.**B-C Hostal Las Espigas**, Miraflores 315, Curacautín, T045-881138, rivaseugenia@hotmail.com. **E** singles. Good rooms with bath, kitchen, breakfast, dinner available on request.

B-C Plaza, Yungay 157, main plaza, Curacautín, T045-881256. Overpriced. Restaurant is okay but pricey.

For an explanation of sleeping and eating price codes used in this guide, see inside the front cover. Other relevant information is found in Essentials, see pages 50-57.

D Residencial Rojas, Tarapacá 249, Curacautín. **F** singles. Without bath, good meals. Recommended.

D Turismo, Tarapacá 140, Curacautín, T045-881116. **F** singles. Clean, good food, comfortable, best value.

Termas and Parque Nacional Tolhuaca *p309*

L Termas de Tolhuaca, Termas de Tolhuaca, T045-881164, www.termasdetolhuaca.cl. With full board, includes use of baths and horse riding, jacuzzi and massage also available. Very good.

D Residencial Roja, Termas de Tolhuaca. **F** singles. Hot water, food, camping near the river, good.

Rerserva Nacional Malalcahuello-Nalcas *p309*

A La Suizandina, Km 28, Curacautín-Lonquimay rd (3 km from Malalcahuello), T045-1973725/09-98849541, www.suiz andina.com. Double rooms, hostel accommodation (price per person) and camping. Laundry, large swiss breakfast with homebaked bread, English and German spoken, TCs accepted, good meals. Hiking, horse riding, travel and trekking tours or just information. Car hire. It has been described as "like being in Switzerland".

C Residencial Los Sauces, in Malalcahuello village, on the edge of the park, T09-98837880. **F** singles with shared bath and use of kitchen, hot water. Also good value cabañas. Full board available. Señora Naomi Saavedra arranges lifts to destinations within the reserve.

D Hospedaje Navidad, Caupolicán 915, Lonquimay, T045-891111. **F-G** singles. More of the same. With restaurant.

D Hostal Lonquimay, Pinto 555, Lonquimay, T045-891324. **F** singles. Basic rooms with shared baths and breakfast.

Parque Nacional Conguillio *p310, map p310*

AL Camping Los Ñirres, southern shore of Lago Conguillio, near the visitors' centre, T045-298213. Campsite with *cabañas* for 4-6 people.

AL La Baita, 3 km south of Laguna Verde, T045-416410/09-97332442, www.labaita conguillio.cl. *Cabañas* with electricity, hot

water, kitchen and wood stove. Charming, lots of information as well as nature trails and a good restaurant. Italian/Chilean owned, recommended.

B-C Centro Turístico Los Pioneros, 1 km east of Melipeuco, T045-581005, turismopioneros@araucaniaandina.cl. Rooms and *cabañas*. Full board available. Tours to the park offered.

C Adela y Helmut, Faja 16000, 5 km north of Temuco-Cunco rd, west of Melipeuco, T09-97244479, www.adelayhelmut.com. **F** singles. Cosy bed and breakfast with central heating and good meals. Tours arranged to Conguillio park. Good value, recommended. Pickups from the main road with advance notice.

D Hospedaje Icalma, Aguirre Cerda 729, Melipeuco, T045-581108. **F** singles. Spacious, basic rooms with bath and breakfast. Recommended.

Camping

There are several campsites in the park, one on the west side of Laguna Captrén and 5 dotted around Lago Conguillio. All are administered by **CONAF**, T045-298213 for information and reservations. There is a free municipal campsite in Melipeuco and **Camping Los Pioneros**, 1 km from Melipeuco, T045-581005. On road to the park, hot water.

7 Eating

For places to eat in Puerto Saavedra, Curacautín and the national parks, see Sleeping, above.

Temuco *p306, map p307*

Those on a very strict budget should make for the **Mercado Municipal**, Aldunate y Portales, where there are several restaurants and fierce touting for business, or the rural bus terminal, where countless restaurants serve very cheap set meals at lunch. *Humitas* are on sale in the street in summer/autumn.

¶¶ Bahía Perú, Alemania y Recreo, near the Mall Mirage, about 10 blocks west of centre. One of several good mid-priced restaurants on Av Alemania (take bus 1), reasonable Peruvian food, good *pisco sours*.

Caletas Restaurante, Mercado Municipal, Aldunate y Portales. One of several in the covered market serving fish and seafood.

La Cumbre del Cerro Ñielol, Cerro Ñielol. Food and dancing on top of the hill, not always open.

La Parrilla de Miguel, Montt 1095, T045-275182. Good for large servings of meat and wine. One of the better restaurants in the town centre.

Las Tranqueras, Alemania 0888, T045-385044. Meat specialists, great grills, but vegetarian options also available.

Otto, V Mackenna 530. German dishes, cakes etc.

El Ceache, Cruz 231. Typical Chilean food. Good value set lunch.

Ñam-Ñam, Portales 802. Good sandwiches and snacks.

Kokaví, Rodríguez y Zenteno, T045-951625. Popular restaurant serving traditional Mapuche food. Gets busy at lunchtime.

Rapa Nui, Aldunate 415. For take-away lunches and snacks, recommended.

Restaurante Temedors, San Martín 827. Good-value lunch.

Cafés

Café Marriet, Prat 451, Local 21. Excellent coffee.

Cafetería Ripley, Prat y Varas. Real coffee.

Dino's, Bulnes 360. Good coffee.

Il Gelato, Bulnes 420. Delicious ice cream.

🍷 Bars and clubs

Temuco *p306, map p307*
Banana bliss, Montt 1031. Bar and disco.

El Túnel, Caupolicán y M Blanco. Restaurant with dancing.

Mr Jones, Bello 844. Pub-café-disco.

Sol y Luna, 10 km south on road to Pucón. Late-night disco.

🎭 Entertainment

Temuco *p306, map p307*
There is a cinema on the south side of the plaza, and another on the 3rd floor of the Almacenes Paris building, Montt y Prat. It is also worth checking out the **Instituto Chileno-Frances**, Varas 736, and the **Instituto Chileno-Norte Americano**, Gen MacKenna 555, for films and events.

🛍 Shopping

Buy supplies in Temuco, Curacautín or Meli-peuco, where they are much cheaper than in the shop in the Parque Nacional Conguillio.

Temuco *p306, map p307*
Crafts
Mapuche crafts and textiles are sold inside and around the **Mercado Municipal**, Aldunate y Portales, and also in the **Casa de la Mujer Mapuche** (see Sights, above).

Food
Frutería Las Vegas, Matta 274. Dried fruit (useful for climbing/trekking).
Las Brisas, Rodríguez 1100 block. Supermarket.
Santa Isabel, Bulnes 279. Supermarket.
Super, Rodríguez 1400 block. Supermarket.
Temuco feria, Lautaro y Aníbal Pinto. This is one of the most fascinating markets in Chile, where people from the surrounding countryside come to sell their wares. You will find excellent cheap fruit and vegetables, local spices such as *merquén* (made from smoked chillies), fish, grains, cheese and honey; there are many inexpensive bars and restaurants nearby.

🏔 Activities and tours

Temuco *p306, map p307*
Most companies in Temuco offer tours to **Parque Nacional Conquillo**, 1 day, US$40; to Puerto Saavedra and Villarrica volcano (US$75), but unless you are in a hurry it is better and cheaper to book a tour closer to the destination. Some also offer skiing and snowboarding trips.
Amity Tour, Bucalemu 01220, T045-285290, www.amitytours.cl. A wide range of tours throughout the region.
Caminos del Sur, Av Alemania 0395, T045-237576, www.caminosdelsur.cl. Añlso sells trekking equipment.
Sur Expediciones, Prat 712, local 6, T045-323632, www.sur-expediciones.com.
Tribu Piren, Lagos 945, T045-236456, www.tribupiren.cl.

Curacautín and around *p308*
Turismo Christopher, Yungay 260, T045-882471.
Turismo Tolhuaca, Calama 240.

⊙ Transport

Temuco *p306, map p307*
Air
LanChile, Bulnes 687, on plaza, T600-5262000, Sky, T600-600 2828, and Aerolíneas del Sur fly to Manquehue Airport from **Santiago**, 1¼ hrs, **Concepción**, 40 mins, **Osorno**, 40 mins, and **Puerto Montt**, 45 mins.

Bus
Local Services to neighbouring towns leave from **Terminal Rural**, Pinto y Balmacedaor from bus company offices nearby: **Erbuc**, Miraflores y Bulnes; **JAC**, **NarBus** and **Igi Llaima**, Balmaceda y Aldunate; **Tur Bus**, Lagos 549.

To **Panguipulli**, Power and Pangui Sur, 3 hrs, US$4. Pangui Sur also has services to **Loncoche**, US$2, **Los Lagos**, US$3, and **Mehuín**, summer only. To **Curacautín** via Lautaro, **Erbuc**, 4 daily, 2½ hrs, US$3, continuing to **Lonquimay**, 3½hrs, US$4. Narbus has hourly services daily to **Nueva Imperial**, **Carahue** and **Puerto Saavedra**. JAC runs buses to **Villarrica** and **Pucón**, many daily 0705-2045, 1½ hrs, US$4, and to **Coñaripe**, 3 hrs, and **Lican Ray**, 2 hrs. Erbuc and Thiele run buses to **Contulmo**, 2 hrs, US$5, **Cañete**, US$5 and **Lebú**. To **Laguna Captren**, Erbuc, Mon and Fri 1645, 4 hrs, US$4. To **Chol Chol**, Huincabus, 4 daily 1100-1800, 1 hr, US$1.50.

Long distance The new long-distance terminal is north of city at Pérez Rosales y Caupolicán; to get there, take buses 2, 7 or 10 from the centre. To **Santiago** several companies, 8-9hrs, many overnight, US$11 (salón cama US$22); to **Castro**, Cruz del Sur, 3 a day; to **Puerto Montt**, Cruz del Sur, 10 a day, 5½ hrs, US$9; to **Valdivia**, JAC, several daily, 2½ hrs, US$5; to **Osorno** 4 hrs, US$5; to **Concepción**, Bío Bío, US$7, 4½ hrs; to **Chillán**, 4 hrs, US$6.

International To **Junín de los Andes** via Pucón, **Igi Llaima** and **Narbus**, daily between them, leaves early morning, advance booking required, US$20. To **Neuquén** via Curacautín, Lonquimay and the Paso Pino Hachado, **Igi Llaima**, **Buses Caraza** and **Buses El Valle**, daily between them, US$25; **Buses Caraza** have connecting services to **Buenos Aires**, **Bahía Blanca** and **Mar del**

Plata, US$50. To **Bariloche** via Osorno, Tas Choapa, daily, US$23.

Car
Car hire from **Automóvil Club de Chile**, Varas 687, T045-248903and at airport; **Budget**, Lynch 471, T045-214911; **Christopher Car**, Varas 522, T/F045-215988; **Dollar**, at airport, T045-336512; **Euro**, MacKenna 426, T045-210311, helpful, good value; **Full Famas**, at airport and in centre T045-215420, recommended; **Hertz**, Las Heras 999, T045-235385, US$45 a day. Several others.

Motorbike/bike
Motorbike mechanic: **Terremoto**, Claro Solar 358, T045-312828. Bicycles parts can be bought at **Oxford**, Andrés Bello 1040, T045-211869; repairs at Bulnes 228,Lautaro 1370, Portales 688. Also many on Balmaceda, nos 1266, 1294 and 1448.

Train
The **station** is at Barros Arana y Lautaro Navarro, T045-233416, www.efe.cl. There is also an additional ticket office at Bulnes 582, T045-233522, open Mon-Fri 0900-1300, 1430-1800, Sun 0900-1300. To **Santiago**, overnight service, daily 2200, 10 hrs, salón US$19-26, preferente US$22-35, Unfortunately the old sleeper service has recently been discontinued (the carriages with wood inlay and velvet upholstery can be seen in Temuco's railway museum). To **Puerto Montt**, via **Osorno**, **Frutillar** and **Puerto Varas**, 2 daily 6½ hrs, US$6.

Puerto Saavedra and around *p308*
To **Temuco** (Terminal Rural), **Narbus**, hourly, 3 hrs, US$2.

Lago Budi *p308*
There are **buses** to **Puerto Domínguez** from Temuco, 3 hrs. The Carlos Schalchli **ferry** leaves Puerto Domínguez for **Isla Huapi**, Mon and Wed 0900 and 1700, returning 0930 and 1730, free, 30 mins.

Curacautín and around *p308*
The **bus** terminal is on the main street, by the plaza. Tur Bus and Inter Sur have daily direct services to **Santiago**. Erbuc services from Temuco and Los Angeles continue on to **Malalcahuello** and **Lonquimay**, see below.

Parque Nacional Tolhuaca *p309*

There are **bus** services from Victoria to **San Gregorio** (19 km from park entrance) Mon, Wed, Fri 1715; return same day 0645.

Reserva Nacional Malalcahuello-Nalcas *p309*

Erbuc runs **bus** services from Temuco via Lautaro and Curacautín, 4 daily, to **Malalcahuello**, 3 hrs, US$3, and **Lonquimay** town, 3 ½ hrs (or 4 hrs via Victoria), US$4.

Parque Nacional Conguillío *p310, map p310*

There are daily **buses** from Temuco to **Cherquenco**, but no onward public transport into the park. **Taxi** from Curacautín to the **northern entrance**, US$28 one way. Transport to the **southern entrance** can be arranged from Melipeuco (ask in grocery stores and *hospedajes*), US$26 one way. For touring, hire a 4WD in Temuco or join an agency tour, see Activities and tours, above.

⊙ Directory

Temuco *p306, map p307*

Banks ATMs at several banks on or around Plaza A Pinto. Also try the following casas de cambio: **Christopher**, Prat 696, Oficina 419; **Comex**, Prat 471; **Inter-Santiago**, Bulnes 443, Local 2 ; **Turcamb**, Claro Solar 733; also at Bulnes 667, Local 202, and at Prat 427. There are many cambios around the Plaza; all deal in dollars and Argentine pesos. **Consulates** Netherlands, España 494, honorary consul, Germán Nicklas, is friendly and helpful. **Internet** Several throughout the city, generally US$0.75 per hr. **Laundry** Alba, Zeneto 480, opposite the church, and at Aldunate 324 and Aldunate 842; **Marva**, M Montt 415 and 1099, Mon-Sat 0900-2030. **Post office** Portales 839. **Telephone** CTC, A Prat just off Claro Solar and plaza, open Mon-Sat 0800-2400, Sun and holidays 1030-2400; **Entel**, Bulnes 303. daily 0830-2200; also call centres at Lautaro 1311 and Montt 631.

Lago Villarrica and around

→ *Colour map 4, B2/3.*

Wooded Lago Villarrica, 21 km long and about 7 km wide, is one of the most beautiful lakes in the region, with the active and snow-capped Villarrica Volcano (2840 m) to the southeast. Visitors should note, though, that its resorts are among the priciest in Chile (although those with the money will find them well worth the expense). ►► *For Sleeping, Eating and other listings, see pages 322-330.*

Villarrica ⊟🚲❀▲⊜⊙ ►► *pp322-330.*

Pleasantly set at the extreme southwest corner of the lake, Villarrica can be reached by a paved road southeast from Freire, 24 km south of Temuco on the Pan-American Highway, or from Loncoche, 54 km south of Freire, also paved. Less significant as a tourist resort than nearby Pucón, it is a little cheaper. Founded in 1552, the town was besieged by the Mapuche in the uprising of 1599: after three years the surviving Spanish settlers, 11 men and 13 women, surrendered. The town was refounded in 1882.

There is a small museum, **Museo Histórico** ⊙ *Pedro de Valdivia 1050 y Zegers, Mon-Sat 0900-1730, 1800-2200, Sun 1800-2200, reduced hrs in winter, US$0.50,* containing a collection of Mapuche artefacts. Next to it is the **Muestra Cultural Mapuche,** featuring a Mapuche *ruca* and stalls selling good quality handicrafts in summer. The **tourist office** ⊙ *Valdivia 1070, T045-411162, open daily in summer, Mon-Fri off season,* has information and maps. There are good views of the volcano from the *costanera*; for a different perspective over the lake, go south along Aviador

Acevedo and then Poniente Ríos towards the **Hostería La Colina**. Just south of town (½ km along Avenida Matta), there is a large working farm, **Fundo Huifquenco** ① *T045-415040, www.fundohuifquenco.cl*, with trails, horse riding, carriage rides and meals (book in advance).

Pucón

On the southeastern corner of the lake, 26 km east of Villarrica, Pucón is one of the most popular destinations in the Lake District, famous above all as a centre for visiting the 2840 m Villarrica Volcano, which dominates the view to the south. Built across the neck of a peninsula, it has two black sand beaches, which are popular for swimming and water sports. Whitewater rafting is also offered on the nearby rivers

Villarrica

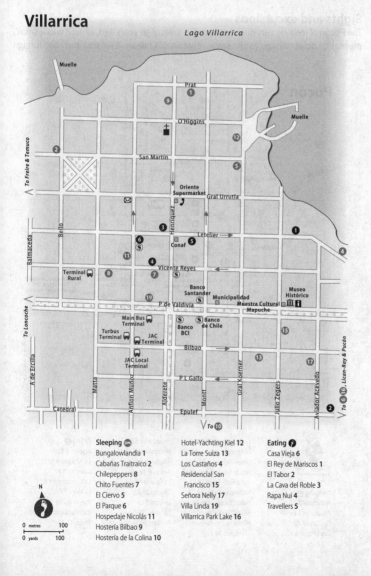

Sleeping
Bungalowlandia 1
Cabañas Traitraico 2
Chilepeppers 8
Chito Fuentes 7
El Ciervo 5
El Parque 6
Hospedaje Nicolás 11
Hostería Bilbao 9
Hostería de la Colina 10

Hotel-Yachting Kiel 12
La Torre Suiza 13
Los Castaños 4
Residencial San
  Francisco 15
Señora Nelly 17
Villa Linda 19
Villarrica Park Lake 16

Eating
Casa Vieja 6
El Rey de Mariscos 1
El Tabor 2
La Cava del Roble 3
Rapa Nui 4
Travellers 5

and excursions can be made into the Parque Nacional Huerquehue or the Cañi Nature Reserve as well as a number of thermal springs, all of which lie east of the town.

Ins and outs

Getting there Pucón is served by one or two daily buses from Puerto Montt and Valdivia and several daily from Santiago. There are regular services from Temuco and Villarrica. The airport 2 km east of Pucón on the Caburga road has several flights a week to/from Santiago in summer.

Getting around Pucón is small enough to walk around on foot. Taxis for out-of-town.

Tourist information Do not confuse the **Municipal Tourist Office** ① *Municipalidad, O'Higgins 483, T045-293002, www.pucon.com*, which provides information and sells fishing licences, with the Chamber of Tourism at the entrance to Pucón from Villarrica. The town also has a **CONAF** office ① *O'Higgins 669*.

Sights and excursions

The Pucón of today is very different from the town of 30 years ago, when it was a small, pleasant, quiet village with some seasonal Chilean tourism, but no foreign

Pucón

0 metres 100
0 yards 100

Sleeping 🛏
Antumalal **2** *C1*
Araucarias **1** *B1*
Del Lago **6** *A2*
Gran Pucón **8** *A2*
Gudenschwager **4** *A1*
Hospedaje Graciela **13** *C2*
Hospedaje Lucía **17** *C2*
Hospedaje M@yra **10** *B3*
Hospedaje Sonia **18** *B2*
Hospedaje Victor **11** *C2*
Hostal Backpackers **3** *C2*
Hostal Gerónimo **26** *B3*
Hostal Puerto Parque
 Tinquilco **19** *B3*
Hostal Willy **5** *C3*
Hostería école **21** *B3*
Interlaken **24** *C1*
Kernayel **12** *C3*
La Posada Plaza-
 Pucón **28** *B1*
La Poza **9** *C1*
La Tetera **29** *B2*
Residencial Lincoyán **16** *B2*

Eating 🍴
Arabian **1** *B2*
En Alta Mar **4** *B2*
Il Baretto **5** *B2*
La Buonatesta **8** *B2*
La Maga **7** *B2*
Puerto Pucón **10** *B2*
Rap Hamburguesa **9** *B3*
Senzo **11** *B2*

backpackers. It is now a thriving tourist centre, full of Chileans in summer and gringos in the autumn. Within easy reach of town are an active climbable volcano where you can also ski in winter, rivers for whitewater rafting and fly-fishing, canopy tours in native forests, quadbike excursions, lakes and waterfalls, two national parks and a private nature sanctuary as well as a dozen thermal springs. This makes Pucón an excellent base for visiting the northern lake district.

Every other house in the town centre seems to offer accommodation, while the main drag is awash with tour operators. Neon signs are forbidden and road signs and telephone kiosks are made of wood, but the streets are full of bars, restaurants, boutiques and *artesanía*. The commercial centre lies between **Avenida O'Higgins**, the main thoroughfare, and the **Gran Hotel Pucón**. Private land (ask for permission at the entrance) leads west from the centre of town to **La Peninsula**, where there are fine views of the lake and volcano, as well as pony rides and golf. There is also a pleasant walk, along the **Costanera Otto Gudenschwager**, starting at the northern end of Calle Ansorena and following the lakeside north.

Boat trips ① *daily 1500 and 1900, summer only, 2 hrs, US$6*, on the lake leave from the landing stage at La Poza at the western end of O'Higgins. Walk a couple of kilometres north along the beach from here to the mouth of the Río Pucón for views of volcanoes. Or take a boat ① *summer only, US$15*, to the mouth of the river from near the **Gran Hotel**.

To cross the Río Pucón, head east out of Pucón along the main road, then turn north on an unmade road leading to a new bridge. There are pleasant walks from here along the north shore of the lake to the Mapuche settlement of **Quelhue** and the village of **Trarilelfú**, or northeast towards **Caburga** (the round trip makes a perfect day's outing by mountain bike). You can also strike up into the hills through farms and agricultural land, with views of three volcanoes and the lake.

From the road to the Villarrica Volcano, a *ripio* road branches off for 5 km to some privately managed *cuevas volcanicas* '(volcanic caves') ① *T045-442002, www.cuevas volcanicas.cl, US$12*, surrounded by a small attractive park with tunnels and a museum, as well as paths through the forest. Entry to the site is expensive, but it's recommended as a bad-weather option.

East of Lago Villarrica

Within easy reach of Villarrica and Pucón are two more lakes, two national parks and several hot springs. Busy with Chilean tourists in summer, these are among the most dramatic spots in the Lake District, and well worth a visit for those in the area.

Parque Nacional Villarrica

This park, which covers 61,000 ha, stretches from Pucón to the Argentine border near Puesco. There are three sectors: Villarrica Volcano sector, Quetrupillán Volcano sector (see page 321) and the Puesco sector, which includes the slopes of the Lanín Volcano on the Argentine border. Each sector has its own entrance and ranger station.

The **Villarrica Volcano**, 2840 m high and still active, lies 8 km south of Pucón. Due to accidents, access to this sector ① *US$5*, is restricted only to groups with a guide – several agencies offer excursions (see Activities and tours, page 327) – and to individuals who can show proof of membership of a mountaineering club in their own country. Entry is refused if the weather is poor. Good boots, crampons and ice picks are essential; these can be rented for US$8 per day from tour operators, but will generally be included in the price of a tour. You should also take sunglasses, sun block, plenty of water and chocolate or some other snack; equipment is checked at the park entrance.

It is a three- to four-hour trek to the summit, but you can skip the first part of the ascent by taking the ski lift (① *US$7*) This is recommended as it saves 400m climbing scree. If the conditions are right, at the summit you can look down into the crater at the bubbling molten lava below, but beware of the sulphur fumes; tour agencies will occasionally provide gas masks, otherwise take a cloth mask moistened with lemon juice. On exceptionally clear days you will be able to see six other volcanoes. Conditions permitting, groups may carry ski and snowboard equipment for the descent; otherwise just slide down.

Between July and September (and occasionally October) it is possible to ski at the **Pucón resort**, which is situated on the eastern slopes of the volcano and reached by a badly maintained track (see page 327).

Lagos Caburga and Colico

Lago Caburga (spelt locally Caburgua) is a very pretty lake in a wild setting 25 km northeast of Pucón. It is unusual for its beautiful white sand beach (other beaches in the area have black volcanic sand), and is supposedly the warmest lake in the Lake District. The western and much of the eastern shores are inaccessible to vehicles, but the village of **Caburga**, at the southern end of the lake, is reached by a turning off the main road to Argentina, 8 km east of Pucón. If walking or cycling, there is a very pleasant alternative route: turn left 3 km east of Pucón, cross the Puente Quelhue, then turn right and follow the track for 18 km through beautiful scenery. Just off the road from Pucón, Km 15, are the **Ojos de Caburga** ① *US$0.60*, beautiful pools fed from underground, which are particularly attractive after rainfall. The northern tip of the lake can be reached by a road from Cunco, which runs east along the northern shore of **Lago Colico**. This is one of the less accessible lakes, and lies north of Lago Villarrica in a remote setting.

> ❧ *Rowing boats for the lake may be hired in Caburga for US$3 per hour.*

Parque Nacional Huerquehue

① *Open officially Jan-Mar, but you can get in at other times, US$4, parking 1½ km along the track, US$1.*

Located a short distance east of Lago Caburga, Parque Nacional Huerquehue covers 12,500 ha at altitudes rising to 1952 m at the **Picos del Caburgua**. It also encompasses about 20 lakes, some of them very small, and many araucaria trees. The entrance and administration is on the western edge, near **Lago Tinguilco**, the largest lake in the park.

Lagos Villarrica, Caburga & Colico

To Cunco · To Cunco
Los Laureles
Río Colico
Lago Colico
Playa Negra
Lago Huillipilún
Lago Caburga
Lago Toro
Lago Verde
Lago Tinguilco
Parque Nacional Huerquehue
Trarileufú
Caburga
Ojos de Caburga
Termas de Quimey-Co
Termas Los Pozones
Quelhue
Reducción de Quelhue
Termas de Huife
Lago Villarrica
Río Llucura
Río Pucón
Villarrica
Pucón
Reserva Forestal Cañi
To Freire
To Loncoche
To Lican-Ray
To Volcán Villarrica & Parque Nacional Villarrica
To Curarrahue & Argentina
To Termas de San Luis

0 km 5
0 miles 5
N

To get there take the Caburga road from Pucón; 3 km before Caburgua turn right along a ripio road to Paillaco, from which another road leads 7 km to the park administration. JAC run a daily bus from Pucón. From the entrance there is a well-signed track north up a steep hill to **Lago Chico**, where the track divides left to **Lago Verde** and right to **Lago Toro**. The lakes are surrounded by trees and are very beautiful. The tracks rejoin at **Lago Huerquehue**, where a further 20 km of trails begin. None of the routes is particularly taxing, making the park a good warm-up for the Volcán Villarrica hike. An adequate map may or may not be provided at entrance. The warden is generally very helpful. People in the park rent horses and boats. Take your own food.

Termas de Quimey-Co, de Huife and los Pozones

South of Parque Nacional Huerquehue and reached via turning off the Pucón-Caburga road are three sets of thermal baths. The most expensive and ostentatious are the **Termas de Huife** ① *Km 33, T045-441222, www.termashuife.cl, US$13*, where entry includes the use of one modern, pleasant pool. Closer to Pucón and rather more low-key are the **Termas de Quimey-Co** ① *Km 29, T045-441607, www.termasquimey co.com, US$7*, while further on are the **Termas los Pozones** ① *Km 35, US$6 per day, US$8 at night*, which have six natural rock pools but little infrastructure and are very popular with travellers.

Reserva Forestal Cañi

① *Park entrance is US$5 per person; see Activities and tours for tour details.*
Situated south of Parque Nacional Huerquehue and accessed from the road to the Termas de Huife, this is a private nature reserve covering 500 ha, owned by the non-profit **Fundación Lahuén**. It is a three-hour trek to its highest peak, **El Mirador**. The first part of the trek to a basic *refugio* at the park entrance is straightforward, along a wide path winding upwards through ancient native forests of coigue and lenga, with occasional views back to Lagos Villarrica and Caburga. Inside the reserve there are 17 small lakes, snow-covered for much of the year. Between these lakes are some of the oldest araucaria trees in Chile. From here it is a steep climb to **El Mirador** (1550 m) from where there are panoramic views over neighbouring parts of Argentina and Chile, including four volcanoes: Lanín, Villarrica, Quetrupillán and Llaima. As the reserve is above the snowline for much of the year, independent visits are normally restricted to summer, although guided visits are possible off season.

Towards Argentina

From Pucón a road runs southeast along the southern bank of the valley of the Río Trancura to **Curarrehue** and the Argentine border, providing access en route to thermal springs and a number of hikeable *saltos* (waterfalls).

At Km 18, a *ripio* road heads south 10 km to the **Termas de Palguín** ① *T045-441968, www.termasdepalguin.cl, US$8*, and the spectacular **Saltos del Puma** and **del León** ① *800 m from the Termas, also accessible at Km 27 on the Pucón-Curarrehue road, US$2 for both*. From the springs a poor rough dirt road runs south to Coñaripe, with access to the Volcán Quetrupillán section of the **Parque Nacional Villarrica**. If you're driving, a high-clearance 4WD vehicle is necessary to reach the national park, and the road is often impassable in winter; but travelling on horseback is best. The treks in this sector are not physically demanding. Palguín is also the starting point for a four- to five-day hike to Puesco (see below), with vistas over the Villarrica and Lanín volcanoes.

Further along the road, on the other side of the park are the new **Termas Geométricas** ① *T02-2141214, www.termasgeometricas.cl, US$18*, 17 architecturally designed pools of different sizes and geometrical shapes. There is a small café.

Back on the Curarrehue road, at Km 23, a turning leads north to the indoor and outdoor pools at **Termas de San Luis** ① *www.sanluis.pucon.com, US$9*, and **Termas**

Trancura ① *www.termastrancura.com, US$9 or US$13 including transport from Pucón*, from where it is 30 minutes' walk to **Lago del León**. At Km 24, the **Salto Palguín** can be seen (but not reached), and beyond that is the impressive **Salto China** ① *Km 26, US$1.50*, where there's a restaurant and camping. At Km 35 another turning leads north for 15 km to the **Termas de Panqui** ① *US$10*, where there are three pools beautifully situated in the mountains as well as accommodation.

Beyond the small town of Curarrehue, 36 km east of Pucón, the road continues unpaved, south to Chilean **immigration and customs** at Puesco ① *16 km from the border, 0800-1900*. The road then climbs via **Lago Quellelhue**, to reach the border at **Paso Mamuil Malal** (Paso Tromen). On the Argentine side it runs south to Junín de los Andes, San Martín de los Andes and Bariloche.

To the south of the pass rises the graceful cone of **Volcán Lanín** (3747 m), one of the world's most beautiful mountains. Although extinct, Lanín is geologically one of the youngest volcanoes in the Andes. It is climbed from the Argentine side. A four-hour hike from Argentine customs (3 km from the border) leads to a *refugio* at 2400 m. The climb from here to the summit is not difficult but crampons and ice axe are needed.

● Sleeping

Villarrica *p316, map p317*
Price codes are based on high season rates (Jan-Feb); off season prices are 30-40% lower. The more upmarket accommodation tends to be on the lakefront.
LL Villarrica Park Lake, Km 13 on road to Pucón, T045-450000, www.villarricaparklake hotel.cl. 5-star. All rooms have balconies overlooking the lake. Conference rooms, banquet halls, spa with pools, sauna, solarium, tours.
AL El Ciervo, Koerner 241, T045-411215, www.hotelelciervo.cl. 4-star. Comfortable rooms with heating. In pleasant grounds. German-style breakfasts. German spoken, pool, terrace Wi-Fi. Recommended.
AL Parque Natural Dos Ríos, 13 km west of Villarrica, T09-94198064, www.dosrios.de. With full board. Tranquil 40 ha nature park with *cabañas* on the banks of the Río Toltén (there is a white sand beach), horseback riding, birdwatching, children-friendly, German, English spoken.
AL-A Hostería de la Colina, Las Colinas 115, overlooking town, T045-411503, www.hosteriadelacolina.comWith breakfast, large gardens, good service, Wi-Fi, good restaurant, views. English spoken. Recommended.
AL-A Hotel y Cabañas El Parque, 3 km east on Pucón road, T045-411120, www.hotelel parque.cl. Lakeside with beach, tennis courts, breakfast, good restaurant with set meals. Highly recommended.

A Bungalowlandia, Prat 749, T045-411635, www. bungalowlandia.cl. *Cabañas* for 2, with *comedor*, good facilities and service. Better value off season.
A Hostería Bilbao, Henríquez 43, T045-411186, www.interpatagonia.com/bilbao. Clean, small rooms, pretty patio, good restaurant.
A-B Cabañas Traitraico, San Martín 380, T045-411064, traitraico@hotmail.com. 100 m from lake, sleep 2-6, TV, heating, kitchenette, parking.
B Hotel-Yachting Kiel, Koerner 153, T045-411631, www. yachtingkiel.cl. All rooms with lake views, clean, friendly, rooms with bath, cable TV and heating. Restaurant. Good value.
B-C La Torre Suiza, Bilbao 969, T045-411213, www.torresuiza.com. F per person in dorms. Some rooms with bath. Excellent breakfast, kitchen and laundry facilities, camping, cycle rental, book exchange. Lots of info. German, English spoken. Recommended.
C Villa Linda, Pedro de Valdivia 678, T045-411392. F singles. Hot water, clean, basic, cheap, good restaurant.
C-D Chilepeppers, Vicente Reyes 546, T045-414694, www.chilepeppers.cl. F per person in dorms. Lively backpackers' hostel with basic cramped dorms. Kitchen facilities, internet, barbeque area.
C-D Hospedaje Nicolás, Anfion Muñoz 477, T045-410232. F singles. Basic rooms with

cable TV and bath. With breakfast. Good value, although the walls are thin. One of several on Muñoz 400 and 500 blocks.

D Chito Fuentes, Vicente Reyes 665, T045-411595. **F** singles. Basic rooms above a restaurant.

C-D Señora Nelly, Aviador Acevedo 725, T045-412299. **F** singles. Hot water all day, good value, camping, recommended.

F-G Residencial San Francisco, Julio Zegers 646. Price per person in dormitories. There are also rooms in private homes usually **C**, or **F** singles; several on Koerner 300 block and O'Higgins 700 and 800 blocks.

Camping

Many sites east of town on Pucón road, but these are expensive and open in season only. It may be cheaper to stay in a *hospedaje*; those nearest to town are **El Edén**, 1 km southeast of centre, T045-412772, US$6 per person, recommended, and **Los Castaños**, T045-412330, US$15 per site.

Pucón *p317, map p318*

Rooms may be hard to find in high season (Dec-Feb) but there are plenty of alternatives in Villarrica. There are also rooms in private houses – look for the signs or ask in bars/restaurants. Price codes are based on high season rates; off season prices are 20-40% lower and it's often possible to negotiate.

LL Antumalal, 2 km west, T045-441011, www.antumalal.com. Very small, picturesque Bauhaus chalet-style, set in 5 ha of parkland, magnificent views of the lake, tennis court, lovely gardens, excellent, with meals, open year round, pool.

LL-L Del Lago, Ansorena 23, T045-291000, www.hoteldellago.cl. Large 5-star on the plaza, pool, health suite, casino, cinema.

LL-L Gran Hotel Pucón, Holzapfel 190, T045-913300, www.granhotelpucon.cl. Restaurant, disco, sports centre. Some rooms have beautiful lake views, although the hotel, once Pucón's best, has seen better days. Shared with **Condiminio Gran Hotel** apartments.

L Interlaken, Caupolicán 720, T045-441276, www.hotelinterlaken.cl. Chalets, pool, water-skiing, tours arranged, no restaurant. Recommended.

AL Araucarias, Caupolicán 243, T045-441286, www.araucarias.cl. Clean, comfortable, indoor pool and spa, wifi area.

AL-A Gudenschwager, Pedro de Valdivia 12, T045-442025, www.hogu.cl. Refurbished 1920s hotel. 20 simple centrally heated rooms some with lake and volcano view. Much cheaper rooms with exterior bathroom. Also good rates off season. Living room with big screen TV and Wi-Fi area. Large breakfast included. Meals served (special needs catered for). English spoken.

AL-A La Posada Plaza-Pucón, Valdivia 191, T045-441088, www.hotelplazapucon.cl. Pleasant rooms with bath, , restaurant, also spacious cabins, gardens and a pool. Cheaper when paying in dollars.

A-B Hostal Gerónimo, Alderete 665, T045-443762, www.geronimo.cl. Recently refurbished. Rooms with bath and cable TV. Comfortable, friendly, quiet, with restaurant, bar and terrace. Recommended.

A Kernayel, 1 km east at Camino International 1510, T045-442164, www.kernayel.cl. 8 rooms with bath heating and cable TV and more expensive *cabañas*, pool, comfortable, but nothing special.

B La Tetera, Urrutia 580, T045-441462, www.tetera.cl. Rooms with and without bath. Good breakfast with real coffee, English spoken, good Spanish classes, book swap, lots of information. Recommended, book in advance.

B-C Hostal Willy, Arauco 565, T045-444578, www.hostalyturismowilly.com. **E** singles. Pleasant carpeted and heated rooms with cable TV and spacious bathrooms. Breakfast available, internet, use of kitchen. Friendly, information given, good value, recommended.

B-C Hostería école, Urrutia 592, T045-441675, www.ecole.cl. **F** per person in dorms without breakfast, some rooms with bath, good vegetarian and fish restaurant, ecological shop, forest treks, rafting, biking, information, language classes, massage, recommended.

C Hospedaje M@yra, Colo Colo 485, T045-442745, www.myhostelpucon.com. **F** singles. Some rooms with bath and cable TV. Kitchen facilities, internet, laundry, parking, information, tours offered. Good backpackers' hostel. Recommended.

C Hospedaje Victor, Palguín 705, T045-443525, www.pucon.com/victor. **F** singles. Some rooms with bath. Kitchen facilities, TV, laundry. Friendly. A decent choice.

C Hostal Backpackers, Palguín 695, T045-441373, hostal@politur.com. Kitchen facilities, internet, cycle hire, information, 10% discount on Politur excursions.

C Hostal Puerto Parque Tinquilco, Arauco 171, www.parquehuerquehue.cl. **E** singles, some with bath. Central location, use of kitchen, internet, also at Parque Huerquehue (see below).

C Residencial Lincoyán, Av Lincoyán 323, T045-441144, www.lincoyan.cl. **E** singles. With bath, cheaper without, clean and comfortable.

C Tr@vel Pucón, Blanco Encalada 190, T045-444093, www.interpatagonia.com/travelpucon. **F** singles. English, German, French spoken, near Turbus terminal, garden, kitchen facilities, Spanish classes.

C-D Hospedaje Graciela, Pasaje Rolando Matus 521 (off Av Brasil). **F** singles. Comfortable rooms, good food.

C-D Hospedaje Lucía, Lincoyán 565, T045-441721. **F** singles. Friendly, quiet, garden, recommended, cooking facilities.

C-D Hospedaje Sonia, Lincoyán 485, T045-441269, www.myhostelpucon.com/sonia. **F** singles. Basic but clean rooms, some with bath. Use of kitchen, noisy and somewhat crowded, friendly. Basic English spoken.

Camping

You should buy supplies in Villarrica where they are cheaper.

Ainoha, 12 blocks north of town centre. Lakeside site.

La Poza, Costanera Geis 769, T045-441435. Hot showers, clean, quiet, good kitchen facilities, open all year. Recommended.

L'etoile, Km 2 towards Volcán Villarrica, T045-442188. Attractive forest site.

Los Boldos, Pasaje Las Rosas. East of town.

Millaray, Km 7 west of Pucón, T045-212336. Lakeside campsite.

Saint John, Km 7 west of Pucón, T045-441165, casilla 154. Beside Lago Villarrica.

Parque Nacional Villarrica p319

There is a refuge without beds 4 km inside the park; it's not secure and is in desperate need of renovation. Below is a campsite with drinking water and toilets.

Lagos Caburga and Colico p320

L-AL Trailanqui, 20 km west of Lago Colico (35 km north of Villarrica), T045-578218, www.trailanqui.com. Luxurious hotel on the riverbank, with suites and restaurant, also fully equipped cabañas, campsite, horse riding and golf course.

C Hostería Los Robles, 3 km from Caburga village, T045-236989. Lovely views, good restaurant; also campsite, expensive in season, but cheap out of season.

B Landhaus San Sebastián, east of Lago Caburga, F045-1972360, www.landhaus-chile.com. With bath and breakfast, tasty meals, laundry facilities, good walking base, English and German spoken, Spanish classes.

Camping

The southern end of Lago Caburga is lined with campsites, but there are no shops, so take your own food. There are 2 sites about half-way along north shore of Lago Colico:

Quichelmalleu, Km 22 from Cunco, T045-573187.
Ensenada, Km 26, T045-221441.

Parque Nacional Huerquehue *p 320*
B-D Refugio Tinquilco, 3½ km from park entrance, T02-7777673, patriciolanfranco @entelchile.net. Doubles with bath available, meals served, cooking facilities, heating.
C Braatz and Soldans, southern end of Lago Tinquilco near the park entrance. 2 German-speaking families offer accommodation, no electricity, food and camping (US$6); they also rent rowing boats on the lake.
C Hostal Carlos Alfredo Richard, southwest shore of Lago Tinquilco, 2 km from park entrance, parque_huerquehue@hotmail. com. Breakfast included. Large rooms, private bathrooms with hot water, restaurant, rowboats for hire.

Camping
There are 2 campsites at the park entrance, US$10, but no camping is allowed in the park.

Termas de Quimey-Co, de Huife and los Pozones *p 321*
L Hostería Termas de Huife, Termas de Huife, T045-1975666, www.termashuife.cl. The most upmarket of the spa hotels.
A Hotel Termas de Quimey-Co, Termas de Quimey-Co, T045-441903, www.termas quimeyco.com. Also a campsite and 2 cabins.

Towards Argentina *p321*
AL Termas de San Luis, T045-443965, www.sanluis.pucon.com. *Cabañas* with TV, heating, sauna, restaurant. Pickup service for hotel guests from Pucón. Cheaper in pesos than in dollars. Extra for full board.
A-F Cabañas La Tranquera, Puesco. Cabins for 6, also dormitory accommodation, restaurant, campsite.
B Hotel Termas de Panqui, T049-94436741, panquihotsprings@hotmail.com. **D** singles. in rooms or tepees that sleep 3. Also camping facilities. Breakfast extra. Good vegetarian meals, trekking, aromatherapy, English spoken.
C Kila Leufu, Km 20, Pucón-Curarrehue road, T09-97118064, www.kilaleufu.cl. **F** per person in shared rooms. Rooms on the

Lake District Lago Villarrica & around Listings

HOTEL
ANTUMALAL
PUCON · CHILE

Located at 2 kms from Pucón.
Lake side setting.
Panoramic Views of Lake.
Fire place in all the rooms
5 acre private park
Swimming Pool, Tennis court,
Privet Beach &
Docks in premises
Personal Activity Coordination

Tel: 56-45-441011
Fax: 56-45-441013
info@antumalal.com
www.antumalal.com

Martínez family farm, contact daughter Margot in advance, friendly, English spoken, full board available including spit-roast lamb in the *ruca* and other home-grown food, also offers trekking information, horse riding and mountain bike hire, camping possible. Recommended.

B Rancho de Caballos, 36 km southeast of Pucón on the dirt road to Coñaripe, T045-441575. Restaurant with vegetarian dishes, laundry and kitchen facilities; also *cabañas* and camping, self-guided trails, horse riding excursions US$70 per day, English and German spoken, recommended.

Camping

There is a CONAF campsite at Puesco and another, 5 km from the frontier near Lago Tromen, free, no facilities.

Eating

For eating options in the national parks and lakes east of Pucón, see Sleeping above.

Villarrica *p316, map p317*
El Tabor, Epulef 1187, T045-411901. Excellent but pricey.
La Cava del Roble, Valentin Letelier 658, piso 2, T045-416446. Excellent grill. Specializes in exotic meat and game. Extensive wine list. Recommended.
El Rey de Mariscos, Letelier 1030. Good seafood.
Hotel Yandaly, Henríquez 401. Good food. Recommended.
Rapa Nui, Vicente Reyes 678. Good and cheap end of the range, closed Sun.
The Travellers, Letelier 753, T045-413617. Varied menu including vegetarian and Asian food, bar, English spoken.
Café 2001, Henríquez 379. Coffee and ice cream, good.
Casa Vieja, Letelier y Muñoz. Good value set lunch. Family run, friendly.
Chito Fuentes, Reyes 665. Chilean fast food.

Pucón *p317, map p318*
For other options, see Sleeping above. Vegetarians should check out the delicatessen at O'Higgins y Fresia, which serves fresh vegetarian food. New boutique restaurants open every year along Fresia, while there are several cheap restaurants around the junction of Urrutia and Ansorena.
Ana María, O'Higgins 865, T045-444288. Classic Chilean food including game and seafood.
En Alta Mar, Urrutia y Fresia. Fish and seafood, very good.
Puerto Pucón, Fresia 251. One of Pucón's older restaurants. Spanish, stylish.
La Buonatesta, Fresia 243, T045-441434. Pucón's original pizzeria. Good, but a little on the expensive side.
La Maga, Fresia 125, T045-444277. Uruguayan Parillada serving possibly the best steak in Chile. So good that imitations have opened up beside it to take the overspill.
Senzo, Fresia 284, T045-449005. Fresh pasta and risotto prepared by a swiss chef.
Arabian, Fresia 354-B, T045-443469. Arab specialities – stuffed vine leaves, falafel etc.
El Refugio, Lincoyán 348. Some vegetarian dishes, expensive wine.
il Baretto, Fresia 124, T045-443515. Stone-baked pizzas. Relatively good value.
Rap Hamburguesa, O'Higgins 625. Freshly made hamburgers, chips and Chilean fast food. Open late.

Cafés

Also try **Hostería école**, see Sleeping above.
Café de la P, O'Higgins y Lincoyán. Real coffee.
Holzapfel Backerei, Holzapfel 524. German café. Recommended.
Patagonia Express, Fresia 223. Chocolates, ice creams, pancakes and snacks as well as coffee.

Bars and clubs

Pucón *p317, map p318*
El Bosque, O'Higgins 524. Lively bar with occasional live jazz music. Wide range of wines and cocktails. Also serves good food. At weekends in summer, there are discos 2-3 km east of town, near the airport:
Kamikaze and **La Playa**. There are several more discotheques in the same area.
Mamas and Tapas, O'Higgins y Arauco. Drink and snacks. There are several others on O'Higgins.

● Entertainment

There is a cinema open to the general public in the Hotel del Lago and occasional concerts in summer.

● Festivals and events

Villarrica *p316, map p317*
Jan-Feb Many events are organized, including music, regattas, rodeo and the Festival Cultural Mapuche, with a market, based around the Muestra Cultural Mapuche, usually in 2nd week of Feb.

Pucón *p317, map p318*
Feb Pucón is home to an international triathlon competition every year.

○ Shopping

Pucón *p317, map p318*
There is a large handicraft market just south of O'Higgins on Ansorena. The local specialities are painted wooden flowers. Camping equipment is available at **Eltit Supermarket**, O'Higgins y Fresia, and from **Outdoors and Travel**,Lincoyán 361. **Pucon Express** , O'Higgins y Colo Colo, is a 24-hr supermarket.

▲ Activities and tours

Villarrica *p316, map p317*
Prices are fairly standard: to **Parque Nacional Villarrica**, US$18; to climb **Volcán Villarrica**, US$40-50; to **Valdivia** US$45; to **Termas de Coñaripe** US$30.
Karina Tour, Letelier 825, T045-412048.
Politur, Henríquez 475, T045-414547. Recommended.
Turismo Coñaripe, P Montt 525, T045-411111.
Vuelatour, Camilo Henríquez 430 local 1, T045-415766. General tour agency. Trips to thermal springs etc, **Navimag, Lan Chile** agent, airport transfer, car hire.

Pucón *p317, map p318*
Canopy
Several agencies offer canopy tours – ziplining from treetop to treetop in native forests. **Bosque Aventura**, O'Higgins 615, T09-93254795, www.canopypucon.cl. Has

one of the longest runs as well as being the most responsible safety-wise.

Fishing

Pucón and Villarrica are celebrated as bases for fishing on Lago Villarrica and on the beautiful Lincura, Trancura and Toltén rivers. The local tourist office will supply details on licences and open seasons etc. Some tourist agencies also offer trips as well as fly-fishing classes. Prices although not cheap are much more reasonable than further south.
Mario's Fishing Zone, O'Higgins 580, T045-444259, www.pucon.com/fishing. Expensive, but good fishing guide.
Off Limits, O'Higgins 560, T045-442681, www.offlimits.cl. Fishing specialists, English and Ialian spoken, offer fly-fishing excursions and courses between half and three days. Recommended. Birdwatching trips also offered as well as cycle hire.

Horse riding

Horse hire is about US$40 half day, US$70 full day; enquire at **La Tetera** in Pucón, or try **Rancho de Callabos** at the Termas de Palguín; for both see Sleeping above.
Centro de Turismo Ecuestre Huepil-Malal, T09-96432673, www.huepil-malal.cl. Small groups, excursions ranging from half-day to 11-day trips to Argentina.

Mountaineering
Outdoor Experience, Urrutia, next to Hostal école, T045-442809, www.outdoorexperience.org. Runs mountaineering trips for people of all levels. Experienced guides. It also organizes excursions to the Cañi nature reserve (see below).

Skiing
Pucón resort, 35 mins from Pucón on the slopes of the Villarrica Volcano, T045-441901, www.skipucon.cl. The resort is owned by **Gran Hotel Pucón**, which can provide information on snow, ski lifts and, perhaps, transport; otherwise consult the tourist office in Pucón. There are 8 lifts (day ticket US$23-33, depending on the season, US$7 to the restaurant only), though rarely do more than 2 or 3 work and piste preparation is mediocre. The snow is generally soft and good for beginners, though more advanced skiers can try the steeper areas. The season

runs from mid-July to mid-Sep (longer during exceptionally good years). The ski centre offers equipment rental (US$20 per day, US$110 per week), ski instruction, first aid, and has a restaurant and bar with wonderful views from the terrace.

Tour operator

Travel Aid, Ansorena 425 local 4, T045-444040, www.travelaid.cl. Helpful general travel agency selling trekking maps, guidebooks, lots of other information, agents for **Navimag** and other boat trips. English and German spoken.

White water rafting and Volcán Villarrica trek

Most operators can arrange a variety of trips, including climbing Villarrica, 12 hrs, US$55-70 including park entry, equipment provided; ski hire and transport to slopes US$25 per person; tours to Termas de Huife, US$25 including entry. Whitewater rafting, Trancura bajo (basic, Grade II-III) US$25, Trancura alto (advanced, Grade III-IV) US$40. Shop around, prices vary, as well as the quality of guides and equipment. Unfortunately, while several agencies offer acceptable levels of service, none is exceptional. To reach the falls, lakes and termasit is cheaper for groups to flag down a taxi and negotiate a price. Also try **Hostería école**, see Sleeping above.
Aguaventura, Palguín 336, T045-444246, www.aguaventura.com. French-run kayaking and rafting specialists.
Anden Sport, O'Higgins 535, T045-441475, www.andensport.cl. Skiing specialists, but also do volcano trips, etc. Slightly disorganized.
Enjoy Tour, Ansorena 123, T045-442303, www.enjoytour.cl. Owned by the upmarket **Hotel del Lago**. Prices are slightly above average, but equipment is generally first rate.
Politur, O'Higgins635, T045-441373, www.politur.com. Good for volcano trek and rafting. A little more expensive than most, but generally responsible.
Ronco Track, O'Higgins 615, esq Arauco, T045-449597, roncotrack@hotmail.com. Small group quadbike excursions from 1½ hrs to 1½ days. Good fun. Also hires out good quality bicycles.
Sol y Nieve O'Higgins, esq Lincoyán, T/F045-441070, www.solynieve.cl. Previously held in high esteem, with guides and equipment, but now some mixed reports about organization. Most guides speak English.
Spirit Palguín 323, T/F045-442481, www.spiritexplora.com. Offers the usual tours as well as diving and canyoning.
Sur Expediciones, O'Higgins 615. One of the better agencies for the volcano trip.
Trancura, O'Higgins 211, T045-443436, www.trancura.com. The biggest agency in Pucón with several branches. Very competitive prices but lax safety record. Recommended for trips to thermal springs but not for any sort of adventure tourism.

Watersports

Equipment for water-skiing (US$13 for 15 mins), dinghy sailing (lasers US$16 per hr) and windsurfing (sailboards US$13 per hr) can be hired in summer at Playa Grande, the beach by the **Gran Hotel**. Rowing boats can also be hired for US$6 per hr. The outlets on La Poza beach are more expensive and not recommended.

Parque Nacional Villarrica p319

Tours from Pucón cost US$40-50, including park entry, guide, transport to park entrance and hire of equipment (no reduction for those with their own equipment). Bargain for group rates. Travel agencies will not start out if the weather is bad and some travellers have experienced difficulties in obtaining a refund: establish in advance what terms apply in the event of cancellation and be prepared to wait a few days. For information on individual guides, all with equipment, ask for recommendations at the tourist office.

Reserva Forestal Cañi p321

Outdoor Experience, Urrutia, next to Hostal école, T045-442809, www.outdoorexper ience.org. Offers good tours of the area.
Hostería école, see Sleeping above. Also offers good tours.

⊖ Transport

Villarrica p316, map p317
Bus

The main terminal is at Pedro de Valdiva y Muñoz; **JAC** has 2 terminals, at Muñoz y Bilbao (long-distance) and opposite for Pucón and Lican-Ray (local). Other services leave from the **Terminal Rural**, Matta y Vicente Reyes.

Buses to **Santiago**, 10 hrs, US$11, several companies; to **Pucón**, both **Vipu-Ray** (main terminal) and **JAC**, every 15 mins in summer, 40-min journey, US$1; to **Puerto Montt**, US$8; to **Valdivia**, JAC, 5 a day, 2½ hrs, US$5; to **Lican-Ray** services in summer, JAC and Vipu-Ray, US$1.50; to **Coñaripe**, US$2, and **Liquiñe** at 1600 Mon-Sat, 1000 Sun; to **Temuco**, JAC, every 30 mins in summer, US$4; to **Loncoche** (Route 5 junction for hitching), US$2. There are also occasional direct buses to **Panguipulli**, via Lican Ray.

To Argentina Buses from Temuco to Junín stop in Villarrica en route to the Tromen Pass; fares are the same as from Temuco, see page 315. If the Tromen pass is blocked by snow buses go via the paso Carirriñe instead of via Villarrica and Pucón.

Car/bicycle
Car hire from **Christopher Car**, Pedro de Valdivia 1061, T/045-F413980; **Castillo Propiedades**, Anfion Muñoz 417, good value. Bike hire from **Mora Bicicletas**, Körner 760, helpful.

Pucón p317, map p318
Air
Lan Express flies to **Santiago**, 4 times weekly in summer. **LanChile**, Urrutia 103 y Caupolican, T045-443516, Mon-Sat 1000-1400, 1800-2200.

Bus
There is no municipal terminal; each company has its own: **JAC**, Uruguay y Palguín; **Tur Bus**, O'Higgins 910, east of town; **Igi Llaima** and **Condor**, Colo Colo south of O'Higgins.

JAC has services to **Villarrica**, every 15 mins, US$1; to **Valdivia**, JAC, 5 daily, US$6; to **Temuco** hourly, 2 hrs, US$4, or rápido, 1½ hrs, US$5; to **Puerto Montt**, 6 hrs, US$9, daily with **Tur Bus**, or change at Valdivia. To **Santiago**, morning and evening, 10 hrs, US$12; salón cama service by **Tur Bus** and JAC, US$33.

To Argentina Buses from Temuco to **San Martín** arrive in Pucón 1000; fares are the same as from Temuco, see page 315. If the Tromen pass is blocked by snow buses

go via the paso Carirriñe instead of via Villarrica and Pucón.

Taxi
Cooperative, T045-441009.

Lagos Caburga and Colico p320
JAC runs buses from Pucón to **Caburga**, several daily, US$1.50; there are also minibuses every 30 mins from Ansorena y Uruguayin Pucón; a taxi day trip costs US$25 return.

Parque Nacional Huerquehue p320
JAC buses from Pucón, 3 daily in summer, 2 in winter, 1½ hrs, US$2. Tour agencies arrange transport for groups, US$10. Taxis cost US$40 return. Minibuses from Ansorena y Brasil.

Termas de Quimey-Co, de Huife and los Pozones p321
A taxi from Pucón costs US$30 return, US$20 one way; **Hostería Termas de Huife** has its own transport and will pick people up from Pucón.

Towards Argentina p321
Several minibuses daily to Curarrehue from Pucón. Daily bus from Pucón to border, 1800, 2 hrs, US$3. To Pucón 0700.

ⓘ Directory

Villarrica p316, map p317
Banks There are ATMs at **Banco BCI**, Pedro de Valdivia y Alderete; **Banco de Chile**, Pedro de Valdiva y Pedro Montt; **Banco Santander**, Pedro de Valdiva 778. In general, rates through casas de cambio are poor. **Carlos Huerta**, Muñoz 417; **Central de Repuestos**, Muñoz 415, good rates; **Cristopher**, Valdivia 1061, good rates for Tcs; **Turcamb**, Henríquez 570, poor rates for TCs.
Internet Cybercafé Salmon, Letelier y Henríquez. **Laundry** Lavacenter, Alderete 770; Lavandería y Lavaseco Villarrica, Andrés Bello 348; Todo Lavado, Urrutia 669.
Post office Muñoz y Urrutia, open Mon-Fri 0900-1300, 1430-1800, Sat 0900-1300.
Telephone CTC, Henríquez 544; Chilesat, Henríquez 473; Entel, Henríquez 440 and 575.

Banks There are 3 or 4 banks with ATMs on o'Higgins. Several casas de cambio on O'Higgins, although rates are universally poor. Much better to change money in Temuco. **Bicycle hire** US$1.50 per hr or US$10 per day from several travel agencies, many on O'Higgins; shop around as quality varies. **Car hire** Prices start at US$27 per day; Christopher Car, O'Higgins 335, T/F045-449013; Hertz, Fresia 220, T045-441664, more expensive; same prices per day at Gran Hotel; Pucón Rent A Car, Camino Internacional 1395, T045-441922, kernayel@cepri.cl; Sierra Nevada, Palguín y O'Higgins, cars and 4WDs, reasonable. **Internet** Several on O'Higgins. **Laundry** atUrrutia 520; Palguín 460; Fresia 224; Colo-Colo 475and 478, several others. All close for 2 hrs for lunch. **Post office** Fresia 183. **Telephone** CTC, Gral Urrutia 472; Entel, Ansorena 299.

The Seven Lakes → *Colour map 4, B2.*

This group of lakes, situated south of Lago Villarrica, provides a beautiful necklace of water, surrounded by thick woods and with views of distant snows giving a picture-postcard backdrop. Six of the lakes lie in Chile, with the seventh, Lago Lacár, in Argentina. After the final peace settlement of 1882 the area around these lakes was reserved for Mapuche settlements. The southernmost lake, Lago Riñihue, is most easily reached from Valdivia and Los Lagos and is dealt with in a later section (see page 340). Most of the lakes have black-sand beaches, although in spring, as the water level rises, these can all but disappear. ▸▸ *For Sleeping, Eating and other listings, see pages 334-335.*

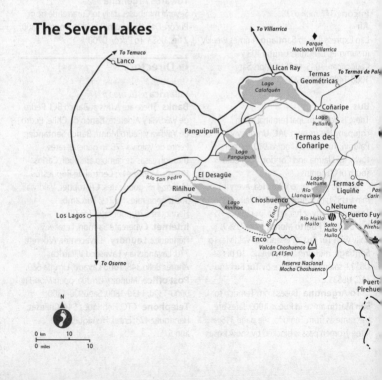

The Seven Lakes

Lago Calafquén ⊟🏊🏕🚌 ➤ pp334-335.

The most northerly of the seven lakes, Lago Calafquén is a popular tourist destination for Chileans, readily accessible by a paved road from Villarrica, along which there are fine views of the Volcán Villarrica. Wooded and dotted with small islands, the lake is reputedly one of the warmest in the region and is good for swimming. A mostly paved road runs around the lake.

Lican-Ray

Situated 30 km south of Villarrica on a peninsula on the north shore, Lican-Ray is the major resort on the lake and is named after a legendary Mapuche woman (see page 333). There are two beaches, one on each side of the peninsula. Boats can be hired ① US$3 per hr, and there are **catamaran trips** ① US$5 per hr or US$18 to the islands. Although crowded in season, Lican-Ray can feel like a ghost town by the end of March, when most facilities have closed. Some 6 km to the east is the river of lava formed when Volcán Villarrica erupted in 1971. There is a **tourist office** on the plaza ① daily in summer, Mon-Fri in winter.

Coñaripe

Lying 21 km southeast of Lican-Ray at the eastern end of Lago Calafquén, Coñaripe is another popular Chilean tourist spot. At first sight the village is dusty and nondescript, but its setting, with a black-sand beach surrounded by mountains, is beautiful. Most services are on the Calle Principal. The **tourist office** on the plaza ① mid Nov-mid Apr daily; late Apr-early Nov Sat and Sun only, can arrange trips to local thermal springs.

From Coñaripe a road (mostly ripio) around the lake's southern shore leads to **Lago Panguipulli**, see below, 38 km west, and offers superb views over Volcán Villarrica, which can be climbed from here. Another dirt road heads northeast through the Parque Nacional Villarrica to Pucón, see page 317; high-clearance vehicles only.

ARGENTINA

To Junín de los Andes

Parque Nacional Lanín

To Junín de los Andes

Paso Huahum

Lago Lascar

San Martín de los Andes

Southeast of Coñaripe

From Coñaripe a road runs southeast over the steep Cuesta Los Añiques offering views of **Lago Pellaifa**, a tiny lake with rocky surroundings covered with vegetation and a small beach. **Termas de Coñaripe** ① Km 16, 2 km from the lakeshore, T063-411407, www.termasconaripe.cl, has four pools, accommodation, restaurant, cycles and horses for hire.

Further south are the **Termas de Liquiñe** ① Km 32, T/F063-317377, US$6-10 per person, with eight thermal springs and accommodation (but little other infrastructure), surrounded by a small native forest. About 8 km north of Liquiñe is a road going southwest for 20 km along the southeast shore of **Lago Neltume** to meet the Choshuenco-Puerto Fuy road.

The **Paso Carirriñe** across the Argentine border ① open 15 Oct-31 Aug, is reached by unpaved road from the Termas de Liquiñe. On the Argentine side the road continues to San Martín de los Andes.

Lake District The Seven Lakes

Lago Panguipulli ➤ *pp334-335.*

Covering 116 sq km, Lago Panguipulli, the largest of the seven lakes, is reached either by paved road from Lanco or Los Lagos on the Pan-American Highway or by *ripio* roads from Lago Calafquén. A road leads along the beautiful northern shore, which is wooded with sandy beaches and cliffs, but most of the lake's southern shore is inaccessible by road.

Panguipulli

The site of a Mapuche settlement, Panguipulli, meaning 'hill of pumas', is situated on a hillside at the northwest corner of the lake. It grew as a railway terminal and a port for vessels carrying timber from the lakesides, and is now the largest town in the area.

On Plaza Prat is the **Iglesia San Sebastián**, built in Swiss style with twin towers by the Swiss Padre Bernabé; its belltower contains three bells from Germany. By the plaza there iss a **tourist office** ① *Dec-Feb daily, otherwise week days only, T063-310435, www.panguipulli.cl.*

From Plaza Prat the main commercial street, Martínez de Rozas, runs down to the lakeshore. In summer, catamaran trips are offered on the lake and excursions can be made to Lagos Calafquén, Neltume, Pirehueico and to the northern tip of Lago Riñihue, see page 340. The road east to Coñaripe, on Lago Calafquén, offers superb views of the lake and of Volcán Villarrica.

Choshuenco and around

Choshuenco lies 45 km east of Panguipulli on the Río Llanquihue, at the eastern tip of the lake and can only be reached by road from Panguipulli or Puerto Fuy. To the south

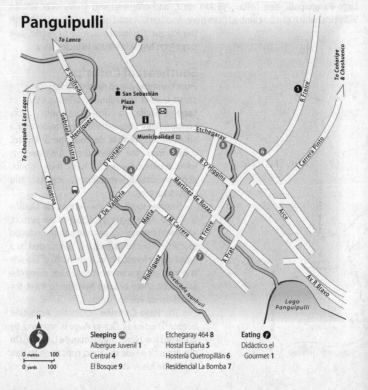

Panguipulli

To Lanco
To Chauquén & Los Lagos
To Coñaripe & Choshuenco

San Sebastián
Plaza Prat
Municipalidad

P Sigifredo
Gabriela Mistral
Henríquez
C Figueroa
D Portales
P De Valdivia
Matta
J M Carrera
R Freire
Rodríguez
Quebrada Nanhuil
Etchegaray
B O'Higgins
Martínez de Rozas
A Prat
Arce
I Carrera Pinto
R Freire
Av R Bravo

Lago Panguipulli

N

| 0 metres | 100 |
| 0 yards | 100 |

Sleeping
Albergue Juvenil **1**
Central **4**
El Bosque **9**

Etchegaray 464 **8**
Hostal España **5**
Hostería Quetropillán **6**
Residencial La Bomba **7**

Eating
Didáctico el
Gourmet **1**

⁞ The legend of Lican-Ray

At the height of the wars between the Spanish and the Mapuche a young Spanish soldier lost the rest of his unit and strayed into the forests near Lago Calafquén. Suddenly he saw a beautiful young Mapuche woman drying her hair in the sun and singing. As he did not want to frighten her he made himself visible at a distance and began to sing along. Singing, smiling and exchanging glances, they fell in love. She called him Allumanche, which means white man in Mapuche, and, pointing to herself, indicated that her name was Lican Rayan, meaning the flower of magic stone. They began to live together near the lake.

Lican Rayan's father, Curtilef, a powerful and fearsome chief, feared she might be dead. One day a boy came to him and said: "Lican Rayan is alive. I have seen her near the lake with a white man but she is not a prisoner: it is clear they are in love".

Lican Rayan saw the warriors coming to look for her. Knowing her father she feared what might happen, so she persuaded the soldier that they should flee. They escaped by riding on logs to one of the islands. There they felt safe, but they could not light a fire against the cold because the smoke would give them away. The weather grew cooler, the north wind blew and it rained heavily. After several days, unable to bear the cold and thinking that the warriors would have given up the search, they lit a fire. The smoke was spotted by Curtilef's men, so Lican Rayan and the solider fled to another island further away but again they were discovered and had to escape. This happened so many times that, although they were never caught, they were never seen again.

In the town of Lican-Ray, it is said that on spring afternoons it is sometimes possible to see a distant column of smoke from one of the islands, where Lican Rayan and the soldier are still enjoying their love after over 400 years.

Abridged and translated from *Lengua Y Costumbres Mapuches* by Orietta Appelt Martin, Imprenta Austral, Temuco, 1995.

is the **Reserva Nacional Mocho Choshuenco** (7536 ha), which includes two volcanoes: Choshuenco (2415 m) and Mocha (2422 m). On the slopes of Choshuenco the **Club Andino de Valdivia** runs a small ski resort and three *refugios*. (The resort is reached by a turning from the road that goes south from Choshuenco to Enco at the east end of Lago Riñihue, see page 340.) From Choshuenco a road leads east to **Neltume** and **Lago Pirehueico**, via the impressive waterfalls of **Huilo Huilo**. The falls are three hours' walk from Choshuenco, or take the Puerto Fuy bus and get off at **Alojamiento Huilo Huilo,** from where it is a five-minute walk to the falls.

Lago Pirehueico ⬤⬤ pp334-335.

Lago Pirehueico is a 36-km long, narrow and deep glacial lake surrounded by virgin *lingue* forest. It is beautiful and largely unspoilt, although there are plans to build a huge tourist complex in Puerto Pirehueico.

There are two ports on the lake: **Puerto Fuy** at the northern end and **Puerto Pirehueico** at the southern end. The ports are linked by a ferry service (the crossing is beautiful; see page 335) and can also be reached by the road that runs east from Neltume to the Argentine border crossing at Paso Huahum. The road south from Puerto Fuy, however, is privately owned and closed to traffic. This is a shame because it is a beautiful route passing around Volcán Choshuenco and through rainforest to Río Pillanleufú, Puerto Llolles on Lago Maihue and Puerto Llifén on Lago Ranco.

Paso Huahum ① *all year, Chilean immigration summer 0800-2100, winter 0800-2000*, is 11 km southeast of Puerto Pirehueico. On the Argentine side the road leads alongside Lago Lacar to San Martín de los Andes and Junín de los Andes.

● Sleeping

Lican-Ray *p331*
There are plenty of options along the north shore of Lago Calafquén towards Coñaripe.
B Hospedaje Los Nietos, Manquel 125, T045-431078. Without breakfast.
B Hostería Inaltulafquen, Casilla 681, Playa Grande, T045-431115, F410028.With breakfast and bath, English spoken.
C Cabañas Cacique Vitacura, Urrutia 825, Playa Grande, T02-2355302, tradesic@inter media.cl. For 2, also larger cabins with kitchen.
C-D Residencial Temuco, G Mistral 515, Playa Grande, T045-431130. **F** singles, with breakfast. Clean, without bath, good.

Camping
There are also 6 sites just west of town.
Foresta, ½ km east of town, T045-211954. Sites for up to 6 people.
Prado Verde,1 km east of town, T045-431161.

Coñaripe *p331*
A Entre Montañas, on the Plaza, T063-408300. Overpriced, poor food.
C Hospedaje Chumay, on Plaza, T063-317287 turismochumay@hotmail.com. **F** singles. Restaurant, internet, tours.

Camping
There are campsites on both north and south sides of the lake, US$15 per site. Free camping is possible on the beach outside town.
Isla Llancahue, 5 km east, T063-317360. Camp- site with cabañason an island in Río Llancahue.

Southeast of Coñaripe *p331*
AL Termas de Liquiñe, Km 32 , T/F063-317377. Price per person, full board, cabins, restaurant, tours offered. There is also accommodation in private houses.

Panguipulli *p332, map p332*
B Hostal España, O'Higgins 790, T063-311166, hostal_espana@elsitio.com. Rooms with breakfast.

B Hostería Quetropillán, Etchegaray 381, T063-311348. Comfortable.
C Residencial La Bomba, J M Carrera y R Freire. Quiet.
C Hotel Central, Valdivia 115, T063-311331/ 09-98823955. **F** singles. Clean, breakfast.
C Etchegaray 464. **F** singles. Clean, good breakfast. Reduced rates for longer stays.
C Hospedaje Familiar, Los Ulmos 62, T063-311483. **F** singles. English and German spoken, kitchen facilities, helpful, good breakfast.
F-G Albergue Juvenil, Gabriela Mistral 1112, T063-311282. Youth hostel opposite bus terminal. Price per person.

Camping
There are also 3 sites at Chauquén, 6 km southeast on the lakeside.
Camping Lago Riñihue, T063-461344, F063-461111.
El Bosque, P Sigifredo 241, T063-311489. Clean, hot water.

Choshuenco and around *p332*
C Hostería Rayen Trai, María Alvarado y O'Higgins. **F** singles. Former yacht club serving good food, open all year.
C Hostería Ruca Pillán, San Martín 85, T063-318220, rucapi@telsur.cl. **F** singles. English spoken, tours.
C-D Choshuenco, Bernabé s/n, T063-318214. **F** singles. Run-down but clean, good meals.
C-D Restaurant Robles, in Neltume, east of Choshuenco. **F** singles without bath.
D Alojamiento Huilo Huilo, Huilo Huilo, near Neltume. **F-G** singles. Basic but comfortable and well situated for walks.

Lago Pirehueico*p333*
Beds are available in private houses, and free camping is possible on the beach.
D Hospedaje Pirehueico Puerto Pirehueico. **F-G** singles.
D Restaurant Puerto Fuy, Puerto Fuy. **F** singles. Cold water, good restaurant.

🍴 Eating

For eating options in Coñaripe, Choshuenco and around, see Sleeping, above.

Lican-Ray *p331*
🍴-🍴 **Café Ñaños**, Urrutia 105. Very good, reasonable prices, helpful owner.
🍴-🍴 **Restaurant-Bar Guido's**, Urrutia 405. Good value.
🍴 **Coyote**, on the plaza. Cheap, open off season.

Panguipulli *p332, map p332*
There are cheap restaurants on O'Higgins 700 block.
🍴 **Didáctico El Gourmet**, Ramón Freire s/n. Restaurant linked to a professional hotel school. Excellent food and wine, mid price but high quality, open in school terms only.
🍴-🍴 **Café Central**, M de Rozas 750. Good cheap lunches, expensive evening meals.
🍴-🍴 **El Chapulín**, M de Rozas 639. Good food, good value, friendly.

🎉 Festivals and events

Panguipulli *p332, map p332*
Last week of Jan La Semana de Rosas, with dancing and sports competitions.

🧭 Activities and tours

Coñaripe *p331*
Hospedaje Chumay, see Sleeping, above, organizes hikes to Villarica volcano and trips to various thermal springs.

Panguipulli *p332, map p332*
Fishing
The following fishing trips on Lago Panguipulli are recommended: **Puntilla Los Cipreses** at the mouth of the Río Huanehue, 11 km east of Panguipulli, 30 mins by boat; the mouth of the **Río Niltre**, on east side of lake. Boat hire US$3, licences: the **Municipalidad**, **Librería Colón**, O'Higgins 528or from the **Club de Pesca**.

Rafting
Good rafting opportunities on the **Río Fuy**, grade IV-V; **Río San Pedro**, varying grades, and on the **Río Llanquihue** near Choshuenco.

🚌 Transport

Lican-Ray *p331*
There is no central **bus** terminal; buses leave from offices around plaza. To **Villarrica**, JAC, frequent, 1 hr, US$1.50; to **Santiago**, Tur Bus and JAC, 11 hrs, US$14, salón cama in summer US$40; to **Temuco**, JAC, 2½ hrs, US$6; to **Coñaripe**, 7 daily (4 off season).

Coñaripe *p331*
Buses run to **Panguipulli**, 7 daily (4 off season), US$2; to **Villarrica**, 16 daily, US$2; to **Lican-Ray**, 45 mins, US$1. Also a nightly bus direct to **Santiago** run by Tur Bus and JAC, 11½ hrs, US$15, salón cama in summer US$40.

Panguipulli *p332, map p332*
The **bus** terminal is at Gabriela Mistral y Portales. To **Santiago** daily, US$15; to **Valdivia**, Mon-Sat, 4 only on Sun, several companies, 2 hrs, US$5; to **Temuco**, frequent, **Power** and **Pangui Sur**, US$5; to **Puerto Montt**, US$8; to **Calafquén**, 3 daily at 1200, 1545 and 1600; to **Choshuenco**, **Neltume** and **Puerto Fuy** (3 hrs), 3 daily, US$4.50; to **Coñaripe**, for connections to Lican-Ray and Villarrica, 7 daily, 4 off season.

Lago Pirehueico *p333*
Bus
Puerto Fuy to **Panguipulli**, 3 daily, 3 hrs, US$4.50; Puerto Pirehueico via Paso Huahum to **San Martín de los Andes**, daily in summer, weekly in winter (out Sat 0930, back Sun 1330).

Ferry
The Hua Hum sails from **Puerto Fuy** across lake to **Puerto Pirehueico**, twice daily in summer, twice a week, other times, 2-3 hrs, foot passengers US$2, cars US$20. For reservations and information see www. panguipulli.cl/pasohuahum/index.html. This is a recommended journey and compares with the famous lakes crossing from Puerto Montt to Bariloche but at a fraction of the price.

📖 Directory

Panguipulli *p332, map p332*
Banks ATM at the BCI, M de Rozas y Matta.

⋮ The 1960 earthquake

Southern Chile is highly susceptible to earthquakes: severe quakes struck the area in 1575, 1737, 1786 and 1837, but the tremor that struck around midday on 22 May 1960 caused the most extensive damage throughout southern Chile and was accompanied by the eruption of four volcanoes and a *maremoto* (tidal wave) that was felt as far away as New Zealand and Japan.

Around Valdivia the land dropped by 3 m, creating new lagunas along the Río Cruces to the north of the clty. The *maremoto* destroyed all the fishing villages and ports between Puerto Saavedra in the north and Chiloé in the south. The earthquake also provoked several landslides. The greatest of these blocked the Río San Pedro, near the point where it drains Lago Riñihue, and the lake, which receives the waters of six other lakes, rose 35 m in 24 hours. Over the next two months all available labour and machinery was used to dig channels to divert the water from the other lakes and to drain off the waters of Lago Riñihue, thus averting the devastation of the San Pedro Valley.

Valdivia and around → *Colour map 4, B2.*

Surrounded by wooded hills, Valdivia is one of the most pleasant cities in southern Chile and a good place to rest after arduous treks in the mountains. In the summer tourist season the city comes to life with activities and events, while off season this is a pleasant verdant city with a thriving café culture. With a high student population (its total population is 127,000), it is also one of the best cities for meeting young Chilenos, who will be at the pulse of anything in the way of nightlife in the city. The city lies nearly 839

km south of Santiago at the confluence of two rivers, the Calle Calle and Cruces, which form the Río Valdivia. To the northwest of the city is a large island, Isla Teja, where the Universidad Austral de Chile is situated. West, along the coast, are a series of important Spanish colonial forts, while to the north are two nature reserves with native forests and a wide range of birdlife. Inland there are two lakes off the beaten tourist path.▶▶ *For Sleeping, Eating and other listings, see pages 341-345.*

Ins and outs

Getting there There are daily flights north to Santiago and Concepción. The bus network is very wide, with numerous daily services to Santiago and south to Puerto Montt, as well as to cities such as Temuco, Pucón, Concepción and Chillán. By road access to the Panamericana is north via Mafil or south via Paillaco.

Valdivia centre

Sleeping 😊	Eating 🍴
Palace 1	Café Haussmann 2
	Camino de Luna 6
	Entrelagos 4

0 metres 100
0 yards 100

Getting around Valdivia is quite sizeable: *colectivos* and buses serve the outlying *barrios*. However, like many Chilean cities, the centre is relatively compact, and few places are beyond walking distance, even those across the river on the Isla Teja.

Tourist information The tourist office ① *Prat 555, by dock, T063-342300, infovaldivia@sernatur.cl, daily in summer, weekdays off season*, has good maps of the region and local rivers, a list of hotel prices and examples of local crafts with artisans' addresses. There's also a **CONAF** office ① *Ismael Váldez 431, T063-218822.*

History

Valdivia was one of the most important centres of Spanish colonial control over Chile. Founded in 1552 by Pedro de Valdivia, it was abandoned as a result of the Mapuche insurrection of 1599 and was briefly occupied by Dutch pirates. In 1645 it was refounded as a walled city and the only Spanish mainland settlement south of the Río Biobío. The Spanish continued to fortify the area around Valdivia throughout the 1600s, developing the most comprehensive system of defence in the South Pacific against the British and Dutch navies. Seventeen forts were built in total. They were reinforced after 1760, but proved of little avail during the Wars of Independence, when the Chilean naval squadron under Lord Cochrane seized control of the forts in two days. From independence until the 1880s Valdivia was an outpost of Chilean rule, reached only by sea or by a coastal route.

Valdivia

The city is centred around the tree-lined **Plaza de la República**. In the cathedral, the **Museo de la Cathedral de Valdivia** ① *Independencia 514, Tue-Sun 1000-1300, 1600-1900 in summer; Mon-Fri 1000-1300, 1600-1900, Sat 1000-1300 in winter*, covers four centuries of Christian history. Three blocks east is the **Muelle Fluvial**, the dock for

Valdivia

Sleeping
A Muñoz 345 **9**
Aires Buenos **13**
Camilo Henríquez 749 **12**
Hospedaje Internacional **5**

Hospedaje Pérez Rosales **1**
Hostal Andwandter **2**
Hostal Casagrande **7**
Hostal Centro Torreón **8**
Hostal Esmeralda **10**
Hostal Prat **16**

Melillanca **14**
Puerta del Sur **3**
Residencial Germania **17**
Villa Beauchef **18**

Eating
Cervecería Kunstmann **2**
La Calesa **1**
Ritual **3**
Sake **4**
Shanghai **5**
Volcán **6**

boat trips down the river. From the Muelle Fluvial there is a pleasant walk north along the *costanera* (Avenida Prat) and under the bridge to Isla Teja and on round the bend in the river (where boats can be hired; US$3.50 per hour) as far as the bus terminal.

On the western bank of the river, **Isla Teja** has a botanical garden and arboretum with trees from all over the world. West of the botanical gardens is the **Parque Saval** ① *open daylight hours, US$0.50*. Covering 30 hectares it has areas of native forest as well as a small lake, the Lago de los Lotos. There are beautiful flowers in spring. Also on the island are two museums. The **Museo Histórico y Antropológico** ① *daily 1000-1300, 1400-1800 in summer; closed Mon off season, US$2*, is beautifully situated in the former mansion of Carlos Andwandter, a leading German immigrant. Run by the university, it contains sections on archaeology, ethnography and German colonization. Next door, in the former Andwandter brewery, is the **Museo de Arte Moderno** ① *Jan-Feb Tue-Sun, 1000-1300, 1400-1800, off season only open for temporary exhibitions, US$2*. Boat trips can be made around Isla Teja, offering views of birds and seals.

Kunstmann Brewery ① *just out of town on the Niebla road, T063-292969, www.cerveza-kunstmann.cl*, offers tours of the working brewery and its beer museum; it also has a good restaurant.

Every Sunday during January and February there is a special **steam train** service ① *departs on Equador 2000, T063-214978, Sun, 1½ hrs, return from Antilhue 2 hrs later, US$5 return, advance booking essential*, to **Antilhue**, 20 km to the east. The train is met by locals selling all sorts of local culinary specialities. The engine dates from 1913. Special additional trips are often made on public holidays; check departure times before travelling.

Along the Río Valdivia → *Colour map 4, B1/2.*

The various rivers around Valdivia are navigable: pleasant journeys can be made by rented motor boat south of town on the Ríos Futa and Tornagaleanes around the **Isla del Rey**, while at the mouth of the Río Valdivia are interesting and isolated villages that can be visited by road or by river boat. The two main centres are **Niebla** on the north bank and **Corral** opposite on the south bank, site of two of the most important 17th-century Spanish forts on the río Valdivia (see History, page 337). There is a frequent boat service between the two towns. In midstream, between Niebla and Corral is **Isla Mancera**, a small island dominated by the Castillo de San Pedro de Alcántara, the earliest of the Spanish forts. Inside the fort there is a small church and convent. The island is a pleasant place to stop over on the boat trips, but it can get crowded when an excursion boat arrives.

Eighteen kilometres west of Valdivia, **Niebla** is a resort with seafood restaurants and accommodation. To the west on a promontory is the **Fuerte de la Pura y Limpia Concepción de Monfort de Lemus** ① *daily in summer 1000-1900, closed Mon in winter, US$1, free on Sun*. It has a museum on Chilean naval history. There's a tourist information office and a telephone office. Around Niebla the north bank is dotted with campsites and *cabañas*. About 6 km further round the coast is **Los Molinos**, a seaside resort set among steep wooded hills. There is a campsite and lots of seaside restaurants including **La Bahía** which has good food but it's not cheap.

Corral lies 62 km west of Valdivia by road and is the main port serving the city. It is much quieter and more pleasant than Niebla, and its fort, **Castillo de San Sebastián**, has a dilapidated, interesting atmosphere. It was built in 1645 as one of the main fortifications on the estuary, and during the 17th century its 3-m thick walls were defended by a battery of 21 guns. Inside is a museum, and in summer re-enactments of the 1820 storming of the Spanish fort by the Chilean Republican forces in period costume are held daily 1200 and 1800. Horses are sometimes found grazing among the ramparts. Entry US$5 Jan-Feb, US$1.50 off season.

Further north near the mouth of the river are pleasant beaches and the remains of two other Spanish colonial forts, the **Castillo San Luis de Alba de Amargos** and the **Castillo de San Carlos**. The coastal walks west and south of Corral, along very isolated and forested roads above the ocean, are splendid and very rarely visited. The friendly tourist office on the pier can provide some trekking information.

North of Valdivia

Some 27 km to the northwest is the **Parque Oncol** ① *To9-96441439, www.parqueoncol.cl, US$1.80, 3 buses weekly, leave early morning; on weekends there is a special service leaving Valdivia 1005, returning 1700, US$7 including park entry, To63-278100 for bookings*. It consists of 754 ha of native Valdivian forest with several trails and lookouts, canopy ziplines, a picnic area and campsite.

Stretching from the outskirts of the city, 30 km north, is the **Santuario de la Naturaleza Carlos Anwandter**, along the Río Cruces which was flooded as a result of the 1960 *maremoto* and now attracts many bird species. Boat trips to the reserve are available from Valdivia aboard the *Isla del Río* ① *daily 1415, 6 hrs, US$22 per person*.

On the Río Cruces, 42 km north of Valdivia, lies the small town of **San José de la Mariquina**. From the town an unpaved road leads west along the north side of the river to the **Fuerte de San Luis de Alba de Cruces** (22 km), a colonial fortification built in 1647 and largely rebuilt according to the original plans.

West of San José, **Mehuín** is a small, friendly resort and fishing port with a long beach. The fishermen here are usually willing to take people out to see the nearby sealion and penguin colonies, and with a little luck dolphins can also be spotted. A clifftop *ripio* road, with fantastic views north and south along the coastline, leads 6 km north to **Queule**, which has a good beach, but which is dangerous for bathing at high tide because of undercurrents. (Bathing is safer in the river near the ferry.) From Queule, a pretty road leads north again to **Toltén**; numerous small ferry

Río Valdivia

crossings provide access to isolated Mapuche communities and there are wonderful beaches along the coast.

East of Valdivia

The route east from Valdivia to the lakes passes through what is, perhaps, the least interesting part of the Lake District, consisting largely of wheatfields and dairy farms. Some 93 km east of Valdivia, beyond Antilhue (where there are picnic sites) and Los Lagos, is **Lago Riñihue**, the southernmost of the Seven Lakes. **Riñihue**, a beautiful but small and isolated village at its western end, is worth visiting but the road around the southern edge of the lake from Riñihue to Enco is poor and there is no road around the northern edge of the lake.

South of Lago Riñihue is **Lago Ranco**, one of the largest lakes, covering 41,000 ha, and also one of the most accessible as it has a road, albeit poor in many places, round its edge. The road is characterized by lots of mud and animals, including oxcarts. However it is worth taking the opportunity to escape the gringo trail and witness an older lifestyle while admiring the beautiful lake, starred with islands, and the sun setting on the distant volcanoes. There is excellent fishing on the southern shore; several hotels organize fishing expeditions.

❧ If you're travelling to Lago Ranco from the south, access is via La Unión and Río Bueno, which are bypassed by the Pan-American Highway.

From the Pan-American Highway the north side of the lake can be reached from Los Lagos or from a better road 18 km further south. These two roads join and meet the road around the lake some 5 km west of **Futrono**. This is the main town on the northern shore and has a daily boat service to **Huapi**, the island in the middle of the lake. From Futrono the road (paved at this point) curves round the north of the lake to **Llifén**, Km 22, a picturesque place on the eastern shore. From Llifén, it is possible visit **Lago Maihue**, 33 km further east, the south end of which is surrounded by native forests. From Llifén the road around Lago Ranco continues via the Salto de Nilahue (Km 14) to **Riñinahue**, Km 23, at the southeast corner, with access to beaches. Further west is **Lago Ranco**, Km 47, an ugly little town on the south shore, which has a museum with exhibits on Mapuche culture. On the western shore is **Puerto Nuevo**, where there are watersports and fishing on the Río Bueno. Further north, 10 km west of Futrono, is **Coique** , where there are more good beaches. Paved roads lead back to the Pan-American Highway from Puerto Bueno and the town of Lago Ranco.

Lagos Ranco & Maihue

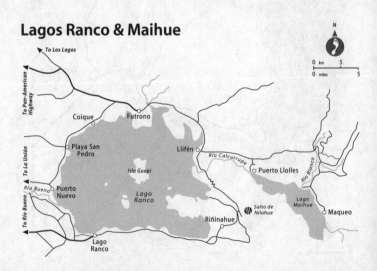

Lord Cochrane

Lord Thomas Alexander Cochrane (1775-1860) was born into a Scottish aristocratic family and began his career in the British navy during the Napoleonic Wars, rising rapidly through the officer ranks. He was elected to Parliament in 1806 as MP for Honiton and in 1807 as MP for Westminster. Cochrane had never been on good terms with his naval superiors, and when he used his position in the House of Commons to accuse the naval commander, Lord Gambier, of incompetence, he precipitated his own downfall. Gambier was court-martialled and acquitted; Cochrane was retired on half-pay and spent the next three years exposing corruption and abuses in the navy. His links with a financial scandal in 1814 provided his enemies with an opportunity for revenge: he was dismissed from the navy, expelled from Parliament and sentenced to 12 months' imprisonment.

Cochrane was recruited for the Chilean armed forces by an agent in London and quickly became friendly with Chile's independence leader Bernardo O'Higgins. He was put in command of the new republic's 'navy', a few ill-equipped vessels that relied on foreign adventurers for experienced sailors, and with this fleet harassed the Spanish-held ports along the Chilean coast. His audacious storming of the fortresses of Corral, San Carlos and Amargos led to the capture of the key Spanish base of Valdivia (see page 337).

Later that year Cochrane transported Peruvian liberation troops, led by José de San Martín, along the Pacific coast to invade Peru, but his relations with San Martin were poor and he became very critical of the Peruvian's cautious strategy. Afterwards Cochrane continued to attack Spanish shipping in the Pacific, sailing as far north as Mexico in 1822.

In 1823 the new government of Brazil appointed Cochrane to head its navy in the struggle for independence from Portugal. Once again leading a motley collection of boats manned largely by foreigners, Cochrane drove the colonial fleet from Bahia and pursued it back to Portugal. In 1825 he fell out with the Brazilian government and returned to Britain. Two years later he volunteered to help the Greeks in their struggle for independence from Turkey. He was reinstated in the British navy in 1832, was promoted to Rear-Admiral and spent much of the rest of his life promoting developments in the use of steam power in shipping.

Sleeping

Valdivia *p336, maps p337 and p336*
Accommodation is scarce during **Semana Valdiviana**. In summer accommodation is widely available in private homes, usually **C**, or **F** singles.
L-AL Puerta del Sur, Los Lingues 950, Isla Teja, T063-224500, www.hotelpuertadelsur. com. 5-star, set in large grounds, all facilities including pool, sauna, restaurant, tennis courts, activities and tours offered, very good.
AL Melillanca, Alemania 675, T063-212509,

www.melillanca.cl. 4-star. Decent business standard. With restaurant, sauna, Wi-Fi zones.
AL Naguilán, Gral Lagos 1927, T063-212851, www.hotelnaguilan.com. Pleasant 4-star, south of the city centre along the river. Clean, quiet, nice views, pool, good restaurant.
A Palace, Chacabuco 308 y Henríquez, T063-213319, hotelpalace@surnet.cl. With breakfast, good, comfortable, central.

B **Hostal Casagrande**, Andtwandter 880, T063-202035, hostalcasagrande@hotmail. com .Heated rooms with bath and cable TV. Attractive old house, recently refurbished. Great views from the breakfast area. Internet and laundry facilities. Recommended.

B **Hostal Centro Torreón**, P Rosales 783, T063-212622, hostorreon@telsur.cl. With breakfast, old German villa with nice atmosphere, cable TV, parking.

B-C **Aires Buenos**, Gral Lagos 1036, T063-206304, www.airesbuenos.cl. F per person in dorms. Some rooms with bath. Refurbished 19th-century house, kitchen facilities, bar, internet, tours, nice common areas, Spanish lessons, Argentine run, English spoken, recommended. HI affiliated.

B-C **Hospedaje Internacional**, García Reyes 660, T063-212015, www.hostalinternacional.cl. Some rooms with bath. E singles. With breakfast, without bath, clean, helpful, use of kitchen, barbeque area, book exchange, tours offered. Recommended; also *cabañas*.

B-C **Hostal Prat**, Prat 595, T063-222020. With good breakfast and bath, cable TV. Views to an industrial zone across the river.

C **Hospedaje Pérez Rosales**, Pérez Rosales 1037, T063-215607, trivinos@surnet.cl. E singles. With or without bath and breakfast. Modern, small rooms, good beds, electricity supply shares a circuit with a welding business next door.

C **Hostal Anwandter**, Anwandter 601, T063-218587, hostalanwandter@hotmail.com. Good value rooms with bath and breakfast. Also cheaper rooms without. Internet and laundry facilities.

C **Villa Beauchef**, Beauchef 844, T063-216044, www.villabeauchef.cl. F singles. Some rooms with or without bath and breakfast, cable TV. Thin walls.

C **Hostal Esmeralda**, Esmeralda 651, T063-215659. F singles. A little run down. Spacious rooms, some with bath, also *cabañas*, parking.

C-D **Camilo Henríquez 749**, casa 6, T063-222574. F singles. Charming tumbledown mansion which survived the 1960 earthquake at the expense of wildly sloping floors. Large basic rooms, kitchen,

laundry, internet. Basic English spoken. Highly recommended.

C-D **Residencial Germanía**, Picarte 873, T063-212405. F singles. With breakfast, without bath, poor beds, clean, German spoken,

D **A Muñoz 345**, opposite bus terminal. F-G singles. Very basic accommodation. Several similar places on the same street or nearby on Picarte.

Camping

Camping Centenario, rowing club on España. Overlooking the river.

Isla Teja, T063-213584. Views over the river.

Along the Río Valdivia *p338*

B **Cabañas Fischer**, Niebla, T063-282007. *Cabañas* and camping. Worth bargaining out of season.

C **Hostería Los Alamos**, Corral. F singles. Perfect for a quiet life.

C **Hostería Mancera**, Isla Mancera, T/F063-216296. Open Dec-Mar, depending on weather, no singles, phone first, no drinking water.

C **Residencial Mariel**, Tarapacá 36, Corral, T063- 471290. F singles. Modern, clean, friendly, good value.

C **Villa Santa Clara**, Niebla, T063-282018. With breakfast, also *cabañas*, cooking and laundry facilities.

North of Valdivia *p339*

The following are all in Mehuín. There are also 2 simple *residenciales* in Queule.

B **El Nogal**, T/F063-451352. With bath and breakfast, good.

D **Hospedaje Marbella**. F-G singles. Clean and the cheapest option.

East of Valdivia *p340*

Some of the houses around Lago Ranco are available for let in summer.

AL **Hotel Puerto Nuevo**, Puerto Nuevo, Lago Ranco, T064-375540, www.hotelpuerto nuevo.cl. Leisure complex in large grounds by the lake, with restaurant.

AL **Hostería Huinca Quinay**, 3 km east of Riñihue, Lago Riñihue, T063-1971811, gcristi@hotmail.com. 4-star *cabañas* with restaurant and lots of facilities.

● *For an explanation of sleeping and eating price codes used in this guide, see inside the*
● *front cover. Other relevant information is found in Essentials, see pages 50-57.*

AL Hostería Riñinahue, Casilla 126,
Riñinahue, near Lago Ranco, T063-491379.
Organizes fishing expeditions.
AL-A Hostería Chollinco, 3 km out of
Llifén, on the road towards Lago Maihue
in the Lago Ranco area, T063-1971979,
www.hosteriachollinco.cl. Remote country
lodge with swimming pool, trekking, horse
riding, fishing, hunting and other activities.
AL-A Riñimapu, northwest edge of Lago
Riñihue, T063-311388, www.rinimapu.cl.
Comfortable rooms and suites with views
over the lake, excellent food.
A Huequecura, Llifén, T09-96535450.
Includes meals and fishing services, good
restaurant.
C-D Hospedaje Futronhue, Balmaceda 90,
Futrono, T063-481265. Good breakfast.

Camping
There are campsites all around Lago Ranco
as well as several on Lago Maihue, though
many are open in summer only and prices
are high.
Bahía Coique, 9 km west of Futrono,
T063-481264. Autocamping, US$50 per site
in summer, US$35 per site off season.
Bahía Las Rosas, 1 km east of Futrono.
US$20 per site.
Camping Lago Ranco, Lago Ranco.
US$18 per site.
Maqueo, eastern shore of Lago Maihue,
US$20 per site.
Nalcahue, 1 km west of Futrono,
T063-481663. US$20 per site.
Playa Ranquil, Riñinahue, US$12 per site.

Eating

For places to eat in the coastal resorts and
around the lakes, see Sleeping above.

Valdivia *p336, maps p337 and p336*.
There are plenty of very cheap restaurants
serving good food down by the waterfront,
facing the boat dock, and in the market.
Restaurante Camino de Luna, Prat s/n.
A floating restaurant next to the *costanera*,
unique in Chile.
Café Haussmann, O'Higgins 394.
A Valdivian institution famous for its
raw meat dishes.

Cervecería Kunstmann, on the road
to Niebla, T063-292969, www.cerveza-kunst
mann.cl. German food, brewery with 5
varieties of beer, recommended.
Delicias, Henríquez 372. Recommended
for meals, cakes and real coffee.
La Calesa, Yungay 735, on the *costanera*.
Peruvian and international cuisine, plus
music and an art gallery. Recommended.
Ritual, Prat 233. Fashionable bar/
restaurant on the waterfront. Varied menu.
Good food.
Sake, Beauchef 629. Claims to be
Japanese, but really serves generic 'oriental'
food. Take away service available.
Shanghai, Andwandter y Muñoz.
Pleasant Chinese.
Café Aruba, Picarte 766. Good value, filling
sandwiches.
Derby, Henríquez 314. Good value.
Restaurant Volcán, Caupolicán y
Chacabuco. *Pichangas*, cazuelas. Great food
at a good price.

Cafés
Café Moro, Independencia y Libertad. Airy
café with a mezzanine art gallery. Popular
bar at night.
Entrelagos, Pérez Rosales 622. Ice cream
and chocolates, expensive.
La Baguette, Libertad y Yungay. Bakery
selling French-style cakes and brown bread.
Repeatedly recommended.
La Ultima Frontera, Pérez Rosales 787 (in
Centro Cultural 787). Real coffee, homemade
cakes and more.

Along the Río Valdivia *p338*
Las Delicias, Niebla, T063-213566. A
restaurant with 'a view that would be worth
the money even if the food weren't good'.
Also *cabañas* and camping.

Bars and clubs

Valdivia *p336, maps p337 and p336*.
Bataclan, Henríquez 326. Live music.
El Cantino, Andwandter 385. Brazilian
bar/restaurant.
Fuerte de Pedro, Caupolicán. Cheap,
new restaurant/bar.
La Bomba, Caupolicán. Pleasant old
Valdivian bar, serves *empanadas*.

LakeLake District Valdivia & around Listings

● Entertainment

Valdivia *p336, maps p337 and p336.*
There's a cinema on Chacabuco 300 block.
Cine Club UACH on the university campus
shows films at the weekend (not in summer).

⊛ Festivals and events

Valdivia *p336, maps p337 and p336.*
Mid-Feb Semana Valdiviana culminates in
Noche Valdiviana on the Sat with a
procession of elaborated decorated boats
which sail past the Muelle Fluvial.

Along the Río Valdivia *p338*
Mid-Feb Niebla hosts a Feria Costumbrista,
with lots of good food including *pullmay,
asado* and *paila marina.*

○ Shopping

Valdivia *p336, maps p337 and p336.*
Bookshops
Librería Andrés Bello, Independencia 635.
Librería/Centro Cultural 787, Pérez Rosales
787. Old mansion with hip bookstore, café
and art exhibitions.
Librería Chiloé, Caupolicán 410.

Supermarkets/malls
There is a shopping mall on Arauco y Beauchef.
Hiper-Unico, Arauco 697.
Las Brisas, Henríquez 522 (on plaza).

▲ Activities and tours

Mi Pueblito Expediciones, San Carlos 169,
T063-245055, www.pueblitoexpediciones.cl,
offers classes and trips in sea kayaks in the
waters around Valdivia, US$20-30 for 4-5 hrs.

● Transport

Valdivia *p336, maps p337 and p336.*
Air
LanChile, Maipú 271, T60-5262000, runs
several flights daily to/from **Santiago** every
day via Temuco or Concepción.

Bus
Terminal at Muñoz y Prat, by the river. For
local services along the Río Valdivia or to
Lago Ranco, see below.

To **Santiago**, several companies, 10 hrs,
most services overnight, US$12 salón cama
US$25; to **Osorno**, every 30 mins, 2 hrs,
several companies, US$4; to **Panguipulli**,
Empresa Pirehueico, about every 30 mins,
US$4; to **Puerto Montt**, many daily, 3 hrs,
US$5; to **Castro**, 7 hrs, US$10; to **Temuco**,
US$4; to **Puerto Varas**, 2¾ hrs, US$5; to
Frutillar, 2¼ hrs, US$5; to **Villarrica**, JAC, 6 a
day direct, 2½ hrs, US$5, continuing to
Pucón, US$6, 3 hrs; to **Mehuin**, 2 hrs,
US$2.50.
  To Argentina to **Bariloche** via Osorno,
7 hrs, Bus Norte, US$19; to **Zapala**,
Igi-Llaima, Mon, Thu, Sat, 2300, change in
Temuco at 0200, arrive Zapala 1200-1500,
depending on border crossing, US$40.

Car
Hire from **Automóvil Club de Chile**, García
Reyes 490, T063-250376; **Autovald,**
Henríquez 610, T063-212786;
Hertz, Picarte 640 and at the airport,
T063-272273/T063-218316; **Turismo
Méndez,** Gral Lagos 1335, T063-213205.

Along the Río Valdivia *p338*
Boat
The tourist boats to **Isla Mancera** and
Corral, depart from the Muelle Fluvial, Av
Prat 555, Valdivia. Several companies offer
trips. They will only leave with a minimum of
10 passengers, so off season organize in
advance. There is a full list of operators in the
tourist information office. Prices per person:
city US$4, **Isla Teja** US$7, **Corral-Mancera**
US$15-30. There are several other
destinations.
  There is an hourly ferry service between
Niebla and **Corral**, 30 mins, US$1.

Bus
Bus to **Niebla** from Chacabuco y Yungay,
Valdivia, roughly every 20 mins between
0730 and 2100, 30 mins, US$1; the service
continues to **Los Molinos.** Also *colectivos.*

Lago Ranco *p, map p*
Buses from Valdivia to **Llifén** via Futrono,
Cordillera Sur, 4 daily, US$2.50; to **Riñihue**
via Paillaco and Los Lagos, frequent; from
Osorno to **Lago Ranco**, Empresa Ruta 5,
6 daily.

Directory

Valdivia *p336, maps p337 and p336*
Banks There are several banks with ATMs throughout the centre. **Turismo Cochrane**, Arauco 435; **Casa de Cambio**, Carampangue 325, T063-213305; **Turismo Austral**, Arauco y Henríquez, Galería Arauco, accepts TCs.

Internet Several throughout the centre, around US$0.80 per hr. **Laundry** Au Chic, Arauco 436; **Lavazul**, Chacabuco 300; slow; coin laundry at **Lavamatic**, Schmidt y Picarte, Mon-Sat 0930-2030; **Manantial**, Henríquez 809. **Telephone** CTC, Independencia 628, T063-252700; **Entel**, Pérez Rosales 601, T063-225334.

Osorno and around → *Colour map 4, B2.*

Situated at the confluence of the Ríos Rahue and Damas, 921 km south of Santiago, Osorno was founded in 1553 before being abandoned in 1604 and refounded by Ambrosio O'Higgins and Juan MacKenna O'Reilly in 1796. It later became one of the centres of German immigration; their descendants are still of great importance in the area. Although Osorno is an important transport hub and a reasonable base for visiting the southern lakes, it is a drab uninspiring city, and is likely to be a place that you will pass through. ▸▸ *For Sleeping, Eating and other listings, see pages 348-350.*

Ins and outs

Getting there Osorno is a key crossroads for bus routes in southern Chile. Passengers heading for Bariloche, Neuquén, Coyhaique or Punta Arenas will pass through here before making for the Puyehue Pass into Argentina; buses tend to leave from Puerto Montt, and travellers from Santiago may well change buses here. There are also hourly local services to Puerto Montt, as well as frequent services north to Temuco and Valdivia.

Osorno

Sleeping
Eduviges **4**
Gran Osorno **6**
Hospedaje de la Fuente **7**
Hostal Bilbao Express **15**
Inter-Lagos **9**
Residencial Bilbao II **16**

Residencial Carillo **17**
Residencial Hein's **5**
Residencial Riga **19**
Residencial San Diego **20**

Eating
Atelier **5**

Club de Artesanos **6**
Dino's **2**
La Paisana **3**
Peter's Kneipe **4**

0 metres 100
0 yards 100

Lake District Osorno & around

Getting around   Most of the places visitors are likely to visit are within easy walking distance. Taxis or *colectivos* may be useful for longer trips.

Tourist information   Information is available from the provincial government office of **Sernatur** ① *Plaza de Armas, O'Higgins s/n, piso 1, T064-234104*. The municipal tourist office is based in the bus terminal and in a kiosk on the Plaza de Armas, both open December to February. There is also a **CONAF** office ① *Rosas 430, T064-234393*.

Osorno

On the large **Plaza de Armas** stands the modern, concrete and glass cathedral, with many arches and a tower that is itself an open, latticed arch with a cross superimposed. West of the centre on a bend overlooking the river is the **Fuerte María Luisa**, built in 1793 and restored in 1977; only the river front walls and end turrets are still standing. East of the main plaza along Calle MacKenna are a number of late 19th-century wooden mansions built by German immigrants, now preserved as national monuments. Two blocks south of the Plaza is the **Museo Histórico Municipal** ① *Matta 809, Mon-Sun 1100-1900 in summer; Mon-Fri 0930-1730, Sat 1500-1800 in winter, US$1.50*, which has displays on natural history, Mapuche culture, the refounding of the city and German colonization. Three blocks southwest of the plaza, in the former train station is the **Museo Interactivo de Osorno (MIO)** ① *T064-212996, www.municipalidadosorno.cl, Mon-Thu 0815-1300, 1445-1815, Fri 0815-1300, 1445- 1715, Sat 1415-1745*, an interactive science museum designed for both children and adults.

North and west of Osorno

Río Bueno, 30 km north, is celebrated for its scenery and fishing. The Spanish colonial fort, dating from 1777, is situated high above the river and offers fine views. Just over 20 km further west on the Río Bueno is **Trumao**, a river port with a river launch service to La Barra on the coast. There are beaches at **Maicolpue**, 60 km west of Osorno, and **Pucatrihue**, which are worth a visit in the summer. Further north is the **Monumento Natural Alerce Costero**, a newly designated park covering 2307 ha in the coastal mountain range and protecting an area of alerce forest (though a fire in 1975 destroyed some of the forest). Access is by a poor ripio road which runs northwest for

Lagos Puyehue & Rupanco

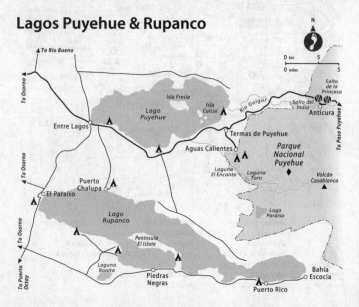

East out of Osorno

From Osorno Route 215 runs east to the Argentine border at the Puyehue Pass via the
south shore of Lago Puyehue, Anticura and the Parque Nacional Puyehue (see below).
Auto Museo Moncopulli ① *Route 215, T064-210744, www.moncopulli.cl, 1000-1900,*
US$2.75, bus towards Entre Lagos, 25 km east of Osorno is the best motor museum in
Chile. Exhibits include a Studebaker collection from 1852 to 1966. There is also a
1950s-style cafeteria.

Lago Puyehue and the Parque Nacional

Surrounded by relatively flat countryside, 47 km east of Osorno, **Lago Puyehue**
extends over 15,700 ha. The southern shore is much more developed than the
northern shore, which is accessible only by unpaved road from **Entre Lagos** at the
western end. On the opposite side of the lake are the **Termas de Puyehue**
① *0900-2000 daily, US$5 outdoor pools, US$18 indoor pools.*

Stretching east from Lago Puyehue to the Argentine border, **Parque Nacional
Puyehue** covers 107,000 ha, much of it in the valley of the Río Golgol. On the eastern
side are several lakes, including Lago Constancia and Lago Gris. There are two
volcanic peaks: **Volcán Puyehue** (2240 m) in the north (access via a private track
US$10) and **Volcán Casablanca** (also called Antillanca, 1900 m). Leaflets on walks
and attractions are available from the park administration at Aguas Calientes and
from the ranger station at Anticura.

At **Aguas Calientes**, 4 km south of the Termas de Puyehue in a thickly forested
valley, is an open-air pool (dirty) with very hot thermal water beside the Río Chanleufú
① *Mon-Fri 0830-1230, 1400-1800 in summer only; Sat, Sun and holidays 0830-2030
all year; outdoor pool US$3, children US$1.50; indoor pool US$8, children US$4.*

From Aguas Calientes the road continues 18 km southeast past three small lakes
and through forests to **Antillanca** on the slopes of Volcán Casablanca. In winter a one-way
traffic system operates on the last 8 km: ascending traffic from 0800 to 1200 and 1400 to
1730; descending traffic from 1200 to 1400 and after 1730. This is a particularly beautiful
section, especially at sunrise, with views over Lago Puyehue to the north and Lagos
Rupanco and Llanquihue to the south, as well as the snow-clad peaks of Calbuco,
Osorno, Puntiagudo, Puyehue and Tronador forming a semicircle. The tree-line on
Casablanca is one of the few in the world made up of deciduous trees (*nothofagus* or
southern beech). From Antillanca it is possible to climb Casablanca for even better views
of the surrounding volcanoes and lakes; there's no path and the hike takes about seven
hours there and back; information from **Club Andino** in Osorno. On the south side of the
volcano there are caves (accessible by road, allow five hours from **Hotel Antillanca**).

The paved Route 215 continues from the Termas de Puyehue to **Anticura**,
northeast of Aguas Calientes. In this section of the park are three waterfalls, including
the spectacular 40-m wide **Salto del Indio**. Legend has it that an Indian, enslaved by
the Spanish, was able to escape by hiding behind the falls. Situated just off the road,
the falls are on a marked path through dense forest which includes a 800-year-old
Coúhue tree known as 'El Abuelo'.

Border with Argentina

The **Chilean border** post is 4 km east of Anticura at Pajaritos ① *immigration open
second Sat in Oct-second Sat in Mar 0800-2100, otherwise 0800-1900*. From here it's
a further 22 km east to the border at **Paso Puyehue**, although this route is liable to
closure after snow. For private vehicles entering Chile, formalities are quick (about 15
minutes), but include a search for fruit, vegetables and dairy produce. On the
Argentine side the road continues to Bariloche.

Lago Rupanco

Lying south of Lago Puyehue and considerably larger, this lake covers 23,000 ha and is far less accessible and less developed for tourism than most of the other larger lakes. Access from the northern shore is via two unpaved roads that branch off Route 215. **El Paraíso** (aka Marina Rupanco), at the western tip of the lake, can be reached by an unpaved road south from Entre Lagos. A 40-km dirt road runs along the southern shore, via **Laguna Bonita**, a small lake surrounded by forest, and **Piedras Negras** to **Bahía Escocia** at the eastern end. From the south, access is from two turnings off the road between Osorno and Las Cascadas.

● Sleeping

Osorno *p345, map p345*

AL Inter-Lagos, Cochrane 515, T064-234695, www.hotelinterlagos.cl. Small 3-star with decent sized rooms,parking, restaurant.

A Gran Hotel Osorno, O'Higgins 615, T064-232171, granhotelosorno@entel chile.net. Cable TV, well furnished. Comfortable 3-star.

B Eduviges, Eduviges 856, T064-235023, www.hoteleduviges.cl. Cheaper rooms with out bath. Spacious, clean, quiet, attractive, gardens, also *cabañas* and restaurant. Laundry and internet facilities. Recommended.

B-C Residencial Riga, Amthauer 1058, T064-232945, resriga@telsur.cl. Clean, pleasant. Internet access. Recommended but heavily booked in season.

C Hostal Bilbao Express, Bilbao 1019, T064-262200, pazla@telsur.cl. With bath and breakfast, parking, restaurant. Also **Residencial Bilbao II**, MacKenna 1205, T064-264444.

C-D Residencial Hein's, Errázuriz 1757, T064-234116. **E** singles. Some rooms with bath. Old- fashioned, spacious, family atmosphere.

There are lots of cheap options near the bus terminal, including the following:

D Hospedaje de la Fuente, Los Carrera 1587. **F** singles. Basic, friendly.

D Residencial Ortega, Colón y Errázuriz. **F** singles. Parking, basic, clean, friendly.

D Residencial San Diego, Los Carrera 1551. **F** singles with breakfast.

D Residencial Carillo, Angulo 454. **F-G** singles. Basic, clean.

Camping

Municipal site off Pan-American Highway near southern entrance to city, open Jan-Feb only, poor facilities, US$9 per site.

North and west of Osorno *p346*

C Hostería Miller, Maicolpue, 60 km west of Osorno, T064-1975360. On the beach, clean, with good service, also a recommended campsite.

Lago Puyehue and the Parque Nacional *p347, map p346*

A private house close to the *termas* provides cheap accommodation, either room only or full board.

LL-L Hotel Termas de Puyehue, Termas de Puyehue, T600-2936000, www.puyehue.cl. Large resort containing 2 thermal swimming pools (one indoors, very clean), theatre, conference centre, well maintained, meals expensive, beautiful scenery, heavily booked Jan-Feb (cheaper May to mid-Dec).

AL Hotel Antillanca, at foot of Volcán Casablanca, T064-235114, www.skiantill anca.com. Attached to the antillanca ski resort, decent restaurant/café, pool, sauna, friendly club-like atmosphere, also *refugio*.

A Cabañas Ñilque, on the southern lake-shore, T064-371218, www.turismonilque.cl. Cabins (half-price May-Oct), fishing trips, watersports, car hire.

B Hospedaje Millaray, Ramírez 333, Entre Lagos, T064-371251. **E** singles. With breakfast, excellent, clean, friendly.

B Hostal y Cabañas Miraflores, Ramírez 480, Entre Lagos, T064-371275, olivia.hostal miraflores@gmail.com. Pleasant rooms and cabins.

B Hostería Entre Lagos, Ramírez 65, Entre Lagos, T064-371225. Rooms with lake view.

D Ruta 215 Gasthaus, Osvaldo Muñoz 148, Entre Lagos, T064-371357. **F** singles with bath and good breakfast. Clean, friendly, German spoken. Good value.

Camping

Camping No Me Olvides, Km 56, on southern lakeshore. US$15, also *cabañas*.
Chanleufu, Aguas Calientes, T064-236988. US$305 per site with hot water, also *cabañas*, an expensive café and a small shop.
Los Derrumbes, 1 km from Aguas Calientes. No electricity, US$25 per site.
Playa Los Copihues, Km 56.5, on southern lakeshore. Hot showers, good.
There is also a **CONAF** *refugio* on Volcán Puyehue (check with CONAF in Anticura whether it is open) and a campsite beside the Río Chanleufú (US$5 per person).

Lago Rupanco *p348, map p*
There is no accommodation on the northern shore of the lake.
L-AL Puntiagudo Lodge, Bahía Escocia, T064-1974731, www.puntiagudolodge.cl. With breakfast, very comfortable, good restaurant, fly-fishing, horse riding, boat excursions. Advance bookings only.
A-B Refugio Club de Pesca y Caza, Sector Islote, 7 km east of Piedras Negras, T064- 232056. Basic *refugio* with breakfast and bath.

Camping

There are several campsites on the southern shore, including at Puerto Rico.
Desague del Rupanco, just south of El Paraíso. No facilities.
Puerto Chalupa, on northern shore, T064-232680. US$32 per site.

🍴 Eating

For other eating options in the area, see Sleeping above. Good cheap restaurants can be found in the market

Osorno *p345, map p345*
The bakery at Ramírez 977 sells good wholemeal bread.
🍴 **Atelier**, Freire 468, T064-213735. Fresh pasta and other Italian delights.
🍴 **Dino's**, Ramírez 898, on the plaza. Good restaurant upstairs, bar/cafeteria/diner downstairs.
🍴 **La Paisana**, O'Higgins 827, piso 2. Arab specialities including vegetarian options.

🍴 **Peter's Kneipe**, M Rodríguez 1039. Excellent German restaurant.
🍴-🍴 **Club de Artesanos**, MacKenna 634. A good choice for hearty traditional Chilean fare.
🍴 **Waldis**, on Plaza de Armas. Real coffee.

Lago Puyehue and the Parque Nacional *p347, map p346*
🍴 **Chalet Suisse**, Km 55, on the southern lakeshore, T064-234073. Restaurant with excellent food.
🍴 **Jardín del Turista**, Entre Lagos, T064-371214. Very good restaurant.
🍴 **Pub del Campo**, Entre Lagos, T064-371220. Highly recommended restaurant.

🛍 Shopping

Osorno *p345, map p345*
There is a mall on C Freire 542 with 3 internet cafés and a bookshop, **CM Books**, which sells some English titles.
Alta Artesanía, MacKenna 1069. Excellent handicrafts, not cheap.
Climet, Angulo 603. Fishing tackle.
Ekono, Colón y Errázuriz. Supermarket.
The Lodge, Los Carrera 1291, local 5. Fishing tackle.

⛰ Activities and tours

Osorno *p345, map p345*
Skiing
Club Andino, O'Higgins 1073, T064-235114. Information and advice on skiing in the area.
Hotel Antillanca, see Sleeping above, is attached to one of Chile's smaller ski resorts; 17 pistes are served by 3 lifts, ski instruction and first aid available. Piste preparation is unreliable. Skiing is not difficult but quality depends on the weather: though rain is common it often does not turn to snow. See www.skiantillanca.cl for information on the state of the pistes.

Lago Rupanco *p348*
Fishing
Lago Rupanco is very popular for fishing.
Bahía Escocia Fly Fishing offers excursions from the **Puntiagudo Lodge** (see Sleeping, above) advance booking required.

⊙ Transport

Osorno *p345, map p345*

Air
LanChile, E Ramírez 802, T600-5262000, flies daily to **Santiago** via Temuco.

Bus
Main terminal 4 blocks from Plaza de Armas at Errázuriz 1400, bus from centre, US$0.50. Left luggage open 0730-2030.

To **Santiago**, frequent, 11 hrs, US$15, salon cama US$35; to **Valparaíso** and **Viña del Mar**, Tas Choapa, US$17; to **Concepción**, US$10; to **Temuco**, US$8; to **Panguipulli**, Buses Pirehueico, 4 a day; to **Pucón** and **Villarrica**, US$10; to **Valdivia**, frequent, 2 hrs, several companies, US$4; to **Frutillar**, US$2, **Llanquihue**, **Puerto Varas** and **Puerto Montt**, every 30 mins, US$4; to **Puerto Octay**, Vía Octay, hourly, US$2; to **Lago Ranco** (town), 6 a day, Empresa Ruta 5, 2 hrs, US$3; to **Punta Arenas**, several each week, US$65; to **Anticura**, 2 or 3 buses daily, 3 hrs, US$6 .

Some local services leave from the Mercado Municipal terminal, 1 block west of the main terminal. To **Entre Lagos**, frequent in summer, reduced service off season, Expreso Lago Puyehue, T064-234919, and Buses Barria, 45 mins, US$1.50; buses by both companies also continue to **Aguas Calientes**, off season according to demand, 2 hrs, US$3. To **Puyehue**, 4-5 daily, 1½ hrs, US$3.50. Also frequent buses to **Río Bueno** and daily services to **Maicolpué** and **Pucatrihue** on the coast.

Car
Car mechanics at **Automotriz Amthauer**, Amthauer 1250; **Automotriz Salfa Sur SA**, Fco Bilbao 857.

Train
The station is 3 blocks west of the Plaza de Armas at Variante Mackenna 555, T600-5855000, www.efe.cl. Two daily services north to **Temuco**, US$4.50 and south to **Puerto Montt**, US$2.75.

North and west of Osorno *p346*

River launches run between **Trumao** on the Río Bueno, 22 km west of Osorno to **La Barra** on the coast, 0900 Wed and Sat only, 5 hrs, return 0900 Thu and Sun, US$12, no service in winter. For bus services from Osorno, see above.

Lago Puyehue and the Parque Nacional *p347, map p346*

Note that buses from Osorno (see above) to **Entre Lagos** and **Aguas Calientes** do not stop at the lakeside (unless you want to get off at **Hotel Termas de Puyehue** and clamber down). There is no public transport from Aguas Calientes to **Antillanca**; hitching is always difficult, but it is not a hard walk.

Border with Argentina *p347*

Several bus companies run daily services from Puerto Montt via Osorno to **Bariloche** along this route (see page 372). Although less scenic than the ferry journey across Lake Todos Los Santos and Laguna Verde this crossing is far cheaper, reliable and still a beautiful trip. Best views are from the right hand side of the bus.

Lago Rupanco *p348, map p*

Bus from Osorno to **Piedras Negras** from the main terminal, leaves 1230 Mon-Fri, 1630 on Sat, returns from Piedras Negras early morning.

⊙ Directory

Osorno *p345, map p345*

Banks Several banks with ATMs around the plaza. Casas de cambio at **Cambio Tur**, MacKenna 1004; **Turismo Frontera**, Ramírez 949, local 11 (Galería Catedral); if stuck try Travels bar in bus terminal. **Internet** Several throughout the city centre. **Laundry** Prat 678, allow at least a day. **Post office** O'Higgins 645. **Telephone** Ramírez at central plaza, Juan MacKenna y Cochrane. **Useful address** Automóvil Club de Chile, Bulnes 463, T064-232269, information and car hire.

Lago Llanquihue → *Colour map 3, C2.*

The second largest lake in Chile and the third largest natural lake in South America, Lago Llanquihue is one of the highlights of the Lake District. Three snowcapped volcanoes can be seen across the vast expanse of water: the perfect cone of Osorno (2680 m), the shattered cone of Calbuco (2015 m), and the spike of Puntiagudo (2480 m), as well as, when the air is clear, the distant Tronador (3460 m). On a cloudless night with a full moon, the snows reflect eerily in the lake and the peace and stillness are hard to match. ▸▸ *For Sleeping, Eating and other listings, see pages 356-361.*

Ins and outs

Getting there Access from the south is from nearby Puerto Montt, while there are direct transport links with Santiago along the Pan-American Highway. The northern tip of the lake is also easily reached from Osorno.

Getting around The largest towns, Puerto Varas, Llanquihue and Frutillar are all on the western shore, linked by the Pan-American Highway and the railway. Although there are roads around the rest of the lake the eastern shore is difficult to visit without transport, and beyond Las Cascadas, the road is narrow with lots of blind corners, necessitating speeds of 20-30 kph at best in places (see below). Beware of lorries that ply the route servicing the salmon farms. There is almost no public transport on this section and hitching is very difficult.

Tourist information There is no general information centre for the lake, but each town has its own municipal tourist office.

Lago Llanquihue

German colonization in the Lake District

The most important area of German agricultural colonization in Chile was around Lago Llanquihue. The Chilean government declared the area as destined for colonisation in 1845, and to encourage settlement and help the new arrivals get started, gave each adult male 75 *cuadras* of land plus an extra 12 *cuadras* for each son, a milking cow, 500 planks of timber, nails, a yoke of oxen, a year's free medical assistance and Chilean citizenship on request.

The first groups of German colonists arrived in the area in 1852: one group settled around Maitén and Puerto Octay, another helped found Puerto Montt. The lives of these early settlers were hard and the risks great, yet within 10 years the settlers had cleared much of the forest round the lake and soon they were setting up small industries. In 1880, when the offer to colonists ended, unsettled land was auctioned in lots of 400-800 ha. By then the lake was ringed by a belt of smallholdings and farms. The legacy of this settlement can be seen in the German-looking farmhouses around Puerto Octay and in many of the older buildings in Frutillar and Puerto Varas.

Valdivia was another centre for German colonization. A relatively small number of German and Swiss colonists settled in the city, exerting a strong influence on the architecture agricultural methods, education, social life and customs of the area. They established most of the industries that made Valdivia an important manufacturing centre until the 1950s. According to an 1884 survey all the breweries, leatherworks, brickworks, bakeries, machine shops and mills in Valdivia belonged to families with German surnames.

Little of the architectural heritage of this period survived the 1960 earthquake, but the city's German heritage can still be seen in some of its best cafés and restaurants and in the names of its streets.

Puerto Octay 🖥🖊🖥 ›› *pp356-361.*

Puerto Octay is a peaceful and picturesque small town at the north tip of the lake 56 km southeast of Osorno, set amid rolling hills, hedgerows and German-style farmhouses with views over Volcán Osorno. Founded by German settlers in 1852, the town enjoyed a boom period in the late 19th century when it was the northern port for steamships on the lake: a few buildings survive from that period, notably the church and the enormous German-style former convent. Since the arrival of railways and the building of roads, the town has declined. Much less busy than Frutillar or Puerto Varas, Puerto Octay offers an escape for those seeking peace and quiet. Rowing boats and pedalos can be hired for excursions on the lake.

Museo el Colono ① *Independencia 591, Tue-Sun 1000-1300, 1500-1900, Dec-Feb only*, has displays on German colonization. Another part of the museum, housing agricultural implements and machinery for making *chicha*, is just outside town on the road towards **Centinela**. This peninsula, about 3 km south (taxi US$2 one way) along an unpaved road, has accommodation, camping, a launch dock, bathing beaches and watersports. It is a very popular spot in good weather, especially for picnics, with fine views of the Osorno, Calbuco and Puntiagudo volcanoes.

East of Puerto Octay ●🍴🏍🛏⛰🚌 ›› *pp356-361.*

Puerto Octay to Volcán Osorno

The eastern lakeside, with Volcán Osorno on your left is very beautiful. From Puerto Octay two roads run towards Ensenada, one *ripio* along the shore, and one paved. (They join up after 20 km.) At Km 10 along the lakeside route is **Playa Maitén**, a lovely beach, often deserted, with a marvellous view of Volcán Osorno. Continue for another 24 km past **Puerto Fonck**, which has fine 19th-century German-style mansions, and you'll reach **Las Cascadas**, surrounded by picturesque agricultural land, old houses and German cemeteries. To reach the waterfalls that give the village its name follow signs along a *ripio* road east to a car park, continue along a footpath over two or three log bridges over a stream, and after a final wade across you will arrive at a 40-m-high natural cauldron, with the falls in the middle. The round trip takes about one-and-a-half hours.

Volcán Osorno

The most lasting image of Lago Llanquihue is the near perfect cone of Volcán Osorno, situated north of Ensenada on the eastern edge of the lake. Although the peak is on the edge of the Parque Nacional Pérez Rosales (see page 362), it is climbed from the western side, which lies outside the park. Access is via two roads that branch off the Ensenada-Puerto Octay road along the eastern edge of Lago Llanquihue: the northern one at Puerto Klocker, 20 km southeast of Puerto Octay; the other 2 km north of Ensenada (turning unmarked, high clearance vehicle necessary).

Guided ascents of the volcano (organized by agencies in Puerto Varas) set out from the *refugio* at **La Burbuja**. From here it is six hours to the summit. The volcano can also be climbed from the north (La Picada); this route is easier and may be attempted without a guide, although only experienced climbers should attempt to climb right to the top as ice climbing equipment is essential.

Ensenada

Despite its lack of a recognizable centre, Ensenada is beautifully situated at the southeast corner of Lago Llanquihue, almost beneath the snows of Volcán Osorno. A good half-day trip from Ensenada itself is to **Laguna Verde**, about 30 minutes from **Hotel Ensenada**, along a beautiful circular trail behind the lake (take first fork to the right behind the information board), and then down the road to a secluded campsite at Puerto Oscuro on Lago Llanquihue.

The western shore ●🍴🏍❀🛏⛰🚌☕ ›› *pp356-361.*

Frutillar

Lying about half-way along the western side of the lake, Frutillar is in fact two towns: **Frutillar Alto**, just off the main highway, and **Frutillar Bajo**, beautifully situated on the lakeside, 4 km away. The latter is possibly the most attractive and expensive town on the lake, with superb views from the *costanera* over the water with volcanoes Osorno and Tronador in the background. The town's atmosphere is very German and somewhat snobbish, but the **tourist office** ① *on the lakeside, T065-420198, summer only,* is helpful. In the square opposite is an open-air chess board and the **Club Alemán** restaurant. A new concert hall is under construction on the lakeside to host the town's prestigious music festival in late January (see Festivals and events, below).

Away from the waterfront, the appealing **Museo Colonial Alemán** ① *off Prat, summer 1000-1930 daily; winter 1000-1330, 1500-1800 Tue-Sun, US$3,* is set in spacious gardens, with a watermill, replicas of two German colonial houses with furnishings and utensils of the period and a blacksmith's shop selling personally engraved horseshoes for US$8. It also has a *campanario*, a circular barn with agricultural machinery and carriages inside, as well as a handicraft shop. At the northern end of the town is the **Reserva Forestal Edmundo Winckler**, run by the Universidad de Chile and extending over 33 ha, with a guided trail through native woods. Named after one of the early German settlers, it includes a very good collection of native flora as well as plants introduced from Europe.

Llanquihue

Twenty kilometres south of Frutillar, Llanquihue lies at the source of the Río Maullín, which drains the lake. The site of a large dairy processing factory, this is the least touristy town on the lake, and makes a cheaper alternative to Puerto Varas and Frutillar. It has uncrowded beaches and hosts a German-style beer festival at the end of January.

Puerto Varas and around 🍴🍷🚻🛏️🚌ℹ️

▶ *pp356-361.*

Situated on the southwestern corner of the lake, Puerto Varas, with a population of 22,000, is the commercial and tourist centre of Lago Llanquihue. It also serves as a residential centre for Puerto Montt, 20 km to the south. In the 19th century Puerto Chico (on the southern outskirts) was the southern port for shipping on the lake. With the arrival of the railway the settlement moved to its current location and is now a resort, popular with Chilean as well as foreign tourists. Despite the numbers of visitors, though, it has a friendly, compact feel, and is one of the best bases for exploring the southern Lake District, near centres for trekking, rafting, canyoning and fly-fishing.

Ins and outs

Getting there Puerto Varas is served by many buses from Puerto Montt; there are also connections north to Osorno, and some that contine on to Valdivia and Temuco. A taxi to Puerto Montt airport costs US$22.

Getting around Puerto Varas is small and easily navigable on foot.

Tourist information The tourist office is in the Municipalidad ① *San Fransisco 413, T065-321330, securismo.puerto varas@munitel.cl.*

Frutillar Bajo

Sleeping 🛏️
Apart Hotel Frutillar 2
Casona del 32 1
Hospedaje Tía Clara 4
Hospedaje Vivaldi 6
Hostal Cinco Robles 5
Hostería El Arroyo 3
Hostería Los Maitenes
   Rincón Alemán 8
Pérez Rosales 590 12
Philippi 451 10
Residenz am See 13
Salzburg 11

Eating 🍴
Andes 1
Casino de Bomberos 2
Club Alemán 3
Selva Negra 4

Parque Philippi, on top of a hill, is a pleasant place to visit, although the views are a bit restricted by trees and the metal cross at the top is unattractive. Also in the park is an electric clock that chimes the quarter-hours during daylight hours. To reach the summit walk up to **Hotel Cabañas del Lago** on Klenner, cross the railway and the gate is on the right. The centre lies at the foot of the hill, but the town stretches east along the lake to **Puerto Chico**, where there are hotels and restaurants. The imposing **Catholic church** was built by German Jesuits in 1918 in baroque-style as a copy of the church in the Black Forest. North and east of the former **Gran Hotel Puerto Varas** (1934) are a number of German-style mansions.

Puerto Varas is a good base for trips around the lake. A paved road runs along the south shore to Ensenada on the southwestern corner of the lake. Two of the best beaches are **Playa Hermosa**, Km 7, and **Playa Niklitschek**, Km 8, where an entry fee is charged. At Km 16 narrow channels overhung with vegetation lead south from Lago Llanquihue to the little lake of **La Poza**. There are boat trips (US$2.50) to the beautiful **Isla Loreley**, an island on the lake, and a channel leads from La Poza to yet another lake, the **Laguna Encantada**. At Km 21 there is a watermill and a restaurant run by the Club Alemán.

Puerto Varas

● Sleeping

Camping wild and having barbecues are forbidden on the lake shore.

Puerto Octay *p352*
L Hotel Centinela, T064-391326, www.hotelcentinela.cl. Built in 1914 as a summer mansion, this hotel has been recently restored. It is idyllically situated and has superb views, 12 rooms, also *cabañas*, restaurant with grand minstrels' gallery and bar, open all year. Edward VIII once stayed here.

C Hospedaje Raquel Mardorf, Germán Wulf 712. **E** singles with enormous breakfast, clean, comfortable.

C Zapato Amarillo, 35 mins' walk north of town, T064-391575, www.zapatoamarillo. 8k.com. **F** per person in shared rooms. Excellent for backpackers and others, use of spotless kitchen, great breakfasts with homemade bread, very friendly, German and English spoken. Lots of information, mountain bike rental, tours, canoes and sailing boat, luggage storage, phone for free pickup from town. Main house has a grass roof or there's the roundhouse next door with restaurant. Highly recommended.

D Hostería La Baja, Centinela, T064-391269, irisbravo1@hotmail.com. **F** singles, with breakfast and bath. Beautifully situated at the neck of the peninsula. Good value.

Camping
Camping Municipal, on lakeside, T064-391326. US$18 per site.
El Molino, beside lake. US$5 per person, clean, friendly, recommended.

Puerto Octay to Volcán Osorno *p353*
Several farms on the road around the north and east side of the lake offer accommodation; look for signs. Camping is possible at the **Centro de Recreación Las Cascadas**, T064-235377, and at **Playa Maitén**.

C Hostería Irma, on lake, 2 km south of Las Cascadas, T064-396227, julietatrivino @yahoo.es. **F** singles. Attractive former residence, good food, very pleasant.

Volcán Osorno *p353*
E There are 2 *refugios*, both of them south of the summit and reached from the southern access road: **La Burbuja**, the former ski-club centre, 14 km north of Ensenada at 1250 m) and **Refugio Teski Ski Club**, just below the snow line. Price per person, meals served.
Refugio La Picada marked on the northern slopes on many trekking maps burned down several years ago.

Ensenada *p353*
LL Yan Kee Way Lodge, T065-212030, www.southernchilexp.com. Plush resort specializing in fly-fishing expeditions. Excellent restaurant.

L-AL Ensenada, Casilla 659, Puerto Montt, T065-212028, www.hotelensenada.cl. With bath, old-world style, good food, good view of lake and Volcán Osorno, runs tours, hires mountain bikes (guests only). Closed in winter. Also much cheaper *hostal* in the grounds with cooking facilities.

AL-B Cabañas Brisas del Lago, Km 42, T065-212012, www.brisasdellago.cl. On beach, rooms and cabins sleeping 2-6, good restaurant nearby. Recommended.

B Hospedaje Ensenada, Km 43, T065-212050, www.hospedajensenada. blogspot.com. **E** singles. Most rooms with bath. Very clean, excellent breakfast.

B-C Hospedaje Arena, km 43, T065-212037. Some rooms with bath. Breakfast. Recommended.

Camping
Montaña, centre of town. Price per site, good beach space.
Playa Larga, 1 km east of **Hotel Ensenada**, US$15 per site.
Puerto Oscuro, 2 km north of Ensenada, US$12 per site.
Trauco, 4 km west of Ensenada, T065-212033. Large site with shops, fully equipped, US$5-10 per person.

Frutillar *p353, map p354*
During the annual music festival accommodation should be booked well in advance; alternatively stay in Frutillar Alto or Puerto Varas. There are several cheap

---

● *For an explanation of sleeping and eating price codes used in this guide, see inside the front cover. Other relevant information is found in Essentials, see pages 50-57.*

options along Carlos Richter (main street) in Frutillar Alto and at the school in Frutillar Alto in Jan-Feb (sleeping bag required).

AL Casona del 32, Caupolicán 28, Frutillar Bajo, T065-421369. With breakfast, comfortable old house, central heating, English and German spoken. Groups only off season. Recommended.

AL Salzburg, Playa Maqui, 7 km north of Frutillar Bajo, T065-421589, www.salzburg.cl. Excellent restaurant, plus sauna, swimming pool, mountain bikes, tours and fishing.

A Hostal Cinco Robles, 1 km north of Frutillar Bajo, T065-421351, www.cinco-robles.com. In pleasant large grounds with views. Rooms with wooden interiors. With breakfast, restaurant, parking.

A Hostería Los Maitenes Rincón Alemán, 3 km north of Frutillar Bajo, T065-330033, www.interpatagonia.com/losmaitenes. In an old country house in 16 ha of land by the lake (private beach), fishing trips, free pickup from terminal. Disabled friendly. Also *cabañas*.

A Residenz am See, Philippi 539, Frutillar Bajo, T065-421539, hotelamsee.cl. Good breakfast and views. Café downstairs serving German specialities.

B Apart Hotel Frutillar, Philippi 1175, Frutillar Bajo, T065-421388, mwikler@vtr.net. Also cabins, good breakfasts, meals available.

B Hospedaje Vivaldi, Philippi 851, Frutillar Bajo, T065-421382. **D** singles. Quiet, comfortable, excellent breakfast and lodging, also family accommodation. Recommended.

B Hostería El Arroyo, Philippi 989, Frutillar Bajo, T065-421560, alarroyo@surnet.cl. With breakfast. Highly recommended.

C Hospedaje Tía Clara, Pérez Rosales 743, Frutillar Bajo, T065-421806. **F** singles, kitchen facilities, very friendly, good value.

C Pérez Rosales 590, Frutillar Bajo. *Cabañas* and excellent breakfast.

C Philippi 451, Frutillar Bajo, T065-421204. Clean accommodation and good breakfast.

C-D Hospedaje Juana Paredes, Aníbal Pinto y Winkler, Frutillar Alto, T065-421407. **F** singles. Recommended, also *cabañas* for up to 5 and parking.

Camping
Los Ciruelillos, 2 km south of Frutillar Bajo, T065-339123. Most services.

Playa Maqui, 7 km north of Frutillar, T065-339139. Fancy, expensive site.
Sr Guido González, Casa 3, Población Vermont, T065-421385. Recommended site.

Llanquihue *p354*
Camping
Baumbach, 1 km north of Llanquihue, T065-242643. On lakeside, meals available.
El Totoral, 8 km north of Llanquihue, T065-339123. Campsite and *cabañas*.
Playa Werner, 2 km north Llanquihue, T065-242114. On lakeside.

Puerto Varas *p354, map p355*
There are many hotels all along the lake front, but in high season they tend to be tourist traps.

LL-AL Cabañas del Lago, Klenner 195, T065-232291, www.cabanasdellago.cl. Recently rebuilt 4-star hotel on Philippi hill overlooking lake, superb views. Also self-catering *cabañas* sleeping 5 (good value for groups), cheaper rates in low season, heating, sauna, swimming pool, games room, bar and restaurant.

L Bellavista, Pérez Rosales 060, T065-232011, www.hotelbellavista.cl. 4 star with good views over the lake, king size beds, restaurant and bar, sauna, parking..

L Colonos del Sur, Estación 505, T065-235555, www.colonosdelsur.cl. Overlooking the town, decent rooms, good restaurant and tea room. Owns another hotel at Del Salvador 24, on the lakeside, which is being refurbished.

L-AL Licarayén, San José 114, T065-232305, www.hotelicarayen.cl. Overlooking lake, comfortable, clean, gym and sauna, 'the perfect place for bad weather or being ill'. Book in season.

AL-A Gran Reserva, Mirador 134, T065-346876, www.granreserva.cl. New boutique hotel overlooking the town and lake. Conference centre and pleasant living room.

A El Greco, Mirador 104, T065-233388, www.hotelelgreco.cl. Recently refurbished German-style mansion with wooden interior and full of artworks. Simple rooms with bath and cable TV. A good choice.

A Terrazas del Lago, Pérez Rosales 1571, T/F065-232622. Good breakfast, views over Volcán Osorno, restaurant.

A-B **Hostería Outsider**, San Bernardo 318, T065-232910, www.turout.com. With bath, breakfast with real coffee, meals, friendly, comfortable. German and English spoken, book in advance.

B **Amancay**, Walker Martínez 564, T065-232201, cabamancay@chile.com. With bath and breakfast. Friendly, German spoken, also *cabañas*, sleep 4. Recommended.

B **Canales del Sur**, Pasage Ricke 224, T065-346620, www.canalesdelsur.com. Very friendly and helpful, tours arranged. Laundry, internet and car hire service.

B-C **Casa Azul**, Manzanal 66 y Rosario, T065-232904, www.casaazul.net. E per person in shared rooms. Some rooms with bath. German/Chilean owners, good buffet breakfast with homemade muesli (US$5 extra), large kitchen, good beds with duvets, central heating, internet, book exchange, comfortable common area, English and German spoken, tours organized, friendly, helpful. Highly recommended.

B-C **Compass del Sur**, Klenner 467, T065-232044, compassdelsur.cl. E per person in shared rooms. Chilean-Swedish run, kitchen facilities, internet, cable TV in comfortable lounge, breakfast with muesli and real coffee, friendly, helpful, lots of information, tours, German, English, Swedish spoken, highly recommended. Also camping, car hire.

B-C **Ellenhaus**, Walker Martínez 239, T065-233577, www.ellenhaus.cl. Some rooms with bath. F per person in dorms. Kitchen and laundry facilities, luggage stored, lounge, tours offered. German and English spoken, recommended.

C **Casa Margouya**, Santa Rosa 318, T065-511648, www.margouya.com. E per person in shared rooms. Bright and colourful hostel in the town centre with breakfast and kitchen facilities. Friendly, lots of info. French run, English spoken.

C **Hospedaje Carla Minte**, Maipo 1010, T065-232880. E singles. Rooms with bath and breakfast in a family home. Cable TV, very comfortable.

C **Las Dalias**, Santa Rosa 707, T065-233277, las_dalias@hotmail.com. E singles. Some rooms with bath. In a family home, peaceful, clean, good breakfast with real coffee, parking, German spoken.

C **Villa Germania**, Nuestra Sra del Carmen 873, T065-233162. E-F singles. Old wooden mansion north of the centre. Also *cabañas*.

D **Hospedaje Don Raúl**, Salvador 928, T065-310897, hospedajedonraul@hotmail.com. F singles. Laundry and cooking facilities, very friendly, garden with hammock, clean. Recommended. Camping by main road.

Camping

Campo Aventura, San Bernardo 318, T065-232910, www.campo-aventura.com. 2 lodges with camping facilities, excellent horse riding, fishing, birdwatching, Spanish classes and vegetarian food.

Los Troncos, 10 km east of Puerto Varas, T09-9206869. US$15 per site, no beach access.

Playa Hermosa, 7 km east of Puerto Varas. Fancy ground, US$22 per site, bargain off season. Recommended. Take own supplies.

Playa Niklitschek, 8 km east of Puerto Varas, T065-338352. Full facilities.

Trauco, Imperial 433, T065-236262. Expensive but central (in Puerto Varas).

Eating

Puerto Octay *p352*

††† **El Rancho del Espanta-Pajaros**, 6 km south on the road to Frutillar, T065-330049. In a converted barn with wonderful views over the lake, serves all kind of spit roasted meat. All you can eat, with salad bar and drinks included, for US$12. Also arranges horse riding trips. Recommended.

††† **Fogón de Anita**, 1 km out of town, T064-391455. Mid-priced grill. Also German cakes and pastries.

† **Restaurante Baviera**, Germán Wulf 582. Cheap and good. Salmon and *cazuelas*.

Ensenada *p353*

†††† **Latitude 42**, Yan Kee Way resort, T065-212030. Expensive, excellent and varied cuisine, very good quality wine list. Views over the lake.

† **Canta Rana**. Recommended for bread and *küchen*.

† **Donde Juanito**, west of Ensenada. Excellent value cheap set lunch.

Frutillar *p353, map p354*

Andes, Philippi 1057, Frutillar Bajo. Good set menus and à la carte.

Club Alemán, Av Philippi 747. Good but not cheap, hostile to backpackers.

Selva Negra, Varas 24 y Philippi, Frutillar Bajo. Located in a traditional German mill, with scores of toy witches hanging from the ceiling, open 1100-2300.

Casino de Bomberos, Philippi 1060, Frutillar Bajo. Upstairs bar/restaurant, open all year, memorable painting caricaturing firemen in action. Great value but service can be poor.

Cafés

There are several German-style cafés on C Philippi, including **Salón de Te Frutillar** at No 775 and **Guten Apetit** at No 1285.

Puerto Varas *p354, map p355*

The expensive motel restaurants at the end of the *costanera* aren't worth visiting, although the service is friendly.

Merlin, Imperial 0605, on the road east out of town, T065-233105, www.merlin restaurant.com. Reputed to be one of the best restaurants in the Lake District, but occasional adverse reports.

Mediterráneo, Santa Rosa 068, T065-237268. On the lakefront, varied and interesting menu with a Mediterranean influence, recommended.

Di Carusso, San Bernardo 318, T065-233478. Italian tratoria. Good fresh pasta dishes on Fri. Recommended.

La Olla, Pérez Rosales 1071, T065-233540. 1 km east of centre along the lakefront. Seafood and traditional Chilean cuisine. Recommended.

Parrilla Don Carlos, Del Salvador 450. Typical Chilean grill.

Donde El Gordito, downstairs in market. Large portions, good range of meat dishes, no set menu.

Don Jorge, San Bernardo 240. Sandwiches and good value lunches.

Cafés

Café Danés, Del Salvador 441. Good coffee and cakes.

Punto Café, Del Salvador 348. Cafe with internet and art gallery.

El Molino, on road to Ensenada, 22 km east. Café next to an old water mill.

🍸 Bars and clubs

Puerto Varas *p354, map p355*
Barómetro, San Pedro 418. Cosy bar serving
Kuntstman beer and food.
Pim's, San Francisco near C Imperial.
Spacious US-style pub with food.

⚙ Festivals and events

Frutillar *p353, map p354*
Jan/early Feb A highly regarded classical
music festival is held in the town; tickets
must be booked well in advance from the
Municipalidad, T065-421290.

Llanquihue *p354*
End Jan A German-style beer festival with
oom-pah music is held here.

⚪ Shopping

Ensenada *p353*
There are several shop selling basic supplies.
Most places are closed off season, other than a
few pricey shops, so take your own provisions.

Frutillar *p353, map p354*
Services and shops are generally much
better in Frutillar Alto, although in Frutillar
Bajo, seek out **Der Volkladen**, O'Higgins y
Philippi, for natural products, including
chocolates, cakes and cosmetics.

Puerto Varas *p354, map p355*
El Libro del Capitán, Martiínez 417. Book
shop with a large selection in German and
English. Also book swap.
Las Brisas, Salvador 451. Supermarket.
Mamusia, San José 316. Chocolates.
VYH Meistur, Walker Martínez. Supermarket
with a good selection, reasonably priced.

🔺 Activities and tours

Most tours operate in season only (Sep-May).

Volcán Osorno *p353*
Weather permitting, agencies in Puerto Varas
organize climbing expeditions with a local
guide, transport from Puerto Montt or Puerto
Varas, food and equipment, US$150 per
person, payment in advance (minimum group

2, maximum 6 with 3 guides). Weather
conditions are checked the day before and a
50% refund is available if the climb is
abandoned due to weather. Those climbing
from La Burbuja must register with **CONAF** at
La Burbuja, and show they have suitable
equipment. Those climbing from the north
(La Picada) are not subject to any checks.

Ensenada *p353*
Southern Chile Expeditions, T065-213030,
www.southernchilexp.com. Expensive
fly-fishing tours.

Frutillar *p353, map p354*
Viajes Frutillar, Richter y Alissandre, Frutillar
Alto. Travel and tour agent.

Puerto Varas *p354, map p355*
Fishing
The area around Puerto Varas is popular for
fishing. A licence (obligatory) is obtainable
from the Municipalidad. Fishing expeditions
are organized by many operators (see
below). The Río Pescado (25 km east of
Puerto Varas) is a good easy alternative for
those who do not want to hire a guide.

Horse riding
Cabañas Puerto Decher, Fundo Molino
Viejo, 2 km north of Puerto Varas,
T065-338033. Guided tours, horse riding,
minimum 2 people, mixed reports.
Campo Aventura, San Bernardo 318,
T065-232910, www.campo-aventura.com.
English and German spoken, offers 1-, 3- and
10-day trips on horseback (see Cochamó,
page 364).

Tour operators
Al Sur, Del Salvador 100, T065-232300,
www.alsurexpeditions.com. Rafting on Rió
Petrohue. Official tour operator to the Parque
Pumalín. Sells trekking maps.
Andina del Sud, Del Salvador 72,
T065-232811, www.andinadelsud.cl.
Operates 'lakes' trip to Bariloche, Argentina
via Lago Todos los Santos, Peulla, Cerro
Tronador, plus other excursions.
Aqua Motion, San Fransisco 328, T065-
232747, www.aquamotion.cl. Rafting,
trekking, mountain biking, fishing,
birdwatching.

Kokayak, San José 320, T065-346433, www.paddlechile.com, French/Chilean run, offers bike hire, white-water rafting and sea kayaking.
Tranco Expeditions, San Pedro 422, T065-311311, www.trancoexpediciones.cl Trekking, rafting and climbing, Norwegian and English spoken, good equipment.
Travel Art, Imperial 0661, T065-232198, www.travelart.coml. General all-inclusive multi-day tours.
Turismo Biker, Café Terranova, on Plaza, turismobiker@yahoo.es. Specialists in downhill mountain bike trips. Not for the fainthearted.

⊜ Transport

Puerto Octay *p352*
Buses to **Osorno**, hourly, US$2; to **Las Cascadas** Mon-Fri 1730, return next day 0700. **Thaebus** runs 5 daily services to **Frutillar**, 1 hr, US$1, **Puerto Varas**, 2 hrs, and **Puerto Montt**, 2¼ hrs, US$2.50.

Ensenada *p353*
Frequent minibuses run from **Puerto Varas** in summer. Buses from Puerto Montt via Puerto Varas to **Cochamó** also stop here. Hitching from Puerto Varas is difficult.

Frutillar *p353, map p354*
Colectivos run between the two towns, 5 mins, US$0.60. Most buses to other destinations leave from opposite the Copec station in Frutillar Alto. **Thaebus** and others have frequent services to **Puerto Varas**, US$1, and **Puerto Montt**, US$1.25. To **Osorno**, Turismosur, 1¼ hrs, US$2.50; to **Puerto Octay**, Thaebus, 5 a day.

There are 2 daily train services north to **Temuco**, US$5 and south to **Puerto Varas** and **Puerto Montt**, US$1.80. Trains leave from the staion at Alessandri s/n.

Car mechanic, **Toirkens**, Los Carrera 1260, is highly recommended.

Puerto Varas *p354, map p355*
Minibuses to **Ensenada** and **Petrohué** leave from San Bernardo y Martínez; regional buses stop on San Fransisco 500 block; long-distance buses leave from their own terminals.

To **Santiago**, Turbus, Igi Llaima, Cruz del Sur and several others, US$20, semi cama US$30, salón cama US$40. **Thaebus, Full Express** and others have services to **Puerto Montt**, every 15 mins, 30 mins, US$1; same companies, same frequency to **Frutillar**, 30 mins, US$1, and **Osorno**, 1 hr, US$3. Same companies hourly to **Petrohue**, US$3. To **Valdivia**, 3 hrs, US$6; to **Temuco**, US$9; to **Cochamó** via Ensenada, 5 a day, US$3. Services from Puerto Montt to **Bariloche** (Argentina) also stop here. For the **Andina del Sud** lakes route via Lago Todos los Santos, see page 366.

There are 2 daily trains north to **Temuco**, US$6 and south to **Puerto Montt**, US$1. Trains leave from the staion at Klenner 350.

Car hire companies include **Adriazola Expediciones**, Santa Rosa 340, T065-233477; **Turismo Nieve**, Gramado 560, T065-346115.

Cycle hire is available from many tour operators, see above, for around $US18 per day; check equipment carefully.

⊙ Directory

Frutillar *p353, map p354*
Banks Banco Santander, Phillippi, at the lakeside, with Redbanc ATM taking Visa and other cards. **Post office** San Martín y Pérez Rosales, Mon-Fri 0930-1230, 1430-1800, Sat 0900-1230. **Telephone** call centre at Phillippi 883. **Useful services** Toilet, showers and changing cabins for beach on O'Higgins.

Puerto Varas *p354, map p355*
Banks Several banks with ATMs in the town centre. Casas de cambio include Exchange Ltda, Del Salvador 257, local 11, Travel Sur, San José 261, local 4; Turismo Los Lagos, Del Salvador 257 (Galería Real, local 11), open daily 0830-1330, 1500-2100, Sun 0930-1330, accepts TCs, good rates. **Internet** Several in the centre, although if you want coffee while you browse try Punt Café, Del Salvador 348. **Laundry** Gramado 1090; Lavandería Delfin, Martínez 323, expensive. **Medical emergencies** Clinica Alemana, Otto Bader 810, T065-232336, emergencies T065-232274, usually has English-speaking doctors. **Post office** San José y San Pedro; Del Salvador y Santa Rosa. **Telephone** Several call centres around town.

Parque Nacional Vicente Pérez Rosales and around → *Colour map 4, C2/3.*

Established in 1926, this is the oldest national park in Chile, stretching east from Lago Llanquihue to the Argentine border. The park is covered in woodland and contains a large lake, Lago Todos los Santos, plus three major volcanic peaks: Osorno, Puntiagudo and Tronador. Several other peaks are visible, notably Casablanca to the north and Calbuco to the south. Near the lake are the Saltos de Petrohué, impressive waterfalls on the Río Petrohué. A memorable journey by road and water takes you through the park from Puerto Montt to Bariloche in Argentina. South of the park is the beautiful Seno de Reloncaví. → *For Sleeping, Eating and other listings, see pages 365-366.*

Ins and outs

Getting there In season, take one of the hourly minibuses from Puerto Montt and Puerto Varas via Ensenada to Petrohué. They generally allow you to break your journey at the waterfalls at no extra cost. It is impossible to reach the national park by public transport out of season: there are buses only as far as Ensenada, little traffic for hitching and none of the ferries takes vehicles. Entrance to the park is free.

Getting around A combination of walking and hitching rides in locals' boats is the best way to explore the park. In wet weather many treks in the park are impossible and the road to Puerto Montt can be blocked.

Parque Nacional Pérez Rosales & the lakes route to Argentina

museum and 3D model of the park. There is also a *guardaparque* office in Puella. No
maps of treks are available in the park; buy them from a tour agency in Puerto Varas
(see page 360).

Lago Todos los Santos ⬤🍴⬤ ⇢ *pp365-366*.

The most beautiful of all the lakes in southern Chile, Lago Todos los Santos is a long,
irregularly shaped sheet of emerald-green water, surrounded by a deeply wooded
shoreline and punctuated by several small islands that rise from its surface. Beyond
the hilly shores to the east are several graceful snow-capped mountains, with the
mighty Tronador in the distance. To the north is the sharp point of **Cerro Puntiagudo**,
and at the northeastern end **Cerro Techado** rises cliff-like out of the water. The lake is
fed by several rivers, including the Río Peulla to the east, the Ríos Techado and Negro
to the north, and the Río Blanco to the south. At its western end
the lake is drained by the Río Petrohue. The lake is warm and
sheltered from the winds, and is a popular location for
watersports, swimming and for trout and salmon fishing. There are
no roads round the lake. The only scheduled vessel on the lake is
the **Andina del Sud** service between Petrohue and Peulla, with
connections to Bariloche (Argentina, see page 364), but private
launches can be hired from locals for trips.

> ❢ *In the national
> parks to the east of the
> Panamerican Highway
> night-time temperatures
> candrop as low as -10°C,
> even in summer.*

Petrohué and around

At the western end of the lake, 16 km northwest of Ensenada, **Petrohué** is a good base
for walking tours with several trails around the foot of Volcàn Osorno, or to the
miradors that look over it, such as Cerro Picada. Near the Ensenada-Petrohué road,
6 km west of Petrohué, is the **Salto de Petrohué** ① *US$2*, which was formed by a
relatively recent lava flow of hard volcanic rock. Near the falls are a snack bar and two
short trails, the **Sendero de los Enamorados** and the **Sendero Carileufú**. Boat trips
from Petrohué visit **Isla Margarita**, the largest island on the lake, with a lagoon in the
middle of it, in summer only, and boats can also be hired to visit the **Termas de Callao**
– actually two large Alerce tubs in a cabin – north of the lake. The boat will drop you at
the uninhabited El Rincón (arrange for it to wait or collect you later), from where it's a
three-and-a-half-hour walk to the baths through forest beside the Río Sin Nombre.
The path twice crosses the river by rickety hanging bridges. Just before the baths is a
house, doubling as a comfortable *refugio*, where you collect the keys and pay.

Peulla and around

Peulla, at the eastern end of the lake, is a good starting point for hikes in the
mountains. The **Cascadas Los Novios**, signposted above the **Hotel Peulla**, are a steep
walk away, but are stunning once you reach them. There is also a good walk to **Laguna
Margarita**, which takes four hours.

Cayutué and around

On the south shore of Lago Todos Los Santos is the little village of **Cayutué**, reached
by hiring a boat from Petrohué ① *US$30*. From Cayutué (no camping on the beach but
there are private sites) it is a three-hour walk to **Laguna Cayutué**, a jewel set between
mountains and surrounded by forest, where you can camp and swim. From the laguna
it is a five-hour hike south to **Ralún** on the Reloncaví Estuary (see page 364): the last
half of this route is along a *ripio* road built for extracting timber and is part of the old
route used by missionaries in the colonial period to travel between Nahuel Huapi in
Argentina and the island of Chiloé.

The lakes route to Bariloche ⊟ ▶▶ *pp365-366.*

This popular and evermore expensive route from Puerto Montt to Bariloche, involving ferries across Lago Todos los Santos, Lago Frías and Lago Nahuel Huapi, is outstandingly beautiful. The journey starts by bus via Puerto Varas, Ensenada and the Petrohué falls (20-minute stop) to **Petrohué**, where you board the catamaran service (1¾ hours) across Lago Todos Los Santos to **Peulla**. During the summer there is a two-hour stop in Peulla for lunch (see Eating, below) and for **Chilean customs** ① *summer 0800-2100 daily; winter 0800-2000 daily*, followed by a two-hour bus ride through the **Paso Pérez Rosales** to Argentine customs in **Puerto Frías**. Then it's a 20-minute boat trip across Lago Frías to **Puerto Alegre**, and a short bus journey (15 minutes) to **Puerto Blest**. A catamaran departs from Puerto Blest for the beautiful one-hour trip along Lago Nahuel Huapi to **Puerto Panuelo**, from where there is a final one-hour bus journey to Bariloche. (The bus drops passengers at hotels, camping sites or in the town centre.)

Bariloche is a popular destination and centre for exploring the Argentine Lake District. Beautifully situated on the south shore of Lago Nahuel Huapi, the streets rise steeply along the edge of a glacial morraine. West of the city on the shores of the lake is the resort of **Llao Llao**, where the famous **Hotel Llao Llao** looks out over chocolate-box scenery. Nearby are two ski resorts. Boat excursions can be made from Bariloche to other parts of the Argentine Lake District. There is a wide range of accommodation as well as air and bus connections to Buenos Aires and other destinations in Argentina.

▶▶ *For more details, consult Footprint Argentina or the South American Handbook.*

Seno de Reloncaví ⊟⊘▲⊟ ▶▶ *pp365-366.*

The Seno de Reloncaví, situated east of Puerto Montt and south of the Parque Nacional Pérez Rosales, is the northernmost of Chile's glacial inlets. It is a quiet and beautiful estuary, often shrouded in mist and softly falling rain, but stunning nonetheless, and recommended for its wildlife, including sea lions and dolphins, and for its peaceful atmosphere. It is relatively easily reached from Puerto Montt by a road that runs along the wooded lower Petrohué Valley south from Ensenada and then follows the eastern shore of the estuary for almost 100 km to join the Carretera Austral.

Ralún and around

A small village situated at the northern end of the estuary, Ralún is 31 km southeast from Ensenada by a poorly paved road. There is a village shop and post office, and on the outskirts are **thermal baths** ① *US$2, reached by boat, US$2.50 across the Río Petrohué*. Ralún is the departure point for a five-hour walk north to **Laguna Cayutué** in the Parque Nacional Vicente Pérez Rosales (see above). From Ralún you can either travel along the eastern shore of the estuary to Cochamó (see below) or take the road that branches off and follows the western side of the estuary south, 36 km to Lago Chapo and the Parque Nacional Alerce Andino (see page 402).

Cochamó and further south

Some 17 km south of Ralún along a poor *ripio* road is the pretty village of Cochamó. It's situated in a striking setting, on the east shore of the estuary with the volcano behind, and has a small, frequently deserted waterfront, where benches allow you to sit and admire the view. Cochamó's fine wooden church dates from 1900 and is similar to those on Chiloé. It has a clock with wooden hands and an unusual black statue of Christ.

Puelo, a most peaceful place. From here the road continues 36 km further southwest to Puelche on the Carretera Austral (see page 403).

Gaucho Trail

The Gaucho Trail east from Cochamó to **Paso León** on the Argentine border was used in the colonial period by the indigenous population, Jesuit priests and later by *gauchos.* It runs along Río Cochamó to La Junta, then along the north side of Lago Vidal, passing waterfalls and the oldest surviving Alerce trees in Chile at El Arco. The route takes three to four days by horse or five to six days on foot, depending on conditions and is best travelled between December and March. A road is due to be built which will allow access by jeep. From the border crossing at Paso León it is a three-hour walk to the main road towards San Carlos de Bariloche.

● Sleeping

Lago Todos los Santos *p363*
The CONAF office in Petrohué can help find cheaper family accommodation.
LL Fundo El Salto, near Salto de Petrohué, fly-fish-chile.com. Very expensive fishing lodge.
L Hotel Peulla, Peulla, T02-1964182, hpeullareservas@terra.cl. Price includes dinner and breakfast, direct personal reservations, cheaper out of season. Beautiful setting by the lake and mountains, restaurant and bar, poor meals, cold in winter, often full of tour groups (tiny shop at back of hotel).
L Hotel Petrohué, T065-212025, www.petrohue.com. Burned down in 2002, but is now rebuilt. Half board available. Magnificent views, log fires, cosy. Sauna and heated swimming pool. Hiking, fishing and other activities arranged.
D Residencial Palomita, 50 m west of Hotel Peulla. Price per person for half board, lunches available. Family-run, simple, comfortable but not spacious, separate shower, book ahead in season.

Camping

In **Petrohué**, there's a campsite beside the lake, US$6 per site, no services (local fishermen will ferry you across for US$2). Camping wild and picnicing is forbidden at Petrohué; car parking US$4 per day.
The campsite in **Peulla** is opposite the CONAF office, US$4 per site. There's also a good campsite 1¾ hrs' walk east of of the village, or ask at the *carabineros* station if you can camp on the beach; no facilities.

Seno de Reloncaví *p364*
Accommodation in Puelo is also available with families.
LL Río Puelo Lodge, Puelo, T02-2298533, www.rio-puelo-lodge.cl. Plush lodge offering all-in fly-fishing packages from US$500.
A Campo Aventura, 4 km south of Coch-amó, T065-232910, www.campo-aventura. com. For details of riding and trekking expeditions, see below. Accommodation is offered at the base camp (signpost on road) with great breakfast, kitchen, sauna. Camping is also possible. Very fresh milk from Campo Aventura's cow, herb garden, expensive but good food using local produce, vegetarian also available, book exchange. There's another base in a renovated mountain house in the valley of La Junta. Write to **Campo Aventura**, Casilla 5, Correo Cochamó for further information.
C-D Cochamó, T065-216212. **F** singles. Basic but clean, friendly, often full with salmon farm workers, good meals, recommended.
C-D Mercado Particular Sabin, Catedral 20, Cochamó. One of several *pensiones*, next to Hotel Cochamó.
C-D Navarrito, Ralún. **F** singles in basic accommodation. Also restaurant.
D Hospedaje Edicar, Cochamó. **F** singles. Breakfast available. Without bath, spacious, recommended.
D Hospedaje Maura, JJ Molina 12, Cochamó. **F** singles. Some rooms with bath. Beautifully situated, good food.
D Posada Campesino, Ralún. **F** singles. Without breakfast, very friendly, simple, clean.

Camping Los Castaños, Cochamó, T065-216212.

Eating

Lago Todos los Santos *p363*
See Sleeping, above, for hotel restaurants. There is a small shop in the **Andina del Sud** building in Petrohué, with basic supplies and some of the houses sell fresh bread, but if you're camping it's best to take your own food.

Seno de Reloncaví *p364*
Eateries in Cochamó include **Donde Payi,** opposite the church and **Reloncaví**, on the road down to the waterfront. On the seafront there is a cheap fish/seafood restaurant, which also hires out canoes, US$1.50 for 30 mins.

Activities and tours

Seno de Reloncaví *p364*
Horse riding/trekking
Campo Aventura, Casilla 5, Correo Cochamó, T065-232910, www.campo-aventura.com. Specializes in all-inclusive riding and trekking expeditions with packhorses along the Gaucho trail between the Reloncaví Estuary and the Argentine border, 2-10 days, roughly US$100 per person, per day; good guides, spectacular scenery, English, French and German spoken, highly recommended. It also organizes other activities including combined sea kayaking-horse riding trips with **Kokayak** in Puerto Varas.
Sebastián Contreras, C Morales, Cochamó, T065-216220. An independent guide who offers tours on horseback and hires out horses, recommended.

Transport

Lago Todos los Santos *p363*
Boat
The Andina del Sud catamaran sails between Petrohué and Peulla, departing Petrohué 1030 Mon-Sat, departing Peulla 1500 Mon-Sat, 2 hrs, US$22 per person one way, bicycles free (book in advance); most seating indoors, no cars carried, commentaries in Spanish and English, expensive refreshments. This is the only public service across the lake and it connects with the **Andina del Sud** tour bus between Puerto Montt and Bariloche (see page 373). Local fishermen also make the trip across the lake and for a group this can be cheaper than the public service, allow 3½ hrs.

Bus
Minibuses from **Puerto Varas** to Ensenada continue to **Petrohué** in summer; last return bus from Petrohue to Puerto Varas, 1800. There is a reduced service to **Ensenada** only in winter.

The lakes route to Bariloche *p364*
The trip may be cancelled if the weather is poor; there are reports of difficulty in obtaining a refund. This journey is operated only by **Andina del Sud** (see page 373) whose buses depart from company offices in **Puerto Montt** daily at 0800; the fare is US$160 one way (not including lunch in Peulla). From 1 May to 30 Aug this trip is done over 2 days with an overnight stay in Peulla. Add another US$140 to the fare for a double room in the **Hotel Peulla**. Baggage is automatically taken here but for cheaper alternatives see Sleeping, above.

Seno de Reloncaví *p364*
Bus
Buses Fierro and Bohle from Puerto Montt via Puerto Varas and Ensenada, to **Ralún**, **Cochamó** and **Puelo**, 5 daily all year.

Boat
In summer boats sail up the estuary from **Angelmó**. Get a group of people together and convince one of the fishermen to take you. For information on (irregular) scheduled trips, contact the Regional Sernatur office in Puerto Montt.

Puerto Montt → *Colour map 4, C2.*

The capital of Región X (Los Lagos), Puerto Montt lies on the northern shore of the Seno de Reloncaví, 1016 km south of Santiago. The jumping-off point for journeys south to Chiloé and Patagonia, it is a busy modern city, the fastest growing in Chile, flourishing with the salmon-farming boom. It was founded in 1853, as part of the German colonization of the area, on the site of a Mapuche community known as Melipulli, meaning four hills. Good views over the city and bay are offered from outside the Intendencia Regional on Avenida X Region. There is a wide range of accommodation, but most people will prefer to stay in Puerto Varas, more picturesque and only 20 minutes' away by bus. ➤➤ *For Sleeping, Eating and other listings, see pages 370-374.*

Ins and outs

Getting there El Tepual Airport is 13 km northwest of town, served by ETM buses ① *T065-294292, 1½ hrs before departure, US$3,* from the bus terminal; there's also a minibus service to/from hotels, US$6 per person. There are several daily flights north to Santiago, Concepción and Temuco, and south to Chaitén, Coyhaique and Punta Arenas. Ferries and catamarans serve Chaitén (four to six times weekly) and Puerto Chacabuco (one or two weekly); there's also a weekly service south to Puerto Natales. Puerto Montt is the departure point for bus services south to Coyhaique and Punta Arenas, and for buses north to Santiago and all the intermediate cities.

Getting around Puerto Montt is quite a large city, with many *colectivos* and buses serving the *barrios* on the hill above the town. The cental area is down by the port, though, and everything here is within walking distance.

Tourist information Sernatur ① *Gobernación Provincial building, Plaza de Armas, summer daily 0900-1300, 1500-1900; winter Mon-Fri 0830-1300, 1400-1800,* has an office. If going to Chiloé, get information here as this is often difficult to obtain on the island. The regional tourist office is in the Intendencia Regional ① *Av Décima Región 480, Casilla 297, T065-254580, infoloslagos@sernatur.cl.* There's an information kiosk ① *till 1800 Sat,* on the Plaza de Armas run by the municipality, which has town maps, but little information on other destinations. **CONAF** is on Ochogavia 458, but cannot supply details of conditions in the national parks. Information on the Parque Pumalín, see page 404, is available from ① *Buin 356, T065-250079, www.pumalinpark.org.*

Puerto Montt

The **Plaza de Armas** lies at the foot of steep hills, one block north of Avenida Diego Portales, which runs east–west parallel to the shore. The **Palacio del Arte Diego Rivera** ① *Quillota 116, off the Plaza de Armas, T065-261817,* hosts temporary exhibitions, concerts and plays. Two blocks west of the square is the **Iglesia de los Jesuitas**, on Calle Gallardo, dating from 1872, which has a fine blue-domed ceiling; behind it on a hill is the **campanario** (clock tower). Further west, near the bus terminal, is the **Museo Regional Juan Pablo II** ① *Diego Portales 997, 1030-1800, US$1,* documenting local history. It has a fine collection of historic photos of the city and memorabilia of Pope John Paul II's visit in 1988.

❖ If driving north out of Puerto Montt (or Puerto Varas, Frutillar, etc), look for signs to 'Ruta 5'.

The little fishing port of **Angelmó**, 2 km west along Avenida Diego Portales, has become a tourist centre thanks to its dozens of seafood restaurants and handicraft shops. Launches depart from Angelmó ① *US$1,* for the wooded **Isla Tenglo**, offshore from Puerto Montt. It's a favourite place for picnics, with views from the summit. The island is famous for its *curanto*, served by restaurants in summer. Boat trips round the island from Angelmó last for 30 minutes and cost US$8. A longer boat trip (two hours) will take you to **Isla Huar**, an island in the Seno de Reloncaví, departing at 1600 and returning from the other end of the island at 0730. If you are lucky you can stay at the church on the island, but it may be best to camp.

West of Puerto Montt

The old coast road west from Puerto Montt is very beautiful. **Chinquihue** (the name means 'place of skunks'), beyond Angelmó, has many seafood restaurants, oysters being a speciality. Further south is **Calbuco**, scenic centre of the fishing industry. It is situated on an island linked to the mainland by a causeway and can be visited direct by boat or by road. West of here is the Río Maullín, which drains Lago Llanquihue, and has some attractive waterfalls and good salmon fishing. At its mouth is the little fishing village of **Maullín**, founded in 1602. On the coast to the southeast is **Carelmapu**, with an excellent beach and *cabañas* at windswept Playa Brava, about 3 km away.

Sea routes south of Puerto Montt

Puerto Montt is the departure point for several popular voyages along the coast of southern Chile. All sailings are from Angelmó; timetables should be checked carefully in advance as schedules change frequently. ➤➤ *For further details, see Transport, page 373, and for ferry routes, refer to the colour maps at the back of the book.*

To Puerto Natales One of the highlights of many journeys to Chile is the 1460-km voyage between Puerto Montt and the southern port of Puerto Natales, made by the Navimag *M/N Puerto Edén*; it is quicker to fly and cheaper to go by bus via Argentina but the voyage by boat is spectacular. The route south from Puerto Montt crosses the Seno de Reloncaví and the Golfo de Ancud between the mainland and the large island of Chiloé, then continues south through the Canal Moraleda and the Canal Errázuriz, which separate the mainland from the outlying islands. It then heads west through the

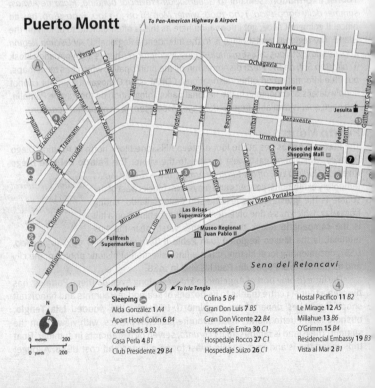

Puerto Montt

Seno del Reloncaví

To Angelmó · To Isla Tenglo

Sleeping	Colina **5** *B4*	Hostal Pacífico **11** *B2*
Alda González **1** *A4*	Gran Don Luis **7** *B5*	Le Mirage **12** *A5*
Apart Hotel Colón **6** *B4*	Gran Don Vicente **22** *B4*	Millahue **13** *B6*
Casa Gladis **3** *B2*	Hospedaje Emita **30** *C1*	O'Grimm **15** *B4*
Casa Perla **4** *B1*	Hospedaje Rocco **27** *C1*	Residencial Embassy **19** *B3*
Club Presidente **29** *B4*	Hospedaje Suizo **26** *C1*	Vista al Mar **2** *B1*

Golfo de Peñas (Gulf of Sorrows) to reach a series of channels – Canal Messier, Angostura Inglesa, Fiordo del Indio and Canal Kirke – which provide one of the narrowest routes for large shipping in the world. There are spectacular views of the wooded fjords, weather permitting, particularly at sunrise and sunset, and a sense of desolate peace pervades everything except the ship, which is filled with cows in transport containers mooing day and night, and people having a good time.

Take seasickness tablets especially for the stretch of open sea towards the Golfo de Penas and for the onward the journey south of puerto Eden.

The only regular stop on this route is at the fishing village of **Puerto Edén** on Isla Wellington, one hour south of the Angostura Inglesa. It has three shops (scant provisions), one off-licence, one café, and a *hospedaje* for up to 20 people (open intermittantly). The population of 185, includes five *carabineros* and a few remaining native Alacaluf people. Puerto Edén is the drop-off point for exploring **Isla Wellington**, which is largely untouched, with stunning mountains. If you do stop here, take all food; maps (not very accurate) are available in Santiago. The onward fare to Puerto Natales is US$70.

This is a ferry that also carries cargo (including cattle and sheep) rather than a cruise liner; standards of service and comfort vary, depending on the number of passengers and weather conditions. Economy class accommodation is basic and near the engine room, in 24-berth dormitories (see box, page 370), and although economy class and cabin passengers eat the same food, they are confined to separate areas (economy class is very cramped). The food is variable, and, apart from videos, organized entertainment on board is limited. Wine is available, but you are welcome to bring your own.

To Puerto Chacabuco and Laguna San Rafael

Navimag also runs a twice weekly ferry service between Puerto Montt and **Puerto Chacabuco**, 80 km west of Coyhaique. This beautiful voyage passes forested cliffs,

seemingly within touching distance, and offers glimpses of distant snows. However, taking this route south means that travellers miss out on the attractions of much of the Carretera Austral. From Puerto Chacabuco there are further services to visit **Laguna San Rafael**. However, it may well be cheaper, and is certainly more comfortable, to take a catamaran service to the Laguna from Puerto Chacabuco (see page 432) or to charter a small plane from Coyhaique. A luxury alternative is to board *Skorpios II* for a cruise to Chiloe and Laguna San Raphael. Generally service is excellent, the food superb and, at the laguna, you chip ice off the face of the glacier for your whisky. After San Rafael the ship visits **Quitralco fjord**, where there are thermal pools and boat trips. The fare varies according to season, type of cabin and number of occupants. There are also four- to six-day tours from Puerto Montt with **Patagonia Connection**, which visit Puerto Chacabuco, Laguna San Rafael and the Termas de Puyuhuapi (see page 432). ▶▶ *For further details, see Transport, page 374.*

Vista Hermosa **24** *C1*

Eating 🍴
Café Haussman **1** *B5*
Café Central **2** *B4*
Café Real **2** *B4*

Centro Español **3** *B5*
Club Alemán **4** *B5*
Club de Yates **8** *C6*
Dino **7** *B4*
Milton Plaza **5** *B5*

Lake District Puerto Montt

❖ On board the *Magellanes* to Puerto Natales

"When the boat began loading there was a mild stampede, especially for us economy-class (or dungeon class) passengers: no-one wanted to end up in one of the top bunks, which require elaborate climbing equipment to reach and which give only three in of headroom. There were two 24-occupant dungeon-class barracks, each equipped with two toilets and one shower, located at the very bottom of the ship, scattered alongside the engine room, the generator, the anchor-chain-dropping room and the rock-concert-amplifier-testing room. It was loud.

What did we do all day? Not much. The ship felt like an airport waiting room. People read, played cards, drank and slept. The scenery was indeed 'breathtakingly beautiful and rugged' but it was too windy and cold to stay outside for long, so we usually settled for glancing out of the ship's tiny windows. At Puerto Edén we were awakened by the release of the anchor, which, in dungeon class, sounded as though it had been dropped through the ceiling. We weren't sure whether to wake up or abandon ship.

Nearly 200 of us decided to go ashore. We each wore a bright orange life jacket so, naturally, we were easily identifiable to the locals who were eager to do business with us. After a few hours stocking up on souvenirs, we went back to the ship and steeled ourselves for the rough sea crossing. The waves, relative to the boat's size, were not threatening, but they hit the boat directly on her port side and created an impressively nauseating effect. Some passengers took seasickness pills and wandered down to their rooms to pass out. Others drank wine or beer till this had the same effect.

Perhaps the highlight of the trip was a tug-o-war on the upper cargo deck against the crew. The passengers, who had spent too much time sitting around and too little time loading cargo ships, were trounced. Team gringo fared better, however, in the ensuing soccer match: adding to the excitement were the obstacles on the 'pitch': huge metal rivets every few metres and a 20-tonne freight elevator."

⬤ Sleeping

Puerto Montt *p367, map p369*
Accommodation is expensive in season, much cheaper off season. There are lots of *cabañas* on the outskirts of the city and in Pelluco.

LL-L Gran Hotel Don Vicente, Varas 447, T065-432900, www.granhoteldonvicente.cl. Business class hotel. Some rooms noisy, restaurant serving seafood, fine views.

L Club Presidente, Portales 664, T065-251666, www.presidente.cl. Comfortable 4-star with breakfast. Large rooms or suites. English spoken.

L-AL Gran Hotel Don Luis, Quillota 146, T065-259001, www.hoteldonluis.cl. Another comfortable 4-star hotel and very good

restaurant as well as a gym and sauna. Recommended.

AL Apart Hotel Colón, Pedro Montt 65, T065-264290, www.aparthotelcolon.cl. Fully furbished studio apartments, good value, especially when paying in dollars.

AL O'Grimm, Gallardo 211, T065-252845, www.ogrimm.com. Pleasant rooms with lounge area, cosy restaurant with occasional live music, central.

A-B Le Mirage, Rancagua 350, T065-255125. A basic business class hotel with breakfast, small rooms, clean.

B Hostal Pacífico, J J Mira 1088, T065-256229. With bath, some rooms a little cramped, breakfast included, cable TV, parking, comfortable. Discounts for foreign tourists.

B Millahue, Copiapó 64, T065-253829, www.hotelmillahue.cl. With breakfast and bath, slightly run down, restaurant, also apartments at Benavente 959, T/F065-254592.

B-C Colina, Talca 81, T065-253502, hotcolina @surnet.cl. With bath. Spacious, restaurant, bar, car hire, can be, noisy, good value. Recommended.

B-C Hospedaje Suizo, Independencia 231, T/F065-252640, rossyoelckers@yahoo.es. F singles, with breakfast. Some rooms with bath. Attractive house near the bus terminal, clean, German and Italian spoken, painting and Spanish classes. Convenient for Navimag. Recommended.

C Alda González, Gallardo 552, T065-253334. F singles. Some rooms with bath, breakfast included, cooking facilities, English and German spoken, good value, near the Plaza de Armas.

C Hospedaje Emita, Miraflores 1281, T065-250725, hospedaje_emita@hotmail.com. persons singles with breakfast, including home-made bread. Some rooms with bath. Clean, friendly, safe, near the bus terminal.

C-D Casa Perla, Trigal 312, T065-262104, www.casaperla.com. F per person in shared rooms. With breakfast. Near the bus terminal, helpful, friendly, meals, laundry, internet, pleasant garden, English spoken, Spanish classes offered, good meeting place. Recommended.

C-D Hospedaje Rocco, Pudeto 233,T/065-272897, www.hospedajerocco.cl. F singles. With breakfast, but without bath, real coffee, English and Italian spoken, friendly atmosphere, laundry. Quiet residential area, convenient for navimag. Recommended.

C-D Residencial Embassy, Valdivia 130, T065- 253533. E singles. Some rooms with bath, clean, stores luggage. Meals served.

C-D Vista al Mar, Vivar 1337, T065-255625, www.hospedajevistaalmar.unlugar.com . F singles. Friendly, helpful, welcoming, good breakfast. Phone for lift from bus terminal.

D Casa Gladis, Ancud y Mira. Some double rooms. F-G per person for dormitory beds, kitchen and laundry facilities, near bus terminal.

D Vista Hermosa, Miramar 1486, T/F065-268001, vistahermosa@mixmail.com. F singles without bath, 10 mins' walk from bus terminal. The room at the front has the best views.

Camping

Wild camping is possible along the sea front. There are also several official sites west of Puerto Montt.

Anderson, 11 km west. American run, hot showers, private beach, home-grown fruit, vegetables and milk products.

El Ciervo, 3 km west. Good site.

Municipal, Chinquihue, 10 km west. Open Oct-Apr, fully equipped with tables, seats, barbecue, toilets and showers, small shop, no kerosene, bus service from town.

West of Puerto Montt *p368*

B Cabañas El Pangal, 5 km from Maullin, T065-451244, m_essedin@hotmail.com. Campsite and cabins on the beach.

B Hotel Colonial, Calbuco, T065-461546, www.hotelcolonial@hotmail.com. One of several decent hotels.

● Eating

Puerto Montt *p367, map p369*

For seafood enthusiasts, the only place to go is **Angelmó**, where there are many small, very popular seafood restaurants in the old fishing port past the fish market, serving excellent lunches only. There is fierce touting for business. Look out for local specialities such as curanto and picoroco al vapor, a giant barnacle whose flesh looks and tastes like a crab, and ask for té blanco (white wine; the stalls are not legally allowed to serve wine). There are more good seafood restaurants on the other side of the city in Pelluco (see page 402). In Puerto Montt itself, try the following eateries:

♥♥♥ Club de Yates, Juan Soler s/n. Excellent, expensive seafood.

♥♥♥-♥♥ Club Alemán, Varas 264, T065252551. Old fashioned, good food and wine.

♥♥ Café Haussman, San Martín y Urmeneta. German-style cakes, beer and *crudos* (raw meat).

♥♥ Centro Español, O'Higgins 233, T065-343753. Decent traditional Chilean and Spanish food. Vegetarian options.

Dino, Varas 550, T065-252785. Restaurant upstairs, snacks downstairs (try the lemon juice). Often has an all you can eat buffet.

Café Central, Rancagua 117, T065-482888. Spartan decor, generous portions (sandwiches and *pichangas*). Giant TV screen for football enthusiasts.

Café Real, Rancagua 137, T065-253750. For *empanadas*, *pichangas*, *congrío frito* and cheap lunches.

Milton Plaza, Urmeneta 326 y O'Higgins, T065-295790. Good seafood and snacks. Doubles as a pool hall. Recommended.

Restaurant de las Antigüedades, Av Angelmó. Attractive and unusual decor, real coffee, interesting menu.

Cheap food is also available at Puerto Montt bus terminal.

Cafés

Asturias, Angelmó 2448. Limited menu but often recommended.

Café Alemana, Rancagua 117. Real coffee, good.

West of Puerto Montt *p368*

Kiel, Chinquihué, T065-255010. Good meat and seafood dishes.

○ Bars and clubs

Puerto Montt *p367, map p369*

Watch out: several of the 'bars' near the port and along Pérez Rosales have more to them than meets the eye.

Star, Ruta 5 north of the city. Disco. Several more in Pelluco, east of Puerto Montt.

○ Shopping

Puerto Montt *p367, map p369*

Woollen goods and Mapuche-designed rugs can be bought at roadside stalls in Angelmó and on Diego Portales opposite the bus terminal. Prices are much the same as on Chiloé, but quality is often lower.

Fullfresh, opposite bus terminal. Supermarket open 0900-2200 daily.

Libros, Diego Portales 580. Bookshop with a small selection of English novels, also maps.

Paseo del Mar, Talca y Antonio Varas. Large modern shopping mall. There is also a new mall, the **Paseo Costanera** on the seafront.

▲ Activities and tours

Puerto Montt *p367, map p369*

There are many agencies. Most offer 1-day excursions to **Chiloé** (US$30) and to **Puerto Varas**, **Isla Loreley**, **Laguna Verde**, and the **Petrohué Falls**: these tours are cheaper from bus company kiosks inside the bus terminal. Some companies offer 2-day excursions along the Carretera Austral to **Hornopirén**, US$100, with food and accommodation.

Alsur, Antonio Varas 445, T/F065-287628, www.alsurexpeditions.com. Rafting and watersports as well as trips to Pumalín Park.

Andina del Sud, Varas 437, close to central tourist kiosk, T065-257797. Sells a variety of tours, and through its subsidiary **Cruce de Lagos** (www.lakecrossing.cl) also offers the lakes trip to Bariloche (see page 364).

Eureka Turismo, Gallardo 65, T065-250412, www.chile-travel.com/eureka.htm. Helpful, German and English spoken.

Kayaking Austral, T09-6980951, or book through **Casa Perla**. Guided sea kayaking.

Petrel Tours, Benavente 327, T065-251780, petrel@telsur.net. Recommended.

Travellers, General Bulnes 1009, 22 de Mayo, T065-262099, www.travellers.cl. Booking office for **Navimag** ferry to Puerto Natales, bespoke excursions, also sells imported camping equipment and runs computerized tourist information service, book swap ("the best south of Santiago"), map display, TV, real coffee, English-run.

West of Puerto Montt *p368*

Marina del Sur (MDS), T/F065-251958, Chinquihué. Sailing courses, notice board for crew (*tripulante*) requests, modern building with bar and restaurant. The MDS charters office specializes in chartering boats for cruising the Patagonian channels: US$3200-10,000 per week depending on size of boat.

⊖ Transport

Puerto Montt *p367, map p369*

Air

LanChile, Sky and Aerolíneas del Sur have several flights daily to **Santiago**, from US$150 return (best one way prices with Aerolíneas del Sur); to **Balmaceda** for Coyhaique, from US$120 return; to **Punta**

Arenas, from US$170 return. In Jan, Feb and Mar you may be told that flights are booked up, however, cancellations are sometimes available from the airport. To **Chaitén**, Cielomar Austral and Aerotaxis del Sur, daily, US$70. To **Bariloche** and **Neuquén** (Argentina), TAN, 2 weekly, 40 mins; to **Port Stanley** (Falkland Islands/Islas Malvinas), from Santiago via Punta Arenas, **LanChile**, Sat, US$700 return.

Airline offices include Aerotaxis del Sur, A Varas 70 , T065-731315, www.aerotaxis delsur.cl; Cielomar Austral, Quillota 245, loc 1, T065-264010; LanChile, O'Higgins 167, T600-5262000; Sky, T600-600 2828 for information.

Bus
The very crowded terminal on the seafront at Diego Portales y Lota has telephones, restaurants, a casa de cambio and left luggage (US$1.80 per item for 24 hrs).

Expreso Puerto Varas, Thaebus and Full Express run minibuses every few mins to **Puerto Varas**, US$1, **Llanquihue** and **Frutillar**, US$1.50, and to **Osorno**, US$2.50. Buses and *colectivos* nos 2, 3 and 20 ply the route to **Anglemo**, US$0.50 each way.

To **Ensenada** and **Petrohué**, several companies, hourly; to **Ralún**, **Cochamó** and **Puelo**, Buses Fierro and Buses Bohle, 5 daily via Puerto Varas and Ensenada; to **Pucón**, several daily, 6 hrs, US$10; to **Santiago**, several companies, 13 hrs, US$20, semi cama US$30, salón cama US$40; to **Temuco**, US$9; to **Valdivia**, US$6; to **Concepción**, US$11. For services to Chiloé, see page 380.

To **Punta Arenas**, Pacheco and Queilen Bus, 1-3 weekly, 32-38 hrs, approximately US$55 (bus goes through Argentina via Bariloche; take US$ cash to pay for meals etc in Argentina); book well in advance in Jan-Feb and check if you need a multiple-entry Chilean visa; also book any return journey before setting out. To **Coyhaique** via Bariloche, 2 weekly, Turibus, US$60.

International To **Bariloche** via Osorno and the Puyehue pass, daily, 7hrs, Andes Mar, Río de la Plata and Tas Choapa, US$17. Andes Mar also has through services to **Buenos Aires**, **Nequén** and **Bahía Blanca**; services are reduced out of season. Buy tickets for international buses from the bus terminal, not through an agency. The best views are from the right hand side of the bus. For the route to Argentina via **Lago Todos los Santos**, see page 364.

Car/motorbike
Hire from **Automotric Angelmó**, Talca 79, cheap and helpful; **Automóvil Club de Chile**, Ensenada 70, T065-254776, and at airport; **Autovald**, Diego Portales 1330, T065-256355, cheap rates; **Avis**, Urmeneta, 1037, T065-253307, and at airport; **Budget**, Gallardo 450, T065-254888 and at airport; **Dollar**, Hotel Vicente Pérez Rosales, Antonio Varas 447; **Egartur**, Benavente 575, loc. 3, T065-257336, egartur@telsur.cl, good service, recommended, will deliver your car to your hotel for free; **First**, Antonio Varas 447, T065-252036; **Full Famas**, Diego Portales 506, T065-258060, F065-259840, and airport, T065-263750, friendly, helpful, good value, has vehicles that can be taken to Argentina; **Hertz**, Antonio Varas 126, T065-259585, helpful, English spoken; **Travicargo**, Urmeneta 856, T065-257137.

For motorcycle repairs, visit **Miguel Schmuch**, Urmeneta 985, T/F065-258877.

Ferry
Shipping offices Bohemia, Antonio Varas 947, T065-254675; Catamaranes del Sur, Diego Portales 510, T065-267533, www.catamaranesdelsur.cl; Navimag, Terminal Transbordadores, Av Angelmó 2187, T065-253318, www.navimag.com; Skorpios, Angelmó 1660 y Miraflores (Castilla 588), T065-252619, www.skorpios.cl; Naviera Austral, Terminal Transbordadores, Angelmó 2187, T065-270400, www.navieraustral.cl.

Train
The station is 2 km north of the city centre at Cuarta Terraza s/n, La Paloma, T600-5855000, www.efe.cl. Two daily services north to **Temuco**, US$6 via **Puerto Varas**, US$1, **Frutillar**, US$1.80 and **Osorno**, US$2.75.

Sea routes south of Puerto Montt *p368*
To Puerto Natales Navimag *Ferry Eden* sails once a week, Nov-Apr, departing Puerto Montt Mon 1600, returning Fri 0400 (although departures are frequently delayed,

or even advanced, by weather conditions), 3½ days, economy from US$555 per person (take sleeping bag), private cabin with view US$1720 (double US$1750), all prices include meals, 10% discount for ISIC holders in cabin class only, fares 10-20% lower Apr-Oct. Book well in advance for cabin class departures Dec-Mar (more than 2 weeks in advance in Feb), especially for the voyage south; Puerto Natales to Puerto Montt is less heavily booked; it is worth putting your name on the waiting list for cancellations at busy periods. Tickets can be bought in advance through **Travellers** in Puerto Montt (see Activities and tours above), from **Navimag** offices in Puerto Montt, Puerto Natales and Punta Arenas, from travel agencies throughout the country, or online at www.navimag.cl.

To Puerto Chacabuco and Laguna San Rafael Navimag ferry *M/V Magallanes* sails this route throughout the year, once or twice a week, 24 hrs, bunks from US$60 to US$200, cars US$180, motorcycles US$40, cycles US$28. In the summer (Sep-Apr) the Magallanes continues once a week (usually at the weekend) from Puerto Chacabuco to **Laguna San Rafael**, 21-24 hrs, return fare Puerto Montt-Laguna San Rafael US$400-800; better offers are available from from Puerto Chacabuco to Laguna San Rafael (see page 432).

Skorpios Cruises luxury ship *Skorpios 2* leaves Puerto Montt Sat 1100 for a 6-day cruise to **Laguna San Rafael**, returning to Puerto Montt Fri, double cabin from US$1100 per person. For further details (and information about routes sailed by Skorpios II , consult www.skorpios.cl).

Raymond Weber, Av Chipana 3435 Pasaje 4, T02-8858250, www.chilecharter.com, charters 2 luxury sailing catamarans to visit Golfo de Ancud and Laguna San Rafael.

Other sea routes To **Chaitén**, Naviera Austral, 4 ferries weekly, 10 hrs, passengers US$25, reclining seat US$33, cars US$120, bicycles US$11; **Catamaranes del Sur** 2 weekly in summer, less frequently off season, catamaran service, 4 hrs, US$35 including transfer to port from company offices.

To **Río Negro**, Isla Llancahué, Baños Cahuelmó and Fiordo Leptepu/Coman, m/n Bohemia, 6 days/5 nights, US$745-920 per person depending on season.

● Directory

Puerto Montt *p367, map p369*
Banks ATMs at several banks and supermarkets in the centre and in both malls; commission charges for TCs vary widely. As for casas de cambio, good rates at Galería Cristal, Varas 595; **Afex**, Portales 516; **La Moneda de Oro**, at the bus terminal, exchanges Latin American currencies Mon-Sat 0930-1230, 1530-1800; **Turismo Los Lagos**, Varas 595, local 13. **Consulates Argentina**, Cauquenes 94, piso 2, T065-253996, quick visa service; **Germany**, Antonio Varas y Gallardo, piso 3, Oficina 306, Tue-Wed 0930-1200; **Netherlands**, Chorillos 1582, T065-253003; **Spain**, Rancagua 113, T065-252557. **Internet** Several in the centre and on Av Angelmó. **Laundry Center**, Antonio Varas 700; **Lavatodo**, O'Higgins 231; **Narly**, San Martín 187, Local 6, high prices, US$7 for 3 kg; **Nautilus**, Av Angelmó 1564, cheaper, good; **Unic**, Chillán 149; **Yessil't**, Edif Caracol, Urmeneta 300, service washes. **Medical services** Seminario s/n, T065-261134. **Post office** Rancagua 126, open 0830-1830 Mon-Fri, 0830-1200 Sat. **Telephone** Several in the centre and along Av Angelmó.

Chiloé

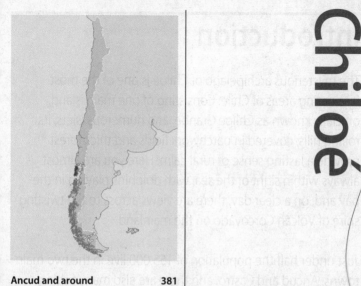

Footprint features

Introduction

The mysterious archipelago of Chiloé is one of the most fascinating areas of Chile. Consisting of one main island, officially known as Chiloé Grande, and numerous islets, its rolling hills, covered in patchwork fields and thick forest provide a lasting sense of rural calm. Here you are almost always within sight of the sea, with dolphins playing in the bay and, on a clear day, there are views across to the twisting spire of Volcán Corcovado on the mainland.

Just under half the population of 155,000 live in the two main towns, Ancud and Castro, and there are also many fishing villages. The Cordillera de la Costa runs at low altitudes along the Pacific side of the island; south of Castro a gap in the range is filled by two connected lakes, Lago Huillinco and Lago Cucao. Thick forests cover most of the sparsely populated western and southern parts of the island; elsewhere hillsides are covered with wheat fields and dark green plots of potatoes and the roads are lined with wild flowers in summer. East of the main island are several groups of smaller islands, where the way of life is even more peaceful.

Chiloé is famous for its legends and rich mythology; here witches are said to fly around at night, identifiable as lights in the dark sky. Chiloé is equally well known for its painted wooden churches, some of them dating back to the late colonial period. In January and February, most towns and villages celebrate their annual fiestas; traditional dishes, such as *curanto*, are served and there are rodeos and dancing, as well as much drinking of local *chicha*.

★ Don't miss...

1 **Parque Nacional Chiloé** Explore the thick forest at the northern end of this remote national park, pages 383 and 393.

2 **Quinchao and Lemuy** Explore these beautiful islets between Chiloé Grande and the mainland. They're easy to get to from Dalcahue and Chonchi respectively, pages 386 and 392.

3 **Iglesia de Quinchao** One of the many fascinating wooden Chilote churches based on Jesuit designs, page 386.

4 **Curanto** Enjoy this and other Chilote specialities in the seafood restaurants by the port at Castro, page 387.

5 **The beach at Cucao** Gallop on horseback along this windswept strand, page 393.

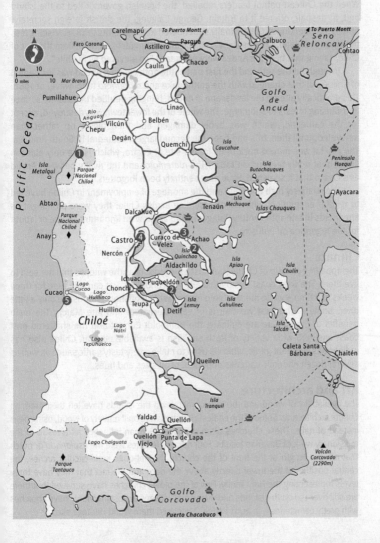

Chiloé

Background

History

The original Chilotes (inhabitants of Chiloé) were the Chonos tribe, who were pushed south by the Huilliches, invading from the north. The first Spanish sighting of the islands was by Francisco de Ulloa in 1553 and, in 1567, Martín Ruiz de Gamboa took possession of the islands on behalf of Spain. The small settler population divided the indigenous population and their lands between them, but the Huilliche uprising after 1598 drove the Spanish out of the mainland south of the Río Biobío, isolating the 200 Spanish settlers on Chiloé. Following a violent earthquake in 1646, the Spanish population asked the viceroy in Lima for permission to leave, but this was refused. Much of Chiloé's distinctive character derives from the subsequent 200 years of separation from the mainstream of Spanish colonial development.

The islanders were the last supporters of the Spanish Crown in South America. When the Chilean patriot leaders rebelled, the Spanish governor fled to the island and, in despair, offered it to Britain. George Canning, the British foreign secretary, turned the offer down; Chiloé finally surrendered to the patriots in 1826. Visiting less than a decade later, Charles Darwin still clearly distinguished Chiloé from the rest of Chile, saying that here the Andes were not nearly "so elevated as in Chile".

Throughout the 19th and the first part of the 20th century, Ancud was the capital of Chiloé. All that changed with the earthquake and *maremoto* (tidal wave) of 1960. This drastically altered the landscape in Ancud, bringing petrified trees to the surface and causing forests to submerge. The whole of the lower town was destroyed, except for the cathedral, which was badly damaged and then blown up rather than renovated; until then, this had been the second largest cathedral in South America. The capital was moved back to its former site at Castro, which is the only place in Chiloé that really feels urban today. The *maremoto*, and the rivalry between Ancud and Castro that it spawned, have never entirely been forgotten.

The relatively high birth rate and the shortage of employment in Chiloé have led to regular emigration, with Chilotes settling across Chile; they were prominent as shepherds in late 19th-century Patagonia and are now an important source of labour for the Argentine oil industry.

Climate

The appalling climate of Chiloé is almost as legendary as the witches that are said to live there. The west coast has particularly vile conditions – it can rain here for three weeks at a time – while the sheltered east coast and offshore islands are only a little drier. Some of the best weather is in early December and late March. The main benefits of the climate are culinary: the Humboldt Current and the sheltered east coast ensure a wide variety of fresh shellfish is available all year. Chiloé also has indigenous elephant garlic, which is used to make a very tasty garlic sauce as well as several dozen endemic varieties of potato, of all sizes and hues.

Art and architecture

The availability of wood and the lack of metals on the islands have left their mark on Chilote architecture. Some of the earliest churches were built entirely of wood, using pegs instead of nails. These churches often displayed German influence as a result of the missionary work of Bavarian Jesuits. Four notable features were the *esplanada* or porch that ran the length of the front of the church, the not-quite semi-circular arches, the central position of the tower directly above the door and the fact that they have three levels representing the Holy Trinity. Few of the oldest churches have survived, but there are still over 150 on the islands and even small villages almost invariably have churches with pretty cemeteries – in 2001 UNESCO declared them World Heritage sites.

ℹ Jesuits in Chiloé

The Jesuits arrived in Chiloé in 1608 and the first Jesuit residence was established four years later. Although in Chiloé they introduced few of the missions for which they became famous in Paraguay, at their expulsion in 1767 there were 79 churches on the island.

The key to the Jesuits' influence lay in their use of *fiscales*: indigenous people who were trained to teach Christian doctrine and to ensure that everyone observed religious duties. One *fiscal* was appointed for every 50 inhabitants. On 17 September each year, two missionaries set sail from Castro in small boats, taking with them statues of saints and other essential supplies. They spent the next eight months sailing round the islands of Chiloé, visiting all the parishes in a set order. In each parish they would spend three days officating at weddings and baptisms, hearing confessions and reviewing the work of the *fiscales*.

Most of the old churches for which Chiloé is famous date from after the expulsion of the Jesuits, but some writers claim that their influence can still be seen, for example in the enthusiasm for education on the island, which has long boasted one of the highest literacy rates in the world. Many villages in Chiloé still have *fiscales* who are, according to tradition, responsible for keeping the church keys.

The *rucas* (houses) of the indigenous population were thatched; thatch continued in widespread use throughout the 19th century. The use of thin *tejuelas* (tiles) made from alerce wood was influenced by the German settlers around Puerto Montt in the late 19th century; these tiles, which are nailed to the frame and roof in several distinctive patterns, overlap to form effective protection against the rain. *Palafitos* or wooden houses built on stilts over the water, were once popular in all the main ports, but are now mainly found at the northern end of Castro, to the west of the Panamericana.

The islands are also famous for their traditional handicrafts, notably woollens and basketware, which can be bought in all the main towns and on some of the smaller islands, as well as in Puerto Montt and Angelmó.

Folklore

Chiloé's distinctive history and its maritime traditions are reflected in the strength of its unique folklore. There is widespread belief in a mermaid (*pincoya*); witches, who are said to meet at caves near Quicaví (between Dalcahue and Quemchi); and a ghost ship, the *Caleuche*, which whisks shipwrecked sailors aboard (see box, page 380). The *Caleuche* is said to transform itself into a log, brought ashore by its crew (who become birds) when it needs repairs. Legend has it that Chiloé's dead are rowed along the reaches of Lago Huillinco and Lago Cucao in a white ship, out into the Pacific. For further information about the myths associated with the islands, read *Casos de Brujos de Chiloé* by Umiliana Cárdenas Saldivia (1989, Editorial Universitaria) and *Chiloé, Manual del Pensamiento Mágico y Creencia Popular* by Renato Cárdenas and Catherine Hall (1989, El Kultrún).

Modern Chiloé

Although fishing and agriculture remain mainstays of the economy, salmon farming has become just as important; seaweed is also harvested for export to Japan. Tourism provides a seasonal income for a growing number of people, especially in Castro, with **agrotourism** increasingly available in rural areas. This consists of staying with

Chiloé Background

❗ Mythical mischiefmakers

Visitors to Chiloé should beware of these four unlikely mythological hazards.

El Trauco A small, ugly and smelly man who wears a little round hat made of bamboo and clothing of the same material; he usually carries a small stone hatchet, with which he is reputed to be able to fell any tree in three strokes. He spends much of his time haunting the forests, sitting on fallen tree trunks and weaving his clothes.

El Trauco specializes in seducing virgins and is – perhaps a little too conveniently – held to be responsible for unwanted pregnancies. He uses his magic powers to give them erotic dreams while they are asleep; they wake and go to look for him in the forest and are seduced by his eyes. Despite his ugliness, he is irresistible and the girl throws herself on the ground. You should be careful not to disturb the Trauco while he is thus occupied: those who do so are immediately deformed beyond recognition and sentenced to die within 12 months.

La Fiura A small ugly woman who lives in the forests near Hualdes, where she is reputed to bathe in the streams and waterfalls, combing her hair with a crystal comb. Known as the indefatigable lover of bachelors, she attracts her victims by wearing colourful clothes. As the man approaches he is put to sleep by her foul breath. After La Fiura has satisfied her desire, the unfortunate man goes insane. Refusing her advances is no escape either: those who do so, whether animals or men, become so deformed that they are unrecognizable.

La Sirena and **El Caleuche** A dangerous double act for those travelling by sea. La Sirena is a mermaid who lies alluringly on rocks and entices sailors to their deaths. Once shipwrecked, sailors are whisked into the bowels of *El Caleuche*, the ghost ship that is said to patrol the channels of the archipelago. Both the Chilean navy and merchant ships have reported sightings of the *Caleuche*. The author of this book has also met several people on Chiloé who claim to have seen the ghost ship; but a word of warning was sounded by an old cynic in Castro: "I knew a fisherman who used to walk along the beach shouting 'I've seen La Sirena'. All the other fishermen fled, and then he stole their fish."

local families and sharing their way of life, whether it be farming or fishing. The host families are invariably friendly and welcoming, and the stays are highly recommended as a fascinating way to immerse yourself in Chilote life. Locations of families offering agrotourism are mentioned in the text; prices per person are all E with breakfast, D for half board and C for full board. Reservations should be made in advance directly, or through the group's office in Ancud ① *Ramírez 207, T065-630247, agroturismochiloe@gmail.com, see also Sernatur, page 381.*

Ins and outs

Getting there

Ferry and catamaran services connect the island with Chaitén and the Carretera Austral (see page 396), but the main sea link is the frequent vehicle ferry service between Pargua on the mainland (55 km southwest of Puerto Montt) across the Chacao straits to Chacao ① *30 mins, cars US$16 one way (more expensive at night),*

foot passengers US$1. Dolphins often follow the boat. There have been plans to build
a bridge to the mainland for a number of years although these have not gone beyond
the planning stages.

Getting around

Frequent bus services, which connect with ferry sailings, operate between Ancud and
Castro (the main towns on Chiloé) and Puerto Montt. It is possible to travel direct to
many cities, including Santiago, Osorno, Valdivia, Temuco and Los Angeles.
Inter-urban bus transport is dominated by **Cruz del Sur**, who also owns **Trans Chiloé**,
operating from their own terminal in Castro. **Cruz del Sur** also operates its own ferries
to the mainland, which give priority to **Cruz del Sur** buses. The only independent bus
operator to the island is **Queilen Bus** (cheaper but less regular). Local services are
crowded, slow and often wet, but provide a good picture of life in rural Chiloé.
Mountain bikes and horses are ideal for travelling slowly through the more remote
parts of the archipelago.

Ancud and around → *Colour map 4, C1.*

*Situated on the northern coast of Chiloé, 34 km west of the Straits of Chacao, Ancud
lies on a great bay, the Golfo de Quetalmahue. It is a little less characterful than some
of the other towns on the island but is nevertheless the best centre for visiting the
villages of northern Chiloé. There is a friendly small-town feel; everyone knows each
other and everything happens in its own time. Tourism is slowly reviving Ancud's
fortunes following the disaster of the* maremoto *in 1960. Within striking distance are
white-sand beaches, Spanish colonial forts and an important colony of Magellanic
and Humboldt penguins.* ▸▸ *For Sleeping, Eating and other listings, see pages 383-385.*

Ins and outs

Getting there There are many buses south to Castro and Quellón (hourly), and also
north to Puerto Montt. **Cruz del Sur** have buses continuing north to Valdivia, Temuco
and Santiago (several daily).

Getting around Ancud is big enough for you to want to take the occasional
colectivo; there are many of these, with their destinations signed on the roof (fares are
rarely over US$0.60). There are some buses serving outlying *poblaciones*, but it is
unlikely that you will need to use them.

Tourist information Sernatur ① *Libertad 665, T065-622800, infochiloe@serna
tur.cl, Mon-Fri 0830-2000, Sat and Sun (summer only) 0900-1800.*

Ancud

The port is dominated by the **Fuerte San Antonio**, the fort where the Spanish
surrendered Chiloé to Chilean troops in 1826. Close to it are the unspectacular ruins
of the Polvorín del Fuerte (a couple of cannon and a few walls). A kilometre north of
the fort is a secluded beach, **Arena Gruesa**, where public concerts are held in
summer. Some 2 km east is a *mirador* offering good views of the island and across to
the mainland. The small fishing harbour at Cochrane y Prat is worth a visit, especially
in the evening when the catch is landed. On the road west, along the coast, you can
see concrete pillars, remnants of the old railway, destroyed by the 1960 earthquake.

Near the Plaza de Armas is the **Museo Regional** ① *Libertad 370, T065-622413,
Tue-Fri 1000-1730, Sat, Sun and holidays 1000-1400, US$1, children US$0.50,* with an
interesting collection on the early history of Chiloé. It also displays a replica of a
traditional Chilote thatched wooden house and of the small sailing ship *Ancud*, which
claimed the Straits of Chacao for Chile, pipping the French to the post by a day. There's

a good craft shop and café on site and activities for children are provided. Excellent wooden toys and clocks are made by **Lucho Troncoso** ① *Prat 342, T099-92639383*.

The **Faro Corona** lighthouse lies 34 km west of Ancud along a beach, which, although unsuitable for swimming (absolutely freezing water, quite apart from the dangerous currents), offers good views with interesting birdlife. There isn't much there so take something to eat and drink. Two or three buses a day ferry passengers from Ancud. To the south is **Fuerte Ahuí**, an old fort with good views of Ancud.

East of Ancud

Most people travelling to Chiloé will arrive in **Chacao** on the north coast. The town has a small, attractive plaza; and there's a pretty church and old wooden houses in Chacao Viejo, east of the port. Black-necked swans arrive here in summer from their winter habitat in Paraguay and Brazil. The Panamericana heads west from here to Ancud, while a coastal road branches south, towards Quemchi. Turn north off the Panamericana along the coast to reach **Caulín**; the road is only passable at low tide. There are good beaches here; in Caulín you can see many black-necked swans in summer and flamingos in autumn.

‡ *Just outside of Chacao, on the road to Ancud, is a shop selling good smoked salmon.*

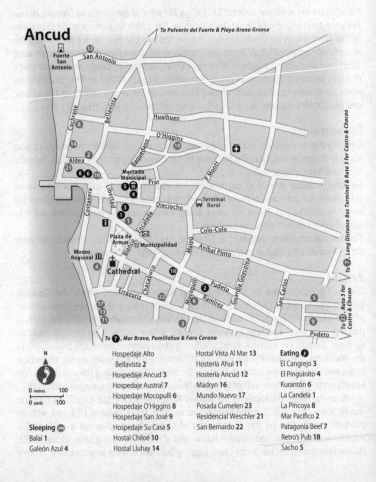

Ancud

To Polvorín del Fuerte & Playa Arena Gruesa

To Long Distance Bus Terminal & Ruta 5 for Castro & Chacao

To Ruta 5 for Castro & Chacao

To ⑳, Mar Brava, Pumillahue & Faro Corona

N

0 metres 100
0 yards 100

Sleeping 🛏
Balai 1
Galeón Azul 4

Hospedaje Alto
  Bellavista 2
Hospedaje Ancud 3
Hospedaje Austral 7
Hospedaje Mocopulli 6
Hospedaje O'Higgins 8
Hospedaje San José 9
Hospedaje Su Casa 5
Hostal Chiloé 10
Hostal Lluhay 14

Hostal Vista Al Mar 13
Hostería Ahui 11
Hostería Ancud 12
Madryn 16
Mundo Nuevo 17
Posada Cumelen 23
Residencial Weschler 21
San Bernardo 22

Eating 🍴
El Cangrejo 3
El Pinguinito 4
Kurantón 6
La Candela 1
La Pincoya 8
Mar Pacífico 2
Patagonia Beef 7
Retro's Pub 18
Sacho 5

Chiloé Ancud & around

Pumillahue

Pumillahue is 27 km southwest of Ancud, on the Pacific coast. About 10 km before is **Mar Brava**, a vast, deserted curved beach, wonderful for horse riding. About 3 km away from Pumillahue there is colony of both Humboldt and Magellanic penguins as well as sea otters, sea lions and a wide range of marine birdlife, situated on an island looked after by the **Otway Foundation** ① *T099-95204121, www.fundacionotway.cl, Otway guided tours in English/German US$7, guided tour with local fishermen (in Spanish with exaggerated hand gestures) US$5*. The penguins are there from November to early March. The best time to see them is in the early morning or evening. For an account of penguin-watching at Pumillahue, read Ben Richards' *The Mermaid and the Drunks* (Weidengeld, 2003). Catch one of the two or three buses that leave daily from Ancud, or hitch.

Chepu and around

South of Ancud, at junction 26 of the Pan-American Highway, a dirt road heads west to the coast at Chepu, famed for its river and sea fishing. It is a base for exploring the drowned forest and the waterways of the Río Chepu and its tributaries (a result of the 1960 *maremoto*). There is a wide range of bird life here and excellent opportunities for boat trips and horse riding. Chepu is also the entrance to the north part of the Parque Nacional Chiloé (see page 393). At **Río Anguay** (also known as Puerto Anguay), en route from Ancud, there is a campsite and *refugio*. From here, it is a 1½-hour walk to **Playa Aulén**, which has superb forested dunes and an extinct volcano.

 Boat trips can be organized in Río Anguay to **Laguna Coluco**, one hour up the Río Butalcura (a tributary of the Río Chepu). Two-day trips, navigating the rivers Grande, Carihueco and Butalcura, usually start further inland and finish at Río Anguay. These can be arranged in Ancud (see page 385). It is possible to reach Chepu on a wild coastal walk from Pumillahue. The route is difficult to follow so take food for three days and wear light-coloured clothes in summer to protect against *tavanos* (horseflies).

● Sleeping

Ancud *p381, map p382*
In summer the school on C Chacabuco is used as a cheap *albergue*. Many people wait at the bus station offering accommodation in private homes. These are generally decent and in the **F-G** range per person.
L-AL Hostería Ancud, San Antonio 30, T065-622340, www.panamericanahoteles.cl. Overlooking bay, wonderful views, attractive, reasonably comfortable, friendly and helpful, restaurant, traditional Chilote carvings, English spoken, tours offered.
AL Galeón Azul, Libertad 751, T065-622543, www.chiloeweb.com/pweb/galeonazul. Cramped rather basic rooms for the price but excellent views. Bright restaurant.
B Balai, Pudeto 169, T065-622541, www.hotelbalai.cl. With heating, laundry, parking, restaurant, cable TV, interesting local paintings, models and artefacts on display. Tours arranged.
B Hostería Ahui, Costanera 906, T065-622415, www.hosteriaahui.cl. With

breakfast, modern, clean, some rooms with splendid views, restaurant.
B-C Madryn, Bellavista 491, T065-622128, www.hotelmadryn.cl. With bath, cable TV and breakfast, also meals, clean. Laundry.
B-C Mundo Nuevo, Costanera 748, T065-628383, www.newworld.cl. **F** per person in dorms. With breakfast, comfortable, great views over the bay, lots of info, heating, good showers, kitchen facilities, bike rental, car hire, one room has a boat-bed. English, German spoken. Highly recommended.
B-C Posada Cumelen, Quintanilla No 5, just off Pudeto 600 block, T/F065-625677, pcorrea2003@yahoo.com. Comfortable rooms, with bath, heating, laundry, good breakfast, free internet, bar, pool table, great views, friendly, tours arranged, recommended.
C Hospedaje Alto Bellavista, Bellavista 449, T065-622384. With bath. **F-G** per person in dorms with shared bath. Good breakfast, very friendly, meals served.

C Hospedaje San José, Las Américas 661, T065-622467, hostalsanjose6@hotmail.com. **E** singles. With breakfast, good family atmosphere, nice views from lounge, clean, hot water, some rooms with bath, use of kitchen, internet, tours offered, bicycle hire, friendly. Recommended.

C Hostal Chiloé, O'Higgins 274, T065-622869, hchiloe@yahoo.es. **F** singles. With bath, large doll collection, food served, laundry service.

C Hostal Vista al Mar , Costanera 918, T065-622617, www.vistaalmar.cl. **F** per person in dorms, also self-catering apartments **B**. Views over the bay, heating, internet, laundry, dinner served in barn in summer.

C-D Hostal Lluhay, Cochrane 458, T/F065-622656, hostallluhay@hotmail.com. Meals served, friendly, attentive, nice lounge. Recommended.

C-E Residencial Weschler, Cochrane 480, T065-625975. With bath, cheaper without. Clean, view of bay.

D Hospedaje Ancud, Los Carrera 821, T065-622296, macriser@latinmail.com. **F** singles. Nice house, clean, friendly, kitchen facilities.

D Hospedaje Austral, Aníbal Pinto 1318, T065-624847, hospedajeaustral@hotmail.com. **F** singles. Cosy wooden house near bus station, with breakfast. laundry and kitchen facilities (US$1 charge).

D Hospedaje O'Higgins 6, O'Higgins 06, T065-622266. With breakfast, bath, spacious, interesting objets d'art, near the sea, nice views, recommended.

D Hospedaje Sra Marta, Lautaro 988, T065-623748, martaalvarado@latinmail.com. **F** singles. With breakfast, TV, kitchen facilities, good beds, good views from some rooms, friendly. Recommended.

D Hospedaje Su Casa, Los Alerces 841, T065-623382. **F** singles. Clean, with bath, TV, with breakfast, friendly. Kitchen and laundry facilities.

D-E Hospedaje Aguilera, Aguilera 756, **F-G** singles. Good beds, nice bathroom.

D-E Hospedaje Lautaro, Lautaro 947, T065-622980. **F-G** singles. Clean, friendly.

D-E Hospedaje Mocopulli, Mocopulli 710 y Ramírez. **F-G** singles. Very friendly, living room full of plants and flowers, full breakfast, quiet.

F-G San Bernardo, Errázuriz 395, T065-622657. Price per person in dorms, clean. Several others on same street.

Camping

Arena Gruesa, Costanera Norte 290, Arena Gruesa beach, at north end of Baquedano, T065-623428, arenagruesa@yahoo.com.

Chiloé, Arena Gruesa beach, at north end of Baquedano, T065-622961.

Playa Gaviotas, 5 km north, T099-96538096. Also has *cabañas*.

Playa Larga Huicha, 9 km north. Hot water and electricity.

Agrotourism

Juan Saldivia and **Corina Huentelicán**, Guapilacuy, near Faro Corona, T099-96539422, produce their own cheese, butter and preserves.

East of Ancud *p382*

A Hotel Caulín, Caulín, 09-96437986, www.caulinlodge.cl. Native Chilote trees grow in the garden, *cabañas* and a sauna also available. Decent restaurant. Horse riding and other trips offered.

Agrotourism

Ariela Bahamonde and **Amador Villagas**, Pulelo, 2 km south of Chacao, T099-98842421. Still use traditional agricultural techniques and make preserves.

Pumillahue *p383*

AL-C Pinguinland Cabañas, at Puñihuil, between Mar Brava and the penguin colony, T099-90194273, pinguinland@hotmail.com. Clean *cabañas* for 5-7 people, also double rooms and expensive meals. Spectacular view if weather is good.

Chepu and around *p383*
Agrotourism

Armando Pérez and **Sonia Díaz**, T099-96539241. Make cheese, tend cattle and sheep, and offer good walks in the Chepu area. To get there from Ancud, travel 26 km south on Route 5, turn right (east) for 5 km to Coipomó, there turn left, and after 3½ km turn right. The farm is on the left after 2 km.

● *For an explanation of sleeping and eating price codes used in this guide, see inside the*
● *front cover. Other relevant information is found in Essentials, see pages 50-57.*

🍴 Eating

Ancud *p381, map p382*

🍴 **Kurantón**, Prat 94, T065-623090. Serves good *curantos* and seafood.

🍴 **Patagonia Beef**, main road leading west from Ancud. Argentine restaurant, lots of meat as the name implies.

🍴-🍴 **Mar Pacífico**, Pudeto 346. Typical Chilote fare.

🍴-🍴 **Sacho**, Mercado Municipal, local 7, T065-622918. Renowned for its *curantos*. Huge portions, not fancy but very reasonable; several similar places in the same arcade.

🍴 **El Cangrejo**, Dieciocho 155. Highly recommended for seafood.

🍴 **El Pinguinito**, off Prat, near the market. Seriously cheap lunches only. Also look in the market area, where there are *colaciones*.

🍴 **El Timón**, Yungay y Allende. Small, cheap and good value.

🍴 **Hamburguería**, Av Prat. Much better than name suggests, good seafood.

🍴 **La Candela**, Pudeto y Libertad. Cosy café serving a nice range of snacks, drinks and light meals.

🍴 **La Pincoya**, Prat 61, T065-622613. Seafood next to harbour.

🍴 **Mar y Velas**, Serrano 2. Beautiful views and good food.

🍴 **Retro's Pub**, Maipú 615, off Pudeto, T065-626410. Appealing ambience, food (including vegetarian fare) and good cocktails. Open Mon-Fri 1100-0300, Sat 2000-0400, Sun 2000-0400 in summer.

East of Ancud *p382*

🍴🍴-🍴🍴 **Ostras Caulín**, Caulín, T099-96437005, www.ostrascaulin.cl. Excellent, very fresh oysters served in any number of ways.

🍴🍴 **Restaurant Pilón de Oro**, Sommermier 20, Chacao, T099-98393651. Good Chilote fare. There's also restaurant and *hospedaje* at Freire 35.

⛰ Activities and tours

Ancud *p381, map p382*

Tours are available from the kiosk on the plaza. For bicycle hire try the shop at Ramírez 311, US$1.50 per hour or US$8 per day.

Aki Turismo, in the bus terminal, oficina12, 2 piso, T065-545253, www.akiturismochiloe.cl. Good-value trips to the penguin colony.

Austral Adventures, Cochrane 432, T065-625977, www.austral-adventures.com. Small group bespoke tours of the archipelago and northern Patagonia (including Parque Pumalín), hiking or by sea, bilingual guides, US run. Recommended.

Paralelo 42, Prat 28, T065-622458. Recommended for tours to the Río Chepu area, including 2-day kayak trips guided by Carlos Oyarzún.

Chepu and around *p383*

For fishing trips around Chepu, try **Alfonso Bergara**, Chepu, T099-95170358. This area also offers great opportunities for horse riding, with long beaches that are perfect for a windswept gallop. Try **Sr Zuñipe** or **Sr Uroa**, US$6 per hr (ask at the *refugio* in Río Anguay).

🚌 Transport

For ferry services between the mainland and Chacao, see page 380.

Bus

Local Buses leave Ancud from Terminal Rural, Pedro Montt 538. To **Pumillahue** and **Mar Brava**, 2 buses daily with **Buses Mar Brava**; to **Quemchi** (via Linao and coast), 2 hrs, US$2.

Long distance Terminal on eastern outskirts of Ancud at Av Prat y Marcos Vera, reached by bus 1 or **Pudeto colectivos**. To **Castro**, frequent, 1½ hrs, **Cruz del Sur** , US$3, or Queilen Bus, US$2.50; to **Chonchi**, US$4; to **Quellón**, Cruz del Sur , 11 daily, US$6.

To **Santiago**, Cruz del Sur, 24 hrs, US$25, salón cama US$40; to **Puerto Montt**, 3 hrs, frequent, with Cruz del Sur, US$4.50 and Queilen Bus, US$4.

☎ Directory

Ancud *p381, map p382*

Banks ATM at Banco BCI, Ramírez, 1 block from the plaza; **Casa de cambio** on same block. **Post office** Pudeto y Blanco Encalada, corner of Plaza de Armas. **Telephone** Plaza de Armas, open Mon-Sat 0700-2200; ENTEL, Pudeto 219, with internet; Los Carrera 823.

Towards Castro

There are two alternative routes from Ancud to Castro: direct along the Pan-American Highway, crossing rolling hills, forest and agricultural land, or the more leisurely route via the east coast. This is a dramatic journey on unpaved roads that plunge up and down forested hills. The route passes through small farming and fishing communities and offers a real insight into rural life in Chiloé. The two main towns along the coastal route, Quemchi and Dalcahue, can also be reached by roads branching off the Pan-American Highway. ▸▸ *For Sleeping, Eating and other listings, see pages 388-392.*

Along the east coast ●❼❀❶▲❸ ▸▸ *pp 388-392.*

Quemchi and around
South of Chacao is the small village of **Hueihue**, where fresh oysters can be bought, US$19 for 100. Further south, before Quemchi, is a small lake with model sailing boats. Quemchi itself is a quiet town with long beaches, overlooking a bay speckled with wooded islands. There is a small tourist information booth in the plaza. A short walk up the road north towards Linao leads to high ground from where there are views to the temperate rainforest on the mainland. Miniature ornamental boats are made in the village. Some 4 km from Quemchi is **Isla Aucar**, once linked by bridge (now ruined), where black-necked swans can be seen.

The road from Quemchi to Dalcahue (50 km) passes many places that are the essence of Chiloé. The road rises up and down steep forested hills, rich with flowers, past salmon farms and views of distant bays. Some 20 km from Quemchi is a turn-off to **Quicaví**, legendary as the home of the witches of Chiloé; a further few kilometres brings you to **Tenaún**, a beautiful village with a church dating from 1837, which is now a UNESCO World Heritage site – trips to neighbouring islands such as Mechuque are easy to arrange here. You will pass numerous small communities with churches and views to the coast before you reach Dalcahue.

Dalcahue and around
Some 74 km south of Ancud via the Pan-American Highway, Dalcahue is more easily reached from Castro, 30 km further south. The wooden church on the main square dates from the 19th century and is a UNESCO World Heritage site. There is a tourist kiosk in season. Dalcahue is one of the main ports for boats to the offshore islands, including Quinchao (see below) and the **Chauques Islands**. These are a group of 16 islands east of Dalcahue, interconnected by sandbars, which are accessible at low tide. The largest is **Mechuque** (reached by bus from Tenaún), which has one village and offers splendid walking country. There are beautiful views of the mainland in good weather.

Quinchao
The island of Quinchao (population 3500) is a short ferry journey from Dalcahue. Passing the pretty village of Curaço de Velez, you reach the main settlement, **Achao**, 25 km southeast of Dalcahue. This is a large fishing village serving the smaller islands offshore, with a boarding school attended by pupils from outlying districts. Its wooden church, built in 1730, is the oldest surviving church in Chiloé. Saved by a change of wind from a fire that destroyed much of the town in 1784, it is a fine example of Chilote Jesuit architecture and contains a small **museum** ① *US$1*. Achao has a seasonal **tourist office** ① *Serrano y Progreso, Dec-Mar only*. A beautiful road leads 9 km south of Achao to the small village of **Quinchao** in a secluded bay at the

foot of a hill; an important religious festival is held in the fine church here on 8 December (see page 390). For more information, see www.islaquinchao.com.

With patience and persistence, boats can be found to take you from Achao to outlying islands, where facilities are basic and shops non-existent but lodging can be found with families; ask around. It is recommended to go with a local friend, if possible.

Castro ›› *pp388-392.*

The capital of Chiloé, with a population of just under 30,000, lies 88 km south of Ancud on a fjord on the east coast. It is a small, friendly town, full of bars and seafood restaurants where Chilotes from remote regions sit drinking *chicha*, eating *cazuela* and swapping tall stories. The centre is on a promontory, from which there is a steep drop to the port. Castro is the major tourist centre on the island.

Ins and outs

Getting there Castro is Chiloé's transport hub. There are many buses south to Quellón (hourly) and north to Ancud and Puerto Montt. **Cruz del Sur** have buses continuing north to Valdivia, Temuco and Santiago (several daily). Many buses serve the more isolated Chilote communities from the Municipal Bus Terminal. Although

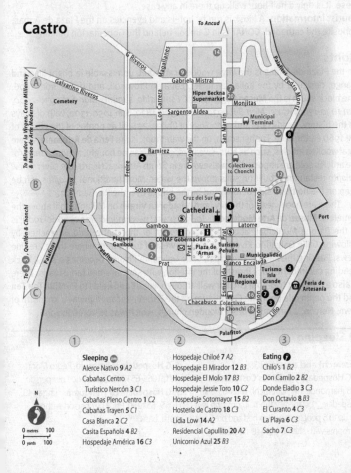

Castro

To Ancud

Galvarino Riveros

Cemetery

To Mirador la Virgen, Cerro Millantuy & Museo de Arte Moderno

Río Gamboa

To S, Quellón & Chonchi

Palafitos

C Riveros

Magallanes

Los Carrera

Gabriela Mistral

Hiper Beckna Supermarket

Sargento Aldea

San Martín

Freire

O'Higgins

Ramírez

Sotomayor

Cruz del Sur

Gamboa

Plazuela Gamboa

CONAF Gobernación

Prat

Plaza de Armas

Turismo Pehuén

Prat

Blanco Encalada

Museo Regional

Turismo Isla Grande

Chacabuco Colectivos to Chonchi

Palafitos

Esmeralda

Thompson

Lillo

Palafitos Pedro Montt

Monjitas

Municipal Terminal

Colectivos to Chonchi

Barros Arana

Serrano

Cathedral

Latorre

Port

Municipalidad

Feria de Artesanía

N

0 metres 100
0 yards 100

⁝ Dish of the day

Particularly associated with Puerto Montt and Chiloé, *curanto* is a very filling fish, meat and seafood stew, which is delicious despite the rather odd combination of ingredients. Though of pre-Hispanic origins, it has developed by adding new ingredients according to new influences. In its original pre-Conquest form, a selection of fish was wrapped in leaves and baked over hot stones in a hole – some specialists wonder if this way of cooking may have come from the Pacific islands, where pit baking is still practised. With the arrival of the Spanish, the dish was modified to include pork, chicken and white wine. Today, it is often cooked in a large pan and advertised as *pullmay* or *curanto en olla*, to distinguish it from the pit-baked form.

most services leave from Quellón, Castro is occasionally used as a port for passenger services to Chaitén and Puerto Montt.

Getting around There are some *colectivos* and public buses serving the *barrios* high above the town near the *media luna*, but it is unlikely that you will need to use these. It is only a half-hour walk up there in any case.

Tourist information A kiosk is run by hotels and agencies on the Plaza de Armas, opposite the cathedral. **CONAF** is in Gamboa behind the Gobernación building.

Sights

On the Plaza de Armas is the large wooden **cathedral**, unmissable in bright lilac and orange, designed by the Italian architect, Eduardo Provosoli, and dating from 1906. One block south is the **Museo Regional** ① *C Esmeralda, summer Mon-Sat 0930-2000, Sun 1030-1300, winter Mon-Sat 0930-1300, 1500-1830, Sun 1030-1300,* with displays on the history, handicrafts and mythology of Chiloé, as well as photos of the effects of the 1960 earthquake. Further south, on the waterfront, is the **Feria de Artesanía**, where local woollen articles, such as hats, sweaters, gloves, can be bought, although many of the articles sold are imported from elsewhere in South America. Nearby are several new *palafito* restaurants, built on stilts above the water. More traditional *palafitos* can be seen on the northern side of town and by the bridge over the Río Gamboa.

There are good views of the city from **Mirador La Virgen** on Millantuy hill above the cemetery. **Museo de Arte Moderno** ① *T065-635454, www.mamchiloe.cl, 1000-1900,* is in the Parque Municipal, about 3 km northwest of the centre, and is reached by following Calle Galvarino Riveros up the hill west of town, from where there are fine views. Passing the Parque Municipal, Calle Galvarino Riveros becomes a small track heading out into the thick forests of the interior, with several small farmsteads. There is also a pleasant two-hour circular walk through woods and fields to **Puntilla Ten Ten** and the peninsula opposite Castro; turn off the Pan-American Highway 2 km north of town. **Nercón**, 4 km south, has a wooden church, which was restored in 1996.

⬭ Sleeping

Quemchi and around *p386*
B-C Hospedaje y Cabañas Costanera, D Bahamonde 141, Quemchi, T065-691230, hospedaje_costanera@latinmail.com. *Cabañas* for up to 5 people, as well as bed and breakfast in rooms with shared bath (E singles).

F-G Hospedaje El Embrujo, Pedro Montt 431, T065-651262. Basic, price per person.
F-G Hospedaje La Tranquera, Yungay 40, T065- 651250. Price per person without bath, basic.

Agrotourism

Guillermo Hernández and **Bernarda Zúñiga**, Huite, 4 km north of Quemchi, T099-96539239. Part of the agrotourism network, in a beautiful spot.

Juan Dougnac and **Evangelina Cordaro**, Tubildad, 2 km north of Quemchi, T065-691305. Salmon fishing in lovely surroundings.

Magali Miranda, Huite, 4 km north of Quemchi, T099-96539245. Produces honey, milk, preserves and smoked salmon. Great location.

María Soto and **Manuel Vásquez**, Tenaún, 32 km south of Quemchi, T099-96539416/96476752. Honey, *chicha* and preserves.

Mirella Montaña and **Guido Vásquez**, Tenaún, 32 km south of Quemchi, T099-6539423/6476750. Butter, preserves, *chicha* and pastries.

Dalcahue and around *p386*

F La Feria, Rodríguez 17, T065-641293. Price per person without bath, basic.

F Residencial Playa, Rodríguez 9. Price per person. Basic.

F-G Hospedaje Mary, Tte Merino 10, T065-641260. Price per person. Also sells handicrafts.

F-G Hospedaje Puteman, Freire 305, T065-641330. Price per person. Clean, basic.

F-G Residencial San Martín, San Martín 1, T065-641207. Price per person. Basic, clean, also meals.

On Mechuque, accommodation is available with the schoolteacher's son or with Señora Dina del Carmen Paillacar, who serves good meals.

Quinchao *p386*

C-D Hostería La Nave, Prat y Aldea, Achao, T065-661219, hosterialanave@latinmail.com. Breakfast provided, cheaper rooms without bath, restaurant with fine views over bay.

C-D Plaza, Plaza de Armas, Achao, T065-661283. With bath and breakfast, clean, good.

D Hospedaje Achao, Serrano 061, Achao, T065-661373. Without bath, good, clean.

D Hospedaje Chilhue, Zañartu 021, Achao. Without bath, with breakfast, clean.

D Hospedaje São Paulo, Serrano 52, Achao, T065-661245. Basic, poor beds, hot water.

Agrotourism

There are 2 options on Quinchao:

Juan Guilquiruca and **Luzmira Barrientos**, Huyar Bajo (turn left before Achao en route from Curaço de Velez), T099-97963697. Butter, preserves and *chicha*.

Ramiro and María Cárcamo, Matao, southeastern tip of the island, T099-96539424. Preserves and *chicha*.

Castro *p387, map p387*

AL Cabañas Centro Turístico Nercón, Km 5 south of Castro, T065-632985. With bath, hot water, heating, restaurant, tennis court.

AL Cabañas Pleno Centro, Los Carrera 346, T065-635092. 2-person *cabañas*, also larger version with kitchen.

AL Unicornio Azul, Pedro Montt 228, T065-632359, www.chiloeweb.com/pweb/unicornioazul/. Good views over bay, comfortable, although has seen better days, restaurant, English spoken.

AL-A Alerce Nativo, O'Higgins 808, T065-632267, hotelalerc@surnet.cl. Heating, breakfast, also has *cabañas* (4 km south of Castro), and restaurant. Helpful.

AL-A Cabañas Trayen, Km 5 south of Castro, T065-633633, www.trayenchiloe.com. Cheaper off season, *cabañas* with lovely views over the Fiordo de Castro.

AL-A Hostería de Castro, Chacabuco 202, T065-632301, www.hosteriadecastro.cl. With breakfast, good restaurant, wonderful views.

A Casita Española, Los Carrera 359, T/F065-635186, casitaespanola@telsur.cl. Heating, cable TV, parking. A little overpriced.

B Casa Blanca, Los Carrera 308, T/F065-632726, nelysald@surnet.cl. With breakfast, cheaper rooms without bath (E per person), clean, modern, warm, also *cabañas*, sleep 6.

C Hospedaje El Mirador, Barros Arana 127, T065-633795, maboly@yahoo.com. F singles. Good breakfast, kitchen facilities, good views, internet, laundry, very clean and friendly, highly recommended.

C Hospedaje Sotomayor, Sotomayor 452, T065-632464. F singles. With breakfast, quiet, small beds.

C Serrano 407. F singles. With breakfast, friendly, warm water.

C-D Hospedaje América, Chacabuco 215, T065-634364. F singles. With breakfast. Friendly, very good food – "our tourists arrive thin and leave fat" – cable TV, shared bath.

C-D **Hospedaje Chiloé**, San Martín 739. **F** singles. With breakfast, clean. Recommended.
C-D **Hospedaje El Molo**, Barros Arana 140, T065-635026. **F** singles. With breakfast, clean, comfortable, cooking facilities, friendly, secure. Recommended.
C-D **Hospedaje Jessie Toro**, Las Delicias 287, off Esmeralda. **F** singles with good breakfast, helpful, clean, spacious, good bathrooms, also *cabañas*. Recommended.
C-D **Residencial Capullito**, San Martín 709. **F** singles. Clean, friendly, quiet.
D **Lidia Low**, San Martín 890. **F-G** singles. With good breakfast, warm showers, use of kitchen.
D **San Martín 879**. **F-G** singles. With big breakfast, central, clean. Recommended.

Camping
Llicaldad, Esmeralda 269, Km 6 south of Castro, T065-635080. One of several sites along road south towards Chonchi. *Cabañas* also available.
Pudú, 10 km north on the Pan-American Highway, T/F065-632476. Hot showers, sites with light, water, children's games, also *cabañas*.

🍽 Eating

Along the east coast *p386*
🍴 **Restaurant Centenario**, Bahamonde 360, Quemchi. Good, cheap fare.
🍴 **Restaurant La Dalca**, Freire 502, Dalcahue. Serves good cheap food. Recommended. There are also numerous small restaurants along the harbour and around the market in Dalcahue, serving excellent and cheap seafood. Note that if you ask for *té*, you will be served a mug of white wine.
For restaurant food on Quinchao, try:
🍴 **Hostería La Nave**, see Sleeping above.
🍴 **Restaurant Central**, Achao. Simple, good.

Castro *p387, map p387*
You may have difficulty tracking down some breakfast before 0900. Palafito restaurants near the Feria Artesanía on the waterfont offer good food and good value, including **Brisas del Mar**, **La Amistad** and **Rapu Nui**. There are also very cheap restaurants by the municipal bus terminal. In the market, try *milcaos*, fried potato cakes with meat stuffing.

🍴🍴 **Anadito**, Plaza de Armas. Good pub and restaurant.
🍴🍴 **Donde Eladio**, Lillo 97. Meat and seafood specialities.
🍴🍴 **La Playa**, Lillo 93. Recommended for fish and meat.
🍴 **Chilo's**, San Martín 459. Good lunches.
🍴 **Don Camilo**, Ramírez 566. Good food, not expensive.
🍴 **Don Octavio**, Pedro Montt 261. Good food, good value.
🍴 **El Curanto**, Lillo 67. Seafood including *curanto*. Recommended.
🍴 **Sacho**, Thompson 213. Good sea views. Recommended.

Cafés
La Brújula del Cuerpo, Plaza de Armas. Good coffee and snacks.
Stop Inn Café, Martín Ruiz shopping centre, Gamboa s/n. Good coffee.

⊕ Festivals and events

Quinchao *p386*
8 Dec People come to the small village of Quinchao from all over Chiloé for **Día de la Virgen** and watch as a huge model of the Virgin is carried with great reverence to the church.

○ Shopping

Dalcahue *p386*
Dalcahue weekly **market** is held Sun 0700-1300. It has quality goods, but bargaining is practically impossible, and in recent years it has become somewhat overrun with tourists; good for *curantos*, though.

Castro *p387, map p387*
CDs of typical Chilote music are widely available around town.
Annay Libros, Serrano 357. Books in Spanish on Chiloé, often cheaper than Santiago bookshops.
El Tren Libros, Thompson 229. Books in Spanish on Chiloé, often cheaper than Santiago bookshops.
Hiper Beckna, Sargento Aldea y O'Higgins. Supermarket with good bakery.
Libros Chiloé, Blanco Encalada 204. Books in Spanish on Chiloé, often cheaper than Santiago bookshops.

Mercado Artesanal, on the wharf. Good-quality woollens at reasonable prices.
Mercado Municipal, Yumbel, off Pilato Samuel Ulloa. Good fish and vegetables.

▲ Activities and tours

Dalcahue *p386*
Altue Active Travel, 3 km south of Dalcahue, reservations from Encomenderos 83, piso 2, Las Condes, Santiago, T02-2321103, www.altue.com. Sea kayaking.

Castro *p387, map p387*
Tour operators usually charge around US$25 to Parque Nacional Chiloé.
Chiotours, Blanco 293, T065-639544. Tours to the Parque Nacional, Quinchao, Lemuy and Queilen. Also boat trips.
Costa Sur, O'Higgins 670, piso 3, oficina 11, T065-632788, costasur@surnet.cl. A variety of tours throughout the island. Also trekking.
Sergio Márquez, Felipe Moniel 565, T065-632617. Very knowledgeable local guide with transport.
Turismo Isla Grande, Thompson 241, Transmarchilay and Navimag agency.
Turismo Pehuén, Blanco Encalada 299 y Esmeralda, T065-635254, www.turismopehuen.cl LanChile agents; also horse riding excursions and trips to the national park, the penguin colony and the smaller islands.
Turismo Queilen, Gamboa 502, T065-632776. Recommended tours to Chonchi and to the National Park.

⊖ Transport

Dalcahue and around *p386*
Buses to **Castro**, hourly, 40 mins, US$1.50; also *colectivos* to **Castro** and to **Achao**, US$2; daily bus to **Puerto Montt**, via Ancud, US$6.
To reach **Mechuque**, catch the bus from Tenaún, departs Wed 1730, returns Thu, 2½ hrs, US$3.50 one way.

Quinchao *p386*
Arriagada buses to **Ancud**, 5 daily; to **Castro**, 4 daily, US$2.50. There's a frequent ferry service to **Dalcahue**, free for pedestrians and cyclists.

Bus
There are 2 bus terminals. **Cruz del Sur** services depart from **Cruz del Sur terminal**, San Martín behind the cathedral, T065-632389. Other services, including most buses to rural communities, leave from the **Municipal Terminal**, San Martín, 600 block (2 blocks further north).

To **Quemchi**, 1 daily, with Quelen Bus; to **Dalcahue**, frequent, with Gallardo and Arriagada, also *colectivos* from San Martín 815; to **Tenaún**, daily 1200; to **Achao** via Dalcahue and Curaço de Vélez, 4 daily Mon-Sat, 3 daily Sun, with Arriagada, US$2.50, last return from Achao 1730.

To **Chonchi**, frequent, with Cruz del Sur, Quelen Bus, minibuses and *colectivos* (from Ramírez y San Martín and Esmeralda y Chacabuco); to **Puqueldón**, 4 daily Mon-Sat, with Gallardo, US$2; to **Queilen**, 6 daily, with Quelen Bus, US$3.50; to **Quellón**, frequent, with Cruz del Sur/Trans Chiloé, US$3.

To **Cucao** for the Parque Nacional Chiloé, 6 daily in summer, 1 daily in winter, with Arroyo and Ocean Bus, US$3, avoid Fri, when the service is crowded with school children.

There are also frequent services to **Ancud**, 1 hr, and **Puerto Montt**, 3 hrs, with Cruz del Sur, Trans Chiloé and Queilen Bus, US$6. Cruz del Sur also runs to **Osorno**, **Valdivia**, **Temuco**, **Concepción** and **Santiago**. Bus Norte serves **Ancud**, **Puerto Montt**, **Osorno** and **Santiago** daily. Quelen Bus runs a weekly service on Mon to **Punta Arenas**, 36 hrs, US$70.

Ferry
If for whatever reason the Quellón ferry port is out of action, the Naviera Austral services to **Chaitén** on the mainland depart from Castro, 4 per week Dec-early Mar, reduced service off season, 5 hrs, passengers US$30, cars US$130, cycles US$13. Some ships continue from Chaitén to **Puerto Montt**. A faster catamaran service is provided by Catamaranes del Sur to **Chaitén**, 2 hrs, US$18, and **Puerto Montt**, 2 or 3 per week in summer, less regularly off season. Again, this service normally leaves from Quellón, but occasionally from Castro. The Transmarchilay ferry Pincoya sails to **Puerto Chacabuco**, irregular service, 24 hrs.

❶ Directory

Castro *p387, map p387*

Banks Banco de Chile, Plaza de Armas, ATM, accepts TCs (at a poor rate); BCI, Plaza de Armas, MasterCard and Visa ATM; **Julio Barrientos**, Chacabuco 286, cash and TCs, better rates than the banks. **Internet** Throughout the town centre.

Laundry Clean Centre, Serrano 440 ; Lavandería Adolfo, Blanco Encalada 96, quick, reasonably priced; Lavaseco Unic, Gamboa 594. **Medical services** Muñoz de Las Carreras, near police station, surgery Mon-Fri 1700-2000, recommended. **Post office** West side of Plaza de Armas. **Telephone** Latorre 289; Entel, O'Higgins between Sotomayor and Gamboa; also private centre at Latorre 275.

Chonchi to Quellón → *Colour maps 4, C1/5, A2.*

The Pan-American Highway continues south to Quellón, the southernmost port in Chiloé, with paved side roads leading east to Chonchi and an unpaved track heading west to Cucao. From Chonchi, a partially paved road continues southeast to Queilen. Winding across forested hills, this is probably the most attractive route on the island, especially in autumn; numerous tracks branch off to deserted beaches where you can walk for hours and hear nothing but the splashing of dolphins in the bay. The ferry to Lemuy is caught from a port on this track. ▸▸ *For Sleeping, Eating and other listings, see pages 394-396.*

Chonchi and around

A picturesque fishing village 23 km south of Castro, Chonchi is a good base for exploring the island. Known as the *Ciudad de los Tres Pisos* (city built on three levels), it was, until the opening of the Panama Canal in 1907, a stopping point for sailing ships. In the years that followed, it was the cypress capital of Chile: big fortunes were made in the timber industry and grand wooden mansions were built in the town. In the 1950s, Chonchi boomed as a free port but, in the 1970s, it lost that status to Punta Arenas. Its harbour is now the supply point for salmon farms almost as far south as Coyhaique. Its population is around 4000.

On the main plaza is the **church**, built in neoclassical style in 1880. Its impressive tower was blown off in a storm in March 2002 and has recently been rebuilt. There is also a **tourist information kiosk** here in summer. From the plaza, **Calle Centenario** drops steeply to the harbour, lined with several attractive but sadly neglected wooden mansions. Fishing boats bring in the early morning catch, which is carried straight into the nearby **market**. The small **Museo de Chonchi Viejo** is located in an old house, with videos on the churches of Chiloé, including the 18th-century church 5 km north of Chonchi at Vilopulli.

In the bay opposite Chonchi lies the island of **Lemuy**. It covers 97 sq km and offers many good walks along quiet unpaved tracks through undulating pastures and woodland. From the ferry dock, a road runs east across the island, passing a fine 19th-century wooden church at **Ichuac** before reaching **Puqueldón**. This is the main settlement on the island and is built on a very steep hill stretching down to the port. There's a post office and a telephone centre here. From Puqueldón, the road continues a further 16 km on a ridge high above the sea, passing small hamlets, with views of the water and the patchwork of fields. There are old churches at **Aldachildo**, 9 km east of Puqueldón, and at **Detif**, in the extreme south of the island.

Some 46 km southeast of Chonchi, **Queilen** is a pretty fishing village on a long finger-shaped peninsula. On the north side is a sandy beach, which curves round the head of the peninsula, while on the south side is the old wooden pier, which doubles as the port. There are fine views across the straits to Tanqui Island and the mainland.

The west coast

West of Chonchi at Km 12 is **Huillinco**, a charming village on Lago Huillinco. Beyond here the *ripio* road continues west to **Cucao**, one of the few settlements on the west coast of Chiloé. The immense 20-km-long beach is battered by thundering Pacific surf and dangerous undercurrents, making it one of the most dramatic places along the whole coast of Chile.

Cucao lies at the edge of the southern sector (35,207 ha) of the **Parque Nacional Chiloé** ① *T065-532501/09-99329193, US$3*. The park, in three sections, covers extensive areas of the wild and uninhabited western side of the island, much of it filled by temperate rainforest. Wildlife includes the Chiloé fox and pudu deer. There are over 110 species of birds resident here, including cormorants, gulls, penguins and flightless steamer ducks.

You can take a car as far as the administration centre at the entrance ① *1 km north of Cucao, T099-99329193, daily*, which has limited information and a guest bungalow for use by visiting scientists; applications to CONAF via your embassy. There are also decent camping facilities. The centre provides maps of the park, but they are not very accurate and should not be used to locate *refugios* within the park.

⁑ The northern sector of the park is accessed via Chepu (see page 383) the third section of the park is the small island of Metalqui and is difficult to reach.

A path, affording great views, runs 3 km north from the administration centre to **Laguna Huelde** and then north for a further 12 km to **Cole Cole**. Once you reach **Río Anay**, 9 km beyond Cole Cole, you can wade or swim across the river to reach a beautiful, secluded beach from where you can enjoy the sight of dolphins playing in the huge breakers. The journey can also be made on horseback; allow nine hours for the round trip. Take lots of water and your own food. There are several other walks in the national park, but signposts are limited and *tavanos* are bad in summer, so wear light-coloured clothing.

Quellón

The southernmost port in Chiloé, located 92 km south of Castro, Quellón has suffered its fair share of misfortunes in recent years. In 2002, the arrival of the lethal *marea*

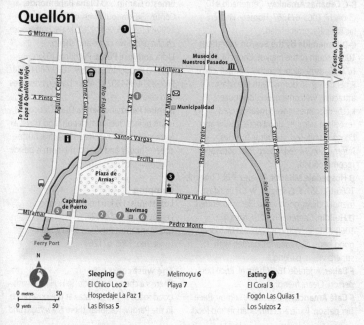

Quellón

Museo de Nuestros Pasados

To Castro, Chonchi & Chaiguao

Municipalidad

Plaza de Armas

Capitanía de Puerto

Navimag

Ferry Port

0 metres 50
0 yards 50

Sleeping	Melimoyu 6	Eating
El Chico Leo 2	Playa 7	El Coral 3
Hospedaje La Paz 1		Fogón Las Quilas 1
Las Brisas 5		Los Suizos 2

Chiloé Chonchi to Quellón

roja micro-organism (see page 53) caused the collapse of the shellfish industry, provoking demonstrations from fishermen and dockers who destroyed part of the pier. As a result, the passenger ferry services from Quellón to Chaitén and Puerto Montt were suspended and have only recently returned to normal. There is not much to interest the traveller here, although the **Museo de Nuestros Pasados** ① *Ladrilleros 225*, includes reconstructions of a traditional Chilote house and mill, and there are pleasant beaches nearby: **Viejo**, 4 km west, where there is an old wooden church; **Punta de Lapa**, 7 km west, and **Yaldad**, 9 km west along a pretty road over the hills. The launch *Puerto Bonito* sails around the bay in summer from the pier, passing Punta de Lapa, Isla Laitec and Quellón Viejo ① *3 times daily in summer, US$16.* A trip can be made to **Chaiguao**, 11 km east, where there is a Sunday morning market.

The far south of the island has been bought by a private foundation and has been turned into a nature sanctuary known as the **Parque Tantauco**. Covering some 120,000 ha of native woodland, wetlands, lagoons and rivers, it is home to a range of endangered wildlife. There are two campsites (no electricity) and 12 shortish trails. At present access is by sea only, from Quellón to **Inio** on the south coast. Transport can be arranged through the park office in Quellón ① *Av La Paz 068, T065-681064, www.fundacionfuturo.cl/parque_chiloe.php.*

● Sleeping

Chonchi and around *p392*
There are also a number of *hospedajes* on Irarrázaval, Chonchi. In Queilen there is also accommodation in the big house beside the pier.
A Posada Antiguo Chalet, Irarrázaval s/n, Chonchi, T065-671221, fco_barrientos@hotmail.com. Cheaper in winter, charming, beautiful location, not great value.
B-C Cabañas Amankay, Centenario 410, Chonchi, T065-671367. Homely, kitchen facilities. Recommended.
C-D Esmeralda by the Sea, on waterfront 100 m south of the market, Chonchi, T065-671328, esmeraldachonchi@hotmail.com. **F** per person in dorms. With breakfast, attractive, welcoming, English spoken, kitchen facilities, cheap meals served (excellent salmon), good beds, canoe and boat trips offered, also rents bicycles, information. Mixed reports, but generally recommended.
D Hospedaje Mirador, Alvarez 198, Chonchi, T065-671351. **F-G** singles. With breakfast, friendly, clean, good value. Recommended.
D Huildín, Centenario 102, Chonchi, T065-671388. Without bath, old fashioned, good beds, also *cabañas*, garden with superb views, parking.
F Baker, Andrade 184, Chonchi. Price per person. Clean, friendly.
F Café Amancay, Puqueldón, Lemuy. Price per person. Basic accommodation and food.

F Restaurant Lemuy, Lemuy. Clean, without bath, good, price per person. Food served only in high season.
F-G Pensión Chiloé, Queilen, is basic, friendly, without bath. Price per person.

Agrotourism
There are several options between Chonchi and Queilen.
Ernesto Gamín and **Diana Bahamonde**, Contuy, 38 km southwest of Chonchi, T099-96539206/96449262. Make butter and *chicha* and have cattle and sheep.
Lidia and José Pérez, Puchilco, 10 km beyond Puqueldón, Lemuy, T099-98842430/98998914/94440252. Make butter, preserves and *chicha*.
Manuel Pérez and **Bertila Díaz**, Dético (4 km before Queilen turn right and travel a further 6 km), T099-99605558. Make butter, cheese, honey and *chicha*; the farm is beside a football pitch.

Camping
Los Isleños, 1½ km from Puqueldón, Lemuy, T099-96548498.
Los Manzanos, Aguirre Cerda y Juan Guillermo, T065-671263.

The west coast *p393*
There's a cheap *residencial* in Huillinco with good food, or you can stay at the post office. In the Parque Nacional, there is a *refugio* and

camping at Cole Cole and another *refugio* at Anay, 9 km further north. The following accommodation is all in Cucao.

F Parador Darwin, at park entrance, Cucao sector, T065-633040. Price per person with breakfast, good food with vegetarian options, real coffee. Highly recommended. Camping also available.

F Posada Cucao, T065-633040/09-8969855. Price per person with breakfast, hot water, meals, friendly.

F Provisiones Pacífico. Small grocery store offering full board or demi-pension, friendly, good, clean, meals and homemade bread, but no hot water. Price per person. Recommended.

Camping

Lago Mar, 2 km east of Cucao, T065-635552, US$15 per site. One of several campsites in the area; check prices carefully first.

Quellón *p393*
The school becomes a cheap *albergue* in summer, with dormitory accommodation.
B Melimoyu, Pedro Montt 369, T065-681250. Clean, good beds, parking.
C El Chico Leo, Pedro Montt 325, T065-681567, elchicoleo@telsur.cl. Cheaper without bath.
C-D Playa, Pedro Montt 427. **F** singles. With breakfast, without bath. Clean.
D Hospedaje La Paz, La Paz 370, T065-681207. **F** singles. With breakfast, hot water.
D Las Brisas, Pedro Montt 555, T065-681413. **F-G** singles. Without bath, basic.

Agrotourism

Mercedes Vargas, 10 km north of Quellón on Route 5 (turn right at Candelaria; the farm is 2 km on the right), T099-6539213. Makes preserves and *chicha*.

Camping

There are 5 sites at Punta de Lapa and sites without services at Chaiguao and Yaldad.

● Eating

Chonchi and around *p392*
¶¶ **La Parada**, Centenario 133. Very friendly, good selection of wines, erratic opening hours. Recommended.
¶ **El Alerce**, Aguirre Cerda 106. Excellent value.
¶ **El Trébol**, Irarrázaval 187. Good views over the harbour.
¶ **La Quila**, Andrade 183. Cheap, good, popular with locals.

The west coast *p393*
¶ **Las Luminarias** in Cucao sells excellent *empanadas de machas* (*machas* are local shellfish).

Quellón *p393*
¶¶ **Fogón Las Quilas**, La Paz 053, T065-681206. Famous for lobster. Recommended.
¶¶ **Los Suizos**, Ladrilleras 399. Swiss cuisine.
¶ **El Coral**, 22 de Mayo. Good, reasonably priced, superb views.
¶ **Rucantú**, Pedro Montt. Good food and value.

● Bars and clubs

Chonchi and around *p392*
Club 88, on the waterfront. Bar/restaurant.
Rockets Disco, near Copec filling station. Open weekends; more often in summer.

● Festivals and events

2nd week of Feb La Semana Chonchina is one of the series of Chilote festivals.

● Shopping

Chonchi and around *p392*
Handicrafts are sold from **Opdech** (Oficina Promotora del Desarrollo Chilote), on the waterfront, and from the parroquia, next to the church (open Oct-Mar only). In the summer many *artesanal* stalls open, a speciality being traditional woollen clothes.

Chiloé Chonchi to Quellón Listings

▲ Activities and tours

The west coast *p393*
Many houses in Cucao rent horses at US$3.50 per hr, US$28 per day. It usually costs US$45 a day for the round trip on horseback to **Río Anay**. Bear in mind that the horses will be of varying tameness, and that if you hire a guide you pay for his horse too.

Quellón *p393*
Horses can be hired US$3.50 per hr; kayaks with a guide, US$4 per hr from the beach at Quellón.

⊖ Transport

Chonchi and around *p392*
Bus
Services depart from the main plaza to **Castro**, frequent, US$1; to **Puerto Montt**, US$7. Services to **Quellón** and **Queilen** (from Castro and Puerto Montt) and to **Cucao** (from Castro) also stop in Chonchi.

There are 4 buses daily Mon-Sat from Castro to **Lemuy**, and 6 daily Mon-Fri, 4 daily Sat, 3 daily Sun, from Castro to **Queilen**, Queilen Bus, 2 hrs, US$3.

Ferry
Services to **Lemuy** depart from Puerto Huicha, 4 km south of Chonchi, approximately every 30 mins, foot passengers travel free.

The west coast *p393*
Six buses a day to **Cucao** from Castro via Chonchi in season, US$2.50, last departure

1600, reduced service off season; hitching is very difficult.

Quellón *p393*
Bus
To **Castro**, frequent, 2 hrs, Cruz del Sur, US$4; also services to **Ancud** and **Puerto Montt**, US$8.

Ferry
Naviera Austral services, , Pedro Montt 457, T065-681331, to **Chaitén** on the mainland depart from Quellón, 4 per week Dec-early Mar, reduced service off season, 5 hrs, passengers US$30, cars US$130, cycles US$13. Some ships continue from Chaitén to **Puerto Montt**. A faster catamaran service is provided by **Catamaranes del Sur** to **Chaitén**, 2 hrs, US$18, and **Puerto Montt**, 2 or 3 per week in summer, less regularly off-season. Transmarchilay ferry, *Pincoya*, sails to **Puerto Chacabuco** , irregular service, 24 hrs. All services leave from Castro when Quellón's port is out of commission. **Navimag** is at Pedro Montt 383.

⊕ Directory

Chonchi *p392*
Casas de cambio Nicolás Alvarez, Centenario 429, cash only. **Telephone** San Martín y Mistral.

Quellón *p393*
Banks Banco del Estado, Ladrilleros. No TCs, credit cards not possible, no commission on US$ cash. **Laundry** Lavandería Ruck-Zuck, Ladrilleras 392.

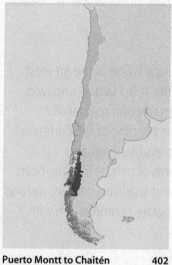

Carretera Austral

Introduction

Travelling along the Carretera Austral is one of the greatest journeys South America has to offer. It is a largely unpaved *ripio* road stretching over 1100 km through spectacular ever-changing scenery. Before the opening of the Carretera, this part of Chile was largely inaccessible; it remains breathtaking. Deep tree-lined fjords penetrate into the heart of a land of spiralling volcanoes and sparkling glaciers, rushing rivers, crystal blue lakes and temperate rainforest rich with southern Chile's unique flora.

The only town of any size, Coyhaique, lies in the valley of the Río Simpson. South of Coyhaique are Lago General Carrera, the largest lake in Chile, and the Río Baker, one of the longest rivers in the country, which reaches the sea at Caleta Tortel. Further south still is Villa O' Higgins and the icefields of the Campo de Hielo Sur, which feed several magnificent glaciers and prevent further road building, although a route (by boat and on foot or mountain bike) exists that goes on to El Chaltén in Argentina. Coyhaique enjoys good air connections with Puerto Montt and Santiago, while nearby Puerto Chacabuco can be reached by ferry or catamaran from Puerto Montt, Chaitén and Chiloé. The most appealing parts of this region, however, can only be visited by travelling along the Carretera Austral.

★ **Don't miss...**

1 **Mountain biking**
   Take to two wheels
   along a stretch of
   the spectacular
   Carretera Austral
   itself, page 402.

2 **Parque Pumalín**
   Not only is it an
   area of outstanding
   beauty, it also gives
   an insight into what
   is widely regarded as
   one of the world's
   most important
   conservation projects,
   page 404.

3 **Trekking** Especially
   near Futaleufú in
   the north and Chile
   Chico in the south,
   pages 409 and 425.

4 **Lago General Carrera**
   Take a ferry ride
   across the huge,
   deep blue expanse
   between Puerto
   Ibañez and Chile
   Chico, page 423.

5 **Laguna San Rafael**
   Sail on a cruise
   ship right up to the
   icebergs at the foot
   of the San Rafael
   glacier, page 430.

Background

The original inhabitants of northern Patagonia were Alacalufes (Kaweshour or *canoeros*), who were coast dwellers living off the sea (see page 520), and Tehuelches (Tzónecas, or Patagones), who lived on the pampa hunting guanacos, *ñandúes* (rheas) and *huemules* (an indigenous deer, now almost extinct; see box, page 426). There are some fine cave paintings in the vicinity of Lago General Carrera, for example at Cueva de la Guanaca, near Lago Lapparent, and Cueva de las Manos, on the Argentine side of the border near Chile Chico.

The Spanish called the region Trapalanda, but initially explored little more than the coast. This was the last territory to be occupied by the Chilean state after Independence from Spain. In the late 19th century, expeditions up the rivers led by George Charles Musters (1869) and Enríque Simpson Baeza (1870-1872) were followed by a failed attempt to found a settlement at the mouth of the Río Palena in 1884. Fearing that Argentina might seize the territory, the Chilean government appointed Hans Steffen to explore the area. His seven expeditions (1892-1902) were followed by an agreement with Argentina to submit the question of the frontier to arbitration by the British crown.

The Chilean government granted concessions to three large cattle companies in an attempt to occupy the area. One of these ranches, on the Río Baker, was managed by E Lucas Bridges, of the Bridges family from Tierra del Fuego and author of *Uttermost Part of the Earth* (for more details, see *South* by AF Tschiffely). Until the 1920s, there were few settlers; early pioneers settled along the coast and brought supplies from Chiloé. The estimated population of northern Patagonia in 1907 was just 197 people. By 1920, this had risen to 1660 and, by 1930, 8886 inhabitants were in the region. Although the first town, Balmaceda (modern-day Coyhaique), was founded in 1917, followed by Puerto Aisén in 1924, the first road, between Puerto Aisén and Coyhaique, was not built until 1936. It was not until the 1960s, when new roads were built and airstrips were opened, that this region began to be integrated with the rest of the country.

Although the road has helped transform the lives of many people in this part of Chile, the motivation behind its construction was mainly geopolitical. Ever since Independence, Chilean military and political leaders have stressed the importance of occupying the southern regions of the Pacific coast and preventing any incursion by Argentina. Building the Carretera Austral was seen by General Pinochet as a means of achieving this aim: a way of occupying and securing territory, just as colonization had been in the early years of the 20th century.

Begun in 1976, the central section of the Carretera Austral, from Chaitén to Coyhaique, was opened in 1983. Five years later, the northern section, linking Chaitén with Puerto Montt, and the southern section, between Coyhaique and Cochrane, were officially inaugurated. Since then, the Carretera has been extended south of Cochrane to Puerto Yungay and Villa O'Higgins. Work is continuing, building branch roads (which currently amount to around 900 km) and paving the most important sections.

Despite recent growth, this remains one of the most sparsely populated areas of Chile, with barely 100,000 inhabitants, most of whom live in Coyhaique or in nearby Puerto Aisén. Agriculture is limited by the climate and poverty of the soil, but fishing remains important as a source of employment in the inland channels, with salmon farming providing most income. Forestry plays a growing role in the economy: wood is used for construction and winter fuel. Zinc, lead and copper are mined, but only zinc is extracted in large quantities. A huge aluminium plant is in the pipeline, which will have both economic and ecological repercussions. Perhaps even more disturbing, the Chilean government sees hydroelectric power as a solution to the petrol and natural gas crises and studies are underway as to the feasibility of damming some of Chile's most spectacular rivers including the Baker and Futaleufú.

⁞ Tips for travelling along the Carretera Austral

Travelling the length of the Carretera Austral can be quite a challenge. The first and most important piece of advice is to take enough cash. While there are Cirrus and MasterCard ATMs in Chaitén and Cochrane, Coyhaique is the only place between Puerto Montt and Villa O'Higgins with Visa ATMs.

Off season much of the northern section of the Carretera is rendered inaccessible when the Arena-Puelche and Hornopirén-Caleta Gonzalo ferries are suspended. You will have to go to Chaitén directly from Puerto Montt or Chiloé instead. If you are driving, take a 4WD vehicle and fill up your tank whenever possible. Take spare parts – the road is unforgiving. After heavy rain, parts of the Carretera are liable to flood, so check the weather carefully and be prepared to be stuck in one place for a few days while conditions improve.

Most of the buses that ply the Carretera Austral are minibuses (and in more than one case converted transit vans) operated by small companies, and often they are driven by their owners. Services are less reliable than elsewhere in Chile and timetables change frequently as operators go out of business and new ones start up. Booking your ticket in advance means that if your bus does not leave, for whatever reason, the company is liable to pay for your accommodation until the bus is ready to depart. Complaints should be directed to SERNAC, the government consumer rights department, in Coyhaique.

Geography and climate

South of Puerto Montt the sea has broken through the coastal *cordillera* and drowned the central valley. The higher parts of the coastal *cordillera* form a maze of islands, stretching for over 1000 km and separated from the coast by tortuous fjords and inlets (*senos*). There is no real dry season near the coast, with annual rainfall of over 2000 mm on the offshore islands. Westerly winds are strong, especially in summer, and temperatures vary little between day and night.

⁞ *January and February are probably the best months for a trip to this area of Chile. From April to September it is bitterly cold inland.*

The Andes are much lower than further north and eroded by glacial action: towards the coast they rise in peaks such as San Valentín (4058 m), the highest mountain south of Talca; inland they form a high steppe around 1000 m, where the climate is drier, warm in summer and cold during the winter months. The shores of Lago General Carrera enjoy a warm microclimate that allows the production of fruit.

To the south of Coyhaique are two areas of highland covered by ice, known as *campos de hielo* (icefields). The Campo de Hielo Norte, over 100 km from north to south and some 50 km from east to west, includes the glaciers (*ventisqueros*) San Rafael, Montt and Steffens. The Campo de Hielo Sur covers a larger area, stretching south from the mouth of the Río Baker towards Puerto Natales.

Five main rivers flow westwards: from north to south these are the Futaleufú or Yelcho, the Palena, the Cisnes, the Simpson or Aisén and the Baker. This last, at 370 km, is the third longest river in Chile. The three largest lakes in this region, Lago General Carrera, Lago Cochrane and Lago O'Higgins, are shared with Argentina.

● Chilote legend ascribes the creation of the myriad islands and fjords south of Puerto Montt to a war between two serpents, one good (on land) and one evil (in the sea).

The road can be divided into three sections: **Puerto Montt to Chaitén** (157 km), plus two ferry crossings; **Chaitén to Coyhaique** (399 km); and **Coyhaique to Villa O'Higgins** (559 km), plus one ferry crossing. There is also a branch that runs along the southern shore of **Lago General Carrera** from Puerto Guadal to Chile Chico as well as branches to Futaleufú, Palena, Puerto Balmaceda, Lago Verde, Puerto Cisnes, Bahía Exploradores and Tortel. The Puerto Montt-Chaitén section can only be travelled in summer, when the ferries are operating, but an alternative route, through Chiloé to Chaitén, exists year round (see page 391). The road is paved just south of Chaitén and around Coyaique, from just north of Villa Mañihuales to Villa Cerro Castillo and Puerto Ibáñez.

The condition of the road can vary dramatically depending on the time of year and amount of traffic. Some sections can be difficult or even impossible after heavy rain or snowfall, and widening/paving/repair work is constantly being undertaken. Although tourist infrastructure is growing rapidly and unleaded fuel is available all the way to Villa O'Higgins, drivers should carry adequate fuel and spares, especially if intending to detour from the main route, and should protect their windscreens and headlamps.

Hitching is popular in summer, but extremely difficult out of season, particularly south of Cochrane. Watching the cloak of dust thrown up by the wheels from the back of a pickup, while taking in the lakes, forests, mountains and waterfalls, is an unforgettable experience, but be prepared for long delays and allow at least three days from Chaitén to Coyhaique.

The Carretera Austral is highly recommended for **cycling** as long as you have enough time and are reasonably fit. A good mountain bike is essential and a tent is an advantage. Most buses will take bicycles for a small charge. An excellent online guide to cycling the Carretera can be found at www.salamandras.cl.

Puerto Montt to Chaitén → *Colour map 4, C2.*

This 242-km section of the Carretera Austral is perhaps the most inaccessible and secluded stretch along the entire route, passing through two national parks and the private Parque Pumalín. Beautiful old trees close in on all sides, the rivers and streams sparkle and, on (admittedly rare) clear days, there are beautiful views across the Golfo de Ancud to Chiloé. ▸▸ *For Sleeping, Eating and other listings, see pages 406-408.*

Ins and outs

This section of the route includes two ferry crossings at La Arena and Hornopirén. Before setting out, it is imperative to check when the ferries are running (generally only in January and February) and, if driving, to make a reservation for your vehicle: do this at the **Transmarchilay** office in Puerto Montt, rather than in Santiago. Hitching to Chaitén takes several days, and there is a lot of competition for lifts: you must be prepared for a day's wait if you find yourself out of luck. The experience of riding in the back of a pickup, however, will make the hanging around worthwhile. An alternative route to Chaitén is by catamaran or ferry from Puerto Montt or Castro/Quellón (see page 391).

South of Puerto Montt

The Carretera Austral heads east out of Puerto Montt through **Pelluco**, where there is a polluted bathing beach with black sand and some good seafood restaurants, and then follows the shore of the beautiful Seno de Reloncaví ('Reloncaví Estuary', see page 364). Between the sound to the south and west and Lago Chapo to the northeast is **Parque Nacional Alerce Andino** ① *entrances 2½ km from Correntoso (35 km west of Puerto Montt) and 7 km west of Lenca (40 km south of Puerto Montt), US$8.* The park covers

39,255 ha of steep forested valleys rising to 1500 m and containing ancient alerce trees, some over 1000 years old (the oldest are estimated to be 4200 years old). There are also some 50 small lakes and many waterfalls in the park. Wildlife includes *pudú*, pumas, *vizcachas*, condors and black woodpeckers. Lago Chapo (5500 ha) feeds a hydroelectric power station at Canutillar, east of the park. There are ranger posts at Río Chaicas, Lago Chapo, Laguna Sargazo and at the north entrance. These can provide very little information, but a map is available from CONAF in Puerto Montt.

Some 4 km south of Puerto Montt (allow one hour), **La Arena** is the site of the first ferry, across the Reloncaví Estuary to **Puelche**. From Puelche there is an unpaved road east to Puelo, from where transport can be found north to Cochamó and Ralún.

Hornopirén and around
Also called Río Negro, **Hornopirén** lies 54 km south of Puelche at the northern end of a fjord. Although a branch of the Carretera Austral runs round the edge of the fjord to Pichanco, 35 km further south, that route is a dead-end. There is excellent fishing in the area and Hornopirén is a base for excursions to the Hornopirén Volcano (1572 m) and to Lago Cabrera, which lies further north. It is also the departure point for the second ferry, to Caleta Gonzalo. At the mouth of the fjord is **Isla Llancahué**, a small island with a hotel and thermal springs. The island is reached by boat ① *T099-6424857, US$50 one way shared between group*; look out for dolphins and fur seals on the crossing.

Parque Nacional Alerce Andino

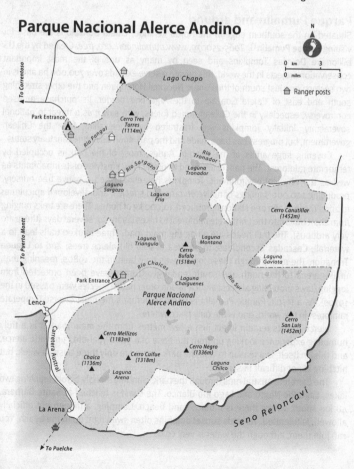

⁝ The price of settlement

In 1937, desperate to encourage settlement in this isolated region, the Chilean government passed a law offering settlers ownership of land provided it was cleared of forest. The people came, and smoke from the forest fires which followed could be seen from the Atlantic coast. The legacies of this law are still apparent to the visitor. Firstly, in the large expanses of burnt tree stumps to be seen, especially around the Río Palena and Mañihuales, and also in the shifting of the port facilities from Puerto Aisén to Puerto Chacabuco, as so much soil was washed into the rivers that the Río Aisén silted up, preventing vessels from reaching Puerto Aisén.

Some 16 km by *ripio* road east of Hornopirén and covering 48,232 ha, **Parque Nacional Hornopirén** includes the Yates Volcano (2187 m) as well as the basins of two rivers, the Blanco and the Negro. The park protects some 9000 ha of alerce forest as well as areas of mixed native forest including lenga and coigue. From the entrance a path leads 8 km east up along the Río Blanco to a basic *refugio*.

Parque Pumalín and around

Situated on the southern edge of the Fiordo Reñihue, **Caleta Gonzalo** is the base for visiting **Parque Pumalín** ① *T065-250079, www.pumalinpark.org, free.* Created by the US billionaire Douglas Tompkins and seen by many as one of the most important conservation projects in the world, this private reserve extends over 700,000 ha and is in two sectors: one just south of the Parque Nacional Hornopirén and the other stretching south and east of Caleta Gonzalo to the Argentine border. Its purchase aroused controversy, especially in the Chilean armed forces, who saw it as a threat to national sovereignty. Initially Tompkins was frustrated by stonewalling from the Chilean government, but progress has been made and the park now has nature sanctuary status.

Covering large areas of the western Andes, most of the park is occupied by temperate rainforest. The park is intended to protect the lifestyles of its inhabitants as well as the physical environment. Tompkins has established a native tree nursery, producing 100,000 saplings of native endangered species, and developed apiculture; in 2002 the Pumalín bee stations produced 30,000 kg of honey. There are treks ranging from short trails into the temperate rainforest to hikes lasting for several days (these are very arduous). The trail heads are all on the main road. Three marked trails lead to a waterfall, **Cascadas Escondidas**; to an area of very old alerce trees; and to **Laguna Tronador**. The road through these forests was only built in the 1980s, meaning that, unlike areas to the north and south, endangered trees have been protected from logging (laws protecting alerces, araucaria and other native species were passed in the 1970s). As a result, Parque Pumalín is home to perhaps the most diverse temperate rainforest in the world, and is the only place where

alerce forests remain intact just a few metres from the main road. It is a truly humbling experience looking up from the base of a 3000-year-old, 3-m-wide alerce, and this, in itself, is a reason to visit the park. There are only three buses a week, but hitching is not difficult in season.

The Carretera Austral runs through the park, climbing steeply before reaching two lakes, **Lago Río Negro** and **Lago Río Blanco**. The coast is reached at **Santa Bárbara**, 48 km south, where there is a black sand beach. Camping, although not officially allowed, is tolerated. Towards sunset dolphins often swim right up to the beach. You can join them, although the water is very cold.

Chaitén

The capital of Palena Province, Chaitén lies in a beautiful spot, with a forest-covered hill rising behind it, and a quiet inlet leading out into the Patagonian channels. In many ways Chaitén is a cultural crossroads. Until relatively recently, the town had more contact with Argentina than the central Chilean mainland, while a Chilote influence is clear in the town's architecture. Indeed until the construction of the Carretera this area was known as Chiloé Continental and was governed as part of the island opposite. Today, although firmly part of Patagonia, Chaitén (with a population of around 4000) is politically administered from Puerto Montt in the Lake District.

The town is important as a **port** for catamarans and ferries to Puerto Montt and to Chiloé (see page 391), and is a growing centre for **adventure tourism**, and trips to the **Parque Pumalín** as well as nearby thermal springs and glaciers. There is excellent **fishing** nearby, especially to the south in the ríos Yelcho and Futaleufú and in lagos Espolón and Yelcho. Fishing licences are sold at the Municipalidad. Visits are also possible to a sea lion colony offshore on **Isla Puduguapi**. There are good views over the Corcovado Bay from Avenida Corcovado. Just east of the town centre, along Carrera Pinto is the **Parque Palena**, formerly a military base and now home to an interesting museum chronicling local history, with emphasis on the building of the Carretera. There is a **waterfall** about 15 minutes beyond the museum.

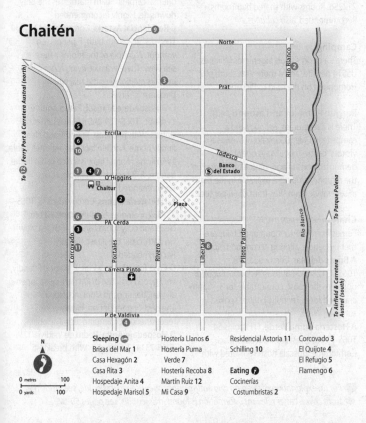

Chaitén

N

0 metres 100
0 yards 100

Sleeping
Brisas del Mar 1
Casa Hexagón 2
Casa Rita 3
Hospedaje Anita 4
Hospedaje Marisol 5

Hostería Llanos 6
Hostería Puma
Verde 7
Hostería Recoba 8
Martín Ruiz 12
Mi Casa 9

Residencial Astoria 11
Schilling 10

Eating
Cocinerías
Costumbristas 2

Corcovado 3
El Quijote 4
El Refugio 5
Flamengo 6

⊜ Sleeping

South of Puerto Montt *p402*

There are basic *refugios* at Río Pangal, Laguna Sargazo and Laguna Fría in the Parque Nacional Alerce Andino, and campsites at Río Chaicas and the northern entrance; no camping is permitted inside the boundaries of the park.

Hornopirén and around *p403*

There are lots of *cabañas* and *residenciales* here, including the following:

A Termas de Llancahue, Llancahue Island, T099-6424857. Full board, good food, access to thermal springs.

B-C Holiday Country, O'Higgins 637, T065-217220. Restaurant, also *cabañas*.

B-C Hostería Catalina, Ingenieros Militares s/n, T065-217359, www.hosteriacatalina.cl. Comfortable rooms with breakfast and bath. Recommended.

C Hornopirén, Carrera Pinto 388, T065-217256. Rooms with shared bathrooms. Recommended, also *cabañas*.

Camping

There's a good site on Ingenieros Militares, US$14 per site, and 4 more sites south of Hornopirén on the road to Pichanco.

Parque Pumalín and around *p404*

There is a restaurant, *cabañas* and a campsite in Caleta Gonzalo, as well as a visitors' centre (not always open) and demonstrations of agricultural techniques in the region. Camping is available in the park at several well-run sites from US$8 per tent.

Chaitén *p405, map p405*

Ferries from Puerto Montt and Chiloé are met by people offering accommodation.

A Brisas del Mar, Corcovado 278, T065-731284, cababrisas@telsur.cl. *Cabañas* opposite the coast, comfortable for 3, slightly cramped for 4. Friendly, English spoken in summer, Wi-Fi.

A Hostería Puma Verde, O'Higgins 54, T065-731184, reservasalsur@surnet.cl. Comfortable upscale hostel affiliated with the Pumalín organization. Furnished and decorated with local products, some of which are for sale in the annexed store. English spoken. There is also an apartment, L, sleeping up to 5.

A Schilling, Corcovado 320, T065-731295. With breakfast, heating, restaurant. No views from rooms despite the location, overpriced, unfriendly. No advance reservations.

B Mi Casa, Av Norte, T065-731285, hmicasa@telsur.cl. On a hill offering fine views. Sauna, gymnasium and restaurant with good value set meal. Recommended.

C Casa Hexagon, Blanco 36, T0-82862950. E singles. Extraordinary hexagonal hostel with a tree trunk at its centre. Very comfortable and with excellent kitchen facilities. There are pleasant walks along the river from the back of the house. Owned by an eccentric German, an origami master, ex-concert guitarist and fly-fishing expert who built the house himself, and has furnished it with contemporary art and oriental carpets. Foam mattresses the only downside. Highly recommended.

C Residencial Astoria, Corcovado 442, T065-731263. With bath, F per person without. A couple of the rooms have a sea view. There is a nice living room upstairs overlooking the sea, where breakfast is served.

C-D Hospedaje Marisol, Pedro Aguirre Cerda 66, T065-731188, rumer@surnet.cl. F singles. With breakfast. Friendly and clean family home. Kitchen facilities, internet, cable TV in living room. There is a nice cabin in the garden, A-B for up to 5 people. Recommended.

C-D Hostería Llanos, Corcovado 378, T065-731332. F Singles. Slightly cramped but clean and cosy rooms, some with sea view. No bath, basic breakfast, friendly. Recommended.

D Casa Rita, Rivero y Prat. F singles. Friendly, very good beds, use of kitchen, clean, open all year, heating, no smoking. Good value. The best budget option, highly recommended. Camping also available.

D Hospedaje Anita, Pedro de Valdivia 129, T065-731413. F singles. With breakfast.

● *For an explanation of sleeping and eating price codes used in this guide, see inside the*
● *front cover. Other relevant information is found in Essentials, see pages 50-57.*

Typical family home. Very low ceilings. Camping possible in the garden.

D Hospedaje Watson, Ercilla 580, T065-731237. **F** singles, including use of kitchen. Clean.

D Hostería Recoba, Libertad 432, T065-731390. **F-G** singles. With breakfast. More doss-house than *hostería*. Cheap and clean but very little privacy – some rooms are separated by just a window that can be opened from either side!

F-G Martín Ruiz, Carretera Austral, 1 km north of Chaitén. Price per person with breakfast. Friendly, nice views.

Camping

Los Arrayanes, Carretera Austral, 4 km north. With hot showers and close to sea, good.

🍴 Eating

South of Puerto Montt *p402*
🍴 **Pazos**, Pelluco, T065-252552. Serves the best *curanto* in the Puerto Montt area.

Chaitén *p405, map p405*
🍴 **Brisas del Mar**, Corcovado 278. T065-731284. Good fish dishes.
🍴 **Corcovado**, Corcovado 408. T065-731221. Run-of-the-mill seafood restaurant.
🍴 **El Refugio**, Corcovado y Ercilla. One of the better seafood restaurants with rustic furniture carved out of tree trunks. Slow service when full.
🍴 **Cocinerías Costumbristas**, Portales 300 block. Several tiny restaurants serving local fare such as *curanto* at reasonable prices and in large portions. Recommended.
🍴 **El Quijote**, O'Higgins 42, T065-731293. Basic food and bar snacks.
🍴 **Flamengo**, Corcovado 218. Popular seafood restaurant.

▲ Activities and tours

Chaitén *p405, map p405*
Chaitur, O'Higgins 67, T/F065-731429, nchaitur@hotmail.com. General travel agent selling bus and boat tickets. Also bespoke excursions, trekking, horse riding, fishing and trips to Parque Pumalín as well as trips to the Termas de Amarillo and Yelcho Glacier. English spoken, friendly and helpful. Lots of information and internet access. Highly

recommended. Another branch at Diego Portales 350. Opposite the bus station is an office of the Parque Pumalín.

⊖ Transport

South of Puerto Montt *p402*
Bus
To reach the northern entrance of the **Parque Nacional Alerce Andino**, take **Fierro** or **Río Pato** bus from Puerto Montt to **Correntoso** (or **Lago Chapo** bus which passes through Correntoso), several daily except Sun, then walk. To reach the southern entrance, take any **Fierro** bus to Chaicas, La Arena, Contau and Hornopirén, US$2.50, getting off at **Lenca** sawmill, then walk (signposted).

Ferry
30-min crossing from La Arena to **Puelche**, 10 daily Dec-Mar, reduced service off season. Arrive 30 mins early for a place; buses have priority, cars US$15, bicycles US$4. See www.transmarchilay.cl for more details.

Hornopirén and around *p403*
Bus
Fierro runs 2 buses daily from Puerto Montt in season. There are no buses south from Hornopirén.

Ferry
In Jan and Feb only, **Naviera Austral** operates a ferry from Hornopirén to **Caleta Gonzalo**, 1600 daily, 6 hrs, return departures 0900 daily, cars US$110 one way, foot passengers US$18, bicycles US$11. Advance booking required: there can be a 2-day wait. See www.navieraustral.cl for more details. **Chaitur** organizes connecting transport between the ferry port in Caleta Gonzalo and Chaitén (see Activities and tours, above).

Chaitén *p405, map p405*
Air
Flights to **Puerto Montt** by Aerosur, Aeropuelche and Aeromet, daily 1200, 35 mins, US$50. **Aeroregional** also flies to **Castro**, irregular service. Bookings can be made through **Chaitur** (see Activities and tours, above). Note, however, that flying in bad weather in a small aircraft is not necessarily safe and there have been a number of accidents in recent years.

Terminal at O'Higgins 67. Several companies run minibuses along the Carretera Austral to **Coyhaique**, 12 hrs, most days direct in summer, 2 a week with overnight stop in La Junta or Puyuhuapi in winter, departures usually 0800-0900. Minibuses usually travel full, so can't pick up passengers en route. Chaitur acts as an agent for all these services (see Activities and tours, above). Or try **Buses Norte**, Libertad 432, T065-731390, with buses to **Coyhaique**, US$30, and intermediate points such as La Junta and Puyuhuapi. To **Futaleufú**, Buses Ebenezer, Mon-Sat 1530, 4 hrs, US$12 (3 weekly off-season); change here for buses to the Argentine border.

Ferry
The ferry port is about 1 km north of town. Schedules change frequently and ferries are infrequent off season. **Naviera Austral**, Corcovado 266, T065-731272, www.navieraustral.cl; **Catamaranes**

del Sur, Riveros y Cerda, T065-731199, www.catamaranesdelsur.cl.

To **Chiloé**, Naviera Austral operates ferry services to Castro or Quellón, 4 per week in summer (Dec-Mar), reduced service off season, 5 hrs, passengers US$30 one way, cars US$130, bicycles US$13. **Catamaranes del Sur** operates catamaran services on the same route for foot passengers only, 2 or 3 weekly in summer, less regularly off season, 2 hrs, US$25.

To **Puerto Montt**, Naviera Austral, 4 weekly, 10 hrs, passengers US$25, car US$120, bike US$11; **Catamaranes del Sur**, 2 weekly weather permitting, 3 hrs, US$35.

❶ Directory

Chaitén *p405, map p405*
Banks Banco del Estado, O'Higgins y Libertad, charges US$10 for changing TCs, ATM accepts MasterCard and Cirrus but not Visa. Rates in general are poor along the Carretera Austral; change money in Puerto Montt.

Chaitén to Coyhaique → *Colour map 5, A3.*

This section of the Carretera Austral, 422 km long, runs through long stretches of virgin rainforest, passing small villages, the perfectly still white waters of Lago Yelcho, and the Parque Nacional Queulat, with its glaciers and waterfalls. Roads branch off east to the Argentine border and west to Puerto Cisnes. Near Coyhaique, the road passes huge tracts of land destroyed by logging, where only tree stumps remain as testament to the depredations of the early colonists. ▶▶ *For Sleeping, Eating and other listings, see pages 411-414.*

Towards Puerto Cárdenas

At Amarillo, 25 km south of Chaitén there is a turning to the **Termas de Amarillo** ① *5 km east, US$3*, which consists of two wooden sheds with a very hot pool inside, and an outdoor swimming pool. There is superb salmon fishing in the nearby rivers. From here, it is possible to hike along the old trail to **Futaleufú** (see below). The hike takes four to seven days and is not for the inexperienced; be prepared for wet feet all the way. The trail follows the Río Michinmawida, passing the volcano of the same name, to **Lago Espolón** (see below). A ferry with a sporadic schedule crosses the lake, taking cargo, foot passengers and bicycles to Futaleufú.

Situated 46 km south of Chaitén and surrounded by forest, **Puerto Cárdenas** lies on the northern tip of **Lago Yelcho**, a beautiful glacial lake on the Río Futaleufú, surrounded by hills and with views of the stunning Yelcho glacier. The lake is frequented by anglers. At Puerto Cárdenas, there is a police post where you may have to register your passport. Further south at Km 60, a path leads to the **Yelcho glacier**, a two-hour walk. There is a campsite here, and the administrator charges people walking to the glacier. Whether he is legally allowed to do this is a contentious issue.

⁑ Taking in the waters

If you want to whitewater raft in Chile, there is no better place than the Río Futaleufú. Only accessible by road since 1982, Futaleufú (big river in the Mapuche language) has quickly grown to be a Mecca for kayakers and whitewater rafters. Every year, hundreds of fanatics travel to spend the southern summer here and there is no shortage of operators offering trips.

The river is an incredible deep-blue colour and offers everything from easy grade II-III sections downstream to the extremely challenging grade V Cañón del Infierno (Hell Canyon), surrounded by a dramatic backdrop of spectacular mountain scenery.

Into Argentina via Futaleufú or Palena

Southeast of Chaitén the Argentine border is reached in two places, Futaleufú and Palena, along a road that branches off the Carretera Austral at **Villa Santa Lucía** (Km 81), where there are 30 houses, a military camp and one small shop; bread is available from a private house. The road to the border is single track, *ripio*, passable in a regular car, but best with a good, strong vehicle; the scenery is beautiful.

At **Puerto Ramírez**, at the southern end of **Lago Yelcho**, the road divides: the north branch runs along the valley of the Río Futaleufú to **Futaleufú**, while the southern one continues to Palena. Futaleufú has established itself as the centre for the finest whitewater rafting in the southern hemisphere. Although only at 350 m, the spectacular mountain scenery makes you feel as if you were up in the High Andes. The Río Espolón provides a peaceful backdrop to this pleasant town, with wide streets lined with shrubs and roses and Chilote-style houses. Tourist information ① *on the plaza, daily in summer, 0900-2100, T065-721241*. **Lago Espolón**, west of Futaleufú, is reached by a turning 41 km northeast of Puerto Ramírez. It is a beautiful lake and enjoys a warm microclimate: 30ºC in the day in summer, 5ºC at night. The lake is even warm enough for a quick dip, but beware of the currents.

Chilean immigration ① *summer 0800-2100; winter 0800-2000*, is on the border, 8 km east of Futaleufú, at the bridge over the Río Grande. If entering Chile, change money in Futaleufú (poor rates but there is nowhere at the border), and then continue from Futaleufú towards Puerto Ramírez; outside Ramírez, take the right turn to Chaitén, otherwise you'll end up back at the border in Palena.

The Chilean immigration post ① *0800-2000*, at Palena lies 8 km west of the border. It is much quieter than the crossing at Futaleufú. Both crossings lead to **Trevelin**, which is 45 km east of Futaleufú, 95 km east of Palena. Trevelin is an offshoot of the Welsh Chubút colony on the Atlantic side of Argentine Patagonia, as featured in Bruce Chatwin's *In Patagonia* (see page 559). It has accommodation,

Futaleufú

El Barranco 5
Hostería Río Grande 6
Los Troncos 7
Posada La Gringa 8
Sur Andes 9

Sleeping
Adolfo B&B 1
Cabañas Río Espolón 2
Cabañas Veranada 3
Continental 4

Eating
Futaleufú 1
Martín Pescador 2
Sur Andes 3

restaurants, tea rooms and a tourist office, but there is a much wider range of services at **Esquel**, 23 km northeast. Esquel is a base for visiting the Argentine Parque Nacional Los Alerces. There are also transport connections to Bariloche and other destinations in Argentine Patagonia.

Into Argentina via La Junta

From Villa Santa Lucía, the Carretera Austral follows the Río Frío and then the Río Palena to **La Junta**, a tranquil, nondescript village at the confluence of Río Rosselot and Río Palena, 151 km south of Chaitén. Fuel is available here. Some 9 km east is **Lago Rosselot**, surrounded by forest and situated at the heart of a *reserva nacional* (12,725 ha). From here, the road continues east, 74 km, to the border crossing at **Lago Verde** ① *summer 0800-2200, winter 0800-2000*, and on to Las Pampas in Argentina. There is also a new road leading northwest from La Junta to **Puerto Raúl Marín Balmaceda** on the coast.

Puyuhuapi and around

From La Junta, the Carretera Austral runs south along the western side of Lago Risopatrón, past several waterfalls, to **Puyuhuapi** (also spelt Puyuguapi), 45 km further south. Located in a beautiful spot at the northern end of the Puyuhuapi fjord, the village is a tranquil stopping place, about halfway between Chaitén and Coyhaique. It was founded by four Sudeten German families in 1935, and its economy is based around fishing, ever-increasing tourism and the factory where Puyuhuapi's famous handmade carpets are produced. By the municipalidad on the main street there is a decent tourist information office ① *Mon-Sat in season, 1000-1400, 1800-2200*. A bus timetable is pinned up here. If you are travelling in your own vehicle ask at the police station about road conditions and temporary road closures.

From Puyuhuapi, the road follows the eastern edge of the fjord along one of the most beautiful sections of the Carretera Austral, with views of the **Termas de Puyuhuapi** ① *18 km southwest of Puyuhuapi, US$20 per person, under-12s US$15*. This resort is on the western edge of the fjord and is accessible only by boat. It has several 40°C springs filling three pools near the beach. Take food and drink. The resort can also be visited on a four- or six-day tour with **Patagonia Connection SA** (see pages 412 and 431). More easily accessible are the new **Termas del Ventisqero**, 6 km south of Puyuhuapi by the side of the Carretera overlooking the fjord. In season the baths are open until 2300 and during the day there is a café.

Covering 154,093 ha of attractive forest around Puyuhuapi, the **Parque Nacional Queulat** ① *administration at the CONAF office in La Junta, T067-314128*, is, supposedly, the former location of the legendary Ciudad de los Césares, a fabulously wealthy mythological city built between two hills made of gold and diamonds and inhabited by immortal beings. According to legend, the city was protected by a shroud of fog and hence was impossible for strangers to discover. The Carretera Austral passes through the park, close to **Lago Risopatrón** north of Puyuhuapi, where boat trips are available. Some 24 km south, a two-hour trek leads to the **Ventisquero Colgante** hanging glacier ① *US$5*. From here the Carretera Austral climbs out of the jungle-like Nalca-filled Queulat valley through a series of narrow hairpin bends offering fine views of the forest and several glaciers. Near the pass (500 m) is the **Salto Pedro García** waterfall, with the **Salto del Cóndor** waterfall some 5 km further on. Steep gradients mean that crossing the park is the hardest part of the Carretera for those travelling by bicycle.

South of the Río Cisnes

Stretching 160 km from the Argentine border to the coast at Puerto Cisnes, the Río Cisnes is recommended for rafting or canoeing, with grand scenery and modest rapids – except for the horrendous drop at Piedra del Gato, about 60 km east of

Puerto Cisnes. Good camping is available in the forest. Possibly the wettest town in Chile, **Puerto Cisnes** is reached by a 33-km winding road that branches west off the Carretera Austral about 59 km south of Puyuhuapi. It is a peaceful fishing port where traditional knitted clothes are made. Fuel is available.

At Km 92, south of **Villa Amengual**, a road branches west 104 km to the **Argentine border** via La Tapera. Chilean immigration ① *summer 0800-2200, winter 0800-2000*, is 12 km west of the border. On the Argentine side, the road continues to meet up with Route 40, the north-south road at the foot of the Andes.

Reserva Nacional Lago Las Torres is 98 km south of Puyuhuapi and covers 16,516 ha. It includes the wonderful **Lago Las Torres**, which offers good fishing and a small CONAF campsite. Further south, at Km 125, a road branches east to El Toqui where zinc is mined. From here the Carretera Austral is paved.

Villa Mañihuales, at Km 148, is a small, nondescript town with a Copec petrol station and a couple of basic *residenciales* and restaurants. Most buses stop here for 15 to 30 minutes. Nearby is the **Reserva Forestal Mañihuales** ① *US$3*. The reserve covers 1206 ha and encompasses a huemul sanctuary. Fires largely destroyed the forests in the 1940s but the views are good.

Sleeping

Towards Puerto Cárdenas *p408*
L-AL Cabañas Yelcho en La Patagonia, Lago Yelcho, 7 km south of Puerto Cárdenas, T065-731337, www.yelcho.cl. Cabins and rooms on the lake shore. Also camping and cafeteria.
L Cabañas CAVI, Lago Yelcho, near Puerto Cárdenas. Sauna, restaurant, video room, laundry. 6 *cabañas* with private bathrooms, hot water, kitchen facilities. Also campsite with electricity, hot showers, drinking water, laundry facilities, barbecue area and fishing boats for hire. Book via **Turismo Austral Ltda**, Santa Magdalena 75, oficina 902, Providencia, Santiago, T02-3341309, F3341328.
A Termas de Amarillo, Termas de Amarillo, T065-731326. Also camping and *cabañas*.
C Residencial Yelcho, Puerto Cárdenas, T065-264429. Clean, full board available.
D Residencial Marcela, Amarillo, T065-264442. Also *cabañas* and camping.

Into Argentina via Futaleufú or Palena *p409, map p409*
LL-L El Barranco, O'Higgins 172, Futaleufú, T065-721314, www.elbarrancochile.cl. Probably the best rooms in town, but still overpriced. There is a bar, restaurant, outdoor swimming pool and free bicycles for the guests. Fishing trips organized. Rather nonchalant staff.
L-AL Hostería Río Grande, O'Higgins 397, Futaleufú, T065-721320, www.pacchile.com. Overpriced though comfortable, en suite

bathrooms, friendly, bar, good restaurant, arranges tours and activities.
AL Posada la Gringa, Sargento Aldea 498, Futaleufú, T065-721260. Elegant and charming guesthouse set in large gardens and with the best view in town. Price includes a large brunch. The owner is of Basque descent and speaks perfect English. Recommended, but she may be moving back to Santiago soon.
A-B Cabañas Veranada, Sargento Aldea 480, Futaleufú, T065-721266. Well-equipped cabins with excellent beds and good kitchens. All have slow-burning wood stoves except one with an open fireplace. Friendly owners. Recommended.
B Cabañas Río Espolón, PA Cerda s/n, 5 mins' walk west of centre, Futaleufú, T065-721216, rioespolon@yahoo.es. Secluded cabins with bar and restaurant overlooking the river, the sound of which is a constant in the background. Book ahead as it often fills up with rafting groups.
B Sur Andes, Cerda 308, Futaleufú, T065-721405, www.surandes.tk. Rustic but tasteful apartment, fully equipped but with no kitchen.
C Adolfo B&B, O'Higgins 302, Futaleufú, T065-721256. E-F singles. Well-kept and friendly family home. With breakfast and kitchen facilities.
C Los Troncos, Carmona 541, Futaleufú, T065-721269. F singles. Basic clean *hospedaje* on the northern edge of town. With breakfast and kitchen facilities.

D Residencial La Chilenita, Pudeto 681, Palena, T065-741212. Simple rooms.
E Continental, Balmaceda 595, Futaleufú, T065-721222. F-G singles. Pokey rooms, creaky floors, squeaky beds and no toilet paper provided, but clean and you can't ask for more at this price.
E Sra Rosalía Cuevas de Ruiz, No 7, Villa Santa Lucía. Basic, meals available. One of several options on the main street; none has hot water.

Camping
Los Copihues, T065-721413, is on the river, 500 m from Futaleufú. Horse-riding trips offered.
Camping Puerto Espolón, T099- 4477448, puertoespolon@latinmail.com.
Futaleufú has a decent, if basic campsite on the west edge of town next to Laguna Espejo, US$5 per person with hot water.

Into Argentina via La Junta *p410*
AL-A Espacio y Tiempo, La Junta, T067-314141, www.espacioytiempo.cl. Attractive garden, English spoken, good restaurant, fishing expeditions and other tours.
C Hostería Patagonia, Lynch 331, La Junta, T067-314120. Good meals, small rooms, limited bathrooms.
C Residencial Copihue, Varas 611, T067-314184. E singles. Without bath, with breakfast, good meals, changes money at very poor rates.
C Residencial Valdera, Varas s/n, T067-314105. E singles. Breakfast and bath, excellent value.

Puyuhuapi and around *p410*
There's a CONAF campsite at Lago Risopatrón.
LL Fiordo Queulat Ecolodge, Seno Queulat, Parque Nacional Queulat, T067-233302, www.aisen.cl. Half board. Has a good reputation, offers hikes and fishing trips. Campsite nearby, US$5.
LL-L Cabañas El Pangue, north end of Lago Risopatrón, Carretera Austral Norte, Km 240, Parque Nacional Queulat, T067-325128, www.elpangue.cl. Cabins sleep 4, private bathrooms, hot water, heating, telephone, parking, swimming pool, fishing trips, horse riding, mountain bikes. Recommended.
LL-L Puyuhuapi Lodge and Spa, T067-325103, www.patagonia-connection.com.

For reservations contact **Patagonia Connection**, Fidel Oteiza 1921, oficina 1006, Santiago. Price depends on season and type of room but always includes use of baths and the boat transfer to/from the hotel. Good restaurant; full board US$50 extra. Recommended. Boat schedule from jetty, 2 hrs' walk from town, frequent in season, US$5 each way, 10-min crossing. Transport to the hotel may be arranged independently via hydroplane from Puerto Montt. See also Activities and tours, page 431.
B Hostería Alemana, Av Otto Uebel 450, T067-325118. A large, comfortable, wooden house on the main road, owned by Señora Ursula Flack Kroschewski. Highly recommended, closed in winter.
B-C Casa Ludwig, Av Otto Uebel s/n, on the southern edge of town, T067-325220, www.contactchile.cl/casaludwig. Excellent, English and German spoken. Highly recommended. Price per person.
D Sra Leontina Fuentes, Llantureo y Circunvalación. F singles. Clean, hot water, good breakfast for US$2.

Camping
CONAF, reservations T067-212125, runs a basic campsite (cold water) 12 km north of Puyuhuapi on the shores of Lago Risopatrón, and another near the Ventisquero Colgante. There is also a dirty campsite by the fjord behind the general store in Puyuhuapi.

South of the Río Cisnes *p410*
AL-B Cabañas Río Cisnes, Costanera 101, Puerto Cisnes, T067-346404. Cabins sleep 4-8. Owner, Juan Suazo, has a boat and offers good sea trout/salmon fishing.
A Manzur, Dunn 75, Puerto Cisnes, T067-346453. *Cabañas*.
C Pensión, Carlos Condell y Dr Steffen, Puerto Cisnes. With breakfast, hot shower, friendly.
E Hospedaje, Café y Restaurante El Encanto, Villa Amengual. One of several cheap options in the town.
E Hostería El Gaucho, Holmberg 140, Puerto Cisnes, T067-346514. With breakfast, dinner available, hot water.
E Residencia Bienvenido, Ibar 248, Villa Mañihuales. Clean, friendly, with a restaurant.
E Villa Mañihuales, E Ibar 200, Villa Mañihuales, T067-234803. Friendly, with breakfast.

○ Eating

Into Argentina via Futaleufú or Palena *p409, map p409*

Martín Pescador, Balmaceda y Rodríguez, Futaleufú, T065-721279. Decent meat and fish.

Futaleufú, Cerda 407, Futaleufú, T065-721295. All the normal Chilean fare plus, of course, trout.

Sur Andes, Cerda 308, Futaleufú, T065-721405, www.surandes.tk. Pleasant little café serving real coffee as well as a variety of cakes, sweets, snacks and light meals. Local handicrafts also sold.

Puyuhuapi and around *p410*

Café Rossbach, Costanera, Puyuhuapi. Limited menu, including excellent salmon; also good for tea and *küchen*; building is in the style of a German Black Forest inn.

Restaurante Marili, Otto Ubel s/n, Puyuhuapi. Cheaper option.

South of the Río Cisnes *p410*

K-Cos Café Restaurante, Prat 270, Puerto Cisnes. Good snacks.

▲ Activities and tours

Fishing

Isla Monita Lodge, near Puerto Cárdenas, offers packages for anglers and non-anglers on a private island on Lago Yelcho (see page 408), as well as fishing in many nearby locations; contact **Turismo Grant**, PO Box 52311, Santiago, T02-6395524, F6337133.

There are also good opportunities for fishing on Río Futaleufú and Lago Espolón (see page 409; ask for the Valebote family's motorboat on the lake) and in the area around Puerto Cisnes (see page 411). For the latter, contact **German Hipp**, Costanera 51, Puerto Cisnes, T067-346587, or **Cabañas Río Cisnes** (see above). For further information contact **Turismo Lago Las Torres**, 130 km Carretera Austral Norte, T067-234242.

Kayaking

Patagonian Waters, main road in Puyuhuapi, T067-314300, www.patagonianwaters.com, offers canoeing and sea kayak trips in the fjord, as well as trekking and horse riding. There is also an office in La Junta.

Into Argentina via Futaleufú or Palena *p409, map p409*

Tour operators in Futaleufú can arrange whitewater rafting (see page 409). Prices start from US$75 per person. There are several local fishing guides who can be contacted in the village.

Earth River, www.earthriver.com. Excellent choice for river rafting and kayaking trips, book in advance.

Expediciones Chile, Mistral 296, Futaleufú, T065- 721386, www.exchile.com. Offers the best multi-day trips. Book in advance. Day trips can be booked on site.

Futaleufú Explore, O'Higgins 772, Futaleufú T065-721411, www.futaleufuexplore.com. Another respected rafting company.

Futaleufú Expediciones, O'Higgins 397, Futaleufú, T/F065-258634. Organizes rafting, canyoning, trekking and horse riding expeditions around Futaleufú.

○ Transport

Into Argentina via Futaleufú or Palena *p409, map p409*

Buses to the **border** depart O'Higgins 234 in Futaleufú, Mon Wed and Fri 0845 and 1815, 30 mins, US$4; from the Argentine side there are connecting services to **Trevelin** and **Esquel**, US$3. Futaleufú to **Chaitén**, daily, 5 hrs.

Transporte Patagonia Norte, T065-741257, runs a weekly service from Palena to **Puerto Montt** via Argentina, Mon 0630, 13 hrs, US$28.

The café on Balmaceda y Prat acts as agent for flights and catamarans to Puerto Montt.

Into Argentina via La Junta *p410*

There is no bus terminal in La Junta. To **Puerto Cisnes**, Buses Emanuel, Manuel Montt, esq Esmeralda, T067-314198, Mon and Fri, US$8. To **Coyhaique**, Buses Emanuel, Tue and Sat, US$16; Buses Daniela, T067-231701, 2 weekly, US$16; Buses Norte, 3 weekly. To **Chaitén**, Buses Emanuel, Mon-Sat, US$11; Transportes Lago Verde, Varas s/n, T067-314108, 3 weekly, US$11; Buses Norte, 3 weekly. To **Lago Verde**, Buses Daniela, 2 weekly. Book all in advance.

Puyuhuapi and around *p410*

Daily buses from Puyuhuapi north to **Chaitén** and south to **Coyhaique**, plus 2 weekly to **Lago Verde**.

South of the Río Cisnes *p410*
Transportes Terra Austral, T067-346757, runs
services from **Puerto Cisnes** to **Coyhaique**,
Mon-Sat 0600, US$11; Buses Norte,
T067-346440, offers the same route once a
week, US$11. There are also daily buses to
Coyhaique from **Villa Mañihuales**, 1½ hrs.

⊙ Directory

**Into Argentina via Futaleufú
or Palena** *p409, map p409*
Banks Banco del Estado, Futaleufú, but no
ATM. Changing foreign currency is difficult,
but US dollars and Argentinian pesos are
accepted in many places.

Coyhaique and around → *Colour map 5, B3.*

*Located 420 km south of Chaitén, Coyhaique (also spelt Coihaique) lies in the broad
green valley of the Río Simpson. The city is encircled by a crown of snow-capped
mountains and, for a few hours after it has rained, the mountainsides are covered in a
fine layer of frost – a spectacular sight. Founded in 1929, it is the administrative and
commercial centre of Region XI and is the only settlement of any real size on the
Carretera Austral (its population is just over 36,000). The constant call of chickens in
people's gardens gives away the fact that much of the population comprises recent
arrivals from a very distinct and slowly disappearing lifestyle in the surrounding
countryside, while the number of bow-legged elderly men making their way slowly
about town is indicative of a generation who feel more comfortable on horseback than
on foot. A rapidly growing and increasingly lively city, it also provides a good base for
day excursions in the area. Rafting down the Río Simpson is a memorable experience,
while in the Reserva Nacional Río Simpson there are picturesque waterfalls and the
occasional sighting of the elusive huemul.* ▸ *For Sleeping, Eating and other listings, see pages
417-422.*

Ins and outs

Getting there There are two **airports** in the Coyhaique area: **Tte Vidal** ⓘ *5 km
southwest of town, taxi US$7*, handles only smaller aircraft; **Balmaceda** ⓘ *56 km
southeast of Coyhaique via paved road, 5 km from the Argentine border at Paso
Huemules, taxi 1 hr, US$8*, is the most direct way into Coyhaique from Santiago or
Puerto Montt, with several flights daily. There's also a weekly flight to Punta Arenas
(more often in summer). There is no bus service between Coyhaique and Balmaceda;
instead minibuses, known as *transfers*, ply this route, stopping at hotels; contact
Travell ⓘ *Parra y Moraleda, T067-230010, US$5*, and **Transfer Valencia** ⓘ *Lautaro
828, T067-233030, US$5*. **Ferries** (one or two a week) make the journey from Puerto
Montt to Puerto Chacabuco, 77 km west of Coyhaique. **Buses** (several weekly) from
Puerto Montt have to take the route via Argentina, which is long and expensive. There
are also one or two weekly buses to Comodoro Rivadavia and south to Punta Arenas.
Within Region XI, Coyhaique is the transport hub. There are minibuses north to
Chaitén and south to Cochrane (both daily), as well as minibuses connecting with the
ferry at Puerto Ibáñez for Chile Chico (five weekly).

Getting around Coyhaique is small enough to be easily covered on foot; taxis are
expensive and only useful for out-of-town excursions.

Tourist information English is spoken at the very helpful **Sernatur** office ⓘ *Bulnes
35, T067-231752, infoaisen@sernatur.cl, Mon-Fri 0830-1700*, which has bus timetables. See www.patagoniachile.net for more information. There's also a kiosk on the
plaza in summer. **CONAF** ⓘ *Ogana 1060, T067-212125, Mon-Fri 0830-1730.*

Coyhaique

Although a visit to the tourist office will throw up far more attractions outside Coyhaique than in the town itself, this is a pleasant, friendly place, perfect for relaxing for a couple of days or as a base for day trips. The town is centred around an unusual pentagonal plaza, on which stand the cathedral, the Intendencia and a handicraft market. The plaza was built in 1945, supposedly inspired by the Place de l'Étoile in Paris. Two blocks northeast of the plaza at Baquedano y Ignacio Serrano, there is a monument to El Ovejero (the shepherd). Further north on Baquedano is a display of old military machinery outside the local regimental headquarters. In the Casa de Cultura the **Museo Regional de la Patagonia Central** ① *Lillo 23, T067-213174, Tue-Sun summer 0900-2000, winter 0830-1730, US$1*, has sections on history, mineralogy, zoology and archaeology, as well as photos of the construction of the Carretera Austral (no information in English). Near the city, on the west bank of the Río Simpson, is the **Piedra del Indio**, a rock outcrop which, allegedly, looks like a face in profile. This is best viewed from the Puente Simpson.

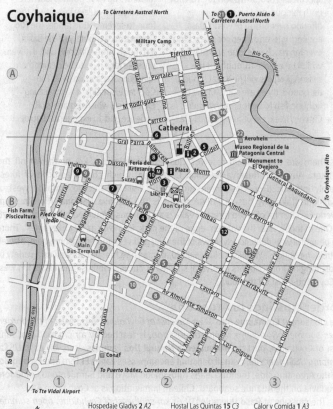

Coyhaique

0 metres	200
0 yards	200

Sleeping 🛏
Albergue Las
 Salamandras **18** *C1*
Cabañas Mirador **1** *B3*
El Reloj **3** *B3*
Hospedaje Gladys **2** *A2*
Hospedaje Lautaro 269 **7** *B1*
Hospedaje María Ester **5** *B2*
Hospedaje Mondaca **8** *C2*
Hospedaje Natti **10** *C2*
Hospedaje Patricio y
 Gedra Guzmán **21** *A3*
Hospedaje Pochi **6** *B2*
Hostal Araucarias **9** *B1*
Hostal Bon **11** *B3*
Hostal Español **13** *B3*

Hostal Las Quintas **15** *C3*
Hostería Coyhaique **12** *B1*
Libanés **14** *C2*
Los Ñires **16** *A3*
Residencial Mónica **20** *C2*
San Sebastián **22** *A3*

Eating 🍴
Café Alemana **5** *B2*
Café Oriente **2** *B2*
Café Ricer **3** *B2*

Calor y Comida **1** *A3*
Casino de
 Bomberos **6** *A2*
Central **4** *B2*
El Mastique **7** *B2*
Histórico Ricer **3** *B2*
La Casona **9** *B1*
La Fiorentino **10** *B2*
La Olla **8** *B2*
Las Piedras **11** *B3*
Yangtse **12** *B3*

Anglers' paradise

The rivers around Coyhaique provide the greatest fishing in Chile; each summer the international fishing fraternity converge on the town for the season, which runs from 15 November to 15 April. Rivers range from the typically English slow chalk stream to the fast-flowing Andean snow-melt torrents, requiring a variety of angling techniques.

On the outskirts of Coyhaique, the spectacular **Río Simpson** teems with both rainbow and brown trout, offering over 60 km of world-class angling. It is renowned for its exciting evening hatches (sedge and mayfly), which take place throughout the season. Anglers will find that, pound for pound, these are some of the best fighting fish to be found anywhere. Catches in excess of five pounds are frequent and rainbow trout weighing over 12 pounds have been landed.

Located near the Argentine border, the **Río Nirehuao** is a fly-fisher's dream. The easy wading and moderate casting distances make this an all-time brown trout favourite.

South of Coyhaique, the **Río Baker** offers a unique fishing experience in its turquoise blue water. The Baker is huge and intimidating, as are its fish: rainbows up to 12 pounds lurk here and anglers regularly take fish in the four- to seven-pound range. The **Río Cochrane**, a tributary of the Baker, also holds large rainbows and, if it were possible for a river to be clearer than 'gin-clear', this would be it. The Cochrane is mainly a 'sight-fishing' experience, which requires skill, patience and an experienced guide.

There are two national reserves close to Coyhaique: 5 km northwest off the Carretera Austral is **Reserva Nacional Coyhaique**, which covers 2150 ha of forest (mainly introduced species), while around the valley of the Río Simpson west of Coyhaique (take any bus to Puerto Aisén) is the **Reserva Nacional Río Simpson**, covering 40,827 ha of steep forested valleys and curiously rounded hills rising to 1878 m. One of these, near the western edge of the park, is known as '*El Cake Inglés*'. There are beautiful waterfalls, lovely views of the river and very good fly-fishing here, as well as trekking options. Wildlife includes pudú, pumas and huemul, as well as a variety of birds, ranging from condors to several species of ducks. Administration is 32 km west of Coyhaique, just off the road.

Border crossings to Argentina

The crossing at **Coyhaique Alto** ① *43 km east of Coyhaique, 6 km west of the border, open summer 0800-2200, winter 0800-2000*, is reached by a *ripio* road that runs east of Coyhaique past the **Monumento Natural Dos Lagunas** ① *25 km east, US$2, camping US$15 per site*, a small park that encompasses Lagos El Toro and Escondido. On the Argentine side, the road leads through Río Mayo and Sarmiento to Comodoro Rivadavia on the Atlantic seaboard. Chilean immigration is at Coyhaique Alto.

The crossing at **Paso Huemules** ① *61 km southeast of Coyhaique, open summer 0800-2200, winter 0800-2000*, is reached by a paved road, Route 245, which runs southeast from Coyhaique, via Balmaceda airport. There is no accommodation at the frontier or at the airport and no public transport from the border to the airport. On the Argentine side, a *ripio* road runs via Lago Blanco (fuel) to join Route 40, 105 km west of Paso Huemules. ▶ *For details of transport between Coyhaique and the crossings, see page 420.*

Puerto Aisén and around

Puerto Aisén lies at the confluence of the rivers Aisén and Palos. First developed in the 1920s, the town grew as the major port of the region although it has now been replaced by Puerto Chacabuco, 15 km further down the river. Few vestiges of the port remain today: boats lie high and dry on the riverbank when the tide is out and the foundations of buildings by the river are now overgrown with fuchsias and buttercups. To see any maritime activity you have to walk a little way out of town to **Puerto Aguas Muertas** where the fishing boats come in.

The town is linked to the south bank of the Río Aisén by the Puente Presidente Ibáñez, once the longest suspension bridge in Chile. From the far bank a paved road leads to **Puerto Chacabuco**; a regular bus service runs between the two. There is a helpful tourist office ⓘ *Prat y Sgto Aldea, Dec-Feb only*, in the Municipalidad.

A good 10-km walk north along a minor road from Puerto Aisén leads to **Laguna Los Palos**, calm, deserted and surrounded by forested hills. En route is a bridge over a deep, narrow river; it's freezing cold but offers the chance for a bracing swim. **Lago Riesco**, 30 km south of Puerto Aisén, can be reached by an unpaved road that follows the Río Blanco. In season, the *Apulcheu* sails regularly from Puerto Chacabuco to **Termas de Chiconal** ⓘ *US$50, 1 hr, on the northern shore of the Seno Aisén*, offering a good way to see the fjord; take your own food.

It is much wetter here than in Coyhaique: local wags say it rains for 370 day of the year. September to January are the driest months.

● Sleeping

Coyhaique *p415, map p415*
The tourist office has a list of all accommodation, but look out for notices in windows since any place with fewer than 6 beds does not have to register with the authorities.
L-AL Hostería Coyhaique, Magallanes 131, T067-231137. Coyhaique's premier hotel. 4-star, though showing its age a little. Set in spacious gardens, decent rooms, doubles have full bathtub. There is a plan to tear the hotel down and build a casino here.
AL El Reloj, Baquedano 828, T067-231108, www.elrelojhotel.cl. In a former saw mill. With good restaurant, nice lounge, conference room, some rooms have wonderful views. English spoken. Highly recommended.
AL-A Cabañas Mirador, Baquedano 848, T067-233191. Fully equipped cabins sleeping 2-4. The last cabin has tremendous views. Advance booking essential in season (deposit required). Long-term lets off season.
AL-A Cabañas Río Simpson, 3 km north of town, T067-232183, www.cabanas-rio-simpson.cl. Fully equipped cabins for 4-9 people. Horse riding, fishing and tours. Several tame alpacas in the grounds.
AL-A Los Ñires, Baquedano 315, T067-232261, www.doncarlos.cl/hotel.htm. With breakfast, small rooms, comfortable, parking.
A Hostal Español, Sargento Aldea 343, T067-242580, www.hostalcoyhaique.cl. New, small family-run hotel. 7 rooms all with views, carpets, bathrooms and cable TV.

Spacious living room downstairs. Recommended.
A San Sebastián, Baquedano 496, T067-233427. Small hotel with spacious rooms, all with view, good breakfast, recommended.
A-B Hostal Araucarias, Vielmo 71, T067-232707. Spacious, slightly creaky rooms with bath and TV, pleasant lounge with good view, quiet.
A-B Libanés, Simpson 367, T067-256262, hlibanes@patagoniachile.cl. With TV, phones, heating, laundry and café, several small lounges, careworn, overpriced.
B Hostal Bon, Serrano 91, T067-231189, hostal_bon@hotmail.com. With breakfast, friendly, clean but cramped rooms, good meals served.
B-C Hospedaje Gladys, Parra 65, T067-251076. **D-E** singles. Clean and well-kept rooms with cable TV. Some with bathrooms. A little dark. Breakfast extra. Doubles as a beauty salon.
B-C Hostal Las Quintas, Bilbao 1208, T067-231173. Spartan, but clean and extremely spacious rooms with bath and breakfast. Some of the rooms are architecturally among the most bizarre of any hostel in Chile.
C Hospedaje María Ester, Lautaro 544, T067-233023. **F** singles. Some rooms with bath and TV. Friendly, local information given, breakfast extra, laundry facilities, kitchen use charged for.

C Hospedaje Patricio y Gedra Guzmán, Baquedano 20, T067-232520, www.balasch. cl/cabanas. Small but comfortable self-contained cabins on the edge of town with extensive views. Good value. Recommended. Preference given to those taking Spanish classes.

C Hospedaje Pochi, Freire 342, T067-256968. **E** singles. Rooms in a family home with bath and cable TV. Breakfast included. Very pleasant owners. English spoken by the daughter. Good value. Recommended.

C Residencial Mónica, Lillo 664, T067-234302. A little dark. Good value singles with bath (**D-E**).

C-D Hospedaje Lautaro 269, T067-237184. **F** singles. Large old wooden house with creaky floors. With parking, internet access and kitchen facilities.

C-D Hospedaje Mondaca, Av Simpson 571, T067-254676. **F** singles. Small (only 3 rooms) but spotless family home. Friendly, breakfast extra, will heat up pre-prepared food.

C-G Albergue Las Salamandras, 2 km south of town, T067-211865, www.salamandras.cl. Double rooms, dorm beds, *cabañas* and camping in attractive forest location. Kitchen facilities, winter sports, trekking and tours. Maps, including good trekking maps, and cycling information provided. English spoken. Excellent website. Highly recommended.

D Hospedaje Natti, Av Simpson 417, T067-231047. **F** singles. Clean, very friendly, kitchen facilities, breakfast US$2 extra. Also good-value camping including access to hot showers. Recommended.

Campsites
Sernatur in Coyhaique (see page 414) has a full list of all sites in Region XI. Also see Albergue las Salamandras and Hospedaje Natti above. There are several other campsites in Coyaique and on the road to Puerto Aisén, including:
Camping Alborada, Km 1 towards Puerto Aisén, T067-238868. US$14, with hot shower.
Camping Río Correntoso, Km 42 towards Puerto Aisén, T067-232005. US$20, showers and fishing. Automobile Club discount.

In the Reserva Nacional Coyhaique, there are basic campsites, US$7, at Laguna Verde and at Casa Bruja, 4 km and 2 km

respectively from the entrance, and a *refugio*, US$2, 3 km from the entrance. There's also a campsite near the turning to Santuario San Sebastián, US$7, in the Reserva Nacional Río Simpson.

Puerto Aisén and around *p416*
Accommodation can be hard to find, most is geared towards workers in the fishing industry in both Puerto Aisén and Puerto Chacabuco. There's no campsite but free camping is easy.

LL Parque Turístico Loberías de Aisén, Carrera 50, Puerto Chacabuco, T067-351112, www.loberiasdelsur.cl. Recently rebuilt 5-star complex, the best hotel serving the best food in this area. Climb up the steps direct from the port for a drink or a meal overlooking boats and mountains before boarding your ferry. Car hire available.

B Hotel Caicahues, Michimalonco 660, Puerto Aisén, T067-336633. With bath, heating, telephone and internet; book in advance.

C Hotel Plaza, O'Higgins 613, Puerto Aisén, T067-332784. **F** singles. Basic, without breakfast, some rooms with no windows.

C Mar Clara, Carrera 970, Puerto Aisén, T067-330945. **F** singles. More expensive with bath. Basic, clean, thin walls, looks nicer from outside than within.

C Roxy, Aldea 972, Puerto Aisén, T067-332704. **E-F** singles. Friendly, clean, large rooms, restaurant. Rooms at the back are quieter and have a view. Recommended.

C-D Moraleda, O'Higgins 82, Puerto Chacabuco, T067-351155. **F** singles, also food.

🍴 Eating

Coyhaique *p415, map p415*
¥¥¥ Restaurant Histórico Ricer, Horn 48 y 40, piso 2, T067-232920. Regional specialities, historical exhibits, recommended, though slightly overpriced.
¥¥¥-¥¥ Calor y Comida, Baquedano 022, T067-25183, yelisa@patagoniachile.cl. Bizarre entrance through someone's house leading to a restaurant with as breathtaking a view as any in Coyaique. Aims for rustic elegance, occasionally at odds with the music they play. Patagonian-Mediterranean cuisine. Abundant portions. Decent food. Wine sold by the glass.

¶¶ **El Reloj**, Baquedano 444, T067-231108. Unusual dishes using all local ingredients. Good service, recommended.

¶¶ **La Casona**, Obispo Vielmo 77, T067-238894. Good lamb and fish dishes, recommended.

¶¶ **La Olla**, Gral Prat 176, T067-242588. Spanish, excellent cuisine, not cheap but there are good-value lunches. Recommended.

¶¶ **Las Piedras**, 21 de Mayo 655, T067-233243. Slightly upmarket but with good-value set lunches. Dishes include venison and emu. Fills up at weekends. Recommended.

¶¶ **Yangtse**, Bilbao 715, T067-242173. Better than average (in Chilean terms) Chinese. You can hear your food being stir-fried fresh to order. Reasonable prices but the quantity of MSG leaves you almost happy to fork out for the exorbitantly expensive drinks.

¶¶-¶ **Casino de Bomberos**, Gral Parra 365, T067-231437. Wide range, large portions, very good value. Slow service, especially if the overdressed tip-hungry waiters are doting on a table of cruise ship tourists.

¶¶-¶ **Restaurant Central**, Freire 319, T067-256885. Decent basic set lunches. Big screen TV. A good place to watch football matches.

¶ **El Mastique**, Bilbao 141. Cheap but good pasta and Chilean food. Recommended.

¶ **La Fiorentina**, Prat 230, T067-238899. Good value pizza and pasta.

Cafés

Café Alemana, Condell 119. Excellent cakes, coffee, vegetarian dishes. Recommended.

Café Oriente, Condell 201 y 21 de Mayo. Good bakery, serves tea.

Café Ricer, Horn 48. Also serves light food.

Puerto Aisén and around *p416*

¶¶ **Café Restaurante Ensenada**, O'Higgins 302, Puerto Chacabuco. Basic grub.

¶¶ **Restaurante La Cascada**, Km 32 between Coyhaique and Puerto Aisén. Waterfalls nearby. Recommended for meat and fish.

¶¶ **Restaurante Martina**, Av Municipal, near bridge, Puerto Aisén. Good Chilean fare. Probably the best place to eat in town.

There are many cheap places on Aldea in Puerto Aisén, between Municipal and Dougnac.

🍷 Bars and clubs

Coyhaique *p415, map p415*

Bar West, Bilbao y 12 de Octubre. Western-style bar.

Kamikaze, Moraleda 428. Disco.

Piel Roja, Moraleda y Condell. Friendly, laid-back atmosphere, meals served, not cheap.

Pub El Cuervo, Parra 72. Good cocktails and snacks, relaxed ambience, live music at weekends.

Puerto Aisén and around *p416*

The following are all in Puerto Aisén. There are a couple of smaller bars on Sargento Aldea; one has a wildly sloping pool table.

Crazzy Pub, Aldea 1170. Make up your own mind how 'crazzy' it is.

Dina's, Carrera 1270. Disco.

Eko Pub, Tte Merino 998.

⊛ Festivals and events

Puerto Aisén and around *p416*

2nd week of Nov Local festival of folklore is held in Puerto Aisén.

🛍 Shopping

Coyhaique *p415, map p415*

Food, especially fruit and vegetables, is more expensive here than in Santiago. For *artesanía* try the **Feria de Artesanía** on the plaza or **Manos Azules**, Riquelme 435. **The Wool House**, Horn 40, loc 101, T067-255107, sells good-quality woollen clothing. Decent camping equipment can be obtained from **Condor Explorer**, Dussen 357, T067-670349. **La Casa del Mate**, Errázuriz 268. Everything for the connoisseur of the South American herb. There are large supermarkets at Prat y Lautaro and Lautaro y Cochrane. Good sheep's cheese is often available from a kiosk by the plaza.

For an explanation of sleeping and eating price codes used in this guide, see inside the front cover. Other relevant information is found in Essentials, see pages 50-57.

▲ Activities and tours

Coyhaique *p415, map p415*

A full list of specialist tours and fishing guides is available from **Sernatur**, see page 414. Excursions and good trekking information is available from **Albergue Las Salamandras** (see Sleeping, page 417). There is also an association of independent local guides who offer (as a rule) good-value and well-informed excursions within the region. See www.escueladeguias.cl for more information.

Fishing

There are excellent opportunities for fishing in the Coyhaique area, especially southwest at Lagos Atrevesado (20 km) and Elizalde (also yachting and camping), and southeast at lagos Frío, Castor and Pollux. In addition to those listed below, most of the general tour operators offer specialist fishing trips.

Alex Prior, T067-234732. Recommended for fly-fishing.

General tours

Aike Bikers, T067-258307, juan.orellanam@ 123mail.cl. Mountain bike tours of the city and surrounding countryside.

Andes Patagónicos, Horn 48 y 40, local 11, T067-216711, www.ap.cl. Trips to local lakes as well as Tortel, historically based tours and bespoke trips all year round. Good, but not cheap. Provides general tourist information.

Aysen Tour, Gral Parra 97, T067-237070, www.aysentour.cl. Typical range of tours along the Carretera Austral.

Camello Patagón, Simpson 169, T067-244327, www.camellopatagon.cl. Trips to Capilla de Marmol in Río Tranquilo.

Condor Explorer, Dussen 357, T067-670349, www.condorexplorer.com. Good small-scale agency who specialize in trekking but also do general Carretera tours. English spoken. Recommended.

El Puesto Expeditions, Moraleda 299, T067-233785, elpuesto@entelchile.net. Hiking, fishing, climbing.

Expediciones Coyhaique, Portales 195, T067-232300, juliomeier@entelchile.net. Tours of local lakes and other sights, Laguna San Rafael trips, fishing and birdwatching trips and excursions down the Río Baker.

Geo Turismo, Lillo 315, T067-237456, www.geoturismopatagonia.cl. Offers wide range of tours throughout the region, English spoken, professional, recommended.

Patagonia Adventure Expeditions, Riquelme 372, T067-219894, www.adventurepatagonia.com. Agency famed for its rafting tours. Various other multi-day adventure tours also offered. English spoken. Recommended.

Turismo Prado de la Patagonia, 21 de Mayo 417, T067-231271, www.turismoprado patagonia.cl. Tours of local lakes and other sights, Laguna San Rafael trips and historical tours. Also offers general tourist information and accepts TCs.

Horse riding

Baltazar Araneda, T067-231047 or book through **Hospedaje Natti** (see Sleeping, page 417). Horse riding trips to lagos Palomo, Azul and Desierto, US$300 per person for 4 days, US$375 for 5 days.

Cabot, Lautaro 339, T067-230101, www.cabot.cl. Horse riding excursions to Cerro Castillo and other tours.

Scenic flights

Patagonia Explorer, T099-8172172, stonepiloto@hotmail.com. Pilot Willy Stone offers charter flights to the Laguna San Rafael, US$250 per person, recommended.

Skiing

El Fraile, office in Coyhaique at Dussen y Plaza de Armas 376, T067-231690. Near Lago Frío, 29 km southeast of Coyhaique, this ski resort has 5 pistes, 2 lifts, a basic café and equipment hire (season Jun-Sep).

Puerto Aisén *p416*

Turismo Rucaray, on the plaza, rucaray@ entelchile.net. Recommended for local tours. Internet access.

◉ Transport

Coyhaique *p415, map p415*
Air

From **Tte Vidal airport**, Don Carlos flies to **Chile Chico**, Mon-Sat, US$50; to **Cochrane**, Mon and Thu, 45 mins, US$75, and to **Villa O'Higgins**, Mon and Thu, US$100, recommended only for those who like flying, have strong stomachs, or are in a hurry. Note that a number of Don Carlos' planes have gone down in the last couple of years. There are also flights to **Tortel**, Wed, US$35, but these are subsidized for residents of the village; foreigners may fly if there's a free seat, but should expect to pay more.

Balmaceda airport is used by LanChile, Sky and **Aerolíneas del Sur** for flights to **Santiago**, several daily, US$130-250 return plus tax (depending on season and flexibility), and **Puerto Montt**, several daily, US$75-150 return plus tax. **LanChile** also flies to **Punta Arenas**, Sat (more often in summer), US$75-150 return plus tax. The best one-way fares are generally with **Aerolíneas del Sur**. For details of transport to/from the airport, see page 414.

Bus

Local A full listing of bus timetables is posted outside the **Sernatur** office (see page 414). The main terminal is at Lautaro y Magallanes but many companies use their own offices. In the terminal are **Bus São Paulo**, T067-237630; **Bus Sur**, T067-211460, www.bus-sur.cl; **Don Oscar**, T067-254335, **Giobbi**, T067-232607; **Interlagos**, T067-240840, www.patagonia interlagos.cl, recommended; **Queilen Bus; Transportes Terra Austral**, T067-254475. Other companies are **Alegría**, Errázuriz 145; **Bus Bronco**, Magallanes 560; **Buses Becker**, Ibáñez 358, T067-35050; **Buses Daniela**, Baquedano 1122, T067-231701; **Bus Norte**, Parra 337, T067-232167; **Don Carlos**, Subteniente Cruz 63, T067-232981; **Suray**, Prat 265, T067-238387; **Turibus**, Baquedano 1171, T067-231333.

Long distance To **Puerto Montt**, via Bariloche, all year, **Turibus**, Tue and Sat 1700, US$40; **Queilen Bus**, Mon, Thu, US$40, with connections to Osorno, Valdivia, Temuco, Santiago and Castro, often heavily booked. To **Punta Arenas** via Coyhaique Alto and Comodoro Rivadavia, **Bus Sur**, Tue, US$55. To **Comodoro Rivadavia** (Argentina), **Turibus**, Mon, Fri, also **Giobbi**, Tue, Sat, from terminal, 12 hrs, US$35.

Carretera Austral Suray, São Paulo, Interlagos and Don Carlos minibuses run to **Puerto Aisén** every 15 mins between them, 1 hr, US$2, with connections for Puerto Chacabuco. There are also a few buses daily

to **Mañihuales**. *Colectivos* to **Puerto Ibáñez** on Lago General Carrera will pick you up at 0700 from your hotel to connect with *El Pilchero* ferry to Chile Chico, 2 hrs, book the day before, US$7; operators include **Colectivos Sr Parra**, T067-251073, Sat and Sun only; **Mini- bus Don Tito**, T067-250280, daily; **Sr Yarnil**, T067-250346, daily, and **Interlagos**, daily.

Bus services further afield vary according to demand: north to **Chaitén** via Puyuhuapi and La Junta, **Don Oscar**, 3 weekly, approximately 12 hrs, US$28. Also **Buses Norte**, **Buses Daniela**, **Buses Becker**, several weekly between them. To **Lago Verde** via La Junta, **Buses Daniela**, Tue, Sat, US$18; also **Bus Bronco**, Wed, Fri, Sat. To **Puerto Cisnes**, **Transportes Terra Austral** and **Alegría**, each Mon-Sat, US$9. South to **Cochrane**, **Interlagos**, 0930 Mon, Wed, Thu, Sat, Sun, US$20, recommended, and **Don Carlos**, 0930 Tue, Thu, Sat, US$17. Buses to Cochrane stop at **Cerro Castillo**, US$5, **Bahía Murta**, US$9, **Puerto Río Tranquilo**, US$12, and **Puerto Bertrand** , US$14.

Bicycle

Bike hire from: **Figón**, Simpson y Colón, T067-234616, check condition first, also sells spares; **Bilbao 500** block, poor supply of spares but good repair service; **Motortech**, Baquedano 131; **Tomás Enrique**, Madrid Urrea, Pje Foitzick y Libertad, T067-252132. Bicycle spares repair services are also available from several shops on Simpson.

Car

Hire from: **AGS**, Av Ogana 1298, T067-235354; **Automóvil Club de Chile**, Carrera 333, T067-231649, rents jeeps and other vehicles; **Automundo AVR**, Bilbao 510, T067-231621; **Río Baker**, Balmaceda airport, T067-272163; **Sur Nativo Renta Car**; Baquedano 457, T067-235500; **Traeger-Hertz**, Baquedano 457, T067-231648; **Turismo Prado**, 21 de Mayo 417, T/F067-231271. Mechanic at **Automotores Santiago**, C Los Ñires 811, T067-238330, T099-6406896, speaks English, can obtain spare parts quickly.

Ferry

Shipping offices are at **Catamaranes del Sur**, Carrera 50, T067-351112, www.catamaranes

delsur.cl; **Naviera Río Cisnes**, Magallanes 303, T067-432702, www.navierariocisnes.cl; **Navimag**, Ibáñez 347, T067-233306, www.navimag.cl; **Skorpios**, Gral Parra 21, T067-213755, www.skorpios.cl.

Taxi

Fares are 50% extra after 2100. *Colectivos* congregate at Prat y Bilbao, fare US$0.70.

Puerto Aisén *p416*

Bus

To **Puerto Chacabuco**, Suray, every 20 mins, US$0.75. For services to **Coyhaique**, see above.

Ferry

Navimag have year-round ferry services from Puerto Chacabuco to **Puerto Montt** via the Canal Moraleda once or twice a week in summer, irregular off season, 24 hrs, from US$55. See also page 391.

Several companies offer trips of varying length to **Laguna San Rafael**. Patagonia Connection SA, Fidel Oteíza 1921, oficina 1006, Providencia, Santiago, T02-225 6489, www.patagonia-connection.com, operates all-inclusive 3-day tours from Puerto Chacabuco to Laguna San Rafael, from US$990 per person, including the Patagonia Express catamaran service from Puerto Chacabuco via **Termas de Puyuhuapi** (see page 410), overnight accommodation at Termas de Puyuhuapi and a day excursion to Laguna San Rafael. Boat information is posted at **Turismo Rucaray**. Also, contact **Agemar**, Tte Merino 909, T067-332716, or **Navimag**, Terminal de Transbordadores, Puerto Chacabuco, T067-351111, www.navimag.cl.

❸ Directory

Coyhaique *p415, map p415*

Airline offices Sky, Prat 203, T067-240826, local calls 600-6002828; **LanChile**, Moraleda 402, T067-231188, local calls 600-5262000; **Don Carlos**, Subteniente Cruz 63, T067-231981; **Aerohein**, Baquedano 500, T067-232772, www.aerohein.cl; **Transportes Aéreos San Rafael**, 18 Septiembre 469, T067-233408. **Banks** Several with Redbanc ATMs in centre, for dollars, TCs and Argentine pesos. Both the following *casas de cambio* are recommended: Casa de Cambio **Emperador**, Bilbao 222, and **Lucía Saldivia**, Baquedano 285. **Hospital** C Hospital 068, T067-233172. **Internet** Ciber Patagonia, 21 de Mayo 525, best value; Entel, Prat 340; Hechizos, 21 de Mayo 460, also cheap; several others. **Language schools** Baquedano Language School, Baquedano 20, T067-232520, www.balasch.cl. US$400 per week, including 4 hrs one-to-one tuition daily, lodging and all meals, other activities organized at discount rates, friendly, informative, highly recommended. **Laundry** Lavaseco Universal, Gral Parra 55; QL, Bilbao 160. **Post office** Cochrane 202, open Mon-Fri 0900-1230, 1430-1800, Sat 0830-1200. **Telephone** Several call centres; shop around as prices are relatively expensive.

Puerto Aisén *p416*

Banks BCI, Prat, for Visa; Banco de Chile, Plaza de Armas, only changes cash, not TCs. There's a Redbanc ATM machine in Puerto Chacabuco. **Post office** South side of bridge. **Telephone** Plaza de Armas, next to Turismo Rucaray; ENTEL, Libertad 408, internet access.

Lago General Carrera → *Colour map 5, B3.*

The section of the Carretera Austral around the north and western sides of Lago General Carrera is reckoned by many people to be the most spectacular stretch of all. Straddling the border with Argentina, this is the largest lake in South America after Lake Titicaca and is now believed to be the deepest lake on the continent; soundings in 1997 established its maximum depth as 590 m.

The lake is a beautiful azure blue, surrounded at its Chilean end by predominantly Alpine terrain and at the Argentine end by dry pampa. The region prides itself on having the best climate in southern Chile, with some 300 days of sunshine a year; much fruit is grown as a result, especially around Chile Chico where rainfall is very low for this area. In general, the climate here is more similar to Argentine Patagonia than to the rest of the Carretera Austral region.

The eruption of Volcán Hudson in 1991 (south of Chile Chico) polluted parts of Lago General Carrera and many rivers. Although the waters are now clear, the effects can still be seen in some places where there is a metre-thick layer of ash on the ground. In Argentine Patagonia, the eruption was even more catastrophic: prevailing winds blew the ash onto farmland, blinding and killing many thousands of sheep. ►► For Sleeping, Eating and other listings, see pages 426-428.

Ins and outs

Getting there The main towns, Puerto Ibáñez on the north shore and Chile Chico on the south, are connected by a ferry, *El Pilchero*. Overland routes between Coyhaique and Chile Chico are much longer, passing either through Argentina, or along the Carretera Austral, which runs west around the lake.

Getting around Minibuses run along the Carretera Austral in summer and air taxis link the small towns of the region.

Reserva Nacional Cerro Castillo and around

Beyond Coyhaique, the Carretera Austral runs southwest through the Reserva Nacional Cerro Castillo, which extends over 179,550 ha. The park is named after the fabulous **Cerro Castillo** (2675 m), which resembles a fairy-tale castle with rock pinnacles jutting out from a covering of snow. It also includes Cerro Bandera (2040 m) just west of Balmaceda and several other peaks in the northern wall of the valley of the Río Ibáñez. The park offers some of the best trekking in the region. There is a *guardería* at the northeastern end of the park near Laguna Chinguay and a **CONAF campsite** ① *T067-237070, US$8 per site*, nearby. At Km 83 the road crosses the **Portezuelo Ibáñez** (1120 m) and drops through the **Cuesta del Diablo**, a series of bends with fine views over the Río Ibáñez.

The principal port on the Chilean section of the lake, **Puerto Ibáñez** (officially Puerto Ingeniero Ibáñez) is reached by taking a paved branch road, 31 km long, from La Bajada 97 km south of Coyhaique. There are some fine waterfalls, including the **Salto Río Ibáñez**, 6 km north. Some 8 km beyond La Bajada along the main Carretera is **Villa Cerro Castillo**, a village where there are several *residenciales*. Near the village is a small local **museum** ① *2 km south of Villa Cerro Castillo, Dec-Mar 0900-1900*, and the **Monumento Nacional Manos de Cerro Castillo**, where traces of ancient rock paintings, estimated to be 10,000 years old, have been found. Various trekking options are available in this area.

◆ Fuel (sold in 5 litre containers) is available in Puerto Ibáñez at Luis A Bolados 461 (house with five laburnum trees).

The road climbs out of the valley, passing the emerald-green **Laguna Verde** and the Portezuelo Cofré. It descends to the boggy Manso Valley, with a good campsite at the bridge over the river; watch out for mosquitoes. This area was seriously affected by the ash from Volcán Hudson.

The western shore

Some 5 km from the Carretera Austral, at Km 203, is **Bahía Murta**, situated on the northern tip of the central arm of Lago General Carrera. This village dates from the 1930s, when it exported timber to Argentina via Chile Chico. From here, the road follows the lake's western shore to **Río Tranquilo** at Km 228 from Coyhaique, where the buses stop for lunch and fuel is available. The lake reflects the mountains that surround it and the clouds above. Close to Río Tranquilo is the unusual **Catedral de Mármol**, a peninsula made of marble, with fascinating caves that can be visited by boat ① *10 mins, US$35 to hire a boat with guide*. The village also has an unusual cemetery. A new branch of the Carretera Austral heads northwest from Río Tranquilo to **Puerto Grosse** on the coast at Bahía Exploradores.

El Maitén and south

At the southwestern tip of Lago General Carrera, at Km 279, is **El Maitén**, from where a road branches off east along the south shore of the lake towards Chile Chico (see below). South of El Maitén, meanwhile, the Carretera Austral becomes steeper and more winding; in winter this stretch is icy and dangerous. **Puerto Bertrand**, 5 km away, is a good place for fishing. Nearby is a sign showing the *Nacimiento del Río Baker*: the place where the gleaming turquoise Río Baker begins. Beyond Puerto Bertrand, the road climbs up to high moorland, passing the confluence of the rivers Neff and Baker, before winding south along the east bank of the Río Baker to Cochrane. The road is rough but not treacherous and the scenery is splendid all the way. Watch out for cattle and hares on the road (and huemuls in winter) and take blind corners slowly.

Lago General Carrera

The southern shore of Lago General Carrerra

Some 10 km east of El Maitén, **Puerto Guadal** is a picturesque town that is a centre for fishing. It also has shops, accommodation, restaurants, a post office and petrol. Further east along the shore, just past the village of **Mallín Grande**, Km 40, the road runs through the **Paso de las Llaves**, a 30-km stretch carved out of the rock face on the edge of the lake. The road climbs and drops, offering wonderful views across the lake and the icefields to the west. At Km 74, a turning runs to **Fachinal**. A further 8 km east, there is an opencast mine, which produces gold and other precious metals.

Chile Chico and around

Chile Chico is a quiet, friendly but dusty town situated on the lake shore 122 km east of El Maitén, close to the Argentine border. The town dates from 1909 when settlers crossed from Argentina and occupied the land, leading to conflict with cattle ranchers who had been given settlement rights by the Chilean government. In the showdown that followed (known as the war of Chile Chico) the ranchers were driven out by the settlers, but it was not until 1931 that the Chilean government finally recognized the town's existence.

Now the centre of a fruit-growing region, it has an annual **festival** at the end of January and a small **museum** (summeronly); outside is a boat that carried cargo on the lake before the opening of the road along the southern shore. There are fine views from the **Cerro de las Banderas** at the western end of town. The **tourist office**, on O'Higgins, is helpful when open.

To the south and west of Chile Chico is good walking terrain, through weird rock formations and dry brush scrub. The northern and higher peak of **Cerro Pico del Sur** (2168 m) can be climbed by the agile from Los Cipres (beware dogs in the farmyard). You will need a long summer's day and the 1:50,000 map. Follow the horse trail until it peters out, then navigate by compass or sense of direction until the volcano-like summit appears. After breaching the cliff ramparts, there is some scrambling and a 10-ft pitch to the summit, from where you'll enjoy indescribable views of the lake and the Andes.

About 20 km south of Chile Chico towards Lago Jeinimeni is the **Cueva de las Manos**, a cave full of Tehuelche paintings, the most famous of which are the *manos azules* (blue hands). From the road, climb 500 m and cross Pedregoso stream. The path is difficult, and partly hidden, so you're recommended to take a guide.

Reserva Nacional Lago Jeinimeni

ⓘ *53 km south of Chile Chico, open all year but access may be impossible Apr-Oct due to high river levels, US$3, camping US$6. Lifts from Chile Chico; see CONAF office.*
This park covers 160,000 ha and includes two lakes, **Lago Jeinimeni** and **Lago Verde**, which lie surrounded by forests in the narrow valley of the Río Jeinimeni. Impressive cliffs, waterfalls and small glaciers provide habitat for huemul deer, pumas and condors. Activities include fishing for salmon and rainbow trout, trekking and rowing. Access is via an unpaved road, which branches south off the road to Los Antiguos and crosses five rivers, four of which have to be forded. At Km 42, there is a small lake, **Laguna de los Flamencos**, where large numbers of flamingos can be seen. The park entrance is at Km 53; just beyond is a ranger station, a campsite and fishing area at the eastern end of Lago Jeinimeni. Take all supplies, including a good map.

Into Argentina

A road runs 2 km east from Chile Chico to the **Argentine border** ⓘ *Chilean immigration Sep-Apr 0730-2200, May-Aug 0800-2000*, and on for 5 km to **Los Antiguos**. This is another fruit-growing town with an annual cherry festival in mid-January. Salmon fishing is also possible. **Perito Moreno**, 67 km east of the border, has a few hotels, a campsite, a restaurant and money exchange services. About 120 km south is another famous **Cueva de las Manos**, where the walls of a series of galleries are covered with painted human hands and animals, 10,000 years old. All but 31 of the 800 hands are left hands.

¡ Deer, oh deer

The Andean **huemul** (*Hippocamelus bisulcus*) is a mountain deer native to the Andes of southern Chile and Argentina. Sharing the Chilean national crest with the Andean condor, the huemul (pronounced 'way-mool') is a medium-sized stocky cervid adapted to survival in rugged mountain terrain. Males grow antlers and have distinctive black face masks.

Human pressures have pushed the huemul to the brink of extinction and current numbers are estimated at 1000-1500. The huemul has become the focal point of both national and international conservation efforts, carried out primarily by CONAF and the Comité pro la Defensa de la Fauna y Flora de Chile (CODEFF).

Your best chance of seeing the huemul is in one of two reserves managed by CONAF: the Reserva Nacional Río Claro, which lies on the southeastern corner of the larger Reserva Nacional Río Simpson just outside Coyhaique, and the Reserva Nacional Tamango, near Cochrane. To visit either of these you will need to be accompanied by a warden: ask in Coyhaique or Cochrane to make sure someone is available.

The Carretera Austral area is also one of the best places for trying to spot the equally rare **pudu**. This miniature creature, around 40 cm tall and weighing only 10 kg, is the smallest member of the deer family in the world. Native to southern Argentina and Chile, the pudu is listed in Chile as vulnerable to extinction, largely due to habitat loss, but also because its unique appearance (the males grow two short spiked antlers) has made it a target for poaching for zoos. Reddish-brown in colour, the pudu is ideally adapted to the dense temperate rainforests of Chile and Argentina, scooting along on trails through the undergrowth, leaving behind minuscule cloven tracks.

● Sleeping

Reserva Nacional Cerro Castillo and around *p423*

B **Cabañas Shehen Aike**, Risopatrón 55, Puerto Ibáñez, T067-423284 www.shehen aike.cl. Children-friendly cabin complex run by a Swiss-Chilean family. Lots of information on the local area as well as horse riding and fishing trips. English, German, French spoken.

D **Hostería Villarrica**, O'Higgins 59, Villa Cerro Castillo. F singles. Basic accommodation, good mid-price meals and a grocery store. Cheap meals are also available at **Restaurante La Querencia**, O'Higgins s/n, Villa Cerro Castillo.

D **Residencial Ibáñez**, Bertrán Dixon 31, Puerto Ibáñez, T067-423227. F singles. Clean, warm, hot water. Similar next door at No 29.

D **Vientos del Sur**, Bertrán Dixon 282, Puerto Ibáñez, T067-423208. F singles. Cheap meals available, good.

Camping

Municipal campsite, Puerto Ibáñez, T067-423234. Open Dec-Mar, US$10 per site.

The western shore *p424*

AL **Hostal el Puesto**, Pedro Lagos 258, Río Tranquilo, T02-1964555, www.elpuesto.cl. No doubt the most comfortable place in Río Tranquilo. The owners can organize a variety of tours.

B **Campo Alacaluf**, Km 44 on the Río Tranquilo-Bahía Exploradores side road, T067-419500. Wonderful guesthouse hidden miles away from civilization and run by a very friendly German family. Recommended.

B-C **Hostal Los Pinos**, 2 Oriente 41, T067-411576, Río Tranquilo. Family run, well maintained, good mid-price meals. Recommended.

C **Cabañas Jacricalor**, 1 Sur s/n, Río Tranquilo, T067-419500. F singles. Tent-sized *cabañas*.

C **Hostería Carretera Austral**, 1 Sur 223, Río Tranquilo, T067-419500, lopezpinuer@yahoo.es. Serves mid-range/cheap meals.

E **Hostería Lago General Carrera**, Av 5 de Abril 647 y Colombia, Bahía Murta, public phone 067-419600. F-G singles. Cheap meals.

E **Residencial Patagonia**, Pasaje España 64, Bahía Murta, public telephone 067-419600. F-G singles. Very basic, without bath.

Free camping is possible by the lake in Bahía Murta, with good views of Cerro Castillo.

El Maitén and south *p424*
L **Mallín Colorado**, 2 km west of El Maitén, T067-2741807, chile@patagonia-pacific.cl. *Cabañas*, adventure activities, horse riding, rafting, fishing, English and German spoken.
A-B **Hostería Campo Baker**, Puerto Bertrand, T067-411477. *Cabañas*, sleep 5.
C **Doña Ester**, Puerto Bertrand. Rooms in a pink house. F singles. Good.
C **Hostería Puerto Bertrand**, Sector Costanera, Puerto Bertrand, T067-419900. E singles. Also meals, *cabañas*, and activities (see below).

Chile Chico and around *p425*
All the following are in Chile Chico:
C **Casa Quinta No Me Olvides**, Camino Internacional s/n. Price per person. Without bath. Clean, cooking facilities. Also camping. Tours arranged to Lago Jeinimeni and Cueva de las Manos.
C **Hostería de la Patagonia**, Camino Internacional s/n, T067-411337, F411414. E singles; full board available. Clean, excellent food, English, French and Italian spoken, trekking, horse riding and whitewater rafting organized, also camping.
C-D **Ventura**, Carrera 290, T067-411311. Modern suites.
D **Plaza**, O'Higgins y Balmaceda, T067-411510. Basic, clean. Recommended.
E **Residencial Don Luis**, Balmaceda 175, T067-411384. F-G singles. Clean, meals available.

Camping
Free campsite at **Bahía Jarra**, 5 km from Chile Chico, then 12 km north. **Camping del Sol** at the eastern end of the town.

🍴 Eating

Hosterías are your best bet for food (see Sleeping, above).

Chile Chico and around *p425*
🍴 **Café Holiday**, C González. Good coffee, friendly service.
🍴 **Cafetería Loly y Elizabeth**, González 25, on plaza. Serves coffee, ice cream and cakes.

🍷 Bars and clubs

Chile Chico and around *p425*
Pub El Minero, Carrera 205. Recommended for a drink.
Zebra, O'Higgins 750 Interior. This disco is the place to be seen in Chile Chico.

✦ Festivals and events

Chile Chico and around *p425*
Last week of Jan The town hosts the Festival Internacional de la Voz.

▲ Activities and tours

The western shore *p424*
El Puesto Expediciones, Lagos 258, Río Tranquilo, T067-233785, www.elpuesto.cl. Fishing trips and other excursions.

El Maitén and south *p424*
Jonathan Leidich, Puerto Bertrand, T067-411330. Lives on the edge of the lake, and is highly recommended for rafting, horse riding and other activities.
La Red de Turismo Río Baker, Hostería Puerto Bertrand, Puerto Bertrand, T067-419900. Rafting, horse riding and other activities.
Patagonia Baker Lodges, Orillas del Río Baker, Puerto Bertrand, T067-411903. Fishing trips on the lake.
Río Baker Lodges, T067-411499. Fishing trips on the lake.

The southern shore *p425*
Hacienda Tres Lagos, Sector El Maitén, Puerto Guadal, T067-411323. Fishing trips.
Playa Guadal, 2 km from Puerto Guadal, T067-411443. Fishing trips.

Chile Chico and around *p425*
Jaime Berrocal, O'Higgins 501. Fishing guide.

Reserva Nacional Cerro Castillo and around *p423*

Bus

Minibuses run between Puerto Ibáñez and **Coyhaique**, 2 hrs, US$7. There is also a road from Puerto Ibáñez to **Perito Moreno** in Argentina, but no public transport. Transportes Amin Ali, O'Higgins s/n, Villa Cerro Castillo, T067-419200, provides transport from Villa Cerro Castillo to **Coyhaique**, US$6.

Ferry

The car ferry, *El Pilchero*, sails from Puerto Ibáñez to **Chile Chico**, Mon 1800, Wed 1000, Thu 1630, Sat 1100, Sun 1700, return departures Mon 0800, Tue 0800, Wed 1600, Fri 1630, Sun 1330, 2½ hrs, cars US$40, passengers US$4.50, motorbikes US$8 and bicycles US$3. The number of passengers is limited to 105; arrive 30 mins before departure. Reserve at least 2 days in advance through **Mar del Sur**, Baquedano 146, Coyhaique, T067-231255. This is a very cold crossing even in summer: take warm clothing. Buses and jeeps meet the ferry in Puerto Ibáñez for connections to Coyhaique (see above).

Chile Chico and around *p425*

Air

Don Carlos flies to **Coyhaique**, 5 weekly, US$50, from an airstrip just outside Chile Chico.

Bus

Transportes Ales, T067-411739, runs minibuses along the south side of the lake to **Puerto Guadal**, Wed, Sat, US$11, and **Cochrane**, US$19. Additional services to Puerto Guadal are provided by **Sr Sergio Haro Ramos**, T067-411251, Wed, Sat, US$13, and **Transportes Seguel**, 2 weekly, US$12.

Minibuses from Chile Chico to **Los Antiguos** (Argentina), 45 mins including formalities, US$4 (payable in Chilean pesos only), are run by **Arcotrans**, T067-411841, and **Transportes Padilla**, T067-411904. The buses depart when they are full – usually about 5 times daily each.

Car

Hire from **Jaime Acuña Vogt**, Grosse 150, T/F067-411553.

Ferry

For services to Puerto Ibáñez, see above.

Into Argentina *p425*

From Los Antiguos buses run weekdays to **Comodoro Rivadavia** via Perito Moreno, 7 hrs, US$25. There are also direct buses to **Río Gallegos** and **El Calafate** from Los Antiguos, and one flight a week to **Río Gallegos** from Perito Moreno.

⊙ Directory

Chile Chico and around *p425*

Banks Generally it's best to change money in Coyhaique or Argentina, but dollars and Argentine pesos can be changed in small amounts (at poor rates) at shops and cafés in Chile Chico, including **Cafetería Loly y Elizabeth**. **Hospital** Lautaro s/n, T067-411334.

Cochrane and further south

→ *Colour map 5, C2/3.*

The final 224-km stretch of the Carretera Austral from Cochrane to Villa O'Higgins has now been completed. Travelling by bus can be frustrating as you will undoubtedly want to stop every 15 minutes to marvel at the views. From Vagabundo, Km 98, boats sail regularly down the Río Baker to Tortel. This is a beautiful trip through thick forest, with vistas of snow-capped mountains and waterfalls. ▶▶ *For Sleeping, Eating and other listings, see pages 430-432.*

Ins and outs

Getting there Cochrane can be reached by aeroplane or bus from Coyhaique, or on a poor unpaved road from Perito Moreno in Argentina. The southern tip of the Carretera at Villa O'Higgins is linked by an erratic ferry service to Calendario Mansilla, from where it is a two-day hike to/from El Chaltén in Argentina.

Getting around Public transport is scarce. Only two weekly buses ply the route from Cochrane to Villa O'Higgins. Hitching is a possibility in summer, but a 4WD vehicle will make getting around much easier. Better still, travel by mountain bike. ▶▶ *For further details, see Transport, page 431.*

Tourist information The office in Cochrane is open only in the summer① *Mon-Sat 0900-1300, 1430-2000*; in winter go to Cochrane Municipalidad at Esmeralda 398.

Cochrane and around

Sitting in a hollow on the northern banks of the Río Cochrane, 343 km south of Coyhaique, Cochrane is a simple place, sunny in summer and good for walking and fishing. There is a small **museum** ① *San Valentín 555, Mon-Fri 0900-1300, 1500-1900*. On the same street is an odd, *mate*-shaped house.

Excursions can be made to **Lago Cochrane**, which straddles the frontier with Argentina (the Argentine section is called Lago Puerredón). The lake, which covers over 17,500 ha, offers excellent fishing all year round; boats can be hired for US$15 per person. On the northern shores of the lake is the **Reserva Nacional Tamango** ① *Dec-Mar 0830-2100, Apr-Nov 0830-1830, US$4, guided visits to see the huemul, Tue, Thu, Sat, US$80 for a group of 6 people.* The reserve covers 6925 ha of lenga forest and is home to one of the largest colonies of the rare huemul as well as guanaco, foxes and lots of birds, including woodpeckers and hummingbirds. There are several marked trails affording views over the town, the nearby lakes and even to the Campo de Hielo Norte to the west. Tourist facilities, however, are rudimentary.

Some 17 km north of Cochrane, a road runs east through Villa Chacabuco to enter Argentina at **Paso Roballos** ① *78 km, Chilean immigration summer 0730-2200, winter 0800-2000*, before continuing on to Bajo Caracoles. There isn't any public transport along this route and, although the road is passable in summer, it is often flooded in spring.

Tortel to Villa O'Higgins

Built on a hill at the mouth of the river 135 km from Cochrane, Tortel has no streets, only wooden walkways; its main industries are wood, for trade with Punta Arenas, and shellfish. The village became famous in October 2000 as the place where British Prince William spent three months working for **Operation Raleigh**; it is also where Rosie Swale ended her epic horseback journey through Chile, as recorded in *Back to Cape Horn* (see page 560). A branch of the Carretera Austral, beginning 2 km south of Vagabundo and reaching south to Tortel, was completed in early 2003, so the village is now accessible by road, and the effect on its character will be enormous. From Tortel, you can hire a boat to visit two spectacular glaciers: **Ventisquero Jorge Montt**, five hours southwest, or **Ventisquero Steffens**, north on the edge of the Parque Nacional San Rafael. On the Río Baker nearby is the **Isla de los Muertos**, where some 100 Chilote workers died in mysterious circumstances early in the 20th century.

The Carretera continues southwards to **Puerto Yungay**, a tiny village with a military post and a pretty church. This section of the road is hilly and in places very bad; it is not advisable to drive along here at night. From Puerto Yungay, there is a **ferry** crossing to Río Bravo run by the army ① *several daily, 45 mins, free, check timetables locally.* If you miss the last boat the *carabineros* will help you find accommodation. After the ferry crossing, the road continues through more spectacular scenery – lakes, moors, swamps, rivers and waterfalls – before arriving at its final destination, Villa O'Higgins.

Carretera Austral Cochrane & further south

Villa O'Higgins lies 2 km from the northeastern end of an arm of **Lago O'Higgins**, which straddles the Argentine border (it's known as Lago San Martín in Argentina). With a population of around 500, the people are friendly, and there is still something of a frontier feel about the town. **Tourist information** ① *T067-211849*, is available in the plaza in summer or from the Municipalidad, which can provide trekking guides.

Behind the town, a *mirador* affords spectacular views of nearby mountains, lakes and glaciers. There are large numbers of icebergs in Lago O'Higgins, which have split off the glaciers of the Campo de Hielo Sur to the west. A six-hour trek from the town goes through native forest to the **Mosco Glacier**. Allow two days for a return trip. Fresh water is plentiful and there is a *refugio* on the way, but the route is difficult after heavy rain.

From Villa O'Higgins, the road continues 7 km south to **Bahía Bahamóndez** on the shores of Lago O'Higgins, from where a boat departs ① *every 2 wks in summer, although frequency is likely to increase (contact the Municipalidad in Villa O'Higgins for details)*, to Chilean immigration at Candelario Mancila. From here, it is a two-day walk or one-day mountain bike ride (you will need to carry the bicycle in places) to **El Chaltén** in Argentina. With the opening of this route, it is now possible to travel along the whole of the Carretera Austral and on to Torres del Paine without having to double back on yourself.

Parque Nacional Laguna San Rafael

Situated west of Lago General Carrera and some 200 km south of Puerto Aisén, Laguna San Rafael is one of the highlights for many travellers to Chile. The **Ventisquero San Rafael**, one of many glaciers from the giant **Campo de Hielo Norte**, flows into the laguna, which, in turn, empties into the sea northwards via the Río Tempano. About 45 km in length and towering 30 m above water level, the deep blue glacier groans and cracks as it carves off icebergs, which are carried across the laguna and out to sea. Around the shores of the lake is thick vegetation and above are snowy mountain peaks.

Laguna San Rafael and the Campo de Hielo Norte are part of the **Parque Nacional Laguna San Rafael** ① *US$6*, which extends over 1,740,000 ha. In the national park are puma, pudu, foxes, dolphins, occasional sea lions and sea otters, and many species of bird. Walking trails are limited (about 10 km in all) but a lookout platform has been constructed, with fine views of the glacier. There is also a small ranger station that provides information, and a pier. The rangers are willing to row you out to the glacier in calm weather, an awesome three-hour adventure, past icebergs and swells created when huge chunks of ice break off the glacier and crash into the laguna.

Sadly, the San Rafael Glacier is rapidly disintegrating and is likely to have disappeared entirely by 2011. While this shrinkage is symptomatic of what has happened to many glaciers in Patagonia, some blame the motorized tourist boats that go too close to the glacier, creating a greater force of erosion against the ice. If the glacier is to be preserved, it is vital that travellers take a proactive stance on this issue and insist that the boats do not go too close to the glacier and further damage this fragile environment.

● Sleeping

Cochrane and around *p429*
In summer it is best to book rooms in advance. The following are all in Cochrane:
AL Ultimo Paraíso, Lago Brown 455, T067-522361. Regarded as the best place to stay. Also arranges fishing trips.
A **Cabañas Rogery**, Tte Merino 502, T067-522264. Cabins sleep 4, with kitchen facilities. Breakfast included.

A **Hotel Wellmann**, Las Golondrinas 36, T067-522171. Hot water, comfortable, warm, good meals. Recommended.
B **Residencial Rubio**, Tte Merino 4, T067-522173. E singles, breakfast included, lunch and dinner extra. With bath. Very good.
C **Hostal Latitud 47 sur**, Lago Brown 564. E singles. Clean, hot water, internet, tours offered.

C **Residencial Cero a Cero**, Lago Brown 464,
T067-522158, ceroacero@ze.cl. **E** singles,
with breakfast, cheaper without bath,
welcoming, recommended.
C **Residencial Sur Austral**, Prat 334, T067-
522150. **E** singles, with breakfast and hot water.
D **Hospedaje Cochrane**, Dr Steffens 451,
T067-522377. **F** singles. Good meals,
camping available. Recommended.
D **Hospedaje Paola**, Lago Brown 150,
T067-522215. **F** singles. Also camping.
D **Residencial El Fogón**, San Valentín 651,
T067-522240. **F** singles. Its pub is one of few
eating places open in the low season.

Camping
In the Reserva Nacional Tamango, there are
campsites and *cabañas* at **Los Correntadas**,
US$14 per site, and **Los Coigües**, US$18 per
site. Details and booking through **CONAF**,
Av Ogana 1060, T067-212125.

Tortel to Villa O'Higgins *p429*
Free accommodation is available at the
Centro Abierto, ask at the Municipalidad,
T067-211876.
C **Doña Berta Muñoz**, Tortel. Full board.
One guest comments: "Expect fresh mutton
meals and if you are squeamish...don't look
out of the window when they butcher the
two lambs a day on the front porch."
C **Sergio Barrio**, Tortel. Full board available,
good food.
D **Casa Rural**, Tortel. Full board or bed
and breakfast.
D **Hospedaje Costanera**, Tortel,
T067-234815. Price includes breakfast (also
open to non-residents). Clean, warm, with
attractive garden, recommended.

Villa O'Higgins *p430*
D **Apocalipsis 1:3**, T067-216927.
F singles. Shared baths, friendly, serves food.
D **Hospedaje Patagonia**, T067-234813.
F singles. Basic accommodation.

🍴 Eating

For other eating options, see Sleeping, above.

Cochrane and around *p429*
🍴 **La Costa**, plaza, Cochrane. A friendly
cheapie. There are a couple of mid-range
options on Tte Merino and San Valentín too.

🍴 **Café Celes Salom**, Tortel. Basic cheap
meals and disco on Sat with occasional
bands.

▲ Activities and tours

Cochrane and around *p429*
Excursions can be arranged through
Guillermo Paso at **Transportes Los Ñadis**
(see Transport, below); fishing tours are
available from **Hotel Ultimo Paraíso** (see
Sleeping, above).
Don Pedro Muñoz, T067-522244. Hires
out horses for excursions in the surrounding
countryside.
Red de Turismo Río Baker, San Valentín
438, T067-522646, trural@patagoniachile.cl.
Offers tours of all kinds within the region.
Samuel Smiol, T067-522487. Offers tours to
the icefields and mountains, English spoken.
Siesta Oppi, 3176 Neuenegg, Switzerland,
T+41-31-7419192. This Swiss canoe shop
organizes canoe trips in Jan and Feb.

Tortel to Villa O'Higgins *p429*
Charter boats can be arranged through
Viviana Muñoz or Hernán Ovando at the
Municipalidad, T067-211876. Prices to
Ventisquero Jorge Montt, speedboat 2 hrs,
US$120 per person; *lancha* 5 hrs, US$150. To
Ventisquero Steffens, speedboat 1 hr,
US$80 per person; *lancha* 2½ hrs, $100.

Villa O'Higgins *p430*
Nelson Henríquez, Lago Cisnes 201.
Fishing trips on the lake.

Parque Nacional Laguna San Rafael *p430*
Patagonia Connection SA, Fidel Oteíza 1921,
Oficina 1006, Providencia, Santiago,
T02-2256489. Operates a 3-night catamaran
tour to Laguna San Rafael via **Puyuhuapi
Lodge and Spa** (see page 410) on board the
Patagonia Express. Also offers special
fly-fishing programmes and other excursions.

🚌 Transport

Cochrane and around *p429*
Air
Don Carlos flies to **Coyhaique**, Mon, Thu,
US$75, from an airstrip just north of town.

To **Coyhaique**, Don Carlos, Prat 344, T/F067-522150, 2 weekly, US$18; Inter Lagos, 6 weekly, US$20, recommended. To **Vagabundo**, US$10, Los Ñadis Los Helechos 490, T/F067-522196, 3 weekly. To **Villa O'Higgins**, Los Ñadis, 1 weekly, US$12.

Tortel to Villa O'Higgins *p429*
Air
Don Carlos to **Coyhaique**, Mon and Wed, US$35. This is a subsidized price for residents of the village. Other travellers must buy a standby ticket and should expect to pay much more.

Boat
To **Vagabundo**, Tue, Sun 0900, 5 hrs, US$3 one way; return trip Tue, Sun 1500, 3 hrs. There is a boat once a fortnight from Tortel to **Puerto Yungay**, or you can arrange a charter for 6-10 people by contacting Viviana Muñoz or Hernán Ovando at the Municipalidad, T067-211876, 8 hrs, US$150 return.

Villa O'Higgins *p430*
Don Carlos air taxi flies to Villa O'Higgins from **Coyhaique**, via Cochrane, Mon, Thu, US$100. There are also 1 or 2 buses weekly to **Cochrane**, US$12.

Parque Nacional Laguna San Rafael *p430*
Air
Aerohein and Don Carlos provide air taxis from **Coyhaique** (addresses under Coyhaique), US$200 each for party of 5; some pilots in **Puerto Aisén** will also fly to the glacier for about US$95 per person, but many are unwilling to land on the rough airstrip. Other air-tour options are available from Coyhaique.

Boats from Puerto Montt
The official cruises from Puerto Montt are run by Skorpios (see page 369). Various private yachts for 6-12 passengers can also be chartered. Other tour companies include: **Compañía Naviera Puerto Montt**, Diego Portales 882, Puerto Montt, T/F065-252547. Runs 6-day, 6-night tours to the Laguna San Rafael, via various ports and channels, on board the *Quellon*, US$900. Office in Santiago at Alameda Bernado O'Higgins 108, local 120, T02-633 0883, and in Puerto Aisén/Puerto Chacabuco, see below.

Pamar, Pacheco Altamirano 3100, T065-256220. Sails Sep-Mar only.

Boats from Puerto Chacabuco
For agency contact details, see page 421. Although it's now nearly as cheap to fly, official cruises to the Laguna are run by Navimag, all year, reduced service off season, 24 hrs, from US$324, and Catamaranes del Sur, 1-3 weekly Sep-Apr, 1-day trips US$299, 3-day trips from $550. Naviera Río Cisnes runs a variety of 5-day cruises from US$300 per person in the *Motonave El Colono*.
Compañía Naviera Puerto Montt, Sgto Aldea 679, Puerto Aisén, T067-332908. Motorized sailing boats, the *Odisea* and the *Visun*, sail Dec-Mar on 6-day trips to the Laguna San Rafael.
Iceberg Express, Av Providencia 2331, oficina 602, Santiago, T02-335 0580. 12-hr luxury catamaran cruises.

Local fishing boats from Puerto Chacabuco/ Puerto Aisén take about 18-20 hrs each way and charge the same as the tourist boats. Try the following: Jorge Prado, ask at the port, takes a minimum of 7, more expensive than others; Andino Royas, Cochrane 129; Justiniano Aravena, Dr Steffen 703; Rodrigo Azúcar, Agemar office T067-332716; or Sr Ocuña, ask at the port. Note that these unauthorized boats may have neither adequate facilities nor a licence for the trip. Trips to Laguna San Rafael out of season are very difficult to arrange, but in Puerto Chaca buco try Edda Espinosa, Sgto Aldea 943.

⊙ Directory

Cochrane and around *p429*
Banks Banco del Estado, on the plaza, changes dollars. ATM accepts MasterCard and Cirrus but not Visa. **Internet** There are 2 on the plaza, one run by nuns (closed Sun). **Supermarket** Melero, Las Golondrinas 148.

Tortel to Villa O'Higgins *p429*
Banks There is no bank in Tortel but a mobile bank comes twice a month. **Medical services** Medical centre staffed by doctors, nurses and dentists visits Tortel monthly. **Post office** Mon-Fri 0830-1330, post leaves Tortel weekly by air.

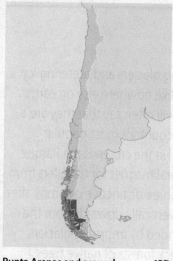

The Far South

Footprint features

Introduction

A spectacular land of fragmenting glaciers and teetering icy peaks, southern Patagonia feels like nowhere else on earth. Although Chileans posted here will often say that they are a 'long way from Chile', this is the country's most popular destination for visitors. The jewel in the crown is the Parque Nacional Torres del Paine, a natural magnet for travellers from all over the world. The 'towers', three distinctive columns after which the park is named, point vertically upwards from the Paine massif-like fingers, surrounded by imposing glaciers, turquoise-coloured lakes and thick forests of native trees.

Nearby, Punta Arenas is a European-style city with a lively Chilote community and remnants of earlier English and Croatian influences. There are numerous other attractions, notably the glaciers that descend from Monte Balmaceda at the southern end of the Parque Nacional Bernardo O'Higgins. On the Argentine side of the border lies more spectacular scenery, including the Perito Moreno Glacier and the mountainous area around Cerro Fitz Roy.

★ Don't miss...

1 **Seno Otway** Pick up a penguin near Punta Arenas, page 441.

2 **Cerro Mirador** One of the only places in the world where you can ski in sight of the sea, page 445.

3 **Parque Nacional Bernardo O'Higgins** Take a boat trip to the glaciers at the bottom of one of the planet's largest non-polar icefields, the Campo de Hielo Sur, page 451.

4 **Parque Nacional Torres del Paine** Complete the seven-day trek through the national park, passing fields of wild flowers, glaciers, mountains, forests and white and turquoise lakes, page 456.

5 **Cerro Fitz Roy** Trek through a stunning part of Argentine Patagonia: "anyone within 500 miles would be a fool to miss it", page 472.

6 **Perito Moreno** Witness the creaking, heaving mass of this Argentine glacier, from which huge chunks of ice regularly break off into Lago Argentino, page 474.

The Far South

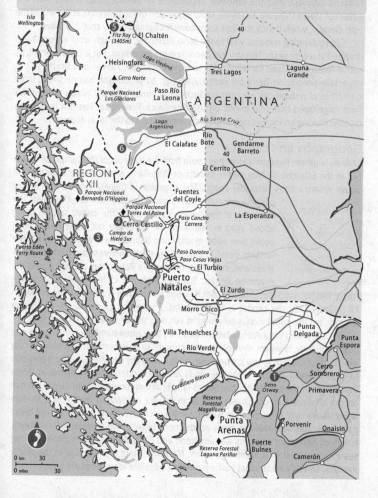

Background

Southern Patagonia was inhabited from the end of the Ice Age, mainly by the Tehuelche people, who roamed from the Atlantic coast to the mountains (see box opposite). The first Europeans did not visit until the 16th century. When Magellan sailed through the Straits in 1520, the strategic importance was quickly recognized: soon Spanish naval and merchant ships were using the route, as were mariners from other countries, including Francis Drake on his world voyage (1578). However, the route became less important after 1616 when the Dutch sailors Jacob le Maire and Cornelius van Schouten discovered a quicker route into the Pacific round Cape Horn.

At Independence, Chile claimed the far southern territories along the Pacific coast but little was done to carry out this claim until 1843 when, concerned at British activities in the area and at rumours of French plans to start a colony, President Bulnes ordered the preparation of a secret mission. The expedition, on board the vessel *Ancud*, established Fuerte Bulnes; the fort was abandoned in 1848 in favour of a new settlement 56 km north, called Punta Arenas. The development of sheep farming in Patagonia and on Tierra del Fuego (with the help of arrivals from the nearby Falkland Islands), and the renewed importance of the Magellan Straits with the advent of steam shipping, led to the rapid expansion of Punta Arenas at the end of the 19th century, when it took the first steps towards being the city that it is today.

Sheep farming remains vital to the local economy, although wool exports have dropped in recent years. Forestry has become more important, but is controversial, as native forests are used for woodchips to export to Japan, Taiwan and Brazil. This is especially serious on Tierra del Fuego. Although oil production has declined, large quantities of natural gas are now produced and about 33% of Chilean coal comes from large open-cast coal mines on the Brunswick Peninsula. Tourism is growing rapidly, making an increasingly important contribution to the local economy.

Geography and climate

Chilean southern Patagonia stretches south from the icefields of the Campo de Hielos Sur to the Estrecho de Magallanes (Straits of Magellan), which separate continental South America from Tierra del Fuego. The coastline is heavily indented by fjords; offshore are numerous islands, few of which are inhabited. The remnants of the Andes stretch along the coast, seldom rising above 1500 m, although the Cordillera del Paine has several peaks over 2600 m and Cerro Balmaceda is 2035 m. Most of the western coast is covered by thick rainforest but further east is grassland, stretching into the arid Patagonian plateau across the Argentine border. Together with the Chilean part of Tierra del Fuego, Isla Navarino and Chilean Antarctica, this part of Chile is administered as Región XII (Magallanes); the capital is Punta Arenas. The region covers 17.5% of Chilean territory, but the population is only around 150,000, under 1% of the Chilean total.

❧ When travelling in this region, protection against the sun is essential at all times, but especially in the spring, when the ozone layer all but disappears.

People from Punta Arenas tell visitors that they often have four seasons in one day. Frequently, however, the only season appears to be winter. Strong, cold, piercing winds, often exceeding 100 km per hour, blow during the summer bringing heavy rain to coastal areas. Further east, the winds are much drier; annual rainfall at Punta Dungeness at the east end of the Straits is only 250 mm compared to over 4000 mm on the offshore islands. Coastal temperatures are moderated by the sea, seldom rising above 15°C in summer. In winter, snow covers the whole region, except those parts near the sea, making many roads more or less impassable. Recent times, however, have seen a general warning trend and Punta Arenas, for example, has not seen heavy snow for a number of years. Moreover there is little wind in the winter months, and this means that tourism remains possible for most of the year.

⁞ The original big foots

The dry Patagonian plateau was originally inhabited by one principal indigenous group, the **Tehuelches**, who lived along the eastern side of the Andes, as far north as modern-day Bariloche, and were hunters of guanaco and rheas. In the 18th century, they began to domesticate the wild horses of the region and sailed down the Patagonian rivers to reach the Atlantic coast.

The Tehuelches were very large: it is said that when the Spanish first arrived in this area, they discovered Tehuelche footprints in the sand, exclaiming *'qué patagón'* ('what a large foot'), hence the name Patagonia.

In the 18th and early 19th centuries, the Tehuelche interacted with European whalers and were patronizingly described as 'semi-civilized'. The granting by the Chilean government of large land concessions in the late 19th century, combined with Argentine President Julio Roca's wars of extermination against Patagonian native peoples in the 1870s, spelled the end for the Tehuelches. They were hunted and persecuted by settlers and only a few survived diseases and the radical change of lifestyle.

Towards the end of the 20th century, a belated sense of moral guilt arose among the colonizers, but it was too late to preserve the Tehuelche way of life. Today only a few isolated groups remain in Argentine Patagonia.

For details of the indigenous groups further south and in the Patagonian fjords, see the Tierra del Fuego chapter and page 534.

Punta Arenas and around

→ *Colour map 7, B1. Population: 116,000.*

Capital of Región XII, Punta Arenas lies 2140 km due south of Santiago. The city was originally named 'Sandy Point' by the English, but adopted the Hispanic equivalent under Chilean colonization. A centre for the local sheep farming and fishing industries as well as an important military base, it is also the home of La Polar, one of the most southerly breweries in the world. Although Punta Arenas has expanded rapidly, it remains a tranquil and pleasant city . The climate and architecture give it a distinctively northern European atmosphere, quite unlike anywhere else in Chile.
▶▶ *For Sleeping, Eating and other listings, see pages 442-448.*

Ins and outs

Getting there Punta Arenas is cut off from the rest of Chile. The only road connections are via Comodoro Rivadavia and Río Gallegos either to Coyhaique and the Carretera Austral (20 hours; one or two buses weekly in summer) or to Bariloche and on to Puerto Montt (36 hours, daily buses in summer); it is quicker, and often cheaper, to take one of the many daily flights to/from Puerto Montt or Santiago instead. Carlos Ibáñez del Campo Airport is 20 km north of town. **Buses Transfer** and **Buses Pacheco** run scheduled services to/from Punta Arenas to meet flights, US$3. Buses from Punta Arenas to Puerto Natales will only stop at the airport if they are scheduled to pick up passengers there. There are also minibuses operated by **Sandy Point** costing US$5 which will drop you anywhere near the city centre. A taxi ordered at the airport costs US$13, but a radio taxi ordered in advance from the city is

⁞ *Many phone numbers in Punta Arenas are being changed at the end of 2006.*

much cheaper. Transport to Tierra del Fuego is on the Melinka ferry to Porvenir (six weekly) or, further north, at Punta Delgada (many daily) to Cerro Sombrero. There are also direct flights to Porvenir, Puerto Williams and Ushuaia. Puerto Natales, 247 km north, is easily reached on a paved road (many buses daily). ▶▶ *For further details, see Transport page 446.*

Getting around Punta Arenas is not a huge city and walking about is a pleasant way of getting to know it. Buses and *colectivos* are plentiful and cheap (US$0.40-0.60): a taxi is only really necessary for out-of-town excursions.

Tourist information The municipal tourist office on the plaza ① *T061-200610*, is good. **Sernatur** ① *Magallanes 960, T061-225385, www.patagonia-chile.com, 0830-1845, closed Sat and Sun off season*, is helpful and has lots of information, English spoken. **CONAF** ① *Bulnes 0309, opposite the shepherd monument, between the racetrack and the cemetery, T061-238544, Mon-Fri*, doesn't have much useful info.

History

After its foundation in 1848, Punta Arenas became a penal colony modelled on Australia. In 1867, it was opened to foreign settlers and given free port status. From the 1880s, it prospered as a refuelling and provisioning centre for steam ships and whaling vessels. It also became a centre for the new sheep *estancias* since it afforded the best harbour facilities. The city's importance was reduced overnight by the opening of the Panama Canal in 1914. Most of those who came to work in the *estancias* were from Chiloé, and many people in the city have relatives in Chiloé and feel an affinity with the island (the *barrios* on either side of the upper reaches of Independencia are known as Chilote areas); the Chilotes who returned north took Patagonian customs with them, hence the number of *maté* drinkers on Chiloé.

Sights

Around the attractive **Plaza Muñoz Gamero** are a number of mansions that once belonged to the great sheep-ranching families of the late 19th century. A good example is the **Palacio Sara Braun** ① *Tue-Sun, US$2*, built between 1894 and 1905 with materials from Europe; the Palacio has several elegantly decorated rooms open to the public and also houses the **Hotel José Nogueira**. In the centre of the plaza is a statue of Magellan with a mermaid and two Fuegian Indians at his feet. According to local wisdom, those who rub or kiss the big toe of one of the Indians will return to Punta Arenas.

Just north of the plaza is the **Museo de Historia Regional Braun Menéndez** ① *Magallanes 949, T061-244216, www.dibam.cl/subdirec_museos/mr_magallanes, Mon-Sat 1030-1700, Sun 1030-1400 (summer); Mon-Sun 1030-1300 (winter), US$2, children half-price*, the opulent former mansion of Mauricio Braun, built in 1905. A visit is recommended. Part of the museum is set out as a room-by-room regional history; the rest of the house has been left with its original furniture. Guided tours are in Spanish only, but a somewhat confusing information sheet in English is also available. In the basement there is a café. One block further north is the **Teatro Cervantes**, now a cinema with an ornate interior.

Three blocks east of the plaza, the **Museo Naval y Maritimo** ① *Pedro Montt 981, T061-205479, terzona@armarda.cl, Tue-Sun 0930-1230, 1400-1700, US$1.50*, houses an exhibition of local and national maritime history with sections on naval instruments, cartography, meteorology , as well as shipwrecks. There is a video in Spanish and an information sheet in English.

● *Punta Arenas is the only city in the whole of Chile where the sun rises over the sea and sets over the land.*

West of the plaza Muñoz Gamero on Waldo Seguel are two reminders of British influence in the city: the **British School** and **St James's Anglican Church** next door. Nearby on Calle Fagnano is the **Mirador Cerro de La Cruz** offering a view over the city and the Magellan Straits complete with its various shipwrecks.

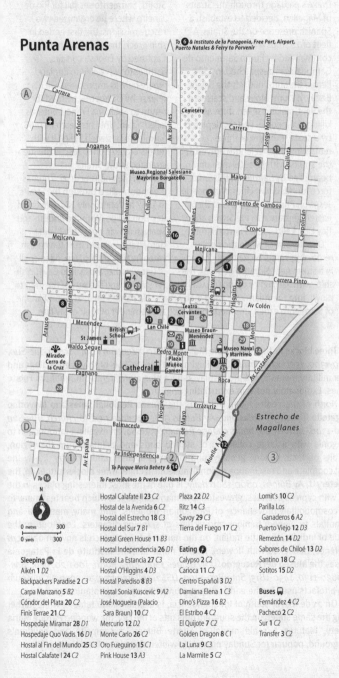

Punta Arenas

To 6 & Instituto de la Patagonia, Free Port, Airport, Puerto Natales & Ferry to Porvenir

Estrecho de Magallanes

N

| 0 metres | 300 |
| 0 yards | 300 |

Sleeping
Aikén 1 *D2*
Backpackers Paradise 2 *C3*
Carpa Manzano 5 *B2*
Cóndor del Plata 20 *C2*
Finis Terrae 21 *C2*
Hospedaje Miramar 28 *D1*
Hospedaje Quo Vadis 16 *D1*
Hostal al Fin del Mundo 25 *C3*
Hostal Calafate I 24 *C2*

Hostal Calafate II 23 *C2*
Hostal de la Avenida 6 *C2*
Hostal del Estrecho 18 *C3*
Hostal del Sur 7 *B1*
Hostal Green House 11 *B3*
Hostal Independencia 26 *D1*
Hostal La Estancia 27 *C3*
Hostal O'Higgins 4 *D3*
Hostal Parediso 8 *B3*
Hostal Sonia Kuscevic 9 *A2*
José Nogueira (Palacio
   Sara Braun) 10 *C2*
Mercurio 12 *D2*
Monte Carlo 26 *C2*
Oro Fueguino 15 *C1*
Pink House 13 *A3*

Plaza 22 *D2*
Ritz 14 *C3*
Savoy 29 *C3*
Tierra del Fuego 17 *C2*

Eating
Calypso 2 *C2*
Carioca 11 *C2*
Centro Español 3 *D2*
Damiana Elena 1 *C3*
Dino's Pizza 16 *B2*
El Estribo 4 *C2*
El Quijote 7 *C2*
Golden Dragon 8 *C1*
La Luna 9 *C3*
La Marmite 5 *C2*

Lomit's 10 *C2*
Parilla Los
   Ganaderos 6 *A2*
Puerto Viejo 12 *D3*
Remezón 14 *D2*
Sabores de Chiloé 13 *D2*
Santino 18 *C2*
Sotitos 15 *D2*

Buses
Fernández 4 *C2*
Pacheco 2 *C2*
Sur 1 *C2*
Transfer 3 *C2*

Port Famine (Puerto Hambre)

In 1582, Felipe II of Spain, alarmed by Drake's passage through the Straits of Magellan, decided to establish a Spanish presence on the Straits. A fleet of 15 ships and 4000 men, commanded by Pedro Sarmiento de Gamboa, was despatched in 1584. Before the ships had left the Bay of Biscay, a storm arose and scattered the fleet, sinking seven ships and killing 800 people. Further depleted by disease, the fleet of three remaining ships at length arrived at the Straits, with just 300 men on board. Led by Sarmiento this small force founded two cities: Nombre de Jesús on Punta Dungeness at the eastern entrance to the Straits and Rey Don Felipe near Puerto Hambre.

Disaster struck when their only remaining vessel broke its anchorage in a storm near Nombre de Jesús; the ship, with Sarmiento on board, was blown into the Atlantic, leaving many of Sarmiento's men stranded on land.

After vain attempts to re-enter the Straits, Sarmiento set sail for Río de Janeiro where he organized two rescue missions: the first ended in shipwreck, the second in mutiny. Captured by English corsairs, Sarmiento was taken to England where he was imprisoned. On his release by Elizabeth I, he tried to return to Spain via France, but was jailed again. Until his death in 1608, Sarmiento besieged Felipe II with letters urging him to rescue the men stranded in the Straits.

When the English corsair Thomas Cavendish sailed through the Straits in 1587 he found only 18 survivors at Rey Don Felipe. With the English and Spanish at war, only one – Tomé Hernández – would trust Cavendish when he first arrived. A sudden spell of fine weather arose, and Cavendish set sail, leaving the rest of the men to die. He named the place Port Famine as a reminder of their grisly fate.

Three blocks further west is the **Museo Militar** ① *Zenteno y Balmaceda, Tue-Sun, 0900-1300, 1500-1700, free*, at the Regimiento Pudeto. Lots of knives guns, flags and other military memorabilia are displayed here plus many items brought from Fuerte Bulnes. Explanatory notes in excruciating English.

North of the centre along Bulnes is the **Museo Regional Salesiano Mayorino Borgatello** ① *Colegio Salesiano, Av Bulnes 374, entrance next to church, Tue-Sun 1000-1300, 1400-1800, hours change frequently, US$4*, an excellent introduction to Patagonia with a large collection of stuffed birds and animals from the region, exhibits on local history, geology, anthropology, aviation and industry. Easily the most complete and fascinating regional museum in Chile. Three blocks further on, the **cemetery** ① *Av Bulnes, 0800-1800 daily*, is one of the most interesting places in the city, with cypress avenues, gravestones in many languages, which bear testimony to the cosmopolitan provenance of Patagonian pioneers, and many mausolea and memorials to pioneer families and victims of shipping disasters. Look out for the statue of Indicito, the little Indian, on the northwest side, which is now an object of reverence, bedecked with flowers. Further north still, the **Instituto de la Patagonia** houses the **Museo del Recuerdo** ① *Av Bulnes 1890, Km 4 north, T061-207056, Mon-Fri 0830-1130, 1430-1815, Sat 0830-1300, US$2, children free*, an open-air museum with artefacts used by the early settlers, pioneer homes and botanical gardens.

On 21 de Mayo, south of Independencia, is a small Hindu temple, while further along the same street, on the southern outskirts of the city, the wooded **Parque María Behety**, features a scale model of Fuerte Bulnes, a campsite and children's playground, popular for Sunday picnics. In winter, there is an ice rink here.

Parque Japonés, extends over 13,500 ha and rises to 600 m. **Viento Sur** (see Activities and tours page 445) offers a scheduled transport service to the reserve, but it can also be reached on foot or by bike: follow Independencia up the hill and take a right turning for Río de las Minas, about 3 km from the edge of town; the entrance to the reserve is 2 km beyond. Here you will find a self-guided nature trail through lenga and coigue trees. The road continues through the woods for 14 km passing several picnic sites. From the top end of the road a short path leads to a lookout over the **Garganta del Diablo** (Devil's Throat), a gorge with views over Punta Arenas and Tierra del Fuego. From here a slippery path leads down to the Río de las Minas Valley and then back to Punta Arenas.

Around Punta Arenas

Reserva Forestal Laguna Parrillar

About 25 km south of Punta Arenas, there is a fork in the road to the right; 21 km further on is the very peaceful Parrillar reserve, covering 18,814 ha and surrounded by snowcapped hills. It has older forest than the Magallanes Reserve and sphagnum bogs, and offers excellent salmon and trout fishing. There is a three-hour walk to the treeline, as well as along poorly marked, boggy paths, and fine views from the Mirador. There are CONAF administered campsites and picnic sites. Note that there is no public transport to the reserve and hitching is virtually impossible; a radio taxi will cost about US$50.

Fuerte Bulnes and further south

Some 56 km south of Punta Arenas, Fuerte Bulnes is a replica of the wooden fort erected in 1843 by the crew of the Chilean vessel *Ancud*. Built in the 1940s and originally designed to house a museum, nearly all the interesting exhibits and artefacts were moved to museums in Punta Arenas and Santiago in 1986 and now only the empty shells of the various buildings remain. Several agencies run half-day tours to here, but hitching is not difficult at weekends or in summer, as there are many holiday camps in the area.

Nearby is **Puerto Hambre**, where there are ruins of the church built by Sarmiento de Gamboa's colonists in 1584. This is a very beautiful area with views towards the towering ice mountains near Pico Sarmiento; it was of Puerto Hambre that Darwin wrote: "looking due southward... the distant channels between the mountains appeared from their gloominess to lead beyond the confines of this world". Southern dolphins can often be seen in the straits around this point.

At the intersection of the roads to Puerto Hambre and Fuerte Bulnes, 51 km south of Punta Arenas, is a small monolith marking the **Centro Geográfico de Chile**, the midway point between Arica and the South Pole. Bypassing Fuerte Bulnes, the road continues past a memorial to Captain Pringle Stokes, Captain of the Beagle, who committed suicide here in 1829, being replaced as captain by Fitz Roy. The road runs out 5 km further on, at San Juan. From here, it is a two-and-half-day hike to **Cape Froward**, the southernmost point of the continent of South America, marked by a 24-metre-high cross. There is no path, and a guide is essential (travellers have died attempting the trek alone); **Bruce Willett**, T099-3602204, has been recommended.

North of Punta Arenas

Some 70 km north of Punta Arenas, **Seno Otway** ⓘ *Oct-mid Mar, US$5*, is the site of a colony of around 11,000 Magellanic penguins. There are beautiful views across the sound to the mountains to the north and rheas skunks and foxes can also be seen. Several agencies offer trips to the colony lasting five hours (US$19 at peak season); if you wish to visit independently, a taxi from Punta Arenas will cost US$50 return. It is best to go early in the day. Try to avoid going at the same time as the large cruise ship tours – it is not much fun having to wait behind 200 people for your turn at the viewing stations.

A small island, 30 km northeast, **Isla Magdalena** is the location of the **Monumento Natural Los Pingüinos**, a colony of 150,000 penguins, administered by CONAF. Deserted apart from during the breeding season from November to early February, Magdalena is one of a group of three islands visited by Drake (the others are Marta and Isabel), whose men killed 3000 penguins for food. Boat trips to the island are run by **Comapa** ① *Tue, Thu, Sat, 1600 (Dec-Feb), 2 hrs each way with 2 hrs on the island, US$30, subject to cancellation if windy (full refund given)*.

Beyond, Route 255 heads northeast via Punta Delgada to the **Argentine border** at Kimiri Aike and then along Argentine Route 3 to Río Gallegos, an unappealing city. For routes to Calafate in Argentina, see page 465.

● Sleeping

Punta Arenas *p437, map p437*
Hotel prices are substantially lower during winter months (Apr/May-Sep). Most hotels include breakfast in the room price. Accommodation is also available in many private houses; ask at tourist office. There are no campsites in or near the city.
LL Cabo de Hornos, Muñoz Gamero 1039 on the plaza, T061-715000, www.hoteles australis.com. 4 star, newly refurbished and comfortable. Bright and spacious rooms. Good views from the 4th floor up, either of the Magellan straights or the plaza.
LL Finis Terrae, Colón 766, T061-228200, www.hotelfinisterrae.com. Typical large hotel; some rooms are small, as are the bathrooms. Expensive suites. Views from the top 2 floors. Best thing about the hotel is the rooftop café/bar. English spoken, parking.
LL José Nogueira, Bories 959, in former Palacio Sara Braun, T061-248840, www.hotel nogueira.com. Beautiful *loggia*. Slightly small rooms, but high ceilings. The rooms on the 2nd floor are best. Good suites, lovely dining room, parking. Probably the nicest hotel in town. Recommended.
L Tierra del Fuego, Colón 716, T061-226200, www.puntaarenas.com. Good breakfast, parking. Decent sized rooms, some rooms with kitchenette. **Café 1900** is downstairs.
AL Hostería Yaganes, Camino Antiguo Norte Km 7.5, T061-211600, www.pehoe.cl/ yaganes.htm. *Cabañas* on the shores of the Straits of Magellan, nice setting.
AL Cóndor del Plata, Colón 556, T061-247987, www.condordeplata.cl. Small hotel often used by polar expeditions. Rooms with cable TV and full bathtubs. Slightly disinterested staff. Cash discounts.
AL Mercurio, Fagnano 595, T061-242300, mercurio@chileaustral.com. Rooms with full

bathtub, TV and phone. Reasonable value.
AL Plaza, Nogueira 1116, piso 2, T061-248613, www. Hotelplaza.cl. Historic building with high ceilings and old-fashioned charm, redone recently. English spoken. Limited parking. Recommended.
AL-A Carpa Manzano, Lautaro Navarro 336, T061-248864, www.hotelcarpamanzano.com. Small hotel with comfortable but slightly cramped carpeted rooms. There is a wild garden at the back. A bit impersonal. Basic English spoken. Overpriced for what is essentially a glorified bed and breakfast.
A Hostal Calafate I, Lautaro Navarro 850, T061-248415, www.calafate.cl. Rooms with TV, cheaper without bath, internet access, clean, overpriced. **Calafate II**, Magallanes 926, T061-241281, www.calafate.cl, is the same price but more impersonal, dirty and also overpriced.
A Hostal Sonia Kuscevic, Pasaje Darwin 175, T061-248543, www.hostalsk.50megs.com. One of the oldest guesthouses in Punta Arenas. Impeccably kept rooms with TV and bath. Very quiet, information given. Good breakfast including omelette. Slightly over-priced but good value offseason or long stays.
A Oro Fueguino, Fagnano 356, T061-249401, www.orofueguino.cl. Recently refurbished, TV and phone. Some rooms with no windows. Good breakfast. Often fills up with groups so book ahead. Cheaper in US$dollars than pesos. Recommended.
A Savoy, Menéndez 1073, T061-247979, www.hotelsavoy.cl. Garish pink carpets and low ceilings. Pleasant rooms but some lack windows, slightly claustrophobic. Acidic receptionist. Better value in US dollars than in pesos.
A-B Monte Carlo, Colón 605, T061-222120, www. Montecarlohotel.cl. Old wooden

building. Rooms are heated, carpeted and have seen better days. The last refit seems circa 1970. Cheaper without bath.

B Hostal de la Avenida, Colón 534, T061-247532. Heated rooms with bath and cable TV. Good breakfast. Homely feel but some staff not so friendly.

B Hostal sel Estrecho, Menéndez 1048, T061-241011, www.chileanpatagonia.com/estrecho. With large breakfast and bath (cheaper without), central heating, cable TV.

B Hostal del Sur, Mejicana 151, T061-227249. Homely and impeccably kept late 19th-century house. The living room is top of the range 1960s, but the rooms are modern. Excellent breakfast with cereal and cakes. Not central, but in a peaceful neighbourhood. Advance booking advised in summer. Highly recommended.

B Hostal La Estancia, O'Higgins 765, T061-249130, www.Hostallaestancia.cl. Simple but comfortable rooms, some with bath. Heating in passageways but not in rooms. Very good kitchen facilities, internet, lots of information, friendly. English spoken. Excellent breakfast with real coffee. A little expensive. Recommended.

B Hostal O'Higgins, O'Higgins 1205, T061-227999. With bath and breakfast, very clean. **E** per person with shared bath.

B Hostal Rubio, España 640, T061-226458, www. Hostalrubio.cl. Small rooms with bath, parking, laundry facilities, helpful. Tours and transport arranged.

B-C Hostal al Fin del Mundo, O'Higgins 1026, T061-710185, www.alfindelmundo.cl. **E** singles. With breakfast. Bright cosy and friendly. Shared baths, central, helpful, laundry service, book exchange, internet, English spoken, helpful, recommended.

B-C Hostal Green House, Angamos 1146, T061-227939, www.hostalgreenhouse.cl. Friendly hostel run by Christina, an anthropologist and Mario, a psychologist. Kitchen facilities, laundry, internet. German and a little English spoken. If Mario is in the mood he will get out his bagpipes! Recommended.

B-C Hostal ParedISo, Angamos 1073, T061-224212. **C-E** singles. Decent rooms with cable TV and heating, with or without bath (some cheaper rooms have no window). Good breakfast, parking, use of kitchen. Friendly, basic information given, some English spoken. Recommended.

B-C The Pink House, Caupolicán 99, T061-222436,pinkhous@ctcinternet.cl. **E** singles. Impeccable rooms with or without bath, breakfast included. Pickup from bus station. English spoken, internet, recommended.

C Hostal Dinka's House, Caupolicán 169, T061-226056, www.dinkashouse.cl. With bath, breakfast, use of kitchen, laundry.

C Hostal Luna, O'Higgins 424, T061-221764, elbosque@patagonia.com. Breakfast included, use of kitchen, laundry facilities; dorm beds available, **F**.

C Hostal Magallanes, Sanhueza 933, T061-221035. **E** singles. With or without bath, clean, heating, modern.

C Residencial Central 1, España 247, T061-222315, r.central@ctcinternet.cl. Comfortable rooms with or without bath. Also at Sanhueza 185, T061-222845.

C Ritz, Pedro Montt 1102, T061-224422. **D** singles. All rooms with shared bathrooms. Breakfast extra. Old, clean and cosy and with a kind of run-down charm. Recommended. (Bruce Chatwin stayed here: check out his name in the guest book.)

C-D Aikén, Errázuriz 612, T061-222629, www.aiken.cl. **F** per person in dorms. Good beds with duvets. Some rooms with view. Large bathrooms, internet, TV lounge, heating, kitchen facilities, friendly, English spoken.

D Backpackers Paradise, Carrera Pinto 1022, T061-240104, backpackersparadise@hotmail.com. **F-G** per person in basic dormitories. Fun cheap backpackers' with cooking facilities, limited bathroom facilities, lots of info, good meeting place, luggage store, internet, laundry service, little privacy, book exchange. Expensive bike rental. Recommended.

D Hospedaje Costanera, Correa 1221, T061-240175. **F** singles. Kitchen facilities, large breakfast, friendly, clean.

D Hospedaje Miramar, Almte Senoret 1190, T061-215446. **G** per person in dorms. Slightly exotic location on the edge of the red-light district. Friendly staff, good views over the bay. Breakfast extra.

D Hospedaje Nena, Boliviana 366, T061-242411, mrivera@aim.cl. **F** singles, with large breakfast. Friendly.

D Hospedaje Quo Vadis, Paraguaya 150, T061-247687. **F** singles. Motorcycle parking, meals, safe, quiet. Recommended.

D **Residencial Roca**, Magallanes 888, piso 2, T061-243903, franruiz@entelchile.net. F singles. More expensive with bath. Clean.

E **Hostal Independencia**, Independencia 374, T061-227572, www.chileaustral.com/independencia. F-G per person in shared rooms. Friendly, small basic rooms. Breakfast extra, kitchen facilities, laundry service, internet, bike rental and cheap camping. Also *cabañas* away from the centre. Good value. Recommended.

● Eating

Punta Arenas *p437, map p437*
Visitors to Punta Arenas and the surrounding region should be especially wary of eating shellfish. In recent years, the nearby waters have been sporadically affected by a *marea roja* (red tide) of poisonous algae. While the *marea roja* only affects bivalve shellfish, infected molluscs can kill humans almost instantly. Mussels should not be picked along the shore of Punta Arenas; foreigners who have done this have died. However, all shellfish sold in restaurants have been inspected and so are theoretically safe.

Lobster has become more expensive and there are seasonal bans on *centolla* (king crab) fishing to protect dwindling stocks; do not purchase *centolla* out of season. *Centolla* fishing is banned at other times, too, if the crabs become infected with a disease that is fatal to humans.

Many eateries are closed on here on Sun.
🍴🍴🍴 **Remezón**, 21 de Mayo 1469, T061-241029, www.patagoniasalvaje.net. Regional specialities such as krill. Very good, and so it should be given the exorbitant prices.
🍴🍴🍴-🍴🍴 **Centro Español**, Plaza Muñoz Gamero 771, above Teatro Cervantes. Large helpings, limited selection, quite expensive. Decent lunch menu.
🍴🍴🍴-🍴🍴 **El Estribo**, Carrera Pinto 762, T061-244714. Specializes in local and exotic dishes such as guanaco.
🍴🍴🍴-🍴🍴 **Sotitos**, O'Higgins 1138. Good service and excellent cuisine. Elegant, expensive. Recommended.
🍴🍴🍴-🍴🍴 **Tierra del Fuego** and **José Nogueira** hotels have good restaurants (see Sleeping).
🍴🍴 **Damiana Elena**, O'Higgins 694, T061-222818. Stylish restaurant serving Mediterranean food with a Patagonian touch. Popular with locals. Advance booking essential at weekends.
🍴🍴 **Golden Dragon**, Señoret 908. Slightly upmarket chinese with views.
🍴🍴 **La Luna**, O'Higgins 1017, T061-228555. Fish and shellfish including local specialities, huge *pisco sours*, lively atmosphere.
🍴🍴 **La Marmite**, Plaza Sampaio. Intimate restaurant decorated in desert pastel colours. Self-styled 'mestizo' restaurant – regional food with an international touch. Friendly service. Good value for Punta Arenas.
🍴🍴 **Parrilla Los Ganaderos**, Bulnes 0977, T061-222818. Best place for spit-roast lamb. It's a long walk past the hippodrome from the town centre. Take a taxi or a *colectivo* going towards the Zona Franca.
🍴🍴 **Puerto Viejo**, O'Higgins 1205, T061-225296. By the port. The most traditional of the seafood restaurants. Slightly tacky decor and surprisingly no views considering its location. Overattentive waiters used to cruise ship clientele speak comedy pigeon English.
🍴🍴 **Santino**, Colón 657, T061-220511. Good pizzas, large bar, good service.
🍴 **Calypso**, Bories 817. Open Sun evening, busy at night, smoky, cheap.
🍴 **Carioca**, Menéndez 600 y Chiloé. Cheap lunches, snacks and beer, good service.
🍴 **Cocinerías**, Lautaro Navarro, south of the port entrance. Stalls serving cheap fish meals.
🍴 **Dino's Pizza**, Bories 557. Good pizzas, huge sandwiches. For something different, try the rhubarb juice. Recommended.
🍴 **El Quijote**, Lautaro Navarro 1087, T061-241225. Good burgers, sandwiches and fish dishes. Good value set lunch. Recommended.
🍴 **La Terraza**, 21 de Mayo 1288. Sandwiches, *empanadas* and beer, cheap and good.
🍴 **Lomit's**, Menéndez 722. A Punta Arenas fast food institution serving cheap snacks and drinks, open when the others are closed, always busy, recommended.
🍴 **Los Años 60 The Mitchel**, Chiloé 1231. One of several along this strip serving economic set lunches.
🍴 **Restaurant de Turismo Punta Arenas**, Chiloé 1280. Good, friendly. Recommended. Also serves beer and 26 varieties of sandwiches, open 24 hrs.
🍴 **Sabores de Chiloé**, Chiloé esq Balmaceda. Chilote food as the name implies.

Cafés

Café 1900, Tierra del Fuego hotel, Colón 716. See Sleeping.

Casa del Pastel, Carrera Pinto y O'Higgins. Very good pastries.

Chocolatta, Bories 852. Probably the best coffee in town.

Coffeenet, Waldo Seguel 670. Proper internet café serving espresso.

Entre Fierros, Roca 875, T061-223436. Small diner that by all accounts has remained unchanged since the 1950s. It is famous for its banana milkshakes and tiny *choripan* (spicy sausage-meat sandwiches). Open until 1900.

La Espiga, Errázuriz 632. Bread, pastries and snacks.

Pancal, 21 de Mayo 1280. Excellent *empanadas*, bread and pastries.

🕪 Bars and clubs

Punta Arenas *p437, map p437*

Be aware that anywhere that calls itself a 'nightclub' is in fact a brothel.

Bar Lunaticos, 21 de Mayo 1262. A dive.

Kamikaze, Bories 655. Disco.

La Taberna del Club de la Unión, Plaza Muñoz Gamero y Seguel. Atmospheric pub in the basement of the **Nogueira** hotel, smoky.

Olijoe, Errázuriz 970. Reasonably plush British-style pub, leather interior, recommended.

Pub 1900, Av Colón esq Bories. Friendly, relaxed atmosphere.

🕸 Festivals and events

Punta Arenas *p437, map p437*

Feb Muestra custumbrista de Chiloe, when the Chilote community celebrates its culture.

21 Jun Carnaval de invierno is the winter solstice marked by a carnival on the weekend closest to 21 Jun.

🅾 Shopping

Punta Arenas *p437, map p437*

Zona Franca, 3½ km north of the centre, on the right-hand side of the road to the airport, take bus E or A from Plaza Muñoz Gamero or a *colectivo*. Punta Arenas has certain free-port facilities. Cheap perfume and

electrical goods are especially worth seeking out, as is camping equipment and cameras. The quality of most other goods is low and the prices little better than elsewhere. Open Mon-Sat 1000-1230, 1500-2000.

Handicrafts and local products

Punta Arenas is famous for the quality of its chocolate. Delicious handmade chocolate is for sale at several shops on Calle Bories.

Artesanía Ramas, Independencia 799. A wide selection of handicrafts.

Casa Diaz, Bories 712/546. Handicrafts.

Chile Típico, Carrera Pinto 1015, T061-225827. Chilean souvenirs

Chocolates Norweisser, Carrera 663. Good chocolate factory.

Patagonia Gourmet, Mejicana 608. Local marmalades and other specialities.

Pingüi, Bories 404. Crafts and books on Tierra del Fuego, Patagonia and Antarctica.

Sports Nativa, Colón 614. Camping and Skiing equipment.

The North Face, Bories 887. Outdoor gear.

The Wool House Patagonia, Fagnano 675, by the plaza. Good quality, reasonably priced woollen clothes.

Supermarkets

Abu Gosch, between Magallanes and Bories north of Carrera Pinto.

Cofrima, Lautaro Navarro 1293 y Balmaceda.

Cofrima 2, España 01375.

Listo, 21 de Mayo 1133.

Marisol, Zenteno 0164.

Super Norte, Salvador Allende y Chorillos.

🔺 Activities and tours

Punta Arenas *p437, map p437*

Golf

There's a 9-hole golf course 5 km south of town on the road to Fuerte Bulnes.

Skiing

Cerro Mirador, 9 km west of Punta Arenas in the Reserva Nacional Magallanes, is one of the few places in the world where you can ski with a sea view. Season Jun to Sep, weather permitting. Daily lift-ticket, US$11; equipment rental, US$9 per adult. There's a mid-way lodge with food, drink and equipment. For crosscountry skiing facilities, contact the **Club Andino**, T061-241479, www.clubandino.tierra.cl. However, the ski centre is often closed due to lack of snow. There's also a good 2-hr hike here in summer; the trail is clearly marked and flora is labelled. Skiing is also available at **Tres Morros**.

Tour operators

Most organize tours to Torres del Paine, Fuerte Bulnes and *pingüineras* on Otway sound. Several also offer bespoke tours: shop around as prices vary. Specify in advance if you want a tour in English. There are many more tour operators than these listed. For more information ask at the Sernatur office.
Arka Patagonia, Magallanes 345, T061-248167, www.arkapatagonia.com. All types of tours, rafting, fishing, etc.
International Tours & Travel, LAN GSA, PO Box 408 Stanley, F1QQ 1ZZ, T+500-22041, www.falklandstravel.com. LanChile agents on the Falkland Islands and organizes tailor-made and special-interest tours.
Kayak Tour, T061-240028, www.kayak tour.cl. Kayak tours in the Magellan Straights.
Pali Alke, Lautaro Navarro 1125, T061-229388, www.turismopaliaike.com. Wide range of tours including horse riding trips.
Sandy Point, Lautaro Navarro 975, T061-222241, www.sandypoint.cl. Offers transport to Seno Otway and Fuerte Bulnes with or without guide. Also has airport shuttlebuses that will pick you up from your lodgings, US$5.
Turismo Aonikenk, Magallanes 619, T061-221982, www.aonikenk.com. Expensive but very good bespoke excursions. Recommended.
Turismo Aventour, Nogueira 1255, T061-241197, www.aventourpatagonia.com.

English spoken, specializes in fishing trips and organizes tours to Tierra del Fuego.
Turismo Comapa, Magallanes 990, T061-200200, www.comapa.com. Tours to Torres del Paine, Tierra del Fuego and Isla Magdalena, also agents for trips to the Falklands/Malvinas, Ushuaia and Cape Horn.
Turismo Pehoé, Menéndez 918, T061-241373, www.pehoe.com. Organizes tours and hotels; enquire here about catamaran services.
Turismo Renta Club Internacional, Carrera Pinto 1142, T061-223371. Cycle hire, US$2 per hr.
Turismo Viento Sur, Fagnano 585, T061-226930, www.vientosur.com. For camping equipment, fishing excursions, sea kayaking, cycle hire, English spoken, good tours.

⊖ Transport

Punta Arenas *p437, map p437*
All transport is heavily booked from late Dec through to Mar; advance booking is advised.

Air
Airline offices Aerovías DAP, O'Higgins 891, T061-223340, www. dap.cl, 0900-1230, 1430-1930; **LanChile**, Bories 884, T600-5262000, www.lan.cl, **Sky Airline**, Roca 933, www.skyairline.cl, **Aerolíneas del Sur**, Fagnano 817.

Flights arrive at **Carlos Ibáñez del Campo Airport**, 20 km north of town.
Local To Balmaceda (for Coyhaique), with LanChile (LanExpress), daily in summer, US$80, otherwise 1 a week or daily via Puerto Montt (more expensive). To **Puerto**

Montt, with **LanChile** (LanExpress), **Aerolíneas del Sur** and **Sky Airline**, 10 daily, from US$160 return. Cheapest one-way tickets with **Aerolíneas del Sur**. To **Santiago**, LanChile (LanExpress), Aerolíneas del Sur and Sky Airline several daily, from US$200 return, via Puerto Montt (sit on the right for views). To **Porvenir**, Aerovías DAP, 2 daily Mon-Sat, US$26 one way, plus other irregular flights, with Twin-Otter and Cessna aircraft. To **Puerto Williams**, Aerovías DAP, daily in summer, US$70 one way.

Long distance To **Ushuaia** (Argentina), Lan Chile, 3 weekly in summer, 1 hr, US$140 one way; reserve well in advance from mid-Dec to Feb. To **Falkland Islands/Islas Malvinas**, LanChile, Sat, US$500 return. **International Tours & Travel**, T+500-22041, www.falklandstravel.com (see Tour operators, above, serves as **LanChile** agents on the Falkland Islands.

Bike and motorbike
Bike parts from **José Aguila Quezada**, Arauco 2675, T061-265399. Motorbike parts from **Violic**, Sanhueza 285, T061-241606, also in the Zona Franca.

Bus
Buses depart from the company offices as follows: **Bus Sur**, Menéndez 565 T061-227145, www.bus-sur.cl; **Buses Sur**, Menéndez 552; **Buses Transfer**, Pedro Montt 966, T061-229613; **Cruz del Sur**, Pingüino and **Fernández**, Sanhueza 745, T061-242313, www.busesfernandez.com; **Gesell**, Menéndez 556, T061-222896; **Ghisoni**, Lautaro Navarro 971, T061-222078, www.ghisoni.terra.cl; **Los Carlos**, Plaza Muñoz Gamero 1039, T061-241321; **Pacheco**, Colón 900, T061-242174, www.busespacheco.com.

Services and frequencies change every year, so check on arrival at the helpful Sernatur office. Timetables are also printed daily in *El Austral*. The services detailed below are for high season only.

Fernández, **Transfer** (cheapest), **Buses Pacheco** and **Buses Sur**, all run several services each day to **Puerto Natales**, 3 hrs, last departure 2000, US$6 one way, US$10.50 return (although this means you have to return with the same company). Buses may pick up at the airport with advance notice.

To **Coyhaique**, 20 hrs, Buses Sur, 1 per week via Argentina, US$55, meals not included. **Cruz del Sur**, **Queilen Bus** and Pacheco have services through Argentina to **Osorno**, **Puerto Montt** and **Castro**, several weekly, 36 hrs to Castro, US$60.

To Argentina To **Río Gallegos**, Pingüino, departs 1245 daily, returns 1300; **Ghisoni**, 4 weekly, departs 1100; **Pacheco**, 5 weekly, departs 1130. All cost US$14 and take about 5 hrs. For services to **Buenos Aires** it is cheaper to go to Río Gallegos and buy an onward ticket from there. **Pacheco** and Ghisoni have buses most days to **Río Grande** via Punta Delgada, 8hrs, US$25, heavily booked. To **Ushuaia** via Punta Delgada, 12-14 hrs, book any return at same time, **Tecni Austral**, Tue, Thu, Sat, Sun 0800 from Ghisoni office, US$34; **Pacheco**, Mon, Wed, Fri 0715, US$46.

Car
Car hire Try looking in the local newspaper for special deals and bargain if you want to hire a car for several days. **Autómovil Club**, O'Higgins 931, T061-243675, F243097, and at the airport; **Budget**, O'Higgins 964, T061-241696; **Econorent**, at the airport, T02-2997103; **EMSA**, Roca 1044, and at the airport, T061-241182, www.emsarentacar.cl. Avis agents; **Hertz**, O'Higgins 987, T061-229049, F244729, English spoken; also at airport T061-210096; **Internacional**, Seguel 443 and at the airport, T061-228323, F226334, recommended; **Lotus Rentacar**, Mejicana 694, T061-241697, F241697; **Lubac**, Magallanes 970, T/F061-242023; **Magallanes Rent a Car**, O'Higgins 949, T/F061-221601; **Payne Rent a Car**, Menéndez 631, T061-240852, payne@ctcinternet.cl, try bargaining, friendly; **Todoauto**, España 0480, T061-212492, F212627; **Willemsen**, Lautaro Navarro 1038, T061-247787, F241083, recommended.

Car mechanic Automotriz Hoopers, Boliviana y Chiloé, T061-241239; **Centro automotriz Crisostomo**, Independencia 377, T061-243731.

Ferry
All tickets on ships must be booked in advance for Jan and Feb. Visits to the beautiful fjords and glaciers of **Tierra del**

Fuego are highly recommended. **Comapa** (Compañía Marítima de Punta Arenas), Magallanes 990, T061-200200, runs a fortnightly 22-hr, 320-km round trip to the 30-km fjord d'Agostino, where many glaciers descend to the sea. The luxury cruiser, *Terra Australis*, sails from Punta Arenas on Sat via Ushuaia and Puerto Williams; details from Comapa. **Navimag**, Magallanes 990, T061-244400, www.navimag.cl, is another operator. Advance bookings (advisable) from **Cruceros Australis SA**, Miraflores 178, piso 12, Santiago, T02-6963211, www.australis.com.

Government supply ships are only recommended for the young and hardy, but take a sleeping bag, extra food and travel pills. For transport on navy supply ships to **Puerto Williams** and **Cape Horn**, enquire at **Tercera Zona Naval**, Lautaro Navarro 1150, but be prepared to be frustrated by irregular sailings (about 1 every 3 months) and inaccurate information. You will almost certainly also need a letter of recommendation. During the voyage across the Drake Passage, albatrosses, petrels, cormorants, penguins, elephant seals, fur seals, whales and dolphins can all be sighted. Most cruise ships to **Antarctica** leave from Ushuaia (Argentina). However, there are a few operators based in Punta Arenas. Try **Antarctic Dream Shipping**, Roca 1016, T061-223676, www.antarctic.cl, or **Antarctica XXI**, Lautaro Navarro 987, Piso 2, T061-228783, www.antarcticaxxi.com.

Taxi
Ordinary taxis have yellow roofs. Reliable service is available from **Radio Alce vip**, T061-710889, and **Taxi Austral**, T061-247710/244409. *Colectivos* (all black) run on fixed routes within the city, US$0.60 for anywhere on the route.

⊙ Directory

Punta Arenas *p437, map p437*
Banks Several on or around Plaza Muñoz Gamero many 24 hrs, all have ATMs. Banks open Mon-Fri 0830-1400, casas de cambio open Mon-Fri 0900-1230, 1500-1900, Sat

0900-1230; outside business hours, try **Buses Sur** (see above), or the major hotels (lower rates); Argentine pesos can be bought at casas de cambio; good rates at **Cambio Gasic**, Roca 915, Of 8, T061-242396. German spoken; **La Hermandad**, Lautaro Navarro 1099, T061-243991, excellent rates, US$ cash for AmEx TCs and credit cards; **Scott Cambios**, Colón y Magallanes, T061-227145; **Sur Cambios**, Lautaro Navarro 1001, T061-225656, accepts Tcs.
Consulates Argentina, 21 de Mayo 1878, T061-261912, open weekdays 1000-1530, visas take 24 hrs; Brazil, Arauco 769, T061-241093; Belgium, Roca 817, Oficina 61, T061-241472; Germany, Pasaje Korner 1046, T061-241082, Casilla 229; Italy, 21 de Mayo 1569, T061-221596; Netherlands, Magallanes 435, T061-248100; Norway, Magallanes 990, T061-241437; Spain, Menéndez 910, T061-243566; Paraguay, Bulnes 0928 Dp14 piso 1, T061-211825; Sweden, Errázuriz 891, T061-224107; UK, Cataratas de Niaguara 01325, T061-211535, helpful, with information on Falkland Islands; Uruguay, José Nogueira 1238, T061-241594.
Dentists Dr Hugo Vera Cárcamo, España 1518, T061-227510, recommended; Rosemary Robertson Stipicic, 21 de Mayo 1380, T061-22931, speaks English.
Hospitals Hospital Regional Lautaro Navarro, Angamos 180, T061-244040, public hospital, for emergency room ask for 'la posta'; Clínica Magallanes, Bulnes 01448, T061-211527, private clinic, medical staff the same as in the hospital but fancier surroundings and more expensive; minimum charge US$45 per visit. A list of English-speaking doctors is available from Sernatur.
Internet Lots of places offer access, including at Magallanes y Menendez, and below Hostal Calafate on Magallanes, ½ block north of Plaza. Prices are generally US$1 per hr. **Laundry** Lavaseco Josseau, Carrera Pinto 766; Lavasol, O'Higgins 969, the only self-service laundry, Mon-Sat 0900-2030, Sun (summer only) 1000-1800, US$6 per machine, wash and dry, good but busy. **Post office** Bories 911 y Menéndez, Mon-Fri 0830-1930, Sat 0900-1400.

Puerto Natales and around

→ *Colour map 6, B3. Population 17,000.*

From Punta Arenas a good paved road runs 247 km north to Puerto Natales through forests of southern beech and prime pastureland; this is the best area for cattle and sheep-raising in Chile. Ñandúes and guanacos can often be seen en route. Puerto Natales lies between Cerro Dorotea (which rises behind the town) and the eastern shore of the Seno Ultima Esperanza (Last Hope Sound), over which there are fine views, weather permitting, to the Peninsula Antonio Varas. Founded in 1911, the town grew as an industrial centre and, until recent years, the town's prosperity was based upon employment in the coal mines of Río Turbio, Argentina. Today, Puerto Natales is the starting point for trips to the magnificent Balmaceda (see page 451) and Torres del

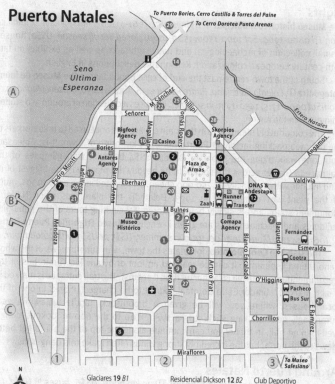

Puerto Natales

To Puerto Bories, Cerro Castillo & Torres del Paine
To Cerro Dorotea Punta Arenas

Seno Ultima Esperanza

N
0 metres 100
0 yards 100

Sleeping
Aquaterra 17 *B2*
Blanquita 1 *B2*
Casa Cecilia 3 *A2*
Casa Teresa 23 *B2*
Charles Darwin 21 *B1*
Costaustralis 5 *B1*
El Refugio 18 *C2*
Glaciares 19 *B1*
Hospedaje Chila 6 *C2*
Hospedaje Nancy 24 *C3*
Hostal Bulnes 2 *B2*
Hostal Sir Francis
  Drake 25 *A2*
Hostel Natales 26 *B1*
Indigo Patagonia 4 *B1*
Juan Ladrilleros 8 *A1*
Lady Florence Dixie 7 *B3*
Los Inmigrantes 9 *C2*
Martín Gusinde 10 *A2*
Natalino 20 *B2*
Patagonia Adventure 11 *B2*
Residencial Dickson 12 *B2*
Residencial
  El Mundial 13 *B2*
Residencial
  Gabriela 14 *B2*
Residencial La Florida 27 *C2*
Residencial Niko's 15 *C3*
Residencial Niko's II 28 *A2*
Residencial Oasis 22 *A2*
Weskar Ecolodge 29 *A2*

Eating
Andrés 1 *B1*
Angelicas 3 *B3*
Club Deportivo
  Natales 4 *B2*
Cristal 5 *B2*
El Asador Patagónico 9 *B2*
El Living 6 *B2*
El Marítimo 7 *B1*
El Rincón de Don Chicho 8
La Casa de Pepe 2 *B2*
La Mesita Grande 11 *B2*
La Oveja Negra 2 *B2*
La Repizza 12 *B3*
La Ultima Esperanza 10 *B2*
Masay 5 *B2*
Parrilla Don Jorge 13 *A2*

Paine national parks (see page 456), and tourism is one of its most important industries; the town centre has a prosperous if somewhat touristy atmosphere. ▸▸ *For Sleeping, eating and other listings see pages 451-456.*

Ins and outs

Getting there Puerto Natales is easily reached by many daily buses from Punta Arenas, as well as by daily buses from Río Turbio (Argentina) and El Calafate. There are also two buses weekly from Río Gallegos. The town is the terminus of the **Navimag** ship to Puerto Montt. If driving between Punta Arenas and Puerto Natales make sure you have enough fuel. ▸▸ *For further details see Transport, page 455.*

Getting around Puerto Natales is small; taxis needed only for journeys out of town.

Tourist office There is a kiosk on the waterfront ⓘ *Av Pedro Montt y Phillipi, T061-412125*; information is also available from the **Municipalidad** ⓘ *Bulnes 285, T061-411263*, and from **CONAF** ⓘ *O'Higgins 584*.

Sights

The **Museo historico municipal** ⓘ *Bulnes 285, T061-411263, museonat@123mail.cl, Mon-Fri 0800-1900, Sat 1000-1300, 1500-1900, closed Sat off season, US$2*, houses a small collection of archaeological and native artefacts as well as exhibits on late 19th-century European colonization. Reasonable descriptions in English.

South of the town centre past the end of calle Baquedano is the **Museo de fauna patagonica** ⓘ *Colegio Salesiano, Padre Rossa 1456, T061-411258, museo@fagnano.cl, Mon-Sat 0900-1315, 1430-1930 in summer*. It houses a collection of around 350 stuffed animals from the region.

The colourful old steam train in the main square was once used to take workers to the the the meatpacking factory at **Puerto Bories**, 5 km north of town. It is a pleasant hour-long walk along the shore to Bories (US$4 by taxi), with glimpses of the Balmaceda Glacier across the sound. In its heyday the plant was the biggest of its kind in Chile with a capacity for 250,000 sheep. Bankrupted in the early 1990s, much of the plant was dismantled in 1993. Belatedly the plant was given National Monument status and is slowly being restored. Fascinating tours of the remaining buildings and machine rooms are given in English. **Museo Frigorífico Puerto Bories** ⓘ *T061-414328, Mon-Sun 1000-1900 in summer, US$5 or US$7 with guided tour*.

The slab-like **Cerro Dorotea** dominates the town, with superb views of the whole Seno Ultima Esperanza. It can be reached on foot or by any Río Turbio bus or taxi (recommended, as the hill is farther off than it seems). The trail entrance is marked by a sign marked 'Mirador Cerro Dorotea'. Expect to be charged US$5-8 in one of the local houses, where you will be given a broomstick handle which makes a surprisingly good walking stick. It is a 1½-trek up to the 600 m lookout along a well-marked trail. In theory you can continue along the top of the hill to get better views to the north, but the incredibly strong winds often make this dangerous.

Around Puerto Natales

Monumento Nacional Cueva Milodón ⓘ *25 km north, US$6, buses JB US$7, taxi US$24 return. Most Torres del Paine tours stop at the cave.*
This is the end point of Bruce Chatwin's travelogue *In Patagonia* (see page 559). The cave, a massive 70 m wide, 220 m deep and 30 m high, contains a plastic model of the prehistoric ground-sloth whose remains were found there in 1895. The remains are now in London, although there is talk of returning them to the site. Evidence has also been found here of occupation by Patagonians some 11,000 years ago. Nearby, a visitors' centre has summaries in English. There's also a restaurant.

Estancia Rosario ⓘ *T061-411273, estancia_rosario@hotmail.com, US$50 for a full day including transport across the sound.*

On the Peninsula Antonio Varas, on the western side of the Seno Ultima Esperanza, is this *estancia* offering lunches, horse riding and other activities. Book in advance.

Parque Nacional Bernardo O'Higgins Often referred to as the **Parque Nacional Monte Balmaceda,** this park covers much of the Campo de Hielo Sur, plus the fjords and offshore islands further west. A three-hour boat trip from Puerto Natales up the Seno de Ultima Esperanza takes you to the southernmost section, passing the Balmaceda Glacier, which drops from the eastern slopes of **Monte Balmaceda** (2035 m). The glacier is retreating; in 1986 its foot was at sea level. The boat docks further north at **Puerto Toro**, from where it is a kilometre walk to the base of the Serrano Glacier on the north slope of Monte Balmaceda. On the trip, dolphins, sea lions (in season), black-necked swans, flightless steamer ducks and cormorants can be seen. Take warm clothes, including a hat and gloves.

There is a route from Puerto Toro along the Río Serrano for 35 km to the Torres del Paine administration centre (see page 457); guided tours are available. It is also possible to travel to the Paine administration centre by boat or zodiac (4 hrs, US$60).

⬤ Sleeping

Puerto Natales *p449, map p449*
Most prices include breakfast. Hotels in the countryside are open only in the summer months; specific dates vary. In season, cheaper accommodation fills up quickly after the arrival of the Navimag ferry from Puerto Montt. Most of the more expensive hotels are much of a muchness give or take the view. Occasionally one of these will have a special offer. Call round for quotes.
LL Costaustralis, Pedro Montt 262, T061-412000, www.costaustralis.com. The most expensive hotel in town. No better than the other big hotels. In effect you are paying for the view, which, to be fair, is the best there is. The rooms facing inland are an expensive waste.
LL Indigo Patagonia, Ladrilleros 105, T061-413609, www.indigopatagonia.com. C singles. Old 3-storey house on the waterfront with fantastic views, recently

expanded and converted into a boutique hotel, together with restaurant (open to the public) and roof-top spa.
L Charles Darwin, Bulnes 90, T061-412478, www.hotelcharlesdarwin.com. Newly refurbished comfortable 3-star standard. Some rooms with partial views. Permanently empty restaurant downstairs.
L-AL Juan Ladrilleros, Pedro Montt 161, T061-411652, afv@entelchile.net. Small basic rooms with great views. With bath, but no TV. Often willing to give discounts on the rack price.
AL Aquaterra, Bulnes 299, T061-412239, www.aquaterrapatagonia.cl Understated design. No frills but thought and effort have gone into it. Not cheap, but unlike many other places in the same price bracket you get the feeling that the staff are there to help and are able to answer any question you might have.

The Far South Puerto Natales & around Listings

Living room upstairs and a resto-bar downstairs. Alternative therapies also offered.

AL Glaciares, Eberhard 104, T061-411452, www.hotelglaciares.co.cl. Another standard 3-star. Comfortable enough and some rooms have a partial view. Good day tours to Torres del Paine.

AL Lady Florence Dixie, Bulnes 655, T061-411158, www.chileanpatagonia.com/florence. 3-star. The standard rooms are a bit cramped and cold, but the superior rooms are bigger, carpeted and reasonable value.

AL Martín Gusinde, Bories 278, T061-412770, www.austrohoteles.cl. Comfy 3-star, although the carpets could do with a change. Good value rates off season.

AL Weskar Ecolodge, Km 1, road to Bories, T061-414168, www.weskar.cl. Quiet lodge overlooking the bay, understated wooden interior. Most rooms with extensive views. There is a restaurant for guests and bike rental. A good out-of-town place to relax.

A Hostal Sir Francis Drake, Phillipi 383, T061-411553, www.chileaustral.com/francisdrake. Simple, smallish but comfortable rooms with bath and cable TV. There is a pleasant living room on the upper floor with views. Recommended.

A Hostel Natales, Ladrilleros 209, T061-411081, www.hostelnatales.cl. **D** per person in dorms. All rooms with bath. Formerly a decent hotel converted into a luxury hostel. The place has been fully refurbished and is very comfortable, if overpriced.

B Residencial Oasis, Señoret 332, resoasis@hotmail. com. Comfortable rooms, with or without bath, cable TV. Breakfast included. Some rooms have no window.

B-C Casa Cecilia, Tomás Rogers 60, T061-411797, www.casaceciliahostal.com. **E** singles. With good breakfast, some rooms with bath, clean, cooking facilities, English, French and German spoken, heating, luggage store, camping equipment rental, information on Torres del Paine, tours organized, bus tickets sold, credit cards accepted. Better value in US dollars. Warmly recommended.

B-C Hostal Bulnes, Bulnes 407, T061-411307, www.hostalbulnes.com. With breakfast, some rooms with bath, laundry facilities, luggage store.

C Blanquita, Carrera Pinto 409, T061-411674. **E** singles. Basic quiet hotel that looks like a giant portacabin. With bath, heating and breakfast, friendly. Recommended.

C Natalino, Eberhard 371, T061-411968. Clean and very friendly. Rooms with bath and breakfast, parking.

C Patagonia Adventure, Tomás Rogers 179, T061-411028, www.apatagonia.com. **F** per person in dorms. Friendly, clean, English spoken, camping equipment for hire, luggage store, book exchange. Good bike and kayak tours offered. Also a general agent selling trips to Torres del Paine. Breakfast is served in the café annex. Recommended.

C-D Residencial Niko's II, Phillipi 528, T061-411500, residencialnicosii@hotmail.com. With good breakfast. Some rooms with bath and cable TV, English spoken, tours, tent hire, book exchange.

D Casa Teresa, Esmeralda 463, T061-410472, freepatagonia@hotmail.com. **F** singles. Good value, warm, cheap meals, quiet, friendly. Tours to Torres del Paine arranged. Recommended.

D El Refugio, O'Higgins 456, T061-414881. **F** singles. Youthful and lively place to stay. Offers tours. Internet access.

D Hospedaje Chila, Carrera Pinto 442, T061-412328. **F** singles. Use of kitchen, welcoming, laundry facilities, luggage store, bakes bread. Recommended.

D Hospedaje Laury, Bulnes 222. **F** Singles. With breakfast, cooking, laundry facilities, clean, warm, friendly.

D Hospedaje Nancy, E Ramírez 540, T061-4510022, www.nataleslodge.cl. **F** singles. Cooking facilities, internet access, laundry service, helpful, tours and lots of information. Good budget option. Recommended.

D Los Inmigrantes, Carrera Pinto 480, T061-413482, losinmigrantes@hotmail.com. **F** singles. Good breakfast, clean, kitchen facilities, equipment rental, luggage store. Recommended.

D Residencial Asturias, Prat 426, T061-412105. **F** singles, breakfast, kitchen facilities, cosy.

D Residencial Centro, Magallanes 258, T061-411996. **F** singles, with bath.

D Residencial Dickson, Bulnes 307, T061-411871, lodging@chilaustral.com. **F** singles. Good breakfast, clean, helpful, cooking and laundry facilities, internet. Recommended.

D Residencial El Mundial, Bories 315, T061-412476, omar@fortalezapatagonia.cl.

F singles. Some rooms with bath. Use of kitchen (if the owners are not using it), good value meals, luggage stored. Recommended.

D Residencial Gabriela, Bulnes 317, T061-411061. F singles. Clean, good breakfast, helpful, luggage store, heating. Recommended.

D Residencial La Florida, O'Higgins 431, T061-411361. F singles. Luggage store, laundry.

D Residencial Lago Pingo, Bulnes 808, T061-411026. F singles. Basic, with breakfast, laundry, use of kitchen, luggage stored, English spoken; similar at O'Higgins 70, 431 and Perito 443.

D Residencial Niko's, Ramírez 669, T061-412810, nikoresidencial@hotmail.com. F singles. With breakfast, basic rooms, some rooms with bath, good meals, also dormitory accommodation, recommended.

D Residencial Ritz, Carrera Pinto 439, T061-412196. F singles. Full board available, friendly.

D Residencial Sutherland, Barros Arana 155, T061-410359. F singles. With bath, welcoming, clean, kitchen facilities.

D Tierra del Fuego, Bulnes 23, T061-412138. F singles. Clean, parking, will store luggage, good.

Around Puerto Natales *p450*
Parque Nacional Bernado O'Higgins
L Hostería Monte Balmaceda, T061-220174. Although the park is uninhabited, guest accommodation is available here.

Road from Punta Arenas
L Hostal Río Penitente, Km 138, T061-331694. In an old *estancia*. Recommended.
AL Hostería Río Verde, Km 90, east off the highway on Seno Skyring, T061-311122. Private bath, heating. Recommended.
A Hostería Llanuras de Diana, Km 215 (30 km south of Puerto Natales), T061-410661. Hidden from road, beautifully situated. Recommended.
B Hotel Rubens, Km 183, T061-226916. Popular for fishing.

North of town
L-AL Cisne de Cuello Negro, 6 km from town, Km 275 near Puerto Bories, for bookings contact Av Colón 782, Punta Arenas, T061-244506, pehoe1@ctcinternet.cl. Clean, excellent cooking. Recommended.
AL Estancia Tres Pasos, 40 km north, T061-221930, www.trespasos.cl. Simple and

beautiful lodge between Puerto Natales and Torres del Paine. Horse riding trips offered.
A Cabañas Kotenk Aike, 2 km north of town, T061-412581. Sleeps 4, modern, very comfortable, great location.

Camping
There is a campsite in town on Esmeralda y Prat with hot water and tent hire.

Eating

Puerto Natales *p449, map p449*
Angelicas, Eberhard 532, T061-410365, angelicas@rest.cl. A sign of how Puerto Natales has turned into a boutique town. Elegant Mediterranean-style restaurant originally from Santiago. Quality ingredients well prepared. Pricy but more than reasonable for Natales, and customers invariably leave satisfied. Staff can be a little flustered when the restaurant is full. Recommended.
El Asador Patagonico, Prat 158 on plaza. Specializes in spit-roast lamb. Recommended.
Parrilla Don Jorge, Bories 430 on plaza, T061-410999. Another restaurant specializing in Cordero al Palo, but also serving fish, etc. The open plan leaves you feeling a little exposed when the restaurant is not full. Decent service.
El Marítimo, Pedro Montt 214. Seafood and salmon, good views, popular.
El Rincón de Don Chicho, Luiz Cruz Martínez 206, T061-414339. All-you-can-eat *parrillada*. Vegetarian options on request. 15 mins' walk from town centre. Recommended.
La Casa de Pepe, Tomas Rogers 131 on the plaza. For those who want to sample the traditional food of central Chile – *pernil*, *pastel de choclo* etc. Uncomfortable seats.
La Caleta Economica, Eberhard 261, T061-413969. Excellent seafood, also meat and chicken dishes, large portions, good value for money.
La Mesita Grande, Prat 196 on the plaza, T061-411571, www.mesitagrande.cl. Fresh pizzas made in a wood-burning clay oven. Also pasta and good desserts. Not much atmosphere, but there's a fantastic antique till.
La Oveja Negra, Tomas Rogers 169, on the plaza. Typical Chilean dishes, book swap.

Ownership of this restaurant seems to change every year.

♔♔ La Ultima Esperanza, Eberhard 354. Recommended for salmon, seafood, huge portions, not cheap but worth it.

♔ Andrés, Ladrilleros 381. Excellent, good fish dishes, good service.

♔ Club Deportivo Natales, Eberhard 332. Very cheap, decent meals

♔ Cristal, Bulnes 439. Tasty sandwiches and salmon, good value.

♔ La Repizza, Blanco Encalada 294, T061-410361. Good-value sarnies and light meals.

♔ Masay, Bulnes 429. Cheap sandwiches.

Cafés

Aquaterra, Bulnes 299. Cosy, good, also a shiatsu and reiki centre.

Café + Books, Blanco Encalada 224. Cosy café with an extensive 2 for 1 book exchange.

El Living, on the plaza. Cosy, British run, with English newspapers and magazines. Wide variety of cakes, good tea and coffee, wine and vegetarian food. Book exchange.

Emporio de la Pampa, Eberhard 226C, T061-510520. Small café/delicatessen selling wine and local gourmet products.

Patagonia Adventure, Tomas Rogers 179 on the plaza. Opens at 0630 for early risers.

Patagonia Dulce, Barros Arana 233, T061-415285, www.patagoniadulce.cl. For the best hot chocolate in town.

◑ Bars and clubs

Puerto Natales *p449, map p449*
There are a couple of discos on Blanco Encalada.

Casino, Bories 314, T061-411834, daily 1300-0400. Modest, tables open from 2100.

El Bar de Ruperto, Bulnes 371. Good, English-run pub with a lively mix of locals and tourists. For a kick, try the chile vodka.

Kaweshkar, Eberhard 161. European style lounge bar.

Iguana, Magallanes y Eberhard. There is invariably a bar here, but it seems to change name and ownership each year.

◎ Shopping

Puerto Natales *p449, map p449*
Camping equipment
Camping gas is available in hardware stores, eg at Baquedano y O'Higgins. Wares tend to

be more expensive than the Zona Franca in Punta Arenas.

Alfgal, Barros Arana 299, T061-413622.
Balfer, Esmeralda y Baquedano.
La Maddera, Prat 297, T061-41331. Outdoor clothing.

Patagonia Adventure and **Casa Cecilia** hire out good-quality gear (see Sleeping, above). Check all equipment and prices carefully. Average charges, per day: tent US$8, sleeping bag US$4-6, mat US$2, raincoat US$1, also cooking gear US$2. Deposits sometimes required: tent US$200, sleeping bag US$100. Note that it is often difficult to hire walking boots.

Food

Food prices are variable so shop around, although everything tends to be more expensive than in Punta Arenas. There's a 24-hr supermarket on the Bulnes 300 block, and at Bulnes 1085. The town markets are also good.

Handicrafts

Ñandu, Eberhard 586. Popular craft store. Another branch at Baquedano y Chorrillos.

▲ Activities and tours

Puerto Natales *p449, map p449*
Reports of the reliability of agencies, especially for their trips to Parque Nacional Torres del Paine, are very mixed. It is better to book tours direct with operators in Puerto Natales than through agents in Punta Arenas or Santiago, where huge commissions may be charged.

Some agencies offer 1-day tours to the Perito Moreno glacier in Argentina (see page 470), 14-hr trip, 2 hrs at the glacier, US$60 excluding food and park entry fee; take US$ cash or Argentine pesos as Chilean pesos are not accepted. However, if you have more time it is better to break the trip by staying in Calafate, and organizing a tour from there.

Antares, Barros Arana 111, T061-414611, www.antarespatagonia.com. Kayaking and trekking.

Bigfoot Expediciones, Bories 206, T061-413247, www.bigfootpatagonia.com. Sea kayaking, trekking, mountaineering and ice-hiking trips on the Grey glacier. Unforgettable if expensive. Recommended.

Chile Nativo, Eberhard 230, casilla 42, T061-411835, www.chilenativo.com. Specializes in multi-day and bespoke tours of Torres del Paine and surroundings.

Comapa, Bulnes 533, T061-411300, www.comapa.cl. Large regional operator offering decent day tours to the park.

Erratic Rock, Baquedano 719, T061-410355, www.erraticrock.com. New agency offering interesting and alternative trekking routes from half a day to 2 weeks.

Estancia Travel, Casa 13B, Puerto Bories (5 km north of Puerto Natales), T061-412221, www.estanciatravel.com. English/Chilean operator offering a different way of experiencing Patagonia – on horseback. Bilingual guides and well-kept horses. Good half-day trips to the cueva del Milodón. Prices start from US$35 for 2 hrs. Multi-day trips only for the well off. Book direct or through agencies in Natales.

Fishing Patagonia, Magallanes 180, T061-410349, www.fishing-patagonia.com. Expensive fly-fishing trips.

Onas, Eberhard 595, T061-414349, www.onaspatagonia.com. Tours of Torres del Paine and kayak trips. Also trips to and from the park down the Río Serrano in zodiac boats to the Serrano glacier in the Parque Nacional Bernardo O'Higgins, and from there on the tour boats to Puerto Natales, US$90 each all inclusive. Book in advance.

Skorpios, Prat 62, T061-412409, www.skorpios.cl. Catamaran trips up to the Fjordo de las montañas. Truly spectacular close up vistas of glaciers and waterfalls given good weather. Two sailings weekly, US$130.

Sendero Aventura, Hostal Patagonia Adventure, Tomás Rogers 179, T061-415636, sendero_aventura@terra.cl. Trekking in Torres del Paine, cycle and kayak trips to the park, boats to Parque Nacional Bernado O'Higgins, camping equipment and bike hire. Recommended.

Turismo 21 de Mayo, Eberhard 554, T061-411476, www.turismo21demayo.cl. Runs boat trips to Parque Nacional Bernado O'Higgins and on to Torres del Paine in motor zodiac. This can be combined in a very long day with a trip to the park returning by bus. US$150 including park entry and food.

Turismo Runner, Eberhard 555, T061-414141, www.turismorunner.cl.

Specializes in day trips to Torres del Paine combined with a boat trip to the face of the Grey Glacier, US$150 per person including park entrance and a decent lunch at the Hostería Grey.

Turismo Zaahj, Prat 236, T061-412260. Day trips of Torre del Paine cost around US$35, excluding park entry.

Transport

Puerto Natales *p449, map p449*
Bike
Hire from **Patagonia Adventure** (see Sleeping, above). Repairs at **El Rey de la Bicicleta**, Ramírez 540; good, helpful.

Bus
Punta Arenas is served by Bus **Fernández**, Eberhard 555, T061-411111; **Bus Sur**, Baquedano 634; **Buses Sur**, Baquedano 558, T061-411325; and **Bus Transfer**, Baquedano 414, T061-421616; several daily, 3 hrs, US$4, book in advance. **Bus Sur** runs to **Coyhaique**, Mon, US$55.

To Argentina Buses Sur has 2 weekly direct services to **Río Gallegos**, US$18. Cootra runs services to **Río Turbio**, 2 hrs (depending on customs), US$5. To **Calafate**, **Buses Sur** and **Bus Zaahj** , 4½ hrs, US$19 both have daily services; **Cootra** also runs a service via Río Turbio, 7 hrs, reserve at least 1 day ahead.

Car
Hire agents can arrange permission to drive into Argentina, but this is expensive and takes 24 hrs to arrange. **Avis**, Bulnes 632, T061-410775; **Motor Cars**, Blanco 330, T061-415593, www.motorcars.cl; **Punta Alta**, Blanco 244, T061-410115, www.puntaalta.cl; **Ultima Esperanza**, Blanco Encalada 206, T061-410461. **Carlos González**, Ladrilleros entre Bories y Eberhard, is a recommended car mechanic.

Ferry
Navimag, Pedro Montt 262, Loc B, Terminal Marítimo, T061-411421, sails *Eden* every Fri in summer to **Puerto Montt**, less frequently offseason (see page 368); confirmation of reservations is advised.

The cutter *21 de Mayo* sails every morning from Puerto Natales to **Parque Nacional Bernardo O'Higgins** in summer, Sun only in the winter, US$60 per person, min 10 people. Book through **Casa Cecilia** (see Sleeping), or through **Turismo 21 de Mayo** (see Activities and tours). Lunch extra, so take own food; snacks and drinks available on board. You can combine the trip with a visit to Torres del Paine.

❶ Directory

Puerto Natales *p449, map p449*

Banks Shop around as some casas offer very poor rates (much better to change money in Punta Arenas). Banks offer poor rates for TCs, which cannot be changed into US$ cash. **Banco Santander Santiago**, Bulnes y Blanco Encalada, MasterCard and Visa, ATM; **Banco de Chile**, Bulnes 544, MasterCard and Visa, ATM; **Cambio Stop**, Baquedano 380; **Enio America**, Blanco Encalada 266, Argentine pesos can be changed here; there are two more at Bulnes 683 and 1087 (good rates, also change Argentine pesos), and others on Prat. **Internet** Concepto Indigo, Hospedaje María José (see Sleeping, above). El Rincón de Tata, Prat 236, **Patagonianet**, Blanco 330. **Laundry** Lavandería Catch, *Bories 218*, friendly service; **Servilaundry**, Bulnes 513. **Post office** Eberhard 417, Mon-Fri 0830-1230, 1430-1745, Sat 0900-1230. **Telephone** CTC, Blanco Encalada 23 y Bulnes; **Entel**, Baquedano y Bulnes, phone and fax service; **Telefonica**, Blanco Encalada y Phillipi.

Parque Nacional Torres del Paine

→ *Colour map 6, B2.*

Covering 242,242 ha, 145 km northwest of Puerto Natales, this national park is a UNESCO Biosphere Reserve and a huge, huge draw for its diverse wildlife and spectacular surroundings. Taking its name from the Tehuelche word Paine, *meaning 'blue', the park encompasses stunning scenery, with constantly changing views of peaks, glaciers and icebergs, vividly coloured lakes of turquoise, ultramarine and grey, and quiet green valleys filled with wild flowers. In the centre of the park is one of the most impressive mountain areas on earth, a granite massif from which rise oddly shaped peaks of over 2600 m, known as the* Torres *(towers) and* Cuernos *(horns) of* Paine. ▸▸ *For Sleeping, Eating and other listings, see pages 462-464.*

Ins and outs

Getting there

The most practical way to get to Torres del Paine is with one of the many bus or tour companies that leave Puerto Natales daily. If you want to drive, hiring a pickup from Punta Arenas or Puerto Natales is an economical proposition for a group (up to nine people), US$400 for four days. The road from Puerto Natales is being improved; it takes about three hours from Puerto Natales to the administration. Petrol is available at Río Serrano, but fill up in case. There is a new road being built to the south side of the park which should cut the journey time to around two hours. ▸▸ *For further details, see Transport, page 464.*

Getting around

Allow a week to 10 days to see the park properly. Most visitors will find that they get around on foot, however, there are minibuses between the CONAF administration and Guardería Laguna Amarga, as well as boats across Lago Pehoé. Roads inside the park are narrow and bendy with blind corners. Rangers keep a check on the whereabouts of all visitors: you are required to register and show your passport when entering the park or setting off on any hike. There are entrances at Laguna Amarga, Lago Sarmiento and Laguna Azul, foreigners US$19 (proceeds are shared between all Chilean national parks), climbing fees US$1000. The park is administered by CONAF, which has an administration centre ① *northern end of Lago del Toro, T061-691931, daily 0830-2000 in summer, 0830-1230, 1400-1830 offseason*. It provides a good slide show at 2000 on Saturday and Sunday and there are also excellent exhibitions on the flora and fauna of the park in Spanish and English. There are six ranger stations (*guarderías*) in the park staffed by *guardaparques*, who give advice and also store luggage (not at Laguna Amarga).

Best time to visit

The weather in the park can change in a few minutes. The warmest time is from December to March, although it can be wet and windy. The spring months of October and November are recommended for wild flowers. Rain and snowfall are heavier the further west you go and bad weather sweeps off the Campo de Hielo Sur without warning. Snow may prevent access in winter, but well-equipped hikers can do some good walking, when conditions are stable. For information in Spanish on weather conditions, phone the administration centre.

Sights

Here, there are 15 peaks above 2000 m, of which the highest is **Cerro Paine Grande** (3050 m). Few places can compare to its steep forested talus slopes topped by 1000-m vertical shafts of basalt with conical caps. These are the remains of frozen magma in ancient volcanic throats, everything else having been eroded. On the western edge of the park is the enormous **Campo de Hielo Sur** icefield. Four main *ventisqueros* (glaciers) – Grey, Dickson, Zapata and Tyndall – branch off it, their meltwater forming a complex series of lakes and streams, which lead into fjords extending to the sea. Two other glaciers, Francés and Los Perros, descend on the western side of the central massif.

A micro-climate exists especially favourable to **plants** and **wildlife**. Over 200 species of plants have been identified and, although few trees reach great size, several valleys are thickly forested and little light penetrates. The grassland here is distinct from the monotony of the pampa and dispersed sclerophyl forest. Some 105 species of birds call the park home, including 18 species of waterfowl and 11 birds of prey. Particularly noteworthy are condors, black-necked swans, rheas, kelp geese, ibis, flamingos and austral parrakeets. The park is also one of the best places on the continent for viewing rheas and guanacos. Apart from the 3500 guanacos, 24 other species of mammals can be seen here, including hares, foxes, skunks, huemules and pumas (the last two only very rarely).

Torres del Paine has become increasingly popular with foreigners and Chileans alike: in 2005 it received around 107,000 visitors, most during the summer months of January and February, which, if possible, should be avoided due to overcrowding, especially at *refugios* and campsites, and the unpredictability of the weather. Many parts of the park are now open all year round; visiting in winter is becoming increasingly popular as, although the temperature is low, there is little wind. Despite efforts to manage the ever-growing number of visitors, the impact of such a large influx is starting to show. Litter has become a problem, especially around *refugios* and camping areas; please take all your rubbish out of the park and remember that this also includes toilet paper. Most importantly, if you are using your own cooking stove, only cook in designated areas. The negligence of one backpacker caused around 14,000 hectares of forest to burn down in the northeastern sector of the park in 2005.

▲ Trekking

There are about 250 km of well-marked trails. Visitors must keep to the trails: cross country trekking is not permitted. It is vital not to underestimate the unpredictability of the weather, nor the arduousness of some stretches on the long hikes. Some paths are confusingly marked and it is all too easy to end up on precipices with glaciers or

Parque Nacional Torres del Paine

churning rivers awaiting below; be particularly careful to follow the path at the Paso John Gadner on El Circuito (see below). The only means of rescue are on horseback or by boat; the nearest helicopter is in Punta Arenas and high winds usually prevent its operation in the park.

In theory, lone walkers are not allowed on this route.

Sleeping
Explora **1**
Hostería Lago Grey **3**
Hostería Las Torres **4**
Hostería Mirador del Payne **2**
Hostería Pehoé **5**
Posada Río Serrano **6**

Refugios
Chileno (Fantástico Sur) **1**
Grey (Andescape) **3**
Lago Dickson (Andescape) **2**
Laguna Verde **7**
Las Torres (Fantástico Sur) **10**
Lodge Paine Grande (Vertice) **9**
Los Cuernos (Fantástico Sur) **8**
Pudeto **11**

Camping
Campamento Británico **1**
Campamento Chileno **3**
Campamento Italiano **4**
Campamento Japonés **5**
Campamento Lago Paine **2**
Campamento Las Carretas **15**
Campamento Las Guardas **6**
Campamento Las Torres **7**
Campamento Paso **8**
Campamento Pingo **16**
Campamento Zapata **17**
Lago Pehoé **14**
Laguna Azul **9**
Las Torres **10**
Los Perros **11**
Serón **13**
Serrano **12**

Ranger stations (guarderías)

Map labels: Lago Cebolla, Lago Azul, Entrance, Laguna Azul, Río Paine, Río Ascencio, Entrance, Laguna Amarga, Río Paine, Entrance, Lago Sarmiento, Laguna Verde, Sierra del Toro, Lago del Toro, To Puerto Natales, To Puerto Natales

0 km 4
0 miles 4

It is essential to be properly equipped against cold, wind and rain. A strong, streamlined, waterproof tent is essential if doing El Circuito (although you can hire camping equipment for a single night at most *refugios*). Also essential are protective clothing, strong waterproof footwear, compass, good sleeping bag and sleeping mat. In summer also take shorts and sunscreen. You are strongly advised to bring all necessary equipment and your own food from Puerto Natales and not to rely on availability at the *refugios* within the park; the small shops at the *refugios* (see below) and at the **Posada Río Serrano** are expensive and have a limited selection. Note that rats and mice are occasionaly a problem around camping sites and the free *refugios*, so do not leave food in your pack (which may be chewed through). The safest solution is to hang food in a bag on a wire. Note that you are not allowed to build fires in the park. A decent map is provided with your park entrance ticket; other maps (US$7) are obtainable in many places Puerto Natales but most have one or two mistakes. The map produced by **Cartographia Digital** has been recommended as more accurate, as is the one produced by **Patagonia Interactiva**.

El Circuito

The most popular trek is a circuit round the Torres and Cuernos del Paine. It is usually done anticlockwise starting from the *guardería* at **Laguna Amarga**, although some walkers advise doing the route clockwise so that you climb to Paso John Gadner with the wind behind you. While some people complete the route in less time, it normally takes five to six days. The circuit is often closed in winter because of snow; major rivers are crossed by footbridges, but these are occasionally washed away. From Laguna Amarga the route is north along the western side of the Río Paine to **Lago Paine**, before turning west to follow the lush pastures of the valley of the Río Paine to the southern end of **Lago Dickson** (it is possible to add a journey to the *campamento* by the Torres on day one of this route); the *refugio* at Lago Dickson lies in a breathtaking position in front of the icy white lake with mountains beyond. From Lago Dickson the path runs along the wooded valley of the **Río de los Perros**, past the Glaciar de los Perros, before climbing through bogs and up scree to **Paso John Gadner** (1241 m, the highest point on the route), then dropping steeply through forest to follow the Grey Glacier southeast to **Lago Grey**, continuing to **Lago Pehoé** and the administration centre. There are superb views en route, particularly from the top of Paso John Gadner.

The longest stretch is between Refugio Laguna Amarga and Refugio Dickson (30 km, 10 hours in good weather; two campsites on the way at Serón and Cairon), but the most difficult section is the very steep, slippery slope from Paso John Gadner down to the Campamento Paso; the path is not well signed at the top of the pass, and some people (including the author) have got dangerously lost and ended up on the Grey Glacier itself. Camping gear must be carried, as some *campamentos* (including Campamento Paso and Campamento Torres) do not have *refugios*.

The W

A popular alternative to El Circuito, this four- to five-day route can be completed without camping equipment as there is accommodation in *refugios* en route. It combines several of the hikes described separately below. From Refugio Laguna Amarga the first stage runs west via **Hostería Las Torres** and up the valley of the **Río Ascensio** via Refugio Chileno to the base of the **Torres del Paine** (see below). From here return to the **Hostería Las Torres** and then walk along the northern shore of **Lago Nordenskjold** via **Refugio Los Cuernos** to **Campamento Italiano**. From here climb the **Valley of the Río del Francés** (see below) before continuing to **Refugio Pehoé**. From here you can complete the third part of the 'W' by walking west along the northern shore of **Lago Grey** to **Refugio Grey** and the Grey Glacier before returning to **Refugio Pehoé** and the boat back across the lake to the **Refugio Pudeto**.

Valley of the Río del Francés

From **Refugio Pehoé** this route leads north across undulating country along the western edge of **Lago Skottberg** to **Campamento Italiano** and then follows the valley of the Río del Francés, which climbs between Cerro Paine Grande and the Ventisquero del Francés (to the west) and the Cuernos del Paine (to the east) to **Campamento Británico**; the views from the mirador an hour's walk above **Campamento Británico** are superb. Allow 2½ hours from **Refugio Pehoé** to **Campamento Italiano**, 2½ hours further to **Campamento Británico**.

Treks from Guardería Grey

Guardería Grey, 18 km west by road from the administration centre, is the starting point for a five-hour trek to **Lago Pingo**, recommended if you want to get away from the crowds, and one of the best routes in the park for birdwatching. From the *guardería* follow the **Río Pingo**, via **Refugio Pingo** and **Refugio Zapata** (four hours), with views south over Ventisquero Zapata (look out for plenty of wildlife and for icebergs in the lake) to reach the lake. **Ventisquero Pingo** can be seen 3 km away over the lake. Note there is a bridge over a river here, marked on many maps, which has been washed away. The river can be forded when it is low, however, allowing access to the glacier.

Two short signposted walks from Guardería Grey have also been suggested: one is a steep climb up the hill behind the ranger post to **Mirador Ferrier**, from where there are fine views; the other is via a suspension bridge across the Río Pingo to the peninsula at the southern end of **Lago Grey**, from where there are good views of the icebergs on the lakes.

To the base of the Torres del Paine

From **Refugio Laguna Amarga**, this six-hour route follows the road west to **Hostería Las Torres** (1½ hours), before climbing along the western side of the **Río Ascensio** via **Refugio Chileno** (two hours) and **Campamento Chileno** to **Campamento Las Torres** (two hours), close to the base of the **Torres del Paine** (be careful when crossing the suspension bridge over the Río Ascensio near **Hostería Las Torres**, as the path is poorly marked and you can end up on the wrong side of the ravine). The path alongside the Río Ascensio is well marked, and the **Campamento Las Torres** is in an attractive wood (no *refugio*). A further 30 minutes up the morraine takes you to a lake at the base of the towers themselves; they seem so close that you almost feel you could touch them. To see the Torres lit by sunrise (spectacular but you must have good weather), it's well worth carrying your camping gear up to **Campamento Torres** and spending the night. One hour beyond **Campamento Torres** is **Campamento Japonés**, another good campsite.

To Laguna Verde

From the administation centre follow the road north 2 km, before taking the path east over the **Sierra del Toro** and then along the southern side of **Laguna Verde** to the Guardería Laguna Verde. Allow four hours. This is one of the easiest walks in the park and may be a good first hike.

To Laguna Azul and Lago Paine

This route runs north from Laguna Amarga to the western tip of **Laguna Azul**, from where it continues across the sheltered **Río Paine** valley past Laguna Cebolla to the Refugio Lago Paine at the western end of the lake. Allow 8½ hours. Good birdwatching opportunities.

● Sleeping

LL Explora, Salto Chico on edge of Lago Pehoé, T061-411247, reservations from Av Américo Vespucci 80, piso 7, Santiago, T02-206 6060, www.explora.com. Ugly building but the most luxurious and comfortable hotel in the park, offering spectacular views, pool, gym, tours and transfer from Punta Arenas.

LL Hostería Lago Grey, T061-410172, reservations T061-229512, www.austro hoteles.cl. Small rooms on edge of Lago Grey with views of the Grey Glacier, decent restaurant.

LL Hostería Las Torres, head office Magallanes 960, Punta Arenas, T061-710050, www.lastorres.com. Probably the best of the hosterías in the park. Recently expanded. Nice rooms, although strangely none has a particularly good view, good restaurant, disabled access, English spoken, horse riding, transport from Laguna Amarga ranger station. There is a imited number of standard rooms which are considerably cheaper.

LL Patagonia Ecocamp, reservations 02-232 9878, www.ecocampo.travel. Luxury all-inclusive tented camp with geodesic design and powered by renewable energy. Offers 4- to 10-day walking and wildlife-watching packages.

LL-L Hostería Lago Tyndall, T061-413139 www.hosterialagotyndall.com. Expensive, cafeteria-style restaurant, electricity during the day only. Not recommended.

LL-AL Hostería Pehoé, 5 km south of Pehoé ranger station, 11 km north of park administration, T061-411390, www.pehoe.com. On an island with spectacular view across the lake to Cerro Paine Grande and Cuernos del Paine, this place does not make the most of its stunning location, run-down, overpriced.

L Hostería Mirador del Payne (Estancia Lazo), on the eastern edge of the park, reservations at Fagnano 585, Punta Arenas, T061-226930, www.miradordel payne.com. Beautifully situated on Laguna Verde with spectacular views and good fishing, restaurant. Recommended but an inconvenient base for visiting the park; own transport essential, or you can trek to it from within the park.

L Posada Río Serrano, reservations advisable; book through Baqueano Zamora, Baquedano 534B, Puerto Natales, T061-412911, www.baqueanozamora.com. An old *estancia*, much improved recently, some rooms with bath, some with shared facilities, breakfast extra, near park administration, with expensive but good restaurant and a shop.

Private refugios

Three companies between them run half of the *refugios* in the park, providing dormitory space only (bring your own sleeping bag or hire one for US$6). Prices are around US$30 per person with full board about US$30 extra. Take US dollars and your passport as you will save 19% tax. *Refugios* have kitchen facilities, hot showers and space for camping. Most will hire out tents for around US$12 per night. In high season accommodation and meals in the non-CONAF *refugios* should be booked in advance in Puerto Natales, or by asking staff in one *refugio* to radio another. In winter most of the *refugios* close, although one or two may stay open depending on the weather. Note that the administration rights for several *refugios* are up for tender in 2007 so the following details may well change.

trips@cascada.travel

ECOCAMP patagonia

Sustainable lodging & Trekking and
wildlife excursions in Torres del Paine

www.ecocamp.travel

Andescape refugios, book through agencies in Puerto Natales or direct at Andescape, Eberhard 599, Puerto Natales, T061-412877, www.andescape.cl. It owns:
Refugio Grey, on the eastern shore of Lago Grey.
Refugio Lago Dickson, on the northern part of the circuit.

Fantástico Sur refugios, book in agencies in Puerto Natales or direct on T061-710050, www.wcircuit.com. It owns:
Refugio Las Torres, next to the Hostería Las Torres (see above).
Refugio Los Cuernos, on the northern shore of Lago Nordenskjold.
Refugio Chileno, valley of the Río Ascensio at the foot of the Torres.

Vertice refugios, book through agencies in Puerto Natales or via www.verticepatagonia.cl. It owns:
Lodge Paine Grande, new and large on the northwestern edge of Lago Pehoe. In theory the most comfortable of all, but in practice has had teething troubles and several complaints regarding customer service.

In addition, there are 6 free *refugios*: Zapata, Pingo, Laguna Verde, Laguna Amarga, Lago Paine and Pudeto. Most have cooking areas (wood stove or fireplace) but Laguna Verde and Pingo do not. These two are in very poor condition.

Campsites

The wind tends to increase in the evening so it is a good idea to pitch tents early (by 1600). Free camping is permitted in 7 other locations in the park; these sites are known as *campamentos*. Fires are not allowed. These restrictions should be observed as forest fires are a serious hazard. Use camping stoves. *Guardaparques* also require campers to have a trowel to bury their waste. Equipment can be hired in Puerto Natales (see Shopping above).

In addition to sites at the private *refugios*, there are the following sites:
Lago Pehoé, run by Turismo Río Serrano (see Sleeping, above), US$20 per site, max 6 persons, hot showers, beware of mice.
Laguna Azul, hot showers.
Las Torres, run by Estancia Cerro Paine, US$4, hot showers.
Los Perros, run by Andescape, with shop and hot showers.
Serón, run by Estancia Cerro Paine, US$4, hot showers.
Serrano, run by Turismo Río Serrano (see Sleeping, above), US$15 per site, maximum 6 persons, cold showers, basic.

▲▲ Activities and tours

Before booking a tour check all the details carefully and get a copy in writing, as there have been increasingly mixed reports of the quality of some tours. Many companies who claim to visit the Grey Glacier, for example, only visit Lago Grey (you see the glacier in the distance). After mid-Mar there is less public transport and trucks are irregular.

Several agencies in Puerto Natales offer 1-day tours by minibus, US$35 plus park entry; these give a good impression of the lower parts of the park, although you spend most of the day in the vehicle and many travellers would argue that you need to stay several days, or at least overnight, in the park

to appreciate it fully. Cheaper tours are also available, but both guide and vehicle may not be as good as the established operators. There are many more operators based in Puerto Natales offering trekking, kayaking, ice-hiking, boat trips and other tours in the park (see page 454).

Cascada Expediciones, T02-861 1777, www.cascada-expediciones.com, based in Santiago, offers small group tours to Torres del Paine.

Chile Nativo, Eberhard 230, Casilla 42, Puerto Natales, T061-411835, www.chile nativo.com. Specialists in tailor-made trips.

Experience Chile, T07977-223326, www.experiencechile.org. Itineraries and accomodation in the region can be arranged by this UK-based operator.

Hostería Grey, see Sleeping, above, provides excursions by boat to the face of the Grey Glacier at 0900 and 1500 daily, 3½ hrs, US$60 per person. Book direct or through **Turismo Runner** in Puerto Natales.

⊖ Transport

Bus

These timetables are likely to change with the opening of the new road to the park in 2007. From early Nov to mid-Apr daily bus services run from Puerto Natales to the park, leaving between 0630 and 0800, and again at around 1430, 2½ hrs to Laguna Amarga, 3 hrs to the administration centre, US$10 one way, US$16 open return (return tickets are not always interchangeable between different companies); return departures are usually around 1300 and 1800. Generally, buses will drop you at Laguna Amarga and pick you up at the administration centre for the return. The buses wait at Refugio Pudeto until the 1200 boat from Refugio Lago Pehoé arrives. Travel between 2 points within the park (eg Pudeto-Laguna Amarga), US$4. Services are provided by **Bus Sur**, Baquedano 534, T061-411325; **JB**, Prat 258, T061-412824; and **Fortaleza**, Prat 258, T061-410595.

At other times, services by travel agencies are subject to demand; arrange your return date with the driver and try to coincide with other groups to keep costs down; **Luis Díaz** has been recommended, about US$17, minimum 3 persons. In season there are minibus connections from Laguna Amarga to the **Hostería Los Torres**, US$4, and from the administration centre to **Hostería Lago Grey**.

To go from Torres del Paine to **Calafate** (Argentina), either return to Puerto Natales and catch a bus, or take a bus or hitch from the park to Villa Cerro Castillo and try to link with the Natales–Calafate bus schedule. In season, there is a direct bus service from the park to Calafate with **Chaltén Travel**, US$50.

Ferry

A boat service runs across **Lago Pehoé** from near the **Lodge Paine Grande** to **Refugio Pudeto**, daily, 30 mins, US$19 one way with 1 piece of baggage free, tickets available on board. Departures from Paine Grande 1000, 1230, 1830; from Pudeto 0930, 1200, 1800. Reduced service off season, no service May-Sep. For information call T061-411380.

Into Argentina

The small Argentine town of El Calafate, the base for visits to the Parque Nacional Los Glaciares, is a short distance from Puerto Natales and can easily be visited. This little town is situated in a beautiful position on the southern shore of Lago Argentino, the largest lake in Argentina, surrounded by mountains. ▶▶ *For Sleeping, Eating and other listings, see pages 467-470.*

Ins and outs → *Argentine phone code: +54.*

Getting there El Calafate is easily accessible from Puerto Natales in Chile (two buses daily in summer, less frequent in winter) via Río Turbio or Cerro Castillo (both roads *ripio*), or along a smooth metalled road from Río Gallegos near the Atlantic coast (several buses daily). There are poorer roads north to El Chaltén and Perito

Moreno. Lago Argentino airport, 22 km east of town, has a paved runway suitable for
jet aircraft. **Aerobus** ① *T02902-492492, US$3* runs from the airport to hotels in town;
a taxi to the town centre costs US$7.

Getting around El Calafate is so small that it's easy to get around the town on foot.

Tourist information The office in the bus terminal ① *T02902-491090, info@cala
fate.com, Oct-Apr daily 0700-2200*, is very helpful, English spoken. For information
on the Parque Nacional los Glaciares, visit the park office ① *Libertador 1302,
T02902-491005, apnglaciares@cotecal.com.ar, Mon-Fri 0800-1500*.

Argentine border

From Puerto Natales, the Argentine border can be crossed at three points, all of which
meet Route 40, which runs north to El Calafate. These crossings are open, subject to
weather conditions, 24 hours a day from September to May and 0700 to 2300 daily
between June and August.

Paso Casas Viejas This crossing, 16 km east of Puerto Natales, is reached by turning
off Route 9 (the Punta Arenas road) at Km 14. On the Argentine side, the road (*ripio*)
runs east to meet Route 40, en route to Río Gallegos (or north to El Calafate). This
crossing is open all year.

Villa Dorotea This crossing is reached by branching off Route 9, 9 km east of Puerto
Natales and continuing north a further 11 km. On the Argentine side, the road (*ripio*)
continues north to Route 40 via **Río Turbio**, see page 465.

Cerro Castillo The most northerly of the three crossings, Cerro Castillo is reached by
turning off the road north to Torres del Paine at Km 65. Chilean customs and
immigration formalities are at Cerro Castillo; Argentine formalities are at Cancha
Carrera, 2 km further east. On the Argentine side of the border, the road meets Route
40 in a very desolate spot – hitching may be possible, but this route is more feasible if
you have your own transport.

Río Turbio

Only 30 km northeast of Puerto Natales, Río Turbio is the site of Argentina's largest
coalfield. Although little-visited by travellers, it is a good centre for trekking and horse
riding. There is a **tourist office** in the Municipalidad on Calle San Martín. Visits can be
made to **Mina Uno** (where the first mine was opened), to the south of the town, and to
the present mining and industrial area, on the eastern outskirts, where there is a
museum, the **Museo del Carbón** ① *Mon-Fri 0700-1200*. About 4 km south of town is
Valdelén, a ski resort situated just inside the border on the slopes of Sierra La Dorotea
(see page 469).

Towards El Calafate

From the border there are two alternative routes to El Calafate. On clear days both
offer fantastic views of Torres del Paine. The longest but easiest route runs north
along Route 40 along beautiful valleys with flowers, woods and grazing horses, to
Cancha Carrerra (the junction with the border crossing from Cerro Castillo), then
follows the Río Coyle to **La Esperanza**, Km 123, where it meets the main El
Calafate–Río Gallegos road, 161 km southeast of El Calafate. The shorter route
continues northwards from Cancha Carrerra along a very poor, desolate *ripio* road,
the continuation of Route 40, which turns off at Km 30 and runs northeast 70 km to
meet the El Calafate–Río Gallegos road at **El Cerrito**, 91 km southeast of El Calafate. In
winter, both the Cerro Castillo crossing and this shorter route are occasionally closed.
For public transport on this route, see page 455.

Founded in 1927, El Calafate, with a population of 8000, has grown rapidly as a tourist centre for the Parque Nacional los Glaciares, 50 km further west. Here you will see no sign of the Argentine economic crisis. The weakness of the peso has led to a boom in tourism. As a result, El Calafate has a distinctly prosperous feel. Given the town's name, it is no surprise that the surrounding hills abound with small calafate bushes.

A straightforward walk behind the town leads up a hill from where there are views of the silhouette of the southern end of the Andes, Lago Argentina and Isla Solitaria. Just west of the town centre is **Bahía Redonda**, a shallow part of Lago Argentino where in winter you can ice-skate and ski. At its eastern edge is **Laguna Nimes**, a bird reserve where there are flamingos, black-necked swans and ducks. There is scope for good hill-walking to the south of town. **Cerro Elefante**, west of Calafate on the road to the Moreno Glacier, is good for rock climbing. **El Galpón** ⓘ *21 km west, T02902-492316,* is an *estancia* and bird sanctuary where 43 species of birds have been identified. There are also sheep shearing displays, horse riding and a barbecue; English spoken.

Punta Gualicho, on the shores of Lago Argentino, some 15 km east of town (or 7 km on foot when cutting across the *pampa*), has badly deteriorated painted caves. The caves are on private property and may soon be closed to the public. There is an entrance fee (US$3). On the same road, 12 km east of El Calafate on the edge of the lake, are fascinating geological formations caused by erosion. Several agencies run two-hour tours to Punta Gualicho for US$6. At **Lago Roca**, 40 km south of El Calafate, there is trout and salmon fishing, climbing, walking and cattle branding in summer.

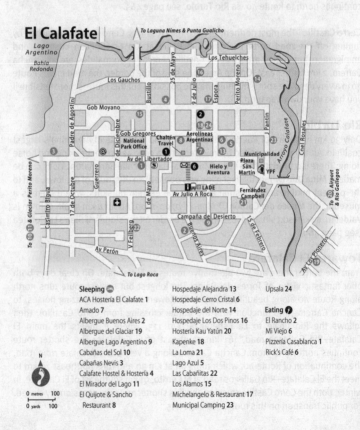

El Calafate

N

0 metres 100
0 yards 100

Sleeping
ACA Hostería El Calafate 1
Amado 7
Albergue Buenos Aires 2
Albergue del Glaciar 19
Albergue Lago Argentino 9
Cabañas del Sol 10
Cabañas Nevis 3
Calafate Hostel & Hostería 4
El Mirador del Lago 11
El Quijote & Sancho
  Restaurant 8

Hospedaje Alejandra 13
Hospedaje Cerro Cristal 6
Hospedaje del Norte 14
Hospedaje Los Dos Pinos 16
Hostería Kau Yatún 20
Kapenke 18
La Loma 21
Lago Azul 5
Las Cabañitas 22
Los Alamos 15
Michelangelo & Restaurant 17
Municipal Camping 23

Upsala 24

Eating
El Rancho 2
Mi Viejo 6
Pizzería Casablanca 1
Rick's Café 6

The calafate

According to local lore, whoever eats the fruits of the calafate, *Berberis buxifolia*, will return to Patagonia. Certainly, he or she is likely to have purple-stained lips and fingers thanks to the plant's edible berries.

This spiny, hardy shrub grows to 2 m in height and has single bright yellow/orange flowers dotted along its arching branches in spring. Also known as the Magellan barberry, its wood is used for making red dye.

Sleeping

Argentine border *p465*
AL-A Hostería El Pionero, Villa Cerro Castillo, 63 km north of Puerto Natales, T061-412911. With bath, good service, horses available for hire.

There are also 2 *hospedajes* in the town.

Río Turbio *p465*
Hotels are almost always full, so reserve your room in advance.
B-F Gato Negro, T02902-4921226. Rooms and dormitory accommodation.
E Hostería de la Frontera, Paraje Mina 1, T02902-421979. Nice *albergue* at Valdelén.

Towards El Calafate *p465*
F Hotel Fuentes del Coyle, Fuentes del Coyle, 31 km east of Cerro Castillo. Cold, dirty.
F Restaurant La Esperanza, La Esperanza. Bunk beds, with bath; also *cabañas* at the YPF service station.

El Calafate *p466, map p466*
In summer, accommodation can be hard to find. Ask at the tourist office, which rents out caravans, tents and 4-berth *cabañas*, showers extra. Credit cards are only welcome at hotels, with high commissions. Many hotels are only open Oct to Apr/May.
L El Mirador del Lago, Libertador 2047, T02902-491213, www.miradordellago.com.ar. Good accommodation on the lakefront just outside town, restaurant, half-board available.
L Hostería Kau-Yatún, 25 de Mayo (10 blocks from town centre), T02902-491059, kauyatun@cotecal.com.ar. Many facilities, old *estancia* house, comfortable, restaurant and barbecues, horse riding tours with guides.
L Los Alamos, Moyano y Bustillo, T02902-491145, www.posadalosalamos.com. Best hotel in town, comfortable, very good service,

excellent restaurant, extensive gardens, single-hole golf course. Recommended.
AL ACA Hostería El Calafate, Av del Libertador 1350, T02902-491004, www. Ubikt.com.ar/usc/hosteriaelcalafate. Good view, open all year.
AL El Quijote, Gob Gregores 1181, T02902-491017, elquijote@cotecal.com.ar. Modern, comfortable. Recommended.
AL Kapenke, 9 de Julio 112, T02902-491093, www.kapenke.com.ar. Modern, with breakfast, good beds, bright, internet, snackbar, overpriced.
A La Loma, Julio Roca 849, T02902-491016, www.lalomahotel.com. Spacious rooms, breakfast, library, restaurant, tea room, games room, gardens. Recommended.
A Michelangelo, Espora y Gob Moyano, T02902-491045, www.michelangelo hotel.com.ar. With breakfast, modern, comforte, excellent restaurant, accepts TCs (poor rates).
B Upsala, Espora 139, T02902-491166, dflella@lacasilla.com.ar. With breakfast, good beds. Recommended.
B-C Cabañas Del Sol, Libertador 1956, T02902-491439, cabadelsol@yahoo.com.ar. Good meals. Recommended.
B-F Albergue del Glaciar, Los Pioneros 251, T02902-491243, www.glaciar.com. Discount for ISIC or IYHA members, open mid-Sep to end-Apr. Price per person with dorms, also doubles with bath and without, kitchen facilities, English, German, Italian spoken, internet, also **El Tempano Errante** restaurant with good-value fixed menu and vegetarian options. Recommended. Their tour agency **Patagonia Backpackers**, a Navimag agent, organizes tours to the Moreno glacier (US$35 per person, good value) and else-where, and runs a free shuttle service from the bus station, book in advance in summer.

C **Amado**, Libertador 1072, T02902-491134, familiagomez@cotecal.com.ar. With bath and breakfast, simple, cable TV.

C **Hospedaje Cerro Cristal**, Gob Gregores 979, T02902-491088. With bath and breakfast, basic.

C **Hospedaje del Norte**, Los Gauchos 813, T02902-491117. Open all year, kitchen facilities, comfortable, owner organizes tours.

C **Las Cabañitas**, V Feilberg 218, T02902-491118, lascabanitas@cotecal.com.ar. Cabins, hot water, kitchen and laundry facilities, helpful. Recommended.

C **Los Lagos**, 25 de Mayo 220, T02902-491170, loslagos@cotecal.com.ar. Very comfortable, with bath and breakfast, good value. Recommended.

D **Cabañas Nevis**, 1 km from town towards glacier, Libertador 1696, T02902-491180. For 4 or 8, some have lake view, full board available, excellent value.

D **Lago Azul**, Perito Moreno 83, T02902-491419. Only 2 double rooms. Highly recommended.

E **Enrique Barragán**, Barrio Bahía Redonda, Casa 10, T02902-491325. Accommodation in a private house. Recommended.

F **Apartamentos Lago Viedma**, Paralelo 158, T02902-491159. Hostel, 4 bunks to a room, cooking facilities.

F **Calafate Hostel**, Gob Moyano 1226, 300 m from bus terminal, T02902-492450, www.hostelspatagonia.com. Price per person in dormitories. Also more expensive rooms with bath. Kitchen facilities, internet, often full.

F **Hospedaje Alejandra**, Espora 60, T02902-491328. Price per person. Without breakfast or bath, good value, kitchen facilities, recommended.

F **La Cueva de Jorge Lemos**, Gob Moyano 839, behind YPF station. Bunk beds, bathroom, showers, kitchen facilities, popular and cheap.

F-G **Albergue Buenos Aires**, Buenos Aires 296, 200 m from terminal, T02902-491147. Kitchen facilities, helpful, good hot showers, luggage store.

F-G **Albergue Lago Argentino**, Campaña del Desierto 1050, T02902-491423. Near bus terminal. Price per person for dormitory accommodation, limited bathrooms, kitchen facilities, helpful.

G **Hospedaje Los Dos Pinos**, 9 de Julio 358, T02902-491271. Price per person for dorm

accommodation, bad beds, cooking and laundry facilities, also cabins(C) and camping. Arranges tours to glacier, popular.

Camping

Camping Lago Roca, T02902-499500. Good campsite in a wooded area beside Lago Roca, US$4 per site, also restaurant/*confitería*.

Camping Río Bote, 35 km, on road to Río Gallegos.

Municipal campsite, behind YPF service station, T02902-492622, campingmunicipal@cotecal.com.ar. Hot water, security, bar, *parillada*, 1 Oct-30 Apr; good meeting place.

❶ Eating

El Calafate *p466, map p466*

❚❚ **Hotel Los Alamos**, Moyana y Bustillo. Inventive menu using local ingredients. Recommended.

❚❚ **Michelangelo**, Espora y Gob Moyano. Magnificent steaks, trout, pastas. Recommended.

❚❚ **Paso Verlika**, Libertador 1108. Cosy and good value.

❚ **Bar Don Diego de la Noche**, Libertador 1603. Lamb and seafood, live music, good atmosphere.

❚ **El Rancho**, 9 de Julio y Gob Moyano. Good-value, generously sized pizzas, popular, free video shows of the glacier. Highly recommended.

❚ **La Loma**, see Sleeping above. Friendly, home-style food.

❚ **Maktub**, Libertador 905. Excellent pastries.

❚ **Mi Viejo**, Libertador 1111. *Parrilla*.

❚ **Pizzería Casablanca**, Libertador y 25 de Mayo. Serves good breakfasts.

❚ **Rick's Café**, Av del Libertador 1105. Popular *tenedor libre* , US$5.

❷ Festivals and events

El Calafate *p466, map p466*

15 Feb People flock from all over the vast Provincia de Santa Cruz to the rural show on **Día del Lago Argentino**. Many wear their finest *gaucho* clothes – *bombachas*, *espuelas* and wide-brimmed hats – and camp out. Revelry includes dances, *asados* and *jineteadas* (a type of rodeo, featuring wild horses ridden by wild men). This is a highly recommended insight into Patagonia's 'wild west'.

10 Nov There are barbecues and rodeos, etc on **Día de la Tradición**.

▲ Activities and tours

Río Turbio *p465*
Skiing
The ski resort at **Valdelén** has 6 pistes and is ideal for beginners. There is also scope for crosscountry skiing nearby. The season runs from early Jun to late Sep, with floodlights to extend the short winter afternoons.

El Calafate *p466, map p466*
Mountain biking
Mountain bikes can be hired from **Bike Way**, Espora 20, T02902-492180, US$7 per day.

Tour operators
Most of theagencies are along Libertador and charge the same rates for excursions: to the **Moreno Glacier**, US$18 plus US$3.50 park entry for a trip leaving early morning or around 1400, 3 hrs at glacier (see page 475); to **Lago Roca**, depart 0930, return 1700, US$20; to **Cerro Fitz Roy**, depart 0600 return 1900, US$30; to **Punta Gualicho**, 2 hrs, US$10.
Cecilia Scarafoni, T02902-493196, ecowalks@cotecal.com.ar. Birdwatching walks 2 km from town, 2 hrs, US$5.
Chaltén Travel, Libertador 1177, T02902-492212, rancho@cotecal.com.ar. Wide range of tours, English spoken, helpful.
Fernández Campbell, Libertador 867, T02902-491155. Combined bus and boat tours to the Upsala glacier.
Hielo y Aventura, Libertador 935, T02902-491053, hieloyaventura@cotecal.com.ar. Organizes 2-hr treks on the Moreno glacier with champagne, US$50, plus US$15 for transport to the glacier. Recommended, book ahead.
Interlagos, Libertador 1175, T02902-491179. Daily bus to Moreno glacier.
Leutz, Libertador 1341, T02902-492316, leutzturismo@cotecal.com.ar. Daily excursion to Lago Roca 1000-1800, US$25 per person, plus US$12 for lunch at Estancia Nibepo Aike.
Santa Cruz, Campo del Desierto 1695, T02902-493166. Helpful.
Several hotels organize tours by minibus including **Albergue del Glaciar** (see Sleeping above), which offers an alternative Moreno glacier tour including some trekking.

⊖ Transport

Río Turbio *p465*
Air
The airport is 15 km southeast near 28 de Noviembre; taxi US$7. LADE flies to **Río Gallegos** on Tue, 45 mins, US$30.

Bus
To **Puerto Natales**, several daily, 1 hr, US$2, with Cootra, Bus Sur and Zaahj. To **Calafate**, several daily, many companies, 4½ hrs, US$7. To **Río Gallegos**, many companies, 4 hrs, US$5.

El Calafate *p466, map p466*
Air
Aerolíneas Argentinas and AIRG have daily services to **Buenos Aires**. To **Ushuaia**, LADE and Aerolíneas Argentinas, several weekly between them, US$50. To **Gob Gregores** and **Perito Moreno**, LADE, weekly, US$35. To **Río Turbio**, LADE, weekly, US$35. LADE also flies twice weekly to **Río Gallegos**, US$40, and **Comodoro Rivadavia**, US$60. To **Puerto Natales**, DAP, daily in summer, US$54. There are many more flights in summer.

Bus
The terminal is on Roca, 1 block from Libertador. Bus schedule changes annually.
   To **Perito Moreno Glacier**, Taqsa and Interlagos, daily, $10 return. To **Río Gallegos**, Interlagos and Taqsa, daily, US$11. To **Río Turbio**, several daily, many companies, 4½ hrs, US$7. For **Ushuaia**, **Buenos Aires** and northern destinations go to Río Gallegos and change.
   Cootra runs to **Puerto Natales** via Río Turbio, daily, 6 hrs including tedious border crossing, US$15 (advance booking recommended). Bus Sur and Zaahj make the journey via Cerro Castillo (a simpler crossing), 5 weekly, 4½-5 hrs, US$15. Chaltén Travel runs regular services in summer to Torres del Paine, US$45.

Taxi
Travel by road to the most interesting spots near El Calafate is limited and may require taxis. Tours can be arranged with taxi drivers at the airport who await arrivals. To **Río Gallegos**, 4 hrs, US$100 for up to 5 people
.

① Directory

El Calafate *p466, map p466*

Banks There are several ATMs in town. Travel agencies such as **Interlagos** change notes; YPF garage, **Chocolate El Calafate** and some other shops give good rates for cash; **Albergue del Glaciar** charges 5% commission on TCs; the **Scorpio** snack bar on Libertador is reported to give the best rates. Many businesses add 10% for credit card transactions. US dollar notes are widely accepted. **Laundry** El Lavadero, Libertador 1474, US$3 a load, also has internet access. **Post office** Libertador; service is quicker from Puerto Natales (Chile). **Telephone** Open Calafate, Libertador 996, good service, with internet.

Parque Nacional Los Glaciares

This park, the second largest in Argentina, covers more than 660,000 ha. Over a third is covered by the hielos continentales, giant icefields that straddle the border with Chile. Of the 47 major glaciers that flow from the icefields, 13 descend into the park to feed two great lakes, Lago Argentino and Lago Viedma. The Río La Leona, flowing south from Lago Viedma, links the two lakes. There are also 190 other smaller glaciers that aren't even connected to the icefields. East of the icefields are areas of forest, which eventually give way to Patagonian steppe. Here, there are over 100 species of bird, among them the condor, the Patagonian woodpecker, the austral parakeet, the green-backed firecrown as well as black-necked swans, Andean ruddy ducks and torrent ducks. Guanacos, grey foxes, skunks and rheas can be seen on the steppe, while the endangered huemul inhabits the forest. ▶▶ *For Sleeping, Eating and other listings, see pages 474-476.*

Ins and outs

Getting there There are two sections of the park, around Lago Argentino and the Perito Moreno Glacier, and around Cerro Fitz Roy. To get to the former, most people take one of the minibuses that leave daily from El Calafate. To get to the latter, take a daily bus from El Calafate to El Chaltén.

Getting around Once in a section of the park, most people walk, but to go from one part of the park to another, it is necessary to return to Calafate first and change buses.

Best time to visit Many facilities are closed off season. The climate is variable. The best time to visit is between October and March. Temperatures in summer reach 20-30°C, so remember your sun block at all times. Rainfall ranges from 2000 mm in the far west to 400 mm in the east, falling mainly between March and late May.

Tourist information Trekking information is available in El Chaltén from the **national park office** ① *across the bridge at the entrance to town, T02962-493004.* The village also has a **tourist office** ① *Guemes 21, T02962-493011, www.el chalten.com, Mon-Fri 0900-2000, Sat and Sun 1300-2000.* Both provide helpful maps of the area, showing paths, campsites, distances and walking times. Lighting fires and camping wild are prohibited throughout the park. Access to the central sector of the park, north of Lago Argentino and south of Lago Viedma, is difficult and there are few tourist facilities, although *estancias*, such as Helsingfors and La Cristina, offer accommodation and excursions. The Helsingfors also offers boat trips to the Viedma Glacier.

Lago Argentino and around

The source of the Río Santa Cruz, one of the most important rivers in Patagonia, Lago Argentino covers some 1400 sq km. At its western end there are two networks of fjords (*brazos*), fed by glaciers (*ventisqueros*). The major attraction in the park is the **Ventisquero Perito Moreno**, which reaches the water at a narrow point in one of the fjords, opposite Peninsula Magallanes, 80 km, west of Calafate.

Spectacular, especially at sunset, the Moreno Glacier is constantly moving and never silent and was, until recently, one of the few in the world still advancing. Five kilometres across, 20 km long and 60 m high, it used to advance across Brazo Rico, blocking the fjord roughly every three years; as the water pressure built up behind it, the ice would break, reopening the channel and sending giant icebergs (*témpanos*) rushing down the appropriately named Canal de los Témpanos. Since February 1988 this has not occurred, possibly because of global warming.

Parque Nacional Los Glaciares

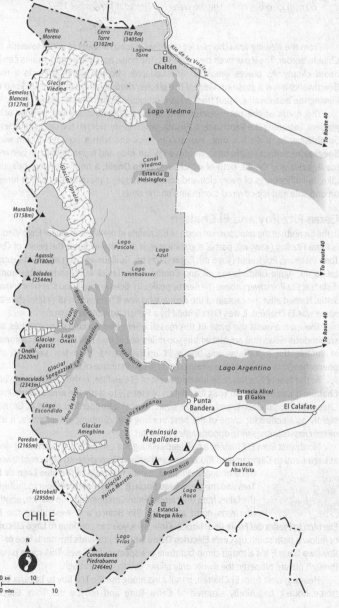

⁞ Beware: flying ice

"One or two of the tourists who ignore the prohibition signs and walk down to the rocks overlooking the channel in front of the glacier always get washed away every season. They all think it won't happen to them, but it does; 60 m of ice break off and hit the water just in front of them. But it isn't the water that kills them, it's the chunks of flying ice."

Carlos Dupáez, Superintendent, Parque Nacional Los Glaciares, interviewed in the *Buenos Aires Herald*, 1 November 1997.

From the viewing area the glacier stretches back in a sheet of white towards the Chilean border. The ice is riven by crevasses; the noise as it cracks and strains can be heard clearly. As pieces break off and collapse into the water, there is a roar. Boardwalks allow a close-up view of the glacier; there is a fine of up to US$250 for leaving the boardwalks, apart from on guided expeditions onto the glacier itself.

The fjords at the northwestern end of Lago Argentino are fed by four other glaciers, including the **Ventisquero Upsala**, which is considered the largest glacier in South America at 60 km long, over 100 m thick and with a frontage 10 km wide. **Spegazzini**, further south, has a frontage 1½ km wide and is 130 m high. In between are **Agassiz** and **Onelli**, both of which feed **Lago Onelli**, a quiet and very beautiful lake, full of icebergs of every size and sculpted shape, surrounded by beech forests on one side and ice-covered mountains on the other.

Cerro Fitz Roy and El Chaltén

In the far north of the park, 230 km north of El Calafate at the western end of Lago Viedma is Cerro Fitz Roy (3405 m), part of a granite massif that also includes the peaks of Cerro Torre (3128 m), Poincenot (3076 m), Egger (2673 m), Guillaumet (2503 m), Saint-Exupery (2600 m), Aguja Bífida (2394 m) and Cordón Adela (2938 m). Clearly visible from a distance, Fitz Roy towers above the nearby peaks, its sides normally too steep for snow to settle. Named after the captain of the *Beagle* who saw it from afar in 1833 (its Tehuelche name was El Chaltén), it was first climbed by a French expedition in 1952.

The area around the base of the massif offers fine walking opportunities and stupendous views that anyone within 500 miles would be a fool to miss. Occasionally at sunrise the mountains are briefly lit up bright red for a few seconds: this phenomenon is known as the *amanecer de fuego* ('sunrise of fire').

At the foot of Fitz Roy, 230 km northwest of El Calafate, is this small village of **El Chaltén**. It was founded in 1985 for military reasons – to settle the area and pre-empt Chilean territorial claims, and still has something of a frontier feel about it. Growing rapidly as a centre for some of the best trekking and climbing in Patagonia, it also offers crosscountry skiing opportunities in winter.

Northwest from El Chaltén, a trail leads via a good campsite with wonderful views at Lago Capri to Campamento Río Blanco and nearby Campamento Poincenot (two to three hours). From here, a path heads up to the blue **Lago de los Tres** and the green **Lago Sucia**; it's a two- to three-hour roundtrip to the lakes from the camps. From Campamento Río Blanco, another trail runs north along the Río Blanco and west along the Río Eléctrico to **Piedra del Fraile** (four hours). From here, you can continue to **Lago Eléctrico** or follow a path south up **Cerro Eléctrico Oeste** (1882 m) towards the north face of Fitz Roy (two hours); it's a tough climb but there are spectacular views. This route passes through private property: the owner only allows you to walk through.

Heading west from El Chaltén, a trail runs along the Río Fitz Roy to **Laguna Torre** (three hours), beautifully situated at Cerro Torre and fed by the Torre Glacier.

⁞ *Do not stray from the paths. A map Is essential, even on short walks.*

Southwest from El Chaltén, meanwhile, a badly marked path leads to **Laguna Toro** (six hours) and the southern entrance of the icefields.

The park information centre (see Ins and outs above) provides photocopied maps of treks, but the best one is published by *Zagier and Urruty*, 1992, US$6; available in shops in El Calafate and El Chaltén.

Lago del Desierto

Some 37 km north of El Chaltén and surrounded by forests, this lake is reached by an unpaved road that leads along the Río de las Vueltas via **Laguna Condor**, where flamingos can be seen. A path runs along the east side of the lake to its northern tip, from where a trail leads west along the valley of the Río Diablo to **Laguna Diablo**. Excursions to Lago del Desierto from El Chaltén are offered by **Chaltén Travel**, daily in summer (see page 469). There are also daily boat trips on the lake on board the *Mariana* ⓘ daily *1030, 1330, 1630, 2 hrs, US$20*.

The Fitz Roy area

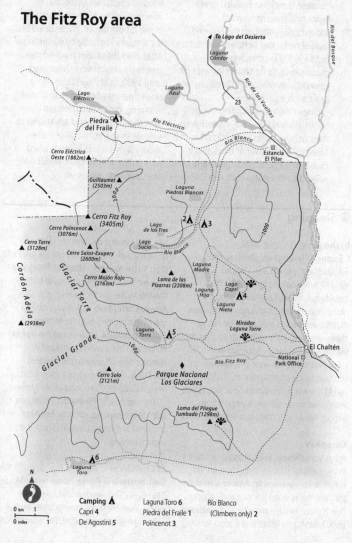

Camping ⛺
Capri 4
De Agostini 5

Laguna Toro 6
Piedra del Fraile 1
Poincenot 3

Río Blanco
(Climbers only) 2

0 km   1
0 miles   1

The advance and retreat of the Moreno Glacier

The Moreno Glacier is frequently said to be in retreat as a result of global warming. Although the glacier no longer blocks Brazo Rico on a three-yearly cycle, such statements must be treated with caution.

Glaciers are usually described by glaciologists as advancing, retreating or stable. However, even a retreating glacier will continue moving slowly forward; its frontage or snout retreats because it melts or breaks up at a faster rate than its forward movement. Although the Moreno Glacier no longer behaves as it did up until 1988, it is considered by glaciologists to be stable: its rates of forward movement and break-up are in a rough equilibrium.

One of the most puzzling things about glaciers is the way they change their behaviour. As far as is known, the Moreno Glacier did not block Brazo Rico until 1917; according to early scientific studies its snout was 750 m away from the Magallanes Peninsula in 1900, a distance that had dropped to 350 m by 1908. In 1917, the small dam formed by the ice broke after a few weeks; the next time the glacier blocked the fjord was in 1934-1935. Between this date and 1988 the glacier moved forward more vigorously; in 1939, when it reached the Magallanes Peninsula again, the waters in Brazo Rico rose 9 m and flooded coastal areas, leading to attempts by the Argentine navy to bomb it from the air. These failed but the waters eventually broke through. After 1939 the glacier reached the peninsula about every three years until 1988. Its changed behaviour since then may be related to global warming, but we also need to know why the glacier started advancing so vigorously in the first place – one theory is that it was being pushed forward by an unknown glacier on the Campo de Hielos Sur.

Sleeping

In the park p470, map p471
L Estancia Helsingfors, shores of Brazo Sur, southern end of Lago Viedma, T02902-420719, www.helsingfors.com.ar. With breakfast, full board available (good food), many treks, boat trips on Lago Viedma and flights over glaciers available, also riding, sheep-shearing, daily sailing across the lake, via the Viedma glacier. Recommended.
L Los Notros, 40 km west of El Calafate on the road to the Moreno glacier, T02902-491437, www.lastland.com. Spacious, rooms with views of the glacier, transport from airport. Breakfast included; other meals extra.

Camping
Apart from those in El Chaltén, all campsites in the national park are free. There are no toilets so bury your waste. A stove is essential for camping as wood is scarce and lighting fires is prohibited in campsites in the national park. Take warm clothes and a good sleeping bag. You can rent equipment in El Chaltén, ask at the park entrance, or from the *artésania* shop on the road past **Albergue Patagonia**.

There are 3 campsites en route from El Calafate to the glacier. Take food to all 3.
Arroyo Correntoso, 10 km east of the glacier. No facilities but nice location.
Bahía Escondida, 7 km east of the glacier. Toilets and hot showers, crowded in summer, free off season but no water.
Río Mitre, near the park entrance, 52 km from El Calafate, 26 km east of the glacier.

The campsite at **Piedra del Fraile**, just outside the park, has *cabañas* (with hot showers) and tent pitches, US$5, plus an expensive shop.

El Chaltén p472, map p473
L-AL Hostería El Puma, Lionel Terray 545, T02962-493095, www.elchalten.com/el puma. With breakfast, comfortable, lounge with log fire, tours arranged. Recommended.

AL La Aldea, Av M Guemes s/n, T02962-493040, www.patagonia-travel.com/aldea.html. Fully furnished apartments sleeping 4-6.

A Hotel Lago del Desierto, T02962-493010, www.elchalten.com/hotellagodeldesierto. Good beds, *comedor*, Italian spoken, camping US$5.

A-D Fitz Roy Inn, San Martin s/n, T02962-493062, www.elchalten.com/fitzroyinn. With breakfast and restaurant. Also shared cabins.

A-E Casa de Piedra, Lago del Desierto s/n, T02962-493015, www.lacasapiedra.com/lacasadepiedra. Shared cabins, also 4-bed cabins with bath, new restaurant, trekking guides (English, French and Italian spoken).

B Estancia La Quinta, 3 km from Chaltén, T02962-493012, info@estancialaquinta.com.ar. Half-board, no heating, prepares lunch for trekkers. Recommended.

C La Base, Lago del Desierto 97, T02962-493031, www.elchalten.com/labase. With bath, nice atmosphere, self-service breakfast, kitchen facilities, video rental, hot water, heating, helpful.

D Cabañas Cerro Torre, Halvorsen 110, T02962-493061, www.elchalten.com/cerrotorre. Built for the Herzog film *El Grito de la Piedra*, fully equipped cabins sleep 4/6, heating, kitchenette.

E Hostería Los Ñires, Lago del Desierto s/n, T02962-493009, www.elchalten.com/losnires. Doubles and dormitories, and camping, US$5.

F Albergue Rancho Grande, San Martín s/n, T02962-493005, rancho@cotecal.com.ar. Price per person in small dormitories, good bathrooms, laundry and kitchen facilities, Hostelling International discounts, English, Italian, French, German spoken, highly recommended, reservations from **Chaltén Travel** in Calafate (see page 469).

F-G Albergue Patagonia, San Martín 493, T02962-461564, www.elchalten.com/patagonia. Price per person for dormitory accommodation, kitchen and laundry facilities, TV and video, book exchange, accepts TCs, comfortable. Hostelling International discounts, mountain bike rental US$10 per day, reservations for local excursions (Lago del Desierto, Lago Viedma boat trip, ice trek on Cerro Torre glacier). Highly recommended. Next door is the **Bar de Ahumados**, which serves regional specialities, homemade pasta and local ice cream.

Camping
These 3 campsites in the village all have hot showers. Showers are also available at the **Albergue Patagonia** and at **Confitería La Senyera** for US$2. There is also a campsite at the southern end of the **Lago del Desierto**.
Del Lago, Lago del Desierto 135, T02962-493010.
El Refugio, San Martín s/n.
El Relincho, San Martín s/n, T02962-493007.

⑦ Eating

El Chaltén *p472, map p473*
🍴 **El Bodegón**, San Martín s/n. Small pub that brews its own beer, also serves reasonable food.
🍴 **Josh Aike**. Excellent *confitería*, homemade food, beautiful building. Recommended.
🍴 **La Senyera del Torre**. Pub/restaurant, excellent bread. Recommended.
🍴 **Ruca Mahuida**, Lionel Terray s/n. Imaginative food using local ingredients.
🍴 **The Wall Pub**. Breakfasts and meals, plus interesting videos of ascents of Fitz Roy and Cerro Torre.
🍴 **Las Lengas**, Güemes y A de Viedma. Large portions, good value.

⊛ Festivals and events

El Chaltén *p472, map p473*
10 Nov The Día de la Tradición is celebrated with *gaucho* events, riding and a barbecue (US$5).

⊙ Shopping

El Chaltén *p472, map p473*
There are several small shops selling food, gas and batteries (**Despensa 2 de Abril** is said to be cheapest) but you're better off buying supplies in El Calafate (cheaper and more choice). Many places bake good bread. Fuel is available.
Viento Oeste, T02962-493021. Rents and sells mountain equipment.

▲ Activities and tours

Lago Argentino and around *p470*
Equip yourself with warm clothes, food and drink for any trip to the glacier.

Tours to Ventisquero Petit Moreno

From El Calafate, in addition to buses by **Interlagos** and **Taqsa** (see page 469), many agencies run minibus tours, US$18 return (plus US$3.50 park entry), leaving around 0800 or around 1430, 6-7 hr trip, allowing 3 hrs at the glacier, return ticket valid if you come back next day (student discount available). Several agencies offer walking excursions on the Ventisquero Moreno, usually finishing with champagne or whisky with ice chipped from the glacier. For contact details, see page 469. It is also possible to visit from Puerto Natales (see page 449), which is cheaper than staying in Argentina.

Out of season, trips to the glacier are difficult to arrange, but you could gather a group and hire a taxi (US$40 for 4 passengers round trip); try **Remise Taxis**, T02902-491745. Ask rangers where you can camp out of season; there are no facilities except for a decrepit toilet block.

You can also arrive by boat. They leave twice daily to the glacier from near the park entrance. Most of the minibus tours are timed to coincide with departure. The boats (with capacity for up to 60 passengers) take you right up to the face of the glacier, 1 hr, US$10, recommended.

Tours to Ventisquero Upsala

Pay in dollars and take food. Out of season it is extremely difficult to get to the glacier. **Fernández Campbell** (see page 469) runs daily bus and boat tours in summer to visit the Upsala glacier, Lago Onelli, the Onelli Glacier and the Spegazzini Glacier (check before going that access to the face of the Upsala glacier is possible). Bus departs 0730 from El Calafate for Punta Bandera, 50 km west, from where the tour boats depart. The price includes bus fares and park entry fees. 1 hr is allowed for a meal at the restaurant near Lago Onelli. Return bus to Calafate at 1930: a tiring day, it is often cold and wet, but memorable. **Upsala Explorer**, 9 de Julio 69, T02902-491034, reservascristinaing@cotecal.com.ar. Organizes tours for US$100, including lunch, 4WD trip and guided hikes around Estancia Cristina with amazing views of the glacier. Reservations can be made through several agencies.

Cerro Fitz Roy *p472, map p473*

Climbing

Base camp for climbing Fitz Roy is **Campamento Río Blanco** (see above). Permits for climbing are available at the national park information office. The best time is mid-Feb to end-Mar; Nov-Dec is very windy; Jan is fair; winter is extremely cold. Most of the peaks in the Fitz Roy massif and the Campo de Hielo Continental (continental icefield), which marks the frontier with Chile, are for very experienced climbers only. For the icefields guides are essential; the terrain is ice and rock and should only be tackled by extremely fit climbers. Necessary gear includes double boots, crampons, pickaxe, ropes, winter clothing; ask **Sr Guerra** in El Chaltén about hiring animals to carry equipment.

Fitz Roy Expediciones, El Chaltén, T02962-493017, www.elchalten.com/fitzroy. Experienced guide Alberto del Castillo organizes adventure excursions, including trekking on the Campo de Hielo Continental and horse riding, English and Italian spoken. Highly recommended.

Horse treks

Prices from El Chaltén to Laguna Capri US$15; Laguna Torre US$20; Río Blanco, Piedra del Fraile and Laguna Toro all US$25 each; contact **Rodolfo Guerra**, T02962-493020, or **El Relincho**, T02962-493007.

⊖ Transport

El Chaltén *p472, map p473*

Bus To **Calafate**, Chaltén Travel, Los Glaciares and Caltur, several daily in summer, less frequent off season, 4 hrs, US$7 one way. Bear in mind that day trips from Calafate involve a lot of travelling and little time to see the area, although some agencies offer deals, for example return travel by regular bus and 1 night's accommodation for US$50. To **Los Antiguos**, north along Ruta 40, **Chaltén Travel**, 3 weekly, 14 hrs, US$40. Best to book return before departure during high season. Off season, travel is difficult and there's little transport for hitching. Agencies charge US$100 1 way for up to 8 people, US$150 return.

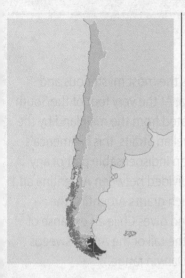

Tierra del Fuego

Footprint features

Introduction

The island of Tierra del Fuego is the most mysterious and captivating part of all Patagonia. At the very foot of the South American continent and separated from the mainland by the intricate waterways of the Magellan Straits, this is America's last remaining wilderness and an indispensable part of any trip to the south. The island is divided between Argentina and Chile by a north-south line, which grants Argentina the Atlantic and southern coasts, and gives Chile an expanse of wilderness to the west, where the tail of the Andes sweeps east in the form of the mighty Darwin range.

The Chilean side is largely inaccessible, apart from the small town of Porvenir, though expeditions can be organized from Punta Arenas to take you hiking and trout fishing. Glaciers and jagged peaks give a dramatic backdrop to the Argentine city of Ushuaia the island's main centre, set in a serene natural harbour on the Beagle Channel, with views of the Dientes de Navarino mountains on the Chilean island of Navarino opposite. Sail from Ushuaia along the channel to the pioneer home of Harberton; to Cape Horn; or even to Antarctica. Head into the small but picturesque Parque Nacional Tierra del Fuego, for hikes around Bahía Lapataia and steep climbs with magnificent views out along the channel. The mountain slopes are covered in lenga forest, and if you visit in autumn you might think the name 'Land of Fire' derives from the blaze of scarlet and orange. Elsewhere on the island, lakes and valleys can be explored on foot or on horseback, and in winter the valleys are perfect for cross-country skiing, while the slopes at Cerro Castor offer good powder snow, and skiing with spectacular views of the end of the world.

★ Don't miss…

1 **Dientes de Navarino** Fly to Isla Navarino and trek the mighty teeth – only for the intrepid, page 484.
2 **Fly-fishing in the Río Grande** Take a trip into the Chilean wilderness, or stay at the famous Argentine Estancia María Behety to fish huge trout, page 488 and 496.
3 **Yámana Museum**, **Ushuaia** The moving story of the island's original inhabitants, now tragically lost, page 492.
4 **The Beagle Channel** Imagine the experiences of those early explorers as you take a comfortable boat to seal islands and the calm haven of Harberton, page 492 and 493.
5 **Parque Nacional Tierra del Fuego** Stroll around the bay for magical views of the end of the world, page 494.

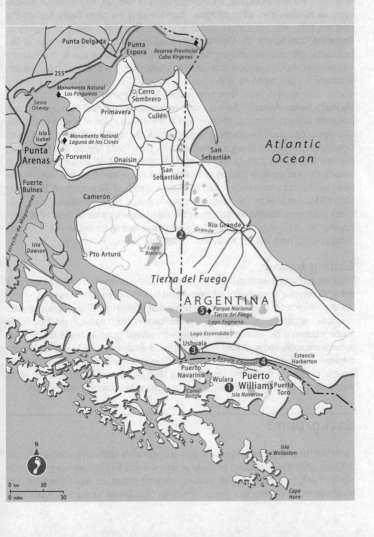

Ins and outs

Getting there

Air The **Argentine Tierra del Fuego** is easy to reach with several flights daily from Buenos Aires to Río Grande and Ushuaia, and less frequent flights from El Calafate, and some other towns in Patagonia. Flights are heavily booked in advance throughout the summer months. **Chilean Tierra del Fuego** is less easily accessed by air, but there are five flights a week from Punta Arenas to Porvenir in the summer, and four a week to Puerto Williams on Isla Navarino, also summer only; it's almost impossible to reach by boat.

Ferry and bus There are two places where ferries cross to Tierra del Fuego: from **Tres Puentes**, just north of Punta Arenas to **Porvenir**, and further east across **Primera Angostura** at Punta Delgada, both crossings on Chilean territory. All buses from mainland Argentina use the quicker and more frequent Punta Delgada crossing, and from Punta Arenas, buses take the road northeast to Punta Delgada, and cross by ferry there. Via **Punta Delgada**, the crossing takes 15 minutes, and boats run roughly every 40 minutes from 0830 to 2300. There's a cosy tea room **Bahía Azul** on the northern side, with hot snacks and toilets. Foot passengers free, US$23 per car.
Argentine/Chile border The Chilean/Argentine border is at the Argentine town of San Sebastián, 128 km south of where the ferry arrives at Punta Espora, and – confusingly – 14 km east of a Chilean town also called San Sebastián. The border at Argentine San Sebastián is open 24 hours, with a basic ACA motel, To2964-425542, and a service station open 0700 to 2300. From here Route 3 is paved to Río Grande.
Via Punta Arenas-Porvenir There is a daily ferry crossing (summer) from Tres Puentes, just north of Punta Arenas to Porvenir, and from here a 225 km road runs east to Río Grande (six hours) via the border at San Sebastián. (By road, Punta Arenas and Punta Delgada are connected by a good road, RN255). From Punta Arenas, bus A or E from Avenida Magallanes goes to Tres Puentes, or *colectivo* 15, US$0.50; taxi US$4. In season, the *Melinka* sails Tuesday to Sunday. Less frequently off season. The crossing takes two hours 20 minutes, and can be rough and cold, US$8 per person, US$12 per bike, US$50 per vehicle. The timetable is dependent on tides and subject to change; check in advance. Reservations are essential especially in summer (at least 24 hours in advance for cars), obtainable from **Transbordadora Austral Broom**, in Punta Arenas, Bulnes 05075, To61-218100, www.tabsa.cl (or To61-580089 in Porvenir).

Getting around

There are good bus links from Punta Arenas to Río Grande in Argentina, with an option of going via Porvenir, along the decent loop of road on the Chilean side. From Porvenir your options are limited to a *ripio* road around Bahía Inútil to near Lago Blanco, though there's no public transport here. Argentine Tierra del Fuego is much easier to get around, via Route 3 between Río Grande and Ushuaia with several buses a day. A fan of roads spreads out south and west from Río Grande to the estancias in the Argentine side, but these are unpaved, and best attempted in a 4WD vehicle. A good *ripio* road leads from 40 km east of Ushuaia to Harberton and Estancia Moat on the south coast, and part of the way along the north coast to Estancia San Pablo; no public transport here either.

Background

Tierra del Fuego's narrated history began with the early 16th-century explorers, but the island had been inhabited for some 10,000 years by four indigenous groups who survived only until the early 20th century, when white settlers wiped them out. The most numerous of these four groups, the Onas (also known as the Selk'nam), were

Shipwrecked in the Magellan Straits

The Estrecho de Magallanes, 534 km long, is a treacherous sea passage with a long history of claiming victims. The hostile conditions are eloquently conveyed in the words of Sir John Narborough: "horrible like the ruins of a world destroyed by terrific earthquakes".

From the Atlantic the first navigational problem facing sailors is simply the difficulty of entering the straits against the fierce westerly gales that prevail. Once in the straits the dangers are far from over: many ships have fallen victim to the notorious Williwaws, winds with the ferocity of tornados that spring up from nowhere; no less vicious are the Pamperos, which blow off the land with enough force to capsize a vessel.

Although in 1520 Magellan succeeded in passing through the straits that bear his name, few others managed to do so in the years that followed; of the 17 ships that attempted the passage in the early 16th century, only one, the *Victoria*, succeeded in reaching the Pacific and returning to Europe. Twelve were lost near the eastern entrance and four returned in failure. The reason these early navigators chose to attempt the dangerous voyage was the lure of a short route between Europe and the spices of the East. Even when it became clear that there was no such short route, the straits still provided a useful means for Europeans to reach the rich Pacific ports of Peru and Chile without disembarking to cross Mexico or Panama overland.

Even with the development of advanced navigation techniques in the 19th century, losses continued: in 1869, for instance, the *Santiago*, an iron paddle-steamer built in Glasgow and owned by the Pacific Mail line, went down off Isla Desolación at the western end of the straits with a cargo of gold and silver. While the Panama Canal now provides a shorter route between the Atlantic and Pacific Oceans, the size of modern ships means that the straits are still a busy shipping route. The most common cargo is now oil; casualties still occur with, of course, the added risk of environmental disaster from oil spillage.

Tierra del Fuego Background

hunter-gatherers in the north, living mainly on guanaco , which they shot with bow and arrow. The southeastern corner of the island was inhabited by the Haus or Hausch, also hunter-gatherers, of whom very little is known. The Yaganes or Yámana lived along the Beagle Channel and on the islands further south, and were seafaring people who survived mainly on seafood, fish and seabirds, physically smaller than the Onas but with a strongly developed upper body for rowing long distances. The fourth group, the Alacalufe, lived in the west of Tierra del Fuego as well as on the Chonos Archipelago, surviving by fishing and hunting seals.

The first Europeans to visit the island came with the Portuguese navigator Fernão Magalhães (Magellan), who, in 1520, sailed through the channel that now bears his name. It was Magellan who named the island Land of Fire when he saw the smoke from many fires lit along the shoreline. As a result of numerous maritime disasters, including the failure of Sarmiento de Gamboa's attempt at colonizing the Straits in 1584, the indigenous population were left undisturbed for three centuries.

Fitzroy and Darwin's visits for scientific surveying in 1832 and 1833 recorded some fascinating interaction with the indigenous peoples. Their visits were a precursor to determined attempts to convert the indigenous groups to Christianity so that the island could be used by white settlers without fear of attack by uncontrolled natives. Several disastrous missions followed, and encountered naturally stiff resistance from the inhabitants; the first successful mission was finally established in 1869 and, in 1884, the Reverend Thomas Bridges (see box, page 493) founded a mission at Ushuaia. But Bridges soon realized that his original task was a destructive one. He was the first European to learn the Yámana language, and soon had many Yámana settled around Ushuaia and compiled his Yámana-English dictionary for the ease of conversion. The purpose of the missionary work had of course been to facilitate lucrative sheep farming on the island. The Ona were attracted to the 'white guanacos' on their land and hunting sheep proved far easier than the faster footed guanaco. The colonists responded by offering two sheep for each Ona that was killed (proof was provided by a pair of Ona ears). The indigenous groups were further ravaged by epidemics of European diseases. In a desperate attempt to save the Ona, Salesian missionaries founded three missions in the Magellan Straits in the early 20th century but, stripped of their land, the Ona lost the will to live; the last Ona died in 1999. The Hausch also died out. One old Yámana lady presently survives near Puerto Williams and there are a few Alacalufe at Puerto Edén in the Chonos Archipelago.

Imprecision in the original colonial land division and the greed of the rush southwards led to border disputes between Argentina and Chile. These still rumble on today. The initial settlement of the dispute in 1883 was followed by a desire by both governments to populate the area by allocating large expanses of land for sheep farming. The main beneficiaries of this policy on Tierra del Fuego were the Menéndez and Braun families, already established in Punta Arenas.

Argentine government tax incentives to companies in the 1970s led to the establishment of new industries in Río Grande and Ushuaia and a rapid growth in the population of both cities; the subsequent withdrawal of incentives has produced rising unemployment and migration. Tourism is increasingly important in Ushuaia.

For a detailed narrative account of Tierra del Fuego, the best book is the classic by Lucas Bridges, *Uttermost Part of the Earth*, out of print, but easily obtained on Abe Books, www.abebooks.co.uk. Colin McEwan's *Patagonia, Natural History, Prehistory and Ethnography at the Uttermost Part of the Earth* (British Museum press, 1997) is brilliantly informative and utterly fascinating. Also recommended is *Savage – The Life and Times of Jemmy Button*. by Nick Hazelwood (Hodder & Stoughton, 2000).

Chilean Tierra del Fuego

The Chilean half of Tierra del Fuego is in two sections: the western half of Isla Grande, the main island, and the whole of Isla Navarino, to the south of the main island. Much less developed than the Argentine side of Tierra del Fuego, there are just two small towns where Chile's Fuegians are mostly concentrated: Porvenir, on Isla Grande, easily reached by ferry from Punta Arenas, and Puerto Williams on Isla Navarino, which can only be reached by a flight from Punta Arenas. The northern part of Isla Grande is flat steppe, but the south is dominated by the Darwin range of mountains, which provide a dramatic visual backdrop, even if you can't easily get to them. Tourism on Chilean territory is very limited, but it's possible to organize trekking tours from Punta Arenas, and there are plenty of fishing lodges offering magnificent trout fishing, particularly on Río Grande.» For Sleeping, Eating and other listings, see pages 486-488.

Porvenir and around 🏨🍴⛰️🚌🚗 » pp486-488. Colour map 6, C3.

Chilean Tierra del Fuego has a population of 7000, most of whom live in the pretty small town of Porvenir (population 5100), the only town on the Chilean half of the main island. Founded in 1894 in the gold boom, when many people came seeking fortunes from Croatia and Chiloe, Porvenir is a quiet place with a wide open pioneer feel, streets of neat brightly painted houses of corrugated zinc, and quaint tall domed trees lining the main avenue. The small museum **Museo Fernando Cordero Rusque** ① *Samuel Valdivieso 402*, has archaeological and photographic displays on the Onas and good displays on natural history and the early gold diggers and sheep farmers. There's little else to do here, but you could stroll around the plaza, with its **Iglesia San Francisco de Sales**, and down to the shoreside promenade, where there's a strange collection of 19th-century farm machinery and a striking wooden monument to the Selknam. **Tourist information** ① *Padre Mario Zavattaro No 424, T/F 061-580094, www.pata goniachile.com*. There's more helpful information at a kiosk on the waterfront, which sells fine handicrafts, kuanip@entelchile.net. There's a bank on the plaza.

Beyond Porvenir

Beyond Porvenir there is wonderfully wild virgin territory to explore. However, if you want an adventure, by far your best bet is to arrange a trip through tour operators in Punta Arenas, since there's still very little infrastructure on the Chilean side of the island. **Turismo Aonikenk** is recommended (see Tour operators, page 486), offering several days' trekking into the remote mountainous south of the island, which is otherwise unreachable, horse riding expeditions and also fly-fishing. There are two tour operators in Porvenir itself, offering fairly traditional tours through the Cordón Baquedano to see the areas where gold was mined – recommended for great views of the Magellan Straits and, and to traditional sheep farming *estancias*.

Until recently the secret haunt of Hollywood stars such as Stallone and Ted Turner (who has his own *estancia* here), it's now possible to stay in several comfortable fishing lodges in Río Grande, Lago Escondido and Lago Blanco. This area is famous for its brown trout, sea-run brook trout and steelheads, weighing 2 to 14 kg. See specialist fly-fishing tour operators, or **Turismo Aonikenk** (page 486). The season runs from 15 October to 14 April, with the best fishing from January to April.

Cameron

About 90 km east of Porvenir, roads head north to San Sebastián and south to **Cameron**. This large farm settlement, which is the only other community of any size on the Chilean part of the island, lies 149 km southeast of Porvenir on the opposite shore of Bahía Inútil. This wonderful windswept bay, with views of distant hills and the snow-capped Darwin range all along the horizon, was named 'useless' by British engineers making a hydrographic survey here in 1827 because it has no useful port. Nevertheless, as you near Cameron, the southern mountains loom ahead and the road passes secluded canyons and bays, interspersed with a few farms, and the whole feel is dramatic, isolated and somehow rather magical. The road has little traffic, but there are a few vehicles daily in summer, so hitching is possible – if you don't mind waiting on an exposed windswept plain for hours. There's not much at Cameron itself, although 650 people live scattered among the farm buildings all around, but at the eastern end of the bay, at **Caleta Josefina**, you can visit a handsome ex-estancia built 1833 by the powerful sheep farming Menéndez family, where some old buildings remain.

From Cameron a road runs southeast past an airfield and on for a further 40 km to a junction, where roads head north to San Sebastián and south to Sección Río Grande (7 km from the junction) and Estancia Vicuña (35 km further on) – there is very little traffic here. The road south climbs into the hills, through woods where guanacos hoot and run off into glades and the banks are covered with red and purple moss. The north shores of **Lago Blanco** can be reached by cutting through the woods from Sección Río Grande, with superb views of the mountains surrounding the lake and the snows in the south, or from Estancia Vicuña. In the centre of the lake is Isla Victoria, which has accommodation. The lake area can be very cold, even in mid-summer; biting winds sweep in from the south, so wrap up warmly. It's essential to organize any trip to this area through a reliable tour operator with the infrastructure.

From **Estancia Vicuña** a trail leads southwest to the **Río Azopardo**, which also offers trout fishing (sleeping at **Estancia Almirantazgo**). South of here trails run across the Darwin Range to the **Estancia Yendegaia** near the Beagle Channel, a wonderful area for horse riding. For trips into this wild and undiscovered country, contact **Aonikenk** in Punta Arenas, www.aonikenk.com.

Isla Navarino ⬛🔋🔺🚌🔵 ➤➤ pp486-488.

Situated on the southern shore of the Beagle Channel, Isla Navarino is totally unspoilt and beautiful, offering great geographical diversity, thanks to the Dientes de Navarino range of mountains, with peaks over 1000 m, covered with southern beech forest up to 500 m and, south of that, great plains covered with peat bogs, and many lagoons abundant in flora. The island was centre of the indigenous Yaganes culture, and there are 500 archaeological sites, the oldest dated as 3000 years old. Guanacos and condors can be seen inland, as well as large numbers of beavers, which were introduced to the island and have done considerable damage. The flight from Punta Arenas is beautiful, with superb views of Tierra del Fuego, the Cordillera Darwin, the Beagle Channel and the islands stretching south to Cape Horn.

Puerto Williams → *Phone code: 061. Colour map 7, C2. Population: 2500.*
The only settlement of any size on the island is Puerto Williams, a Chilean naval base situated about 50 km east of Ushuaia in Argentina, across the Beagle Channel. Puerto Williams is the southernmost permanently inhabited town in the world; 50 km east-southeast is Puerto Toro, the southernmost permanently inhabited settlement on earth. Some maps mistakenly mark a road from Puerto Williams to Puerto Toro, but it doesn't exist; access is only by sea. Due to the long-running border dispute with Argentina here, Puerto Williams is controlled by the Chilean Navy. Outside the Naval headquarters, you can see the bow section of the *Yelcho*, the tug chartered by Shackleton to rescue men stranded on Elephant Island (see box, page 485).

Your main purpose for visiting the island is likely to be the trekking on the Dientes de Navarino, but you should take time to explore the indigenous heritage here too. It's beautifully documented in the **Museo Martín Gusinde** ① *Mon-Thu 1000-1300, 1500-1800, Sat and Sun 1500-1800, US$1*, known as the **Museo del Fin del Mundo** (End of the World Museum) which is full of information about vanished indigenous tribes, local wildlife and the famous voyages by Charles Darwin and Fitzroy of the *Beagle*. A visit is highly recommended. A kilometre west of the town is the yacht club (one of Puerto Williams' two nightspots), whose wharf is made from a sunken 1930s Chilean warship. **Tourist information** ① *Municipalidad de Cabos de Hornos, Presidente Ibañez 130, T061-621011, isotop@mitierra.cl*. Ask for maps and details on hiking. The town also has a bank, supermarkets and hospital.

Exploring the island
For superb views, climb **Cerro Bandera**, which is reached by a path from the dam 4 km west of the town (a three- to four-hour round trip, it's steep, and you'll need warm clothes). There is excellent trekking around the Dientes de Navarino range, the southernmost trail in the world, through impressive mountain landscape, frozen lagoons and snowy peaks, giving superb views over the Beagle Channel. It's a challenging hike, over a distance of 53 km in five days, possible only from December to March, and a good level of fitness is needed. There is no equipment rental on island; ask for information in the tourist office at Puerto Williams, but it's best to go with an organized expedition from Punta Arenas. There are views of Cape Horn in clear weather but conditions change quickly and it can snow on the hills, even in summer. Charter flights are available over Cape Horn and to King George Island on the northern

⋮ Endurance in the Antarctic

Ernest Shackleton's 1914-1916 Antarctic expedition is one of the epics of polar exploration. Shackleton's vessel, *Endurance*, which left England in August 1914 with 28 men aboard, became trapped in pack-ice in January 1915. After drifting northwards with the ice for eight months, the ship was crushed by the floes and sank. With three boats, supplies and the dogs, the group camped on an ice floe which continued to drift north for eight months. In April 1916, after surviving on a diet largely of seals and penguins, the party took to the boats as the ice broke up. After seven days at sea they reached Elephant Island. From there, Shackleton and five other men sailed 1300 km to South Georgia, where there were whaling stations. At first Shackleton, from whom nothing had been heard for 18 months, was not recognized.

The British government sent a rescue vessel to Elephant Island. After ice had prevented three rescue attempts Shackleton persuaded the Chilean authorities to permit a fourth attempt using the tug *Yelcho*. Leaving Punta Arenas on 25 August 1916, the small vessel encountered thick fog but, unusually for the time of year, little ice and it quickly reached Elephant Island where the men, who had endured an Antarctic winter under upturned boats, were down to four days of supplies.

Although the expedition failed to cross Antarctica, Shackleton's achievement was outstanding: the party had survived two Antarctic winters without loss of life. Shackleton himself returned to the region in 1921 to lead another expedition but, in January 1922, aged only 47, he suffered a fatal heart attack in South Georgia.

tip of the Antarctic peninsula, where you can see the curvature of the earth on the horizon, with excursions to penguin and sea lion colonies.

Beyond Cerro Bandera, a road leads 56 km west of Puerto Williams to Puerto Navarino. There is little or no traffic on this route and it is very beautiful, with forests of lengas stretching right down to the water's edge. You can also visit **Villa Ukika**, 2 km east of town, the place where the last descendants of the Yaganes people live, relocated from their original homes at Caleta Mejillones, which was the last indigenous reservation in the province, inhabited by hundreds of Yagana descendents. At **Mejillones**, 32 km from Puerto Williams, is a graveyard and memorial to the Yámana people. Just before Estancia Santa Rosa (10 km further on), a path is said to cross the forest, lakes and beaver dams to Wulaia (four to six hours), where the *Beagle* anchored in 1833; however, even the farmer at Wulaia gets lost following this track.

At **Puerto Navarino** there are a handful of marines and an abandoned police post, where you may be allowed to sleep. There are beautiful views across to Ushuaia and west to icebound Hoste Island and the Darwin Massif. A path continues to a cliff above the Murray Narrows; blue, tranquil and utterly calm. If trekking alone in wild parts of the island, beware of sinking mud caused by beaver dams; note also that there is quite a high incidence of rabies among domestic and wild animals (including beavers).

Cape Horn

You can catch a boat from Isla Navarino to Cape Horn (the most southerly piece of land on earth apart from Antartica). There's a pebbly beach on the north side of the island; boats anchor in the bay and passengers are taken ashore by motorized dinghy. A rotting stairway climbs the cliff above the beach to the building where three marines run the naval post. A path leads to the impressive monument of an albatross over looking the churning waters of the Drake Passage below. ▸▸ *For further details, see Transport, page 487.*

● Sleeping

Porvenir *p482*

A Hostería Los Flamencos, Tte Merino 018, T061-580049, www.hosterialosflamen cos.com. One of the town's best places to stay with wonderful views of the bay, good food, and a pleasant place for a drink. Recommended. Also organizes tours.

C Hostería y Turismo Yendegaia, Croacia 702, T061-581665, www.turismoyendegaia.com. A charming, bright yellow house just 2 blocks from the plaza, built by a Croatian pioneer in 1926, this has 7 comfortable and light rooms, all with bath and TV, a good restaurant, and plenty of tourist information from the travel company which is also housed here. Recommended.

C Rozas, Phillipi 296, T061-580088. With bath, hot water, heating, restaurant and bar, internet, laundry facilities. Recommended.

D Hostel Kawi, Pedro Silva 144, T061-581638, www.tierradelfuegoandtrouts.com. A comfortable hostal, with rooms for 3, all with bath, and offering fly-fishing trips on the island.

D Restaurant y Hostal El Chispa, Señoret 202, T061-580 054. Simple rooms, some with shared bath, and a good restaurant, serving seafood and other Chilean dishes.

E España, Croacia 698, T061-580160. Price per person. Some rooms with bath, breakfast extra. Good restaurant with fixed-price lunch.

Beyond Porvenir *p483*

If you get stuck in the wilds, note that it is almost always possible to camp or bed down in a barn at an *estancia*.

B-E Hostería de la Frontera, San Sebastián, T061-696004, escabini@tie.cl. Rooms with bath and a decent restaurant. Avoid the more basic accommodation in an annexe.

B-E Hostería Tunkelen, Cerro Sombrero, 46 km south of Primera Angostura, T061-345001, hosteria_tunkelen@hotmail.com. Rooms and dormitory accommodation. Recommended.

E Posada Las Flores, Km 127 on the Porvenir-San Sebastián road. Reservations via **Hostal de la Patagonia** in Punta Arenas.

F Pensión del Señor Alarcón, Cerro Sombrero, 46 km south of Primera Angostura. Good, friendly.

F Refugio Lago Blanco, Lago Blanco, T061-241197. The only accommodation on the lake.

Puerto Williams *p484*

You can also stay at private houses.

A-B Hostería Wala, on the edge of Lauta bay, 2 km out of town, T061-621114. Splendid walks in the area. Very hospitable.

C Pensión Temuco, Piloto Pardo 244, T061-621113. Price per person for full board, comfortable, good food, hot showers. Slightly overpriced, but recommended. Good breakfasts.

D Hostería Camblor, T061-621033, hosteria camblor@terra.cl. Price per person for full board. Gets very booked up. Good value.

E Hostal Yagan, Piloto Pardo 260, T061-621334, hostalyagan@hotmail.com. Price per person. Single and double rooms. Good meals available. Clean and comfortable, friendly, tours offered.

E Jeanette Talavera, Maragaño 168, T061-621150, www.simltd.com. Small dormitories, shared bathrooms, kitchen and laundry facilities, also organizes sailing trips, treks and other activities.

E Residencial Onashaga, Uspashun 15, T061-621564, run by Señor Ortiz – everyone knows him. Price per person. Accommodation is basic, but the welcomes is warm. Good meals, helpful, full board available.

● Eating

Porvenir *p482*

Fishermen will prepare lobster on the spot.

♥ Hostería Los Flamencos, Tte Merino 018. Very good food.

♥ Hostería y Turismo Yendegaia, Croacia 702 Great range of seafood.

♥Club Croata, Senoret y Phillippi. On waterfront, good food, lively.

♥Restaurante Puerto Montt, Croacia 1169. Recommended for seafood.

Puerto Williams *p484*

There are several grocery stores; prices are high because of the remoteness.

▲ Activities and tours

Porvenir *p482*

For adventure tourism and trekking, it's best to go through tour operators in Punta Arenas:

Turismo Aonikenk, Magallanes 619, T061-221982, www.aonikenk.com. An excellent company offering adventures and hiking on Ilsa Navarino and also south of Porvenir and mainland Chile. Superb expedition around the Dientes de Navarino, fly-fishing and horse riding.

Turismo Cordillera de Darwin, Croacia 675, T061-580206, www.explorepatagonia.cl For tours of the island from a day to a week.

Hostería y Turismo Yendegaia, Croacia 702, T 061-581665, www.turismo yendegaia.com. Lots of conventional tours in the area and some fishing too.

Puerto Williams *p484*

There is no trekking/outdoors equipment available on Isla Navarino, so stock up in Punta Arenas before you arrive.

Sailing

Captain Ben Garrett offers recommended adventure sailing in his schooner *Victory* in Dec and Jan, including special trips to Ushuaia, cruises in the canals and voyages to Cape Horn, the glaciers, Puerto Montt and Antarctica. Write to **Victory Cruises**, Annex No 1 Puerto Williams; or call collect to Punta Arenas and leave a message with the Puerto Williams operator.

⊖ Transport

Porvenir *p482*
Air

Aerovías DAP, Señoret s/n, Porvenir, T061-580089, www.aeroviasdap.cl, fly from **Punta Arenas** (weather and bookings permitting), twice daily Mon-Sat, US$50 one way. Heavily booked so make sure you have your return reservation confirmed.

Bus

Buses from Punta Arenas to Ushuaia don't take on passengers here. **Transportes Gessell**, Duble Almeyda 257, T061-580488 (also in Punta Arenas at José Menéndez 556, T061-222896) runs buses to **Río Grande** (Argentina), Tue and Sat 1400, 5 hrs, US$20; return service Wed and Sun 0800. Local buses run to **Cameron** from Manuel Señor, in theory Mon and Fri 1700, US$13.

Ferry

The *Melinka* sails from **Tres Puentes** (5 km north of Punta Arenas; catch bus A or E from

Av Magallanes, US$1; taxi US$3) to Bahía Chilota, 5 km west of Porvenir, Tue-Sun 0900 with an extra afternoon sailing Tue-Thu in season, 2½ hrs, pedestrians US$8, cars US$50. The boat returns from Porvenir in the afternoon Tue-Sun. Timetable dependent on tides and subject to change; check in advance. The crossing can be rough and cold; watch for dolphins. Reservations are essential especially in summer (at least 24 hrs in advance for cars); obtainable from **Transbordadora Austral Broom**, Bulnes 05075, Punta Arenas, T061-218100 (T061-580089 in Porvenir), www.tabsa.cl.

The ferry service from **Punta Delgada** on the mainland to Punta Espora, 80 km north of Porvenir, departs usually every 40 mins 0830-2300 (schedules vary with the tides) and takes just 15 mins, pedestrians US$4, cars US$25. This is the principal route for buses and trucks between Ushuaia and mainland Argentina. Before 1000 most space is taken by trucks.

Puerto Williams *p484*
Air

Aerovías DAP, Centro Comercial s/n, T061-621051, www.aeroviasdap.cl, flies 20-seater Cessna aircraft from **Punta Arenas** Mon-Sat, departure time varies, 1¼ hrs, US$64 one way. Book well in advance; there are long waiting lists. Luggage allowance 10 kg (US$2 per kg extra). **Aeropetrel** will charter a plane from **Puerto Williams** to Cape Horn (US$2600 for 8-10 people).

Ferry

Despite its proximity, there are no regular sailings to Isla Navarino from Ushuaia (Argentina). The following all depart from **Punta Arenas**: Austral Broom ferry Cruz Australis, www.tabsa.cl, once a week, 36 hrs, US$130 for a reclining seat, US$170 for a bunk, meals included; Navarino (contact Carlos Aguilera, 21 de Mayo 1460, Punta Arenas, T061-228066), 3rd week of every month, 12 passengers, US$180 one way; Beaulieu cargo boat, once a month, US$350 return, 6 days. Some cruises to **Ushuaia** also stop at Puerto Williams.

Cape Horn *p485*

Crucero Australis cruises from **Ushuaia** stop at Cape Horn. In addition, the naval vessel *PSG Micalvi*, which sails once every 3 months from

Punta Arenas via **Puerto Williams**, may take passengers to Cape Horn for US$250 (letters of recommendation will help). Navy and port authorities in Puerto Williams may deny any knowledge, but everyone else knows when a boat is due; ask at the Armada in Punta Arenas. Otherwise ask at the yacht club about hitching a ride to Cape Horn.

⚙ Directory

Porvenir *p482*
Banks Currency exchange is available at Estrella del Sur, Santos Mardones.

Puerto Williams *p484*
Post Closes 1900. **Telephone** CTC, Mon-Sat 0930-2230, Sun 1000-1300, 1600-2200.

Argentine Tierra del Fuego

Argentine Tierra del Fuego belongs to the province of Tierra del Fuego, Antártida y Las Islas del Atlántico Sur, the capital of which is Ushuaia. The population of the Argentine sector is around 85,000, most of whom live in the two towns of Río Grande and Ushuaia. Both bigger and more developed than the Chilean side of the island, it provides good territory for guided explorations of the wilderness. ⟫ *For Sleeping, Eating and other listings, see pages 495-502.*

Río Grande 🚌🚕🚻🚠🚉⚙ ⟫ *pp 495-502. Colour map 6, C4.*

Río Grande is a sprawling modern coastal town (population 53,000), the centre for a rural sheep-farming community which grew rapidly in the oil boom of the 1970s, and with government tax incentives. The new population was stranded when benefits were withdrawn in recent years, leading to increasing unemployment and emigration, and leaving a rather sad, windy dusty town today. The people are friendly but there's little culture, and you're most likely to visit in order to change buses. There are a couple of good places to stay, however, and a small museum worth seeing, as well as the splendid historical Estancia Viamonte nearby. And if you're keen on fishing, Río Grande's legendary monster brown trout can be plucked from the water at Estancia María Behety.

Sights
The city's architecture is a chaotic mixture of smart new nouveau riche houses and much humbler wooden and tin constructions. It seems to have defied municipal efforts at prettification, and the series of peeling and graffitied concrete 'sculptures' along some of the avenues do little to cheer it up. But if you do get stuck here, you could trace the city's history through sheep, missions, pioneers and oil in its interesting, small **Museo de la Ciudad** ① *Alberdi 555, T02964-430414, Tue-Fri 1000-1700*. The city was founded by Fagnano's Salesian mission in 1893, and you can visit the original building **La Candelaria** ① *11 km north, T02964-421642, Mon-Sat 1000-1230, 1500-1900, Sun 1500-1900, US$1.50, afternoon teas, US$3*, whose museum has displays of natural history and indigenous artefacts, with strawberry plantations, piglets and an aviary. The **tourist office** ① *Rosales 350, T02964-431324, www.tierradelfuego.org.ar, Mon-Fri 0900-2100, Sat 1000-1700*, is small but helpful in the blue-roofed hut on the plaza.

Estancia Viamonte, on the coast 40 km south, is a working sheep farm with a fascinating history. Here, Lucas Bridges (see box, page 493) built a home to protect the large tribe of indigenous Onas, who were fast dying out. The estancia is still inhabited by his descendents, who can take you riding and to see the life of the farm. There's also a house to rent and superb accommodation. Highly recommended. **Estancia María Behety**, built by the sheepfarming millionaire José Menéndez, is a heaven for brown trout fishing.

From Río Grande to Ushuaia

From Río Grande, several roads fan out south west to the heart of the island, though this area is little inhabited, with just a few estancias. The paved main road south, Route 3, continues across wonderfully open land, more forested than the expanses of Patagonian steppe further north, and increasingly hilly as you near Ushuaia. After around 160 km, you could turn left along a track to the coast, to find **Estancia Cabo San Pablo**, 120 km from Río Grande. A simple working estancia in a beautiful position, owned by the charming Apolinaire family, with beautiful native woodland for walking and riding, birdwatching and fishing. Also other trips to places of interest within reach. Open all year, but reserve in advance. Route 3 then climbs high above Lago Fagnano and Tolhuin.

Tolhuin and around → *Phone code: 02964.*

A friendly, small, growing settlement close to shore of Lago Fagnano, a large expanse of water, right at the heart of Tierra del Fuego, with a stretch of beach close to the village, which remains quiet and little exploited. There's a YPF service station just off the main road, but it's worth driving into the village itself for the wonderful, famous bakery **La Unión**, where you can buy all kinds of bread, great *empanadas* and delicious fresh *facturas* (pastries). It's also the source of all information in the village. There's a tiny, friendly **tourist office** ① *open 0900-1500*, with very helpful staff, near the YPF station. Handicrafts are available at El Encuentro including fine leather goods, just half a block from tourist information. For **horse riding** in the area, contact **Sendero del Indio**, ① *T02964-15615258 sonia@netcombbs.com.ar*. From the village a road leads down to the tranquil lake shore, where there are a couple of good places to stay. Further along Route 3, 50 km from Ushuaia, a road to the right swoops down to **Lago Escondido**, a long, fjord-like lake with steep, deep green mountains descending into the water on all sides.

Ushuaia ⊜🕖🕗⛰️🚌🍴🎕 »pp 495-502. Colour map 6, C4.

The most southerly town in the world, Ushuaia's (population 45,000) setting is spectacular. Its brightly coloured houses look like toys against the dramatic backdrop of vast jagged mountains. Opposite are the forbidding peaks of Isla de Navarino and, between flows, the serene green Beagle Channel. Sailing those waters you can just imagine how it was for Darwin, arriving here in 1832, and for those early settlers, the Bridges, in 1871. Though the town has expanded in recent years, sprawling untidily along the coast, Ushuaia still retains the feel of a pioneer town, isolated and expectant. There are lots of places to stay, which fill up entirely in January, a fine museum, and some great fish restaurants. There is spectacular landscape to be explored in all directions, with good treks in the accessible Parque Nacional Tierra del Fuego just to the west of the city, and more adventurous expeditions offered into the wild heart of the island, trekking, climbing or riding. There's splendid cross-country skiing nearby in winter, as well as downhill skiing too, at Cerro Castor. And to the east, along a beautiful stretch of coastline, is the historic *estancia* of Harberton, which you can reach by a boat trip along the Beagle Channel. » *See Sleeping, Eating and other listings, page 495-502.*

Ins and outs

Getting there Flights are daily from Buenos Aires and Río Gallegos, frequent flights from El Calafate and Punta Arenas, and weekly from other Patagonian towns to Ushuaia's airport, on a peninsula in the Beagle Channel, close to the centre. Airport information T02901-423970. A taxi to the centre costs US$3. Buses and minibuses from Río Grande arrive at their respective offices: **Tecni Austral** (also from Punta Arenas, Río Gallegos and Comodoro Rivadavia) ① *Tolkar, Roca 157, T02901-431408, www.tolkarturismo.com.ar*, **Líder** ① *Gobernador Paz 921, T02901-436421*, and **Montiel** ① *Marcos Zar 330, T02901-421366.* » *See Transport, page 501 for further details.*

Getting around It's easy to walk around the town in a morning, since all its sights are close together, and you'll find banks, restaurants, hotels and shops along San Martín, which runs parallel to the shore, a block north of the coast road, Maipú. Boat trips leave from the Muelle Turístico (tourist pier) by a small plaza, 25 de Mayo. Ushuaia is very well organized for tourism, and there are good local buses to the national park and other sights, as well as many boat trips.

Best time to visit Ushuaia is at its most beautiful in autumn, when the dense forests all around are turned rich red and yellow, and there are many bright clear days. Summer is best for trekking, when maximum temperatures are around 15°C, but try to avoid January, when the city is swamped with tourists, both Argentines, and even more foreigners. Late February is much better, and still pleasant enough to go walking. The ski season is from mid-June to October, when temperatures hover around zero, but the wind drops.

Tourist information ① *San Martín 674, corner with Fadul, T/F02901-432000, www.tierradelfuego.org.ar, www.e-ushuaia.com, Mon-Fri 0800-2200, Sat, Sun and holidays 0900-2000. Also an office at the pier (Muelle Turístico), T02901-437666, and a desk at the airport, T423970.* Quite the best tourist office in Argentina, the friendly and helpful staff here speak several languages between them, and will hand you a map with all accommodation marked and find you somewhere to stay, even in the busiest period. They also have a great series of leaflets in English, French, German and Portuguese, about all the things to see and do, and bus and boat times. The **Tierra del Fuego National Park Office** ① *San Martín 1395, T02901-421315,* has a basic map of the park.

Ushuaia

Sleeping
Albergue Cruz del Sur 1
Amanecer de la Bahía 4
Antártica 2
Apart Hotel Cabo
San Diego 6
B&B Nahuel 5

Cabañas del Martial 20
Canal Beagle 7
Cap Polonio &
Marcopolo Restaurant 8
César 9
Cumbres del Martial 19
Familia Velásquez 11

Galeazzi-Basily 12
Hostal Malvinas 13
Hostería Posada Fin
del Mundo 14
Las Hayas 15
Los Cauquenes 21
Los Ñires 17

History

Founded in 1884 after missionary Thomas Bridges had established his mission in these inhospitable lands (see box, page 493) Ushuaia attracted many pioneers in search of gold. Keen to populate its new territory, the government set up a penal colony on nearby Staten Island, which moved to the town in 1902, and the town developed rapidly. Immigration was largely Croatian and Spanish, together with those shipwrecked on the shores, but the town remained isolated until planes arrived in 1935. As the prison closed a naval base opened, and in the 1970s, a further influx arrived, attracted by job opportunities in assemblage plants of electronic equipment that flourished thanks to reduced taxes. Now the city is capital of Argentina's most southerly province, and though fishing still is a traditional economic activity, Ushuaia has become an important tourist centre, particularly as the departure point for voyages to Antarctica.

Sights

There are several museums worth looking at. The most fascinating is **Museo del Fin del Mundo** ① *seafront at Maipú y Rivadavia, T02901-421863, www.tierradelfuego.org.ar/museo, Nov-Apr daily 0900-2000; May-Oct Mon-Sat 1200-1900, US$ 3.50*, in the 1912 bank building, which tells the history of the town through a small collection of carefully chosen exhibits on the indigenous groups, missionaries, pioneeers and shipwrecks, together with nearly all the birds of Tierra del Fuego (stuffed), and you can get an 'end of the world museum' stamp in your passport. There are helpful and informed staff, and also an extensive reference library. Recommended. Further east, the old prison, Presidio, at the back of the Naval Base ① *Yaganes y Gobernador Paz, daily 1000-2000, US$8.50, www.museomaritimo.com*, houses the **Museo Marítimo**, with models and artefacts from seafaring days, and, in the cells of most of the five wings of the huge

Los Troncos **18**
Tolkeyen **16**
Yakush **3**

Eating 🍴
Barcleit 1912 **1**
Bodegón Fueguino **9**

Café Tante Sara **2**
El Turco **3**
Kaupé **5**
La Baguette **6**
La Cabaña **4**
La Estancia **7**
Moustacchio **10**

Parrilla La Rueda **11**
Tanta Sara Pizzas & Pastas **12**
Tía Elvira **13**
Volver **15**

Bars & clubs 🍸
Café de la Esquina **17**

Che, qué potito! **16**
Küar **14**
Lennon Pub **8**

building, the **Museo** Penitenciario, which details the history of the prison. Excellent guided visits (in Spanish only) show a replica of the lighthouse that inspired Jules Verne's novel. Recommended. Much smaller is **Museo Yámana** ① *Rivadavia 56, T02901-422874, www.tierradelfuego.org.ar/mundoyamana, daily 1000-2000 high season (1200-1900 in low season), US$ 1.70,* has interesting scale models showing scenes of everyday life of Yamana people and the geological evolution of the island, also recommended.

Whatever you do, unless it's pouring with rain, take the chairlift up to **Cerro Martial**, about 7 km behind the town, for exhilarating views along the Beagle Channel and to Isla Navarino opposite. From the top of the lift, you can walk 90 minutes through lenga forest to Glaciar Martial. There are also a splendid tea shop, *refugio* and *cabañas* at the Cerro. The **aerosilla** (chairlift) runs daily 1000-1800 (1030-1630 in winter), US$ 3.50. To reach it, follow Magallanes out of town; allow 1½ hours walking, or take a bus; several companies run minibus services from the corner of Maipu and Roca, frequently in summer, US$3-4 return. Last buses return at 1900 and 2100. Taxis charge US$5 to the base, from where you can walk down and all the way back.

Parque Nacional Tierra del Fuego (see below) just outside Ushuaia, is easily accessible by bus and offers superb walks for all levels of fitness. The **Tren del Fin del Mundo** is the world's southernmost steam train, running new locomotives and carriages on track first laid by prisoners to carry wood to Ushuaia. It's a totally touristy experience with relentless commentary in English and Spanish, but it might be fun for children, and is one way of getting into the national park to start a walk. ① *The train runs for 50 mins from the Fin del Mundo station, 8 km west of Ushuaia, into Tierra del Fuego National Park. Two departures daily in summer, one in winter. US$20 (tourist), US$ 35 (first class), US$50 (exclusive service) return, plus US$ 7 park entrance and transfer to the station. Tickets at station, from Tranex Turismo, T02901-431600, www.trendelfindelmundo.com.ar, or from travel agencies in town. Sit on left outbound for the best views. Buses to reach the train station with companies Kaupen and Pasarela, leaving from the corner of Maipú and Roca, at unreliable times; better take a taxi, US$3.*

Excursions can also be made to Lagos Fagnano and Escondido: agencies run seven-hour tours for US$25 per person without lunch (US$32 lunch included); or check list of cheaper but rather unreliable minibuses going there, at tourist office. Tour agencies offer many good packages which include trekking, canoeing, birdwatching and horse riding in landscape accessible only by 4WDs. See Tour operators, page 500, and the tourist office's list of excursions, indicating which companies go where.

Estancia Harberton and Museo Akatushún

① *T02901-422742, www.acatushun.org, daily 15 Oct-15 Apr, except Christmas, 1 Jan and Easter. Tour of the estancia US$ 5, museum entrance US$2.*

The Estancia Harberton, 85 km from Ushuaia, is the oldest *estancia* in Tierra del Fuego. It was built in 1886 on a narrow peninsula overlooking the Beagle Channel. Its founder, the missionary Thomas Bridges (see box, page 493) was granted the land by President Roca for his work amongst the indigenous peoples and for his help in rescuing victims of numerous shipwrecks in the channels. Harberton is named after the Devonshire village where his wife Mary was born, and the farmhouse was pre-fabricated there by her carpenter father and assembled on a spot chosen by the Yámana peoples as the most sheltered. The English connection is evident in the neat garden of lawns, shrubs and trees between the jetty and the farmhouse. Behind the buildings is a large vegetable garden, a real rarity on the island, and there's noticeably more wildlife here than in the Tierra del Fuego National Park, probably owing to its remoteness.

Still operating as a working farm, mainly with cattle and sheep, Harberton is run by Thomas Goodall, great-grandson of the founder, whose wife Natalie has created an impressive museum of the area's rich marine life with a thriving research centre. Visitors receive a guided tour either of the museum, or of farm buildings and grounds with reconstructions of the Yámana dwellings. Tea or lunch (if you reserve ahead) are

Building bridges

The story of the first successful missionary to Tierra del Fuego, Thomas Bridges and his son Lucas, is one of the most stirring in the whole history of pioneers in Argentina. An orphan from Bristol, Thomas Bridges was so called because he was found as a child under a bridge with a letter 'T' on his clothing. Adopted by Reverend Despard, he was taken as a young man to start a Christian mission in the Tierra del Fuego, and brought his young wife and daughter to establish the mission, after Despard left following the massacre of the Christians by the indigenous inhabitants. Until his death in 1898, Bridges lived near the shores of the Beagle Channel, first creating the new settlement of Ushuaia and then at Harberton, devoting his life to his work with the Yámanas (Yaghanes) and compiling a dictionary of their language. His son Lucas (1874-1949), one of six children, spent his early life among the Yámanas and Onas, living and hunting as one of them, learning their languages, and even, almost fatally, becoming involved in their blood feuds and magic rituals. Lucas became both defender and protector of the indigenous peoples, creating a haven for them at Harberton and Estancia Viamonte (see page 496) when most sheep farmers were more interested in having them shot. His memoirs, *Uttermost Part of the Earth* (1947), trace the tragic fate of the native population with whom he grew up. (Out of print, try second-hand shops).

served in the Manacatush tea room overlooking the bay, and you may well be tempted to rent one of the two simple cottages on the shore. There are wonderful walks along the coast, and nowhere in Argentina has quite the feeling of peace you'll find here. Highly recommended.

The impressive **Museo Akatushún**, has skeletons of South American sea mammals, the result of 23 years' scientific investigation in Tierra del Fuego, with excellent tours in English. You can camp free, with permission from the owners, or stay in cottages (see below). Access is from a good unpaved road (Route 33, ex 'J') which branches off Route 3, 40 km east of Ushuaia and runs 25 km through forest before the open country around Harberton; marvellous views, about two hours (no petrol outside of Ushuaia and Tolhuin!). **Boat trips** to Harberton run twice weekly in summer, and allow one or two hours on the *estancia*. Regular daily minibus service with Ebenezer from Avenida Maipú and 25 de Mayo, US$ 20 return. Agency tours by land cost US$40 plus entrance.

Boat trips

All these trips are highly recommended, but note that the Beagle Channel can be very rough. Food and drink on all boats is pricey. Excursions can be booked through most agencies, or at the Muelle Turístico where boat companies have their ticket offices; boats leave from the Muelle Turístico, with a few excursions leaving from Muelle AFASYN (next to the old airport). If going to Harberton (see above), check that your tour actually visits the *estancia* and not just the bay, as some do.

Popular excursions visit the small islands southeast of Ushuaia in 2½ to three hours, passing next to the sea lion colony at **Isla de los Lobos**, **Isla de los Pájaros** and **Les Eclaireurs lighthouse**. They can add an hour or so for a landing on **Bridges island**. Prices vary if trips are made on big catamarans (US$30), more exclusive sailing boats (from US$40), or the charming old boat *Barracuda*, with excellent commentary, US$25. A few pricier services include lunch, otherwise a light snack or a coffee is served. In summer additional services are added, with some going further east past the islands and lighthouse mentioned above, to the **Isla Martillo penguin colony,** and to the Estancia Harberton, six to nine hours round trip on catamaran, US$ 60, includes packed lunch and entrance. A few excursions going west to the National Park in about 5½ hours.

Winter sports ›› *For more information, see Activities and tours, page 500.*

Ushuaia is becoming popular as a winter resort with several centres for skiing, snowboarding and husky sledging. There's good powder snow, thanks to the even temperatures (between 5 and -5ºC) and the climate isn't as cold as you'd think, despite the latitude, because winter is the least windy season here. The season runs between mid-June and mid-October, but late August to late September is recommended as days are lighter and the snow is still good. The most developed resort is **Cerro Castor complex** ① *27 km from town, T02901-499302, www.cerrocastor.com.* With 20 km of pistes of all grades – plenty for intermediate skiers – and vertical drop of 772 m, it's bettered only by Las Leñas and Bariloche. There's an attractive centre with complete equipment rental for skiing, snowboarding and snowshoeing, ski school, cafés and a hotel, and restaurants on the pistes. Ski pass US$ 35 per day. Three regular buses run per day. There's excellent cross-country skiing in the area, with various new centres strung along the main road Route 3 at 18-36 km east of Ushuaia, of which **Tierra Mayor** ① *T02901-423240,* 21 km from town, is recommended. In a beautiful wide valley between steep-sided mountains, the centre offers half- and full-day excursions on sledges with huskies for hire, as well as cross-country skiing and snow shoeing. Equipment hire and cosy restaurant with wood stoves. In the city itself, **Martial Glacier Winter Sports Centre**, 7 km from the centre, has a single piste. The **Haruwen Winter Sports** complex is 35 km east on Route 3 also offers winter sports activities.

Parque Nacional Tierra del Fuego 🚌 ›› *pp495-502.*

Covering 63,000 ha of mountains, lakes, rivers and deep valleys, this small but beautiful park stretches west to the Chilean border and north to Lago Fagnano, though large areas have been closed to tourists to protect the environment. Public access is at the park entrance 12 km west of Ushuaia, where you'll be given a basic map with marked walks.

Parque Nacional Tierra del Fuego

There's good camping in a picturesque spot at Lago Roca, with a *confitería*. All walks are best early morning or afternoon to avoid the tour buses. You'll see lots of geese, the beautiful torrent duck, Magellanic woodpeckers and austral parakeets.

Ins and outs

The park **entrance** is 12 km west of Ushuaia, on the main road west (a continuation of the coast road) signposted from the town centre. The **park administration** ① *San Martín 1395, Ushuaia, T02901-421315, entry for non-Argentines is US$7*. In summer, various buses and minibuses run an hourly service, US$ 5 return to Lago Roca, US$ 8 return to Bahía Lapataia, leaving from Ushuaia's tourist pier at the corner of Maipú and Roca or from Maipú and 25 de Mayo. Returning from either Bahía Lapataia or Lago Roca, hourly until last bus 2000 or 2100 in summer. Ask at the tourist office for bus details and map of park, with walks. There are no legal crossing points to Chile. Wear warm, waterproof clothing; in winter the temperature drops to as low as -12°C, and although in summer it can reach 25°C, evenings can be chilly. There's a most helpful *guardaparque* (ranger) at Lago Roca.

For a longer hike, or for a really rich experience of the park, go with **guides** who know the territory well and can tell you about wildlife. Inexpensive trips for all levels with the highly recommended **Compañía de Guías de Patagonia** ① *hostel El Nido de los Cóndores, Gobernador Campos 795, y 9 de Julio, T02901-437753, www.companiade guias.com.ar*, and **All Patagonia** ① *Juana Fadul 48, T02901-430725*.

⛰ Walks

Leaflets provided at the entrance show various walks; the following are recommended:
Senda Costera 6½ km, three hours each way. This lovely easy walk along the shore gives you the essence of the park, its rocky coastline, edged with a rich forest of beech trees, and glorious views of the low islands with a backdrops of steep mountains. Start at Bahía Ensenada (where the boat trips start, and where the bus can drop you off). Follow a well-marked path along the shoreline, and then rejoin the road briefly to cross Río Lapataia (ignoring signs to Lago Roca to your right). After crossing the broad green river and a second stretch of water (where there's a small camping spot and the *gendarmería*), it's a pleasant stroll inland to the beautifully tranquil **Bahía Lapataia**, an idyllic spot, with views across the sound.

Senda Hito XXIV Along Lago Roca, 4 km, 90 minutes one way. This is another easy walk, beside this peaceful lake, with lovely pebble beaches and through dense forest at times, with lots of bird life. It is especially recommended in the evening, when most visitors have left. Get off the bus at the junction for Lago Roca, turn right along the road to the car park (passing the *guardaparque*'s house) and follow the lake side.

Cerro Guanaco 4 km, four hours one way. Challenging hike up through the very steep forest to a mirador at the top of a hill (970 m) with splendid views over Lago Roca, the Beagle Channel and far-off mountains. The ground is slippery after rain: take care and don't rush. Allow plenty of time to return in light, especially in winter. The path branches off Senda Hito XXIV (see above) after crossing Arroyo Guanaco.

⊜ Sleeping

Río Grande *p488*
Book ahead, as there are few decent choices.
B **Posada de los Sauces**, Elcano 839, T02964-432895, info@posadadelossauces. com.ar. By far the best choice. Breakfast included, beautifully decorated and

comfortable rooms, good restaurant and cosy bar. Recommended.
C **Apart Hotel Keyuk'n**, Colón 630, T02964-424435. A good apart hotel, with simple well-equipped flats for 2-4.

C **Hotel Atlántida**, Belgrano 582, T02964-431915, atlantida@netcombbs.com.ar. A modern, rather uninspiring place, with plain comfortable rooms all with bath and cable TV, but good value with breakfast included.
D **Hotel Isla del Mar**, Güemes 963, T02964-422883, www.hotelguia.com/hotel isladelmar. Right on the sea shore, looks very bleak in bad weather and is frankly run-down, but cheap, with bathrooms and breakfast included, and the staff are welcoming.
F **Hotel Argentina**, San Martín 64, T02964-422546, hotelargentino@yahoo.com. Price per person. Quite the best cheap place to stay. Much more than the backpackers youth hostel it claims to be, in a beautifully renovated 1920s building close to the sea front. Kitchen facilities, a bright sunny dining room with space to sit, owned by the welcoming Graciela, who knows all about the local area. Highly recommended.

Estancias around Río Grande
LL **Estancia María Behety**. Established in 1897, 15 km from Río Grande, on a 40 km stretch of the river that has become legendary for brown trout fishing, with comfortable accommodation for 18 anglers, and good food. At US$5350 per week, this is one of the country's priciest fishing lodges, apparently deservedly so! Reservations through the **Fly shop**, www.flyfishingtravel.com, guides, equipment and accommodation included.
L **Estancia Viamonte**, some 40 km southeast on the coast, T02964-430861, www.estanciaviamonte.com. For a really authentic experience of Tierra del Fuego, stay as a guest here. Built in 1902 by pioneer Lucas Bridges, see box, page 493, this working *estancia* is run by his descendants. You'll be warmly welcomed as their guest, in traditional, beautifully furnished rooms, with comfortable bathrooms, and delicious meals (extra cost for these). Also a spacious cottage to let, US$315 for 7. Join in the farm activities, read the famous book by blazing fires, ride horses over the estate and completely relax. Warmly recommended. Reserve a week ahead.
L **Estancia Rivadvia**, 100 km from Río Grande, on the route H, www.estanciarivadavia.com, T02901-492186. A 10,000-ha sheep farm, owned by descendents of the original Croatian pioneer who built the place.

Luxurious accommodation in a splendid house near the mountains and lakes at the heart of Tierra del Fuego, where you can enjoy a trip around the *estancia* to see wild horses and guanacos, good food, and trekking to the trout lake of Chepelmut and Yehuin.

Camping
Club Náutico Ioshlelk-Oten, Montilla 1047, 2 km from town on river. Clean, cooking facilities, camping in heated building in cold weather. YPF petrol station has hot showers.

Tolhuin and around *p489*
A **Hostería Petrel**, RN 3, Km 3186, Lago Escondido, T02901-433569, hpetrel@ infovia.com.ar. The only place to stay in this idyllic spot. In a secluded position amidst forest on a tranquil beach of the lake, with decent rooms with bath, and a good restaurant overlooking the lake which serves delicious lamb (pricey at US$7), open to non-residents. There are also tiny basic *cabañas* right on the water, US$40 for 2-4 people.
D **Cabañas Khami**, T02964-1561 1243, T/F422296 www.cabaniaskhami.com .ar. Isolated in a lovely open spot at the head of the lake on low-lying and very comfortable and well-equipped *cabañas*, nicely decorated and with great views of the lake. Good value at US$40 per day for 6. Recommended.
D **Terrazas del Lago**, RN 3, Km 2938, T02964-1560 4851, terrazas@uol.com.ar. A little way from the shore, smart wooden *cabañas*, well decorated, and also a *confitería* and *parrilla*.
D **Parador Kawi Shiken**, off the main road on the way to Ushuaia, 4 km south of Tolhuin on RN 3, Km 2940, T02964-1561 1505, www.hotelguia .com/hoteles/kawi-shiken/. A rustic place with 3 rooms, shared bathrooms, *casa de té* and restaurant. Ring them to arrange for local *cordero al asador* (barbecued lamb). Also horse riding.
F **Refugio Solar del Bosque**, RN 3, Km 3020, Lago Escondido, T02964-453276, T156-06176, solardelbosque@tierradelfuego.org.ar. Price per person. Further along the road 18 km from Ushuaia is a basic hostel for walkers, with shared bathrooms in dorms for 4, breakfast included.

Camping

Camping Hain del Lago, T02964-425951, 156-03606, robertoberbel@hotmail.com. Lovely views, fireplaces, hot showers, and a *quincho* for when it rains.

Camping La Correntina, T156-05020, 17 km from Tolhuin. In woodland, with bathrooms, and horses for hire.

Ushuaia *p489, map p490*

The tourist office has lists of all accommodation, and can help find you somewhere to stay, but in Jan you must reserve before you come. On the road to the Glaciar Martial overlooking the city are:

LL Las Hayas, Camino Glaciar Martial, Km 3, T02901-430710, www.lashayas.com.ar. A 5-star hotel, in a spectacular setting, high up on the mountainside with outstanding views over the Beagle Channel. Light, tasteful, impeccable rooms. Breakfast included and use of pool, sauna, gym, squash court, 9-hole golf course, shuttle from town in high season, and transfer from airport. A lovely calm atmosphere, friendly staff, recommended.

L Cumbres del Martial, Luis F Martial 3560, T02901-424779, www.cumbresdelmartial. com.ar. This charming cottage by a mountain stream in the forested slopes of Martial range has very comfortable rooms with balconies for viewing the Beagle Channel. A homely feel prevails in this small, relaxed and secluded place 7 km away from town. There are also 4 *cabañas*, in which rustic materials contrast with a cosy interior. All have a fireplace and big windows open onto the woods. Superb fondues are served in its restaurant and tea room.

L Los Cauquenes, C Reinamora, Barrio Bahía Cauquen, T02901-441300, www.loscau quenesushuaia.com.ar. A 5-star by the sea. Wonderfully set on the shores of the Beagle Channel, this large and stylish hotel is an exclusive retreat 7 km west of Ushuaia. Wood and stone are predominant in its architecture, while a relaxing minimalist decor prevails inside, in standard and larger superior rooms. Suites have their own private balconies on to the sea. There is a restaurant, a spa and vans going frequently to the town centre.

AL Canal Beagle, Maipú y 25 de Mayo, T02901-432303, www.hotelcanalbeagle. com.ar. Good ACA hotel (discounts for members) with a small pool, gym and sauna,

with clear views over the channel from some of its comfortable and tastefully decorated rooms, and a good, reasonably priced restaurant.

A Tolkeyen, Del Tolkeyen 2145, 4 km from town towards national park, T02901-445315, www.tolkeyenhotel.com. A lovely traditional rustic place in a superb setting, with open views from its rooms, which vary between plain and flouncy, but are all spacious and comfortable. Lots of land to walk in, and close to the national park, with free buses into town, and free room service. Also an excellent restaurant, serving king crab and Fuegian lamb. Very relaxing. Recommended.

A Cabañas del Martial, L F Martial 2109, T02901-430475, www.delmartial.com.ar. Wonderful views from these comfortable and well-equipped *cabañas*, set on wooded slopes. Price quoted for 5 people.

A Los Ñires, Av de los Ñires 3040, T02901-443781, www.nires.com.ar. The setting is the feature here, with lovely views, comfortable rooms in simple rustic style, and a good restaurant. Transfers and breakfast included.

B Apart Hotel Cabo San Diego, 25 de Mayo 368, T02901-435600, www.cabosandiego .com.ar. Really comfortable and spacious apartments, spick and span, well equipped for cooking, good bathrooms and comfortable beds. Great for couples or families. Excellent value.

B Cap Polonio, San Martín 746, T02901-422140, www.hotelcappolonio. com.ar. A smart central modern city hotel with very comfortable minimalist rooms, all with bath, phone, TV, internet; some have views of the canal. There's a chic restaurant café downstairs.

B César, San Martín 753, T02901-421460, www.hotelcesarhostal.com.ar. Very central, this big tourist place is often booked by groups, but is reasonable value. Simple rooms with bath, breakfast included.

B Hostal Malvinas, Gobernador Deloqui 615, T/F02901-422626, www.hostalmalvinas.net. Neat, comfortable if rather small rooms with excellent bathrooms, and good views, in this central and well-run town house hotel. Breakfast is included, and all day tea and coffee. Recommended.

B Hostería Posada Fin del Mundo, Gobernador Valdez 281, T02901-437345, www.posadafindelmundo.com.ar. A relaxed family atmosphere in a quiet residential area close to centre, homely rooms, and friendly staff. Good value.

D B&B Nahuel, 25 de Mayo 440, T02901-423068. byb_nahuel@yahoo.com.ar. A family house with views over channel, with brightly painted and tastefully decorated rooms, and a lovely welcome from the charming and talkative owner. Great value. Recommended.

E-F Amanecer de la Bahía, Magallanes 594, T02901-424405, www.ushuaiahostel.com.ar. Price per person. A light, spacious, impeccably kept *hostal*, with shared rooms for 4 and cramped for 6, also a good double and triples with shared bath. Internet, living rooms, breakfast included.

F Albergue Cruz del Sur, Deloqui 636, T02901-434099, www.xdelsur.com.ar. Price per person. There's a very friendly atmosphere in this relaxed small Italian-owned *hostal*, with cosy dorms, use of kitchen, and a lovely quiet library room for reading. A place to make friends. Recommended.

F Antárctica, Antártida Argentina 270, T02901-435774, www.antarcticahostel.com. Price per person. Welcoming and central hostel with a spacious chill-out room and an excellent bar open till late. Dorms are rather basic and cramped, with **C** larger private doubles. Cooking facilities, breakfast and the use of internet are included. Cycles for hire.

F Yakush, Piedrabuena y San Martín, T02901-435807, www.hostelyakush.com.ar. Price per person. A very well-run hostel with spacious rooms to share and a few private ones, a light kitchen and dining room, and a steep tiny garden with views. If a cheerful atmosphere prevails, there are also comfy and more secluded corners for oneself.

Private homes

D Galeazzi-Basily, Gobernador Valdez 323, T02901-423213, www.avesdelsur.com.ar. The best option by far. A cosy and stylish family home, with welcoming owners Frances and Alejandro, who speak excellent English, in a pleasant residential area 5 blocks from the centre. Delicious breakfast included. There are also excellent- value 4- and 5-bed *cabañas* in the garden. Highly recommended.

D Familia Velásquez, Juana Fadul 361, T02901-421719. Basic rooms with breakfast in cosy cheerful pioneer family home, where the kind owners look after you.

D Los Troncos, Gobernador Paz 1344, T02901-421895, lostroncos@speedy.com.ar. A welcoming house run by charming Mrs Clarisa Ulloa, with simple rooms, breakfast, TV and free internet.

Estancias

L Estancia Rolito, Route 21 (ex 'A'), Km 14, T02901-492007, rolitotdf@hotmail.com. A magical place on the wooded heart of the island, with cosy accommodation in traditionally built houses, and friendly hosts Annie and Pepe, booked through **Turismo de Campo** (see page 501). Also day visits with recommended walks or horse rides in mature southern beech forest.

LL Harberton, T02901-422742, estancia harberton@tierradelfuego.org.ar. 2 impeccably restored historical buildings on the tranquil lakeside, giving space and privacy from the main house. Simple accommodation, but wonderful views, and beautiful walks on the *estancia*'s coastline. 90 km east of Ushuaia, along RN 3 and 33, a spectacular drive. Price given for 6 people. Open mid-Oct to mid-Apr.

Camping

La Pista del Andino, Leandro N Alem 2873, T02901-435890, www.lapistadelandino. com.ar. Set in the **Club Andino** ski premises in a woodland area, it has wonderful views over the town and channel. Electricity, hot showers, a tea room and a grocery store, US$3 per person.

Kawi Yoppen, RN 3 Km 3020, heading to Río Grande, T02901-435135, 10 km from Ushuaia, US$2 per person.

Camping del Solar del Bosque, RN 3, Km 19, heading to Río Grande, T02901-421228. US$2.50 per person. At a small ski resort that in summer offers plenty of activities. Hot showers, and also a large dorm with good facilities.

Camping Haruwen, Haruwen Winter Sports complex (Km 36), en route to Río Grande, T02901-431099. US$3 per tent, electricity, shop, bar, restaurant in a winter sports centre, open also in summer for outdoor activities.

Parque Nacional Tierra del Fuego
p494, map p494
Camping
Camping Lago Roca, T02901-433313 (entry fee US$ 7), 21 km from Ushuaia. By the

forested shore of tranquil Lago Roc, this is a beautiful site with good facilities, reached by bus Jan-Feb, expensive small shop, cafetería, US$4 per person.

There are also various sites with no facilities: Bahía Ensenada Camping, 14 km from Ushuaia; Río Pipo, 16 km from Ushuaia, and Camping Las Bandurrias, Cauquenes and Camping Laguna Verde, 20 km from Ushuaia.

🍴 Eating

Río Grande p488
🍴 **La Nueva Colonial**, Fagnano 669. Half a block from the plaza, next to Casino Club, where the locals go for delicious pasta in a warm family atmosphere.
🍴 **La Rueda**, Islas Malvinas 954, 1st floor. Excellent *parrilla* in a welcoming place.
🍴 **La Nueva Piamontesa**, Belgrano y Mackinlay, T02964-423620, to the side of the charming 24-hr grocery store. Cheap set menus and also delivers food.
🍴 **Leymi**, 25 de Mayo 1335. Cheap fixed menu.

Tolhuin and around p489
Pizzería Amistad, on the same block as the famous La Unión bakery. Pizzas 24 hrs daily except Mon 2400-Tue 0600.
La Posada de los Ramírez, a cosy restaurant and *rotisería*. 3 courses will cost you US$4, weekends only, lunch and dinner.
Parrilla La Victoria, Koshten 324, T02964-4922970. Open daily, with beef and lamb on the *asado*, and also pizzas, call before for delicious Fuegian lamb.

Ushuaia p489, map p490
🍴🍴🍴 **Bodegón Fueguino**, San Martín 859. In a stylishly renovated 1896 house in the main street, this stands out from the crowd by serving *picadas* with delicious and imaginative dips, good roast lamb, and unusual *cazuelas*, *picadas* and dips. A buzzy atmosphere and welcoming staff.
🍴🍴🍴 **Kaupé**, Roca 470 y Magallanes, T02901-437396. The best restaurant in town, with exquisite food. King crab and meat dishes all beautifully served, in a lovely environment – a great treat.
🍴🍴🍴 **La Cabaña**, Luis F Martial 3560, T02901-424779. The cosy restaurant and tea room of Cumbres del Martial hotel serves several excellent types of fondue for dinner,

that may be preceded at teatime by a rich list of cakes, scones and brownies.
🍴🍴🍴 **Marcopolo**, San Martín 746. A chic modern international-style café restaurant for seafood and everything else. Soothing decor, good service.
🍴🍴🍴 **Tía Elvira**, Maipú 349. Retains its reputation for excellent seafood, with a good choice of fresh fish and views over the channel.
🍴🍴🍴 **Volver**, Maipú 37. In an atmospheric old 1898 house, with ancient newspaper all over the walls (read intriguing fragments while you eat). Cosy stoves and an intimate atmosphere. Delicious salmon and *arroz con mariscos*.
🍴🍴 **Barcleit 1912**, Juana Fadul 148. Serves good Italian food, pizzas and pastas.
🍴🍴 **La Estancia**, San Martín 253. Cheery and good-value **parrilla tenedor libre**. Packed in high season.
🍴🍴 **Moustacchio**, San Martín y Gobernador Godoy. Long-established, good for seafood in a cosy atmosphere. Next door is a cheaper all-you-can-eat sister restaurant.
🍴🍴 **Parrilla La Rueda**, San Martín y Rivadavia. A good *tenedor libre* for beef, lamb and a great range of salads.
🍴🍴 **Tante Sara Pizzas and Pastas**, San Martín 137. A brightly-lit functional place with tasty filling food. Also take-away.
🍴 **El Turco**, San Martín 1410. One of few good and cheap places, popular with locals, serves generous *milanesas*, pastas, steaks and pizzas.

Cafés
Café Tante Sara, Fadul y San Martín. The most appealing of the cafés on San Martín. Smart and modern with an airy feel, serving good coffee and tasty sandwiches.
La Baguette, Don Bosco y San Martín. The best fresh takeaway sandwiches, and also delicious *empanadas* and *facturas* (pastries).

🍷 Bars and clubs

Ushuaia p489, map p490
Café de la Esquina, 25 de Mayo y San Martín. Light meals and drinks, in a good atmosphere.
¡Che, qué potito!, San Martín 452. A lively place with Mexican and Brazilian food.
Küar, Av Perito Moreno 2232, east of town. Great setting by the sea, restaurant, bar and brewery open from 1800.
Lennon Pub, Maipú 263. A lively friendly atmosphere and live music.

❀ Festivals and events

Río Grande *p488*

Jan The sheep shearing festival is definitely worth seeing, if you're in the area.

2nd week of Feb Rural exhibition with handicrafts.

1st week of Mar Shepherd's day, with impressive sheepdog display.

Jun 20/21 Winter solstice, the longest night, has fireworks and ice skating contests, though this is a very inhospitable time of year.

▲ Activities and tours

Río Grande *p488*
Tour operators
Fiesta Travel, 9 de Julio 663, T02964-431800, fiestatravel@arnet.com.ar.
Mariani Travel Rosales 259, T02964-426010, mariani@netcombbs.com.ar.
Techni Austral, Moyano 516, T02964-430610. Bus tickets to Ushuaia.

Ushuaia *p489, map p490*
Fishing
The lakes and rivers of Tierra del Fuego offer great fishing, for brown and rainbow trout, and stream trout in Lago Fagnano. Both fly-casting and spinning are allowed, and permits must be bought. The trout season is 1 Nov- Apr (though this varies slightly every year), licences US$10 per day (an extra fee is charged for some rivers and lakes). Contact Asociación de Caza y Pesca at Maipú 822, T02901-423168, cazapescush@infovia.com.ar.
Fly Casting, T02901-423340. Offer a range of fishing excursions, provide equipment.
Yishka, Gobernador Godoy 62, T02901-437606, www.yishkaevt.com.ar. Arranges fishing excursions to Lago Fagnano.

Skiing, hiking, climbing
Club Andino, Fadul 50, T02901-422335, www.clubandinoushuaia.com.ar. For skiing, hiking, climbing information. Maps and trekking guidebooks for sale, free guided walks once a month in summer. Winter sports resorts along RN 3 (see below) are an excellent base for summer trekking and many arrange excursions.
Nunatak, 19½ km from Ushuaia, nunatak@tierradelfuego.org.ar, is a small centre from where amazing day treks to nearby glaciers

and lakes are possible. To get to the more remote areas of the island from Ushuaia, it's worth going on an expedition with an agency. See Tour operators, below, for some excellent packages and day hikes.

Tour operators
Lots of companies now offer imaginative adventure tourism expeditions. All agencies charge the same fees for excursions; ask tourist office for a complete list: Tierra del Fuego National Park, 4 hrs, from US$ 17 (entry fee US$ 7 extra); Lagos Escondido and Fagnano, 7-8 hrs, US$25 without lunch. With 3 or 4 people it might be worth hiring a taxi.
All Patagonia, Juana Fadul 60, T02901-433622, www.allpatagonia.com/Eng. A wonderful range of tours, sailing, hiking, birdwatching, all making the most of the wild land around Ushuaia. Ask about the birdwatching trip to the centre of the island, and the 6-day trip crossing the Fuegian cordillera. Also Antarctic trips. Well organized and recommended.
Canal Fun & Nature, Rivadavia 82, T02901-437395, www.canalfun.com. Oriented to young people, it offers a huge range of activities, including trekking, canoeing, horse riding, 4WD excursions. And they also run their own bar **Küar**. Recommended.
Comapa, San Martín 245, T02901-430727, www.comapa.com. A complete range of excursions and accommodation arrangements in Chile, including tickets for **Buses Pacheco** (to Punta Arenas), **Cruceros Australis** (to Cabo de Hornos and **Punta Arenas**), and **Navimag** ferries (Puerto Natales-Puerto Montt); also trips to Antarctica.
Compañía de Guías de Patagonia at Posada Nido de Cóndores, Gobernador Campos 795 (y 9 de Julio), T02901-437753, www.companiade guias.com.ar. The best walking guides. Well-run expeditions for all levels to the national park, and also to more inaccessible places, for the day, or several days, including the beautiful 3-day walk along the Lucas Bridges path, some equipment and food included. Also ice climbing (training and equipment provided) to Cerro Alvear. Professional, friendly and knowledgeable. Highly recommended.
Rumbo Sur, San Martín 350, T02901-421139, www.rumbosur.com.ar. Flights, buses and all the conventional tours, including Harberton,

fishing excursions, plus wonderful Antarctic expeditions, mid-Nov to mid-Mar, friendly, English spoken.

Tolkar Viajes y Turismo, Roca 157, T02901-431412, www.tolkarturismo.com.ar. Flights, bus tickets to Punta Arenas, Río Grande and Río Gallegos, conventional and adventure tourism, including a full-day mountain biking and canoeing trip in Lago Fagnano and Lago Escondido area.

Travel Lab, San Martín 1444, T02901-436555, www.travel-labpatagonia-com.ar. *Tren del fin del Mundo*, unconventional tours, mountain biking, trekking, etc. English and French spoken, very helpful.

Turismo de Campo, Fuegia Basket 414, T02901-437351, www.turismodecampo.com.ar. Adventure tourism in small groups with English/French speaking guides. Boat and trekking combinations in the National Park, and trekking for all levels in other remoter places, visiting Estancia Rolito, birdwatching tours, fishing excursions, horse riding in central Tierra del Fuego woodlands, sailing in the Beagle Channel. Also Antarctica. Highly recommended.

⊕ Transport

Río Grande *p488*
Book ahead in summer when buses and planes fill up fast. Take passport when buying ticket.

Air
Airport 4 km west of town, T02964-420600. Taxi US$2. To **Buenos Aires**, Aerolíneas Argentinas daily, 3½ hrs direct. To **Ushuaia** , LADE once a week to **Ushuaia** and **Patagonian towns**.
    Airline offices Aerolíneas Argentinas, San Martín 607, T02964-424467.

Bus
Buses leave from terminal at Elcano y Güemes, T02964-420997, or from **Tecni Austral's** office Moyano 516, T02964-430610. To **Porvenir** , Chile, 5 hrs, US$9, **Gesell**, Wed, Sun, 0800, passport and luggage control at San Sebastián. To **Punta Arenas**, Chile, via Punta Delgada, 10 hrs, **Pacheco**, Tue, Thu, Sat 0730, US$15, To **Río Gallegos**, 3 times a week, US$15. To **Ushuaia**, Tecni Austral, 3-4 hrs, 2 daily (heavily booked in sumnmer), US$12, also **Tolkeyen**, US$7.

Car hire
Hertz Annie Millet, Libertad 714, T02964-426534, hertzriogrande@netcombbs.com.ar. **Al Rent a Car International**, Belgrano 423, T02964-430757, ai.rentcar@carletti.com.ar. Also rents 4WDs and *camionetas*.

Ushuaia *p489, map p490*
Air
Aeropuerto Internacional Malvinas Argentinas, 4 km from town, taxi, US$3 (no bus). Schedules tend to change from season to season, so call offices for times and prices. Book ahead in summer, as flights fill up fast. In winter, poor weather often delays flights.
    Airline offices LADE, San Martín 542, shop 5, T/F421123. **Aerolíneas Argentinas**, Roca 116, T421218, T0810-2228 6527. **Aerovías DAP**, Gobernador Deloqui 555 piso 4, T02901-431110.
    Airport tourist information, T02901-423970. Offices: Aerolíneas Argentinas, Roca 116, T02901-421218. LADE, San Martín 542, Loc 5, T02901-421123. To **Buenos Aires**, 3½ hrs, **El Calafate**, 1 hr, in summer, both with **Aerolíneas** and LADE. Flights are also available daily to **Río Gallegos**, 1 hr, and **Río Grande**, 1 hr, several a week, but check with agents. To **Punta Arenas**, 1 hr, Aerovías DAP. Note that departure tax must be paid to cities in Argentina, US$ 5.

Bus
To **Río Grande** 3½-4 hrs, Mon-Sat 0530, US$8.50 with bus **Tecni Austral**. Book through **Tolkar**, Roca 157, T02901-431412. Combis **Líder**, Gob Paz 921, T02901-436421, and **Montiel**, Marcos Zar 330, T02901-421366, US$8.50-10. To **Río Gallegos**, Tecni Austral, 11½ hrs, US$30. To **Punta Arenas**, Tecni Austral, Mon, Wed, Fri 0530, US$30, and Buses Pacheco, San Martín 245 (at Comapa agency), T02901-430727, www.busespacheco.com, twice a week. From **Río Gallegos**, several buses daily to **El Calafate**, 4 hrs.

Car hire
Most companies charge around US$45 per day including insurance and 150 km per day, though check for promotional rates almost always available at most agencies. **Hertz**, at the airport, T02901-432429. **Wagen**, San Martín 1222, T02901-430739.

DTT Cycles Sport, San Martín 905. **Seven Deportes**, San Martín y 9 de Julio.

Sea

Cruceros Australis, www.australis.com, operates 2 luxury cruise ships (one weekly each) from Ushuaia to **Punta Arenas**, via Puerto Williams and around Cabo de Hornos, 4-5 days, from US$1100 per person in summer (book through Comapa agency), frequently recommended. **Ushuaia Boating**, Godoy 190, T02901-436193, www.ushuaia boating.com.ar, operates all year round a channel crossing to **Puerto Navarino**, 40 mins (subject to weather conditions), plus the bus transfer that completes the journey to **Puerto Williams**, US$100. From Puerto Williams there are frequent ferries to **Punta Arenas**. At Muelle AFASYN (next to the old airport), T02901-435805, ask about possible crossings with a club member to **Puerto Williams**, about 4 hrs, from US$80, or if any foreign sailing boat is going to **Cabo de Hornos** or to **Antarctica**.

Antarctic expeditions Ushuaia is the starting point for a number of excellent expeditions to Antarctica. These can be informative, adventurous, wonderful experiences. The expeditions run Oct-Mar, usually 8- to 12-day trips to the western shores of the Antarctic peninsula, the South Shetland Islands and the Wedell sea, some offering extra activities such as camping and kayaking. It's not a luxury cruise, and there's informal, simple accommodation usually in non-tourist boats used for scientific explora-tion, so the food is fine but not excessive. The expedition leader organizes lectures during the 3-day journey to reach the Antarctic, with at least 2 disembarkations a day in a zodiac to see icebergs and penguins. There's most ice in Nov and Dec, but more baby penguins in Jan and Feb, and whales in Mar. The landscape is always impressive. A longer trip, 18- 20 days, combines the Antarctic with the Malvinas/Falklands and South Georgia islands. It's worth turning up and asking for availability; there's a reasonable discount if you book last minute, only available if bought in Ushuaia, when the price starts at about US$3400 per person (in a twin cabin); cheapest fares are offered by Antarpply, on her ship Ushuaia, www.antarpply.com. Weekly departures in season. For more information on Antarctica in Ushuaia, visit Oficina Antártica, Maipú 505 (at Muelle Turístico), T02901-421423, for general information with a small library that keeps navigational charts. Several travel agencies in Ushuaia sell tickets for trips to Antarctica.

Taxi

For taxis, call T02901-422007 or T02901-440225. **Remise Carlitos**, T02901-422222. Reliable.
Bahía Hermosa, T02901-422233. Reliable.

Train

For *Tren del Fin del Mundo*, see page 492.

⊕ Directory

Río Grande *p488*
Banks ATMs: 4 banks on San Martín between 100 and 300. **Banco de la Nación Argentina**, San Martín 219. **Bansud**, Rosales 241. Cash advance on Visa. Cash exchange Thaler Rosales 259. **Post office** Piedra buena y Ameghino. Locutorio, San Martín at 170 and 458.

Ushuaia *p489, map p490*
Banks Open 1000-1500 (in summer). ATMs are plentiful all along San Martín, using credit cards is by far the easiest, as changing TCs is difficult and expensive. Changing money and TCs: **Banco de Tierra del Fuego**, San Martín 396, **Agencia de Cambio Thaler**, San Martín 788, also open weekends, 1000-1300, 1700-2030. **Consulates** Chile, Jainén 50, T02901-430909. Finland, Gobernador Paz 1569. Germany, Rosas 516. Italy, Calle de la Pradera 1889, Barrio Casas del Sur.
Internet Many broadband cybercafés along **San Martín**. **Post office** San Martín y Godoy, Mon-Fri 0900-1900, Sat 0900-1300.
Telephone *Locutorios* all along San Martín.

Chilean Pacific Islands

Introduction

Far out in the Pacific are two Chilean island possessions, the Juan Fernández Islands, famed for Alexander Selkirk's enforced stay in the 17th century (the inspiration for Defoe's *Robinson Crusoe*), and the Polynesian island of Rapa Nui, better known as Easter Island, the most isolated inhabited spot on earth. Both possess dramatic views of the Pacific. Juan Fernández is famous for the huge cliffs that rise sheer from the ocean, while Easter Island is home to hundreds of mysterious and imposing *Moai*. Although the cost of getting to these islands is prohibitive for many visitors to Chile, both can be reached relatively easily by air from Santiago.

Islas Juan Fernández

→ *Phone code: 032. Colour map 3, B2. Population: 500.*

Situated 667 km west of Valparaíso, this group of small volcanic islands is a national park administered by CONAF and was declared a UN World Biosphere Reserve in 1977. There are three islands: Isla Alejandro Selkirk (4952 ha), the largest; Isla Robinson Crusoe (4794 ha), and Isla Santa Clara (221 ha), the smallest. The islands enjoy a mild climate and the vegetation is rich and varied: the Juan Fernández palm, previously used widely for handicrafts, is now a protected species, but the sandalo (sandalwood tree), once the most common tree on the islands, is now extinct owing to its overuse for perfumes. Fauna includes wild goats, hummingbirds and seals. The islands are famous for langosta de Juan Fernández *(a pincerless lobster) that is prized on the mainland. In summer, a boat goes once a month between Robinson Crusoe and Alejandro Selkirk if the* langosta *catch warrants it, so you can visit either for a few hours or a whole month.* ▸▸ *For Sleeping, Eating and other listings, see pages 506-507.*

Background

The islands are named after João Fernández, a Portuguese explorer in the service of Spain, who was the first European to visit them in 1574. For the next 150 years, they were frequented by pirates and *corsairs* resting up before attacking the coast of Spanish America. In 1704, Alexander Selkirk, a Scottish sailor, quarrelled with his captain and was put ashore from HMS *Cinque Ports* on what is now Isla Robinson Crusoe, where he stayed alone until 1709, when he was picked up by a privateer, the *Duke*; his experience became the inspiration for *Robinson Crusoe*.

It was not until after 1750 that the Spanish took steps to defend the archipelago, founding San Juan Bautista and building seven fortresses. During the Wars of Independence the islands were used as a penal colony for Chilean independence leaders captured after the Battle of Rancagua. In 1915, two British destroyers, HMS *Kent* and *Glasgow* cornered the German cruiser, *Dresden*, in Bahía Cumberland. The German vessel was scuttled and still lies on the bottom; a monument on shore commemorates the event and, nearby, unexploded shells are embedded in the cliffs. Some of the German crew are buried in the cemetery.

Legends of buried pirate treasure have abounded over the years and several attempts have been made to find it. In 2005 a team using a Chilean-built robot with a penetrative sensor claimed to have discovered signs of the treasure, leading to massive media interest, but at the time of writing they have yet to unearth anything of interest.

Isla Robinson Crusoe

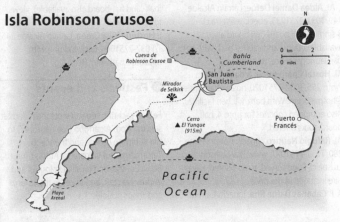

Chilean Pacific Islands Islas Juan Fernández

Getting there   The best time for a visit is between October and March. Air taxis from Santiago land on an airstrip in the west of the island, from where passengers are taken by boat to San Juan Bautista. (The boat tranfer should be included in the price of the air ticket.) There are also boats to the islands from Valparaíso.

Getting around   Isla Robinson Crusoe is small enough to explore on foot. You will need a boat the other islands. Take insect repellent.

Tourist information   San Juan Bautista has a **CONAF office** ① *Mon-Fri 0800-1800*, with information and advice on the island.

Sights

The only settlement in the archipelago is **San Juan Bautista**, a fishing village of simple wooden frame houses, located on Bahía Cumberland on the north coast of Isla Robinson Crusoe: it has a church, schools, post office, police station and radio station. San Juan Bautista is overlooked by the remains of the **Fuerte Santa Bárbara**, the largest of the Spanish fortresses, while in the village itself is a **Casa de la Cultura** ① *Mon-Fri 1000-1300, 1700-2100*, with exhibition rooms. Nearby are the **Cuevas de los Patriotas**, home to the deported Chilean independence leaders. The island's other famous cave, where Alexander Selkirk spent his years of isolation, is about 4 km north west of the village and can be visited by boat.

South of the village is the **Mirador de Selkirk**, the hill where Selkirk lit his signal fires. A plaque was set in the rock at the lookout point by British naval officers from *HMS Topaze* in 1868; nearby is a more recent plaque placed by Selkirk's descendants. The mirador is the only easy pass between the north and south sides of the island. A footpath leads further south to the anvil-shaped **El Yunque**, 915 m, the highest peak on the island, where Hugo Weber, a survivor from the *Dresden,* lived as a hermit for 12 years: some remains of his dwelling can be seen. The only sandy beach on Robinson Crusoe is **Playa Arenal**, in the extreme southwest corner, two hours by boat from San Juan Bautista.

● Sleeping

Lodging with villagers is difficult.

LL-L Hostería El Pangal, east of San Juan in the Caleta Pangal, T02-2731458, www. robinsoncrusoetours.cl. With half board. Owned by one of the airlines. Great views, pool, bar and restaurant, best on the island.

L-AL Aldea Daniel Defoe, Larraín Alcalde 449, T032-2751233, ebeeche@terra.cl. B singles. Half board (full board also available), rooms and cabins, both with bath, bar, laundry service, tours offered.

AL Hostal Charpentier, Ignacio Carrera Pinto 256, T032-2751020, hostalcharpentier @hotmail.com. With bath, kitchen facilities, Also equipped *cabañas* for upto 4, half board, tours offered.

AL Refugio Nautico, Ignacio Carrera Pinto 280, T032-2751077, www.islarobinson crusoe.cl. Food served, tours offered, kayak hire included in the price.

A-B Cabañas Dafne Rita, Ignacio Carrera

Pinto 118, T/F032-2751042, ritachamorro_g @hotmail.com. Wooded *cabañas* for 2, with views, laundry facilities.

A-B Hostería Martínez Green, El Castillo 116, T032-2751039, www.hosteriamartinez green.cl. Rooms with bath and TV, restaurant (half- and full-board also available), views, tours offered.

B Hostería Villa Green, Larraín Alcalde 246, T/F032-2751044. Basic lodging with breakfast, bath and TV.

● Festivals and events

Feb   A yachting regatta visits the islands. It sets out from Algarrobo (see page 147) to Isla Robinson Crusoe and thence to Talcahuano and Valparaíso. At this time, Bahía Cumberland is full of colourful and impressive craft, and prices in restaurants and shops double.

▲ Activities and tours

The following all offer all-inclusive packages, some including flights:

Ecoturismo Los Colonos, El Castillo s/n, T032-2751216, www.colonosdejuan fernandez.cl.

Endémica Expeditions, Sector del Muelle s/n, T032-2751023, www.endemica.com.

Marooned, La Falda s/n, T032-2751030, lactorisfernandeziana@hotmail.com, offers guided day hikes. English spoken.

Refugio Nautico, see under Sleeping, offers all-inclusive packages.

Rutas de Robinson Crusoe, Larraín Alcalde 390, T032-2751023, www.rutasdeirc.cl.

⊖ Transport

Air

Air taxis from **Santiago**, 2½ hrs, are operated by 2 companies: services can be erratic, especially off season. All leave from Tobalaba Aerodrome in La Reina (eastern outskirts of the city). Prices are about US$250-300 one way, US$500-600 return, luggage allowance 10 kg. **Línea de Aeroservicios SA** (Av Larraín 7941, La Reina, Santiago, T02-2738179, www.robinsoncrusoetours.cl); **Aerolíneas ATA** (11 de septiembre 2115 Torre B, Of 1107, Providencia, Santiago, T02-2343389, aerolineasata.cl).

Ferry

Boats from **Valparaíso** are operated by **Naviera del Sur** of Valparaíso (Blanco Encalada 1623, oficina 602, Valparaíso, T032-2594304, www.navieradelsur.cl), US$300 return including meals, leaving in the first week of each month; preference is given to islanders, and passages are sometimes difficult to obtain.

The Chilean Navy has 4 boats a year to the islands and may take passengers with appropriate credentials; contact the **Armada**, Prat 620, Valparaíso, T032-2252094.

To explore the archipelago, it is possible to charter the municipal launch, *Blanca Luz*, which goes to different places including Selkirk Island; contact Larraín Alcalde 320, T032-2751001. The fishermen's union has several launches between them, some of which can be hired.

❶ Directory

There are no exchange facilities on the island. No credit cards, no TCs; only pesos and US$ cash are accepted. The post office is at Alcalde Larraín s/n.

Rapa Nui (Easter Island)

→ *Phone code: 032. Population 3800.*

Isla de Pascua or Rapa Nui lies in the Pacific Ocean just south of the Tropic of Capricorn and 3790 km west of Chile; its nearest neighbour is Pitcairn Island. The island is triangular in shape, with an extinct volcano at each corner. The original inhabitants called the island Te Pito o te Henua, 'the navel of the world'. The unique features of the island are the many ahu *(ceremonial altars) on top of some of which stand 600 (or so)* moai, *huge stone figures up to 10 m in height and broad in proportion, representing the deified ancestors of the Rapa Nui people. The islanders have preserved their indigenous songs and dances and are extremely hospitable.* ⇥ *For Sleeping, Eating and other listings, see pages 512-516.*

Background

It is now generally accepted that the island was colonized from Polynesia about AD 800. Thor Heyerdahl's theories that the first inhabitants came from South America are less widely accepted than they used to be and South American influence is now largely discounted.

Indigenous Polynesian society, for all its romantic idylls, was competitive and it seems that the five clans that originally had their own lands on Rapu Nui demonstrated their strength by erecting complex monuments representing deceased leading figures of the tribes facing inwards as to protect his tribesfolk. These *Moai* were sculpted at the Rano Raraku quarry and transported on wooden rollers over more or less flat paths to their final locations; their red topknots were sculpted at Puna Pau and then brought to the coast. Rounded pebbles were all collected from the same beach at Vinapu and laid out checkerboard fashion at the *ahu*. The sculptors and engineers were paid out of the surplus food produced by the sponsoring family. The population grew steadily until around the 16th or 17th century it passed the limits of the islands natural resources, causing a century of warfare and famine between the tribes during which most of the *Moai*, seen to have failed their descendents, were destroyed or at the very least knocked off their plinths. At one point the population was reduced to as little as 111 inhabitants. War was finally ended with the introduction of the cult of the Bird man at Orongo, and the population slowly recovered.

European contact with the island began with the visit of the Dutch admiral, Jacob Roggeven, on Easter Sunday 1722, who was followed by the British navigator James Cook in 1774 and the French sailor Le Perouse in 1786. The population of the island remained stable at 4000 until the 1850s, when Peruvian slavers, smallpox and emigration to Tahiti (encouraged by plantation owners) reduced the numbers. Between 1859 and 1862, over 1000 islanders were transported as slaves to work in the Peruvian guano trade. The island was annexed by Chile in 1888 and from 1895 to 1952 most of it was leased to a private company, which bred sheep on its grasslands: a wall was built around the Hanga Roa area and the islanders were forbidden to cross.

Nowadays, about half the island of low round hills with groves of palms and eucalyptus, is used for grazing and agriculture, while the other half constitutes a national park. Of the current population, about 1000 are from the mainland. Tourism has grown rapidly since the air service began in 1967 and the islanders have profited greatly from the visits of North Americans: a Canadian medical expedition left a mobile hospital on the island in 1966 and, when a US missile-tracking station was abandoned in 1971, vehicles, mobile housing and an electricity generator were left behind. Many of the *Moai* have now been restored to their original positions.

Rapa Nui - Easter Island

Volcanoes (extinct)

Easter Island geology and the making of the *Moai*

In geological terms Easter Island is not very old; potassium argon dating shows that its oldest part is under 2.5 million years old. It is located above a tectonic 'hot spot', an active upwelling of liquid rock emerging from beneath the crust of the earth and solidifying. Enough molten rock has poured out to form a mountain nearly 3000 m high, the altitude of the Easter Island volcano if measured from the sea bed. There are, however, no records of volcanic activity since human occupation of the island began. The three high peaks are all volcanic in origin and consist mainly of basalt. In the cliffs of Rano Kau different layers of basalt can be identified, indicating the existence of distinct lava flows.

Caves have been formed where the lava has solidified on the outside but continued to flow downhill on the inside. On Terevaka, where the roofs of some of these caves have collapsed, long caverns up to 10 m high can be seen.

The volcanic nature of the island contributed to the carving of the *Moai*. Extremely hard basalt from Terevaka was used to make the tools for carving and sharp-edged implements were fashioned using obsidian, volcanic glass formed by lava cooling very rapidly. The *Moai* themselves were carved from tuff, a porous rock much softer than basalt but also volcanic in origin, which can be found at Rano Raruka, a secondary cone on the side of Terevaka.

Ins and outs

Getting there The high tourist season is from September to April, although there are tourists throughout the year. The only way to reach the island is by **Lanchile** plane from Santiago. Easter Island's airport is just south of Hanga Roa. Most flights continue from Easter Island to Tahiti.

Getting around There are numerous taxis available on the island and an unreliable summer bus service. Horses, bicycles, motorbikes and cars can all be hired.

Tourist information Sernatur ① *Tu'u Maheke, T032-2100255, Mon-Fri 0830-1300, 1400-1730, Sat 1000-1300, 14300-1730.* English spoken.

Climate Unlike most Polynesian islands, Easter Island has no coral reef as winter temperatures are too cold for coral to survive. As a result, the coastline has been eroded in parts to form steep cliffs, around Poike, Rano Kao and on the northern side of Terevaka. There is no high central plateau and consequently little gully erosion, which would normally lead to the development of streams and rivers. Moreover much of the island's rainfall drains away underground into the huge caverns formed by the collapse of basalt caves. As a result, although annual rainfall is usually above 1000 mm, there is always a severe shortage of water and in many years several months of drought. Humidity is usually high, while the rainy season is March to October, with the wettest weather in May. Average monthly temperatures range from 15-17°C in August to 24°C in February, the hottest month.

Hanga Roa and around

There is one village on the island, Hanga Roa, where most of the population live. The **Museo Antropológico Sebastián Englert** ① *T032-2551020, www.museorapanui.cl, Tue-Fri 0930-1230, 1400-1730, Sat and Sun 0930-1230, US$2, US$1 concessions,*

● In 1947, the Norwegian ethnologist Thor Heyerdahl constructed a reed and balsawood boat, the Kon Tiki, and sailed it from the coast of Chile to Easter Island in order to prove that such a migration would have been possible.

valid for unlimited visits within a 30-day period, has good descriptions of island life, although most of the objects are reproductions, because the originals were removed from the island. Free guided visits are available with advance notice. There is also an interesting modern church with locally stylized religious art and carvings, mixing catholic themes with elements of the cult of the birdman. Services are held on Sundays with hymns sung in Rapa Nui. A taxi journey within any two points in town should not cost more than US$3.

A six-hour walk from Hanga Roa north along the west coast passes **Ahu Tahai**, just outside town, where there is a cave house and a *moai* with eyes and topknot in place. Two caves can be reached north from here: the one inland appears to be a ceremonial centre, while the other (nearer the sea) has two 'windows' (take a strong flashlight and be careful). Further north is **Ahu Te Peu**, with a broken *moai* and ruined houses. Beyond here you can join the path to Hanga o Teo (see below), or turn right, inland to **Te Pahu** cave and the seven *moai* at **Akivi**. Either return to Hanga Roa or continue to the **Puna Pau** crater (two hours), where the *moai*'s distinctive red topknots were carved.

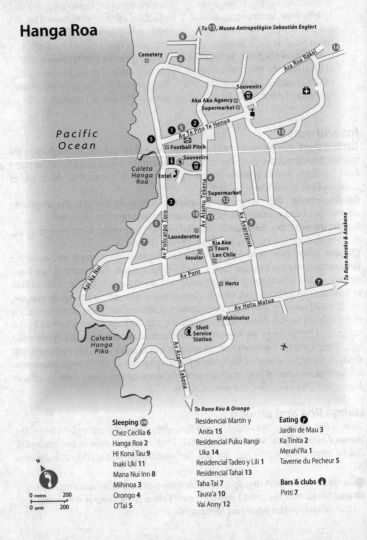

Hanga Roa

Sleeping
Chez Cecilia 6
Hanga Roa 2
HI Kona Tau 9
Inaki Uki 11
Mana Nui Inn 8
Mihinoa 3
Orongo 4
O'Tai 5

Residencial Martín y
  Anita 15
Residencial Puku Rangi
  Uka 14
Residencial Tadeo y Lili 1
Residencial Tahai 13
Taha Tai 7
Taura'a 10
Vai Anny 12

Eating
Jardín de Mau 3
Ka Tinita 2
Merahi'Ra 1
Taverne du Pecheur 5

Bars & clubs
Piriti 7

Bird man cult of Orongo

Far from being the passive recipient of external influences, Easter Island shows the extent of unique development possible for a people left wholly in isolation. Its older altars (*ahu*) are similar to those of French Polynesia, and its older statues (*Moai*) similar to those of the Marquesas Islands, but the very precise stone fitting of some of the *ahu*, and the tall gaunt *Moai* with elongated faces and ears for which Easter Island is best known were later developments.

The bird man cult represented at Orongo developed in the early 18th century after the islanders had lost their clan territoriality and were concentrated at Hanga Roa, but still needed a non-territorial way to simulate inter-clan rivalry. The central feature of the birdman cult was an annual ceremony in which the heads of the clans, or their representatives, raced to the islets of Motu Nui, Motu Iti and Motu Kao off the southwest coast of Rapa Nui to obtain the first egg of the sooty tern (known as the Manutara), a migratory seabird that nests there. The winning chief was then named Bird Man, Tangata Manu, for the following year.

It appears that, in the cult, the precious egg of the tern represented fertility, although the actual status of the Tangata Manu on the island is less clear. The petroglyphs at Orongo depict the half-man, half-bird Tangata Manu, the creator god Make Make and the symbol of fertility, Komari.

South of Hanga Roa is **Rano Kau**, the extinct volcano where the curious Orongo ruins can be seen. The road south out of Hanga Roa passes the two caves of **Ana Kai Tangata**, one of which has paintings, and continues southeast, if, however, you're on foot, take the path just past the CONAF sign for a much shorter route to the impressive Rano Kau crater. A lake with many reed islands lies 200 m below the rim of the crater. Locals occasionally scramble down to collect medicinal herbs. On the seaward side of the volcano is **Orongo** ① *US$6*, one of the most important sites on the island with many ruined buildings and petroglyphs, where the bird man cult flourished (see box, above). Out to sea are the 'bird islets', Motu Nui, Motu Iti and Motu Kao. It is very windy at the summit, with good views at sunset or under a full moon. It is easy to follow the road back to Hanga Roa in the dark.

If you are driving, visit the sites from south to north since travel agencies tend to start their tours in the north.

Rest of the island

A tour of the main part of the island can be done on foot, but this would need at least two days, returning to Hanga Roa on the first day and setting out again the next day. For more extensive exploration you could hire either a bicycle, horse or a car (see below). A high-clearance vehicle is better suited to the smaller roads than a normal car. From Hanga Roa, take the road going southeast past the airport; at the oil tanks turn right to **Vinapu**, where there are two *ahu* and a wall whose stones are joined with Inca-like precision. Head back northeast along the south coast to reach **Vaihu**, an *ahu* with eight broken *Moai* and a small harbour, **Akahanga**, an *ahu* with toppled *Moai*, and **Hanga Tetenga**, a toppled *Moai* and an *ahu*, with bones visible inside. Beyond is **Ahu Tongariki**, largest platform on the island with a row of 15 *Moai*, which was damaged by a tidal wave in 1960 and later restored with Japanese aid. Turn left here to **Rano Raraku** (2 km), the volcano where the *Moai* were originally carved (see box above) and where many statues can still be seen. In the crater is a small lake surrounded by reeds; swimming is possible beyond the reeds.

⦂ Tapati or Semana Rapa Nui

Held each year in late January/early February, Tapati is organized as a huge competition between groups, many of them families, each of which elects a beauty queen. It begins slowly but keeps on getting better as the fortnight goes on. Families score points by participating in a wide variety of competitions, including gastronomy, necklace-making, sculpting *Moai*, body painting, dancing, singing, horse racing, swimming, modified decathlon. In the most spectacular event, men, dressed only in the traditional thong and with their bodies painted, compete to slide down the side of a volcano, sitting on a kind of sledge made from the trunks of two banana plants. Only for the tough guys!

Lots of tourists, especially from the Chilean mainland, visit at this time. It is best to stay in Hanga Roa, since it is easy to hitch from here to activities elsewhere on the island.

The road heads north past 'the trench of the long ears'; an excursion can be made from here east to **Poike** headland to see the open-mouthed statue that is particularly popular with local carvers. Ask the farmer for permission to cross his land. At the northeast end of the headland is the cave where a virgin was kept before marriage to the victor of ceremonies during the time of the bird man cult; ask someone for directions.

The road along the north coast passes **Ahu Te Pito Kura**, where the 10-m-tall *Moai* is one of the largest ever brought to a platform. The road continues to **Ovahe** where there is a very attractive beach with pink sand and some rather recently carved faces and a cave.

From Ovahe, you can return direct to Hanga Roa or continue to the palm-fringed, white-sand beach at **Anakena**, the site of the village of the island's first king, Hotu Matua, and the spot where Thor Heyerdahl landed in 1955; his visit is commemorated with a plaque. The *moai* here has been restored to its probable original state. There is a picnic area and a stall selling barbequed meat and fish on a skewer, US$7 (the tuna is excellent). From Anakena a coastal path of variable quality runs west, passing beautiful cliff scenery and interesting remains. At **Hanga o Teo**, there appears to be a large village complex, with several round houses, while further on is a burial place, built like a long ramp with several ditches containing bones. From Hanga o Teo the path goes west then south, inland from the coast, to meet the road north of Hanga Roa.

◔ Sleeping

Hanga Roa and around *p509, map p510*
Unless it is a particularly busy season there is no need to book in advance; some mainland agencies make exorbitant booking charges. That said, the advantage of an advance booking is that you will be met at the airport, given a traditional welcome necklace and a free transfer to your hotel or hostel. Flights are met by large numbers of hotel and *residencial* representatives but it is often cheaper to look for yourself. There are even reports of touts approaching passengers at

Santiago airport prior to their flight to the island. Accommodation is much more expensive than anywhere else in Chile, ranging from about US$25-150 per person for bed and breakfast. There is no accommodation outside Hanga Roa. The tourist office has a full list of accommodation and prices.
LL-L Hanga Roa, Av Pont s/n, T032-2100299, www.hotelhangaroa.cl. In its time the best hotel on the island. Lack of investment has given it a run-down, tatty feel, although the staff are helpful and there is a good buffet

‼ Money matters

When travelling to Easter Island make sure you take both dollars and Chilean pesos in cash. Most purchases can be made in either currency, but in some cases it is much better to pay in one and in other cases the other. Always ask for the price in dollars and pesos and see which is better value. Credit card transactions have a 10% surcharge added.

breakfast and it is in an excellent location. It has recently been bought, however, and a full refit is promised.

LL-L Taha Tai, Api Na Nui s/n, T032-2551192, www.hoteltahatai.cl. Well kept bright hotel with ceramic floors and cabins with a sea view. There is a small swimming pool, and expensive tours are offered. English spoken.

L-AL O'Tai, Te Pito Te Henua s/n, T032-2100250, otairapanui@entelchile.net. Great location 2 mins from sea, lovely gardens, pool, restaurant. English spoken. Rooms vary in quality. The better rooms have a terrace and a/c; 133-137 are the most spacious.

L-AL Taura'a, C Principal s/n, T032-2100463, www.tauraahotel.cl. Upmarket B&B. Comfortable rooms with good beds and spacious bathrooms. Good breakfast, pleasant garden. English and French spoken, good service, tours offered. Recommended.

AL Mana Nui Inn, Tahai s/n, opposite the cemetery, T032-2100811, www.rapanuiweb.com/mananui. **B** singles. Pleasant cabins on the north edge of town with fine views. Friendly, good breakfast with local specialities, tours offered.

AL Residencial Martín y Anita, Simon Paoa s/n, opposite hospital in Hanga Roa, T032-2100593, www.hostal.co.cl. With breakfast, clean, good food, tours offered.

AL Residencial Tadeo y Lili, Apina Ichi s/n, T032-2100422, tadeolili@entelchile.net. Simple but clean French/Rapa Nui run. All rooms have sea view and a small terrace. Excellent location, good breakfast, tours offered including excursions on horseback. Recommended.

AL-A Chez Cecilia, near Tahai Moai, T032-2100499, www.rapanuichezcecilia.com. With breakfast, speaks English and French, excellent food, also *cabañas* and good value camping. Nice view from the grounds.

Discounts for students.
AL-A Orongo, Atamu Tekena s/n, T/F032-2100572, www.hotelorongo.com. Half-board available (excellent restaurant), good service, nice garden.

A HI Kona Tau, Avareipua s/n s/n, T032-2100321, www.konataurapanui.com. D per person in dorms. Hostelling International affiliated. All rooms with bath and breakfast. Kitchen facilities, meals served, terrace with interesting views inland.

A Inaki Uki, C Principal s/n, opposite Taura'a, www.inakiuki.cl. **C** singles. Simple but clean rooms with shared bathrooms and kitchen facilities. No breakfast. Central, and a good budget option.

A Residencial Puku Rangi Uka, Puku Rangi Uka s/n, T032-2100405, www.rapanuiweb.com/puku rangiuka. Simple but spacious rooms, some with bath.

A Residencial Tahai, Sector Tahai s/n, T032-2100395. With breakfast, full board available, nice garden. Good value.

B Vai Anny, Tuki Haka He Viri s/n, T032-2100650, www.vaianny.com. Good value, family run *cabañas*.

B-C Mihinoa, Av Pont s/n, T032-511593, www.mihinoa.com. This is a campsite that also has a few rooms, breakfast extra, excellent fresh fish barbeques, clean, kitchen facilities, hot showers, laundry, internet, very friendly and exceptional value. Fishing trips also offered. Recommended.

Camping
Camping is only officially allowed in **Hanga Roa**, where there are several sites. Many people have campsites in their gardens, US$8-12 per person, check availability of water first; some families also provide food.
Mihinoa, Av Pont s/n, T032-511593, www.mihinoa.com. Campsite with good facilities and friendly owners. Also hire out camping equipment. Recommended.

🍴 Eating

Food, wine and beer are expensive, often twice the price of the mainland, because of freight charges, but local fish, vegetables, fruit and bread are cheap and vegetarians will have no problems on the island. Average prices: coffee/tea US$1.50, meals about US$10 or more, bread and fruit US$2 per kg, beer/cola US$3 in most bars and restaurants. Bring all you can from the mainland, but not fruit. Fish can be bought from the *caleta* for around US$5.50 per kg. Restaurants tend to serve their fish well done. If you don't want to be chewing leather, ask for it *no tan cocido*.

Some *residenciales* offer full board at an extra cost. Coffee is generally instant. It is worth booking a table in advance for evening meals.

🍴🍴 **Jardín de Mau**, Atanu Tekena s/n. Pasta/fusion using mostly local ingredients. Some of the pasta is made fresh. Excellent tuna carpaccio. Clean, friendly staff, sea view, better wine list than most.

🍴🍴 **Taverne du Pecheur**, Caleta Hanga Roa. By far the most expensive restaurant on the island – the prices are in line with the owner's ego – this is the self-proclaimed "best restaurant in Chile"! To be fair the food is excellent – lobster, fish and meat all cooked to a tee with inventive sauces using ingredients brought specially from all over the world. Full selection of wines and spirits.

🍴🍴 **Ka Tinita**, Te Pito Te Henua s/n. Closed Sun. Fish, prepared simply but well, large salads and side dishes. Good value by island standards.

🍴🍴 **Merahi'Ra**, Te Pito Te Henua s/n. Closed Thu. Well known for its fish. Service can be a bit lax.

🍴 **Klosk**, by football pitch. *Empanadas* and cheap sandwiches.

🍸 Bars and clubs

There are 2 discos in Hanga Roa. The action begins after 0100. Drinks are expensive: a *pisco sour* costs US$5, canned beer US$3. **Piriti**, near airport. Open Thu-Sat. **Toroko**, by the coast in Caleta Hanga Roa. Open daily.

🎭 Entertainment

There are shows of traditional dancing from the island at **Hotel Hanga Roa** (see Sleeping above), and at **Kopakabana Restaurant**. Music at the **church**, Av Te Pito Ote Henua, for the 0900 Sunday mass has been described as 'enchanting'.

🎉 Festivals and events

Jan-Feb Tapati, or Semana Rapa Nui starts at the end of Jan and lasts 2 weeks, see box, page 512.

🛍 Shopping

On **Av Policarpo Toro**, the main street, there are lots of small shops and market stalls, which close when it rains, and a couple of supermarkets; the cheapest are **Kai Nene** or **Tumukai**. Some local produce can be found free, but ask first. This includes wild guava fruit, fish, '*hierba luisa*' tea and wild chicken. Film is readily available but cannot be developed on the island.

Handicrafts and souvenirs

Wood carvings and stone *Moai* are sold throughout Hanga Roa. Good pieces cost between US$50-200. Bargaining is only possible if you pay cash. The municipal market, left of the church, will give you a good view of what is available and there's no compunction to buy. The cheapest handicrafts are available from the jail, behind the airport where the prisoners earn money by carving and then selling semi-finished items to market stall owners. With a couple of days notice you can ask for practically any design at modest prices.

There are several souvenir shops on Av Policarpo Toro including **Hotu Matuu's Favorite Shoppe** where prices have been described as 'top dollar and she will not bargain', but she does have the best T-shirts. Handicrafts are also sold at Tahai, Vaihu, Rano Raraku and Anakena. The airport shop is expensive.

▲ Activities and tours

Hiking

Allow at least a day to walk the length of the island, one way, taking in all the sites. It is 5 hrs' easy walk from Hanga Roa to Rano Raraku; 5 hrs to Anakena. You can hitch back to Hanga Roa, especially at weekends, although there are few cars at other times. Anyone wishing to spend time exploring the island would be well advised to speak to CONAF first (T032-2100236); they also give good advice on special interests (biology, archaeology, handicrafts etc). Maps are sold on Av Policarpo Toro for US$15-18.

Riding

This is the best way to see the island, provided you are fit. Horses can be hired for US$65 a day (including a guide; cheaper without).
Pantu Cabalgatas, T032-100577, www.pantupikerauri.cl, is the only officially licenced operators, although several other local guides can be hired privately and charge a little less. Ask at the tourist office.

Tours

Over 20 agencies as well as several *residenciales* and local individuals arrange excursions around the island. Some provide transport (tour prices around US$35 per person per day). others will accompany tourists in hired vehicles (usually around US$100 for a full day). The English of tour guides is often poor.
Recommended operators include:
Aku-Aku Tours , Tu'U Koihu s/n, T032-210070, akuakuturismo.cl. Wide range of half and full day tours.
Archaeological Travel Service, Tu' U Koihi s/n, T032-2100364, archeots@rapanui.cl. Archaeological and scientific tours. English, French, German spoken.
Hanga Roa Travel, T032-2100158, hfritsch@entelchile.net. English, German and Spanish spoken, good-value all-inclusive tours. Recommended.

Tour operators

Mike Rapu, Caleta Hanga Roa, T032-2551055, www.mikerapu.cl. Offers diving expeditions and courses as well as fishing trips.
Orca, Caleta Hanga Roa, T032-100375, www.seemorca.cl. Offers guided diving trips as well as excursions by boat, kayaking and windsurfing. English and French spoken.

⊙ Transport

Air

LanChile flies from **Santiago**, 4 to 6 times a week, depending on the season, 5-5½ hrs. Some flights continue to Papeete on Tahiti. LanChile will not allow you to fly to Easter Island unless you have a confirmed flight off the island (note that planes to Tahiti are more crowded than those back to Santiago). You should reconfirm your booking on arrival on the Island.

If booked well in advance, the cheapest fare in 2006 was approximately US$655 return from Santiago, with occasional special deals available through travel agents. Special deals may be available on flights originating outside Chile, or for those booking in advance. Under 24s and over 65s are often eligible for a 28% discount on some fares.

Flying from Santiago to Easter Island incurs the domestic tax of US$16. The airport tax for international flights from Easter Island to Tahiti is US$9. Don't take pesos to Tahiti, they are worthless in French Polynesia.
LanChile, Poilcarpo Toro Y Av Pont, T032-2100279.

Bicycle/motorcycle

Bicycles (some in poor condition) are available for rent for US$12 per day on main street or from *residenciales*. Motorbikes can be hired for about US$25 a day plus fuel (Suzuki or Honda 250 are recommended because of the rough roads).

Boat

Many pacific cruises stop off at Easter Island. There is no scheduled passenger services to Easter Island from the mainland. Freight is brought by sea 3 times a year.

The runway south of Hanga Roa has been extended to provide an emergency landing site for US space shuttles.

Cars and jeeps are available from *residenciales* and hotels as well as hire companies. There are many different companies (Policarpo Toro is a good place to start) and vehicles vary in size and condition, so shop around. Jeep hire US$50 per day, US$100 with driver. There is no insurance available, drive at your own risk (be careful at night, many vehicles drive without lights). US$5-10 will buy enough fuel for a one-day trip around the island.

Taxi

Taxis can be hired to take you around but it is much better value either to take a tour or hire some means of transport.

ⓘ Directory

Banks There is one bank on Atamu Tekena s/n with an ATM. Accepts MasterCard and Cirrus but not visa. Cash can be exchanged in shops, hotels, etc, at about 5% less than in Santiago. Poor rates on TCs at **Afex** on the main street but no commission. Credit cards are widely accepted, but all transactions incur a 10% service charge. **Internet** Broad band has recently reached the island and there are several internet cafes which, although expensive, have good connections.
Medical services There is a 20-bed hospital as well as 3 resident doctors, a trained nurse and 1 dentist on the island.
Post office Mon-Fri 0900-1300, 1430-1800, Sat 0900-1200.
Telephone ENTEL, Atamu Tekena s/n. Phone calls to the Chilean mainland are subsidized, at US$0.50 per minute. Calls to Europe cost US$1 per min.

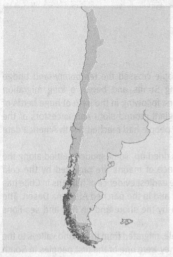

History

Origins

Some 50,000 years ago, the very first people crossed the temporary land bridge spanning Asia and America at the Bering Straits and began a long migration southwards. They were hunters and foragers, following in the path of huge herds of now extinct animals, such as mammoth, giant ground sloth and ancestors of the camel and horse. The first signs that these people had reached South America date from around 14,000 BC, if not earlier.

As sources of game in forested valleys dried up, some groups settled along the coasts, particularly drawn by the abundance of marine life provided by the cold Humboldt current in the Pacific. Some of the earliest evidence of humans in Chile has been found in the north, both on the coast and in the parched Atacama Desert. The coastal people lived on shellfish gathered by the shore and on fish and sea-lions speared from inflated seal-skin rafts.

One such group, the Las Conchas people, migrated from the inland valleys to the coast near Antofagasta around 7500 BC. They were one of the first peoples in South America to take hallucinogenic drugs. Many graves excavated in this region contain mortars, which may have been used to grind up seeds also found nearby. These seeds contained an alkaloid similar to that found in the ayahuasca plant, which is still used for its hallucinogenic effects by the Shuar in Peru – indeed, the Shuar are believed by some to be descendants of these Atacameño peoples, having migrated to the Amazon in order to hide from the Spanish. Some specialists believe that the many geoglyphs of the Atacama Desert (see box, page 240) – the most famous ones being the Nazca Lines in Peru – were maps for shamans undergoing the hallucinatory experience of flight after taking drugs such as ayahuasca. Other objects found in graves include bags, trays and tubes, which were used for inhaling the drug in the form of snuff, a method still employed in curing and divination practices in the Andean region and coastal Brazil. Some of the trays and tubes found were decorated with images of supernatural beings and anthropomorphic figures, such as bird-headed angels, styles that are also common in the Andean regions of present-day Peru and Bolivia.

The beginnings of agriculture

Gradually, the settled life of agricultural subsistence took over from the more nomadic hunting lifestyle. Remains of slingshot stones and what seem to be *bolas* (weights attached to cords used to bring down prey by entangling their legs) have been found alongside bones of mastodons in Monte Verde, near Puerto Montt. Other remains found nearby included agricultural tools and medicinal plants, hearths and house foundations, all indications that the site was inhabited for some time by one community. Crop seeds have also been found, including those of potatoes, evidence of very early contact with cultures from as far afield as the Central Andes. Some of these remains were found in a remarkable condition, owing to being buried in a peat bog; mastodon bones even had traces of meat on them. It is widely agreed that the site was settled 10,000 years ago, although lower levels have been controversially dated from as early as 34,000 years ago.

By about 2500 BC, agriculture was practised throughout much of Chile, as it was across the rest of the continent. Maize, beans and squash have been found in northern Chile from as early as 5000 BC. However, people in the south only turned definitively to agriculture at a much later date. In Araucanía, horticulture was not practised until around AD 500. These people also had unusual burial practices, placing the body in an urn inside a funerary canoe, perhaps reflecting the local

66 99 Specialists believe that geoglyphs were maps for shamans undergoing the hallucinatory experience of flight after taking drugs such as ayahuasca...

dependence on fishing for their livelihood. Elaborate artefacts found in some graves, such as stone and copper jewellery and ceramic offerings, suggest a stratified society of both rich and poor.

Northern influences

In the north, the extremely dry climate is a great preservative, allowing archaeologists to build up a detailed picture of early life. The people in the Atacama lived in solidly built adobe houses, arranged in complexes around inner courtyards and corridors, such as can be seen in the village of Tulor near San Pedro de Atacama.

These northern peoples had contact with neighbouring highland communities, shown by the presence there of plants and other goods found only in the adjacent regions. The important *altiplano* culture of **Tiahuanaco** in present-day Bolivia is thought to have had particularly close links with northern Chile, helping to stimulate the growth of settlements such as that at San Pedro de Atacama. Trade with Tiahuanaco, through llama caravans bringing highland goods and produce, boosted the wealth and cultural development of the desert people. Some very fine textiles were found in this area, showing distinct design similarities with those of Tiahuanaco. The textiles were hand-spun and coloured with vegetable and cochineal dyes. Clothing and jewellery adornments containing feathers suggested contact even with tropical regions, although these may have been obtained through their *altiplano* intermediaries. Local ceramics were mostly plain and highly polished, but some items decorated with elaborate dragon-like figures had probably been traded with Tiahuanaco.

Mummification was practised from as early as 2500 BC by coastal peoples and was also common further north in present-day Peru as practised by the Chinchorro people. They buried their dead stretched out straight, in contrast to the foetal position used by other Chilean and Peruvian cultures. Internal organs and the brain were removed and the body was stuffed with a variety of materials to preserve it. Sticks were attached to the limbs to keep them straight. A mask was placed over the face and a wig of real human hair was attached to the head. The body was then coated in a layer of clay and wrapped in animal skins or mats. According to the person's status, they were often buried with their personal possessions: clothing, jewellery, musical instruments and copper items.

In the period AD 500-900 the association between San Pedro de Atacama and Tiahuanaco had become even stronger. In return for trading their agricultural produce and other goods, it is thought that the Tiahuanaco people sought copper, semi-precious stones and the use of grazing lands in northern Chile. As with the Araucanía in the south, some graves from this period contained bodies with more elaborate clothing, jewellery, imported ceramics and other valuables, suggesting the existence of a wealthy elite, which was also common in central Andean cultures.

Following the demise of Tiahuanaco in about AD 1100, a number of cultures arose in the adjacent area bordering southern Bolivia, northern Chile and Argentina, practising derivative agriculture, with terraces and irrigation, and producing ceramics in similar styles. In the Quebrada de Humahuaca in present-day Argentina, several small defensive towns were built with fortified walls and stone houses. Grave remains have revealed that metallurgy was well developed here; some bodies were adorned with pectorals, bracelets, masks and bells, made of copper, silver and gold. Shells from the Pacific and ceramics from present-day Bolivian cultures, such as the Huruquilla, show the existence of widespread trade links.

Inca expansion

The next major empire to touch northern Chile was that of the Incas, which, at the peak of its growth in the 16th century, stretched as far south as the Aconcagua Valley near modern-day Santiago. The advancing armies of Inca Topa Yupanqui suppressed resistance in the valleys of the central region and replaced local structures with their own military administration. They were finally stopped by hostile forest tribes at the Río Maule near present-day Talca. This was the southernmost limit of the Inca Empire, some 3840 km south of the equator and the deepest that any imperial movement had penetrated into the southern hemisphere.

One major group that survived the Inca incursion and resisted conquest by the Europeans right up until the 19th century was the **Mapuche** (see box, page 305). They were concentrated in the central valley south and east of the Cordillera de Nahuelbuta. The Mapuche were primarily farmers but also hunted and fished, both inland and along the coasts and lake shores. Their large cemeteries contained a variety of burial sites, some in canoes or stone chambers and some in simple earthen graves. Grave goods were plentiful, with elaborate ceramics, wooden and stone artefacts and jewellery made of copper and semi-precious stones.

The far south

Despite the apparently inhospitable conditions, these regions were home to a sizeable population of hunting, fishing and gathering peoples from very early times continuously up to the 19th century AD. Bones of horses and extinct giant sloths, dating from approximately 8000 BC, have been found near to stone arrowheads in sites such as Fells's Cave and Pali Aike Cave on the Magellan Straits – evidence of the earliest hunters.

Four distinct cultures developed here: the Haush, Ona, Yámana and Alacalufe. The oldest of these was the **Haush**, nomadic hunters of the guanaco mainly confined to the farthest southeastern tip of Tierra del Fuego, in present-day Argentina. The Haush hunted with bows and arrows, using guanaco skins for clothing and sometimes for covering their stick-framed houses. They also gathered shellfish and caught fish by the shore, using spears and harpoons.

The **Ona** people also hunted guanaco, ranging on foot across most of the Isla Grande de Tierra del Fuego in family groups. They were strong runners and tall people, some of them 6 ft tall; in fact, all these hunters and gatherers are thought to have been the tallest of the first South American peoples. They wore guanaco skin robes, fur side out, and also guanaco fur moccasins, known as *jamni*. They made open-topped shelters out of guanaco skins, which were weatherproofed with a coating of mud and saliva, and sometimes painted red. The Ona did not use harpoons or spears and only collected shellfish from beaches at low tide.

The **Yámana** were nomadic coastal hunters, travelling in canoes up and down the coasts of the Beagle Channel and around the islands southwards to Cape Horn. They caught otters, fish and seals, using spears and harpoons, and used slings and snares to catch birds. The Yámana houses were simple, made of sticks and grass, and they wore little clothing, perhaps a small seal skin and skin moccasins in winter.

Like the Yámana, the **Alacalufes** were also nomadic coastal peoples, roaming from Puerto Edén in the Chilean channels, to Yendegaia in the Beagle Channel. There was some contact with the Yámana, with whom they would sometimes exchange goods and inter-marry. The Alacalufes had similar lifestyles to the Yámana but developed various additions, such as raising a sail on their canoes and using a bow and arrow in addition to the sling when hunting birds or guanaco.

Town planning in the 16th century

Perhaps the most obvious influence of Spanish colonial settlement for a visitor is the characteristic street plan of towns and cities. Colonial cities were founded by means of an official ceremony, which involved tracing the central square and holding a mass. A series of Royal Ordinances issued in Madrid in 1573 laid down the rules of town planning: the four corners of the main plaza had to face the four points of the compass; the plaza and the main streets had arcades and, away from the plaza, the streets were traced out with a cord and ruler in the now-familiar grid-pattern. Once this was done, building lots near the plaza were distributed, allocated by lottery to those settlers who had rights to be there.

The Ordinances specified the principles underlying the distribution of the major public buildings. Churches were to be distant from the plaza and built on high ground, so that they were easy to see and people had to climb up to them on steps, thereby forcing a greater reverence. The *cabildo* and the customs house were to be built nearby, while the hospital of the poor and those sick with non-contagious diseases was to be north-facing, planned so that the inmates could enjoy southern exposure.

The Ordinances also advised settlers on how to deal with local suspicion and hostility: "While the new town is being built the settlers … shall try to avoid communication and intercourse with the Indians. Nor are the Indians to enter the circuit of the settlement until the latter is complete and in condition for defence and the houses built, so that when the Indians see them they will be filled with wonder and will realize that the Spaniards are settling there permanently and not temporarily."

'Royal Ordinances Governing the Laying Out of New Towns' by Zelia Nuttall, *Hispanic American Historical Review*, May 1922.

Spanish conquest and early settlement

The first Spanish expeditions to Chile were led by **Diego de Almagro** and **Pedro de Valdivia**, both of whom followed the Inca road from Peru to Salta and then west across the Andes. Almagro's expedition of 1535-1537, which included 100 Spaniards, African slaves, crypto-Jews and some thousands of indigenous Americans – many of whom perished – reached the heartland but, bitterly disappointed at not finding gold, returned to Peru almost immediately. Valdivia's expedition then carried out what initially appeared to be a swift and successful conquest, founding Santiago in February 1541 and a series of other settlements in the following years. But, in the 1550s, these Spanish settlements were shaken by a Mapuche rebellion, which led to the death of Valdivia.

The two major indigenous figures in this early resistance to the Spaniards were the *caciques* Lautaro and Caupolicán. Lautaro was an interesting case: initially an adjutant of Pedro de Valdivia (known by the conquistador as Felipe), he turned against Validivia and led the expedition that captured him in 1553. Lautaro went on to lead several successful campaigns, before being killed by the Spaniards in the Mataquito Valley in 1557. Caupolicán fought alongside Lautaro, but was eventually captured in the *cordillera* in 1558 and impaled on a stake by the Spaniards. Nevertheless, the two Mapuche heros had successfully undermined the Spanish colony and their struggles set the tone for the colonial period in Chile. Lacking precious minerals, threatened by the warlike Mapuche and never less than four months' journey from Europe, the colony was of relatively little importance to Spain, except as a frontier zone.

The motivation of these early expeditions – as in Mexico and Peru – was greed. The Spanish crown did nothing to finance the ventures, so all the risk was shouldered by those who participated, who therefore had a pressing need to find silver and gold to recompense themselves. Nevertheless, a fifth of all gold and silver that was found in the New World went into the royal coffers; an influx of precious metal that was urgently needed to prop up the falling value of coinage in Europe at this time.

The greedy motivations of the early arrivals made control in distant Chile difficult for the Castillian crown to exercise. Chile was effectively run by men such as **Francisco de Aguirre**, a conquistador who had accompanied Pedro de Valdivia's initial expedition. As one of the first Spaniards on the scene, Aguirre was made Governor of Tucumán – just across the Andes in modern-day Argentina – and later founded La Serena. He was, however, deeply anti-clerical and proclaimed himself "Pope and King" in Chile, saying that he would rather have a farrier than a priest. The Inquisition eventually caught up with Aguirre in the Río de la Plata in the 1570s and he died poor, bitter and disgraced in La Serena.

In addition to trying to exert effective control over the Spaniards in their territory, one of the main concerns of Chile's Spanish governors after Valdivia was the war against the Mapuche successors to Lautaro and Caupolicán. Known by the Spanish as Araucanos, the Mapuche were fearsome opponents. In 1598, they began a general offensive that destroyed all of the Spanish settlements south of the Río Biobío, revealing the weakness of a colony whose Spanish population was under 8000. Pushed back into the northern part of the Central Valley, the Spanish were forced to build a string of forts along the Río Biobío, guarded by a frontier army of 2000 men, the only force of its type in Spanish America, financed by a special subsidy from the viceregal capital of Lima. However, Chile was not important enough to warrant a full-scale Spanish assault on the Mapuche and, for the rest of the colonial period, the Spanish presence south of the river would be limited to the island of Chiloé and to the coastal city of Valdivia.

The Chilean colony

As in the other colonies in the Americas, Chilean society under Spanish rule was not the two-sided world of Spanish settlers and Amerindian peoples that official histories would have us believe. From very early on, two other groups became increasingly important: *marranos* – or forced converts from Judaism to Christianity, who had fled Inquisitiorial persecution in Spain and Portugal – and slaves from West Africa. The *marranos* controlled large parts of the trade in South America and suffered bouts of persecution from the Inquisitional office in Lima (see box, opposite), while the Africans did much of the manual labour in the colony. Although both groups eventually became absorbed into Chile, the legacy of their presence can perhaps be felt today in the widespread stereotyping of Africans and Jews in mainstream Chilean society.

African slaves started arriving from very early on in the colonial period, principally because the Spanish found that the indigenous people were not hardy enough to do the work required of them. By the end of the 16th century, Africans in Chile were working as cattle ranchers and as *stevedores*, and as blacksmiths, tailors, carpenters and servants in every city. They were mostly sold as contraband, brought over from Buenos Aires instead of through the 'official' port of entry at Cartagena, Colombia, and originated from all parts of the West African coast, from Senegambia to Angola.

By the turn of the 17th century, much of the trade of the fledgling colony was in the hands of the *marranos*, who were prohibited from holding positions of authority. Their main port of entry was Buenos Aires, from where they travelled overland to Potosí and Lima by way of Tucumán.

In the following years, colonial Chile achieved a degree of stability and developed as a compact society; most of its population inhabited the Central Valley and most trade was through Valparaíso. By the end of the 17th century, there were few

No one expects the Spanish Inquisition

The activities of the Spanish Inquisition were not restricted to Spain, they spread to every corner of the Spanish Empire during the colonial period. In Latin America, the Inquisition is best known for a few large show trials and burnings. At a conflagration in Lima in 1639, 11 people were burnt and one person was tortured to death. Even beyond these headline events, its influence was pervasive and enduring on colonial life. It operated in every corner of the American continent, persecuting alleged Jews and avowed Protestants for the 'irregularities' of their faith. The Inquisition was not permitted to inquire into the faith of indigenous peoples, as they were not thought to have sufficient 'mental maturity' but its influence on the colonial population was pervasive. As well as engendering fear among the settlers, it was capable of impounding the goods of anyone who was suspected of heresy, thereby affecting payment for goods and services over networks that ranged from Mexico to Chile. The force of the Inquisitorial inquiries at this date has been blamed by some historians for the economic decline in South America at this time. As most people of Judaic origin were merchants, this had a significant knock-on effect in small provincial towns.

Furthermore, the essential requirements of keeping a 'pure' faith were underlined by the processions that took place in every town at three-year intervals on the first Sunday in Lent. Every Spanish settler had to attend the procession, at which Inquisitorial officials, wearing the habit of St Peter, with a green cross encased in silver and a crown hanging from their necks, read out the 'edicts of faith'. The settlers were told that they had to denounce anyone observing Judaic practices, which the Inquisitors would then list.

Genuine crypto-Jews who wished to profess their faith were moved to crisscross the continent in search of sanctuary. Santiago was one of the last significant strongholds of the crypto-Jews in the Spanish American colonies, lasting into the 18th century. Elsewhere, Jews sought sanctuary in Colombia's Antioquia region, Suriname, Curação and, for a time, in northern Brazil. Although it was usually the crypto-Jews who suffered the burnings, Protestants were often punished as well; victims included Francis Drake's cousin, John, who spent three years in a monastery near Lima repenting his Lutheran 'crimes' in the late 1580s.

In Chile – as in the whole of Latin America – the Inquisition was finally abolished only at the time of Independence. However, the torture practices of the DINA – the secret police under Pinochet – were eerily resonant of the Inquisition's methods of extracting confessions of heresy. It could be argued that the legacy of the Inquisition once more reared its ugly head in South America during the 1970s, as much of the continent became taken over by repressive regimes, many of which had a penchant for torture.

people of pure indigenous blood, most having died, inter-married or escaped south of the Río Biobío. The majority of the population was *mestizo* (mixed race), though the society was dominated by a small white elite. Chile was, however, highly isolated, being cut off from the rest of the continent in winter. People dared not use the lower passes to the south for fear of the Mapuche, and the high passes near Mendoza and Santiago were blocked by snow for months at a time.

⁞ War of the Pacific, 1879-1883

One of the few major international wars in Latin America after Independence, the War of the Pacific had its roots in a dispute between Chile and Bolivia over national boundaries in the Atacama Desert. There had already been one military conflict in 1836-39, when Chile defeated Peru and Bolivia, but relations were further complicated by the discovery of nitrates in the Atacama in the 1860s, particularly in the then-Bolivian province of Antofagasta.

The War also has to be put into the wider international context of the late 1870s. The years 1873-75 saw a serious recession, with plunging commodity prices around the world. This was followed in 1876 by one of the most severe El Niño weather patterns the world has ever seen, leading to the deaths of tens of millions of people from famine. Santiago had its lowest ever barometric reading in 1877, Peru suffered widespread floods and there were devastating droughts in the Bolivian *altiplano*.

The Bolivian government was forced to impose port taxes to support its weak economy and, in 1878, attempted to tax the Chilean-owned Antofagasta Railroad and Nitrate Company. When the company refused to pay, its assets were seized, sparking claims of foul play by the Chilean government. Peru announced that it would honour a secret alliance with Bolivia, so the Chilean president, Aníbal Pinto, declared war on both states.

None of these three countries was prepared for military conflict; they lacked skilled officers and adequate weapons. Control of the sea was vital: when the Chileans blockaded the Peruvian nitrate port of Iquique with two wooden ships, the *Esmeralda*

and the *Covadonga*, Peru retaliatied with her two best iron-clad ships, the *Huáscar* and the *Independencia*. In the Battle of Iquique, 21 May 1879, the *Esmeralda* was sunk, but the *Independencia* ran aground and was captured, thus altering the balance of power between the two navies. Later in October 1879, the two Chilean iron-clads, *Blanco Encalada* and *Cochrane*, captured the *Huáscar* off Angamos, near Antofagasta. (The ship can now be visited in the harbour at Talcahuano.)

Rather than attack the Peruvian heartland, the Chileans invaded the southern Peruvian province of Tarapacá and then took the town of Tacna, in May 1880, before capturing Arica, further south. In January 1881, fresh Chilean armies seized control of Lima. Bolivia signed a ceasefire, giving up her coastal province, and eventually, under the 1883 peace settlement, Peru gave up Tarapacá to Chile.

The provinces of Tacna and Arica were occupied by Chile for 10 years, and it was not until 1929 that an agreement was reached under which Tacna was returned to Peru.

The war gave Chile a monopoly over the world's supply of nitrates and enabled her to dominate the southern Pacific coast. Some idea of its importance in official Chilean history can be gained by the number of streets and squares named after the war heroes, especially Arturo Prat and Aníbal Pinto, and after the two Chilean vessels *Esmeralda* and *Blanco Encalada*. Chile's relations with her northern neighbours, however, remain sour. There is widespread racism in Chile towards the indigenous peoples in Peru and Bolivia, while signs in Bolivia proclaim that the Pacific coastline is still Bolivian.

During the colonial period, the *hacienda*, or landed estate, was the most important feature of rural society in the Central Valley. In the 17th century, Chilean agriculture expanded to meet demands for wheat, tallow, salted beef and cattle hides from Peru; hides were also sent to Potosí and mules to the great fair in Salta. These exports and the need to feed the frontier army led to the development of large-scale agriculture. As the *haciendas* grew, small farmers and tenants were gradually forced to become *inquilinos*, a class of peasants tied to the land. The *inquilino* is regarded as the ancestor of the *huaso*, the Chilean cowboy, a figure seen as resourceful, astute, cunning and archetypally Chilean.

Although *haciendas* grew in response to food shortages, they were very self contained, with their own supplies of food and clothing, their own vineyards, forges and workshops. Ownership of a *hacienda* was one of the clearest marks of upper-class status, although many were the property of religious orders. The *hacienda* remained at the centre of rural life in the Central Valley and social relations between landowners and *inquilinos* changed little until the Agrarian Reforms of the 1960s. Although no colonial *haciendas* remain, a few dating from the 19th century can be visited, notably Villa Huilquilemu, near Talca (see page 278).

Chile was governed as part of the Viceroyalty of Peru, with its capital in Lima; until the 18th century, all trade with Spain had to pass via Lima and trade with other countries was forbidden. This led to uncontrolled smuggling and, by 1715, there were 40 French vessels trading illegally along the Chilean coast. In 1740, direct trade with Spain was permitted for the first time and, in 1750, Chile was allowed to mint her own currency.

The War of Independence

Independence came to Spanish America as a direct result of Napoleon's invasion of Spain. As Spanish guerrilla forces fought to drive the French out, these events led the colonial elites to debate where their loyalties lay: to Napoleon's brother Joseph, now officially King? Or to the overthrown king, Ferdinand VII, now in a French prison? Or to the Spanish resistance parliament in Cádiz?

In 1810, a group of leading Santiago citizens appointed a Junta to govern until Ferdinand returned to the throne. Although they protested loyalty to Ferdinand, their move was seen as a challenge to the crown by the viceregal government in Lima, which sent an army to Concepción. War broke out between the Chilean Patriots and the Royalist troops supporting Lima. The defeat of the Patriot army led by **Bernardo O'Higgins** at Rancagua in October 1814 led to a restoration of colonial rule, but O'Higgins was able to escape across the Andes to join forces with Buenos Aires' liberation hero, José de San Martín. The turning point came in 1817, with the invasion of Chile from Mendoza by San Martín's Army of the Andes, a force of 4000 men, which defeated the Royalists at Chacabuco on 12 February 1817. A Royalist counter-attack was defeated at Maipó, just south of Santiago, on 5 May 1818, putting an end to Royalist power in the Central Valley. The victory of the small Patriot navy led by **Lord Cochrane** (see box, page 341) at Valdivia in January 1820 helped clear the Pacific coast of Royalist vessels and paved the way for San Martín to launch his seaborne invasion of Peru.

Nineteenth-century expansion

In most of former Spanish America, Independence was followed by a period of political turmoil, marked by civil wars and dictatorship, which in some cases lasted until the 1860s. Many Independence heroes had tragic ends: disgusted at the chaos, San Martín retired to France; Simon Bolívar died penniless and in hiding in a boarding house in Santa Marta, Colombia; and O'Higgins was quickly overthrown. O'Higgins' demise was followed by a brief period of instability in Chile but, in 1830, conservative forces led by Diego Portales restored order and introduced the Constitution of 1833, which created a strong government under a powerful president. Portales, a

Valparaíso merchant, who never became president, explained his actions thus: "If one day I took up a stick and gave tranquillity to the country it was only so that the bastards and whores of Santiago would let me get on with my work in peace."

Chile became famous throughout Latin America as the great example of political stability: the army was reduced to 3000 men and kept out of politics; after 1831, four successive presidents served the two five-year terms permitted under the constitution. However, this stability had another side: civil liberties were frequently suspended, elections rigged, opponents exiled and power lay in the hands of a small landowning elite. Neither was the stability perfect: there were short civil wars in 1851, 1859 and 1891.

The latter half of the 19th century saw Chile's great period of expansion. In 1881, when victory over Peru in the War of the Pacific was assured (see box, page), the much-enlarged army was sent to put an end to Mapuche independence and thus secure continuous Chilean control over the entire Pacific coastline south of Arica. In the few short years between 1879 and 1883, Chilean territory had expanded both northwards and southwards. However, some Chileans still argue that the victory over Peru and Bolivia came at the price of losing both the region around Mendoza and most of Patagonia to Argentina; according to some, this should, by dint of colonial land divisions under the Viceroyalty, be Chilean territory. It is certainly true that maps from the early 19th century show Chilean territory crossing the Andes and advancing halfway to the Atlantic Ocean, while early colonial documents speak of "the city of Mendoza in Chile".

From the 1860s onwards, conflict between President and Congress became a constant feature of political life. The War of the Pacific brought the Chilean government a new source of income through the tax levied on nitrate exports coming from the new territories of the Atacama (see box, page 524) but it also increased rivalry for control of this income. When, in 1890, Congress rejected the budget, President Balmaceda announced he would use the 1890 budget for 1891. Congressional leaders denounced this as illegal and fled to Iquique, where they recruited an army, which defeated Balmaceda's forces and seized the capital. Balmaceda took refuge in the Argentine embassy, where he committed suicide. His defeat was important: between 1891 and 1924 Chilean presidents were weak figures and real power lay with Congress, ruled by the elite.

Twentieth-century politics

In the years before the First World War, the income from nitrates helped build a large railway network, roads and ports and the best education system on the continent. However, the collapse of the industry during the First World War led to worker and student unrest, which brought down the constitutional system in 1924 when the military intervened. A new constitution restored the strong presidency, which had apparently served Chile so well in the 19th century, but the Great Depression brought further economic stress, which resulted in a series of short-lived governments, including a military-led 100-day Socialist Republic in 1932.

As economic conditions recovered in the 1930s, Chile once again became a model of political stability. Between 1932 and 1970, Chile developed a complex multiparty system: two left-wing parties, the Socialists and Communists, representing the urban workers and miners; the Conservative and Liberal parties, dating from the 19th century, representing the landowners; and the Radicals, a centre party representing the middle classes. The Radicals became the key to power, winning the presidency in 1938, 1942 and 1946. However, one major group remained excluded from political life: the peasants, whose votes, controlled by their landlords, gave the Liberals and Conservatives their representation in Congress and enabled the landlords to block rural reform.

⁘ Salvador Allende Gossens

Born in 1908 into an upper-middle-class Valparaíso family, Salvador Allende's childhood ambition was to be a doctor, like his grandfather Ramón Allende Padín, a respected Radical politician who became Serene Grand Master of the Chilean freemasons. While studying medicine, Salvador discovered first-hand the appalling living conditions of the poor and the links between poverty and disease. Even before he qualified as a doctor, he became active in politics and was briefly imprisoned during the Ibáñez dictatorship. He was a founder member of the Chilean Socialist party in 1933; at about the same time he also became active in the Freemasons.

Elected to Congress for Valparaíso at the age of 29, he served as Minister of Health in Aguirre Cerda's Popular Front government of 1939-1942 and was elected to the Senate in 1945, becoming Senate president in 1965. Allende was a candidate in four presidential elections. In 1952, he gained only 5.45% of the votes but, in 1958, as candidate of the Front for Popular Action, an alliance between the Socialists and Communists,

he lost narrowly to the right-wing candidate, Jorge Alessandri. Easily defeated in 1964 by the Christian Democrat, Eduardo Frei, he finally won the presidency in 1970. However, without a majority in Congress, heading a broad but divided coalition of eight parties, and facing the hostility of much of the Chilean population and of Washington, Allende found himself with increasingly little room for political manoeuvre.

When news of the military revolt came through in the early hours of 11 September 1973, Allende went to the Moneda Palace and spoke twice on the radio before communications were cut. Although he was offered a flight out of the country in return for his resignation, Allende refused, and the Palace was bombed by three Hawker Hunter jets. Most accounts now accept that Allende committed suicide. He was buried in an unmarked grave in Viña del Mar. In September 1990, following the return to civilian rule, his body was exhumed and transported to Santiago for a state funeral, thousands of people lining the route from the coast.

Background History

In the 1958 election, the Socialist **Salvador Allende** (see box, page 527) only narrowly failed to defeat the Conservative Jorge Alessandri. This shook both the right-wing parties and (in the aftermath of the Cuban Revolution), the US government. In 1964, the US and the Chilean right-wing threw their weight behind **Eduardo Frei Montalva**, a Christian Democrat who promised a 'revolution in freedom'. Frei Montalva's achievements in office were impressive: state ownership of 51% of the copper industry; minimum wage and unionization rights for agricultural workers; and the 1967 agrarian reform, which began replacing the *haciendas* with family farms. However, these measures raised hopes that could not be satisfied, especially in the countryside where workers now enjoyed rights and pushed for faster land reform. Hostility from the landowners was reflected in Congress where the National Party, formed in 1966 by the merger of the Conservatives and Liberals, denounced the government. The President's Christian Democrat Party was divided between supporters and opponents of reform. Nevertheless, Frei Montalva has been an enduringly popular President – his memory was widely seen as a key factor in the landslide victory of his son, Eduardo Frei Ruiz-Tagle, in the 1993 presidential elections.

The 1970 election was narrowly won by Salvador Allende, polling just over 36.3% of the vote, with the electorate split in three. Allende headed a left-wing alliance called Unidad Popular, which launched an ambitious programme of reforms: banking, insurance, communications, textiles and other industries were taken over in the first year and the nationalisation of copper was completed (this last even with the support of the right-wing parties). After that, the government ran into major problems: the nationalisations had depleted Chile's currency reserves, while hostility by domestic business groups and the US caused capital flight and a US-led boycott on international credit. In Congress, an alliance between the Christian Democrats and National Party impeached several ministers. At grassroots level, a series of anti-government strikes by truck drivers and professional groups brought the country to a halt in October 1972 and again in August 1973, while the supplies in shops were unable to keep pace with the wider purchasing power of many social classes, leading to long queues for foodstuffs and a rise in annual inflation to over 300% in 1973.

Despite these negative effects, Allende's Socialist experiment did have a measure of success: agricultural production increased and, by 1972, there were 27% more foodstuffs available in Chile than there had been in 1970. However, even this increase in supply was outstripped by the demand caused by a real rise in wages among the poor. This was a sign that Allende's goal of eradicating poverty was bearing some fruit, with per capita consumption rising for all foodstuffs except red meat. The upper and middle classes who bemoaned the queues in the shops were, in fact, venting frustration that their customary position at the head of affairs was finally being usurped.

The Pinochet era

Allende's popularity in some quarters was demonstrated by the March 1973 Parliamentary elections, at which the Unidad Popular polled 43.4% of the vote, 7% more than in 1970. Nevertheless, the coup of 11 September 1973, led by **General Augusto Pinochet** (born 1915), was widely expected, the armed forces having received open encouragement from Allende's opponents in Congress, including the Christian Democrats, and from opposition groups on the streets; it later became clear that the CIA had had a major role in fomenting the unrest that led to the pre-coup stand-off.

The brutality of the coup shocked people who were accustomed to Chile's peaceful traditions. Left-wing activists and people mistakenly identified as leftists were arrested, thousands were executed, torture was widespread, with at least 7000 people held in the national football stadium, and, by 1978, there were 30,000 Chilean exiles in Western Europe alone. With political parties and labour unions banned, the government adopted neo-liberal economic policies under the influence of the 'Chicago Boys' – local economists who had been trained at the University of Chicago under the tutelage of Milton Friedman.

Pinochet installed himself as the undisputed head of a military junta. Those who did not approve of his methods often met grisly ends, including the former head of the Army, Carlos Prats, who was assassinated by a car bomb in Buenos Aires in 1974. Pinochet increased his hold on power by his control over the regime's notorious secret police, the DINA, which was headed by a close colleague, General Manuel Contreras, while silencing exiles and international critics through Operation Condor, an international anti-leftist terrorist movement. Under a new constitution, adopted in 1980, Chile became a 'protected democracy' based on the exclusion of political parties and the 'guardianship' of the armed forces, who put forward a single candidate for an eight-year presidential term in 1981. To no one's surprise that candidate was Pinochet, who, during his second term (1981-1989) became the longest-serving Chilean president. With his stern features enhanced by dark glasses, Pinochet became the stereotype of the South American dictator. Often seen as a bluff, no-nonsense character, he was also noted for his astuteness, his suspicious mind, his ruthlessness, his hatred of communism and distrust of democracy.

It would be wrong to see his dominance as merely the result of repression and fear. For many Chileans, who had hated Allende and feared his liberal policies, the human rights abuses and destruction of democracy were seen as a price worth paying. In spite of his widespread vilification in much of the Western press, Pinochet retained popularity among many Chileans, polling 44% of the vote in a plebiscite in 1988. This bid for a further eight-year term was unsuccessful but, when the first results came in, the military government initially tried to maintain that the 'si' vote (yes to Pinochet) had triumphed. Even when this position became untenable, the constitution of 1980 ensured that Pinochet still had 18 months before he had to relinquish power.

Eventually, presidential and congressional elections were held in 1989. A veteran Christian Democrat politician, **Patricio Aylwin Azócar**, the candidate of the Coalition of Parties for Democracy (CPD, or Concertación), was elected President and took office in March 1990 in a peaceful transfer of power. General Pinochet remained as Army Commander, although other armed forces chiefs were replaced. The new Congress set about revising many of the military's laws on civil liberties and the economy, but in December 1990, questions in Congress and in the press about financial scandals involving army officers and Pinochet's own son-in-law led the Army Commander to order all troops to report to barracks. In May 1993, Pinochet surrounded the Ministry of Defence with soldiers and ordered generals to wear battle dress to work for a day.

In 1991, the National Commission for Truth and Reconciliation (the RETTIG Commission) published a report detailing those who had been killed under the military regime. The RETTIG commission established that 3,197 people had died as the result of the violation of human rights, but opposition by the armed forces and an amnesty law protecting members of the military prevented mass human rights trials. At this time, prosecution of those guilty of human rights abuses in Chile was widely seen as impossible.

Presidential elections in December 1993 resulted in victory for the Christian Democrat, Eduardo Frei Ruiz-Tagle, candidate of the Concertación coalition but, in congressional elections held at the same time, the Concertación failed to achieve the two-thirds majority required to reform the constitution, replace the heads of the armed forces and end the system of designated senators whose votes enabled the right-wing parties and the military to block reform. As a result Frei's presidency became an exercise in balancing the demands of the parties of the Concertación against the entrenched power of the military and the right-wing. Although the Concertación won a comfortable victory in congressional elections in December 1997, it still failed to achieve the majority necessary to break the deadlock; the position of the military was strengthened in March 1998 when General Pinochet retired as Army Commander-in-Chief and, as a former president who had held office for six years, took up his lifetime seat in the Senate.

In October 1998, General Pinochet was arrested in London at a private clinic, while recovering from a back operation. The arrest warrant had been issued by a Spanish judge, Baltasar Garzón, for murder and torture of Spanish citizens under the military regime. Pinochet's arrest put the Frei government under great pressure: Pinochet's supporters demanded action, while some of the government's supporters, especially those in the Socialist party, were privately delighted. Meanwhile, the families of those who had disappeared during Pinochet's regime continued to demand news of the whereabouts of the victims' corpses, and the prosecution of those responsible. Combined with the worsening economic situation and the choice of the first Socialist to head the Concertación into presidential elections, these dramatic events made the December 1999 poll unexpectedly close. The Concertación candidate, Ricardo Lagos, eventually won with a tiny majority in a second-round ballot against the populist Mayor of Las Condes, Joaquín Lavín (one of the bright young 'Chicago boys' of the 1970s), although Lavín had won more votes in the first round of polling.

The ructions caused by the Pinochet affair were significant. Having allowed the extradition process to continue, Jack Straw, the British Home Secretary, permitted Pinochet to return to Chile on grounds of ill health in March 2000. However, a legal case started by Judge Juan Guzmán Tapia in the Chilean courts in January 1998 meant that Pinochet still faced a legal challenge. In July 1999, the Supreme Court ruled that, in cases where the fact of death could not be certified, amnesty did not apply, thereby laying Pinochet and the military open to charges regarding the 'disappeared'. This was followed in June 2000 by an Appeal Court ruling that stripped Pinochet of his immunity from trial. The decision was confirmed by the Supreme Court in August, and Pinochet was finally indicted by Judge Guzmán on 29 January 2001. The charges of kidnapping and murder related to the infamous 'caravan of death' in 1973, when many political detainees 'disappeared' in the north of the country. However, in July 2001, the court ruled narrowly that Pinochet's worsening health meant that he was not capable of mounting a proper defence and that the case could not be continued. Judge Guzmán was soon forced to take sick leave as a result of stress induced by the case. Although appeals were mounted by the families of victims of the military government, Pinochet eventually won the right not to stand trial under a Supreme Court Ruling in July 2002, although he resigned his position as senator for life.

Recent history

It appeared that the July 2002 ruling would finally allow some distance to be put between Chile and its troublesome former President. However over the next two years a series of human rights abuse charges were made against Pinochet. Each followed the same course as the last; first Pinochet had to be stripped of immunity for a particular charge, then he was indicted and placed under house arrest before being ruled too infirm to stand trial. For some time Chileans had been cynical about the prospects of 'Pinocchio' ever being brought to justice and the ruling simply seemed to confirm most people's suspicions. Indeed, 'the old man' still retained sizeable support amongst large sectors of the population who maintained that his acts were justified in as much as they were borne of patriotic ideals and served to save Chile from communism and transform it into the modern country of today. However all this changed in 2004 when it was discovered that Pinochet had stashed away US$27 million in secret foreign bank accounts. He was charged along with his wife and four of his children (one of whom laughably tried to claim political asylum in the US) for tax evasion and holding false passports. Now, suddenly, the same people who had defended Pinochet's murders were aghast at the idea that he may have been stealing money from them. To add further fuel to the fire, in July 2006, Manuel Contreras, the former head of the DINA, claimed that Pinochet made this money by the large-scale production and sale of cocaine to Europe and North America. Whatever the outcome of this new case, the long, drawn-out legal wranglings will make it impossible for Pinochet to end his life with the respect and authority he spent so long developing.

Meanwhile, President Lagos urgently needed to concentrate on important national economic issues: in particular, the impact of the economic meltdown in neighbouring Argentina – Chile's main trading partner and the source of the majority of its overseas visitors. As political uncertainty increased across the continent – with coups and counter-coups in Venezuela, the collapse of Argentina and the victory of the left in presidential elections in Brazil – 2002 was a difficult year to be steering the Chilean ship. The government's decision in August 2002 to freeze the minimum wage in an effort to reduce unemployment caused widespread protests, largely because most people's experience of economic realities did not match the government's subsequent statements as to the "improving situation".

The early months of 2003, however, saw Lagos able to reassert his statesmanship through his renewed importance on the global stage: Chile now occupied one of the 15 seats on the UN Security Council. As the international crisis over Iraq reached a head, Lagos did not desert his old support base, with Chile proving to be one of the most intractable of the "six undecided council members", and putting forward a strong case against pre-emptive military invasion. This resistance to pressure from the 'yanquis' and the Brits reflected the mood in the country and enhanced Lagos's popularity. But opposition to war in Iraq did not come without a price; the Americans subsequently postponed signing a free trade agreement with Chile.

In his last two years of office, president Lagos concentrated on important social and democratic themes. The Plan Auge aimed to create a more European style healthcare system heavily subsidising treatment for an increasing number of illnesses to low income families and in some cases allowing them access to private clinics, while the justice system was shaken up in an effort to speed up processes that had often seen prisoners on remand for longer than they were finally sentenced for. Agreement was finally reached to phase out the system of appointed senators, paving the way for a return to true democracy, while in 2005 the president was at last given the authority to dismiss leaders of the armed forces, once again making the military subordinate to democratic institutions. When President Lagos finally stepped down he ejoyed the highest popularity rating of any Chilean leader.

The most recent elections, at the end of 2005 threw up a three way contest. The Concertación put forward the Socialist Michelle Bachelet, while the right put up two candidates, Joaquín Lavín for the UDI and Sebastián Piñera for the RN. After Lavín was knocked out in the first round the final result seemed too close to call. Over a series of television debates Piñera , owner of Chile's national airline and a major television channel came across as a slightly false patronising and domineering figure and in the end Bachelet won by a comfortable seven percent.

In many ways Bachelet has broken the mould in Chilean politics. A woman president in a still very much male dominated country, Bachelet was not a career politician. Tortured along with her father (a military man who had remained loyal to Allende), she worked for many years as a paediatrician before being made health and then defence minister under Lagos. Although she has had a quiet start to her presidency she has promised to continue the progressive reforms of her predecessor, promising, for example to reform the state pension system. On the domestic front she has the advantages of record copper prices filling the treasury coffers, while internationally she has to balance Chile's reputation as a stable neo-liberal trading partner with her relations with ever more left-leaning populist governments in the region.

Modern Chile

An overview

The Pinochet affair forced Chileans to confront their recent past. Although old wounds reopened, the increasing political apathy of the young, which was apparent in the early 1990s, was nipped in the bud. While the presidencies of the Concertación continued the Pinochetista neo-liberal policies that made Chile such a banker's favourite in the 1980s, these have been accompanied by a genuine attempt at more inclusive government, including significant increases in the national minimum wage, at rates well above that of inflation. With a pension system on which countries such as Britain have modelled their own 'stakeholder' schemes, urban Chile is now, for the most part, modern and dynamic.

There are, however, several problems that the government needs to address. While there has been a limited rise in living standards among the inhabitants of Santiago's *callampas* (shanty towns), urban poverty remains widespread. Problems in Santiago are due in large part to the over-centralisation of the country: over a third of the population live in the capital or the surrounding Región Metropolitana, and Chile's unusual geography means that Santiago is a natural focal point, on which the rest of the country is all too dependent.

Chile managed to weather the short '*crisis económica*' at the beginning of the decade caused largely by weaknesses among Chile's main trading partners: the crisis in the Far East had major ramifications in Chile, while the devaluation in Brazil, followed by the subsequent economic crisis in Argentina, led to the temporary rise of the US dollar against the Chilean peso from 2001 to 2004. The government did extremely well to stave off the inflationary pressures of these developments, and buoyed by the rise in copper prices the steady constant growth and prosperity that characterised the 1990s is in some senses back. However, although this might be the case on a macro level and although Chile's economy remains the most stable in South America, the economic situation of the lower and middle classes remains tough. There is an all too apparent wealth gap, while the working week is a hefty 45 hours (reduced from 48 by Lagos). In order to avoid having to make redundancy payments jobs are all too often offered on short term contracts, and it is not surprising that people talk about the difficulty of finding – and keeping – work.

Chile's income tax system is symptomatic of the country's traditional conservatism. Direct income tax is exceptionally low and business tax is almost non-existent. While Chile's lower and middle classes can clearly not afford to pay more income tax, this is far from true of the country's upper classes. The inability of recent governments to tackle this subject is evidence both of the oligarchic stranglehold that the Chilean aristocracy retains on the state and of the taboo status of even the slightest economic redistribution – thanks to the 'anti-Communist wars' waged by the military government in the 1970s and 1980s and to the psychological scars caused by the Allende government's economic policies and their consequences.

Perhaps the most fundamental long-term problem, however, is that Chile's wealth depends in part on the ongoing rape of its extensive natural resources, often by multinational companies; industries such as logging and intensive fishing, while successful at present, have the potential to ruin Chile's future. One example is the ongoing plan of a Canadian multinational to build a vast aluminium smelting plant in the Aysen region in the far south, which would contaminate the pristine ecosystems of Chilean Patagonia, while in the mountains of the Atacama in the north plans have been made do divert a glacier to dig a gold mine. In both cases there has been widespread local opposition (see, for example, www.greenpeace.org/chile for more details). According to one estimate, Chile lost 80% of its marine life in the 1980s and its native forests continue to disappear at alarming rates. Environmentalists have joined forces with farmers to highlight the environmental damage caused by introduced species such as the eucalyptus, which extracts most of the goodness from the soil, and by plantations of pine, which acidify the soil. Chile's Free Trade Agreements with Europe and North America are not seen as beneficial in all quarters.

However, these moves are symbolic of Chile's increasingly outward-looking mentality. After four centuries characterized by isolation and insularity, the ramifications of Chile's recent history have put the country onto the international map in an unprecedented manner. Whereas, until recently, Chileans compared themselves to Europeans, they now take increasing national pride in their own achievements. Even though Pinochet was not put on trial in Chile, the case and its consequences mean that the country is at the vanguard of one of the most significant human rights movement in history; one that, in a short space of time, has already had repercussions for repressive former heads of state in the Central African Republic and Yugoslavia.

Constitution and government

Chile is governed under the 1980 Constitution, introduced by the military government of General Pinochet and approved in a plebiscite on 11 September 1980, although important amendments were made during the transition to civilian rule in 1989-1990. The constitution provided for an eight-year non-renewable term for the President of the Republic, a bicameral legislature with a Congress and a Senate and an independent judiciary and central bank, although it was only after the rejection of Pinochet in the 1988 vote that most of the provisions of the constitution come into operation. A two-thirds majority in both houses of legislature is required to reform the constitution. In February 1994, the legislature cut the presidential term of office from eight years to six, and in 2006 it was further reduced to four years. Presidents are prohibited from holding two consecutive terms of office.

The legislature is composed of a 120-seat Chamber of Deputies and a 47-seat Senate, eight of whose members are nominated rather than elected. Among the nominated senators is one former head of each of the armed forces and any former presidents who have completed a full six-year term. After agreement between the parties these nominated senators are now being phased out.

The dominant political party in Chile is the Christian Democrats, a centre party which grew rapidly after its foundation in 1957. The Christian Democrats welcomed the overthrow of Allende but later became the focus of opposition to the dictatorship. Not strong enough to rule on its own, since 1990 the party has contested elections in an alliance known as the **Concertación**. The other members are the Socialists, a centre-left party traditionally split between the Radicals and the Partido por la Democracía, a centre-left grouping led by ex-Socialists. The main opposition to the Concertación comes from the right wing, which is divided into two main parties, Renovación Nacional and the ever stronger Unión Democrática Independiente. In recent elections, they have formed an alliance called the **Alianza para Chile**.

Chile is divided into 13 regions, usually referred to by Roman numerals (although they also have names). The government of each region is headed by an intendente, who is appointed by the president.

Economy

Chile's economy is dependent on the mining sector. Mineral ores account for half of total export revenue. Copper is the most important mineral, with Chile being the world's largest producer. Although the Pinochet government of 1973-1990 sold off most state- run industries to the private sector, CODELCO (the state copper mining company) was not touched. The biggest new mine is La Escondida, where production began in 1990, which produces an output of 800,000 tonnes a year, making it the world's leading mine (see page 222), while Chuquicamata is the biggest open cast mine in the world. Other mineral resources in Chile include a quarter of the world's known molybdenum ore reserves and around 40% of the world's lithium reserves. Fluctuations in world prices for minerals can have a great impact on the country's balance of payments.

The country's diverse environment means that agriculture is also of great importance. Traditional crops, such as cereals, pulses and potatoes, and industrial crops, such as sugar beet, sunflower seed and rape seed, account for about a third of the value of agriculture, while vegetables account for a quarter. Fruit growing has expanded rapidly, with fresh fruit now accounting for over US$1 billion in exports a year, while timber and wood products make up the third place in exports. Chile is the most important fishing nation in Latin America and the largest producer of fishmeal in the world; it is also one of the world's leading salmon farmers.

Chile is fortunate in possessing reserves of oil, natural gas and coal, and abundant hydroelectricity potential. Almost all the country's hydrocarbon reserves are in the extreme south, on Tierra del Fuego, in the Strait of Magellan. Two pipelines are planned and six new gas-fired power plants have recently been built. Manufacturing activity is mostly food processing, metalworking, textiles, footwear and fish processing.

The government follows anti-inflationary policies, accompanied by structural adjustment and reform. Privatisation has been widespread, although certain key companies, such as *Codelco*, remain in state hands. Rising investor confidence has brought reasonably stable economic growth since the late 1980s and the Chilean model has been held up as an example for other debtor countries.

Society

Chile is a deeply conservative country: it was the first newly independent state in Latin America fully to embrace the Catholic church and has the most stable 'democratic' (or, until the 1950s, oligarchic) tradition in the region.

There is less racial diversity in Chile than in most Latin American countries. Over 90% of the population of 15.2 million is *mestizo* (mixed race). There are hardly any people of African origin – in sharp contrast to, say, Brazil or Colombia – and there has been much less immigration from Europe than in Argentina and Brazil. The German, French, Italian and Swiss immigrants came mostly after 1846 as small farmers in the forest zone south of the Biobío. Between 1880 and 1900, gold-seeking Serbs and Croats settled in the far south and the British took up sheep farming and commerce in the same region.

There is disagreement over the number of indigenous people in Chile. Survival International estimate the **Mapuche** population to be one million, but other statistics – including the official ones – put it at much less. There are also 45,000-50,000 **Aymara** in the northern Chilean Andes and 4500 **Rapa Nui** on Easter Island. A political party, the Party for Land and Identity, unites many indigenous groupings, and legislation is proposed to restore indigenous people's rights.

The population is far from evenly distributed: Middle Chile, from La Serena to Concepción, consisting of 20% of the country's area, is home to over 77% of the population, with the Metropolitan Region of Santiago containing, on its own, about 40% of the total. Population density in 2002 ranged from 393 per sq km in the Metropolitan Region to 0.84 per sq km in Región XI (Aisén). Since the 1960s, heavy migration from the countryside has led to rapid urbanisation. By 2002, 86.6% of the population lived in urban areas.

According to the 2002 census the population is 70% Catholic and 15% Protestant. Membership of Evangelical Protestant churches has grown rapidly in recent years. There are also small Jewish communities in Santiago and Temuco especially.

Chilean literacy rates are higher than those of most other South American states; according to the 2002 census over 95% of the population above the age of 10 is literate. Census returns also indicated that, among the over-25s, 16% had completed higher education, 52% had completed secondary education and 41% had only completed primary education. Higher education provision doubled in the 1980s through the creation of private universities.

In November 2004, and to the consternation of the catholic church and most conservative politicians Chile became one of the last countries in the world to legalise divorce . Until then, couples that wanted to separate had to go through the farcical process of getting a notary to swear that they were married in an inappropriate municipality and that their marriage certificate is therefore invalid. Even now the process is not cheap and the upshot for impoverished rural populations is that divorce – and remarriage – is still, in effect, impossible.

Culture

Chilean culture is rooted in the nation's hybrid soul. European guitars blend with panpipes and *queñas*; religious art flourishes alongside traditional crafts; literature scales the heights of modernism, while never losing track of the natural beauty from which it is born.

Traditional arts and crafts

Chile's traditional crafts are often specific to particular places and all have a long history. Present-day handicrafts represent either the transformation of utilitarian objects into works of art, or the continued manufacture of pieces that retain symbolic value. A number of factors threaten these traditions: the loss of types of wood and plant fibres through the destruction of forests; the mechanisation of farm labour, reducing the use of the horse; other agricultural changes, which have, among other things, led to reductions in sheep farming and wheat growing; and migration from the countryside to the city. On the other hand, city dwellers and tourists have created a demand for 'traditional' crafts so their future is to some degree assured.

Basketry Mapuche basketry is made for domestic, agricultural and fishing uses in Lago Lanalhue and the Cautín region. Apart from the Mapuche areas, one of the great centres of basket-making is Chimbarongo, just south of San Fernando in the Central Valley. Here, weaving is done in almost every household, usually by the men. One of the main materials used is willow, which is collected in June when it is still green and then soaked in water for four months, at the end of which the bark peels off. The lengths of willow are split into four and finished with a knife. Baskets, chairs and lamps are the most common objects made. Willow is not the only fibre used. Many items are made from different types of straw, including little boxes made of wheat; although the latter are produced throughout the country, the most famous are from La Manga, Melipilla. Note also the yawl made for fishing, typical of Chiloé. Other important centres of basket-making are Ninhue-Hualte in Ñuble (Región VIII), Hualqui, 24 km south of Concepción, and San Juan de la Costa, near the coast of Osorno, Región X.

Carving and woodwork The people of the Atacama region edge trays with cactus wood and make little churches – traditionally the doors of the old churches were made of cactus – and they also use cactus for drums, while bamboo is used for flutes of various sizes. Different types of wood are used in the construction of guitars, *guitarrones*, harps and *rabeles* (fiddles), mainly in the Metropolitan Region. Villarrica (see page 316) is a major producer of wooden items: plates, kitchen utensils, but especially decorative objects like animals and birds, jointed snakes and *picarones* (small figures, which, when picked up, reveal their genitals). Wooden ships in bottles are made in Coronel, while in Loncoche, south of Temuco, a workshop specialises in fine carvings, in native wood, of country and Mapuche scenes. Another craft from the Mapuche region is the carving of horn or antler (*asta*) in Temuco, to make animals, birds, cups, spoons, etc.

Ceramics The two most famous places for ceramics are Quinchamalí near Chillán, where the traditional black ware is incised with patterns in white, and Pomaire, west of Santiago (see page 110), which is renowned for heavy terracotta household items that are used in many Chilean homes. Less well known is the pottery of the Atacama zone, the clay figures of Lihueimo (Región VI), the household items, clay figurines and model buildings of Pilén de Cauquenes-Maule (Región VII) and the scented pottery of the nuns of the Comunidad de Santa Clara (Convento de Monjas

Claras in Santiago and Los Angeles). These highly decorated pieces have been made since colonial times, when they achieved great fame.

Cowboy equipment and clothing Items can be found in any part of the country where there are *huasos*: Rancagua, San Fernando, Chillán, Curicó, Colchagua, Doñihue and also in Santiago. Saddles of leather, wood and iron, carved wooden stirrups in the old style, leather reins, spurs (some of them huge and very elaborate – *huasos* are always proud of their spurs) and hats of straw or other materials are the types of equipment you will see. The clothing comprises ponchos (long, simple in colour and design, often with one or two coloured stripes), *mantas* (shorter, divided into four with a great variety of colour), *chamantos* (luxurious *mantas*, double-sided, decorated with fine patterns of vines, leaves, flowers, small birds etc) and sashes/*fajas* (either single or tri-coloured, made to combine with *mantas* or *chamantos*).

Knitwear and textiles Chiloé is famous for its woollen goods, hand-knitted and coloured with natural dyes. With the atrocious weather, clothing (such as sweaters, knitted caps, *mantas*, socks) is very popular; this and rugs, blankets and patch dolls are all sold locally and in Puerto Montt. The main knitting centres are Quinchao, Chonchi and Quellón. Other crafts of Chiloé are model boat building and basketware from Quinchao and Quellón, where mats and figurines such as birds and fish are also made.

The Mapuche are also weavers of sheep's wool, making ponchos, *mantas*, sashes (*fajas*), reversible rugs (*lamas*) with geometric designs and bedspreads (*pontros*). The colours come from natural dyes. The main producing areas are around Lago Lanalhue, Chol Chol, Nueva Imperial and other small settlements in the Mapuche heartland between Temuco and the coast.

Silverware Although silverware is one of the traditional crafts of the Mapuche, its production is in decline owing to the cost of the metal. Traditional women's jewellery includes earrings, headbands, necklaces, brooches and *tupus* (pins for fastening the *manta* or shawl). Nowadays, the most common items to be found for sale are *chawai* (earrings), but these are smaller and in simpler shapes than those traditionally worn by Mapuche women. It is a matter of debate whether Mapuche silversmiths had perfected their skills before the arrival of the Spaniards; certainly the circulation of silver coins in the 18th century gave great impetus to this form of metalwork. The Universidad Católica in Temuco is in charge of a project to ensure the continuance of the art.

Specialist crafts The Mapuche make musical instruments: the *trutruca*, a horn 1½ to 4 m long; *pifilka* (or *pifüllka*), a wooden whistle; the *kultrún* drum; *cascahuilla*, a string of bells; and *trompe*, similar to a Jew's harp. The village of Rari, near the Termas de Panimávida, some 25 km northeast of Linares (Región VII), specialises in beautiful, delicate items made from dyed horsehair: bangles and brooches in the shape of butterflies, little hats, flowers, etc.

Mined in the Cordillera de Ovalle, lapis lazuli is a blue stone, only found otherwise in Afghanistan. It is set in silver to make earrings, necklaces and bracelets. Many shops in Santiago sell the semi-precious stone and objects that incorporate it. Of growing popularity in recent years, combarbalita is a smooth, marble-like stone found only around the remote town of Combarbalá in Región IV. A very beautiful stone that comes in a variety of hues, it is used to make everything from jewellery and cutlery holders to bedside tables and can be very good value.

The colonial period

There was little home-grown art during the colonial period in Chile but trade with other regions was extensive and Santiago in particular has good collections of non-Chilean art. The Catholic church inevitably dominated fine art and sculpture; the new religious foundations needed images of Christ and the saints to reassure Christian settlers and also to instruct new converts. The importation of works from Spain was very costly, so most patrons relied instead on the major colonial artistic centres of Cuzco, Potosí and Quito.

The churches and monasteries of Santiago give a vivid sense of the thriving art market in colonial Spanish America: sculptures were shipped down the coast from Lima and from Quito via Guayaquil; canvasses were carried across the Andes on mule trains from Cuzco and Potosí; and occasionally an itinerant Spanish-trained artist would pass through in search of lucrative commissions. Extensive cycles of the lives of Christ, the Virgin and selected saints were popular: a cycle of 40 or 50 large canvasses representing the exploits of, say, St Francis, provided instant cover for large expanses of bare plaster, a good clear narrative and an exemplary life to follow.

San Francisco in Santiago (see page 79) has a cycle of 53 paintings of the life of St Francis painted in Cuzco in the late 17th century. These are based on a similar cycle in the Franciscan monastery in Cuzco by the indigenous artist Basilio de Santa Cruz Pumacallao, which is in turn derived from a series of European engravings. One of the Santiago paintings, the Funeral of St Francis of 1684, is signed by **Juan Zapaca Inca**, an indigenous artist and follower of Santa Cruz, who probably oversaw production of the whole series. Wherever possible the artist has introduced bright-coloured tapestries and rich fabrics embellished with lace and gold embroidery, a mark of the continuing importance of textiles in Andean culture. This is a typical pattern for colonial art: a set of European engravings forms the basis for a large painted cycle which in turn becomes the source for further copies and derivatives. The narrative content and general composition remain constant, while the setting, attendant figures, costume and decorative detail are often translated into an Andean idiom.

There are, of course, many different categories of colonial art. The big painted cycles were produced more for the educated inhabitants of the monastic establishments than for a lay audience, and were intended for edification rather than devotion. Popular devotion tends to create increasingly decorated and hieratic images. A good example is that of the so-called Cristo de Mayo. Early in the 17th century Pedro de Figueroa, a friar of the Augustinian monastery in Santiago, carved a figure of the crucified Christ, which still hangs in the church of **San Agustín** (Estado 170, not far from Cerro Santa Lucía). This passionate, unusually defiant image was credited with miraculous powers after it survived a serious earthquake in Santiago in May 1647 (hence the popular name *de Mayo*). The only damage was that the crown of thorns slipped from Christ's head and lodged around his neck. A cult quickly grew up around the image, creating a demand for painted copies, which are identifiable by the upward gaze, the distinctive necklace of thorns and the evenly distributed lash marks across the body. The Carmelite convent of San José has a locally produced 18th-century example of the Cristo de Mayo that includes attendant saints and garlands of bright flowers, the latter like pious offerings. The Jesuits established a school of sculpture on Chiloé, where, up until the late 19th century, native craftsmen continued to produce boldly expressive Christian images.

In the 19th century, Chile's distance from the old colonial centre of viceregal power worked to its advantage in the field of art. The Lima-born artist **José Gil de Castro** (died 1841), known as El Mulato Gil, accompanied Bernardo O'Higgins on the campaign for Chilean Independence from 1814, working both as engineer and map-maker and as a portrait painter. His portrait of O'Higgins of 1820 in the **Museo Histórico Nacional** in Santiago represents the hero as a towering giant of a man, immovable as the rocky mountains behind him. Another 1818 painting in the **Municipalidad of La Serena** shows San Martín standing beside a writing desk, his hand inside his jacket in a distinctively Napoleonic pose.

The 19th century also brought European traveller-artists to Chile, who helped to confirm the Chilean landscape, peoples and customs as legitimate subjects for paintings, including the German Johann Moritz Rugendas, who lived in Chile from 1833 to 1845, and the Englishman Charles Wood (in Chile from 1819 to 1852). Examples of both artists' work can be seen in the **Museo Nacional de Bellas Artes** (see page 78). The Frenchman Raymond Monvoisin also spent many years in Chile, from 1843 to 1857. His perceptive portraits of members of the government and the literary élite are interesting for the way in which they link the Chilean tradition of Gil de Castro with European sources. After his return to France he produced the first major painting dedicated to an event from colonial history, the Mapuche hero Caupolicán taken prisoner by the Spaniards (1859). Caupolicán was celebrated in Chile 10 years later in a bronze statue by Nicanor Plaza (1844-1914) erected on the Cerro Santa Lucía in Santiago, and although it originated as an entry for a competition organized by the US government for a statue to commemorate the Last of the Mohicans, it represents the incorporation of indigenous people into the national mythology.

The **Chilean Academy of Painting** was founded in 1849 and, although its first presidents were mediocre European artists, they too helped to make Chilean subject matter respectable. The Academy also acted as a focus for aspiring young artists. **Antonio Smith** (1832-1877) rebelled against the rigidity of the academic system, working as a political cartoonist as well as a painter, but his dramatic landscapes grew out of the gradual awakening of interest in Chilean scenery. He transformed the picturesque view into a heroic vision of mountains and valleys, full of air and space and potential. Cosme San Martín (1850-1906), Pedro León Carmona (1853-1899), Pedro Lira (1845-1912), Alfredo Valenzuela Puelma (1856-1909) and English-born Thomas Somerscales (1842-1927) extended the range of possible national subjects in the fields of landscape, portraiture, history and genre. The late 19th century saw a number of important commissions for nationalistic public statuary including the peasant soldier El Roto Chileno in Santiago's Plaza Yungay by Nicanor Plaza's pupil Virginio Arias (1855-1941), and several monumental works by Rebecca Matte (1875-1929).

The 20th century

From the later 19th century until well into the 20th century, Chilean painting was dominated by refracted versions of Impressionism. Artists such as **Juan Francisco González** (1853-1933) and **Alfredo Helsby** (1862-1933) introduced a looser technique and more luminous palette to create landscapes full of strong contrasts of sunlight and shadows, a tradition continued by, for example, **Pablo Burchard** (1873-1964), **Agustín Abarca** (1882-1953), **Arturo Gordon** (1883-1944) and **Camilo Mori** (1896-1973).

The Chilean avant garde has been dominated by artists who have lived and worked for long periods abroad, many as political exiles. After studying with Le Corbusier in Switzerland and encountering the Surrealists in Paris, **Roberto Matta** (born 1911) moved to New York in 1939 and began painting uniquely unsettling space-age monsters and machines that circulate in a multi-dimensional chaos; he is perhaps the most famous artist to have come from Chile. **Nemesio Antúnez** (1918-1993) developed more earth-bound abstractions of reality: volcanic landscapes viewed through flames and falling rocks, or milling crowds, faceless and powerless.

The younger generation includes **Eugenio Dittborn** (born 1943), who sends 'Airmail Paintings' around the world in an exploration of ideas of transition and dislocation and, because many contain photographs of victims of political violence, of anonymity and loss. **Alfredo Jaar** (born 1956) creates installations using maps and photographs to document the destructive exploitation of the world's resources, both human and natural – most recently focusing on the aftermath of the Rwandan genocide.

In recent years many exiles have returned home and Santiago is now a cultural centre of growing importance, with women particularly well represented (for example **Carmen Valbuena**, born 1955, and **Bernarda Zegers**, born 1951). Chile is the home of an interesting ongoing project called **'Cuerpos Pintados'** (Painted Bodies), whereby artists from Chile and other Latin American countries are invited to Santiago to paint nude models in the colours and designs of their choice. It is worth watching out for exhibitions of the stunning photographs that are the project's permanent outcome; and also for one-off exhibitions up and down the country of the many very talented local artists (especially in cultural centres such as Valparaíso and Concepción).

Literature

From colonial times to Independence

The long struggle of the Spaniards to conquer the lands south of their Peruvian stronghold inspired one of the great epics of early Spanish American literature, *La Araucana* by **Alonso de Ercilla y Zúñiga** (1533-1594). Published in three parts (1569, 1578 and 1589), the poem tells of the victories and defeats of the Spaniards. Nothing like an apologia, the work endures because it recognises the brutal actions of the Spaniards. Like a subsequent work, *Arauco domado* (1596), by the *criollo* **Pedro de Oña** (1570-1643), the point of view is that of the conquering invader, not a celebration of Chilean, or American identity, although Ercilla does show that the people who resisted the Spaniards were noble and courageous. After Ercilla, literature written in what was to become Chile concentrated on chronicling either the physical or the spiritual conquest of the local inhabitants.

Writers in the 18th and early 19th centuries tended to mirror the colonial desire to consolidate the territory that was in Spanish, rather than Mapuche hands. Post-Independence, the move was towards the establishment of the new republic. To this end, the Venezuelan **Andrés Bello** (1781-1865) was invited to Santiago from London in 1829 to oversee the education of the new elite. Already famous for his literary journals and strong views on Romantic poetry, Bello made major contributions to Chilean scholarship and law. His main work was *Gramática de la lengua castellana destinada al uso de los americanos* (1847). As Jean Franco says, "He was one of the first of many writers to see that a general literary Spanish could act as an important cohesive factor, a spiritual tie of the Hispanic peoples".

A cultural haven

Chile's relative political stability in the 19th century helped Santiago to become a cultural centre that attracted many foreign intellectuals, such as the Argentine Diego Sarmiento and the Nicaraguan Rubén Darío. At this time, Chilean writers were establishing a national literary framework to replace the texts of the colonial era. This involved the spreading of *buenas costumbres*, a movement to shift literary subject matter onto Chilean territory, a republican education for the middle classes and the founding of a national identity. Realist fiction captured the public interest. **José Victorino Lastarria** (1817-1888) wrote *costumbrista* stories, portraying national scenes and characters, while **Alberto Blest Gana** (1829-1904) enjoyed two periods of success as a novelist, heavily influenced by Balzac. His most popular novel was *Martín Rivas* (1862), the love story of a young man who wins a wife of a higher class. For some, Blest Gana's presentation of Santiago and its class structure is a worthy imitator of the French *comédie humaine*; for others, his realism fails either to unite his themes to his sketches of Chilean life or to rise above a pedestrian style.

Twentieth-century prose writing

Realism remained the dominant mode of fiction until well into the 20th century, but it appeared in several guises. **Baldomero Lillo** (1867-1923) wrote socialist realist stories about the coal miners of Lebu: *Sub terra* (1904) and *Sub sole* (1907). Lillo and other regionalist writers shifted the emphasis away from the city to the countryside and the miserable conditions endured by many Chileans. Other novelists, including **Luis Orrego Luco** (1866-1948) and **Joaquín Edwards Bello** (1887-1968), concentrated on the crisis of aristocratic values and the gulf between the wealthy and the deprived.

Another strand was *criollismo*, a movement seeking to portray Chile and the tribulations of Chileans without romanticism, championed especially by short story writers like **Mariano Latorre** (1886-1955). His main interest was the Chilean landscape, which he described almost to the point of overwhelming his characters. A different emphasis was given to regionalism and *criollismo* by **Augusto d'Halmar** (Augusto Goeminne Thomson, 1882-1950), whose stories in *La lámpara en el molino* (1914) were given exotic settings and were labelled *imaginismo*. D'Halmar's followers, the Grupo Letras (1920s and 1930s), became openly antagonistic towards the disciples of Latorre: **Luis Durand** wrote books in the 1920s and 1940s that described *campesino* life in detail. Another branch of realism was the exploration of character through psychology in the books of **Eduardo Barrios** (1884-1963), such as *El niño que enloqueció de amor* (1915), *El hermano asno* (1922) and *Los hombres del hombre* (1950).

The anti-fascist views of a group of writers known as the Generation of 1938 (**Nicomedes Guzmán**, 1914-1965, **Juan Godoy**, **Carlos Droguett**, born 1915, and others) added a politically committed dimension, which coincided with the rise to power of the Frente Popular, a Socialist movement. At the same time, *Mandrágora*, a journal principally dedicated to poetry, introduced many European literary ideas, notably those of the surrealists. Its influence, combined with a global decline in Marxist writing after the Second World War and the defeat of the Frente Popular, contributed to the rise of a new generation of writers in the 1950s, whose main motivation was the rejection of all the '*ismos*' that had preceded it. These novelists, short story writers and dramatists were characterised by existential individualism and political and social scepticism. Many writers started publishing in the 1950s; among them was **Volodia Teitelboim** (born 1916), a communist exiled to the USSR after 1973, whose novels *Hijo del salitre* (1952) and *La semilla en la arena* (1957) were portrayals of the struggles of the Chilean masses. In 1979 he published *La guerra interna*, which combined real and imaginary characters in a vision of post-coup Chile.

From the 1920s on, a significant development away from *criollismo* was the rise of the female voice. The first such novelist to achieve major recognition was **Marta Brunet** (1901-1967), who brought a unique perspective to the rural themes she handled (including the need to value women), but who has also been described as a writer of the senses (by Nicomedes Guzmán). Her books include *Montaña adentro* (1923), *Aguas abajo* (1943), *Humo hacia el sur* (1946) and *María Nadie* (1957). Also born in 1901, **María Flora Yáñez** wrote about the alienation of women with great emphasis on the imagination as an escape for her female protagonists from their routine, unfulfilled lives (*El abrazo de la tierra*, 1934; *Espejo sin imágen*, 1936; *Las cenizas*, 1942). **María Luisa Bombal** (1910-1980) took the theme of alienated women even further (*La última niebla*, 1935; *La amortajada*, 1938, and various short stories): her narrative and her characters' worlds spring from the subconscious realm of female experience and are expressed through dreams, fantasies and journeys loaded with symbolic meaning.

Manuel Rojas (1896-1972) was brought up in Argentina, but his family moved to
Chile in 1923. His first short stories, such as *Hombres del sur* (1926), *Travesía* (1934)
and the novel *Lanchas en la bahía* (1932) were undoubtedly *criollista* in outlook, but
he devoted a greater importance to human concerns than his *criollista*
contemporaries. By 1951, Rojas' style had changed dramatically, without deserting
realism. *Hijo de ladrón* (1951) was perhaps the most influential 20th-century Chilean
novel up to that time. It describes the adventures of Aniceto Hevía, the son of a
Buenos Aires jewel thief, who crosses the Andes to Valparaíso, ending up as a
beachcomber. Nothing in his life is planned or motivated by anything other than the
basic necessities. Happiness and intimacy are only brief moments in an
unharmonious, disordered life. Aniceto's adventures are continued in *Mejor que el
vino* (1958), *Sombras contra el muro* (1963) and *La obscura vida radiante* (1971). To
describe the essential isolation of man from the inside, Rojas relaxes the temporal
structure of the novel, bringing in memory, interior monologue and techniques to
multiply the levels of reality (to use Fernando Alegría's phrase).

The demise of *criollismo* coincided with the influence of the US Beat Generation
and the culture epitomized by James Dean, followed in the 1960s by the protest
movements in favour of peace, and black and women's rights. The Cuban Revolution
inspired Latin American intellectuals of the left and the novel-writing 'boom' gained
momentum. At the same time, the national political process which led ultimately to
Salvador Allende's victory in 1970 was bolstered by writers, folk singers and painters
who questioned everything to do with the Chilean bourgeoisie.

José Donoso (1924-1996) began publishing stories in 1955 (*Veraneo y otros
cuentos*), followed two years later by his first novel, *Coronación*. This book describes
the chaos caused by the arrival of a new maid into an aristocratic Santiago household
and introduces many of Donoso's recurring themes: the closed worlds of old age and
childhood, madness, multiple levels of reality, the inauthenticity of the upper classes
and the subversion of patriarchal society. The stories in *Charleston* (1960), *El lugar
sin límites* (1966), about a transvestite and his daughter who live in a brothel near
Talca, and *Este domingo* (1966) mark the progression from *Coronación* to *El obsceno
pájaro de la noche* (1970), a labyrinthine novel (Donoso's own term) narrated by a
schizophrenic, throwing together reality, dreams and fantasy, darkness and light.
Donoso achieved the same status as Gabriel García Márquez, Julio Cortázar and
Mario Vargas Llosa with this, his most experimental novel. Between 1967 and 1981 he
lived in Spain; in the 1970s he published several novels, including *Casa de campo*
(1978), which relates the disintegration of a family estate when the children try to take
it over. Back in Chile, he published, among others, *El jardín de al lado* (1981), which
chronicles the decline of a middle-aged couple in exile in Spain, *Cuatro para Delfina*
(1982), *La desesperanza* (1986) about the return of a left-wing singer from Paris to the
daily horrors of Pinochet's regime.

Another writer who describes the bad faith of the aristocracy is **Jorge Edwards**
(born 1931). His books include *El patio* (1952), *Los convidados de piedra* (1978), *El
museo de cera* (1980), *La mujer imaginaria* (1985) and *Fantasmas de carne y hueso*
(1993). His book *Persona non grata* (1973) describes his experiences as a diplomat,
including his expulsion from Cuba. **Fernando Alegría** (born 1918) spans all the
movements since 1938, with a variety of work including essays, highly respected
literary criticism, poetry and novels. He was closely associated with Salvador Allende
and was his cultural attaché in Washington 1970-1973. *Recabarren* was published in
1938, after which followed many books, among them *Lautaro, joven libertador del
Arauco* (1943), *Caballo de copas* (1957), *Mañana los guerreros* (1964), *El paso de los
gansos* (1975), about a young photographer's experiences in the 1973 coup, *Coral de
guerra* (1979), also about brutality under military dictatorship, *Una especie de
memoria* (1983), Alegría's own memoir of 1938 to 1973, and *Allende: A Novel* (1992).
Having been so close to Allende, Alegría could not write a biography, he had to

⦂ Ariel Dorfman

As expressed in the subtitle of his fascinating recent memoir, *Heading South, Looking North* (1998), the literary and political career of Ariel Dorfman has taken the form of a 'bilingual journey', between the United States and South America, between English and Spanish. Born in Buenos Aires in 1942, as the son of Russian Jewish immigrants, Dorfman and his family were expelled from Argentina in the mid-1940s due to his father's political activism. They took up residence in New York, until McCarthyism sent the Dorfmans once more south in 1954, this time to Chile. Here, the monolingual, English-speaking adolescent gradually focused his attention on the Spanish language and on Chilean politics and culture, until the military coup of 1973 drove Dorfman once again into exile, where he became one of the most articulate, bilingual voices against the military regime.

Since the return to civilian government in 1990, Dorfman has divided his time between Santiago and a professional post at Duke University, writing and broadcasting in both Spanish and English. Dorfman's work, as a poet, novelist, short story writer, essayist, playwright and more recently scriptwriter, is concerned, in his words, with, "on the one hand, the glorious potential and need of human beings to tell stories and, on the other, the brutal fact that in today's world, most of the lives that should be telling those stories are generally ignored, ravaged and silenced". He is perhaps best known for his early critique of US cultural imperialism, *How to Read Donald Duck* (1971) and for *Death and the Maiden* (1990), later filmed by Roman Polanski, which deals with torture and resistance.

He often adapts his own work to different genres: *Widows* started as a poem, became a novel and later a play. Much of the work focuses on torture, disappearance, censorship and the exile condition, but also demonstrates staunch rebellion and resistance and optimism for our future. For further details, see page 560.

fictionalise it, he said. But the rise and fall of Allende becomes a realisation that history and fiction are intimately related, particularly in that Chilean epoch.

The death of Salvador Allende in 1973, and with it the collapse of the left's struggle to gain power by democratic means, was a traumatic event for Chilean writers. Those who had built their careers in the 1960s and early 1970s were for the most part exiled, forcibly or voluntarily, and thus were condemned to face the left's own responsibility in Allende's failure. René Jara says that before 1970 writers had not managed to achieve mass communication for their ideas and 1970-1973 was too short a time to correct that. Once Pinochet was in power, the task became how to find a language capable of expressing the usurping of democracy without simplifying reality. Those in exile still felt part of Chile, a country temporarily wiped from the map, where their thought was prohibited.

There are many other contemporary male novelists who deserve mention: **Antonio Skármeta** (born 1940) was exiled in Germany until 1980, writing short stories and novels and directing theatre and film. His short-story collections include *El entusiasmo* (1967), *Desnudo en el tejado* (1969), *Tiro libre* (1973) and his novels *Soñé que la nieve ardía* (975), *No pasó nada* (1980), *Ardiente paciencia* (1985) and *Match-ball* (1989). *Ardiente paciencia*, retitled *El cartero de Neruda* after its successful filming as *Il postino*, is a good example of Skármeta's concern for the enthusiasms and emotions of ordinary people, skilfully weaving the love life of a postman and a bar owner's daughter into the much bigger picture of the death of Pablo Neruda and the fall of Allende. A different take entirely on the legacy of Neruda and Chilean letters in general is provided by **Roberto Bolaño** – also an exile – whose satirical novel *Nocturno de Chile* (2003 – English translation, *By Night in Chile*) provides both an understanding of the fate of the Chilean literary world under Pinochet and of the nature of that world itself.

Another famous Chilean exile is **Ariel Dorfman** (see box, page 542), whose work exemplifies the struggle of the exile to find a bridge between their social reality overseas and their Chilean identity. His prolific output includes the novels *Moros en la costa*, 1973 (Hard Rain), *La última canción de Manuel Sendero*, 1982 (The Last Song of Manuel Sendero), *Mascara*, 1988, *Viudas*, 1981 (Widows), *Konfidenz*, 1995 and *The Nanny and the Iceberg*, 1999; the plays *Death and the Maiden*, *Reader* (1995), *Widows* (1997) and two further dramas co-written with his son Rodrigo; several volumes of essays and many poems (some collected in English as *Last Waltz in Santiago and other poems of Exile and Disappearance* (1988). Most of Dorfman's work is currently in print in English.

The most successful Chilean novelist today is **Isabel Allende** (born 1942). Her book *La casa de los espíritus* (1982) was a phenomenally successful novel worldwide. Allende, a niece of Salvador Allende, was born in Peru and went into exile in Venezuela after the 1973 coup. *The House of the Spirits*, with its tale of the dynasty of Esteban Trueba interwoven with Chilean history throughout much of the 20th century, ends with a thinly disguised description of 1973. It was followed in 1984 by *De amor y de sombra*, a disturbing tale set during the Pinochet regime. The main motivation behind these novels is the necessity to preserve historical reality (see the brief prologue to *Of Love and Shadows*, "Here, write it, or it will be erased by the wind"). The same thing applies in *Paula* (1994), Allende's letter to her daughter in a coma, where possible salvation from the devastation of not being able to contact Paula comes through the "meticulous exercise of writing". She has also written *Eva Luna* (1987) and *Los cuentos de Eva Luna* (1990), about a fictional Venezuelan storyteller and her stories, *El plan infinito* (1991), *Daughter of Fortune* (1998), *Portrait in Sepia* (2002), and her most recent work , *Mi país inventado* (2002), a look at Chile and her people.

Like her predecessors, Allende employs the marvellous and the imaginary to propose alternatives to the masculine view of social and sexual relations. The same is true of **Lucía Guerra** (born 1942), who published *Más allá de las máscaras* in exile in 1984. Another example might be **Daniela Eltit** (born 1949), who did not leave Chile after 1973 and was actively involved in resistance movements. Her provocative, intense fiction confronts issues of exploitation, violence, the oppression of women and volatile mental states. In *Vaca sagrada* (1991) at least, the protagonist's vulnerability is expressed through her body, by her blood, her two lovers' effects upon it, the brutality inflicted upon it and her obsession with her heartbeat. The main characters live out their obsessions and fears in a city in which there are no jobs and no warmth. Three earlier novels, *Lumpérica* (1983), *Por la patria* (1986) and *El cuarto mundo* (1988) maintain the same experimental, challenging approach to contemporary Chilean society.

Twentieth-century poetry

In many ways, poetry is the lifeblood of Chilean culture; the country's poetic output is prodigious, with poetry circles thriving even in remote rural areas. In the first half of the 20th century, four figures dominated Chilean poetry, Gabriela Mistral, Vicente Huidobro, Pablo Neruda (see box, page 544) and Pablo de Rokha. The three men were all socialists, but their politics and means of expression followed different trajectories. Neruda overshadows all other Chilean poets on an international level, and for this reason he is discussed in the accompanying box (see page 544).

⁞ Pablo Neruda

Pablo Neruda was born in Parral on 12 June 1904 as Ricardo Neftalí Reyes. Two months later, his mother died and his father and stepmother subsequently moved the family to Temuco. Neruda's childhood memories were dominated by nature and, above all, rain, "my only unforgettable companion", as he described it in *Confieso que he vivido*. Among his teachers in Temuco was Gabriela Mistral. In 1921, he went to study in Santiago, but he had already decided on a literary career. His first book of poems *Crepusculario* (1923), was published under the pseudonym Neruda, borrowed from a Czech writer; it was postmodernist in style but did not yet reveal the poet's own voice. His next volume, *Veinte poemas de amor y una canción desesperada* (1924) catapulted him into the forefront of Latin American poetry. The freedom of the style and the natural, elemental imagery invoking the poet's two love affairs, made the collection an immediate success. Three books followed in 1926 before Neruda was sent to Rangoon as Chilean consul in 1927. His experiences in the Orient, including his first marriage, inspired one of his finest collections, *Residencia en la tierra*, in which the inherent sadness of the *Veinte poemas* becomes despair at the passing of time and human frailty. Reinforcing this theme is a kaleidoscope of images, seemingly jumbled together, yet deliberately placed to show the chaos and fragmentary nature of life.

In the 1930s, Neruda moved to Spain, where he met many poets. The Civil War, especially the death of Federico García Lorca, affected him deeply and his poetic vision became more direct, with a strong political orientation. 'Explico algunas cosas' in *Tercera residencia* (1947) explains the move towards militancy.

Between 1938 and the election of Videla to the Chilean presidency, Neruda worked with the Frente Popular and was consul general in Mexico. He also composed his epic poem of Latin American and Chilean history, from a Marxist stance, *Canto general* (1950). Its 15 cantos chronicle the natural and human life of the Americas, from the conquered pre-Columbian inhabitants to the 20th-century labourers. One of its most famous sections is 'Alturas de Machu Picchu', which mirrors the poet's own development: from the universal to 'minuscule life' from introspection to a new- found role as the voice of the oppressed. 'Canto general' defined Neruda's subsequent enormous output.

The political commitment remained but did not submerge his respect for and evocation of nature in *Odas elementales* (1954), *Nuevas odas elementales* (1957) and *Tercer libro de odas* (1959), which begins with 'El hombre invisible'. He also never tired of writing lyric verse, such as *Los versos del capitán* (1950), *Cien sonetos de amor* (1959), and wrote memoirs such as *Memorial de Isla Negra* (1964) and *Confieso que he vivido* (1974). *Extravagaria* (1958), whose title suggests extravagance, wandering and variety, is full of memory, acceptance and a world-weary joy.

Neruda was awarded the Nobel Prize in 1971 but died of cancer two years' later. His death was hastened by the coup and the military's heartless removal of him from Isla Negra to Santiago. The poet's three houses were either ransacked or shut up by the dictatorship, but many of the Chileans for whom the poet spoke visited Isla Negra to leave messages of respect, love and hope until democracy returned. See Ariel Dorfman's 'Afterword' in *The House in the Sand*, translated by Dennis Maloney and Clark Zlotchew, 1990, Milkweed).

Gabriela Mistral wrote poetry that rejected elaboration in favour of a simple style using traditional metre and verse forms. Her poetry derives from a limited number of personal roots: she fell in love with Romelio Ureta who blew his own brains out in 1909. This inspired the *Sonetos de la muerte* (1914), which were not published at the time. She never lost the grief of this tragic love, which was coupled with her love of God and her "immense martyrdom at not being a mother". Frustrated motherhood did not deprive her of tenderness, nor of a deep love for children. The other main theme was her appreciation of nature and landscape, not just in Chile, but also in North and South America and Europe, which she visited as a diplomat. Her three principal collections are *Desolación* (1923, but re-edited and amplified frequently), *Tala* (1938) and *Lagar* (1954). She also wrote many poems for children.

If Gabriela Mistral relied on tradition and verse to present her unique view of a lone woman trying to find a place in a male-oriented world, **Vicente Huidobro** (1893-1948) wanted to break with all certainties. He made grand claims for the poet's role as nothing short of a quest for the infinite and for the language to liberate it. From Santiago he moved to Buenos Aires, then Paris, where he joined the Cubists, collaborated with Apollinaire and others, began to write in French and got involved in radical politics. Between the 1920s and 1940s he moved from Europe to the USA to Chile, back to Spain during the Civil War, before retiring to Llolleo to confront time and death in his last poems, *Ultimos poemas*, 1948. Huidobro considered himself at the forefront of the avant garde, formulating *creacionismo*, a theory that the poet is not bound by the real world, but is free to create and invent new worlds through the complete freedom of the word. Nevertheless, all the experimentation and imagery which "unglued the moon", was insufficient to achieve the language of revelation. So in 1931 he composed *Altazor*, a seven-canto poem which describes simultaneously the poet's route to creation and the ultimate frustration imposed by time and the human condition.

Pablo de Rokha (Carlos Díaz Loyola, 1894-1968) was deeply concerned for the destiny of the Chilean people and the advance of international socialism. His output was an uncompromising epic search for Chilean identity and through his work, for all its political commitment, there runs a deep sense of tragedy and inner solitude (especially true in *Fuego negro*, 1951, written after the death of his wife). *Los gemidos* was his first major book (1922); others included *Escritura de Raimundo Contreras* (1929), a song of the Chilean peasant, *Jesucristo* (1933) and *La morfología del espanto* (1942).

Although these poets, and Neruda especially, furthered the Chilean poetic tradition, those who came after were not necessarily keen to emulate his style or his politics. From the 1950s, poets were still critical of society but, taking their cue from **Nicanor Parra**, they did not elevate the writer's role in denouncing inhumanity, alienation and the depersonalisation of modern life. Instead writer and reader are placed on the same level; rhetoric and exuberant language are replaced by a conver- sational, ironic tone. **Parra** (born 1914; see also box, page 551), a scientist and teacher, called this attempt to overcome the influence of Neruda *antipoesía* (anti-poetry). In the poem 'Advertencia al lector' in *Poemas y antipoemas* (1954), he writes:

> *According to the doctors of the law this book should not be published:*
> *The word rainbow does not appear in it,*
> *Let alone the word grief,*
> *Chairs and tables, yes, there are aplenty,*
> *Coffins! Writing utensils!*
> *Which fills me with pride*
> *Because, as I see it, the sky is falling to bits.*

Obra gruesa anthologises his work to 1969, followed by *Emergency Poems* (1972, bilingual edition, New York), which contain a darker humour and satire, but remain compassionate and socially committed, *Artefactos* (1972) and *Artefactos II* (1982), *Sermones y prédicas del Cristo de Elqui* (1979) and *Poesía política* (1983).

The adherents of *antipoesía* continually sought new means of expression, so that the genre never became institutionalised. There are too many poets to list here, but **Gonzalo Rojas** (born 1917), **Enríque Lihn** (1929-1988), **Armando Uribe** (born 1933) and **Miguel Arteche** (born 1926) are perhaps the best known.

Another poetic development of the 1950s onwards was *poesía lárica*, or *de lares*, poetry of one's place of origin (literally, of the gods of the hearth). Its founder and promoter was **Jorge Teillier** (1935-1996), whose poems describe a precarious rural existence, wooden houses, fencing, orchards, distant fires, beneath changing skies and rain. The city dweller is an exile in space and time who returns every so often to the place of origin. See especially 'Notas sobre el último viaje del autor a su pueblo natal', which evokes the lost frontier of his youth, the changed countryside and his city life. As for the future, "if only it could be as beautiful as my mother spreading the sheets on my bed", but it is only an unpaid bill; "I wish the UFOs would arrive." In his later poems, the violence of the city and the dictatorship invade the *lares*. Among Teillier's books are *Para angeles y gorriones* (1956), *Para un pueblo fantasma* (1978), *Cartas para reinas de otras primaveras* (1985) and *Los dominios perdidos* (1992). A variation on this type of poetry comes from **Clemente Riedemann** (born 1953), whose *Karra Maw'n* deals with the Mapuche lands and German immigration in the area.

Many poets left Chile after 1973 but others stayed to attack the dictatorship from within through provocative, experimental works. In a country with such a strong poetic tradition and such a serious political situation, poets understood that their verses had to mutate in order to reflect and comment on their contemporary realities. A more experimental and opaque poetry developed as a result, dealing with themes such as the reaffirmation of colloquialism, the city (developed through the slang of *antipoesía*), and poetry itself, unravelling contexts and bridging the past and the present. Several writers were members of the Grupo Experimental de Artaud, including Daniela Eltit (see above), Eugenia Brito, Rodrigo Cánovas and **Raúl Zurita**, perhaps the most celebrated poet in Chile today: his verse is a complex and at times difficult union of mathematics and poetry, logical, structured and psychological. *Purgatorio* (1979) had an immediate impact and was followed by *Anteparaíso* (1982), *El paraíso está vacío* (1984), *Canto a su amor desaparecido* (1986) and *El amor de Chile* (1987). 'Pastoral de Chile' in *Anteparaíso* reveals most of Zurita's obsessions: Chilean landscapes, love, Chile's distress, sin and religious terminology.

Other significant poetic works of the 1980s include *La Tirana* (1985) by **Diego Maquieira**, a complex, multireferential work, dealing with a Mapuche virgin, surrounded by a culture that oppresses her and with which she disguises herself. It is irreverent; a 'black mass', threatening to the régime. Carmen Berenguer's *Bobby Sands desfallece en el muro* (1983) is a homage to the IRA prisoner and thus to all political prisoners. She also wrote *Huellas del siglo* (1986) and *A media asta* (1988). Carla Grandi published *Contraproyecto* in 1985, an example of feminine resistance to the coup.

Poetry continues to be significant in Chile. There are numerous workshops and organisations for young poets; the *Taller de Poesía de la Fundacion Pablo Neruda* is particularly influential. There are also important underground literary movements. Interesting contemporary poets include **Carolina Cerlis** and **Javier del Cerro**, both maintaining the experimental and free verse tradition of Zurita and others.

Not many months after the first screening organized by the Lumière brothers in Paris in December 1895, moving pictures were exhibited in Chile on 25 August 1896. Initially all the films were imported, but from 1902 local artists and entrepreneurs began to produce short documentaries. The first narrative movie, *Manuel Rodríguez*, was screened in September 1910. From about 1915, with European production semi-paralysed by war, the pre-eminence of Hollywood cinema was established. The modern dreams of Hollywood were often more complex, technologically superior and more entertaining than the products of rudimentary national cinemas. The historian of Chilean silent films, Eliana Jara Donoso, quotes a publicity handout for a local movie that read, "it's so good that it doesn't seem Chilean".

But despite the overwhelming presence of Hollywood, local film-makers in the silent era could still establish a small presence in the market. In the main they made documentaries, for this was a niche free of international competition: regional topics, football competitions, civic ceremonies, military parades. Almost 100 feature films were also made, but these are the domain of the film historian, since only one such movie has survived (carefully restored by the University of Chile in the early 1960s): *El húsar de la muerte* (The Hussar of Death), directed by Pedro Sienna in 1925. It was, like many movies in Latin America at the time, a historical melodrama, exploring the fight for Chilean independence from Spanish rule in the 1810s through the heroic exploits of the legendary Manuel Rodríguez. It achieved great box office success in a year when 16 Chilean films were screened. Never again would so many national movies be produced annually.

The coming of synchronized sound created a new situation in Latin America. In those countries with a large domestic market – in particular Mexico, Argentina and Brazil – investment was made in expensive machinery, installations and rudimentary studios. Elsewhere, and Chile is a telling example, sound devastated local production due to its cost and complexity. Local entrepreneurs were usually unwilling to make the risky capital investment, and the history of Chilean cinema thereafter is littered with tales of self-sacrifice on the part of cast and crew. The first non-silent film made in Chile was *Norte y Sur*, directed by **Jorge Délano** in 1934, telling the story of a love triangle where a woman is the object of the attentions of a Chilean and an American engineer. It was a rare example of sophisticated cinema at a time when Chilean film output was reverting to often formulaic stories of young men seducing innocent ladies, or the naïve idealisation of rural landscapes. Délano stood out in this age – another film of his, *Escándalo* (1940) was almost unique in dealing with the lives of the middle class, rather than those of the aristocracy or the peasantry. Nevertheless, Tobías Barros, an important director of the time, summed up the mood when he sarcastically described his *Río Abajo* as a film "where there are neither illegitimate nor lost children".

An attempt was made in the 1940s to stimulate cinema through state investment. The state agency CORFO saw cinema as an important growth industry and in 1942 gave 50% finance to set up **Chile Films**. Costly studios were erected, but the plan proved over-ambitious and Argentine film-makers ended up using most of the facilities; by 1947 Chile Films had collapsed. In 1959, however, the Universidad de Chile set up a Centre for Experimental Cinema under the direction of a documentary film-maker Sergio Bravo, which trained aspirant directors from Chile and elsewhere in Latin America (notably the Bolivian Jorge Sanjinés).

Cinema became intricately involved in the wider political discussions of the 1960s. The years 1968-1969 saw the maturity of Chilean cinema. Five features came out: **Raúl Ruiz**'s *Tres tristes tigres* (Three Sad Tigers); Helvio Soto's *Caliche sangriento* (Bloody Nitrate); Aldo Francia's *Valparaíso mi amor* (Valparaíso My Love); Miguel Littín's *El chacal de Nahueltoro* (The Jackal of Nahueltoro) and Carlos Elsesser's *Los testigos* (The

Witnesses). These film-makers came from different ideological and aesthetic tendencies, from the inventive maverick Raúl Ruiz to the sombre neo-realism of Francia, but they can be seen as a group, working with very scarce resources: the films by Ruiz, Elsesser, Francia and Littín were made, consecutively, with the same camera; furthermore, many of the directors sought to break down the traditionally melodramatic themes of Chilean cinema, employing more realistic language and situations more reflective of everyday social problems. Aldo Francia, a doctor by profession, also organized a famous 'Meeting of Latin American Film-makers' at the Viña del Mar film festival in 1967. This would be one of the key events to cause growing awareness of cineastes across the continent that they were working with similar ideas and methods, producing 'new cinemas'.

The narrow victory of the Popular Unity parties in the election of 1970 was greeted by film-makers with an enthusiastic manifesto penned by **Miguel Littín**; Littín himself was put in charge of the revived state institution Chile Films. He lasted for only 10 months, tiring of bureaucratic opposition and inter-party feuding, as the different members of Popular Unity all demanded a share of very limited resources. Few films were made between 1970 and 1973; Raúl Ruiz was the most productive film-maker of the period, with a number of films in different styles. Littín was working on an historical feature *La tierra prometida* (The Promised Land) when the 1973 coup occurred and post-production took place in Paris.

The most ambitious film to trace the radicalization of Chile in 1972 and 1973 was Patricio Guzmán's three-part documentary *La batalla de Chile* (The Battle of Chile), which was edited in exile in Cuba. In the first years of exile, this film became Chile's most evocative testimony abroad and received worldwide distribution. Paradoxically, Chilean cinema, which had little time to grow under Popular Unity, strengthened in exile.

Policies following the coup practically destroyed internal film production for several years. Film personnel were arrested, tortured and imprisoned and many escaped into exile. Severe censorship was established: even *Fiddler on the Roof* was banned for displaying Marxist tendencies. It is from the exiled directors that the continuity of film culture can be seen. Littín took up residence in Mexico, supported by Mexican President, Echeverría, and became an explicit spokesman for political Latin American cinema, making the epic *Actas de Marusia* (Letters from Marusia) in 1975 and several other features in Mexico and later in Nicaragua. In the mid-1980s he returned clandestinely to Chile with several foreign film crews to make the documentary *Acta General de Chile* in 1986, a perilous mission documented by Gabriel García Márquez in his reportage *Clandestine in Chile* (1986). Raúl Ruiz took a less visible political role, but since his exile to France, he has produced a body of work that has earned him a reputation as one of the most innovative directors in Europe, the subject of a special issue in 1983 of France's distinguished journal *Cahiers du Cinéma*. He makes movies with great technical virtuosity and often great speed: on a visit to Santiago to celebrate the return to civilian rule in 1990, he shot a film, entitled *La telenovela errante* (The Wandering Soap Opera), in less than a week for US$30,000. Other exile directors to make their mark include Ruiz's wife Valeria Sarmiento, Gastón Ancelovici and Carmen Castillo, all based in France, Patricio Guzmán in Spain, Marilú Mallet in Canada, Angelina Vásquez in Scandinavia, Sebastián Alarcón in the Soviet Union and Antonio Skármeta in Germany.

Inside Chile, the output under censorship varied from maritime adventures such as *El Último Grumete* to Silvio Caiozzi's *Julion comienza en julio* (Julio begins in July, 1979), one of the first films made in the period, set carefully in a turn-of-the-century historical location and self-financed through Caiozzi's work in commercials. It would take him a further 10 years to produce a second feature, *La luna en el espejo* (The Moon in the Mirror), evocatively set in Valparaíso, which was screened in 1990. An example of increased critical debate within Chile in the last years of the Pinochet régime can be found in Pablo Perelman's *Imagen latente* (Latent Image, 1987) which tells of a photographer's search for a missing brother who disappeared after the coup; although the film was not released in Chile until 1990, it was possible to make the film in the country in the mid-1980s. Another case is that of *Hijos de la Guerra Fría* by Gonzalo Justiniano (1985), which is replete with metaphors of a society asphyxiated by a repressive system.

The return to civilian rule had some benefits for film-makers, most notably the easing of censorship. The Viña del Mar Film Festival was symbolically reinstated after 20 years and saw the emotional return of many exiled directors, but that, in itself, could not solve the problems of an intellectual community dispersed around the world and the chronic underfunding and under-representation of Chilean films in the home market. New names have emerged and some internationally successful films have been made, most notably Ricardo Larraín's *La Frontera* (The Frontier, 1991), one of the best Chilean films ever made, which tells of a school teacher's internal exile in the spectacular scenery of southern Chile in the late 1980s, which as Gustavo Graef-Marino's *Johnny Cien Pesos* (1993), which deals with violence in Chilean society. The latter was produced by Chile Films, a short-lived production company made up of film directors and producers financed by a State Bank credit loan. The loan was withdrawn, however, when other productions failed at the box office.

The last few years have seen the screening of one or two Chilean features a year, the best received being the political thriller *Amnesia* (1994), directed by Gonzalo Justiniano, Andrés Wood's vogue-ish *Historias de Futbol* (1997) and Sergio Castillo's 1997 *Gringuito*, which focuses on the problems of children brought up in exile, returning as foreigners to Chile. This gentle comedy of reintegration has been made to seem somewhat tame by the demonstrations in Chile surrounding the Pinochet extradition process. Larraín's latest feature *El entusiasmo* (Enthusiasms, 1999) did not live up to its title among local audiences but it garnered international recognition, as did Andrés Wood's new films, *Loco Fever,* an engaging comedy about two conmen's frenzied search for as many 'locos' – the shellfish, not the crazies – as possible, and most recently *Machuca,* a socio-political drama centred around the friendship of two boys, one rich and one poor, during the final doomed days of Allende's regime. While there are many talented young filmmakers, and although government art grants are becoming more available, the increasing globalisation of the culture industry, however, means that the pattern of scarce local production is likely to continue.

Music and dance

Traditional forms

As far as **traditional dance** goes, at the very heart of Chilean music is the *cueca*, a courting dance for couples, both of whom make great play with a handkerchief waved aloft in the right hand. The man's knees are slightly bent and his body arches back; in rural areas, he stamps his spurs together for effect. Guitar and harp are the accompanying instruments, while handclapping and shouts of encouragement add to the atmosphere. The dance has a common origin with the Argentine *zamba* and Peruvian *marinera* via the early 19th-century *zamacueca*, in turn descended from the Spanish fandango. The most traditional form of song is the *tonada*, with its variants the *glosa*, *parabienes*, *romance*, *villancico* (Christmas carol) and *esquinazo* (serenade), in common with the *custon* in Argentina, this may be heard in the form of a *contrapunto* or *controversia*, a musical duel. Among the most celebrated groups are **Los Huasos Quincheros**, Silvia Infante with **Los Condores** and the **Conjunto Millaray**, all of which are popular at rural dances, with their poignant combination of formal singing and rousing accordian music. Famous folk singers in this genre are the **Parra family** from Chillán (see box, page 551), **Hector Pávez** and **Margot Loyola**.

⁘ Facing the music

There are many famous Chilean groups whose music is still widely distributed and available internationally. These include Illapu, Inti Illimanni, Quilapayún and the late Victor Jara. All these groups were involved in some way in the movement of *La Nueva Canción*, and went into exile after the military coup.

One of the best albums is Illapu's *Despedida del Pueblo*, of which the most popular and resonant song is 'Vuelvo', dealing with the emotions of the returning exile. Compilations of Victor Jara are usually good, and the collection of *Cantos de Pueblos Andinos* by Inti Illimanni is a haunting, melodic introduction to their music.

Among the standard bearers of *La Nueva Canción* and one of Inti Illimanni's most popular songs was 'El pueblo unido jamás será vencido' ('The people, united, will never be divided') – a good old-fashioned protest song. Later Inti Illimanni music demonstrates the influence of dance rhythms from the Caribbean, yet retains its Chilean roots – a good example is 'Andadas'.

As far as pop music goes, the Chilean national scene has been dominated in recent years by the rock band La Ley. Los Prisioneros, an older band, were more political, producing music that expressed the feelings of the Chilean youth that grew up in the 1980s under the Pinochet dictatorship.

In the north of the country the music is Amerindian and closely related to that of Bolivia. Groups called 'Bailes' dance the *huayño*, *taquirari*, *cachimbo* or *rueda* at carnival and other festivities as well as pre-Columbian rites like the *cauzulor* and *talatur*. Instruments are largely wind and percussion, including *zampoñas* (pan pipes), *lichiguayos*, *pututos* (conch shells), *queñas* (flutes) and *clarines*. There are some notable religious festivals that attract large crowds of pilgrims and include numerous groups of costumed dancers. The most outstanding of these festivals are those of the **Virgen de La Tirana** near Iquique (see box, page 238), the **Virgen de la Candelaria** of Copiapó (see page 186) and the **Virgen de Andacollo** (see page 162).

In the south the Mapuche nation have their own songs, dance-songs and magic and collective dances, accompanied by wind instruments like the great long *trutruca* horn, the shorter *pifilka* and the *kultrún* drum. Further south still, Chiloé has its own unique musical expression: wakes and other religious social occasions include collective singing, while the recreational dances, all of Spanish origin – such as the *vals*, *pavo*, *pericona* and *nave* – have a heavier and less syncopated beat than in central Chile. Accompanying instruments here are the *rabel* (fiddle), guitar and accordion.

Nueva canción

The most famous Chilean movement on the international stage was that of the *nueva canción*, or new song, which arose in the late 1960s and early 1970s under such luminaries as **Violeta Parra** (see box, page 551) and **Victor Jara**. This movement, which scorned commercialism and sought to give a political meaning to its songs – whether overt or suggested – gave a whole new dimension to the Chilean musical scene, and was part of a wider movement across the continent, involving people such as Mercedes Sosa in Argentina and Sílvio Rodríguez in Cuba.

Beginning as an underground movement, faraway from the usual round of publicity and radio stations, the *nueva canción* protagonists rose to prominence during the 1970 election campaign, which resulted in the victory of Salvador Allende. Although related to folk rhythms, the movement sought to be dynamic and not

Violeta Parra

Violeta Parra was brought up in Chillán as one of 11 children. Her father, Nicanor, was a music teacher, while her mother, Clarisa, was a seamstress who played the guitar and sang. Violeta sang with her sister Hilda in Santiago bars for several years. She also worked in the circus. Another child, Nicanor, became a professor of maths and physics, and a poet (see page 545).

Violeta travelled the length of Chile and abroad with the Chilean poet Pablo de Rokha (see page 545), collecting material and promoting their idea of Chilean-ness. While de Rokha expressed himself in the lyrical epic, Violeta sang, wrote songs, made tapestries, ceramics, paintings and sculpture. All her work was based on a philosophy of helping those in need. In France she was recognized as a great artist and her works were exhibited in the Louvre in 1964, but at home recognition was only grudgingly given.

In the 1960s Violeta set up La Carpa de la Reina as a centre for popular art in the capital. It was here, in February 1967, that she committed suicide, her head resting on her guitar. The national grief at her funeral far outweighed the acclaim given her during her life. Neruda called her 'Santa Violeta'; the Peruvian novelist Jose María Arguedas described her as 'the most Chilean of all Chileans I could possibly know, but at the same time the most universal of all Chile'.

For Violeta, folklore was a form of class struggle. Her influence on a whole generation of Latin American folk singers was enormous and long-lasting. Without her, Salvador Allende would not have had the folkloric backing of Victor Jara, Inti-Illimani, Los Quilapayún and the Parras themselves. After Violeta's death, her brother Nicanor published *Décimas*, a sort of autobiography in verse, full of simple humanity.

confined to any particular style. Violeta Parra's suicide and the subsequent coup of 1973 forced its protagonists into exile – Inti Illimanni to Italy, Illapu to France. But Victor Jara was imprisoned in the National Stadium after the coup and was hauled to his death, singing Violeta Parra's famous song, 'Gracias a la vida' (I give thanks to life). Now back in Chile, the ageing Intis and other nueva canción folk groups of the early 1970s still play regular concerts throughout the country.

Land and environment

Chile is smaller than all other South American republics except Ecuador, Paraguay, Uruguay and the Guianas. It is 4329 km long and, on average, no more than 180 km wide. In the north Chile has a short (150 km) east-west border with Peru. In the far north its eastern frontier is with Bolivia – 750 km long – but from San Pedro de Atacama south to Tierra del Fuego it shares over 3500 km of border with Argentina. In the main this frontier follows the water margin of the Andes but, in the far south, where the Andes are lower, or where icefields cover the border area, there have been frequent frontier disputes with Argentina; these still rumble on. Chilean sovereignty over the islands south of Tierra del Fuego gives it control over Isla Navarino, on which Puerto Williams is the most southerly permanent settlement in the world (apart from scientific bases in Antarctica). Various island archipelagos in the Pacific, including Easter Island/Rapa Nui and the Juan Fernández group, are under Chilean jurisdiction.

Glacial landscapes

Southern Chile provides some of the best examples of glacial landscapes on earth. One common sign of the region's glacial past is the U-shaped valleys. Good examples can be seen throughout the south, but perhaps one of the best is the Río Simpson between Coyhaique and Puerto Aisén. High above these valleys, sharp mountain ridges can often be seen, which have been caused by the eroding action of the ice on two or more sides. In some places, the resulting debris or 'moraine' formed a dam, blocking the valley and creating a lake, as in the Lake District at Lagos Calafquén, Panguipulli and Riñihue.

The drowned coastline south of Puerto Montt also owes its origin to glaciation. The ice that once covered the southern Andes was so heavy that it depressed the relatively narrow tip of South America. When the ice melted and the sea level rose, water broke through, leaving the western Andes as islands and creating the Chilean fjords, glaciated valleys carved out by the ice and now drowned.

Geology

The Quaternary Period, 1.6 million years ago, was marked by the advance and retreat of the Antarctic Ice Sheet which, at its maximum extent, covered all of the Chilean Andes and the entire coastline south of Puerto Montt. However, although there are surface remnants of older rock formations, most have disappeared with the dramatic creation of the Andes, which started around 80 million years ago and continues to this day. The South American Plate, moving westwards, meets the Nazca and Antarctic Plates, which are moving eastwards and sinking below the continent. These two plates run more or less parallel between 26°S and 33°S and the friction between them creates a geologically unstable zone, marked by frequent earthquakes and volcanic activity. The area of Concepción has been particularly susceptible to both land and undersea quakes and the city was twice destroyed by tidal waves in the 18th century before being moved to its present site.

All of the Chilean Pacific islands were formed by underwater volcanoes associated with fracture zones between the Nazca and Antarctic Plates. Easter Island gained its characteristic triangular shape from the joining together of three lava flows.

Northern desert

Northern Chile has a similar form to Peru immediately to the north: the coastal range rises to 1000-1500 m; inland are basins known as bolsones, east of which lie the Andes. The Atacama Desert is, by most measures, the driest area on earth, and some meteorological stations near the coast have never reported precipitation. Water is therefore at a premium as far south as Copiapó; it is piped in from the east and, in the Andean foothills, streams flow into alluvial fans in the inland basins, which can act as reservoirs and may be tapped by drilling wells. One river, the Río Loa, flows circuitously from the Andes to Calama and then through the coastal range to the coast; however, for most of its length it is deeply entrenched and unsuitable for agriculture. East of Calama and high in the Andes are the geysers of El Tatio, more evidence of volcanic activity, which are fed by the summer rains that fall in this part of the Andes.

In the past, notably as the ice sheets retreated, there were many lakes in the depressions between the Coastal Range and the Andes. These dried out, leaving one of the greatest concentrations of salts in the world, rich in nitrates: there has been extensive mining activity here since the late 19th century.

Central Chile

South of Copiapó the transition begins between the Atacama and the zone of heavy rainfall in the south. At first, the desert turns to scrub and some seasonal surface water appears. The Huasco and Elqui rivers follow deep trenches to reach the sea, allowing valley bottoms inland to be irrigated for agriculture. Further south, near Santiago, the Central Valley between the Coastal Range and the Andes reappears, the rivers flowing westwards across it to reach the Pacific. Further south is the Lake District, with its many lakes formed by glaciation and volcanic activity, its attractive mountain scenery, its rich volcanic soils and fertile agricultural land.

Southern Chile

South of Valdivia, the Coastal Range becomes more broken until near Puerto Montt it becomes a line of islands as part of a 'drowned coastline' that extends all the way south to Cape Horn. The effects of glaciation can be seen in the U-shaped valleys and the long deep fjords stretching inland. This is a land of dense forests with luxuriant undergrowth that is virtually impenetrable and difficult to clear owing to the high water content. Further south in Chilean Patagonia, coniferous forests are limited in expanse because glaciers have stripped the upper slopes of soil. Some of the remaining glaciers reach sea level, notably the San Rafael, which breaks off the giant icefields of the *Campo de Hielo Norte*.

The Andes

The whole of Chile is dominated by this massive mountain range, which reaches its highest elevations in the border region between Chile and Argentina. In the north, near the Peruvian border, the ranges that make up the Andes are 500 km wide, but the western ranges, which mark the Chilean border, are the highest. Sajama, the highest peak in Bolivia, lies only 20 km east of the border, along which are strung volcanoes including Parinacota (6330 m). Further south, to the southeast of San Pedro de Atacama, lies the highest section of the Andes, which includes the peaks of Llullaillaco (6739 m) and Ojos del Salado (altitude 6864 m or 6893 m depending on your source). Still further south, to the northeast of Santiago and just inside Argentina, lies Aconcagua (6960 m).

South of Santiago, the Andes begin to lose altitude. In the Lake District, the mountain passes are low enough in places for crossing into Argentina. South of Puerto Montt, the Andes become more inhospitable, however, as lower temperatures bring the permanent snowline down from 1500 m at Volcán Osorno near Puerto Montt to 700 m on Tierra del Fuego. Towards the southern end of the Andes stand Mount Fitzroy (3406 m) – in Argentina – and the remarkable peaks of the Paine massif in Chilean territory.

Climate

It is only to be expected that a country that stretches over 4000 km from north to south will provide a wide variety of climatic conditions. Annual rainfall varies from zero in northern Chile to over 4000 mm on the offshore islands south of Puerto Montt. Rainfall is heavier in the winter months (May to August) throughout the country, except for in the northern *altiplano* where January and February are the wettest months.

Variations in the Chilean climate are concentrated by two significant factors: altitude and the cold waters of the Humboldt Current. The Andes, with their peaks of over 6000 m, are rarely more than 160 km from the coastline. On average, temperatures drop by 1°C for every 150 m you climb. The Humboldt Current has perhaps even more impact. The current flows in a northeasterly direction from Antarctic waters until it meets the southern coast of Chile, from where it follows the coastline northwards. Cold polar air accompanies the current on its journey, eventually colliding with warmer air moving in from the southwest. The lighter warm air is forced to rise over the dense cold air, bringing rainfall all year round to the area south of the Río Biobío and rain in winter further north in the Central Valley.

Paradoxically, the ocean also has a moderating effect on temperatures, which are not generally extreme and decrease less than might be expected from north to south. As a result of the Humboldt Current, temperatures in northern Chile are much lower than they are for places at corresponding latitudes, such as Mexico. In the far south, the oceans have the opposite effect and temperatures rarely fall below -6°C despite the high latitude. Detailed temperature and rainfall patterns are given in the text.

Flora

The diversity of Chilean flora reflects the geographic length and climatic variety of the country. Although the Andes constitute a great natural barrier, there are connections between the flora of Chile and that of the eastern side of the mountain range, most notably in the far north with the Bolivian *altiplano* and in the south with the temperate forests of Argentina.

Far north

The arid central plain of northern Chile forms one of the driest areas on earth. Vegetation is limited to cacti, among them the *cardon* (Echinopsis atacamensis) and, in the Pampa de Tamarugal around Iquique, the *tamarugo* (Proposis tamarugo), a tree specially adapted to arid climates. On the western slopes of the Andes, ravines carry water, which has permitted the establishment of small settlements and the planting of crops. The only native tree of this area, *queñoa* (Polylepis tomentella) – heavily overexploited in the past – grows in sheltered areas, mainly near streams, at altitudes between 2000 and 3500 m. Among cacti are the *candelabros* (genus Browningia) and, at higher altitudes (between 3000 and 4000 m) the *ayrampus* (genus Opuntia).

The northern *altiplano* supports only sparse vegetation. Many plants found in this area, such as the *llareta* (genus Laretia) and the *tola* (genus Baccharis) have deep root systems and small leaves. Near streams, there are areas of spongy, wet salty grass, known as *bofedales*.

To the west of the central plain, the Pacific coastal area is almost complete desert, although in places the influence of the Humboldt Current is offset by the *camanchaca*, an early morning coastal fog that comes off the sea and persists at low altitudes, permitting the growth of vegetation, notably in the Parque Nacional Pan de Azúcar, north of Chañaral, and around Poposo, south of Antofagasta, where about 170 flowering plants, including shrubs, bromeliaceae and cacti can be found.

Norte Chico

Lying between the northern deserts and the matorral of central Chile, the Norte Chico is a transition zone: here annual rainfall averages from 30 to 100 mm, increasing southwards. In the main dry areas native flora, such as *pingo-pingo* (Ephedra andina), *jarilla* (Larrea nitida) and *brea* (Tessaria absinthoides) can be found. On the rare occasions when there is spring rainfall, the desert comes to life in a phenomenon known as the 'flowering of the desert' (see box, page 182). The central plain is crossed by rivers; in the valleys irrigation permits the cultivation of fruit, such as chirimoya, papaya and grapes.

On the coast near Ovalle, sea mists support a forest of evergreen species, including the *olivillo* (Aextoxicon punctatum), *canelo* or winter's bark (Drimys winteri) and *arrayán* (Luma chequen or Myrtus chequen) in the Parque Nacional Fray Jorge.

Central Chile

The Central Valley, with its dry and warm summers and mild winters, is home to the *matorral*, a deciduous scrubland ecologically comparable to the chaparral in California and consisting of slow-growing drought-resistant species with deep roots and small spiny sclerophyllous leaves. The original plant cover has been modified by human impact, particularly in the form of livestock agriculture, charcoal-burning and irrigation. In many areas, from the Río Limari in the north to the Río Laja in the south, the result is *espinal* (Acacia cavan), usually considered to be a degraded form of the original matoral and characterised by open savanna scattered with *algarrobo* trees (Prosopis chilensis). Along ravines and on western facing slopes, there are areas of evergreen sclerophyllous trees, including the *peumo* (Cryptocarpa alba), *litre* (Lithrea caustica) and *boldo* (Peumos boldos) and, along the banks of the great rivers, the *maiten* (Maytenus boaria or Maytenus chilensis) and a local species of willow can be found.

Towards the coast more hygrophilous species grow on hills receiving coastal fogs: among these are *avellano*, *lingue* (Persea lingue), *belloto* or northern acorn (Beilschmiedia miersii) and *canelo* as well as bromeliads and epiphytic lichens and mosses. Species of southern beech (Nothofagus) and the formerly endemic Chilean or ocoa palm (Jubea chilensis), grow under protection in the Parque Nacional La Campana between Santiago and Valparaíso.

Subantarctic temperate forests

As a result of the fragmentation of the great landmass of Gondwana some 120 million years ago, some of the species in these forests (Araucaria araucana, Nothofagus and Podocarpus salingus) share affinities with flora found in Australia and New Zealand as well as with fossils uncovered in Antarctica. Similar affinities of some insect groups have also been established. However the isolation of these subantarctic forests, with the nearest neighbouring forests 1300 km away in northwestern Argentina, has led to the evolution of many unique endemic species, with volcanic activity also having had an important influence.

Nowadays these forests are mainly of broad-leafed evergreen species; in contrast to temperate forests in the northern hemisphere there are few species of conifers. The dominant genus is the Nothofagus or southern beech, of which eight species are found in Chile. In the Maule area *roble* (Nothofagus obliqua) and *hualo* (Nothofagus glauca) can be found, while further south there is a gradual transitional change via the Valdivian rainforest (see below), to the southern deciduous Nothofagus forests. The latter, which can also be found at higher altitudes along the Andes, include the Patagonian and Magellanic forests. From the Valdivian forest south to the Magellanic forests all species of Nothofagus attract fungis from the genus Cyttaria and, especially in the south, the *misodendron* or South American mistletoe.

Around the Río Biobío, the Valdivian rainforest predominates. This is a complex and diverse environment, which includes ferns, bromeliads, lichens including old man's beard, and mosses, as well as a variety of climbing plants including the *copihue* or Chilean bell flower (Lapageria rosea), the national flower of Chile. Colourful flowering plants that can easily be identified include the firebush or *ciruelillo* (Embothrium coccineum), several species of alstroemeria and berberis and the fuschia. Near the Andes, for example in the Parque Nacional Puyehue, the forests are dominated by two species of Nothofagus, the evergreen *coihue* or *coigüe* (Nothofagus dombeyi) and the deciduous *lenga* (Nothfagus pumilio) as well as by the Podocarpus (Podocarpus salingus) and, near water, myrtle trees like the *arrayán*. The under-storey is dominated by tall *chusquea* bamboos. However many of these endemic species of flora are currently under threat from the proposed damming of the Río Biobío by Endesa, the Chilean electricity company, in violation of a law of 1993 which safeguards people from signing away their lands if they do not want to.

In the northern parts of the Valdivian forest, at altitudes mainly between 900 m and 1400 m, there are forests of monkey puzzle trees (Araucaria araucana), Chile's national tree. The most important of these forests are in the Parque Nacional Nahuelbuta in the coastal *cordillera* and in the Parque Nacional Huerquehue in the Andean foothills (see also box, page 309).

Other species include the giant larch (Fitzroya cupressoides), known as the *alerce* or *lahuén*, which has some of the oldest individual specimens on earth (3600 years). Athough this conifer grew extensively as far south as the 43° 30' south, excessive logging has destroyed most of the original larch forest. Some of the best examples of *alerce*, which is now a protected species, can be seen in the Parque Nacional Andino Alerce and in the Parque Pumalín.

The Patagonian and Magellanic forests are less diverse than their Valdivian counterpart, mainly due to lower temperatures. The Magellanic forest, considered the southernmost forest type in the world, includes the evergreen Nothofagus betuloides, the deciduous *lenga* (Nothofagus pumilio) and Nothofagus antarctica, and the *canelo*. Firebush and berberis can also be found, as well as several species of orchids and beautiful species of Calceolaria or slipper plants. Shrubland in the south is mainly characterised by mounded shrubs, usually found in rocky areas. Common species include *mata barrosa* (Mullinum spinosum), a yellow-flowered shrub, and *mata guanaco* (Anartrophyllum desideratum), a red-flowered shrub of the legume family.

The Pacific Islands

In both the Juan Fernández Islands and Easter Island there are endemic species. In the forests of the Juan Fernández Archipelago, at altitudes above 1400 m, important species of ferns can be found, as well as tree species such as *luma*, *mayu-monte*, giant naranjillo and the *yonta* or Juan Fernández palm, which, along with the ocoa palm, is one of only two palms native to Chile. The native forests of Easter Island were destroyed, first by volcanic activity and later by human impact, leaving land covered partially with pasture. Although native species, such as the *toromiro*, can be found, introduced species,such as the eucalyptus, are more common.

Fauna

Chile is an ecological island. Fauna that is commonplace in neighbouring countries has not been able to migrate here because of the Andes, the desert, the ice and the sea. This explains why there are no land tortoises, squirrels, jaguars or poisonous snakes in the country. Surrounded by natural barriers on all sides, its isolation has contributed to a range of endemic wildlife – something that Darwin glimpsed in microcosm on Chiloé in 1835, when he observed a fox unique to that island.

The one geographical constant from top to bottom of the country is the **Pacific Ocean**, the world's richest ocean for marine species. Coldwater species live near Chile's mainland, feeding off the rich nutrients in the Humboldt Current, while subtropical species inhabit the warmer waters around the Juan Fernández archipelago, and tropical species can be found in the waters around Easter Island. This explains the diversity of Chilean marine life, from hake, swordfish, bream and bass to countless shellfish, such as abalones, mussels, sea urchins, lobsters and a variety of crabs. Nine of the world's 18 species of **penguins** also live in Chile. The Humboldt penguins can be found between Arica and Chiloé, while the King, Adelia and Emperor penguins live solely in Antarctica. There are numerous colonies of sea-lions up and down the coast; dolphins are often seen off the shore of Chiloé and even killer whales abound.

Inland, there are some 680 species of mammals, amphibians, reptiles and birds. In the north, the **camelids** predominate among mammals: the alpacas, guanacos, llamas and vicuñas, with the guanaco also being found as far south as Tierra del Fuego.

These South American camels are adapted for the mountainous terrain by having narrower feet than the desert forms of the species. All four species can be seen in Chile, although three are found only in the north. Like horses and donkeys, all the camelids can breed with one another, arising to some confusion as to their origins. There is a long-held view that both the llama and the alpaca are descended from wild guanaco.

Guanaco, coffee coloured with a dark head and tail and weighing up to 55 kg, were once found throughout Chile except in rainforest areas. Both grazers and browsers, they live in deserts, shrub land, savannah and occasionally on forest fringes. In many areas hunted to extinction, an estimated 20,000 now survive in the far north, especially in the Parque Nacional Lauca, in coastal and mountain areas between Antofagasta and Lago Rapel and in parts of the far south, such as the Parque Nacional Torres del Paine.

Vicuña, weighing up to 20 kg, are like half-sized guanaco, although with a much finer yellower coat and coffee-coloured head and tail. Hunted almost to extinction, there were only around 400 in Chile in 1970. Protection has increased their numbers to around 12,000, mainly in the far north at altitudes of 3700-4800 m.

Alpaca are domesticated animals, weighing 20-30 kg, but seeming to be much larger because of their wool. Colours vary between black, coffee coloured, mahogany, grey and white. An estimated 20,000 can be found in drier parts of the northern *altiplano*.

Llama are also domesticated and are usually found with alpacas. Larger than alpacas and weighing up to 55 kg, their wool varies in colour but is shorter than that of alpacas. They are found only in the area of their domestication, which first occurred around Lake Titicaca some 4000-5000 years ago. Used as pack animals, males can carry loads of up to 40 kg. There are some 40,000 in the Tarapacá and Antofagasta regions of Chile.

Perhaps surprisingly, the north is also one of the avian capitals of Chile, with three of the world's six species of **flamingo** – the James, Chilean and Andean – all to be found around the saltpans of the Atacama. The **Parque Nacional Lauca** is also exceptional for birdlife, with over 120 species of either resident or migrant birds (see box, page 250).

As the land becomes more humid, south of the desert, there are naturally many changes in wildlife. One of the few constants is the famous **puma**, which is found in the *cordillera* all the way from Arica to the Straits of Magellan, albeit in increasingly small numbers; the puma is understandably shy of humans, and is rarely spotted. There are several species of fox, particularly in the mountains, and the Central Valley is also a haven for spiders, including dangerous **arañas de rincón** and tarantulas.

Further south, in the lush forests of the Lake District and down towards the Carreterra Austral, two of the most interesting creatures are the **huemul** and the **pudú**. Both are species of deer. The huemul's northernmost group is found around Chillán; it is a medium-sized stocky creature, well adapted for the rigours of life in the mountains. The pudú is an extraordinary creature, a deer just 40 centimetres high, very shy and extremely difficult to spot, although it can sometimes be seen in the more remote parts of Chiloé and the Carreterra Austral (see box page 426).

The **Parque Nacional Torres del Paine** is a haven for wildlife, sheltering guanacos, condors, pumas and foxes. On Isla Magdalena and Seno Otway, both near Punta Arenas, there are famous Magellanic penguin colonies, while Isla Navarino has a colony of beavers (unintentionally introduced from Canada), as well as some fantastic birdlife including petrels and even – on a good day – albatrosses.

Background Land & environment

⁝ An aristocratic tradition

The cultivation of grapes in Chile dates back almost to the Spanish conquest, the first recorded vineyard being established in 1551 in La Serena by Francisco de Aguirre. One of the major motives for early vine-growing was to supply wine for the celebration of mass. In the 18th century, the efforts of Madrid to restrict the planting of new vines in order to prevent competition with Spanish wines were largely ignored and vineyards became common on *haciendas* and villages throughout the Central Valley as far south as the Río Biobío.

Some of the most famous Chilean wines are closely associated with major names in the Chilean elite of the 19th century, among them the Errázuriz, Cousiño, Subercaseaux and Undurraga families. With the introduction of direct steamship services to Europe, the heads of

many of these families travelled to France and returned with French and German grape varieties. New cultivation techniques were also introduced from France. French experts were employed to design the cellars with double walls to prevent temperature fluctuations; some of them can be visited today. The largest and most famous of these vineyards were situated just south of Santiago in the floodplains of the Ríos Pirque and Maipo, which were adapted for commercial agriculture by the building of a network of canals.

Defended by natural frontiers, the Pacific, the Andes and the Atacama Desert, Chile also benefited by being one of the very few wine-growing areas in the world not to suffer the devastation of the phylloxera louse, which destroyed the vineyards of Europe after 1863.

Wine

Chile is a major producer and exporter of fine wines. The fine wine-producing area stretches from the valley of the Río Aconcagua in the north to the Maule Valley in the south. Grapes are also produced outside this area, notably around Ovalle and in the Elqui Valley near La Serena, which is the main production centre for *pisco*, a clear distilled spirit commonly drunk with lemon as *pisco sour* (see box, page 55), although the distillery that many hold to be the best is Alto del Carmén, in the upper reaches of the Huasco Valley.

The great majority of Chilean wines come from the Central Valley. The hot, dry summers guarantee exceptionally healthy fruit. Chilean wine is famous for being free from diseases such as downy mildew and phylloxera. As a result, growers are spared the costs of spraying and of grafting young vines onto phylloxera-resistant rootstocks.

There are eight denominated wine-growing regions, based around the valleys of the Ríos Limarí, Aconcagua, Casablanca, Maipo, Cachapoal, Colchagua, Curicó, Maule and Biobío. The heartland of Chilean red wine production is the Maipo Valley, just south of Santiago, which is home to many of the most prestigious names in Chilean wine. Although the Maipo produces far less wine than the regions to the south, it is considered by many experts to produce the best wines in Chile as a result

● ‍'120' one of Chile's most popular wines, commemorates the 120 patriot soldiers who hid in
● the Santa Rita cellars in 1814 after their defeat at Rancagua. 'Castillero del Diablo'
meanwhile was a favourite of the founder of Concho y Toro company, who kept intruders
away from this cellar by spreading the rumour it was haunted by the devil.

of the lime content of its soils. For visits to vineyards in this area, see page 111. In recent years the Casablanca Valley has emerged as a fine producer of Chardonnay and crisp Sauvignon blancs, while the recent rediscovery of the lost Carmenere grape is helping to give Chilean wine its own identity.

The main harvest period begins at the end of February, for early maturing varieties such as Chardonnay, and runs through to the end of April for Cabernet Sauvignon, although there are regional variations. Harvest celebrations are often accompanied by two drinks: *chicha*, a partly fermented grape juice, and *vino pipeño*, an unfiltered young wine which contains residue from the grapes and dried yeast.

Although the vine was introduced to Chile in the mid-16th century by the Spanish, the greatest influence on Chilean vineyards and wine making has been exerted by the French. In the 1830s, one prominent Frenchman, Claudio Gay, persuaded the Chilean government to establish the *Quinta Normal* in Santiago as a nursery for exotic botanical specimens including vines. In the 1970s domestic consumption of wine dropped and wine prices fell, leading to the destruction of many vineyards. In the last two decades, however, large-scale investment, much of it from the United States and Europe has led to increases in wine production, increasingly of quality wines destined for export. Chilean wines are now widely available around the world; they are also very popular within Latin America.

Chileans are justly proud and are increasingly becoming connoisseurs of their wines. More and more top-end wines are sold on the domestic market each year. However, there remains a marked distinction between these fine wines and wines sold in tetrapacks and grown exclusively for mass domestic consumption. The most commonly planted grape variety is stlii the dark-skinned *Pais*, found only in Chile, and thought to be a direct descendant of cuttings imported by Spanish colonists. Although Chilean wines, especially those produced for export, are typically very clean and fruity, they have only recently developed a full-bodied structure. Most export wines are red Cabernet Sauvignon, Merlot and Carmenere and white Chardonnay and Sauvignon Blanc.

Four large companies now account for 80% of all the wine sold inside Chile: Concha y Toro, Santa Rita, San Pedro and Santa Carolina. There are perhaps a hundred other smaller producers, many of which concentrate on the export market.

Books

Travelogues

Beckett, Andy, *Pinochet in Piccadilly* (2002), Faber. Part travelogue, part reprise of almost two centuries of relations between England and Chile, seen through the prism of the Pinochet affair. A handful of factual errors aside, one of the best books by an English writer on Chile for a long time – highly recommended.

Chatwin, Bruce, *In Patagonia* (1977), Pan. A modern classic for those visiting the far south, although it concentrates mainly on Argentina.

Cooper, Marc, *Pinochet and Me* (2001), Verso. Fascinating account of the 1973 coup by Salvador Allende's English translator, intermingled with his account of Chile today and the coup's legacy.

Darwin, Charles, *The Voyage of the Beagle* (1989), Penguin. Still fascinating reading of the great naturalist's voyage and adventures from Cape Horn to Copiapó in the 1830s.

Giménez Hutton, Adrian, *La Patagonia de Chatwin* (1999), Editorial Sudamericana. Interesting Argentine perspective on Chatwin and Patagonia (both Argentine and Chilean).

Green, Toby, *Saddled with Darwin* (2000), Phoenix House. A former author of this book retraces Darwin's route in South America on horseback.

Keenan, Brian and McCarthy, John, *Between Extremes* (2000), Black Swan. The two friends from Lebanon travel together again, this time through Chile.

Lucas Bridges, E, *Uttermost Part of the Earth* (1948), Hodder & Stoughton. Brilliant and beautiful account of his adventurous life in Tierra del Fuego with the Yámana and Ona peoples; the classic text on Tierra del Fuego.

Pilkington, John, *An Englishman In Patagonia* (1991), Century. Heavily critical of Chatwin.

Reding, Nick, *The last cowboys at the end of the world* (2001), Random House. Quirky yet evocative and highly readable account of the lives of the dying breed of Gauchos in central Patagonia.

Souhami, Diana, *Selkirk's Island* (2001), Weidenfeld & Nicolson. The extraordinary story of Alexander Selkirk and his island, inspirations for Robinson Crusoe and for the community of San Juan Bautista on modern-day Isla Robinson Crusoe. A prize-winning account.

Swale, Rosie, *Back to Cape Horn* (1988), Fontana. Swale tells of her epic journey from Antofagasta to Cape Horn on horseback.

Wheeler, Sara, *Travels in a Thin Country* (1994), Little, Brown & Co. Popular account of the author's 6-month stay in Chile.

Fiction and poetry

Allende, Isabel, the doyenne of modern Chilean letters. Her books include: *The House of the Spirits* (1994), Black Swan. Brilliant, evocative, allegorical magical-realist account taking the reader through 20th-century Chilean history. *Of Love and Shadows* (1988), Black Swan. Painful story about a journalist uncovering evidence of military atrocities under the military regime. *Paula* (1996), Flamingo. A beautiful 'letter' written from Allende to her daughter, who is stuck in a coma after a car accident, taking in the modern history of Chile and Allende's emotional roots. More recent books include *Daughter of Fortune* (2000), Flamingo, and *Portrait in Sepia* (2002), Flamingo, both of which are lyrical prequels to the story that made Allende's name: *The House of the Spirits*.

Bolaño, Roberto, *By Night in Chile* (2003), Harvill. A caustic, brilliant novel, as an ageing Chilean priest lives through the last night of his life, and recalls teaching Marxism to General Pinochet and various surreal encounters with the Chilean literary establishment – thereby exposing the complicity of so many in the 'normality' that accompanied the military government. If you read one novel about Chile, make sure it's this one.

Donoso, José, *The Garden Next Door* (1994), Grove Press. Evocative novel that deals with the ageing process of a couple in Spain. *The Obscene Bird of the Night* (1995), Grove Press. Donoso's most famous, experimental novel, which gained him international acclaim across Latin America.

Dorfman, Ariel, *Death and the Maiden* (1996), Nick Hern Books (also in the collected volume *The Resistance Trilogy*; 1998). Subtle, moving tale of torture and resistance, an allegory for the state of Chile. *The Nanny and the Iceberg* (1999), Sceptre. Cross-cultural story of Chile and North America told with Dorfman's usual eloquence.

Neruda, Pablo, *Selected Poems* (trans/ed Ben Bellit (1961), New York Grove Press. Bilingual anthology of the master's work.

Richards, Ben, *The Mermaid and the Drunks* (2003), Weidenfeld & Nicolson. A recent English novel set in Chile, which gives an entertaining picture of modern Chile from the perspective of a longtime friend of the country.

Skármeta, Antonio, *Il Postino* ('The Postman', 1996), Bloomsbury. Beautiful novel about the relationship between Neruda and his postman while the poet is in exile in Italy, made into a famous film. *Watch Where the Wolf is Going* (1991), Readers' International. Another novel in Skármeta's trademark style of eloquence and emotional honesty.

Adventure sports

Biggar, John, *The High Andes* (1996), Castle Douglas, Kirkudbrightshire. Andes contains three chapters with information on Chilean peaks.

CONAF, *Guía de Parques Nacionales y Otras Areas Silvestres Protegidas de Chile*, US$12, a very useful guide to the main parks, with information on access, campsites, flora and fauna. It also publishes *Chile Forestal*, a monthly magazine with articles on the parks and ecological issues.

Fagerstrom, René Peri, *Cuentos de la Carretera Austral*, on the Camino Austral. *Regata*, a monthly sailing magazine. Climbers will also find *Cumbres de Chile* of interest: two books with accompanying tapes, each covering 20 peaks.

Mantellero, Alberto, *Una Aventura Navegando Los Canales del Sur de Chile*, a guide to sailing the southern coast, with maps.

Reference and background

Almarza V, Claudio, *Patagonia* (Punta Arenas: GeoPatagonia). A book of photographs, with text, on the region.

Araya, B and Millie, G, *Guía de Campo de Las Aves de Chile*. Bird-lovers will appreciate this guide to Chile's feathered population.

Bahn, Paul and Flenley, John, *Easter Island, Earth Island* (1992), Thames and Hudson. A comprehensive appraisal of Easter Island's archaeology.

Cárdenas Saldivia, Umiliana, *Casos de Brujos de Chiloé* (1989), Editorial Universitaria. Fascinating tales of witchcraft on Chiloé.

Castillo, Juan Carlos (ed) *Islas Oceánicas Chilenas* (1987), Ediciones Universidad Católica de Chile. Much information on the natural history and geography of Juan Fernández and Easter Islands.

Clissold, Stephen, *Chilean Scrapbook* (1952), The Cresset Press. Gives an evocative historical picture of Chile, region by region.

Collier, S and Sater, WF, *A History of Chile 1808-2002* (2004), Cambridge University Press. The definitive single volume history of Chile in English.

Coña, Pascal, *Memorias de un Cacique Mapuche* (1930), publisher unmarked. An account of Mapuche traditions and history by a Mapuche chief in his 70s.

Constable, Pamela and Valenzuela, Arturo, *Chile: A Nation of Enemies* (1991), Norton. Excellent and readable take on the Pinochet years.

Dinges, John, *The Condor Years* (2004), The New Press. Thorough examination of the Condor anti-leftist terrorist operation set up by South American dictators including Pinochet.

Dorfman, Ariel, *Unending Terror: The Incredible Unending Trial of General Augusto Pinochet* (2003), Pluto Press. A gripping account of the Pinochet affair from one of the most perceptive living writers on Chile. His memoir *Heading North, Looking South* (1998) is also essential reading.

Goni, Uki, *The Real Odessa: How Perón Brought the Nazi War Criminals to Argentina* (2002), Granta. Although based on the Argentine hiding of Nazi war criminals, this book has a continent-wide significance, as it reveals how this movement shaped the fascist attitudes of military governments of the 1970s.

Haslam, Jonathan, *The Nixon Administration and the Death of Allende's Chile* (2005), Verso. This book examines the involvement of Nixon and the CIA in the 1973 coup.

Hazlewood, Nick, *Savage: The Life and Times of Jemmy Button* (2001), Sceptre. Interesting if hyperbolic history of Jemmy's tale.

Heyerdahl, Thor, *Aku-Aku, The Art of Easter Island* (1975), New York: Doubleday.

Kornbluh, Peter, *The Pinochet File* (2003), The New Press. Declassified CIA documents together with editorial explanations relating to US government involvement and collusion in the 1973 coup.

Montecino, Sonia, *Historias de Vida de Mujeres Mapuches* (1985), Centro de Estudios de la Mujer. Interviews with Mapuche women giving a real insight into their lives.

O'Shaughnessy, Hugh, *Pinochet: The Politics of Torture* (2000), Latin American Bureau. Informed and up-to-date analysis of the whole Pinochet affair.

Porteous, J Douglas, *The Modernization of Easter Island* (1981), Department of Geography, University of Victoria, BC, Canada. A very thorough illustrated book.

Read, Jan, *The Wines of Chile* (1994), Mitchell Beazley. A gazetteer of the vineyards and wineries of Chile, ideal for the discerning specialist.

Rector, John, *TheHistory of Chile* (2005), Palgrave MacMillan. A readable general history of Chile.

South American Explorers Club, *The South American Explorer* (126 Indian Creek Road, Ithaca, New York 14850, USA). This journal regularly publishes articles on Chile including Easter Island.

Spooner, MH, *Soldiers In A Narrow Land* (1994), University of California Press. A readable account of the Pinochet dictatorship by a North American journalist resident in the country at the time.

Wearne, Philip, *Return of the Indian: Conquest and Revival in the Americas* (1996), Cassell/Latin America Bureau. Information on the Mapuche within the entire Amerindian context.

Maps and guidebooks

The **Turistel** guide, **Turiscom**, *Av Santa María 0120, Providencia, Santiago, T02-3658800, turiscom@chilesat.net* is very useful for roads and town plans, but not all distances are exact. It is published annually in three parts, *Norte, Centro*, and *Sur* (in Spanish only), alongside a separate volume listing campsites. It contains a wealth of maps covering the whole country and neighbouring tourist centres in Argentina, and is well worth getting, particularly for those with their own transport. Each volume costs around US$10, but buying the whole set is better value. Available from bookshops and from newspaper kiosks in the centre of Santiago or directly from the publisher.

Sernatur publishes a free *Guía Turística/ Tourist Guide* in Spanish and English, with good maps, useful text, while **CONAF** publishes a series of illustrated booklets in Spanish/English on Chilean trees, shrubs and flowers, as well as *Juventud, Turismo y Naturaleza*, which lists national parks, their facilities and the flora and fauna of each.

A recommended series of general maps are published by **International Travel Maps** (ITM), *345 West Broadway, Vancouver, V5Y 1P8, Canada, T604-8793621*, compiled with historical notes, by Kevin Healey.

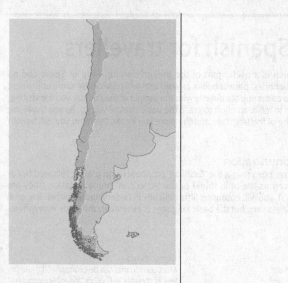

Basic Spanish for travellers

Learning Spanish is a useful part of the preparation for a trip to Spain and no volumes of dictionaries, phrase books or word lists will provide the same enjoyment as being able to communicate directly with the people of the country you are visiting. It is a good idea to make an effort to grasp the basics before you go. As you travel you will pick up more of the language and the more you know, the more you will benefit from your stay.

General pronunciation

Whether you have been taught the 'Castilian' pronunciation (*z* and *c* followed by *i* or *e* are pronounced as the *th* in think) or the 'American' pronunciation (they are pronounced as *s*), you will encounter little difficulty in understanding either. Regional accents and usages vary, but the basic language is essentially the same everywhere.

Vowels

a	as in English *cat*
e	as in English *best*
i	as the *ee* in English *feet*
o	as in English *shop*
u	as the *oo* in English *food*
ai	as the *i* in English *ride*
ei	as *ey* in English *they*
oi	as *oy* in English *toy*

Consonants

Most consonants can be pronounced more or less as they are in English. The exceptions are:

	before *e* or *i* is the same as *j*
h	is always silent (except in *ch* as in *chair*)
j	as the *ch* in Scottish *loch*
ll	as the *y* in *yellow*
ñ	as the *ni* in English *onion*
rr	trilled much more than in English
x	depending on its location, pronounced *x, s, sh* or *j*

Spanish words and phrases

Greetings, courtesies

hello	*hola*
good morning	*buenos días*
good afternoon/evening/night	*buenas tardes/noches*
goodbye	*adiós/chao*
pleased to meet you	*mucho gusto*
see you later	*hasta luego*
how are you?	*¿cómo está?¿cómo estás?*
I'm fine, thanks	*estoy muy bien, gracias*
I'm called...	*me llamo...*
what is your name?	*¿cómo se llama? ¿cómo te llamas?*
yes/no	*sí/no*
please	*por favor*
thank you (very much)	*(muchas) gracias*
I speak Spanish	*hablo español*
I don't speak Spanish	*no hablo español*
do you speak English?	*¿habla inglés?*
I don't understand	*no entiendo/no comprendo*
please speak slowly	*hable despacio por favor*
I am very sorry	*lo siento mucho/disculpe*
what do you want?	*¿qué quiere? ¿qué quieres?*
I want	*quiero*
I don't want it	*no lo quiero*
leave me alone	*déjeme en paz/no me moleste*
good/bad	*bueno/malo*

Basic questions and requests

have you got a room for two people?	*¿tiene una habitación para dos personas?*
how do I get to_?	*¿cómo llego a_?*
how much does it cost?	*¿cuánto vale? ¿cuánto es?*
I'd like to make a long-distance phone call	*quisiera hacer una llamada de larga distancia*
is service included?	*¿está incluido el servicio?*
is tax included?	*¿están incluidos los impuestos?*
when does the bus leave (arrive)?	*¿a qué hora sale (llega) el autobús?*
when?	*¿cuándo?*
where is_?	*¿dónde está_?*
where can I buy tickets?	*¿dónde puedo comprar boletos?*
where is the nearest petrol station?	*¿dónde está la bomba de bencina más cercana?*
why?	*¿por qué? ¿para qué?*

Basic words and phrases

bank	*el banco*
bathroom/toilet	*el baño*
to be	*ser, estar*
bill	*la cuenta*
cash	*el efectivo*
cheap	*barato/a*
credit card	*la tarjeta de crédito*
exchange house	*la casa de cambio*
exchange rate	*el tipo de cambio*
expensive	*caro/a*
to go	*ir*
to have	*tener, haber*
market	*el mercado/la feria*
note/coin	*el billete/la moneda*
police (policeman)	*la policía/los carabineros*
post office	*el correo*
public telephone	*el teléfono público*
shop	*la tienda*
supermarket	*el supermercado*
there is/are	*hay*
there isn't/aren't	*no hay*
ticket office	*la boletería*
traveller's cheques	*los cheques de viajero/los travelers*

Getting around

aeroplane	*el avión*
airport	*el aeropuerto*
arrival/departure	*la llegada/salida*
avenue	*la avenida*
block	*la cuadra*
border	*la frontera*
bus station	*la terminal de buses*
bus	*el bus/el autobús/el camión*
collective/fixed-route taxi	*el colectivo*
corner	*la esquina*
customs	*la aduana*
diesel	*el petróleo*
left/right	*izquierda/derecha*
ticket	*el boleto*
empty/full	*vacío/lleno*
highway, main road	*la carretera*
immigration	*la inmigración*
insurance	*el seguro*
insured person	*el asegurado/la asegurada*

to insure yourself against	*asegurarse contra*
luggage	*el equipaje*
motorway, freeway	*el autopista/la carretera*
north, south, west, east	*el norte, el sur, el oeste (poniente), el este (oriente)*
oil	*el aceite*
to park	*estacionarse*
passport	*el pasaporte*
petrol/gasoline	*la bencina/la gasolina*
puncture	*el pinchazo/la ponchadura*
street	*la calle*
that way	*por allí/por allá*
this way	*por aquí/por acá*
ticket	*el boleto/pasaje*
tourist card/visa	*la tarjeta de turista/visa*
tyre	*el neumático/la llanta*
waiting room	*la sala de espera*
to walk	*caminar/andar*

Accommodation

air conditioning	*el aire acondicionado*
all-inclusive	*todo incluido*
bathroom, private	*el baño privado*
bed, double/single	*la cama matrimonial/sencilla*
blankets	*las frazadas*
to clean	*limpiar*
dining room	*el comedor*
guesthouse	*la casa de huéspedes*
hotel	*el hotel*
noisy	*ruidoso*
pillows	*las almohadas*
power cut	*el apagón/corte*
restaurant	*el restaurante*
room/bedroom	*el cuarto/la habitación*
sheets	*las sábanas*
shower	*la ducha/regadera*
soap	*el jabón*
toilet	*el baño/sanitario/excusado*
toilet paper	*el papel higiénico*
towels, clean/dirty	*las toallas limpias/sucias*
water, hot/cold	*el agua caliente/fría*

Health

altitude sickness	*el saroche/la puna*
aspirin	*la aspirina*
blood	*la sangre*
chemist	*la farmacia*
condoms	*los preservativos, los condones*
contact lenses	*los lentes de contacto*
contraceptives	*los anticonceptivos*
contraceptive pill	*la píldora anticonceptiva*
diarrhoea	*la diarrea*
doctor	*el médico*
fever/sweat	*la fiebre/el sudor*
pain	*el dolor*
head	*la cabeza*
period/sanitary towels	*la regla/las toallas femeninas*
stomach	*el estómago*
altitude sickness	*el soroche*

Family

family	*la familia*
brother/sister	*el hermano/la hermana*
daughter/son	*la hija/el hijo*
father/mother	*el padre/la madre*
husband/wife	*el esposo (marido)/la esposa*
boyfriend/girlfriend	*el novio/la novia*
friend	*el amigo/la amiga*
married	*casado/a*
single/unmarried	*soltero/a*

Months, days and time

January	*enero*
February	*febrero*
March	*marzo*
April	*abril*
May	*mayo*
June	*junio*
July	*julio*
August	*agosto*
September	*septiembre*
October	*octubre*
November	*noviembre*
December	*diciembre*
Monday	*lunes*
Tuesday	*martes*
Wednesday	*miércoles*
Thursday	*jueves*
Friday	*viernes*
Saturday	*sábado*
Sunday	*domingo*
at one o'clock	*a la una*
at half past two	*a las dos y media*
at a quarter to three	*a cuarto para las tres/a las tres menos quince*
it's one o'clock	*es la una*
it's seven o'clock	*son las siete*
it's six twenty	*son las seis y veinte*
it's five to nine	*son cinco para las nueve/las nueve menos cinco*
in ten minutes	*en diez minutos*
five hours	*cinco horas*
does it take long?	*¿tarda mucho?*

Numbers

one	*uno/una*
two	*dos*
three	*tres*
four	*cuatro*
five	*cinco*
six	*seis*
seven	*siete*
eight	*ocho*
nine	*nueve*
ten	*diez*
eleven	*once*
twelve	*doce*
thirteen	*trece*
fourteen	*catorce*

fifteen	*quince*
sixteen	*dieciséis*
seventeen	*diecisiete*
eighteen	*dieciocho*
nineteen	*diecinueve*
twenty	*veinte*
twenty-one	*veintiuno*
thirty	*treinta*
forty	*cuarenta*
fifty	*cincuenta*
sixty	*sesenta*
seventy	*setenta*
eighty	*ochenta*
ninety	*noventa*
hundred	*cien/ciento*
thousand	*mil*

Food

avocado	*la palta*
baked	*al horno*
bakery	*la panadería*
banana	*el plátano*
beans	*los porotos*
beef	*la carne de res*
beef steak or pork fillet	*el lomo*
boiled rice	*el arroz blanco*
bread	*el pan*
breakfast	*el desayuno*
butter	*la mantequilla*
cake	*el pastel*
chewing gum	*el chicle*
chicken	*el pollo*
chilli pepper or green pepper	*el ají/el chile/el pimiento*
clear soup, stock	*el caldo*
cooked	*cocido*
dining room	*el comedor*
egg	*el huevo*
fish	*el pescado*
fork	*el tenedor*
fried	*frito*
garlic	*el ajo*
goat	*el chivo*
grapefruit	*la toronja/el pomelo*
grill	*la parrilla*
guava	*la guayaba*
ham	*el jamón*
hamburger	*la hamburguesa*
hot, spicy	*picante*
ice cream	*el helado*
jam	*la mermelada*
knife	*el cuchillo*
lime	*el limón*
lobster	*la langosta*
lunch	*el almuerzo/la comida*
meal	*la comida*
meat	*la carne*
minced meat	*la carne molida*
onion	*la cebolla*
orange	*la naranja*

pasty, turnover	*la empanada/el pastelito*
pork	*el cerdo*
potato	*la papa*
prawns	*los camarones*
raw	*crudo*
restaurant	*el restaurante*
salad	*la ensalada*
salt	*la sal*
sandwich	*el bocadillo/el sandwich*
sauce	*la salsa*
sausage	*la longaniza/el chorizo*
scrambled eggs	*los huevos revueltos*
seafood	*los mariscos*
soup	*la sopa*
spoon	*la cuchara*
squash	*la calabaza*
squid	*los calamares*
supper	*la cena*
sweet	*dulce*
to eat	*comer*
toasted	*tostado*
turkey	*el pavo*
vegetables	*los legumbres/vegetales*
without meat	*sin carne*
yam	*el camote*

Drink

beer	*la cerveza*
boiled	*hervido/a*
bottled	*en botella*
camomile tea	*té de manzanilla*
canned	*en lata*
coffee	*el café*
coffee, white	*el café con leche*
cold	*frío*
cup	*la taza*
drink	*la bebida*
drunk	*borracho/a*
firewater	*el aguardiente*
fruit milkshake	*el batido/licuado*
glass	*el vaso*
hot	*caliente*
ice/without ice	*el hielo/sin hielo*
juice	*el jugo*
lemonade	*la limonada*
milk	*la leche*
mint	*la menta/la hierbabuena*
rum	*el ron*
soft drink	*el refresco/la bebida*
sugar	*el azúcar*
tea	*el té*
to drink	*beber/tomar*
water	*el agua*
water, carbonated	*el agua mineral con gas*
water, still mineral	*el agua mineral sin gas*
wine, red	*el vino tinto*
wine, white	*el vino blanco*

Glossary

adobe a sun-dried mixture of silt and clay used as a building material in the country

alfajores flaky biscuits filled with *manjar* (caramelised condensed milk)

almuerzo lunch

altiplano the high plateau found in the northern Andes

cabaña chalet, usually rented out to families in the south and on the coast

cama bed

carabineros police

cerro hill

chicha type of homemade fermented drink, usually made of apples (in the south) or grapes (in the north)

Copec National Petrol Company

Codeff national body campaigning to protect flora and fauna

colectivo a collective taxi

comedor dining room

CONAF national body overseeing the running and administration of Chile's national parks and reserves

congrio not to be confused with conger eel (although Iberian Spanish uses *congrio* in this way). It is, in fact, a type of ling

cordillera mountain range

costanera waterfront

cuadra block (in a city)

curanto stew from Chiloé with shellfish, pork and potatoes

estancia sheep farm in the far south

fundo old-style farm in the Central Valley

huasos Chilean cowboys

humitas crushed corn paste stuffed into corn leaves, often sweetened

kuchen cakes in German style (usually found in the south)

pampa flat, desert or semi-desert landscape (found in the Atacama and also in Patagonia)

pebre spicy chilli and tomato sauce found in any restaurant worthy of the name as a relish

peñas restaurant or bar with live folkloric performances

pudú small indigenous deer, very rare, found in the southern Andes

restaurant bailable restaurant with live music and dancing. Sometimes it is necessary to pay a cover to enter.

seno gulf, inlet

s/n (*sin número*) 'without number', to denote that a place is on a particular street, but with no street number

Sernatur National Tourist Board, usually very helpful

tábanos horseflies (found in the south)

Index

Map index

Map symbols

Administration

☐ Capital city
○ Other city, town
⌇ International border
⌇ Regional border
⌇ Disputed border

Roads and travel

═══ Motorway
─── Main road (National highway)
─── Unpaved or *ripio* (gravel) road
- - - - Track
······· Footpath
⊶▪ Railway with station
✈ Airport
🚍 Bus station
Ⓜ Metro station
- - - - Cable car
╫╫╫╫ Funicular
⛴ Ferry

Water features

≋ River, canal
⬭ Lake, ocean
᭐ Seasonal marshland
▦ Beach, sandbank
⣿ Waterfall
⌇ Reef

Topographical features

⬭ Contours (approx)
▲ Mountain, volcano
⇋ Mountain pass
᠁ Escarpment
▨ Gorge
▨ Glacier
▨ Salt flat
⚬ Rocks

Cities and towns

═══ Main through route
═══ Main street

Minor street
━━━ Minor street
╤╤╤ Pedestrianized street
Ƹ Ɛ Tunnel
→ One way-street
▥▥▥ Steps
≕ Bridge
▬▬ Fortified wall
▦ Park, garden, stadium
● Sleeping
❷ Eating
❶ Bars & clubs
▬ Building
▪ Sight
✝✝ Cathedral, church
🏮 Chinese temple
卐 Hindu temple
⚘ Meru
🕌 Mosque
△ Stupa
✡ Synagogue
ℹ Tourist office
🏛 Museum
✉ Post office
Ⓟ Police
Ⓢ Bank
@ Internet
♪ Telephone
🏪 Market
✚ Medical services
Ⓟ Parking
⚑ Petrol
⛳ Golf
Ⓐ Detail map
◁Ⓐ Related map

Other symbols

∴ Archaeological site
♦ National park, wildlife reserve
✹ Viewing point
⋀ Campsite
⌂ Refuge, lodge
🏰 Castle, fort
🤿 Diving
🌲🌴 Deciduous, coniferous, palm trees
⌂ Hide
🍇 Vineyard
⚗ Distillery
⛵ Shipwreck
⨯ Historic battlefield

Major domestic air routes

Advertisers' index

Credits

Footprint credits

Editor: Stephanie Lambe
Map editor: Sarah Sorensen

Publisher: Patrick Dawson
Editorial: Sophie Blacksell, Alan Murphy, Felicity Laughton, Nicola Gibbs, Angus Dawson
Cartography: Robert Lunn, Kevin Feeney
Series development: Rachel Fielding
Design: Mytton Williams and Rosemary Dawson (brand)
Sales and marketing: Andy Riddle, Vassia Efstathiou
Advertising: Debbie Wylde
Finance and administration: Elizabeth Taylor

Photography credits

Front cover:
Alamy (Atacama Desert)
Back cover:
Alamy (fish market at Valparaíso)
Inside colour section:
Alamy, Jamie Marshall, Rick Senley, South American Pictures, Superstock, Wines of Chile

Print

Manufactured in Italy by LegoPrint
Pulp from sustainable forests

Footprint feedback

We try as hard as we can to make each Footprint guide as up to date as possible but, of course, things always change. If you want to let us know about your experiences – good, bad or ugly – then don't delay, go to www.footprintbooks.com and send in your comments.

Publishing information

Footprint Chile
5th edition
© Footprint Handbooks Ltd
November 2006

ISBN 1 904777 73 2
CIP DATA: A catalogue record for this book is available from the British Library

® Footprint Handbooks and the Footprint mark are a registered trademark of Footprint Handbooks Ltd

Published by Footprint

6 Riverside Court
Lower Bristol Road
Bath BA2 3DZ, UK
T +44 (0)1225 469141
F +44 (0)1225 469461
discover@footprintbooks.com
www.footprintbooks.com

Distributed in the USA by
Publishers Group West

Neither the black and white nor coloured maps are intended to have any political significance.

Every effort has been made to ensure that the facts in this guidebook are accurate. However, travellers should still obtain advice from consulates, airlines etc about travel and visa requirements before travelling. The authors and publishers cannot accept responsibility for any loss, injury or inconvenience however caused.

About the author

Janak Jani was born in London and spent part of his childhood in France and East Africa, before going on to read Philosophy at Cambridge. He lived, worked and travelled in over 20 countries in four continents until, enchanted by the magic of Valparaíso, he decided to settle down. He now owns and runs a guesthouse there with his wife, Lorena.

Acknowledgements

Many people have helped in making this book as precise and relevant as possible. Wholehearted thanks go to all the regional SERNATUR offices from Iquique to Punta Arenas as well as to the CONAF and municipal tourist offices who gave their time, expertise and local knowledge to ensure that information on their area was thorough and complete.

Special thanks go to the following for providing help and information:
Mariela Lara and family for their kind hospitality in Arica; Orlando for his good company and for seeing me through a bad bout of altitude sickness in the altiplano; Martin and Co in San Pedro; Sergio in Chañaral; the old copper miner in the Copiapó Valley; Patricio Valenzuela for much-needed help in Santiago; Ben Box, editor of the *South American Handbook*, for help and advice; Toby Green for all his work on previous editions; Cristabelle Dilks and Nicolás Kugler for updating the Tierrra del Fuego section; Stephanie Lambe, Sarah Sorensen, Felicity Laughton and everyone at Footprint for working tirelessly and to a very tight schedule on the production of this book and to the countless readers whose letters have helped to make this guide as up-to-date as possible.

The Health section was written by Professor Larry Goodyer Head of the Leicester School of Pharmacy and director of Nomad Medical.

Finally thanks to Juan Carlos, Christelle, Angela, Gustavo and Rubén for holding the fort at Luna Sonrisa during my travels and to my wonderful wife Lorena for all her help and support.

Bibliography

Sources for the section on Arts and Crafts are: Artesanía tradicional de Chile, Serie El Patrimonio Cultural Chileno, Ministerio de Educación, 1978; 'Visión estética de la cerámica de Quinchamalí', by Luis Guzmán Molina, Atenea, No 458 (Universidad de Concepción, 1988), pages 47-60; Mapudungun, lengua y costumbres Mapuches, by Orietta Appelt Martín (Temuco: Magin, 1995); Arts and Crafts of South America, by Lucy Davies and Mo Fini (Bath: Tumi, 1994). Tumi, a Latin American Craft Centre in Britain, specializes in Mexican and Andean products and produces cultural and educational videos for schools: at 23/24 Chalk Farm Road, London NW1 8AG, 8/9 New Bond Street Place, Bath BA1 1BH, 1/2 Little Clarendon Street, Oxford OX1 2HJ, 82 Park Street, Bristol BS1 5LA.

A great many sources have been consulted in the preparation of the section on Literature. Apart from those already mentioned, reference is made to: Cedomil Goic, La novela chilena. Los mitos degradados (Santiago: Universitaria, 1991); Kenneth Fleak, The Chilean Short Story. Writers from the Generation of 1950 (New York: Peter Lang, 1989); René Jara, El revés de la arpillera, perfil literario de Chile (Madrid: Hiperión, 1988); Jean Franco, Spanish American Literature since Independence (London: Ernest Benn, 1973); Eugenia Brito, Campos minados. Literatura post-golpe en Chile (Santiago: Mujeres Cuarto Propio, 1990); Poesía chilena de hoy. De Parra a nuestros días, selected by Erwin Díaz (Santiago: Ediciones Documentas, 1989); Lautaro Silva, Vida y obra de Gabriela Mistral (Buenos Aires: Andina, 1967); Gordon Brotherston, The Emergence of the Latin American Novel (1977) and Latin American Poetry. Origins and Presence (Cambridge University Press, 1975); Darío Villanueva y José María Viña Liste, Trayectoria de la novela hispanoamericano actual (Madrid: Austral, 1991); Jason Wilson, Traveller's Literary Companion: South and Central America (Brighton: In Print, 1993); Gerald Martin, Journeys through the Labyrinth (London: Verso, 1989); Poesía Chilena Para el Siglo XXI (Dirección de Bibliotécas, Archivos y Museos, 1996). A key text for English readers is Steven White's Poets of Chile (Unicorn Press, 1986).

Footnotes Bibliography

Complete title listing

Footprint publishes travel guides to over 150 destinations worldwide. Each guide is packed with practical, concise and colourful information for everybody from first-time travellers to travel aficionados. The list is growing fast and current titles are noted below. Available from all good bookshops and online Www.footprintbooks.com

(P) denotes pocket guide

Latin America & Caribbean
Antigua & Leeward Islands (P)
Argentina
Barbados (P)
Discover Belize, Guatemala & Southern Mexico
Discover Patagonia
Discover Peru, Bolivia & Ecuador
Bolivia
Brazil
Caribbean Islands
Mexico & Central America
Chile
Colombia
Costa Rica
Cuba
Cuzco & the Inca heartland
Dominican Republic (P)
Ecuador & Galápagos
Havana (P)
Jamaica (P)
Nicaragua
Peru
Rio de Janeiro (P)
St Lucia (P)
South American Handbook
Venezuela

North America
Discover Western Canada
New York (P)
Vancouver (P)

Africa
Cape Town (P)
East Africa
Egypt
Kenya
Libya
Marrakech (P)
Morocco
Namibia
South Africa
Tanzania
Tunisia
Uganda

Middle East
Dubai (P)
Israel
Jordan
Syria & Lebanon

Australasia
Australia
Discover East Coast Australia
New Zealand
Sydney (P)
West Coast Australia

Asia
Bali
Bangkok & the Beaches
Bhutan
Borneo
Cambodia
Discover Vietnam, Cambodia & Laos
Goa
Hong Kong (P)
India
Indonesia
Laos
Malaysia & Singapore
Nepal
Northern Pakistan
Rajasthan
South India
Sri Lanka
Sumatra
Thailand
Tibet
Vietnam

Europe
Andalucía
Barcelona (P)
Belfast & the north of Ireland (P)
Berlin (P)
Bilbao (P)
Bologna (P)
Britain
Cardiff (P)
Copenhagen (P)

Costa de la Luz (P)
Croatia
Dublin (P)
Edinburgh (P)
England
European City Breaks
Glasgow (P)
Ireland
Lisbon (P)
London
London (P)
Madrid (P)
Naples & the Amalfi Coast (P)
Northern Spain
Paris (P)
Reykjavík (P)
Scotland
Scotland Highlands & Islands
Seville (P)
Siena & the heart of Tuscany (P)
Spain
Tallinn (P)
Turin (P)
Turkey
Valencia (P)
Verona (P)
Wales

Lifestyle guides
Diving the World
Snowboarding the World
Surfing Britain
Surfing Europe
Surfing the World
Wine Travel Guide to the World

Also available
Traveller's Handbook (WEXAS)
Traveller's Healthbook (WEXAS)
Traveller's Internet Guide (WEXAS)

What the papers say...

"I carried the South American Handbook from Cape Horn to Cartagena and consulted it every night for two and a half months. I wouldn't do that for anything else except my hip flask."
Michael Palin, BBC Full Circle

"My favourite series is the Handbook series published by Footprint and I especially recommend the Mexico, Central and South America Handbooks."
Boston Globe

"If 'the essence of real travel' is what you have been secretly yearning for all these years, then Footprint are the guides for you."
Under 26 magazine

"Who should pack Footprint—readers who want to escape the crowd."
The Observer

"Footprint can be depended on for accurate travel information and for imparting a deep sense of respect for the lands and people they cover."
World News

"The guides for intelligent, independently-minded souls of any age or budget."
Indie Traveller

Mail order
Available worldwide in bookshops and on-line. Footprint travel guides can also be ordered directly from us in Bath, via our website www.footprintbooks.com or from the address on the imprint page of this book.

Check out...

WWW...

100 travel guides, 100s of destinations,
5 continents and 1 Footprint...
www.footprintbooks.com

The Footprint story

It was 1921
Ireland had just been partitioned, the British miners were striking for more pay and the federation of British industry had an idea. Exports were booming in South America – how about a Handbook for businessmen trading in that far away continent? The *Anglo-South American Handbook* was born that year, written by W Koebel, the most prolific writer on Latin America of his day.

1924
Two editions later the book was 'privatised' and in 1924, in the hands of Royal Mail, the steamship company for South America, became the *South American Handbook*, subtitled 'South America in a nutshell'. This annual publication became the 'bible' for generations of travellers to South America and remains so to this day. In the early days travel was by sea and the Handbook gave all the details needed for the long voyage from Europe. What to wear for dinner; how to arrange a cricket match with the Cable & Wireless staff on the Cape Verde Islands and a full account of the journey from Liverpool up the Amazon to Manaus: 5898 miles without changing cabin!

1939
As the continent opened up, the *South American Handbook* reported the new Pan Am flying boat services, and the fortnightly airship service from Rio to Europe on the Graf Zeppelin. For reasons still unclear but with extraordinary determination, the annual editions continued through the Second World War.

1970
From the 1970s, jet aircraft transformed travel. Many more people discovered South America and the backpacking trail started to develop. All the while the Handbook was gathering fans including literary vagabonds such as Paul Theroux and Graham Greene who once sent some updates addressed to **'The publishers of the best travel guide in the world, Bath, England'**.

1990s
During the 1990s Patrick and James Dawson, the publishers of the *South American Handbook* set about developing a new travel guide series using this legendary title as the flagship. By 1997 there were over a dozen guides in the series and the Footprint imprint was launched.

2000-2006
Footprint travel guides now cover more than 150 destinations in Latin America, the Caribbean, Africa, the Indian sub-continent, Southeast Asia, the Middle East, Australasia and Europe. In addition, Footprint has launched a series of activity and lifestyle guides focusing on diving, surfing, snowboarding and wine tourism.

The future
There are many more travel and activity guides in the pipeline. To keep up-to-date with the latest releases check out the Footprint website for publishing news and information, **www.footprintbooks.com**

Notes

Am Exp.
RA 604 . 352 . 044 $100
RA 604   357 . 043 $100

Subway → Vicente Valdes
↑ Baquedano to line 1 red
directa San Pablo get off at
Universidad de Santiago . - bus
terminal buses to Valparaiso every
15 mins.

Visit Museo La Sebastiana
        Concepcion Hill - elevator
        Cerro Alegre - elevator el rural
        Artilleria Hill
                - Pase de 21 Mayo
                - Naval Museum

        En el Plano
                a) Muelle Prat.
                b) Plaza Sotomayor
                c) Reloj Turri

    Stay Concepcion Hill
            Rec Casa Latina
                            32-249-4622
    Rest Cinzano - local bar   Papudo 46
        383 delicatessen.

020 8947 4770

594

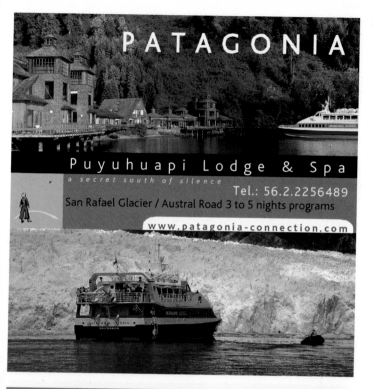

Chile

Pacific

Ocean

Islas Juan Fernández

To Rapa Nui ←

PERU ①

Iquique ○

BOLIVIA

Antofagasta ○

②

Copiapó ○

La Serena ○

③

Valparaíso ○

SANTIAGO □

Rancagua ○

Talca ○

Concepción ○   ARGENTINA

④

Temuco ○

Puerto Montt ○

⑤

Coyhaique ○

Atlantic

Ocean

⑥   ⑦

Punta
Arenas ○

N

0 km   200

0 miles   200

—— Major road

—— Unpaved or *ripio* road

—— Railway

–·–·– Ferry between Puerto Montt &
Puerto Natales (Puerto Edén)

········· Ferry between Puerto Montt &
Puerto Chacabuco/Laguna
San Rafael

–·–·– Ferry between Quellón & Chaltén

⬭ Salt plains

Altitude in metres

4000
3000
2000
1000
500
200
0

Neighbouring
country

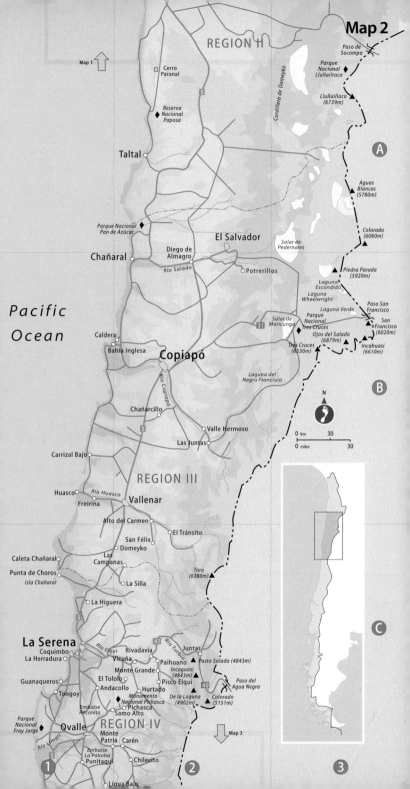

Map 3

Map 2

Punitaqui
Chilecito
Ligua Bajo
Combarbalá

REGION IV

Canela Baja
Illapel
Reserva Nacional
Las Chinchillas

Salamanca
Limpo
Los Vilos
Loma Blanca (1868m)
Morado (4114m)
Vizcachar (1969m)
Caimanes
Jorquera (3743m)
Río Quilimarí

Pichidangui
Petorca
Los Molles

La Ligua
Cabildo
Papudo
Zapallar
Cachagua
REGION V
Monumento Natural
Isla Cachagua
Maitencillo
Putaendo
Termas de Jahuel
Horcón
San Felipe
La Calera
Los Andes
Quintero
Llaillay
Portillo
Concón
Parque Nacional
La Campana
Tunnel Chacabuco
Quillota
La Campana
Viña del Mar
Limache
Valparaíso
Termas de Colina
Reserva Nacional
Lago Peñuelas
Santuar
Naturaleza
Casablanca
Lampa
Colina
La Parva
El Quisco
Algarrobo
Curacaví
Las Condes
El Co
Isla Negra
Farellones
Cartagena
Peñaflor
SANTIAGO
San Antonio
Pomaire
Puente
Lagun
Rocas de
Santo Domingo
Llolleo
Bajo
Alto
San José
Melocot
Melipilla
Parque
Nacional
Río Clarillo
Baños Morales
Paine
El Volcán
Rapel
San Francisco
de Mostazal
Chapa
Verde
Navidad
Villa
Alhué
Machalí
Sewell
Río Rapel
Doñihue
Lago
Rapel
Rancagua
Lítueche
REGION VI
Márchihue
Pichilemu
Peumo
Rengo
Peralillo
San Vicente de
Tagua Tagua
Peleguén
El Portillo (4986m)
Bucalemu
Santa Cruz
Los Lingues
San Fernando
Llico
Chimbarongo
Lago Vichuquén
Lolol
Vichuquén
Rauco
Sierra
Belle Vista
Tinguiririca (4280m)
Iloca
Licantén
Hualañé
Romaral
Termas del
Río Mataquito
Curicó

*Pacific
Ocean*

Pudú
Molina
REGION VII
Cumpeo
Paso Vergara
del Planchón
Área Protección
Radal
Siete Tazas
Constitución
Talca
Pelarco
Vol
Descabezado (3850m)
Río Maule
Aurora
Reserva
Nacional
Altos de Lircay
Maule
Vilches
Área de
Protección
Vilches
Área Silvestre
Laguna Reloca
San Javier
San
Clemente
El Colorado
Reserva Nacional
Fredrico Albert
Chanco
Colbún
Lago
Colbún
Armerillo
Villa Alegre
Termas de
Panimávida
Curanipe
Reserva Nacional
Los Ruiles
Putagán
Villa Seca
El Boldo
Longaví
Linares
Hualve
Copihue
Miraflores
Cauquenes
Quella
Retiro
Aduana Pejerrey
Cobquecura
Perquilauquén
Parral
Laguna
de Maule
Quirihue
Níquén
Termas de Catillo
San
Gregorio
Paso Pehueche
Coelemu
San Carlos
Dichato
Magdalena
Termas del
Tomé
Quinchamalí
Chillán
San Fabián de Alico
Talcahuano
Lirquén
Rucapequén
Coihueco
Lama
Penco
Bulnes
Pinto
Esperanza
Map 4
Colorado
Concepción
Recinto
Termas
de Chillán
REGION VIII
Río Itata
Pemuco
Las Trancas
Coronel
Monte Águila

0 km   30
0 miles   30

N

Juan
Fernández
Islands

1   **2**   **3**

A

B

C

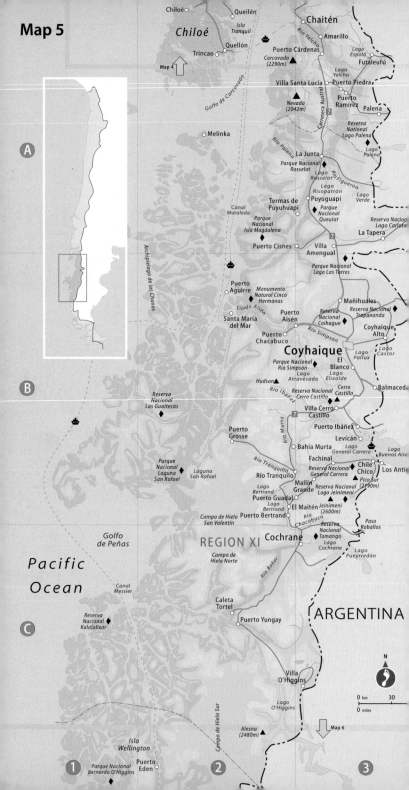

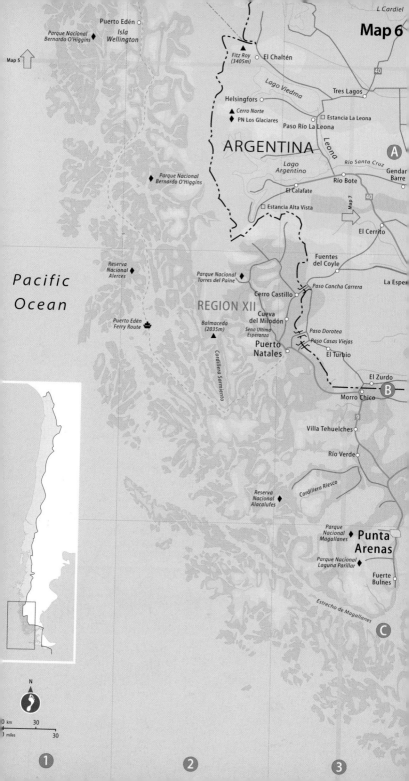

Footprint

Wine Travel Guide
to the World

Robert Joseph

Published in association with Montana Wine.

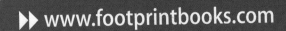

▶▶ www.footprintbooks.com

A guide specifically conceived and written for anyone who travels and enjoys wine.

In Margaux, I want to tread the warm, well-drained gravel outcrops... I want to see the Andes water gushing down off the mountains into the fertile vineyards of Chile's Maipo Valley. I want to feel the howling mists chill me to the bone in California's Carneros, and then feel the warm winds of New Zealand's Marlborough tugging at my hair. I want it all to make sense. *Oz Clarke*

Available now for £19.99 from all good bookshops and online at www.footprintbooks.com

SBN 1 904777 85 6

Footprint
Travel guides